Posttraumatic Stress Disorder

Posttraumatic Stress Disorder

Scientific and Professional Dimensions

Second Edition

Julian D. Ford
Department of Psychiatry,
University of Connecticut Health Center,
Farmington, USA

Damion J. Grasso
Department of Psychiatry,
University of Connecticut Health Center,
Farmington, USA

Jon D. Elhai
Department of Psychology and Psychiatry,
University of Toledo, Ohio, USA

Christine A. Courtois
Independent Practice, Washington, USA;
National Clinical Trauma Consultant
Elements Behavioral Health, LLC, CA, USA

ELSEVIER

AMSTERDAM • BOSTON • HEIDELBERG • LONDON
NEW YORK • OXFORD • PARIS • SAN DIEGO
SAN FRANCISCO • SINGAPORE • SYDNEY • TOKYO
Academic Press is an imprint of Elsevier

Academic Press is an imprint of Elsevier
525 B Street, Suite 1800, San Diego, CA 92101-4495, USA
The Boulevard, Langford Lane, Kidlington, Oxford OX5 1GB, UK

First Edition 2009
Second Edition 2015

ISBN: 978-0-12-801288-8

British Library Cataloguing-in-Publication Data
A catalogue record for this book is available from the British Library

Library of Congress Cataloging-in-Publication Data
A catalog record for this book is available from the Library of Congress

For information on all Academic Press publications
visit our website at http://store.elsevier.com/

Typeset by MPS Limited, Chennai, India
www.adi-mps.com

Transferred to Digital Printing in 2015

Contents

Preface

The published literature on posttraumatic stress disorder (PTSD) has grown rapidly over the past 25 years, almost doubling in size since the 2009 first edition of this book. Now there are more than 10,000 journal articles and hundreds of books on this topic that are widely read by scientists, clinicians, educators, trainees, and laypersons—and increasingly by policy makers, judges and attorneys, organizational leaders, and opinion leaders in the media and popular and political culture. PTSD offers a widely accepted framework for understanding the effects of experiencing potentially traumatic events such as terrorism, domestic and community violence, physical and sexual assault, child maltreatment, human trafficking, refugee adversity homicide, disaster, life-threatening illness and accidents, torture, genocide, and the injury done to both civilians and military combatants in war. Public as well as professional awareness has grown commensurately as most people now recognize the profound impact of psychological trauma and the need for proactive and scientifically based approaches to timely prevention, humanitarian relief, and evidence-based treatment for traumatized persons, communities, and nations.

As a result, scholars, researchers, and educators in the social, biological, medical, political, and behavioral sciences need a current and comprehensive source on PTSD for their studies and teaching. *The Handbook of PTSD, Second Edition* (Friedman, Keane, & Resick, 2014) and *The Encyclopedia of Trauma* (Figley, 2012) provide snapshots of key issues and topics in the PTSD field, but practitioners, clinicians, students, and trainees in the health care and human and social services need a concise and complete overview of PTSD as their source of authoritative information on PTSD. This Second Edition of *Posttraumatic Stress Disorder: Science and Practices* was designed to meet that need for a comprehensive yet concise textbook on PTSD that will be useful to researchers, educators, clinicians, and trainees in graduate and advanced undergraduate courses in the mental health, health care, social and human services, and criminal justice fields.

This text covers all major topics in the traumatic stress field, from etiology to neurobiology to assessment and diagnosis to evidence-based treatment and prevention. All topics covered in the two comprehensive *Encyclopedias* on PTSD (Figley, 2012; Reyes, Elhai, & Ford, 2008) are addressed in this text. A balanced view of each topic includes (i) material relevant to scientific researchers and clinical practitioners; (ii) multiple theoretical vantage points; (iii) answers to questions that aspiring trainees have about becoming a traumatic stress researcher or clinician; (iv) key points for educators to use in teaching; (v) recognition in every section of the book (and special emphasis in Chapter 11) of the critical role that ethnicity, culture, gender and sexual identity, and legal and economic factors have in influencing PTSD and its assessment, treatment, and prevention; and (vi) a developmental focus on the nature of PTSD across the life span from infancy to older adulthood.

The book is written at the level suitable for both advanced undergraduate and graduate trainees, as well as for educators, clinicians, or researchers seeking an overview of the traumatic stress field. The text uses language that is free of technical jargon except for key terms that are supplemented with nontechnical definitions and examples. The focus is on describing state-of-the-art research and clinical methodologies in down-to-earth terms with interesting examples and both research and clinical case studies. The text introduces the major issues, controversies, and findings in the field, as well as highlights what is not yet known and how researchers and clinicians are (or can) make further discoveries.

Chapter 1, Understanding Psychological Trauma and Posttraumatic Stress Disorder (PTSD), describes the history of scientific knowledge and popular conceptions of psychological trauma from the earliest writings several thousand years ago to modern definitions and diagnoses. Controversies such as the nature and validity of memories of childhood traumatic exposure, potential bias in diagnosis and treatment of females and persons of color, gender and ethnocultural differences in the experience and impact of psychological trauma, major expansion in the field's understanding of the range of problems involved in PTSD and diagnostic definitions of PTSD in the United States (the 2014 *Diagnostic and Statistical Manual of Mental Disorders, Fifth Edition, DSM*-5) and internationally (the 2016 *International Classification of Diseases, Eleventh Edition, ICD-11*), and the interplay of mind and body (including genetics and brain development) in psychological trauma are highlighted. Each major topic from subsequent chapters is previewed.

Chapter 2, The Impact of Psychological Trauma, provides a description of the longitudinal course of psychological trauma and PTSD: the unfolding impact of traumatic stress from initial exposure[s] through the following months, years, and decades, and across generations. Acute reactions to psychological trauma and their biological, psychological, and sociocultural bases are described, followed by a description of positive trajectories (e.g., resistance, resilience) and problematic trajectories (e.g., acute posttraumatic stress problems, PTSD, complex PTSD) in the wake of psychological trauma—including the different manifestations of formal diagnoses of PTSD and comorbid disorders as they occur at different developmental epochs and over time.

Chapter 3, Etiology of PTSD: What Causes PTSD?, provides an overview of scientific knowledge and clinical and popular theories of the causes of PTSD. Risk factors for developing PTSD and related behavioral health disorders or sociovocational and legal problems are summarized. Protective factors and contexts that promote stress "resistance" or "resilience" are summarized. An integrative model that takes into account risk and protective factors and the impact of different types of psychological trauma at different developmental phases is presented in order to provide the reader with a unified approach to understanding how PTSD develops and can be effectively treated (discussed in Chapters 7 and 8) or potentially prevented (discussed in Chapter 9). The role of family, community, culture, and service systems in increasing risk of, or resilience/recovery from, traumatic stress disorders is illustrated through case examples.

Chapter 4, Epidemiology of PTSD, describes research on the incidence (how often something occurs) and prevalence (how commonly something is found in a population) of exposure to different types of psychological trauma, Acute Stress Disorder, PTSD, and comorbid psychiatric/addictive disorders and sociovocational and legal problems among children and adults. Differences in the extent and nature of traumatic stressor exposure and PTSD are highlighted across community, clinical (mental health), medical, and criminal justice (juvenile and adult) populations. Approaches to increasing the accuracy and completeness of epidemiological studies of psychological trauma and PTSD are discussed.

Chapter 5, Neurobiology of Traumatic Stress Disorders and Their Impact on Physical Health, distills the extensive animal and human research literatures on the biological foundations of stress and posttraumatic stress in a summary that addresses (i) alterations in the body's stress response systems; (ii) alterations in brain chemistry, structure, and functioning; (iii) the role of genetics and epigenetics (changes in genes caused by life experiences) in PTSD; and (iv) the impact of psychological trauma and traumatic stress disorders on physical health. Classic and contemporary studies on the physiology, neurobiology, and alterations in brain functioning that may contribute to PTSD are highlighted to bring to life the complex biological underpinnings of psychological trauma and its impact on physical as well as psychological health.

Chapter 6, Assessment of Psychological Trauma and PTSD, presents an overview of approaches to clinical and research assessment of people's life history of exposure to traumatic stressors and past or current PTSD. Measures with the strongest evidence base are described, along with concise definitions of the psychometric criteria (the standards for accurate measurement) that are required for assessment to be considered to be reliable, valid, and clinical useful. Approaches to the following aspects of assessment are described: (i) screening to identify individuals who may have experienced trauma and may be suffering traumatic stress symptoms; (ii) structured interview assessment of psychological trauma history and traumatic stress disorders; (iii) standardized questionnaires assessing trauma history, PTSD and its symptoms, and key comorbid psychosocial problems; (iv) psychophysiological and neuropsychological assessment of trauma survivors; and, (v) forensic (juvenile and criminal justice, civil law) assessment of psychological trauma survivors.

Chapters 7 and 8, Treatment of Adults with PTSD and Treatment of Children and Adolescents with PTSD, describe the classic three-phase model of treatment for PTSD and discuss the essential clinical and ethical/legal ingredients that transcend any single therapeutic theory or intervention (such as engagement, working alliance, confidentiality/privilege, mandated reporting, crisis prevention and management, identifying and therapeutically addressing severe dissociation). Then, approaches with the strongest evidence base for traumatic stress treatment are described, including cognitive behavioral therapies (CBT), PTSD affect and interpersonal regulation (PAIR) therapies, psychodynamic and experiential therapies, marital and family therapies, group therapies, and pharmacotherapy (medication).

Chapter 9, Prevention of PTSD, begins with a discussion of why, even though the best approach to prevention is to prevent psychological trauma from occurring, it is not completely possible to prevent traumatic stressors from occurring given the ubiquity of accidents, disasters, social upheaval, and violence. The innovative array of interventions designed for secondary/tertiary or selected/indicated prevention of PTSD are described. These prevention approaches are designed to increase the ability of people and communities to cope effectively with and recover with resilience from traumatic stress and include Hobfoll's Conservation of Resources (COR), Saxe's Trauma Systems Therapy (TST), Brom and Kleber's Minimal Learning Model (MLM), De Jong's Multisystemic Model, and Zatzick's Collaborative Care Model. Specific prevention interventions are described that address community and school-based violence and abuse prevention; psychological first aid in the wake of disaster and terrorism; and social and culturally based humanitarian programs and advocacy.

Chapter 10, Forensic Issues in the Traumatic Stress Field, describes how psychological trauma and PTSD play an important role in the criminal, civil, and juvenile justice systems, and are ubiquitous in the lives of most persons who are involved in these systems. An overview is provided of the challenges facing traumatic stress professionals while conducting research, providing expert and clinical evaluations and testimony, and developing and conducting treatment, rehabilitation, and prevention interventions, in the justice and family services systems, including:

a. the child welfare and child protective services systems (e.g., child abuse/neglect);
b. the family law courts (e.g., divorce and child custody, parental competence);
c. the juvenile justice system (e.g., juvenile courts, detention, probation, incarceration);
d. the adult criminal justice system (e.g., courts, jails, prisons, parole/probation);
e. the immigration/naturalization system (e.g., refugee asylum hearings).

Issues such as the role of PTSD as a mitigating factor in criminal culpability of victimized persons, the credibility of witness and defendant memories, political asylum, and the rehabilitation and community reentry of incarcerated youth and adults are discussed with reference to empirical research, practice parameters, and clinical case studies.

Chapter 11, Social, Cultural, and Other Diversity Issues in the Traumatic Stress Field, describes how the impact of psychological trauma differs, depending on the social and cultural context and the social and cultural resources available to individuals, families, and communities. Disadvantaged persons and communities such as those experiencing poverty, stigma and discrimination, homelessness, political repression, communal/societal violence (including military and gang warfare), forced immigration (refugees), interrogation and torture, terrorism, and genocide are given special attention as victims of traumatic stress. Ethical issues facing traumatic stress professionals and scientists as they seek to provide services, conduct research, and influence policy regarding these and other vulnerable groups (e.g., children, older adults, incarcerated persons) are described.

Chapter 12, Careers and Ethical Issues in the Traumatic Stress Field, describes the opportunities and challenges provided by careers that focus on traumatic stress, including the scientist/researcher (in basic, clinical, and translational sciences), the mental health and social work clinician, the public health and medical professional, the educator, and the program director. Real-life examples are used to illustrate the kinds of work, rewards, and dilemmas involved in each career path. Particular emphasis is given to understanding the impact that working with persons or communities suffering from traumatic stress has on the professional (described as "vicarious or secondary trauma" or "compassion fatigue" and "posttraumatic growth") and approaches to understanding and preventing professional burnout and promoting personal and professional resilience. Ethical issues in PTSD research, assessment, and treatment also are described.

References

Figley, C. (Ed.). (2012). *Encyclopedia of trauma*. Thousand Oaks, CA: Sage Publications.

Friedman, M. J., Keane, T. M., & Resick, P. A. (Eds.). (2014). *Handbook of PTSD: Science and practice* (2nd ed.). New York, NY: Guilford Press.

Reyes, G., Elhai, J. D., & Ford, J. D. (Eds.). (2008). *Encyclopedia of psychological trauma*. Englewood Cliffs, NJ: John Wiley & Sons.

Understanding psychological trauma and posttraumatic stress disorder (PTSD)

1

Traumatic stressors and the resultant psychological trauma have been sources of both horror and fascination for thousands of years. Both have been documented in many different art forms and in written histories across the ages. Events or experiences that confront a person—or an entire community or society—with actual or imminent death or destruction are terrifying and life-changing. Something unique happens when you are overwhelmed and "see your life flash before your eyes"—and that "something" is a biological, psychological, communal/social, and spiritual shock that is called *traumatic stress*. Exposure to traumatic stressors most often results in post-traumatic reactions, but when these reactions become persistent and debilitating, they are no longer just "normal reactions to abnormal circumstances"; they have become a *posttraumatic* stress disorder (PTSD).

Technically, PTSD is a psychiatric disorder that affects as many as one in 14 adults and adolescents at some time in their lives and as many as 1 in 20 children before they begin kindergarten. Trauma-related disorders were the second or third most costly health problem in the United States in every year surveyed from 2000 to 2012. (the most recent year for which costs have been officially tallied), according to the federal Agency for Healthcare Research and Quality (Box 1.1, Figures 1.1 and 1.2). Only heart disease was consistently more costly than trauma-related disorders, and cancer was generally slightly less costly (except in 2004). This was true even though the cost per person was three to four times higher for heart disease and cancer (due to expensive high-technology and pharmacological treatments and the high rates of death or total disability). This means many more persons suffer from trauma-related disorders than from either heart disease or cancer, and the costs, including treatment, to both them and society exceed those of any other disorder or illness except heart disease.

This book explains how and why exposure to traumatic stressors can cause psychological trauma (both reactions and symptoms) and how and for whom these events or experiences can lead to the debilitating disorder of PTSD (which actually is a biological as well as psychological phenomenon). With this knowledge, it is possible to make informed decisions about how to conduct further research on PTSD, how to accurately assess and effectively treat PTSD in clinical practice, and how to prevent trauma survivors from developing and suffering from the symptoms of PTSD. The large and rapidly growing published scientific and clinical literature on psychological trauma and PTSD is cited as a scholarly evidence base for rigorous discussion of these crucial issues, as well as a guide for readers interested in learning more about PTSD and its treatment. Many questions about PTSD, its origins, prevention, and

Posttraumatic Stress Disorder. DOI: http://dx.doi.org/10.1016/B978-0-12-801288-8.00001-7

Box 1.1 Top 5 Most Costly Medical Conditions in the United States in 2012

Condition	Cost ($ billions)
1. Heart conditions	101
2. Trauma disorders	93
3. Cancer	88
4. Mental disorders	87
5. Asthma	76

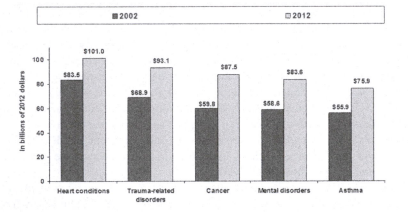

Figure 1.1 Expenditures for the five most costly conditions, 2002 and 2012.
Center for Financing, Access, and Cost Trends, AHRQ, Household Component of the
Medical Expenditure Panel Survey, 2012.

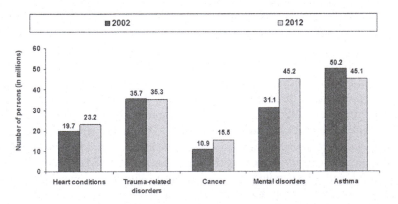

Figure 1.2 Number of persons with expenses for the top five most costly conditions,
2002 and 2012.
Center for Financing, Access, and Cost Trends, AHRQ, Household Component of the
Medical Expenditure Panel Survey, 2012.

Source: Soni, A. *Trends in the Five Most Costly Conditions among the U.S. Civilian Noninstitutionalized Population, 2002 and 2012*. Statistical Brief #470. April 2015. Agency for Healthcare Research and Quality, Rockville, MD. http://www.meps.ahrq.gov/mepsweb/data_files/publications/st470/stat470.shtml. Accessed April 13, 2015

treatment that remain unanswered are covered to provide information about hypotheses that are still being tested or will be tested by future generations of researchers and psychotherapists.

This chapter provides a survey of the history and current state of scientific knowledge and popular conceptions of psychological trauma, from the earliest writings several thousand years ago to modern definitions and diagnoses. Controversies are highlighted, such as whether infants can experience traumatic stress responses and if they remember psychological traumas, whether military personnel can be protected from PTSD and if their lives (and those of civilian victims) are ever the same after experiencing the horrors of war, whether PTSD is a psychiatric disorder or a "normal response to abnormal events," whether trauma survivors have to return to the past and confront terrifying memories if they are to recover from PTSD, and whether psychological trauma can lead to growth. This chapter also touches on the major topics covered in subsequent chapters. As we do in all of the chapters, we begin with a real-life case example and evidence-based facts. These case studies are based on the lives of real people, disguised to preserve the privacy of each individual. These examples show how experiencing psychological trauma and living with PTSD affect people from every walk of life, of all genders and in all developmental stages, every sexual orientation, ethnocultural and socioeconomic background, and nationality. We will see important differences based on these diverse characteristics in the specific ways in which potentially traumatizing events occur and subsequent PTSD symptoms develop, but there are also universal features in the events that threaten people's lives (and those of the people they rely on for safety and intimacy) and in our reactions to these close encounters with the specter of death that occur biologically simply because we all share an essential humanness.

"Is there a life after trauma?": The case of Marian M.

Marian is a 55-year-old woman of mixed racial background who grew up in a family that was going through the throes of transition from living in the "Old World"—a family tree with branches of many generations before World War II in Eastern Europe and the Middle East—to the postwar modern Western world. Her parents were the first generation to grow up in the United States with English as their primary language and a secular view of religion. Her mother's parents had survived the Holocaust and emigrated after losing all of their family members in Nazi death camps. Her father's parents had experienced genocide as children in Armenia. Marian's parents grew up "poor but safe" in New York during the Great Depression and became the first generation in their families to attend college. Her mother was a teacher, and her father was a successful businessman. Marian was the youngest of three daughters, and when she was born, her parents were still struggling to acquire the "American Dream" of a car, a house in Levittown (the prototype for postwar suburbia), and good schools for their children.

For many years, Marian believed that her first brush with psychological trauma, in this relatively sheltered life, was a dramatic incident in which she was caught in a terrorist attack when she was attending the 1972 Munich Olympics as a college student traveling through Europe on summer vacation. While visiting a friend in the Olympic village, they happened to be walking past the Israeli team's residence just as it was being attacked by terrorists. Years later, in therapy, Marian could vividly describe the sudden contrast between the soft, happy sounds of a summer evening and the explosive staccato of gunfire and the screams of people running for their lives. Although she can't exactly recall how much time passed because everything seemed both to grind to a halt and race past in a blur, she also remembered the wailing as people carried out bodies and horribly wounded young men to the ambulances. The next hours and days continued to be "a blur," but somehow Marian found her way to the airport, and 2 days later, she was back in New York. Marian decided not to tell her parents about her experience. Although her family and friends were intensely interested in what she had seen on her travels, Marian felt oddly detached and emotionally empty. She explained, "I told them what had happened like I was a narrator in a movie. It didn't really bother me to tell it again and again, and that's what bothers me now. How could I be so cold and unfeeling? I wasn't like that before." She spent the next year finishing college, "right on schedule, as if nothing had happened," but she spent most of her time alone in the library, in contrast to having been "always around other people, talking, laughing, very social" in the past.

After that incident, Marian began to have nightmares in which she was being hunted, captured, and tortured. She would wake up screaming for help. She said, "It was nothing like either of the experiences, just these mixed-up, jump-right-out-of-your-skin visions of being pursued, trapped, and annihilated, again and again each night—until I just couldn't really go to sleep, always staying just alert enough to catch the beginning of that dream and wake myself up so I wouldn't have to go through it." She learned that the only way to sleep was to "drink myself under the table," and she preferred the inevitable hangover to being in a daze because of sleeplessness. She remained determined to complete college and did so with great effort despite feeling like her mind had become "a sieve." Marian said she felt like "everything I read or heard at lectures just went right down the drain, where I used to have an absolute steel-trap mind and memory, never had to read anything twice or take notes, and now I could barely retain information long enough to pass a test, and only then if I went over all of my notes again and again." The library was her sanctuary. Gradually she was able to cope with the emotional "ups and downs," bad dreams, and mental "Swiss cheese. She got a job as an art museum curator, married, and had children.

When her youngest child turned 20, he decided to travel through Europe for the summer before completing college. Marian's stress reactions returned with a vengeance, for no apparent reason: "My life was wonderful, not without the usual hassles, and I worried about everything, always 'doom and gloom,' as my husband and children would say affectionately. So I was a worrier, it could be worse, but I was happy and ready to enjoy life as an empty nester. Then Eric went off on his trek, and I fell apart. I really was happy to have him out of the house and have some peace and quiet for the whole summer, after years of the endless noise that is the curse and blessing of a family. But I wasn't happy. I was miserable—nightmares of terrorists, drunk drivers, worse than 35 years ago! My heart would start pounding, and I'd break into a sweat—and it wasn't the change of life because I'd already been through that. It wasn't this bad if someone just walked up behind me and I didn't know they were there. My husband learned fast to send a clear signal before he came within five feet of me. It was like being in that car all over again and someone's about smash into me even though it's just someone walking over to say Hi." Marian became intensely fearful that all of her children were going to be killed, even though she knew there was little danger now. For the first time in her adult life, she couldn't get up and face the day. She began to miss work and then social activities with friends and family, until she felt like she was trying to isolate herself completely.

Marian was experiencing a return of her original PTSD, which had been dormant for years but was reactivated when she experienced the trigger of her son's European travels. Her experience illustrates how seemingly innocuous life circumstances, events, and transition can lead to a new episode of PTSD long after its traumatic origins, even when the disorder appears to have been completely resolved. Marian did in fact recover from her original PTSD. However, like many other traumatized but resilient individuals, she remained at risk for the disorder to flare up again. Had she experienced a new traumatic event, such as her son actually being attacked or killed in an accident (as she feared might happen, based upon her past traumatic experience), she would have been even more likely to develop a severe episode of PTSD based upon the combination of the prior and current traumatizations. But it does not take a traumatic event to trigger the reemergence of PTSD, and that is why it is crucial to prepare individuals who experience PTSD so they are not blindsided if PTSD symptoms reappear years or even decades after they have fully recovered from the disorder. Like other chronic health problems—for example, malaria—PTSD is never fully cured but can be overcome with effective treatment (see Chapters 7 and 8), and recurrences can be minimized and managed with preventive precautions (see Chapter 9).

History of popular and scientific conceptions of psychological trauma and PTSD

The term *trauma* originates from the Greek word for "injury" or "wound" (Mattox, Moore, & Feliciano, 2013). It originally was used to describe physical injury, but today it also includes "the psychic wounding that can potentially follow a traumatic episode" (Dass-Brailsford, 2007, p. 3). As Ford and Courtois (2009, p. 15) explain, *trauma* has been used "interchangeably (and confusingly) to refer to (1) the *traumatic stressor event(s)*, including *the individual's experience during exposure to the stressor(s)*, or (2) the individual's *response*, whether *peritraumatic* (occurring during *or in the immediate aftermath of* the experience) or *posttraumatic* (occurring weeks, months, or years afterwards)." In this book, the term *trauma* is used in several distinct ways with different meanings (Box 1.2). Most important, (Box 1.3) physical trauma is distinguished from psychological trauma, with the latter defined as a *traumatic stressor* in order to emphasize that *stress is the key factor in psychological trauma*

Box 1.2 Key Points

1. Trauma-related disorders were the second most costly health problem in the United States, costing $72 billion annually in the United States according to a 2008 estimate of the federal government's Agency for Healthcare Research and Quality.
2. PTSD affects 1 in 10 men and 1 in 5 women at some point in their lives, about half of whom experienced PTSD at some time in their childhood.
3. PTSD is one of the two psychiatric diagnoses that requires that the person has experienced stressful event(s) in addition to having distressing symptoms and problems in functioning.
4. In PTSD, a "traumatic" stressor is an event that involves directly experiencing or witnessing an immediate threat to one's own or someone else's life or the violation of the integrity of one's own or someone else's bodily integrity (including sexual or physical assault or abuse).
5. PTSD has been recognized as a problem throughout human history, but it was not technically defined as a psychiatric diagnosis until 1980 in the third revision of the American Psychiatric Association's *Diagnostic and Statistical Manual of Mental Disorders (DSM-III)*.
6. PTSD symptoms must last for at least 1 month and must include "intrusive reexperiencing" (unwanted memories or reminders of traumatic experiences while awake or asleep), "avoidance and emotional numbing" (attempts to actively avoid trauma memories or reminders, or reduced range or ability to experience emotions), and "hyperarousal" (feeling physically and mentally tense, on edge, excessively watchful for danger, irritable, or easily startled, or unable to sleep).
7. Although there is no single established cause, PTSD appears to involve several interrelated changes in the body's stress response system and the brain's emotion regulation systems that are associated with extreme sensitivity to danger (potential as well as actual) that results in the person essentially becoming stuck in "survival mode" and unable to participate as fully and productively in relationships, school or work, and daily life as they otherwise would be.
8. Memories of events that were life-threatening or violations of bodily integrity may differ in quality and organization from other memories as a result of the heightened activation of the body and brain's stress response system during and after traumatic experiences.
9. Survivors of traumatic stressors may not fully or accurately remember those experiences, but there is no evidence that trauma memories are typically, let alone always, false. False memories of exposure to traumatic stressors are not the same as incomplete or partially inaccurate memories. However, a trauma memory may be false if the "recovery" of trauma memory is unduly influenced by social psychological coercion or "contagion" or if there is clear evidence that memories have been purposefully made up or exaggerated for personal gain.
10. The currently accepted symptoms of PTSD are based on clinicians' insights and scientific theory and research that show that, *after a traumatic event* (PTSD diagnosis Criterion A), when distressing memories or troubling reactions to reminders of the event persist (PTSD diagnosis Criterion B) despite the person's attempts to avoid reminders (Criterion C, avoidance), over time this leads emotional distress and exhaustion as well as changing the individual's core beliefs because of never feeling safe (Criterion D, altered emotions and cognitions) and to being on guard mentally and on edge and tense, reactive, and alternatively defensive or aggressive (Criterion E) or severely detached and shut down mentally (dissociative subtype).

Box 1.3 Trauma Terminology

Trauma: events or experiences that are severely damaging to an individual or society.

Physical Trauma: bodily illness or injury that places a person's life in jeopardy or causes potentially irreparable damage to the body.

Psychological Trauma: experiences that place a person's life or bodily integrity in jeopardy.

Traumatic Stressor: an event that places a person's life or bodily integrity in jeopardy directly or indirectly (as a witness) and elicits feelings of extreme fear, helplessness, or horror.

Traumatic Stress: biological and psychological reactions to psychological trauma or a traumatic stressor, including acute traumatic stress reactions and posttraumatic stress symptoms.

Posttraumatic Stress: persistent problematic biological and psychological adaptations following exposure to a traumatic stressor, including intrusive memories, avoidance, negative or numbed emotions, detachment from relationships, and hypervigilance, combined with hyperarousal or dissociation (the latter represents a dissociative subtype of PTSD).

PTSD: posttraumatic stress reactions persist for at least 1 month and interfere significantly with personal adjustment and functioning.

Complex PTSD: a proposed diagnosis that is not accepted by the American Psychiatric Association (in the *DSM*-5) but may be included by the World Health Organization (WHO) (in the *ICD-11*), including three additional types of symptoms along with PTSD: difficulty in expressing or recovering from extreme negative emotions, self-image as damaged by trauma, and social isolation or highly unstable relationships.

Acute Traumatic Stress Reactions: biological and psychological reactions to exposure to a traumatic stressor during or within the first month after this exposure.

ASD: multiple types of acute traumatic stress reactions occur within the first month after exposure to a traumatic stressor and persist for more than the first 3 days following exposure, interfering significantly with personal adjustment and functioning.

Trauma Survivor: a person exposed to a traumatic stressor, including as a direct victim of abuse, assault, war, or disaster; as a direct witness (or an emergency responder who repeatedly is exposed to the harm done) to other persons who are being victimized; or as the bereaved close friend or family member of someone who is murdered or dies unexpectedly.

Trauma-Related Disorders: psychological and medical problems that begin or are substantially worsened by exposure to psychological trauma. Numerous psychiatric disorders other than PTSD have been found to be related to (although not caused by) exposure to traumatic stressors, including anxiety, affective, substance use, dissociative, somatoform, eating, disruptive behavior, psychotic, personality, and childhood psychiatric disorders.

(as opposed to trauma that is physical in nature, such as an orthopedic injury when a bone is broken or damage to the brain due to a traumatic brain injury). Psychological trauma can often occur as a consequence of a physical trauma, but it may occur without any evident physical injury, as in the case of a violent threat or sexual assault.

The oldest known description of traumatic stress was found inscribed on clay tablets 5000 years ago. The Sumerian *Epic of Gilgamesh* describes a Babylonian king who was terrified and distraught after the unexpected death of his closest friend, Enkidu. Gilgamesh's reactions reflect several classic symptoms of PTSD and traumatic grief (e.g., terrifying memories, inability to sleep, anger, sense of foreshortened future; Birmes, Hatton, Brunet, & Schmitt, 2003). The 10th tablet describes Gilgamesh's ordeal:

> *I was terrified by his appearance, I began to fear death, and roam the wilderness. How can I stay silent, how can I be still! My friend whom I love has turned to clay! Am I not like him! Will I lie down never to get up again! That is why I must go on, to see… "the Faraway." That is why sweet sleep has not mellowed my face, through sleepless striving I am strained, my muscles are filled with pain. (www.ancienttexts. org/library/mesopotamian/gilgamesh/)*

Gilgamesh's psychological experience of trauma was not the result of any physical injury but of the death of his closest friend. Interestingly, the most recent update of the definition of PTSD in the American Psychiatric Association's (2013) guidebook to mental disorders (*Diagnostic and Statistical Manual of Mental Disorders*, Fifth Edition, *DSM-5*) has added precisely this kind of tragic loss to the list of events that may be considered traumatic: "learning that … traumatic event(s) [such as] the actual or threatened death of a close family member or close friend [that is violent or accidental] occurred" (p. 271). Traumatic events, whether we are the victims or only witness harm to the key people in our lives confront us in a shocking manner with the reality of death and the fragility of life and security. When the result is intolerable fear or grief, it can lead to profound psychic (and often also, as Gilgamesh describes, physical) pain, causing the victim to feel emotionally tortured while both awake and asleep—as if life has become a "wilderness" through which he or she must endlessly "roam." These are the devastating and relentless symptoms of PTSD.

Two millennia later, famous Greek and Roman storytellers and authors captured the essence of traumatic stress and grief (Birmes et al., 2003). Homer's *Illiad* describes the rageful loss of control of Achilles in the siege of Troy (Shay, 1994). Homer's *Odyssey* depicts chronic PTSD when describing Odysseus as emotionally unable to return home after experiencing traumatic betrayal and loss (Shay, 2002). The Greek historian Herodotus and Roman historian Pliny the Younger graphically described acute traumatic stress reactions, such as dissociation in combatants at the battle of Marathon (490 BC) and people trapped in the eruption of Mount Vesuvius (AD 79). Across the ages, war has often been glorified and its victors celebrated. The horrific psychological cost and impact of war on individuals—civilians trapped in the melee as well as the combatants, not to mention their families, and entire societies—tragically often is overlooked or viewed as the unavoidable "collateral damage" of warfare or other forms of humanmade or natural violence. Yet, the most chronic damage caused by war or disasters, often persisting for years or decades after communities and countries have been rebuilt and revitalized, come from psychic wounds that remain open and never fully healed in the form of PTSD.

Less common, but equally poignant, are ancient stories of women who suffer traumatic stressors. For example, the biblical tale of a brother's incestuous rape of

King David's daughter, Tamar, describes her "wisdom, courage, and unrelieved suffering" (Trible, 1984): "Tamar took ashes upon her head and the long robe that was upon her she tore. She put her hand upon her head ... and she wept. ... So Tamar dwelt, and she was desolate, in the house of her [other] brother Absalom" (Samuel 13: 19–20). More than a millennium later, in the fifteenth to seventeenth centuries, Renaissance and Reformation paintings offered representations of traumatic events, and literature and theater produced vivid accounts of psychological trauma and its aftermath, such as Shakespeare's portrayals of the traumatic impact of natural disasters (e.g., *The Tempest*), rape (e.g., *The Rape of Lucrece*), domestic violence (e.g., *Othello, The Winter's Tale*), war (e.g., *Titus Andronicus; Henry the IV/V/VI*), political violence and exile (*As You Like It, Antony and Cleopatra, The Merchant of Venice*), and murder (e.g., *Antony and Cleopatra, Romeo and Juliet, Othello, The Winter's Tale, Macbeth, Richard II*).

It was not until the eighteenth century, when medicine first became a science-based profession, that traumatic stress was first technically described and treated. Trauma was viewed primarily as involving physical injury and related infection that presented physicians and surgeons with the challenge of preventing death due to infection (Moore & Feliciano, 2004). In the 1860s, physicians began to describe chronic physical and psychological syndromes characterized by fatigue, tremors, pain, anxiety, and depression following life-threatening injuries and exposures. John Eric Erichsen's (1866) *On Railway and Other Injuries of the Nervous System* described a condition known as "railway spine" that originally was thought to be the result of physical trauma sustained in train crashes. A quarter century later, the Jewish German neurologist Hermann Oppenheim reconceptualized the phenomenon as a "traumatic neurosis" caused by exposure to life-threatening events rather than due to physical injury.

During that same time period, British and American cardiologists Arthur B. R. Myers (1870) and Jacob Mendez DaCosta (1871) almost simultaneously published descriptions of combat soldiers with or without physical injuries who suffered from chronic anxiety and dysphoria, which they attributed to the cardiologic defect of an "irritable soldier's heart." In 1918, at the end of World War I, the syndrome was classified by the US Surgeon General as *neurocirculatory asthenia*, meaning a muscular weakness caused by some combination of neurological and cardiologic/circulatory disease. The 1916 War Congress of the German Association for Psychiatry similarly determined that anxiety and exhaustion among soldiers were due to "hysteria," "feeble-mindedness," and factitious claims made to obtain a disability pension (Lerner et al., 2003). Seemingly consistent with this view, "neurasthenia" in large military and civilian medical case samples was found to occur not only after war combat but also among others with mild or no combat exposure and a predisposition to complain of exhaustion and anxiety. Thus, with the exception of Oppenheim's formulation of a traumatic neurosis, early clinical observations of chronic posttraumatic stress were attributed to medical trauma or disease, hysteria (both male and female), or malingering.

During this period, Freud began to formulate the psychoanalytic approach to the treatment of hysterical neuroses, beginning with discussions with an internal medicine colleague, Josef Breuer (the case of Anna O.). The patient was a young woman who suffered from what at the time was labeled as female "hysteria"—symptoms that today would be considered forms of severe dissociation such as paralysis, anesthesia, visions, aphasia, fugue states, and alternation between complete indifference and extreme distress. Her symptoms subsided when Breuer helped her to reconstruct events that she recalled as preceding their onset. She (her real name was Bertha Pappenheim) later became a renowned social worker and actually was the inventor of the widely used colloquial description of psychoanalysis, "the talking cure"—which she also imaginatively described as psychological "chimney sweeping." The case was described in Breuer and Freud's (1893) classic monograph "On the Psychic Mechanisms of Hysterical Phenomena." In a series of papers that outlined what came to be known as the "seduction theory" of "psychoneuroses" such as hysteria, Freud described these disorders as not just symptoms but fundamentally altered "personality structures resulting from defensive attempts to deal with traumatic experiences in childhood that predispose the individual to later psychopathology" (Davis, 1994, p. 492) (Box 1.4).

However, foreshadowing the contemporary controversy about "false memories" of childhood trauma, Freud subsequently radically altered his position from suspecting that childhood sexual trauma had actually occurred to assuming that emotionally troubled patients (most of whom were women) were only imagining childhood sexual traumas as a way to justify or gain sympathy for what otherwise would be viewed by "polite society" as aberrant emotional and behavioral excesses. Then, as now, discrediting (and either implicitly or explicitly blaming) troubled individuals as either unable to deal with reality or flat-out dishonest was cruel and often damaging not only to those who actually had been molested or otherwise traumatized as children but also to those whose suffering was real even if not actually the result of childhood trauma.

The position of automatically disbelieving disclosures of childhood trauma by assuming that they are merely fantasies or sexualized and romanticized longings for the parent of the opposite sex is not consistent with research showing that many, if not most, disclosures of past traumatic events are true—including memories that appear to emerge after a period of years or decades (Dalenberg et al., 2012). It is important to recognize that all memories fluctuate in their availability to our conscious awareness, depending on both the original (i.e., at the time of the event(s)) and current circumstances, and that most memories are not in our conscious awareness most of the time simply because our brains have a finite information processing capacity. Trauma memories also tend to be different from ordinary memories: more vivid perceptually and in the automatic bodily reactions and behaviors they elicit but less precise and organized as a story-like "narrative" (Brewin, 2014; Goodman, Marsh, Peterson, & Packard, 2014; Hitchcock, Nixon, & Weber, 2014). Thus, while Freud initially recognized the potential severe psychological harm that has been scientifically and clinically documented to result from childhood sexual abuse (Courtois, 2010), his repudiation of the seduction theory is consistent with other research that has shown that current emotional distress increases the likelihood of recalling past experiences as traumatic (Bryant, 2008b) but inconsistent with the extensive research documenting the traumatic toll of actual experiences of childhood sexual abuse and other forms of childhood maltreatment—including not only PTSD but also other severe problems with anxiety, depression, addiction, dissociation, self-injury and suicidality, risk-taking, revictimization, and physical illness (D'Andrea, Ford, Stolbach, Spinazzola, & van der Kolk, 2012).

Box 1.4 The False Memory Syndrome Controversy

Precisely how psychologically traumatic events are remembered and whether memories of traumatic stressors are different from, and in particular less accurate or more prone to being either "repressed" or falsely created than, memories of other events and experiences have been a major controversies not only in the traumatic stress field but in the larger arenas of politics, law, ethics, child welfare, and health care. Freud hypothesized that his patients repressed memories of childhood events that were psychically intolerable and only were able to "recover" these memories with the help of psychoanalysis. Janet described a similar phenomenon—dissociative amnesia—that he believed occurred unconsciously when memories that overwhelmed the person's psychic capacities were removed from conscious awareness.

The false memory controversy arose in the 1980s when survivors of childhood abuse (and other forms of particularly horrific traumas such as prolonged violence, captivity, or torture) reported that they became able much later to recall some traumatic experiences that they did not consciously remember for a period of time after the event. *The Courage to Heal* (Bass & Davis, 1988) was a popular book that described these as "repressed" memories of childhood sexual abuse. At that time, some clinicians actively encouraged clients to attempt to "recover" memories of childhood abuse in therapy. However, most such memories are very difficult to corroborate, and some people who had been accused of perpetrating abuse not only denied the allegations but started or joined organizations such as the False Memory Syndrome Foundation (FMSF) in order to lobby against laws and court decisions that upheld those accusations. The controversy had a major impact on laws prosecuting childhood sexual abuse, with increases in the statute of limitations for reporting past abuse extended from a few years to as long as decades in 37 states (Lindblom & Gray, 2008). Some researchers have contested the truthfulness of those memories, not necessarily accusing the trauma survivors of lying but citing evidence that the memories may not be borne out by legal records or testimony (as occurred in the infamous McMartin Preschool case of purported satanic child abuse in the 1980s) and that people often think they are remembering events that actually did not happen at all (Loftus, 2001). These examples suggest that false memories can result when investigators or therapists suggest to witnesses or clients that they should confess or admit that terrible events happened, using techniques of emotional and psychological coercion.

Research on ordinary memory has shown that amnesia is not synonymous with normal forgetting, that memories often are incompletely entered into memory ("encoding" errors) and therefore cannot be fully or accurately recalled ("retrieved" from long-term memory), and that when people avoid thinking about memories (as occurs by definition in PTSD), they may unintentionally fail to report memories they truly possess. Bryant (2008a) describes an experimental paradigm for studying memory with trauma survivors, called the "directed

(Continued)

Box 1.4 Continued

forgetting paradigm." This involves being shown trauma-related, positive, or neutral words with the instruction to either forget or remember the word. Adults who experienced childhood sexual abuse do not show a different pattern of forgetting or remembering trauma-related words, but people with ASD are particularly able to forget trauma-related words. Bryant (2008b) notes that ASD involves both recent exposure to traumatic stressors and dissociative symptoms that may include amnesia. Bryant (2008a) notes that adults with PTSD may not recall trauma-related information (or may recall events as if they were a detached observer) due to their avoidance of trauma memories or reminders and that their recall months or years later of details of traumatic events and acute stress reactions may exaggerate the severity of the events and reactions (compared to what they reported at the time; McNally, 2003). Bryant (2008a) concludes that the theory that trauma survivors repress trauma memories is not supported because "there is not sound empirical evidence that people ... dissociate trauma memories to the extent proposed by dissociative amnesia theories. ... People tend to recall their trauma memories too vividly, although there may be some mechanisms that result in preferential forgetting of other trauma-related information."

Lindblom and Gray (2008) define *repression* as "a defensive mechanism rooted in psychoanalytic theory that represents an inability to consciously access stored memories for events characterized by intense negative emotions" and *forgetting* as "an inability to access memories due to processes of encoding, storage and retrieval that are universal across memories." They also distinguish "false" versus "recovered" memories, defining a recovered memory as one that involved an actual experience that the person could not recall for a period of time but then became able to recall.

Based on the complexity of this controversy and the potential for harm to either people who have been traumatized or others who are potentially unfairly accused of having perpetrated abuse, Lindblom and Gray (2008) recommend that clinicians should not assume that clients who are troubled by symptoms that are similar to PTSD have "repressed memories" as a result of psychogenic amnesia if they have no clear memory of traumatic events. Techniques such as hypnosis that therapists have used to "help" clients "recover" trauma-related memories should not be used for this purpose because of the risk of influencing clients to falsely recall what they do not really remember. In addition, only forensically trained mental health experts should provide evidence in courts of law concerning trauma survivors' memories. It also is important to remember that the completeness and accuracy of memories are always in flux and that many types of memories can become accessible after periods of being forgotten. Thus, it is entirely possible for trauma survivors to "recover" memories (which may not have been remembered for many reasons, not just repression) from years or decades before. When this occurs, the critical challenge is to determine if the remembering has been influenced in ways that might undermine the accuracy of the memory and how best to help the person use the memory in constructive rather than destructive ways.

In 1915, during World War I, the British physician Charles Myers described the hysterical neuroses among returning soldiers as "shell shock." Based on three cases of "loss of memory, vision, smell, and taste" subsequent to exposure to exploding shells, Myers noted that the soldiers' hearing was intact, but other senses and memory were lost or distorted (i.e., a "dissociated complex"), consistent with contemporary descriptions of psychological and somatoform dissociation (Leys, 1994). Another British physician, William Brown, treated more than 3000 shell-shocked soldiers using Breuer and Freud's approach of encouraging a detailed retelling of the specific events occurring just prior to the emergence of the hysterical symptoms. In a 1920 presentation, "The Revival of Emotional Memories and Its Therapeutic Value," to the British Psychological Society, Brown noted that when vivid, even "hallucinatory," memories were described in detail, the patient's symptoms disappeared due to "a re-synthesis of the mind of the patient [in which] the amnesia has been abolished" (Leys, 1994, p. 625).

Like Freud, Brown viewed *catharsis*, a liberation of repressed emotional distress, as the therapeutic mechanism. Charles Myers and William McDougall provided commentary in which they proposed that the critical factor was that the patient was able to articulate rather than avoid the traumatic memory and thereby to create a psychologically coherent narrative description of the formerly fragmented and intolerable memory (Leys, 1994). The Myers and McDougall conceptualization is similar to Pierre Janet's 1925 formulation of "presentification" after "disagregation" (dissociation)—that is, the reconstruction of traumatic memories in a meaningful narrative (Van der Hart & Friedman, 1989)—which Janet developed after earlier attempts to help patients "erase" or continue to dissociate their troubling memories (Leys, 1994). Brown also noted that the treatment was less effective in both eliciting vivid recall and reducing hysterical symptoms if done after the soldier left the war zone and returned home. Thus, Brown's clinical work and the Myers/McDougall and Janet conceptualizations foreshadowed the later development of cognitive-behavioral therapy for acute stress disorder (ASD) and PTSD, as well as narrative and self-reconstructive therapies for Complex PTSD (Herman, 1992).

Additional conceptualizations of PTSD have been formulated in response to war or major sociopolitical upheavals (Lasiuk & Hegadoren, 2006). During World War II, prevention in the US military was attempted by predeployment screening to identify and refuse to enroll "at-risk" men as soldiers, a strategy that failed due to the numerous psychiatric casualties that resulted to even the "healthy" recruits when they were faced with the horror, terror, and deprivations that occur to combatants in war. During and after World War II and the Korean conflict, military psychiatrists such as Abraham Kardiner and Herbert Spiegel described psychiatric casualties as "war neurosis," "combat stress reaction," or "combat fatigue." They formulated principles of immediate prevention and treatment that emphasized the affected soldier's temporary removal from danger, rest, and the maintenance of ongoing contact with the combat unit.

As discussed above, before World War II, there was no single accepted diagnosis for the problems experienced by people exposed to an extreme (psychologically traumatic) stressor. Several conditions such as "railway spine" and "soldier's heart," which appear to reflect posttraumatic stress, were described in the medical literature in the late nineteenth and early twentieth centuries.

The Vietnam War was singularly important in codifying what would become known as PTSD. In Vietnam, young men from the United States and several other countries (e.g., France, the United Kingdom, Australia) were conscripted and deployed in a war whose purpose and legitimacy became increasingly controversial on the home front and among the combatants themselves. Returning military personnel who had suffered extreme exposure fighting the war or in equally hazardous supportive duties (such as medical corpsmen, nurses, and physicians; convoy truck drivers; and logistical personnel stationed on bases that came under attack) were given less than welcoming homecomings, and the war itself ended ignominiously. These veterans suffered a higher rate of posttraumatic and psychiatric symptoms than had been previously associated with any conflict (Kulka et al., 1990). The US Veterans' Administration was inundated and began to research the symptoms and to find treatment methods that were effective in ameliorating them. A "post-Vietnam traumatic syndrome" began to be identified among returning soldiers.

The time period surrounding Vietnam was rife with major societal change and turmoil. The assassinations of President Kennedy, Robert Kennedy, and Martin Luther King Jr. left an indelible imprint of violence and loss on the entire nation. The civil rights, feminist, and human rights movements in the 1960s and 1970s galvanized the recognition of social inequalities and violence against various populations worldwide, including women and children, both in the home and in the community. Millions died internationally as the result of political oppression, and tens of millions suffered life-threatening deprivations and life-altering stigma and discrimination as a result of their race, ethnicity, culture, nationality, religion, gender, and political and personal beliefs. Mental health professionals and advocates documented traumatic syndromes in the aftermath of rape, child physical and sexual abuse, and other forms of violence (i.e., "rape trauma syndrome," "battered child syndrome," "battered woman syndrome"), as well as among survivors of genocide, torture, and other forms of mass violence.

"Post-Vietnam syndrome" (Kulka et al., 1990) was identified as including symptoms that were similar to those identified by the psychiatrist Abraham Kardiner after World War II, in three major groupings: reexperiencing, in which memories or flashbacks of the traumatic events recurred, often repeatedly and with great intensity and distress; emotional numbing, in which the individual was emotionally detached and deadened; and hyperarousal, in which the individual experienced hypervigilance (i.e., feeling constantly on guard for danger) and increased irritability and physiological reactivity. In response to social and political pressure to include a posttraumatic diagnosis, the American Psychiatric Association incorporated a new diagnosis based on symptoms from these three domains—PTSD—in the 1980 third edition of the *Diagnostic and Statistical Manual (DSM-III)*.

In the *DSM-I*, the diagnosis most comparable to PTSD was "Gross Stress Reactions," which was a subtype within a broader group of "Transient Situational Personality Disturbances" (Wilson, 1989). The condition was considered to be temporary, in contrast to more permanent neuroses or psychoses, in response to "overwhelming fear" created by exposure to "severe physical demands or extreme emotional stress such as in combat or in civilian catastrophe (fire, earthquake, explosion, etc.).'' The definition next adds a key clarification: "In many instances, this diagnosis applies to previously more or less 'normal' persons who have experienced intolerable stress.'' Although limiting the symptoms to an undefined "transient" period of time, the definition foreshadows subsequent views of PTSD as a response by an otherwise "normal" person to abnormally stressful events or circumstances.

In the *DSM-II*, that diagnosis was dropped and replaced with "Adjustment Reaction of Adult Life'' (Wilson, 1989). Although the forms that these "adjustment reactions" might take were not specified, this diagnosis can be viewed as a step in the direction of PTSD by eliminating the reference to "personality" and providing an extensive listing of specific types of stressors potentially severe enough to elicit clinically significant problems in adjustment. However, in addition to combat stress reactions, only two additional examples of stressors and adjustment reactions were provided in the main text of the *DSM-II*, one of which was quite rare (inaccurate testimony provided by a person sentenced to death), while the other reflected what appears to be sexist bias (hostility and suicidality associated with an unwanted pregnancy).

In the *DSM-III*, PTSD was explicitly defined as involving three types of symptoms "to a recognizable stressor that would evoke significant symptoms of distress in almost everyone" (American Psychiatric Association, 1968). The emergence of social movements and protest in the 1960s and 1970s brought the previously hidden or overlooked problems of sexual assault, domestic violence, and war trauma vividly into public awareness. Whether these stressors occurred only once (such as an isolated physical or sexual assault) or repeatedly and chronically (such as in child maltreatment or war), their adverse effects were not "transient" for many people. The *DSM-III* PTSD symptoms included unwanted memories ("intrusive reexperiencing," including "flashbacks"), numbing of emotions and detachment from relationships, and completely unprecedented changes in personality (such as survivor guilt or problems with sleep). Although the diagnosis was lauded by its advocates as a major advance in understanding mental illness, detractors decried a diagnosis that was included in response to pressure from antiwar psychiatrists and other advocates. Moreover, although the diagnosis was adopted by clinicians and researchers studying child abuse and other forms of domestic and community violence against women and children, they soon raised concerns that the diagnostic criteria based on war trauma experienced mostly by male soldiers in late adolescence/adulthood varied substantially from symptoms seen in these other traumatized populations (Herman, 1992).

Judith Herman (1992) described forms of traumatic stressors that were repetitive and prolonged experiences of captivity, coercion, torture, or other forms of profound violation or humiliation (see the description of an alternative diagnosis of "enduring personality change after catastrophic experience" in Box 1.5). She described these as "complex trauma" and proposed a new diagnostic conceptualization based on the accumulating research findings regarding the aftereffects of domestic trauma, which she termed "Complex PTSD" (see below for further discussion of this). Three other diagnoses are not necessarily related to exposure to traumatic stressors but tend to often be related to early childhood psychological trauma. The first are the dissociative disorders, such as Dissociative Amnesia (*DSM* 300.12), Depersonalization/ Derealization Disorder (*DSM*-5 300.6), or Dissociative Identity Disorder (DID)

Box 1.5 America Versus the World: Competing Systems for Defining the Diagnosis of PTSD

Internationally, the WHO has established an *ICD* with diagnoses for all psychiatric as well as medical illnesses. Although the *ICD* tends to be accepted worldwide for medical diagnoses, in the mental health field, the American Psychiatric Association created its *DSM* as a separate system of diagnoses from the *ICD*. When PTSD was first established as a diagnosis in the late 1970s and early 1980s, there were few differences between its definition in the *DSM* and the *ICD*. However, as clinical and scientific understand of PTSD has evolved over the past 4 decades, the two systems have diverged in important ways in how they define and describe PTSD.

As early as 1837, the British medical statistician William Farr first articulated principles for a system to classify all types of diseases. At the Second International Statistical Society meeting in 1855, Farr presented a *Report on Nomenclature and Statistical Classification of Diseases*, in which he proposed classifying diseases in five categories: epidemic diseases, constitutional illnesses affecting the entire body, local diseases affecting specific anatomical sites, developmental diseases of childhood or old age, and, of greatest relevance to PTSD, diseases directly caused by violence. In 1860, Florence Nightingale urged the Fourth International Statistical Society conference to adopt Farr's system in her *Proposals for a Uniform Plan of Hospital Statistics*. However, no classification system was widely affirmed until 1900, when 26 countries, including North American nations represented by the American Public Health Association, adopted Bertillon's *International Classification of Causes of Death*. This classification system was updated every 10 years, and at the fifth decennial international conference in 1938, it was proposed to develop a companion system to classify diseases. Many nations developed systems for classifying diseases, but finally in 1946, at the International Health Conference, the WHO was designated as responsible for convening experts to create a consensus sixth revision of the classification system of causes of death. This was unveiled in 1948 as the *Manual of the International Statistical Classification of Diseases, Injuries, and Causes of Death*.

In 1955, 1965, 1975, and 1990, international conferences were held by the WHO to initiate the seventh, eighth, ninth, and tenth (current) revisions of what became known more simply as the *ICD*. The *ICD-10* was put online in 2003 and has had nine updates to this version, with the most recent occurring in 2015. Each diagnosis in the *ICD* is a distinct physical condition for which there is a numerical code (e.g., I21 is the code for a myocardial infarction (heart attack), and C50 is the code for breast cancer). In the mental health field, *ICD* diagnoses exist for mental disorders ranging from conditions primarily beginning in childhood (such as attention deficit hyperactivity disorder or pervasive developmental disorder) to conditions involving problems with impaired reality orientation (such as schizophrenia), mood regulation (such as major depressive episodes or bipolar disorder), eating (such as anorexia or bulimia nervosa), dissociation (such as DID), substance use (such as alcohol dependence or cocaine abuse), and anxiety (such as PTSD, phobias, or social anxiety disorder).

The way in which PTSD has been defined and described in the *ICD* has changed over its several editions, just as it has in the *DSM*. In the 1955 *ICD-7* and the 1968 *ICD-8a*, the only stressor-related disorder involved transient rather than chronic stress reactions, paralleling the *DSM-I* Gross Stress Reactions and *DSM-II* Adjustment Reactions of Adult Life diagnoses. The *ICD* diagnosis of PTSD was established in the *ICD-9* in 1978, under the heading of "Adult Onset Adjustment Reaction." A separate category of "Acute Reaction to Stress" also was set forth in the *ICD-9*, including separate subcategories reflecting reactions characterized by disturbance of emotions, consciousness, or psychomotor functions. The *DSM-III* did not distinguish acute and chronic posttraumatic stress reactions (categorizing them all as PTSD), and *DSM-III-R* provided no diagnosis for traumatic stress reactions in the first 30 days after a traumatic stressor. Thus, in describing Acute Stress Reaction as severe symptoms in the immediate wake of experiencing a traumatic stressor, the *ICD-9* was more precise and complete than its *DSM* counterparts.

An updated description of PTSD and Acute Stress Reaction was provided in the most recent (*ICD-10*) edition, which was published at approximately the same time (1992) that the *DSM-IV* (American Psychiatric Association, 1994) was being finalized (Lasiuk & Hegadoren, 2006). The *ICD-10* and *DSM-IV* PTSD and Acute Stress Reaction (*ICD-10*) or Disorder (*DSM-IV*) diagnoses involved very similar but not exactly identical definitions of the stressor criterion, symptom criteria, and duration and functional impairment criteria. However, there are several important differences between the *ICD-10* and the *DSM-IV*, some of which foreshadow changes in the *DSM* that occurred 20 years later in the *DSM-5*. In the *ICD-10*:

- Both the PTSD and Acute Stress Reaction diagnoses were placed in the "Reactions to Severe Stress and Adjustment Disorders" category, while the *DSM-IV* continued to describe them (as did the *DSM-III and III-R*) as "Anxiety Disorders."
- The Acute Stress Reaction diagnosis involves a variety of possible symptoms that tend to ebb and flow rather than remaining constant, in the immediate (i.e., up to 3 days) wake of a traumatic experience—including anxiety, depression, anger, grief, hyperarousal, intrusive reexperiencing, avoidance/withdrawal, and dissociation. The *DSM-IV* required at least one intrusive reexperiencing and three dissociative symptoms in addition to avoidance, emotional numbing, and hyperarousal symptoms, despite evidence that no single set of symptoms characterizes most or all persons who are adversely affected in the acute aftermath of traumatic stressors (Marshall, Spitzer, & Liebowitz, 1999).
- An entirely new Disorder of Adult Personality and Behavior was added: called "enduring personality change after a catastrophic experience." EPCACE must be chronic (i.e., lasting for at least 2 years), and it involves "a hostile or distrustful attitude toward the world, social withdrawal, feelings of emptiness or hopelessness, a chronic feeling of 'being on edge' as if constantly threatened, and estrangement" following exposure to "concentration camp experiences, disasters, … torture, … [or] prolonged … exposure to terrorism … [or] captivity with an imminent possibility of being killed." EPCACE includes some similar symptoms to PTSD (such as emotional numbing, avoidance, and hyperarousal) but is a more chronic existential syndrome that parallels Herman's (1992) Complex PTSD.

(*DSM* 300.14) or "multiple personality disorder" in the *International Classification of Diseases (ICD)* (F44.8). The second is a personality disorder diagnosis labeled "borderline personality disorder" in the *DSM* (BPD; 301.83) and the *ICD*'s "emotionally unstable personality disorder" (F60.3). A number of other psychiatric disorders have been found to be associated with a history of exposure to traumatic stressors (such as addictive, anxiety, disruptive behavior, eating, mood, psychotic, sexual, and somatoform disorders) and often occur comorbidly with PTSD, as we will discuss in greater detail in Chapter 3.

From stress reactions to traumatic stressors and posttraumatic disorders

Traumatic events and circumstances were originally considered to be abnormal or atypical (i.e., "outside the range of normal human experience," as described originally in Criterion A (i.e., the traumatic stressor) of the *DSM-III-R* (American Psychiatric Association, 1987)); however, as epidemiological evidence has accumulated to demonstrate that a majority of adults (e.g., Kessler, Sonnega, Bromet, & Hughes, 1995) and a substantial minority of children (e.g., Copeland, Keeler, Angold, & Costello, 2007; McLaughlin et al., 2013) are exposed to or experience traumatic events, there has been a shift to defining traumatic events without any qualifications about their normalcy. The types of stressors specified in this and all previous and subsequent *DSM* definitions involve physical exposure to death and dying or to grotesque physical injury, with the unwanted pregnancy in *DSM-II* as the only (and, unfortunately, a highly stigmatizing for women) exception. Remarkably absent are high-impact interpersonal stressors such as childhood maltreatment, rape, or intimate partner violence.

After PTSD first officially appeared in the third edition of the *DSM* (1980) as an Anxiety Disorder (and in the *ICD*-9 as an Adjustment Reaction Disorder), it was revised to provide a more detailed specification of the diagnostic criteria in the revision of the *DSM* published in 1987 (*DSM-III-R*). PTSD in the *DSM-III-R* included five components that continued to be the basis for the diagnosis (albeit in altered forms), until an important expansion occurred in the most recent version (the *DSM*-5). The first component ("Criterion A") of the PTSD diagnosis is the "traumatic stressor," which was defined in the *DSM-III* as exposure to a stressor or set of stressors that are "generally outside the range of usual human experience" (American Psychiatric Association, 1980, p. 236) and that "evoke significant symptoms of distress in almost everyone" (American Psychiatric Association, 1980, p. 238; see Lasiuk & Hegadoren, 2006). Exposure to a traumatic stressor need not be recent; it may have occurred many years or even decades earlier.

The next three elements or "criteria" for the *DSM-III-R* PTSD diagnosis referred to symptoms of distress that the person is experiencing at the time of the diagnosis. These three criteria included more detailed definitions of symptoms than in the *DSM-III* and the removal of a symptom reflecting memory impairment and relocating of the avoidance symptoms to include them with emotional numbing. The *DSM-III-R* organization of symptoms into three domains remained as the core structure of the PTSD diagnosis for more than 25 years.

The first symptom criterion of the *DSM-III-R* PTSD diagnosis ("Criterion B") required the current persistent reexperiencing of the traumatic stressor in at least one of four ways.

- B1: memories of the traumatic event(s) that are recurrent (i.e., repetitive), intrusive (i.e., unwanted and involuntary), and distressing;
- B2: repeated distressing dreams of the traumatic event(s);
- B3: suddenly acting as if the traumatic event was happening all over again (often in the form of a dissociative episode called a "flashback"), which may occur when intoxicated but also when not under the influence of any substances;
- B4: severe distress when reminded of the traumatic event(s): "intense psychological distress at exposure to events that symbolize or resemble an aspect of the traumatic event, including anniversaries."

The second symptom criterion of the *DSM-III-R PTSD* diagnosis ("Criterion C") required that the person was experiencing at least *three* symptoms involving the avoidance of reminders of the traumatic stressor event(s) and a substantial reduction in the ability to feel emotions, such as enjoyment of pleasurable activities, closeness or love in relationships, and optimism about the future (i.e., "emotional numbing"). The symptoms must *not* have been present before the person was exposed to the stressor(s). The symptoms could have occurred in any combination and did not have to include all of the symptoms at the same time. The first two "C" symptoms are the avoidance symptoms, and the third through seventh "C" symptoms are the emotional numbing symptoms:

- C1: efforts to avoid thoughts or feelings associated with the traumatic event(s);
- C2: efforts to avoid activities or situations that evoke memories of the event(s);
- C3: inability to recall an important aspect of the event(s) ("psychogenic amnesia");
- C4: markedly diminished interest in significant activities ("anhedonia"), which in young children may take the form of regression in previously established developmental skills such as toilet training or receptive or expressive language;
- C5: feeling emotionally detached or estranged from people ("social detachment");
- C6: limited ability or unable to feel most emotions, such as loving feelings ("emotional numbing");
- C7: expecting to have one's life cut short, such as not expecting to have or complete a career, family, or long life ("sense of a foreshortened future").

The third symptom criterion for the *DSM-III-R* PTSD diagnosis ("Criterion D") required at least *two* symptoms of persistent excessive physical arousal that were not present before the stressor(s) occurred. As with avoidance and emotional numbing symptoms, the "hyperarousal" symptoms may occur in any combination and need not include every symptom simultaneously.

- D1: difficulty falling or staying asleep;
- D2: irritability or outbursts of anger;
- D3: problems with mental concentration;
- D4: feeling watchful and on guard even when not necessary ("hypervigilance");
- D5: easily startled, including an exaggerated physical and behavioral reaction;
- D6: physically reactive to reminders of the stressor event(s).

The fifth or "duration" criterion ("E") for PTSD in the *DSM-III-R* required that the B, C, and D criterion symptoms had to be experienced for a period of *at least 30 days*. Not all of the symptoms had to be experienced every day during this period. In fact, some of the symptoms may have occurred as infrequently as only once as long as the total of the PTSD symptoms caused "impairment or "disturbance" to the person for that entire duration. The diagnosis may be applicable for periods of time much longer than a month—potentially for decades.

The diagnosis also specified that it was possible for the PTSD symptoms to have a "delayed onset"—that is, to not begin until at least 6 months after exposure to the stressor. This onset specification is not a requirement to diagnose PTSD but provides a description of a difference in the development of the disorder that can help the clinician or researcher to distinguish between people who began to suffer PTSD symptoms relatively soon after experiencing psychological trauma (acute reaction) versus others who appeared to be relatively symptom free for a long period and then developed PTSD (delayed onset or expression) (see Chapter 2). In turn, both of these can develop into chronic PTSD. For example, PTSD has been observed to develop in trauma-exposed individuals who are apparently symptom-free or at most mildly symptomatic and not functionally impaired if changes occur in their lives that subject them to other major stressors, whether traumatic or not (such as widowhood, retirement, job or residence changes, the birth or developmental transitions of children) that serve as reminders of the trauma or to new incidents of the same or different traumatic stressors.

The subsequent fourth edition of the *DSM* (*DSM-IV* in 1994, and the "text revision" of and *DSM-IV-TR*; American Psychiatric Association, 1994, 2000), as well as the 10th revision of the *ICD* (first in use in 1994) retained the basic structure of the *DSM-III-R* and *ICD-9* PTSD diagnoses, but it made significant modifications in the traumatic stressor criterion and some revisions in the specification and placement of symptoms in the B, C, and D criteria. The requirement that traumatic events must be outside the range of usual human experience was deleted and replaced by a two-part Criterion A that included both an *objective* definition of the traumatic stressor (a life-threatening event or a violation of bodily integrity, called "Criterion A1") and a subjective response at the time or soon after of extreme fear, helplessness or horror (called "Criterion A2"). The objective aspect (Criterion A1) was expanded in the *DSM-IV* to include events that were *witnessed or indirectly experienced*, as well as events directly occurring to the person. In addition, the *DSM-IV* added a sixth criterion ("Criterion F") that required that the symptoms had an adverse effect on social, occupational, or other important aspects of the person's ability to have a successful and satisfying life ("healthy functioning"). *DSM-IV* also specified the disorder's chronicity. "Acute" PTSD was defined as having a duration of less than 3 months. "Chronic" PTSD required a duration of 3 or more months. Finally, the *DSM-IV* also added ASD as a diagnosis (see Box 1.4 for a description of "Acute Stress Reaction" in the *ICD-10*), similar to PTSD but with more focus on dissociative symptoms and with the requirement that it must begin within 3 days and end within 30 days of experiencing the traumatic stressor (see Chapter 2 for additional discussion).

The changes in the PTSD diagnosis in *DSM-IV* and *DSM-IV-TR* are based to a large extent on clinicians' observations of how people exposed to traumatic stressors coped or became impaired, as well as scientific research that has tested various hypotheses based on clinical observation. For example, it is apparent clinically that few people have every PTSD symptom at any one point in time. This is consistent with other *DSM* psychiatric diagnoses, none of which requires that *every* symptom be present. Scientists describe this as "equifinality," which means that there are many different but equal ("equi") ways in which a person may finally suffer a psychiatric disorder ("finality"). Many factors determine whether, and how exactly, each person with a psychiatric disorder such as PTSD actually experiences symptoms, based on individual differences in biology and genetics, personality, cultural and religious beliefs, personal and family background and experiences, age, gender, and socioeconomic opportunities and barriers (see Chapter 3). For PTSD specifically, research studies have shown that the symptoms within each of the three Criterion (B, C, and D) sets tend to occur in combination even though they do not usually all occur simultaneously. The PTSD symptom criteria also reflect theory (Hobfoll, 2012; Horowitz and Smit, 2008) and research (see Chapters 3 and 4) that indicate that persistent stress reactions after a traumatic event tend to occur when distressing memories of the event persist (Criterion B) despite the person's attempts to avoid reminders (Criterion C, avoidance) and that over time this leads to a kind of emotional exhaustion (Criterion C, emotional numbing) and a state of being on guard mentally and on edge physically due to never feeling really safe and, as a result, coping with hypervigilance (Criterion D).

Complex PTSD: can traumatic stress affect a person's core self?

Traumatic events take many forms. Terr (1991) distinguished between "Type I" single-incident trauma (e.g., an event that is "out of the blue" and thus unexpected, such as a traumatic accident or a natural disaster, a terrorist attack, a single episode of abuse or assault, or witnessing violence) and "Type II" complex or repetitive trauma (e.g., ongoing abuse, domestic violence, community violence, war, or genocide). Type II trauma is more prevalent than typically recognized (i.e., affecting as many as 1 in 7 to 1 in 10 children), more often occurs in combination or cumulatively (i.e., "poly-victimization"; Finkelhor, Ormrod, & Turner, 2007), and usually involves a fundamental betrayal of trust in primary relationships because it is often interpersonal, perpetrated by someone known or related to the victim. Complex or "Type II" trauma not only is associated with a much higher risk (33–75%) for the development of PTSD than Type I trauma (10–20%) (Copeland et al., 2007; Kessler et al., 1995), but it also may compromise or alter a person's psychobiological and socioemotional development when it occurs at critical developmental periods. Such "developmentally adverse interpersonal traumas" (Ford, 2005) are "complex" (Herman, 1992) because they place the person at risk not only for recurrent anxiety (e.g., PTSD; other anxiety disorders) but also for interruptions and breakdowns in the most fundamental outcomes of healthy psychobiological development: the integrity of the body, the development of a healthy identity and a coherent personality, and secure attachment leading to the ability to have healthy and reciprocal relationships (Cook et al., 2005; Courtois & Ford, 2013; van der Kolk, 2005).

Complex traumatic stressors therefore are a subset of the larger universe of traumatic stressors that have as their unique trademark a *compromise of the individual's self-development and psychophysiological integrity*. The timing of its occurrence—in critical windows of development during childhood when self-definition and self-regulation are being formed and consolidated—and the very nature of complex trauma—the disruption or distortion of fundamental attachment security due to betrayal of the developing child's security and trust in core relationships (often called attachment or relational trauma)—distinguish complex trauma from all other forms of psychological trauma. Complex trauma thus involves not only the shock of fear but also more fundamentally a violation of and challenge to the fragile and newly emerging self and immature mind-body. Complex trauma often leaves the child unable to self-regulate (i.e., to control her or his feelings, beliefs, intentions, and actions), to achieve a sense of self-integrity (i.e., the feeling and belief that one is a unique, whole, coherent, and worthy individual, inherently loveable and capable of being loved), or to experience relationships as nurturing and reliable resources that support self-regulation and self-integrity.

Due to compromised self-regulation, self-integrity, and attachment security, complex trauma creates objective threats not only to physical survival—as is the case in all forms of psychological trauma—but moreover to the development and survival of the self. The nature of the objective threat involved in complex traumas often encompasses features that go beyond obvious instances of a threat of death or violation of bodily integrity as currently defined in Criterion A1 of the PTSD diagnosis in the *DSM-IV TR* and *DSM*-5 (American Psychiatric Association, 2000, 2013). For example, when emotional abuse by an adult caregiver involves systematic attacks upon the psychological integrity and the very selfhood of a child, it may not be immediately life-threatening and may not involve violent or sexual violations of the child's bodily integrity, but nevertheless it may lead to longstanding problems with self-regulation that are associated with psychobiological stress dysregulation and reactivity (Spinazzola et al., 2014; Teicher, Samson, Polcari, & McGreenery, 2006). Thus, the threat to self-integrity posed by developmentally adverse interpersonal stressors, particularly when interwoven into a developing child's primary family/caregiver relationships, may induce long-term biological as well as psychosocial stress reactivity even in the absence of threat to life or violation of bodily integrity (Ford, 2005). Consistent with these findings, a diagnosis of "Developmental Trauma Disorder" (DTD; Ford et al., 2013)—proposed to but not included by the *DSM*-5 workgroup—requires exposure to "developmentally adverse interpersonal trauma" (e.g., abuse, betrayal, abandonment, threats to bodily integrity) as its objective (A1) criterion.

Similarly, in complex trauma the individual's subjective reactions during stressful experiences extend beyond those that define psychological trauma in the *DSM-IV TR* PTSD Criterion A2 (i.e., extreme fear, helplessness, or horror). For example, "resignation" and "defeat" might be cognates for helplessness, as might "rage" or "betrayal" for horror. However, the DTD A2 criteria provide more than just a better detailed operationalization of the subjective sense of traumatization than that used in the traditional definition of PTSD. DTD's more complex subjective reactions articulate aspects of psychological shock that are not clearly implied solely by the emotional responses of fear, helplessness, or horror. The inclusion of betrayal is derived from clinical and theoretical work done on the distinct phenomenology and clinical sequelae of "betrayal trauma" (Freyd, DePrince, & Gleaves, 2007). Including shame also expands the clinician's focus from fear or anxiety to the sense of a damaged self and negative self-worth (Feiring, Taska, & Lewis, 2002). Including rage is consistent with research suggesting that children exposed to traumatic victimization may be defiantly oppositional and victimizing toward others as well as anxious and that these responses may extend into adolescence (Ford, Steinberg, Hawke, Levine, & Zhang, 2012) and adulthood (Ford & Gomez, 2015).

Identifying complex trauma as a distinct subset of other types of traumatic events and circumstances thus provides the clinician and researcher with a basis for identifying individuals who have experienced not only the reactions of extreme fear, helplessness, and horror but also disruption of the emergent capacity for psychobiological self-regulation and secure attachment. In addition to hyperarousal and hypervigilance in relation to *external* danger, complex trauma poses the *internal* threat of being unable to self-regulate, self-organize, or draw upon relationships to regain self-integrity. Traumatized individuals might then rely on external behaviors and substances (i.e., self-injury, suicidality, sexual behavior, drugs, alcohol, food) to regulate these internal states (Ford & Gomez, 2015; Ford, Steinberg, & Zhang, 2011).

As defined by Herman (1992), Complex PTSD symptoms include:

1. *extreme emotional instability and distress* that differ from depression or manic-depressive illness ("emotion dysregulation");
2. pathological *dissociation* (see Box 1.5);
3. physical health problems that cannot be explained or fully treated medically (*"somatization"*; see Chapter 6);
4. *fixed and virulently negative beliefs* about (i) oneself (such as viewing self as fundamentally psychologically damaged), (ii) relationships (such as expecting to be horribly betrayed, exploited, or totally abandoned), and (iii) spirituality (such as a fundamental loss of spiritual faith or hope).

The emotion dysregulation symptoms as defined are quite similar to the primary symptoms of BPD and to a comparable personality disorder in the *ICD* ("emotionally unstable personality disorder, borderline type"). Interestingly, these diagnoses are consistent with research findings from a national study in the United States of patients diagnosed with BPD who were found to be more likely to have severe dysphoria and episodes of dissociation and self-harm and to generally be functionally impaired if they had experienced sexual abuse in childhood (Zanarini et al., 2002). They have also been shown to have histories of invalidation by primary caregivers in addition to experiences of more frank abuse and neglect (Ford & Courtois, 2014). Studies of military veterans with PTSD also have shown that two personality dimensions— "negative emotionality" and "disconstraint" (i.e., difficulty inhibiting strong emotional or behavioral impulses)—lead people with chronic PTSD to be more prone to drug and alcohol use disorders (Miller, Vogt, Mozley, Kaloupek, & Keane, 2006).

A combination of extreme negative emotionality and impulsive lack of self-control with PTSD thus may distinguish complex PTSD (or the *ICD* "enduring personality changes" diagnosis) from those that make up the *DSM* borderline and *ICD* emotionally unstable—borderline personality disorders. In a recent review of the literature on BPD and Complex PTSD, Ford and Courtois (2014) found them to be distinct diagnoses but with considerable overlap. However, individuals with BPD are hypervigilant and reactive about real or perceived threats of abandonment and rejection by other people, whereas individuals with Complex PTSD tend to be hypervigilant and reactive about real or perceived threats of a broader range of types of victimization (such as violence, violation, or exploitation) and loss (such as accidental or unintentional separations or unexpected death).

PTSD becomes complex in the DSM-5

The revised fifth edition of the DSM was published in 2013 amidst considerable controversy. In terms of the posttraumatic disorders, on the basis of research findings, they were moved from being categorized as anxiety-based disorders to a new category of Trauma and Stressor-Related Disorders. The ASD diagnosis remains in a similar form. The PTSD diagnosis was changed and expanded to include four main criteria (it was formerly three; avoidance was placed in its own category apart from numbing and combined with trauma-related changes in belief systems and cognitions), and it now includes several symptoms found in the proposed Complex PTSD and DTD diagnoses. In addition, based on new research findings, two new subtypes of PTSD were added: *dissociative subtype* (Lanius, Brand, Vermetten, Frewen, & Spiegel, 2012; Lanius et al., 2010) and *preschool-age subtype* (Scheeringa, Zeanah & Cohen, 2011). The dissociative subtype emphasizes a shutdown or blunted reaction to traumatic stressors characterized by dissociation, which has been shown to be related to different patterns of brain activation as well as in bodily reactivity than the hyperarousal and active avoidance symptoms that have classically been used to define PTSD. The dissociative subtype also features prominent symptoms that are very similar to those described in DTD for children and youth and Complex PTSD for adults. The preschool PTSD subtype adds that dissociative intrusive reexperiencing (such as flashbacks) may occur in play and does not include persistently altered beliefs or self-harm (because these do not tend to crystallize as fixed and consciously articulated attitudes or behaviors at this young age). In part due to the smaller set of symptoms, and because avoidance behaviors can be difficult to distinguish from developmentally normative shyness or aversions in early childhood, the preschool criteria for PTSD also require only one symptom of avoidance or "negative alterations in cognitions"— and rather than relying upon children's stated thoughts to assess "cognitions," they are defined in terms of problems with negative or positive emotions, constricted play, or social withdrawal (Box 1.6).

The types of events that qualify as traumatic stressors have been expanded in the American Psychiatric Association's (2013, p. 271) *DSM*-5. Traumatic stressors include actual or threatened physical and sexual assaults, abuse, or injury; witnessing severe violence or death (or learning about this occurring to a close family member

Box 1.6 Understanding Dissociation

Dissociation has been defined by the *DSM*-5 as "a disruption of and/or discontinuity in the usually integrated functions of consciousness, memory, identity, emotion, perception, body representation, motor control, and behavior" (American Psychiatric Association, 2013, p. 291). However, in common usage, even by clinicians and researchers, dissociation is often oversimplified as a state of mental detachment that involves feeling "spaced out," "in a daze," "as if in a dream," "on automatic pilot," "looking down from out of your body," or "blanking out" and "losing time" (i.e., having gaps in one's memory). These are potential side effects of dissociation and are experiences that can happen to anyone.

However, pathological (i.e., clinically severe) dissociation is more than just experiencing an altered state of consciousness. In the *DSM*-5, dissociative symptoms are defined as "(a) unbidden intrusions into awareness and behavior, with accompanying losses of continuity in subjective experience (i.e., "positive" dissociation symptoms such as fragmentation of identity, depersonalization, and derealization) and/or (b) inability to access information or to control mental functions that normally are readily available to access or control (i.e., "negative" dissociative symptoms such as amnesia" (American Psychiatric Association, 2013, p. 291). The *DSM*-5 also notes that "dissociative disorders are frequently found in the aftermath of trauma" and purposefully placed the listing of dissociative disorders immediately adjacent to but (because it has not been established scientifically or clinically that exposure to traumatic stressors is a necessary precondition for dissociative disorders) separate from the class of "Trauma- and Stressor-Related Disorders" in which PTSD (and ASD) are located in *DSM*-5.

Van der Hart, Nijenhuis, & Steele, (2006), after extensive historical and clinical research, defined pathological dissociation as "a division of the personality into two types of dissociative parts," with each of these part-selves functioning as if it was the entire person, with very distinct "ideas of the world and their relation to this world." Thus, dissociation can be understood as a fragmentation of the self into parts, not just a temporary loss of consciousness or normal awareness. However, this does *not* mean that anyone who experiences dissociative symptoms will have separate "multiple personalities" or "dissociative identities." Multiple personality disorder, currently described in the *DSM-IV* as DID, is a very rare form of extreme dissociative fragmentation. Most people who experience even quite significant problems with dissociation do *not* develop alternate selves ("alters") but instead develop a split in their self and personality that leads them periodically—typically when experiencing a stress reaction or emotional distress—to not be able to maintain an organized identity or self. Dissociation is a form of disorganization of the self, which in extreme cases such as DID may involve relying on artificially divided parts of the self as if they were not only distinct states of mind but interchangeable and distinct personalities.

(Continued)

Box 1.6 Continued

The origins of pathological dissociation are not fully understood, but research studies have shown that children and adults who experience pathological dissociation commonly have had to survive severe interpersonal trauma in childhood. Complex trauma in childhood often involves a breakdown in primary relationships (such as when a parent is severely neglectful or abusive, or violent toward other family members) that lead a child to understandably question whether they can trust those whom they otherwise would love and most fundamentally depend on. As a self-protective strategy, the child may adopt a detached attitude of silence, secrecy, or denial.

This circumstance has been labeled the *second injury* (Symonds, 1975) or *betrayal trauma* (DePrince & Freyd, 2007). Children, more than adults, are prone to use dissociation to cope with such overwhelming circumstances (Putnam, 2003), and it is now hypothesized that this style transforms the personality, preventing the child from developing a complete and organized identify and self. Young children exposed to betrayal trauma by caregivers often develop what has been described as a *disorganized/dissociative* attachment style in childhood (Lyons-Ruth, Dutra, Schuder, & Bianchi, 2006). This means that the child relates to the people with whom she or he should feel emotionally closest and most secure as if they are always about to do something upsetting or even seriously harmful. Instead of feeling "securely" attached to these close relationships, the child alternates between one moment feeling and acting desperately needy and dependent, the next moment outraged and defiant, and the next moment withdrawn and indifferent.

These rapid, and apparently unconscious, shifts in the child's core feelings and beliefs can lead to the psychological equivalent of fault lines in the child's identity. When a child's identity is fragmented in this manner, she or he is experiencing the pathological form of dissociation that is more than just a problem with attention or mood or anxiety.

The result is a child—and later an adult—who maintains a dissociation, or split, between the "front" that she or he presents to the world—an "as-if" or "apparently normal" personality that seems functional but is numb to and even unaware of traumatic experiences or stress reactions—and a deeply injured and dysregulated "emotional" personality that is chronically overwhelmed by ordinary life because of struggling to survive every moment as if it was a new catastrophe (Van der Hart, Nijenhuis, & Steele, 2006). The child's very personality and identity have been split apart, in stark contrast to the joining together of disparate parts of the personality that occurs as a child grows into adolescence and adulthood with healthy psychological development. Note that this disassociation, or splitting apart, of the self and personal identity is not something that a child chooses to do or does on purpose. Extremely traumatized children who are psychologically precocious may be aware of the dissociative splitting that occurs as they attempt to adapt to and survive extremely dangerous or violating experiences, and they may come to believe that they actually chose to develop different "selves" or to hide their true self behind a false front.

However, there is substantial evidence from biological studies (see Chapter 6) of traumatized children and dissociative adults that posttraumatic dissociation is an automatic defensive reaction and not a conscious choice. A major problem with posttraumatic dissociation is that it cannot be turned on and off at will, although the person often thinks he or she has that ability. This is similar to PTSD's unwanted memories, which are "intrusive" because they intrude despite being unwanted and cannot be turned on and off by simply trying to forget or not think about them. In fact, intrusive trauma memories and dissociation both tend to be prolonged and worsened rather than improved or eliminated by attempts to avoid or mentally control the troubling memories or the self-protective shifts from one state of mind or self to another.

Dissociation is not definitely caused by psychological trauma, and most people who have experienced traumatic stressors (including those who develop PTSD) do not have severe problems with dissociation. However, dissociation is not formally assessed when diagnosing PTSD, except if the person describes intrusive reexperiencing symptoms that take the form of "flashbacks." A flash-back is an unwanted memory that occurs so vividly that the person feels as though the past event is happening to her at that very moment. This feeling of being lost in a past experience may be dissociative (e.g., if the person feels as if she is more like who she was at a time in the past when the traumatic event was occurring) but need not necessarily involve dissociation (e.g., if the ter-rible event seems as though it is happening all over again, but the person is able to recognize that it is really only a memory and stays aware of her cur-rent circumstances and self). Dissociation may occur in other ways, however, that are not included as symptoms of PTSD. Therefore, in both clinical and research assessment with people who have experienced psychological trauma, particularly if the traumatic stressors involved a betrayal of trust by caregivers in childhood, it is important to also include dissociative disorder symptoms rather than assuming that dissociation is not a problem. The International Society for the Study of Trauma and Dissociation originally did not include "trauma" in its name, but the well-documented connection between traumatic stress and dissociation is reflected in its current name and its focus on research and treatment to help traumatized persons to recover from severe problems with dissociation.

or friend); or "experiencing repeated or extreme exposure to aversive details of [these types of] traumatic event(s) (e.g., first responders collecting human remains, police officers repeatedly exposed to details of child abuse)" (Figure 1.3).

Experiences involving the unexpected or premature death of a primary caregiver fit this definition, but it is not clear whether abandonment by a caregiver—which can have profound adverse effects on child development and adolescent and adult

Posttraumatic Stress Disorder

Diagnostic Criteria   **309.81 (F43.10)**

Posttraumatic Stress Disorder

Note: The following criteria apply to adults, adolescents, and children older than 6 years. For children 6 years and younger, see corresponding criteria below.

A. Exposure to actual or threatened death, serious injury, or sexual violence in one (or more) of the following ways:

1. Directly experiencing the traumatic event(s).
2. Witnessing, in person, the event(s) as it occurred to others.
3. Learning that the traumatic event(s) occurred to a close family member or close friend. In cases of actual or threatened death of a family member or friend, the event(s) must have been violent or accidental.
4. Experiencing repeated or extreme exposure to aversive details of the traumatic event(s) (e.g., first responders collecting human remains; police officers repeatedly exposed to details of child abuse).

   Note: Criterion A4 does not apply to exposure through electronic media, television, movies, or pictures, unless this exposure is work related.

B. Presence of one (or more) of the following intrusion symptoms associated with the traumatic event(s), beginning after the traumatic event(s) occurred:

1. Recurrent, involuntary, and intrusive distressing memories of the traumatic event(s).

   Note: In children older than 6 years, repetitive play may occur in which themes or aspects of the traumatic event(s) are expressed.
2. Recurrent distressing dreams in which the content and/or affect of the dream are related to the traumatic event(s).

   Note: In children, there may be frightening dreams without recognizable content.
3. Dissociative reactions (e.g., flashbacks) in which the individual feels or acts as if the traumatic event(s) were recurring. (Such reactions may occur on a continuum, with the most extreme expression being a complete loss of awareness of present surroundings.)

   Note: In children, trauma-specific reenactment may occur in play.
4. Intense or prolonged psychological distress at exposure to internal or external cues that symbolize or resemble an aspect of the traumatic event(s).
5. Marked physiological reactions to internal or external cues that symbolize or resemble an aspect of the traumatic event(s).

C. Persistent avoidance of stimuli associated with the traumatic event(s), beginning after the traumatic event(s) occurred, as evidenced by one or both of the following:

1. Avoidance of or efforts to avoid distressing memories, thoughts, or feelings about or closely associated with the traumatic event(s).
2. Avoidance of or efforts to avoid external reminders (people, places, conversations, activities, objects, situations) that arouse distressing memories, thoughts, or feelings about or closely associated with the traumatic event(s).

D. Negative alterations in cognitions and mood associated with the traumatic event(s), beginning or worsening after the traumatic event(s) occurred, as evidenced by two (or more) of the following:

1. Inability to remember an important aspect of the traumatic event(s) (typically due to dissociative amnesia and not to other factors such as head injury, alcohol, or drugs).

Figure 1.3 *DSM*-5 criteria for the PTSD diagnosis.
From National Center for PTSD, http://www.ptsd.va.gov/professional/PTSD-overview/dsm5_criteria_ptsd.asp (American Psychiatric Association, 2013).

2. Persistent and exaggerated negative beliefs or expectations about oneself, others, or the world (e.g., "I am bad," "No one can be trusted," "The world is completely dangerous," "My whole nervous system is permanently ruined").
3. Persistent, distorted cognitions about the cause or consequences of the traumatic event(s) that lead the individual to blame himself/herself or others.
4. Persistent negative emotional state (e.g., fear, horror, anger, guilt, or shame).
5. Markedly diminished interest or participation in significant activities.
6. Feelings of detachment or estrangement from others.
7. Persistent inability to experience positive emotions (e.g., inability to experience happiness, satisfaction, or loving feelings).

E. Marked alterations in arousal and reactivity associated with the traumatic event(s), beginning or worsening after the traumatic event(s) occurred, as evidenced by two (or more) of the following:
1. Irritable behavior and angry outbursts (with little or no provocation) typically expressed as verbal or physical aggression toward people or objects.
2. Reckless or self-destructive behavior.
3. Hypervigilance.
4. Exaggerated startle response.
5. Problems with concentration.
6. Sleep disturbance (e.g., difficulty falling or staying asleep or restless sleep).

F. Duration of the disturbance (Criteria B, C, D, and E) is more than 1 month.

G. The disturbance causes clinically significant distress or impairment in social, occupational, or other important areas of functioning.

H. The disturbance is not attributable to the physiological effects of a substance (e.g., medication, alcohol) or another medical condition.

Specify whether:

With dissociative symptoms: The individual's symptoms meet the criteria for posttraumatic stress disorder, and in addition, in response to the stressor, the individual experiences persistent or recurrent symptoms of either of the following:
1. **Depersonalization:** Persistent or recurrent experiences of feeling detached from, and as if one were an outside observer of, one's mental processes or body (e.g., feeling as though one were in a dream; feeling a sense of unreality of self or body or of time moving slowly).
2. **Derealization:** Persistent or recurrent experiences of unreality of surroundings (e.g., the world around the individual is experienced as unreal, dreamlike, distant, or distorted).

Note: To use this subtype, the dissociative symptoms must not be attributable to the physiological effects of a substance (e.g., blackouts, behavior during alcohol intoxication) or another medical condition (e.g., complex partial seizures).

Specify if:

With delayed expression: If the full diagnostic criteria are not met until at least 6 months after the event (although the onset and expression of some symptoms may be immediate).

Figure 1.3 (Continued)

functioning (D'Andrea et al., 2012) and may lead to added trauma exposure or adversities such as multiple out-of-home placements (Ford, 2009)—constitutes a traumatic stressor. "Betrayal traumas" (Freyd, 1994) that do not involve death or the threat of death or severe physical injury, such as emotional abuse and childhood neglect, also do not technically constitute traumatic stressors despite clearly constituting serious risks to child health and development (D'Andrea et al., 2012). However, the *DSM*-5 eliminated the requirement that a traumatic exposure must be accompanied by a reaction of fear, helplessness, or horror (A2) based on research showing that almost all individuals who meet the symptom criteria for PTSD also recall experiencing severe peritraumatic distress: therefore, it is impossible to discern clinically or scientifically whether this recollection of past reactions is accurate or partially or fully a by-product of the current PTSD symptoms (Brewin, Lanius, Novac, Schnyder, & Galea, 2009; O'Donnell, Creamer, McFarlane, Silove, & Bryant, 2010). More important, the subject emotional impact of experiencing traumatic stressors was not lost in the *DSM*-5 PTSD operationalization because it is captured by newly added symptom items.

With regard to symptoms, PTSD requires exhibiting at least one (of five potential) reexperiencing symptom (Criterion B), at least one (of two potential) avoidance symptoms (Criterion C), two or more (of seven potential) "negative alterations in cognitions or mood associated with the traumatic events," and two or more (of six potential) hyperarousal "and reactivity" symptoms (Criterion E) (American Psychiatric Association, 2013, p. 271). The intrusive reexperiencing symptoms include repeated unwanted memories, recurrent frightening dreams (which, in the *DSM*-5 revision, may include affect/emotion related to traumatic events or, for children, may be nightmares "without recognizable content"), flashbacks (i.e., feeling as if the trauma is happening all over again in the present moment, or reenacting traumatic experience(s)), or intense psychological distress or physiological reactivity in response to stimuli that resemble or symbolize the traumatic event(s). Efforts to avoid reminders of traumatic memories may take the form of avoiding the memories (or related thoughts or feelings) themselves or "external reminders (people, places, conversations, activities, objects, situations) that arouse distressing memories, thoughts, or feelings about or closely associated with the traumatic event(s)" (American Psychiatric Association, 2013, p. 271).

Of particular importance in the *DSM*-5, many of the symptoms of emotional numbing that were grouped together with avoidance symptoms in prior *DSM*s (i.e., inability to recognize positive emotions, amnesia about some or all important parts of the traumatic event(s), feeling detached from relationships, and believing one's life will be cut short) are now listed with new symptoms under the rubric of a new Criterion D. The added symptoms represent trauma-related beliefs and emotional dysregulation that extend beyond fear and anxiety. Hence, PTSD is no longer grouped in the *DSM*-5 with anxiety disorders as it was in the *DSM-III* and *DSM-IV* but is now in a new class of "trauma and stressor-related disorders" (American Psychiatric Association, 2013, p. 271). The newly added symptoms reflect negative changes in beliefs and emotions that began during or worsened after traumatic events (persistent negative beliefs about oneself; distorted blame of self or others for the traumatic events; and emotional distress in the form of anger, guilt, shame, or horror, as well as, or instead of, fear and anxiety). With these new negative mood/cognition symptoms, PTSD now encompasses the trauma-related impairments in self-regulation that hundreds of research studies have shown to be aftereffects of exposure to interpersonal traumatic stressors in childhood (e.g., abuse, violent or sexual victimization, family violence) and in some cases in adulthood as well (e.g., genocide, torture, intimate partner violence) (D'Andrea et al., 2012). This is particularly relevant to understanding how and why traumatized youth are at risk for substance use disorders, because the new PTSD dysregulation symptoms are well known to be risk factors for, and contributors to, the severe and treatment refractory substance use disorders (Ford, Hartman, Hawke, & Chapman, 2008).

Several important additions also have been made in the *DSM-5* to the final set of PTSD symptoms: those reflecting hyperarousal and hypervigilance. The original symptoms in this category from the *DSM-III, III-R*, and *IV* are retained: severe sleep difficulties, anger and irritability, concentration problems, scanning the environment for threats (hypervigilance), and exaggerated startle responses. To these have been added one expansion of a prior symptom (i.e., verbal or physical aggression as a component of posttraumatic anger problems) and an entirely new symptom: reckless or self-destructive behavior. Here, too, as with the new negative mood/cognition symptoms, PTSD's problems with hyperarousal now include risk factors for substance use disorders (e.g., impulsivity, disregard of consequences, aggression).

Complex PTSD emerges as a (proposed) subtype of PTSD in the ICD-11

In the *ICD-11*, which at this writing is still in the decision-making process and proposed for finalization in 2017, PTSD has been simultaneously simplified in its core symptoms and expanded to include an alternative Complex PTSD diagnosis (Cloitre, Garvert, Brewin, Bryant, & Maercker, 2013):

> *Proposed ICD-11 Complex PTSD is a disorder that requires PTSD symptoms [of intrusive reexperiencing, avoidance of trauma reminders, and hypervigilance]… but also includes three additional features that reflect the impact that trauma can have on systems of self-organization, specifically problems in affective, self-concept, and relational domains.…The affective domain problems are characterized by emotion dysregulation as evidenced by heightened emotional reactivity, violent outbursts, reckless or self-destructive behavior, or a tendency toward experiencing prolonged dissociative states when under stress. In addition, there may be emotional numbing and a lack of ability to experience pleasure or positive emotions. Self-disturbances are characterized by negative self-concept marked by persistent beliefs about oneself as diminished, defeated, or worthless [possibly] accompanied by deep and pervasive feelings of shame or guilt.… Interpersonal disturbances are defined by persistent difficulties in sustaining relationships [due to a tendency to either] avoid, deride, or have little interest in relationships [or] occasionally experienc[ing] close or intense relationships but [having] difficulty maintaining emotional engagement. (p. 2)*

From trauma exposure to developing (and recovery from) traumatic stress disorders

Marian M.'s experience at the time of the traumatic incidents vividly illustrates "acute stress *reactions*" that are so common as to be almost universal when a life-threatening shock occurs. In the first days and weeks after the first traumatic incident, the stress reactions play themselves out and seem to abate and disappear. In fact, this is the most typical scenario for the response of adults to the experience of single-event traumatic stress: *approximately 75% do not go on to develop a traumatic stress disorder,* making PTSD the atypical response. However, additional exposure, especially to intentional harm inflicted by others (especially betrayal-based interpersonal trauma), often causes stress reactions to became amplified rather than diminished, resulting in symptoms of either "ASD" and an acute (early) form of PTSD or other psychiatric or psychosocial problems. In Chapter 2, acute traumatic stress reactions and ASD are more fully defined and described.

When PTSD does develop, it results from an extremely strong and dysregulated physiological response to the threat of the trauma that does not remit. Unlike the stress response associated with more low-intensity or nonsevere traumatic stressors, where the body's physiology returns to baseline or homeostasis, the traumatized body's response remains elevated or in a condition of dysregulation that has been described as allostasis (McEwen, 2006). The impact of traumatic stressors may be felt for many years, even decades, depending on how the survivor adapts after experiencing the traumatic stressor. PTSD may develop almost immediately and persist for decades (becoming chronic), particularly if the person had a previous history of childhood relational or attachment problems or additional traumatization predating the additional exposure. PTSD may develop immediately or soon after a traumatic exposure (acute form or meeting criteria for ASD). However, it may also occur after a period of a few months or years. Even after an extended period of being asymptomatic—usually due to the distractions and responsibilities of other life events (as occurred in Marian's case)—or absent due to the use of dissociation and resultant amnesia—PTSD can return in delayed form. Whatever the type, survivors may recover as a result of informal assistance relationships with individuals who offer secure attachment and emotional support, professional help that is also founded on safety of attachment and involves processing of the trauma, or natural and spiritual forms of healing—in the process regaining some or all of their adaptive capacities and quality of life.

Epidemiology of PTSD: how often (and to whom) does PTSD occur?

As noted at the beginning of this chapter, traumatic stressors occur more often than most of us would expect to more than half of adults at some time in their lives (Kessler et al., 1995) and to as many as two in three children by the age of 16 (Copeland et al., 2007; McLaughlin et al., 2013). Overall only about *one in eight* traumatized children develop PTSD, but many more experience emotional, learning, memory, behavioral, and physical health problems that persist into adulthood (D'Andrea et al., 2012) and between 33% and 40% of children who suffer the violent death of a loved one or sexual assault develop persistent posttraumatic stress symptoms (Copeland et al., 2007). PTSD develops fully for *1 in 20* men and *1 in 10* women at some point in their lives, and for as many as *two in three* men and *almost half* of all women who experienced sexual assault or childhood physical abuse (Foa & Tolin, 2006; Kessler et al., 1995). Other types of traumatic events may lead to PTSD (or persistent posttraumatic distress for children), typically for between 10% and 25% of the children or adults who are exposed to them.

The fact that many adults experience traumatic stressors but never develop PTSD or persistent posttraumatic distress has spurred a great deal of research on the "epidemiology" of PTSD. Epidemiology is the study of how often and to whom illnesses occur in large populations. As described in Chapter 3, PTSD is indeed an epidemic illness worldwide, considering that it occurs more often with children, adolescents, and young and midlife adults than any serious medical illness. Chapter 3 also describes how samples of people are selected to participate in epidemiology studies in order to obtain scientifically valid estimates of how often and to whom PTSD occurs. Epidemiological research has demonstrated that PTSD is one of two psychiatric disorders (bipolar disorder is the other) that are particularly likely to be accompanied by other psychiatric and medical illnesses. Therefore, Chapter 3 also describes the combinations of "comorbid" disorders, illnesses, and problems that most often occur along with PTSD.

Etiology of PTSD: potential causes and risk factors for developing PTSD

Experiencing a traumatic stressor was originally believed to be the "cause" of PTSD. By definition, PTSD can only occur if the traumatic event or experience results in psychological trauma. However, research has shown that exposure to a traumatic stressor is a necessary but not sufficient condition for the development of PTSD. This is evident from the fact that many people who experience traumatic stressors never develop PTSD. It also is clear that each traumatic stressor is unique and therefore that the experience and outcomes of potentially traumatic events such as violence, abuse, or disaster may be radically different, depending on the exact nature and circumstances of their occurrence. For example, one person may experience a single sexual assault by a stranger, while another might be repeatedly sexually assaulted by a close family member, teacher, or clergy. Although these two "rape" survivors have some things in common, there are still many differences in what happened to them (and therefore in their subsequent reactions and symptoms). The complicated nature of traumatic stressors, as well as the many different circumstances in which, and persons to whom, they occur, requires a detailed examination in order to understand the causes of PTSD.

Research summarized in Chapter 4 indicates that there is no single or definite cause of PTSD. However, there are specific features of traumatic events and victims that substantially increase the likelihood that PTSD will occur. These are called "risk factors" because they increase the person's risk of developing PTSD. Risk factors do not necessarily "cause" a disorder; instead, they either contribute to causing it or are highly related to (and therefore serve as "red flags" or warnings of) factors that cause the disorder. Thus, the question that is the focus of Chapter 4 is, what is it about the traumatic event, the person to whom it occurs, and the preceding and subsequent circumstances of that person's life that places a person at greatest risk for developing PTSD? In addition to these "risk" factors, research has shown that certain features of the person and their life circumstances may *reduce* the likelihood of developing PTSD. Chapter 4 therefore also describes these "protective" factors, which may serve as a basis for prevention or treatment interventions to reduce the likelihood that traumatized persons will suffer from PTSD.

Biology of PTSD: alterations in the body and in physical health associated with PTSD

All of the emotions, thoughts, and actions that a person experiences are preceded and accompanied by changes in the biology of the body. Although DesCartes asserted that the body and mind are fundamentally different, he (and philosophers and scientists for centuries since) recognized that the biology of the body is highly related to the activity of the mind. PTSD is a good example. Scientific studies described in Chapter 5 have shown that people suffering from PTSD are biologically different than other people, although it is not yet fully understood whether (and when) those biological differences are the causes or effects of PTSD or are the by-products of other disorders that occur along with PTSD ("comorbidities"). Chapter 5 summarizes the rapidly growing scientific evidence base that has shown that PTSD is associated with three essential types of biological changes: alterations in the body's stress response systems; alterations in brain chemistry, structure, and functioning; and physical health problems or diseases.

Research and clinical assessment of psychological trauma and PTSD

Many methods can be used to gather information and make a clinical or research determination that psychological trauma and PTSD have (or have not) occurred. This is understandable in light of the complexity of traumatic stressors, the risk and protective factors that influence the likelihood of developing traumatic stress disorders, and the several types of traumatic stress disorders (and comorbid disorders and problems) themselves. Therefore, Chapter 6 describes (and provides samples of) scientifically validated measures for the clinical and research assessment of psychological trauma and traumatic stress disorders. Following a brief overview of the criteria that are used in determining if an assessment measure provides reasonably (although never perfectly) accurate and valid information about trauma history and traumatic stress disorders, four purposes for PTSD assessment are discussed: screening to identify individuals who may have experienced trauma and may be suffering traumatic stress symptoms; structured interview assessment of psychological trauma history and traumatic stress (and comorbid) disorders; standardized questionnaire assessment of psychological trauma history, traumatic stress symptoms and disorders, and comorbid psychiatric symptoms and psychosocial and physical health problems; and psychophysiological, neuropsychological, and projective assessment of trauma survivors. PTSD assessment information may be used for a variety of purposes, including identifying individuals with undetected and untreated PTSD, documenting the severity of a person's (or group's) PTSD symptoms, and determining whether a prevention or treatment intervention for PTSD leads to improvement in PTSD; related symptoms; and social, occupational/educational, and recreational functioning and quality of life.

Treatment and prevention of PTSD

PTSD can be successfully treated, and it may be preventable. Once PTSD has developed, two basic approaches to treatment are available, each with many specific options that can be deployed to best address the needs and circumstances of the person who is seeking help. Psychotherapy is the best researched treatment approach for PTSD, for children as well as adults. Pharmacotherapy—the use of therapeutic medications—is the other major approach to treating PTSD, with wide usage of medications, most of which were originally developed to treat depression, other anxiety disorders, seizure disorders, and medical conditions such as hypertension.

The spectrum of PTSD psychotherapies is broad, including cognitive behavioral therapies (CBT), present-centered and emotion regulation therapies, psychodynamic and experiential therapies, body and movement therapies, marital and family therapies, and group therapies. The CBT approach to psychotherapy has the strongest scientific evidence of efficacy for the treatment of PTSD—that is, research showing that the treatment is directly responsible for improvements in the disease condition, in this case PTSD. However, no one size fits all, and there is growing evidence that other psychotherapy approaches may be efficacious for (and in some cases, better accepted by) persons of different backgrounds and circumstances who are seeking help for PTSD. Across all approaches to psychotherapy, both clinicians and researchers have found that certain core treatment goals and practices can help in the successful resolution of PTSD.

A three-phase approach to PTSD psychotherapy has become the gold standard. Each phase represents a core treatment goal: (i) ensuring that the recipient is sufficiently safe and psychologically prepared to be free from further exposure to traumatic stressors (such as abuse or domestic or community violence) or serious crises (such as suicide or relapse into alcohol or drug addiction); (ii) enabling the recipient to understand and therapeutically change the persistent stress reactions that are the biological and psychological source of PTSD; and (iii) empowering the recipient to begin, or resume, living a fuller and more personally rewarding life by utilizing psychological capacities and social resources (family relationships, friendships, and work and recreation pursuits) with which PTSD has interfered (Ford & Courtois, 2009, 2013).

Exciting new medication options are being developed, researched, and approved by the US Food and Drug Administration and similar safety regulatory agencies in countries worldwide for PTSD treatment. Medications that are efficacious for depression are the most widely approved and used pharmacotherapy agents for PTSD, not surprisingly in light of the frequent comorbidity of PTSD and depression and the fact that PTSD emotional numbing symptoms overlap with the symptoms of depression. However, many other medicines are being applied to PTSD treatment based on the growing research on the biology of PTSD. For example, an antihypertensive drug, Prazosin, was first shown to help people with PTSD who suffer from nightmares and recently has been found to be helpful to many people with the chronic daytime anxiety and tension that occur in PTSD's hyperarousal symptoms (Arnsten, Raskind, Taylor, & Connor, 2014). Pharmacotherapy most often is done in conjunction with psychotherapy when PTSD has been diagnosed, because PTSD involves a number of anxiety, mood, and behavioral problems that are sufficiently complex to be difficult to treat with medication alone.

Before PTSD occurs, the opportunity to prevent this disorder is clearly suggested by the scientific evidence showing that most people who experience acute traumatic stress reactions do not develop PTSD (or do so gradually or only after a delay of months or years). Psychotherapy in conjunction with some antianxiety and antihypertensive medications has been found to be helpful for people who develop the precursor of PTSD: ASD (Bryant, 2008a). CBT is the best-validated treatment for ASD, and as such, it is a promising approach to preventing PTSD. Other prevention approaches (called "psychological first aid") also have been developed for people whose communities suffer natural or humanmade disasters.

In Chapters 7–9, the full array of treatment and prevention interventions for PTSD is described, beginning with psychotherapy, pharmacotherapy, and prevention models for adults in Chapter 7, an equally diverse and promising spectrum of treatments for traumatized children and adolescents (and their parents and families) in Chapter 8, and the approaches to PTSD prevention in Chapter 9. With the rapid growth of treatment and prevention options, it is crucial to be able to provide the best possible help in the most timely and efficient manner to the most adults and children who are at the highest risk of developing PTSD. Chapters 7—9 therefore also provide an overview of research studies that are being conducted to establish an "evidence base"—that is, a record of the efficacy and effectiveness (the real-world benefits) of the rapidly expanding array of PTSD treatments and prevention interventions.

Forensic issues in the PTSD field

Psychological trauma and PTSD play an important role in the criminal, civil, and juvenile justice systems and are ubiquitous in the lives of most persons who are involved in these systems. Traumatic stress professionals face critical challenges while conducting research, providing expert and clinical evaluations and testimony, and developing and conducting treatment, rehabilitation, and prevention interventions, in the justice systems, including:

a. the child welfare and child protective services systems (e.g., child abuse/neglect);
b. the family law courts (e.g., divorce and child custody, parental competence);
c. the juvenile justice system (e.g., juvenile courts, detention, probation, incarceration);
d. the adult criminal justice system (e.g., courts, jails, prisons, parole/probation);
e. the immigration/naturalization system (e.g., refugee asylum hearings).

In Chapter 10, forensic issues such as the role of PTSD as a mitigating factor in criminal culpability of victimized persons, the credibility of witness and defendant memories of traumatic events, the traumatic stress experienced by refugees seeking asylum after emigrating to a new country, the impact of PTSD on the rehabilitation and community reentry of incarcerated youth and adults, and testifying in court as an expert witness regarding PTSD are discussed.

Social, cultural, and ethical issues in the PTSD field

The impact of psychological trauma differs, depending on the social and cultural context in which traumatic stressors occur and the social and cultural resources available to individuals, families, and communities in the wake of experiencing traumatic stressors. Disadvantaged persons and communities such as those experiencing poverty, stigma, and discrimination; homelessness; political repression; communal/societal violence (including military and gang warfare); forced immigration (refugees); interrogation and torture; terrorism; and genocide are particularly likely to be victims of psychological trauma and to develop PTSD as a result of exposure to cumulative adversities that may worsen the negative impact of traumatic stressors:

- socioeconomic disparities (poverty, limited access to education or jobs);
- discrimination and racism faced by ethnoracial minority groups;
- discrimination based on gender or sexual identity/orientation;
- discrimination based on mental or medical illness or addiction;
- discrimination based on age;
- political repression, genocide, "ethnic cleansing," torture, or displacement;
- sexual or physical harassment and assaulted on the job or in the ranks;
- workplace pressures and constraints on personal autonomy;
- repeated exposure to grotesque death and suffering;
- legal proceedings and incarceration;
- homelessness.

These social and cultural challenges facing vulnerable groups whose members also often are subjected to traumatic stressors pose several fundamental ethical challenges for clinicians and scientists who conduct assessment, treatment, and prevention services addressing PTSD. Relevant ethical principles are discussed in relation to these vulnerable groups, including the first principle of the healing arts, "first do no harm," as well as the guiding principles of caring, respect, diversity, justice, empowerment, and integrity (freedom from conflict of interest).

Careers in the PTSD field and impact of psychological trauma on the professional

The book's final chapter describes the opportunities and challenges provided by careers that focus on traumatic stress, including the scientist/researcher (in basic, clinical, and translational sciences), the mental health and social work clinician, the public health and medical professional, the educator, the social/humanitarian advocate, and the criminal justice professional. Real-life examples are used to illustrate the kinds of work, rewards, and dilemmas involved in each career path. Particular focus is placed on understanding the impact that working with persons or communities suffering from PTSD has on the professional. PTSD is not contagious, but helping or studying people who are experiencing PTSD often brings clinicians and scientists face-to-face with the painful reality that psychological trauma can strike at any time and can have a devastating effect on anyone who is victimized. Compassionate therapists and researchers are affected by the distress that their patients and study participants are experiencing due to PTSD. This is called vicarious or secondary trauma or compassion fatigue. Approaches to maximizing the benefits of working in careers in the PTSD field are discussed, including ways to understand and prevent vicarious/secondary trauma and compassion fatigue from turning into professional burnout and workplace problems that can spill over into all areas of personal life. The professionals working in the PTSD field tend to have remarkable personal and professional resilience, and these strengths provide a basis for making careers in the PTSD field a source of lasting satisfaction and fulfillment, as well as an important contribution to bettering the world.

References

American Psychiatric Association, (1968). *Diagnostic and statistical manual of mental disorders* (2nd ed.). Washington, DC: American Psychiatric Press.

American Psychiatric Association, (1980). *Diagnostic and statistical manual of mental disorders* (3rd ed.). Washington, DC: American Psychiatric Association Press.

American Psychiatric Association, (1987). *Diagnostic and statistical manual of mental disorders* (3rd ed. revised). Washington, DC: American Psychiatric Press.

American Psychiatric Association, (1994). *Diagnostic and Statistical manual of mental disorders* (4th ed.). Washington, DC: American Psychiatric Press.

American Psychiatric Association, (2000). *Diagnostic and statistical manual of mental disorders* (4th ed. Text Revision). Washington DC: American Psychiatric Press.

American Psychiatric Association, (2013). *Diagnostic and statistical manual of mental disorders* (5th ed.). Washington, DC: American Psychiatric Press.

Arnsten, A., Raskind, M., Taylor, F., & Connor, D. (2014). The effects of stress exposure on prefrontal cortex: Translating basic research into successful treatments for post-traumatic stress disorder. *Neurobiology of Stress, 1*, 89–99.

Bass, E., & Davis, L. (1988). *The courage to heal.* New York: Harper & Row Publisher.

Birmes, P., Hatton, L., Brunet, A., & Schmitt, L. (2003). Early historical literature for post-traumatic symptomatology. [Print Electronic; Print]. *Stress and Health: Journal of the International Society for the Investigation of Stress, 19*(1), 17–26.

Breuer, J., & Freud, S. (1893). On the psychical mechanism of hysterical phenomena: Preliminary communication. In J. Breuer & S. Freud (Eds.), *Studies on hysteria* (pp. 3–17). New York: Basic Books.

Brewin, C. R. (2014). Episodic memory, perceptual memory, and their interaction: Foundations for a theory of posttraumatic stress disorder. *Psychological Bulletin, 140*(1), 69–97.

Brewin, C. R., Lanius, R. A., Novac, A., Schnyder, U., & Galea, S. (2009). Reformulating PTSD for DSM-V: Life after Criterion A. *Journal of Traumatic Stress, 22*(5), 366–373. http://dx.doi.org/10.1002/jts.20443.

Bryant, R. (2008a). Acute stress disorder. In G. Reyes, J. D. Elhai, & J. D. Ford (Eds.), *Encyclopedia of psychological trauma* (pp. 12–14). Hoboken, NJ: Wiley.

Bryant, R. (2008b). Memory. In G. Reyes, J. D. Elhai, & J. D. Ford (Eds.), *Encyclopedia of psychological trauma* (pp. 424–426). Hoboken, NJ: Wiley.

Cloitre, M., Garvert, D. W., Brewin, C. R., Bryant, R. A., & Maercker, A. (2013). Evidence for proposed ICD-11 PTSD and complex PTSD: A latent profile analysis. *European Journal of Psychotraumatology, 4.* http://dx.doi.org/10.3402/ejpt.v4i0.20706.

Cook, A., Spinazzola, P., Ford, J., Lanktree, C., Blaustein, M., Cloitre, M., et al. (2005). Complex trauma in children and adolescents. *Psychiatric Annals, 35*(5), 390–398.

Copeland, W. E., Keeler, G., Angold, A., & Costello, E. J. (2007). Traumatic events and post-traumatic stress in childhood. *Archives of General Psychiatry, 64*, 577–584.

Courtois, C. A. (2010). *Healing the incest wound* (2nd ed.). New York, NY: W. W. Norton.

Courtois, C. A., & Ford, J. D. (2013). *Treating complex trauma: A sequenced relationship-based approach.* New York: Guilford.

DaCosta, J. M. (1871). On irritable heart; a clinical study of a form of functional cardiac disorder and its consequences. *American Journal of the Medical Sciences, 61*, 17–52.

Dalenberg, C. J., Brand, B. L., Gleaves, D. H., Dorahy, M. J., Loewenstein, R. J., Cardena, E., et al. (2012). Evaluation of the evidence for the trauma and fantasy models of dissociation. *Psychological Bulletin, 138*(3), 550–588.

D'Andrea, W., Ford, J. D., Stolbach, B., Spinazzola, J., & van der Kolk, B. A. (2012). Understanding interpersonal trauma in children: Why we need a developmentally appropriate trauma diagnosis. *American Journal of Orthopsychiatry, 82*(2), 187–200. http://dx.doi.org/10.1111/j.1939-0025.2012.01154.x.

Dass-Brailsford, P. (2007). *A practical approach to trauma: Empowering interventions.* London: Sage Publications.

Davis, D. A. (1994). A theory for the 90s: Traumatic seduction in historical context. *Psychoanalytic Review, 81*, 627–640.

DePrince, A. P., & Freyd, J. J. (2007). Trauma-induced dissociation. In M. J. Friedman, T. M. Keane, & P. A. Resick (Eds.), *Handbook of PTSD: Science and practice* (pp. 135–150). New York: Guilford.

Erichsen, J. E. (1866). *On railway and other injuries of the nervous. system.* London: Walton and Maberly.

Feiring, C., Taska, L., & Lewis, M. (2002). Adjustment following sexual abuse discovery: The role of shame and attributional style. *Developmental Psychopathology, 38*, 79–92.

Finkelhor, D., Ormrod, R. K., & Turner, H. A. (2007). Poly-victimization: A neglected component in child victimization. *Child Abuse & Neglect, 31*, 7–26.

Ford, J. D. (2005). Treatment implications of altered affect regulation and information processing following child maltreatment. *Psychiatric Annals, 35*(5), 410–419.

Ford, J. D. (2009). Translation of emerging neurobiological and developmental findings to the clinical conceptualization and treatment of complex psychological trauma. In C. A. Courtois & J. Ford (Eds.), *Treating complex traumatic stress disorders: An evidence-based guide* (pp. 31–58). New York: Guilford.

Ford, J. D., & Courtois, C. A. (2009). Introduction. In C. A. Courtois & J. D. Ford (Eds.), *Treating complex traumatic stress disorders: An evidence-based guide* (pp. 1–9). New York: Guilford.

Ford, J. D., & Courtois, C. A. (Eds.). (2013). *Treating complex traumatic stress disorders in children and adolescents: Scientific foundations and therapeutic models.* New York: Guilford.

Ford, J. D., & Courtois, C. A. (2014). Complex PTSD, affect dysregulation, and borderline personality disorder. *Borderline Personality Disorder and Emotion Dysregulation, 1*, 9.

Ford, J. D., & Gomez, J. M. (2015). Dissociation and posttraumatic stress disorder (PTSD) in non-suicidal self-injury and suicidality: A review. *Journal of Trauma and Dissociation, 16*(5), 487–522.

Ford, J. D., Grasso, D., Greene, C., Levine, J., Spinazzola, J., & van der Kolk, B. (2013). Clinical significance of a proposed developmental trauma disorder diagnosis: Results of an international survey of clinicians. *Journal of Clinical Psychiatry, 74*(8), 841–849. http://dx.doi.org/10.4088/JCP.12m08030.

Ford, J. D., Hartman, J. K., Hawke, J., & Chapman, J. (2008). Traumatic victimization, posttraumatic stress disorder, suicidal ideation, and substance abuse risk among juvenile justice-involved youths. *Journal of Child and Adolescent Trauma*, *1*, 75–92.

Ford, J. D., Steinberg, K. L., Hawke, J., Levine, J., & Zhang, W. (2012). Randomized trial comparison of emotion regulation and relational psychotherapies for PTSD with girls involved in delinquency. *Journal of Clinical Child and Adolescent Psychology*, *41*(1), 27–37. http://dx.doi.org/10.1080/15374416.2012.632343.

Ford, J. D., Steinberg, K. L., & Zhang, W. (2011). A randomized clinical trial comparing affect regulation and social problem-solving psychotherapies for mothers with victimization-related PTSD. *Behavior Therapy*, *42*(4), 560–578. http://dx.doi.org/S0005-7894(11)00048-7 [pii]; http://dx.doi.org/10.1016/j.beth.2010.12.005.

Freyd, J. (1994). Betrayal trauma: Traumatic amnesia as an adaptive response to childhood abuse. *Ethics & Behavior*, *4*(4), 307–329.

Freyd, J. J., DePrince, A. P., & Gleaves, D. H. (2007). The state of betrayal trauma theory: Reply to McNally--Conceptual issues and future directions. *Memory*, *15*, 295–311.

Goodman, J., Marsh, R., Peterson, B. S., & Packard, M. G. (2014). Annual research review: The neurobehavioral development of multiple memory systems—implications for childhood and adolescent psychiatric disorders. *Journal of Child Psychology and Psychiatry*, *55*(6), 582–610.

Hitchcock, C., Nixon, R. D., & Weber, N. (2014). A review of overgeneral memory in child psychopathology. *British Journal of Clinical Psychology*, *53*(2), 170–193.

Hobfoll, S. E. (2012). Conservation of resources and disaster in cultural context: The caravans and passageways for resources. *Psychiatry*, *75*, 227–232.

Horowitz, M., & Smit, M. (2008). Stress response syndromes. In G. Reyes, J. D. Elhai, & J. D. Ford (Eds.), *Encyclopedia of psychological trauma* (pp. 629–633). Hoboken, NJ: John Wiley & Sons.

Kessler, R. C., Sonnega, A., Bromet, E., & Hughes, M. (1995). Posttraumatic stress disorder in the National Comorbidity Survey. *Archives of General Psychiatry*, *52*, 1048–1060.

Kulka, R. A., Schlenger, W. E., Fairbank, J. A., Hough, R. L., Jordan, B. K., Marmar, C. R., et al. (1990). *Trauma and the Vietnam war generation: Report of findings from the National Vietnam Veterans Readjustment Study*. Philadelphia, PA: Brunner/Mazel.

Lanius, R. A., Brand, B., Vermetten, E., Frewen, P. A., & Spiegel, D. (2012). The dissociative subtype of posttraumatic stress disorder: Rationale, clinical and neurobiological evidence, and implications. *Depression and Anxiety*, *29*(8), 701–708. http://dx.doi.org/10.1002/da.21889.

Lanius, R. A., Vermetten, E., Loewenstein, R. J., Brand, B., Schmahl, C., Bremner, J. D., et al. (2010). Emotion modulation in PTSD: Clinical and neurobiological evidence for a dissociative subtype. *American Journal of Psychiatry*, *167*(6), 640–647. http://dx.doi.org/10.1176/appi.ajp.2009.09081168.

Lasiuk, G. C., & Hegadoren, K. M. (2006). Posttraumatic stress disorder part I: Historical development of the concept. *Perspectives on Psychiatric Care*, *42*, 13–20.

Lerner, A. G., Gelkopf, M., Skladman, I., Rudinski, D., Nachshon, H., & Bleich, A. (2003). Clonazepam treatment of lysergic acid diethylamide-induced hallucinogen persisting perception disorder with anxiety features. *International Clinical Psychopharmacology*, *18*, 101–105.

Leys, R. (1994). Traumatic cures - shell-shock, janet, and the question of memory. *Critical Inquiry*, *20*, 623–662.

Lindblom, K., & Gray, M. (2008). Memories of traumatic experiences. In G. Reyes, J. D. Elhai, & J. D. Ford (Eds.), *Encyclopedia of psychological trauma* (pp. 412–424). Hoboken, NJ: Wiley.

Loftus, E. F. (2001). Imagining the past. *The Psychologist*, *14*(11), 584–587.

Lyons-Ruth, K., Dutra, L., Schuder, M. R., & Bianchi, I. (2006). From infant attachment disorganization to adult dissociation: Relational adaptations or traumatic experiences? *Psychiatric Clinics of North America*, *29*, 63–86.

Marshall, R. D., Spitzer, R., & Liebowitz, M. R. (1999). Review and critique of the new DSM-IV diagnosis of acute stress disorder. *American Journal of Psychiatry*, *156*(11), 1677–1685.

Mattox, K. L., Moore, E. E., & Feliciano, D. V. (2013). *Trauma* (7th ed.). New York, NY: McGraw Hill.

McEwen, B. (2006). Stress, adaptation, and disease. *Annals of the New York Academy of Sciences*, *840*(1), 33–44.

McLaughlin, K. A., Koenen, K. C., Hill, E. D., Petukhova, M., Sampson, N. A., Zaslavsky, A. M., et al. (2013). Trauma exposure and posttraumatic stress disorder in a national sample of adolescents. *Journal of the American Academy of Child and Adolescent Psychiatry*, *52*(8) 815-830.e814. http://dx.doi.org/10.1016/j.jaac.2013.05.011.

McNally, R. J. (2003). *Remembering trauma*. Cambridge, MA: Belknap Press/Harvard University Press.

Miller, M. W., Vogt, D. S., Mozley, S. L., Kaloupek, D. G., & Keane, T. M. (2006). PTSD and substance-related problems: The mediating roles of disconstraint and negative emotionality. *Journal of Abnormal Psychology*, *115*, 369–379.

Moore, E. E., Feliciano, D. V., & Mattox, K. L. (2004). *Trauma* (5th ed.). New York: McGraw-Hill.

Myers, A. B. R. (1870). *On the aetiology and prevalence of diseases of the heart among soldiers*. London: Churchill.

O'Donnell, M. L., Creamer, M., McFarlane, A. C., Silove, D., & Bryant, R. A. (2010). Should A2 be a diagnostic requirement for posttraumatic stress disorder in DSM-V? *Psychiatry Research*, *176*(2–3), 257–260. http://dx.doi.org/S0165-1781(09)00195-4 [pii]; http://dx.doi.org/10.1016/j.psychres.2009.05.012.

Putnam, F. W. (2003). Ten-year research update review: Child sexual abuse. *Journal of the American Academy of Child and Adolescent Psychiatry*, *42*, 269–278.

Scheeringa, M. S., Zeanah, C. H., & Cohen, J. A. (2011). PTSD in children and adolescents: Toward an empirically based algorithm. *Depression and Anxiety*, *28*(9), 770–782. http://dx.doi.org/10.1002/da.20736.

Shay, J. (1994). *Achilles in Vietnam: Combat trauma and the undoing of character*. New York: Atheneum.

Shay, J. (2002). *Odysseus in America: Combat trauma and the trials of homecoming*. New York: Scribner.

Spinazzola, J., Hodgdon, H., Liang, L., Ford, J. D., Layne, C., Pynoos, R., et al. (2014). Unseen wounds: The contribution of psychological maltreatment child and adolescent mental health and risk outcomes. *Psychological Trauma: Theory, Research, Practice & Policy*, *6*, 518–528.

Symonds, J. D. (1975). Modeling effectiveness as a function of the similarity of the learner to personal characteristics of the model. *Dissertation Abstracts International*, *36*(2-A), 799–800.

Teicher, M. H., Samson, J. A., Polcari, A., & McGreenery, C. E. (2006). Sticks, stones, and hurtful words: Relative effects of various forms of childhood maltreatment. *American Journal of Psychiatry*, *163*, 993–1000.

Terr, L. C. (1991). Childhood traumas: An outline and overview. *American Journal of Psychiatry*, *148*, 10–20.

Tolin, D. F., & Foa, E. B. (2006). Sex differences in trauma and posttraumatic stress disorder: A quantitative review of 25 years of research. *Psychological Bulletin*, *132*, 959–992.

Trible, P. (1984). *Texts of terror: Literary-feminist readings of Biblical narratives*. Philadelphia: Fortress Press.

Van de Hart, O., Nijenhuis, E. R. S., & Steele, K. (2006). *The haunted self: Structural dissociation and the treatment of chronic traumatization*. New York: Norton.

Van der Hart, O., & Friedman, B. (1989). A reader's guide to Pierre Janet on dissociation: A neglected intellectual heritage. *Dissociation: Progress in the Dissociative Disorders, 2*(1), 3–16.

Van der Hart, O., & Nijenhuis, E. (2008). Dissociation. In G. Reyes, J. D. Elhai, & J. D. Ford (Eds.), *Encyclopedia of psychological trauma* (pp. 216–224). Hoboken, NJ: Wiley.

van der Kolk, B. A. (2005). Developmental trauma disorder: Toward a rational diagnosis for children with complex trauma histories. *Psychiatric Annals, 35*(5), 401–408.

Wilson, J. P. (1989). *Trauma, transformation, and healing*. New York: *Brunner/Mazel*.

Zanarini, M. C., Yong, L., Frankenburg, F. R., Hennen, J., Reich, D. B., Marino, M. F., et al. (2002). Severity of reported childhood sexual abuse and its relationship to severity of borderline psychopathology and psychosocial impairment among borderline inpatients. *Journal of Nervous and Mental Disorders, 190*, 381–387.

The impact of psychological trauma

2

In this chapter, we examine how people adapt in the wake of experiencing psychological trauma. This is called the "longitudinal" (i.e., over a period of time) or "prospective" (i.e., beginning with a particular time or event and continuing into the future) course of posttraumatic adaptation. Traumatic stressors have an impact that is not limited to when they are occurring or the immediate aftermath. Experiencing psychological trauma affects how people adjust and carry on with the rest of their lives, beginning with traumatic events but continuing in the subsequent months, years, and even decades. Like the aftershocks of an earthquake, the impact of traumatic stressors may be felt in many ways for many years, and in ways that are not entirely predictable.

The chapter begins by describing what makes a stressor traumatic and considering the acute (immediate) reactions that people have to psychological trauma (Bovin & Marx, 2011), both of which are based upon a number of biological, psychological, and sociocultural factors. Next, several patterns of positive and negative adaptation following exposure to traumatic stressors are examined. The impact of traumatic stressors includes a variety of changes in the pathway that a person's life takes that occur as time passes, including positive trajectories that have been described as "resistance," "resilience," "recovery," and "posttraumatic growth (PTG)." Posttraumatic stress disorder (PTSD) is the result of individual differences (Yehuda & LeDoux, 2007) that lead to negative trajectories of adaptation (Yehuda & Flory, 2007) that can take the form of "stable maladaptive functioning" (such as preexisting psychiatric or addictive disorders or chronic problems with relationships, school, work, the law, or illness), "persistent posttraumatic distress" (i.e., new forms of dysfunction that begin during or soon after the traumatic stressor and worsen or remain severe problems long afterward), or "posttraumatic decline" (such as a worsening of stress symptoms that initially are manageable but become sufficiently severe to constitute PTSD) (Box 2.1).

When the other shoe falls: What makes stressful events traumatic?

Most people are fortunate to not have the experience of frequently experiencing traumatic stressors during their lives. (Note that this is not the case for tens of millions of people in wartorn and desperately impoverished areas of the world, for whom traumatic stress and PTSD are everyday realities; see the discussion on complex PTSD among survivors of traumatic communities and cultural-political systems in

Posttraumatic Stress Disorder. DOI: http://dx.doi.org/10.1016/B978-0-12-801288-8.00002-9

Box 2.1 Key Points

1. Traumatic stressors are events or experiences that are unpredictable, uncontrollable, and confront the person with actual or potential death or irreparable violence or loss.

2. Every individual reacts differently to stressful events, based upon the person's biological and psychological characteristics and social history and support system, as well as the exact nature, combination and timing, and circumstances (the "context") of the events. Events or experiences that are traumatic for one person may not be traumatic for another person, and or they may not be traumatic for the same person if the event or experience occurs in a different form, timing, or context previously or subsequently.

3. Some stressful events are psychologically traumatic for almost anyone. These include rape, childhood sexual or physical abuse or life-threatening neglect, gruesome injuries or death in war (either as a combatant or a civilian victim), genocide, torture, or prolonged isolation and dehumanization while being physically or sexually assaulted or held captive or hostage (including chronic entrapment in a violent intimate partner relationship).

4. Even when an event or experience is psychologically traumatic. most people do not develop PTSD. Across a range of traumatic stressors, about 10% of men or boys develop PTSD at some future time, versus about 20% of women or girls. However, a much higher proportion of people (up to 67–75%) develop PTSD when confronted by the types of events that are traumatic for almost anyone (see #3). This gender difference may be partially, but not entirely, explained by the unfortunate fact that girls or women are more likely than boys or men to be victims of sexual or domestic violence trauma. Boys and men are more often exposed to combat or physical assault traumas than girls or women.

5. Acute reactions during and immediately after exposure to a traumatic stressor include dissociation, unwanted ("intrusive") memories or reminders of the event and its impact, attempts to avoid these unwanted memories, extreme states of physical arousal or exhaustion, preoccupation with identifying other potential dangers ("hypervigilance"), difficulties with mental concentration, memory, problem solving, and decision making.

6. Although it is typical for some or all of these acute stress reactions to occur within the first hours or days after a psychologically traumatic experience, if they persist or worsen within the first month after the traumatic stressor, the individual may develop an "ASD" (see Figure 2.1). ASD is a psychiatric diagnosis that can be made only between 3 days and 1 month after a traumatic experience. The 3-day "grace period" is provided because the stress reactions are almost universal in the first 2 days following psychological trauma. The 1 month outer limit for an ASD diagnosis reflects the fact that when stress reactions persist and interfere with a person's life for more than a month they can no longer be considered "acute" and instead are better described as "posttraumatic stress" reactions (or, if severe, as PTSD).

7. The most common outcomes following a traumatic stressor are positive in nature and are referred to with three Rs (see Figure 2.2). *Resistance* involves successful coping with acute stress reactions such that the person experiences no more than mild and brief difficulties in work, relationships, and psychological and physical health. *Resilience* refers to successful coping with more severe acute stress reactions and problems in living following exposure to a traumatic stressor, such that the person

adjusts and functions well despite having distinct posttraumatic stress symptoms and even PTSD. *Recovery* is the regaining of healthy functioning after suffering severe posttraumatic problems. A fourth positive trajectory is less common, or possibly quite common but simply not often recognized: "PTG" involves the development of new knowledge, abilities, relationships, or hope and confidence following a traumatic stressor in addition to recovering successfully from acute stress reactions.

8. PTSD and associated severe biopsychosocial problems may occur along several negative trajectories that can begin prior to exposure to a traumatic stressor or in the aftermath and that may continue or fluctuate significantly over the following years (Figure 2.2). PTSD is not the only serious problem that can occur in the wake of psychological trauma. Several other psychiatric disorders occur more often following exposure to traumatic stressors than if psychological trauma does not occur, including complicated bereavement (debilitating grief), depression, other anxiety disorders (such as fears or phobias), serious mental illness (such as bipolar disorder or schizophrenia), addictive disorders, eating disorders, dissociative disorders, and personality disorders. Chronic problems with anger, violence, suicidality, poor school and work outcomes, troubled relationships, and serious medical illness also have been linked to exposure to traumatic stress (especially when this occurs in childhood and undermines healthy relationships and development) and PTSD.

9. Psychological trauma does not "cause" these disorders and problems. Surprisingly, even PTSD may not be "caused" solely or primarily by exposure to traumatic stress. Exposure to traumatic stress increases the individual's risk of developing PTSD and psychosocial, behavioral, and medical problems. When other risk factors are sufficient, or protective factors (such as the person's genetic, familial, or socioeconomic resources) are lacking or lost, traumatic stress may "tip the scales" and lead to a negative life trajectory.

10. Preventing PTSD or helping people to recover from PTSD requires an individualized approach to providing protective resources through interventions such as education or treatment in order to enable the person to regain a positive life trajectory.

Chapter 11.) The rarity of traumatic stressors actually contributes to their impact, because it is easier to cope with a stressor that is relatively expected than with one that is unexpected and comes "out of the blue." However, surprise is only one element in traumatic stress, and in some cases traumatic stressors actually are expectable, such as in a war zone where the next attack is always imminent or in a family where violence is a common occurrence.

Before we define traumatic stressors and examine their effects on people's lives, we first need to consider the question of how to define the larger domain of all types of "stressors" and what constitutes "stress." *Stressors* are events or circumstances that require living organisms to adapt (i.e., to allocate resources such as energy, thought, and action) in order to maintain their physical (and for humans and some other animals) integrity (i.e., health, well-being, functioning, development). Chiriboga and Dean (1978) identified nine areas of life in which stressors may occur: family, marriage, home, personal, habits, financial, legal, work, and nonfamily. *Stress* is the amount of demand that adaptation places on our physical and psychological resources, ranging from minimal (but not zero) when we are confronted by stressors to which our bodies can adapt successfully with limited effort (and thought)—essentially on automatic pilot—to the other extreme of high stress when stressors require large and/ or rapid deployment of resources. *Stress reactions* are physical, emotional, cognitive, and behavioral responses to stressors that are intended to achieve a successful adaption by deploying resources from those domains to either protect against harm (the classic fight-or-flight response), achieve a valued goal (goal-directed actions such as problem solving, learning, or reward seeking), or gain access to additional resources (mobilizing help in the form of instrumental, emotional, or social support). The goal of stress reactions is *allostasis*—adapting to not only meet the demands of a stressor but also to maintain one's overall health, or *homeostasis*. *Stasis* means being in a state, and *homeo* means healthy, so *homeostasis* means being in a state of good health. *Allo* means the *allocation* of resources, so *allostasis* means allocating resources to maintain a healthy state.

Although we tend to think of stress and stress reactions as negative in nature and impact, they actually often are beneficial and may even be pleasurable when they enable us to achieve positive outcomes in our lives. Indeed, stressors themselves may be of a positive nature (e.g., celebrations, successes, opportunities) or neutral (e.g., innocuous changes in the environment, casual social encounters, natural transitions in daily routines) as well as negative (e.g., pressures, injuries, problems, threats). We often are less aware of the demands that positive or neutral stressors place upon our physical and psychological resources than we are of the strain and drain caused by adaptation to negative stressors. This can make us unprepared for or inefficient at using our resources to adapt to positive and neutral stressors, which can lead to particularly problematic complications when those stressors are traumatic.

If stressors, stress reactions, and stress are a normal part of everyday life, and stressors are events or circumstances that can be positive or neutral as well as negative, why do stress and stress reactions seem to be such a problem? The answer is that stress reactions are a problem only when the physical and psychological resources expended (i.e., the stress) in adapting to a stressor (i.e., the stress reactions) *exceed an individual's (or group or community's) resource capacity* (i.e., the amount of energy, time, thought/knowledge, ability to act, and social support they have available and are willing and able to allocate to meet this challenge). When adapting to stressors requires more resources than are available or than can be deployed, the attempt to adapt is likely to be at best only partly successful (and it may fail entirely).

The partial or complete failure to cope with a stressor leads to several interrelated problems. First, there are the *stress reactions*, which take the form of beliefs and behaviors that are intended to cope with or resolve the challenge posed by the stressor. Stress reactions can be allostatic (i.e., effective in preserving or restoring health, or homeostasis). However, when stress reactions are only partially effective, or fail completely, as a result of insufficient resources, this can compound problems and compromise health—for example, attempting to avoid problems rather than constructively facing them, blaming or distrusting self or others, hopelessness, or pursuing goals that are based on revenge, aggression, or disregard for one's own or other people's safety.

Second, there is the experience of *stress*, which neuroscientist Bruce McEwen has described as "allostatic load" (McEwen & Lasley, 2003). Allostatic load refers to the strain or damage to the individual's or group's health that results when the resources necessary to cope with stressors exceed the individual's (or group's) capacities. When stressors require only a modest expenditure of resources compared to the overall stockpile of resources that the individual or group has available, the allostatic load caused by stress reactions is manageable, and health is either unaffected or maybe even improved by the effort to cope. However, when stress reactions require more resources than are available or deployable, the expenditure of resources may be so great that health is compromised or there are not sufficient resources left over to deal with subsequent stressors or simply to continue to preserve good health.

Moreover, even if the individual or group can achieve positive solutions to cope with stressor(s), the third consequence of having insufficient resources to meet the demands of a stressor is the exhaustion of available resources. This is particularly likely to happen when a stressor is intensely challenging or dangerous and the stress reactions necessary to successfully adapt (or in the case of traumatic stressors, to survive) require substantial resources. But it also can occur when stress reactions involve expending amounts or types of resources that are not commensurate with the actual adaptations needed to respond successfully to a stressor. The latter dilemma is precisely what occurs when posttraumatic stress reactions occur in response to nontraumatic stressors: the stress reaction that is commensurate with the demands of surviving a traumatic stressor is almost always more than is necessary to meet the demands of ordinary daily stressors. Thus, PTSD can be understood as a disorder of stress reactions that create an extreme allostatic load because they are adaptive in coping with traumatic stressors but are in excess of and poorly matched to the actual demands of subsequent ordinary, day-to-day nontraumatic stressors. Coping with a traumatic stressor demands extreme amounts of personal resources—bodily, emotional, and mental strength and energy. When that allocation of personal resources continues in the form of PTSD long after the traumatic stressor has ended, personal resources become severely depleted. In his theory of PTSD, psychologist Stevan Hobfoll calls this a failure of "conservation of resources" (see Box 2.2).

When the defining features of traumatic stressors are understood as the unpredictable and uncontrollable confrontation with actual or potential life-threatening injury or loss, PTSD can be understood as a chronic state of attempting to regain safety and a sense of life as predictable and controllable—but doing so as if survival continues to be threatened when it is not. Thus, PTSD involves being trapped in a never-ending state of extreme stress (i.e., high levels of allostatic load) that begins with adaptive survival reactions that become self-perpetuating stress reactions. The attempt to escape danger becomes a self-imposed (but entirely unintended) virtual prison in which stress reactions continue unabated because they seem to be the only path to escape, but they leave unsolved the fundamental problem of regaining safety and control. PTSD symptoms thus can be understood as extreme variations of the four basic types of stress reactions: freezing (not being able to remember aspects of traumatic

Box 2.2 PTSD as a Disorder of Diminished Resources

More than 25 years ago, Stevan Hobfoll proposed a new theory of stress based on "the supposition that people strive to retain, project, and build resources and that what is threatening to them is the potential or actual loss of these valued resources" (Hobfoll, 1989, p. 513). Since then, dozens of research studies have been conducted demonstrating that what makes stressors stressful is when events or experiences prevent people from achieving the primal goal of conserving precious personal resources. Moreover, many of these studies have shown that the traumatic impact of stressors that threaten the lives or bodily integrity of victims or their loved ones is compounded by—and may in fact be directly due to, at least in part—the loss of or barriers to regaining crucial personal resources such as an intact family, home, community, school, job, or income.

Hobfoll (2001) defines resources as "objects, personal characteristics, conditions, or energies that are valued in their own right, or that are valued because they act as conduits to the achievement or protection of valued resources" (p. 339). Thus, resources include tangible items (e.g., a house, food, clothing), socioeconomic factors (e.g., income, employment), interpersonal factors (e.g., intimacy, social support), and intrapersonal factors (e.g., self-esteem, hope). A study of Somali refugee youth and families identified five crucial resources that promoted successful resettlement in the United States after exposure to genocide and the dissolution of their entire communities and society: religious faith, healthy family communication, support networks, and peer support (Betancourt et al., 2015).

A study of 752 Palestinian adults living in the West Bank, Gaza Strip, and East Jerusalem who were interviewed four times at 6-month intervals found that loss of psychological (e.g., self-esteem, self-confidence) or interpersonal (e.g., social support, access to family and friends) resources predicted increased depression and PTSD symptoms, and the symptoms predicted further resource loss. More specifically, psychological distress predicted resource loss across shorter, 6-month time periods, but resource loss predicted psychological distress across longer, 12-month intervals. The results supported a corollary of Conservation of Resources theory that posits that loss of resources and psychological distress escalate each other over time in what comes to be a spiraling increase in posttraumatic stress. When only symptoms are assessed, chronic PTSD may appears to reach a steady-state of very high symptom severity, but these findings suggest that continuing resource loss may lead to further spikes in PTSD and depression symptoms, as well as potentially maintaining the severe symptoms by constant or periodic reactivation of intrusive memories of past traumatic experiences and attempts to avoid those memories, as well as and PTSD's depressive emotions and beliefs.

A study with 691 women attending a university at which a mass shooting occurred found that resource loss predicted PTSD symptoms 8 months after the shooting (Littleton, Kumpula, & Orcutt, 2011). Other potential contributing factors to PTSD symptoms, including previous exposure to other traumatic stressors, symptoms of PTSD, anxiety, and depression in the first month after the shooting, and being in the line of fire during the shooting, were predictive of more severe PTSD symptoms 8 months later. However, loss of resources since the shooting was significantly predictive of PTSD symptoms at that follow-up assessment over and above the contributions of these other trauma exposure, PTSD, and psychological distress factors. Thus, it appears that it is not only the immediate traumatic shock of experiencing a life-threatening stressor but also the subsequent loss of key personal resources, that contributes to the development of PTSD.

events or being unable to feel positive emotions), fight (anger, hypervigilance, blaming self or others), flight (avoiding reminders, detachment from relationships, difficulty sustaining concentration), and shutting down (dissociation, emotional numbing, pervasive negative beliefs and emotions, anhedonia).

Living organisms tend to be biologically oriented to avoid death, except when a stronger innate imperative overrides the survival instinct (e.g., suicidality; sacrifice for the lives of others). Traumatic events confront people with the reality of their own death, even though they may only be a witness to someone else's actual or potential death and not personally injured or even in harm's way. The aphorism "There but for the grace of God go I" captures how being a witness to death, the threat of death, or terrible suffering can confront a person with her own mortality. It can be equally or even more terrifying to helplessly witness others face death or extreme suffering than it is to experience it oneself. When others die or suffer, people often experience a form of guilt known as "survivor guilt," which is a particularly insidious feeling of having failed to protect others from trauma or death. At the core of survivor guilt is a sense of terror, horror, and helplessness that may not actually be guilt so much as it is a sense of identification with the traumatized individual(s) as if their terrible fate was one's own. Either directly surviving a near-death experience or witnessing others survive or succumb to death can create an extreme sense of terror, horror, and helplessness that fundamentally changes the person.

Traumatic stressors may not objectively change the course of a person's life, but the sense of having narrowly escaped death inevitably changes a person's outlook on life. As such, traumatic stressors are unique among all other stressors in that they fundamentally involve an alteration (or ending) in the course of the lives of victims and witnesses that could not be more than partially anticipated (e.g., in war, one knows that being mortally wounded is possible—in some cases even inevitable—but one never knows exactly when or how or to whom this will happen.). As such, traumatic stressors are inherently uncontrollable, even by highly trained and prepared survivors (e.g., even elite military, law enforcement, or emergency responder personnel cannot prevent or even mitigate many tragic deaths, losses, or life-changing catastrophes) (Box 2.3).

Box 2.3 Definition of a "Traumatic Stressor"

Traumatic stressors are events or experiences that are defined as follows by the American Psychiatric Association's (2013) *Diagnostic and Statistical Manual of Mental Disorders* (fifth edition, p. 271). A "traumatic event" involves: "Exposure to actual or threatened death, serious injury, or sexual violence in one (or more) of the following ways): 1. Directly experiencing the traumatic event(s); 2. Witnessing, in person, the event(s) as it occurred to others. 3. Learning that the traumatic event(s) occurred to a close family member or close friend. In cases of actual or threatened death of a family member or friend, the event(s) must have been violent or accidental. 4. Experiencing repeated or extreme exposure to aversive details of the traumatic event(s) (e.g., first responders collecting human remains; police officers repeatedly exposed to the details of child abuse. *Note:* [This] does not apply to exposure through electronic media, television, movies, or pictures, unless the exposure is work-related."

Twenty-five years ago, psychologist Bonnie Green (1990) anticipated this definition by describing eight defining features of traumatic stressors:

1. threat to one's life or bodily integrity;
2. severe physical harm or injury;
3. intentional injury/harm (such as physical or sexual assaults or abuse);
4. exposure to the grotesque (such as corpses or human remains in war or a disaster);
5. violent/sudden loss of a loved one;
6. witnessing or learning of violence to a loved one;
7. learning of exposure to a noxious agent (such as poison gas, nuclear radiation, or HIV);
8. causing death or severe harm to another.

The final two features in this list are important special instances of the first subtype of traumatic stressor as defined by the American Psychiatric Association (direct exposure to actual or threatened death or serious injury). Whether the "noxious" effects of being contaminated by a harmful biological agent are immediate (e.g., exposure to poison gas or chemical weapons) or delayed (e.g., exposure to a virus such as HIV or Ebola), the pain and suffering that results is not only physical but may be even more extreme psychologically. The certainty of death or extreme physical suffering is compounded by the uncertainty of exactly when and how these horrifying consequences will occur and the sense of helplessness because it may not be possible to stop this apparently inevitable progression to death and disfigurement. If antidotes, preventive vaccines, curative treatments, or agents that slow or halt the progression of the contamination are available, such exposures are still frightening but not overwhelmingly so.

The final feature of perpetration of harm was first identified when soldiers returned from war bearing the emotional burden and guilt of having committed atrocities such as killing innocent bystanders (especially children) or executing helpless combatants. The My Lai killing of virtually the entire population of a Vietnamese village by an army company led by Lieutenant William Calley in the

1970s was a highly publicized atrocity, but hundreds more have been disclosed from many wars before and since that conflict (Yager, Laufer, & Gallops, 1984). Such acts usually are not premeditated but occur in "the heat of battle" or as reprisals for deaths of comrades, yet they appear to leave a particularly intractable "moral injury" (Litz et al., 2009) when the perpetrator views the acts as a violation of fundamental ethical and spiritual principles. Perpetrating harm has been found to be associated with particularly severe and complex PTSD among military personnel (Ford, 1999; Maguen et al., 2013).

So, ultimately, what makes a stressor such an extreme drain on personal resources that it should be considered not just stressful but "traumatic"? Three factors are consistently found to be crucial in research studies: severe (life-altering) injury, unpredictability, and uncontrollability.

- *Confrontation with irreparable violence or loss*: traumatic stressors involve violence (either intentional or accidental) or losses that threaten the person's *own life or bodily integrity*, or the that of other persons whom they either directly *witness* being severely harmed (or its horrific aftermath) or with whom they have *an intimate relationship* and learn that that person was the victim of a sudden or violent death or life-threatening assault. The common denominator is that the person is faced with the reality (directly or vicariously) that their own life and body, and the relationships that they depend on for security and happiness, have been or could be permanently taken away or damaged beyond repair. In this way, traumatic events shatter an illusion of invulnerability that serves as a crucial buffer against suffering and hardship and a source of hope and optimism for all human beings—unless or until a traumatic confronted immediately and inescapably with the reality of death and loss. Traumatic assaults and losses may be of a violent or sexual nature or both, and may occur by chance (as in a severe accident or natural disaster) or due to actions intentionally perpetrated (as in abuse, rape, torture, kidnapping, genocide, intimate partner or gang attacks, or war).
- *Unpredictability*: danger is always most dangerous when you never know when it's going to happen. It also takes a lot of mental and physical resources to stay on alert and be prepared when you can't anticipate exactly when or how a stressor will occur. Before they actually happen, unpredictable stressors evoke anticipatory anxiety, a sense of vigilance and dread that lead a person to feel on edge, vulnerable, worried, and simultaneously preoccupied with adverse future possibilities and unable to concentrate on the present moment. When a stressor actually occurs unexpectedly, even if it turns out to be positive in nature and outcome, there is a sense of surprise or shock that comes from feeling unprepared to handle it effectively or caught off guard and blindsided. In such events, the resultant stress is higher than if the situation or circumstances were predicted and the individual had a plan that she or he could be easily and confidently put into action: the additional stress is due to having to expend personal resources to simply regain one's balance and develop a plan on the spur of the moment when taken by surprise (i.e., "building an airplane while flying it"). Most assaults and permanent losses are not predictable—even when military, law enforcement, or emergency medical personnel knows they are about to face life threatening violence, or a child is trapped in a chronically abusive situation from which she or he cannot escape, the exact timing and nature of assaults and losses cannot be predicted.

(*Continued*)

Box 2.3 Continued

• *Uncontrollability*: a loss or injury, even when severe and unexpected, often can be coped with if there is a way to have some influence over what happens or the outcome. Most stressors are not entirely controllable—we cannot prevent life from happening, and we often can't dictate the terms of events or other people's actions. Control is always a matter of degree, the extent to which we can have some meaningful input into decisions and actions that affect us even if most of what happens is beyond our ability to influence. Traumatic stressors render people largely if not completely powerless, unable to protect themselves or others and unable to change the course or ultimate outcome of events. The victim of a sexual assault may be able to resist or attempt to escape, but even when the worst is avoided or cut short, it is not possible to undo the sense of shock, disbelief, rage, or helplessness that occurs when someone else violently or coercively assets control over a person's body and strips them of their privacy and their trust in other human beings. The classic stress reaction of "freeze, fight, and flight" is an attempt by the body to regain control, and when a stressor neutralizes or takes all of these options away the expectable result is a form of physical and psychological shutting down that is the last vestige of control: this is not giving up (although it typically feels like that to the victim) but is instead a largely involuntary way of preserving just enough inner resources to survive.

Some stressful events are psychologically traumatic for almost everyone. For example, Rothbaum, Foa, Riggs, and Murdock (1992) found that 94% of women who had been raped within the past month reported symptoms consistent with PTSD. Rape was the stressor that was most likely to be followed by PTSD among men (65%) and women (46%) even years or decades later (Kessler, Sonnega, Bromet, Hughes, & Nelson, 1995). Childhood sexual or physical maltreatment, combat or war trauma (either as a military or civilian participant or victim), genocide or atrocities, disasters that obliterate an entire community or involve biological or chemical contamination, and torture or severe physical assault are other stressors that are highly likely to lead to PTSD.

In the beginning: acute traumatic stress reactions and acute stress disorder

Acute traumatic stress reactions

When people experience horrifying threats to their lives or the lives of others, or deliberate exploitation and violation of their sexual, physical, or psychological integrity and privacy, the shocking harm caused by these events triggers a cascade of self-protective reactions. Acute traumatic stress reactions are, first and foremost, instinctive attempts to survive in the face of potentially life-threatening or psychologically overwhelming harm or danger. Thus, it is not surprising that acute traumatic stress reactions occur commonly; they have been called a "normal reaction to abnormal circumstances" (Herman, 1992) in order to emphasize the adaptive nature of stress reactions during and soon after experiencing a traumatic event. For example:

- Disbelief and emotional shock (feeling emotionally numb or dazed and detached from the experience, as if in a dream; seeing with tunnel vision and laser-like clarity) may provide an emotional buffer or anesthesia similar to the physical numbing that occurs when an injury causes a biological state of shock.
- Hyperarousal (the "adrenaline rush" experience of having one's heart pounding, muscles tensing, sweating, rapid breathing, and being jumpy and easily startled) may mobilize the physical energy needed to respond rapidly and forcefully to a threat.
- Hypervigilance (being extremely on guard, watchful, and alert for danger) may enable the person to anticipate and react rapidly and purposefully to additional stressors.
- Dissociation (feeling as if you don't know who you are or as if the experience can't be real; having gaps in one's memory) may provide a form of psychological escape hatch when the enormity of adversity or the resultant fear, grief, horror, rage, or pain become overwhelming.
- Intrusive memories (unwanted recollections that may include feeling as if the trauma is actually happening all over again—"flashbacks"—or thoughts, images, sounds, or other reminders or "replays" of what happened and one's immediate reactions) may enhance the person's ability to mentally and emotionally confront and make sense of the experience and prepare for or prevent similar dangers or harm.
- Avoiding reminders (such as people, places, or activities) and thoughts of a traumatic experience may assist in shifting focus from bad things in the past toward positive personal goals and pursuits that can enrich one's life and relationships in the present.

Particularly intense acute traumatic stress reactions are a risk factor for developing persistent posttraumatic distress and PTSD (Brewin et al., 2002; Bryant, 2008; Bryant, Creamer, O'Donnell, Silove, & McFarlane, 2008). This means that the more severe a person's stress reactions during or soon after experiencing a traumatic event, the more likely that person is to develop lasting posttraumatic distress or PTSD. Because most people do not develop lasting posttraumatic distress or PTSD, this "risk" should *not* be interpreted to mean that a person with severe acute stress reactions is destined to develop prolonged problems or PTSD. However, more intense acute stress reactions can be thought of as a warning sign that the person's biological and psychological reaction to a psychologically traumatic experience may be strong enough to become a lasting rather than temporary stress reaction.

This risk relationship between acute traumatic stress reactions and subsequent PTSD may seem to suggest that people who are experiencing, or have recently experienced, psychologically traumatic events should attempt to keep their stress reactions as mild as possible. However, it is not possible to control the exact nature and intensity of acute traumatic stress reactions simply by attempting to be calm or to react less strongly. Stress management skills that have shown promise in helping people deal with nontraumatic stressors may be beneficial for some trauma survivors, but the severity, unpredictability, and uncontrollability of danger or loss involved in traumatic stressors appears to trigger relatively automatic self-protective biological reactions that are less amenable to stress management skills than other stress reactions (see Chapter 5).

Acute stress disorder

When acute stress reactions are destabilizing rather than a source of helpful physical and psychological readjustment, they may become symptoms of a disorder that has been formally included by the American Psychiatric Association as a diagnosis warranting mental health treatment. "Acute Stress Disorder" (ASD; Figure 2.1) is precisely the same set of acute stress reactions but with the added kick of persisting beyond the first few days following traumatic stress exposure and becoming sufficiently severe to compromise the person's functioning in one or several important domains of life (such as family, friendships, work, school, or health).

The first edition of the *DSM*, published in 1952 (APA, 1952), included the stress-related diagnosis Gross Stress Reaction (GSR), which was defined as a "transient situational personality disorder" that could occur when essentially "normal" individuals experienced "severe physical demands or extreme emotional stress." However, GSR was dropped from the second edition of the *DSM* (APA, 1968) and subsumed within the category of Adjustment Reactions—acute responses to environmental stress of any severity—thereby diminishing the specificity of the diagnosis (Brett, 1996). Twelve years later, with the publication of the *DSM-III* (APA, 1980), the extreme emotional stress of the GSR resurfaced in an altered form as PTSD, this time with the recognition of the chronic reactions that can occur in response to trauma and differentiation between adjustment and traumatic stress disorders (Brett, 1996). Advocacy efforts by and on behalf of Vietnam War veterans (Jones & Wessely, 2007) and women who had experienced "rape trauma syndrome" (Burgess & Holmstrom, 1974) were decisive in both restoring a stress-related diagnosis to the formal psychiatric classification system and linking it specifically to the experience of exposure to extreme or traumatic stressors (Breslau & Davis, 1987).

Further, in an effort to provide a more valid and reliable guide to diagnosis, the *DSM-III* introduced a phenomenological approach to diagnosis, and as such provided specific symptom criteria for the diagnosis of PTSD. Trauma exposure (Criterion A) was defined as the "existence of a recognizable stressor that would evoke significant symptoms of distress in almost everyone" (APA, 1980, p. 238). Colloquially, this has been described as a stressor that was outside the range of normal human experience, a distinction that was solidified in the *DSM-III-R* revision (APA, 1987). Twelve possible PTSD symptoms were described, based on early research and clinical observations that identified unwanted and severely distressing memories of traumatic events (technically designated as "intrusive reexperiencing") and extreme states of physiological and emotional arousal (technically designated as "hyperarousal") as core symptoms of PTSD (Horowitz & Smit, 2008). However, there was no diagnosis specifically for severe stress reactions in the acute aftermath of exposure to traumatic stressors.

In a 1994 revision, the *DSM-IV* added subjective features (a response of "intense fear, helplessness, or horror") to the traumatic exposure (Criterion A2). The *DSM-IV* also for the first time included an ASD diagnosis. Like PTSD, ASD required a Criterion A traumatic event and includes similar symptom criteria to those constituting PTSD (Criteria B through D). However, ASD could not be diagnosed unless symptoms and associated impairment last at least 2 days (so as to exclude those with immediate but transient "peritraumatic" reactions, which are almost universal)

Acute Stress Disorder

Diagnostic Criteria	308.3 (F43.0)

A. Exposure to actual or threatened death, serious injury, or sexual violation in one (or more) of the following ways:

1. Directly experiencing the traumatic event(s).
2. Witnessing, in person, the event(s) as it occurred to others.
3. Learning that the event(s) occurred to a close family member or close friend. **Note:** In cases of actual or threatened death of a family member or friend, the event(s) must have been violent or accidental.
4. Experiencing repeated or extreme exposure to aversive details of the traumatic event(s) (e.g., first responders collecting human remains, police officers repeatedly exposed to details of child abuse).

Note: This does not apply to exposure through electronic media, television, movies, or pictures, unless this exposure is work related.

B. Presence of nine (or more) of the following symptoms from any of the five categories of intrusion, negative mood, dissociation, avoidance, and arousal, beginning or worsening after the traumatic event(s) occurred:

Intrusion Symptoms

1. Recurrent, involuntary, and intrusive distressing memories of the traumatic event(s). **Note:** In children, repetitive play may occur in which themes or aspects of the traumatic event(s) are expressed.
2. Recurrent distressing dreams in which the content and/or affect of the dream are related to the event(s). **Note:** In children, there may be frightening dreams without recognizable content.
3. Dissociative reactions (e.g., flashbacks) in which the individual feels or acts as if the traumatic event(s) were recurring. (Such reactions may occur on a continuum, with the most extreme expression being a complete loss of awareness of present surroundings.) **Note:** In children, trauma-specific reenactment may occur in play.
4. Intense or prolonged psychological distress or marked physiological reactions in response to internal or external cues that symbolize or resemble an aspect of the traumatic event(s).

Negative Mood

5. Persistent inability to experience positive emotions (e.g., inability to experience happiness, satisfaction, or loving feelings).

Dissociative Symptoms

6. An altered sense of the reality of one's surroundings or oneself (e.g., seeing oneself from another's perspective, being in a daze, time slowing).
7. Inability to remember an important aspect of the traumatic event(s) (typically due to dissociative amnesia and not to other factors such as head injury, alcohol, or drugs).

Avoidance Symptoms

8. Efforts to avoid distressing memories, thoughts, or feelings about or closely associated with the traumatic event(s).
9. Efforts to avoid external reminders (people, places, conversations, activities, objects, situations) that arouse distressing memories, thoughts, or feelings about or closely associated with the traumatic event(s).

Arousal Symptoms

10. Sleep disturbance (e.g., difficulty falling or staying asleep, restless sleep).
11. Irritable behavior and angry outbursts (with little or no provocation), typically expressed as verbal or physical aggression toward people or objects.
12. Hypervigilance.
13. Problems with concentration.
14. Exaggerated startle response.

C. Duration of the disturbance (symptoms in Criterion B) is 3 days to 1 month after trauma exposure.

Note: Symptoms typically begin immediately after the trauma, but persistence for at least 3 days and up to a month is needed to meet disorder criteria.

D. The disturbance causes clinically significant distress or impairment in social, occupational, or other important areas of functioning.

E. The disturbance is not attributable to the physiological effects of a substance (e.g., medication or alcohol) or another medical condition (e.g., mild traumatic brain injury) and is not better explained by brief psychotic disorder.

Figure 2.1 *DSM*-5 diagnostic criteria for ASD (308.3).
© American Psychiatric Association, www.psychiatryonline.com.

and not more than 4 weeks following exposure to the traumatic stressor. ASD also included symptoms of dissociation (i.e., derealization, depersonalization) that were not included in PTSD until the next *DSM* revision (*DSM*-5).

During the five decades of evolution of the traumatic stress diagnoses in the American *DSM* diagnostic system, there has been a parallel process of refinement in the definition of ASD in the World Health Organization's *International Classification of Diseases* (*ICD*), with several important points of difference. Like the *DSM*, the earliest references in the *ICD* to stress-related responses described transient rather than chronic stress reactions (WHO, 1948, 1955, 1965). The first reference to PTSD appeared in the *ICD-9* in 1978 under the heading of Adult Onset Adjustment Reaction, which described responses to chronic stress. A separate category of "Acute Reaction to Stress" also was set forth in the *ICD-9* to describe transient responses to "exceptional stress," including separate subcategories reflecting reactions character-ized by disturbance of emotions, consciousness, or psychomotor functions (Turnbull, 1998). Thus, in contrast to the *DSM-III*'s failure to distinguish acute and chronic posttraumatic stress reactions (categorizing them all as PTSD) and to the absence of a diagnosis for severe acute traumatic stress reactions in the *DSM-III-R*, the *ICD-9* was more precise and complete than its *DSM* counterparts (and anticipated the addition of ASD to the *DSM-IV*) by describing Acute Reaction to Stress as severe symptoms in the immediate wake of exposure to a traumatic stressor.

An updated description of PTSD and Acute Stress Reaction was provided in the most recent (*ICD-10*) edition, which was published at approximately the same time (1992) that the *DSM-IV* (APA, 1994) was being finalized (Lasiuk & Hegadoren, 2006). The *ICD-10* and *DSM-IV* PTSD and Acute Stress Reaction (*ICD-10*) or Disorder (*DSM-IV*) diagnoses involved very similar but not exactly identical definitions of the stressor criterion, symptom criteria, and duration and functional impairment criteria. However, there are several important differences between the *ICD-10* and the *DSM-IV*, some of which foreshadow changes in the *DSM* that occurred 20 years later in the *DSM*-5. While the *DSM-IV* continued to describe both PTSD and Acute Stress Reaction diagnoses as Anxiety Disorders (as did the *DSM-III* and *III-R*), the *ICD-10* placed these diagnoses in the "Reactions to Severe Stress and Adjustment Disorders" category. In addition, while the Acute Stress Reaction diagnosis in the *ICD-10* involves a variety of possible symp-toms that tend to ebb and flow rather than remain constant, in the immediate (i.e., for at least 3 days) wake of a traumatic experience, the *DSM-IV* requires a more prescribed set of required symptoms. This description of acute posttraumatic stress reactions is consistent with research evidence that no single set of symptoms characterizes most or all persons who are adversely affected in the acute aftermath of traumatic stressors (Marshall, Spitzer, & Liebowitz, 1999). That view, as we shall see, was adopted in the *DSM*-5 but not in the definition of ASD in the *DSM-IV*.

ASD in both the *DSM-IV* and the *DSM*-5 has a Criterion A (traumatic stressor) identical to that in PTSD, but it differs from "acute" PTSD in several important ways. First, ASD must occur within 1 month of exposure to the stressor event(s) and may be diagnosed as soon as 2 (in the *DSM-IV*) or 3 (in both the *DSM*-5 and *ICD-10*) days afterward. Thus, ASD represents a traumatic stress disorder that can be diagnosed almost immediately—although not within the first few days after psychological trauma, because most people should not be diagnosed with a traumatic stress disorder when (as is typical) they experience extreme stress reactions in the first hours or days after a traumatic event but go on to recover without developing persistent symptoms or impairment. ASD and PTSD were designed to be complementary diagnoses such that PTSD could first be diagnosed almost exactly when ASD no longer can be diagnosed—at the point in time when 1-month has passed since the traumatic event(s).

Another important difference between ASD and PTSD is that ASD includes fewer symptoms (14 in the *DSM*-5) than PTSD (22 in the *DSM*-5, including the two optional dissociative symptoms). However, every ASD symptom is also a PTSD symptom, or a combination of several PTSD symptoms. For example, in the *DSM*-5, the two PTSD intrusive reexperiencing symptoms involving intense or prolonged psychological distress or marked physiological reactions in response to reminders of traumatic events are collapsed into a single ASD symptom. The two optional PTSD dissociative symptoms of depersonalization and derealization also are combined into a single ASD symptom. Several PTSD symptoms that typically do not develop until more than a month following exposure to traumatic stressors are not included in ASD in the *DSM*-5: persistent negative beliefs, blame of self or others, negative emotion states, loss of interest (anhedonia), and feelings of detachment from others.

The most controversial feature of ASD in the *DSM-IV*—which was dropped in the *DSM*-5—was the requirement that at least three of five symptoms of pathological dissociation had to occur either during or after experiencing the stressor event(s). Dissociation is common during and soon after exposure to psychological trauma; this is called "peritraumatic dissociation" because "peri" signifies that dissociation is occurring close in time to the stressor event(s). Although peritraumatic dissociation is a common acute traumatic stress reaction, research has shown that it is neither the only nor the most important such reaction in determining or predicting who will develop PTSD (Bryant, 2011). Research also points to three key forms of peritraumatic dissociation as most prevalent and predictive of adverse outcomes, each of which involves more than a transient feeling of shock or confusion. These do not include feeling emotionally numbed or detached or "in a daze," which is an expected and immediate reaction to a psychological shock. Instead, they include feeling a sense of unreality ("derealization") or being an outside observer of oneself ("depersonalization"), or being unable to recall important aspects of the event(s) ("psychogenic amnesia"). When those dissociative symptoms occur peritraumatically, the risk of developing PTSD is increased, and therefore they are the only dissociative symptoms included in the *DSM*-5 version of ASD— with the possible exception of a PTSD intrusive reexperiencing symptom of suddenly feeling as if the traumatic event(s) are happening all over again—flashbacks—which in their most extreme form appear to involve dissociation.

Some key questions are whether and how often ASD leads to PTSD. Richard Bryant (2008) and his colleagues conducted extensive studies on ASD, and, based on a review of these and other teams' studies, concluded that "approximately three-quarters of trauma survivors who display ASD subsequently develop PTSD." However, Bryant also notes that 50% of those who develop PTSD did *not* have sufficient symptoms or impairment to qualify earlier for ASD: "Whereas the majority of people who develop ASD are at high risk for developing subsequent PTSD, there are also many other people who will develop

PTSD who do not initially meet ASD criteria. It seems that the major reason for people who are high risk for PTSD not meeting ASD criteria is the requirement of dissociative symptoms." In other words, many people who do not have sufficiently severe symptoms of dissociation in the first 4 weeks after experiencing a traumatic event to qualify for a diagnosis of ASD later develop PTSD. This is consistent with other research that has shown that it is the severity of initial PTSD symptoms (which do not include dissociative symptoms, except for flashbacks) that is the major warning sign of a risk of developing PTSD a month or more after a traumatic event (Brewin & Holmes, 2003).

These findings have led to the retention of ASD as a diagnosis in the *DSM*-5, while including only symptoms that are predictive of subsequent PTSD or other psychiatric disorders (Bryant, Creamer, O'Donnell, Silove, & McFarlane, 2012). There is a clear need for an ASD diagnosis because when people who have this diagnosis receive help in the form of "cognitive behavior therapy" (see Chapters 7 and 8) designed specifically to efficiently (typically in five sessions) eliminate or reduce ASD symptoms, 80% of them do *not* subsequently develop PTSD (compared to only 25% without this therapy) (Bryant, 2008, 2011).

Life after trauma: Positive and problematic trajectories of adaptation

That traumatic stress is a process of adaptation is highlighted by the fact that most people who experience psychological trauma do not develop persistent clinically significant impairment (Charney, 2004), and those who do often report periods of relatively quiescent symptoms on any given day (Frueh, Elhai, & Kaloupek, 2004) and in some cases for periods of weeks, months, or years of "remission" (i.e., without symptoms or with symptoms that are mild or manageable).

In fact, a recent study with military veterans found that several factors that were predictive of developing PTSD in the first place (such as the person's education and income before entering the military, the severity of the person's acute sense of threat and dissociation during or soon after traumatic events, and subsequent traumatic experiences) were *not* associated with the "maintenance" (i.e., persistence) of PTSD over a period of many years (Schnurr, Lunney, & Sengupta, 2004). Both developing and having persistent PTSD were associated with the person's sense of not having emotional support in relationships. Having experienced or been involved in acts of abusive violence was the sole unique predictor of chronic PTSD (i.e., of not recovering from PTSD). On the other hand, military personnel from some ethnic groups (Native Hawaiian and Japanese American) were not less likely to develop PTSD but were *more* likely to recover from PTSD than those of Hispanic, African American, or white ethnic backgrounds.

Thus, most people can and do recover from acute traumatic stress reactions, although few people escape entirely unscathed (i.e., without any acute distress). Acute stress reactions may provide trauma survivors with an opportunity to learn from and cope with the distress, shock, and emotional or physical harm caused by a traumatic event. From that perspective, acute traumatic stress reactions, while not something to wish upon anyone, nevertheless can be the beginning of, or a chance to shift back to, a positive trajectory in life after being thrown off course by traumatic event(s).

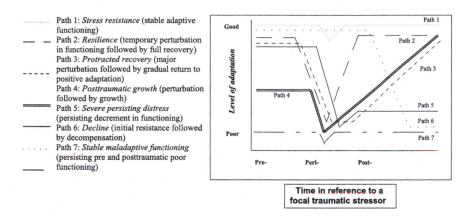

Path 1: *Stress resistance* (stable adaptive functioning)
Path 2: *Resilience* (temporary perturbation in functioning followed by full recovery)
Path 3: *Protracted recovery* (major perturbation followed by gradual return to positive adaptation)
Path 4: *Posttraumatic growth* (perturbation followed by growth)
Path 5: *Severe persisting distress* (persisting decrement in functioning)
Path 6: *Decline* (initial resistance followed by decompensation)
Path 7: *Stable maladaptive functioning* (persisting pre and posttraumatic poor functioning)

Figure 2.2 Trajectories of adaptation following stressful or traumatic life events. Reprinted with permission of the author and publisher from Layne et al. (2007).

Four positive posttraumatic life trajectories have been identified by Layne et al. (2008), each of which can be traced back to the individual's acute traumatic stress reactions. Figure 2.2 shows these and three negative trajectories, with each trajectory represented by a line running from left to right along the horizontal (*x*) axis, beginning prior to the traumatic stressor, continuing during and shortly after the trauma (the "peri"-traumatic period, where "peri" means near in time to the traumatic stessor), and going on for days, weeks, months, and years in the posttraumatic period. The higher the line for a trajectory is on the vertical (*y*) axis ("Level of Adaptation"), the better the person's functioning and quality of life.

There is not yet sufficient research evidence to enable us to estimate the most likely trajectory for any specific individual in the wake of a traumatic stressor. It is not possible as yet to estimate the general percentages of trauma survivors whose lives will follow each posttraumatic trajectory except in very general terms, in large part because the events and the individuals involved are unique. With additional research on the risk factors (including genetics) that lead people to be vulnerable to problematic posttraumatic life trajectories and PTSD and the "protective" factors that are related to more positive posttraumatic life trajectories, greater precision will no doubt be achieved. With those caveats in mind, consider the following four potential positive posttraumatic trajectories that represent ways in which people are able to go on with their lives and avoid entirely or put to rest or learn to live with the symptoms of PTSD and associated problems.

Positive posttraumatic life trajectories

"Stress resistance" involves successful coping with acute stress reactions such that the person experiences no more than mild and brief difficulties in work, relationships, and psychological and physical health (represented by the shallow dip in the line during the peritraumatic period during and soon after the traumatic stressor, as shown in the light solid line at the top of Figure 2.2). Stress resistance is common following ordinary life stressors that are upsetting, worrisome, or challenging but neither traumatic nor particularly persistent or burdensome. Stress resistance is less common following traumatic stressors and is most likely to occur:

1. when the traumatic event is relatively brief and does not involve severe emotional or physical damage or suffering (such as a motor vehicle accident that happens quickly and despite potentially being disastrous actually does not cause any major injuries or the death of anyone involved);
2. when intentional acts of cruelty or exploitation such as abuse, purposeful violence, or sexual violation are not involved (such as an accidental injury);
3. when the traumatic event does not cause prolonged adversity in its aftermath (such as a natural disaster in which most people were able to safely survive and keep their homes and community intact);
4. where the individual did not feel helpless and unable to take steps, either during or soon after the event, to prevent harm from occurring, reduce the severity of harm, or to hasten successful recovery for self and others (such as military combat in which the combatant is able to prevent an ambush from occurring or respond to the attack in ways that prevented severe harm or death from occurring to comrades or other friendly personnel and civilians).

"Resilience" refers to successful coping with acute stress reactions and problems in living following exposure to a traumatic stressor, such that the person adjusts and functions well even if these acute posttraumatic stress reactions are intense. The person who is resilient in the wake of psychological trauma may be terrified, shocked, confused, grief stricken, or even horrified by the events and their aftermath, but she or he is able to regain emotional and mental balance and focus over the subsequent days such that PTSD does not develop or is at most a relatively temporary condition.

"Recovery" involves suffering PTSD or other severe posttraumatic problems and then later regaining healthy functioning. Psychological, psychiatric, or social interventions have been designed specifically to help people recover from PTSD (see Chapters 7 and 8). However, many people who do not receive special treatment or assistance are able to recover from PTSD for reasons that are not fully understood. Several theories have been advanced to explain how psychosocial resources such as innate resilience or intelligence, supportive relationships, and economic and social "capital" may lead some persons (and communities) to recover from posttraumatic impairment without receiving formal treatment for PTSD (see Chapter 9). As noted earlier in this chapter, as many as 80% of people who receive an evidence-based CBT for ASD (and 25% of those who do not receive this targeted therapy) do not develop PTSD and therefore can be considered to be "early recovers."

"PTG" is a fourth positive trajectory that is less common (or possibly more common than suspected, but often unrecognized, because growth is not typically expected to occur in the wake of traumatic experiences). PTG involves the development of new knowledge, abilities, relationships, or hope and confidence following a traumatic stressor in addition to recovering successfully from acute stress reactions. For example, people whose homes and communities are devastated by disasters such as hurricanes, cyclones, tornados, or earthquakes at times are able to not only rebuild or relocate successfully but also to develop a keen appreciation for their relationships, work, personal activities, or spiritual faith that is beyond what they had experienced prior to the traumatic disaster. Whether or not this is personal growth due specifically to the traumatic stressor that they experienced remains controversial (see Box 2.4), but their sense of having grown often is very strong and is associated with resistance, resilience, and recovery from PTSD.

Box 2.4 PTG: Can Traumatic Stressors Produce Personal Growth?

For many years, survivors of psychological trauma have described feeling a sense of psychological, emotional, or spiritual growth as a result of enduring and overcoming adversities such as war, genocide, family violence, child abuse, and life-threatening accidents, disasters, or illnesses. Trauma survivors have described feeling as if they have been given a second chance and as a result have a keener appreciation of the opportunities that they have in their lives and relationships. Experiences that previously seemed mundane or went unnoticed in the rush to meet deadlines and follow habitual routines might seem to have a new significance. The survivor might feel able, or even inwardly compelled, to "stop and smell the roses"—that is, to mindfully pay attention to and find value in every experience. Some say that they feel a sense of clarity of vision and purpose, or a revised set of priorities, where they had been stagnating or living reflexively before (Salter & Stallard, 2004). A classic example is Dr. Viktor Frankl's (1946) observations of spiritual and existential inspiration during the Holocaust in Nazi concentration camps. Clinicians working with survivors of psychological trauma have been deeply affected by similar personal stories of personal and spiritual renewal in the face of trauma, leading to a challenge to the dominant pathologizing view of psychological trauma (that traumatic stress damages the body, mind, and relationships): perhaps experiencing traumatic stressors can lead to personal PTG (Joseph & Linley, 2008; Tedeschi & Calhoun, 2004).

Research on PTG has resulted in factor analyses of the data from a number of self-report questionnaires that have been developed to assess PTG (see Joseph & Linley, 2008). These studies have yielded a primary ("higher order") factor reflecting a wide range of positive changes following exposure to stressors or psychological trauma, and three secondary ("lower order") factors that represent the positive components of posttraumatic adaptation: (i) enhanced relationships, (ii) new beliefs and understanding about oneself, and (iii) change in life philosophy (Joseph & Linley, 2008). Additional analyses of scores from PTG self-report measures suggest that the positive adaptations in the wake of psychological trauma may represent a unique dimension of posttraumatic adjustment that is distinct from negative changes such as PTSD symptoms rather than merely the opposite end of a single positive-negative continuum of posttraumatic adaptation (Joseph & Linley, 2008).

Numerous studies have attempted to measure positive posttraumatic adaptations using PTG questionnaires (e.g., 39 studies reviewed by Joseph & Linley, 2008). However, some important limitations in the methodologies of these studies limits the conclusions that can be drawn about using PTG as the organizing construct for positive posttraumatic adaptation. Three methodological issues are of particular concern (Ford, Tennen, & Albert, 2008). First, each measure of PTG has different questions and response formats and requirements, so it is difficult to compare results across studies. Second, PTG almost always is

(Continued)

Box 2.4 Continued

assessed by self-report, which means that what is being studied is the survivor's subjective view rather than more objective evidence of actual personal growth. Third, there are few studies that measure PTG at several periods over time ("longitudinal" studies; see Research entry, this volume) and that include measures of the individual's pretraumatic event status in the areas of purported "growth."

Concerning the measurement of PTG, most (27/39) of the studies reviewed by Linley and Joseph (2004) did not use well-validated measures of PTG. In addition, of the seven published instruments that were used to measure PTG in those studies, only two—the Changes in Outlook Questionnaire and the Revised Stress-Related Growth Scale—inquire about negative as well as positive change (Joseph & Linley, 2008). Thus, respondents may overreport positive changes simply because they are only asked about positive change. On the encouraging side, broadening the field of measurement to include positive as well as the more often assessed negative sequelae of traumatic experiences is an important advance in the traumatic stress field. However, assessment tools for PTG should be designed either to include or to be copresented with other measures of negative changes, and to assess threats to validity such as is done with the "validity scales" that are used in many psychological questionnaires (Ford et al., 2008).

PTG questionnaires also do not differentiate between positive states or outcomes that are an extension or continuation of prior psychological growth or development, versus changes that represent the qualitatively distinct discontinuities in the person's development that are necessary in order to demonstrate that the PTG is actually related to experiencing trauma (Ford et al., 2008). Frazier and Kaler (2006) note that retrospective self-report measures of PTG are vulnerable to error because of the well-documented difficulty that people have inaccuracy recalling past states or attributes, making it unlikely that they can accurately compare current states or attributes to past ones when estimating the nature or extent of "growth." PTG measures also do not rule out alternative explanations for outcomes that are supposedly the product of exposure to psychological trauma: for example, growth following psychological trauma may be due to survivors receiving unusual amounts of social support from family, friends, community, or professional helpers, or to the opportunity (born of necessity) to temporarily suspend their usual life routines and responsibilities in the aftermath of psychological trauma (Ford et al., 2008). Thus, growth that seems to be a response to psychological trauma actually may be due to other associated changes that are at most indirectly related to experiencing trauma per se.

People also may be influenced by wishful thinking and denial, particularly in the wake of stressful events (Frazier & Kaler, 2006). McFarland and Alvaro (2000) found that psychological trauma survivors tended to rate their preevent functioning less favorably than did other observers, and therefore rated their postevent functioning as more improved simply because they viewed themselves in a less favorable light before the traumatic event. Smith and Cook (2004) suggest that this downplaying of strengths prior to psychological trauma and the corresponding increase in estimates of the positive change experienced in the wake of traumatic events may be an example of the concept of a "positive illusion." Such an illusion—the belief that PTG has occurred when there may be very little actual change—could help survivors cope with the negative impact of psychological trauma. Specifically, altering one's self-perceptions might increase a sense of control following a traumatic event. This could be a positive posttraumatic adaptation, but it might not reflect "growth" and might provide an increase in self-efficacy that could be transient and vulnerable to breaking down if negative posttraumatic changes become pronounced or if further stressors are encountered in the recovery period (Ford et al., 2008).

Some descriptions of positive outcomes following exposure to psychological trauma may reflect survivors' relief rather than growth. For instance, Salter and Stallard (2004) interpreted statements by children who had experienced a traumatic accident such that they felt "lucky" to be alive or that, "Anything you want, go for it quicker as you never realize when you are going to go." These statements may reflect an attempt to cope with the heightened realization of mortality that is a hallmark symptom of PTSD (i.e., sense of foreshortened future; Ford et al., 2008). This attitude also may reflect a personality trait that Rabe, Zollner, Maercker and Karl (2006) describe as "goal-related approach tendencies" (p. 883). In a study with survivors of life-threatening motor vehicle accidents on average 5 years later, Rabe et al. (2006) found that scores on the Posttraumatic Growth Inventory (PTGI) subscales that represented a tendency to seek control and find meaning were associated with patterns of activation the brain that are likely to be related to an enduring trait of setting goals and seeking personal control and meaning. Thus, Rabe et al.' (2006) findings suggest that "growth" may be a preexisting trait and not a posttraumatic change—an adaptation based primarily on preexisting capacities rather than a response caused by the experience of psychological trauma per se.

The ultimate evidence of growth following exposure to psychological trauma would come from studies in which people who experience psychological trauma had already been assessed prior to experiencing traumatic events (see Longitudinal Research studies section, this chapter). The optimal scenario would include a series of assessments over a period of months or years prior to trauma exposure, rather than no pretrauma baseline or only a single measurement of pretrauma status. This is an ambitious approach that has not yet been reported in the published research on psychological trauma. It would provide evidence of not only their pretrauma status at one time-point but whether there already was evidence of "growth" (or stability, or a decline) along potential pathways or trajectories of posttraumatic adaptation that include the many areas of psychological functioning that are assessed following the traumatic event(s). Then it would be possible to test survivors again using the same or similar measures over a

(*Continued*)

Box 2.4 Continued

period of time following the traumatic event(s) in order to determine if there is evidence of change and if there is an increase in the rate of positive change following the traumatic events compared to their rate of change prior to trauma exposure. No such studies have as yet been reported.

Linley and Joseph (2004) identified three longitudinal studies of PTG, but none of them measured preevent functioning. Two other longitudinal studies have included pretrauma baseline measures, however. Davis, Nolen-Hoeksema, and Larson (1998) assessed bereaved adults during a hospice program on average 3 months prior to a loved one's death, and then for the next 18 months. Controlling for preloss distress levels, they found that making sense of the loss was associated with less distress in the first year postloss, and reporting benefiting from the experience was associated with less distress more than a year after the loss. However, it is not clear that the "preloss" distress levels were a true baseline because the loss was imminent and the stress of caregiving often already was protracted at the time of the baseline assessment (Ford et al., 2008). It also is not clear that the "benefit" was associated with loss per se, as opposed to other factors such as social support or preexisting resilience (Ford et al., 2008).

In the second longitudinal study with a pretrauma baseline, Ickovics et al. (2006) obtained an assessment of psychological distress from inner-city adolescent girls who were sexually active (half of whom were pregnant), and reinterviewed them every 6 months, for a total of 18 months. Trauma history and PTG were assessed at the 12-month assessment by open-ended responses to a question asking about the "hardest thing [they] ever had to deal with" and by the PTGI subscales reflecting a tendency to seek positive experiences in life. Controlling for baseline distress levels, PTGI at 12 months predicted reduced emotional distress 6 months later. However, the traumatic events may have occurred at any point in the girls' lives, so there actually was no pretrauma baseline. Stability or change in PTGI was not assessed, nor were other factors such as stable personality traits and social support. Therefore, the PTG's apparent relationship to emotional distress 6 months later may be due to many factors, and whether the PTGI scores actually reflected growth due to traumatic adversity is unknown.

Overall, methodological weaknesses in these studies makes any conclusions premature with regard to whether PTG actually occurs, what factors increase or decrease the likelihood of PTG, how PTG occurs psychologically and neurobiologically, and what temporary or lasting benefits are associated with PTG. Nevertheless, PTG remains a plausible form of posttraumatic adaptation, given the abundance of testimonials of PTG in popular culture and by clinicians who work with psychological trauma survivors, and the many studies attempting to measure PTG. As Ford et al. (2008) summarize, growth may occur as a result of overcoming adversity, but the evidence is not conclusive as to whether " PTG" constitutes (i) actual sustained growth; (ii) temporary changes in mood, expectancies, and lifestyle; (iii) reappraisals to compensate for distress (e.g., positive illusions); (iv) the restoration of prior capacities following an adaptive shift from ordinary to survival-based self-regulation (i.e., resilience); or (v) measurement artifact.

Whether positive reinterpretation and acceptance coping are manifestations of actual growth, and not enduring personality traits, and change that has been catalyzed by experiencing traumatic stressors (as opposed to transient attempts to maintain emotional balance and hope in the wake of psychological trauma), remains unknown. The fact that some psychological trauma survivors feel that they have been given a second chance or a new lease on life, and in some cases are able to parlay this sense of relief and renewal into positive adaptations in their lives and relationships, is undeniable and serves as an inspiring reminder of the remarkable resilience that has made possible some of humanity's greatest accomplishments despite—and perhaps in part due to—the adversities of psychological trauma.

Problematic posttraumatic life trajectories

The most familiar problematic posttraumatic life trajectory has been described by Layne et al. (2008) as "severe persisting distress." In this case, the trauma-exposed individual develops acute traumatic stress reactions that persist (or worsen) over time in the form of severe problems such as PTSD, other anxiety disorders, depression, substance abuse, conflict at work and in relationships, legal or financial problems, or physical illness or disability. This trajectory is the classic form of PTSD, representing a sudden and lasting change in the person's ability to manage stress and anxiety that begins during or soon after experiencing a traumatic stressor. For example, people whose homes and communities are destroyed by a natural or manmade disaster may experience a shattering or paralyzing sense of loss and panic that can become a persistent problem with unresolved grief (especially if they cannot rebuild or if they are forced to relinquish important relationships), anxiety (including PTSD and other anxiety disorders), or related disorders such as depression or substance abuse. If acute posttraumatic distress is severe (as discussed earlier in this chapter) and key sources of social support are lost or unavailable (see Chapter 3), a sense of fearfulness, helplessness, or hopelessness may ensue that can take the form of persistent PTSD, depression, or other serious emotional and interpersonal problems. For the individual who has never struggled with this degree of psychological distress, developing PTSD may be not only upsetting and burdensome but also terrifying: "What has happened to me? Am I no longer the same person I used to be? Have I lost my ability to cope? Will I ever get back to being able to keep my emotions in balance and my life on track?" These fears are based upon a change in their bodies (see Chapter 6) and mental/emotional state for which previously healthy people typically have no benchmarks or road maps to help them see signs of recovery and a path to regaining their former ways of thinking, feeling, and handling life's challenges. This is why PTSD can be so devastating; it not only involves distressing memories and a body that is extremely reactive to even mild stressors but also a fundamental sense of being trapped by these symptoms with no way to see (or get to) a light at the end of the tunnel.

A similar dilemma of feeling trapped by symptoms of unprecedented and unanticipated severity and persistence occurs when people experience a similar problematic trajectory, only after a period (often as long as months, years, or decades after a traumatic stressor) of positive functioning (i.e., resistance or resilience). Layne et al. (2008) describe this trajectory as one of "decline," because PTSD or associated severe problems emerge only after a delay and then lead to a reduction (or decline) in the person's ability to function that is severe and chronic (Zlotnick, Bruce, Shea, & Keller, 2001).

This trajectory is, unfortunately, seen quite often among emergency or disaster first responders who may be highly effective in their work for lengthy careers and multiple traumatic experiences but at some point seem to lose their "edge" or "nerve" or ability to handle horrific situations with an attitude of cool professional detachment. Studies of first responders have shown that they tend to deny any "chinks in their armor" (such as feelings of anxiety, depression, or demoralization), but their spouses often report concern about them having difficulty with anger, sleep, becoming emotionally detached, or being tense, on edge, unable to relax, and using alcohol to cope with these likely symptoms of posttraumatic stress (Norris, Friedman, & Watson, 2002). These stress-related problems often go unnoticed and may be well managed by the individual and the family for many years—and they do not inevitably lead to sufficiently severe impairment to threaten the responder's work or relationships. However, when a particularly gruesome or heart-wrenching incident occurs (such as the death of a young child), this can be the "last straw" and lead to a decline in the responder's emotional or mental state that may be gradual or very steep.

First responders also may experience posttraumatic decline in the absence of a new traumatic experience as the result of the cumulative impact (see Chapter 3) of repeated exposure to the horrific details of injury and death, as well as at times themselves becoming victims. Warning signs such as an increase in the frequency or amount of alcohol use, sleep problems, and irritability with or withdrawal from family or friends often are the best ways to detect posttraumatic decline among such an extraordinarily resistant and resilient group of individuals. Even first responders, however, have limits to their capacity to adapt to repeated traumatic stressor exposures, and it is essential to provide them as well as other trauma survivors with help before the decline becomes severe (see Chapter 9 for a discussion of prevention interventions for stress-resilient trauma survivors).

From this perspective, it might seem that people who already are struggling with emotional or psychiatric problems before experiencing a traumatic stressor could actually be better prepared to resist or recover from acute traumatic stress reactions because they have some familiarity with this challenge—and because they may have fewer positive illusions (Taylor, 2007) about their own safety or ability to handle stressors without severe distress. There is anecdotal evidence to support this view, such as reports from disaster-affected communities such as New York City immediately after September 11, 2001, of persons with psychiatric disorders offering to relinquish their own treatment temporarily so that their mental health clinicians could devote themselves to helping the victimized survivors and bereaved families. However, the consistent research finding is that both adults and children who have preexisting psychiatric or emotional disorders are prone to have *similar or worsened problems in the wake of psychological trauma*. Their life trajectory, unfortunately, may be one of "stable maladaptive functioning" (Layne et al., 2008) that involves brief periods of resilience or growth. More often, the result of experiencing traumatic stressors is a worsening of their ongoing symptoms and a further decline (or even crisis) in their functioning as a result of the addition of PTSD symptoms.

Chronic psychiatric disorders range from severe mental illness (such as schizophrenia, bipolar disorder, severe dysthymia or depression, anorexia, obsessive-compulsive disorder, dissociative identity disorder, or personality disorders) to less debilitating but persistent anxiety, mood, and addictive disorders. Tragically, people with severe mental illnesses are more likely to experience traumatic stressors in their ongoing daily lives (such as violence) than other people (Goodman et al., 2001; Mueser et al., 2004). People with chronic but less severe psychiatric problems also are more likely to have experienced traumatic stressors and PTSD at some point in their lives than other people, although they are not necessarily more susceptible to *new* traumas (Breslau, Peterson, & Schultz, 2008).

More complicated variations of these posttraumatic trajectories may occur as well. For example, the stress-resistance trajectory may be fundamentally altered by a "delayed onset" of PTSD (Andrews, Brewin, Philpott, & Stewart, 2007). Delayed onset means that the individual develops PTSD after a prolonged period of positive adaptation and functioning.

For example, a former World War II combat soldier experienced PTSD symptoms for the first time more than 50 years after the war, having had only mild and manageable acute stress reactions despite participating in numerous battles in which many other soldiers on both sides died or were badly wounded. This soldier epitomized stress resistance, having been highly effective as a fighter and a leader for other soldiers and going on to have a very successful and happy family and career after the war. Shortly after he retired, he began to experience severe PTSD symptoms that included intense anxiety, hypervigilance, nightmares, irritability, and avoidance of and loss of interest in formerly meaningful relationships and personal pastimes.

Exactly why the severe PTSD symptoms emerged after such a long delay—and despite his remarkable stress resistance—is not certain, but the loss of the prestige, satisfaction, rewarding relationships, and structure and time involvement that had been provided by his work may have led to a major reduction in several protective factors that are known to reduce the risk of PTSD. These factors include social support, self-efficacy, and involvement in activities that are rewarding and consistent with the person's core values and life goals. This example illustrates how PTSD may emerge as a disorder after a delay of years or decades. However, it is uncommon for this to occur unless the person experienced some (often severe, but temporary) acute stress or posttraumatic stress symptoms previously (Andrews et al., 2007). Thus, when meeting with a patient who presents with delayed onset PTSD, the possibility that some of his or her PTSD symptoms actually appeared earlier would need to be ruled out. This septuagenarian military veteran entered treatment with full PTSD symptoms and impairment after almost 50 years of high functioning after having experienced substantial combat trauma in World War II. Upon inquiry, it was clear that this man had substantial acute traumatic stress reactions during and shortly after the war but that his role as a leader and his responsibilities to family and work after the war had provided a focus that enabled him to cope with these symptoms effectively. Several stressful changes in his life, including retirement and an unprecedented reminder of very specific war trauma experiences, appeared to have intensified his traumatic stress symptoms at time when he was less able to refocus on immediate life goals and roles. With a brief course of narrative exposure and cognitive processing therapy (see Chapter 7), the man was able to understand his symptomatic reactions, and he achieved a positive reduction in their severity to the prior level (i.e., mild and manageable symptoms).

It also is possible that aging may have played an indirect role. Although older adults are actually *more* stress resistant or resilient in the wake of traumatic events than midlife or younger adults or adolescents, older age also often is a time of reflection on one's life that may lead to the revival of memories and emotions that have been placed on hold while dealing with the responsibilities of family and work. This healthy normative process of "life review" occurs as older adults address the developmental challenge of making sense of and coming to terms with their lives, which Erik Erikson described as "integrity versus despair." This man found that after retirement he spontaneously spent more time than ever before reflecting on memories from all throughout his life. He took great pleasure in recalling distant but significant encounters with family members, friends, and work colleagues, almost as if reviewing a movie of his life. When he began to experience sudden unprecedented waves of anxiety, he felt as though a floodgate had opened and distressing memories from his combat experiences poured into his mind against his will. He had thought of those experiences as over and done with, and he had felt genuinely at peace about them, despite knowing that they had been terrifying and emotionally horrifying at the time.

Research on the impact of traumatic stress on the course of people's lives

Over the past 25 years scientists have focused a great deal of energy and thought on studying the question that is at the heart of this chapter: What is the lasting impact of psychological trauma over the course of people's lives? We know that some *but not most* people will develop ASD, many of whom will subsequently develop PTSD, while others will be resistant or resilient in the face of acute stress reactions but nevertheless develop PTSD as a result of posttraumatic decline or stable maladaptive functioning. And overall, *most* people who suffer a psychological trauma will *not* develop

PTSD, although they may experience distressing acute traumatic stress reactions, and they also may develop other psychiatric or psychological problems with or without PTSD. In the next chapter, we discuss the factors that place people at risk for developing PTSD or for being resistant, resilient, or able to recover or even grow personally in the wake of experiencing a traumatic stressor ("protective" factors). Before we turn to those matters, a brief discussion of the way that researchers have formulated theories and scientific methods to study the longitudinal course of posttraumatic adaptation is provided in order to encourage readers to consider becoming involved in this fruitful and very important area of traumatic stress research.

Dan and Lynda King are psychologists who have been leaders in the field of longitudinal studies of PTSD during the exciting period of growth in this field over the past 25 years. In their entry in the *Encyclopedia of Psychological Trauma* on research methods in the traumatic stress field, they describe the state-of-the-art methods regarding prospective studies of trauma survivors. They begin by reminding readers that "the ultimate goal of any scientific endeavor is to unambiguously demonstrate a cause-effect relationship between an independent variable and a dependent variable. It is generally accepted that three conditions must obtain to establish such causality: (a) covariation (that an independent variable, or variations in it, is accompanied by changes in a dependent variable); (b) temporal precedence (the putative cause must precede the outcome in time); and (c) the elimination of any alternative explanations (also known as "third variables") that could explain the association between cause and effect."

For example, the research question might be to discover what causes people to be resistant or resilient (as opposed to developing PTSD on a trajectory of severe persistent distress or delayed decline) following exposure to traumatic stressors. The dependent variable in this case is PTSD. If we focus on the most frequently studied potential cause of PTSD, then the type of traumatic stressor and the extent of a person's exposure to that stressor could be the independent variables. These independent variables are known to be associated with PTSD; indeed, PTSD can occur only after exposure to a traumatic stressor. Therefore, these independent variables must also occur before the dependent variable, because exposure to a traumatic stressor is the first precondition for PTSD. Additionally, we might hypothesize that several other variables might be the cause—or at least contribute to the development—of PTSD— for example whether the person has had PTSD or other psychiatric disorder(s) prior to experiencing the psychological trauma (as discussed in relation to the "stable maladaptive functioning" trajectory, earlier in this chapter).

The most common approach to studying exactly this question has been to conduct what is called an "observational cross-sectional" study (King & King, 2008). As King and King (2008) describe it, such a study is "based on data collected at a single point in time, with after-the-fact ('retrospective') reports of events and circumstances before, during, and after the occurrence of psychological trauma. While such designs can demonstrate a covariation between psychological trauma or other independent variables and posttraumatic outcomes, establishing temporal precedence and eliminating alternative explanations are serious problems for these types of research methodologies. Indeed, with regard to temporal precedence, ambiguity about the direction of cause and effect frequently has surfaced as a challenge to research findings." King and King describe how people's "faulty recollections ... combined with current mental health problems may lead research participants who are suffering from PTSD or other mental health problems to unintentionally describe themselves as having more or worse past experiences of psychological trauma than others who are not suffering from those problems. In that case, the correct research finding would not be that actual exposure to psychological trauma might cause PTSD or mental health problems. Psychological trauma might, in fact, cause PTSD or mental health problems, but the research design simply does not allow the scientist to rule out the alternative possibility that memories of trauma might be "caused" to be worse (although not necessarily to occur) by suffering from PTSD or other mental health problems."

Thus, when people are asked to recall traumatic experiences from the past, even when they are asked to be as precise and objective as possible (see Chapter 6 on the assessment of trauma history), their recollections may be affected by their current state of mind, and if they have PTSD they may unintentionally be biased toward recalling experiences as more traumatic because their current PTSD or other psychiatric symptoms leads them to emphasize the traumatic nature of past events. This would not necessarily be a "false memory" (see Chapter 1), but it would result in current PTSD "causing" the person to highlight the traumatic nature of past experiences, rather than the actual extent of traumatic stress in the past "causing" the person to have PTSD now.

The only real solution to this dilemma of "state-dependent" recollection (i.e., a bias toward recalling memories that is affected by (dependent on) the person's current state of mind) is to conduct research in which measurements are collected at several time-points and information is obtained from or about the participants only related to their current experiences and functioning. Ideally, longitudinal research begins with measurements *before* a traumatic stressor occurred, and then continues with periodic measurements over time as participants carry on with their lives. This is an ambitious goal, because it presupposes the prescience to know when and from whom to collect data in advance of event(s) that have not yet occurred.

Such "longitudinal naturalistic" research (i.e., studies conducted over time and following the "natural" course of change in people's lives) are rare in science generally and in the PTSD field specifically. Most often such studies have been possible when researchers have collected measurements from large samples of people in either community or clinical epidemiological studies (see Chapter 4) and then returned to those study groups to readminister the same measures or to collect new measures several times over a period of months or years later. In some cases, these longitudinal studies compare participants who did versus did not report experiencing a traumatic stressor in the first (and subsequent) measurement period(s). For example, Norris and Murrell (1988) reassessed a sample of older adults who had been involved in a years-long study on aging after a natural disaster that had devastated many of their homes and communities. Silver et al. (2002) were able to reassess a national sample of adults who had participated in an internet survey months before September 11, 2001, at several time-points in the months following the terrorist incidents in order to identify risk factors for subsequent PTSD and related problems. Breslau et al. (2008) surveyed a community sample of young adults in a midwestern health maintenance organization at several time-points over more than a decade, each time asking about their recent traumatic experiences and their current PTSD symptoms in order to establish that repeated exposure to traumatic stressors increases the likelihood that a healthy adult will develop PTSD but that PTSD does not increase the likelihood that those adults will suffer further psychological traumas.

Another approach to naturalistic longitudinal research is to identify people who are likely to be in harm's way and survey them several times, beginning as early as possible in their lives. For example, separate studies by Lyons-Ruth, Dutra, Schuder, and Bianchi (2006), Putnam and Trickett (1997), Widom et al. (Koenen & Widom, 2009; Widom, Czaja, Bentley, & Johnson, 2012; Widom, Czaja, & Dutton, 2008; Wilson & Widom, 2009), and Briggs-Gowan et al. (Briggs-Gowan et al. 2010; Briggs-Gowan, Carter, & Ford, 2012; Grasso, Ford, & Briggs-Gowan, 2013) assessed high-risk children's exposure to maltreatment and other traumatic stressors beginning at age 1 and then reassessing their development and further exposure to traumatic stressors (i.e., revictimization) several times over the course of their childhood and adolescence, and even into adulthood, including when some of them had become parents themselves. Exposure to maltreatment and family violence in early childhood increases the risk that severe behavioral, emotional, interpersonal, and physical health problems will develop—including PTSD, although the trajectory of traumatized children tends to involve a variety of symptoms that ebb and flow over time as they pass through the phases of childhood development and does not lead to chronic PTSD for many until they reach adolescence (McLaughlin et al., 2013) or adulthood. Moreover, severely traumatized children are at high risk for revictimization, including not only subsequent reexposure to the same type(s) of traumatic stressors but also to new types of victimization (e.g., childhood abuse survivors who are sexually assaulted as adults; Miron, Orcutt, & Kumpula, 2014; Box 3.6).

Morgan et al. (Morgan & Taylor, 2013) and Vasterling et al. (2010) applied this prospective approach to military personnel, measuring their bodily and psychological stress reactivity while they are in training and subsequently after returning from deployment to hazardous war duty. Exposure to potentially traumatic deployment stressors (such as firefights, explosions, sniper attacks, or patrolling or escorting convoys through hazardous areas) was associated with PTSD (including dissociative reactions), as expected. However, the adverse impact of combat stressors was greatest for personnel who had higher levels of PTSD symptoms prior to deployment, suggesting that preexisting vulnerability and revictimization play an important role in the development of military PTSD. Additionally, in highly stressful training exercises, the most elite personnel (e.g., Marine Special Forces) tended to not only disclose having dissociative reactions but to describe them as intentional and adaptive for fighting. Whether dissociative reactions actually are intentional and adaptive in war or war-like scenarios is uncertain, but peritraumatic dissociation is known to place traumatized individuals at risk for PTSD and related psychosocial problems (see Box 1.6), so any short-term benefit may come at the cost of adverse long-term consequences for highly trained and effective military personnel.

A more imperfect but nevertheless potentially informative approach to longitudinal PTSD research involves identifying people soon after exposure to traumatic stressors and conducting repeated follow-up assessments with them over time. For example, longitudinal studies by Shalev and Yehuda (1998) and Zatzick et al. (2005) with adults and Daviss et al. (2000a, 2000b), Saxe et al. (2001), and Winston et al. (2002) with children began with assessments of emergency department patients' stress reactions (and those of their parents as well in the latter studies), injuries, treatment, and medical outcomes at discharge, and then followed with assessments of ASD, PTSD, and stress reactivity over a period of months. Similar research has been done in a number of longitudinal studies that began with assessments of victims (and in some cases, similar people in nonaffected or less-affected communities) soon after natural or humanmade disasters (Norris et al., 2002; Norris, 2008) or traumatic accidents (Hickling & Blanchard, 2001), and continued with repeated measurements for months or years.

A parallel form of longitudinal research involves "clinical trials" of treatment interventions for PTSD or related psychological or psychiatric problems. In order to determine if a treatment is the "cause" of recovery from PTSD, it is necessary to measure a dependent variable such as the severity of PTSD before and again after treatment has been provided. It also is necessary to randomly assign participants to either receive the treatment or an alternative experimental condition (such as a placebo medication or an alternative therapeutic intervention) in order for the designated treatment (or its theoretically beneficial elements) to be the independent variable. Contemporary clinical trials research on PTSD treatments typically involves several posttherapy assessments over a several-month time period in order to establish the durability of positive outcomes (Cloitre, Koenen, Cohen, & Han, 2002; Davidson, 2006; Foa et al., 2005; Ford, Steinberg, & Zhang, 2011; Resick, Nishith, Weaver, Astin, & Feuer, 2002; Taylor, Asmundson, & Carleton, 2006). These studies often include measurements taken repeatedly *during* as well as before and after treatment, thus providing not only an evidence base for PTSD treatment (see Chapters 7 and 8) but also valuable information about the natural history of change in PTSD treatment—that is, when, how, and for whom symptoms improve in treatment.

Studies of the impact of traumatic stressor exposure on changes in genes and their activity—the science of epigenetics (i.e., the influence of experience, "epi," on genetics)—is a novel focus for prospective longitudinal research on traumatic stress and PTSD. Yehuda et al. (2009) found that not only are levels of the stress hormone cortisol lower among adults with chronic PTSD but that lower levels of both cortisol and its metabolites (bodily chemicals that are produced when cortisol is metabolized, or processed, within the body) predict poorer response to psychotherapy for PTSD (among survivors of the September 11, 2001, World Trade Center attack). Because cortisol tends to be produced by the body when stressors occur, it seems counterintuitive at first glance to find that a condition of chronic stress reactivity like PTSD would be associated with lower rather than higher levels of cortisol. A possible explanation is that PTSD may involve the suppression of the responsiveness of the body's stress system as a result of extreme stress reactivity, either exhausting the body's capacity to produce stress hormones or leading to a negative feedback loop of hypersensitivity of the receptors that are activated by cortisol and lower production of cortisol due to its increased ability to activate those receptors. Further studies have supported the hypersensitivity hypothesis (Sriram, Rodriguez-Fernandez, & Doyle, 2012), and this raises the question of what has changed in the body that could account for this effect of PTSD.

Evidence of the transmission of PTSD from one generation to the next provided a clue to a potential answer. Yehuda and Bierer (2008) described results of studies showing that children of Holocaust survivors whose parents developed PTSD were not only at risk for developing PTSD themselves but also tended to have lower levels of cortisol even if they did not have symptoms qualifying for PTSD. This research group also reported evidence that infants of mothers who developed PTSD following the World Trade Center attack also had lower cortisol levels than their peers, suggesting that experiencing PTSD in a primary caregiver may lead to altered stress reactivity very early in childhood (Yehuda & Bierer, 2008). A potential biological mechanism for this cross-generational transmission of stress reactivity was identified in subsequent studies with adults who were the offspring of Holocaust survivors: those whose mother and father both had PTSD also had an alteration in the activity (called "methylation") of genes that set the sensitivity of receptors for cortisol (called "glucocorticoid receptors") (Lehrner et al., 2014; Yehuda et al., 2014). Similar alterations in genes related to glucocorticoid receptors also were found among military veterans with PTSD, indicating that direct exposure to traumatic stressors also can cause epigenetic changes in stress reactivity that may be biological underpinnings of PTSD (Yehuda et al., 2015). Research on epigenetic "markers" (i.e., indicators) of PTSD psychotherapy outcome with military veterans demonstrated that the activity of one gene that controls glucocorticoid receptor sensitivity before therapy predicted who did or did not benefit from treatment (Yehuda et al., 2013). Also, as further evidence of the influence of experience on genetic activity, the study also found that a different epigenetic marker related to glucocorticoid receptor sensitivity actually changed when PTSD symptoms improved! Thus, prospective longitudinal research across generations and across the course of PTSD treatment is yielding remarkable insights into the biological as well as psychological features of PTSD.

King and King (2008) described several precautions that guide researchers in conducting longitudinal traumatic stress research: "Perhaps the most important caution is to be sure that the schedule of repeated assessments is controlled by the researcher and not by study participants. In the latter case, a third variable (e.g., participants avoiding assessment when they are feeling particularly healthy or ill, or participants with the least resources tending to delay or cancel appointments) [may be the true cause of variations in the dependent variable]. In addition, it is wise to target more frequent assessments at critical points of expected change and fewer assessments during periods of expected relative stability in the characteristics being monitored.

Moreover, it goes without saying that longitudinal research should use the same assessment devices and measures at every time-point. If changes in measures are deemed necessary (as might be the case in studying traumatic stress in children and then into adolescence and young adulthood), measures must be checked statistically to ensure they are comparable. ... Finally, for research efficiency and in order to prevent participants from being unduly burdened, longitudinal traumatic stress studies can utilize methods that allow some participants to be exempted at some time-points, using "planned missingness" designs (Graham, Taylor, Olchowski, & Cumsille, 2006). In such designs, the researcher purposefully assigns subgroups of participants to provide data at targeted subsets of assessment occasions (no single person is assessed on all occasions)."

From this brief overview and sampling of representative studies, it should be apparent that prospective longitudinal research on the impact of experiencing a traumatic stressor over the course of subsequent months and years is scientifically and practically both highly challenging and potentially highly rewarding. It is not enough to simply ask people retrospectively whether they have had distressing experiences and how they've adjusted since that time. Care must be taken to design repeated measurements that collect scientifically reliable and valid data (see Chapter 6) from the same people over long time periods. Despite, or perhaps because of, the challenges, research on the impact of psychological trauma is rapidly and creatively evolving.

References

American Psychiatric Association, (1952). *Diagnostic and statistical manual of mental disorders* (1st ed.). Washington, DC: American Psychiatric Press.

American Psychiatric Association, (1968). *Diagnostic and statistical manual of mental disorders* (2nd ed.). Washington, DC: American Psychiatric Press.

American Psychiatric Association, (1980). *Diagnostic and statistical manual of mental disorders* (3rd ed.). Washington, DC: American Psychiatric Press.

American Psychiatric Association, (1994). *Diagnostic and statistical manual of mental disorders* (4th ed.). Washington, DC: American Psychiatric Press.

American Psychiatric Association, (2013). *Diagnostic and statistical manual of mental disorders* (5th ed.). Washington, DC: American Psychiatric Press.

Andrews, B., Brewin, C. R., Philpott, R., & Stewart, L. (2007). Delayed-onset posttraumatic stress disorder: A systematic review of the evidence. *American Journal of Psychiatry*, *164*, 1319–1326.

Betancourt, T. S., Abdi, S., Ito, B. S., Lilienthal, G. M., Agalab, N., & Ellis, H. (2015). We left one war and came to another: Resource loss, acculturative stress, and caregiver-child relationships in Somali refugee families. *Cultural Diversity & Ethnic Minority Psychology*, *21*, 114–125. http://dx.doi.org/10.1037/a0037538.

Bovin, M. J., & Marx, B. P. (2011). The importance of the peritraumatic experience in defining traumatic stress. *Psychological Bulletin*, *137*(1), 47–67.

Breslau, N., & Davis, G. C. (1987). Posttraumatic stress disorder. The stressor criterion. *Journal of Nervous and Mental Disease*, *175*(5), 255–264.

Breslau, N., Peterson, E. L., & Schultz, L. R. (2008). A second look at prior trauma and the posttraumatic stress disorder effects of subsequent trauma: A prospective epidemiological study. *Archives of General Psychiatry*, *65*(4), 431–437.

Brett, E. A. (1996). The classification of posttraumatic stress disorder. In B. A. van der Kolk, A. C. McFarlane, & L. Weisarth (Eds.), *Traumatic stress: The effects of overwhelming experience on mind, body, and society* (pp. 117–128). New York, NY: Guilford.

Brewin, C. R., & Holmes, E. A. (2003). Psychological theories of posttraumatic stress disorder. *Clinical Psychology Review*, *23*(3), 339–376.

Brewin, C. R., Rose, S., Andrews, B., Green, J. D., Tata, P., McEvedy, C., et al. (2002). Brief screening instrument for post-traumatic stress disorder. *British Journal of Psychiatry*, *181*(2), 158–162.

Briggs-Gowan, M. J., Carter, A. S., Clark, R., Augustyn, M., McCarthy, K. J., & Ford, J. D. (2010). Exposure to potentially traumatic events in early childhood: Differential links to emergent psychopathology. *Journal of Child Psychology and Psychiatry and Allied Disciplines*, *51*(10), 1132–1140.

Briggs-Gowan, M. J., Carter, A. S., & Ford, J. D. (2012). Parsing the effects violence exposure in early childhood: Modeling developmental pathways. *Journal of Pediatric Psychology*, *37*(1), 11–22.

Bryant, R. (2008). Acute stress disorder. In G. Reyes, J. D. Elhai, & J. D. Ford (Eds.), *Encyclopedia of psychological trauma* (pp. 12–14). Hoboken, NJ: Wiley.

Bryant, R. A. (2011). Acute stress disorder as a predictor of posttraumatic stress disorder: A systematic review. *Journal of Clinical Psychiatry*, *72*(2), 233–239. http://dx.doi.org/10.4088/JCP.09r05072blu.

Bryant, R. A., Creamer, M., O'Donnell, M., Silove, D., & McFarlane, A. C. (2012). The capacity of acute stress disorder to predict posttraumatic psychiatric disorders. *Journal of Psychiatric Research*, *46*(2), 168–173. http://dx.doi.org/10.1016/j.jpsychires.2011.10.007.

Bryant, R. A., Creamer, M., O'Donnell, M. L., Silove, D., & McFarlane, A. C. (2008). A multisite study of the capacity of acute stress disorder diagnosis to predict posttraumatic stress disorder. *Journal of Clinical Psychiatry*, *69*, 923–929.

Burgess, A. W., & Holmstrom, L. L. (1974). Rape trauma syndrome. *American Journal of Psychiatry*, *131*, 981–986.

Charney, D. S. (2004). Discovering the neural basis of human social anxiety: A diagnostic and therapeutic imperative. *American Journal of Psychiatry*, *161*, 1–2.

Chiriboga, D. A., & Dean, H. (1978). Dimensions of stress: Perspectives from a longitudinal study. *Journal of Psychosomatic Research*, *22*(1), 47–55.

Cloitre, M., Koenen, K. C., Cohen, L. R., & Han, H. (2002). Skills training in affective and interpersonal regulation followed by exposure: A phase-based treatment for PTSD related to childhood abuse. *Journal of Consulting and Clinical Psychology*, *70*, 1067–1074.

Davidson, J. R. T. (2006). Pharmacologic treatment of acute and chronic stress following trauma: 2006. *Journal of Clinical Psychiatry*, *67*, 34–39.

Davis, C. G., Nolen-Hoeksema, S., & Larson, J. (1998). Making sense of loss and benefiting from the experience: Two construals of meaning. *Journal of Personality and Social Psychology*, *75*, 561–574.

Daviss, W. B., Mooney, D., Racusin, R., Ford, J. D., Fleischer, A., & McHugo, G. J. (2000a). Predicting posttraumatic stress after hospitalization for pediatric injury. *Journal of the American Academy of Child and Adolescent Psychiatry*, *39*(5), 576–583. http://dx.doi.org/10.1097/00004583-200005000-00011.

Daviss, W. B., Racusin, R., Fleischer, A., Mooney, D., Ford, J. D., & McHugo, G. J. (2000b). Acute stress disorder symptomatology during hospitalization for pediatric injury. *Journal of the American Academy of Child and Adolescent Psychiatry*, *39*(5), 569–575. http://dx.doi.org/10.1097/00004583-200005000-00010.

Foa, E. B., Hembree, E. A., Cahill, S. P., Rauch, S. A., Riggs, D. S., Feeny, N. C., et al. (2005). Randomized trial of prolonged exposure for posttraumatic stress disorder with and without cognitive restructuring: Outcome at academic and community clinics. *Journal of Consulting and Clinical Psychology*, *73*, 953–964.

Ford, J. D. (1999). Disorders of extreme stress following war-zone military trauma: Associated features of posttraumatic stress disorder or comorbid but distinct syndromes? *Journal of Consulting and Clinical Psychology*, *67*(1), 3–12.

Ford, J. D., Steinberg, K. L., & Zhang, W. (2011). A randomized clinical trial comparing affect regulation and social problem-solving psychotherapies for mothers with victimization-related PTSD. *Behavior Therapy, 42*(4), 560–578.

Ford, J. D., Tennen, H., & Albert, D. (2008). A contrarian view of growth following adversity. In S. Joseph & P. Linley (Eds.), *Trauma, recovery, and growth: Positive psychological perspectives on posttraumatic stress* (pp. 297–324). Hoboken, NJ: Wiley.

Frankl, V. E. (1946). *Man's search for meaning*. New York: Bantam.

Frazier, P. A., & Kaler, M. E. (2006). Assessing the validity of self-reported stress-related growth. *Journal of Consulting and Clinical Psychology, 74*(5), 859–869.

Frueh, B. C., Elhai, J. D., & Kaloupek, D. G. (2004). Unresolved issues in the assessment of trauma exposure and posttraumatic reactions. In G. M. Rosen (Ed.), *Posttraumatic stress disorder: Issues and controversies* (pp. 63–84). New York: Wiley.

Goodman, L. A., Salyers, M. P., Mueser, K. T., Rosenberg, S. D., Swartz, M., Essock, S. M., et al. (2001). Recent victimization in women and men with severe mental illness: Prevalence and correlates. *Journal of Traumatic Stress, 14*(4), 615–632. http://dx.doi.org/10.1023/A:1013026318450.

Graham, J. W., Taylor, B. J., Olchowski, A. E., & Cumsille, P. E. (2006). Planned missing data designs in psychological research. *Psychological Methods, 11*, 323–343.

Grasso, D. J., Ford, J. D., & Briggs-Gowan, M. J. (2013). Early life trauma exposure and stress sensitivity in young children. *Journal of Pediatric Psychology, 38*(1), 94–103.

Green, B. L. (1990). Defining trauma: Terminology and generic stressor dimensions. *Journal of Applied Social Psychology, 20*, 1632–1642.

Herman, J. L. (1992). *Trauma and recovery*. New York: Basic Books.

Hickling, E. J., & Blanchard, E. B. (2007). Motor vehicle accidents and psychological trauma. In E. K. Carll (Ed.), *Trauma psychology: Issues in violence, disaster, health, and illness, Vol 2: Health and illness* (pp. 1–25). Westport, CT: Praeger Publishers/Greenwood Publishing Group.

Hobfoll, S. E. (1989). Conservation of resources. A new attempt at conceptualizing stress. *American Psychologist, 44*(3), 513–524.

Hobfoll, S. E. (2001). The influence of culture, community, and the nested-self in the stress process: Advancing conservation of resources theory. *Applied Psychology: An International Review, 50*, 337–421.

Horowitz, M., & Smit, M. (2008). Stress response syndromes. In G. Reyes, J. D. Elhai, & J. D. Ford (Eds.), *Encyclopedia of psychological trauma* (pp. 629–633). Hoboken, NJ: John Wiley & Sons.

Ickovics, J. R., Meade, C. S., Kershaw, T. S., Milan, S., Lewis, J. B., & Ethier, K. A. (2006). Urban teens: Trauma, posttraumatic growth, and emotional distress among female adolescents. *Journal of Consulting and Clinical Psychology, 74*, 841–850.

Jones, E., & Wessely, S. (2007). A paradigm shift in the conceptualization of psychological trauma in the 20th century. *Journal of Anxiety Disorders, 21*(2), 164–175. http://dx.doi.org/10.1016/j.janxdis.2006.09.009.

Joseph, S., & Linley, P. (Eds.). (2008). *Trauma, recovery, and growth: Positive psychological perspectives on posttraumatic stress*. Hoboken N.J.: Wiley.

Kessler, R. C., Sonnega, A., Bromet, E., Hughes, M., & Nelson, C. B. (1995). Posttraumatic stress disorder in the National Comorbidity Survey. *Archives of General Psychiatry, 52*, 1048–1060.

King, D., & King, L. (2008). Research methodology. In G. Reyes, J. D. Elhai, & J. Ford (Eds.), *Encyclopedia of psychological trauma* (pp. 575–584). Hoboken, NJ: Wiley.

Koenen, K. C., & Widom, C. S. (2009). A prospective study of sex differences in the lifetime risk of posttraumatic stress disorder among abused and neglected children grown up. *Journal of Traumatic Stress, 22*(6), 566–574.

Lasiuk, G. C., & Hegadoren, K. M. (2006). Posttraumatic stress disorder part I: Historical development of the concept. *Perspectives on Psychiatric Care, 42*, 13–20.

Layne, C., Beck, C., Rimmasch, H., Southwick, J., Moreno, M., & Hobfoll, S. (2008). Promoting 'resilient' posttraumatic adjustment in childhood and beyond. In D. Brom, R. Pat-Horenczyk, & J. D. Ford (Eds.), *Treating traumatized children: Risk, resilience, and recovery* (pp. 13–47). London: Routledge.

Layne, C. M., Beck, C. J., Rimmasch, H., Southwick, J., Moreno, M., & Hobfoll, S. (2007). Promoting "resilient" posttraumatic adjustment in childhood and beyond: "unpacking" life events, adjustment trajectories, resources, and interventions. In D. Brom, R. Pat-Horenczyk, & J. D. Ford (Eds.), *Treating traumatized children: Risk, resilience and recovery* (pp. 13–40). London, Great Britain: Routledge.

Lehrner, A., Bierer, L. M., Passarelli, V., Pratchett, L. C., Flory, J. D., Bader, H. N., et al. (2014). Maternal PTSD associates with greater glucocorticoid sensitivity in offspring of Holocaust survivors. *Psychoneuroendocrinology, 40*, 213–220.

Littleton, H., Kumpula, M., & Orcutt, H. (2011). Posttraumatic symptoms following a campus shooting: The role of psychosocial resource loss. *Violence and Victims, 26*(4), 461–476.

Litz, B. T., Stein, N., Delaney, E., Lebowitz, L., Nash, W. P., Silva, C., et al. (2009). Moral injury and moral repair in war veterans: A preliminary model and intervention strategy. *Clinical Psychology Review, 29*(8), 695–706.

Lyons-Ruth, K., Dutra, L., Schuder, M. R., & Bianchi, I. (2006). From infant attachment disorganization to adult dissociation: Relational adaptations or traumatic experiences? *Psychiatric Clinics of North America, 29*, 63–86.

Maguen, S., Madden, E., Bosch, J., Galatzer-Levy, I., Knight, S. J., Litz, B. T., et al. (2013). Killing and latent classes of PTSD symptoms in Iraq and Afghanistan veterans. *Journal of Affective Disorders, 145*(3), 344–348.

Marshall, R. D., Spitzer, R., & Liebowitz, M. R. (1999). Review and critique of the new DSM-IV diagnosis of acute stress disorder. *American Journal of Psychiatry, 156*(11), 1677–1685.

McEwen, B., & Lasley, E. N. (2003). Allostatic load: When protection gives way to damage. *Advances in Mind-Body Medicine, 19*(1), 28–33.

McFarland, C., & Alvaro, C. (2000). The impact of motivation on temporal comparisons: Coping with traumatic events by perceiving personal growth. *Journal of Personality and Social Psychology, 79*, 327–343.

McLaughlin, K. A., Koenen, K. C., Hill, E. D., Petukhova, M., Sampson, N. A., Zaslavsky, A. M., et al. (2013). Trauma exposure and posttraumatic stress disorder in a national sample of adolescents. *Journal of the American Academy of Child and Adolescent Psychiatry, 52*(8) 815–830.e814. http://dx.doi.org/10.1016/j.jaac.2013.05.011.

Miron, L. R., Orcutt, H. K., & Kumpula, M. J. (2014). Differential predictors of transient stress versus posttraumatic stress disorder: Evaluating risk following targeted mass violence. *Behavior Therapy, 45*(6), 791–805. http://dx.doi.org/10.1016/j.beth.2014.07.005.

Morgan, C. A., III, & Taylor, M. K. (2013). Spontaneous and deliberate dissociative states in military personnel: Are such states helpful? *Journal of Traumatic Stress, 26*(4), 492–497.

Mueser, K. T., Salyers, M. P., Rosenberg, S. D., Goodman, L. A., Essock, S. M., Osher, F. C., et al. (2004). Interpersonal trauma and posttraumatic stress disorder in patients with severe mental illness: Demographic, clinical, and health correlates. *Schizophrenia Bulletin, 30*(1), 45–57.

Norris, F. H. (2008). Disasters. In G. Reyes, J. D. Elhai, & J. D. Ford (Eds.), *Encyclopedia of psychological trauma* (pp. 211–214). Hoboken, NJ: Wiley.

Norris, F. H., Friedman, M. J., & Watson, P. J. (2002). 60,000 disaster victims speak: Part II. Summary and implications of the disaster mental health research. *Psychiatry, 65*, 240–260.

Norris, F. H., & Murrell, S. A. (1988). Prior experience as a moderator of disaster impact on anxiety symptoms in older adults. *American Journal of Community Psychology, 16,* 665–683.

Putnam, F. W., & Trickett, P. K. (1997). Psychobiological effects of sexual abuse. A longitudinal study. In R. Yehuda & A. C. McFarlane (Eds.), *Psychobiology of posttraumatic stress disorder* (Vol. 821, pp. 150–159). Annals of the New York Academy of Sciences.

Rabe, S., Zollner, T., Maercker, A., & Karl, A. (2006). Neural correlates of posttraumatic growth after severe motor vehicle accidents. *Journal of Consulting and Clinical Psychology, 74,* 880–886.

Resick, P. A., Nishith, P., Weaver, T. L., Astin, M. C., & Feuer, C. A. (2002). A comparison of cognitive-processing therapy with prolonged exposure and a waiting condition for the treatment of chronic posttraumatic stress disorder in female rape victims. *Journal of Consulting and Clinical Psychology, 70,* 867–879.

Rothbaum, B. O., Foa, E. B., Riggs, D. S., & Murdock, T. (1992). A prospective examination of post-traumatic stress disorder in rape victims. *Journal of Traumatic Stress, 5,* 455–475.

Salter, E., & Stallard, P. (2004). Posttraumatic growth in child survivors of a road traffic accident. *Journal of Traumatic Stress, 17,* 335–340.

Saxe, G., Stoddard, F., Courtney, D., Cunningham, K., Chawla, N., Sheridan, R., et al. (2001). Relationship between acute morphine and the course of PTSD in children with burns. *Journal of the American Academy of Child and Adolescent Psychiatry, 40,* 915–921.

Schnurr, P. P., Lunney, C. A., & Sengupta, A. (2004). Risk factors for the development versus maintenance of posttraumatic stress disorder. *Journal of Traumatic Stress, 17,* 85–95.

Shalev, A. Y., & Yehuda, R. (1998). Longitudinal development of traumatic stress disorders. In R. Yehuda (Ed.), *Psychological trauma* (pp. 31–66). Washington, DC: American Psychiatric Association.

Silver, R. C., Holman, E. A., McIntosh, D. N., Poulin, M., & Gil-Rivas, V. (2002). Nationwide longitudinal study of psychological responses to September 11. *Journal of the American Medical Association, 288,* 1235–1244.

Smith, S. G., & Cook, S. L. (2004). Are reports of posttraumatic growth positively biased? *Journal of Traumatic Stress, 17*(4), 353–358.

Sriram, K., Rodriguez-Fernandez, M., & Doyle, F. J., III (2012). Modeling cortisol dynamics in the neuro-endocrine axis distinguishes normal, depression, and post-traumatic stress disorder (PTSD) in humans. *PLoS Computational Biology, 8*(2), e1002379.

Taylor, S. (2007). *Posttraumatic stress disorder: A decade of progress-and controversy* (Vol. 52). Washington, DC: American Psychological Association.

Taylor, S., Asmundson, G. J., & Carleton, R. N. (2006). Simple versus complex PTSD: A cluster analytic investigation. *Journal of Anxiety Disorders, 20,* 459–472.

Tedeschi, R. G., & Calhoun, L. G. (2004). Posttraumatic growth: Conceptual foundations and empirical evidence. *Psychological Inquiry, 15,* 1–18.

Turnbull, G. J. (1998). A review of post-traumatic stress disorder. Part 1: Historical development and classification. *Injury, 29*(2), 87–91.

Vasterling, J. J., Proctor, S. P., Friedman, M. J., Hoge, C. W., Heeren, T., King, L. A., et al. (2010). PTSD symptom increases in Iraq-deployed soldiers: Comparison with nondeployed soldiers and associations with baseline symptoms, deployment experiences, and postdeployment stress. *Journal of Traumatic Stress, 23*(1), 41–51.

Widom, C. S., Czaja, S. J., Bentley, T., & Johnson, M. S. (2012). A prospective investigation of physical health outcomes in abused and neglected children: New findings from a 30-year follow-up. *American Journal of Public Health, 102*(6), 1135–1144.

Widom, C. S., Czaja, S. J., & Dutton, M. A. (2008). Childhood victimization and lifetime revictimization. *Child Abuse and Neglect, 32*(8), 785–796.

Wilson, H. W., & Widom, C. S. (2009). A prospective examination of the path from child abuse and neglect to illicit drug use in middle adulthood: The potential mediating role of four risk factors. *Journal of Youth and Adolescence, 38*(3), 340–354.

Winston, F. K., Kassam-Adams, N., Vivarelli-O'Neill, C., Ford, J. D., Newman, E., Baxt, C., et al. (2002). Acute stress disorder symptoms in children and their parents after pediatric traffic injury. *Pediatrics, 109*, e90.

World Health Organization, (1948). *International classification of diseases, 6th Revision.* Geneva, Switzerland: Author.

World Health Organization, (1955). *International classification of diseases, 7th Revision.* Geneva, Switzerland: Author.

World Health Organization, (1965). *International classification of diseases, 8th Revision.* Geneva, Switzerland: Author.

Yager, T., Laufer, R., & Gallops, M. (1984). Some problems associated with war experience in men of the Vietnam generation. *Archives of General Psychiatry, 41*(4), 327–333.

Yehuda, R., & Bierer, L. M. (2008). Transgenerational transmission of cortisol and PTSD risk. *Progress in Brain Research, 167*, 121–135.

Yehuda, R., Daskalakis, N. P., Desarnaud, F., Makotkine, I., Lehrner, A. L., Koch, E., et al. (2013). Epigenetic biomarkers as predictors and correlates of symptom improvement following psychotherapy in combat veterans with PTSD. *Frontiers in Psychiatry, 4*, 118.

Yehuda, R., Daskalakis, N. P., Lehrner, A., Desarnaud, F., Bader, H. N., Makotkine, I., et al. (2014). Influences of maternal and paternal PTSD on epigenetic regulation of the glucocorticoid receptor gene in Holocaust survivor offspring. *American Journal of Psychiatry, 171*(8), 872–880.

Yehuda, R., & Flory, J. D. (2007). Differentiating biological correlates of risk, PTSD, and resilience following trauma exposure. *Journal of Traumatic Stress, 20*(4), 435–447.

Yehuda, R., Flory, J. D., Bierer, L. M., Henn-Haase, C., Lehrner, A., Desarnaud, F., et al. (2015). Lower methylation of glucocorticoid receptor gene promoter 1 in peripheral blood of veterans with posttraumatic stress disorder. *Biological Psychiatry, 77*, 356–364.

Yehuda, R., & LeDoux, J. (2007). Response variation following trauma: A translational neuroscience approach to understanding PTSD. *Neuron, 56*(1), 19–32.

Yehuda, R., Schmeidler, J., Labinsky, E., Bell, A., Morris, A., Zemelman, S., et al. (2009). Ten-year follow-up study of PTSD diagnosis, symptom severity and psychosocial indices in aging holocaust survivors. *Acta Psychiatrica Scandinavica, 119*(1), 25–34. http://dx.doi.org/ACP1248 [pii]. http://dx.doi.org/10.1111/j.1600-0447.2008.01248.x.

Zatzick, D. F., Russo, J., Pitman, R. K., Rivara, F., Jurkovich, G., & Roy-Byrne, P. (2005). Reevaluating the association between emergency department heart rate and the development of posttraumatic stress disorder: A public health approach. *Biological Psychiatry, 57*, 91–95.

Zlotnick, C., Bruce, S. E., Shea, M. T., & Keller, M. B. (2001). Delayed posttraumatic stress disorder (PTSD) and predictors of first onset of PTSD in patients with anxiety disorders. *Journal of Nervous and Mental Disease, 189*(6), 404–406.

Etiology of PTSD: What causes PTSD?

Although most people will encounter a traumatic stressor at least once, and often several times, in their lives, most people who experience a traumatic stressor do *not* develop PTSD (Breslau, 2002; Kessler et al., 2005; Kessler, Sonnega, Bromet, & Hughes, 1995). Therefore, the question of what causes PTSD cannot simply be answered by referring to its definition: a disorder whose symptoms occur following exposure to a traumatic stressor. In fact, there is controversy as to whether PTSD symptoms really are caused by exposure to traumatic stressors, because all of the symptoms, except for memories, flashbacks, and nightmares of traumatic events, could occur regardless of whether a person has experienced a traumatic stressor. The PTSD symptoms that are not by definition tied to a traumatic stressor—even the two symptoms that are defined as psychological or physical distress due to reminders of past stressful events—actually are also symptoms of other psychiatric disorders as well as of PTSD. Thus, it is important to scientifically examine the assumption that PTSD is caused by exposure to traumatic stressors (Box 3.1). Scientific evidence indicating that PTSD is most likely to occur not just when a traumatic stressor has occurred—but *when the objective severity of exposure to traumatic danger or harm is more extreme*—provides important (albeit not definitive) support for the view that exposure to a traumatic stressor plays a key role in PTSD, as is discussed later in this chapter (see section on the Impact of Stressor Exposure).

In this chapter, a more nuanced view of the causes of PTSD is presented than the commonsense version that PTSD is "caused" simply by exposure to a traumatic stressor. Research demonstrates that PTSD is a "multicausal" phenomenon, meaning that it is the product of a combination of a number of potential causes. Rather than describing the factors that contribute to the development of PTSD as "causes," it is clearer and more factual to describe them as "risk factors" and "protective factors"— that is, things that increase a person's risk of developing PTSD and things that reduce (or protect against) the risk of developing PTSD. As you will see, risk factors include not only exposure to a traumatic stressor but also biological, psychological, and social factors that influence whether PTSD will occur and that can protect against (but not necessarily prevent) the development of PTSD (Box 3.2).

Box 3.1 Key Points

1. The "etiology" of PTSD refers to the study of the "causes of PTSD." Psychological phenomena such as PTSD are rarely, if ever, "caused" by a single factor or any single specific combination of factors (such as specific genes or personality traits or life

(Continued)

Posttraumatic Stress Disorder. DOI: http://dx.doi.org/10.1016/B978-0-12-801288-8.00003-0

Box 3.1 Continued

experiences) but instead are the product of complex interrelationships among many different biological, environmental, and life experience factors.

2. PTSD is *not* "caused" solely by exposure to traumatic stressors. Although, by definition, PTSD can only occur if a person has been exposed to a traumatic stressor, most people—about 80–90%—who are exposed to traumatic stressors do *not* develop PTSD. Therefore, exposure to a traumatic stressor is a *necessary* but *not sufficient* cause that contributes to—but does not alone account for—PTSD.

3. PTSD is the result of large number of different combinations of "risk" and "protective" factors that influence a person's life trajectory (see Chapter 2) after exposure to a traumatic stressor. Risk factors increase, and protective factors decrease, the likelihood that PTSD will occur.

4. Some "risk" and "protective" factors begin before a traumatic stressor occurs. These "preevent" factors include the person's genetic characteristics (including gender and ethnocultural background, as well as subtler variations in specific genes associated with memory, learning, motivation, and emotional and behavioral problems) that are just beginning to be understood in relation to PTSD. Preevent risk factors also include age (although both children and older adults actually are at *lower* risk generally, compared to adolescents or young and midlife adults). Other preevent risk factors for PTSD are the person's and their family members' previous exposure to traumatic events and past episodes of PTSD, psychiatric or addiction problems, and interpersonal conflicts. A key preevent protective factor that lowers the risk of PTSD is access to socioeconomic resources, most importantly as a result of a higher education level and social support.

5. Female gender is a risk factor, and male gender is a protective factor, for PTSD. However, it is not certain that this is directly related to genetically inborn differences between females and males, because research has shown that females and males may be exposed to different types of traumatic stressors and related risk factors (such as gender bias) as a result of social and political factors that are independent of their biological sex.

6. Persons from ethnoracial minority backgrounds may be more vulnerable (i.e., at greater risk) for developing PTSD than those of majority ethnocultural backgrounds. However, this may be a by-product of social and economic factors (such as racial stigma and discrimination, or poverty) rather than due to a person's ethnicity per se.

7. The specific experience of psychological trauma differs in many ways that may increase or protect against the risk of developing PTSD. Traumatic stressors that involve betrayal or violation of the basic safety of key relationships (such as physical or sexual abuse, family violence, cruel and inhumane imprisonment, or torture), especially if this occurs during the formative years of childhood, increase the risk of PTSD 75% or more.

8. When traumatic events occur directly to the person, and when severe physical injury or pain result, the risk of or "vulnerability" to PTSD is higher—although witnessing very horrific events or their aftermath, especially if this occurs to someone close or on a mass scale (such as genocide or war), can lead to a high risk of PTSD (see Chapter 11).

9. In addition to the nature of the traumatic event, certain reactions immediately or soon after the traumatic event(s) are risk factors. These are called "peritraumatic" risk factors because they occur during or soon after ("peri") a traumatic event). High levels of initial distress (including large increases in physiological stress, such as

blood pressure) or dissociation (i.e., becoming mentally and physically shut down and profoundly disoriented) are the primary peritraumatic risk factors demonstrated by research.

10. Social support and coping self-efficacy (the belief that it is possible to effectively cope with and overcome adversity) are key postevent protective factors against PTSD.

Box 3.2 "Is PTSD Caused by Traumatic Stress?"

This provocative and timely question was the title of an article by Bodkin et al. (2007) in a special issue of the *Journal of Anxiety Disorders*. They report the results of a study in which adults who were receiving antidepressant medications were assessed for trauma history and PTSD using the *Structured Clinical Interview for DSM-IV Axis I Disorders* (First, Spitzer, Gibbon, & Williams, 1996). More than half of the participants reported experiences that qualified as traumatic stressors, and most of them (78%) also reported sufficient symptoms to be diagnosed with PTSD. However, an equivalent proportion (78%) of the participants who did *not* report any past exposure to a traumatic stressor nevertheless reported sufficient symptoms to be diagnosed with PTSD. The authors conclude that it was not necessary to have experienced a traumatic stressor in order to have substantial symptoms of PTSD and that therefore (at least among people seeking treatment for a psychiatric disorder—depression in this case), there is reason to doubt that traumatic stressors "cause" PTSD.

Another study used a thorough trauma history interview and the *Structured Clinical Interview for DSM-III-R* to assess PTSD symptoms (see Chapter 6) with men and women who were diagnosed with one or more personality disorders and were receiving outpatient mental health treatment (Golier et al., 2003). As expected, participants who reported a history of having been physically assaulted as an adult or abused as a child or adolescent were more likely than other patients to be diagnosed with PTSD and also with borderline personality disorder. Those reporting other (accident, disaster, or war-related) traumatic stressors in adulthood were *not* more likely to be diagnosed with either PTSD or borderline personality disorder, but they were more likely to be diagnosed with a paranoid personality disorder. However, patients with PTSD or either personality disorder were more likely to *not* report having experienced each of these types of psychological trauma than to report each type of psychological trauma. Thus, while traumatic stressors involving assault or abuse were definitely related to PTSD, they did not appear to singularly determine who developed PTSD, and they were equally or more related to the two personality disorders as to PTSD. This is consistent with research showing that risk and protective factors, including genetics, personality, anxiety-proneness, intelligence, education, and social support, influence the likelihood and severity of PTSD in addition to trauma exposure.

(Continued)

Box 3.2 Continued

Thus, it is clear that exposure to traumatic stressor(s) does not alone cause PTSD and that PTSD-like symptoms may occur to people who do not report any exposure to traumatic stressors. However, these facts do not add up to a conclusion that PTSD is a pseudo-disorder (i.e., a false and misleading diagnosis). Rosen and Taylor (2007) consider the question of whether "pseudo-PTSD" can occur and note that people can pretend to have a trauma history and PTSD symptoms when they really do not ("malingering")—often in an attempt to get benefits such as a disability pension—or can genuinely but falsely believe that they experienced traumatic stressors and are suffering from PTSD symptoms when they really are not ("factitious PTSD"). Weeding out these individuals is very important for clinical, legal, and research purposes (e.g., to prevent misuse of workers compensation, veterans' benefits, and civil law systems), although in practice, even with the best tools (see Chapter 10), it is "almost impossible" (Rosen & Taylor, 2007, p. 204; see also Spitzer, First, & Wakefield, 2007, for a discussion of preventing malingering in PTSD).

McHugh and Treisman (2007) press the point that PTSD is not caused by exposure to traumatic stressors by examining historical accounts (see also Chapter 1; Jones & Wessely, 2007) of stress reactions that preceded the first formal diagnoses of traumatic stress disorders (Gross Stress Reactions in the 1952 *Diagnostic and Statistical Manual*; Posttraumatic Stress Disorder in the 1980 *Diagnostic and Statistical Manual*, 3rd ed.). They argue that the PTSD diagnosis should be eliminated because the symptoms reflect either natural processes of adaptation following exposure to a traumatic stressor (and therefore should not be considered a psychiatric "disorder") or a misclassification of another psychiatric disorder whose symptoms overlap with those of PTSD (such as major depressive disorder or anxiety disorders).

In response, Spitzer et al. (2007) wrote a rejoinder on "saving PTSD from itself in *DSM-5*" recommending several specific changes in the wording of PTSD criteria to clarify the link between exposure to a traumatic stressor and the PTSD symptoms. Spitzer et al. (2007) more fundamentally propose eliminating symptoms from the list of 17 that make up PTSD that are not specific to PTSD—that is, that are identical or highly similar to symptoms of other psychiatric disorders: "irritability, insomnia, difficulty concentrating, and markedly diminished interest" (p. 237). Subsequently, research studies testing the effects of removing these items (and combining PTSD avoidance, emotional numbing, and hyperarousal items into a single set) have found that there would be at most small changes in how often PTSD was diagnosed and in how often PTSD occurred in combination with depression or anxiety disorders (Elhai & Palmieri, 2011; see also Ford et al., 2000 for an earlier study).

The fact that a diagnosis can be faked or mistakenly asserted and incorrectly documented does not render the diagnosis unusable or unnecessary—these problems affect every medical and psychiatric diagnosis (Rosen & Taylor, 2007). Nor should overlap in symptoms of PTSD with those of other diagnoses disqualify the diagnosis, as this would eliminate many other medical and psychiatric diagnoses that share symptoms. The fundamental issue raised by the study by Bodkin et al. (2007) is not whether the PTSD symptoms could constitute a meaningful diagnosis but whether the diagnosis should include the requirement of a relationship between the symptoms and exposure to a traumatic stressor.

However, a major uncertainty in that study is whether the absence of *reporting* a traumatic stressor can be considered evidence of an absence of *actual exposure* to a traumatic stressor. The assessment instrument used, the *SCID*, is widely used for the diagnosis of PTSD but has been criticized as flawed in several ways. First, *SCID* questions used to ascertain exposure to traumatic stressors are brief and vague and do not systematically and specifically ask about the wide range of potentially traumatic stressors. By comparison, thorough and precise trauma history interviews or questionnaires such as the TESI (see Chapter 6) provide a complete survey of potentially traumatic events that reduces the risk of inadvertent underreporting.

Second, *SCID* questions do not guide the evaluator or interviewee in distinguishing between events that are objectively life-threatening or sexual violations versus those that are distressing or stressful but not technically traumatic. This could lead to either an overreporting of traumatic exposure or an underreporting—in the latter case, because events that may not clearly involve death or severe injury may nevertheless involve substantial danger or life threat that is not evident to either the respondent or the interviewer. Third, *SCID* symptom questions do not enable the interviewer to precisely assess the frequency and intensity of each PTSD symptom; instead, symptoms must be judged as "clinically significant," "subthreshold" (present but not serious), or not present. The distinction between clinically significant and subthreshold symptoms often is very difficult and can lead to over- or underreporting of the PTSD symptoms by the interviewer. For these reasons, it is unclear whether the determination of who had experienced a traumatic stressor and of who warranted a PTSD diagnosis was accurate in Bodkin and colleagues' study.

Evidence from an unexpected source—a study with laboratory rats—suggests that PTSD can occur despite the individual having no conscious memory of traumatic events. This is especially relevant for people who were exposed to maltreatment or family or community violence in the first years of life and subsequently develop PTSD symptoms. Although brain development in infancy is not sufficient at that preverbal stage to support more than fragmentary sensory memories—because words can at most be repeated or named but not yet used to form narrative story-like descriptions of complete events—infants definitely form nonverbal memories that can be virtually permanent. Traumatic events are likely to involve intense sensory experiences and thus to evoke strong and potentially long-lasting memories that could result in any of the PTSD symptoms except verbally describable recall of the traumatic events themselves (the first type of intrusive reexperiencing symptom). Consistent with this view, the

(Continued)

Box 3.2 Continued

animal study showed that rats that were exposed to painful foot shocks at an early age (19 days old, comparable to infancy for humans) did not react in adulthood with fear in the context in which the shocks occurred. There was no evidence of what in humans would be a conscious memory of the traumatic event. However, they had extreme startle reactions when given foot shocks as adults, and they displayed several biological and behavioral signs of persistent anxiety, including abnormal fluctuations in stress hormones, a surplus of stress-related (glucocorticoid) receptors in the amygdala, a high level of sensitivity to threats, avoidance of open areas in their environment, and even an aversion to odors that had been present when they were shocked in early life (Poulos et al., 2014). Thus, without evidence of remembering the foot shocks, these rats had changes in their behavior and in the areas in their brains and bodies that match those found in humans who have PTSD.

However, the question still remains whether people can develop PTSD despite never actually having been exposed to traumatic stressor(s). Studies have shown that people report levels of PTSD-like symptoms that are as high, or higher, in relation to distressing but not traumatic life events (such as divorce, job loss, burglary, or chronic illness) as to traumatic events (Anders, Frazier, & Frankfurt, 2011; Mol et al., 2005) and that PTSD symptoms occur along a continuum of severity from relatively mild reactions to nontraumatic stressors to severe reactions to traumatic stressors (Mulder, Fergusson, & Horwood, 2013). Results suggesting that milder "PTSD" symptoms may be quite different than symptoms of true PTSD comes from a study of adult twin pairs. The severity of psychiatric symptoms reported by men who had PTSD related to having been in military combat was substantially worse than for either his identical twin who had not been in combat (ruling out the effects of genetically based vulnerability to psychiatric problems) or for other combat-exposed men who did not have PTSD (Gilbertson et al., 2010). Thus, although people may report high levels of symptoms consistent with PTSD despite not having experienced a traumatic stressor, the symptoms appear to reflect a general sense of distress that has a less severe impact on the person's overall mental state (and potentially also their brain's and body's stress response systems; Poulos et al., 2014) than when PTSD follows exposure to traumatic stressor(s).

Further evidence of the role of traumatic stressors in the development of PTSD comes from a study that addressed the question of whether PTSD symptoms should be assessed with reference to only one traumatic stressor (presumably the past event that was the worst, or that is currently most distressing to recall) or to all traumatic stressors that have ever occurred in the individual's life (Elhai et al., 2009). The study included three groups of college students, all of whom rated their own PTSD symptoms, based on (i) all past traumatic events in their life; (ii) the one past traumatic event they found most distressing to recall currently; and (iii) other nontraumatic stressors in their life (this group had not experienced a traumatic stressor). The key finding was that the PTSD symptoms reported by the first two groups (all past trauma and one worst past trauma) tended to be organized in a consistent manner, but the symptoms reported by the third group (no past trauma) were more scattered and did not fit a single PTSD profile. The profile of PTSD symptoms also differed between the all past trauma group and the one worst past trauma group in an interesting way. The all past trauma group reported a symptom profile similar to the *DSM-IV* definition of PTSD, except that avoidance and emotional numbing symptoms formed two separate factors instead of being a single combined group. The one worst past trauma group reported a symptom profile more similar to that of the *DSM*-5 PTSD structure, with a separate factor for persistently altered negative emotions ("dysphoria"). The take-home message is that PTSD symptoms "hold together" better for people who actually have been exposed to traumatic stressors than others who have not, which suggests that traumatic exposure may play an important role in the development of PTSD that can be distinguished from the mere presence of PTSD-like symptoms as reported by people who have never been traumatized. Thus, the overall evidence suggests it is unlikely that true PTSD can occur without a traumatic stressor.

Understanding etiology: causes? Or risk and protective factors?

"Etiology," derived from the Greek word for "cause," is the study of the causes of diseases. Psychiatric disorders and psychosocial problems such as PTSD are "multi-determined"—that is, they are the product not of any single "cause" but instead of a complex interplay (Carlson, Dalenberg, & Muhtadie, 2008) of "nature," which is a person's inborn or acquired biological and psychological characteristics, and "nurture," which involves the influences in the physical and social environments that promote or interfere with healthy adaptation or illness, learning or disability, and growth or developmental delays. Regardless of the role played by exposure to traumatic stressors in PTSD, there is convincing scientific evidence that PTSD is caused in part by certain other "risk factors"—or at least that PTSD is more likely to develop when such "risk factors" have occurred.

The term "risk factor" is used because it is virtually impossible scientifically to isolate the exact "cause" of any phenomenon. As an example from the medical field, we know that infection by the human immunodeficiency virus (HIV) can lead to acquired immunodeficiency syndrome (AIDS); thus, HIV could be considered the "cause" of AIDS. However, not everyone who is exposed to HIV develops AIDS, and even among those who do contract AIDS, the timing of developing the illness, its symptoms, and the severity of the symptoms vary greatly from person to person and for the same person at different times. Several "risk factors" can hasten the onset of AIDS and increase its severity and lethality, particularly other conditions that compromise the body's defenses against infection (the immune system)—for example, other sexually transmitted diseases such as syphilis or herpes. Thus, the "cause" of AIDS, which usually is described as contracting HIV through unprotected sex, needle use or sticks, infected blood transfusions, or mother-child transmission, is more complicated than this. In order to understand the full causes of AIDS and to prevent the disease, it is essential to know about risk factors that may "tip the balance" between having HIV and developing AIDS.

The analogy to PTSD is fairly direct. Exposure to traumatic stressors is the counterpart of exposure to HIV, leading to the risk of developing, respectively, PTSD or AIDS. Therefore, in order to understand, prevent, or treat PTSD, it is essential to know the risk factors that contribute to the development of PTSD and "tip the balance" in a positive or negative way when people are exposed to traumatic stressors. However, it is not enough to know what places a person at risk for a disease, because even when risk factors are present, some individuals still do not develop the disease or do so more slowly or with lesser severity. This suggests that some people may have a kind of "resistance" or even "invulnerability" to disease even when exposed to its causes or risks (Figure 3.1).

The positive side of disease prevention and treatment is that there are "protective factors" that reduce the likelihood of developing diseases. The most important protective factor is any condition or attribute that prevents (or reduces the likelihood) of a person encountering the active biological agent(s) (called "pathogens") that are involved in the disease. Thus, key protective factors for the prevention of AIDS include knowledge about risky behaviors (such as unprotected sex or sharing needles) and safer alternatives, societal and peer-group norms and relationships that support the use

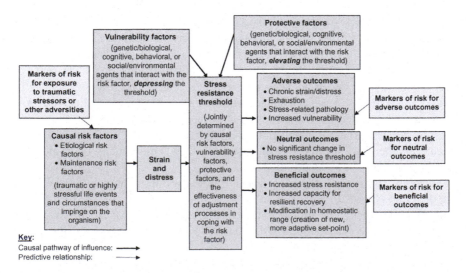

Figure 3.1 The role of risk and protective factors in the etiology of psychological "outcomes" such as PTSD.
Reprinted with permission of the author and publisher from Layne et al. (2008).

of safer alternative practices, and access to activities and practical tools that are necessary in order to engage in safer alternative practices. Other protective factors increase a person's resistance to the disease if infected, such as a particular gene (*CCL3L1*) that has been identified in HIV-resistant individuals, or timely access to prophylactic (preventive) and therapeutic medicines (such as antiretroviral drugs for HIV).

Here, again, there is a direct analogy to protective factors for PTSD. Just as the best way to prevent AIDS is to increase safe practices, PTSD is best prevented by reducing people's exposure to traumatic stressors. Although exposure to traumatic stressors cannot be entirely eliminated (just as it is impossible to absolutely ensure that accidental exposure to HIV will never happen), it is important to create conditions that reduce the risk of traumatic stressors (such as programs aimed at preventing violence or abuse; see Chapter 9). As with HIV, traumatic stressors also are less likely to be encountered when a person's family, peer-group, community, work or school, and societal support systems promote safety and discourage risky behaviors such as violence or actions that lead to serious accidents (such as drunk driving or driving without a seatbelt). In addition to social norms and support, there are protective factors that reduce the risk that a person will develop PTSD after encountering a traumatic stressor. These include biological protective factors (although, unlike HIV/AIDS, no specific genes have been identified that are protective against PTSD—but research is headed in that direction; see Chapter 6), as well as other person-specific protective factors, and social and environmental protective factors.

Thus, the best way to understand the "cause(s)" of PTSD is not to look for a single (or few) villains that can be defeated or enemies that can be eradicated, but instead to develop a broader understanding of how risk and protective factors lead to the posttraumatic trajectories (see Chapter 2) that result in either PTSD or freedom or recovery from PTSD. Figure 3.2 provides an overview of a "causal model" (i.e., the

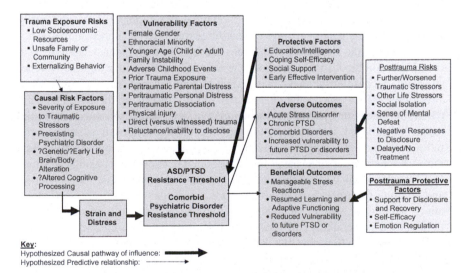

Figure 3.2 Factors influencing PTSD following stressful or traumatic life events.

theoretical connections among the potential "causes") of PTSD developed by Layne et al. (2008). Three types of risk factors are distinguished. The first are "causal risk factors," which are presumed to be directly responsible for a disease or problem (such as HIV with AIDS and exposure to traumatic stressors with PTSD). Causal risk factors have a direct negative effect on the individual biologically and psychologically, increasing the "strain" on the person's resources (e.g., depleting the immune system's capacities or leading to a psychological sense of hopelessness) and the "distress" experienced by the person (e.g., the physical illness symptoms of AIDS or the anxiety of PTSD).

"Vulnerability factors" are the second type of risk factor, including aspects of the individual or the environment that make a person more likely to either experience a causal risk factor or to develop the disease or problem after having experienced the causal risk factor. For AIDS, engaging in unprotected sex or needle use and having a compromised immune system are vulnerability factors. Several vulnerability factors for exposure to traumatic stressors and PTSD are discussed later in the chapter. An interesting bimodal vulnerability factor for PTSD—age—is highlighted in Box 3.3. Vulnerability factors often do not increase strain or distress, but instead contribute to disease or problems by decreasing resistance to the adverse outcomes.

Box 3.3 Age as a Risk or Protective Factor for PTSD

Age may be either a risk or protective factor for PTSD, depending on the stage of emotional, social, and cognitive development of a person exposed to a traumatic stressor. Chronological age appears to be less important in determining risk of PTSD than the developmental stage and the challenges facing the individual at that stage. In addition, at certain points in the life span, there are *transitions* between stages of biological and psychological development that temporarily shake up a person's familiar ways of handling stressors. The upheaval that inevitably occurs in developmental transitions (such as in early latency, adolescence, or midlife adulthood) increases both the risk of exposure to traumatic or other stressors (because of the inevitable change in routines and relationships) and of developing PTSD (due to the demand that simply traversing the developmental transition places on the coping capacities that are needed to recover from the impact of exposure to traumatic stressors). As each transition is completed, the individual gains additional social resources (e.g., the wider array of relationships that develops as a person expands his or her social network) and coping capacities (e.g., increased knowledge and skills that come with maturation, independence, and learning from life experiences). Yet, the transitions also are times of uncertainty and change, which can amplify the impact of a traumatic stressor and lead to increased vulnerability to PTSD regardless of the person's chronological age.

Consistent with this view that developmental transitions confer risk for PTSD, childhood generally is a period of less risk for PTSD than adolescence (Carlson et al., 2008). Childhood is a developmental period when the biological and cognitive capacities needed for complete narrative (story-like) memories that shape our core beliefs about self/identity and the world/relationships are incomplete and rapidly evolving. Children also tend not to question beliefs and expectations that they hold at any particular moment, while adolescents are constantly reconsidering their view of themselves, relationships, and the future. In addition, children tend to both rely upon and receive more immediate help from primary caregivers than adolescents in coping with stressors. Hormonal changes, accelerated brain development, and increased social, educational, and personal independence and responsibility make adolescence an often tumultuous time in which stress reactivity commonly increases drastically (albeit temporarily). Adolescents also more often report exposure to interpersonal violence than younger children or adults (Boney-McCoy & Finkelhor, 1996; Kessler et al., 2005, 1995), and more than 20% of both girls and boys report new incidents of victimization by interpersonal violence in as short a time period as 15 months (Boney-McCoy & Finkelhor, 1996) and 33% report multiple forms of exposure to interpersonal violence ("polyvictimization," Finkelhor, Ormrod, & Turner, 2007).

Therefore, although children have less well-developed coping capacities, their relatively greater degree of developmental continuity compared to adolescents may actually protect them from developing PTSD—especially if they have reliable and emotionally attuned primary caregiving to support their recovery from exposure to stressors (traumatic and otherwise).

However, young children can be profoundly impacted emotionally and behaviorally when exposed to traumatic stressors (Briggs-Gowan et al., 2010; Briggs-Gowan, Carter, & Ford; 2012; Grasso, Greene, & Ford, 2013). This is particularly true when traumatic stressors occur on an ongoing basis or as a series of events that occur over a lengthy period of time. Such chronic or cumulative traumatic exposure (see Box 3.4) can place a young child at high risk for PTSD or related psychosocial problems as a result of overwhelming their (and their caregivers') capacities to cope and also lead them to develop core beliefs and expectations that are tainted by anxiety, hypervigilance, and despair. Young children are particularly vulnerable to PTSD when they experience chronic or recurrent traumatic stressors at the same time that major disruptions are occurring in their relationships with primary caregivers (such as sexual or physical abuse or severe neglect), placing them at risk for severe emotional and behavioral problems, including PTSD (D'Andrea et al., 2012; English, Graham, Litrownik, Everson, & Bangdiwala, 2005; Ford et al., 2000; Kaplow, Dodge, Amaya-Jackson, & Saxe, 2005; Kaplow & Widom, 2007; Keiley, Bates, Dodge, & Pettit, 2001).

Transitional vulnerability may play a role in adults' vulnerability to PTSD as well. Adults are more likely to develop PTSD if they are exposed to psychological trauma in middle adulthood than either as young adults or in older adulthood (Ford, Adams, & Dailey, 2007). For example, in the National Comorbidity Study-Replication, the prevalence of PTSD among adults rose from 6% among 18–29 year olds (which was very similar to the prevalence among teenagers,

(*Continued*)

Box 3.3 Continued

McLaughlin et al., 2013) to 8% among 30–44 year olds, and 9% among 45–59 year olds (Kessler et al., 2005). Two in three cases of PTSD had an initial onset between age 15 and 53, indicating that late adolescence and midlife adulthood appear to be particularly high-risk developmental periods for PTSD. Beyond the turmoil of adolescence, in middle adulthood additional hormonal changes (such as menopause and decreasing levels of testosterone) and an accumulation of work, family, and financial responsibilities (such as job promotion and midlife career challenges and changes, raising children and caring for aging parents, and increasing costs due to providing for a growing family's needs and children's educations and health care) also may increase stress reactivity and reduce coping resources.

Culture and ethnicity also may play a role in influencing the risk of PTSD for persons of different ages. Norris, Friedman, and Watson (2002) surveyed adults following a hurricane in the United States, a different hurricane in Mexico, and a flood in Poland. In the United States sample, midlife adults were most likely to report PTSD symptoms; in Mexico, younger adults were most likely to report PTSD symptoms; and in Poland, older adults were most likely to report PTSD symptoms. Thus, there was no single relationship between age and PTSD symptoms, suggesting that the different ethnoracial backgrounds, cultures, and social support resources of the three cohorts of disaster survivors may have led to the differences reported by adults of different ages within each cohort resist or recover from PTSD symptoms.

Third, there are "outcome risk factors," which are factors that increase the likelihood that adverse outcomes will be severe if they occur. Developing an increasing viral "load" (level of HIV in the blood system) or repeated unprotected exposure to HIV are examples of HIV/AIDS outcome risk factors. Later in this chapter several PTSD outcome risk factors (risk factors associated with more severe and prolonged PTSD symptoms) identified by scientific research are discussed.

Protective factors counteract or counterbalance the effects of risk factors by increasing the person's ability to "resist" (prevent) or to be "resilient" in coping with and "recovering" from adverse outcomes. Protective factors may indirectly increase beneficial outcomes, but their primary function is to reduce the resistance threshold— that is, to increase the likelihood that the person will successfully access biological or psychosocial resources that reduce exposure to causal risk factors, vulnerability, and the development of severe disease or problems.

Causal risk factors for PTSD

One causal risk factor for PTSD has been strongly established by scientific research: the "dose" or severity of exposure to traumatic stressors. We next consider the one necessary—but not sufficient (see Box 3.1)—causal risk factor for PTSD: exposure to traumatic stressor(s). Then we explore the evidence regarding three other types of potential causal risk factors for PTSD that were identified in a review of 54 prospective longitudinal studies of risk factors for PTSD: psychiatric disorders, and associated coping and personality styles and family adversities; vulnerability in brain/body stress response systems related to genetics or early life experiences; and limitations or deficits in cognitive abilities (DiGangi et al., 2013).

Degree or severity of exposure to traumatic stressor(s)

The causal risk factor for PTSD that has been most consistently documented in scientific research is the *degree of exposure to traumatic stressor(s)* (Brewin, Andrews, & Valentine, 2000; Carlson et al., 2008; Ford, 2009; Norris & Slone, 2007; Ozer, Best, Lipsey, & Weiss, 2003; Vogt, King, & King, 2007). This has been termed the "dose response relationship" because the greater the "dose" (in this case of exposure to harm or threat), the greater the likelihood that the exposed person will subsequently suffer PTSD. There is no *a priori* way to define or measure "degree of exposure" to a traumatic stressor. It is not as simple as saying that certain events seem "worse," "more horrible," or "more painful" than others. Exactly how the "dose" or "event exposure" is defined and measured varies greatly, however (Vogt et al., 2007). It may be defined as the severity of the threat to the person's (or someone else's) life (Ozer et al., 2003). It may be defined as the extent of physical injury (Acierno, Resnick, Kilpatrick, Saunders, & Best, 1999) or of the cruelty or violence or destruction inflicted upon affected persons (Kessler et al., 1995). It also may be defined as the extent of destruction to the family, home, or community in the wake of a natural or humanmade disaster or mass-casualty incident (Norris & Slone, 2007). The survivor's subjective response of terror or horror (Brewin et al., 2000; Bryant, 2005) or dissociation (Ozer et al., 2003) at the time of the event or soon afterward (the "peritraumatic" period) also have been used to operationalize trauma exposure and found to be predictive of developing PTSD (see Vulnerability Factors in this chapter).

Aspects of traumatic stressors have been identified and shown to be associated with more severe immediate stress reactions, which in turn are associated with a greater likelihood of developing PTSD or other psychiatric disorders (Brewin et al., 2000, 2002). These include:

- intentional physical or sexual violence perpetrated by another person or group (such as domestic, war, or community violence; terrorist attacks; or torture);
- betrayal by a person or organization responsible for protecting the safety and rights of vulnerable individuals (such as physical or sexual abuse by a caregiver or priest);
- violation of victims' bodies or selves or homes by extreme violence or destruction (such as war atrocities, rape, or destruction of home and community in a disaster);
- coercion used to destroy people's self-respect and will to resist (such as combined physical and emotional abuse, domestic violence, or torture; see Chapter 11);
- prolonged complete isolation from human contact and social interaction (such as solitary confinement of prisoners of war, kidnapping victims, or abused children);

- Lengthy duration or numerous repetitions of exposure to traumatic stressors, or of uncertainty in the face of imminent exposure (such as chronic abuse, violence, or premature deaths, or living in a violent family, war-zone, or disaster-prone area; Boxes 3.4 and 3.5).

Box 3.4 Cumulative Traumatic Stress: Retraumatization, Childhood Adversity, and Polyvictimization

When people experience a series of stressors, simultaneously or one at a time over a period of days, weeks, months, or years, there is a "cumulative" impact (Grasso et al., 2013), similar to that of a boxer who is hit by a rapid sequence of blows and by many blows over the course of a long fight. People who have already been exposed to a traumatic stressor tend to be at risk for exposure to another traumatic stressors. Three distinct lines of theory and research have evolved in an attempt to understand cumulative traumatic stress: retraumatization, childhood adversity, and polyvictimization.

Retraumatization. There is substantial evidence that being multiply exposed to traumatic stressors places an individual at increasing risk of developing PTSD and related psychosocial and physical health problems in childhood and across the life span (Follette & Vijay, 2008). However, exactly what constitutes retraumatization has not been rigorously defined. There is no specified period of time or context in which the subsequent exposure to additional psychological trauma(s) must occur in order for retraumatization to have occurred. Once the initial, or "index," psychological trauma has occurred, any subsequent exposure to traumatic stressors may result in retraumatization. Retraumatization can occur regardless of whether the environmental or contextual factors of the first traumatic exposure are different at the time of the later traumatic exposures or remain consistent. Thus, if the first traumatic experience is childhood sexual abuse (CSA), retraumatization can occur through exposure to very different types of traumatic stressors, such as a natural disaster, war, or interpersonal violence (Whitfield, Anda, Dube, & Felitti, 2003). Whether different combinations (or timings) of index and subsequent traumatic stressors have different causal or vulnerability effects in relation to PTSD has not been established by research.

In some cases the term *retraumatization* has been used to describe acute exacerbations of PTSD-related distress by reminders of past psychological traumas. For example, involvement in the judicial system can prove retraumatizing to crime victims when they are forced to recount their experience or are mandated to testify in trials. In such cases, the person is not exposed to additional psychological trauma but experiences increased posttraumatic distress as a result of encountering reminders of the past traumatic stressors. It is important to distinguish between this usage of the term *retraumatization* from repeated exposure to traumatic stressors usage because, while the results may be similar, the second case does *not* actually involve exposure to traumatic stressors. If this difference is not carefully noted, experiences or events that are stressful but not traumatic may be misconstrued as being traumatic stressors. Such confusion could lead to the false conclusion that stressful experiences such as court proceedings inevitably are traumatic stressors, as opposed to being highly stressful.

Research has shown that repeated exposures to the same or different psychological traumas is associated with an increased risk of developing PTSD and more severe PTSD symptoms compared to a single exposure to a traumatic event (Follette and Vijay, 2008). Over the course of a lifetime, 67% of women who have been victimized by interpersonal violence will report at least one additional incident of victimization (Cloitre, Cohen, & Koenen, 2006). The factors associated with increased risk for sexual revictimization/retraumatization include having a history of child or adolescent sexual abuse and the characteristics of previous victimization (the severity and frequency of those abuses, the age at which the abuse began, the nature of the abusive sexual contact, the victim's relationship with the abuser, the duration and number of exposures to victimization; Follette and Vijay, 2008). A history of CSA is a risk factor for sexual victimization as an adult: women with a history of CSA have been found to be twice as likely as other women to be assaulted in adulthood (Nishith, Mechanic, & Resick, 2000), and men with a CSA history are 5.5 times more likely than other men to be assaulted as an adult (Classen, Palesh, & Aggarwal, 2005). The combination of CSA and adult victimization is a key risk factor for adult PTSD (Nishith et al., 2000). Follette and Vijay (2008, pp. 588–589) notes:

Intrapersonal variables, which include psychological disorders, substance use, and sexual practices, can also put an individual at risk for retraumatization by affecting the ways they are able to respond to subsequent stressful events. ... For example, an individual who utilizes dissociation as a form of coping with posttraumatic stress problems is at significantly greater risk to experience another traumatic event.

Although individual risk factors are an important consideration, this should not be misinterpreted as "blaming the victim." In most such cases, the traumatized individual does not intentionally cause the occurrence of additional traumas, but she or he may be less careful or more prone to taking risks as a result of experiencing posttraumatic distress or dissociation—or the person may simply live in circumstances that are unavoidably dangerous (such as violent communities or families). Environmental or contextual factors also seem to increase risk of retraumatization as well. Factors such as poverty or neglect can increase the likelihood of a person being exposed to multiple potentially traumatic events, including childhood abuse and family and community violence. Poverty may also be a risk factor for retraumatization among people exposed to disasters, because they are more likely than more affluent people to lose (or simply not have access to) vital resources that facilitate postdisaster recovery.

An example of the kind of study needed in order to more definitively establish whether and how repeated exposure to traumatic stressors leads to a greater likelihood or severity of PTSD is the 10-year follow-up conducted by Breslau, Peterson, and Schultz (2008) of a survey of a sample of generally healthy young adults in a midwestern U.S. health maintenance organization. They found that

(Continued)

Box 3.4 Continued

retraumatization (i.e., having a subsequent exposure to a traumatic stressor after having had a prior experience of psychological trauma) was associated with an increase in the risk of PTSD only if PTSD had occurred following the first traumatic exposure. Thus, it was not simply the cumulative impact of repeated exposure to traumatic stressors but that "retraumatization" *in combination with vulnerability to PTSD* that resulted in the increased risk of PTSD that has been associated with retraumatization.

Adverse Childhood Experiences (ACEs). The ACEs Study was a large-scale epidemiological (see Chapter 4) investigation that has gained professional and public recognition by demonstrating that adversities experienced in childhood may substantially increase the risk of many physical and mental health problems in adulthood (Anda, Butchart, Felitti, & Brown, 2010; Felitti et al., 1998). The study originally was based on information obtained from more than 17,000 young and midlife adults who completed a routine health screening while receiving health care services in the California Kaiser Permanente Health Maintenance Organization. (80% white; 54% female; average age 57 years old). Participants completed a 10-item yes-or-no questionnaire telling whether they had experienced each of the following ACEs before the age of 18: physical abuse, verbal abuse, sexual abuse, physical neglect, emotional neglect, an alcoholic parent, witnessing domestic violence of their mother, a family member jailed, a mentally ill family member, and loss of a parent due to divorce, death, or separation.

Each participant was assigned a score based on the number of ACE categories endorsed. Nearly two-thirds of the participants reported at least one ACE, and one in six people experienced four or more ACEs. Women were 50% more likely than men to have experienced five or more ACE categories. Disturbingly high proportions reported traumatic adversity in childhood: 18% of men and 25% of women reported CSA; 22% of men and 20% of women reported childhood physical abuse; 12% of men and 15% of women had witnessed maternal battering. Almost 90% of those who reported any one ACE reported at least one additional ACE, so more than half experienced the cumulative impact of multiple childhood adversities. Three times as many (65%) individuals who had witnessed domestic violence (versus 23% of those not exposed to domestic violence in childhood) also had an alcoholic parent while growing up. Similarly, more than four times as many (81%) people who reported emotional abuse (versus 20% who did not) also reported physical abuse as a child.

Therefore, the ACEs study explored the relationship of *the number of ACEs* experienced to a wide variety of adverse outcomes in adulthood. The result was a "dose-response" relationship where *every additional ACE* reported increased the risk of serious physical and mental health problems in adulthood (including smoking, obesity, physical inactivity, depression, suicide attempts, alcoholism, drug abuse, sexual promiscuity, sexually transmitted disease) and also major medical illnesses (heart disease, cancer, stroke, chronic bronchitis, COPD, diabetes, hepatitis, and skeletal fractures). Some of the more dramatic and serious public health findings of the ACEs study included:

- People reporting five or more ACEs were *10 times* as likely to have attempted suicide, and those reporting seven or more ACEs were *30 times* more likely. After accounting for other risk factors for suicide (alcoholism, depression, street drug use), people with ACE scores of 7 or higher were still *17 times* more likely to have attempted suicide than people reporting no ACEs.
- Besides the occurrence of psychiatric disorders, their complexity and severity (as measured by the number of psychiatric medications prescribed) were also related to the number of ACEs.
- The risk of developing often fatal or extremely severe medical illnesses, such as heart disease, lung cancer, or autoimmune diseases, was directly related to the number of ACEs reported.
- Subsequently, the 10 ACEs questions were included by the Centers for Disease Control (Bynum et al., 2010) in a random sampling of the adult populations of five states in the United States, and the original findings from the Kaiser Permanente study were replicated; with each additional ACE, physical and mental health risk behaviors and illnesses were several times more likely to occur in childhood or adulthood.

Polyvictimization. The National Survey of Children's Exposure to Violence (NatSCEV) interviewed 2030 10- to 17-year-old children and adolescents who represented a cross section of all youth in the United States. Victimization experienced in the past year was measured using the Juvenile Victimization Questionnaire (JVQ) to survey 34 different types of victimization. Although noninterpersonal events (e.g., accident, natural disaster) could be viewed as "victimizing" survivors or witnesses, in these studies victimization was defined as including only interpersonal events (e.g., physical or sexual assault, abuse, or witnessed violence). Youth were defined as having been "polyvictimized" if they endorsed exposure to four or more victimization types on the JVQ. This is similar to the ACEs score in that it is based on the number of different *types* of victimization rather than the number of times or chronicity or severity of any single type of victimization. However, the NatSCEV assessed a much larger number of more specifically defined types of victimization than the 10 ACEs. Victimization also was assessed based only on the past year, rather than as recalled several decades later, which would be expected to increase the accuracy of the respondent's recall of victimization. Despite these definitional and procedural differences, the findings regarding polyvictimization from the NatSCEV were remarkably similar to the findings from the ACEs studies.

Nearly one in four youths surveyed who had experienced any victimization were polyvictims. Polyvictims tended to be older and male, although a large number of girls also were polyvictims (Finkelhor et al., 2005). Polyvictims were on average four times more likely to be revictimized in the year following the study, and nearly half of polyvictims at baseline were categorized as polyvictims again in the second year (Finkelhor et al., 2007). While referred to as "persistent

(Continued)

Box 3.4 Continued

polyvictims" in the NatSCEV, these youths definitely could be considered likely to have experienced retraumatization. In addition, consistent with the ACEs studies' results, the persistently polyvictimized youths tended to live in families in which violence occurred, to have experienced childhood maltreatment, and to have had family members who abused alcohol and drugs or a parent who was unemployed. Thus, persistent polyvictimization of children involves not only exposure to multiple types of potentially traumatizing victimization but also living in a family context of maltreatment and relational adversity. Retraumatized polyvictim children encounter adversity across multiple contexts where violence is pervasive, inflicted by a variety of perpetrators: physically and emotionally maltreatment by caregivers; bullying by peers; sexual abuse by caregivers, mentors, or acquaintances; and witnessing a host of violent and traumatic incidents in the home, school, and community (Cuevas, Finkelhor, Clifford, Ormrod, & Turner, 2010). On the other hand, the more friends a youth has, the lower the risk of persistent polyvictimization (Finkelhor et al., 2007)—except if the friends are involved in risky behaviors or lifestyles, such as juvenile delinquency (Cuevas, Finkelhor, Turner, & Ormrod, 2007; Ford, Elhai, Connor, & Frueh, 2010). The latter findings echo the results of studies showing that social support can be either a protective or risk factor, depending on its nature (see Box 3.5).

Ultimately, four pathways to polyvictimization were identified by the NatSCEV: (i) residing in a dangerous community, (ii) living in a dangerous family, (iii) living in a nondangerous but chaotic and multiproblem family environment, and (iv) having emotional problems that lead to risky behavior, foster antagonism, and increase the likelihood of being victimized (Finkelhor, Ormrod, Turner, & Holt, 2009). The first (dangerous community) pathway to polyvictimization was most common among children who became polyvictims before 10 years of age, and these children most often became polyvictims at about the age of entry to elementary school (i.e., when their contact with the larger community sharply expanded). The other age at which many youth became polyvictims was at about the age of entry into high school, which may be a vulnerable period both due to the turmoil of adolescence and contact with an even broader spectrum of peers that occurs in the typically large and diverse high school context. The vulnerability that occurs at those two key points of developmental transition is consistent with the research evidence showing that such transitions are risky times for PTSD (see Box 3.3).

Box 3.5 Pathways from Victimization to Revictimization

As many as three in four women who report a history of having been victimized by CSA also report experiencing sexual assault in adulthood (Roodman & Clum, 2001), and they are two to three times more likely to report an adult sexual assault than other women (Classen et al., 2005). Many factors have been hypothesized to account for this high risk of revictimization, including early developmental production of sex hormones, increased sexual activity and engaging in risky sexual behavior, and attempting to use sex to cope with depression or other forms of psychological distress (Noll, Trickett, & Putnam, 2003; Orcutt, Cooper, & Garcia, 2005). However, sexual abuse often occurs in combination with other forms of childhood maltreatment (such as physical or emotional abuse or neglect), each of which has been shown to be associated with adult revictimization (D'Andrea et al., 2012). For example, a prospective study of high-risk children in adulthood found that not only CSA but also physical abuse and neglect predicted physical and sexual revictimization (Widom, DuMont, & Czaja, 2007).

A study with young women found that the relationship between CSA and revictimization over a 6-year period of time could be explained in part by a tendency toward depression, anxiety, and attempts to manage these negative emotions and beliefs by using sex (Orcutt et al. 2005). Pervasive negative emotional states and beliefs are a core PTSD symptom that is consistently associated with all forms of childhood maltreatment (D'Andrea et al., 2012). Adolescents may be at risk for sexual revictimization due to a developmentally normative tendency to use sex to manage these types of distress. For example, a study with a community sample of adolescents who reported their reasons for engaging in sex immediately after sexual encounters found that they reported using sex to cope with negative emotions if they felt a sense of low self-esteem or anxiety, and for boys there was indirect evidence that using sex to manage negative emotions provided a buffer against feeling depressed (Dawson, Shih, de Moor, & Shrier, 2008).

These findings raise the question of whether adolescents and young adults who have been victimized in childhood actually are trapped by posttraumatic distress in ways that might lead them to be vulnerable to revictimization (see Box 3.4). Therefore, a study was done with college women who reported whether they had experienced childhood sexual (CSA), physical (CPA), or emotional (CEA) abuse and then approximately 2 months later reported whether they had been sexually assaulted in that time period (ASA) (Miron & Orcutt, 2014). One in nine of the women reported a sexual assault (11%), and there appeared to be several potential pathways from the childhood abuse to revictimization. EA was directly predictive of ASA. Women who had experienced CSA and also sexual abuse in adolescence also were at risk for ASA. And women who had experienced CPA were at risk for ASA if they were subsequently sexually abused in adolescence and felt depressed in adulthood. In addition, CPA victims also were at risk for ASA even if they had never been previously sexually assaulted but if they used sex to manage negative emotions and were likely to agree to have sex after a casual encounter. The four pathways to sexual revictimization identified in this study may be only a subset of the ways in which survivors of childhood traumatic stressors are at risk for further traumatization. However, despite the brief time frame in which adult victimization was assessed (on average 2 months), the

(Continued)

Box 3.5 Continued

findings demonstrate that revictimization is a prevalent problem and point to the role that PTSD—in the form of negative emotions and beliefs, and risky attempts to manage this distress—may play when sexual or physical abuse has occurred in the life of a child or youth.

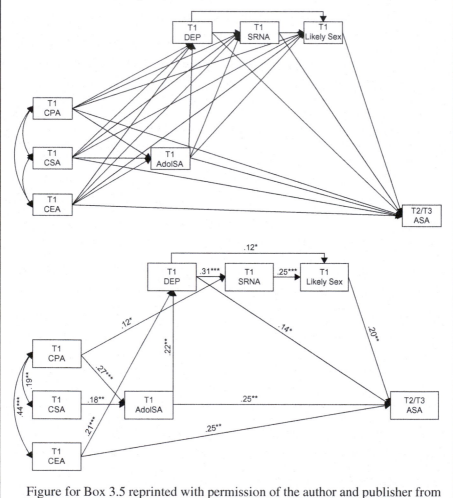

Figure for Box 3.5 reprinted with permission of the author and publisher from Miron and Orcutt (2014).

These "event" or "exposure" risk factors have several common denominators despite their many differences. Actual or imminent severe physical injury or "violation" (by sexual assault or disfigurement or dismemberment) is explicit or implicit in each exposure causal risk factor. In addition, several exposure causal risk factors involve witnessing or suffering the loss of primary relationship(s) due to someone else's untimely death or experiencing one's own (or witnessing someone else's) imminent death. The reality or imminent threat of death is likely to elicit the biological survival reaction that appears to become fixed and chronic in PTSD (see Chapter 6), and this biological shift could explain how the threat of death or witnessing the death or near death of someone else can have a psychologically "traumatic" impact.

Another common denominator among the exposure causal risk factors is the terror elicited by extreme violence such as war or torture, and the horror elicited by extreme "violation," such as sexual assault or abuse (D'Andrea, Ford, Stolbach, Spinazzola & van der Kolk, 2012). Although individuals' subjective reactions will differ even to what seem to be objectively severely terrifying or horrifying events, a number of scientific studies have shown that more severe violence or violation that is intentionally inflicted on victim(s) is associated with a higher likelihood of directly disclosed or indirectly expressed terror and horror (Marx, Forsyth, Gallup, Fuse, & Lexington, 2008; Pat-Horenczyk, 2008).

A third common denominator among exposure causal risk factors is the extent to which they are "sudden, uncontrollable, and have an extremely negative valence" (Carlson et al., 2008). To this could be added the unpredictability of the stressor (Foa, Zinbarg, & Rothbaum, 1992). A sudden and unpredictable stressor is likely to occur too rapidly and with too little warning for the affected person to "act to either physically protect himself/herself from harm or to psychologically prepare for a negative outcome" (Carlson et al., 2008). If the stressor also is largely or completely beyond the person's ability to control what happens or influence the outcome, the combination of *suddenness, unpredictability, and uncontrollability* of the event is likely to take the affected person by surprise, which may result in a sense of shock, disbelief, and confusion. Such events provide minimal opportunity to defend oneself physically or psychologically, leading to greater risk of being unprotected and injured (and to be unable to protect others from being injured).

When events happen rapidly and without warning or an opportunity to influence their course or outcome, it is more difficult to think clearly because the person has little or no preparation to provide a foundation for a thoughtful appraisal and even less time to think analytically about what is happening, what it means, and what to do. Not surprisingly, therefore, people with PTSD often describe feeling particularly distressed—frightened, helpless, guilty, ashamed—by intrusive memories of traumatic events because they believe that they were powerless to prevent or stop terrible things from happening ("I never saw it coming, and when it did, I couldn't stop it") or that they should have been vigilant and prepared but had failed to do so ("I should have known it was going to happen and been ready so I wouldn't have been so helpless when it happened").

Preexisting psychiatric disorders

A second type of potential causal risk factor is a *preexisting psychiatric illness*. Adults with chronic and severe mood disorders (such as major depression or bipolar disorder), anxiety disorders (such as obsessive-compulsive, panic, or generalized anxiety disorder), psychotic disorders (such as schizophrenia or schizoaffective disorder), dissociative disorders, eating disorders (such as anorexia or bulimia nervosa), or personality disorders (such as borderline or paranoid personality disorder) often report a history of exposure to psychological trauma and both past (14–66%) and current (i.e., 12–35%) PTSD (see Chapter 4) (Mueser, Essock, Haines, Wolfe, & Xie, 2004; Mueser et al., 2001). Adults with psychiatric disorders report substantial recent exposure to victimization traumas (such as abuse or domestic violence; Goodman et al., 2001; Neria, Bromet, Sievers, Lavelle, & Fochtmann, 2002; Sells, Rowe, Fisk, & Davidson, 2003), but the most common time of first victimization is in childhood (Follette and Vijay, 2008; Neria et al., 2002).

Not only is PTSD prevalent among adults with psychiatric disorders (see Chapter 4), but it also is associated with more severe symptoms of those disorders and worse impairment in relationships and work than is found when adults with psychiatric disorders do not also have PTSD. For example, Mueser et al. (2004) reported that 16% of patients with psychiatric disorders in a study of three vocational rehabilitation programs met research criteria for current PTSD, and those with PTSD had more severe psychiatric symptoms, worse self-reported health, lower self-esteem, lower subjective quality of life, and poorer employment outcomes (lower rates of competitive work, fewer hours worked, fewer wages earned) *even when these patients had received the most effective rehabilitation intervention*. Similarly, a study of more than 1000 depressed adults who had been treated in inpatient psychiatric programs showed that PTSD was associated with more severe hostility and depression at discharge from the hospital and more discharges against medical advice (Holtzheimer, Russo, Zatzick, Bundy, & Roy-Byrne, 2005).

Psychiatric disorders also may be risk factors for PTSD even when the disorders are relatively mild and not severe mental illnesses. For example, Sandweiss et al. (2011) showed that military personnel injured during deployment were 2.5 times as likely to screen positive for PTSD if they had any psychiatric disorder prior to the injury; the severity of the injury also was correlated with the risk of PTSD, but this had only one-tenth as strong a relationship to PTSD as did prior psychiatric disorder. A prospective longitudinal study of children followed over 3 decades into adulthood found that all new cases of PTSD and 93.5% of participants who had ever had PTSD by age 26 also had a psychiatric disorder (most of which began by age 15) between ages 11 and 21 years old (Koenen et al., 2008). This study systematically assessed psychiatric disorders periodically in childhood and adolescence, thus identifying many mild to moderate severity cases that would never have been detected under ordinary circumstances (because most of those individuals would not have sought mental health treatment). While these results do not definitely establish that psychiatric disorders contribute to causing PTSD, they strongly suggest that having a psychiatric disorder makes a person vulnerable to developing PTSD.

One potential explanation for these findings is that PTSD may precede and exacerbate other psychiatric disorders. Consistent with this evidence, patients with psychiatric disorders who report having experienced interpersonal psychological traumas such as abuse in childhood often report particularly severe hallucinations, paranoia, mania, depression, severe anxiety, suicidality, hostility, suspiciousness, and dissociation

(Leverich et al., 2001; Lysaker, Meyer, Evans, Clements, & Marks, 2001; Lysaker, Nees, Lancaster, & Davis, 2004). Perkonigg, Kessler, Storz, and Wittchen (2000) also found that agoraphobia, dysthymic disorder, generalized anxiety disorder, and somatoform disorder were more likely to occur after PTSD had occurred.

However, another possibility is that the symptoms of psychiatric disorders may make people vulnerable to PTSD or may even serve as a causal risk factor and contribute to causing PTSD. Perkonigg et al. (2000) found that several psychiatric disorders *preceded* first exposure to a traumatic stressor and PTSD in most (64–71%) cases, including specific phobia, social phobia, and somatoform disorder. These disorders also increased the likelihood that PTSD would occur following exposure to a traumatic stressor, although major depression was the best predictor of PTSD after exposure to a traumatic stressor, increasing the risk of developing PTSD more than 23 times. Substance use disorders were particularly likely to occur before exposure to a traumatic stressor, but they did not to lead to an increased risk of PTSD (Perkonigg et al., 2000). A number of studies have shown that emotional and behavioral difficulties that are commonly found in psychiatric disorders—anxiety, anger, dysphoria, and rumination (persistent nagging worry or distress)—are risk factors for PTSD (DiGangi et al., 2013). Several other studies have found that a family history of emotional or behavioral problems, which place offspring at risk for psychiatric disorders, are risk factors for PTSD (Copeland, Keeler, Angold, & Costello, 2007; Inslicht et al., 2010; Koenen, Moffitt, Poulton, Martin, & Caspi, 2007). Thus, psychiatric problems both on an individual and intergenerational (see Chapter 2) level may increase trauma-exposed persons' risk of developing PTSD.

How might a psychiatric disorder lead a person to be vulnerable to PTSD? A study of 500 male military veterans who had varying degrees of exposure to a natural disaster (Hurricane Katrina) found that those with PTSD were more likely than others to have a psychiatric illness that was diagnosed before the disaster (Constans et al., 2012). After the disaster, veterans who developed PTSD also were more likely than others to endorse trauma-related beliefs (see Altered Cognitive Processes in this chapter). Having trauma-related beliefs also was more strongly related to PTSD than the extent of the individual's exposure to traumatic stressors or damage to his home during the disaster or his social support after the disaster. A trajectory was identified leading from preexisting psychiatric illness to trauma-related beliefs and from those beliefs to PTSD, although the beliefs did not fully account for the relationship between psychiatric illness and postdisaster PTSD. Thus, one possible pathway from a preexisting psychiatric disorder to PTSD may be fearful beliefs that, if apparently confirmed by a traumatic event, could develop into persistent PTSD symptoms such as nightmares, avoidance, or hypervigilance.

The complicated relationship between other psychiatric disorders and PTSD is illustrated by studies that suggest that psychosis may increase the risk of PTSD and that exposure to traumatic stressors increases the risk of psychosis (Morrison, Frame, & Larkin, 2003). As an example of the first point, Shaw, McFarlane, Bookless, and Air (2002) conducted interviews with patients hospitalized for psychotic disorders and concluded that psychotic symptoms were sufficiently distressing to potentially lead to a "post-psychosis PTSD." Whether the psychotic symptoms indeed were sufficiently distressing to lead to the development of PTSD symptoms was not established. It is possible that psychosis may contribute to PTSD instead by increasing the distress associated with PTSD symptoms that preexisted the psychotic disorder and were due to an actual traumatic stressor that had not been identified—that is, a delayed form of PTSD that psychotic symptoms did not cause but that may have been exacerbated by the psychosis. It also is possible that symptoms co-occurring with psychoses that are thought to represent PTSD actually are symptoms of other disorders such as depression. These two possibilities are illustrated by the findings of a study of adults in pharmacotherapy studies who were diagnosed with depression and reported substantial PTSD symptoms despite not reporting any past exposure to traumatic stressors (Bodkin, Pope, Detke, & Hudson, 2007). The "PTSD" symptoms may have been due to traumatic stressors that they did not recall or chose not to report, or to their depression rather than to PTSD.

Indirect support for the hypothesis that psychiatric disorders may serve as a causal risk factor for PTSD may be found by comparing the results of neuroimaging (brain scan) studies for PTSD with those for other psychiatric disorders such as major depression (Gotlib & Hamilton, 2008), bipolar disorder (Strakowski, Delbello, & Adler, 2005), schizophrenia (Brunet-Gouet & Decety, 2006), obsessive-compulsive disorder (Remijnse, van den Heuvel, & Veltman, 2005), dissociative disorders (Peres, Moreira-Almeida, Caixeta, Leao, & Newberg, 2012), and personality disorders (Reinders et al., 2014). While there are numerous specific differences in the integrity and size and patterns of neural activation in different areas in the brain across these disorders, a consistent finding is impaired activation in the brain areas involved in regulating emotions and making executive decisions (such as the medial and dorsolateral prefrontal cortices) and abnormal size or neural activity patterns in the areas of the brain associated with stress reactivity and emotional distress (such as the amygdala in the limbic system), screening, and organizing perceptual and cognitive information (such as the thalamus, striatum, and hippocampus). As is discussed in greater detail in Chapter 6, these brain areas and psychological functions have been found to be altered or impaired in PTSD.

A study with patients diagnosed with dissociative identity disorder (formerly called multiple personality disorder) shed further light on the possibility that altered patterns of brain activation may underlie both PTSD and other psychiatric disorders (Reinders et al., 2014). When patients were in a state of anxiety ("hyperaroused"), their brains showed high levels of stress response activation and low levels of emotion regulation and executive functioning activation, directly paralleling what occurs in PTSD. However, when they were emotionally and mentally shut down ("hyperaroused") their brains had almost the opposite pattern of activation—directly parallel to neuroimaging findings for the dissociative subtype of PTSD (Lanius et al., 2010).

Thus, it is possible that the fundamental biological and psychological capacities that are compromised in PTSD may already have been compromised by preexisting psychiatric disorders. However, preexisting psychiatric disorders could not be the primary cause of PTSD, because most individuals who develop PTSD, particularly when it begins within a few weeks or months after exposure to a traumatic stressor, do not have a preexisting psychiatric disorder (particularly children (Copeland et al., 2007) but also including adults (Kessler et al., 2005)). PTSD may precede other psychiatric disorders. Therefore, the alterations in brain structure and activity observed in psychiatric disorders may be a prior causal risk or vulnerability factor for many psychiatric disorders—including but not limited to PTSD. It may not be psychiatric disorders per se but preexisting alterations in brain activation that underlie the psychiatric disorders that contribute to the etiology of PTSD. Given the differences in specific symptoms and specific brain alterations that exist between psychiatric disorders, including PTSD, it remains necessary to determine what other risk or vulnerability factors lead to specific brain alterations and symptoms that distinguish each psychiatric disorder (including PTSD) from all others.

Currently, the evidence for psychiatric disorders as risk factors for PTSD is strong in terms of a vulnerability factor (because people with psychiatric disorders more often report both exposure to traumatic stressors and PTSD than people with no psychiatric disorder) but at best preliminary in terms of psychiatric disorder symptoms serving as a causal risk factor (because it is not clear that psychiatric symptoms either can serve as a traumatic stressor or involve alterations in brain structure or function that may subsequently lead to PTSD). It also is not known whether more basic risk or vulnerability factors (such as altered brain structure or function) may play a role in the etiology of all psychiatric disorders, including PTSD, rather than the psychiatric disorders serving as risk or vulnerability factors for PTSD or vice versa.

Potential genetic or biological causal risk factors

A third potential causal risk factor is a genetic predisposition that may underlie alterations in brain structure and function that may in turn result in specific symptoms of PTSD. Family and twin studies suggest that PTSD may be "heritable" (i.e., inborn genetic differences may predispose people to develop PTSD; Goenjian et al., 2008; Guffanti et al., 2013; Liberzon et al., 2014; Sumner et al., 2014; White et al., 2013). The potential heritability of PTSD does not mean that people who share the same or similar genetic inheritance automatically or inevitably will develop PTSD—only that when one of two twins or family members who share some or all of the same genes develops PTSD, it is more likely that the other twin or family member also has had, or will have, PTSD than if neither of them develop PTSD. Whether this is actually the result of genetic inheritance or other related factors (such as a shared family environment) has not been definitively established, but it does appear that shared genetic inheritance is associated with a correlated risk of both exposure to traumatic stressors (Stein, Jang, Taylor, Vernon, & Livesley, 2002) and developing PTSD (Guffanti et al., 2013; Koenen et al., 2007; White et al., 2013).

A study of 200 members from 12 multigenerational families from Armenia, who 20 years earlier had survived the massive Spitak earthquake (which led to 17,000 deaths and destroyed more than half the city of Gumri), demonstrated that 41% of the risk of developing PTSD was due to genetic factors (Goenjian et al., 2008). A profile of the objective impact of the earthquake was compiled for each person, including factors such as whether their home was destroyed, deaths of relatives, seeing dead bodies, being injured, and witnessing the injury of another person. After statistically accounting for the effects of these factors, age, and other variables that were related to the likelihood of developing PTSD (female gender, pre-earthquake traumatic experiences), the extent to which family members shared common genes was strongly related to their risk of developing PTSD (as well as to resilience and recovery from PTSD). Exposure to earthquake traumatic stressors also played a role in the risk of developing a depressive or other anxiety disorder, although the contribution of genetic inheritance to those disorders was stronger (66% and 61%, respectively) than for PTSD. While specific genes were not identified, it appeared that the same or very similar genes were responsible for the risk of developing any or all of the PTSD, anxiety, or depressive disorders.

If there is a genetic causal risk factor for PTSD, a specific genetic source of the risk will have to be identified (i.e., specific genes or portions of a genes that are different among people with and without PTSD). This is unlikely to be a single gene or portion thereof because PTSD is a "phenotypically complex" phenomenon—that is, PTSD involves several alterations in behavior, cognition, emotion, and physiology. Groups or complexes of genes are typically needed to orchestrate complex psychobiological conditions such as PTSD. To add to the complication, the same genes that are associated with depression, other anxiety disorders (such as generalized anxiety disorder and panic disorder), and substance or alcohol dependence also appear to be associated with PTSD because the genetic contribution to PTSD seems to share most of its variance with the genetic contribution to depression and to other anxiety disorders (Koenen et al., 2007). Thus, the same or similar genetic alterations might underlie several psychiatric disorders that share anxiety, depression, and emotion dysregulation symptoms—and not just PTSD.

Genetically transmitted biological alterations that might be responsible for an increased risk for PTSD include those involved in emotion regulation (Harrison and Tunbridge, 2008) and cognitive abilities (Kremen et al., 2007). Problems in each of these areas of psychological functioning are associated with specific brain structures and processes (see Chapter 6), and both could either increase the likelihood of exposure traumatic stressors or reduce the ability of the impaired individual to cope emotionally with stressors once exposed. Therefore, in order to fully account for genetic causal risk factors, the many ways in which PTSD alters behavior (such as avoidance of reminders of stressful events, problems with sleep, withdrawal from relationships), cognition (such as hypervigilance, blame of self and others, difficulty sustaining concentration on mental tasks, and difficulty accessing verbal memory to solve problems), emotion (such as anxiety, irritability and anger, and dysphoria), and physiology (such as hyperarousal, tendency to startle easily, difficulty with sleep, and physical reactivity to reminders of stressful experiences) each will have to be linked to specific genetic locations or complexes.

Two biological characteristics that have been linked to PTSD are dysregulation of the hypothalamic-pituitary-adrenal (HPA) axis and altered size and function of the hippocampus in the brain (see Chapter 6). The most consistent HPA axis alteration in PTSD is low levels of cortisol (hypocortisolism), which is the brain chemical that "turns down" the body's stress response. These findings suggested that PTSD may be caused in part, biologically, by a stress response system that cannot be slowed down. A study of Swedish soldiers found that those with lower prewar levels of cortisol were at risk for developing PTSD (Aardal-Eriksson, Eriksson, & Thorell, 2001). However, a metaanalysis of dozens of studies concluded that there were no systematic differences in cortisol levels between people with PTSD and controls (Meewisse, Reitsma, De Vries, Gersons, & Olff, 2007). It also is not clear whether cortisol levels of children (Yehuda et al., 2007) or adults (Delahanty, Nugent, Christopher, & Walsh, 2005) are altered as the result of: (i) genetic inheritance, (ii) early life parent-child or family interactions, (iii) exposure to a traumatic stressor (such as in the first hours after a severe accident or assault), (iv) developing PTSD, or (v) some combination of these factors. Thus, neither genetics nor an abnormality in the body's stress response system can be assumed be a causal risk factor for PTSD; either genetics or biological abnormalities may contribute to PTSD or may be only indirectly or secondarily related to PTSD.

A second example of the potential but as yet uncertain role of genetics and biology in PTSD is provided by studies on the hippocampus, a brain region that is thought to play an important role in creating and retrieving personal ("autobiographical") memories, and numerous studies have shown evidence of smaller hippocampi among people PTSD (and one recent study showed a correlated reduction in the activation of the hippocampus in laboratory experiences; Astur et al., 2006; see Chapter 6). Findings of smaller hippocampi in PTSD, and evidence that chronic stress is associated with loss of neurons in animals' hippocampi (McEwen, 2006) led to speculation that traumatic stressor exposure or having PTSD might cause atrophy in the hippocampus. However, rigorous scientific studies did not support the hypothesis that PTSD caused atrophy of the hippocampus (Neumeister, Henry, & Krystal, 2007). Studies of the size (volume) of the hippocampus in twins indicate that smaller hippocampi may be a risk factor for PTSD that is not inborn but results from adverse prenatal and early childhood environmental factors such as poor nutrition, exposure to toxins, or imbalances of maternal hormones during the early period of brain development in utero and in infancy (Woodward et al., 2007). Thus, what appear to be genetically based alterations a brain area involved in memory and PTSD may actually be due to environmental factors that are causal risk or vulnerability factors for PTSD.

Longitudinal studies of genetics and exposure to adverse experiences have shown that genetic factors may have a causal risk effect by interacting with potentially traumatic experiences rather than directly causing adverse outcomes such as PTSD. For example, a prospective study from birth to adulthood of a large sample of males in New Zealand (Segman, Shalev, & Gelernter, 2007) found that a particular genetic characteristic interacted with maltreatment experiences such that boys with the characteristic who were maltreated showed more aggressive violence as adults than those who were not maltreated (Caspi et al., 2002; Segman et al., 2007). A different gene variant was found to interact with stressful life experiences (including childhood abuse) in determining the risk of depression in adulthood (Kaufman et al., 2004), and to interact with the extent of exposure to Hurricane Katrina and adequacy of social support to determine the risk of PTSD (Kilpatrick et al., 2007; White et al., 2013).

Most interestingly, variants of genes that are directly involved in the body's stress response systems have been particularly likely to be associated with risk of PTSD. Studies showed that genes that control the production and effects of cortisol and related HPA stress hormones were associated with PTSD risk in hurricane survivors (White et al., 2013) and interacted with a history of childhood abuse trauma (but not with childhood exposure to other types of traumatic stressors) in determining the risk of PTSD symptoms in a large sample of adults in nonpsychiatric health care (Binder et al., 2008). Another gene variant that is involved in adrenaline responses to stressors was found to interact with childhood exposure to traumatic stressors in determining risk versus resilience to PTSD in two very different samples: primarily Caucasian male military veterans and African American women (Liberzon et al., 2014). Consistent with these findings, the pretrauma exposure physiological characteristics that have been shown to be risks for PTSD involve stress reactivity: startle reactivity (Orr et al., 2012; Sijbrandij, Engelhard, Lommen, Leer, & Baas, 2013), muscle tension (EMG) reactivity (Guthrie & Bryant, 2006; Sijbrandij et al., 2013), high levels of a metabolite of adrenaline (MHPG) in saliva (which also were related to peritraumatic distress; Apfel et al., 2011), difficulty in extinguishing conditioned fear responses (Lommen, Engelhard, Sijbrandij, van den Hout, & Hermans, 2013), and the number of brain receptors in for stress hormones (glucocorticoids) (van Zuiden, Geuze, et al., 2012; van Zuiden et al., 2011; van Zuiden, Heijnen, et al., 2012). Only one physiological marker for stress reactivity—cortisol levels—has not been found to be a PTSD risk factor, and it also was not related to peritraumatic distress *but* was predictive of dissociative symptoms and acute stress disorder (Inslicht et al., 2011). Thus, the path to PTSD may begin with a biological tendency to stress reactivity, except among individuals who are more prone to dissociation (who may instead develop the "shut-down" form of dissociative PTSD).

Genetic factors related to biological stress reactivity thus play a crucial role in determining the risk of or resilience to PTSD when people are exposed to traumatic stressors. The specific type of stress reactivity (e.g., hypo- versus hyperarousal) may be greatly influenced by these genetic characteristics. Moreover, it is not genetics alone but the interaction of genes with different types of exposure to traumatic stressors—particularly childhood maltreatment, but also adult exposure to violence or severe natural disasters—that is crucial in PTSD etiology (and related disorders such as depression) and will be the subject of study for many years to come.

Cognitive processing capacities

Clinicians and scientists (as well as philosophers, historians, and writers) have long observed that life-altering experiences often are followed by profound changes in a person's beliefs that include a sense of alienation from and loss of faith in self, other people, social institutions, and spirituality (Frankl, 1946). Psychological trauma can shatter the assumptions of invulnerability (Janoff-Bulman, 1992) and trust (Freyd, 1994) that are psychologically sustaining "positive illusions" (Taylor, 1989). More specifically, recent theories have hypothesized that exposure to traumatic stressors may alter not just beliefs but the underlying cognitive processes that are the basis for creating, sustaining, or changing a person's knowledge and fundamental beliefs.

Psychological research has demonstrated that beliefs are based on "schemas," which are ideas ("mental representations") that organize everything that a person knows (the "knowledge base") (Fiske & Taylor, 1991). Schemas are like filters or "blueprints" (Dalgleish, 2004) that people use to match what they experience on a sensory level with what they know from prior experience in order to create perceptions ("what I see, hear, touch, taste, and feel"), emotions ("how I feel"), and thoughts ("what I know, wish, hope, believe, or plan"). For example, "safety" is a schema that includes different elements for different people, involving family and friends for one person or self-reliance and physical or mental prowess for another person. Schemas are always in the background when people perceive, feel, think, and act, and rarely are actually observed except in activities that encourage intensive self-reflection (such as some approaches to psychotherapy or psychological research, philosophical inquiry, or spiritual renewal). Traumatic stressors tend to contradict most commonly held schemas (such as safety, trust, and self-confidence), potentially leading to rapid radical shifts in not just beliefs but basic assumptions about self and the world (Foa, Ehlers, Clark, Tolin, & Orsillo, 1999; Janoff-Bulman, 1992). However, schemas are relatively resistant to change, so it has been hypothesized that the contradictory information provided by psychological trauma may be sequestered separately from existing schemas in what Horowitz (1997) describes as "active memory." This could account for the common experience described by persons with PTSD that it seems as if they have two divided consciousnesses—one in which they experience themselves and the world as they were before a traumatic stressor occurred and the other in which they experience a more threatening and dangerous world and powerless or ineffective self.

This potential posttraumatic psychological conflict between long-held schemas and newly learned contradictory—and emotionally highly charged and negative—information also could account for the cardinal symptoms of PTSD. Intrusive reexperiencing could be due to periodic episodes of unwanted awareness of new information in "active memory." Hyperarousal could be the physical and emotional distress due to not being able to integrate the traumatic information that is in "active memory" into existing schemas. Avoidance and numbing of emotions could be automatic attempts to remove trauma-related knowledge and associated emotional distress from "active memory" in order to reduce or eliminate awareness of these painful thoughts, images, and feelings (Horowitz, 1997). Thus, the psychological conflict between the security provided by preexisting schemas and the traumatic stress reactions triggered by memories of traumatic events could be an underlying cause or major contributor to PTSD.

However, numerous research studies suggest that persons with PTSD have such profoundly altered beliefs that it appears more accurate to characterize them as having adopted new schemas rather than experiencing a psychological conflict between preexisting schemas and traumatic information (Foa et al., 1999). Foa and Rothbaum (1998) hypothesize that the underlying mental structure of knowledge—what they call the "associative network," which is the interconnected ("associated") collection of perceptions, emotions, and thoughts that each person develops based on life experiences—can be altered by exposure to traumatic stressors. A new associative network is believed to emerge when PTSD develops, organized around distressing (principally either anxiety or anger) or absent ("numbed") emotions (Foa & Rothbaum, 1998) and corresponding new schemas (or "appraisals"; Ehlers & Clark, 2000) that are organized around core guiding beliefs that the world is dangerous and the self is powerless or ineffective.

The possibility that altered knowledge ("active memory"; Horowitz, 1997) or schemas ("fear network" or fear-based appraisals; Ehlers & Clark, 2000; Foa & Rothbaum, 1998) might cause or contribute to the development or persistence of PTSD raises a basic question: how does exposure to traumatic stressors differ from other types of life experiences sufficiently to create not just new knowledge or modifications in existing schemas but new knowledge that is painfully intrusive or new schemas that are completely based on fear rather than other positive (such as confidence or hope) or negative (such as sadness or guilt) emotions and guiding beliefs?

Brewin (2001) and Dalgleish (2004) attempt to answer this question by postulating that fundamental changes in how a person processes information cognitively occur as a result of demands placed upon the mind by psychologically traumatic events. Brewin (2001) theorizes that human beings have two modes of information processing, one of which enables us to make sense of and recall autobiographically (i.e., as a personal life "story") ordinary experiences in life based on conscious awareness and brief verbal summaries of experiences; this is described as "verbally accessible memory" (VAM). The second form of information processing—"situationally accessible memory" (SAM)—is viewed as a largely automatic nonconscious intake and storage of memories in the form of sensory and bodily reactions to experiences (such as in the form of images, sounds, or bodily feelings). Both VAM and SAM are unique and complementary sources of information processing that together provide complete and meaningful memories in every life experience. Brewin (2001) hypothesizes that traumatic stressors shift the ordinary balance between VAM and SAM such that SAM dominates and VAM becomes impoverished. This is consistent with research findings indicating that if VAM is interrupted and SAM is relatively enhanced in an experiment, healthy young adults report more "intrusive" (unexpected, spontaneous) memories of experimental activities than when VAM is intact or SAM is interrupted (Holmes, Brewin, & Hennessy, 2004). VAM and SAM also are consistent with the cognitive processes that are associated with brain activation patterns that have been identified with, respectively, healthy trauma survivors or nontraumatized adults (VAM) and adults with PTSD (SAM) (Brewin, 2001; see also Chapter 5).

Dalgleish (2004) incorporates elements from each of these information processing theories of the alterations in PTSD in the schematic, propositional, analogue, associative representational system (SPAARS) theoretical model. PTSD is theorized to be the result of alterations in verbal information processing (similar to Brewin's VAM), including schemas (S), propositions (i.e., basic beliefs or appraisals, P), and analogue information processing (i.e., nonverbal sensory-perceptual knowledge, A, which is similar to Brewin's SAM). When these alterations in information processing are sufficient to change the person's basic associative representational systems, PTSD is theorized to result (Dalgleish, 2004). Although there are numerous research studies

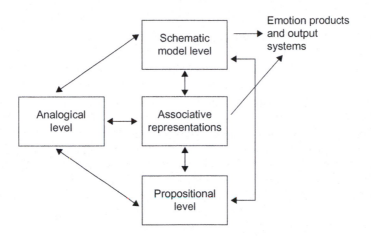

Figure 3.3 SPAARS model of altered information processing in PTSD.
From Power and Dalgleish (1997). Copyright 1997 by Psychology Press. Reproduced with permission.

that indirectly support the SPAARS and related theoretical models of altered information processing in PTSD (Dalgleish, 2004), definitive studies showing whether exposure to traumatic stressors is preceded or followed by these cognitive alterations, and when and for whom such alterations lead to PTSD, are needed before altered information processing can be considered to be established as a causal risk factor (versus a by-product) of PTSD (or correlated but separate phenomenon) (Vogt et al., 2007) (Figure 3.3).

Limitations in cognitive capacities have been consistently found to be a general risk factor for PTSD. The most consistent finding is that individuals with lower levels of childhood verbal IQ (Betts, Williams, Najman, Bor, & Alati, 2012; Koenen et al., 2007—although possibly only females) or adult verbal IQ (Orr et al., 2012; Parslow & Jorm, 2007) and cognitive processing and memory (Parslow & Jorm, 2007) abilities are vulnerable to developing PTSD. Research on anxiety disorders has identified a specific cognitive mechanism that may be a causal risk factor for PTSD: "attention bias to threat" refers to a tendency to pay more attention to either recognizing or avoiding awareness of potential threats (Pine, 2007). These two reactions could help to explain the PTSD symptoms of hypervigilance (the bias toward paying attention to threats) and avoidance (the bias to shifting attention away from threats). A study with adults who had experienced traumatic stressors showed that those with PTSD were more prone to shift their attention toward or away from stimuli associated with threats. Of particular importance, those with PTSD had a unique pattern of brain activity. They had generally higher levels of activation of the "executive" area of the brain (the dorsolateral prefrontal cortex), which suggests that they were making a conscious effort to focus their attention (similar to what would be expected if an individual is hypervigilant). In addition, when they avoided paying attention to threats, the adults with PTSD had higher levels of activation in the "emotion processing" areas of the brain, the ventromedial prefrontal cortex and the anterior cingulate (Fani et al., 2012).

Another study similarly found that adults with PTSD were found to more often direct their attention toward or away from laboratory stimuli that were associated with threat and comparable adults who had experienced traumatic events but did not develop PTSD or who had never been exposed to traumatic events (Iacoviello et al., 2014). However, military personnel who either were or were not deployed to hazardous assignments did not differ before deployment but diverged during the deployment period, with the hazardous duty group showing greater attentional bias toward and away from threat than nondeployed personnel—and the greater the extent of attentional bias, the greater the likelihood of developing PTSD and depression symptoms. Further analyses of the civilian adult sample by Fani et al. (2013) revealed that individuals who showed a bias in attention toward or away from threat also had a genetic variation that affects the body's stress reactivity (the *FKBP5* gene that regulates brain receptors activated by cortisol)—and the shape and activity of the brain area that is crucial to forming and retrieving memories—the hippocampus—also was different for those individuals compared to similar adults. Thus, attention bias related to threat may be a by-product of a genetic difference that either results from or is a pretrauma causal risk factor for PTSD. Either way, altering this attention bias could be an important aspect of preventing or treating PTSD. For example, a study showed that cognitive training for military veterans with PTSD to shift their attention toward neutral (rather than toward or away from threat-related) stimuli substantially enhanced the benefits of other evidence-based psychotherapies and pharmacotherapy (Kuckertz et al., 2014).

Potential risk factors for exposure to traumatic stressors

There have been fewer studies on the factors that place a person at risk for exposure to traumatic stressors than on risk and vulnerability factors for PTSD itself. Two consistent predictors or correlates of exposure to traumatic violence (primarily violence in the community among children (Finkelhor, Ormrod, Turner, & Hamby, 2005) or adults (Briggs-Phillips & Hobfoll, 2006; Schumm, Rayburn et al., 2005) or due to war or terrorism as a noncombatant (Ford, 2008), and secondarily to traumatic family violence (Dutton, 2008)), are living in an unsafe community (or family) and having impoverished socioeconomic resources (such as due to economic poverty, unemployment, or homelessness; Kim et al., 2010).

Another potential risk factor for exposure to traumatic stressors is externalizing behavior, which refers to behaviors that "act out" (or "externalize") emotions such as frustration or anger. Externalizing behavior disorders include childhood attention deficit hyperactivity disorder (ADHD), oppositional-defiant disorder (ODD), and conduct disorder (CD), as well as adult antisocial personality disorder (ASPD). It has been found that children diagnosed with ADHD are not more likely than other children to have histories of exposure to traumatic stressors, but those diagnosed with ODD appear to have a substantially increased likelihood of having been exposed to traumatic violence and victimization (Ford & Connor, 2009).

One study found that adults who were diagnosed with CD as children or adolescents have a greater risk of subsequent exposure to traumatic stressors and of developing PTSD than other adults (Koenen et al., 2005). Another study showed that young adults (ages 20–23 years old) who were identified by their first-grade teachers as exhibiting problematic aggressive or disruptive behavior were 2.6 times more likely to subsequently experience traumatic physical violence or threats of violence than other youths. However, aggressive/disruptive behavior problems in first grade were not associated with an increased risk of PTSD (Storr, Ialongo, Anthony, & Breslau, 2007). PTSD was more likely among young adults who as first graders reported high levels of symptoms of depression or anxiety. A longitudinal study of children who were assessed for ADHD and then reassessed 10 years later found that both childhood ADHD and maternal smoking during pregnancy (which is associated with physical health and behavioral problems in offspring; Huijbregts, Seguin, Zoccolillo, Boivin, & Tremblay, 2008; Li, Langholz, Salam, & Gilliland, 2005; Riedel et al., 2014) were independent risk factors that increased the likelihood of PTSD in late adolescence or early adulthood, by a factor of 225% and 350%, respectively (Biederman et al., 2014). Thus, behavior problems seem to put children at risk for victimization by traumatic violence, but it is not clear whether such acting out or an underlying sense of dysphoria and anxiety that puts children at risk for PTSD. Replication of these studies also is needed to definitively determine the sequence of externalizing behavior disorders, exposure to traumatic stressors, and PTSD. Severe externalizing behaviors involving aggression and illegal activities are a risk factor for exposure to traumatic stressors, but childhood victimization trauma also may precede such behavior problems (Ford, Chapman, Mack, & Pearson, 2006).

Genetic inheritance also may be a risk factor for exposure to traumatic stressors. A study with more than 400 adult twins found that genetic inheritance (comparing monozygotic and dizygotic twins; see Chapter 5) played a role in determining whether "assaultive" traumatic stressors had occurred, but not for "nonassaultive" traumatic stressors (Stein et al., 2002). "Assaultive" refers to psychological traumas involving interpersonal violence, including physical, sexual, domestic, and community violence (but not combat or war, although a relationship with combat or war trauma cannot be ruled out because it happened too rarely to be adequately tested in this study). The genetic influence on exposure to interpersonal violence was equivalent for both genders, although the findings suggested that different genetic locations were likely to be involved in the risk for females and males. The study sample, although large, was not large enough to permit a more definitive investigation of specific gene variations associated with traumatic assaults.

Vulnerability factors for PTSD

A variety of other "preevent" and "postevent" factors have been demonstrated by research studies to serve as "risk" or "vulnerability" factors for PTSD (see Figure 3.2). These characteristics of the person and their social environment prior to exposure to traumatic stressors are associated with a higher likelihood of subsequently developing PTSD (Vogt et al., 2007). A first subgroup of vulnerability factors are characteristics of the individual, including:

- age (see Box 3.3);
- female gender (see Chapter 4);
- ethnoracial minority status (see Chapter 4).

Another subgroup of vulnerability factors for PTSD involves stressful events experienced prior to a new traumatic stressor. Although it has been speculated that facing traumatic stressors might "toughen up" or "inoculate" people against the ill effects of subsequent stressors, in fact research studies with adults and children consistently indicate that stressors (particularly if they occur persistently in childhood or if they are traumatic at any point in the lifespan; Box 3.6) deplete rather than increase people's psychological and biological coping abilities and resources. Therefore, the following pretraumatic stressor events increase vulnerability to PTSD:

- prior exposure to other potentially traumatic adversities in childhood such as family mental illness, loss, family violence, poverty, or abuse (Boxes 3.4 and 3.5);
- prior exposure to other traumatic stressors (see Boxes 3.4 and 3.5).

Box 3.6 Social Support: Protective Against PTSD? Or a Potential Problem?

Coping with traumatically stressful events is seldom a solitary task and typically requires considerable amounts of assistance and support from other people. "Social support" refers to those social interactions that provide people with *actual assistance* and *embed them* into a web of social relationships *perceived to be* loving, caring, and readily available in times of need. There are a variety of ways in which social support may benefit psychological well-being and physical health. For example, people who care for us may prevent the occurrence of stress or reduce its severity. Social support networks can facilitate more accurate appraisal of ambiguous stressful encounters and assist in the reappraisal of ongoing stressors. Social support most routinely serves directly to meet demands caused by consequences of the stressor, such as when people provide material aid and other necessities to disaster survivors. Physical presence of other people may hasten a return to physiological equilibrium (e.g., closely embracing a victim of terror). Concerned helpers may also suggest coping options, such as persuading a victim of crime to seek professional help. These expressions of support may help to sustain self-efficacy, self-esteem, optimism, and other psychological resources severely threatened by exposure to stress. Helpful relationships may validate emotional reactions and support cognitive processing of stressful experiences. Family and friends facilitate recovery of emotional equilibrium through continuous expressions of caring, as well as by simply creating opportunities for diversions (Kaniasty & Norris, 2008).

The strongest and most consistent protective factor that reduces the risk of developing PTSD following exposure to a variety of traumatic stressors is social support (Brewin et al., 2000; Vogt et al., 2007). Social support is a source of both emotional (e.g., companionship, moral support) and instrumental (e.g., access to money, help in rebuilding a home or finding a job) resources (Hobfoll, 2001; see Box 2.2). After a traumatic experience, social support can help restore a person's belief that life can be predictable, controllable, and safe after exposure to traumatic stressors has shaken or shattered these sustaining beliefs (Foa et al., 1999).

Social support can be provided by family, friends, or even by strangers in the form of sympathetic media depictions of and demonstrations of support for persons who are directly and indirectly affected by traumatic stressors. The opposite of social support, "social constraints," on the other hand, are reductions or limitations in the amount or quality of social support available to persons affected by traumatic stressors (Hobfoll, 2001). Social constraints can interfere with resistance to or recovery from exposure to traumatic stressors by increasing emotional distress, emotional or physical injuries, and damaging people's sense of self-efficacy and trust, as well as by limiting people's abilities to understand and resolve their distress or injuries. Koenen et al. (2007) showed that children who grow up in poverty, when followed prospectively with assessments over the next 3 decades, were at high risk for developing PTSD.

Financial resources are a form of both instrumental support and social belongingness that can influence recovery because they make it possible for persons affected by a traumatic stressor to obtain more social support, such as by traveling to visit with family or friends, rebuilding a community destroyed in a disaster, resuming an interrupted education, or getting help from a medical or mental health professional. Financial resources can also result in reduced stress by making it possible for victims or family members to rest and recover without suffering problems that undermine their instrumental and emotional social support and social embeddedness, such as job loss, being unable to meet living expenses, or having to forego costly but needed health care.

In some cases, social "support" actually may be unhelpful and burdensome for survivors of traumatic stressors, depending on who provides the support and when and how it is provided. Studies of children and adults who were exposed to a range of potentially traumatic stressors including war, community violence, disasters, and law enforcement stressors showed that social support was *not* protective against adverse outcomes such as depression or PTSD for some individuals or when perceived to be at a high level or by nonfamily members (Kaniasty & Norris, 2008). Social support also has been found to take different forms and to have different degrees of protective value, depending on gender (Tolin & Foa, 2006) and ethnococultural background (Pole, Gone, & Kulkarni, 2008), when individuals or entire communities face traumatic stressors.

Moreover, social interactions that are objectively or subjectively "unhelpful" (especially if they are rejecting or conflictual in nature) have been found to

(Continued)

Box 3.6 Continued

increase vulnerability to PTSD in the wake of exposure to traumatic stressors—
and also depression and complicated bereavement ("traumatic grief") in the
wake of deaths or losses of important relationships (Maercker & Muller, 2004;
Ullman & Filipas, 2001). Thus, it is important to build or find genuinely helpful
sources of social support in order to protect people from developing or being
unable to recover from PTSD, rather than simply telling people that they "need
to" ask for help in order to cope with the effects of a traumatic stressor and the
other stressors that often follow in its aftermath.

Conflict within a traumatized individual's social network may diminish the
positive effects of social support on well-being, and these effects may be felt
particularly acutely within vulnerable populations of persons who face complex
stressors and have limited resources. For example, a study with homeless women
who were parenting children examined the impact of conflict and social support
on parenting behaviors over time in a sample of mothers who are homeless and
were involved in a study of case management interventions of varying intensity
(Marra et al., 2009). Homeless women who reported high levels of helpful
emotional and instrumental social support self-reported greater improvements in
parenting consistency over time than those who reported lower levels of support.
However, when they experienced conflict in support networks this was a risk
factor for harsh parenting practices if they also had lower levels of instrumental
social support. Thus, social support may enhance homeless mothers' ability to
provide consistent parenting, and this may in turn may reduce the adverse intergenerational effect on their children if they (the mothers) are coping with PTSD
(see Chapter 2). However, when conflict occurs in the support network of highly
stressed and vulnerable individuals, such as homeless mothers, and they also
have little access to practical resources and help (instrumental social support),
this combination of stressful relationships and limited resources may undermine
their ability to provide consistent positive parenting and increase their risk of
their parenting in a harsh manner.

Furthermore, social support often begets more social support, when it is provided in a timely and genuinely helpful manner in the wake of traumatic stressors. Kaniasty and Norris (2008) have developed a *social support deterioration
deterrence model* based on research showing that it was not only a limitation
or absence of social support that failed to protect people exposed to traumatic
stressors from developing PTSD or other psychiatric or psychosocial problems
but the *progressive diminishment* (or "deterioration") of social support over time
following a traumatic stressor. They found that hurricane survivors who received
early helpful social support were not only more likely to be relatively resistant
to adverse psychological outcomes but also to maintain a positive perception of
the social support available to them.

In addition, the conditions of the most basic support system—the family—can lead to increased vulnerability to PTSD. When family relationships are unpredictable, uncontrollable, and negative in their emotional tone, traumatic stressors are more likely to lead to PTSD (Koenen et al., 2007; Smith & Fischer, 2008). Family conflict or disorganization alone cannot cause PTSD, but it can increase vulnerability to PTSD. It also can lead to exposure to traumatic stressors, including childhood maltreatment and domestic violence. Poor psychological stability of family members, and of their relationships, therefore are vulnerability factors for the development of PTSD, particularly in childhood, specifically:

- family history of psychiatric illness (Inslicht et al., 2010);
- family instability (Copeland et al., 2007).

Finally, the nature of the person's immediate ("peritraumatic") reactions to traumatic stressors (in the first hours and several days) have consistently been found to be predictive of—but not to guarantee or absolutely "cause"—the subsequent risk of PTSD (see Chapter 2). In addition to the individual's own peritraumatic distress (or dissociation, although dissociation has been less well established as a vulnerability factor than extreme anxiety and intrusive reexperiencing; Brewin et al., 2002; Bryant, 2007), for children the severity of their parent(s)' peritraumatic distress is associated with increased risk of PTSD (Ford, 2008). Severe physical injuries also tend to be associated with a greater risk of subsequent PTSD, although this is not always the case (Daviss et al., 2000). Similarly, directly experiencing a traumatic accident, illness, disaster, assault, or loss tends to be more strongly associated with the development of PTSD than witnessing the same or similar traumatic stressor, although witnesses may suffer from other problems such as bystander guilt. Finally, people who are unable psychologically or practically to talk with supportive others about their traumatic experiences are at increased risk of developing PTSD (Schnurr, Lunney, & Sengupta, 2004).

The peritraumatic vulnerability factors for PTSD thus include:

- peritraumatic parental distress (the parents' own personal (vicarious) distress when their child is exposed to traumatic event(s)) (Lambert, Holzer, & Hasbun, 2014);
- peritraumatic personal distress (Sugar & Ford, 2012);
- peritraumatic dissociation (Sugar & Ford, 2012);
- physical injury and associated pain (Norman, Stein, Dimsdale, & Hoyt, 2008);
- direct (versus witnessed) trauma;
- reluctance/inability to disclose traumatic experiences in the aftermath.

Except for female gender, each of these pretrauma or peritraumatic (during or soon after the trauma) factors has been found to have a relatively small—but nevertheless statistically significant—and positive relationship with the risk of developing PTSD (Brewin et al., 2000; Ozer et al., 2003). Some studies have failed to find a relationship between each preevent factor and the risk of subsequent PTSD (and no study has found more than a moderate correlation between any preevent vulnerability factor and developing PTSD), indicating that *none* of these characteristics *inevitably* destines a person to suffer PTSD if exposed to a traumatic stressor.

Outcome risk factors

When PTSD persists for several months, it often becomes a chronic condition that can last for years, or even decades. Treatment of chronic PTSD is much more difficult and generally less successful than when PTSD is treated early (see Chapters 7–9; Galatzer-Levy et al., 2013). Factors that have been found to be associated with an increased risk of persistent PTSD include several of the potential causal and vulnerability risk factors: severity of both exposure to traumatic stressors and acute PTSD symptoms (Schnurr et al., 2004), psychiatric disorders and problems such as addictions, depression, and anger (Koenen, Stellman, Stellman, & Sommer, 2003; Schindel-Allon, Aderka, Shahar, Stein, & Gilboa-Schechtman, 2010), ethnocultural minority status (Boscarino and Adams, 2009; Schnurr et al., 2004), and gender (Kessler et al., 1995). Two key protective factors also have been found to be associated with reduced risk of persistent PTSD: social support (Koenen et al., 2003; Schnurr et al., 2004) and self-efficacy (Boscarino & Adams, 2009). However, none of these studies assessed a comprehensive set of risk factors, and therefore it is not possible to determine which of these factors are necessary and sufficient to accurately identify who is at risk for chronic PTSD.

Rona et al. (2012) conducted the first comprehensive assessment of risk factors for persistent PTSD, comparing military personnel who reported severe PTSD symptoms following a hazardous deployment and also at a reassessment 3 years later ("persistent PTSD") to those who initially reported severe symptoms but had only mild symptoms 3 years later ("remitted PTSD"). Older personnel and those who had experienced multiple hazardous events during deployment were more likely to have persistent PTSD than to be remitted. However, the strongest risk factors included an 11 times greater risk of persistent PTSD if they felt unsupported on return from deployment, 5 times greater risk if they were separated from the comrades with whom they trained when they were deployed, and 3 times greater risk if they had been discharged from military service, had college level education, or were in poor physical health. The finding that older (typically midlife) individuals were at greater risk than younger adults is consistent with evidence that this period of transition in adulthood is a time of vulnerability to PTSD (see Box 3.3). The finding concerning education is the opposite of results from studies on risk factors for PTSD itself (where education generally is protective against PTSD), suggesting that, like age, education may increase *or* reduce the risk of PTSD, depending on the specific circumstances and whether new or persistent PTSD is the focus. The finding that poor physical health was associated with persistent PTSD parallels epidemiological evidence that PTSD often is accompanied by physical health problems (see Chapter 3): thus, not only do poor health and PTSD often go together because PTSD can compromise a person's physical health, but poor health also may contribute to the persistence of PTSD.

Perhaps most importantly, the results of the Rona et al. (2012) study highlight the important protective role that social support plays in increasing the likelihood not only that PTSD will not occur but also that, in the event it does occur, it does not become a lasting problem. Social support both during a period of exposure to traumatic events (in this case, hazardous military deployment) and in the aftermath (during the postdeployment homecoming, including both continued contact with military comrades and support from family, friends, and society more generally) were strongly related to the likelihood of recovery from PTSD. Put the opposite way, when those crucial sources of support were not available, PTSD was highly likely to become chronic once it had developed. This provides a segue into the next section on protective factors that mitigate against the development (and in this case, persistence) of PTSD.

The study authors add one additional caveat that is an important reminder that risk factors increase the probability of PTSD but do not definitely destine a person to develop PTSD or to have PTSD become persistent. The actual likelihood that any individual with any one of the risk factors—even ones with high-risk levels such as poor homecoming support or deployment with an unfamiliar team—would have persistent PTSD was not much greater than chance. Rona et al. (2012) concluded that there are many factors that may contribute to the persistence of PTSD, but no single risk factor should be used to predict this for any individual. When multiple risk factors are present, the likelihood of persistent PTSD increases substantially, however, and it is those individuals who most can benefit from treatment so that PTSD does not become chronic.

Protective factors

When traumatic stressors strike, three factors have been identified by clinical observation and validated in scientific research studies as "protective factors"—that is, sources of a *reduced* risk of PTSD. Or in terms of the types of resources described in Chapter 9 and the trajectories of posttraumatic adaptation described in Chapter 2, these are personal and environmental resources that increase the likelihood of resistance to PTSD or resilience or recovery when PTSD develops.

The first protective factor is intelligence (Macklin et al., 1998; McNally & Shin, 1995), reading ability (Storr et al., 2007), or education (Schnurr et al., 2004). This does not mean that "smarter" or better-educated people are invulnerable to developing PTSD, because scientific studies of PTSD etiology (and epidemiology; see Chapter 4) demonstrate that adults and children of *all levels of intelligence, reading levels, and education* can develop PTSD. Intelligence or education are highly correlated with socioeconomic resources, again *not* because more economically affluent people are smarter or more able to succeed in school than people who have lower incomes or material resources, but because economic and material resources provide access to opportunities (such as high quality schools and the time and financial support required to access them) necessary for the kinds of learning tested by psychological measures used to assess intelligence (so-called tests of intellectual functioning or IQ tests).

Education and intelligence therefore are likely to represent the effects of a much wider range of socioeconomic resources, rather than simply a strength (or deficit) in a specific individual. Intelligence and education therefore are part of a network of socioeconomic resources that also are likely to increase a person's access to the other two protective factors against PTSD (self-efficacy and social support). In addition, there are many types or levels of intelligence and education, so it is unlikely that simply testing above average on an IQ test or having a college education *alone* reduces the adverse impact of exposure to a traumatic stressor. For example, the ability to use and remember information presented in a verbal form (i.e., in words, or "verbal information processing") is more likely to be impaired among people with PTSD than "nonverbal information processing" abilities to use and recall information presented in forms other than words, such as by pictures (Bremner, 2008). With regard to education, Schnurr et al. (2004) found that either a high school or college education was protective against developing PTSD in a large survey of military war veterans but that only college education was associated with recovery from PTSD.

The second protective factor is coping self-efficacy (Waldrep & Benight, 2008). Self-efficacy is the person's belief in her or his ability to effectively both set and achieve goals and succeed in handling stressful challenges. The latter aspect of self-efficacy is "coping self-efficacy," and it is particularly relevant to resisting or resiliently recovering from PTSD. For example, Waldrep and Benight (2008) describe how, after a traumatic incident, people have to cope with many high-stress demands related to recovery, including dealing with insurance companies, finding transportation, dealing with possible injuries, and managing the traumatic aspects of the accident itself. Several scientific studies following major natural disasters (hurricanes, wildfires, earthquakes, and floods), terrorist bombings, bereavement due to a spouse's death, and military combat have shown coping self-efficacy in the immediate aftermath of the traumatic stressor to be consistently associated with a lower risk of PTSD or other psychiatric or psychosocial problems (Waldrep & Benight, 2008). Coping self-efficacy also has been shown scientifically to be a bridge (in technical terms, a "mediator" variable) between other risk factors (such as peritraumatic distress or loss of social resources) or protective factors (such as social support and general self-efficacy or optimism) and reduced mental health problems in the wake of a variety of types of traumatic stressors (Waldrep & Benight, 2008). Thus, the deceptively simple—but actually quite complex and powerful—positive belief in one's own ability to successfully cope with and recover from the adverse effects of traumatic stressors may help create a positive cycle of hope and recovery in place of the vicious cycle in PTSD of anxiety, avoidance, and PTSD.

Several scientific studies have reported a protective relationship between self-efficacy more generally and resistance to or recovery from PTSD. A study of persons exposed to violence in the community that conducted three repeated longitudinal assessments over a 12-month period following exposure to a violent traumatic stressor reported that self-efficacy at the first time point was correlated with the extent of perceived positive social support at that time, as well as predicting (lesser) severity of PTSD at subsequent assessments (Johansen, Wahl, Eilertsen, & Weisaeth, 2007). Thus, self-efficacy and social support are likely to often be interrelated. People with more confidence in themselves are more likely to seek and receive social support, and people with strong social support networks are more likely to feel and be effective in coping with stressors—and to contribute jointly as well as separately to lowering the risk of PTSD.

The third and most consistently scientifically supported protective factor mitigating against the development or persistence of PTSD is social support (see Box 3.6).

Social support may take any or all of three different forms (Kaniasty & Norris, 2008): "*emotional support, informational support*, and *tangible support.* Each of these types of support may be linked to specific sources, such as kin relations (spouse, family, relatives), nonkin informal networks (friends, neighbors, coworkers), and people outside the immediate support circles (charitable organizations, professional service providers)." Most often, social support is measured in terms of people's *perception* or *appraisal* of the amount and quality of social support that they have available—confidence that adequate support would be available if needed or to characterize the extent to which potential sources of support are helpful and cohesive (Kaniasty & Norris, 2008). Schnurr et al. (2004) found that military veterans who had higher levels of perceived "emotional sustenance," "instrumental assistance" (such as family or friends from whom they could get practical or financial help), and "structural support" (i.e., access to tangible social and economic resources) were less likely than comparable veterans to develop PTSD. Interestingly, only emotional and tangible support were protective in the form of increasing the likelihood of recovery if PTSD did develop, suggesting that practical "instrumental" help may be less beneficial for recovery from PTSD than emotional support and socioeconomic resources.

Social support also may be measured more objectively in terms of the actual help that a person receives from others ("received" social support) or of the closeness and position of the person in relationship to a network of potential sources of social support ("social embededness"; Kaniasty & Norris, 2008). Koenen et al. (2003) found that military veterans who were more involved in their communities were less likely to have chronic PTSD years or even decades following war-zone deployment, consistent with a view that social embededness is an important protective factor against persistent PTSD. An additional resource that can serve as a protective factor is the receipt of early effective intervention to prevent or reduce the severity of ASD or PTSD (see Chapter 9).

Conclusion

Many factors in a person's psychological and biological makeup, relationships and resources, and life experiences (including nontraumatic and supportive experiences as well as traumatic stressors) influence the path or trajectory that will lead that person to encounter traumatic stressors and to resist, recover from, or persistently suffer from PTSD. Fortunately, many people never encounter a traumatic stressor in their lives, but most (children as well as adults) will experience at least one and often two or more traumatic stressors. Even then, PTSD is far from inevitable, occurring only for 10–20% of people exposed to a traumatic stressor. The person's strengths and limitations, and those of her or his family, community, and society, play a key role in determining whether PTSD will occur and, if so, whether recovery will occur. The risk, vulnerability, and protective factors identified through careful clinical observation and rigorous scientific research studies provide a basis for developing assessment measures (Chapter 6) and treatment (Chapters 7 and 8) and prevention (Chapter 9) interventions that can further reduce the risk of PTSD and enhance recovery from PTSD.

References

Aardal-Eriksson, E., Eriksson, T. E., & Thorell, L. -H. (2001). Salivary cortisol, posttraumatic stress symptoms, and general health in the acute phase and during 9-month follow-up. *Biological Psychiatry, 50*, 986–993.

Acierno, R., Resnick, H., Kilpatrick, D. G., Saunders, B., & Best, C. L. (1999). Risk factors for rape, physical assault, and posttraumatic stress disorder in women: Examination of differential multivariate relationships. *Journal of Anxiety Disorders, 13*, 541–563.

Anda, R. F., Butchart, A., Felitti, V. J., & Brown, D. W. (2010). Building a framework for global surveillance of the public health implications of adverse childhood experiences. *American Journal of Preventive Medicine, 39*(1), 93–98.

Anders, S. L., Frazier, P. A., & Frankfurt, S. B. (2011). Variations in Criterion A and PTSD rates in a community sample of women. *Journal of Anxiety Disorders, 25*(2), 176–184.

Apfel, B. A., Otte, C., Inslicht, S. S., McCaslin, S. E., Henn-Haase, C., Metzler, T. J., et al. (2011). Pretraumatic prolonged elevation of salivary MHPG predicts peritraumatic distress and symptoms of post-traumatic stress disorder. *Journal of Psychiatric Research, 45*(6), 735–741.

Astur, R. S., St Germain, S. A., Tolin, D., Ford, J. D., Russell, D., & Stevens, M. (2006). Hippocampus function predicts severity of post-traumatic stress disorder. *Cyberpsychology and Behavior, 9*(2), 234–240.

Betts, K. S., Williams, G. M., Najman, J. M., Bor, W., & Alati, R. (2012). Pre-trauma verbal ability at five years of age and the risk of post-traumatic stress disorder in adult males and females. *Journal of Psychiatric Research, 46*(7), 933–939.

Biederman, J., Petty, C., Spencer, T. J., Woodworth, K. Y., Bhide, P., Zhu, J., et al. (2014). Is ADHD a risk for posttraumatic stress disorder (PTSD)? Results from a large longitudinal study of referred children with and without ADHD. *World Journal of Biological Psychiatry, 15*(1), 49–55.

Binder, E. B., Bradley, R. G., Liu, W., Epstein, M. P., Deveau, T. C., Mercer, K. B., et al. (2008). Association of FKBP5 polymorphisms and childhood abuse with risk of posttraumatic stress disorder symptoms in adults. *JAMA: Journal of the American Medical Association, 299*(11), 1291–1305. http://dx.doi.org/10.1001/jama.299.11.1291.

Bodkin, J. A., Pope, H. G., Detke, M. J., & Hudson, J. I. (2007). Is PTSD caused by traumatic stress? *Journal of Anxiety Disorders, 21*, 176–182.

Boney-McCoy, S., & Finkelhor, D. (1996). Is youth victimization related to trauma symptoms and depression after controlling for prior symptoms and family relationships? A longitudinal, prospective study. *Journal of Consulting and Clinical Psychology, 64*, 1406–1416.

Boscarino, J. A., & Adams, R. E. (2009). PTSD onset and course following the World Trade Center disaster: Findings and implications for future research. *Social Psychiatry and Psychiatric Epidemiology, 44*(10), 887–898.

Bremner, J. D. (2008). Hippocampus. In G. Reyes, J. D. Elhai, & J. D. Ford (Eds.), *Encyclopedia of psychological trauma* (pp. 313–315). Hoboken, NJ: Wiley.

Breslau, N. (2002). Epidemiologic studies of trauma, posttraumatic stress disorder, and other psychiatric disorders. *Canadian Journal of Psychiatry, 47*, 923–929.

Breslau, N., Peterson, E. L., & Schultz, L. R. (2008). A second look at prior trauma and the posttraumatic stress disorder effects of subsequent trauma: A prospective epidemiological study. *Archives of General Psychiatry, 65*(4), 431–437.

Brewin, C. R. (2001). A cognitive neuroscience account of posttraumatic stress disorder and its treatment. *Behaviour Research and Therapy, 39*(4), 373–393.

Brewin, C. R., Andrews, B., & Valentine, J. D. (2000). Meta-analysis of risk factors for post-traumatic stress disorder in trauma-exposed adults. *Journal of Consulting and Clinical Psychology*, *68*(5), 748–766.

Brewin, C. R., Rose, S., Andrews, B., Green, J., Tata, P., McEvedy, C., et al. (2002). Brief screening instrument for post-traumatic stress disorder. *British Journal of Psychiatry*, *181*(2), 158–162.

Briggs-Gowan, M. J., Carter, A. S., Clark, R., Augustyn, M., McCarthy, K. J., & Ford, J. D. (2010). Exposure to potentially traumatic events in early childhood: Differential links to emergent psychopathology. *Journal of Child Psychology and Psychiatry and Allied Disciplines*, *51*(10), 1132–1140. http://dx.doi.org/10.1111/j.1469-7610.2010.02256.x.

Briggs-Gowan, M. J., Carter, A. S., & Ford, J. D. (2012). Parsing the effects violence exposure in early childhood: Modeling developmental pathways. *Journal of Pediatric Psychology*, *37*(1), 11–22. http://dx.doi.org/10.1093/jpepsy/jsr063.

Brunet-Gouet, E., & Decety, J. (2006). Social brain dysfunctions in schizophrenia: A review of neuroimaging studies. *Psychiatry Research*, *143*, 75–92.

Bryant, R. A. (2005). Predicting posttraumatic stress disorder from acute reactions. *Journal of Trauma & Dissociation*, *6*(2), 5–15.

Bynum, L., Griffin, T., Ridings, D. L., Wynkoop, K. S., Anda, R. F., Edwards, V. J., et al. (2010). Adverse childhood experiences reported by adults — Five States, 2009. *Morbidity and Mortality Weekly Report*, *59*(49), 1609–1613.

Carlson, E. B., Dalenberg, C., & Muhtadie, L. (2008). Etiology. In G. Reyes, J. D. Elhai, & J. D. Ford (Eds.), *Encyclopedia of psychological trauma* (pp. 257–264). Hoboken, NJ: Wiley.

Caspi, A., McClay, J., Moffitt, T. E., Mill, J., Martin, J., Craig, I., et al. (2002). Role of genotype in the cycle of violence in maltreated children. *Science*, *297*, 851–854.

Classen, C. C., Palesh, O. G., & Aggarwal, R. (2005). Sexual revictimization: A review of the empirical literature. *Trauma, Violence, and Abuse*, *6*, 103–129.

Cloitre, M., Cohen, L. R., & Koenen, K. C. (2006). *Treating survivors of childhood abuse: Psychotherapy for the interrupted life*. New York: Guilford.

Constans, J. I., Vasterling, J. J., Deitch, E., Han, X., Teten Tharp, A. L., Davis, T. D., et al. (2012). Pre-Katrina mental illness, postdisaster negative cognitions, and PTSD symptoms in male veterans following Hurricane Katrina. *Psychological Trauma: Theory, Research, Practice, and Policy*, *4*(6), 568–577.

Copeland, W. E., Keeler, G., Angold, A., & Costello, E. J. (2007). Traumatic events and post-traumatic stress in childhood. *Archives of General Psychiatry*, *64*, 577–584.

Cuevas, C. A., Finkelhor, D., Clifford, C., Ormrod, R. K., & Turner, H. A. (2010). Psychological distress as a risk factor for re-victimization in children. *Child Abuse and Neglect*, *34*(4), 235–243.

Cuevas, C. A., Finkelhor, D., Turner, H. A., & Ormrod, R. K. (2007). Juvenile delinquency and victimization: A theoretical typology. *Journal of Interpersonal Violence*, *22*(12), 1581–1602. http://dx.doi.org/22/12/1581 [pii]. http://dx.doi.org/10.1177/0886260507306498.

Dalgleish, T. (2004). Cognitive approaches to posttraumatic stress disorder: The evolution of multirepresentational theorizing. *Psychological Bulletin*, *130*, 228–260.

D'Andrea, W., Ford, J. D., Stolbach, B., Spinazzola, J., & van der Kolk, B. A. (2012). Understanding interpersonal trauma in children: Why we need a developmentally appropriate trauma diagnosis. *American Journal of Orthopsychiatry*, *82*(2), 187–200. http://dx.doi.org/10.1111/j.1939-0025.2012.01154.x.

Daviss, W. B., Racusin, R., Fleischer, A., Mooney, D., Ford, J. D., & McHugo, G. J. (2000). Acute stress disorder symptomatology during hospitalization for pediatric injury. *Journal of the American Academy of Child & Adolescent Psychiatry*, *39*, 569–575.

Dawson, L. H., Shih, M. C., de Moor, C., & Shrier, L. (2008). Reasons why adolescents and young adults have sex: Associations with psychological characteristics and sexual behavior. *Journal of Sex Research, 45*, 225–232.

Delahanty, D. L., Nugent, N. R., Christopher, N. C., & Walsh, M. (2005). Initial urinary epinephrine and cortisol levels predict acute PTSD symptoms in child trauma victims. *Psychoneuroendocrinology, 30*, 121–128.

DiGangi, J. A., Gomez, D., Mendoza, L., Jason, L. A., Keys, C. B., & Koenen, K. C. (2013). Pretrauma risk factors for posttraumatic stress disorder: A systematic review of the literature. *Clinical Psychology Review, 33*(6), 728–744.

Ehlers, A., & Clark, D. M. (2000). A cognitive model of posttraumatic stress disorder. *Behaviour Research and Therapy, 38*, 319–345.

Elhai, J. D., Engdahl, R. M., Palmieri, P. A., Naifeh, J. A., Schweinle, A., & Jacobs, G. A. (2009). Assessing posttraumatic stress disorder with or without reference to a single, worst traumatic event: Examining differences in factor structure. *Psychological Assessment, 21*(4), 629–634.

Elhai, J. D., & Palmieri, P. A. (2011). The factor structure of posttraumatic stress disorder: A literature update, critique of methodology, and agenda for future research. *Journal of Anxiety Disorders, 25*(6), 849–854.

English, D. J., Graham, J. C., Litrownik, A. J., Everson, M., & Bangdiwala, S. I. (2005). Defining maltreatment chronicity: Are there differences in child outcomes? *Child Abuse & Neglect, 29*, 575–595.

Fani, N., Gutman, D., Tone, E. B., Almli, L., Mercer, K. B., Davis, J., et al. (2013). FKBP5 and attention bias for threat: Associations with hippocampal function and shape. *JAMA Psychiatry, 70*(4), 392–400.

Fani, N., Jovanovic, T., Ely, T. D., Bradley, B., Gutman, D., Tone, E. B., et al. (2012). Neural correlates of attention bias to threat in post-traumatic stress disorder. *Biological Psychology, 90*(2), 134–142.

Felitti, V. J., Anda, R. F., Nordenberg, D., Williamson, D. F., Spitz, A. M., Edwards, V., et al. (1998). Relationship of childhood abuse and household dysfunction to many of the leading causes of death in adults - The adverse childhood experiences (ACE) study. *American Journal of Preventive Medicine, 14*, 245–258.

Finkelhor, D., Ormrod, R., Turner, H., & Holt, M. (2009). Pathways to poly-victimization. *Child Maltreatment, 14*(4), 316–329.

Finkelhor, D., Ormrod, R. K., & Turner, H. A. (2007). Re-victimization patterns in a national longitudinal sample of children and youth. *Child Abuse and Neglect, 31*(5), 479–502.

Finkelhor, D., Ormrod, R. K., Turner, H. A., & Hamby, S. L. (2005). Measuring poly-victimization using the Juvenile Victimization Questionnaire. *Child Abuse and Neglect, 29*(11), 1297–1312.

First, M. B., Spitzer, R. L., Gibbon, M., & Williams, J. (1996). *Structured Clinical Interview for Axis I and II DSM-IV Disorders - Patient Edition (SCID-IV/P)*. New York: New York State Psychiatric Institute.

Fiske, S. T., & Taylor, S. E. (1991). *Social cognition* (2nd ed.). New York: Mcgraw-Hill.

Foa, E. B., Ehlers, A., Clark, D. M., Tolin, D. F., & Orsillo, S. M. (1999). The Posttraumatic Cognitions Inventory (PTCI): Development and validation. *Psychological Assessment, 11*, 303–314.

Foa, E. B., & Rothbaum, B. O. (1998). *Treating the trauma of rape: Cognitive-behavioral therapy for PTSD*. New York: Guilford.

Foa, E. B., Zinbarg, R., & Rothbaum, B. O. (1992). Uncontrollability and unpredictability in post-traumatic stress disorder: An animal model. *Psychological Bulletin, 112*, 218–238.

Follette, V., & Vijay, A. (2008). Retraumatization. In G. Reyes, J. D. Elhai, & J. D. Ford (Eds.), *Encyclopedia of psychological trauma* (pp. 586–589). Hoboken, NJ: Wiley.

Ford, J. D. (2009). Translation of emerging neurobiological and developmental findings to the clinicalconceptualization and treatment of complex psychological trauma. In C. A. Courtois & J. Ford (Eds.), *Treating complex traumatic stress disorders: An evidence-based guide*. New York: Guilford.

Ford, J. D., Adams, M. L., & Dailey, W. F. (2007). Psychological and health problems in a geographically proximate population time-sampled continuously for three months after the September 11th, 2001 terrorist incidents. *Anxiety Stress Coping, 20*, 129–146.

Ford, J. D., Chapman, J., Mack, M., & Pearson, G. (2006). Pathway from traumatic child victimization to delinquency: Implications for juvenile and permanency court proceedings and decisions. *Juvenile and Family Court Journal, 57*(1), 13–26.

Ford, J. D., & Connor, D. (2009). ADHD and posttraumatic stress disorder (PTSD). *Current Attention Disorder Reports, 1*, 61–66.

Ford, J. D., Elhai, J. D., Connor, D. F., & Frueh, B. C. (2010). Poly-victimization and risk of posttraumatic, depressive, and substance use disorders and involvement in delinquency in a national sample of adolescents. *Journal of Adolescent Health, 46*(6), 545–552. http://dx.doi.org/S1054-139X(09)00636-3 [pii]. http://dx.doi.org/10.1016/j.jadohealth.2009.11.212.

Ford, J. D., Racusin, R., Ellis, C. G., Daviss, W. B., Reiser, J., Fleischer, A., et al. (2000). Child maltreatment, other trauma exposure, and posttraumatic symptomaology among children with oppositional defiant and attention hyperactivity disorders. *Child Maltreatment, 5*, 205–217.

Frankl, V. E. (1946). *Man's search for meaning*. New York: Bantam.

Freyd, J. (1994). Betrayal trauma: Traumatic amnesia as an adaptive response to childhood abuse. *Ethics & Behavior, 4*, 307–329.

Galatzer-Levy, I. R., Ankri, Y., Freedman, S., Israeli-Shalev, Y., Roitman, P., Gilad, M., et al. (2013). Early PTSD symptom trajectories: Persistence, recovery, and response to treatment: results from the Jerusalem Trauma Outreach and Prevention Study (J-TOPS). *PLoS One, 8*(8), e70084.

Gilbertson, M. W., McFarlane, A. C., Weathers, F. W., Keane, T. M., Yehuda, R., Shalev, A. Y., Harvard/VA PTSD Twin Study Investigators, (2010). Is trauma a causal agent of psychopathologic symptoms in posttraumatic stress disorder? Findings from identical twins discordant for combat exposure. *Journal of Clinical Psychiatry, 71*(10), 1324–1330.

Goenjian, A. K., Noble, E. R., Walling, D. P., Goenjian, H. A., Karayan, I. S., Ritchie, T., et al. (2008). Heritabilities of symptoms of posttraumatic stress disorder, anxiety, and depression in earthquake exposed Armenian families. *Psychiatric Genetics, 18*(6), 261–266.

Golier, J. A., Yehuda, R., Bierer, L. M., Mitropoulou, V., New, A. S., Schmeidler, J., et al. (2003). The relationship of borderline personality disorder to posttraumatic stress disorder and traumatic events. *American Journal of Psychiatry, 160*(11), 2018–2024.

Goodman, L. A., Salyers, M. P., Mueser, K. T., Rosenberg, S. D., Swartz, M., Essock, S. M., et al. (2001). Recent victimization in women and men with severe mental illness: Prevalence and correlates. *Journal of Traumatic Stress, 14*(4), 615–632. http://dx.doi.org/10.1023/A:1013026318450.

Gotlib, I. H., & Hamilton, J. P. (2008). Neuroimaging and depression: Current status and unresolved issues. *Current Directions in Psychological Science, 17*, 159–163.

Grasso, D., Greene, C., & Ford, J. D. (2013). Cumulative trauma in childhood. In J. D. Ford & C. A. Courtois (Eds.), *Treating complex traumatic stress disorders in children and adolescents: An evidence based guide*. New York, NY: Guilford.

Guffanti, G., Galea, S., Yan, L., Roberts, A. L., Solovieff, N., Aiello, A. E., et al. (2013). Genome-wide association study implicates a novel RNA gene, the lincRNA AC068718.1, as a risk factor for post-traumatic stress disorder in women. *Psychoneuroendocrinology*, *38*(12), 3029–3038.

Guthrie, R. M., & Bryant, R. A. (2006). Extinction learning before trauma and subsequent post-traumatic stress. *Psychosomatic Medicine*, *68*(2), 307–311.

Harrison, P. J., & Tunbridge, E. M. (2008). Catechol-O-methyltransferase (COMT): A gene contributing to sex differences in brain function, and to sexual dimorphism in the predisposition to psychiatric disorders. *Neuropsychopharmacology*, *33*, 3037–3045.

Hobfoll, S. E. (2001). Conservation of resources: A rejoinder to the commentaries. *Applied Psychology: An International Review*, *50*, 419–421.

Holmes, E. A., Brewin, C. R., & Hennessy, R. G. (2004). Trauma films, information processing, and intrusive memory development. *Journal of Experimental Psychology General*, *133*, 3–22.

Holtzheimer, P. E., III, Russo, J., Zatzick, D., Bundy, C., & Roy-Byrne, P. P. (2005). The impact of comorbid posttraumatic stress disorder on short-term clinical outcome in hospitalized patients with depression. *American Journal of Psychiatry*, *162*, 970–976.

Horowitz, M. J. (1997). *Stress response syndromes: PTSD, grief, and adjustment disorders* (3rd ed.). Lanham, MD: Jason Aronson.

Huijbregts, S. C., Seguin, J. R., Zoccolillo, M., Boivin, M., & Tremblay, R. E. (2008). Maternal prenatal smoking, parental antisocial behavior, and early childhood physical aggression. *Development and Psychopathology*, *20*(2), 437–453.

Iacoviello, B. M., Wu, G., Abend, R., Murrough, J. W., Feder, A., Fruchter, E., et al. (2014). Attention bias variability and symptoms of posttraumatic stress disorder. *Journal of Traumatic Stress*, *27*(2), 232–239.

Inslicht, S. S., McCaslin, S. E., Metzler, T. J., Henn-Haase, C., Hart, S. L., Maguen, S., et al. (2010). Family psychiatric history, peritraumatic reactivity, and posttraumatic stress symptoms: A prospective study of police. *Journal of Psychiatric Research*, *44*(1), 22–31. http://dx.doi.org/10.1016/j.jpsychires.2009.05.011.

Inslicht, S. S., Otte, C., McCaslin, S. E., Apfel, B. A., Henn-Haase, C., Metzler, T., et al. (2011). Cortisol awakening response prospectively predicts peritraumatic and acute stress reactions in police officers. *Biological Psychiatry*, *70*(11), 1055–1062.

Janoff-Bulman, R. (1992). *Shattered assumptions: Towards a new psychology of trauma*. New York: Free Press.

Johansen, V. A., Wahl, A. K., Eilertsen, D. E., & Weisaeth, L. (2007). Prevalence and predictors of post-traumatic stress disorder (PTSD) in physically injured victims of non-domestic violence. A longitudinal study. *Social Psychiatry and Psychiatric Epidemiology*, *42*, 583–593.

Jones, E., & Wessely, S. (2007). A paradigm shift in the conceptualization of psychological trauma in the 20th century. *Journal of Anxiety Disorders*, *21*, 164–175.

Kaniasty, K., & Norris, F. H. (2008). Longitudinal linkages between perceived social support and posttraumatic stress symptoms: Sequential roles of social causation and social selection. *Journal of Traumatic Stress*, *21*, 274–281.

Kaplow, J. B., Dodge, K. A., Amaya-Jackson, L., & Saxe, G. N. (2005). Pathways to PTSD, Part II: Sexually abused children. *American Journal of Psychiatry*, *162*, 1305–1310.

Kaplow, J. B., & Widom, C. S. (2007). Age of onset of child maltreatment predicts long-term mental health outcomes. *Journal of Abnormal Psychology*, *116*, 176–187.

Kaufman, J., Yang, B. Z., Douglas-Palumberi, H., Houshyar, S., Lipschitz, D., Krystal, J. H., et al. (2004). Social supports and serotonin transporter gene moderate depression in maltreated children. *Proceedings of the National Academy of Sciences USA*, *101*(49), 17316–17321.

Keiley, M. K., Bates, J. E., Dodge, K. A., & Pettit, G. S. (2001). Effects of temperament on the development of externalizing and internalizing behaviors over 9 years. In F. (2001).

Columbus (Ed.), *Advances in psychology research* (Vol. 6, pp. 255–288). Hauppauge, NY: Nova Science Publishers.

Kessler, R. C., Berglund, P., Demler, O., Jin, R., Merikangas, K. R., & Walters, E. E. (2005). Lifetime prevalence and age-of-onset distributions of DSM-IV disorders in the National Comorbidity Survey Replication. *Archives of General Psychiatry, 62*(6), 593–602.

Kessler, R. C., Sonnega, A., Bromet, E., & Hughes, M. (1995). Posttraumatic stress disorder in the National Comorbidity Survey. *Archives of General Psychiatry, 52*, 1048–1060.

Kilpatrick, D. G., Koenen, K. C., Ruggiero, K. J., Acierno, R., Galea, S., Resnick, H. S., et al. (2007). The serotonin transporter genotype and social support and moderation of post-traumatic stress disorder and depression in hurricane-exposed adults. *American Journal of Psychiatry, 164*, 1693–1699.

Kim, M. M., Ford, J. D., Bradford, D. W., & Ferron, J. (2010). Assessing trauma, substance abuse and mental health in a sample of homeless men. *Health & Social Work, 35*, 39–48.

Koenen, K. C., Fu, Q. J., Lyons, M. J., Toomey, R., Goldberg, J., Eisen, S. A., et al. (2005). Juvenile conduct disorder as a risk factor for trauma exposure and posttraumatic stress disorder. *Journal of Traumatic Stress, 18*(1), 23–32.

Koenen, K. C., Moffitt, T. E., Caspi, A., Gregory, A., Harrington, H., & Poulton, R. (2008). The developmental mental-disorder histories of adults with posttraumatic stress disorder: A prospective longitudinal birth cohort study. *Journal of Abnormal Psychology, 117*(2), 460–466.

Koenen, K. C., Moffitt, T. E., Poulton, R., Martin, J., & Caspi, A. (2007). Early childhood factors associated with the development of post-traumatic stress disorder: Results from a longitudinal birth cohort. *Psychological Medicine, 37*(2), 181–192.

Koenen, K. C., Stellman, J. M., Stellman, S. D., & Sommer, J. F., Jr. (2003). Risk factors for course of posttraumatic stress disorder among Vietnam veterans: A 14-year follow-up of American Legionnaires. *Journal of Consulting and Clinical Psychology, 71*, 980–986.

Kremen, W. S., Koenen, K. C., Boake, C., Purcell, S., Eisen, S. A., Franz, C. E., et al. (2007). Pretrauma cognitive ability and risk for posttraumatic stress disorder. *Archives of General Psychiatry, 64*, 361–368.

Kuckertz, J. M., Amir, N., Boffa, J. W., Warren, C. K., Rindt, S. E., Norman, S., et al. (2014). The effectiveness of an attention bias modification program as an adjunctive treatment for post-traumatic stress disorder. *Behaviour Research and Therapy, 63C*, 25–35.

Lambert, J. E., Holzer, J., & Hasbun, A. (2014). Association between parents' PTSD severity and children's psychological distress: A meta-analysis. *Journal of Traumatic Stress, 27*(1), 9–17.

Lanius, R. A., Vermetten, E., Loewenstein, R. J., Brand, B., Schmahl, C., Bremner, J. D., et al. (2010). Emotion modulation in PTSD: Clinical and neurobiological evidence for a dissociative subtype. *American Journal of Psychiatry, 167*(6), 640–647. http://dx.doi.org/10.1176/appi.ajp.2009.09081168.

Layne, C., Beck, C., Rimmasch, H., Southwick, J., Moreno, M., & Hobfoll, S. (2008). Promoting 'resilient' posttraumatic adjustment in childhood and beyond. In D. Brom, R. Pat-Horenczyk, & J. D. Ford (Eds.), *Treating traumatized children: Risk, resilience, and recovery* (pp. 13–47). London: Routledge.

Layne, C. M., Beck, C. J., Rimmasch, H., Southwick, J., Moreno, M., & Hobfoll, S. (2009). Promoting "resilient" posttraumatic adjustment in childhood and beyond: "unpacking" life events, adjustment trajectories, resources, and interventions. In D. Brom, R. Pat-Horenczyk, & J. D. Ford (Eds.), *Treating traumatized children: Risk, resilience and recovery* (pp. 13–40). London, Great Britain: Routledge.

Leverich, G. S., Nolen, W. A., Rush, A. J., McElroy, S. L., Keck, P. E., Denicoff, K. D., et al. (2001). The Stanley Foundation bipolar treatment outcome network. I. Longitudinal methodology. *Journal of Affective Disorders, 67*, 33–44.

Li, Y. F., Langholz, B., Salam, M. T., & Gilliland, F. D. (2005). Maternal and grandmaternal smoking patterns are associated with early childhood asthma. *Chest, 127*(4), 1232–1241.

Liberzon, I., King, A. P., Ressler, K. J., Almli, L. M., Zhang, P., Ma, S. T., et al. (2014). Interaction of the ADRB2 gene polymorphism with childhood trauma in predicting adult symptoms of posttraumatic stress disorder. *JAMA Psychiatry, 71*(10), 1174–1182.

Lommen, M. J., Engelhard, I. M., Sijbrandij, M., van den Hout, M. A., & Hermans, D. (2013). Pre-trauma individual differences in extinction learning predict posttraumatic stress. *Behaviour Research and Therapy, 51*(2), 63–67.

Lysaker, P. H., Meyer, P. S., Evans, J. D., Clements, C. A., & Marks, K. A. (2001). Childhood sexual trauma and psychosocial functioning in adults with schizophrenia. *Psychiatric Services, 52*, 1485–1488.

Lysaker, P. H., Nees, M. A., Lancaster, R. S., & Davis, L. W. (2004). Vocational function among persons with schizophrenia with and without history of childhood sexual trauma. *Journal of Traumatic Stress, 17*, 435–438.

Macklin, M. L., Metzger, L. J., Litz, B. T., McNally, R. J., Lasko, N. B., Orr, S. P., et al. (1998). Lower precombat intelligence is a risk factor for posttraumatic stress disorder. *Journal of Consulting and Clinical Psychology, 66*, 323–326.

Maercker, A., & Muller, J. (2004). Social acknowledgment as a victim or survivor: A scale to measure a recovery factor of PTSD. *Journal of Traumatic Stress, 17*, 345–351.

Marra, J. V., McCarthy, E., Lin, H. J., Ford, J., Rodis, E., & Frisman, L. K. (2009). Effects of social support and conflict on parenting among homeless mothers. *American Journal of Orthopsychiatry, 79*(3), 348–356.

Marx, B. P., Forsyth, J. P., Gallup, G. G., Fuse, T., & Lexington, J. M. (2008). Tonic immobility as an evolved predator defense: Implications for sexual assault survivors. *Clinical Psychology: Science and Practice, 15*, 74–90.

McEwen, B. (2006). Stress, adaptation, and disease. *Annals of the New York Academy of Sciences, 840*(1), 33–44.

McHugh, P. R., & Treisman, G. (2007). PTSD: A problematic diagnostic category. *Journal of Anxiety Disorders, 21*(2), 211–222.

McLaughlin, K. A., Koenen, K. C., Hill, E. D., Petukhova, M., Sampson, N. A., Zaslavsky, A. M., et al. (2013). Trauma exposure and posttraumatic stress disorder in a national sample of adolescents. *Journal of the American Academy of Child & Adolescent Psychiatry, 52*(8) 815–830.e814. http://dx.doi.org/10.1016/j.jaac.2013.05.011.

McNally, R. J., & Shin, L. M. (1995). Association of intelligence with severity of posttraumatic stress disorder symptoms in Vietnam combat veterans. *American Journal of Psychiatry, 152*, 936–938.

Meewisse, M. -L., Reitsma, J. B., De Vries, G., Gersons, B. P. R., & Olff, M. (2007). Cortisol and post-traumatic stress disorder in adults: Systematic review and meta-analysis. *British Journal of Psychiatry, 191*, 367–392.

Miron, L., & Orcutt, H. (2014). Pathways from childhood abuse to prospective revictimization: Depression, sex to reduce negative affect, and forecasted sexual behavior. *Child Abuse & Neglect, 38*, 1848–1859.

Mol, S. S., Arntz, A., Metsemakers, J. F., Dinant, G. J., Vilters-van Montfort, P. A., & Knottnerus, J. A. (2005). Symptoms of post-traumatic stress disorder after non-traumatic events: Evidence from an open population study. *British Journal of Psychiatry, 186*, 494–499.

Morrison, A. P., Frame, L., & Larkin, W. (2003). Relationships between trauma and psychosis: A review and integration. *British Journal of Clinical Psychology*, *42*(Pt 4), 331–353.

Mueser, K. T., Essock, S. M., Haines, M., Wolfe, R., & Xie, H. (2004). Posttraumatic stress disorder, supported employment, and outcomes in people with severe mental illness. *CNS Spectrums*, *9*(12), 913–925.

Mueser, K. T., Rosenberg, S. D., Fox, L., Salyers, M. P., Ford, J. D., & Carty, P. (2001). Psychometric evaluation of trauma and posttraumatic stress disorder assessments in persons with severe mental illness. *Psychological Assessment*, *13*, 110–117.

Mulder, R., Fergusson, D., & Horwood, J. (2013). Post-traumatic stress disorder symptoms form a traumatic and non-traumatic stress response dimension. *Australian and New Zealand Journal of Psychiatry*, *47*(6), 569–577. http://dx.doi.org/10.1177/0004867413484367.

Neria, Y., Bromet, E. J., Sievers, S., Lavelle, J., & Fochtmann, L. J. (2002). Trauma exposure and posttraumatic stress disorder in psychosis: Findings from a first-admission cohort. *Journal of Consulting and Clinical Psychology*, *70*, 246–251.

Neumeister, A., Henry, S., & Krystal, J. H. (2007). Neurocircuitry and neuroplasticity in PTSD. In M. J. Friedman, T. M. Keane, & P. A. Resick (Eds.), *Handbook of PTSD: Science and practice* (pp. 151–165). New York: Guilford.

Nishith, P., Mechanic, M. B., & Resick, P. A. (2000). Prior interpersonal trauma: The contribution to current PTSD symptoms in female rape victims. *Journal of Abnormal Psychology*, *109*, 20–25.

Noll, J. G., Trickett, P. K., & Putnam, F. W. (2003). A prospective investigation of the impact of childhood sexual abuse on the development of sexuality. *Journal of Consulting and Clinical Psychology*, *71*(3), 575–586.

Norman, S. B., Stein, M. B., Dimsdale, J. E., & Hoyt, D. B. (2008). Pain in the aftermath of trauma is a risk factor for post-traumatic stress disorder. *Psychological Medicine*, *38*, 533–542.

Norris, F. H., Friedman, M. J., & Watson, P. J. (2002). 60,000 disaster victims speak: Part II. Summary and implications of the disaster mental health research. *Psychiatry*, *65*, 240–260.

Norris, F. H., & Slone, L. B. (2007). The epidemiology of trauma and PTSD. In M. J. Friedman, T. M. Keane, & P. A. Resick (Eds.), *Handbook of PTSD: Science and practice* (pp. 78–98). New York US: Guilford.

Orcutt, H. K., Cooper, M. L., & Garcia, M. (2005). Use of sexual intercourse to reduce negative affect as a prospective mediator of sexual revictimization. *Journal of Traumatic Stress*, *18*(6), 729–739.

Orr, S. P., Lasko, N. B., Macklin, M. L., Pineles, S. L., Chang, Y., & Pitman, R. K. (2012). Predicting post-trauma stress symptoms from pre-trauma psychophysiologic reactivity, personality traits and measures of psychopathology. *Biology of Mood and Anxiety Disorders*, *2*(1), 8.

Ozer, E. J., Best, S. R., Lipsey, T. L., & Weiss, D. S. (2003). Predictors of posttraumatic stress disorder and symptoms in adults: A meta-analysis. *Psychological Bulletin*, *129*, 52–73.

Parslow, R. A., & Jorm, A. F. (2007). Pretrauma and posttrauma neurocognitive functioning and PTSD symptoms in a community sample of young adults. *The American Journal of Psychiatry*, *164*(3), 509–514.

Pat-Horenczyk, R. (2008). Child development. In G. Reyes, J. D. Elhai, & J. D. Ford (Eds.), *Encyclopedia of psychological trauma* (pp. 112–119). Hoboken, NJ: Wiley.

Peres, J. F., Moreira-Almeida, A., Caixeta, L., Leao, F., & Newberg, A. (2012). Neuroimaging during trance state: A contribution to the study of dissociation. *PLoS One*, *7*(11), e49360.

Perkonigg, A., Kessler, R. C., Storz, S., & Wittchen, H. -U. (2000). Traumatic events and post-traumatic stress disorder in the community: Prevalence, risk factors and comorbidity. *Acta Psychiatrica Scandinavica*, *101*, 46–59.

Pine, D. S. (2007). Research review: A neuroscience framework for pediatric anxiety disorders. *Journal of Child Psychology and Psychiatry*, *48*(7), 631–648.

Pole, N., Gone, J. P., & Kulkarni, M. (2008). Posttraumatic stress disorder among ethnoracial minorities in the United States. *Clinical Psychology: Science and Practice*, *15*, 35–61.

Poulos, A. M., Reger, M., Mehta, N., Zhuravka, I., Sterlace, S. S., Gannam, C., et al. (2014). Amnesia for early life stress does not preclude the adult development of posttraumatic stress disorder symptoms in rats. *Biological Psychiatry*, *76*(4), 306–314.

Power, M. J., & Dalgleish, T. (1997). *Cognition and emotion: From order to disorder*. Hove, England: Psychology Press.

Reinders, A. A., Willemsen, A. T., den Boer, J. A., Vos, H. P., Veltman, D. J., & Loewenstein, R. J. (2014). Opposite brain emotion-regulation patterns in identity states of dissociative identity disorder: A PET study and neurobiological model. *Psychiatry Research*, *223*(3), 236–243. http://dx.doi.org/10.1016/j.pscychresns.2014.05.005.

Remijnse, P. L., van den Heuvel, O. A., & Veltman, D. J. (2005). Neuroimaging in obsessive-compulsive disorder. *Current Medical Imaging Reviews*, *1*, 331–351.

Riedel, C., Schonberger, K., Yang, S., Koshy, G., Chen, Y. C., Gopinath, B., et al. (2014). Parental smoking and childhood obesity: Higher effect estimates for maternal smoking in pregnancy compared with paternal smoking–a meta-analysis. *International Journal of Epidemiology*, *43*(5), 1593–1606.

Rona, R. J., Jones, M., Sundin, J., Goodwin, L., Hull, L., Wessely, S., et al. (2012). Predicting persistent posttraumatic stress disorder (PTSD) in UK military personnel who served in Iraq: A longitudinal study. *Journal of Psychiatric Research*, *46*(9), 1191–1198.

Roodman, A. A., & Clum, G. A. (2001). Revictimization rates and method variance: A meta-analysis. *Clinical Psychology Review*, *21*, 183–204.

Rosen, G. M., & Taylor, S. (2007). Pseudo-PTSD. *Journal of Anxiety Disorders*, *21*, 201–210.

Sandweiss, D. A., Slymen, D. J., Leardmann, C. A., Smith, B., White, M. R., Boyko, E. J., Millennium Cohort Study Team, (2011). Preinjury psychiatric status, injury severity, and postdeployment posttraumatic stress disorder. *Archives of General Psychiatry*, *68*(5), 496–504.

Schindel-Allon, I., Aderka, I. M., Shahar, G., Stein, M., & Gilboa-Schechtman, E. (2010). Longitudinal associations between post-traumatic distress and depressive symptoms following a traumatic event: A test of three models. *Psychological Medicine*, *40*(10), 1669–1678.

Schnurr, P. P., & Green, B. L. (2004). Understanding relationships among trauma, posttraumatic stress disorder, and health outcomes. In P. P. Schnurr & B. L. Green (Eds.), *Trauma and health: Physical health consequences of exposure to extreme stress* (pp. 247–275). Washington, DC: American Psychological Association.

Schnurr, P. P., Lunney, C. A., & Sengupta, A. (2004). Risk factors for the development versus maintenance of posttraumatic stress disorder. *Journal of Traumatic Stress*, *17*, 85–95.

Segman, R., Shalev, A. Y., & Gelernter, J. (2007). Gene-environment interactions: Twin studies and gene research in the context of PTSD. In M. J. Friedman, T. M. Keane, & P. A. Resick (Eds.), *Handbook of PTSD: Science and practice* (pp. 190–206). New York, NY: Guilford Press.

Sells, D. J., Rowe, M., Fisk, D., & Davidson, L. (2003). Violent victimization of persons with co-occurring psychiatric and substance use disorders. *Psychiatric Services*, *54*, 1253–1257.

Shaw, K., McFarlane, A. C., Bookless, C., & Air, T. (2002). The aetiology of postpsychotic posttraumatic stress disorder following a psychotic episode. *Journal of Traumatic Stress*, *15*, 39–47.

Sijbrandij, M., Engelhard, I. M., Lommen, M. J., Leer, A., & Baas, J. M. (2013). Impaired fear inhibition learning predicts the persistence of symptoms of posttraumatic stress disorder (PTSD). *Journal of Psychiatric Research*, *47*(12), 1991–1997.

Smith, D., & Fischer, P. (2008). Family systems. In G. Reyes, J. D. Elhai, & J. D. Ford (Eds.), *Encyclopedia of psychological trauma* (pp. 277–278). Hoboken, NJ: Wiley.

Spitzer, R. L., First, M. B., & Wakefield, J. C. (2007). Saving PTSD from itself in DSM-V. *Journal of Anxiety Disorders, 21*, 233–241.

Stein, M. B., Jang, K. L., Taylor, S., Vernon, P. A., & Livesley, W. J. (2002). Genetic and environmental influences on trauma exposure and posttraumatic stress disorder symptoms: A twin study. *American Journal of Psychiatry, 159*, 1675–1681.

Storr, C. L., Ialongo, N. S., Anthony, J. C., & Breslau, N. (2007). Childhood antecedents of exposure to traumatic events and posttraumatic stress disorder. *American Journal of Psychiatry, 164*, 119–125.

Strakowski, S. M., Delbello, M. P., & Adler, C. M. (2005). The functional neuroanatomy of bipolar disorder: A review of neuroimaging findings. *Molecular Psychiatry, 10*, 105–116.

Sugar, J., & Ford, J. D. (2012). Peritraumatic reactions and posttraumatic stress disorder in psychiatrically impaired youth. *Journal of Traumatic Stress, 25*(1), 41–49.

Sumner, J. A., Pietrzak, R. H., Aiello, A. E., Uddin, M., Wildman, D. E., Galea, S., et al. (2014). Further support for an association between the memory-related gene WWC1 and posttraumatic stress disorder: Results from the Detroit Neighborhood Health Study. *Biological Psychiatry, 76*(11), e25–e26.

Taylor, S. E. (1989). *Positive illusions: Creative self-deception and the healthy mind.* New York: Basic Books.

Tolin, D. F., & Foa, E. B. (2006). Sex differences in trauma and posttraumatic stress disorder: A quantitative review of 25 years of research. *Psychological Bulletin, 132*, 959–992.

Ullman, S. E., & Filipas, H. H. (2001). Correlates of formal and informal support seeking in sexual assaults victims. *Journal of Interpersonal Violence, 16*, 1028–1047.

van Zuiden, M., Geuze, E., Willemen, H. L., Vermetten, E., Maas, M., Amarouchi, K., et al. (2012). Glucocorticoid receptor pathway components predict posttraumatic stress disorder symptom development: A prospective study. *Biological Psychiatry, 71*(4), 309–316.

van Zuiden, M., Geuze, E., Willemen, H. L., Vermetten, E., Maas, M., Heijnen, C. J., et al. (2011). Pre-existing high glucocorticoid receptor number predicting development of posttraumatic stress symptoms after military deployment. *American Journal of Psychiatry, 168*(1), 89–96.

van Zuiden, M., Heijnen, C. J., Maas, M., Amarouchi, K., Vermetten, E., Geuze, E., et al. (2012). Glucocorticoid sensitivity of leukocytes predicts PTSD, depressive and fatigue symptoms after military deployment: A prospective study. *Psychoneuroendocrinology, 37*(11), 1822–1836.

Vogt, D. S., King, D. W., & King, L. A. (2007). Risk pathways for PTSD: Making sense of the literature. In M. J. Friedman, T. M. Keane, & P. A. Resick (Eds.), *Handbook of PTSD: Science and practice* (pp. 99–115). New York: Guilford.

Waldrep, E., & Benight, C. C. (2008). Social cognitive theory. In G. Reyes, J. D. Elhai, & J. D. Ford (Eds.), *Encyclopedia of psychological trauma* (pp. 604–606). Hoboken, NJ: Wiley.

White, S., Acierno, R., Ruggiero, K. J., Koenen, K. C., Kilpatrick, D. G., Galea, S., et al. (2013). Association of CRHR1 variants and posttraumatic stress symptoms in hurricane exposed adults. *Journal of Anxiety Disorders, 27*(7), 678–683.

Whitfield, C. L., Anda, R. F., Dube, S. R., & Felitti, V. J. (2003). Violent childhood experiences and the risk of intimate partner violence in adults—assessment in a large health maintenance organization. *Journal of Interpersonal Violence, 18*(2), 166–185.

Widom, C. S., DuMont, K., & Czaja, S. J. (2007). A prospective investigation of major depressive disorder and comorbidity in abused and neglected children grown up. *Archives of General Psychiatry, 64*, 49–56.

Woodward, S. H., Kaloupek, D. G., Streeter, C. C., Kimble, M. O., Reiss, A. L., Eliez, S., et al. (2007). Brain, skull, and cerebrospinal fluid volumes in adult posttraumatic stress disorder. *Journal of Traumatic Stress, 20*, 763–774.

Yehuda, R., Teicher, M. H., Seckl, J. R., Grossman, R. A., Morris, A., & Biere, L. M. (2007). Parental posttraumatic stress disorder as a vulnerability factor for low cortisol trait in offspring of Holocaust survivors. *Archives of General Psychiatry, 64*, 1040–1048.

Epidemiology of PTSD

Exposure to traumatic stressors can happen at any time in a person's life. Although some age groups are more susceptible to exposure to certain types of traumatic stressors (e.g., young adults are more likely to encounter war-related traumatic stressors than younger or older people because that is the developmental period in which military service most often occurs), all traumatic stressors can occur at any point in the life span. Therefore, with each passing year of life, the probability of having been exposed to a traumatic stressor increases, until in midlife or older adulthood it is rare to find a person who has *not* ever been exposed to a traumatic stressor.

Fortunately, only a small proportion of individuals exposed to most types of traumatic stressors go on to develop posttraumatic stress disorder (PTSD) (although many experience some of the symptoms of PTSD). For this reason, the term *potentially traumatic event* is the most accurate way to describe events or experiences that could be psychologically traumatizing. When a potentially traumatic event fulfills the first criterion for PTSD (i.e., Criterion A) as defined in the *Diagnostic and Statistical Manual of Mental Disorders*, 5th edition (American Psychiatric Association, 2013), we will refer to it as a *traumatic stressor*. Symptoms can only be counted toward a diagnosis of PTSD if they occur following a person's exposure to a traumatic stressor. Recall from Chapter 3 that "PTSD" symptoms can occur even when a traumatic stressor has not been experienced, either as reactions to stressors that have an impact despite not being life-threatening or due to related disorders such as depression.

The reason for this reprise of the definition and terminology of traumatic stressors and PTSD is that it is important to be very clear about these terms in order to describe precisely when and for whom PTSD occurs—which is what the field of epidemiology does. Epidemiology is the scientific study of the occurrence of important phenomena (including physical and mental health conditions such as PTSD) in large populations such as entire nations or geographic regions or large groups (subpopulations) with common characteristics such as children, adults, ethnoracial groups, or people with physical health or psychiatric disorders. The term *epi* means on, about, or around; *demic* means a biological population; and *ology* means the study of. Thus, the epidemiology of exposure to traumatic stressors and PTSD is the study of when, for whom, and with what other disorders (called comorbidity: the co-occurrence of disease conditions (morbidities)), traumatic stressors, and PTSD occur in large groups of people (Box 4.1).

In this chapter, the methods and results of many epidemiological studies on exposure to traumatic stressors and PTSD are described, including studies conducted not only in the United States but also in other areas of the world, with entire nations or special subpopulations. The result is a growing understanding of when and to whom PTSD occurs, the so-called *incidence*, and how common or rare PTSD is for people

Posttraumatic Stress Disorder. DOI: http://dx.doi.org/10.1016/B978-0-12-801288-8.00004-2

Box 4.1 Key Points

1. The "epidemiology" of PTSD refers to the study of the characteristics and experiences of large populations in which PTSD occurs to some but not all persons: "epi" means on, about, or around; "demic" means a biological population; and "ology" means to study.

2. Traumatic stressors occur more often than most of us would expect, to more than half of adults at some time in their and to as many as two in three children by the age of 16.

3. Witnessing severe injury or death (36% of men, 14.5% of women) or being in a life-threatening accident (25% of men, 14% of women) is the most prevalent type of psychological trauma according to a survey of adults in the United States. Similar results have been found in surveys of adults in other industrialized countries.

4. Traumatic stressors involving interpersonal violence or victimization (such as physical assault or rape, 11–12% of men, 9–16% of women; past childhood abuse, 3% of men, 5–12% of women) generally are less prevalent than accidental but conferred greater risk of PTSD than accidental/disaster or witnessed traumas (see Chapter 3). Intentional forms of psychological trauma (such as abuse or family, community, or war violence) may be as common as accidental traumatic stressors in more impoverished areas of the world.

5. PTSD develops fully for only 0.5% of children by the age of 16. Distressing memories and symptoms occur for as many as 13% of children, but for as many as 33–40% of children who suffer the violent death of a loved one or sexual assault.

6. PTSD develops for one in 20 men and one in 10 women at some point in their lives, and for as many as two in three men and almost half of all women who experienced sexual assault, and half of all women who report having experienced childhood physical abuse.

7. Prevalence estimates of recent or current PTSD (i.e., at the time of the survey or within the past 6–12 months) tend to be lower, ranging from 1% to 5%.

8. More than 80% of adults with PTSD meet criteria for at least one other psychiatric diagnosis. The psychiatric disorders occur most often in combination with PTSD (i.e., the "comorbidities" of PTSD—where "morbidity" means illness and "co" means occurring together) among adults are mood disorders (including major depressive disorder and dysthymic disorder), other anxiety disorders (including panic disorder, agoraphobia, social and specific phobia, generalized anxiety disorder, and obsessive compulsive disorder (OCD)), and substance use, somatoform, eating, and dissociative disorders.

9. In the United States and other industrialized countries, PTSD is rare among young (ages 0–4) children (about 1 child in every 167) and school-age and adolescent children (about 1 child in every 100, and perhaps as few as 1 in 1000). However, 13% (1 in 7) children in a community sample in the United States reported some PTSD symptoms, and children who had been exposed to psychological trauma also often had depression and anxiety disorders, as well as disruptive behavior disorders (such as oppositional-defiant disorder).

10. Among children, PTSD often is accompanied by other anxiety disorders, depression, and behavioral disorders, and is associated more severe problems in psychological development, learning and school involvement, peer and family relationships, and (among older children and adolescents) risky and illegal behaviors.

of different backgrounds and characteristics, the so-called *prevalence*, exposed to different types of traumatic stressors.

The primary purpose of this chapter is to discuss research findings on the incidence and prevalence of exposure to traumatic stressors and PTSD in large populations and as influenced by factors such as the identity of the group(s), culture(s), or populations that are being studied, the different characteristics of each individual within those groups or populations (such as age, gender, race or ethnicity, language, socioeconomic status, or family background), and the different characteristics of the type(s) of traumatic stressors being investigated as potential sources of PTSD. In addition to determining the prevalence of PTSD, epidemiology studies also assess and estimate how likely it is that the phenomenon will occur depending on these characteristics of the population, the individual, and the traumatic stressor. This estimate is referred to by a third important term in epidemiology, the *conditional probability*, which is the likelihood of PTSD occurring when certain characteristics or conditions are present. Although exposure to a traumatic stressor is necessary for PTSD, it is not sufficient to guarantee that PTSD will occur (because, as just noted, many people exposed to traumatic stressors do not develop PTSD or do so only after a lengthy delay). Therefore, the conditional probability of PTSD given the occurrence of a traumatic stressor is a very important question. In order to determine who is most at risk for PTSD, it is essential to know not only what traumatic stressor(s) have been experienced but also the conditional probability of PTSD for of the stressors.

In addition, differences between individuals or entire populations can affect the conditional probability of PTSD occurring following exposure to the same or similar traumatic stressors. These are called "pretrauma" characteristics when they were present before exposure to traumatic stressor(s) (such as age, gender, personality, genetics, or family constellation) or "posttrauma" characteristics when they begin or change after exposure to traumatic stressor(s) (such as the social support military personnel receive or the work or financial pressures they must deal with during homecoming after serving in a war zone, or that occur in the lives of civilians who have been exposed to a life-threatening disaster or accident). In many cases, the pre- and posttrauma and traumatic stressor characteristics have a compounding effect on conditional probability of PTSD; for example, children with different genetic backgrounds (pretrauma characteristic) may differ in the probability that they will have PTSD following exposure to different types of traumatic stressors (traumatic stressor characteristics), depending on the type and amount of caregiver or peer social support they have afterward (posttrauma characteristic).

Research on the incidence and prevalence of exposure to traumatic stressors and PTSD, and comorbid mental and physical health, sociovocational, and legal problems among children, adolescents, and adults is summarized. Differences in the incidence and prevalence of traumatic stressor exposure and PTSD are highlighted across community, clinical (mental health), medical, criminal justice, and child welfare populations. It is worth noting that the majority of the epidemiological studies discussed in this chapter define PTSD based on the former *DSM-IV* criteria for PTSD because the new *DSM*-5 criteria, published in 2013, have not been available to researchers long enough for large epidemiological studies on the "new" PTSD.

Epidemiology of exposure to traumatic stressors

Research suggests that different types of traumatic stressors are more or less likely to occur for people at different ages and stages of development. For example, infants and toddlers, who spend much of their time at home and are highly dependent on adult caregivers, most often experience traumatic stressors within the family context (e.g., witnessing partner conflict, experiencing child abuse; Briggs-Gowan, Carter, & Ford, 2012; Briggs-Gowan, Ford, Fraleigh, McCarthy, & Carter, 2010). As children begin to attend school and are spending more time outside of the home and forming relationships with other adult figures (e.g., teachers, coaches), the likelihood increases that they will be exposed to traumatic stressors outside of the family (e.g., community or school violence, serious injury, physical or sexual assault by a nonrelative) (Costello, Erkanli, Fairbank, & Angold, 2002). Adolescents, with increasing independence and freedom to dictate their whereabouts and activities, and their tendency to engage in riskier behaviors, may place themselves in situations in which they are exposed to other types of accidental traumatic stressors or victimization (e.g., accidents in sports or automobiles, sexual assault community violence, witnessing peers' death or severe injury). Adults may be exposed to certain types of traumatic stressors, depending on factors such as their occupations (e.g., military, firefighters, police officers), lifestyle choices (e.g., recreational drug or alcohol use), and family situations (e.g., parent of a child exposed to trauma). In addition, adults are more likely to experience the tragic loss of a loved one or close friend. Moreover, older adults face other life challenges, including increased risk of relational losses and medical illnesses. The rest of this section organizes its discussion of the epidemiology of exposure to traumatic stressor by life stage: early childhood, school-age, adolescence, and adulthood (Figure 4.1).

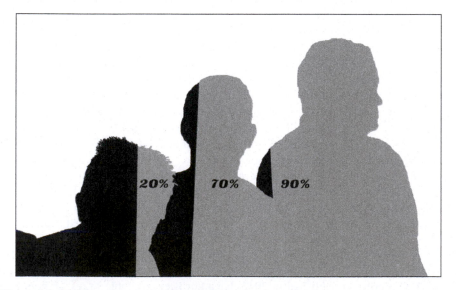

Figure 4.1 Lifetime exposure to a potentially traumatic event.

Traumatic stressor exposure in early childhood

In recent years there has been increased awareness of the occurrence and impact of early childhood trauma exposure by both researchers and clinical practitioners. While epidemiological studies of young children are still few in number compared to studies of adolescents and adults, the prevalence rates are alarming. In a recent examination of the prevalence of trauma exposure in a large study group of 1152 1- to 3-year-old children drawn from the northeastern United States, researchers found that one in six (16.9%) children experienced one or more types of traumatic events (Briggs-Gowan et al., 2010). The types of events experienced included both interpersonal events, involving the intentional act of other persons (e.g., maltreatment, witnessing partner violence), and noninterpersonal events (e.g., serious accident, dog bite). This distinction is important given that interpersonal types of traumatic stressors have a higher conditional probability of negative outcomes (Briggs-Gowan et al., 2010; De Young, Kenardy, & Cobham, 2011), as will be discussed later. Also notable is that the lifetime prevalence of traumatic stressor exposure among these children increased by more than 50% when re-evaluated when they were 1 year older (Briggs-Gowan et al., 2010). Thus, many children who had not experienced traumatic stressors in infancy were newly exposed while they were still toddlers.

Another study examined 36 different types of victimization or interpersonal traumas in a large, nationally representative US sample of 2030 children and adolescents between the ages of 2 and 17 years (Finkelhor, Ormrod, Turner, & Hamby, 2005). By caregiver report, in the youngest subsample of children, ages 2–5 years old, about 47% experienced a physical assault, 1.5% experienced sexual victimization, 18.2% witnessed some form of violence, and 7.5% experienced caregiver perpetrated maltreatment (Finkelhor et al., 2005). Within each broader category there were specific types of events that were more prevalent. For example, physical assault was more often perpetrated by a sibling (70.1% of children who experienced physical assault) as opposed to a peer (26.4%). For sexual victimization, children were more often exposed to sexual content (40%) than were victims of attempted or completed rape (6.7%).

Another source of epidemiological data on exposure to traumatic stressors in early childhood is the National Child Traumatic Stress Network (NCTSN) Core Data Set. The NCTSN is a US federally funded initiative to increase access to services for trauma-exposed children and their families. The sample is comprised of 14,088 youth between the ages of 0 and 21 years old. Because these youth were treatment referred or treatment seeking, they were more likely to have been exposed to traumatic stressors than children in the community general population.

The data were collected using a Trauma History Profile, which included information from multiple sources (e.g., caregiver report, treatment records) about age of exposure to traumatic events. In one analysis of these data, Pynoos et al. (2014) compared children from three different age ranges: 0–5, 6–12, and 13–18 (see Figure 3.2). The types of traumatic stressors that occurred between 0 and 5 years of age were largely characterized by child-directed or child-witnessed violence in the home, including witnessing partner violence (72%) and physical abuse (58.3%), as well as other childhood adversity, including physical neglect (78%), emotional abuse (64%),

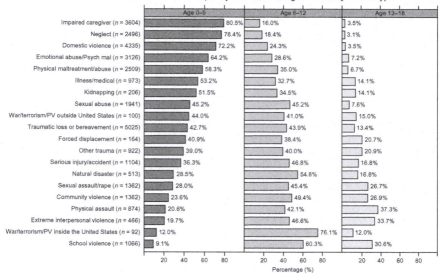

Figure 4.2 Trauma exposure in the NCTSN Core Data Set.

and having an impaired caregiver (80.5%; i.e., alcohol/drug abuse, serious mental illness (SMI)), which often co-occur with traumatic events (Pynoos et al., 2014). Rates of these exposures in the 0- to 5-year-old age range were exponentially greater than rates associated with the 6- to 12-year-old and 13- to 18-year-old age ranges. For example, the rate of witnessing partner violence in the 0- to 5-year-old age range was about three times higher than the rate in the 6- to 12-year-old age range, and about 20 times greater than in the 13- to 18-year-old age range. These findings reflect the complete dependence of young children on their caregivers and their lack of control over their environments. If their caregiver is a perpetrator or victim of violence, young children are a captive audience and/or become another target of violence (Figure 4.2).

Traumatic stressor exposure among school-age children

Compared to younger children, school-age children (6–12 years old) are more likely to be exposed to traumatic stressors outside of the home, including sexual victimization, physical assault, and community or school violence. Within this age range children begin to spend much of their day outside of the home and under the care of other adults—in school, on sports teams, and in other nonfamily activities. This means that there is a higher likelihood that children will be the victim of violence perpetrated by someone outside of the family context, witness violence in the community, or encounter a traumatic experience occurring outside of the home.

In the Finkelhor et al. (2005) survey, school-age children, relative to young children, had a higher rate of exposure to physical assault (57% versus 47%), sexual victimization (5% versus 1.5%), and witnessing community violence (13% versus 7%).

In another study of 536 African American school-age children drawn from an urban population, a high proportion of children were exposed to severe violence outside of the home, including witnessing a shooting (26%), stabbing (30%), or severe beating (78%; Bell & Jenkins, 1993). This study illustrates the higher prevalence of exposure to violence in certain high-risk environments. Indeed, these rates are much higher than the 7.4% of witnessing an assault with a weapon and 7% of witnessing a beating with an injury reported in this age group by Finkelhor et al. (2005).

The Great Smoky Mountain Study (GSMS) was another large epidemiological study involving a randomly selected sample of 1420 children, approximately 49% female, residing in rural North Carolina (Copeland, Keeler, Angold, & Costello, 2007; Costello et al., 2002). Three-month and lifetime trauma exposure and PTSD were assessed. Lifetime trauma exposure among children ages 9–13 years was 54%, and the rate of trauma exposure during the past 3 months was 5%. Rates of exposure among girls and boys were approximately equivalent; however, types of exposures differed, with girls more likely to be exposed to sexual trauma (Copeland et al., 2007).

In the aforementioned NCTSN Core Data Set of clinically referred youth, children in the 6- to 12-year-old age range, relative to the 0- to 5-year-old age range, had higher rates of exposure to various traumatic events occurring outside of the home, including sexual assault (45.4% versus 28%), witnessing community violence (49% versus 23.6%), physical assault (42% versus 20.6%), extreme interpersonal violence (46.6% versus 20%), and school violence 60% versus 9%).

Traumatic stressor exposure in adolescence

Adolescents are a particularly vulnerable group because of their emerging independence, heightened risk-taking behavior, physical body changes, access to potentially dangerous drugs and activities, and increased sexuality. Rates of exposure to a number of traumatic stressor types tend to be at least equivalent to that of school-age children, and in several cases higher.

A larger number of epidemiological studies regarding traumatic stressor exposure have been conducted with adolescents than with younger children. In the 1990s, the National Survey of Adolescents (NSA; Kilpatrick et al., 2003) surveyed 4023 12- to 17-year-old youth with prevalence estimates of 39% for witnessing interpersonal violence, 17% for being a victim of physical assault, and 8% for being a victim of sexual assault. Nearly 20 years later, the National Comorbidity Study Replication Adolescent Supplement (NCSR-A; McLaughlin et al., 2013) surveyed a nationally representative sample of 6483 US adolescents aged 13–17 years, with prevalence estimates of nearly two-thirds of the youths (62%) exposed to at least one traumatic stressor, and one-third (33%) had been exposed to two or more *types* of traumatic stressors. The traumatic stressors most frequently reported were unexpected death of a loved one (28%), manmade/natural disasters (15%), witnessing death/serious injury (12%), learning of a traumatic exposure of a loved one (9%), and life-threatening accidents, being mugged or threatened with a weapon, or witnessing family violence (each 8%). Being kidnapped, physically abused by caregiver, or witnessing domestic violence tended to have the earliest age of onset (i.e., the age at which the traumatic

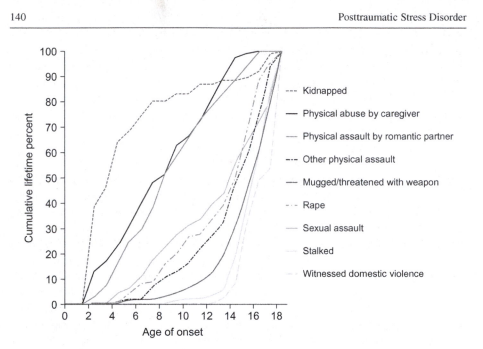

Figure 4.3 Age of first exposure to potentially traumatic experiences (PTEs) involving interpersonal violence in the NCSR-A among adolescents exposed to each PTE ($N = 6483$).

stressor first occurred), while being stalked, mugged, in a life-threatening automobile accident, or victimized by a violent intimate partner tended not to occur until middle adolescence (Figures 4.3 and 4.4).

In the GSMS (Copeland et al., 2007; Costello et al., 2002), researchers found that by the time youths reached the age of 16 years, the majority (>68%) had been exposed to one or more traumatic events in their lifetime. This prevalence estimate is consistent with, but slightly higher than, that for lifetime exposure to one or more traumatic events by adolescents in the NCSR-A (McLaughlin et al., 2013). Across the entire GSMS sample, the most commonly reported trauma was noninterpersonal or nonintentional trauma (33%) involving physical illness, serious accident, natural disaster, or fire, followed by physical violence exposure (25%), either direct or indirect, and sexual trauma (11%). Of exposed youth, more than half (54.6%) had been exposed to two or more trauma types.

Similar to the urban study of school-age children mentioned in the previous section (Bell & Jenkins, 1993), a large study of 2248 adolescents in an urban school system found that 41% had witnessed serious interpersonal violence in the past year that included stabbings and shootings (Schwab-Stone et al., 1995). Once again, this study highlights the high level of prevalence of exposure to victimization trauma in a high-risk population.

In the Finkelhor et al. (2005) survey, several types of victimization were more often reported by adolescents than by younger children. The prevalence of sexual victimization more than tripled from the school-age (5%) to the adolescents (17%).

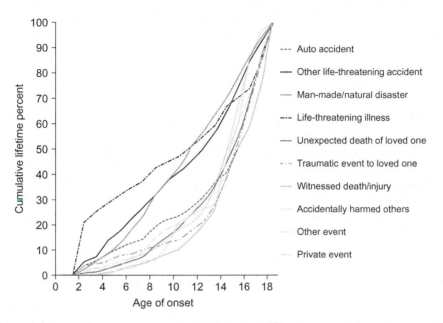

Figure 4.4 Age of first exposure to other PTEs in the NCSR-A among adolescents exposed to each PTE ($N = 6483$).

The prevalence of witnessing physical domestic violence was comparable for school-age and adolescent youths (3% versus 4%), but adolescents were much more likely than school-age children to witness assaults (41% versus 13%) or shootings (9% versus 4%), and to know someone close who was murdered (5.5% versus 1%). About 1% of adolescents actually witnessed a murder. These results reflect the higher risk of exposure to life-threatening violence in adolescence compared to earlier in childhood.

Traumatic stressor exposure in adulthood

Few adults can say that they have never been exposed to a potentially traumatic event. One large epidemiological study conducted in the United States is the 1996 Detroit Area Survey of Trauma, which surveyed 2181 individuals between the ages of 18 and 45 years in the Detroit metropolitan area. The overall lifetime prevalence of trauma exposure was 89.6% (Breslau, 2008). The prevalence of exposure to one or more traumatic events was higher in males than females (92% versus 87%); however, women were more likely to have been exposed to sexual violence (Breslau, 2009). This finding is consistent with results of other epidemiological studies (Kessler et al., 2005; Kessler, Sonnega, Bromet, Hughes, & Nelson, 1995; Resnick, Kilpatrick, Dansky, Saunders, & Best, 1993; Stein, Walker, Hazen, & Forde, 1997). Across all of these studies, the period of 16–25 years old was the time when most traumatic exposures occurred, again highlighting the increased risk of exposure faced during adolescence and into young adulthood. After the age of 20, assaultive violence exposure prevalence declined at every year of age up to 45 years of age (Breslau, 2009).

A more recent epidemiological study of prevalence rates of trauma exposure and PTSD in the Netherlands yielded similar exposure prevalence estimates (de Vries & Olff, 2009). The study included 1087 adults ages 18–80 drawn from the general population of the Netherlands. Lifetime prevalence of exposure to one or more traumatic event(s) was 81%, with tremendous variability in prevalence for different types of traumatic events. Experiencing the sudden death of a loved one was most common (i.e., 54%), followed by injury or disaster (43%), witnessing injury or violence (32%), and physical or sexual assault (27%) (de Vries & Olff, 2009).

Other studies outside of the United States have revealed varied prevalence estimates of traumatic stressor exposure, although all still exceeded 50% with one exception. In Australia, 65% of men and 50% of women reported having experienced at least one traumatic event in their lifetime (Creamer, Burgess, & McFarlane, 2001). Witnessing severe injury or death (38% of men, 16% of women), being in life-threatening accidents (28% of men, 14% of women), and being in a disaster (20% of men, 13% of women) were the most prevalent trauma stressor types. A study in Europe (Belgium, France, Germany, Italy, the Netherlands, Spain; Darves-Bornoz et al., 2008) found that 64% of adults (67% of men, 60.5% of women) reported at least one traumatic event in their lives. The most frequently reported traumatic stressor differed in this European study, compared to the American and Australian studies; it was the unexpected death of a loved one (25% prevalence). However, witnessing severe injury or death (21% prevalence) or being in life-threatening accidents (12–20% prevalence rates) were the second and third most prevalent types of trauma reported, which was consistent with the American and Australian studies.

The one exception in Western nations was a study of adolescents and young adults in another country (Germany), who reported much lower prevalence estimates for females (18%) and males (26%) (Perkonigg, Kessler, Storz, & Wittchen, 2000). Whether that difference is due to characteristics of the country's population, environment, or history (e.g., the intense awareness of the harm caused by traumatic violence in World War II and the Holocaust) is an interesting but unanswerable question. However, in a follow-up assessment after 3–4 years, another 20% of the respondents reported experiencing a new traumatic event (Stein et al., 2002); this incidence estimate was higher than the earlier lifetime prevalence estimate, suggesting that exposure to traumatic stressors was more common than the original prevalence finding indicated. Youth and young adults who had a preexisting anxiety disorder or were using illicit drugs had a 35–200% increased conditional probability of exposure to a traumatic stressor, with the highest conditional probability for exposure to a sexual traumatic stressor (Stein et al., 2002).

Epidemiological studies in developing countries report higher prevalence estimates for exposure to traumatic stressors, consistent with the higher levels of poverty and violence often present in those societies (Norris & Slone, 2007). Adults in Mexico reported 76% prevalence of exposure to violent trauma (83% of men, 71% of women). Adults in Cambodia, Algeria, Ethiopia, and Gaza (de Jong et al., 2003) reported an extremely high prevalence of exposure to traumatic violence, including war violence (59–92%), torture (8–29%), and domestic violence (29–55%), as did Jewish and Arab adults living in Israel during the 2003 Al Aqsa *Intifada* (75% exposure to terrorism or war violence; Tracy, Hobfoll, Canetti-Nisim, & Galea, 2008) and Arab adults living in the Gaza Strip (Thabet, Abu Tawahina, El Sarraj, & Vostanis, 2008). In addition, some areas of the world have very high prevalence estimates of sexual violence against women. Based on 7232 studies conducted in 56 countries of the prevalence of non-partner sexual violence against women (Abrahams et al., 2014), the highest estimates were those from central (21%) and southern (17.4%) sub-Saharan Africa, Australasia (16.4%), and Latin and South America (16.4%; Abrahams et al., 2014).

Traumatic stressor exposure among older adults

Nearly all adults older than 65 have experienced at least one traumatic stressor (Hankin, Spiro, Miller, & Kazis, 1999; Norris, 1992). Older adults have lived longer and thus have had more opportunity to become exposed to traumatic stressors. In addition, historical events and family and gender norms have influenced the prevalence of trauma among older adults. For example, a large proportion of older male adults living in the United States has had military experience and may still be coping with memories of combat experiences. In addition, in a community sample of older women, 72% had been exposed to at least one type of interpersonal violence in their lives, including childhood physical or sexual abuse or physical or sexual assault (Higgins & Follette, 2002). This is a higher prevalence than the approximately 50% estimate that has been found in surveys of younger women's exposure to interpersonal trauma in their lifetime (Iverson et al., 2013). In particular, older women are more likely than younger women to have experienced intimate partner violence during their lifetime and to have remained in a violent relationship for a longer period of time (Vinton & Wilke, 2014).

Poly-victimization

A commonality among all epidemiological studies discussed so far is those who have been exposed to a traumatic stressor are more likely to have been exposed to *more than one type* of traumatic stressor rather than only to a single type. This is in part due to fact that children who are traumatically maltreated or exposed to family or community violence are highly likely to experience other forms of traumatic events and to be re-victimized both in childhood and adulthood (Duckworth & Follette, 2012; Weisel, 2005). For example, adults with histories of childhood sexual abuse are more likely to experience sexual assault in adulthood than adults who were not victimized sexually in childhood (Desai, Arias, Thompson, & Basile, 2002; Noll, Trickett, & Putnam, 2003). In addition, types of interpersonal traumatic stressor exposure tend to co-occur; for example, children who are physically abused often also witness domestic violence. This makes sense, unfortunately, given that a child growing up in a violent household is likely to experience multiple forms of violence. Likewise, individuals living in high-crime neighborhoods are likely to witness and directly experience multiple forms of violence. In addition, individuals exposed to interpersonal violence are more likely than other people to experience noninterpersonal or nonintentional types of traumatic stressors such as life-threatening accidents or traumatic losses.

The relationship between exposure to violence and experiencing traumatic losses is understandable because everyone living in violent families and communities is more likely to die or to be severely harmed than people who live in safer circumstances. It is not known why violence survivors also are at risk for accidental traumatic stressors, but this may be due to multiple other risk factors, including insufficient resources to provide for safety or the unintended adverse effects of PTSD symptoms such as hyper-arousal and defensive coping (which in the *DSM-5* also include a research-documented tendency to act recklessly or carelessly) (Hobfoll, Canetti-Nisim, & Johnson, 2006).

In the previously discussed study by Finkelhor et al. (2005), the term *polyvictimiza-tion* emerged as a reference to individuals exposed to multiple types of violence. In their nationally representative sample, nearly 25% of youths were considered *polyvictims*, the largest portion being male adolescents. Polyvictims were on average four times more likely to be revictimized the following year. Moreover, nearly half of polyvictims based on 1 year's worth of exposure met criteria for polyvictimization in the subsequent year (Finkelhor, Ormrod, & Turner, 2007a, 2007b). These youth, considered to have persistent polyvictimization, were more likely to reside in a family inflicted with violence, experience child maltreatment, be exposed to familial alcohol or drug abuse, and have an impaired caregiver. Polyvictims encounter adversity across multiple contexts of their lives—at home, in their community, at school—such that there is little respite from violence. The onset of polyvictimization was disproportionately likely to occur either in the year prior to turning 7 years old or prior to turning 15 years old, approximate to a youth's entry into elementary and high school, respectively (Finkelhor, Ormrod, & Turner, 2009). As discussed later, polyvictims are at much higher risk of developing deleterious mental health problems, including PTSD and other functional impairments.

Researchers used statistical techniques to examine patterns of traumatic stressor exposure in the NCTSN Core Data Set in order to identify patterns of exposure that constituted polyvictimization in each of the three different age ranges presented earlier: 0–5, 6–12, and 13–18 years old (Grasso, Dierkhising, Branson, Ford, & Lee, submitted). Results revealed a polyvictimization profile in each of the age categories; however, the types of traumatic stressors that constituted polyvictimization varied depending on the age group. Consistent with the preceding research epidemiology results, poly-victimization in early childhood was mainly comprised of adversities experienced in the home and perpetrated by a caregiver. Increasingly complex patterns of traumatic stressor exposure were observed in older age groups, with polyvictimization in the school-age and adolescent age ranges characterized by multiple types of traumatic stressors—as expected, many that occurred outside of the home. Also, new profiles were identified in the 6–12 time period. One profile (15% of the sample) was distin-guished by a higher proportion of girls and by high prevalence estimates of exposure to sexual abuse (>50%) or assault (32%). This finding is consistent with other studies suggesting increased risk for sexual victimization during middle childhood (Trickett, Noll, Reiffman, & Putnam, 2001). Another subgroup that occurred only among school-age and adolescent youths (11%) and not younger children was distinguished by 100% exposure to traumatic loss (including due to deaths or to prolonged separation from a caregiver). The risk conferred by traumatic loss is understudied but potentially highly important (Koenen, Moffitt, Poulton, Martin, & Caspi, 2007; Box 4.2).

Box 4.2 When a Loss Is Traumatic

The death of a loved one or close friend or family member always is emotionally stressful (and often extremely painful), but when this occurs unexpectedly as the result of physical or sexual violence (particularly when this is intentional, such as a murder or assault, but also when it is the result of a natural or humanmade disaster or accident), the shock can be psychologically traumatic. Kaplow et al. (2013) developed a multidimensional grief theory in order to "shed light on adaptive and maladaptive grief responses, theorized causal risk factors, causal consequences, key mediators and moderators, and developmentally linked manifestations of grief is thus needed to guide the field" (p. 326). Three dimensions of distress reactions involved in grief are described: *separation*, *existential/identity alterations*, and *preoccupation with the circumstances of the death*. Each of these domains represents a dimension that extends from normative (expectable) reactions to maladaptive (impairing) distress (Figure 4.5).

Regarding separation distress, when a loved one or close friend, family member, or mentor dies, it is natural to feel sad and a yearning to be reunited with that person. "In contrast, 'maladaptive' manifestations of separation distress may involve persisting suicidal ideation (motivated by a wish to be reunited in an afterlife with the person who died); identifying with unhealthy or dysfunctional elements of the deceased's life, values, habits, or behaviors as a way of feeling close to him/her; and developmental slowing or regression (motivated by desires to stay connected with the deceased by remaining rooted in the same developmental stage, life circumstances, or immature/self-defeating behavior patterns one was in while he or she was still alive)" (Kaplow et al., 2013, p. 327).

The death of key person always involves adjustments that may include major changes in a person's routines, roles, and responsibilities (such as becoming

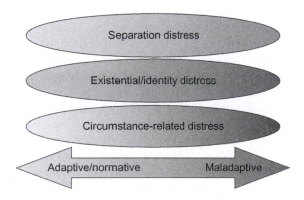
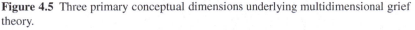

Figure 4.5 Three primary conceptual dimensions underlying multidimensional grief theory.
Reprinted with permission from Kaplow, Layne, Saltzman, Cozza, and Pynoos (2013).

(Continued)

Box 4.2 Continued

a single parent or primary breadwinner when a spouse/partner dies, or coping with the absence of companionship, security, and guidance when a primary adult caregiver, close friend, or mentor dies). "In contrast, maladaptive manifestations of existential/identity distress are theorized to involve a severe and sustained personal existential or identity crisis brought about by the loss. This crisis may be manifest by a perceived loss of personal identity (e.g., 'I feel like a big part of me died with him/her'); nihilism (e.g., 'I've lost what I cared about most, so nothing else matters'); the sense that one's 'real' fate has been thwarted by remaining alive ('I should have died with my buddies, so I shouldn't still be here'); or hopelessness, despair, or resignation in anticipation of a grim future that is blighted by the physical absence of the deceased (e.g., 'Without Mom, I'll always be alone with no one to help me'; no longer investing in personally gratifying relationships or activities" (Kaplow et al., 2013, p. 329).

Reflection on the circumstances of the death of a person with whom one has an emotionally important relationship is expected, and when the circumstances are sudden, unexpected, or involve violence, gruesome physical injury or pain, or a betrayal of trust—many of the features that may make the death a traumatic stressor—peritraumatic shock, distress, and even dissociation are normative reactions as long as they neither substantially impair the individual's functioning (e.g., constituting an acute stress disorder for a period of time between 3 days and 4 weeks after the loss, an episode of major depression if they are severe for at least 2 weeks, or PTSD when the symptoms persist for at least 1 month). Maladaptive circumstance-related distress, on the other hand, involves persistent extreme negative emotions (such as rage, shame, or despair), beliefs (such as guilt, hopelessness, or suicidality), or behaviors (such as reckless self-endangerment, abandonment of important responsibilities, or rejection or isolation from close supportive relationships)—all related to an inability to accept that the circumstances of the death were either unavoidable or understandable despite being extremely regrettable or even tragic.

With a multidimensional theory, grief can be understood as a continuum of reactions that involves a challenge to the individual's ability to carry on in life, after a key person's death, in three core domains: security, identity, and acceptance. The theory points to the importance of assessing all three domains and change over time from the first few days after the loss over the next year or more in order to accurately characterize the impact that loss has on an individual.

For example, assessing the circumstances domain can help to clarify how different people are affected differently by the nature of a death. This has implications for PTSD because it calls into question whether unpredictable or unexpected and violent or accidental circumstances are necessary for the development of PTSD after a loss. This question was posed in a study in which 63 children and 38 adult caregivers who were bereaved due to the death of a parent/partner were interviewed (Kaplow, Howell, & Layne, 2014). Children who lost a caregiver due to a lengthy illness reported higher levels of both maladaptive grief and PTSD symptoms compared to children who lost a caregiver due to sudden natural death (such as a heart attack). Although the cause of death was unrelated to bereaved adult caregivers' maladaptive grief or PTSD symptoms, those bereaved by sudden natural death reported higher levels of depression than those bereaved by prolonged illness. Thus, an anticipated death of a parent that involves prolonged illness may be traumatic for a child but not for an adult partner/spouse, while a sudden unexpected death even in the absence of violence or accident may lead to depression for the adult partner/spouse.

Clearly, much more research is necessary in order to define the different forms and adverse psychosocial consequences of loss. The *DSM-5* includes a proposed (not yet formally accepted) diagnosis of Persistent Complex Bereavement Disorder (PCBD) with criteria that begin simply with an exposure criterion of experiencing "the death of someone with whom he or she had a close relationship" (American Psychiatric Association, 2013, pp. 789–790). Unlike the PTSD traumatic stressor exposure criterion involving loss, neither violence nor an accident is required, only a death. PCBD may include a preoccupation with the deceased person or the circumstances of the death or intense sorrow related to the death (similar to PTSD's intrusive reexperiencing symptoms). But, consistent with multidimensional grief theory, PCBD alternatively may involve a yearning for the deceased (as opposed to PTSD's avoidance symptoms). PCBD also includes symptoms of "reactive distress to the death," which are similar to PTSD's intrusive reexperiencing, persistent negative emotions and beliefs (such as self-blame, difficulty with positive reminiscing, disbelief, and emotional numbness), hyperarousal (such as anger), and avoidance (of reminders of the loss) symptoms. Moreover, PCBD involves social detachment and anhedonia symptoms similar to PTSD's persistent negative emotions and beliefs and confusion about or a diminished sense of one's own identity in the absence of the deceased person (which may be similar to the depersonalization or derealization symptoms in the dissociative subtype of PTSD). In addition to the yearning symptoms, PCBD also includes a symptom of desiring to die in order to join the deceased person, which is distinct from PTSD. The other major difference between the diagnoses is that PCBD requires a minimum of 6 months for children and 12 months for adults of symptoms occurring more days than not, so it is clearly more consistent with a chronic rather than acute or short-term form of PTSD.

On balance, PCBD and PTSD share the vast majority of their symptoms, although PCBD is more explicit and specific in referencing the impact of grieving consistent with the proposed multidimensional theory of grief. Further research is needed to determine if PCBD may provide either a subtype of PTSD associated with traumatic loss or a comorbid disorder that can enable epidemiologists and clinicians to better describe the impact of exposure to traumatic loss.

Epidemiology of PTSD

Criterion A: evidence of trauma exposure

PTSD is unique among other mental health disorders given that it is necessary to identify an environmental stressor—the traumatic event—prior to determining whether a
person meets criteria for clinical symptoms. In order for an event to be identified as
a traumatic stressor in the *DSM*-5 (American Psychiatric Association, 2013), it must
meet one of the following criteria:

> *Exposure to actual or threatened death, serious injury, or sexual violation in one
> (or more) of the following ways:*
> 1. *Directly experiencing the traumatic event(s).*
> 2. *Witnessing, in person, the event(s) as it occurred to others.*
> 3. *Learning that the traumatic event(s) occurred to a close family member or close
>   friend. In cases of actual or threatened death of family member or friend, the
>   event(s) must have been violent or accidental.*
> 4. *Experiencing repeated or extreme exposure to aversive details of the traumatic
>   event(s) (e.g., first responders collecting human remains; police officers
>   repeatedly exposed to details of child abuse).*

These criteria are notably different from the criteria used in the *DSM-IV* (American
Psychiatric Association, 2000):

> *The person has been exposed to a traumatic event in which both of the following
> were present:*
> 1. *The person experienced, witnessed, or was confronted with an event or events
>   that involved actual or threatened death or serious injury, or a threat to the
>   physical integrity of self or others.*
> 2. *The person's response involved intense fear, helplessness, or horror. Note: In
>   children, this may be expressed instead by disorganized or agitated behavior.*

The first noticeable difference is the absence of Criterion A2 in the *DSM*-5.
Although how a person responds during a potentially traumatic stressor or immediately afterward is an important peritraumatic risk factor, assessing a person's
emotional response at the time of the traumatic event by asking the person to recall
his response months or years later ("retrospectively") has proven to be unreliable.
Retrospective report of emotional responses and other psychological phenomena
tend to be weakly correlated with "concurrent" measures of the same phenomenon
(i.e., with the person's self-report or behavior at the actual time of the event) (Henry,
Moffitt, Caspi, Langley, & Silva, 1994). Retrospective recall of emotional state during a traumatic event is particularly complicated given the many complicating factors
(such as peritraumatic stress reactions) that can interfere with accurate memory at the
time or with recall at a later time.

Another difference in these sets of criteria pertains to how PTSD symptoms are
assessed in relation to exposure to traumatic stressors. The *DSM-IV* criteria implied
that symptoms should be assessed in reference to a specific worst event (this is called

the *index traumatic stressor* because the symptoms are "indexed" with reference to that event). Indeed, most PTSD measures based on the *DSM-IV* assessed symptoms based on their association to what the person recalls as the worst past experience they'd had in their life as long as the experience also met the requirements that define what constitutes a traumatic stressor (Naifeh & Elhai, 2010). People often say that the worst experience of their life was an event that was deeply disturbing but not actually life-threatening or a sexual violation (such as a painful divorce or a failure or disappointment in school or work). Those "worst" stressors may have serious adverse effects (such as leading to episodes of severe depression or suicidality), but if they do not threaten someone's life or expose the person to gruesome details of a death or severe injury, the individual is not likely to activate the biological survival reactions (Ford, 2009) that are the core feature of PTSD.

One argument against using a *worst event* method when assessing PTSD is that limiting symptom assessment to one event relies on the assumption that all PTSD symptoms are equally likely to be triggered by any type of traumatic stressor. However, this is not the case, because the conditional probability of PTSD and of specific PTSD symptoms differs, depending upon the specific type of traumatic stressor. Therefore, a person reporting on PTSD symptoms with reference to the impact of a single worst event may only report symptoms characteristic of that event despite also having other PTSD symptoms associated with other types of traumatic stressors that he or she has experienced. Proponents of the worst-event method argue that it captures the majority of PTSD cases (Naifeh & Elhai, 2010), with one study reporting having identified 84% of PTSD diagnoses based on respondents' worst event, while having missed only 16% of cases whose diagnoses hinged on their second or third self-identified event (Breslau, Davis, Peterson, & Schultz, 1997). Those results suggest that epidemiology studies that use the worst-event method will misclassify a small (but not unsubstantial) number—one in six—of actual PTSD cases as not having PTSD. Therefore, the *DSM*-5 criteria for PTSD allow respondents to report PTSD symptoms that are associated with any or all of their past traumatic events. Whether this alternative method of assessing PTSD will alter the prevalence estimates remains to be tested in epidemiological studies now that the *DSM*-5 criteria are the standard.

Finally, another change in criteria involves the exclusion of some of the acceptable events defined in the Criterion A1 of the *DSM-IV*. Specifically, the *DSM*-5 no longer allows unexpected deaths from natural causes to be counted as a traumatic stressor for the family or loved ones of the deceased individual. Whereas in the *DSM-IV* any unexpected death of others was accepted as a traumatic stressor, the *DSM*-5 criteria specify that deaths must *have been violent or accidental*.

Because the *DSM*-5 criteria are very new, little is known about how this change in criteria will affect prevalence rates. One exception is a study by Kilpatrick et al. (2013) that examined the prevalence of PTSD in a national sample of 2953 adults from the United States, using both sets of criteria. When using the *DSM-IV* traumatic stressor exposure criteria, 94% of the sample was identified as having experienced one or more past traumatic stressors, compared to 90% when using the *DSM*-5 criteria. This seemingly small (4%) decrease in the prevalence of past exposure to one or more traumatic stressors could be important both clinically and economically, because with recent estimates of the lifetime prevalence of *DSM-IV* PTSD among adolescents and adults as 10.1% (Kessler, Petukhova, Sampson, Zaslavsky, & Wittchen, 2012), this reduction in traumatic stressor exposure prevalence could lead to a 4% lower PTSD prevalence estimate (based on the likely source of the lower exposure prevalence being the elimination of unexpected natural death as a potentially traumatic event (Kilpatrick et al., 2013) and the conditional probability of PTSD based on such deaths as approximate 10%). Such a change from 10.1% to 9.7% might seem minimal, but in a population of 250 million adolescents and adults in the United States alone, that could translate into a prevalence estimate of one million fewer cases of PTSD.

This section discusses the epidemiology of PTSD, once again organized by key age groups. Many of the *DSM-IV* epidemiological studies discussed in the traumatic stressor exposure serve as the basis for our current understanding of when and for whom PTSD occurs.

PTSD in early childhood

Few studies have explored PTSD in early childhood (<5 years old). PTSD is difficult to assess in this age group because it is entirely based on caregiver report. Young children cannot report symptoms, but, rather, symptoms must be observable by parents. For example, young children cannot describe experiencing intrusive memories of the trauma; however, this may be implied by children's engagement in trauma-related play or trauma reenactments. In fact, some argued that the *DSM-IV* PTSD criteria were not developmentally sensitive enough to detect symptoms in young children, and this led to the development of a modified set of criteria for diagnosing PTSD in infants and young children (Scheeringa, Zeanah & Cohen, 2011). Prevalence studies using *DSM-IV* criteria yielded very low estimates of PTSD prevalence among young children, ranging from 0.0% to 0.1% in community samples (for whom exposure to traumatic stressors was rare), to 0.0% to 1.7% in accident survivors, and as high as 3% to 20% among survivors of domestic violence, abuse, polyvictimization (Levendosky et al., 2004; Meiser-Stedman, Smith, Glucksman, Yule, & Dalgleish, 2008; Scheeringa, Zeanah, & Cohen, 2011; Scheeringa, & Zeanah, 2001). When PTSD was reevaluated using alternative criteria that essentially represented the new standard in the *DSM*-5, the prevalence estimates increased to 0.6% in the community sample, 10–25% among accident victims, and 26–69% among violence survivors and polyvictims (Scheeringa et al., 2011). Thus, PTSD may be no more prevalent among young children generally when the *DSM*-5 revised criteria are utilized but much more prevalent than previously recognized among young children who experience traumatic accidents or violence.

Two additional studies provide evidence consistent with this possibility that PTSD is more common among young children who are exposed to traumatic accidents or violence than previously recognized. A study with 130 Australian children ages 1–6 years of age who were unintentionally burned found that 25% met criteria for PTSD 1 month after the incident, and 10% met criteria for PTSD at 6 months, using the modified criteria for preschool children (De Young, Kenardy, & Cobham, 2011).

Another study found PTSD to be highly prevalent among 232 Israeli children ages 1.5–5 years old living near the Gaza Strip, where they were repeatedly exposed to war-related violence (Feldman & Vengrober, 2011). The prevalence of PTSD among these children was 38%. When further differentiated, 26% of toddlers (≤3 years) were diagnosed with PTSD compared to 44.6% of preschool-age children, which is either suggestive of greater risk of PTSD among older children or greater detection of PTSD among older children.

PTSD in school-age children and adolescents

Surprisingly, fewer studies of PTSD epidemiology have been done with school-age children than with younger children or adolescents. In the GSMS, the prevalence estimate of PTSD for youth ages 9–16 years was 5.6% within the past 3 months, with a lifetime estimate of 31% (Copeland et al., 2007). Higher conditional probabilities (in some cases, >50% for lifetime PTSD) were associated with exposure to violent and sexual traumatic stressors than with noninterpersonal traumatic stressors, such as accidental injuries.

Turning to adolescents, in the NSA in the United States, 5% had experienced PTSD at some point in their lifetime, with 50% more girls (6%) than boys (4%) meeting PTSD criteria (Kilpatrick & Saunders, 1997). Adolescents exposed to violent traumatic stressors involving their families or adult caregivers tended to be polyvictims (i.e., to have experienced between five and seven *types* of traumatic stressors) and had much higher conditional probabilities of meeting criteria for PTSD (31.5% when sexual traumatic stressors were involved; 35% when physical abuse was involved) (Ford, Elhai, Connor, & Frueh, 2010). In comparison, adolescents who were exposed to traumatic violence outside the home also often were polyvictims but had a lower (although still high) conditional probability of PTSD (14%), while those who had experienced only a traumatic accident or had witnessed but not directly been the victim of violence had approximately 5% conditional probability of PTSD.

Similarly, the PSD prevalence estimate in the National Comorbidity Study Adolescent Supplement was 5%, again with females (7%) having a higher conditional probability of PTSD than males (2%) (McLaughlin et al., 2013). Also, the prevalence of PTSD increased with each 2-year increment in age, with the lowest estimates for youth 13–14 years old (4%), followed by 15–16 years old (5%) and 17–18 years old (7%). The conditional probability of PTSD was highest for exposure to traumatic stressors involving interpersonal violence: almost half (41%) of those for whom rape was the worst traumatic stressor met criteria for PTSD, while approximately one-third met criteria for PTSD if the worst traumatic stressor was physical abuse by a primary caregiver or sexual assault (31%), and 9% and 7% met criteria for PTSD with a worst traumatic event of being stalked or domestic violence, respectively. Experiencing a traumatic loss (9%) or automobile accident (7%) were the other traumatic stressors that often led to PTSD (see Box 4.2). Predictors of PTSD among PTE-exposed adolescents included female gender, prior PTE exposure, and preexisting fear and distress disorders. One-third (33.0%) of adolescents with lifetime PTSD continued to meet criteria within 30 days of interview. Poverty, US nativity, bipolar disorder, and PTE exposure occurring after the focal trauma predicted nonrecovery.

Studies outside of the United States found that among 10th--grade students, a much higher (25%) proportion of a South African sample than in a Kenyan sample (5%) met criteria for PTSD (Seedat, Nyamai, Njenga, Vythilingum, & Stein, 2004), while a much lower proportion of 14- to 24-year olds in a German community sample met criteria for PTSD (Perkonigg et al., 2000). The Kenyan estimate matches that from epidemiological studies in the United States. The exact reason for the substantially higher prevalence estimate in the South African sample could not be determined, but youth in that country were still subject to the political and community violence of apartheid, and youth of color were additionally subjected to economic discrimination and poverty. The low estimate from the German study appeared to be due to the low prevalence estimates for traumatic stressor exposure in that study, but when milder forms of PTSD and recent traumatic stressor exposures from a 3- to 4-year follow-up reassessment (more than doubling the prevalence of exposure) were included, the PTSD prevalence estimates were consistent with or higher than those from the US epidemiological studies (5–10%) (Stein et al., 2002).

PTSD among adults

Prevalence estimates of recent or current PTSD among adult samples range from 1% to 5% (Creamer et al., 2001; Darves-Bornoz et al., 2008; Kessler et al., 2005; Perkonigg et al., 2000; Stein et al., 1997). The prevalence of PTSD among adults who report having experienced a traumatic stressor, or the conditional probability, is approximately 20% for women and 10% for men (Breslau et al., 1998; Creamer et al., 2001; Darves-Bornoz et al., 2008; Kessler et al., 1995, 2005). Certain types of traumatic stressors have particularly high conditional probabilities of developing PTSD, including rape (65% of men and 46% of women), childhood sexual or physical abuse, physical assault, combat, and unexpected death of a loved one (30–55%; Kessler et al., 1995). In addition, a European epidemiological study found that the death of a child and being the victim of domestic violence were particularly likely to lead to PTSD and that being kidnapped was the traumatic event that, while extremely rare, most increased the risk of PTSD (i.e., 10-fold; Darves-Bornoz et al., 2008).

Researchers are just beginning to estimate the prevalence of PTSD based on the new *DSM-5* criteria. One study compared prevalence rates based on *DSM-IV* and *DSM-5* criteria in a convenience sample of 185 trauma-exposed adults and found that 50% met criteria based on *DSM-IV* criteria, and 52% met criteria using *DSM-5* criteria (Calhoun et al., 2012). In a study comparing the two sets of criteria, 5% met criteria for past-year PTSD based on *DSM-IV* criteria, and 7% met criteria based on *DSM-5* criteria (Kilpatrick et al., 2013). Using both sets of criteria, PTSD was higher in women than in men (9% versus 5% *DSM-IV*; 7.3% versus 3.2% *DSM-5*). For individuals who met criteria for PTSD based on *DSM-IV* but not *DSM-5*, the biggest contributor was the exclusion of sudden death by natural causes (Kilpatrick et al., 2013).

Finally, a review of several studies compared prevalence estimates of PTSD based on direct exposure to a traumatic event as defined in the *DSM-5* criteria (Santiago et al., 2013). The prevalence of PTSD across all studies was 29% at 1 month and 17% at 12 months. There were notable differences between intentional and nonintentional trauma types, with the median 12-month prevalence of PTSD 23% for intentional trauma and 14% for nonintentional trauma (Santiago et al., 2013). Across the studies reviewed, about 40% of those with PTSD presented with a chronic course, while 35% remitted after 3 months (Santiago et al., 2013).

PTSD among older adults

Older adults are an increasing segment of the population in Western nations and in many developing nations. Most studies of traumatic stressors and PTSD in older adults have been done with military veterans who experienced combat or imprisonment in World War II or the Korean War, civilian survivors of the Holocaust, and older adults who have experienced a disaster such as hurricanes, floods, earthquakes, or terrorist incidents. Study findings include that PTSD in older adults usually is less frequent and intense than found with younger adults exposed to comparable traumatic stressors (O'Donnell & Cook, 2008). Older adults also may experience different symptoms or exhibit differences in coexisting disorders—for example, dissociation appears to be less persistent over time (O'Donnell & Cook, 2008). Studies also have shown that former prisoners of war or Holocaust survivors may have substantial impairments in memory, attention, learning, and executive functioning many decades after they experienced these chronic traumatic stressors (Sutker, Vasterling, Brailey, & Allain, 1995; Yehuda & Flory, 2007).

Although older adults tend to be very resilient in the face of disaster (Ford, Trestman, Wiesbrock, & Zhang, 2007), vulnerabilities of some older adults have been highlighted by studies of survivors of catastrophic events in the United States of the past decade, including Hurricane Katrina and the terrorist attacks of September 11, 2001. For example, frail or disabled older adults may have substantial problems with health and independent living in the wake of traumatic incidents, and older adults were disproportionately likely to die as a result of Hurricane Katrina because a substantial number could not be evacuated from independent living facilities, particularly nursing homes, and those who were housebound quickly became trapped (O'Donnell & Cook, 2008). Similarly, after September 11, 2001, many homebound older adults residing in lower Manhattan were left waiting for up to 7 days to receive health services because they were inaccessible to home health care providers, and their meals or medications were not delivered. Emergency disaster preparedness for these subpopulations of older adults is paramount to future response and recovery endeavors (O'Donnell & Cook, 2008).

Comorbid psychiatric and medical disorders

More than 80% of adults with PTSD meet criteria for at least one other psychiatric diagnosis—approximately 88% of men and 79% of women (Breslau et al., 1998; Creamer et al., 2001; Kessler et al., 1995; Perkonigg et al., 2000). The psychiatric disorders that are most commonly comorbid with PTSD among adults are mood disorders (including major depressive disorder and dysthymic disorder), other anxiety disorders (including panic disorder, agoraphobia, social and specific phobia, generalized anxiety disorder, and OCD), and substance use, somatoform, eating, and dissociative disorders. Almost half (44%) of the women and more than half of the men (59%) in the National Comorbidity Study who were diagnosed with PTSD also met criteria for at least *three* other psychiatric disorders (Kessler et al., 1995). Bipolar and psychotic disorders are less common comorbidities of PTSD but tend to co-occur with PTSD much more often than among adults who do not have PTSD (Boxes 4.3 and 4.4).

Box 4.3 Epidemiology of Psychiatric Disorders Often Comorbid with PTSD

The National Comorbidity Study-Replication (NCS-R; Kessler et al., 2005) provides estimates of the prevalence of psychiatric disorders in the US adult population. Almost half (46%) of respondents had an estimated lifetime history of at least one *DSM-IV* disorder, with 28% of respondents having a lifetime history of two or more disorders and 17% having three or more disorders. The most prevalent disorders were anxiety disorders (29%), followed by impulse-control disorders (25%), mood disorders (21%), and substance use disorders (15%). The most prevalent individual lifetime disorders were major depressive disorder (17%), alcohol abuse (13%), specific phobia (12.5%), and social phobia (12%). The most prevalent disorder was specific phobia (9%), social phobia (7%), and major depressive disorder (7%). Among classes, anxiety disorders are the most prevalent (18%), followed by mood disorders (9.5%), impulse-control disorders (9%), and substance disorders (4%). The 12-month prevalence of any psychiatric disorders is estimated to be 26%, with most of the cases (14% of the total sample) having only one disorder and smaller proportions having two (6%) or more (6%) disorders.

Psychotic disorders affect 1–2% of all adults—primarily schizophrenia (Mueser & McGurk, 2004), schizoaffective disorder (Averill et al., 2004), and acute/transient psychotic disorders (Marneros, Pillman, Haring, Balzuweit, & Bloink, 2003). Schizophrenia is the most disabling psychiatric disorder, accounting for 50% of all inpatient psychiatric admissions and ranking as one of the world's 10 most costly (in disability-adjusted life years) economic and social problems (Mueser & McGurk, 2004). Schizophrenia involves several subtypes and syndromes that differ in the severity of positive, negative, and cognitive impairment symptoms and the corresponding risk of the presence of depression and hostility (Mohr et al., 2004).

Bipolar disorder involves two subtypes—bipolar I (depression and full mania) and bipolar II (depression and hypomania)—which are estimated to affect, respectively, 1% (Kessler, Rubinow, Holmes, Abelson, & Zhao, 1997) and 1–5% (Hadjipavlou, Mok, & Yatham, 2004) of adults at some point in their lifetime, with 0.5–1.5% combined prevalence in the past year (Mitchell, Slade, & Andrews, 2004). Bipolar disorders occur equally for men and women (Kessing, 2004), and more often among adults younger than 45 years old versus older adults (Morgan, Mitchell, & Jablensky, 2005). Most adults with bipolar disorder have recurrent episodes (70%) or a chronic course with no remission (25%)—(0.40 episodes per year, versus 0.20 for major depression; Angst, Gamma, Sellaro, Lavori, & Zhang, 2003)—with prevalent suicidal ideation (>75%), and less functional impairment but more service utilization than schizophrenia (Morgan et al., 2005). Bipolar disorder shows evidence of greater comorbidity overall, and impairment (e.g., suicide attempts, disability days, social isolation), than unipolar major depression (Mitchell et al., 2004). Although not intrinsic to mania or depression and not a negative prognostic factor (Keck et al., 2003), psychosis is present in 10% of first manic episodes in bipolar disorder and is associated bipolar illness severity and recurrence (Ketter, Wang, Becker, Nowakowska, & Yang, 2004). Nearly two in three bipolar II (63%) and 33% of unipolar major depression patients have interepisode mood lability—"frequent up and down fluctuations" (Benazzi, 2004) that are associated with both duration of illness and risk of recurrent episodes in both disorders. Nearly one quarter of the time between bipolar I episodes involves "partial impairment" (Miller, Uebelacker, Keitner, Ryan, & Solomon, 2004). Most adults with bipolar disorder report having had mental health treatment, but less than half report currently being in treatment (Kessler et al., 1997). Thus, providing interepisode treatment (e.g., when symptoms or impairment are sufficiently reduced to permit step-down from partial hospital to outpatient care) may be important in preventing bipolar illness relapse.

Bipolar disorder also may occur in children and adolescents, with children who are maltreated being at particularly high risk for bipolar disorder as well as comorbid borderline personality disorder (Dvir, Ford, Hill, & Frazier, 2014). Although there have been no published studies systematically examining the association between childhood exposure to traumatic stressors and childhood onset bipolar disorder, a history of exposure to traumatic stressors is reported in about half of adult patients with bipolar disorder (Dvir et al., 2014). Adults with bipolar disorder and a history of childhood exposure to interpersonal traumatic stressors also have a higher severity level of bipolar symptoms than other adults with bipolar disorder. A study with a clinical sample of children and adolescents found those with bipolar disorder to be more likely to have comorbid PTSD than those with disruptive behavior and negative mood dysregulation disorders such as attention deficit hyperactivity disorder and unipolar depression.

Unipolar major depression is prevalent (i.e., 16% lifetime; 7% past year; Kessler et al., 2003), undertreated (i.e., 52% of past-year cases report receiving treatment, but only 22% received adequate treatment; Kessler et al., 2003), and associated with substantial interpersonal and vocational burden (i.e., on average 4 hours of lost productive time per week; Stewart, Ricci, Chee, Hahn, & Morganstein, 2003). Although genetics and family history influence the etiology of depression (Hudson et al., 2003; Kendler, Karkowski, & Prescott, 1999), exposure to stressors may precede and precipitate episodes of depression in children (Kaufman and Charney, 2001) and adults (Ehlert, Gaab, & Heinrichs, 2001). An interaction of genetic vulnerability (i.e., a short allele of the serotonin transporter gene) and stressful life events recently was reported to be associated with the risk of depression and suicidality (Caspi et al., 2003). Depressed persons also may differentially select or be exposed to traumatic events (Kendler et al., 1999), including accidents (Guastello, Gershon, & Murphy, 1999), domestic violence (Riggs, Caulfield, &

(*Continued*)

Box 4.3 Continued

Street, 2000), and assault (Whitbeck, Hoyt, & Yoder, 1999). "Dysfunctional" beliefs and coping styles (e.g., hopelessness, avoidance; Brown & Beck, 2002) are characteristic of persons with depression, similar to beliefs and coping associated with PTSD (Amir et al., 1997; Foa, Ehlers, Clark, Tolin, & Orsillo, 1999).

OCD, although relatively rare (0.6–1.3% 12-month prevalence, 0.7–2.5% lifetime; Crino, Slade, & Andrews, 2005), is associated with high levels of functional impairment (ranked 20th among all causes of disability-adjusted life years lost among developed countries; Crino et al., 2005), has a recurrent course with infrequent full recovery (Eddy, Dutra, Bradley, & Westen, 2004), and tends to be resistant to medication and psychotherapy treatment (despite promising results in specific behavioral and pharmacotherapy modalities; Eddy et al., 2004). When diagnosed with stringent *DSM-IV* criteria, OCD's severity and chronicity are similar to that of psychotic and affective SMIs (Crino et al., 2005).

Substance use disorders often co-occur with bipolar and unipolar depression and with psychotic disorders, substantially increasing the severity of psychiatric symptoms and the social and vocational/educational impairment (Compton, Thomas, Stinson, & Grant, 2007; Hasin, Stinson, Ogburn, & Grant, 2007; McMillan, Enns, Cox, & Sareen, 2009). The National Epidemiologic Survey on Alcohol and Related Conditions surveyed more than 43,000 US adults (ages 18 years and older) and determined that most mood and anxiety disorders are not directly caused by substance use disorders but that substance use disorders and independent mood and anxiety disorders were highly comorbid (Grant, Stinson, Dawson, Chou, Dufour, et al., 2004). A cross-national epidemiological study in the United States and South Korea found comparable patterns of comorbidity such that the prevalence estimates of mood and anxiety disorders were consistently the highest among persons with alcohol dependence (Chou et al., 2012). Personality disorders also were found in the US study to be prevalent among adults with a current alcohol use disorder (28.6%) or a current drug use disorder (48%) (Grant et al., 2004). One in six (16.4%) adults with at least one personality disorder had a current alcohol use disorder, and 6.5% had a current drug use disorder. Alcohol use disorders were most strongly related to antisocial (odds ratio (OR), 4.8; 95% CI, 4.1–5.6), histrionic (OR, 4.7; 95% CI, 3.8–5.8), and dependent (OR, 3.0; 95% CI, 1.9–4.8) personality disorders—that is, individuals with alcohol use disorders were between three and five times more likely than adults with no such disorder to have each of those personality disorders. Drug use disorders were even more highly associated with antisocial (OR, 11.8; 95% CI, 9.7–14.3), histrionic (OR, 8.0; 95% CI, 6.0–10.7), and dependent (OR, 11.6; 95% CI, 7.1–19.1) personality disorders. Women with alcohol or drug abuse disorders were more likely than men to also have obsessive-compulsive, histrionic, schizoid, and antisocial personality disorders. Men with alcohol or drug abuse disorders were more likely than women to have dependent personality disorders. Thus, alcohol and other substance use disorders often occur comorbidly with most psychiatric disorders, with some gender differences that may require differential approaches to clinical assessment and treatment.

Box 4.4 Psychological Trauma and PTSD Among Persons with SMI

Adults with chronic and severe mood disorders (such as major depression or bipolar disorder), anxiety disorders (such as obsessive-compulsive, panic, or generalized anxiety disorder), psychotic disorders (such as schizophrenia or schizoaffective disorder), dissociative disorders, eating disorders (such as anorexia or bulimia nervosa), or personality disorders (such as borderline or paranoid personality disorder) are more likely (Ford, 2012; Ford & Courtois, 2014; Ford & Gómez, 2015; Golier et al., 2003; Mueser, Essock, Haines, Wolfe, & Xie, 2004; Sells, Rowe, Fisk, & Davidson, 2003) than adults in community samples (Kessler et al., 1995) to report: (i) a history of exposure to psychological trauma (with estimated prevalence of 61–98% versus 50–60%), (ii) particularly to childhood abuse (32–53% versus 10–20%), and (iii) violent victimization as a child or adult (43–81% versus 20–25%).

Although most persons with psychiatric disorders who have experienced trauma do not develop PTSD (similar to findings from community samples, Kessler et al., 1995), comorbid PTSD is more commonly detected by structured assessment among persons with psychiatric disorders than in community samples, both in the past (i.e., 14–66% versus 5–10%) and currently (i.e., 12–35% versus 1–2%) (Mueser, Essock, et al., 2004; Mueser et al., 2001). Adults with psychiatric disorders report substantial recent exposure to victimization traumas (such as abuse or domestic violence; Goodman et al., 2001; Neria, Bromet, Sievers, Lavelle, & Fochtmann, 2002; Sells et al., 2003), but the most common time of first victimization is in childhood (Neria et al., 2002). Not only is PTSD is prevalent among adults with SMI, but it also is associated with more severe symptoms of those disorders and worse impairment in relationships and work than is found when adults with psychiatric disorders do not also have PTSD (Mueser et al., 2004).

Adults with SMI report substantial recent exposure to victimization traumas (such as abuse or domestic violence; Goodman et al., 2001; Neria et al., 2002; Sells et al., 2003), but the most common time of first victimization is in childhood (Neria et al., 2002). Consistent with the extensive scientific evidence that exposure to traumatic stressors that disrupt development in early childhood is associated with severe and often lifelong psychiatric symptoms and impairment, patients with SMI who are abuse survivors often report hallucinations, paranoia, mania, depression, severe anxiety, suicidality, hostility, interpersonal sensitivity, sociovocational impairment, somatization, and dissociation (Goodman et al., 2001; Leverich et al., 2002; Lysaker, Meyer, Evans, Clements, & Marks, 2001; Lysaker, Nees, Lancaster, & Davis, 2004).

PTSD also often is accompanied by comorbid medical illness, especially chronic PTSD and increasingly as adults grow older and medical illnesses become more prevalent generally (Schnurr & Green, 2004). Adults with PTSD have been found to have 50–150% higher rates for many chronic diseases, including circulatory, nervous system, digestive, musculoskeletal, and respiratory diseases (Boscarino, 2008). Gynecological illnesses and endocrinological conditions (such as chronic fatigue syndrome and fibromyalgia) also have been found to be associated with exposure to traumatic stressors and PTSD (Schnurr & Green, 2004). Boscarino (2008) conducted a unique prospective study showing that male military veterans who developed PTSD 15–20 years following military service during the Vietnam War were twice as likely as other veterans to develop cardiovascular disease and 20% more likely to die as a result of cardiovascular disease during a 15-year follow-up period (i.e., when they were between mid-30s and mid-50s in age) as those without PTSD. Veterans with PTSD were more likely to be smokers and to be clinically depressed, but neither of these factors was as strongly associated with cardiovascular disease and death as PTSD. PTSD also has been found to increase the risk of military veterans developing multisystemic disorders that may be primarily due to toxic exposure in war zones, such as "Gulf War syndrome" (Box 4.5). Thus, PTSD may serve as a risk factor or a vulnerability factor, or both, for serious medical as well as psychiatric illness.

Box 4.5 Military PTSD: Comorbidity with "Gulf War Syndrome" and Traumatic Brain Injury

Neurotoxin exposure, PTSD, and the Persian Gulf War syndrome

An unexpectedly high prevalence of medical and psychiatric conditions of uncertain etiology and diagnosis was reported among the 693,826 military personnel who served in the Persian Gulf War between August 1990 and July 1991. Approximately 15,000 Operation Desert Storm military personnel who served in the Persian Gulf were found by US Department of Veterans Affairs physicians to exhibit persistent but diagnostically unexplained physical symptoms with onset in or after Persian Gulf military service, as were approximately 13,000 veterans evaluated by the Department of Defense Comprehensive Clinical Evaluation Program.

Compared to military personnel who were on active duty during the Persian Gulf War but were not stationed in the war zone, Persian Gulf War veterans show a significantly higher prevalence of symptoms of physical illness (including chronic fatigue, bronchitis, asthma), cognitive impairment, and psychological distress (including depression, anxiety), as well as poorer overall health and greater health-related physical and psychosocial functional impairment.

At least one in seven, and perhaps as many as one in three, Persian Gulf War veterans have been found to suffer from these diverse and persistent medical and psychiatric symptoms. Clinical examinations often revealed complex wide ranging complaints, suggesting that psychological as well as biological factors warrant investigation in order to better understand the nature and etiology of unexplained health problems and to identify veterans at risk.

Exposure to neurotoxicants in the Persian Gulf has been linked to Persian Gulf War veterans' medical problems. Psychological stressors and disorders, including war zone trauma and PTSD, also were implicated as potential contributory factors in Gulf War veterans' unexplained illnesses, although these factors do not appear to entirely account for the reported physical health problems. Haley et al. attributed neurotoxic causation to the psychological aspects of this so-called "Gulf War syndrome," concluding that, due to problems of measurement error, the prevalence of PTSD is effectively nil among Gulf War veterans. However, studies assessing PTSD using validated questionnaires reported current PTSD prevalence estimates of 2–17% among Persian Gulf military veterans. A distinct adverse trajectory of high and progressively increasing PTSD symptoms was identified as characterizing a subgroup of combat-exposed Gulf War military veterans (Orcutt, Erickson, & Wolfe, 2004). The prevalence estimates reported in these studies are comparable to or greater than levels reported for current PTSD and lifetime PTSD in epidemiologic studies of US adults. In samples of male World War II and Korean military veterans and Dutch resistance fighters, and of midlife Vietnam-era male and female military veterans, a PTSD diagnosis or PTSD symptom severity (PTSS) were consistently correlated with the severity of military veterans' self-reported health problems.

Thus, it seemed premature to rule exposure to traumatic stressors or PTSD either in or out as a contributor to the health problems of Gulf War veterans. One possibility is that PTSS rather than the full diagnostic syndrome of PTSD may influence physical health problems. PTSS has been shown to be associated with substantial psychosocial impairment even in the absence of full PTSD. Therefore, a study was conducted to determine if Persian Gulf War military veterans' medically documented but unexplained symptoms were associated with PTSS, independent of other potential correlates of physical health problems, including education level, age, substance abuse, stressful events, psychiatric symptoms, self-reported health, energy/fatigue, pain, and bodily problems, and health-related impairment in work and relationships.

The study (Ford et al., 2001) involved medical and psychological examination of 1119 of 2022 randomly sampled US Persian Gulf War veterans who were screened by the investigators. Of these respondents, 237 Gulf War syndrome cases and 113 controls (veterans who did not report medically unexplained health problems) were identified by medical examination. The study therefore was a case-control study comparing Persian Gulf War military veterans with or without medically unexplained symptoms ("Gulf War syndrome"). Statistical analyses were conducted with half of the sample and then repeated with the other half as a "cross-validation" in order to determine whether PTSS and other potential factors in health problems were more common among veterans with medically unexplained health problems.

(Continued)

Box 4.5 Continued

The study findings were that PTSS and somatic complaints were independently associated with case status, as were (although less consistently) war zone traumatic stressor exposure and depression. Age, education, and self-reported health, stress-related preoccupation with bodily problems, pain, energy/fatigue, illness-related functional impairment, recent life stressors, and anxiety were associated with having a diagnosed Gulf War syndrome, but were not risk factors when PTSS, somatic complaints, depression, and war trauma exposure were accounted for statistically. Thus, the study's findings showed that PTSD symptoms related to war zone traumatic stressor exposure were a potential contributor to the often debilitating physical health problems experienced by Persian Gulf War veterans diagnosed with the Gulf War syndrome.

Afghanistan and Iraq military operations 2002–2015: PTSD and blast injuries
A decade following the Gulf War, military personnel from many countries, including millions of American personnel, were deployed to Afghanistan and Iraq in the aftermath of the September 11, 2001, terrorist incidents in the United States. Pugh et al. (2014) reported an epidemiological study with almost 192,000 US military veterans who received health care from the Department of Veterans Affairs in 2007–2010 following deployment to Afghanistan or Iraq in Operations Enduring and Iraqi Freedom or Operation New Dawn. They described a "polytrauma clinical triad" (PCT) that consists of traumatic brain injury (TBI), PTSD, and used the latent class statistical methodology to determine how well this profile fit the symptoms and disabilities reported in the clinical records of these veterans' treatment. They found that actually the patterns of comorbidity were more complex than a single triad of problems, with six identifiable subgroups of health care problems:

1. Cluster 1: PCT and chronic medical illness (5%);
2. Cluster 2: PCT alone (9%);
3. Cluster 3: mental health and substance abuse disorders other than PTSD, TBI or chronic physical pain (24%);
4. Cluster 4: Sleep problems and chronic illness following amputation of limb(s) (4%);
5. Cluster 5: moderate to severe PTSD alone (6%);
6. Cluster 6: relatively healthy individuals (53%).

As expected, health care utilization was highest in veterans with chronic severe medical and stress-related problems (Clusters 1, 2, and 4), and also substantially higher in veterans with co-occurring mental health and substance use disorders or PTSD (Clusters 3 and 5) compared to the healthy majority of patients. Combat and blast exposure were likely to have preceded the development of the comorbidities associated with the highest utilization subgroups, and exposure to combat or other adverse events were associated with the PTSD-only cluster.

Thus, while PTSD was prevalent (affecting an estimated 20% of the patients, in Clusters 1, 2, and 4), it typically occurred comorbidly with TBI (following blast injuries) and physical pain rather than in isolation. In about one-third of the complex comorbidity PCT cases, chronic medical illnesses also had developed (similar in prevalence, although not in form, to the Gulf War syndromes). However, PTSD did occur for 6% of these postdeployment military veterans, suggesting that programs for screening for PTSD and evidence-based treatment of PTSD are necessary in the primary medical care of postdeployment military veterans in order to identify those who may be free of brain injury, pain, or medical illnesses but still impaired as the result of persistent traumatic stress reactions related to hazardous military service. For the PCT veterans, this study clearly points out the crucial need for assessment and treatment services that assist them in dealing with complex physical health problems while also providing treatment for the common comorbidity of PTSD.

PTSD substantially interferes with adults' work performance and attendance, as much as the often debilitating condition of major depression—although slightly less than panic disorder, which is a major source of disability but less costly overall due to being less prevalent than PTSD or depression (Brunello et al., 2001). PTSD also increases the risk of numerous serious vocational, educational, and interpersonal problems, including unemployment (150% increase), marital instability (60% increase), high school or college failure (40% increase), and becoming a teenage parent (30% increase) (Brunello et al., 2001).

Gender and the epidemiology of PTSD

As briefly discussed earlier, girls and women who experience traumatic stressors consistently report a larger number of and more severe PTSD symptoms (as well as other types of distress, such as symptoms of other anxiety disorders, dissociative disorders, depression, and eating disorders) than comparably trauma-exposed boys or men (Tolin & Foa, 2006). However, the accuracy of this finding and whether it reflects a true gender difference is controversial.

Men and boys are more likely to report having experienced a traumatic stressor than women and girls, as has been described earlier in this chapter in the review of PTSD epidemiological studies. Men and boys are more likely than women and girls to report having experienced physical assault, community and political violence, automobile accidents, combat exposure, and being threatened with a weapon or taken prisoner. Women and girls are more likely than men or boys to report experiencing rape and childhood sexual or physical abuse.

Despite the greater likelihood of men to report exposure to a traumatic stressor, the likelihood of PTSD is consistently *double* for women or girls than for men or boys. (For an exception, however, see Box 4.6, section on Youth in the Juvenile Justice System.) The severity of risk and vulnerability involved in the traumatic events to

Box 4.6 Exposure to Traumatic Stressors and PTSD in the Justice Systems

Involvement in the criminal or juvenile justice systems faces adults or youths with many potentially traumatic stressors, particularly when they are incarcerated. However, even before they become involved with law enforcement or confined to jail, detention, or prison, these adults and youth are likely to have experienced traumatic stressors and more likely than their peers to be suffering from PTSD (typically without the condition being recognized or treated).

Incarcerated adults
An estimated two million adults (http://www.ojp.usdoj.gov/bjs/whtsnw2.htm) are incarcerated in the United States, and an estimated 16% of state prison inmates, 7% of federal inmates, and 16% of jail prisoners suffer from a psychiatric disorder (Ditton, 1999). More precise epidemiological research estimates of current and lifetime prevalence of psychiatric disorders among men (Teplin, 1990; Teplin, Abram, & McClelland, 1994; Trestman, Ford, Zhang, & Wiesbrock, 2007) and women (Jordan, Schlenger, Fairbank, & Cadell, 1996; Teplin, Abram, & McClelland, 1996) in jail or prison indicate that psychiatric disorders are substantially more prevalent among incarcerated adults than in community studies. Most incarcerated adults with psychiatric disorders have comorbid substance use disorders (Abram, Teplin, & McClelland, 2003), yet fewer than 25% receive any (Teplin, Abram, & McClelland, 1997) or adequate treatment (Jordan et al., 2002). Brief psychiatric screening measures therefore have been developed for incarcerated adults (Boothby & Durham, 1999; Ford et al., 2007; Steadman, Scott, Osher, Agnese, & Robbins, 2005; Teplin & Swartz, 1989). However, no brief mental health screening measures as yet has been evaluated for the detection of incarcerated adults with PTSD.

Despite the many risk factors for exposure to violence and other traumatic stressors faced by incarcerated adults, PTSD has only recently been studied in adult correctional populations. A study of a representative sample of newly incarcerated adults who had not been identified as having any psychiatric disorder found that 12% met criteria for current PTSD and 29% for lifetime PTSD (Trestman et al., 2007), with women having double the risk of men, comparable to findings from studies of pretrial female jail detainees (Teplin et al., 1996) and newly incarcerated female felons (Jordan et al., 1996). Goff, Rose, Rose, and Purves (2007) identified four studies of adults incarcerated in prison from four countries (Australia, Canada, New Zealand, the United States) that estimated the current prevalence of PTSD to be between 4% and 21% for men and between 10% and 21% for mixed gender samples. These current PTSD prevalence estimates, while varying in their definition of timing (e.g., past month, 6 months, or year), consistently exceed the 2% (Stein et al., 1997) to 2.8% (Kessler et al., 1995) estimates for current PTSD prevalence in the community. Further evidence of the potential importance of identifying PTSD among incarcerated adults comes from studies showing that approximately 90% of youths detained in juvenile justice system report exposure to psychological trauma (Abram et al., 2004; Ford, Hartman, Hawke, & Chapman, 2008), as well as that more than 10% meet criteria for current PTSD (Abram et al., 2004) and 25–50% meet criteria for lifetime PTSD (Abram et al., 2004; Arroyo, 2001; Cauffman, Feldman, Waterman, & Steiner, 1998).

Youth involved in the juvenile justice system

The estimates of the prevalence of PTSD among youth in the juvenile justice population vary widely, and these variations are attributable to the lack of standardized instruments used across studies and differences in study methodologies (Ford, Chapman, Hawke, & Albert, 2007). Despite these variations, evidence suggests that most youth involved with the juvenile justice system have experienced traumatic events and a disproportionate number suffer from PTSD. Selected studies conducted among youth involved in the juvenile justice system have found that:

- More than one in three youth incarcerated by the California Youth Authority met full criteria for PTSD and 20% met partial criteria for PTSD.
- The incidence of PTSD among youth in the juvenile justice system is similar to youth in the mental health and substance abuse systems, but up to eight times higher than comparably aged youth in the general, community population.
- The prevalence of PTSD is higher among incarcerated female delinquents (49%) than among incarcerated male delinquents (32%), and both estimates are *6–40 times higher* than the estimated prevalence of PTSD (including those with the full diagnosis of PTSD and those who do not meet criteria for PTSD but have significant symptoms) among youths in the community (Copeland et al., 2007).

While the prevalence of PTSD is high, the prevalence of self-reported exposure to traumatic experiences is even higher—as high as 93% in juvenile detention centers. A number of sources note that traumatic experience symptoms are higher among girls than boys in the juvenile justice system. Additionally, different types of traumatic experiences are reported by boys and girls, with girls more likely than boys to report sexual abuse and physical punishment. While boys in the juvenile justice system more often report witnessing violence, girls involved in juvenile justice more often report experiencing violence (including sexual assault and abuse).

African American and Latino/Hispanic youth are disproportionately placed in the juvenile justice system, but they tend to report that they are not more likely to have been previously exposed to traumatic stressors than white youth. Among boys in a representative sample from a large urban juvenile detention facility, white youth were more likely than African American youths to report having been physically assaulted or severely beaten (58% versus 32%), with 44% of Hispanic boys reporting violence exposure. Whether these are accurate estimates or biased by the reluctance of ethnoracial minority youth to report traumatic exposure is not known.

(Continued)

Box 4.6 Continued

Traumatized adolescents typically do not lack a sense of self or values but are often too anxious, angry, or confused to rely upon these important psychological resources because they are struggling with a sense of being in constant danger. Although most youth who experience psychological trauma recover healthy functioning, as many as half of the youth in the juvenile justice system experience chronic health and psychological impairments related to traumatic stress reactions and PTSD. These youth face not only traumatic stressors but many causal risk and vulnerability factors, often without the protection of positive social support and a sense of self-efficacy, and therefore are particularly at risk to develop PTSD (Feierman & Ford, 2015). In particular, traumatic stressors that involve interpersonal violence (victimization) is more likely than other forms of trauma to lead to impairment in psychosocial functioning and physical. Although not every delinquent youth has experienced traumatic victimization, clinical and epidemiological studies indicate that at least *three in four youths in the juvenile justice system* have been exposed to potentially traumatic victimization.

Ford and Blaustein (2013) outline a systemic approach to creating trauma-informed juvenile justice services. The pathways from psychological trauma exposure to confinement in juvenile justice residential facilities are multidetermined. Two key factors are crucial to understanding how traumatic stress can contribute to youths' offending and recidivism. These are an unstated code of behavior—often a "survival code"—that differs from the established rules of majority society, and the impact of traumatic stress on emotional, physiological, and behavioral factors that place youth at increased risk of committing offenses. The experience of traumatic victimization, in many ways, violates the "social contract" that lies at the heart of societal laws and structures: the contract that suggests that good deeds and behavior are rewarded, that perpetrating harm should and will be punished, and that maintaining order is mutually beneficial. For youth who have experienced repeated violence and violation in their homes and communities, often in the absence of societal response, this is a direct, immediate life experience that violates this implicit social contract. It is little wonder, then, that multiply psychologically traumatized youth may apply different standards in decision making and in action. For these youth, the rubric of *survival* ("What will get my needs met?") is likely to trump *legality* ("Is this behavior appropriate within the laws of our society?").

In addition to shifting social paradigms and violating the social contract of fairness and justice, psychological trauma—particularly when chronic and experienced early in life—has a core impact on regulatory processes, or the capacity to effectively manage behavior, emotions, body sensations, and interpersonal relationships (Ford, 2005). As a result, youth who have experienced multiple forms of developmentally adverse interpersonal trauma are at risk for substance use, violent or impulsive behaviors, vulnerability to negative social influence, and high-risk activities (Finkelhor et al., 2007a, 2007b; Ford, Elhai, et al., 2010).

These factors both coincide with the presence of diagnosable mental health conditions, and leave youth vulnerable to engaging in criminal activity. In prospective studies of youth examining factors increasing risk for committing crime in young adulthood, childhood psychiatric disorder—even excluding conduct disorder—substantially increases the likelihood of later involvement with the criminal justice system (Copeland et al., 2007). Even as compared with youth with other significant psychiatric disturbances, those with PTSD are at higher risk of demonstrating delinquent behavior and of risks such as running away from home (Mueser & Taub, 2008).

These two factors—the altered social paradigm and the dysregulation of core self-capacities—influence not just the behaviors leading to detention and adjudication of youth but also to their behaviors and experiences while in care, along with a parallel influence on staff and programs. Consider, for instance, the influence of these factors on a detained adolescent living in close quarters with a member of a rival gang, who has nonetheless been advised by staff of the importance of following programmatic rules. It is not difficult to appreciate that, for this adolescent, "street rules"—those that have previously dictated survival—will at times trump program rules. Imagine a situation in which the adolescent perceives some threat signal from his historical rival—a direct stare, a hand gesture. In the lives of these youth, threat signals are often subtle yet significant, and survival has been predicated on early detection of and strong response to these cues. In the face of this perceived danger, the adolescent enters "survival mode" ("If I am to survive, I must react to this threat"), triggering a cascade of physiological arousal and behavioral responses that are biologically driven and experientially reinforced.

Witnessing his increased agitation and aggressive posturing, a staff member—whose own mandate includes maintaining order and safety—approaches the adolescent, ordering the youth to calm down. The adolescent perceives the staff member as an increased threat and escalates. The staff member—who now similarly perceives threat—also enters survival mode, leading to increased arousal and diffuse distress, decreased awareness of adaptive alternatives, and limited inhibition of survival-based behavioral responses. As the staff member enters further into the adolescent's space, in an effort to gain psychological and behavioral control, both staff and youth experience the other's presence as a danger, leading to heightened arousal and efforts at self-empowerment. Ultimately, the ensuing crisis will reinforce for each the importance of his or her own set of rules: for the adolescent, the importance of maintaining vigilance and survival at all costs, and for the staff member, the importance of exerting control and authority.

As illustrated by this example, juvenile justice facility staff recurrently interact with detained youth around the issue of how to balance self-interest with respect for other persons, individually and collectively. When staff or administrators adopt a stance of requiring that youths behave the way they (the adults) require without any meaningful validation of youths' preferences or best interests, this can

(Continued)

Box 4.6 Continued

communicate a message and model that "people who have authority and power can make other people do whatever they want," and "people who do not have authority or power have no say," and "it doesn't matter what people feel or think, only the rules are important." If a class teaches that it is important to take other people's perspectives seriously (i.e., empathy), or a twice-weekly group emphasizes that youths should express themselves honestly and be open to feedback about ways in which they can improve themselves, these rehabilitative/therapeutic approaches to responsible community participation and self-improvement may be inadvertently contradicted by the example set and messages sent by the day-to-day behavior of the adult role models in the detention milieu. This discrepancy could introduce "cognitive dissonance" interfering with adoption of new learning, as well as the perception of threat and loss of control, which tends to elicit emotional distress in youths who already are affectively volatile as a result of both being in the adolescent stage of development and typically experiencing many life stressors (e.g., past or current family or peer group rejection of conflict, school, and financial pressures).

This dilemma—a divergence between what adults do versus what they say (and hold youths accountable for)—is understandable in light of the often incompatible and contradictory requirements that working in a detention facility places on staff and administrators. On the one hand, detention staff are required to ensure safety and prevent harm from occurring to detained youth, other staff, and the general public—with groups of youths who often behave unsafely and are capable of causing substantial harm to one another and to staff and community members. On the other hand, they typically hope that the detained youths they supervise will do better in their lives, and see and appreciate the good qualities and strengths in these youths that all too often have gone unrecognized or not been supported by other adults in the youths' lives. Thus, there can appear to be an imperative need to impose control on the youths' lives so that they will learn how to be more responsible by obeying the rules and directives of people and a justice system that is better able to "know what's best for them" than what the youths know for themselves.

If the dilemmas faced by trauma-impacted youth and by vicariously and directly traumatized program staff and milieus are viewed as the result of a dysregulation of core self-regulatory competences, then enhancement of self-regulation can provide a focus for trauma-informed juvenile justice residential services at all levels. Self-regulation is acquired through social learning—that is, by modeling (observational learning) and reinforcement (consequences that enhance the motivational value of behavior) from key persons in youths' support systems. Specific educational or mental health services (e.g., groups, classes, counseling, therapy) can provide youths with preparation and guidance for self-regulation (e.g., teaching basic concepts or skills, coaching to facilitate practice and application of skills, enhancing motivation and trust, medications that reduce affective, cognitive, or biological instability). However, the primary source of social learning for youth in detention is the example set by adult staff and the milieu, which in turn substantially sets the tone for a second critical influence: peer role modeling.

Staff in juvenile justice facilities either acquire, or fail to develop, job-relevant self-regulatory capacities through similar mechanisms. The actions of supervisors and administrators, and the formal and informal performance expectations and evaluation processes, and policies and procedures, in place in juvenile justice residential facilities provide powerful sources of modeling and reinforcement for staff as they respond to work stressors and challenges. When these sources consistently set an example that encourages self-regulation (e.g., modeling mindful responses to stressful events, providing meaningful recognition of staff when they manage challenges in a self-regulated manner), they increase staff capacity to manage the at-times dysregulating nature of the juvenile justice environment. Specific educational practices (psychoeducation, supervision, and skills development) can increase staff capacity to apply concrete skills including self-regulatory coping strategies along with youth support, coaching, and deescalation strategies.

A self-regulation framework for correction and rehabilitation of detained juveniles is compatible with two contemporary criminal justice philosophies that have evolved as credible alternatives to the punitive retribution or viral quarantine (i.e., confinement as a way to prevent "carriers" from spreading the pathology of crime) models. The *criminogenic risk/needs* model focuses on identifying and modifying attitudes, circumstances, and behaviors that increase the risk of or need for juvenile crime involvement. Self-regulation can reduce the tendency to reflexively, rigidly, impulsively, and overemotionally or unemotionally (i.e., callously or indifferently) espouse criminogenic attitudes, choose criminogenic circumstances, and engage in illegal or dangerous behaviors. The *restorative justice* model emphasizes redressing the harm to victims and society caused through criminal acts by having those who violate the social contract (by committing crimes) take responsibility and make restitution to victims so as to restore justice in the society-at-large. Enhancing juvenile offenders' ability to self-regulate can enable them to meaningfully engage in honest self-reflection and empathic dialogue with victims, as well as to successfully assume the responsibilities of citizens in society. From a parallel perspective, enhancing juvenile justice program's and staff's capacity to self-regulate can decrease reflexive, impulsive, and over- or underemotional responses to youth behaviors, and increase their capacity to empathically and planfully support youth in engaging in desired skills.

Self-regulation involves the ability to deploy several basic psychobiological competences in order to achieve "allostatic" (homeostasis-promoting; see Chapter 1) balance in body state, psychological state, and relationship to the physical and interpersonal environment. Thus, there is a pivotal role for self-regulation in increased adaptive functioning across a wide range of outcomes

(Continued)

Box 4.6 Continued

(e.g., social competence, academic achievement, maintaining or regaining emotional equilibrium). Markers of successful self-regulation in youth are not just superficially or transiently compliant behavior but an enhanced ability to cope with stressors without self-defeating (e.g., impulsive, perseverative, aggressive) or interpersonally ineffective (e.g., callous, manipulative, defiant) attitudes and behavior.

Self-regulation requires the intentional deployment of attention to gathering and processing information so as to selectively and successfully pursue goals that, when achieved, increase the overall well-being of both the individual and her or his social and physical environment. Active pursuit of goals requires a complex harnessing of self-organizational and emotion regulation capacities. In order to effectively organize behavior so as to achieve goals, it is necessary to shift from being either passive (unresponsive) or reflexively reactive ("automatic response tendency") to finding and selectively activating a planful action strategy ("contextually appropriate response") that is not interrupted or distorted by habitual reactions ("automatic response tendencies") but draws on the person's past successful responses ("general response bias"). Put more basically, to be self-regulated is to be able to (i) "stop and think," (ii) "learn from past experiences," and (iii) "ready and aim before firing."

Self-regulation thus involves the ability to (i) consciously focus attention; (ii) be aware of the environment and one's own physical and emotional body states; (iii) draw on memory in order to learn from the past and adapt effectively in the present; and (iv) maintain or regain emotion states that provide a genuine sense of well-being and lead to further self-regulation. Although these competences may seem obvious, they are deceptively difficult for traumatized youth to actually achieve on a reliable basis. Structuring juvenile justice residential programs to elicit, support, and foster the independent use of these self-regulation competences by detained youths, therefore, is a direct way to both help youths recover from complex trauma and to make the milieus—and the communities and families to which youths return—safer and healthier.

which women are more often exposed than men, such as sexual assault or childhood abuse, appears to partially account for this "gender" difference. For example, a single incident of physical assault by a stranger and chronic exposure to intimate partner violence could each be categorized as physical assault. The more severe and prolonged traumatic exposure involved in domestic violence is more commonly reported by women, while single-incident assaults are more often reported by men. When risk and vulnerability severity criteria are used to measure the extent of trauma exposure rather than simply using the basic type of traumatic stressor, men no longer have more extensive exposure to traumatic stressors than women—and women's risk of developing PTSD is closer to (although still higher than) that of men (Tolin & Foa, 2006). Thus, while women and girls are more likely than men or boys to develop PTSD, this difference has more to do with the nature and extent of exposure to traumatic stressors than to gender per se. Additionally, Kimerling, Mack, and Kendra (2008, pp. 291–292) also note the following:

> *While trauma characteristics (type, frequency, severity) may partially explain gender differences in PTSD, gender roles and social context also show some explanatory power, though less research attention has been devoted to these issues. Gender differences in PTSD appear to be more pronounced in traditional cultures or developing countries, and are thought to be exacerbated by traditional gender roles. For example, cultural norms that discourage emotional expression in men may result in underreporting PTSD symptoms in this population. In cultures that establish women as the sole caregiver and where women are dependent on close social networks for their livelihood, trauma may differentially impact the development of PTSD among women more than men. Outcomes associated with natural disaster, often thought to be a "gender-neutral" event, revealed gender-specific risk factors for PTSD, such as the social roles of wife or mother.*

Ethnocultural and socioeconomic background and the epidemiology of PTSD

Although African American, Native American, and Hispanic/Latino ethnoracial minority statuses have been found to be associated with a high risk of developing PTSD in some studies, particularly with military personnel who served in war zones: (i) numerous studies fail to find this relationship; (ii) it is not clear whether this is the result of other factors than race per se, such as discrimination and socioeconomic deprivation; (iii) it also is possible that the differences may be due to the ethnoracial minority persons having been subjected to different levels of event exposure (e.g., more often being assigned to combat or other forms of hazardous military duty than white personnel); and, (iv) some ethnoracial minority groups may be the *least* likely to develop PTSD (such as Native Hawaiians or Japanese Americans) (Pole, Gone, & Kulkarni, 2008).

Every individual, family, and community has a heritage that includes a distinctive blend of racial, ethnic, cultural, and national characteristics. Within this heritage there often also is a legacy of personal or familial exposure to psychological trauma. Psychological trauma and PTSD occur across the full spectrum of racial, ethnic, and cultural groups in the United States. Trauma and PTSD are epidemic internationally as well, particularly for ethnoracial minority groups (which include a much broader range of ethnicities and cultures and manifestations of PTSD than are typically recognized in studies of PTSD in the United States; de Jong, Komproe, Spinazzola, van der Kolk, & Van Ommeren, 2005). The scientific and clinical study of prevalence, impact, and treatment of PTSD among ethnoracial minority groups is of great importance, especially given the disparities, adversities, and traumatic stressors to which ethnoracial minorities have been subjected historically—and to which they continue to be.

Although Latino (and possibly African Americans) persons are at greater risk than European Americans for PTSD (Pole et al., 2008), it is possible that the elevated prevalence may be due to differential exposure to psychological trauma (including prior traumas that often are not assessed in PTSD clinical or epidemiological studies—e.g., Eisenman, Gelberg, Liu, & Shapiro, 2003) or to differences in exposure to other risk or protective factors such as poverty or education (e.g., Turner & Lloyd, 2003, 2004).

The interactive effects of psychological trauma, PTSD, and racism and discrimination are complex. Racism may constitute: (i) a risk factor for exposure to traumatic stressors, (ii) a moderator that may exacerbate the impact of psychological traumas and increase the risk of PTSD or other posttraumatic disorders, or (iii) a form of psychological trauma in and of itself (Box 4.7).

Box 4.7 Racism and Risk of Trauma Exposure and PTSD

No studies have been reported that directly examine racism as a risk factor for exposure to psychological trauma. Studies based in the United States and elsewhere (e.g., Australia; MacDonald, Chamberlain, & Long, 1997) suggest that racial discrimination may have played a role in placing military personnel from ethnoracial minority groups at risk for more extensive and severe combat trauma exposure. Studies of survivors of the holocaust and other episodes of ethnic annihilation provide particularly graphic and tragic evidence of the infliction of psychological trauma en masse in the name of racism (Yule, 2000). Studies are needed that systematically compare persons and groups who are exposed to different types and degrees of racism in order to test whether (and under what conditions) racism specifically accounts for increased risk of trauma exposure.

In addition, one study found that self-reported experiences of racial discrimination increased the risk of PTSD among Latino police officers particularly (and also African Americans) (Pole, Best, Metzler, & Marmar, 2005). However, the investigation's cross-sectional self-report data prevent any firm conclusions about the actual (as opposed to self-reported) causal or prospective (as opposed to correlational) association of racial discrimination and PTSD. When racism leads to the targeting of ethnoracial minority groups for violence, dispossession, or dislocation, the risk of PTSD increases in proportion type and degree of psychological trauma involved in these adverse experiences. Another study with Asian American military veterans from the Vietnam War era showed that exposure to multiple race-related stressors that met PTSD criteria for psychological trauma was associated with more severe PTSD than when only one or no such race-related traumas were reported (Loo, Fairbank, & Chemtob, 2005). This study more precisely operationalized racism than any prior study, utilizing two psychometrically validated measures of race-related stressors and PTSD. However, as in the Pole et al. (2005) study, the stressors/traumas and PTSD symptoms were assessed by self-report contemporaneously, so it is unclear whether the relationship was an artifact of the measurement method or was the actual extent of racism experienced in each distinct incidence. In order to extend the valuable work these studies have begun, it will be important to utilize measures based on operationally specific criteria for categorizing and quantifying exposure to discrimination (e.g., Wiking, Johansson, & Sundquist, 2004) as distinct adversities or stressors that can be assessed separately from as well as along with exposure to psychological trauma.

As noted earlier, racism also may lead to pervasive disparities in access to socioeconomic resources such as education, income, political influence, and health care. Research is needed to determine to what extent the adverse outcomes of racial disparities are the direct result of racism as a stressor (e.g., racially motivated stigmatization, subjugation, and deprivation), as opposed to the indirect effects of racism as a diathesis reducing access to protective socioeconomic resources that buffer against the adverse effects of stressors such as poverty or pollution and exposure to traumatic stressors such as accidents or crime.

It is important to determine whether PTSD is the product of either the direct (stressor) and indirect (diathesis) effects of racism, particularly given its demonstrated association with other psychiatric disorders (e.g., depression) and with increased risk of physical illness (e.g., cardiovascular disease) in ethnoracial minorities (e.g., American Indians; Sawchuk et al., 2005).

Education is a particularly relevant example of a socioeconomic resource to which ethnoracial minorities often have restricted access and that is a protective factor mitigating against the risk of PTSD (Dirkzwager, Bramsen, & Van Der Ploeg, 2005) and overall health problems (Wiking et al., 2004). Racial disparities in access to education are due both to direct influences (e.g., lower funding for inner city schools that disproportionately serve ethnoracial minority students) and indirect associations with other racial disparities (e.g., disproportionate juvenile and criminal justice confinement of ethnoracial minority persons). Racial disparities in education have a potentially cumulative adverse effect on vulnerability to PTSD because they are both the product of and a contributor to reduced access by ethnoracial minorities to other socioeconomic and health resources (e.g., income, health insurance; Harris et al., 2006). When investigating risk and protective factors for PTSD, it is essential, therefore, to consider race and ethnicity in the context not only of ethnocultural identity and group membership but also of racial disparities in access to socioeconomic resources.

Although ethnoracial subgroups are disproportionately disadvantaged, disparities in access to vital resources and over violence and loss due to displacement from home, community, and national origins have occurred historically across all racial and ethnocultural lines in the United States as well as in other parts of the world (e.g., massively displaced populations in the Balkans, central Asia, and Africa). When primary social ties are cut or diminished as a result of violence and coercion, the challenge expands beyond survival of traumatic life-threatening danger to preserving a viable developmental trajectory in the face of life-altering loss

(Continued)

Box 4.7 Continued

(Garbarino & Kostelny, 1996; Rabalais, Ruggiero, & Scotti, 2002). A recurring theme in these studies is that trauma inflicted in the service of racial discrimination not only may lead to PTSD but also to a range of insidious psychosocial impairments that result from adverse effects upon the psychobiological development of the affected persons. When families and entire communities are destroyed or displaced, the impact on the psychobiological development of children (Ford, 2005) and young adults (Ford, 1999) may lead to complex variants of PTSD that involve not only persistent fear and anxiety but also core problems with relatedness and self-regulation of emotion, consciousness, and bodily health (de Jong et al., 2005).

A critical question posed but not yet answered by studies of PTSD and racial discrimination (Pole et al., 2005) and race-related stress (Loo et al., 2005), as well as by the robust literature demonstrating intergenerational transmission of risk for PTSD (Kellerman, 2001), is whether racism constitutes a "hidden" (Crenshaw & Hardy, 2006) or "invisible" (Franklin, Boyd-Franklin, & Kelly, 2006) form of traumatization that may be transmitted across generations. Recent research findings demonstrate uniquely adverse effects of emotional abuse in childhood (Teicher, Samson, Polcari, & McGreenery, 2006) are consistent with a view that chronic denigration, shaming, demoralization, and coercion may constitute a risk factor for severe PTSD. Research is needed to operationalize the emotional as well as physical violence in racism, as well as to empirically examine the unique and interactive effects this may have not only on directly victimized persons and their families and communities but also on their descendants across several generations.

References

Abrahams, N., Devries, K., Watts, C., Pallitto, C., Petzold, M., Shamu, S., et al. (2014). Worldwide prevalence of non-partner sexual violence: A systematic review. *Lancet*, *383*(9929), 1648–1654. http://dx.doi.org/10.1016/S0140-6736(13)62243-6.

Abram, K. M., Teplin, L. A., Charles, D. R., Longworth, S. L., McClelland, G. M., & Dulcan, M. K. (2004). Posttraumatic stress disorder and trauma in youth in juvenile detention. *Archives of General Psychiatry*, *61*, 403–410.

Abram, K. M., Teplin, L. A., & McClelland, G. M. (2003). Comorbidity of severe psychiatric disorders and substance use disorders among women in jail. *American Journal of Psychiatry*, *160*, 1007–1010.

American Psychiatric Association, (2000). *Diagnostic and statistical manual of mental disorders* (4th ed. Text Revision). Washington, DC: American Psychiatric Press.

American Psychiatric Association, (2013). *Diagnostic and statistical manual of mental disorders* (5th ed.). Washington, DC: American Psychiatric Press.

Amir, M., Kaplan, Z., Efroni, R., Levine, Y., Benjamin, J., & Kotler, M. (1997). Coping styles in post-traumatic stress disorder (PTSD) patients. *Personality and Individual Differences*, *23*, 399–405.

Angst, J., Gamma, A., Sellaro, R., Lavori, P. W., & Zhang, H. P. (2003). Recurrence of bipolar disorders and major depression - A life-long perspective. *European Archives of Psychiatry and Clinical Neuroscience*, *253*, 236–240.

Arroyo, W. (Ed.). (2001). *PTSD in children and adolescents in the juvenile justice system*. Washington, DC: American Psychiatric Association.

Averill, P. M., Reas, D. L., Shack, A., Shah, N. N., Cowan, K., Krajewski, K., et al. (2004). Is schizoaffective disorder a stable diagnostic category: A retrospective examination. *Psychiatric Quarterly*, *75*, 215–227.

Bell, C. C., & Jenkins, E. J. (1993). Community violence and children on Chicago's southside. *Psychiatry*, *56*(1), 46–54.

Benazzi, F. (2004). Inter-episode mood lability in mood disorders: Residual symptom or natural course of illness? *Psychiatry and Clinical Neurosciences*, *58*(5), 480–486.

Boothby, J. L., & Durham, T. W. (1999). Screening for depression in prisoners using the Beck Depression Inventory. *Criminal Justice and Behavior*, *26*, 107–124.

Boscarino, J. A. (2008). Psychobiologic predictors of disease mortality after psychological trauma: Implications for research and clinical surveillance. *Journal of Nervous and Mental Disease*, *196*, 100–107.

Breslau, N. (2009). The epidemiology of trauma, PTSD, and other posttrauma disorders. *Trauma Violence & Abuse*, *10*(3), 198–210. http://dx.doi.org/10.1177/1524838009334448.

Breslau, N., Davis, G. C., Peterson, E. L., & Schultz, L. (1997). Psychiatric sequelae of post-traumatic stress disorder in women. *Archives of General Psychiatry*, *54*(1), 81–87.

Breslau, N., Kessler, R. C., Chilcoat, H. D., Schultz, L. R., Davis, G. C., & Andreski, P. (1998). Trauma and posttraumatic stress disorder in the community: The 1996 Detroit Area Survey of Trauma. *Archives of General Psychiatry*, *55*, 626–632.

Breslau, N., Peterson, E. L., & Schultz, L. R. (2008). A second look at prior trauma and the posttraumatic stress disorder effects of subsequent trauma: A prospective epidemiological study. *Archives of General Psychiatry*, *65*(4), 431–437.

Briggs-Gowan, M. J., Carter, A. S., Clark, R., Augustyn, M., McCarthy, K. J., & Ford, J. D. (2010). Exposure to potentially traumatic events in early childhood: Differential links to emergent psychopathology. *Journal of Child Psychology and Psychiatry and Allied Disciplines*, *51*(10), 1132–1140. http://dx.doi.org/10.1111/j.1469-7610.2010.02256.x.

Briggs-Gowan, M. J., Carter, A. S., & Ford, J. D. (2012). Parsing the effects violence exposure in early childhood: Modeling developmental pathways. *Journal of Pediatric Psychology*, *37*(1), 11–22. http://dx.doi.org/10.1093/jpepsy/jsr063.

Brown, G. P., & Beck, A. T. (Eds.). (2002). *Dysfunctional attitudes, perfectionism, and models of vulnerability to depression*. Washington, DC: American Psychological Association.

Brunello, N., Davidson, J. R., Deahl, M., Kessler, R. C., Mendlewicz, J., Racagni, G., et al. (2001). Posttraumatic stress disorder: Diagnosis and epidemiology, comorbidity and social consequences, biology and treatment. *Neuropsychobiology*, *43*, 150–162.

Calhoun, P. S., McDonald, S. D., Guerra, V. S., Eggleston, A. M., Beckham, J. C., & Straits-Troster, K. (2010). Clinical utility of the Primary Care--PTSD Screen among U.S. veterans who served since September 11, 2001. *Psychiatry Research*, *178*(2), 330–335. http://dx.doi.org/S0165-1781(09)00425-9 [pii]; http://dx.doi.org/10.1016/j.psychres.2009.11.009.

Caspi, A., Sugden, K., Moffitt, T. E., Taylor, A., Craig, I. W., Harrington, H., et al. (2003). Influence of life stress on depression: Moderation by a polymorphism in the 5-HTT gene. *Science*, *301*, 386–389.

Cauffman, E., Feldman, S. S., Waterman, J., & Steiner, H. (1998). Posttraumatic stress disorder among female juvenile offenders. *Journal of the American Academy of Child and Adolescent Psychiatry*, *37*, 1209–1216.

Chou, S. P., Lee, H. K., Cho, M. J., Park, J. I., Dawson, D. A., & Grant, B. F. (2012). Alcohol use disorders, nicotine dependence, and co-occurring mood and anxiety disorders in the United States and South Korea-a cross-national comparison. *Alcoholism, Clinical and Experimental Research*, *36*(4), 654–662.

Compton, W. M., Thomas, Y. F., Stinson, F. S., & Grant, B. F. (2007). Prevalence, correlates, disability, and comorbidity of DSM-IV drug abuse and dependence in the United States: Results from the national epidemiologic survey on alcohol and related conditions. *Archives of General Psychiatry*, *64*(5), 566–576.

Copeland, W. E., Keeler, G., Angold, A., & Costello, E. J. (2007). Traumatic events and posttraumatic stress in childhood. *Archives of General Psychiatry*, *64*, 577–584.

Costello, E. J., Erkanli, A., Fairbank, J. A., & Angold, A. (2002). The prevalence of potentially traumatic events in childhood and adolescence. *Journal of Traumatic Stress*, *15*, 99–112.

Creamer, M., Burgess, P., & McFarlane, A. C. (2001). Post-traumatic stress disorder: Findings from the Australian National Survey of Mental Health and Well-Being. *Psychological Medicine*, *31*, 1237–1247.

Crenshaw, D. A., & Hardy, K. V. (Eds.). (2006). *Understanding and treating the aggression of traumatized children in out-of-home care*. New York: Guilford.

Crino, R., Slade, T., & Andrews, G. (2005). The changing prevalence and severity of obsessive-compulsive disorder criteria from DSM-III to DSM-IV. *American Journal of Psychiatry*, *162*, 876–882.

Darves-Bornoz, J. M., Alonso, J., de Girolamo, G., de Graaf, R., Haro, J. M., Kovess-Masfety, V., et al. (2008). Main traumatic events in Europe: PTSD in the European study of the epidemiology of mental disorders survey. *Journal of Traumatic Stress*, *21*(5), 455–462. http://dx.doi.org/10.1002/jts.20357.

de Jong, J., Komproe, I. H., Spinazzola, J., van der Kolk, B. A., & Van Ommeren, M. H. (2005). DESNOS in three postconflict settings: Assessing cross-cultural construct equivalence. *Journal of Traumatic Stress*, *18*, 13–21.

de Jong, J. T. V. M., Komproe, I. H., & Van Ommeren, M. (2003). Common mental disorders in postconflict settings. *The Lancet*, *361*(9375), 2128–2130.

de Vries, G. J., & Olff, M. (2009). The lifetime prevalence of traumatic events and posttraumatic stress disorder in the Netherlands. *Journal of Traumatic Stress*, *22*(4), 259–267. http://dx.doi.org/10.1002/jts.20429.

De Young, A. C., Kenardy, J. A., & Cobham, V. E. (2011). Trauma in early childhood: A neglected population. *Clinical Child and Family Psychology Review*, *14*(3), 231–250. http://dx.doi.org/10.1007/s10567-011-0094-3.

Desai, S., Arias, I., Thompson, M. P., & Basile, K. C. (2002). Childhood victimization and subsequent adult revictimization assessed in a nationally representative sample of women and men. *Violence and Victims*, *17*(6), 639–653.

Dirkzwager, A. J. E., Bramsen, I., & Van Der Ploeg, H. M. (2005). Factors associated with posttraumatic stress among peacekeeping soldiers. *Anxiety, Stress & Coping*, *18*, 37–51.

Ditton, P. M. (1999). Corporate Author U. S. & Bureau of Justice Statistics. *Mental health and treatment of inmates and probationers*. Special report; Variation: Special report. United States. Bureau of Justice Statistics.

Duckworth, T., & Follette, V. (Eds.). (2012). *Retraumatization*. New York, NY: Routledge.

Dvir, Y., Ford, J. D., Hill, M., & Frazier, J. A. (2014). Childhood maltreatment, affective dysregulation, and psychiatric comorbidities. *Harvard Review of Psychiatry*, *22*, 149–161.

Eddy, K. T., Dutra, L., Bradley, R., & Westen, D. (2004). A multidimensional meta-analysis of psychotherapy and pharmacotherapy for obsessive-compulsive disorder. *Clinical Psychology Review*, *24*(8), 1011–1030.

Ehlert, U., Gaab, J., & Heinrichs, M. (2001). Psychoneuroendocrinological contributions to the etiology of depression, posttraumatic stress disorder, and stress-related bodily disorders: The role of the hypothalamus-pituitary-adrenal axis. *Biological Psychology*, *57*, 141–152.

Eisenman, D. P., Gelberg, L., Liu, H., & Shapiro, M. F. (2003). Mental health and health-related quality of life among adult Latino primary care patients living in the United States with previous exposure to political violence. *Journal of the American Medical Association*, *290*, 627–634.

Feierman, J., & Ford, J. D. (2015). Trauma-informed juvenile justice systems and approaches. In K. Heilbrun, D. DeMatteo, & N. Goldstein (Eds.), *Handbook of psychology and juvenile justice*. Washington, DC: American Psychological Association.

Feldman, R., & Vengrober, A. (2011). Posttraumatic stress disorder in infants and young children exposed to war-related trauma. *Journal of the American Academy of Child and Adolescent Psychiatry*, *50*(7), 645–658. http://dx.doi.org/10.1016/j.jaac.2011.03.001.

Finkelhor, D., Ormrod, R., Turner, H., & Hamby, S. L. (2005). The victimization of children and youth: A comprehensive, national survey. *Child Maltreatment*, *10*, 5–25.

Finkelhor, D., Ormrod, R. K., & Turner, H. A. (2007a). Poly-victimization: A neglected component in child victimization. *Child Abuse & Neglect*, *31*, 7–26.

Finkelhor, D., Ormrod, R. K., & Turner, H. A. (2007b). Re-victimization patterns in a national longitudinal sample of children and youth. *Child Abuse & Neglect*, *31*(5), 479–502. http://dx.doi.org/S0145-2134(07)00083-X [pii]; http://dx.doi.org/10.1016/j.chiabu.2006.03.012.

Finkelhor, D., Ormrod, R. K., & Turner, H. A. (2009). The developmental epidemiology of childhood victimization. *Journal of Interpersonal Violence*, *24*(5), 711–731. http://dx.doi.org/0886260508317185 [pii]; http://dx.doi.org/10.1177/0886260508317185.

Foa, E. B., Ehlers, A., Clark, D. M., Tolin, D. F., & Orsillo, S. M. (1999). The Posttraumatic Cognitions Inventory (PTCI): Development and validation. *Psychological Assessment*, *11*, 303–314.

Ford, J. D. (1999). Disorders of extreme stress following war-zone military trauma: Associated features of posttraumatic stress disorder to comorbid but distinct syndromes? *Journal of Consulting and ClinicalPsychology*, *67*(1), 3–12.

Ford, J. D. (2005). Treatment implications of altered affect regulation and information processing following child maltreatment. *Psychiatric Annals*, *35*(5), 410–419.

Ford, J. D. (2009). Translation of emerging neurobiological and developmental findings to the clinicalconceptualization and treatment of complex psychological trauma. In C. A. Courtois & J. Ford (Eds.), *Treating complex traumatic stress disorders: An evidence-based guide*. New York: Guilford.

Ford, J. D. (2012). Posttraumatic stress disorder and psychological trauma. In J. Verster, K. Brady, M. Galanter, & P. Conrod (Eds.), *Drug abuse and addiction in medical illness: Causes, consequences, and treatment* (pp. 335–342). Totowa, NJ: Springer/Humana Press.

Ford, J. D., & Blaustein, M. (2013). Systemic self-regulation: A framework for trauma-informed services in residential juvenile justice programs. *Journal of Family Violence*, *28*, 655–677.

Ford, J. D., Campbell, K. A., Storzbach, D., Binder, L. M., Anger, W. K., & Rohlman, D. S. (2001). Posttraumatic stress symptomatology is associated with unexplained illness attributed to Persian Gulf War military service. *Psychosomatic Medicine*, *63*, 842–849.

Ford, J. D., Chapman, J. F., Hawke, J., & Albert, D. (2007). *Trauma among youth in the juvenile justice system: Critical issues and new directions*. Albany, NY: National Center for Mental Health and Juvenile Justice.

Ford, J. D., & Courtois, C. A. (2014). Complex PTSD, affect dysregulation, and borderline personality disorder. *Borderline Personality Disorder and Emotion Dysregulation*, *1*, 9.

Ford, J. D., Elhai, J. D., Connor, D. F., & Frueh, B. C. (2010). Poly-victimization and risk of posttraumatic, depressive, and substance use disorders and involvement in delinquency in a national sample of adolescents. *Journal of Adolescent Health*, *46*(6), 545–552. http://dx.doi.org/S1054-139X(09)00636-3 [pii]; http://dx.doi.org/10.1016/j.jadohealth.2009.11.212.

Ford, J. D., & Gómez,, J. M. (2015). Self injury & suicidality: the impact of trauma and dissociation. *Journal of Trauma & Dissociation* (just-accepted).

Ford, J. D., Hartman, J. K., Hawke, J., & Chapman, J. (2008). Traumatic victimization posttraumatic stress disorder, suicidal ideation, and substance abuse risk among juvenile justice-involved youths. *Journal of Child and Adolescent Trauma*, *1*, 75–92.

Ford, J. D., Trestman, R. L., Wiesbrock, V., & Zhang, W. L. (2007). Development and validation of a brief mental health screening instrument for newly incarcerated adults. *Assessment*, *14*, 279–299.

Franklin, A. J., Boyd-Franklin, N., & Kelly, S. (2006). Racism and invisibility: Race-related stress, emotional abuse and psychological trauma for people of color. *Journal of Emotional Abuse*, *6*(2), 9–30.

Garbarino, J., & Kostelny, K. (1996). The effects of political violence on Palestinian children's behavior problems: A risk accumulation model. *Child Development*, *67*, 33–45.

Goff, A., Rose, E., Rose, S., & Purves, D. (2007). Does PTSD occur in sentenced prison populations? A systematic literature review. *Criminal Behavior and Mental Health*, *17*(3), 152–162.

Golier, J. A., Yehuda, R., Bierer, L. M., Mitropoulou, V., New, A. S., Schmeidler, J., et al. (2003). The relationship of borderline personality disorder to posttraumatic stress disorder and traumatic events. *American Journal of Psychiatry*, *160*, 2018–2024.

Goodman, L. A., Salyers, M. P., Mueser, K. T., Rosenberg, S. D., Swartz, M., Essock, S. M., et al. (2001). Recent victimization in women and men with severe mental illness: Prevalence and correlates. *Journal of Traumatic Stress*, *14*, 615–632.

Grant, B. F., Stinson, F. S., Dawson, D. A., Chou, S. P., Dufour, M. C., Compton, W., et al. (2004). Prevalence and co-occurrence of substance use disorders and independent mood and anxiety disorders: Results from the national epidemiologic survey on alcohol and related conditions. *Archives of General Psychiatry*, *61*(8), 807–816.

Grant, B. F., Stinson, F. S., Dawson, D. A., Chou, S. P., Ruan, W. J., & Pickering, R. P. (2004). Co-occurrence of 12-month alcohol and drug use disorders and personality disorders in the United States: Results from the national epidemiologic survey on alcohol and related conditions. *Archives of General Psychiatry*, *61*(4), 361–368.

Grasso, D. J., Dierkhising, C. B., Branson, C. E., Ford, J. D., & Lee, R. (in review). Developmental patterns of adverse childhood experiences and current symptoms and impairment in youth referred for trauma-specific services.

Guastello, S. J., Gershon, R. R. M., & Murphy, L. R. (1999). Catastrophe model for the exposure to blood-borne pathogens and other accidents in health care settings. *Accident Analysis and Prevention*, *31*, 739–749.

Hadjipavlou, G., Mok, H., & Yatham, L. N. (2004). Bipolar II disorder: An overview of recent developments. *Can J Psychiatry*, *49*, 802–812.

Hankin, C. S., Spiro, A., III, Miller, D. R., & Kazis, L. (1999). Mental disorders and mental health treatment among U.S. Department of Veterans Affairs outpatients: The Veterans Health Study. *American Journal of Psychiatry*, *156*(12), 1924–1930. http://dx.doi.org/10.1176/ajp.156.12.1924.

Harris, R., Tobias, M., Jeffreys, M., Waldegrave, K., Karlsen, S., & Nazroo, J. (2006). Racism and health: The relationship between experience of racial discrimination and health in New Zealand. *Social Science and Medicine, 63*, 1428–1441.

Hasin, D. S., Stinson, F. S., Ogburn, E., & Grant, B. F. (2007). Prevalence, correlates, disability, and comorbidity of DSM-IV alcohol abuse and dependence in the United States: Results from the national epidemiologic survey on alcohol and related conditions. *Archives of General Psychiatry, 64*(7), 830–842.

Henry, B., Moffitt, T. E., Caspi, A., Langley, J., & Silva, P. A. (1994). On the "Remembrance of things past": A longitudinal evaluation of the retrospective method. *Psychological Assessment, 6*, 92–101.

Higgins, A. B., & Follette, V. M. (2002). Frequency and impact of interpersonal trauma in older women. *Journal of Clinical Geropsychology, 8*, 215–226.

Hobfoll, S. E., Canetti-Nisim, D., & Johnson, R. J. (2006). Exposure to terrorism, stress-related mental health symptoms, and defensive coping among Jews and Arabs in Israel. *Journal of Consulting and Clinical Psychology, 74*(2), 207–218.

Hudson, J. I., Mangweth, B., Pope, H. G., Jr., et al., De Col, C., Hausmann, A., Gutweniger, S., et al. (2003). Family study of affective spectrum disorder. *Archives of General Psychiatry, 60*, 170–177.

Iverson, K. M., Litwack, S. D., Pineles, S. L., Suvak, M. K., Vaughn, R. A., & Resick, P. A. (2013). Predictors of intimate partner violence revictimization: The relative impact of distinct PTSD symptoms, dissociation, and coping strategies. *Journal of Traumatic Stress, 26*(1), 102–110. http://dx.doi.org/10.1002/jts.21781.

Jordan, B. K., Federman, E. B., Burns, B. J., Schlenger, W. E., Fairbank, J. A., & Caddell, J. M. (2002). Lifetime use of mental health and substance abuse treatment services by incarcerated women felons. *Psychiatric Services, 53*, 317–325.

Jordan, B. K., Schlenger, W. E., Fairbank, J. A., & Caddell, J. M. (1996). Prevalence of psychiatric disorders among incarcerated women: Convicted felons entering prison. *Archives of General Psychiatry, 53*, 513–519.

Kaplow, J. B., Howell, K. H., & Layne, C. M. (2014). Do circumstances of the death matter? Identifying socioenvironmental risks for grief-related psychopathology in bereaved youth. *Journal of Traumatic Stress, 27*(1), 42–49.

Kaplow, J. B., Layne, C. M., Saltzman, W. R., Cozza, S. J., & Pynoos, R. S. (2013). Using multidimensional grief theory to explore the effects of deployment, reintegration, and death on military youth and families. *Clinical Child and Family Psychology Review, 16*(3), 322–340.

Kaufman, J., & Charney, D. (2001). Effects of early stress on brain structure and function: Implications for understanding the relationship between child maltreatment and depression. *Development and Psychopathology, 13*(3), 451–471.

Keck, P. E., McElroy, S. L., Havens, J. R., Altshuler, L. L., Nolen, W. A., Frye, M. A., et al. (2003). Psychosis in bipolar disorder: Phenomenology and impact on morbidity and course of illness. *Comprehensive Psychiatry, 44*, 263–269.

Kellerman, N. P. (2001). Psychopathology in children of Holocaust survivors: A review of the research literature. *Israeli Journal of Psychiatry and Related Sciences, 38*(1), 36–46.

Kendler, K. S., Karkowski, L. M., & Prescott, C. A. (1999). Causal relationship between stressful life events and the onset of major depression. *American Journal of Psychiatry, 156*, 837–841.

Kessing, L. V. (2004). Gender differences in the phenomenology of bipolar disorder. *Bipolar Disorders, 6*, 421–425.

Kessler, R. C., Berglund, P., Demler, O., Jin, R., Koretz, D., Merikangas, K. R., et al. (2003). The epidemiology of major depressive disorder: Results from the National Comorbidity Survey Replication (NCS-R). *Journal of the American Medical Association, 289*(23), 3095–3105.

Kessler, R. C., Berglund, P., Demler, O., Jin, R., Merikangas, K., & Walters, E. E. (2005). Lifetime prevalence and age-of-onset distributions of DSM-IV disorders in the National Comorbidity Survey Replication. *Archives of General Psychiatry, 62,* 593–602.

Kessler, R. C., Petukhova, M., Sampson, N. A., Zaslavsky, A. M., & Wittchen, H. U. (2012). Twelve-month and lifetime prevalence and lifetime morbid risk of anxiety and mood disorders in the United States. *International Journal of Methods in Psychiatric Research, 21*(3), 169–184.

Kessler, R. C., Rubinow, D. R., Holmes, C., Abelson, J. M., & Zhao, S. (1997). The epidemiology of DSM-III-R bipolar I disorder in a general population survey. *Psychological Medicine, 27,* 1079–1089.

Kessler, R. C., Sonnega, A., Bromet, E., Hughes, M., & Nelson, C. B. (1995). Posttraumatic stress disorder in the National Comorbidity Survey. *Archives of General Psychiatry, 52,* 1048–1060.

Ketter, T. A., Wang, P. W., Becker, O. V., Nowakowska, C., & Yang, Y. S. (2004). Psychotic bipolar disorders: Dimensionally similar to or categorically different from schizophrenia? *Journal of Psychiatric Research, 38,* 47–61.

Kilpatrick, D. G., Resnick, H. S., Milanak, M. E., Miller, M. W., Keyes, K. M., & Friedman, M. J. (2013). National estimates of exposure to traumatic events and PTSD prevalence using DSM-IV and DSM-5 criteria. *Journal of Traumatic Stress, 26*(5), 537–547. http://dx.doi.org/10.1002/jts.21848.

Kilpatrick, D. G., Ruggiero, K. J., Acierno, R., Saunders, B. E., Resnick, H. S., & Best, C. L. (2003). Violence and risk of PTSD, major depression, substance abuse/dependence, and comorbidity: Results from the National Survey of Adolescents. *Journal of Consulting and Clinical Psychology, 71*(4), 692–700.

Kimerling, R., Mack, K., & Kendra, K. (2008). Gender. In G. Reyes, J. D. Elhai, & J. Ford (Eds.), *Encyclopedia of psychological trauma* (pp. 291–299). Hoboken, NJ: Wiley.

Koenen, K. C., Moffitt, T. E., Poulton, R., Martin, J., & Caspi, A. (2007). Early childhood factors associated with the development of post-traumatic stress disorder: Results from a longitudinal birth cohort. *Psychological Medicine, 37,* 181–192.

Levendosky, A. A., Bogat, G. A., Theran, S. A., Trotter, J. S., von Eye, A., & Davidson, W. S., III (2004). The social networks of women experiencing domestic violence. *American Journal of Community Psychology, 34*(1-2), 95–109.

Leverich, G. S., McElroy, S. L., Suppes, T., Keck, P. E., Denicoff, K. D., Nolen, W. A., et al. (2002). Early physical and sexual abuse associated with an adverse course of bipolar illness. *Biological Psychiatry, 51,* 288–297.

Loo, C. M., Fairbank, J. A., & Chemtob, C. M. (2005). Adverse race-related events as a risk factor for posttraumatic stress disorder in Asian American Vietnam veterans. *Journal of Nervous and Mental Disorders, 193,* 455–463.

Lysaker, P. H., Meyer, P. S., Evans, J. D., Clements, C. A., & Marks, K. A. (2001). Childhood sexual trauma and psychosocial functioning in adults with schizophrenia. *Psychiatric Services, 52,* 1485–1488.

Lysaker, P. H., Nees, M. A., Lancaster, R. S., & Davis, L. W. (2004). Vocational function among persons with schizophrenia with and without history of childhood sexual trauma. *Journal of Traumatic Stress, 17,* 435–438.

MacDonald, C., Chamberlain, K., & Long, N. (1997). Race, combat, and PTSD in a community sample of New Zealand Vietnam War veterans. *Journal of Traumatic Stress, 10,* 117–124.

Marneros, A., Pillman, F., Haring, A., Balzuweit, S., & Bloink, R. (2003). Features of acute and transient psychotic disorders. *European Archives of Psychiatry and Clinical Neuroscience*, *253*, 167–174.

McLaughlin, K. A., Koenen, K. C., Hill, E. D., Petukhova, M., Sampson, N. A., Zaslavsky, A. M., et al. (2013). Trauma exposure and posttraumatic stress disorder in a national sample of adolescents. *Journal of the American Academy of Child and Adolescent Psychiatry*, *52*(8), 815–830. e814.

McMillan, K. A., Enns, M. W., Cox, B. J., & Sareen, J. (2009). Comorbidity of axis I and II mental disorders with schizophrenia and psychotic disorders: Findings from the national epidemiologic survey on alcohol and related conditions. *Canadian Journal of Psychiatry*, *54*(7), 477–486.

Meiser-Stedman, R., Smith, P., Glucksman, E., Yule, W., & Dalgleish, T. (2008). The posttraumatic stress disorder diagnosis in preschool- and elementary school-age children exposed to motor vehicle accidents. *American Journal of Psychiatry*, *165*(10), 1326–1337. http://dx.doi.org/appi.ajp.2008.07081282 [pii]; http://dx.doi.org/10.1176/appi.ajp.2008.07081282.

Miller, I. W., Uebelacker, L. A., Keitner, G. I., Ryan, C. E., & Solomon, D. A. (2004). Longitudinal course of bipolar I disorder. *Comprehensive Psychiatry*, *45*, 431–440.

Mitchell, P. B., Slade, T., & Andrews, G. (2004). Twelve-month prevalence and disability of DSM-TV bipolar disorder in an Australian general population survey. *Psychological Medicine*, *34*, 777–785.

Mohr, P. E., Cheng, C. M., Claxton, K., Conley, R. R., Feldman, J. J., Hargreaves, W. A., et al. (2004). The heterogeneity of schizophrenia in disease states. *Schizophenia Research*, *71*, 83–95.

Morgan, V. A., Mitchell, P. B., & Jablensky, A. V. (2005). The epidemiology of bipolar disorder: Sociodemographic, disability and service utilization data from the Australian National Study of Low Prevalence (Psychotic) Disorders. *Bipolar Disorders*, *7*, 326–337.

Mueser, K. T., Essock, S. M., Haines, M., Wolfe, R., & Xie, H. (2004). Posttraumatic stress disorder, supported employment, and outcomes in people with severe mental illness. *CNS Spectrums*, *9*(12), 913–925.

Mueser, K. T., & McGurk, S. R. (2004). Schizophrenia. *Lancet*, *363*(9426), 2063–2072.

Mueser, K. T., Rosenberg, S. D., Fox, L., Salyers, M. P., Ford, J. D., & Carty, P. (2001). Psychometric evaluation of trauma and posttraumatic stress disorder assessments in persons with severe mental illness. *Psychological Assessment*, *13*, 110–117.

Mueser, K. T., & Taub, J. (2008). Trauma and PTSD among adolescents with severe emotional disorders involved in multiple service systems. *Psychiatric Services*, *59*(6), 627–634.

Naifeh, J. A., & Elhai, J. D. (2010). An experimental comparison of index traumatic event queries in PTSD assessment. *Journal of Anxiety Disorders*, *24*(1), 155–160. http://dx.doi.org/10.1016/j.janxdis.2009.10.003.

Neria, Y., Bromet, E. J., Sievers, S., Lavelle, J., & Fochtmann, L. J. (2002). Trauma exposure and posttraumatic stress disorder in psychosis: Findings from a first-admission cohort. *Journal of Consulting and Clinical Psychology*, *70*, 246–251.

Noll, J. G., Trickett, P. K., & Putnam, F. W. (2003). A prospective investigation of the impact of childhood sexual abuse on the development of sexuality. *Journal of Consulting and Clinical Psychology*, *71*(3), 575–586.

Norris, F. H. (1992). Epidemiology of trauma: Frequency and impact of different potentially traumatic events on different demographic groups. *Journal of Consulting and Clinical Psychology*, *60*(3), 409–418.

Norris, F. H., & Slone, L. B. (2007). The epidemiology of trauma and PTSD. In M. J. Friedman, T. M. Keane, & P. A. Resick (Eds.), *Handbook of PTSD: Science and practice* (pp. 78–98). New York US: Guilford.

O'Donnell, C., & Cook, J. (2008). Geriatrics. In G. Reyes, J. D. Elhai, & J. D. Ford (Eds.), *Encyclopedia of psychological trauma* (pp. 297–299). Hoboken, NJ: Wiley.

Orcutt, H. K., Erickson, D. J., & Wolfe, J. (2004). The course of PTSD symptoms among Gulf War veterans: A growth mixture modeling approach. *Journal of Traumatic Stress, 17*(3), 195–202.

Perkonigg, A., Kessler, R. C., Storz, S., & Wittchen, H. U. (2000). Traumatic events and posttraumatic stress disorder in the community: Prevalence, risk factors and comorbidity. *Acta Psychiatrica Scandinavica, 101*(1), 46–59.

Pole, N., Best, S. R., Metzler, T., & Marmar, C. R. (2005). Why are hispanics at greater risk for PTSD? *Culture, Diversity, Ethnicity, and Minority Psychology, 11*(2), 144–161.

Pole, N., Gone, J. P., & Kulkarni, M. (2008). Posttraumatic stress disorder among ethnoracial minorities in the United States. *Clinical Psychology: Science and Practice, 15*, 35–61.

Pugh, M. J., Finley, E. P., Copeland, L. A., Wang, C. P., Noel, P. H., Amuan, M. E., et al. (2014). Complex comorbidity clusters in OEF/OIF veterans: The polytrauma clinical triad and beyond. *Medical Care, 52*(2), 172–181.

Pynoos, R., Steinberg, A., Layne, C., Liang, L., Vivrette, R., Briggs, E. C., et al. (2014). Modeling constellations of trauma exposure in the National Child Traumatic Stress Network Core Data Set. *Psychological Trauma: Theory, Research, Practice & Policy, 6*(Suppl. 1), S9–S17. http://dx.doi.org/10.1037/a0037767.

Rabalais, A. E., Ruggiero, K. J., & Scotti, J. R. (2002). Multicultural issues in the response of children to disasters. In W. K. Silverman & A. M. La Greca (Eds.), *Helping children cope with disasters and terrorism* (pp. 73–99). Washington, DC US: American Psychological Association.

Resnick, H. S., Kilpatrick, D. G., Dansky, B. S., Saunders, B. E., & Best, C. L. (1993). Prevalence of civilian trauma and posttraumatic stress disorder in a representative national sample of women. *Journal of Consulting and Clinical Psychology, 61*, 984–991.

Riggs, D. S., Caulfield, M. B., & Street, A. E. (2000). Risk for domestic violence: Factors associated with perpetration and victimization. *Journal of ClinicalPsychology, 56*, 1289–1316.

Santiago, P. N., Ursano, R. J., Gray, C. L., Pynoos, R. S., Spiegel, D., Lewis-Fernandez, R., et al. (2013). A systematic review of PTSD prevalence and trajectories in DSM-5 defined trauma exposed populations: Intentional and non-intentional traumatic events. *PLoS One, 8*(4), e59236. http://dx.doi.org/10.1371/journal.pone.0059236.

Sawchuk, C. N., Roy-Byrne, P., Goldberg, J., Manson, S., Noonan, C., Beals, J., et al. (2005). The relationship between post-traumatic stress disorder, depression and cardiovascular disease in an American Indian tribe. *Psychological Medicine, 35*, 1785–1794.

Scheeringa, M. S., & Zeanah, C. H. (2001). A relational perspective on PTSD in early childhood. *Journal of Traumatic Stress, 14*, 799–815.

Scheeringa, M. S., Zeanah, C. H., & Cohen, J. A. (2011). PTSD in children and adolescents: Toward an empirically based algorithm. *Depression and Anxiety, 28*(9), 770–782. http://dx.doi.org/10.1002/da.20736.

Schnurr, P. P., & Green, B. L. (2004). Understanding relationships among trauma, posttraumatic stress disorder, and health outcomes. In P. P. Schnurr & B. L. Green (Eds.), *Trauma and health: Physical health consequences of exposure to extreme stress* (pp. 247–275). Washington, DC: American Psychological Association.

Schwab-Stone, M. E., Ayers, T. S., Kasprow, W., Voyce, C., Barone, C., Shriver, T., et al. (1995). No safe haven: A study of violence exposure in an urban community. *Journal of the American Academy of Child and Adolescent Psychiatry, 34*(10), 1343–1352. http://dx.doi.org/10.1097/00004583-199510000-00020.

Seedat, S., Nyamai, C., Njenga, F., Vythilingum, B., & Stein, D. J. (2004). Trauma exposure and post-traumatic stress symptoms in urban African schools: Survey in CapeTown and Nairobi. *British Journal of Psychiatry, 184*, 169–175.

Sells, D. J., Rowe, M., Fisk, D., & Davidson, L. (2003). Violent victimization of persons with co-occurring psychiatric and substance use disorders. *Psychiatric Services, 54*, 1253–1257.

Steadman, H. J., Scott, J. E., Osher, F., Agnese, T. K., & Robbins, P. C. (2005). Validation of the brief jail mental health screen. *Psychiatric Services, 56*, 816–822.

Stein, M. B., Hofler, M., Perkonigg, A., Lieb, R., Pfister, H., Maercker, A., et al. (2002). Patterns of incidence and psychiatric risk factors for traumatic events. *International Journal of Methods in Psychiatric Research, 11*(4), 143–153.

Stein, M. B., Walker, J. R., Hazen, A. L., & Forde, D. R. (1997). Full and partial posttraumatic stress disorder: Findings from a community survey. *American Journal of Psychiatry, 154*, 1114–1119.

Stewart, W. F., Ricci, J. A., Chee, E., Hahn, S. R., & Morganstein, D. (2003). Cost of lost productive work time among US workers with depression. *Journal of the American Medical Association, 289*, 3135–3144.

Sutker, P. B., Vasterling, J. J., Brailey, K., & Allain, A. N. (1995). Memory, attention, and executive deficits in POW survivors: Contributing biological and psychological factors. *Neuropsychology, 9*(1), 118–125.

Teicher, M. H., Samson, J. A., Polcari, A., & McGreenery, C. E. (2006). Sticks, stones, and hurtful words: Relative effects of various forms of childhood maltreatment. *American Journal of Psychiatry, 163*, 993–1000.

Teplin, L. A. (1990). The prevalence of severe mental disorder among male urban jail detainees: Comparison with the Epidemiologic Catchment Area Program. *American Journal of Public Health, 80*, 663–669.

Teplin, L. A., Abram, K. M., & McClelland, G. M. (1994). Does psychiatric disorder predict violent crime among released jail detainees? A six-year longitudinal study. *American Psychologist, 49*, 335–342.

Teplin, L. A., Abram, K. M., & McClelland, G. M. (1996). Prevalence of psychiatric disorders among incarcerated women: 1. Pretrial jail detainees. *Archives of General Psychiatry, 53*, 505–512.

Teplin, L. A., Abram, K. M., & McClelland, G. M. (1997). Mentally disordered women in jail: Who receives services? *American Journal of Public Health, 87*, 604–609.

Teplin, L. A., & Swartz, J. (1989). Screening for severe mental disorder in jails: The development of the Referral Decision Scale. *Law and Human Behavior, 13*, 1–18.

Thabet, A. A., Abu Tawahina, A., El Sarraj, E., & Vostanis, P. (2008). Exposure to war trauma and PTSD among parents and children in the Gaza strip. *European Child and Adolescent Psychiatry, 17*(4), 191–199.

Tolin, D. F., & Foa, E. B. (2006). Sex differences in trauma and posttraumatic stress disorder: A quantitative review of 25 years of research. *Psychological Bulletin, 132*, 959–992.

Tracy, M., Hobfoll, S. E., Canetti-Nisim, D., & Galea, S. (2008). Predictors of depressive symptoms among Israeli Jews and Arabs during the Al Aqsa Intifada: A population-based cohort study. *Annals of Epidemiology, 18*, 447–457.

Trestman, R. L., Ford, J., Zhang, W., & Wiesbrock, V. (2007). Current and lifetime psychiatric illness among inmates not identified as acutely mentally ill at intake in Connecticut's jails. *Journal of the American Academy of Psychiatry and Law, 35*, 490–500.

Trickett, P. K., Noll, J. G., Reiffman, A., & Putnam, F. W. (2001). Variants of intrafamilial sexual abuse experience: Implications for short- and long-term development. *Development and Psychopathology, 13*(4), 1001–1019.

Turner, R. J., & Lloyd, D. A. (2003). Cumulative adversity and drug dependence in young adults: Racial/ethnic contrasts. *Addiction, 98*, 305–315.

Turner, R. J., & Lloyd, D. A. (2004). Stress burden and the lifetime incidence of psychiatric disorder in young adults: Racial and ethnic contrasts. *Archives of General Psychiatry, 61*, 481–488.

Vinton, L., & Wilke, D. J. (2014). Are collaborations enough? Professionals' knowledge of victim services. *Violence Against Women, 20*(6), 716–729. http://dx.doi.org/10.1177/1077801214539857.

Weisel, D. L. (2005). Analyzing repeat victimizations The Office of Community Oriented Policing Services (Ed.), *Problem oriented guides for police: Problem-solving tool series*. Washington, DC: U.S. Department of Justice.

Whitbeck, L. B., Hoyt, D. R., & Yoder, K. A. (1999). A risk-amplification model of victimization and depressive symptoms among runaway and homeless adolescents. *American Journal of Community Psychology, 27*, 273–296.

Wiking, E., Johansson, S. E., & Sundquist, J. (2004). Ethnicity, acculturation, and self reported health. A population based study among immigrants from Poland, Turkey, and Iran in Sweden. *Journal of Epidemiology and Community Health, 58*, 574–582.

Yehuda, R., & Flory, J. D. (2007). Differentiating biological correlates of risk, PTSD, and resilience following trauma exposure. *Journal of Traumatic Stress, 20*, 435–447.

Yule, W. (2000). From pogroms to "ethnic cleansing": Meeting the needs of war affected children. *Journal of Child Psychology and Psychiatry, 41*, 695–702.

Neurobiology of traumatic stress disorders and their impact on physical health

5

Every emotion, thought, and action that a person experiences is preceded and accompanied by changes in the biology of the body. Although DesCartes asserted that the body and mind are fundamentally different, he (and philosophers and scientists for centuries since) recognized that the biology of the body is highly related to the activity of the mind. Indeed, every mental act—that is, every form of thinking—and every mental product—that is, our thoughts, emotions, goals, intentions, and plans of action—is the result of physiological activity in our brain (which in turn is always connected to biological activity in the rest of our body). The inherent inter-connection of the body and mind are of particular importance in understanding posttraumatic stress disorder (PTSD).

As you have seen in the prior chapters, PTSD involves complex changes in a person's state of mind: disturbing memories and emotions (intrusive reexperiencing and persistent negative emotions); thoughts dominated by an attempt to anticipate and avoid further danger or harm (hypervigilance and avoidance); and beliefs about the world, other people, and oneself that are focused on distrust and feeling disconnected and damaged (persistent negative beliefs, emotional and interpersonal detachment, dissociation). In this chapter, we discuss how the mental (and emotional, behavioral, and interpersonal) alterations involved in PTSD are grounded in parallel changes in the brain and the rest of the body. These profound changes begin with the intense visceral (that is, bodily) impact that is a universal reaction to experiencing a traumatic stressor.

Traumatic stressors are a physical as well as psychological shock, a threat, and an injury no matter whether they involve obvious physical injuries. Scientific studies have shown that people suffering from PTSD are biologically different than other people in a number of ways. However, the key physical change from which all other posttraumatic alterations in the body flow is a radical shift in the brain and body's stress response systems. Although it is not yet fully understood whether (and when) those biological changes are the causes or effects of PTSD—or the by-products of other disorders that occur along with PTSD ("comorbidities"; see Chapter 4)—the evidence is clear that PTSD involves a dramatically heightened level of physiological and neurological reactivity to stressors. This chapter therefore summarizes the rapidly growing scientific evidence base that has shown that PTSD is associated with three essential types of biological changes: (i) alterations in the body's stress response systems; (ii) alterations in brain structure, functioning, and chemistry that are associated with stress reactivity and PTSD; (iii) the role of genetics in PTSD; and (iv) physical

Posttraumatic Stress Disorder. DOI: http://dx.doi.org/10.1016/B978-0-12-801288-8.00005-4

health problems or medical diseases that are related to PTSD and its heightened stress reactivity.

There has been an explosion of scientific research on the biology of PTSD in the past two decades, much of which was the fortuitous by-product of a decision by the National Institute of Mental Health (NIMH) in the United States (and also other governmental, philanthropic, and corporate organizations that sponsor research studies in other countries as well as in the United States) to designate the 1990s as the "Decade of the Brain." At that time the NIMH strategic plan was to "promote discovery in the brain and behavioral sciences to fuel research on the causes of mental disorders." At the end of the next decade, NIMH launched a new initiative called the Research Domain Criteria (RDoC) project, with the goal of "integrat[ing] multiple scientific disciplines in a translational manner to identify 'fundamental behavioral components' that may play a role in a number of mental health disorders and that can be linked to neurobiological circuitry, (to) delineate dimensions of these fundamental behavioral components that range from normal to abnormal, (and to) establish standardized, reliable, and valid measures of these components in order to facilitate continuity across research studies" (Cuthbert & Kozak, 2013, pp. 928–929).

The RDoC framework laid out five mental and biological domains to be considered when scientifically studying psychological health and disorders: (i) Negative Valence Systems (sources and expressions of negative emotions), (ii) Positive Valence Systems (sources and expressions of positive emotions), (iii) Cognitive Systems (the mental abilities of attention, memory, information processing, decision making, and problem solving), (iv) Systems for Social Processes (social relationships), and (v) Arousal Systems (the bodily capacities to regulate physical arousal in order to preserve health, manage stress, and initiate and sustain effective behavior). Although PTSD involves all of these domains, the Negative Valence domain is of particular relevance because it emphasizes psychobiological reactions to three types of threat. Traumatic stressors are by definition a severe threat that evokes the first kind of psychobiological reaction: *acute* stress reactions. PTSD is a continuation of this initial psychobiological reaction to threat based on the traumatized individual's *anticipation* of further threats (i.e., hypervigilance), because the shock of the traumatic stressor makes what previously was a distant possibility of something terrible happening an all too real reality. "Once burned, twice shy" is a colloquial expression that captures the shift that occurs in PTSD such that a person becomes preoccupied with anxiety about possible future threats and no longer feels safe even when there is no obvious threat. The third type of threat is danger that does not just occur once or briefly but continues on a *sustained* basis such that the person becomes constantly on edge and fearful rather than just temporarily shocked. This corresponds to the traumatic stressors that are most likely to lead to PTSD due to persisting (or occurring periodically) over long periods of time, such as abuse or war. The RDoC concepts of negative valence experiences involving acute, anticipated, and sustained threat and psychobiological reactions to these threats will guide our exploration of the biology of PTSD.

Many of the symptoms of PTSD are characteristic of a dysregulated or hyperreactive bodily stress response system. We begin by discussing the stress response at the level of the autonomic nervous system (ANS), which consists of neural pathways that maintain bodily arousal and ready the body to respond to environmental threat—instigating the *fight-or-flight* response when appropriate. Several autonomic abnormalities associated with PTSD have been identified. Then we discuss how the brain or central nervous system (CNS) is responsible for detecting threat, orchestrating the body's response to threat, and regulating the body's recovery and return to homeostasis. A number of structural (i.e., the size and shape of areas of the brain) and functional (i.e., the biological activation of areas of the brain) abnormalities in the areas in the brain involved in stress response system have been linked to PTSD. Finally, we present a brief summary of research on stress-related genetic and epigenetic correlates of PTSD.

In general, you will notice that more research in this area has been conducted on adults with PTSD relative to children and adolescents. In addition, most of these works are cross-sectional, meaning that they collect data at one time point, and therefore tell us very little about changes in biological correlates of PTSD over time. In particular, very few studies have examined changes in biology prospectively beginning before traumatic stressors have occurred (pretrauma) and continuing afterward (posttrauma). This is not surprising given the practical difficulties in conducting long-term studies. Thus, it is difficult to know whether biological correlates of PTSD reflect premorbid risk factors (see Chapter 3) that increase the risk of developing PTSD symptoms or whether they are biological consequences of exposure to traumatic stressors and subsequent development of PTSD. The studies we will review often compare trauma-exposed individuals with PTSD either to others never exposed to traumatic stressors (i.e., nonexposed) or others who were exposed to traumatic stressors but who do not have PTSD (i.e., healthy trauma-exposed control participants). This is an important distinction in order to understand whether an observed biological anomaly is related to trauma exposure or PTSD or both.

Alterations in the body's stress response systems in PTSD

The body's stress response system is the product of neural pathways called "the ANS." The ANS maintains bodily arousal (i.e., energy, alertness, readiness to respond) at optimum levels by adjusting homeostatically to input from other body systems and from structures deep within the brain and the CNS that automatically monitor bodily integrity (such as the cerebellum; brainstem, midbrain, and network connecting the hypothalamus and the pituitary, and the adrenal glands—the "hypothalamus-pituitary-adrenal (HPA) axis"). The ANS has two "branches." The *sympathetic ANS* produces the "flight-or-flight" stress response (Mayes, 2000; Southwick et al., 1999). The *parasympathetic ANS* can be seen as a regulator or "brake" that maintains levels of sympathetic ANS arousal at levels high enough to permit effective thought and action but low enough to prevent excessive strain on the body (Mayes, 2000, p. 275). The acute threat response results from brain-activated responses by both branches of the ANS.

The ANS also controls the body's arousal levels to achieve a balance of mobilization and restoration of bodily energy and organ activity. The SNS branch of the ANS (so-called "adrenergic" functions regulated by noradrenaline or norepinephrine, NE) in controls the brain and body systems' (e.g., cardiovascular, pulmonary, gastrointes-tinal) arousal levels. The PNS branch of the ANS system operates via the vagus nerve and by restraining the SNS's activation enables the body to conserve energy and prevent overuse of critical organ systems. Rather than working independently, the SNS and PNS are intertwined in a relationship that is complex, reflecting the marriage of antagonistic influences striving to maintain homeostasis or *biological balance* in the face of environmental demands (Kandel & Squire, 2000).

When the SNS portion of the ANS is persistently activated, this state of chronic arousal tends to become extreme (this is called hyperarousal, which is a PTSD symptom). The stress response system tends to override and interfere with the body's immune system defenses (what McEwen has described as "allostatic load"; see Chapter 1) and also the brain systems that are necessary for three key aspects of learning: seeking novelty and rewards (which centers on areas deep in the brain, particularly governed by the neurotransmitter dopamine), tolerating and managing distress (which center on the emotional brain areas known as the limbic system and ventromedial cortex, particularly governed by the neurotransmitter serotonin), and problem-solving and goal-directed actions (which center on the prefrontal cortex). This helps to explain why PTSD may involve reckless or addictive behaviors, persistent negative emotion states, and difficulties with mental concentration, decision making, and avoidance.

ANS reactivity in PTSD

The physiological abnormality most consistently found to be associated with chronic PTSD (Delahanty & Boarts, 2008) is SNS hyperreactivity in response to reminders of traumatic events and to startling stimuli (such as a sudden loud noise) and lower than normal levels of a stress chemical secreted by the adrenal gland: cortisol. The high levels of arousal caused by SNS reactivity may help to explain PTSD's hyperarousal symptoms (and possibly also the anxious arousal involved in intrusive reexperiencing symptoms). Studies with recently traumatized people reveal patterns of posttraumatic physiological stress reactivity that shift over time. High initial levels of sympathetic ANS activation (often assessed by resting heart rate measurements taken in hospital emergency departments; Bryant, 2006) and low cortisol levels (Delahanty & Boarts, 2008) soon after experiencing traumatic accidents or violence are associated with greater risk of being diagnosed with PTSD at follow-up assessments between 1 month and 2 years later. However, heart rate measures taken later (1–4 months after traumatic events) and blood pressure measures taken soon after or months after traumatic exposure, were unrelated to the risk of PTSD 6 months later (Shalev & Yehuda, 1998). Abnormally high heart rates also predict later PTSD among children, but for children, *higher* cortisol levels were related to the risk of PTSD in direct contrast to findings with adults. Overall, elevated sympathetic ANS activation as measured by heart rate levels above 95 beats per minute soon after psychological trauma has been hypothesized to lead to stronger fear conditioning (and thus more intractable intrusive reexperiencing symptoms), which may lead to PTSD in some but not all cases (Bryant, 2006).

A number of studies have detected autonomic abnormalities in adults with PTSD compared to those without. Most consistently, studies have found PTSD to be associated with sympathetic hyperactivity and parasympathetic hypoactivity such that the part of the nervous system responsible for carrying out defensive responses to perceived threat dominates the part of the nervous system responsible for putting the brakes on the defense cascade (Pole, 2007). Laboratory paradigms for studying autonomic responses to perceived threat in individuals with PTSD include measuring physiological responses (e.g., heart rate, skin conductance, muscular activity) while participants are subjected to various aversive stimuli. These include loud tones (i.e., ≥100 dB), startling air puffs delivered to the larynx, images or videos that convey threat (e.g., angry or fearful faces, violence, mutilation), and cues that are specific to a person's traumatic experiences (e.g., associated images or words, trauma narrative or script).

The most consistent findings point to greater increases in heart rate and skin conductance by persons with PTSD in response to perceived threats in laboratory paradigms (i.e., the second stage of the defense cascade). For example, one study reported greater heart rate acceleration in reaction to unpleasant pictures in trauma-exposed refugees with PTSD compared to refugees without PTSD and nonexposed participants (Adenauer, Catani, Keil, Aichinger, & Neuner, 2010). In another study, trauma-exposed Israeli college students who reported greater PTSD symptom severity exhibited greater peak heart rates when listening to a narrated script about their traumatic experiences (Arditi-Babchuk, Feldman, & Gilboa-Schechtman, 2009). These researchers also reported less vagal tone activation as PTSD severity increased, suggesting less parasympathetic control or ability to put the brakes on the stress response (Arditi-Babchuk et al., 2009). Another study measured skin conductance responses in patients with PTSD and trauma-exposed individuals without PTSD presented with groups of words, some of which included a trauma-relevant word (Felmingham, Rennie, Manor, & Bryant, 2011). Compared to trauma-exposed adults without PTSD, adults with PTSD had a greater increase in skin conductance when shown threat-related words (Felmingham et al., 2011).

There have been far fewer studies on this topic in children and adolescents, with some consistency with adult studies. For example, one study examined heart rate responses in trauma-exposed preschool children subjected to a 3-minute conversation about the trauma compared to a nonexposed group involved in a conversation about a hypothetical car crash (Scheeringa, Zeanah, Myers, & Putnam, 2004). The researchers reported elevated heart rate responses during the trauma/car crash condition in trauma-exposed children with and without PTSD compared to nonexposed children (Scheeringa et al., 2004). Another study compared trauma-exposed children and adolescents with PTSD and nonexposed youth in a laboratory task measuring heart rate and skin conductance responses to standardized threat-related pictures and loud tones. Heart rate deceleration was greater and heart rate recovery smaller in the PTSD than in the control group within 3 seconds of picture onset, suggesting a more sustained period of attention (or freezing) for children with PTSD (Grasso & Simons, 2009). In addition, both the PTSD and control groups showed greater skin conductance responses to threat-related pictures; however, this effect was more sustained for children with PTSD, whereas the control children appeared to habituate to these stimuli (Grasso & Simons, 2009).

A few studies examined prospective relationships between autonomic responses to laboratory stressors and development of PTSD symptoms. These studies suggest that dysregulated autonomic functioning may increase a person's vulnerability to developing symptoms following trauma exposure. For example, Bryant, Creamer, O'Donnell, Silove, and McFarlane (2008) reported that traumatically injured patients assessed upon admission to the hospital were more likely to develop PTSD 3 months later if they had had higher resting heart rates and respiration rates at intake. Guthrie and Bryant (2005) found that greater skin conductance responses to loud tones in trainee firefighters prior to trauma-exposure positively predicted traumatic stress symptoms assessed within 4 weeks of an identified trauma exposure. Pole et al. (2009) found that greater skin conductance responses to loud tones in police cadets were positively associated with PTSD symptom severity following a trauma exposure. Pineles et al. (2013) found that heart rate responses to personalized trauma cues measured within 1 month of physical or sexual assault were correlated with the severity of PTSD symptoms when the traumatized individuals were reassessed 3 months later.

Two prospective studies in children examined the predictive value of the resting heart rate on PTSD symptoms. One study measured resting heart rates in children hospitalized for traumatic injury and found that an elevated heart rate during hospitalization predicted the development of PTSD 6 months later (Bryant, Salmon, Sinclair, & Davidson, 2007). This study is consistent with evidence linking resting heart rates and PTSD in adults by the same group (Bryant et al., 2008). Similarly, another prospective study reported a significant positive association between resting heart rates and acute stress symptoms in children and adolescents assessed within 4 weeks of a traumatic injury; however, they did not find that resting heart rate significantly predicted PTSD assessed 6 months later (Nixon et al., 2010). Although prospective studies are difficult to conduct, they have the potential to identify important early predictors of PTSD that may inform how we prevent the development of symptoms in individuals who are exposed to trauma.

Other studies have found autonomic differences when comparing trauma-exposed or maltreated youth to nonexposed youth, without considering PTSD. A study of physically and sexually abused children in a pediatric psychiatric inpatient facility reported a decrease in the resting heart rate and systolic blood pressure immediately (i.e., within minutes) after a routine blood draw in physically abused, but not sexually abused, boys (Ford, Fraleigh, Albert, & Connor, 2010). The authors interpreted this hyporesponsivity in physically abused adolescents as evidence of tonic immobility or autonomic deceleration (freezing), likened to "playing dead" (Ford et al., 2010). Pollak, Vardi, Putzer Bechner, and Curtin (2005) examined changes in heart rate in physically abused and nonabused children during an active anger condition (i.e., angry conversation in the background) and a silent, unresolved anger condition immediately following the conversation. Both groups displayed heart rate deceleration during the active anger and unresolved conditions; however, the physically abused children exhibited greater heart rate deceleration than the nonabused children during the unresolved anger condition, suggestive of tonic immobility or freezing when the threat is unpredictable and imminent (Pollak et al., 2005).

Although PTSD's persistent hyperarousal does not appear to involve some ANS-related systems (such as blood pressure), it is not limited to the cardiovascular system: skin conductance (which is manifested as sweating) and a subtle form of startle responses (eyeblink) both are associated with PTSD. Police officer trainees who developed PTSD in the first year of active duty could be distinguished from those who did not by higher levels of subjective fearfulness and sympathetic ANS reactivity to a startling stimulus when anticipating a shock, but this was true only for skin conductance but and not for heart rate (Pole et al., 2009). Those who developed PTSD also were slower to reduce this ANS reactivity—called "habituation"—that is, to become used to and less affected by the startling stimulus—when anticipating a shock. Skin conductance and heart rate may differ, despite both being influenced by sympathetic ANS activation, in that the former is particularly associated with anxiety and the latter with the fight-or-flight fear response. Thus, the physiology of PTSD may involve a variety of alterations that share the common feature of increased stress reactivity and reduced ability to regain an optimum (neither too high nor too low) level of arousal, but that differ in which phase of the stress response is involved (Box 5.1).

Some biological markers of hyperarousal (such as skin conductance) are particularly malleable via classical conditioning (see Box 5.2) and may in part account for PTSD's general stress reactivity (Orr et al., 2000). Other physiological features associated with PTSD (such as startle eyeblink) are primarily affected by the overall circumstances ("context"; Grillon, Morgan, Davis, & Southwick, 1998), and may thus reflect or contribute to PTSD's hypervigilance. These findings from physiological research indicate that PTSD involves not one but many changes in the body's stress response systems. PTSD's hyperarousal also appears to involve physiological (ANS and HPA) reactivity that does not occur all the time ("tonically") but primarily only when reminders or memories of traumatic experiences occur ("phasically"; Southwick et al., 2007).

Stress hormones and PTSD

Stress induces the release of corticotrophin-releasing hormone by the hypothalamus, which in turn stimulates the pituitary gland to excrete adrenocorticotropic hormone, and this triggers the adrenal gland to produce hormones called a "glucocorticoid" that is called cortisol. Cortisol triggers a cascade of physiological changes to ready the body to respond adaptively to the stressor. Cortisol acts as a brake on the HPA system by signaling the hypothalamus to reduce its production of other stress chemicals that are associated with sympathetic ANS activation; thus, lower levels of cortisol (which are accompanied by a higher than normal level of these other arousal-increasing stress chemicals and brain receptors for them, called "glucocorticoids") may reflect a breakdown in the brain's regulation of stress-related physiological arousal in PTSD—by analogy, a vehicle that is out of control because of a stuck accelerator (high levels of sympathetic ANS activity) and a broken braking system (low levels of cortisol; Yehuda & LeDoux, 2007).

Because measuring cortisol in the human brain is not practically feasible, cortisol is typically measured in the peripheral nervous system—most commonly in urine,

Box 5.1 Key Points

1. People suffering from PTSD are biologically different than other people, although it is not yet fully understood whether (and when) those biological differences are the causes or effects of PTSD or the by-products of other disorders that occur along with PTSD ("comorbidities").

2. PTSD is associated with three essential types of biological changes: alterations in the body's stress response systems; alterations in brain chemistry, structure, and functioning; and physical health problems or diseases.

3. Animal studies that involve severe (but not actually life-threatening) stressors have shown that there are four basic phases in the biological stress response: freezing to prepare for danger; flight (attempting to escape danger); fight (attempting to fend off aggressors); and "tonic immobility" (an involuntary shutdown of the body's defensive systems). PTSD involves similar biological and behavioral reactions, particularly when the traumatic stressor is an intentional assault that also involves being trapped (such as rape or bullying).

4. Areas of the brain that are highly involved in the response to stressors include those that regulate the person's arousal level (such as the "locus coeruleus," deep at the base of the brain) and those that are activated when emotions are experienced (such as the "limbic system" structures known as the "amygdala," "hippocampus," and "anterior cingulate").

5. The locus coeruleus and amygdala interact to create an "alarm" reaction that is the hallmark of PTSD (such as being easily startled or often tense and on edge).

6. The hippocampus and amygdala are areas in the brain's "limbic system" that are important in the formation, storage, and recall ("retrieval") of memories. The amygdala is particularly crucial to the memories of fear that are characteristic of PTSD. The hippocampus is crucial to forming and being able to access more ordinary memories, especially those that involve sequences of events that make up a "narrative" (or story) of one's life. The hippocampus may be damaged (before or as a result of PTSD), and also may be forced "off-line" by intense activation of the amygdala when PTSD occurs.

7. The front area of the brain's frontal cortex (the "prefrontal cortex") and the nearby front ("anterior") portion of the cingulate (a bridge between the frontal cortex and the limbic system) play a key role in conscious thinking, planning, and knowing—including thinking about and knowing one's own emotions and formulating action plans to effectively deal with both stressors and emotions ("emotion regulation"). Growing evidence suggests that these areas in the brain are underactivated when PTSD occurs.

8. Genetic studies show that there is no single gene or combination of genes that specifically lead to PTSD, but several "candidates" (genes that appear likely to contribute to PTSD) have been identified and are being studied. These studies usually are "gene by environment interaction" studies, meaning that they involve identifying genes (or portions of genes) that lead a person to be more vulnerable to PTSD if the person experiences a traumatic stressor (i.e., if the environment has sufficient danger or causes sufficient harm to be traumatic).

9. The body's stress response system tends to be inversely related to the body's immune system: when stress reactivity occurs, the immune system's ability to protect against biological threats that may cause or exacerbate illness is reduced.

10. PTSD is associated with an increase in the risk of stress-related or stress-exacerbated medical conditions (such as cardiovascular disease and diabetes), stress-related behaviors that place the person at risk for medical illness (such as smoking), and "somatic dissociation" (the conversion of unexpressed or unconscious psychological distress into physical symptoms).

Box 5.2 Biological/Behavioral Models of PTSD Based on Research with Animals

PTSD involves chronic states of fear that are not unique to human beings. Animals from many species behave in ways that reflect a similar state of fearfulness. Researchers therefore have studied the behavior and biological responses in a variety of animals in order to better understand when and how fear occurs and persists. Although the thoughts and beliefs that are an integral part of protracted states of fear cannot be expressed in words by animals, their behavior and the changes in their bodies (especially in the brain) that occur when animals are exposed to severe danger or to painful stimuli may be similar enough to what humans experience in PTSD to provide a window into the causes and changes associated with PTSD. Medical research has included studies of animals for many centuries in order to enable scientists to better understand and physicians to better treat illnesses. Psychologists also have tested animals in order to gain insights into the role of biology and the environment in learning, memory, emotions, disorders, relationships, and development. These studies with animals are called "preclinical" research because they provide a basis for hypotheses to guide studies with humans ("clinical" research). They also are called "analogue" or "comparative" research because the physiological and behavioral responses of animals are similar ("analogous") enough to those of humans to enable scientists to make "comparisons" that inform and accelerate research with humans. In the PTSD field, studies with animals have led to important new insights into the nature of PTSD that have been translated into innovations in the diagnosis and treatment of PTSD.

The first consideration in conducting research with animals is that the animals should always be treated in a humane manner (see the American Psychological Association's *Guidelines for Ethical Conduct in the Care and Use of Animals*, http://www.apa.org/science/anguide.html). Exactly how this should be done and whether research should involve subjecting animals to pain, deprivation, fear, or death (as in studies in which animals are euthanized in order to dissect and study their body chemistry and organs) remain a matter of controversy.

In order for research with animals to provide useful insights and hypotheses for research and treatment with humans, two basic conditions must be met (Ronan & Summers, 2008). The first is "face validity"—whether the experimental conditions and the animal's responses are similar to those of the human experience or disorder of interest. The second is predictive validity—whether changes in the experimental conditions lead to changes in the animal's responses that reflect either a worsening or improvement in the animal's responses that would be expected based on the theoretical hypotheses being tested. The third is construct validity—whether the behavioral and biological processes observed in the animal's responses are consistent with those of the human experience or disorder of interest. The following examples illustrate how preclinical research has developed and refined theoretical models and insights about the nature of PTSD.

(Continued)

Box 5.2 Continued

Classical Conditioning of Fear. The Russian physiologist Pavlov conducted studies with dogs early in the twentieth century that led to the formulation of the paradigm of learning known as "classical conditioning." Pavlov discovered that when a neutral stimulus (such as a light) was made to occur just prior to the receipt of food, dogs would begin to salivate when that neutral ("conditioned") stimulus was presented even if they did not receive food (the "unconditioned stimulus"). Researchers subsequently have shown that a variety of species reflexively learn to fear a neutral stimulus if it repeatedly precedes the presentation of a painful or dangerous unconditioned stimulus (Ronan & Summers, 2008). For example, the "social predator" model involves exposing animals to stimuli that indicate the presence of a dangerous predator (such as the smell of cat urine for rats). The "social defeat" or "resident-intruder" model involves having a more dominant or aggressive animal from the same species placed in an animal's territory. These stressors have face validity because they are "ecologically relevant" (Ronan & Summers, 2008)—that is, they represent extreme forms of danger similar to the life-threatening events that are required for a human stressor to be "traumatic" when they happen in the natural environment. The paradigms have predictive validity because neutral stimuli associated with the unconditioned danger stimuli reliably elicit fear reactions, and changes in the circumstances that are associated with safety tend to reduce the likelihood and intensity of fear reactions (this is called "extinction" of learned fear; Bouton, 2002). These paradigms also have construct validity because the animals consistently behave and react physically in ways that parallel PTSD's terror when reminded of a traumatic stressor ("intrusive reexperiencing") and extreme guardedness ("hypervigilance"), even when the stimulus signaling the presence of a predator or the actual intruder are not present.

An innovative recent theoretical model derived from research with animals using the predator paradigm is the "tonic immobility" theory of PTSD following sexual assault (Marx, Forsyth, Gallup, Fuse, & Lexington, 2008). These researchers observed that when animals are not only confronted by a predator (such as a cat placed in a cage that is separate from but adjacent to another cage in which a rodent resides, or introducing stimuli indicating the presence of a cat into the rodent's space) but also placed in a position that prevents them from fighting back or escaping (such as a rodent being rolled over onto its back), a predictable sequence of reactions ensues. First, the threatened and restrained animal tends to "freeze"—that is, to cease moving, while experiencing a dramatic upsurge in sympathetic nervous system arousal (e.g., accelerated heartbeat, tremor). Next, the animal will attempt to flee or escape, continuing to experience high levels of arousal. Third, if unable to escape, the animal will redirect toward the predator in an attempt to regain dominance (displaying rage, struggling, or fighting). If neither of the "fight-or-flight" reactions are successful in terminating the danger, a fourth stage of "tonic immobility" ensues. Tonic immobility is a state of involuntary behavioral paralysis and physiological down-regulation. That is, the animal appears to abruptly stop all behaviors and to collapse physically such that it may actually appear to be dead. The physiological down-regulation seems involve a shift from intense sympathetic nervous system arousal in the freeze, flight, and fight phases to an equal an opposite activation of the parasympathetic nervous system. Thus, tonic immobility is a state of high stress reactivity in which the animal appears paradoxically to no longer be reacting but instead to have given up. In the natural ecology, tonic immobility may promote survival by leading predators to cease attacking or lose interest because the "prey" is no longer trying to escape or fight back.

Applying the tonic immobility paradigm to humans, researchers have noted striking parallels to the reaction of sexual assault victims (Marx et al., 2008). While the research is not conclusive, rape victims often describe going through a sequence of responses both during the assault and when experiencing PTSD symptoms when having unwanted memories or reminders of the rape. An initial reaction of stunned disbelief or feeling "frozen with fear" is common, often followed by an intense desire to escape or struggle to defend oneself. If the assailant is able to restrain or trap the victim more than briefly, victims often describe feeling as if their body simply gives out and they shut down and give up mentally. A sense of helplessness and apathy tends to ensue, which can lead to feelings of guilt, failure, and self-blame by the victim and social stigma ("S/he should not have stopped trying to fight back if s/he really didn't want this to happen"). The tonic immobility model provides an important alternative perspective: rather than faulting the victim, it is more accurate to recognize that a self-protective stress reaction over which the victim had no control took place. This is consistent with research with animals and humans showing that when no other response is available, the body's stress response system shifts into a mode of conserving physical resources (and perhaps signaling to aggressors to cease causing harm) that redirects the body's energies toward healing (the immune system) and staying alive rather than flight or fight.

Instrumental Conditioning of Avoidance. Another important model of learning and stress reactivity derived from research with animals was pioneered by B. F. Skinner (1938; Ferster & Skinner, 1957) in landmark works on "contingencies of reinforcement" affecting the behaviors of animals such as rats and pigeons. Skinner observed that animals tend to increase the rate of behaviors that are followed by certain changes in their environment. He called this phenomenon "reinforcement" that occurs due to the animal's learning that there is a "contingent" relationship between doing that behavior (e.g., pecking or pushing a lever in the cage) and receiving a desired outcome (the reinforce—for example, a pellet of food). Behavior that might previously have been rare or sporadic can become regular and frequent if the contingency of reinforcement is set up to teach the animal that the behavior seems to produce the reinforcer. This is another form of conditioned learning, which is called instrumental conditioning

(Continued)

Box 5.2 Continued

because the animal learns that a behavior is "instrumental" in increasing the likelihood that a reinforcer will occur.

The form of reinforcement that is most relevant to PTSD is negative reinforcement. Negative reinforcement involves learning that doing a certain behavior will result in the removal of an undesirable or distressing stimulus from the environment. For example, dogs will instinctively try to run away if placed in a cage in which they are periodically subjected to an electric shock, and they will rapidly learn to do apparently extraneous behaviors (such as touching a particular spot on the wall with a paw) if that "turns off" the shock (or, better yet, prevents it from occurring in the first place) even if they cannot escape the cage. Negative reinforcement thus involves learning ways to escape or avoid an aversive stimulus, which is just as "instrumental" as learning to use other behaviors to get desired reinforcers. The absence or termination of the aversive consequence (the shock and the resultant pain, as well as the anxiety of anticipating this) is the reinforcer in the case of negative reinforcement. The avoidance and hypervigilance symptoms of PTSD are classic examples of behavior that seems to result from negative reinforcement. By avoiding thinking, talking about, or going places and doing things that are reminders of traumatic stressors, and by being hypervigilant for signs of further danger, the person with PTSD becomes trapped in a vicious cycle in which avoidance and hypervigilance become extremely ingrained because they seem to be the only way to escape or avoid the unwanted memories, the intense stress reactions that are triggered by reminders of traumatic experiences, and the threat of further harm from additional traumatic experiences. Negative reinforcement therefore may lead to a worsening and chronicity of PTSD rather than promoting safety or preventing PTSD.

Dual Conditioning Models. A combination of classical and instrumental conditioning was described by O. H. Mowrer (1947) as a "two factor theory" of learning. Mowrer observed that animals (and humans) learn to respond based on both stimulus-stimulus relationships (i.e., classical conditioning) and stimulus-response-consequence relationships (i.e., instrumental conditioning). Twenty years later, D'Amato, Fazzaro, and Etkin (1968) elaborated the two factor model and applied it specifically to the learning of avoidance behavior. D'Amato and colleagues observed that animals learn to avoid both stimuli that elicit anticipatory anxiety as well as those that signal objective danger and that their avoidance behavior was associated with negative reinforcement resulting from a reduction in anticipatory anxiety as well as in objective danger.

An additional extension of conditioning theories of particular relevance to PTSD is provided by Bouton's (2002) research with animals on mechanisms of a second form of learning related to fear: extinction. Bouton observed that animals do not "un-learn" or "forget" fear established by classical conditioning, but they can learn that a stimulus that previously was associated with danger no longer signals an actual threat. For example, if rodents repeatedly experience an unpleasant shock to their feet preceded by a particular sound or light, they will tend to show signs of fear by "freezing" behaviorally and of avoidance if they are able to terminate or escape the shock by doing certain behaviors that signal that the shock will *not* occur. If the avoidance behavior is prevented and a new series of experiences occurs repeatedly in which the warning signal occurs and is not followed by the shock, the animal may learn that the former warning signals no longer indicate imminent danger and may cease to "freeze" when those signals occur. This new learning that what formerly signaled danger no longer does so is extinction. Bouton also noted, however, that extinction learning is easily reversed under several circumstances: the conditioned fear ("freezing" behavior) may resume when the warning signal occurs if (i) a period of time passes without any exposure to the warning signal ("spontaneous recovery"); (ii) the animal's environmental context changes, particularly in ways that are similar to the context in which the original fear conditioning took place ("renewal"); or (iii) the shock is administered again, whether preceded ("reacquisition") or not ("reinstatement") by the warning signal.

Applied to PTSD, the dual conditioning models suggest the hypothesis that PTSD symptoms involve both classically conditioned anxiety (i.e., distress elicited by stimuli associated with memories or reminders of traumatic experiences) and instrumentally conditioned avoidance (i.e., negative reinforcement as a result of relief from PTSD memories and stress reactions; Foa & Kozak, 1986). Further, recovery from PTSD requires new learning that reminders or memories of the traumatic event are tolerable and need not be avoided—that is, extinction of the learned fear. The PTSD treatment models with the strongest evidence of efficacy were derived initially from these animal research dual conditioning models of PTSD (see Chapters 7 and 8).

saliva, or plasma, which can only provide a rough estimate of cortisol in the brain. Newer studies are examining cortisol derived from hair samples. There are a number of ways to examine cortisol, including quantifying baseline circulating levels, charting diurnal fluctuations in cortisol levels, and examining cortisol reactivity and recovery in the context of a laboratory stress paradigm.

In general, studies examining baseline cortisol levels in individuals with PTSD are mixed with some studies reporting *higher* than normal levels associated with PTSD (Pitman & Orr, 1990; Young & Breslau, 2004), others reporting *lower* cortisol levels (Yehuda et al., 2000), and several not finding an association (Meewise, Reitsma, De Vries, Gersons, & Olff, 2007). Elevated cortisol levels may reflect the body's attempt to regulate a hyperactive stress response system (Yehuda & LeDoux, 2007; Young & Breslau, 2004). Lower cortisol levels may be the result of chronically high stress reactivity that ultimately exhausts the HPA axis system. In fact, one meta-analysis demonstrated an effect for reduced cortisol levels following a period of elevated stress (Miller, Chen, & Zhou, 2007). There are also studies suggesting differences in direction (lower versus higher) according to age, with children with PTSD showing lower than normal levels of cortisol (Carrion et al., 2002; De Bellis et al., 1999) and the opposite for adults with childhood trauma and PTSD (Yehuda, 2002). Thus, another complicating factor is the influence of developmental processes on cortisol functioning. Finally, subtypes of PTSD or different profiles of symptoms may be associated with differential functioning of the HPA axis and associated cortisol levels. For example, while lower cortisol may be associated with symptoms characteristic of avoidance and depression, higher cortisol may be associated with reexperiencing and hyperarousal symptoms.

Prospective research suggests that abnormal cortisol levels may be a premorbid factor that increases individuals' vulnerability to developing symptoms. Consistent with this notion is a recent study that examined plasma cortisol in patients admitted to a level 1 trauma center following injury, then assessed PTSD symptoms 6 weeks and 6 months posttrauma (Mouthaan et al., 2014). The authors reported that lower levels of cortisol predicted PTSD symptoms at both time points, controlling for a number of variables. The authors speculated that low levels of cortisol might fail to activate the negative feedback loop, thereby maintaining the adrenergic stress response and intensifying the traumatic experience and trauma memory formation (Mouthaan et al., 2014). While this finding is promising and is consistent with some prospective studies (Aardal-Eriksson, Eriksson, & Thorell, 2001; Delahanty, Raimonde, & Spoonster, 2000; Ehring, Ehlers, Cleare, & Glucksman, 2008; McFarlane, Atchison, & Yehuda, 1997; McFarlane, Barton, Yehuda, & Wittert; 2011), it should be interpreted alongside other prospective studies that have failed to find a significant association between cortisol and PTSD symptom development (Bonne et al., 2003; McFarlane et al., 1997; Resnick, Yehuda, Pitman, & Foy, 1995; Shalev et al., 2008).

A small number of studies have examined PTSD in relation to cortisol reactivity using laboratory "stress challenges" that may take the form of cognitive, social, or physical (such as the cold pressor task) stressors, or showing the individual trauma-related stimuli or personalized trauma narratives (descriptions of specific traumatic events that have occurred to the person). For the most part, with some exceptions (Bremner et al., 2003; Elzinga, Schmahl, Vermetten, van Dyck, & Bremner, 2003), there appears not to be a significant association between PTSD and cortisol reactivity to a laboratory stressor (Klassens, Giltay, Cuijpers, van Veen, & Zitman, 2012). However, given the small number of investigations and the extent to which methodological approaches differ, it is hard to draw a conclusion based on these data. However, there are a number of studies indicating that children who experienced prolonged traumatic adversity are prone as adults to recurrent depression that may be accompanied by either low (Bockting et al., 2012; Suzuki, Poon, Papadopoulos, Kumari, & Cleare, 2014) or heightened (when accompanied by dissociation; Carvalho Fernando et al., 2012) levels of cortisol reactivity. Whether these adults also are experiencing PTSD and whether their depression symptoms and altered cortisol responses are related to or separate from the symptoms of PTSD are questions that remain to be answered.

Alterations in brain structure, functioning, and chemistry in PTSD

Neuroimaging technology allows researchers to examine brain structure, as well as brain activity, accomplished by conducting brain scans while participants are engaged in a task designed to activate relevant brain areas. Brain scans yield excellent spatial resolution at the expense of temporal resolution, which means that, although we get a good picture of the structure of the brain, we cannot examine changes in brain functioning that occur very rapidly (on the order of milliseconds or seconds). Several neuroimaging studies have been conducted comparing the brains of individuals with and without PTSD. Brain areas implicated in the body's stress response system have been consistently associated with PTSD and include parts of the lower brain (the locus coeruleus, caudate, and reticular formation), the limbic system (the amygdala, hippocampus, and insula), the anterior cingulate cortex, and the frontal cortex (ventromedial/orbital and dorsolateral prefrontal cortices).

Brain structure and PTSD

Brain areas that most consistently are found to be related to PTSD are in the brainstem (the locus coeruleus; see Box 5.3), the limbic system (the amygdala and the hippocampus; see Box 5.4), and the frontal cortex (ventromedial/orbital and dorsolateral prefrontal cortices; see Box 5.5). Neuroimaging studies—that is, brain scans—have used several technologies to examine the structure—typically the size or volume—of these brain areas in people with and without PTSD, including magnetic resonance imaging (MRI), positron emission tomography (PET), or single-photon emission computed tomography.

Numerous neuroimaging studies have shown that adults (but not children) with PTSD tend to have smaller hippocampi on both the left and right sides of the brain than non-trauma-exposed adults without PTSD (Bremner, 2007). However, there are contradictory findings concerning hippocampal size of persons with PTSD in comparison with people who have experienced comparable psychological traumas but who do not have PTSD, and evidence that people who develop PTSD may have smaller hippocampi *before* exposure to psychological trauma and the development of PTSD (Bremner, 2008). Thus, a smaller hippocampus may be a vulnerability factor for PTSD rather than a consequence (Yehuda & LeDoux, 2007).

Few structural neuroimaging studies have been reported examining amygdala volume in PTSD. Depue et al. (2014) found that combat military veterans with PTSD and traumatic brain injuries (TBI) had smaller amygdalas than combat military veterans who had neither PTSD nor TBI, and that smaller amygdala size was correlated with more severe PTSD symptoms and greater difficulty in inhibiting impulsive behaviors. A study of women psychiatric patients diagnosed with borderline personality disorder, half of whom had a history of PTSD, reported that these women had 22% smaller amygdalas than women who were not receiving psychiatric treatment, did not have borderline personality disorder, and rarely (<10%) had histories of PTSD (Schmahl,

Box 5.3 The Locus Coeruleus (LC) and PTSD

The LC is a small, bluish nucleus (self-contained structure) located on each side of the pons in the brainstem (Bracha & Maser, 2008). The LC provides as much as 90% of the body's supply of the neurotransmitter that acts most directly on the ANS: norepinephrine/noradrenaline (NE). Not surprisingly, medications that interfere with the production of NE in the LC (such as the "beta adrenergic receptor blocker" propanolol, or inderol) were originally developed to reduce high blood pressure but more recently have shown promise in reducing the severity of physiological reactivity to trauma memory reminders months after a traumatic experience (see Chapter 9).

The LC transmits neural signals throughout most of the brain, primarily increasing the level of activation in ways that may be manifested behaviorally as a cardinal symptom of PTSD: startle reactions. The LC also sends neural signals to activate the sympathetic ANS via the spinal cord and to inhibit the parasympathetic ANS via the vagus nerve. The LC thus triggers most of the physical symptoms of fear: rapid heart rate, skin conductance, hyperventilation, dilated pupils, gut pain, dry mouth, muscle tension, and in severe cases, tonic immobility (see Box 5.1).

The LC receives neural signals that reduce its activation ("inhibitory afferents") from the anterior cingulate, the medulla, and the Raphe nuclei, and those that increase its activation ("excitatory afferents") from the amygdala and a midbrain area involved in pain and defensive behaviors (the periaqueductal gray). These findings are consistent with the view that the LC plays a vital role in activating defensive stress reactions (triggered by the amygdala) unless its activity is inhibited by the ventromedial prefrontal cortex (specifically the anterior cingulate).

A postmortem study of three World War II veterans with war-related PTSD found them to have 30% fewer neurons than four healthy veterans, suggesting that PTSD may involve excessive LC activation that can "burn out" the LC from overuse (Bracha & Maser, 2008).

Box 5.4 The Hippocampus and PTSD

The limbic system, often referred to as the "emotional brain," is an area deep in the middle of the brain that is in many ways a bridge between brain areas that lie in the brainstem (such as the locus coeruleus; see Box 5.3) and the frontal cortex (ventromedial/orbital and dorsolateral prefrontal cortex; see Box 5.5). The limbic system is a collection of distinct but interconnected brain regions that play several important roles in fear, stress reactivity, learning, and memory. Hence, it is not surprising that limbic system areas are intimately involved in PTSD.

The hippocampus is a small seahorse-shaped brain area that has been shown to be damaged in studies of animals that are exposed to chronic stressors (Bremner, 2008). Studies with animals and humans reveal that the hippocampus is critical for memory, particularly for storing new memories in long-term memory ("encoding") and recalling them ("retrieval") when they involve language ("verbal" or "declarative" memory), environmental contexts ("contextual" memory), or visual perception of three-dimensional environments ("spatial" memory). Individuals with PTSD have been shown to have problems with these types of memory, using both neuropsychological tests (such as the Wechsler Memory Scale, the visual and verbal components of the Selective Reminding Test, the Auditory Verbal Learning Test, Paired Associate Recall, the California Verbal New Learning Test, and the Rivermead Behavioral Memory Test; Bremner, 2008) and virtual reality tasks such as a virtual water maze (Astur et al., in review; see Figure 5.2). The specific function of the hippocampus is suggested by findings that visual memory and overall intellectual functioning (which are not specifically related to the hippocampus, although it may have some indirect roles in those functions) do *not* tend to be impaired in PTSD.

Several studies have shown that PTSD patients have deficits in hippocampal activation while performing a verbal declarative memory task or a virtual water maze task. The water maze task is known to specifically activate the hippocampus. Both hippocampal atrophy and hippocampal-based memory deficits have been found to be successfully reversed with treatment with the selective serotonergic reuptake inhibitor antidepressant medication paroxetine, which has been shown to promote the formation of neurons (neurogenesis) in the hippocampus in studies with animals. Phenytoin, an anticonvulsant (seizure) medication, also has been shown to be associated with increased hippocampal volume in PTSD patients. Therefore, it is possible that medications for PTSD may have their effects in part by positively affecting the hippocampus.

Results of functional imaging studies measuring brain function with PET and functional magnetic resonance imaging (fMRI) are consistent with the possibility that PTSD is associated with dysfunction of the hippocampus. Stimulation of the noradrenergic system with a substance called yohimbine resulted in a failure of activation in several frontal lobe regions, as well as decreased function in the hippocampus. Because stressful events are associated with norepinephrine release in the brain, and because high levels of norepinephrine release are associated with decreased brain function, these findings suggest that high levels of norepinephrine release in PTSD may be associated with decreased hippocampal function during everyday stressors, with associated cognitive impairment (Bremner, 2008).

The possibility that reduced hippocampal functioning plays a role in PTSD was further supported by studies showing that the deficits in declarative memory that are characteristic of many people with PTSD are associated with biological measures indicating poorer hippocampal functioning (Bremner, 2008).

(Continued)

Box 5.4 Continued

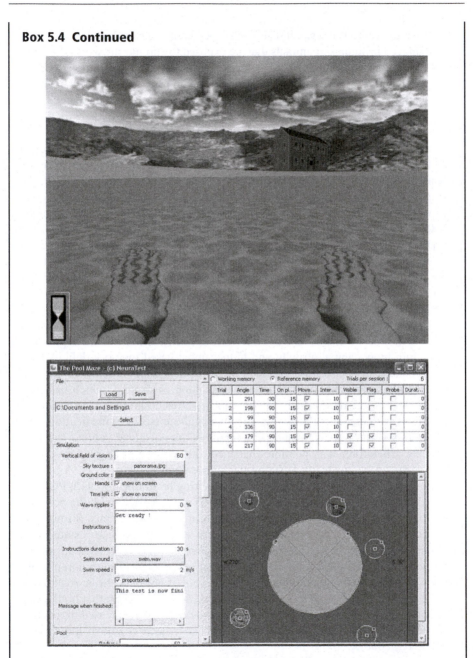

Figure 5.1 Virtual Morris water task. The pool maze is a computerized virtual version of the classical Morris water maze typically used in rodents to assess spatial memory. It is user friendly, versatile, and fully configurable without the assistance of a computer programmer. The software is designed to generate comparable testing procedures and paradigms to those employed with the Morris water maze in rodents.
© 2009 NeuraTest http://www.neuratest.com/services/software/the_pool_maze.html.

Furthermore, studies by Bremner (2008) and colleagues showed that when childhood sexual abuse survivors listened to scripts they had written describing their abuse experiences, they reported an increase in PTSD symptoms and showed a decrease in blood flow in the hippocampus (as measured by PET scans). When other women with PTSD due to childhood abuse were asked to remember emotionally charged words such as "rape-mutilate," researchers observed decreases in blood flow in the left hippocampus (but also in other brain regions). Thus, while it is not yet known whether a smaller or less optimally functioning hippocampus may lead people to be vulnerable to developing PTSD (Gilbertson et al., 2002) or whether the chronic physiological stress states involved in PTSD can actually damage the hippocampus (Bremner, 2008), this brain area is an important focus for further PTSD research. Another study reported smaller hippocampi soon after trauma exposure in adults who had acute PTSD versus those who did not (Wignall et al., 2004), also suggesting that a smaller hippocampus may be a vulnerability factor for PTSD rather than a consequence.

In a recent meta-analysis of cross-sectional studies examining hippocampal volume and PTSD, the combined effect across studies indicated that individuals with PTSD had significantly smaller bilateral hippocampal volumes than healthy controls and smaller left hippocampal volumes than trauma-exposed controls without PTSD. Studies comparing individuals with PTSD and healthy controls have reported 5–26% volume differences in individuals with PTSD (Bremner et al., 1995, 1997; Britton et al., 2005; Gurvits, Shenton, Hokama, & Ohta, 1996; Stein, Koverola, Hanna, Torchia, & McClarty, 1997). Notably, however, several studies have not replicated these findings (Bonne et al., 2003; Carrion et al., 2001; Corbo, Clement, Armony, Pruessner, & Brunet, 2005; Corcoran & Maren, 2001; De Bellis et al., 1999), indicating that not everyone meeting diagnostic criteria for PTSD has a relatively smaller hippocampus.

Contrary to these results in adult studies, there has not been strong evidence of smaller hippocampal size in children and adolescents who have been exposed to traumatic stressors or who have PTSD (Karl, Schaefer, et al., 2006). A meta-analytic review examined effects from four studies of children with maltreatment-related PTSD and found no significant differences compared to volumes in nonmaltreated children (Woon & Hedges, 2008). In fact, one of the studies revealed slightly larger hippocampal volumes in maltreated children compared to nonmaltreated children (De Bellis et al., 1999). Another study by the same group failed to find differences in maltreated children with PTSD compared to healthy controls (De Bellis et al., 2002). In a reanalysis of data obtained by pooling subjects from their previous studies, however, an effort to achieve a larger sample size and more statistical power, these researchers reported a significant group difference, with larger hippocampal volume controlling for cerebral volume in children with PTSD compared to healthy controls (Tupler & De Bellis, 2006). However, an earlier prospective study showed a progressive reduction in the size of the hippocampus in maltreated youth with PTSD over the course of 12–18

(*Continued*)

Box 5.4 Continued

months and that the severity of PTSD and related symptoms and cortisol levels were higher initially in the children who were maltreated and whose hippocampi appeared to shrink in size as time passed (Carrion, Weems, & Reiss, 2007).

There have been few studies examining how exposure to traumatic stressors or PTSD are related to the activity ("functional status") of the hippocampus A fMRI neuroimaging study found that children who had experienced traumatic stressors such as abuse or violence and were troubled by PTSD symptoms had lower levels of activation of their hippocampi when engaging in a memory task, compared to other children who had not experienced traumatic (Carrion, Haas, Garrett, Song, & Reiss, 2010). Thus, children with PTSD symptoms may be less able to use their hippocampus to retrieve memories—which could lead them to have difficulties in school or in simply being able to draw on their past experiences when thinking about the consequences of different actions (and vulnerable to acting in ways that are careless, reckless, or irresponsible).

Several studies with adults suggest that it may not be the size or capacity of the hippocampus that is altered in PTSD but instead the relationship between the hippocampus and its close neighbor in the limbic area, the amygdala. These studies examine the strength of the neural pathways or connections between different brain areas and have shown that areas near the hippocampus (the "para-hippocampus") and another nearby brain area that plays a key role in recognize emotions (the "insula") are more strongly connected in people with PTSD than in other adults (Rabinak et al., 2011; Sripada et al., 2012a, 2012b). While there is much more to be learned about how PTSD affect (or is affected by) subtle relationships such as these between brain areas that play key important roles in memory, emotion, and stress reactivity, these initial findings suggest that PTSD may involve heightened connections among those brain areas that could help to explain the tendency of people with PTSD to be troubled by unwanted memories that are very stressful (PTSD's intrusive reexperiencing symptoms).

Box 5.5 The Prefrontal Cortex and PTSD

In addition to the body and brain's stress response systems (such as the hypothalamus, locus coeruleus, and pituitary gland in the brain, and the adrenal gland and ANS in other areas of the body) and the limbic system amygdala and hippocampus, the very frontmost outer area of the brain—the "prefrontal cortex"—appears to play a key role in PTSD (Frewen & Lanius, 2008; Shin, Rauch, & Pitman, 2006). The prefrontal cortex (PFC) lies just behind the forehead and is the last area of the brain to fully develop as a child matures into adulthood. The PFC is commonly considered to be the seat of many of the most complex forms of human cognitive, affective, and social information processing. For example, dorsolateral (the upper and outside) frontal cortex is thought to implement many higher-order cognitive processes involved in working memory and problem solving that facilitate effective coping with stress, whereas more medial (middle) and ventrolateral (lower and outside) aspects of the frontal cortex are thought to oversee our ability to regulate our emotions and self-reflect about our goals. If the PFC is not activated adequately or capable of functioning optimally, a person under stress may have difficulty recognizing and managing their emotions and thinking clearly enough to draw useful conclusions and formulate and execute plans to deal with the stressor. The PFC, particularly the medial area (Milad et al., 2007), plays a key role in reducing the activation of the limbic "alarm" center, the amygdala, under stressful conditions (or when strong emotions are activated). Thus, if the PFC cannot "apply the brakes" to reduce the potentially high levels of amygdala activation experienced under stress by people with PTSD, the person may become trapped in a state of bodily hyperarousal (as the amygdala signals the locus coeruleus and hypothalamus to release "stress chemicals" such as norepinephrine and precursors of cortisol).

The PFC is closely linked anatomically and in function to a slightly more interior portion of the brain that runs almost exactly parallel to the brain's outer cortex at the front of the head, called the "anterior cingulate cortex (ACC)"— so much so that the ACC may be considered part of one portion of the PFC, the "medial" (middle) PFC (Shin & Handwerger, 2008). The ACC, which is highly interconnected with the amygdala and hippocampus, is implicated in the appraisal of the emotional significance of internal and external stimuli (Kalisch, Wiech, Herrmann, & Dolan, 2006; Ochsner & Gross, 2005; Rushworth, Buckley, Behrens, Walton, & Bannerman, 2007), including error and conflict monitoring (Holroyd & Coles, 2002). Some have proposed that the ACC, along with the medial prefrontal cortex, serves to modulate the limbic system so as to regulate emotion (Etkin, Egner, Peraza, Kandel, & Hirsch, 2006; Ochsner & Gross, 2005; Quirk & Beer, 2006; Schiller & Delgado, 2010). Three studies with adults and one with children have found evidence that individuals with PTSD have a smaller anterior cingulate than control participants who do not have PTSD (Rauch et al., 2006). However, the exact area of the ACC that is reduced in size has been found to differ across the studies (including rostral (front), dorsal (top) "subgenual" portions of the ACC), and one study reported a difference in the shape more than the size of the ACC in persons with PTSD.

The human brain's frontal lobe is commonly considered to be the seat of many of the most complex forms of human cognitive, affective, and social information processing. For example, dorsolateral aspects of the frontal cortex are thought to implement many higher-order cognitive processes involved in working memory and problem solving that facilitate effective coping with stress, whereas more medial and ventrolateral aspects of the frontal cortex are thought to mediate our ability to regulate our emotions and self-reflect about our goals. Accordingly, alterations in the structure or the functioning of the frontal cortex have been

(Continued)

Box 5.5 Continued

studied in conjunction with the cognitive, affective, and social effects of traumatic life experiences using neuroimaging technology, most notably MRI and PET. Specifically, neuroscientists generally believe that human learning takes place through modifications of brain structure and function, and many traumatologists hypothesize accordingly that traumatic experiences may alter normal brain development in pathological ways. For example, threatening and aversive experiences may sensitize the brain to such stimuli, causing one to be hypervigilant and expect harm even when it may be less warranted (Frewen & Lanius, 2008, pp. 286–287).

Thus, if the PFC is not activated adequately or capable of functioning optimally due to PTSD, when a person with PTSD experiences stressors in his current life, he may have difficulty recognizing and managing his emotions (the medial PFC) and think clearly enough to draw useful conclusions and formulate and execute plans to deal with the stressor (the dorsolateral PFC). Although traumatic memories play a prominent role in PTSD, the reactivation of such memories does not appear to impair some high-level cognitive functions such as working memory (Jelinek et al., 2008). Thus, difficulty coping with stress reactions rather than traumatic memories per se may be the primary biological and psychological problems in PTSD.

Consistent with these hypotheses, neuroimaging (such as fMRI or PET) studies of PFC functioning have shown that the PFC may be smaller and less functional in general, and less fully activated under stressful circumstances, among persons with PTSD compared to other people (Frewen & Lanius, 2008; Magnea & Lanius, 2008; Shin & Handwerger, 2008).

Specifically, the medial prefrontal lobe and ACC are involved in many important cognitive and emotional operations, such as generating and modulating emotional arousal and self-referential processing (e.g., "Is this important to me?"; "Can I handle this?"). Consistent with this conjecture, reliable differences have been observed with respect to functional responses within the frontal cortex to specific cognitive and emotional tasks. Several studies have investigated how trauma-exposed individuals with versus without PTSD respond to verbally scripted reminders of their traumatic memories have shown that individuals with PTSD reliably exhibit less response in bilateral ACC, medial orbitofrontal cortex, and dorsomedial prefrontal cortex (than people without PTSD or than when they are confronted with a less distressing task; Frewen & Lanius, 2008, p. 288).

Although research to date strongly suggests that the PFC does not function optimally when people with PTSD experience stressors and that this may be associated with high levels of reactivity on the part of the amygdala, there are contradictory findings and exceptions that make it premature to conclude that PTSD always involves a faulty or underperforming PFC (Frewen & Lanius, 2008). What seems clear is that PTSD treatments that could enhance the biological or psychological integrity and capacity of the PFC warrant further development, while research continues to unravel the complex relationships between the PFC and PTSD.

Vermetten, Elzinga, & Bremner, 2003). However, a subsequent study with women psychiatric patients failed to find evidence of smaller amygdalas among those with comorbid PTSD and borderline personality disorder (Schmahl et al., 2009). A study with women showed that those who had experienced traumatic stressors and were diagnosed with borderline personality disorder had 22–34% smaller amygdalas than comparable women who had not been exposed to traumatic stressors and did not have borderline personality disorder (Weniger, Lange, Sachsse, & Irle, 2009). However, amygdala size of the women in that study did not differ depending on whether or not they had PTSD. A study with male military combat veterans found evidence of reduced size of the anterior cingulate (see Box 5.5) and brain areas responsible for coordinating perception and emotion (the caudate and insula) but not the amygdala (Herringa, Phillips, Almeida, Insana, & Germain, 2012). Thus, the relationship between PTSD and reduced amygdala size is not clear. Other factors such as brain injury or personality disorders may explain the smaller amygdalas rather than PTSD. One additional interesting finding was reported by Pavlisa, Papa, Pavic, and Pavlisa (2006), who tested 11 adults with chronic PTSD and found that their amygdalas on the right side of their brains were smaller than on the left side of their brains (like many other brain structures, the amygdala extends across both sides of the brain).

Brain functioning and PTSD

Results from functional neuroimaging studies—that is, brain scans that are done while the individual is engaged in tasks designed to activate relevant brain areas—have led to a preliminary but generally well supported theoretical model of how brain activity is altered in PTSD (see Figure 5.1). The neurocircuitry of PTSD (Neumeister, Henry, & Krystal, 2007; Rauch, Shin, & Phelps, 2006; Teicher & Samson, 2013) is hypothesized to involve hyperresponsivity by the amygdala to perceptual input from the thalamus and sensory association cortices that are reminders of traumatic experiences, leading to hyperactivation of the locus coeruleus, the HPA axis, and the sympathetic ANS. This "alarm" reactivity optimally is reduced or reversed by inhibitory neural and chemical signals from the ventromedial prefrontal cortex (including the anterior cingulate) and the hippocampus to the amygdala. However, in PTSD, neuroimaging studies indicate that ventromedial prefrontal cortex and hippocampus are underactivated (Neumeister et al., 2007; Rauch et al., 2006). Authors of a review of hundreds of neuroimaging studies of the relationship between childhood maltreatment, PTSD, and the brain concluded (Teicher & Samson, 2013, p. 1127):

Briefly, the thalamus and sensory cortex process threat[s] … and convey this information to the amygdala. Prefrontal regions … modulate amygdala response, turning it down with the realization that something is not actually a threat or … irrationally amplifying it. The hippocampus also processes this information and plays a key role in retrieving relevant explicit memories … [and] modulates … response to psychological stressors.… The amygdala integrates this information and signals [lower brain areas, e.g., locus coeruleus], which regulates autonomic, [HPA], and noradrenergic response.

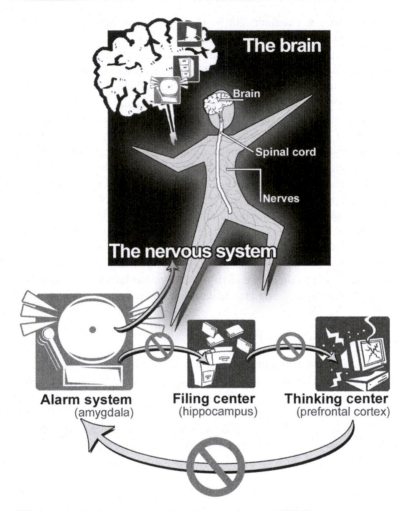

Figure 5.2 Areas in the brain associated with stress, fear, and PTSD.
© University of Connecticut 2001–2009.

The amygdala's role as the alarm center in the brain is well documented. An animal study showed that rats who were exposed to inescapable shocks demonstrated PTSD-like freezing behavior when stimulated by stress hormones and also showed PTSD-like deficits in rapid eye movement sleep—except these PTSD-like reactions did not occur if their amygdalas were inactivated prior to the traumatic exposure to shocks (Wellman, Fitzpatrick, Machida, & Sanford, 2014). Another animal study with rats found that, after recalling a fearful memory, the memory persisted (this is known as resistance to extinction) if the amygdala was stimulated with stress hormones immediately afterward but did not persist if the amygdala's activation was blocked right after the recall. Thus, amygdala activation was crucial to a PTSD-like symptom, very similar to intrusive reexperiencing (Dębiec, Bush, & LeDoux, 2011). Consistent with these findings, adults with PTSD have been shown to have higher levels of amygdala activation than healthy controls in laboratory tasks in which they also show a tendency to focus their attention on detecting or avoiding potential threats (consistent with hypervigilance; El Khoury-Malhame et al., 2011).

Furthermore, there is growing evidence that the amygdala's alarm signals in PTSD impair the hippocampus's ability to process memories and override the modulating signals from the prefrontal cortex. Animal studies indicate that heightened levels of amygdala activation in tasks that evoke fear impair the functioning of the hippocampus (Tsoory et al., 2008). Studies of adults with PTSD (compared to healthy trauma survivors or nontraumatized persons) have shown that the fear-activating neural connections from the amygdala to the visual cortices and ventromedial prefrontal cortex are stronger than the reciprocal inhibitory (calming) connections from the prefrontal cortex to the amygdala (Brown et al., 2014; Gilboa et al., 2004; Mazza et al., 2013; Rabinak et al., 2011; Sripada et al, 2012a; Stevens et al., 2013; Williams et al., 2006; Yan et al., 2013). Of critical importance for PTSD treatment (Chapters 7 and 8) and prevention (Chapter 9), there also is evidence that strong connectivity between the prefrontal cortex and the amygdala is a characteristic of adults who are resilient to depression and PTSD despite having experienced maltreatment in childhood (Cisler et al., 2013; Van der Werff et al., 2013).

As just noted, PTSD involves brain activation patterns consistent with hypervigilance as well as with intrusive reexperiencing symptoms. Adults challenged by a task requiring vigilance for nontraumatic stimuli (rather than the typical paradigm of exposing participants to reminders of traumatic events) showed enhanced activation of the left hemisphere amygdala and also of the dorsal and rostral anterior cingulate (ACC) if they had PTSD (Bryant et al., 2005). Military combat veterans were found to be prone to high levels of ACC activation during laboratory tasks involving potential threat, but only if they had experienced other traumatic stressors in adulthood or childhood addition to their combat experiences (Herringa, Phillips, Fournier, Kronhaus, & Germain, 2013). Thus, the ACC may play a key role in PTSD's hypervigilance symptoms (see Box 5.5).

A more nuanced understanding of brain activation and PTSD was provided by a study that found different patterns of activation in the anterior cingulate and in other portions of the ventromedial (underside middle) prefrontal cortex. Combat veterans with PTSD deactivated the rostral anterior cingulate, while combat veterans without PTSD and men with no combat history deactivated other areas in the ventromedial prefrontal cortex when they imagined personal experiences that were psychologically traumatic or highly stressful (Britton, Phan, Taylor, Fig, & Liberzon, 2005). The rostral anterior cingulated cortex is associated with conscious monitoring of distressing emotions, while the other areas in the ventromedial prefrontal cortex are associated with interpreting emotions in relation to oneself. PTSD may involve altered brain activation related to being aware of one's own emotional distress (Davidson, 2002) without sorting out the feelings by thinking about their personal meaning or how to deal with them. Consistent with these findings, a study of adults with PTSD showed that, compared to adults who did not have PTSD, they displayed a unique pattern in which amygdala activation was highly synchronized with activation of a "default mode" network of areas located toward the middle and back of the brain that is involved in spontaneous daydreaming-like reflections on the personal meaning of experiences. Further, the PTSD participants' amygdalas were highly activated by stressful challenges, but their default mode networks were extremely underactivated (Sripada et al., 2012b).

Brain Activation When PTSD and Pain Co-occur. The neurobiology of pain in PTSD is not well understood, although PTSD and chronic physical pain appear to be mutually exacerbating in Moeller-Bertram, Keltner, and Strigo (2012). Yet, PTSD also has been found to be associated with reduced sensitivity to externally induced acute pain (Geuze et al., 2007). Neuroimaging studies have shown that military veterans with PTSD exhibit increased activation in the hippocampus, insula, and putamen, and decreased PfC and amygdala activation in reaction to externally induced acute pain (Geuze et al., 2007). Women with PTSD secondary to interpersonal violence showed increased activity in both the insula and PfC during acute pain but reduced insula activation with repeated pain induction (Strigo et al., 2010). When physical pain was induced following script-based recall of traumatic events, PTSD symptom severity was found to be associated with activation in brain areas related to stress-induced analgesia (such as the caudate and thalamus), and dissociative symptoms were correlated inversely with activation of the putamen and amygdala (Mickleborough et al., 2011). Thus, the neurobiology of pain in PTSD is complicated and appears to take several forms, including acute analgesia (associated with dissociation) or chronic severe pain (associated with emotional distress and hyperarousal).

Event-Related Potential Studies of Brain Activity in PTSD. Unlike neuroimaging techniques, event-related brain potential (ERP) methodology offers high temporal resolution, on the order of milliseconds, at the expense of spatial resolution. This methodology supplements the neuroimaging literature by allowing us to examine changes in brain activity immediately following a stimulus. Within milliseconds, the brain recognizes potential threat and triggers the ANS to respond. Because of its fine temporal resolution, the measurement of ERPs is a fruitful method for studying perception and information processing.

ERPs are measured by electroencephalography at the scalp and reflect the activity of a population of neurons in response to internal or external events, which may include biological, environmental, or psychological events. They are characterized by their temporal position and polarity along the waveform following stimulus onset. To measure an ERP, it is necessary to average data from several event-based trials (e.g., 30 or more), which functions to reduce noise, capitalize on the common signal, and increase the signal-to-noise ratio. An ERP component is thought to reflect a merger of brain processes and potential neural generators. Statistically informed source localization techniques may provide a clue about the source of the activity; however, they do not compare to neuroimaging techniques in this respect.

Early (i.e., < 200 ms) ERP components (e.g., components called N1, P1, N170) are thought to reflect information processing of relatively simple stimulus features and stimulus discrimination (Schupp et al., 2006), whereas later components (i.e., >200 ms) like the P3 and late positive potential (LPP) are associated with higher-order cognitive processes involved in working memory and context updating (Donchin &

Coles, 1988). More specifically, studies have detected enhanced late positivity (i.e., P3, LPP) but not early positivity (e.g., P1, P2) in response to stimuli that are task-relevant or targeted, novel or improbable, arousing, or emotionally or motivationally significant relative to neutral or nonsignificant stimuli (Olofsson, Nordin, Sequeira, & Polich, 2008). Given the sensitivity of late positive components to emotionally and motivationally significant events, it has been the focus of much psychological research. Although there are many possible neural sources of late positivity, the focus has been on temporo-parietal and prefrontal brain cortex regions, as well as the hippocampus (Karl, Malta, & Maercker, 2006).

Given its sensitivity to the motivational significance of stimuli, these LPPs are studied in experimental paradigms designed to learn more about the sensory-perceptual dysfunction and nonadaptive responses to specific environmental triggers associated with PTSD. A meta-analytic review of ERP studies involving PTSD highlighted a number of irregularities in sensory information processing in individuals with PTSD (Karl, Malta, et al., 2006). Several of these studies examined the LPP in the context of an oddball task, a paradigm in which participants are instructed to attend to target or "oddball" stimuli within a series of nontarget or "distractor" stimuli and to indicate whether each stimulus is a target or not by pushing one of two buttons. Larger LPP amplitudes to target stimuli have been associated with superior attention and memory performance (Karl, Malta, et al., 2006).

Ten of the studies reviewed reported reduced LPPs to target stimuli in individuals with PTSD compared to controls, suggesting attentional and memory deficits (Karl, Malta, et al., 2006). In fact, there is a large body of research demonstrating inhibitory and attention regulation deficits in PTSD, with many studies suggesting that these deficits may predate trauma exposure and serve as risk factors for PTSD development (Aupperle, Melrose, Stein, & Paulus, 2011). For example, one line of work has associated PTSD with problems disengaging attention away from one stimulus to attend to more task-relevant stimuli (Aupperle et al., 2011). Although it is adaptive to be able to quickly orient toward a novel stimulus, it is also adaptive to then disengage from that stimulus in order to stay focused on the task at hand (Aupperle et al., 2011).

To examine another aspect of attention, three studies reviewed in the meta-analysis had modified the oddball task so that traumatic stressor-related stimuli occurred at the same frequency as target stimuli (e.g., 20%) and functioned as motivational distractors. In these studies, individuals with PTSD displayed LPP responses to threat-related distractors that resembled responses to target stimuli (Karl, Malta, et al., 2006). Interestingly, in the context of threat-related distractors, individuals with PTSD showed the opposite patterns than when threat-related distractors were not included—greater LPPs to target stimuli, relative to neutral stimuli, than controls (Karl, Malta, et al., 2006). These context-dependent findings suggest that the inclusion of threat may prime individuals' fear network to be more responsive to emotionally salient stimuli more broadly. This seems to fit with the heightened awareness of traumatic memory reminders, reexperiencing of traumatic memories, and the hyperarousal typically reported in PTSD.

Far fewer studies have examined ERPs in children and adolescents with PTSD. In a study comparing maltreated and nonmaltreated children's responses to angry, happy, and neutral facial expressions, maltreated children exhibited larger LPP components to angry faces than happy and neutral faces, relative to controls (Pollak, Cicchetti, Klorman, & Brumaghim, 1997). In another study by this research group, physically abused and nonabused children participated in a modified oddball task in which they pushed a button when viewing a target image, a facial picture of a parent or stranger posing a happy expression, and withheld pushing the button when viewing a nontarget image, a facial picture of a parent/stranger posing a sad or angry expression, while simultaneously ignoring an emotionally congruent or incongruent verbal cue from a parent or stranger (Shackman, Shackman, & Pollak, 2007). Physically abused children showed larger LPPs to angry facial pictures, which were pronounced for pictures of their parents, relative to controls, but no difference in response to happy or sad faces (Shackman et al., 2007).

Acoustic Startle Reflex and PTSD. The acoustic startle reflex is a biological reflex that, unlike muscle reflexes, is controlled entirely by the CNS via a well-established and relatively simple pathway. Synapses in the cochlear nucleus (in the inner ear) and the reticularis pontis caudalis (brainstem areas that control physical movement) activate the startle reflex when they receive signals from the amygdala (Quevedo, Smith, Donzella, Schunk, & Gunnar, 2010). This pathway is ubiquitous across species, and, if damaged eliminates the startle reflex (Quevedo et al., 2010). The startle reflex is elicited by sudden, intense stimuli such as loud tones (e.g., 90–100 dB) and air puffs. It is typically measured by electromyographically recording muscular activity, most commonly the orbicularis oculi beneath the eye, resulting from rapid eye closure, a reliable component of the startle response (Lang & Bradley, 2008).

The startle reflex has been used in numerous studies examining fear and defensive motivation in normal and patient populations. Studies of adults have consistently found elevated acoustic startle reflexes in patients with anxiety disorders, including PTSD (Grillon, 2002; Pole, 2007). The Griffin (2008) study reported enhanced startle reflexes in victims of physical or sexual assault 6 months after the assault. Another study reported a positive correlation between acoustic startle reflexes and a measure of perceived childhood maltreatment in a primarily African American sample (Jovanovic et al., 2009). In two studies, the context of the stimulus presentation moderated responses. Grillon (2008) reported that PTSD patients displayed greater startle reflexes to air-puff startle probes relative to a healthy control group and a GAD group when presentation of aversive sounds (e.g., fire alarm) was uncued (i.e., unpredictable threat) but no difference when the sounds were cued. Additionally, Pole et al. (2007) found that police cadets with histories of childhood trauma exhibited greater startle reflexes to acoustic startle probes than nonexposed cadets during high threat of shock but no differences during low threat.

In contrast to studies of adults, one study found no evidence of enhanced acoustic startle reflexes in adolescent girls with PTSD symptoms (61% who met full criteria), largely associated with sexually assault, compared to nonexposed healthy female controls (Lipschitz et al., 2005). Also contrary to adult studies, Ornitz and Pynoos (1989) reported diminished acoustic startle reflexes in a small sample of children who developed PTSD after witnessing a sniper attack compared to nonexposed children. The authors, however, reported diminished prepulse inhibition in the PTSD group (Ornitz & Pynoos, 1989). A third study reported results consistent with adult studies showing that children and adolescents with PTSD exhibited greater acoustic startle reflexes to loud sounds compared to nonexposed youth (Grasso & Simons, 2009).

Other studies have examined startle reflexes in maltreated compared to nonmaltreated children and adolescents regardless of PTSD status. Klorman, Cicchetti, Thatcher, and Ison (2003) found that maltreated school-age boys, primarily physically abused, exhibited smaller amplitude startle reflexes to startling sounds. Patterns in maltreated girls, primarily sexually abused, however, were mixed. Younger girls mimicked the boys' pattern, and older girls exhibited larger amplitude startle reflexes to startling sounds (Klorman et al., 2003).

At present, no clear explanation exists for the diversity of findings within the child and adolescent literature, as well as between child and adult samples. Whereas adult studies more consistently report elevated acoustic startle reflexes for PTSD patients, studies of children and adolescents reveal mixed findings.

Brain chemistry and PTSD

Consistent with the structural and functional studies of brain alterations in PTSD, studies of the neurochemistry of PTSD indicate that the disorder is related to imbalances in the production and activity (the neural "receptors") of neurochemicals that amplify the signals and heighten the activity of the amygdala and reduce the ability of the prefrontal cortex and hippocampus to inhibit amygdale activation (Bonne, Grillon, Vythilingam, Neumeister, & Charney, 2004; Southwick et al., 2007). Specifically, PTSD involves increased levels of the excitatory amino acid glutamate and its receptors in the amygdala, which animal research suggests will heighten the intensity of alarm reactions and fear memories (Tronel & Alberini, 2007). PTSD also involves hyperproduction of noradrenaline by the LC and depleted levels of an inhibitory chemical that reduces LC neural activity (neuropeptide Y), such that "the amygdala, hippocampus, and prefrontal cortex become flooded with NE" (Southwick et al., 2007, p. 181). PTSD also appears to involve increased levels of serotonin and impaired receptors, which is associated with hostility, irritability, and aggression (Southwick et al., 2007). Dopamine and its receptors are important in the extinction and may be abnormal in PTSD (Bonne et al., 2004). Thus, neurochemical alterations in PTSD are consistent with the disorder's symptoms of intrusive memories, emotional distress, and hyperarousal.

Finally, receptors for the brain's endogenous (internal) opioids (called "u-opioid receptors), which can reduce fear, anxiety, and avoidance, have been studied in relation to PTSD. Dysregulation of the opioid system may be associated with PTSD's flashbacks as well as with comorbid substance abuse disorders. The study (Liberzon et al., 2007) found evidence of reduced activity by u-opioid receptors in the orbitofrontal cortex and anterior cingulate, and increased activity in the amygdala among combat veterans with PTSD (compared either to combat veterans without PTSD or men with no combat experience). These alterations may reflect "an inadequate initial opioid response" to distress "and subsequent down-regulation of u-opioid receptors" that could play a role in PTSD's persistent anxiety (Liberzon et al., 2007, p. 1036).

Putting it all together: the learning brain versus the survival brain in PTSD

One way of thinking about how exposure to traumatic stressors and PTSD might interfere with brain development and functioning is to view PTSD as a shift from a brain (and body) focused on *learning* to a brain (and body) focused on *survival* (Ford, 2009, chap. 2). The learning brain is engaged in exploration (i.e., the acquisition of new knowledge and neuronal/synaptic connections) driven and reinforced by a search for an optimal balance of novelty and familiarity. The survival brain seeks to anticipate, prevent, or protect against the damage caused by potential or actual dangers, driven and reinforced by a search to identify threats and an attempt to mobilize and conserve bodily resources in order to maintain this vigilance and defensive adjustments to maintain bodily functioning. The learning brain and survival brain are only figures of speech. In actuality, they are the same brain with the same capability neural networks and pathways, but their orientations to the environment and their use of neural networks are critically different.

The survival brain relies on rapid automatic processes that involve primitive portions of the brain (e.g., brainstem, midbrain, parts of the limbic system such as the amygdala) while largely bypassing areas of the brain that are involved in more complex adaptations to the environment (i.e., learning). The learning brain utilizes more complex and potentially consciously controlled areas in the outer areas of the brain, which are the last areas to develop fully (e.g., the anterior cingulate, insula, prefrontal cortex, other parts of the limbic system such as the hippocampus).

A survival brain operates automatically to defend against external threats, but in so doing, it diverts crucial resources from brain/body systems that are essential in order to prevent the body from succumbing to exhaustion, injury, or illness and to promote learning (e.g., reward seeking, distress tolerance, emotion awareness, problem solving, narrative memory). PTSD represents a dominance of the survival brain over the learning brain. PTSD, therefore, is a biological tradeoff in which avoiding harm takes priority over facilitating healthy growth, rejuvenation, and learning (Neumeister et al., 2007). This tradeoff is highly adaptive in life-threatening danger, where rapid automatic self-protective reactions may be lifesaving. However, it comes at a great cost to the person's peace of mind, happiness, health, and success in relationships, education, and work. The biological basis for PTSD is survival, but PTSD prevents people from living full lives.

The survival brain is fixated on automatic nonconscious scanning for and escape from threats, thereby altering two core psychological processes (Ford, 2005): the ability to manage emotions ("emotion regulation") and to think and remember clearly ("information processing").

Emotion Regulation. Areas within the brain that develop primarily prenatally and in infancy and toddlerhood account for the core components of experiencing, expressing, and modulating emotion (Lewis, 2005, pp. 258–259). *Experiencing* core emotion states (e.g., anger, fear, sadness, joy, love, interest) involves brainstem (medulla, pons, midbrain, locus coeruleus; Bracha & Maser, 2008) areas that activate the ANS neurally and chemically (via neurotransmitters such as noradrenaline and dopamine). *Expressing* emotions in mood states and action (e.g., aggression, reward seeking, mating) involves striatal (putamen, caudate, nucleus accumbens) brain areas that are activated by input (afferents) from the cortex and selectively alter sensory perception (via the thalamus) and intentional behavior, as well as by the hypothalamus (Heim, Newport, Mletzko, Miller, & Nemeroff, 2008), which modulates body states by producing or triggering production of neuropeptides (e.g., stress hormones, oxytocin, vasopressin) and engaging the ANS. *Modulation* (adjustment, utilization as information) of emotions involves the limbic system, which focuses sustained attention and triggers automatic (via the brainstem and hypothalamus) and conscious (via the cortex) responses based on the emotional significance of perceptual and memory information (coordinated by the amygdala; Milad et al., 2007) and coordinates these responses based on the overall context, including both past experiences (episodic memory) and current environmental circumstances (coordinated by the hippocampus; Rudy & Matus-Amat, 2005).

Information Processing. The entire brain plays a role in learning, memory, and thinking. The brain's outer layer, the cortices, however, do the following:

> [The cortices coordinate these information processing functions] through a matrix
> of associations, comparisons, synthesis across modalities, planning, reflection,
> and sometimes, but not always, conscious control. These operations take time,
> and emotions maintain a coherent orientation to the world during that period of
> time. For example, deliberate action is guided by attention to alternative plans
> and anticipatory attention is constrained by emotions concerning the pursuit
> of particular goals ... and a continuously refined model of the world achieved
> by selecting, comparing, and pursuing particular plans while integrating the
> information fed back by the world.
>
> Lewis (2005), p. 259

Several areas of the brain's outer layer (the cortex) are involved in organizing what we sense and feel in an intuitive way into perceptions and thoughts that can be described in words. However, two cortical areas toward the front of the brain that are highly interconnected with each other and also closely linked to the limbic system (therefore called "paralimbic" structures) are critical to synthesizing and processing information in the form of conscious thought (consciousness). The middle (medial) and underside (ventral or orbital) parts at the very front of the frontal cortex (the so-called orbital or ventromedial prefrontal cortex) and the hippocampus in the brain's inner limbic system are closely interconnected and crucial to many aspects of information processing. Of relevance to PTSD, the ventromedial prefrontal cortex and hippocampus have been shown to be key for animals and humans in overcoming fear (i.e., "fear extinction"; Milad et al., 2007; Quirk, Garcia, & Gonzalez-Lima, 2006).

Genetics and PTSD

The alterations in body physiology and brain chemistry, structure, and function in PTSD may be the product not only of exposure to traumatic experiences but also of the genetic makeup of the person who experiences psychological trauma. A first step in establishing a relationship between any disorder, including PTSD, and genetics is to determine if people with similar (such as children and parents) or the same (such as identical twins) genetic inheritances have a similar propensity to develop the disorder. "Family" studies of PTSD have shown that parents of a child who develops PTSD are more likely to suffer PTSD than other parents, and that children whose parent develops PTSD are more likely to suffer PTSD than other children (Koenen, Moffitt, Poulton, Martin, & Caspi, 2007). A classic study by Yehuda, Halligan, and Bierer (2001) found that adult children of Holocaust survivors whose parents had PTSD were more likely to develop PTSD than other adult children of Holocaust survivors whose parents did not have PTSD.

Studies comparing identical twins versus fraternal twins provide a more specific test of the role of genetics in PTSD than family studies, because any differences between these two types of twins is more likely to be due to the unique genetic equivalence of identical twins than to other risk or protective factors for PTSD that family members might share in common, such as their family life experiences when growing up or the socioeconomic status of their families. Twin studies enable researchers to precisely estimate the extent to which genetics contribute to PTSD because identical (monozygotic) twins share 100% of their genes, while fraternal (dizygotic) twins share on average 50% of their genes, and twins (unless separated from each other) share the same family environment (although, of course, there may be differences in each twin's exact family experiences). Twin studies have shown that genes account for approximately 30–45% of the risk of developing PTSD (Koenen et al., 2007; Sartor et al., 2012). These findings help to explain why not all people who are exposed to the same or similar psychological traumas develop PTSD: like most medical or psychiatric conditions, each person's biological strengths and vulnerabilities play a role in determining whether exposure to traumatic stressors will lead to PTSD or not, as well as whether PTSD will persist or be recovered from once it occurs.

Locating the precise genes that play a role in PTSD requires more detailed studies of the specific molecules that make up genes. There are approximately 20,000–25,000 genes in the human genome, but most (more than 99%) are shared by all human beings. However, differences between people are not based simply on a specific gene but on small portions of genes that are called "single nucleotide polymorphisms" (SNPs for short)—of which there are approximately 3 million in humans—and combinations of SNPs called "alleles." Alleles are differences in the structure of genes (such as shorter vs longer) that may lead the same gene to operate differently. Given the enormous quantity of small, but potentially significant, differences in human genes (alleles), the search for the most likely "candidate genes" that may lead to PTSD is very challenging. Fortunately, genes can be distinguished based upon their function in regulating brain chemistry and functions, such as whether they influence the production or action of neurochemicals (e.g., noradrenaline, serotonin, or dopamine) that in turn influence the function of brain areas (such as the HPA axis, locus coeruleus, and the limbic system and prefrontal cortex) that are known to be associated with PTSD.

Numerous candidate genes have been studied in relation to PTSD (31 candidate genes) with positive, negative, and contradictory findings (Voisey, Young, Lawford, &

Morris, 2014). There have also been four genome wide association studies (GWAS) that have identified four genes as being associated with PTSD, including *RORA* (Logue et al., 2013), *incRNA* (Guffanti et al., 2013), intergenic SNP (Xie et al., 2013), and *SLC18A2* (Solovieff et al., 2014). GWAS studies are powerful because they examine a very large number of candidate genes and their associated SNPs; however, consequently, they require very large sample sizes (e.g., >1000). Conducting these studies will require combining data sets across different project sites and forming collaborative relationships among researchers—a direction that many genetic researchers have begun to take.

In the past decade, a further refinement of behavioral genetics research—that is, the study of the role of genetics in behavior, emotion, and thinking—has shown promise for identifying gene differences that may be associated with PTSD and related problems (such as depression and aggression). A particular allele of a gene that influences the activity of serotonin in the brain—called the "short-short" allele of the "serotonin transporter" gene 5HTTLPR—has been shown to distinguish individuals who develop depression in adulthood after experiencing adversity in childhood (such as abuse, poverty, or violence; Caspi et al., 2003) and people who developed PTSD after experiencing Hurricane Katrina from those who did not (Kilpatrick et al., 2007). The short-short serotonin transporter gene allele also was associated with increased risk of depression among maltreated children, but only those who had low social support (Kaufman et al., 2004). A study of the dopamine transporter gene found that a certain allele was associated with PTSD only among individuals with high levels of alcohol consumption (Young et al., 2002). Thus, it may be that posttraumatic problems (including depression as well as PTSD) are most likely when people who are exposed to traumatic stressors have both a genetic vulnerability and either additional risk factors (such as alcohol abuse) or deficient protective factors (such as social support).

While it is clear that genetic vulnerability plays a role in PTSD, much has yet to be learned about the specific genes/alleles that are involved and how they interact with the person's environment and experience before and after exposure to psychological trauma. For example, an Australian study found that maltreatment experienced before age 10 was associated with conduct disorder, aggression, and antisocial personality in adolescence and early adulthood, especially for people with an allele of a gene that reduces the body's production of a chemical, monoamine oxidase A (MAO-A), which metabolizes (i.e., activates) neurotransmitters that have been linked to PTSD as well as to aggression: dopamine, norepinephrine, and serotonin (Caspi et al., 2002). However, a study with adolescents in treatment for conduct disorder and substance abuse failed to find that maltreated children with this allele had more severe conduct problems (Young et al., 2006). Thus, not only the specific allele but also the specific group of people studied, the type of traumatic adversity, and the type of posttraumatic problem may lead to very different gene-environment interactions. Because genes tend to be highly specific in their effects on bodily processes and functioning, studies are most likely to be effective in identifying key relationships if they aim to predict more specific outcomes than PTSD per se. PTSD is a complex phenotype (Segman, Shalev, & Gelernter, 2007)—that is, PTSD involves not only 17 different symptoms but also many behavioral, cognitive, affective, and biological alterations and comorbidities (see Chapter 4). Types of problems involved in PTSD, such as aggressive or impulsive behavior, anxiety or dysphoria, or hypervigilance and startle response, may be the most fruitful outcomes to examine in the search for a better understanding of how genetic differences interact with psychological trauma to result in PTSD and other posttraumatic problems. Because genetic factors may confer strengths and resilience as well as vulnerability, the question of how gene-trauma-environment interactions lead to favorable posttraumatic trajectories such as resilience or recovery (Chapter 2) is an area that remains to be explored.

PTSD and physical health problems and medical illness

The body's stress response system directly influences the body's immune system activity, generally reducing its level of activity and potentially compromising its ability to detect and fight off pathogens and promote tissue and organ healing, while increasing autoimmune responses that can lead to vulnerability to illness (Kendall-Tackett, 2007). Individuals who are exposed to psychological trauma often report problems with physical health and associated pain and functional limitations (such as problems with mobility or work), particularly if they develop and chronically suffer from PTSD. Although psychological factors may play a role in the health problems associated with PTSD, this does *not* mean that these bodily problems are actually (or are the result of) "mental" problems such as excessive worry, self-doubt, guilt, low self-esteem, emotional conflicts, or excessive or suppressed/repressed anger. Research suggests that somatic complaints associated with exposure to psychological trauma or PTSD may result from any of the following sources, separately or in combination:

1. medically-diagnosable illnesses or injury-related conditions, and stress-related or stress-exacerbated medical conditions that appear to have biological causes but are not included in current medical diagnoses
2. stress-related behaviors that place the person at risk for medical illness ("behavioral risk factors"), and
3. conversion of unexpressed or unconscious psychological distress into physical symptoms or dissociative splits of the personality.

PTSD and medical illness

People are at heightened risk for diagnosed medical illnesses if they have experienced traumatic stressors, particularly if this occurred in developmentally adverse interpersonal experiences in childhood (Ford, 2005) and when PTSD (see Schnurr & Green, 2004) or complex PTSD develop following traumatic exposure(s). Prospective longitudinal studies have not yet been done but are needed in order to determine, beginning in childhood and continuing through adolescence and adulthood with the same representative sample of persons, how exposure to psychological trauma and the development of PTSD (Fairbank et al., 2007) precede, follow, or co-occur with changes and problems in physical health and serious medical illnesses. Until such a study is done, it is not clear whether experiencing psychological trauma and PTSD actually can cause or contribute to the development of medically diagnosed illnesses or whether medical illness or genetic or environmental factors that lead people to be vulnerable to medical illness precede and contribute to (or simply co-occur with) exposure to psychological trauma and PTSD.

The largest study with a relatively representative sample of adults (all of whom were patients in the Kaiser Health Maintenance Organization) whose medical health and illness status was known based on medical examinations, tests, and diagnoses is the "Adverse Childhood Experiences Study" (ACES; Felitti et al., 1998). The ACES and large-scale epidemiologic research studies (Chartier, Walker, & Naimark, 2007) concluded that adults who report having either or both socioeconomic adversities (such as living in poverty) or psychological traumas in childhood have between 2 and more than 16 times greater risk than other adults of having obesity, sexually transmitted disease, cancer, stroke, ischemic heart disease, diabetes, or chronic bronchitis or emphysema. These findings suggest that even when other risk factors such as age, ethnicity, gender, and health risk behaviors (see below) are taken into account, experiencing adversity—particularly multiple forms of potentially traumatic adversity—in childhood leads to a heightened risk of not just somatic complaints but serious medical illness in adulthood.

Findings of the ACES and similar studies have led clinicians and researchers to question how psychological trauma and PTSD could cause, or more likely contribute to, the development of serious medical illnesses. These clearly are not just "complaints" but potentially life-altering or life-threatening disruptions in the body's self-regulation and physiological and neurochemical functioning. Friedman and McEwen (2004) surveyed the research on the biological changes that occur as a result of psychological trauma and PTSD (see also Neumeister et al., 2007; Southwick et al., 2007) and found that they share a common factor, which McEwen described as "allostatic load." They identify a number of stress-related medical illnesses that include not only several of the serious illnesses already described as potential risks following childhood psychological trauma but also several other stress-related biological abnormalities.

1. Disorders involving dysregulation of the hypothalamus-pituitary-adrenal (HPA) Axis, including hypercortisolism, Cushings syndrome, reproductive abnormalities and inflammatory/autoimmune disorders.
2. Disorders involving dysregulation of the sympathetic branch of the ANS, the brain's adrenergic systems, and the cardiovascular system (including myocardial infarction, stroke, atherosclerosis, hypertension, and cardiac arrhythmias).
3. Disorders of the opioid systems, including chronic pain and headaches.
4. Disorders of the endocrine and metabolic systems, including hyperthyroidism, dyslipidemia, Type II diabetes, and osteopenia/osteoporosis.
5. Disorders of the immune system, including immunosuppression (insufficient immune response) and inflammatory and autoimmune diseases, such as irritable bowel syndrome (IBS), chronic fatigue syndrome, fibromyalgia, Type I diabetes, multiple chemical sensitivity, and rheumatoid arthritis.

Each of the biological systems involved in these stress-related medical conditions has been found to be dysregulated among adults with PTSD as a result of the chronic state of physiological reactivity (e.g., hyperarousal, irritability, sleeplessness involved in PTSD). While Friedman et al. (2004) do not claim that PTSD causes these medical conditions, they demonstrate that PTSD's chronic physiological arousal may contribute to the dysregulation of the underlying biological systems and may therefore increase the risk of developing biological abnormalities that could lead to a variety of somatic complaints. To the extent that somatic complaints associated with PTSD, such as fatigue, pain, and tension, are related to the biological adaptation necessitated by chronic states of stress (allostasis; Friedman et al., 2004), these complaints reflect real medical problems and not simply mental distress or anxiety.

Exposure to traumatic stressors, PTSD, and health risk behaviors

Somatic complaints related to exposure to traumatic stressors and the development of PTSD could be the result of biological alterations that result from engaging in behaviors that are known to increase the risk of illness. These health risk behaviors prominently include smoking and excess alcohol consumption, as well as poor diet (e.g., excess or insufficient consumption, foods with high levels of red meats, trans fats, and simple carbohydrates), lack of exercise, risky sexual behaviors, insufficient sleep, and limited or conflictual social support systems. Exposure to psychological trauma, particularly to violence, and PTSD have been found to be associated with each of these health risk behavior patterns (Haglund, Nestadt, Cooper, Southwick, & Charney, 2007; Kendall-Tackett, 2007). Therefore, somatic complaints associated with psychological trauma exposure or PTSD may be, in part, the result of chronic behavior patterns that increase the allostatic load (Friedman et al., 2004) on the body and predispose the person to biologically based medical problems.

Health risk behavior patterns may begin long before an individual is exposed to psychological trauma and may increase in frequency or amount as a result of traumatic stress reactions or PTSD, but they also may develop in reaction to exposure to psychological trauma. For example, increased alcohol consumption was found to occur among a small subgroup of adults living near New York City within the first 3 months following the September 11, 2001, terrorist attacks. Those individuals also tended to report higher levels of emotional distress immediately after the incidents and to more often seek support in the following year than other adults in that community sample (Ford, Adams, & Dailey, 2006). Thus, somatic complaints may emerge following psychological trauma as a result of continued, increased, or newly developed patterns of behavior that reflect attempts to cope with traumatic stress reactions (such as anxiety, irritability, or hypervigilance) but that also place the person's physical health at risk.

Somatic complaints related to exposure to psychological trauma and the development of PTSD also may be due to physical symptoms that cannot be explained by medical examination, testing, and diagnosis. Roelofs and Spinhoven (2007) review the scientific research and clinical theories that have been developed in an attempt to explain the origins of medically unexplained physical symptoms. These physical symptoms include physical health problems and limitations related to chronic pelvic pain, IBS, and "conversion" or somatization disorders (historically referred to as hysterical disorders; Brown, Schrag, & Trimble, 2005). A subspecialty within the medical profession, psychosomatic medicine, developed largely based on a need to understand and treat medical patients who reported ("complained of") pain (often in the pelvic area, but also in the form of migraine or tension headaches) and discomfort (often due to gastrointestinal conditions such as IBS), or strange changes in their body's capabilities (such as paralysis or pain that move from place to place in the body without any neurological basis). The symptoms are considered to be a "conversion" of emotional distress into physical disability or pain, and thus as a way of indirectly expressing emotions via the body ("somatic" expressions of the psychological distress—hence the term *psychosomatic*). Research on these conditions has demonstrated that women who report chronic pelvic pain, IBS, or conversion symptoms are more often survivors of childhood sexual, physical, and emotional abuse than women who do not report those psychosomatic problems (Roelofs & Spinhoven, 2007). Sexual, not physical, abuse appears to be particularly associated with these conditions rather than with other types of pain, including medically or neurologically explained pain disorders. A tendency to express emotional distress in bodily symptoms (or somatization) was found to be involved in IBS and in conversion disorders, but only in two studies that require replication.

Research or clinical reports describing medically unexplained physical symptoms among men is scarce and primarily has been done with military personnel or veterans. A study was done with military veterans who had been deployed in Operation Desert Storm (Persian Gulf War, 1990–1991) and were tested between 5 and 7 years later, 85% of whom were men. The results showed that they reported medically documented but unexplained chronic fatigue syndrome symptoms or neurological, gastrointestinal, orthopedic, or dermatologic symptoms (Ford et al., 2001; see Box 4.6). In addition to somatization, symptoms of PTSD or depression and having experienced potentially traumatic combat duties were associated with the presence of these medically unexplained physical health problems (compared to a matched healthy control group). Thus, not only childhood abuse trauma but also war trauma and associated PTSD or depression may be a factor in the development or persistence of medically unexplained symptoms, at least for men.

With regard to personality, the trait of "anxiety sensitivity" or "neuroticism" has been shown to be associated with an increased tendency to express somatic complaints that cannot be medically explained among adults with PTSD (Jakupcak et al., 2006). Thus, somatic complaints expressed by survivors of psychological trauma and persons with PTSD may be related to cultural norms or personality traits that lead people to express traumatic stress reactions and emotional distress in terms of bodily symptoms.

Exposure to traumatic stressors, PTSD, and somatic dissociation

When psychological trauma occurs at developmentally sensitive periods in a person's life (particularly in early childhood) and compromises or prevents the development of a secure attachment relationship with primary adult caregivers such as parents, a cascade of biological changes may occur that disrupt or block the development of the two key psychological capabilities that enable children to develop a healthy and durable sense of self—that is, the abilities to regulate physical arousal and emotions and to use attention, working and long-term memory, verbal/declarative and narrative/ autobiographical memory, and executive problem-solving and decision-making skills to think clearly when stressed (Ford, 2005). When infants, toddlers, or preschool-age children develop a secure attachment bond with their primary caregivers, they learn the core emotion regulation and information processing skills by practicing ways to feel good (physically and emotionally) and think clearly while they play and inter-act with caregivers who model the same skills and nonverbally guide the child in using them. The result is that the child becomes able to recognize and utilize bodily reactions (feelings of energy, hunger, or fatigue) while experiencing self as an effec-tive agent. This is the beginning of achieving a sense of psychological integration. However, when psychological trauma leads to, or occurs along with, an undepend-able or unresponsive (or at worst, a neglectful or abusive) relationship with primary caregiver(s), the child may not develop this integration of mind/emotions and body and may instead be unable to not only regulate emotions and think clearly but also to tolerate and manage bodily reactions.

In these adverse circumstances, children often develop a range of minor and serious health problems that may persist into adulthood and take the form of serious medical illnesses and that are either more severe or chronic than can be medically explained (i.e., somatization; see Haugaard, 2004; Waldinger, Schulz, Barsky, & Ahern, 2006). These somatic complaints are the physiological counterpart to psychological disso-ciation, because they are the result of a fragmentation (rather than integration) of the child's self and personality but in the form of a breakdown of the child's ability to mentally organize and regulate bodily reactions. This form of dissociation is called "somatoform dissociation" (Nijenhuis, van der Hart, Kruger, & Steele, 2004), and it is particularly associated with both childhood abuse and adult somatization (Brown et al., 2005). Somatoform dissociation includes symptoms reflecting bodily states of disorganization such as tics; pseudoseizures (seizure-like states that do not involve abnormal brain wave activity); medically unexplainable pain, anesthesia, or paraly-sis; intense physical impulses to act without regard to safety; and distorted auditory, visual, tactile, and gustatory (taste) sensory experiences (e.g., bodily feelings that are extremely intense, opposite to those expected in the current environment, rapidly changing, or entirely absent). Somatoform dissociation tends to persist and become progressively more severe as children grow into adolescence and adulthood and to lead to somatic complaints that are very difficult to treat unless their links to develop-mental trauma and attachment failures are addressed (Nijenhuis et al., 2004).

Somatic complaints and medical illness as precipitants for PTSD

Although experiencing and expressing somatic complaints often are highly stressful, especially if the symptoms and associated distress and discomfort are persistent and medically unexplained (and therefore more difficult for the medical provider to treat and for the patient to develop an internal sense of control, efficacy, and optimism), they are not psychologically traumatic per se unless they are actually (or perceived to be) life-threatening. Not surprisingly, therefore, even an illness such as cancer is not necessarily psychologically traumatic and may not lead to the development of PTSD for most children who experience it, but often their parents are psychologically traumatized (i.e., experience traumatic stress reactions), and these parents are more likely to develop PTSD than parents of other less severely medically ill or healthy children. Older children and adolescents who have recovered from cancer are thought to be more in need of (or better able to benefit from) treatment for posttraumatic stress than younger pediatric cancer patients or those of any age who are recently diagnosed with cancer and still in the early or intensive phases of medical treatment for the illness (Kazak et al., 2005).

However, serious medical illness—particularly when this is discovered in a manner that is emotionally shocking to the person and her support system (e.g., Ford et al., 2004)—may be a psychologically traumatic stressor that can lead to PTSD. Patients with cardiovascular/coronary heart disease who have experienced a myocardial infarction (heart attack) or cardiac surgery are somewhat more likely than patients with less severe somatic complaints or healthy individuals to develop PTSD, although the severity of the illness per se does not predict the likelihood of developing PTSD (Tedstone & Tarrier, 2003). The best predictor of PTSD among adult medical patients was receiving intensive care unit (ICU) treatment and human immunovirus (HIV) infection (Tedstone & Tarrier, 2003), regardless of specific medical illnesses. At the time that the studies reviewed by Tedstone and Tarrier were conducted (i.e., 1980–1990s), HIV+ status was considered a relatively virulent infection that almost inevitably led to an untreatable and lethal disease state (AIDS). Thus, the lethality of the condition and the low likelihood of being able to prevent or control its adverse progression made HIV/AIDS a highly life-threatening stressor. With the advent of more effective approaches to managing HIV infection and preventing AIDS, it will be important to determine whether this condition remains as strongly associated with PTSD as in these earlier studies.

ICU treatment is required when illness is acute and therefore likely to be dangerous, painful, and disorienting, all of which can lead to a sense of life threat and the subjective reactions of intense fear, helplessness, or horror that are the cardinal features of psychological trauma. ICU treatment also exposes the patient to a chaotic and overwhelming multiplicity of often frantic and fragmented sights, sounds, smells, and bodily sensations (e.g., hearing other patients screaming or moaning, seeing one's own or other patients' severe bodily damage and profuse bleeding, hearing and seeing medical personnel working under conditions of high stress, and invasive and painful medical procedures). Thus, the relationship between ICU care and psychological trauma or PTSD is likely to be more an association between traumatic events and traumatic stress reactions than a traumatic reaction to medical illness.

Conclusion

Psychological trauma and PTSD involve profound impairments in the body's stress response systems and the brain's self-regulation systems. Physical health problems, whether medically explainable or not, often accompany PTSD and also may be a source of traumatic stress or PTSD, particularly if they are shocking or life-threatening. These biological alterations and health problems provide a basis for an understanding of PTSD that integrates the body and the mind and for assessment and treatment protocols that address the entire person rather than just the psychological distress associated with PTSD. Interventions designed to address the biological basis for intrusive traumatic memories, self-defeating avoidance, emotional numbing, and hyperarousal are essential in order to not only facilitate recovery from PTSD but also to ensure that the costs of health care services for people with PTSD are not so excessive as to prevent people from receiving timely and effective preventive and treatment services when they are at risk for or have developed PTSD (Zatzick & Roy-Byrne, 2006).

References

Aardal-Eriksson, E., Eriksson, T. E., & Thorell, L. -H. (2001). Salivary cortisol, posttraumatic stress symptoms, and general health in the acute phase and during 9-month follow-up. *Biological Psychiatry*, *50*, 986–993.

Adenauer, H., Catani, C., Keil, J., Aichinger, H., & Neuner, F. (2010). Is freezing an adaptive reaction to threat? Evidence from heart rate reactivity to emotional pictures in victims of war and torture. *Psychophysiology*, *47*(2), 315–322. http://dx.doi.org/10.1111/j.1469-8986.2009.00940.x.

Arditi-Babchuk, H., Feldman, R., & Gilboa-Schechtman, E. (2009). Parasympathetic reactivity to recalled traumatic and pleasant events in trauma-exposed individuals. *Journal of Traumatic Stress*, *22*(3), 254–257.

Astur, R. S., St Germain, S. A., Tolin, D., Ford, J. D., Russell, D., & Stevens, M. (2006). Hippocampus function predicts severity of post-traumatic stress disorder. *Cyberpsychology and Behavior*, *9*(2), 234–240.

Aupperle, R. L., Melrose, A. J., Stein, M. B., & Paulus, M. P. (2011). Executive Function and PTSD: Disengaging from Trauma. *Neuropharmacology*. http://dx.doi.org/10.1016/j.neuropharm.2011.02.008.

Bockting, C. L., Lok, A., Visser, I., Assies, J., Koeter, M. W., Schene, A. H., DELTA Study Group, (2012). Lower cortisol levels predict recurrence in remitted patients with recurrent depression: A 5.5 year prospective study. *Psychiatry Research*, *200*(2–3), 281–287.

Bonne, O., Gilboa, A., Louzoun, Y., Brandes, D., Yona, I., Lester, H., et al. (2003). Resting regional cerebral perfusion in recent posttraumatic stress disorder. *Biological Psychiatry*, *54*(10), 1077–1086.

Bonne, O., Grillon, C., Vythilingam, M., Neumeister, A., & Charney, D. S. (2004). Adaptive and maladaptive psychobiological responses to severe psychological stress: Implications for the discovery of novel pharmacotherapy. *Neuroscience & Biobehavioral Reviews*, *28*, 65–94.

Bouton, M. E. (2002). Context, ambiguity, and unlearning: Sources of relapse after behavioral extinction. *Biological Psychiatry*, *52*, 976–986.

Bracha, H. S., & Maser, J. D. (2008). Anxiety and posttraumatic stress disorder in the context of human brain evolution: A role for theory in DSM-V? *Clinical Psychology: Science and Practice*, *15*(1), 91–97.

Bremner, J. D. (2007). Functional neuroimaging in post-traumatic stress disorder. *Expert Reviews in Neurotherapy*, *7*, 393–405.

Bremner, J. D. (2008). Hippocampus. In G. Reyes, J. D. Elhai, & J. D. Ford (Eds.), *Encyclopedia of psychological trauma* (pp. 313–315). Hoboken, NJ: Wiley.

Bremner, J. D., Licinio, J., Darnell, A., Krystal, J. H., Owens, M. J., Southwick, S. M., et al. (1997). Elevated CSF corticotropin-releasing factor concentrations in posttraumatic stress disorder. *American Journal of Psychiatry*, *154*(5), 624–629.

Bremner, J. D., Randall, P., Scott, T. M., Bronen, R. A., Seibyl, J. P., Southwick, S. M., et al. (1995). MRI-based measurement of hippocampal volume in patients with combat-related posttraumatic stress disorder. *American Journal of Psychiatry*, *152*(7), 973–981.

Bremner, J. D., Vythilingam, M., Anderson, G., Vermetten, E., McGlashan, T., Heninger, G., et al. (2003). Assessment of the hypothalamic-pituitary-adrenal axis over a 24-hour diurnal period and in response to neuroendocrine challenges in women with and without childhood sexual abuse and posttraumatic stress disorder. *Biological Psychiatry*, *54*(7), 710–718.

Britton, J. C., Phan, K. L., Taylor, S. F., Fig, L. M., & Liberzon, I. (2005). Corticolimbic blood flow in posttraumatic stress disorder during script-driven imagery. *Biological Psychiatry*, *57*, 832–840.

Brown, R. J., Schrag, A., & Trimble, M. R. (2005). Dissociation, childhood interpersonal trauma, and family functioning in patients with somatization disorder. *American Journal of Psychiatry*, *162*, 899–905.

Brown, V. M., Labar, K. S., Haswell, C. C., Gold, A. L., Mid-Atlantic, M. W., Beall, S. K., et al. (2014). Altered resting-state functional connectivity of basolateral and centromedial amygdala complexes in posttraumatic stress disorder. *Neuropsychopharmacology*, *39*, 351–359.

Bryant, R. A. (2006). Longitudinal psychophysiological studies of heart rate: Mediating effects and implications for treatment. *Annals of the New York Academy of Sciences*, *1071*, 19–26.

Bryant, R. A., Creamer, M., O'Donnell, M. L., Silove, D., & McFarlane, A. C. (2008). A multisite study of the capacity of acute stress disorder diagnosis to predict posttraumatic stress disorder. *Journal of Clinical Psychiatry*, *69*, 923–929.

Bryant, R. A., Felmingham, K. L., Kemp, A. H., Barton, M., Peduto, A. S., Rennie, C., et al. (2005). Neural networks of information processing in posttraumatic stress disorder: A functional magnetic resonance imaging study. *Biological Psychiatry*, *58*, 111–118.

Bryant, R. A., Salmon, K., Sinclair, E., & Davidson, P. (2007). Heart rate as a predictor of posttraumatic stress disorder in children. *General Hospital Psychiatry*, *29*(1), 66–68. http://dx.doi.org/S0163-8343(06)00174-5 [pii]; http://dx.doi.org/10.1016/j.genhosppsych.2006.10.002.

Carrion, V. G., Haas, B. W., Garrett, A., Song, S., & Reiss, A. L. (2010). Reduced hippocampal activity in youth with posttraumatic stress symptoms: An fMRI study. *Journal of Pediatric Psychology. Special Issue: Health Consequences of Child Maltreatment*, *35*(5), 559–569. http://dx.doi.org/10.1093/jpepsy/jsp112.

Carrion, V. G., Weems, C. F., Patwardhan, A., Brown, W., Ray, R. D., & Reiss, A. L. (2001). Attenuation of frontal asymmetry in pediatric posttraumatic stress disorder. *Biological Psychiatry*, *50*, 943–952.

Carrion, V. G., Weems, C. F., Ray, R. D., Glaser, B., Hessl, D., & Reiss, A. L. (2002). Diurnal salivary cortisol in pediatric posttraumatic stress disorder. *Biological Psychiatry*, *51*(7), 575–582.

Carrion, V. G., Weems, C. F., & Reiss, A. L. (2007). Stress predicts brain changes in children: A pilot longitudinal study on youth stress, posttraumatic stress disorder, and the hippocampus. *Pediatrics*, *119*(3), 509–516. http://dx.doi.org/10.1542/peds.2006-2028.

Carvalho Fernando, S., Beblo, T., Schlosser, N., Terfehr, K., Otte, C., Lowe, B., et al. (2012). Associations of childhood trauma with hypothalamic-pituitary-adrenal function in borderline personality disorder and major depression. *Psychoneuroendocrinology, 37*(10), 1659–1668.

Caspi, A., McClay, J., Moffitt, T. E., Mill, J., Martin, J., Craig, I., et al. (2002). Role of genotype in the cycle of violence in maltreated children. *Science, 297,* 851–854.

Caspi, A., Sugden, K., Moffitt, T. E., Taylor, A., Craig, I. W., Harrington, H., et al. (2003). Influence of life stress on depression: Moderation by a polymorphism in the 5-HTT gene. *Science, 301,* 386–389.

Chartier, M. J., Walker, J. R., & Naimark, B. (2007). Childhood abuse, adult health, and health care utilization: Results from a representative community sample. *American Journal of Epidemiology, 165,* 1031–1038.

Cisler, J. M., James, G. A., Tripathi, S., Mletzko, T., Heim, C., Hu, X. P., et al. (2013). Differential functional connectivity within an emotion regulation neural network among individuals resilient and susceptible to the depressogenic effects of early life stress. *Psychological Medicine, 43*(3), 507–518.

Corbo, V., Clement, M. -H., Armony, J. L., Pruessner, J. C., & Brunet, A. (2005). Size versus shape differences: Contrasting voxel-based and volumetric analyses of the anterior cingulate cortex in individuals with acute posttraumatic stress disorder. *Biological Psychiatry, 58*(2), 119–124. http://dx.doi.org/10.1016/j.biopsych.2005.02.032.

Corcoran, K. A., & Maren, S. (2001). Hippocampal inactivation disrupts contextual retrieval of fear memory after extinction. *The Journal of Neuroscience, 21*(5), 1720–1726.

Cuthbert, B. N., & Kozak, M. J. (2013). Constructing constructs for psychopathology: The NIMH research domain criteria. *Journal of Abnormal Psychology, 122*(3), 928–937.

D'Amato, M. R., Fazzaro, J., & Etkin, M. (1968). Anticipatory responding and avoidance discrimination as factors in avoidance conditioning. *Journal of Experimental Psychology, 77,* 41–47.

Davidson, R. J. (2002). Anxiety and affective style: Role of prefrontal cortex and amygdala. *Biological Psychiatry, 51,* 68–80.

De Bellis, M. D., Baum, A. S., Birmaher, B., Keshavan, M. S., Eccard, C. H., Boring, A. M., et al. (1999). Developmental traumatology: I. Biological stress systems. *Biological Psychiatry, 45*(10), 1259–1270.

De Bellis, M. D., Keshavan, M. S., Shifflett, H., Iyengar, S., Beers, S. R., Hall, J., et al. (2002). Brain structures in pediatric maltreatment-related posttraumatic stress disorder: A sociodemographically matched study. *Biological Psychiatry, 52*(11), 1066–1078.

Dębiec, J., Bush, D. E., & LeDoux, J. E. (2011). Noradrenergic enhancement of reconsolidation in the amygdala impairs extinction of conditioned fear in rats—a possible mechanism for the persistence of traumatic memories in PTSD. *Depression and Anxiety, 28*(3), 186–193.

Delahanty, D., & Boarts, J. (2008). Biology, physiology. In G. Reyes, J. D. Elhai, & J. D. Ford (Eds.), *Encyclopedia of psychological trauma* (pp. 100–102). Hoboken, NJ: Wiley.

Delahanty, D. L., Raimonde, A. J., & Spoonster, E. (2000). Initial posttraumatic urinary cortisol levels predict subsequent PTSD symptoms in motor vehicle accident victims. *Biological Psychiatry, 48*(9), 940–947. http://dx.doi.org/10.1016/S0006-3223(00)00896-9.

Depue, B. E., Olson-Madden, J. H., Smolker, H. R., Rajamani, M., Brenner, L. A., & Banich, M. T. (2014). Reduced amygdala volume is associated with deficits in inhibitory control: A voxel- and surface-based morphometric analysis of comorbid PTSD/mild TBI. *Biomed Research International, 2014,* 691505.

Donchin, E., & Coles, M. G. (1988). Is the P300 component a manifestation of context updating? *Behavioral and Brain Sciences, 11*(3), 357–427.

Ehring, T., Ehlers, A., Cleare, A. J., & Glucksman, E. (2008). Do acute psychological and psychobiological responses to trauma predict subsequent symptom severities of PTSD and depression? *Psychiatry Research, 161*(1), 67–75.

El Khoury-Malhame, M., Reynaud, E., Soriano, A., Michael, K., Salgado-Pineda, P., Zendjidjian, X., et al. (2011). Amygdala activity correlates with attentional bias in PTSD. *Neuropsychologia, 49*(7), 1969–1973.

Elzinga, B. M., Schmahl, C. G., Vermetten, E., van Dyck, R., & Bremner, J. D. (2003). Higher cortisol levels following exposure to traumatic reminders in abuse-related PTSD. *Neuropsychopharmacology, 28*(9), 1656–1665. http://dx.doi.org/10.1038/sj.npp.1300226.

Etkin, A., Egner, T., Peraza, D. M., Kandel, E. R., & Hirsch, J. (2006). Resolving emotional conflict: A role for the rostral anterior cingulate cortex in modulating activity in the amygdala. *Neuron, 51*(6), 871–882.

Fairbank, J. A., Putnam, F. W., & Harris, W. W. (2007). The prevalence and impact of child traumatic stress. In M. J. Friedman, T. M. Keane, & P. Resick (Eds.), *Handbook of PTSD: Science and practice* (pp. 229–251). New York: Guilford.

Felitti, V. J., Anda, R. F., Nordenberg, D., Williamson, D. F., Spitz, A. M., Edwards, V., et al. (1998). Relationship of childhood abuse and household dysfunction to many of the leading causes of death in adults. The Adverse Childhood Experiences (ACE) Study. *American Journal of Preventive Medicine, 14*(4), 245–258.

Felmingham, K. L., Rennie, C., Manor, B., & Bryant, R. A. (2011). Eye tracking and physiological reactivity to threatening stimuli in posttraumatic stress disorder. *Journal of Anxiety Disorders, 25*(5), 668–673. http://dx.doi.org/10.1016/j.janxdis.2011.02.010.

Ferster, C. B., & Skinner, B. F. (1957). *Schedules of reinforcement.* New York: Appleton-Century-Crofts.

Foa, E. B., & Kozak, M. J. (1986). Emotional processing of fear: Exposure to corrective information. *Psychological Bulletin, 99*, 20–35.

Ford, J. D. (2005). Treatment implications of altered affect regulation and information processing following child maltreatment. *Psychiatric Annals, 35*(5), 410–419.

Ford, J. D. (2009). Neurobiological and developmental research: Clinical implications. In C. Courtois & J. D. Ford (Eds.), *Treating complex traumatic stress disorders: An evidence-based guide* (pp. 31–58). New York, NY: Guilford.

Ford, J. D., Adams, M. L., & Dailey, W. F. (2006). Factors associated with receiving help and risk factors for disaster-related distress among Connecticut adults 5-15 months after the September 11th terrorist incidents. *Social Psychiatry and Psychiatric Epidemiology, 41*, 261–270.

Ford, J. D., Campbell, K. A., Storzbach, D., Binder, L. M., Anger, W. K., & Rohlman, D. S. (2001). Posttraumatic stress symptomatology is associated with unexplained illness attributed to Persian Gulf War military service. *Psychosomatic Medicine, 63*, 842–849.

Ford, J. D., Fraleigh, L. A., Albert, D. B., & Connor, D. F. (2010). Child abuse and autonomic nervous system hyporesponsivity among psychiatrically impaired children. *Child Abuse & Neglect, 34*, 507–515.

Ford, J. D., Schnurr, P. P., Friedman, M. J., Green, B. L., Adams, G., & Jex, S. (2004). Posttraumatic stress disorder symptoms, physical health, and health care utilization 50 years after repeated exposure to a toxic gas. *Journal of Traumatic Stress, 17*(3), 185–194. http://dx.doi.org/10.1023/B:JOTS.0000029261.23634.87.

Frewen, P., & Lanius, R. (2008). Frontal cortex. In G. Reyes, J. D. Elhai, & J. D. Ford (Eds.), *Encyclopedia of psychological trauma* (pp. 286–290). Hoboken, NJ: Wiley.

Friedman, M. J., & McEwen, B. S. (2004). Posttraumatic stress disorder, allostatic load, and medical illness. In P. P. Schnurr & B. L. Green (Eds.), *Trauma and health: Physical health consequences of exposure to extreme stress.* Washington, DC: American Psychological Association.

Geuze, E., Westenberg, H. G., Jochims, A., de Kloet, C. S., Bohus, M., Vermetten, E., et al. (2007). Altered pain processing in veterans with posttraumatic stress disorder. *Archives of General Psychiatry, 64*(1), 76–85.

Gilbertson, M. W., Shenton, M. E., Ciszewski, A., Kasai, K., Lasko, N. B., Orr, S. P., et al. (2002). Smaller hippocampal volume predicts pathologic vulnerability to psychological trauma. *Nature Neuroscience*, *5*, 1242–1247.

Gilboa, A., Shalev, A. Y., Laor, L., Lester, H., Louzoun, Y., Chisin, R., et al. (2004). Functional connectivity of the prefrontal cortex and the amygdala in posttraumatic stress disorder. *Biological Psychiatry*, *55*, 263–272.

Grasso, D. J., & Simons, R. F. (2009). Electrophysiological abnormalities in traumatized children with PTSD. *Psychophysiology*, *46* S153–S153.

Griffin, M. G. (2008). A prospective assessment of auditory startle alterations in rape and physical assault survivors. *Journal of Traumatic Stress*, *21*(1), 91–99. http://dx.doi.org/10.1002/jts.20300.

Grillon, C. (2002). Startle reactivity and anxiety disorders: Aversive conditioning, context, and neurobiology. *Biological Psychiatry*, *52*(10), 958–975.

Grillon, C. (2008). Models and mechanisms of anxiety: Evidence from startle studies. *Psychopharmacology*, *199*(3), 421–437. http://dx.doi.org/10.1007/s00213-007-1019-1.

Grillon, C., Morgan, C. A., III, Davis, M., & Southwick, S. M. (1998). Effects of experimental context and explicit threat cues on acoustic startle in Vietnam veterans with posttraumatic stress disorder. *Biological Psychiatry*, *44*, 1027–1036.

Guffanti, G., Galea, S., Yan, L., Roberts, A. L., Solovieff, N., Aiello, A. E., et al. (2013). Genome-wide association study implicates a novel RNA gene, the lincRNA AC068718. 1, as a risk factor for post-traumatic stress disorder in women. *Psychoneuroendocrinology*, *38*(12), 3029–3038.

Gurvits, T. V., Shenton, M. E., Hokama, H., & Ohta, H. (1996). Magnetic resonance imaging study of hippocampal volume in chronic, combat-related posttraumatic stress disorder. *Biological Psychiatry*, *40*(11), 1091–1099. http://dx.doi.org/10.1016/s0006-3223(96)00229-6.

Guthrie, R. M., & Bryant, R. A. (2005). Auditory startle response in firefighters before and after trauma exposure. *American Journal of Psychiatry*, *162*(2), 283–290. http://dx.doi.org/162/2/283 [pii]; http://dx.doi.org/10.1176/appi.ajp.162.2.283.

Haglund, M. E. M., Nestadt, P. S., Cooper, N. S., Southwick, S. M., & Charney, D. S. (2007). Psychobiological mechanisms of resilience: Relevance to prevention and treatment of stress-related psychopathology. *Development and Psychopathology*, *19*, 889–920.

Haugaard, J. J. (2004). Recognizing and treating uncommon behavioral and emotional disorders in children and adolescents who have been severely maltreated: Somatization and other somatoform disorders. *Child Maltreatment*, *9*, 169–176.

Heim, C., Newport, D. J., Mletzko, T., Miller, A. H., & Nemeroff, C. B. (2008). The link between childhood trauma and depression: Insights from HPA axis studies in humans. *Psychoneuroendocrinology*, *33*, 693–710.

Herringa, R., Phillips, M., Almeida, J., Insana, S., & Germain, A. (2012). Post-traumatic stress symptoms correlate with smaller subgenual cingulate, caudate, and insula volumes in unmedicated combat veterans. *Psychiatry Research*, *203*(2–3), 139–145.

Herringa, R. J., Phillips, M. L., Fournier, J. C., Kronhaus, D. M., & Germain, A. (2013). Childhood and adult trauma both correlate with dorsal anterior cingulate activation to threat in combat veterans. *Psychological Medicine*, *43*(7), 1533–1542.

Holroyd, C. B., & Coles, M. G. H. (2002). The neural basis of human error processing: Reinforcement learning, dopamine, and the error-related negativity. *Psychological Review*, *109*(4), 679–709. http://dx.doi.org/10.1037/0033-295x.109.4.679.

Jakupcak, M., Osborne, T., Michael, S., Cook, J., Albrizio, P., & McFall, M. (2006). Anxiety sensitivity and depression: Mechanisms for understanding somatic complaints in veterans with posttraumatic stress disorder. *Journal of Traumatic Stress*, *19*, 471–479.

Jelinek, L., Moritz, S., Randjbar, S., Sommerfeldt, D., Puschel, K., & Seifert, D. (2008). Does the evocation of traumatic memories confound subsequent working memory performance in posttraumatic stress disorder (PTSD)? *Depression and Anxiety*, *25*, 175–179.

Jovanovic, T., Blanding, N. Q., Norrholm, S. D., Duncan, E., Bradley, B., & Ressler, K. J. (2009). Childhood abuse is associated with increased startle reactivity in adulthood. *Depression and Anxiety*, *26*(11), 1018–1026. http://dx.doi.org/10.1002/da.20599.

Kalisch, R., Wiech, K., Herrmann, K., & Dolan, R. J. (2006). Neural correlates of self-distraction from anxiety and a process model of cognitive emotion regulation. *Journal of Cognitive Neuroscience*, *18*(8), 1266–1276.

Kandel, E. R., & Squire, L. R. (2000). Neuroscience: Breaking down scientific barriers to the study of brain and mind. *Science*, *290*(5494), 1113–1120.

Karl, A., Malta, L. S., & Maercker, A. (2006). Meta-analytic review of event-related potential studies in post-traumatic stress disorder. *Biological Psychology*, *71*(2), 123–147.

Karl, A., Schaefer, M., Malta, L. S., Dörfel, D., Rohleder, N., & Werner, A. (2006). A meta-analysis of structural brain abnormalities in PTSD. *Neuroscience & Biobehavioral Reviews*, *30*(7), 1004–1031.

Kaufman, J., Yang, B. Z., Douglas-Palumberi, H., Houshyar, S., Lipschitz, D., Krystal, J. H., et al. (2004). Social supports and serotonin transporter gene moderate depression in maltreated children. *Proceedings of the National Academy of Science*, *101*(49), 17316–17321.

Kazak, A. E., Simms, S., Alderfer, M. A., Rourke, M. T., Crump, T., McClure, K., et al. (2005). Feasibility and preliminary outcomes from a pilot study of a brief psychological intervention for families of children newly diagnosed with cancer. *Journal of Pediatric Psychology*, *30*, 644–655.

Kendall-Tackett, K. A. (2007). Inflammation, cardiovascular disease, and metabolic syndrome as sequelae of violence against women: The role of depression, hostility, and sleep disturbance. *Trauma Violence Abuse*, *8*(2), 117–126.

Kilpatrick, D. G., Koenen, K. C., Ruggiero, K. J., Acierno, R., Galea, S., Resnick, H. S., et al. (2007). The serotonin transporter genotype and social support and moderation of posttraumatic stress disorder and depression in hurricane-exposed adults. *American Journal of Psychiatry*, *164*, 1693–1699.

Klaassens, E.R., Giltay, E.J., Cuijpers, P., van Veen, T., & Zitman, F. G. (2012). Adulthood trauma and HPA-axis functioning in healthy subjects and PTSD patients. a meta-analysis. *Psychoneuroendocrinology*, *37*(3), 317–331.

Klorman, R., Cicchetti, D., Thatcher, J. E., & Ison, J. R. (2003). Acoustic startle in maltreated children. *Journal of Abnormal Child Psychology*, *31*(4), 359–370.

Koenen, K. C., Moffitt, T. E., Poulton, R., Martin, J., & Caspi, A. (2007). Early childhood factors associated with the development of post-traumatic stress disorder: Results from a longitudinal birth cohort. *Psychological Medicine*, *37*, 181–192.

Lang, P. J., & Bradley, M. M. (2008). Emotion and the motivational brain. *Biological Psychology* [In press, Accepted Manuscript].

Lewis, M. D. (2005). Self-organizing individual differences in brain development. *Developmental Review*, *25*, 252–277.

Liberzon, I., Taylor, S. F., Phan, K. L., Britton, J. C., Fig, L. M., Bueller, J. A., et al. (2007). Altered central micro-opioid receptor binding after psychological trauma. *Biological Psychiatry*, *61*, 1030–1038.

Lipschitz, D. S., Mayes, L. M., Rasmusson, A. M., Anyan, W., Billingslea, E., Gueorguieva, R., et al. (2005). Baseline and modulated acoustic startle responses in adolescent girls with posttraumatic stress disorder. *Journal of the American Academy of Child & Adolescent Psychiatry*, *44*(8), 807–814.

Logue, M. W., Baldwin, C., Guffanti, G., Melista, E., Wolf, E. J., Reardon, A. F., et al. (2013). A genome-wide association study of post-traumatic stress disorder identifies the retinoid-related orphan receptor alpha (RORA) gene as a significant risk locus. *Molecular Psychiatry, 18*(8), 937–942.

Magnea, G., & Lanius, R. (2008). Biology, brain structure, and function, adult. In G. Reyes, J. D. Elhai, & J. Ford (Eds.), *Encyclopedia of psychological trauma* (pp. 84–90). Hoboken, NJ: Wiley.

Marx, B. P., Forsyth, J. P., Gallup, G. G., Fuse, T., & Lexington, J. M. (2008). Tonic immobility as an evolved predator defense: Implications for sexual assault survivors. *Clinical Psychology: Science and Practice, 15*, 74–90.

Mayes, L. C. (2000). A developmental perspective on the regulation of arousal states. *Seminars in Perinatology, 24*, 267–279.

Mazza, M., Tempesta, D., Pino, M. C., Catalucci, A., Gallucci, M., & Ferrara, M. (2013). Regional cerebral changes and functional connectivity during the observation of negative emotional stimuli in subjects with post-traumatic stress disorder. *European Archives of Psychiatry and Clinical Neuroscience, 263*(7), 575–583.

McFarlane, A. C., Atchison, M., & Yehuda, R. (1997). The acute stress response following motor vehicle accidents and its relation to PTSD. *Annals of the New York Academy of Sciences, 821*(1), 437–441.

McFarlane, A. C., Barton, C. A., Yehuda, R., & Wittert, G. (2011). Cortisol response to acute trauma and risk of posttraumatic stress disorder. *Psychoneuroendocrinology, 36*(5), 720–727.

Meewisse, M. -L., Reitsma, J. B., De Vries, G., Gersons, B. P. R., & Olff, M. (2007). Cortisol and post-traumatic stress disorder in adults: Systematic review and meta-analysis. *British Journal of Psychiatry, 191*, 367–392.

Mickleborough, M. J., Daniels, J. K., Coupland, N. J., Kao, R., Williamson, P. C., Lanius, U. F., et al. (2011). Effects of trauma-related cues on pain processing in posttraumatic stress disorder: An fMRI investigation. *Journal of Psychiatry & Neuroscience, 36*(1), 6–14.

Milad, M. R., Wright, C. I., Orr, S. P., Pitman, R. K., Quirk, G. J., & Rauch, S. L. (2007). Recall of fear extinction in humans activates the ventromedial prefrontal cortex and hippocampus in concert. *Biological Psychiatry, 62*, 446–454.

Miller, G. E., Chen, E., & Zhou, E. S. (2007). If it goes up, must it come down? Chronic stress and the hypothalamic-pituitary-adrenocortical axis in humans. *Psychological Bulletin, 133*(1), 25–45.

Moeller-Bertram, T., Keltner, J., & Strigo, I. A. (2012). Pain and post traumatic stress disorder—review of clinical and experimental evidence. *Neuropharmacology, 62*(2), 586–597.

Mouthaan, J., Sijbrandij, M., Luitse, J. S., Goslings, J. C., Gersons, B. P., & Olff, M. (2014). The role of acute cortisol and DHEAS in predicting acute and chronic PTSD symptoms. *Psychoneuroendocrinology, 45*, 179–186.

Neumeister, A., Henry, S., & Krystal, J. H. (2007). Neurocircuitry and neuroplasticity in PTSD. In M. J. Friedman, T. M. Keane, & P. A. Resick (Eds.), *Handbook of PTSD: Science and practice* (pp. 151–165). New York: Guilford.

Nijenhuis, E. R. S., van der Hart, O., Kruger, K., & Steele, K. (2004). Somatoform dissociation, reported abuse and animal defence-like reactions. *Australian and New Zealand Journal of Psychiatry, 38*, 678–686.

Nixon, R. D., Nehmy, T. J., Ellis, A. A., Ball, S. A., Menne, A., & McKinnon, A. C. (2010). Predictors of posttraumatic stress in children following injury: The influence of appraisals, heart rate, and morphine use. *Behaviour Research and Therapy, 48*(8), 810–815. http://dx.doi.org/10.1016/j.brat.2010.05.002.

Ochsner, K. N., & Gross, J. J. (2005). The cognitive control of emotion. *Trends in Cognitive Sciences*, *9*(5), 242–249.

Olofsson, J. K., Nordin, S., Sequeira, H., & Polich, J. (2008). Affective picture processing: An integrative review of ERP findings. *Biological Psychology*, *77*(3), 247–265.

Ornitz, E. M., & Pynoos, R. S. (1989). Startle modulation in children with posttraumatic stress disorder. *American Journal of Psychiatry*, *146*(7), 866–870.

Orr, S. P., Metzger, L. J., Lasko, N. B., Macklin, M. L., Peri, T., & Pitman, R. K. (2000). De novo conditioning in trauma-exposed individuals with and without posttraumatic stress disorder. *Journal of Abnormal Psychology*, *109*, 290–298.

Pavlisa, G., Papa, J., Pavic, L., & Pavlisa, G. (2006). Bilateral MR volumetry of the amygdala in chronic PTSD patients. *Collegium Antropologicum*, *30*(3), 565–568.

Pineles, S. L., Suvak, M. K., Liverant, G. I., Gregor, K., Wisco, B. E., Pitman, R. K., et al. (2013). Psychophysiologic reactivity, subjective distress, and their associations with PTSD diagnosis. *Journal of Abnormal Psychology*, *122*(3), 635–644. http://dx.doi.org/10.1037/a0033942.

Pitman, R. K., & Orr, S. P. (1990). Modulation of the startle response in children with PTSD. *American Journal of Psychiatry*, *147*(6), 815–816.

Pole, N. (2007). The psychophysiology of posttraumatic stress disorder: A meta-analysis. *Psychological Bulletin*, *133*(5), 725–746. http://dx.doi.org/10.1037/0033-2909.133.5.725.

Pole, N., Neylan, T., Otte, C., Henn-Hasse, C., Metzler, T. J., & Marmar, C. R. (2009). Prospective prediction of posttraumatic stress disorder symptoms using fear potentiated auditory startle responses. *Biological Psychiatry*, *65*(3), 235–240.

Pole, N., Neylan, T. C., Otte, C., Metzler, T. J., Best, S. R., Henn-Haase, C., et al. (2007). Associations between childhood trauma and emotion-modulated psychophysiological responses to startling sounds: A study of police cadets. *Journal of Abnormal Psychology*, *116*(2), 352–361. http://dx.doi.org/10.1037/0021-843X.116.2.352.

Pollak, S. D., Cicchetti, D., Klorman, R., & Brumaghim, J. T. (1997). Cognitive brain event-related potentials and emotion processing in maltreated children. *Child Development*, *68*(5), 773–787.

Pollak, S. D., Vardi, S., Putzer Bechner, A. M., & Curtin, J. J. (2005). Physically abused children's regulation of attention in response to hostility. *Child Development*, *76*, 968–977.

Quevedo, K., Smith, T., Donzella, B., Schunk, E., & Gunnar, M. (2010). The startle response: Developmental effects and a paradigm for children and adults. *Developmental Psychobiology*, *52*(1), 78–89. http://dx.doi.org/10.1002/dev.20415.

Quirk, G. J., & Beer, J. S. (2006). Prefrontal involvement in the regulation of emotion: Convergence of rat and human studies. *Current Opinion in Neurobiology*, *16*(6), 723–727.

Quirk, G. J., Garcia, R., & Gonzalez-Lima, F. (2006). Prefrontal mechanisms in extinction of conditioned fear. *Biological Psychiatry*, *60*, 337–343.

Rabinak, C. A., Angstadt, M., Welsh, R. C., Kenndy, A. E., Lyubkin, M., Martis, B., et al. (2011). Altered amygdala resting-state functional connectivity in post-traumatic stress disorder. *Frontiers in Psychiatry*, *2*, 62.

Rauch, S. L., Shin, L. M., & Phelps, E. A. (2006). Neurocircuitry models of posttraumatic stress disorder and extinction: Human neuroimaging research--past, present, and future. *Biological Psychiatry*, *60*, 376–382.

Resnick, H. S., Yehuda, R., Pitman, R. K., & Foy, D. W. (1995). Effect of previous trauma on acute plasma cortisol level following rape. *American Journal of Psychiatry*, *152*(11), 1675–1677.

Roelofs, K., & Spinhoven, P. (2007). Trauma and medically unexplained symptoms: Towards an integration of cognitive and neuro-biological accounts. *Clinical Psychology Review*, *27*, 798–820.

Ronan, P., & Summers, C. (2008). Biology, animal models. In G. Reyes, J. D. Elhai, & J. D. Ford (Eds.), *Encyclopedia of psychological trauma* (pp. 80–83). Hoboken, NJ: Wiley.

Rudy, J. W., & Matus-Amat, P. (2005). The ventral hippocampus supports a memory representation of context and contextual fear conditioning: Implications for a unitary function of
the hippocampus. *Behavioral Neuroscience*, *119*, 154–163.

Rushworth, M. F., Buckley, M. J., Behrens, T. E., Walton, M. E., & Bannerman, D. M. (2007).
Functional organization of the medial frontal cortex. *Current Opinion in Neurobiology*,
17(2), 220–227.

Sartor, C. E., Grant, J. D., Lynskey, M. T., McCutcheon, V. V., Waldron, M., Statham, D. J., et al.
(2012). Common heritable contributions to low-risk trauma, high-risk trauma, posttraumatic
stress disorder, and major depression. *Archives of General Psychiatry*, *69*(3), 293–299.

Scheeringa, M. S., Zeanah, C. H., Myers, L., & Putnam, F. (2004). Heart period and variability
findings in preschool children with posttraumatic stress symptoms. *Biological Psychiatry*,
55(7), 685–691.

Schiller, D., & Delgado, M. R. (2010). Overlapping neural systems mediating extinction, rever-
sal and regulation of fear. *Trends in Cognitive Sciences*, *14*(6), 268–276.

Schmahl, C., Berne, K., Krause, A., Kleindienst, N., Valerius, G., Vermetten, E., et al. (2009).
Hippocampus and amygdala volumes in patients with borderline personality disorder with
or without posttraumatic stress disorder. *Journal of Psychiatry & Neuroscience: JPN*,
34(4), 289.

Schmahl, C. G., Vermetten, E., Elzinga, B. M., & Bremner, J. D. (2003). Magnetic resonance
imaging of hippocampal and amygdala volume in women with childhood abuse and borderline personality disorder. *Psychiatry Research*, *122*(3), 193–198.

Schnurr, P. P., & Green, B. L. (2004). Understanding relationships among trauma, posttraumatic stress disorder, and health outcomes. In P. P. Schnurr & B. L. Green (Eds.), *Trauma
and health: Physical health consequences of exposure to extreme stress* (pp. 247–275).
Washington, DC: American Psychological Association.

Schupp, H. T., Stockburger, J., Codispoti, M., Junghöfer, M., Weike, A. I., & Hamm, A. O.
(2006). Stimulus novelty and emotion perception: The near absence of habituation in the
visual cortex. *Neuroreport*, *17*(4), 365–369. 310.1097/1001.wnr.0000203355.0000288061.
c0000203356.

Segman, R., Shalev, A. Y., & Gelernter, J. (2007). Gene-environment interactions: Twin studies
and gene research in the context of PTSD. In M. J. Friedman, T. M. Keane, & P. A. Resick
(Eds.), *Handbook of PTSD: Science and practice* (pp. 190–206). New York: Guilford.

Shackman, J. E., Shackman, A. J., & Pollak, S. D. (2007). Physical abuse amplifies attention to
threat and increases anxiety in children. *Emotion*, *7*(4), 838–852.

Shalev, A. Y., Videlock, E. J., Peleg, T., Segman, R., Pitman, R. K., & Yehuda, R. (2008). Stress hormones and post-traumatic stress disorder in civilian trauma victims: A longitudinal study. Part
I: HPA axis responses. *International Journal of Neuropsychopharmacology*, *11*(3), 365–372.
http://dx.doi.org/S1461145707008127 [pii]; http://dx.doi.org/10.1017/S1461145707008127.

Shalev, A. Y., & Yehuda, R. (1998). Longitudinal development of traumatic stress disorders.
In R. Yehuda (Ed.), *Psychological trauma* (pp. 31–66). Washington, DC: American
Psychiatric Association.

Shin, L. M., & Handwerger, K. (2008). Anterior cingulate cortex. In G. Reyes, J. D. Elhai, &
J. D. Ford (Eds.), *Encyclopedia of psychological trauma* (pp. 31–32). Hoboken, NJ: Wiley.

Shin, L. M., Rauch, S. L., & Pitman, R. K. (2006). Amygdala, medial prefrontal cortex, and
hippocampal function in PTSD. *Annals of the New York Academy of Sciences*, *1071*, 67–79.

Solovieff, N., Roberts, A. L., Ratanatharathorn, A., Haloosim, M., De Vivo, I., King, A. P., et al.
(2014). Genetic association analysis of 300 genes identifies a risk haplotype in SLC18A2
for post-traumatic stress disorder in two independent samples. *Neuropsychopharmacology*,
39(8), 1872–1879.

Southwick, S. M., Bremner, J. D., Rasmusson, A., Morgan, C. A., Arnsten, A., & Charney, D. S. (1999). Role of norepinephrine in the pathophysiology and treatment of posttraumatic stress disorder. *Biological Psychiatry, 46*, 1192–1204.

Southwick, S. M., Davis, L. L., Aikins, D. E., Rasmusson, A. M., Barron, J., & Morgan, C. A. (2007). Neurobiological alterations associated with PTSD. In M. J. Friedman, K. T. Martin, & P. A. Resick (Eds.), *Handbook of PTSD: Science and practice* (pp. 166–189). New York: Guilford.

Sripada, R. K., King, A. P., Garfinkel, S. N., Wang, X., Sripada, C. S., Welsh, R. C., et al. (2012a). Altered resting-state amygdala functional connectivity in men with posttraumatic stress disorder. *Journal of Psychiatry and Neuroscience, 37*(4), 241–249.

Sripada, R. K., King, A. P., Welsh, R. C., Garfinkel, S. N., Wang, X., Sripada, C. S., et al. (2012b). Neural dysregulation in posttraumatic stress disorder: Evidence for disrupted equilibrium between salience and default mode brain networks. *Psychosomatic Medicine, 74*(9), 904–911.

Stein, M. B., Koverola, C., Hanna, C., Torchia, M. G., & McClarty, B. (1997). Hippocampal volume in women victimized by childhood sexual abuse. *Psychological Medicine, 27*(4), 951–959. http://dx.doi.org/10.1017/S0033291797005242.

Stevens, J. S., Jovanovic, T., Fani, N., Ely, T. D., Glover, E. M., Bradley, B., et al. (2013). Disrupted amygdala-prefrontal functional connectivity in civilian women with posttraumatic stress disorder. *Journal of Psychiatric Research, 47*(10), 1469–1478.

Strigo, I. A., Simmons, A. N., Matthews, S. C., Grimes, E. M., Allard, C. B., Reinhardt, L. E., et al. (2010). Neural correlates of altered pain response in women with posttraumatic stress disorder from intimate partner violence. *Biological Psychiatry, 68*(5), 442–450.

Suzuki, A., Poon, L., Papadopoulos, A. S., Kumari, V., & Cleare, A. J. (2014). Long term effects of childhood trauma on cortisol stress reactivity in adulthood and relationship to the occurrence of depression. *Psychoneuroendocrinology, 50*, 289–299.

Tedstone, J. E., & Tarrier, N. (2003). Posttraumatic stress disorder following medical illness and treatment. *Clinical Psychology Review, 23*, 409–448.

Teicher, M. H., & Samson, J. A. (2013). Childhood maltreatment and psychopathology: A case for ecophenotypic variants as clinically and neurobiologically distinct subtypes. *American Journal of Psychiatry, 170*(10), 1114–1133. http://dx.doi.org/10.1176/appi.ajp.2013.12070957.

Tronel, S., & Alberini, C. M. (2007). Persistent disruption of a traumatic memory by postretrieval inactivation of glucocorticoid receptors in the amygdala. *Biological Psychiatry, 62*, 33–39.

Tsoory, M. M., Vouimba, R. M., Akirav, I., Kavushansky, A., Avital, A., & Richter-Levin, G. (2008). Amygdala modulation of memory-related processes in the hippocampus: Potential relevance to PTSD. *Progress in Brain Research, 167*, 35–51.

Tupler, L. A., & De Bellis, M. D. (2006). Segmented hippocampal volume in children and adolescents with posttraumatic stress disorder. *Biological Psychiatry, 59*(6), 523–529. http://dx.doi.org/10.1016/j.biopsych.2005.08.007.

Van der Werff, S., Pankekoek, J., Veer, I., van Tol, M., Aleman, A., Veltman, D., et al. (2013). Resilience to childhood maltreatment is associated with increased resting-state functional connectivity of the salience network with the lingual gyrus. *Child Abuse & Neglect, 37*, 1021–1029.

Voisey, J., Young, R. M., Lawford, B. R., & Morris, C. P. (2014). Progress towards understanding the genetics of posttraumatic stress disorder. *Journal of Anxiety Disorders, 28*(8), 873–883. http://dx.doi.org/10.1016/j.janxdis.2014.09.014.

Waldinger, R. J., Schulz, M. S., Barsky, A. J., & Ahern, D. K. (2006). Mapping the road from childhood trauma to adult somatization: The role of attachment. *Psychosomatic Medicine, 68*, 129–135.

Wellman, L. L., Fitzpatrick, M. E., Machida, M., & Sanford, L. D. (2014). The basolateral amygdala determines the effects of fear memory on sleep in an animal model of PTSD. *Experimental Brain Research*, *232*(5), 1555–1565.

Weniger, G., Lange, C., Sachsse, U., & Irle, E. (2009). Reduced amygdala and hippocampus size in trauma-exposed women with borderline personality disorder and without posttraumatic stress disorder. *Journal of Psychiatry and Neuroscience*, *34*(5), 383–388.

Wignall, E. L., Dickson, J. M., Vaughan, P., Farrow, T. F., Wilkinson, I. D., Hunter, M. D., et al. (2004). Smaller hippocampal volume in patients with recent-onset posttraumatic stress disorder. *Biological Psychiatry*, *56*, 832–836.

Williams, L. M., Kemp, A. H., Felmingham, K., Barton, M., Olivieri, G., Peduto, A., et al. (2006). Trauma modulates amygdala and medial prefrontal responses to consciously attended fear. *Neuroimage*, *29*, 347–357.

Woon, F. L., & Hedges, D. W. (2008). Hippocampal and amygdala volumes in children and adults with childhood maltreatment-related posttraumatic stress disorder: A meta-analysis. *Hippocampus*, *18*(8), 729–736. http://dx.doi.org/10.1002/hipo.20437.

Xie, P., Kranzler, H. R., Yang, C., Zhao, H., Farrer, L. A., & Gelernter, J. (2013). Genomewide association study identifies new susceptibility loci for posttraumatic stress disorder. *Biological Psychiatry*, *74*(9), 656–663.

Yan, X., Brown, A. D., Lazar, M., Cressman, V. L., Henn-Haase, C., Neylan, T. C., et al. (2013). Spontaneous brain activity in combat related PTSD. *Neuroscience Letters*, *547*, 1–5.

Yehuda, R. (2002). Clinical relevance of biologic findings in PTSD. *Psychiatric Quarterly*, *73*(2), 123–133.

Yehuda, R., Bierer, L. M., Schmeidler, J., Aferiat, D. H., Breslau, I., & Dolan, S. (2000). Low cortisol and risk for PTSD in adult offspring of Holocaust survivors. *American Journal of Psychiatry*, *157*, 1252–1259.

Yehuda, R., Halligan, S. L., & Bierer, L. M. (2001). Relationship of parental trauma exposure and PTSD to PTSD, depressive and anxiety disorders in offspring. *Journal of Psychiatric Research*, *35*, 261–270.

Yehuda, R., & LeDoux, J. (2007). Response variation following trauma: A translational neuroscience approach to understanding PTSD. *Neuron*, *56*, 19–32.

Young, E. A., & Breslau, N. (2004). Cortisol and catecholamines in posttraumatic stress disorder: An epidemiologic community study. *Archives of General Psychiatry*, *61*, 394–401.

Young, R. M., Lawford, B. R., Noble, E. P., Kann, B., Wilkie, A., Ritchie, T., et al. (2002). Harmful drinking in military veterans with post-traumatic stress disorder: Association with the D2 dopamine receptor A1 allele. *Alcohol and Alcoholism*, *37*, 451–456.

Young, S. E., Smolen, A., Hewitt, J. K., Haberstick, B. C., Stallings, M. C., Corley, R. P., et al. (2006). Interaction between MAO-A benotype and maltreatment in the risk for conduct cisorder: Failure to confirm in adolescent patients. *American Journal of Psychiary*, *163*, 1019–1025.

Zatzick, D., & Roy-Byrne, P. P. (2006). From bedside to bench: How the epidemiology of clinicalpractice can inform the secondary prevention of PTSD. *Psychiatric Services*, *57*, 1726–1730.

Assessment of psychological trauma and PTSD

There are many ways to gather information and make a clinical or research determination that psychological trauma and posttraumatic stress disorder (PTSD) have or have not occurred. This is understandable in light of the complexity of traumatic stressors, the risk and protective factors that influence the likelihood of developing traumatic stress disorders, and the several types of traumatic stress disorders in addition to PTSD and comorbid disorders and problems. Psychological trauma and PTSD, as defined in the American Psychiatric Association's (2013) *Diagnostic and Statistical Manual* (5th edition), require the presence of events that are objectively "traumatic" and a menu of symptoms that include ones closely tied to memories of those events ("intrusive reexperiencing"); reactions to those memories, reminders, or fears of those or similar events ("avoidance," "hypervigilance"); and general impairments in mood ("emotional numbing," loss of interest ("anehdonia"), "anger/irritability"), mental acuity ("impaired concentration"), and physical relaxation and energy ("exaggerated startle," "hyperarousal"). PTSD assessment must address each of these components of PTSD in order to accurately determine if traumatic events have occurred and symptoms are sufficiently present (and persistent) to constitute a serious problem for the individual.

Therefore, this chapter describes and provides samples of scientifically validated measures for the clinical and research assessment of psychological trauma and PTSD. Following a brief overview of the scientific and clinical criteria that are used to ensure that psychological trauma and PTSD assessment are as safe and effective as possible, four purposes for PTSD assessment are discussed: past exposure to psychological trauma, PTSD symptoms and diagnosis, related (comorbid) psychosocial and physical health problems, and screening to identify people with undetected and untreated PTSD.

Scientific criteria for PTSD assessment

There are many ways for a therapist or researcher to learn about people's experiences of psychological trauma or PTSD symptoms. Assessment measures may take several forms. First, there are "self-report questionnaires," which are lists of questions that the patient or research participant reads and then answers by selecting the best response (for "closed-ended" questionnaires, which provide a menu of specific possible answers) or by filling in an answer (for "open-ended" questionnaires, which allow respondents to create their own answer). Most self-report questionnaires assessing PTSD or psychological trauma are closed-ended measures that ask the respondent to either answer "yes" or "no" (e.g., "Did you ever witness an accident

Posttraumatic Stress Disorder. DOI: http://dx.doi.org/10.1016/B978-0-12-801288-8.00006-6

Box 6.1 Key Points

1. Research has shown that asking about potentially traumatic experiences is only mildly and manageably upsetting for most respondents. Many persons who are asked about their past potentially traumatic experiences say that they appreciate being asked about such important personal experiences and feel that they benefited from the opportunity to talk about traumatic experiences with a concerned and supportive professional clinician.

2. Assessment of PTSD can be done in several ways, including self-report questionnaires, ratings by people who know the person well ("collateral" or "clinician" ratings), and structured interviews conducted by a clinical or research assessor.

3. The accuracy of assessments of PTSD is evaluated in research studies of the "reliability" and "validity" of each assessment measure, which must be done before any assessment measure can be used with confidence by clinicians.

4. Several questionnaires have demonstrated reliability and validity for the assessment of past exposure to traumatic stressors, including ones that cover a wide range of potentially traumatic experiences (such as the TESI) and others that focus on more specific time periods (such as the CTQ) or types of traumatic stressors (such as the CTS2). Some of these tests were specifically designed also to be used as structured interviews (such as the TESI).

5. Caution is required when attempting to assess past potentially traumatic experiences, because memory is imperfect and recollection of past distressing experiences may be distorted (either unintentionally or intentionally) by a person's current emotional state and motivations. When possible, the best approach is to obtain additional confirmation—for example, through legal, child welfare, or medical records—by the independent report of persons who are knowledgeable concerning the assessee's life experiences (such as parents). However, official records and "close informants" reports also are not infallible. For example, records may be incomplete, and a parent may not know that her son or daughter encountered a traumatic stressor experience. Therefore, the best approach to the assessment of a person's "trauma history" is to collect information from as many sources as possible and to make a determination based upon the overall evidence with the likely accuracy of each source taken into account.

6. Well-validated and reliable questionnaire and structured interview measures are widely used to assess the severity of PTSD symptoms (typically questionnaires such as the PCL) and also to diagnose PTSD (which must be done with structured interviews such as the CAPS).

7. PTSD also may be assessed and formally clinically diagnosed by reliable and well-validated larger structured interviews that have a section for PTSD among several other sections for other psychiatric disorders (such as the adult Structured Clinical Interview for *DSM*-5 (SCID-5); or the Diagnostic Interview Schedule for Children, DISC).

8. Brief screening questionnaires have been found to be reliable and valid for identifying persons who are likely to be experiencing PTSD, such as the Primary Care PTSD test (PC-PTSD). Screening measures cannot establish the precise severity of PTSD symptoms or the diagnosis of PTSD, but they can narrow down the potential group of persons who should receive a more thorough PTSD questionnaire or structured interview.

9. People who are most likely to benefit from PTSD screening and assessment are those who are known to have experienced severe traumatic stressors—such as children who receive protective services due to having been abused; women who are extricating themselves from domestically violent relationships; survivors of natural or humanmade disasters who have lost their homes, communities, or loved ones; and emergency first responders and military personnel who deal with death on a regular basis. For these individuals, the primary question is determining the exact nature of the traumatic stressor experience for each unique person and whether his or her recovery was impeded by PTSD.

10. The goal of PTSD assessment in both arenas is to obtain the most reliable and valid information possible about (i) how an individual's past exposure to traumatic stressors and current PTSD symptoms are related; (ii) how PTSD symptoms currently (or at important past time points) affect(ed) the person's health and functioning (i.e., the ability to be successful in relationships, work, school, and other key life experiences); (iii) how PTSD symptoms ebb and flow over time, across developmental periods, and life changes; (iv) how PTSD symptoms are intertwined with symptoms of other psychiatric or medical disorders and other life problems (such as difficulties in school or work, or financial or legal problems); and (v) how PTSD prevention or treatment interventions lead to changes in an individual's risk of developing PTSD or success in recovering from PTSD (see Chapters 7–9).

in which someone died?" Yes No) or to select a numerical rating that best reflects their answer (e.g., "On a scale from $0 = $ Never, $1 = $ Once, $2 = $ Once a week, $3 = $ Several times each week, $4 = $ Every day, how often in the past month have you felt as though the traumatic event was actually happening all over right now, even when it really wasn't?"). Self-report questionnaires may be scored by adding up the numerical scores to provide a total score (e.g., the sum of the 0–4 ratings on a questionnaire with several items like the preceding example could be used to calculate the severity of PTSD symptoms) or by counting each "yes" as evidence of a particular symptom or type of psychological trauma.

Questionnaires also may be used to get information about a person from another person, such as when a parent or teacher is asked to describe the frequency or severity of a child's or student's PTSD symptoms based on what he or she has observed, or if a parent is asked to describe potentially traumatic events that he or she knows (or directly observes) the child has experienced. In this case, the questionnaires are being used not as self-reports but as "collateral" (meaning, provided by a separate person) ratings/reports. Therapists also may make ratings of a patient based on their observations of a patient's behavior in therapy sessions and patients' descriptions of themselves.

Structured interviews are designed very similarly to questionnaires, but the questions are read to the respondent (who may be the person being assessed or a rater such as a parent or teacher) by a therapist or a research interviewer. Interviews are called "structured" for two reasons. First, the questions are "standardized"—that is, the exact (or close to exact) same question wording is used with every patient or interviewee, just as the questions on assessment questionnaires are exactly the same for every respondent. Second, the interviewee's answers may be open-ended, but the interviewer sums up each answer in the form of a numerical score—usually in the same form as that used by questionnaires (i.e., most often, either "yes-no" or a numerical scale). The benefits of structured interviews, compared to questionnaires, include that interviewers can help interviewees by (i) assisting them if they cannot read the questionnaire (e.g., young children or someone having difficulty reading due to language barriers or intellectual functioning limitations); (ii) rephrasing questions or redefining specific terms in a question using language that is more familiar or understandable to the interviewee; or (iii) identifying inconsistencies in responses to different items or between answers and the interviewee's actual behavior. However, when questions are sensitive for interviewees, such as often is the case with questions about traumatic stressors or memories, some respondents are more comfortable and willing to disclose information fully if they can do so without having to actually talk about the stressor or symptoms.

Psychosocial and psychiatric assessment measures and methods must meet certain clinical and scientific standards in order to provide accurate and meaningful information for treatment and research purposes (see the American Psychological Association's, 2014, *Standards for Educational and Psychological Testing*). Although there are several different ways in which measures of psychological trauma and PTSD are scored, these scientific standards apply to all tests and measures that are used for the assessment of psychological trauma exposure and PTSD.

Reliability. Questionnaire and structured interview assessments are considered to be accurate from a scientific perspective (and for clinical purposes) if they produce "reliable" results. There are three separate types of measurement reliability. First, when a total score is calculated based on answers to a series of questions, the "internal consistency" reliability is the extent to which the questions all measure aspects of the same overall phenomenon (such as the PCL, which has 17 questions that all assess different aspects of the same basic phenomenon, PTSD). Second, test-retest reliability is the extent to which the same person gives approximately the same answers in the interview or on the questionnaire if the measure is readministered after a short time period (e.g., repeated measurements using the test within a month of each other). This is also called "temporal stability," referring to the equivalency (stability) of the scores on the measure when it is reassessed at two different time (temporal) points. Third, interviews or collateral ratings also can be evaluated for interrater reliability, which is the extent to which two independent interviewers or raters agree in their scores for the same person on the same measure.

Reliability is calculated using statistics that reflect the extent of the measure's accuracy when administered to a number of respondents or interviewees. Several specific reliability statistics can be calculated, depending on the type of reliability, but generally they yield a reliability estimate that ranges between 0 (completely unreliable) and 1.00 or 100% (perfect reliability). The lowest level of reliability that is considered acceptable varies, depending on the specific statistic, but generally a reliability of 0.70 or 80% or higher is the goal for accurate measurement.

Validity. In addition to being accurate, a test should provide information that is as close to the actual truth as possible. Validity is the degree to which a questionnaire, collateral rating, or interview produces results that describe the actual events (in the case of assessment of traumatic stressors) or symptoms (in the case of PTSD) that a respondent or interviewee has experienced. There are several types of measurement validity, beginning with "face" or "content" validity, which reflects the extent to which the test's questions and answer options are consistent with the phenomena being measured. For example, a measure assessing traumatic stressors would have greater face or content validity if its items describe events that involve definite threat to the life of the interviewee or others than if the items describe events that are not life-threatening, because a traumatic stressor by definition must involve a potential life threat (except for sexual trauma).

More stringent requirements are involved in concurrent, criterion, discriminant, and construct validity. These forms of validity reflect the test's ability to produce results that are statistically comparable to those of other measures of the same or similar phenomena ("concurrent validity"), that match a "gold standard" (i.e., a definitive representation of the phenomenon of interest, "criterion validity"), and that are statistically distinct ("discriminant") from results of measures of other phenomena. For example, if a questionnaire measuring PTSD symptom severity produces scores that are highly correlated with scores produced by another PTSD measure and weakly correlated with scores produced by a measure of a different phenomenon (such as an unrelated psychiatric disorder), and that match diagnoses of PTSD provided by a well-validated interview, it would be said to have evidence of concurrent, discriminant, and criterion validity. Construct validity is the measure's overall ability to measure the construct (phenomenon) of interest, and it is evaluated in several ways, most basically by combining the results from all other validity types. Validity is assessed using statistical calculations based upon administering the questionnaire or interview to a number of respondents, using similar statistical metrics to those for reliability.

For a more detailed discussion of scientific standards of assessment measures for traumatic stressors and PTSD see Keane, Brief, Pratt, and Miller (2007), and Frueh, Elhai, Grubaugh, and Ford (2012). In this chapter, reliability and validity of measures of psychological trauma and PTSD are described in brief as "demonstrated" (when findings from several rigorous studies indicate high levels of reliability and validity), "uncertain" (when findings are mixed), or "unknown" (when no data are reported).

Clinical issues in PTSD assessment: 1. Assessing trauma history

Assessment of psychological trauma and PTSD is relevant for mental health, addictions, social work, marriage and family therapy, and other counseling professions and researchers in those fields because it is highly likely in clinical practice that a significant proportion of patients will have been exposed to psychological trauma; between 50% and 60% of the adult population has reported at least one traumatic stressor at some point in their lives (Kessler, Sonnega, Bromet, Hughes, & Nelson, 1995; Wittchen, Gloster, Beesdo, Schonfeld, & Perkonigg, 2009) and similar numbers of children and adolescents (Copeland, Keeler, Angold, & Costello, 2007; McLaughlin et al., 2013). Screening for a history of exposure to traumatic stressors enables clinicians to identify individuals who should be assessed for PTSD (and provided with specialized treatment if they have PTSD).

However, most children and adults who experience traumatic stressors do not develop PTSD or other clinically significant psychiatric problems (see Chapter 2). Clinicians may therefore question whether it is appropriate to routinely screen for psychological trauma, because asking about such experiences might cause clients significant distress (Elhai, Ford, & Naifeh, 2010). However, research has shown that asking about potentially traumatic experiences is not more than mildly and manageably upsetting for most respondents (Newman & Kaloupek, 2004; Zajac, Ruggiero, Smith, Saunders, & Kilpatrick, 2011). In fact, those who feel distressed typically say they do not regret responding to the questions, and many say that they appreciate being asked about such important personal experiences and feel that they benefited from the opportunity to talk about traumatic experiences with a concerned and supportive professional clinician (Newman & Kaloupek, 2004).

Despite these findings, it is important to be cautious when asking clients to disclose traumatic experiences. Laypersons (and many professionals) often incorrectly assume that trauma history assessment involves a detailed "dredging up" of memories of horrible experiences. Thus, it is important to clearly state at the outset of screening that the interviewee should only answer questions if he or she feels ready and able to disclose sensitive personal information. Questions should be as free from vague expressions or technical jargon as possible, particularly language that may be anxiety-provoking or subject to many different interpretations. For example, asking if a person has ever been "abused" or has witnessed "domestic violence" may be problematic because these colloquial expressions do not assist the person to describe *her actual experience*, and the emotionally charged nature of these terms may lead people to either decline to answer (or deny events that actually happened) or to become emotionally distressed. Thus, the precise concerns that clinicians often raise about asking any questions about trauma history are most likely to be a problem not so much *if* the questions are asked as if the questions are asked poorly.

In order to avoid these pitfalls, experts recommend that clinicians use standardized, behaviorally specific questions that briefly and matter-of-factly describe features of stressful experiences that research suggests are likely to be psychologically traumatic (Elhai et al., 2010). For example, rather than asking, "Were you physically abused as a child?," it is better to ask, for example, "When you were less than 18 years old, did anyone who was in charge of you (e.g., babysitter, relative, etc.) ever hit, slap, shove, kick, burn, or punch you in a way that left a mark/bruise or led you to miss school or go to the doctor?" Instruments that provide these types of psychological trauma history questions are described later in this chapter.

It also is important to therapeutically guide patients when they disclose potentially traumatic experiences so that they do not come away from the assessment feeling emotionally overwhelmed or stigmatized by their disclosure. The first step in this process is to clearly explain to each client why traumatic stressors are being discussed. This explanation should communicate the importance of obtaining a complete understanding of the patient's life experiences (the "psychosocial history") and should help the patient to anticipate but feel confident rather than fearful about handling any transient emotional distress that might occur. If these difficulties are explained as "healthy reactions to severe threats to your or someone else's life or safety," it helps patients to recognize that even problematic symptoms are an understandable (and in many ways resilient) adaptation to severe threat. The other critical step is to inform the patient that it is best to disclose highly stressful experiences gradually, and only as the patient feels ready. Specifically, the patient should feel free to "pass" on disclosing any event(s) or aspects of events that he or she prefers not to think about or describe at the time of assessment. This provides the patient with a way to feel (and be) in control of what is remembered (Harvey, 1996) and disclosed, rather than feeling in any way coerced or pressured. Some patients may spontaneously describe traumatic experiences in great detail, even when cautioned to disclose selectively and gradually. It usually is most helpful in such cases to empathically reflect the seriousness and distressing nature of the experience(s), while simultaneously helping the patient to more consciously decide how much, how fast, and what to disclose rather than indiscriminately "telling all" and feeling overwhelmed.

Often the purpose of inquiring about patients' or research participants' histories of trauma exposure is to establish whether they have a diagnosis of PTSD. Without a careful review of potentially traumatic experiences, a diagnosis of PTSD may either be incorrectly given (if no specific traumatic experiences can be documented; Rosen and Taylor, 2007) or inaccurately assumed not to be present (Elhai et al., 2010). Thus, while it is not necessary to know every detail of every distressing experience in a patient's or research participant's life in order to determine if he or she is eligible for a diagnosis of PTSD, it is necessary to get a reliable and valid "trauma history." Even with the best measures, people have difficulty accurately reporting the details of their trauma history and often provide different answers if they are asked more than once to recall and report the traumatic events they have experienced; technically this is referred to as low temporal reliability (Frueh, Elhai, & Kaloupek, 2004). In most cases, unless the individual is motivated to change his or her answers (e.g., when seeking disability or making a legal claim; see Chapter 10), these changes in what is reported occur simply because human memory is imperfect; thus, what people recall and report about all kinds of past experiences tend to change over time. Therefore, it always is best if possible to obtain corroboration of psychological trauma exposure using medical, educational, military, police, or other public records, if possible, while using caution because those records also are not always accurate and complete.

It also is important to remember that several factors may motivate people to under- or overreport experiencing psychological trauma. Underreporting may occur due to wanting to preserve one's family (when the alleged perpetrator lives with, and even financially supports the victim), fear of retribution by a perpetrator, fear of being stigmatized or blamed as a trauma "victim," little support in important personal relationships for disclosing traumatic experiences, or fear of emotionally falling apart (Acierno, Kilpatrick, & Resnick, 1999). Reasons to overreport traumatic stressors include assuming that events were worse than they actually were due to suffering from PTSD, depression, or anxiety currently, or a desire to get emotional or financial compensation (such as from litigation or disability) (Guriel & Fremouw, 2003). Note however that overreporting of psychological trauma exposure does not necessarily mean that the person did not experience any traumatic stressors; it could be due to overstating the extent, severity, or nature of actual traumatic stressors that really were experienced (Elhai et al., 2010).

Assessing past exposure to traumatic stressors (trauma history)

Based on these scientific and clinical considerations, experts recommend the following preparation for patients or research participants before inquiring about their history of exposure to potentially traumatic events. Asking about trauma exposure involves sensitive questions. Therefore, it is wise to begin with a preface statement that familiarizes the respondent with the types of questions and wording used to inquire about past traumatic experiences. This conveys the clinician's understanding that the questions may elicit distress but also confidence in being able to help the respondent handle distress effectively and sufficient knowledge to recognize that, although traumatic stressors are atypical events, most people nevertheless have experienced traumatic stressors at some point. It also is important to communicate that stress reactions following such exposure are not uncommon, may occur immediately or after a delay, and reflect a healthy self-protective attempt to survive and be prepared for any future similar threats.

Finally, patients and research participants benefit from reassurance that it is only when stress reactions interfere with a person's well-being or functioning that treatment is needed and that the effective treatments require that the clinician knows just enough about the client's past traumatic experiences to teach the patients ways to cope with the specific stress reactions that have become problematic. This overview demonstrates that the clinician is empathic and concerned about how difficult events have affected the client and will use the trauma history to enable the client to manage traumatic stress reactions effectively in her or his present-day life (Acierno et al., 1999).

Several questionnaires and structured interviews instruments have been developed for clinical and research assessment of people's past exposure to traumatic stressors. Each measure has both advantages and disadvantages. A sampling of measures is described here, selected based on their wide usage in the field and demonstrated evidence of reliability and validity (Briere, 2004; Briere & Spinazzola, 2009; Nader, 2008). Most of these measures were developed for assessing PTSD under *DSM-IV*, and some are in the process of being revised for *DSM-5*. At the present time, the only measures discussed here that have been developed and validated for *DSM-5* PTSD are the Life Events Checklist (LEC), PTSD Checklist (PCL), and Clinician-Administered PTSD Scale (CAPS).

Trauma history measures

Detailed descriptions of questionnaires and interviews that screen for past exposures to traumatic stressors may be found in books by Briere and Spinazzola (2009); Ford, Nader, and Fletcher (2013); Frueh et al. (2012); and Nader (2008).

The LEC (Gray, Litz, Wang, & Lombardo, 2004) is a questionnaire that asks respondents to answer "yes" or "no" to whether any of 17 potentially traumatic events has (i) happened to them, (ii) been witnessed by them, or (iii) been learned about by them. The LEC was designed originally to assess the PTSD diagnosis A criterion (exposure to a traumatic event) for a PTSD symptom/diagnosis structured interview that is discussed following (CAPS; Weathers, Keane, & Davidson, 2001). The LEC can be obtained (at no charge) by ordering the CAPS through the National Center for PTSD's assessment website (www.ptsd.va.gov/professional/assessment/overview) or purchased through Western Psychological Services (www.wpspublish.com). Each LEC item is used as a separate score indicating whether that type of potentially traumatic event had ever happened to or been witnessed by the respondent. Although the LEC items have been shown to have good temporal stability reliability and convergent and criterion validity, the LEC cannot provide a definitive assessment of exposure to traumatic stressors because the items do not specify whether events were objectively or subjectively traumatic. For example, items are worded as follows: "a fire or explosion" and "physical assault (such as being attacked, hit, slapped, kicked, beaten up)." It is not possible to determine if these events were life-threatening (PTSD Criterion A1). Therefore, the LEC can serve as a preliminary screening instrument that would need to be followed up with more detailed inquiry in order to determine if events that the respondent endorses (reports having happened directly or having witnessed) meet *DSM* criteria for traumatic stressors.

The Stressful Life Events Screening Questionnaire (SLESQ; Briere, Kaltman, & Green, 2008; Goodman, Corcoran, Turner, Yuan, & Green, 1998) asks if any of 12 potentially traumatic events has ever occurred. A 13th question is included to provide respondents with a way to describe other experiences that were "extremely frightening or horrifying." Detailed follow-up questions (called "probes") are included to briefly determine the nature of each event (such as at what age(s) it occurred, who else was involved, the specific type of injury/harm). However, other than the 13th question, there is no inquiry about the subjective aspect of trauma (*DSM-IV-TR* PTSD Criterion A2: whether the person felt extreme fear, helplessness, or horror).

The Trauma History Questionnaire (THQ; Mueser et al., 2001) is a longer version of the SLESQ and asks about 24 specific potentially traumatic events. However, the THQ does not ask in detail about the events. The SLESQ and THQ can be obtained at no charge from Bonnie L. Green, Ph.D., Department of Psychiatry, Georgetown University Medical School, 310 Kober Cogan Hall, Washington, DC 20007, 202-687-6529, bgreen01@georgetown.edu.

Like the THQ, the Traumatic Life Events Questionnaire (TLEQ; Kubany et al., 2000) asks about exposure to 23 potentially traumatic events. The TLEQ includes probe questions about the specific nature of the events, similar to the SLESQ, and assesses subjective responses (*DSM-IV-TR* PTSD Criterion A2). The TLEQ has demonstrated evidence of reliability and validity, and it is available for purchase from Western Psychological Services.

The Traumatic Events Questionnaire (Lauterbach & Vrana, 2004) and the Traumatic Stress Schedule (Norris, 1990) are two other screening questionnaires that inquire about a smaller number of specific types of potentially traumatic events (Box 6.1).

Questions from the SLESQ and THQ have been combined and supplemented with additional traumatic stressor and probe questions from an omnibus trauma history structured interview: the Traumatic Events Screening Instrument (TESI). Versions of the TESI have been developed and demonstrated to have reliability and validity for adults (TESI-A; Ford, 2008; Ford & Fournier, 2007) and for children or adolescents, the latter either as an interview with the child or as an interview in which a parent reports on the child's experiences (TESI-C and TESI-PRR; Daviss et al., 2000; Ford et al., 2000). The TESI inquires about 18 discrete types of traumatic events that can be summarized in 10 composite categories: accident/disaster trauma (direct or witnessed), medical/illness trauma, traumatic loss, community violence, physical assault, domestic violence, childhood physical abuse, childhood sexual abuse, and trauma due to a drunk driver. Items are phrased to elicit endorsement only if *DSM-IV* PTSD Criterion A1 is met, and a probe follows each item to document *DSN-IV-TR* PTSD Criterion A2. Detailed probes follow each item to determine the specific nature of each potentially traumatic event. On the TESI-A, the developmental epoch(s) in which event(s) occurred also are assessed, including before age 6, ages 6–12, ages 13–17, age 18 or older, and in the past year. Items involving intentional interpersonal stressors (e.g., violence, abuse) also include probes for the specific relationship of the perpetrator(s) to the respondent. A self-report version of the TESI has been developed and shown to be reliable and valid for children and adolescents ages 10 or older (TESI-C/SR; Ford et al., 2008). The TESI-C is available at no charge from the National Center for PTSD (www.ptsd.va.gov), and the other versions of the TESI are available at no charge from Julian Ford, Ph.D., jford@uchc.edu (Box 6.2).

A more detailed assessment of potential exposure to past physical, sexual, and emotional abuse is provided by the Childhood Trauma Questionnaire (CTQ; Scher, Stein, Asmundson, McCreary, & Forde, 2001). The CTQ has demonstrated reliability and validity for adolescents 12 or older and adults, but it does not specifically assess *DSM-IV-TR* PTSD Criterion A1 or A2 and thus cannot definitively determine whether abuse was psychologically traumatic. The CTQ may be purchased from Pearson Assessments (www.pearsonassessments.com).

A more detailed assessment of potential exposure to physical or sexual violence is provided by the Conflict Tactics Scale-2 (CTS-2; Straus, 2012; Straus, Hamby, Boney-McCoy, & Sugarman, 1996). This 78-item questionnaire inquires about physical assault, physical injury, psychological assault, sexual coercion, and negotiation tactics that the person has used or been subjected to in a primary dyadic relationship (such as marriage). A version (CTSPC) has been developed to assess tactics used by the respondent as a parent toward a child, including physical assault (with corporal

Box 6.2 Sample Items from the TESI

1.1 Has your child ever **been in** a serious accident where someone could have been (or actually was) severely injured or died? (like a serious car or bicycle accident, a fall, a fire, an incident where s/he was burned, an actual or near drowning, or a severe sports injury)	❑ Yes ❑ No ❑ Unsure

If YES ❖   Identify the type of
       accident(s):_____
       Victim's relationship to your child:_____ Did anyone die? ❑ yes ❑ no ❑ unsure
       How old was your child? The first time:_____ The last time:_____ The most stressful:_____
       Was your child strongly affected by one or more of these experiences? *(By strongly affected we mean: did your child seem: a) to be extremely frightened; b) to be very confused or helpless; c) to be very shocked or horrified; d) to have difficulty getting back to her or his normal way of behaving or feeling when it was over, OR e) to behave differently in important ways after it was over.)* ❑ yes ❑ no ❑ unsure	

1.2 Has your child ever **seen** a serious accident where someone could have been (or actually was) severely injured or died? (like a serious car or bicycle accident, a fall, a fire, an incident where someone was burned, an actual or near drowning, or a severe sports injury)	❑ Yes ❑ No ❑ Unsure

If YES ❖   Identify the type of accident(s) _____
       Victim's relationship to your child:_____ Did anyone die? ❑ yes ❑ no ❑ unsure
       How old was your child? The first time:_____ The last time:_____ The most stressful:_____
       Was your child strongly affected by one or more of these experiences? ❑ yes ❑ no ❑ unsure	

1.3 Has your child ever been in a natural disaster where someone could have been (or actually was) severely injured or died, or where your family or people in your community lost or had to permanently leave their home (like a tornado, fire, hurricane, or earthquake)?	❑ Yes ❑ No ❑ Unsure

If YES ❖ Type of disaster:_____ Did anyone die? ❑ yes ❑ no
   ❑ unsure   How old was your child? The first time:_____ The last time:_____ The most stressful:_____
   Was your child strongly affected by one or more of these experiences? ❑ yes ❑ no ❑ unsure	

1.4a Has your child ever experienced the severe illness or injury of someone close to him/her?	❑ Yes ❑ No ❑ Unsure

IF YES ❖ What was this person's relationship to your child?_____
     How old was your child? The first time:_____ The last time:_____ The most stressful:_____
     Was your child strongly affected by one or more of these experiences? ❑ yes ❑ no ❑ unsure	

1.4b Has your child ever experienced the death of someone close to him/her?	❑ Yes ❑ No ❑ Unsure

IF YES ❖ What was this person's relationship to your child?_____
     How old was your child? The first time:_____ The last time:_____ The most stressful:_____
     Was the death(s) due to: *(check all that apply)* ❑ natural causes ❑ illness ❑ accident ❑ violence ❑ unknown
     Was your child strongly affected by one or more of these experiences? ❑ yes ❑ no ❑ unsure	

1.5 Has your child ever undergone any serious medical procedures or had a life threatening illness? Or been treated by a paramedic, seen in an emergency room, or hospitalized overnight for a medical procedure?	❑ Yes ❑ No ❑ Unsure

IF YES ❖ Describe _____
     How old was your child? The first time:_____ The last time:_____ The most stressful:_____
     Was your child strongly affected by one or more of these experiences? ❑ yes ❑ no ❑ unsure	

1.6 Has your child ever been separated from you or another person who your child depends on for love or security for more than a few days OR under very stressful circumstances? For example due to foster care, immigration, war, major illness, or hospitalization.	❑ Yes ❑ No ❑ Unsure

IF YES ❖ Who was your child separated from: _____
     How old was your child? The first time:_____ The last time:_____ The most stressful:_____
     Was your child strongly affected by one or more of these experiences? ❑ yes ❑ no ❑ unsure	

1.7 Has someone close to your child ever attempted suicide or harmed him or herself?	❑ Yes ❑ No ❑ Unsure

IF YES ❖ What was this person's relationship to your child?_____
     How old was your child? The first time:_____ The last time:_____ The most stressful:_____
     Was your child strongly affected by one or more of these experiences? ❑ yes ❑ no ❑ unsure	

2.1 Has someone ever physically assaulted your child, like hitting, pushing, choking, shaking, biting, or burning? Or punished your child and caused physical injury or bruises. Or attacked your child with a gun, knife, or other weapon? (This could be done by someone in the family or by someone not in your child's family).	❑ Yes ❑ No ❑ Unsure

IF YES ❖ What was this person's relationship to your child?_____
     Was a weapon used? ❑ unsure ❑ no ❑ yes (type)
     How old was your child? The first time:_____ The last time:_____ The most stressful:_____
     Was your child strongly affected by one or more of these experiences? ❑ yes ❑ no ❑ unsure	

2.2 Has someone ever directly threatened your child with serious physical harm?	❑ Yes ❑ No ❑ Unsure

IF YES ❖ What was this person's relationship to your child? _____
     Did they threatened to use a weapon? ❑ unsure ❑ no ❑ yes (type)_____
     How old was your child? The first time:_____ The last time:_____ The most stressful:_____
     Was your child strongly affected by one or more of these experiences? ❑ yes ❑ no ❑ unsure	

2.3 Has someone ever mugged or tried to steal from your child? Or has your child been present when a family member, other caregiver, or friend was mugged?	❑ Yes

(Continued)

Box 6.2 Continued

IF YES⬦Who was mugged? (If not your child indicate the person's relationship to your child.) _____	❑ No ❑ Unsure
Was a weapon used? ❑ unsure ❑ no ❑ yes (type)_____	
How old was your child? The first time:_____ The last time:_____ The most stressful:_____	
Was your child strongly affected by one or more of these experiences? ❑ yes ❑ no ❑ unsure	
2.4 Has anyone ever kidnapped your child? (including a parent or relative) Or has anyone ever kidnapped someone close to your child?	❑Yes ❑ No ❑ Unsure
IF YES⬦Who was kidnapped? (If not your child indicate the person's relationship to your child.) _____	
What was the kidnapper's relationship to your child? _____	
How old was your child? The first time:_____ The last time:_____ The most stressful:_____	
Was your child strongly affected by one or more of these experiences? ❑ yes ❑ no ❑ unsure	
2.5 Has your child ever been attacked by a dog or other animal?	❑Yes ❑ No ❑ Unsure
IF YES⬦How old was your child? The first time:_____ The last time:_____ The most stressful:_____	
Was your child seriously physically hurt as a result of the attack? ❑yes ❑ no ❑ unsure	
Was your child strongly affected by one or more of these experiences? ❑ yes ❑ no ❑ unsure	
3.1 Has your child ever seen, heard, or heard about people *in your family* physically fighting, hitting, slapping, kicking, or pushing each other. Or shooting with a gun or stabbing, or using any other kind of dangerous weapon?	❑Yes ❑ No ❑ Unsure
IF YES⬦What were these people's relationships to your child? _____	
Was a weapon used? ❑ unsure ❑ no ❑ yes (type)_____	
How old was your child? The first time:_____ The last time:_____ The most stressful:_____	
Did your child see what happened? ❑yes ❑ no ❑ unsure	
Was your child strongly affected by one or more of these experiences? ❑ yes ❑ no ❑ unsure	
3.2 Has your child ever seen or heard people *in your family* threaten to seriously harm each other?	❑Yes ❑ No ❑ Unsure
IF YES⬦What were these people's relationships to your child _____	
Did they threatened to use a weapon? ❑ unsure ❑ no ❑ yes (type)_____	
How old was your child? The first time:_____ The last time:_____ The most stressful:_____	
Was your child present when the threat was made? ❑yes ❑ no ❑ unsure	
Was your child strongly affected by one or more of these experiences? ❑ yes ❑ no ❑ unsure	
3.3 Has your child ever known or seen that a family member was arrested, jailed, imprisoned, or taken away (like by police, soldiers, or other authorities)?	❑Yes ❑ No ❑ Unsure
IF YES⬦What was this person's relationship to your child?_____	
How old was your child? The first time:_____ The last time:_____ The most stressful:_____	
Was your child there when the police came? ❑yes ❑ no ❑ unsure	
Was your child strongly affected by one or more of these experiences? ❑ yes ❑ no ❑ unsure	
4.1 Has your child ever seen or heard people *outside your family* fighting, hitting, pushing, or attacking each other? Or seen or heard about violence such as beatings, shootings, or muggings that occurred in settings that are important to your child, such as school, your neighborhood, or the neighborhood of someone important to your child?	❑Yes ❑ No ❑ Unsure
IF YES⬦What were these people's relationship to your child? _____	
Was a weapon used? ❑ unsure ❑ no ❑ yes (type)_____ Where did this happen? _____	
How old was your child? The first time:_____ The last time:_____ The most stressful:_____	
Did your child see what happened? ❑ yes ❑ no ❑ unsure	
Was your child strongly affected by one or more of these experiences? ❑ yes ❑ no ❑ unsure	
4.2 Has your child ever been directly exposed to war, armed conflict, or terrorism?	❑Yes ❑ No ❑ Unsure
IF YES⬦How old was your child? The first time:_____ The last time:_____ The most stressful:_____	
Was your child strongly affected by one or more of these experiences? ❑ yes ❑ no ❑ unsure	
4.3 Has your child ever seen or heard acts of war or terrorism on the television or radio?	❑Yes ❑ No ❑ Unsure
IF YES⬦How old was your child? The first time:_____ The last time:_____ The most stressful:_____	
Was your child strongly affected by one or more of these experiences? ❑ yes ❑ no ❑ unsure	
5.1 Has someone ever *made* your child see or do something sexual (like touching in a sexual way, exposing self or masturbating in front of the child, engaging in sexual intercourse)	❑Yes ❑ No ❑ Unsure
IF YES⬦What were these people's relationships to your child? _____	
Was a weapon used? ❑ unsure ❑ no ❑ yes (type)_____	
How old was your child? The first time:_____ The last time:_____ The most stressful:_____	
Did your child see what happened? ❑yes ❑ no ❑ unsure	
Was your child strongly affected by one or more of these experiences? ❑ yes ❑ no ❑ unsure	
IF YES⬦What was this person's relationship to your child? _____	❑Yes ❑ No ❑ Unsure
Was physical violence used? ❑ unsure ❑ no ❑ yes Was a weapon used? ❑ unsure ❑ no ❑ yes	
(type)_____	
How old was your child? The first time:_____ The last time:_____ The most stressful:_____	
Was your child strongly affected by one or more of these experiences? ❑ yes ❑ no ❑ unsure	

punishment and physical abuse subscales), psychological aggression, nonviolent discipline, neglect, and sexual abuse. Questions are answered based on the frequency of the behavior, ranging from 1 = Once in past year to 6 = More than 20 times in past year. The internal consistency and temporal stability reliability and validity of the CTS-2 and CTSPC have been demonstrated in numerous studies, although some studies show less than optimal reliability due to very infrequent endorsement of violent behavior. Nevertheless, the CTS-2 yields more reports of violent behavior than comparable surveys (Straus et al., 1996) and thus may be subject to underreporting but potentially less so than less detailed and specific measures of violent acts. The CTS-2 is available from Western Psychological Services.

Assessment of PTSD: identifying symptoms and confirming the diagnosis

Several additional clinical and scientific issues arise when going beyond assessment of exposure to traumatic stressors to assess PTSD symptoms and diagnosis (Frueh et al., 2012). PTSD symptoms usually are assessed in reference to a specific traumatic event. However, most people who report experiencing a traumatic stressor describe a history of more than one type of traumatic stressor (Kessler et al., 1995). Therefore, PTSD symptoms can be assessed in relation to the respondent's trauma history in total rather than to a specific event (Elhai et al., 2010).

Some measures assess PTSD symptoms during a particular time in the respondent's life if it has been established that traumatic stressors occurred intermittently in that time period. Other measures ask about PTSD symptoms without referencing a particular traumatic stressor or time frame, but this is not advised because it leaves open the possibility that symptoms will be misclassified as PTSD (Box 6.3 discusses "pseudo-PTSD") when they actually are better described in terms of other psychiatric disorders that often occur comorbidly with PTSD (see Chapter 4)—for example, major depressive disorder, panic disorder, attention deficit hyperactivity disorder, or borderline personality disorder (Ford & Courtois, 2014).

The best practice recommendation for clinical assessment is to explicitly link each PTSD symptom either in onset or content to one or more specific traumatic stressors (Elhai & Naifeh, 2012). A link to onset is established by asking if the symptom began to occur or became distinctly more frequent or severe after the traumatic stressor(s) occurred (compared to before). A link based on content is established by asking if the symptom specifically is related to memories or reminders of aspects of specific traumatic stressor(s). For example, if nightmares became more frequent and disturbing starting within the month following a psychologically traumatic assault and continued to be distressing for at least a month, a link between that traumatic event and the onset of sleep problems as a PTSD symptom is reasonably likely. If the nightmares involve being threatened by aggressors or monsters, even if these are not exactly the person(s) who perpetrated the assault and even if they do not actually involve being physically attacked, the similarity to the traumatic experience is likely sufficient to

Box 6.3 The PCL *DSM*-5 Version (PCL-5) (www.va.ptsd.gov)

[Instructions: Below is a list of problems and complaints that people sometimes have after stressful experiences where they were severely threatened, assaulted or injured, or sexually abused, or witness someone killed or severely assaulted or injured. Please read each one carefully, then circle one of the numbers describing how much you have been bothered by that problem in the past month.

The stressful event that currently is most troubling for you may have happened at any time in your life. The past event that *currently is most troubling for you* was: _____ and it happened when you were age ____.
  (event)   (years old)

In the past month, how much were you bothered by:	Not at all	A little bit	Moderately	Quite a bit	Extremely
1. Repeated, disturbing, and unwanted memories of the stressful experience. This includes repeating similar experiences in play or other activities.	1	2	3	4	5
2. Repeated disturbing or frightening dreams?	1	2	3	4	5
3. Suddenly feeling or acting as if the stressful experience were actually happening again (as if she or he was actually back there reliving it)? This includes acting out the experience in play.	1	2	3	4	5
4. Feeling very upset when something reminded her or him of the stressful experience?	1	2	3	4	5
5. Having strong physical reactions when something reminded her or him of the stressful experience (for example, heart pounding, trouble breathing, sweating, or stomach aches)?	1	2	3	4	5
6. When reminded of the stressful experience, trying not to think about it, not feel emotionally upset, or not have physical reactions (for example by doing something distracting or pretending to be okay)?	1	2	3	4	5
7. Avoiding people, places, conversations, objects, activities, or situations that may be reminders of the stressful experience?	1	2	3	4	5
8. Not being able to remember important parts of the stressful experience?	1	2	3	4	5
9. Feeling like a very bad or messed up person, or like no one can be trusted, or that the world is completely dangerous?	1	2	3	4	5
10. Feeling guilty or ashamed about the stressful experience or bad things that happened after it?	1	2	3	4	5
11. Not being able to stop feeling scared, sad, angry, guilty, ashamed, or emotionally mixed up.	1	2	3	4	5
12. Not being able to enjoy activities that she or he used to enjoy?	1	2	3	4	5
13. Not being able to feel emotionally close to or cared for by other people?	1	2	3	4	5
14. Not having positive feelings, for example, being unable to feel happy, enthusiastic, or loving).	1	2	3	4	5
15. Feeling irritable or angry or acting aggressively?	1	2	3	4	5
16. Doing dangerous things without being careful or actually trying to get hurt?	1	2	3	4	5
17. Being "superalert" or watchful or on guard?	1	2	3	4	5
18. Feeling jumpy or easily startled?	1	2	3	4	5
19. Having difficulty concentrating?	1	2	3	4	5
20. Having trouble falling or staying asleep?	1	2	3	4	5

establish that the symptom is at least partially a posttraumatic stress reaction. The *DSM*-5 specifically permits clinicians to classify a nightmare as a PTSD symptom even when its content is not identical to what happened in a traumatic event as long as the nightmare's emotional content is an expectable reaction to the traumatic event. If physical assaults actually occur in the nightmare or if the person recalls feeling a similar feeling of terror or helplessness in the nightmares as they did in a traumatic assault, the link between the nightmare and the traumatic stressor would be even more strongly established.

There are two important reasons to link PTSD symptom inquiries to a single specific traumatic stressor event rather than globally assessing symptoms (Elhai & Naifeh, 2012). First, when PTSD symptoms are assessed without referencing a specific traumatic stressor, the respondent may mistakenly endorse a PTSD symptom that did not arise from exposure to a traumatic stressor but that instead arose from other causes. For example, *DSM*-5 PTSD symptom D1 (difficulty remembering aspects of the traumatic stressor) can be caused by normal forgetting or by age-related cognitive impairment. Symptom E6 (sleep difficulties) can be caused by other disorders (such as depression, anxiety, or substance use disorders) or stressors (such as change in work or school schedules or responsibilities, or conflict or separations in relationships). Symptoms E1 and E5 (problems with anger, irritability, or aggression; difficulty concentrating) may be the result of depression, anxiety, frustrating life experiences that are not traumatic, medical illnesses, or sleep deprivation. In fact, evidence suggests that when asking individuals to rate PTSD symptoms based on having experienced life events that are not technically traumatic stressors, relatively high levels of PTSD severity can result (Long et al., 2008). This suggests that what appear to be PTSD symptoms may actually be reactions to psychosocial or physical health problems that are not traumatic stressors (see Box 2.1). Second, some of PTSD's symptoms overlap with other mood and anxiety disorders (Elhai, Grubaugh, Kashdan, & Frueh, 2008), and thus the primary means of distinguishing these other disorders from PTSD is based on whether the symptoms are linked to past exposure to a specific traumatic stressor. For a diagnosis of PTSD, all of the symptoms must be satisfied in reference to at least one traumatic event, but it is not permissible to include some symptoms that are related to one traumatic stressor and other symptoms that are unrelated to that stressor but instead are related to a different traumatic stressor (e.g., nightmares that are related to an assault but avoidance symptoms that are related to memories of experiencing a natural disaster) (American Psychiatric Association, 2013).

However, linking PTSD symptoms to a single traumatic stressor is not always easy and requires some compromises. There is no evidence that trauma survivors can reliably and validly link PTSD symptoms to one, and only one, specific traumatic stressor. An unwanted memory or flashback about a rape might be distinguishable from an unwanted memory or flashback of experiencing a natural disaster. However, intrusive reexperiencing symptoms often include unwanted memories or distress due to reminders that include a mixture of several events or elements of the events—for example, the feeling of being stunned and physically battered or trapped and helpless may be related to a disaster as well as to an assault—or to both. Symptoms of emotional numbing and hyperarousal such as feeling empty emotionally or angry and irritable may be due to several traumatic stressors rather than only to one particular traumatic stressor.

Therefore, it is good practice clinically and in research to help the respondent pinpoint the past traumatic stressor that currently (in the past month) is most distressing to recall or that the person currently tries hardest to avoid remembering or being reminded of. This approach enables the assessor to hone in on the individual's reactions related to that specific traumatic stressor. This makes it clear that the person currently has either (or both) intrusive reexperiencing and avoidance PTSD symptoms right off the bat. Then the assessor can continue to assess the rest of the PTSD symptoms in reference to that currently troubling traumatic stressor. This can include asking the respondent to decide whether symptoms that could be related to other causes are still attributable (at least in part) to that "index" traumatic stressor because (i) they began, or become noticeably more severe, after that traumatic stressor occurred; (ii) they are similar to reactions the person had during or soon after experiencing that traumatic stressors; or (iii) they occur when the person is reminded of that traumatic experience currently.

Even though the diagnosis of PTSD is most accurate when symptoms are carefully related to one traumatic stressor, when an individual has experienced more than one traumatic stressor it is important to include symptoms that are not clearly related to the primary traumatic stressor in the overall clinical assessment. It is possible for people to have PTSD related to more than one traumatic stressor, especially when they have experienced the multiple emotional blows of being retraumatized or revictimized (see Boxes 3.4 and 3.5). It also is possible for people who have experienced multiple traumatic stressors to have severe symptoms related to some of those stressor experiences that do not add up to PTSD but that still should be addressed in treatment because of having an adverse impact on their life and functioning. For example, an adult who was sexually abused as a child and raped in college may have deeply troubling flashbacks or intrusive memories related to each of these experiences that are emotionally paralyzing at times but that are not accompanied by avoidance symptoms. Although this person would not qualify for a PTSD diagnosis based on either of those traumatic stressors, the symptoms he or she is experiencing nevertheless appear to be sufficiently connected to those experiences that trauma-focused therapy interventions should be included in the treatment plan for this individual (see Chapter 7).

Experts recommend that structured interviews should be used in order to firmly establish a diagnosis of PTSD (Frueh et al., 2012), because interviews allow for more detailed inquiry and clarification by the interviewer than is possible with questionnaire. Although questionnaires should not be the sole basis for determining a PTSD diagnosis, it is possible to estimate whether a PTSD diagnosis is likely (although not definitely established) using questionnaires as screening tools for the identification of individuals who are likely to have PTSD.

PTSD symptom and diagnosis assessment is done not only at the outset of treatment (or the beginning of research studies, the so-called "baseline"), but again periodically over time in order to establish the "trajectory" (see Chapter 2) of PTSD and recovery "outcomes" for each individual. In treatment, PTSD assessment is repeated throughout all phases of treatment in order to monitor the therapy's outcomes (and, as necessary, revise the plan, goals, or interventions).

In research, assessment may be conducted once (for a study investigating the relationship between psychological trauma and PTSD and other phenomena at one point in time) or repeatedly (if the study's goal is to describe or explain changes in psychological trauma, PTSD, or related phenomena over time—"longitudinal" studies; see King & King, 2008). For research purposes, results of repeated PTSD assessments can be combined for many participants (this is called "aggregating" the data) in order to scientifically identify a number of different trajectories of PTSD that may occur (see Figures 3.1 and 3.2).

The optimal sequencing and combination of PTSD assessments differ for each patient or study. The goal of PTSD assessment in both arenas is to obtain the most reliable and valid information possible. This includes determining: (i) how an individual's past exposure to traumatic stressors and current PTSD symptoms are related; (ii) how PTSD symptoms currently (or at important past time points) affect(ed) the person's health and functioning (i.e., the ability to be successful in relationships, work, school, and other important life experiences); (iii) how PTSD symptoms ebb and flow over time, across developmental periods, and as changes occur in life circumstances; (iv) how PTSD symptoms are intertwined with symptoms of other psychiatric or medical disorders and other life problems (such as difficulties in school or work, or financial or legal problems); and (v) how PTSD prevention or treatment interventions lead to changes in an individual's risk of developing PTSD or success in recovering from PTSD.

Many PTSD symptom and diagnosis measures use binary "yes"/"no" PTSD ratings. However, clinicians should consider not only determining whether PTSD symptoms are present but also ascertaining their frequency and severity. Using a "yes"/"no" rating format makes it difficult to track gradations of symptom improvement over the course of treatment. Additionally, without information on the severity of PTSD symptoms, affirmative responses may be incorrectly judged to be "clinically significant" when the symptom(s) may actually cause only mild distress or impairment. For example, reporting having daily trauma-related nightmares might be considered a clinically significant PTSD symptom. But what if the nightmares are readily recovered from and forgotten, or if they occur slightly less frequently but still regularly (such as once or twice a month)? There is no universal agreement on which various levels of symptom severity meet criteria for being a "clinically significant" symptom, and *DSM-IV* provides no assistance in arriving at such a determination. Clinical judgment often is required, and this is likely to be most reliable and valid if a detailed measure of PTSD symptom frequency and severity is obtained.

On the other hand, from a clinical standpoint, the effect of PTSD symptoms on a client's well-being and functioning may be very different for different combinations of frequency and intensity. For example, a flashback that occurs only once every few months but is so intense that the client requires acute psychiatric hospitalization may be quantitatively no more severe than a series of moderately disabling flashbacks that occur several times a week. However, treatment for these two "comparably severe" PTSD symptoms is likely to be quite different (e.g., crisis prevention and emotion regulation as a focus in the first case, versus stress inoculation and exposure therapy in the latter case; Elhai et al., 2009). Therefore, it is important to carefully define PTSD symptom "severity" with specific reference to the frequency, intensity, or both symptom dimensions, rather than simply globally labeling the symptoms as more or less severe.

As is true when assessing past traumatic experiences, during the assessment of PTSD symptoms, these may be minimized or underreported, or exaggerated and overreported. For clinical and research purposes, overreporting of PTSD symptoms is particularly problematic. Underreported PTSD symptoms may lead some people to be judged to be functioning better or less in need of treatment than is actually the case, which may lead to problems in the long run if their PTSD symptoms worsen and become chronic (which bodes more poorly for successful treatment than earlier-identified PTSD). However, overreporting creates immediate costs and burdens, including financial compensation for a work-related traumatic injury or disability application, acquittal from a criminal trial, or discharge from the military (Demakis & Elhai, 2011; Guriel & Fremouw, 2003), as well as excessive use of costly treatment (Elhai & Ford, 2007). Overreporting PTSD does not necessarily mean that respondents have no PTSD symptoms or does not warrant a PTSD diagnosis; instead, it could indicate that they are in some emotional distress and exaggerating or overreporting the severity of genuine PTSD symptoms.

PTSD assessment with children

Assessment with children and adolescents includes collecting data based on observing their behavior (typically via ratings by parents or other adult caregivers, teachers, or the therapist), as well as structured interview and questionnaire measures completed with the child. In addition to parent/caregiver/teacher/therapist rating measures, direct observation in the home or clinical settings can provide valuable information to corroborate or revise these ratings. For school-age children and adolescents, self-report questionnaires assessing externalizing (aggression, attention problems, conduct problems, hyperactivity, learning problems) and internalizing (anxiety, atypicality (psychosis), depression, somatization, withdrawal) problems and several domains of self-regulation and social competence (daily activities, adaptability, functional communication, leadership, social skills, study skills) are an important addition to the perspective of the parent or caregiver and the teacher. For preadolescents and adolescents, it is important to assess key risks (e.g., self-harm (Ford & Gomez, 2015), substance use problems (Ford, 2013a)), and competences (e.g., impulse control, consideration for others and responsibility, emotion regulation, self-efficacy and optimism), as well as PTSD and related symptoms.

It is particularly crucial to obtain input and records (with appropriate consent from guardians and assent from the child) from all accessible sources (such as health care providers, therapists, schools, legal or child protection agencies or representatives). In special settings, such as psychiatric inpatient, residential, or day treatment programs; special education classrooms or programs; or the juvenile justice system, assessment measures should be either specifically developed or adapted and normed and validated for the children in those distinct subpopulations (Ko et al., 2008). For example, juvenile justice and child protective service systems have custodial, school, treatment, and rehabilitative programs where screening for psychological trauma history and PTSD may be important for legal decisions (Ford, 2012). Across all age groups in childhood and adolescence, thorough assessment of the family system (Josephson and the AACAP Work Group on Quality Issues, 2007) and the school environment and peer group (Bullock & Dishion, 2007) is essential in order to create treatment or services that fit the primary context(s) for children's and youths' behavioral and emotional problems and competences.

PTSD symptom and diagnosis measures

Numerous questionnaires and structured interviews are available to assess PTSD symptoms and establish (by interview) or estimate the likelihood of (by questionnaire) a PTSD diagnosis with adults (Briere & Spinazzola, 2009; Keane et al., 2007) and children/adolescents (Nader, 2008). Several measures with demonstrated reliability and validity are discussed here.

The PCL (Weathers, 2008) assesses the 17 PTSD symptoms by asking respondents to describe how frequently they have occurred in the past month. The PCL has versions for civilians (PCL-C), military personnel (PCL-M), ratings in relation to a specific stressor event (PCL-S), and for parent ratings of their child's symptoms (PCL-C/ PR; Ford et al., 2000). The PCL has been revised for *DSM*-5 criteria (the PCL-5; see Box 6.3) and may be obtained at no cost on the National Center for PTSD website (www.ptsd.va.gov).

The PTSD Symptom Scale (PSS) also measures PTSD symptom frequency but does so in the past 2 weeks rather than the past month, and on a scale ranging from 0 = Never or only once to 3 = Five times a week or always (Long & Elhai, 2008). The PSS may be used as an interview, and it has been adapted for children in the Children's PTSD Scale (CPDS; Foa, Johnson, Feeny, & Treadwell, 2001) and the Modified PTSD Symptom Scale (MPSS-SR; Falsetti, Resnick, Resick, & Kilpatrick, 1993). The MPSS-SR is available at no charge from Sherry Falsetti, Ph.D., Department of Family and Community Medicine, College of Medicine at Rockford, University of Illinois at Chicago, 1221 East State Street, Rockford, IL 61104, falsetti@uic.edu. The PSS and CPDS may be obtained at no charge from Edna Foa, Ph.D., Department of Psychiatry, University of Pennsylvania, 3535 Market Street, 6th Floor, Philadelphia, PA 19104, 215-746-3327, foa@mail.med.upenn.edu.

The Structured Trauma-Related Experiences and Symptoms Screener for *DSM*-5 (STRESS) is a comprehensive screening questionnaire for children's history of exposure to traumatic stressors and PTSD symptoms (Box 6.4). Children report whether they ever have experienced 25 types of potentially traumatic events and how often in the past week they have experienced each of the *DSM*-5 PTSD symptoms, as well as whether the symptoms have interfered with their lives in three key arenas (family, school, and peer relationships). A parent or other adult caregiver can complete a parallel form to describe the traumatic events and PTSD symptoms that they have observed, or know of, the child experiencing. The STRESS may be obtained from

Box 6.4 Structured Trauma-Related Experiences and Symptoms Screener for *DSM*-5

Structured Trauma-Related Experiences and Symptoms Screener for *DSM-5* (STRESS)

Child Report Version

Grasso, Reid-Quinones, Felton, & DeArellano (2013) v.1.4 All Rights Reserved

Child Name: _____ (circle) Male / Female Age: _____ Date: _____

INSTRUCTIONS PART I

We are going to go through a list of very scary things that sometimes happen to people. Circle **YES** if the thing happened to you or circle **NO** if it has not happened to you.

1. Have you ever been in a really bad storm or disaster, like a flood, earthquake or hurricane?
2. Have you or anyone in your family been in an actual war?
3. Have you ever been in a serious fire or lost your home in a fire?
4. Have you ever been in a really bad car accident?
5. Have you ever had to stay in the hospital because you were really sick or badly injured?
6. Has anyone in your family ever had to stay in the hospital because they were really sick or badly injured?
7. Has anyone ever beaten you up so badly that you had bruises, cuts, or injuries?
8. Have adults in your home ever slapped, punched, or kicked you?
9. Have adults in your home ever hit you so hard you had bruises or red marks?
10. Have you ever been really hungry because your family did not have enough to eat?
11. Do the adults in your home always make sure you go to school?
12. Have you ever been homeless?
13. Have you ever been separated from someone who you depend on for love or safety for more than a few days?
14. Have you ever known or seen a family member being arrested, put in jail, or taken away by police?
15. Have you ever been told over and over that you were no good or that people you live with would leave you or send you away?
16. Have you ever seen or hear adults in your home beat each other up or throw things at each other?
17. Have you ever seen or heard people in your neighborhood get badly hurt or killed?
18. Has anyone ever told you so much about how someone you loved died that you pictured it in your head?
19. Has anyone ever told you they were going to hurt or kill you?
20. Has anyone ever made you feel so scared that you thought they might badly hurt or kill you?
21. Have you ever thought that someone was going to really hurt or kill someone you love?
22. Has anyone ever tried to touch your private body parts or tried to make you touch their private body parts when you did not want to?
23. Has anyone ever touched your private body parts or made you touch their private body parts when you did not want to?
24. Has anyone much older than you ever touched your private body parts, whether you wanted them to or not?
25. Has anything else really scary or very bad ever happen to you?

For all 'YES' responses, write your age when the scary or bad thing happened next to the 'YES'.

Structured Trauma-Related Experiences and Symptoms Screener for *DSM-5* (STRESS)

Child Report Version

Grasso, Reid--⊠Quinones, Felton, & DeArellano (2013) v.1.4 All Rights Reserved

INSTRUCTIONS PART II

The next questions ask about problems some people have after scary or bad things happen to them. Please think about a scary or bad thing that happened to you and how you have been thinking, feeling, or acting in the past week when answering these questions. Circle or check your answer:

None   1 Day   2-3 Days   Most Days

26. How often did thoughts or memories about what happened pop up into your mind?
27. When something reminded you about what happened, how often did it make your body feel bad or sick, like your stomach or head hurt?
28. In the past week, how often was it hard to remember parts of what happened?
29. How often were you bored doing things you usually like to do?
30. In the past week, how often did you look around a lot, just in case something bad might happen?
31. How often did you have scary dreams or nightmares?
32. How often did you try to keep your body from feeling ways that reminded you of what happened?
33. How often did you think the world is a bad place or not as good as it used to be?
34. In the past week, how often did you feel lonely, even when you were around friends or family?
35. How often did you get really scared when you heard or saw something you were not expecting to happen?
36. How often did memories about what happened make you lose track of time or forget where you were?
37. How often did you try to stop yourself from having thoughts, memories, or feelings about what happened?
38. In the past week, how often did you think that a part of what happened was your fault?
39. How often did you feel really grumpy?
40. How often did you feel like you could not focus on things?
41. How often did you get really upset when you saw, heard, or felt something like what happened?
42. How often did you try to get away when you were in a place or saw something that reminded you of what happened?
43. How often did you feel really bad, like mad, scared, or sad for most of the day?
44. How often did you do things that other people think are dangerous or not safe?
45. In the past week, how often did you wake up in the middle of the night and have trouble falling back to sleep?
46. How often was it hard for you to feel happiness or love?
47. How often did it feel like you didn't know yourself or your own body, like you were seeing a stranger when you looked in the mirror?
48. How often did you feel like people or places around you seemed totally strange, like you were in a dream even though you were awake?
49. Have you had these problems for at least the past month?
50. Since the scary or bad thing or things happened, is it harder to
        a. make or keep friends? **YES NO**
        b. get along with other kids your age? **YES NO**
        c. do schoolwork? **YES NO**
        d. get along with your teachers? **YES NO**
        e. get along with people you live with? **YES NO**
        f. get your chores done? **YES NO**
YOU ARE FINISHED

Damion Grasso, Ph.D., Department of Psychiatry, University of Connecticut Health Center, MC1400, 263 Farmington Ave., Farmington CT 06030, dgrasso@uchc.edu.

The Impact of Event Scale-Revised (IES-R) is a 22-item questionnaire that originally assessed only the intrusive reexperiencing and avoidance/emotional numbing aspects of PTSD but was expanded to include hyperarousal symptoms. The original IES used ratings of the frequency of symptoms, but the revised version has respondents rate the *degree of distress* caused by each symptom in the past 7 days. The original IES used a complicated response format that was modified in the IES-R to: 0 = Not at all, 1 = A little bit, 2 = Moderately, 3 = Quite a bit, 4 = Extremely. IES scores are calculated for each of the three subscales (corresponding to Criteria B, C, and D of the PTSD diagnosis), with some *DSM-IV* PTSD symptoms assessed by more than one item. The IES-R is widely used as a brief measure of the recent severity of PTSD symptoms, including change in symptoms following treatment, but not for diagnosis of PTSD. The IES-R is available at no cost on the National Center for PTSD website (www.ncptsd.org).

The Mississippi PTSD Scale (Keane, Caddell, & Taylor, 1989) is a questionnaire originally developed for PTSD studies of Vietnam War and earlier military combat veterans (Mississippi Scale for Combat PTSD) and subsequently revised for Persian Gulf/Operation Desert Storm military veterans (Mississippi Scale for ODS), as well as for civilians (Revised Civilian Mississippi Scale for PTSD, RCMS; Norris, 2008). The questionnaire asks for ratings on a numerical scale from 1 = Never/Not at all/Rarely true to 5 = Always/Very/Very frequently true, with no time frame specified. The scale's original 35 items fell into four categories, three corresponding to the *DSM-III-R* Criteria B, C, and D for PTSD (intrusion, avoidance/numbing, and hyperarousal symptoms) and a fourth for symptoms of guilt and suicidality. The ODS revision added four items related to specific military experiences. The RCMS has 30 items, the first 18 items anchored to a specific event (such as "Since the event, my dreams at night are so real that I waken in a cold sweat and force to stay awake"); the last 12 items are phrased in general terms ("I am able to get emotionally close to others"). The Mississippi PTSD Scales are available at no cost on the National Center for PTSD website (www.ptsd.va.gov).

The Trauma Symptom Inventory (TSI; Briere, 1996) is a 100-item questionnaire that assesses 3 validity scales (Response Level, Atypical Response, and Inconsistent Response) and 10 clinical scales (Anxious Arousal, Depression, Anger/Irritability, Intrusive Experiences, Defensive Avoidance, Dissociation, Sexual Concerns, Dysfunctional Sexual Behavior, Impaired Self-Reference, and Tension Reduction Behavior). Answers are scored from 0 = Never to 3 = Often, with a time frame of the past 6 months. More recently, a revised version was developed (TSI-2; Briere, 2011). Adaptations of the TSI have been developed for children/adolescents, the Trauma Symptom Checklist for Children (TSCC) and Trauma Symptom Checklist for Young Children (TSCYC). The TSCC is a 54-item scale and was developed for 8- to 16-year-olds, with minor normative adjustments for 17-year-olds (Wolpaw, Ford, Newman, Davis, & Briere, 2005). The TSCC has two validity scales (Underresponse and Hyperresponse) and six clinical scales: Anxiety, Depression, Anger, Posttraumatic Stress, Sexual Concerns (with two subscales), and Dissociation (with two subscales). An alternate form (the TSCC-A) excludes items related to sexuality. TSCYC is a

90-item scale developed for 3- to 12-year-olds (Briere, 2005) that has two validity scales (Response Level and Atypical Response) and nine clinical scales: Posttraumatic Stress–Intrusion, Posttraumatic Stress–Avoidance, Posttraumatic Stress–Arousal, Posttraumatic Stress–Total, Sexual Concerns, Anxiety, Depression, Dissociation, and Anger/Aggression. The TSI, TSCC, and TSCYC are available for purchase from Psychological Assessment Resources (www.parinc.com).

The Minnesota Multiphasic Personality Inventory-2 (MMPI-2; Butcher et al., 2001) is a 567-item questionnaire answered on a true/false basis that assesses 10 primary clinical scales and 3 "validity" scales (i.e., scores indicating whether the respondent appears to be answering inaccurately for psychological reasons). The clinical scales are described as "elevated" if a respondent's score is more than two standard deviations away from the average score, reflecting psychiatric problems (but not a specific diagnosis). Respondents diagnosed with PTSD tend to have elevated scores on MMPI-2 subscales for depression (subscale 2), anxiety (subscale 7), and "schizophrenia" (subscale 8, which is thought to assess agitation rather than psychosis per se), as well as on one of the three validity scales that assesses exaggerated distress (subscale F) (Forbes, 2008). Two "supplementary" scales have been developed by identifying MMPI items that best distinguish Vietnam military veterans with PTSD from other persons, the PK and PS scales, of which the PK is most frequently used (Forbes, 2008). The PK subscale included 49 items from the MMPI and was revised to include 46 items from the MMPI-2. Persons with PTSD also may have elevations on other MMPI subscales, including hypochondriasis (scale 1), hysteria (scale 3), psychopathic deviate (scale 4), paranoia (scale 6), hypomania (scale 9), and social introversion (scale 0). The PK subscale is more accurate than the MMPI-2 clinical and validity scales in identifying military personnel with PTSD (Forbes, 2008).

The CAPS (Box 6.5) is the most comprehensive and widely used PTSD interview (Elhai, Gray, Kashdan, & Franklin, 2005). It includes a LEC to assess traumatic stressor exposure, and it is the only PTSD interview that assesses both the frequency *and* intensity of each PTSD symptom. The CAPS also has the most precise and specific descriptions of each rating category for every PTSD symptom (Weathers et al., 2001). Additional items are included to assess the "associated features" of PTSD, such as dissociation and emotion dysregulation (complex PTSD). An adaptation has been created for children/adolescents as young as 7 years old (CAPS-CA). However, the CAPS can be lengthy to administer, usually 40–60 minutes unless the respondent has relatively few or mild symptoms. The CAPS has recently been revised for *DSM*-5. The different versions of the CAPS can be obtained at no charge from the National Center for PTSD website (www.ptsd.va.gov).

The Structured Interview for PTSD (SIP; Davidson, Kudler, & Smith, 1990) assesses either the frequency or intensity of each PTSD symptom, with specific descriptions of each rating category to enhance interrater reliability. The SIP requires 20–30 minutes of administration time. It can be obtained at no charge from Jonathan Davidson, MD, Department of Psychiatry, Box 3812, Duke University Medical Center, Durham, NC 27710-3812, 919-684-2880.

The Children's PTSD Inventory takes 15–20 minutes of administration time and includes a preface about typical traumatic events, and subsequently assesses PTSD

Box 6.5 CAPS for *DSM*-5 (CAPS-5)

The CAPS is the gold standard in PTSD assessment. The CAPS-5 is a 30-item structured interview that can be used to:

- make current (past month) diagnosis of PTSD;
- make lifetime diagnosis of PTSD;
- assess PTSD symptoms over the past week.

In addition to assessing the 20 *DSM*-5 PTSD symptoms, questions target the onset and duration of symptoms, subjective distress, impact of symptoms on social and occupational functioning, improvement in symptoms since a previous CAPS administration, overall response validity, overall PTSD severity, and specifications for the dissociative subtype (depersonalization and derealization).

For each symptom, standardized questions and probes are provided. Administration requires identification of an index traumatic event to serve as the basis for symptom inquiry. The LEC for *DSM*-5 (LEC-5) is recommended in addition to the Criterion A inquiry included in the CAPS-5.

The CAPS was designed to be administered by clinicians and clinical researchers who have a working knowledge of PTSD, but it can also be administered by appropriately trained paraprofessionals. The full interview takes 45–60 minutes to administer.

Changes from previous CAPS for *DSM-IV*

Several important revisions were made to the CAPS in updating it for *DSM*-5:

- CAPS for *DSM-IV* asked respondents to endorse up to three traumatic events to keep in mind during the interview. *CAPS-5 requires the identification of a single index trauma to serve as the basis of symptom inquiry.*
- *CAPS-5 is a 30-item questionnaire, corresponding to the DSM-5 diagnosis for PTSD.* The language of the CAPS-5 reflects both changes to existing symptoms and the addition of new symptoms in *DSM*-5. CAPS-5 asks questions relevant to assessing the dissociative subtype of PTSD (depersonalization and derealization), but it no longer includes other associated symptoms (e.g., gaps in awareness).
- As with previous versions of the CAPS, CAPS-5 symptom severity ratings are based on symptom frequency and intensity (except for amnesia and diminished interest, which are based on amount and intensity). However, *CAPS-5 items are rated with a single severity score in contrast to previous versions of the CAPS that required separate frequency and intensity scores.*

Scoring

Detailed scoring information is included with the CAPS-5 and should be reviewed carefully before administering it. Briefly, the assessor combines information about frequency and intensity of an item into a single severity rating. The CAPS-5 total symptom severity score is calculated by summing severity scores for the 20 *DSM*-5 PTSD symptoms. Similarly, CAPS-5 symptom cluster severity scores are calculated by summing the individual item severity scores for symptoms corresponding to a given *DSM*-5 cluster: Criterion B (items

1–5); Criterion C (items 6–7); Criterion D (items 8–14); and Criterion E (items 15–20). A symptom cluster score may also be calculated for dissociation by summing items 29 and 30. PTSD diagnostic status is determined by first dichotomizing each symptom as "present" or "absent," and then following the *DSM*-5 diagnostic rule. A symptom is considered present only if the corresponding item severity score is rated 2 ("moderate/threshold") or higher. The *DSM*-5 PTSD diagnostic rule requires:

- at least one Criterion B symptom;
- at least one Criterion C symptom;
- at least two Criterion D symptoms;
- at least two Criterion E symptoms;
- Criterion F is met (disturbance has lasted 1 month);
- Criterion G is met (disturbance causes either clinically significant distress or functional impairment).

Sample item

In the past month, have you had any <u>unwanted memories</u> of (EVENT) while you were awake—in other words, not counting dreams?

How does it happen that you start remembering (EVENT)?

[If not clear:] (*Are these* <u>unwanted</u> *memories, or are you thinking about [EVENT] on purpose?*)

How much do these memories bother you?

Are you able to put them out of your mind and think about something else?

How often have you had these memories in the past month? Number of times_____.

Severity rating

1. *Absent*: The respondent denied the problem, or the respondent's report doesn't fit the *DSM*-5 symptom criterion.
2. *Mild/subthreshold*: The respondent described a problem that is consistent with the symptom criterion but isn't severe enough to be considered clinically significant. The problem doesn't satisfy the *DSM*-5 symptom criterion and thus doesn't count toward a PTSD diagnosis.
3. *Moderate/threshold*: The respondent described a clinically significant problem. The problem satisfies the *DSM*-5 symptom criterion and thus counts toward a PTSD diagnosis. The problem would be a target for intervention. This rating requires a minimum frequency of 2 × month or some of the time (20–30%) PLUS a minimum intensity of *Clearly Present*.
4. *Severe/markedly elevated*: The respondent described a problem that is above threshold. The problem is difficult to manage and at times overwhelming, and it would be a prominent target for intervention. This rating requires a minimum frequency of 2 × week or much of the time (50–60%) PLUS a minimum intensity of *Pronounced*.
5. *Extreme/incapacitating*: The respondent described a dramatic symptom, far above threshold. The problem is pervasive, unmanageable, and overwhelming, and it would be a high-priority target for intervention.

(Continued)

Box 6.5 Continued

Versions

There are three versions of the CAPS-5 corresponding to different time periods: past week, past month, and worst month (lifetime). The past week version of the CAPS-5 should be used only to evaluate PTSD symptoms over the past week. PTSD diagnostic status should be evaluated with the past month (for current PTSD) or worst month (for lifetime PTSD) versions of the CAPS-5.

A version for children and adolescents (CAPS-CA for *DSM-IV*) is also available. The CAPS-CA is currently being revised to correspond to *DSM-5*.

Citation

Weathers et al. (2013)

Source: http://www.ptsd.va.gov/professional/assessment/adult-int/caps.asp

---

symptoms, albeit using binary items (e.g., Saigh et al., 2000), available for purchase from Pearson Assessments (www.pearsonclinical.com).

Assessment of psychiatric problems commonly comorbid with PTSD

When assessing trauma history and PTSD, it is important to determine if respondents have other psychiatric disorders or problems that may be exacerbated by exposure to traumatic stressors or by PTSD *and* that may worsen the intensity and frequency of PTSD symptoms (see Chapter 4). In selecting potential psychiatric disorders to evaluate along with PTSD, experts recommend starting with a broadband structured interview for psychiatric disorders, and then follow up with specific assessments of the intensity, frequency, or impairment caused by symptoms of any disorders that are identified (Elhai et al., 2010). For example, a diagnosis of major depressive disorder could cue the clinician to administer a questionnaire measure of depression.

Several psychiatric diagnosis structured interviews for adults include a section (module) for PTSD, such as the *Structured Clinical Interview for DSM-IV* Axis I Disorders (SCID-I), the Composite International Diagnostic Interview (CIDI), the Diagnostic Interview Schedule for *DSM-IV* (DIS-IV), the Mini International Neuropsychiatric Interview (MINI), and the Anxiety Disorders Interview Schedule-IV. The CIDI and DIS also have brief but thorough trauma history assessments. For children, similarly, the most widely used and best-researched structured interviews for psychiatric diagnosis have PTSD modules, including the Diagnostic Interview for Children and Adolescents-Revised (DICA-R), the Diagnostic Interview Schedule for Children (DISC), and the Kiddie-Schedule of Affective Disorders and Schizophrenia (K-SADS). These instruments have not yet been finalized in revision for *DSM-5* at this time.

The SCID-I (First, Spitzer, Gibbon, & Williams, 1996) can be purchased from www.scid4.org. The World Health Organization's CIDI (Haro et al., 2006) can be downloaded from http://www.hcp.med.harvard.edu/wmhcidi/instruments.php. The MINI (Sheehan et al., 1998) is notable for its brevity and brief administration time (15–20 minutes, compared to 90–120+ minutes for most other structured interviews for psychiatric disorders), while still demonstrating reliability and validity. The MINI is modeled after other psychiatric diagnosis structured interviews, but it is streamlined with skip-out rules to substantially reduce administration time and required paperwork and is available at no charge from www.medical-outcomes.com.

The DICA-R (Reich, 2000) is a semistructured interview and takes about 2–3 hours to administer. It is available for purchase in an electronic delivery format from Mental Health Resources (www.mhs.com). The DISC (Shaffer, Fisher, Lucas, Dulcan, & Schwab-Stone, 2000) is highly structured and takes about 70–120 minutes to administer and can be purchased from the Columbia DISC Development Group, Division of Child and Adolescent Psychiatry, 1051 Riverside Drive, New York, NY 10032, 888-814-DISC, disc@worldnet.att.net. The K-SADS (McLeer, Deblinger, Henry, & Orvaschel, 1992) is a semistructured instrument and typically takes at least 2 hours to administer. It is available at no charge for not-for-profit uses (or with permission for other uses) from the University of Pittsburgh's Department of Psychiatry, http://www.psychiatry.pitt.edu/node/8233.

Assessment of posttraumatic dysregulation

Posttraumatic stress reactions extend beyond the primary symptoms of anxiety and dysphoria that characterize PTSD and include alterations in emotional regulation, information processing, biological self-regulation, and relational engagement (Ford, 2011). Assessment of posttraumatic stress dysregulation first requires an understanding of healthy biopsychosocial self-regulation (Kim & Hamann, 2007). There is a relatively clear consensus that self-regulation involves a set of adaptive capacities, or "an integrated set of abilities or skills that draw from both executive function and emotion regulation capacities, which are invoked in the service of accomplishing both proximal and distal goals" (Buckner, Mezzacappa, & Beardslee, 2009, p. 19).

Posttraumatic dysregulation takes many forms that include the symptoms of psychiatric comorbidities (see prior section) but also extends to a larger universe of biospsychosocial problems that do not neatly fall within any specific psychiatric disorder (Ford, 2009, 2013b; Ford, Blaustein, Habib, & Kagan, 2013). For example, posttraumatic dysregulation may take the form of profound emotional instability, dissociation, somatization, suicidality, eating and body image problems, sleep problems, substance use problems, externalizing behavior problems, and physical health problems. Posttraumatic dysregulation causes (and also greatly exacerbates) impairments in psychological development and functioning that include (i) ruptures in attachment in primary relationships (such as with parents, spouse/partner, or close friends); (ii) conflict in or withdrawal from social support relationships; (iii) deficits in information processing (attention and concentration, working, procedural, and narrative memory, executive functions); (iv) problems in maintaining physical and legal safety; and (v) problems in school or work performance.

Scientific and clinical studies suggest that a syndrome described as "Developmental Trauma Disorder" (DTD; Ford, Grasso, et al., 2013; van der Kolk, 2005) could provide a basis for assessing posttraumatic dysregulation. DTD (see Chapter 1) includes symptoms of affective, somatic, cognitive, behavioral, interpersonal, and self-identity dysregulation. Based on results of an international survey of mental health, health care, social work, and education professionals (Ford, Grasso, et al., 2013) and a comprehensive review of the research and clinical evidence on the impact of childhood traumatization on self-regulation and dysregulation across the life span (D'Andrea, Ford, Stolbach, Spinazzola, & van der Kolk, 2012), a structured clinical interview was designed to assess DTD (Box 6.6). The DTD Structured Interview is being used in a national study testing its psychometric reliability and validity, with early results indicating that it provides clinicians with information about posttraumatic dysregulation that can enable them to address problems that extend beyond the symptoms of the psychiatric disorders that are described in the *DSM*-5 (Ford, Spinazzola, van der Kolk, & Grasso, 2014; van der Kolk, Ford, & Spinazzola, 2014).

Screening for PTSD

Screening for PTSD is important, particularly because PTSD is prevalent and costly, but it is not possible to ask more than a few brief questions (Ehring, Klein, Clark, Foa, & Ehlers, 2007) in most settings in which PTSD could be identified (such as pediatric or primary health care, schools, or workplaces). Brief screening measures have been developed to identify persons with or at risk for PTSD and have been tested in psychiatric, medical, community, and school settings (Box 6.7).

Breslau, Peterson, Kessler, and Schultz (1999) developed a seven-item *DSM-IV* PTSD screen based on results from computer-assisted telephone interviews derived from the National Institute of Mental Health Diagnostic Interview Schedule for DSM-IV and the World Health Organization Composite International Diagnostic Interview, version 2.1. In a community sample ($n = 2181$) between ages 18 and 45 years old, best-subset regression analysis and receiver operator characteristic analyses were used to select a subset that most efficiently predicted PTSD diagnoses. The final screen includes five avoidance and numbing items and two hyperarousal items. A score of 4 or greater showed it was able to identify adults with undiagnosed PTSD with more than 80% accuracy. Lang and Stein (2005) selected the two intrusive reexperiencing, two avoidance, and two hyperarousal symptoms from the PCL (Weathers, 2008) that best correlated with the total score for its respective PTSD symptom cluster, for a PTSD screen with primary care patients. The PCL screen was more than 80% accurate in identifying patients with undiagnosed PTSD.

Brewin et al. (2002) developed the 10-item Trauma Screening Questionnaire (TSQ) by using the five intrusive reexperiencing and five hyperarousal symptom

Box 6.6 DTD Structured Interview

POSTTRAUMATIC STRESS DISORDER:
SCIENCE AND PRACTICE 2ND EDITION Chapter 6
Julian D. Ford, Damion J. Grasso, Christine A. Courtois, Jon D. Elhai

---

Box 6.6

Developmental Trauma Disorder Structured Interview

Ford and the Developmental Trauma Disorder Work Group (2014) All Rights Reserved

---

A. Exposure
The child has experienced or witnessed multiple or prolonged adverse events for *at least one year*, including BOTH A1 and A2 (*assessed by Traumatic Events Screening Instrument, TESI*):

A1. Direct experience or witnessing of repeated and severe episodes of interpersonal violence;
A2. Significant disruptions of protective caregiving due to primary caregiver changes, separation, or emotional abuse.

General Guide for Interviewer Symptom Ratings

First read the initial item verbatim with pauses. Do **not** read aloud text in boxes or parentheses.

Use spontaneous answers to rate items in shaded area on the right. Ask probe questions in shaded area as necessary.

Stop asking questions once you are able to rate symptom as *Not Present* or *Threshold*.

Not Present – No symptom, or developmentally expectable problems.

Threshold – Symptom causes significant emotional distress or shut-down or problems in functioning that are *at times unmanageable* or *at best partially manageable with effort* or harm to self/others or other behavioral, emotional, or interpersonal crises. Be sure to indicate whether emotional distress and/or shut-down are present. Consider what is developmentally normative for her/his age when judging the child's ability to manage distress.

IF INTERVIEWEE DOES NOT ANSWER QUESTION ("PASS"):
Check whether s/he Prefers Not to Answer (PNA) or Does Not Understand (DNU) the question.

FOR BOTH PAST/WORST MONTH AND LIFETIME, CHECK EITHER NOT PRESENT OR THRESHOLD

NOTE: Several items are noted with an asterisk (B.1a., B.1b., B.2a., B2b., C1.a., C.1b., C.2a.,

D.2a., D.3b., D.4.) and ask interviewers to assess symptom presence in a dimensional manner

(e.g., high and/or low expression of a given symptom). For these questions, if only one

dimension is present in the Past/Worst Month, make sure to ask about the other dimension

for Lifetime

(Continued)

Box 6.6 Continued

Developmental Trauma Disorder Structured Interview

Ford and the Developmental Trauma Disorder Work Group (2014) All Rights Reserved

| **Verbatim Introduction:** |

I have some questions about your feelings and how you've been getting along with other people, in the past/worst month, that is, since (identify start and end dates covering one month; then describe or ask for examples of specific dates/holidays or events relevant to interviewee to focus just on the **past/worst month**).

If this wasn't a problem in the past/worst month, I'll ask if it ever was a problem for you in your life. You can say **Pass (P)** if you **prefer not to answer** or **do not understand.**

Let's start with feelings.

B. Affective and Physiological Dysregulation
Impaired developmental competencies related to affect or
arousal regulation, generally and during life transitions

B.1. Inability to modulate or tolerate extreme affect states (e.g.,
fear, anger, shame, grief), including extreme tantrums or
immobilization

*__B.1a__. Everyone feels scared, mad, sad, or frustrated
sometimes. These feelings can get so big that you blow
up or just totally shut down. Has this happened to you?
What happened? How did you feel?

_____

_____

_____

_____

☐ YES *(If Yes)* How often did this happen in the past/worst month?

☐ Daily or almost daily ☐ 2 - 3 times per week ☐ Once a week or less

☐ NO *(If No)* Have there <u>ever</u> been any serious problems with this?

☐ Yes (Lifetime) ☐ No

Instructions: Mark any rating for which child
spontaneously provides sufficient information. If
more data are needed to rate a symptom, ask probes
BUT STOP IF YOU HAVE ENOUGH
INFORMATION TO RATE SYMPTOM AS
PRESENT (OR NOT). Y=Yes N= No

When felt upset in the past/worst month …

(Y) (N) Did you blow up or go into a rage?
(Y) (N) Did you hit people or animals?
(Y) (N) Did you hit or break things?
(Y) (N) Did you break down crying?
(Y) (N) Did you yell or scream?
(Y) (N) Did you totally shut down?
(Y) (N) Did you feel scared/terrified?
(Y) (N) Did you feel sad/unhappy?
(Y) (N) Did you feel mad/angry/resentful?
(Y) (N) Did you feel disgusted?
(Y) (N) Did you feel guilty/embarrassed?
(Y) (N) Did you feel ashamed/humiliated?
(Y) (N) Did you feel hopeless/like giving up?
(Y) (N) Did you feel helpless/powerless?
(Y) (N) Did you feel out of control?
(Y) (N) Did you or anyone else get badly hurt?
(Y) (N) Did you or anyone else get into serious
 trouble such as being arrested, suspended,
 overdosing, or feeling suicidal?
(Y) (N) Did you go to the hospital or a doctor?
(Y) (N) Could you get along with friends?
(Y) (N) Could you get along with your family?
(Y) (N) Could you get along with other people in
 your neighborhood, at school, or at work?
(Y) (N) Could you still do activities that you like to
 do, such as sports or clubs or parties?
(Y) (N) Could you watch TV or listen to music?
(Y) (N) Could you go to school and do the work?
(Y) (N) Could you sleep okay at night?
(Y) (N) Could you eat okay?

PASS: ☐ Prefers Not to Answer ☐ Does Not Understand *(If Pass, move on to next item (B.1b.))*

<u>**Severity Rating of Symptom for B.1a.**</u>

Not Present - Developmentally normative negative affect/distress.

Threshold - Child experienced severe emotional **DISTRESS** <u>and/or</u> **SHUT-DOWN** that
was unmanageable for the youth, and that at times led to physical harm to self or others or
serious negative consequences such as arrest, school suspension, or acute crises.

Past/Worst Month: ☐ Not Present ☐ DISTRESS ☐ SHUT-DOWN

<u>NOTE: If only one dimension is present for Past Month, ask about the other dimension for Lifetime.</u>

Lifetime: ☐ Not Present ☐ DISTRESS ☐ SHUT-DOWN

(Continued)

Box 6.6 Continued

*B.1b. When people feel that upset, sometimes they can't calm down for a long time. Or sometimes they feel totally shut down for a long time. Has that happened to you? What happened?

When you couldn't calm down or stop feeling totally shut down emotionally…

(Y) (N) Did you yell or scream for a long time?
(Y) (N) Did you keep hitting people/animals or hitting/breaking things for a long time?
(Y) (N) Were you totally shut down a long time?
(Y) (N) Did you or anyone else get badly hurt?
(Y) (N) Did you or anyone else get into serious trouble such as being arrested, suspended, overdosing, or feeling suicidal?
(Y) (N) Did you go to the hospital or a doctor?
(Y) (N) Could you get along with friends?
(Y) (N) Could you get along with your family?
(Y) (N) Could you get along with other people in your neighborhood, at school, or at work?
(Y) (N) Could you still do activities that you like to do, such as sports or clubs or parties?
(Y) (N) Could you watch TV or listen to music?
(Y) (N) Could you go to school and do the work?
(Y) (N) Could you sleep okay at night?
(Y) (N) Could you eat okay?

_____

_____

_____

_____

☐ YES *(If Yes)* How often did this happen in the past/worst month?

  ☐ Daily or almost daily ☐ 2 - 3 times per week ☐ Once a week or less

☐ NO *(If No)* Have there <u>ever</u> been any serious problems with this?

                    ☐ Yes (Lifetime) ☐ No

PASS: ☐ Prefers Not to Answer   ☐ Does Not Understand   *(If Pass, move on to next item (B.2a.))*

<u>Severity Rating of Symptom for B.1b.</u>

Not Present - No (or at most developmentally normative) difficulty recovering from episodes of severe distress or emotional shut-down

Threshold – At times unable to recover from emotional **DISTRESS** <u>and/or</u> emotional **SHUT-DOWN** without great effort, long delays, or crises/harm to self/others

Past/Worst Month: ☐ Not Present ☐ DISTRESS   ☐ SHUT-DOWN

  <u>*NOTE: If only one dimension is present for Past Month, ask about the other dimension for Lifetime*</u>

Lifetime: ☐ Not Present ☐ DISTRESS   ☐ SHUT-DOWN

B.2. Inability to modulate/recover from extreme bodily states

*B.2a. Sometimes people can't stand to be touched by anyone. Have you felt that way in the past/worst month? Or were there times when you could not stand certain sounds or noises, or other kinds of physical contact? What bothered you about this? What did you do?
(Rule out unwanted sexual contact, being physically assaulted or corporally punished, or accidental contact that causes injury.)

_____

_____

_____

_____

☐ **YES** *(If Yes)* **How often did this happen in the past/worst month?**

☐ **Daily or almost daily** ☐ **2 - 3 times per week** ☐ **Once a week or less**

☐ **NO** *(If No)* Have there <u>ever</u> been any serious problems with this?

☐ **Yes (Lifetime)** ☐ **No**

PASS: ☐ **Prefers Not to Answer** ☐ **Does Not Understand**
(If Pass, move on to next item (B.2b.))

Severity Rating of Symptom for B.2a.

Not Present - No discomfort, or developmentally normative discomfort about sensory experiences in some (but not all) ways by some (not all) people

Threshold - Experienced persistent or episodic emotional **DISTRESS** <u>and/or</u> **SHUT-DOWN** to actual or anticipated sensory experiences of sufficient severity or impairment that child could cope only partially or not at all.

Past/Worst Month: ☐Not Present ☐ DISTRESS ☐ SHUT-DOWN

NOTE: If only one dimension is present for Past Month, <u>ask about the other dimension for Lifetime</u>

Lifetime: ☐Not Present ☐DISTRESS ☐ SHUT-DOWN

When you couldn't stand anyone touching you...

(Y) (N) Was this with everyone in your life?
(Y) (N) Was this for every kind of touching?
(Y) (N) Did you wear clothes that covered you up so no one could touch you?
(Y) (N) Did you do things to your body so that no one would want to touch you?
(Y) (N) Did you not let anyone get close enough to you to be able to touch you?
(Y) (N) Did you threaten or yell or scream at anyone who tried to touch you?
(Y) (N) Did you hit, push, or physically attack anyone who tried to touch you?
(Y) (N) Did you get totally shut down emotionally or space out if anyone touched you?
(Y) (N) Did have to go to the hospital or a doctor?
(Y) (N) Could you get along with friends?
(Y) (N) Could you get along with your family?
(Y) (N) Could you get along with other people in your neighborhood, at school, or at work?
(Y) (N) Could you still do activities that you like to do, such as sports or clubs or parties?
(Y) (N) Could you watch TV or listen to music?
(Y) (N) Could you go to school and do the work?
(Y) (N) Could you sleep after being touched?
(Y) (N) Could you eat okay after being touched

When you couldn't stand some sounds or noises or couldn't stand having things too quiet ...

(Y) (N) Was it because noises seemed too loud?
(Y) (N) Was it because things seemed too quiet?
(Y) (N) Was it a specific kind of sound you hate (briefly describe _____)?
(Y) (N) Did you get really mad or blow up?
(Y) (N) Did you feel really scared or terrified?
(Y) (N) Did you feel confused or mixed up?
(Y) (N) Did you feel emotionally shut down?
(Y) (N) Did you go to the hospital or a doctor?
(Y) (N) Could you get along with friends?
(Y) (N) Could you get along with your family?
(Y) (N) Could you get along with other people in your neighborhood, at school, or at work?
(Y) (N) Could you still do activities that you like to do, such as sports or clubs or parties?
(Y) (N) Could you watch TV or listen to music?
(Y) (N) Could you go to school and do the work?
(Y) (N) Could you sleep okay at night?
(Y) (N) Could you eat okay?

(Continued)

Box 6.6 Continued

*B.2b. Sometimes people's bodies feel all messed up, like hurting a lot or not working right. Has that ever happened to you? When? What was the matter with your body? Were you sick and then got better? Did you get hurt and then get well again?

(Rule out body pain/symptoms reasonably attributable or proportionate to specific known physical injury or illness.)

When your body felt all messed up ...

(Y) (N) Was this almost all of your body?
(Y) (N) Was this certain parts of your body
         (briefly describe _____)?
(Y) (N) Did your body hurt or ache a lot?
(Y) (N) Did your body not work right, like not
         being able to walk or move parts of your
         body?
(Y) (N) Did you shake or twitch, or have
         cramps?
(Y) (N) Did you have trouble peeing like
         accidentally letting go or trouble controlling
         your bowel movements?
(Y) (N) Did you feel really scared or terrified?
(Y) (N) Did you feel helpless?
(Y) (N) Did you feel like no one was helping
         you?
(Y) (N) Did you feel emotionally shut down?
(Y) (N) Did you have to go to the hospital or a
         doctor?

_____

_____

_____

☐ YES *(If Yes)* How often did this happen in the past/worst month?

   ☐ Daily or almost daily ☐ 2 - 3 times per week ☐ Once a week or less

☐ NO *(If No)* Have there <u>ever</u> been any serious problems with this?

        ☐ Yes (Lifetime) ☐ No

PASS: ☐ Prefers Not to Answer   ☐ Does Not Understand
      (If Pass, move on to next item (B.3a.))

(Y) (N) Could you get along with friends?
(Y) (N) Could you get along with your family?
(Y) (N) Could you get along with other people
         in your neighborhood, at school, or at work?
(Y) (N) Could you still do activities that you
         like to do, such as sports or clubs or parties?
(Y) (N) Could you watch TV or listen to music?
(Y) (N) Could you go to school and do the work?
(Y) (N) Could you sleep okay?
(Y) (N) Could you eat okay?

<u>Severity Rating of Symptom for B.2b.</u>
  Not Present - No physical health problems, or developmentally normative physical health
      problems that are proportionate to medical illness or injury

Threshold – Physical complaints, problems, or limitations not fully explained by or worse/more
      difficult to treat than expectable due to medical illness or physical injury which caused
      severe emotional **DISTRESS/CRISES** and/or complete emotional **SHUT-DOWN**

Past/Worst Month: ☐ Not Present ☐ DISTRESS/CRISES ☐ SHUT-DOWN

   NOTE: If only one dimension is present for Past Month, ask about the other dimension for Lifetime

Lifetime: ☐ Not Present ☐ DISTRESS/CRISES ☐ SHUT-DOWN

B.3. Diminished awareness/dissociation of emotions or body feelings

B.3a. Sometimes people just don't have any feelings at all. They don't feel upset—scared or mad or sad or guilty—and they don't feel happy. They just don't feel anything at all, except maybe bored. Has this happened to you? What was it like? How long did it last?

When you didn't have any feelings ...
(Y) (N) Was it like all your feelings just stopped or all just went away?
(Y) (N) Or you were just empty inside?
(Y) (N) Could you feel any feelings, even a little (briefly describe _____)?
(Y) (N) Were you mixed up or confused?
(Y) (N) Did you feel empty inside?
(Y) (N) Did you not care about anyone/thing?
(Y) (N) Did you not care what happened to anyone, even if it was really good or bad?
(Y) (N) Did you get physically hurt or into serious trouble such as being arrested or suspended from school?
(Y) (N) Did you go to the hospital or a doctor?
(Y) (N) Could you get along with friends?
(Y) (N) Could you get along with your family?
(Y) (N) Could you get along with other people in your neighborhood, at school, or at work?
(Y) (N) Could you still do activities that you like to do, such as sports or clubs or parties?
(Y) (N) Could you watch TV or listen to music?
(Y) (N) Could you go to school and do the work?
(Y) (N) Could you sleep okay at night?
(Y) (N) Could you eat okay?

_____

_____

_____

_____

☐ **YES** *(If Yes)* **How often did this happen in the past/worst month?**

☐ **Daily or almost daily** ☐ **2 - 3 times per week** ☐ **Once a week or less**

☐ **NO** *(If No)* Have there <u>ever</u> been any serious problems with this?

☐ Yes (Lifetime) ☐ No

PASS: ☐ **Prefers Not to Answer**   ☐ **Does Not Understand**   *(If Pass, move on to next item (B.3b.))*

<u>**Severity Rating of Symptom for B.3a.**</u>

Not Present - Emotions generally present, with developmentally normative periods of numbing, boredom, or frustration

Threshold - Child consistently or always appears to have no emotions at all (except boredom or frustration), or episodically appears so for extended periods

Past/Worst Month: ☐ **Not Present** ☐ **Threshold**

<u>*NOTE: If symptom not present for Past Month, ask about it for Lifetime*</u>

Lifetime: ☐ **Not Present** ☐ **Threshold**

(Continued)

Box 6.6 Continued

B.3b. Sometimes people can't feel anything in parts of their body. Like when your fingers, toes, or face get completely numb if it's really cold. Has that ever happened to you *when it wasn't cold*? What was it like? Was it hard to do normal things when it happened? Did it get better?
(Rule out anesthesia or impairment attributable to a specific known physical injury or illness, or environmental or climatic conditions.)

When you couldn't feel your body, or your body wasn't working right …

(Y) (N) Was this due to an accident or illness?
(Y) (N) Was this due to extreme cold or heat?
(Y) (N) Was this certain parts of your body
        (briefly describe _____)?
(Y) (N) Did the feelings come back after a while?
(Y) (N) Did you feel really scared or terrified?
(Y) (N) Did you feel ashamed or embarrassed?
(Y) (N) Did you feel really mad or angry?
(Y) (N) Did think it would never get better?
(Y) (N) Did you feel emotionally shut down?
(Y) (N) Did have to go to the hospital or a doctor?
(Y) (N) Could you get along with friends?
(Y) (N) Could you get along with your family?
(Y) (N) Could you get along with other people in
        your neighborhood, at school, or at work?
(Y) (N) Could you still do activities that you like
        to do, such as sports or clubs or parties?
(Y) (N) Could you watch TV or listen to music?
(Y) (N) Could you go to school and do the work?
(Y) (N) Could you sleep okay?
(Y) (N) Could you eat okay?

_____

_____

_____

_____

☐ YES *(If Yes)* How often did this happen in the past/worst month

☐NO *(If No)* Have there <u>ever</u> been any serious problems with this?

☐ Yes (Lifetime)   ☐ No

PASS: ☐ Prefers Not to Answer   ☐ Does Not Understand   *(If Pass, move on to next item (B.4a.))*

<u>Severity Rating of Symptom for B.3b.</u>

Not Present - Body feelings generally present, with developmentally normative or
   illness/climate-related times of temporary numbing

Threshold - Consistently or always unable to feel or use some parts of her/his body

Past/Worst Month: ☐ Not Present ☐ Threshold

   <u>*NOTE: If symptom not present for Past Month, ask about it for Lifetime*</u>

Lifetime: ☐ Not Present ☐ Threshold

> **B.4.** Impaired capacity to describe emotions or bodily states

B.4a. Sometimes people can't tell what they're feeling even though they're acting emotional like crying or shouting. Or they don't know what words to use to describe the emotions they're feeling. Has this happened to you? What was it like? Were you able to figure out what you were feeling, or how to describe your feelings, afterward? *(Rule out alexithymia due to developmentally normative hiding or lack of understanding or familiarity with specific emotions.)*

When you were having some feelings but didn't know what you were feeling ...
(Y) (N) Did you know what your were feeling but not know the words to describe them?
(Y) (N) Were you too excited to know what you were feeling??
(Y) (N) Were you too upset to know what you were feeling?
(Y) (N) Were you too sleepy or exhausted to know what you were feeling?
(Y) (N) Were you crying or laughing or talking really fast or loud, but you didn't know why?
(Y) (N) Were you running or jumping or climbing all over, but you didn't know why?
(Y) (N) Did you feel like you wanted to die?
(Y) (N) Did you go to the hospital or a doctor?
(Y) (N) Could you get along with friends?
(Y) (N) Could you get along with your family?
(Y) (N) Could you get along with other people in your neighborhood, at school, or at work?
(Y) (N) Could you still do activities that you like to do, such as sports or clubs or parties?
(Y) (N) Could you watch TV or listen to music?
(Y) (N) Could you go to school and do the work?
(Y) (N) Could you sleep okay at night?

_____

_____

_____

_____

☐ YES *(If Yes)* **How often did this happen in the past/worst month?**

☐ **Daily or almost daily** ☐ **2 - 3 times per week** ☐ **Once a week or less**

☐ NO *(If No)* Have there <u>ever</u> been any serious problems with this?

☐ **Yes (Lifetime)** ☐ **No**

PASS: ☐ **Prefers Not to Answer** ☐ **Does Not Understand** *(If Pass, move on to next item (B.4b.))*

Severity Rating of Symptom for B.4a.

Not Present - Able to identify/describe/express emotions with developmentally normative limitations in awareness/vocabulary

Threshold – Always or consistently does not or cannot show/express emotions

Past/Worst Month: ☐ **Not Present** ☐ **Threshold**

> *NOTE: If symptom not present for Past Month, ask about it for Lifetime*

Lifetime: ☐ **Not Present** ☐ **Threshold**

(Continued)

Box 6.6 Continued

B.4b. Sometimes people know they're feeling something in their body but can't tell what this feeling is, or can't find the words to describe it. Has that happened to you? What was it like? How long did it last? Were you able later to figure out what your body was feeling?
(Rule out anesthesia likely attributable to a specific known physical injury or illness or environmental/weather conditions.)

_____

_____

_____

_____

When you couldn't tell what your body was feeling or didn't know how to describe it …

(Y) (N) Was this due to an accident or illness, or to being somewhere very hot or cold?
(Y) (N) Was this certain parts of your body (briefly describe _____)?
(Y) (N) Could you describe what those parts of your body were feeling if you tried hard?
(Y) (N) Did you feel too upset or excited be able to know what your body was feeling?
(Y) (N) Did you know what your body was feeling but just not know the words to describe it?
(Y) (N) Did you feel too mixed up/confused to be able to describe what your body was feeling?
(Y) (N) Did you feel like your body, or those parts of your body, didn't really belong to you?
(Y) (N) Did you have to go to the doctor/hospital?
(Y) (N) Did you do anything that got you badly hurt or in very serious trouble?

☐ **YES** *(If Yes)* **How often did this happen in the past/worst month?**

☐ **Daily or almost daily** ☐ **2 - 3 times per week** ☐ **Once a week or less**

☐ **NO** *(If No)* Have there <u>ever</u> been any serious problems with this?

☐ **Yes (Lifetime)** ☐ **No**

PASS: ☐ **Prefers Not to Answer** ☐ **Does Not Understand** *(If Pass, move on to next item (C.1a.))*

<u>Severity Rating of Symptom for B.4b.</u>

Not Present - Able to identify/describe physical/body feelings with developmentally normative limitations on awareness/vocabulary

Threshold - Always/consistently detached from or unaware of body feelings including pain

Past/Worst Month: ☐ **Not Present** ☐ **Threshold**

NOTE: If symptom not present for Past Month, ask about it for Lifetime

Lifetime: ☐ **Not Present** ☐ **Threshold**

C. Attentional or Behavioral Dysregulation
Impaired developmental competencies for attentional or
behavioral self-regulation

C.1. Attention-bias toward or away from potential threats

*C.1a. Sometimes people can't stop thinking about bad
things that have happened, or that could happen. Has
this happened to you? What was it like? How long did it
last? Could you think about anything else then?

_When you couldn't stop thinking about bad things
that happened or could happen…_

(Y) (N) Were the bad things really over and
probably not going to happen again?
(Y) (N) Were you able to remember that the
bad things were over and wouldn't happen
again?
(Y) (N) Were you able to think of ways to
handle the bad things if they ever did
happen again?
(Y) (N) Were you able to put the bad things
out of your mind by doing things you enjoy?
(Y) (N) Were you able to put the bad things
out of your mind by doing hard work or
exercising?
(Y) (N) Were you able to put the bad things out of
your mind by being with people you like?
(Y) (N) Could you get along with friends?
(Y) (N) Could you get along with your family?
(Y) (N) Could you get along with other people
in your neighborhood, at school, or at work?
(Y) (N) Could you still do activities that you
like to do, such as sports or clubs or parties?
(Y) (N) Could you watch TV or listen to music?
(Y) (N) Could you go to school and do the work?
(Y) (N) Could you sleep okay at night?
(Y) (N) Could you eat okay?
(Y) (N) Did you go to the hospital or a doctor?

_____

_____

_____

_____

☐ **YES** *(If Yes)* **How often did this happen in the past/worst month?**

☐ **Daily or almost daily** ☐ **2 - 3 times per week** ☐ **Once a week or less**

☐ **NO** *(If No)* Have there <u>ever</u> been any serious problems with this?

☐ **Yes (Lifetime)** ☐ **No**

PASS: ☐ **Prefers Not to Answer** ☐ **Does Not Understand** *(If Pass, move on to next item (C.1b.))*

Severity Rating of Symptom for C.1a.

Not Present – Developmentally normative memories of upsetting past events and vigilance
about potential future dangers/problems

Threshold - Persistent or episodic distressing/impairing **RUMINATIVE RECALL**
about past threats or harm <u>and/or</u> persistent or episodic **PERSEVERATIVE**
WORRY/UNWARRANTED FEARS about potential future dangers or harm

Past/Worst Month: ☐ **Not Present** ☐ **RECALL** ☐ **WORRY/FEARS**

<u>NOTE: If only one dimension is present for Past Month, ask about the other dimension for Lifetime</u>

Lifetime: ☐ **Not Present** ☐ **RECALL** ☐ **WORRY/FEARS**

(Continued)

Box 6.6 Continued

*C.1b. Sometimes people don't like to think about danger. They might change the topic or stop listening if someone talks about danger. Has that happened to you? What was it like? What made it hard for you to relax then? Or they might not take care to make sure they are safe. Like crossing the street in traffic without looking, or using tools without being careful. Has that happened to you? What was it like? Did anything bad happen because you weren't being careful enough about being safe?

When you didn't feel safe ...
(Y) (N) Did you feel tense or worried even though people you trust told you it was safe?
(Y) (N) Did you feel calmer if you did something to take your mind off the worries?
(Y) (N) Did you feel safer if you were with someone who cares about you?

When you weren't being careful enough ...?
(Y) (N) Did anything bad happen?

If either of these happened ...
(Y) (N) Could you get along with friends?
(Y) (N) Could you get along with your family?
(Y) (N) Could you get along with other people in your neighborhood, at school, or at work?
(Y) (N) Could you still do activities that you like to do, such as sports or clubs or parties?
(Y) (N) Could you watch TV or listen to music?
(Y) (N) Could you go to school and do the work?
(Y) (N) Could you sleep okay?
(Y) (N) Could you eat okay?
(Y) (N) Did you go to the hospital or a doctor?

_____

_____

_____

_____

☐ **YES** *(If Yes)* **How often did this happen in the past/worst month?**

☐ **Daily or almost daily** ☐ **2 - 3 times per week** ☐ **Once a week or less** ☐
NO *(If No)* Have there <u>ever</u> been any serious problems with this?
☐ **Yes (Lifetime)** ☐ **No**

PASS: ☐ **Prefers Not to Answer** ☐ **Does Not Understand** *(If Pass, move on to next item (C.2a.))*

<u>**Severity Rating of Symptom for C.1b.**</u>
Not Present - Developmentally normative distraction or carelessness
Threshold – Persistent or episodic **AVOIDANCE OF THINKING** about past or potential
    future dangers/harm <u>and/or</u> **UNAWARENESS OF ACTUAL DANGER/THREATS**

Past/Worst Month: ☐ **Not Present** ☐ **AVOIDANCE**   ☐ **UNAWARENESS**

  <u>*NOTE: If only one dimension is present for Past Month, ask about the other dimension for Lifetime*</u>

Lifetime: ☐ **Not Present** ☐ **AVOIDANCE**   ☐ **UNAWARENESS**

| **C.2.** Impaired capacity for self-protection, including extreme risk-taking, thrill-seeking, or provocation of anger/aggression from others |

*C.2a. Sometimes people do really dangerous things such as fighting with weapons or driving too fast or jumping from high places. Or they go places that are so dangerous that they could get badly hurt or killed, such as where gangs are fighting or people are drinking too much or doing drugs, or running in front of trains or cars. Did you ever do that?

Or they go places with people they don't know? Did you? Or they don't check back with their parents when they go places or stay out late? Did you? What happened? Did you try to protect yourself?

_____

_____

_____

_____

☐ YES *(If Yes)* How often did this happen in the past/worst month?

  ☐ Daily or almost daily ☐ 2 - 3 times per week ☐ Once a week or less

☐ NO *(If No)* Have there <u>ever</u> been any serious problems with this?

        ☐ Yes (Lifetime) ☐ No

When you did dangerous things or were around dangerous places or people …

(Y) (N) Did this involve violent people?
(Y) (N) Did this involve dangerous weapons?
(Y) (N) Did this involve vehicles like cars or trains, or equipment or tools that cut or crush?
(Y) (N) Did this involve drinking or drugs?
(Y) (N) Did this involve jumping or falling from high places, including extreme sports?
(Y) (N) Did this involve stealing or other illegal actions such as breaking and entering?
(Y) (N) Or prostitution (sex for money)?
(Y) (N) Or having unprotected sex?
(Y) (N) Did this involve selling drugs?
(Y) (N) Were you seriously physically hurt?
(Y) (N) Did you not care if you got badly hurt?
(Y) (N) Did you hope you'd be seriously hurt?
(Y) (N) Was anyone else badly hurt or killed?
(Y) (N) Did anyone get arrested for doing this?
(Y) (N) Did you go to the hospital or a doctor?
(Y) (N) Did you plan ahead so you'd be safe?
(Y) (N) Did your plan include having protection that really could keep you from getting hurt?
(Y) (N) Did you avoid doing things that could get you badly hurt or in trouble (e.g., arrested)?

PASS: ☐ Prefers Not to Answer ☐ Does Not Understand *(If Pass, move on to next item (C.2b.))*

Severity Rating of Symptom for C.2a.

Not Present - Developmentally normative risks or thrill-seeking

Threshold – Persistent or frequent **EXPOSURE OF SELF TO POTENTIAL SERIOUS HARM** with insufficient or no precautions <u>and/or</u> persistent or frequent **FAILURE TO MAINTAIN CONTACT WITH CAREGIVERS**

Past/Worst Month: ☐ Not Present ☐ EXPOSURE TO HARM ☐ FAIL TO CONTACT

  <u>NOTE: If only one dimension is present for Past Month, ask about the other dimension for Lifetime</u>

Lifetime: ☐ Not Present ☐ EXPOSURE TO HARM ☐ FAIL TO CONTACT

(Continued)

Box 6.6 Continued

C.2b. Sometimes people go looking for trouble, like starting fights on purpose, or confronting people who have power like police, teachers, coaches, or gang leaders. Did you ever do that? What happened?

When you were looking for trouble, or picked a fight or confronted someone powerful ...

(Y) (N) Were you seriously physically hurt?
(Y) (N) Did you go to the hospital or a doctor?
(Y) (N) Did you know you'd get badly hurt?
(Y) (N) Did you not care if you got badly hurt?
(Y) (N) Did you hope you'd be seriously hurt?
(Y) (N) Did you get in serious trouble (such as being arrested, expelled, on probation)?
(Y) (N) Did you hope you'd get in bad trouble?
(Y) (N) Did you get so mad you couldn't stop?
(Y) (N) Did you think you had to do so people would know they can't push you around?
(Y) (N) Did you think you had to do so people would respect or be afraid of you?
(Y) (N) Did you think you had to do it so people wouldn't think you were a coward or a punk?
(Y) (N) Did you want to get revenge (pay back)?
(Y) (N) Did you want to teach a lesson to some one who hurt or bullied you or other people?

_____

_____

_____

_____

☐ **YES** *(If Yes)* **How often did this happen in the past/worst month?**

☐ **Daily or almost daily** ☐ **2 - 3 times per week** ☐ **Once a week or less**

☐ **NO** *(If No)* Have there <u>ever</u> been any serious problems with this?

☐ **Yes (Lifetime)** ☐ **No**

PASS: ☐ **Prefers Not to Answer**   ☐ **Does Not Understand**   *(If Pass, move on to next item (C.3.))*

<u>**Severity Rating of Symptom for C.2b.**</u>

Not Present - Developmentally normative assertiveness in response to perceived hypocrisy, unfairness, or bullying/intimidation by others

Threshold – Persistent or frequent risky challenging or confrontation of others with disregard for own/others' safety or to establish dominance

Past/Worst Month: ☐ **Not Present** ☐ **Threshold**

<u>*NOTE: If symptom not present for Past Month, ask about it for Lifetime*</u>

Lifetime: ☐ **Not Present** ☐ **Threshold**

> **C.3.** Maladaptive attempts at self-soothing

C.3. People do different things to try to feel better when they feel upset or bored. What do you do? … When you feel frustrated or mad? … scared or worried? … sad or depressed? … hopeless? … in a lot of pain? Can you stop doing those things if you need to?

When coping with feeling upset, you …
(Y) (N) Eat junk foods or so much you get sick?
(Y) (N) Stop or severely limit eating?
(Y) (N) Exercise so hard or much you get sick?
(Y) (N) Watch TV or play videogames so much you don't sleep or do anything else?
(Y) (N) Skip school, cut classes, or not do school assignments or studying?
(Y) (N) Skip (or not start) organized activities like sports, arts/music, school clubs, church group?
(Y) (N) Pretend you are someone else important or famous so much that you believes it's true?
(Y) (N) Start yelling or screaming and can't stop?
(Y) (N) Start sobbing or crying and can't stop
(Y) (N) Attack or lash out physically at people?
(Y) (N) Damage or destroy objects or property?
(Y) (N) Pick fights with friends, family, teachers, or other people: _____? **(see C2b)**
(Y) (N) Stay out all night with friends/partying?
(Y) (N) Run away for days or weeks at a time?
(Y) (N) Have sex a lot or without protection?
(Y) (N) Do things that little kids do to comfort themselves, like rocking or thumbsucking?
(Y) (N) Drink alcohol
(Y) (N) Use street drugs
(Y) (N) Use prescription drugs against the rules

☐ **YES** *(If Yes)* **How often did this happen in the past/worst month?**

☐ **Daily or almost daily** ☐ **2 - 3 times per week** ☐ **Once a week or less**

☐ **NO** *(If No)* Have there _ever_ been any serious problems with this?

☐ **Yes (Lifetime)** ☐ **No**

PASS: ☐ **Prefers Not to Answer** ☐ **Does Not Understand** *(If Pass, move on to next item (C.4.))*

Severity Rating of Symptom for C.3.

Not Present - Developmentally normative self-soothing, distraction, or active coping (e.g., seeking contact with friends/family, engaging in sports, avocations, job/school, work, or enjoying music/reading)

Threshold – Relies on self-soothing or avoidant coping that has severe adverse effects on safety, health, relationships, or achievement and is unable to stop, limit, or change these behaviors (or only with great effort)

Past/Worst Month: ☐ **Not Present** ☐ **Threshold**

NOTE: If symptom not present for Past Month, ask about it for Lifetime

Lifetime: ☐ **Not Present** ☐ **Threshold**

(Continued)

Box 6.6 Continued

> **C.4.** Habitual (intentional or automatic) or reactive self-harm

C.4 Sometimes people try to hurt their body on purpose because they feel bad, or because it helps them vent or feel better for a while. They might cut, scratch, poke, bite, stab, or burn parts of their body. Or pull out their hair. Or punch or kick a wall. Or stick things in their body? Have you ever done this? What happened? How did you feel? How often do you feel like doing this but not actually do it?

When you hurt your body on purpose …
(Y) (N) Was this certain parts of the body
   (briefly describe _____)?
(Y) (N) Was this an accident and not on purpose?
(Y) (N) Can you cope with feeling upset without
   doing these things if you try not to do them?
(Y) (N) Can you stop before causing serious or
   permanent damage, illness, or
   disfigurement?
(Y) (N) Were you very upset right before doing
   it?
(Y) (N) Were you obsessed or preoccupied with
   thoughts of doing this before actually
   doing it?
(Y) (N) Did you have a lot of urges to do this,
   whether you actually did it or not?
(Y) (N) Did you seem to want to damage your
   body or make yourself ill or in pain?
(Y) (N) Did this cause bruises or scars?
(Y) (N) Did this cause infection/broken bones?
(Y) (N) Did this cause you to be very sick?
(Y) (N) Was medical/hospital care provided?
(Y) (N) Was medical/hospital care not provided
   but it should have been?
(Y) (N) Did you feel a lot of pain?

_____

_____

_____

_____

☐ YES *(If Yes)* How often did this happen in the past/worst month?

    ☐ Daily or almost daily ☐ 2 - 3 times per week ☐ Once a week or less

☐ NO *(If No)* Have there <u>ever</u> been any serious problems with this?

        ☐ Yes (Lifetime) ☐ No

PASS: ☐ Prefers Not to Answer ☐ Does Not Understand *(If Pass, move on to next item (C.5.))*

<u>**Severity Rating of Symptom for C.4.**</u>

Not Present – No self-harm or minor inadvertent self-harm

Threshold – Proactive self-harm (behavior intended to injure, cause pain, or maim or disfigure
   body) <u>or</u> reactive self-harm which causes permanent physical injury or disfigurement and the
   child says (or evidence indicates) s/he usually cannot intentionally stop, limit, or prevent

Past/Worst Month: ☐ Not Present ☐ Threshold

    <u>NOTE: If symptom not present for Past Month, ask about it for Lifetime</u>

Lifetime: ☐ Not Present ☐ Threshold

> **C.5.** Inability to initiate or sustain goal-directed behavior

C.5. Sometimes people have a hard time getting started on activities or finishing them unless someone else reminds them or makes them do it. Or they won't start or finish anything unless someone helps them or does it for them. Has that happened to you? Are there times that you do start and finish activities all on your own?

_____

_____

_____

_____

☐ YES *(If Yes)* **How often did this happen in the past/worst month?**

   ☐ **Daily or almost daily** ☐ **2 - 3 times per week** ☐ **Once a week or less**

☐ NO *(If No)* Have there <u>ever</u> been any serious problems with this?

   ☐ **Yes (Lifetime)**   ☐ **No**

When you don't start or finish activities unless someone reminds you, makes you, or helps you ..

(Y) (N) Do you usually find a way to get started even if you put it off a long time (procrastinate)?

(Y) (N) Do you usually find a way to finish what you start even if it takes a long time?

(Y) (N) Do you only start activities if someone else reminds you or helps you get started?

(Y) (N) Do you only start activities if someone else makes you do it or does most of it for you?

(Y) (N) Do you only finish activities if someone else makes you do it or does most of it for you?

(Y) (N) Do stop activities before your finished for no reason at all, even if you planned to finish?

(Y) (N) Do you give up and not start because you feel like you'll just fail if you try?

(Y) (N) Do you give up after you've started things because you're sure you'll fail or look stupid?

(Y) (N) Do you refuse to start anything boring?

(Y) (N) Do you stop doing things if you find them boring, frustrating, or stupid?

(Y) (N) Do you avoid starting most activities?

(Y) (N) Do you not finish most activities?

PASS: ☐ **Prefers Not to Answer**   ☐ **Does Not Understand**   *(If Pass, move on to next item (D.1.))*

Severity Rating of Symptom for C.5.

Not Present – Developmentally normative difficulties with starting or completing activities due to procrastination, multitasking, boredom

Threshold – Rarely starts or finishes certain (or most) activities, or does so only if most planning/work is accomplished by someone else

Past/Worst Month: ☐ **Not Present** ☐ **Threshold**

   NOTE: If symptom not present for Past Month, ask about it for Lifetime

Lifetime: ☐ **Not Present** ☐ **Threshold**

(Continued)

Box 6.6 Continued

D. Self and Relational Dysregulation
Impaired developmental competencies in personal identity and
involvement in relationships

D.1. Persistent extreme negative self-perception, including self-
loathing or view self as damaged/defective.

D.1. Sometimes people don't like themselves or don't feel
good about themselves. Do you ever feel that way? How bad
do you feel? Please give a brief example.

_____

_____

_____

_____

☐ YES *(If Yes)* **How often did this happen in the past/worst month?**

  ☐ **Daily or almost daily** ☐ **2 - 3 times per week** ☐ **Once a week or less**

☐ NO *(If No)* Have there <u>ever</u> been any serious problems with this?

                        ☐ **Yes (Lifetime)** ☐ **No**

PASS: ☐ Prefers Not to Answer   ☐ Does Not Understand   *(If Pass, move on to next item (D.2a.))*

<u>**Severity Rating of Symptom for D.1.**</u>
Not Present – Developmentally normative difficulty with self-esteem
Threshold – Views self almost entirely as bad, damaging or damaged, defective, unlovable, or physically deformed, and has serious difficulties with relationships, activities, self-care, or self-image as a result.
Past/Worst Month: ☐ Not Present ☐ Threshold
NOTE: If symptom not present for Past Month, ask about it for Lifetime
Lifetime: ☐ Not Present ☐ Threshold

D.2. Attachment insecurity: parentified attempts to care for
caregivers or difficulty tolerating reunion after separation from
primary caregiver(s)

When you don't feel good about yourself ...
(Y) (N) Do you think you are dirty/disgusting?
(Y) (N) Do you think you are horribly ugly?
(Y) (N) Do you think no one could ever like you?
(Y) (N) Do you think there's something terribly
    wrong about you?
(Y) (N) Do you think you're messed up or
    damaged because of things that have happened?
(Y) (N) Do you think you're stupid and dumb?
(Y) (N) Do you think you're no good at anything?
(Y) (N) Do you think you never do anything right?
(Y) (N) Do you think you're no good for anyone?
(Y) (N) Do you think you're a liar or a faker?
(Y) (N) Do some people think these bad things
    about you or say these bad things to you?
(Y) (N) Does anyone say you're better than that?
(Y) (N) Do you remember good things about you?
(Y) (N) Can you get along with friends?
(Y) (N) Can you get along with your family?
(Y) (N) Can you get along with other people in your
    neighborhood, at school, or at work?
(Y) (N) Can you still do activities that you like
    to do, such as sports or clubs or parties?
(Y) (N) Can you watch TV or listen to music?
(Y) (N) Can you go to school and do the work?
(Y) (N) Can you sleep okay?
(Y) (N) Can you eat okay?

*D.2a. Sometimes kids try hard to protect or look after the people who are supposed to take care of them, like their mother or father. They might try really hard to make them feel better. Or they might try hard to never do anything that makes them more upset or unhappy. Have you ever done this? For whom? How did you try to help [caregiver]?

_____

_____

_____

_____

☐ **YES** *(If Yes)* **How often did this happen in the past/worst month?**

   ☐ **Daily or almost daily** ☐ **2 - 3 times per week** ☐ **Once a week or less**

☐ **NO** *(If No)* Have there <u>ever</u> been any serious problems with this?

   ☐ **Yes (Lifetime)** ☐ **No**

PASS: ☐ **Prefers Not to Answer** ☐ **Does Not Understand** *(If Pass, move on to next item (D.2b.))*

When you tried to protect or take care of people who should take care of you …
(Y) (N) Was this for a parent: _mother _father?
(Y) (N) For a parent-figure: _____?
(Y) (N) Did you worry about her/him being safe?
(Y) (N) Did you feel you had to protect her/him?
(Y) (N) Did you worry that s/he was sad/upset?
(Y) (N) Did you feel you had to comfort her/him?
(Y) (N) Did you feel you had to be the parent by looking after your family members and home?
(Y) (N) Did you feel you had to earn money so your family had food, clothes, and a home?
(Y) (N) Did you have to fight someone to do this?
(Y) (N) Did you have to skip school to do this?
(Y) (N) Did you have to break the law (steal)?
(Y) (N) Did you still spend time with friends?
(Y) (N) Did you have a good family life?
(Y) (N) Did you still spend time with people in your neighborhood, at school, or at work?
(Y) (N) Did you still do activities that you like to do, such as sports or clubs or parties?
(Y) (N) Could you watch TV or listen to music?
(Y) (N) Did you go to school and do the work?
(Y) (N) Could you sleep okay at night?
(Y) (N) Could you eat okay?

<u>**Severity Rating of Symptom for D.2a.**</u>

Not Present - Developmentally normative concerns about and attempts to help caregivers

Threshold – Experiences severe distress or impairment
   DUE TO WORRIES ABOUT CAREGIVERS' SAFETY OR WHEN ATTEMPTING TO PROTECT CAREGIVERS
   <u>and/or</u>
   WHEN FEELS SYMPATHETIC CONCERN OR GUILT IN REACTION TO A DISTRESSED CAREGIVER

Past/Worst Month: ☐Not Present ☐WORRY ABOUT SAFETY ☐CONCERN/GUILT

   <u>NOTE: If only one dimension is present for Past Month, ask about the other dimension for Lifetime</u>

Lifetime: ☐ Not Present ☐WORRY ABOUT SAFETY ☐CONCERN/GUILT

(Continued)

Box 6.6 Continued

D.2b. Sometimes kids can't be with someone important who should be looking after them, like their mother or father. Maybe they went away, or maybe you had to go away. Has that happened to you in the past/worst month? What happened? Now here's the question: when you got back together with them again, did you sometimes still feel very upset or angry, like you want to hit them or run away?

When you were upset after being separated
from someone who looks after you …
(Y) (N) Was this for a parent: _mother _father?
(Y) (N) For a parent-figure: _____?
(Y) (N) Did you worry about her/him being safe?
(Y) (N) Did you feel you couldn't trust her/him?
(Y) (N) Did you not care about her/him anymore?
(Y) (N) Did you have no feelings at all (see B3)?
(Y) (N) Did you feel scared s/he'd leave again?
(Y) (N) Did you feel mad at her/him?
(Y) (N) Did you feel guilty like it was your fault?
(Y) (N) Did you feel sad or bad about yourself, like
   you didn't deserve to be with her/him?
(Y) (N) Did you feel you didn't deserve to
   count on anyone to love and take care of
   you?
(Y) (N) Did you feel upset a long time (see B2)?
(Y) (N) Did you still spend time with friends?
(Y) (N) Did you have a good family life?
(Y) (N) Did you still spend time with people in
   your neighborhood, at school, or at work?
(Y) (N) Did you still do activities that you like
   to do, such as sports or clubs or parties?
(Y) (N)Could you watch TV or listen to music?
(Y) (N) Did you go to school and do the work?
(Y) (N) Could you sleep okay at night?
(Y) (N) Could you eat okay?

_____

_____

_____

_____

□ YES *(If Yes)* **How often did this happen in the past/worst month?**

  □ **Daily or almost daily** □ **2 - 3 times per week** □ **Once a week or less**

□ **NO** *(If No)* Have there <u>ever</u> been any serious problems with this?

                    □ **Yes (Lifetime)** □ **No**

PASS: □ **Prefers Not to Answer** □ **Does Not Understand**   *(If Pass, move on to next item (D.3a.))*

<u>Severity Rating of Symptom for D.2b.</u>
Not Present – No separations or reunions, or at most developmentally normative moderate
   intensity of distress due to separation/reunion
Threshold – Experiences prolonged (e.g. more than a few days) severe distress or impairment
   during/after reunion after separations from caregiver(s)

Past/Worst Month: □ **Not Present** □ **Threshold**

       NOTE: If symptom not present for Past Month, ask about it for Lifetime

Lifetime: □ **Not Present** □ **Threshold**

D.3. Extreme persistent distrust, defiance or lack of reciprocal behavior in close relationships

D.3a. Sometimes people feel that close friends or family, or people you used to look up to (like a teacher, coach, priest/minister/rabbi), can't be trusted. Have you felt this way? About whom? What did they do? Were you ever able to trust them again?

When you don't trust people you used to trust…

Who was this? _____
(Y) (N) Was it because they didn't tell the truth?
(Y) (N) Was it because they didn't keep their word and didn't do what they said they'd do?
(Y) (N) Was it because they didn't help you when you really needed their help?
(Y) (N) Was it because they didn't stand up for you when you needed them on your side?
(Y) (N) Was it because they took advantage of you for their own selfish reasons?
(Y) (N) Was it because they told you they cared about you and then did things that hurt you?
(Y) (N) Was it because they told you they cared for you but then were mean or uncaring?
(Y) (N) Were you never able to trust them again?
(Y) (N) Did you not trust people who were nice to you or acted like they cared about you?
(Y) (N) Could you get along with friends?
(Y) (N) Could you get along with your family?
(Y) (N) Could you get along with other people in your neighborhood, at school, or at work?
(Y) (N) Could you still do activities that you like to do, such as sports or clubs or parties?
(Y) (N) Could you watch TV or listen to music?
(Y) (N) Could you go to school and do the work?
(Y) (N) Could you sleep okay at night?
(Y) (N) Could you eat okay?

☐ **YES** _(If Yes)_ **How often did this happen in the past/worst month?**

☐ **Daily or almost daily** ☐ **2 - 3 times per week** ☐ **Once a week or less**

☐ **NO** _(If No)_ Have there <u>ever</u> been any serious problems with this?

☐ **Yes (Lifetime)** ☐ **No**

PASS: ☐ **Prefers Not to Answer** ☐ **Does Not Understand** _(If Pass, move on to next item (D.3b.))_

Severity Rating of Symptom for D.3a.

Not Present – No betrayals of trust or developmentally normative disappointments or frustrations in close or mentoring relationships

Threshold – Perceived betrayals are unrepaired or continue to cause severe distress or inability to trust trustworthy people or relationships

Past/Worst Month: ☐ **Not Present** ☐ **Threshold**

**NOTE: If symptom not present for Past Month, ask about it for Lifetime**

Lifetime: ☐ **Not Present** ☐ **Threshold**

(Continued)

Box 6.6 Continued

*D.3b. Sometimes people think other people are always trying to push them around or take advantage of them. Has that happened to you? What were people doing to push you around or take advantage of you? What did you do? How did it work out?

When felt you had to attack someone because they were doing bad things or being unfair ...

(Y) (N) Did you stand up to them or try to make them stop without really attacking them?
(Y) (N) Did you teach them a lesson by being calm and strong but not really attacking them?
(Y) (N) Did you start to attack them but then calm down before any serious problem happened?
(Y) (N) Did you get so mad that you attacked them even when they weren't doing anything to hurt or disrespect you or anyone else?
(Y) (N) Did you get so mad you couldn't calm down and stop yelling/saying bad things?
(Y) (N) Did you get so mad you couldn't calm down and stop physically attacking them?
(Y) (N) Did you get so mad that you did serious things to hurt them or get revenge?
(Y) (N) Did this cause problems with friends?
(Y) (N) Did this cause problems with family?
(Y) (N) Did this cause problems at school, work, or in activities?

_____

_____

_____

_____

☐ **YES** *(If Yes)* **How often did this happen in the past/worst month?**

  ☐ **Daily or almost daily** ☐ **2 - 3 times per week** ☐ **Once a week or less**

☐ **NO** *(If No)* Have there <u>ever</u> been any serious problems with this?

                              ☐ **Yes (Lifetime)** ☐ **No**

PASS: ☐ **Prefers Not to Answer**   ☐ **Does Not Understand**
         (If Pass, move on to next item (D.4.))

Severity Rating of Symptom for D.3b.

Not Present – No oppositionality or defiance; or developmentally normative assertiveness when coping with actual coercion/pressures

Threshold – Either:
    DEFIANTLY OPPOSES people even if they are not coercive, controlling, or threatening; or generalizes oppositionality to most relationships
    and/or
    Is consistently **RESENTFUL, REVENGE SEEKING, PASSIVE RESISTANT, OR OVERTLY PHYSICALLY OR VERBALLY AGGRESSIVE** if s/he perceives coercion

Past/Worst Month: ☐ **Not Present** ☐ **DEFIANT** ☐ **RESENTFUL/AGGRESSIVE**

  NOTE: If only one dimension is present for Past Month, ask about the other dimension for Lifetime

Lifetime: ☐ **Not Present** ☐ **DEFIANT** ☐ **RESENTFUL/AGGRESSIVE**

D.4. Reactive physical or verbal aggression

*D.4. Sometimes people feel that they have to attack anyone who they think is unfair, or who hurt, mistreat, or disrespect them or other people. They might do this to stop or prevent bad things. Or to get back at or teach a lesson to people. Have you done that? What happened? What did you do?

When you felt that people were trying to push you around or take advantage of you…

(Y) (N) Were there ever times when they were fair and not pushy or trying to take advantage?

(Y) (N) Were there other people who treated you fairly and didn't try to take advantage of you?

(Y) (N) Did you argue or refuse to do whatever people wanted no matter how they treated you?

(Y) (N) Did you refuse to do anything that almost anyone wanted you to do?

(Y) (N) Did you give in but then get revenge **(see D4)**?

(Y) (N) Did you give in but feel mad or depressed?

(Y) (N) Did you act like you gave in but then not do what they were trying to make you do?

(Y) (N) Did get so mad you physically attacked or couldn't stop screaming at them **(see D4)**?

(Y) (N) Could you get along with friends?

(Y) (N) Could you get along with your family?

(Y) (N) Could you get along with other people in your neighborhood, at school, or at work?

(Y) (N) Could you still do activities that you like doing, such as sports or clubs or parties?

_____

_____

_____

_____

☐ **YES** *(If Yes)* **How often did this happen in the past/worst month?**

  ☐ **Daily or almost daily** ☐ **2 - 3 times per week** ☐ **Once a week or less**

☐ **NO** *(If No)* Have there <u>ever</u> been any serious problems with this?

          ☐ **Yes (Lifetime)** ☐ **No**

PASS: ☐ **Prefers Not to Answer** ☐ **Does Not Understand** *(If Pass, move on to next item (D.5a.))*

<u>**Severity Rating of Symptom for D.4.**</u>

Not Present – No aggressive behavior or developmentally normative assertiveness when coping with actual threats/harm

Threshold – REACTS AGGRESSIVELY EVEN WHEN NOT ATTACKED, THREATENED, BULLIED, OR DISRESPECTED <u>and/or</u> **REACTS WITH DYSCONTROLLED AGGRESSION TO ACTUAL THREATS OR HARM TO SELF/OTHERS,** causing serious impairment or harm to self/others

Past/Worst Month: ☐Not Present ☐REACTS WHEN NOT ATTACKED ☐REACTS TO ACTUAL THREAT/HARM

    <u>*NOTE: If only one dimension is present for Past Month, ask about the other dimension for Lifetime*</u>

Lifetime: ☐ Not Present ☐ REACTS WHEN NOT ATTACKED ☐ REACTS TO ACTUAL THREAT/HARM

(Continued)

Box 6.6 Continued

D.5. Psychological boundary deficits: inappropriate (excessive or promiscuous) intimate contact (including physical or sexual), or excessive reliance on peers or adults for safety and reassurance

When you try to be close to people…

D.5a. Sometimes people need to be close to people or to have people show they care about them a lot, even with strangers. They might try to make people they know hug, touch or kiss them. Or they might hug, touch or kiss strangers. Or go places with strangers. Have you done that? What happened? Where did you go?

(Y) (N) Do you only do this with people you know well and feel close to?
[if ≥ 16] (Y) (N) If this includes having sex, is it only with people who are your age own age?
(Y) (N) Do you stop if the other person says stop?
(Y) (N) Are your careful not to go anywhere with people unless you know and trust them?
(Y) (N) Do you stop if the other person is upset?
(Y) (N) Do you stop if you could get hurt or in bad trouble?
(Y) (N) Do you keep trying to hug, touch, or kiss people no matter how upset they get?
(Y) (N) Do you let strangers who are your age or older than you hug, touch, of kiss you?
(Y) (N) Do you go places with strangers where you could have gotten hurt or in bad trouble?
[if ≥ 16] (Y) (N) If this includes having sex, is it with adults or people a lot older than you?
[if ≥ 16] (Y) (N) If this includes having sex, is it with younger kids?

_____

_____

_____

_____

☐ YES *(If Yes)* **How often did this happen in the past/worst month?**

☐ **Daily or almost daily** ☐ **2 - 3 times per week** ☐ **Once a week or less**

☐ NO *(If No)* Have there <u>ever</u> been any serious problems with this?

☐ Yes (Lifetime)   ☐ No

PASS: ☐ **Prefers Not to Answer**   ☐ **Does Not Understand**   *(If Pass, move on to next item (D.5b.))*

<u>**Severity Rating of Symptom for D.5a.**</u>

Not Present – Definite developmentally appropriate boundaries physically and sexually (including consensual same-age sex if ≥ 16)

Threshold – Limited or no concern about personal boundaries when seeking contact or affection, with potentially or actually dangerous or serious adverse consequences.

Past/Worst Month: ☐ **Not Present** ☐ **Threshold**

NOTE: If symptom not present for Past Month, ask about it for Lifetime

Lifetime: ☐ **Not Present** ☐ **Threshold**

D.5b. Sometimes people need a lot of reassurance if they feel upset. Like not being able to calm down or feel better unless someone pays a lot of attention to them or tells them that everything's okay. Have you felt that way? Did you try to feel better on your own? Who did you want to reassure you? What did you do to get them to reassure you?

When you needed a lot of reassurance …

(Y) (N) Did you feel better if someone told you it would be okay?
(Y) (N) Did you help yourself feel better by remembering that it would be okay?
(Y) (N) Did you feel upset no matter how much other people reassured or helped you?
(Y) (N) Did you feel like no one cared enough about you to help you feel okay?
(Y) (N) Were you able to calm down or feel better again before too long?
(Y) (N) Did you feel so bad you couldn't get along with or be with your friends?
(Y) (N) Did you feel so bad you couldn't get along with or be with your family?
(Y) (N) Did you feel so bad you couldn't get along with or be with other people in your neighborhood, at school, or at work?
(Y) (N) Was it hard to sleep or eat?
(Y) (N) Was it hard to enjoy TV or music?

_____

_____

_____

_____

☐ **YES** *(If Yes)* **How often did this happen in the past/worst month?**

  ☐ **Daily or almost daily ☐ 2 - 3 times per week ☐ Once a week or less**

☐ **NO** *(If No)* Have there <u>ever</u> been any serious problems with this?

                    ☐ **Yes (Lifetime)   ☐ No**

PASS: ☐ **Prefers Not to Answer   ☐ Does Not Understand**   *(If Pass, move on to next item (D.6a.))*

Severity Rating of Symptom for D.5b.

Not Present – Developmentally normative desire for reassurance

Threshold – Intense and developmentally immature need for reassurance with minimal ability to restrain or calm/reassure self, or resulting in serious impairment due to over-reliance on others for reassurance

Past/Worst Month: ☐ **Not Present ☐ Threshold**

           NOTE: If symptom not present for Past Month, ask about it for Lifetime

Lifetime: ☐ **Not Present ☐ Threshold**

(Continued)

Box 6.6 Continued

D.6. Impaired capacity to regulate empathic arousal: (a) lacks empathy for, or intolerant of, expressions of distress of others, or (b) excessive responsiveness to the distress of others.

D.6a. Sometimes it's hard for people to feel sympathy for someone who's hurt or needs help. They might feel disgusted because those people seem stupid or whiny or they're acting like babies when they should stop complaining and get over it. Have you felt that way? Who was hurt or needed help? What did you do?

When you don't feel sympathy or like you want to help someone who's hurt or wants help...

(Y) (N) Do you think it's too bad that they're hurt or need help, but that it's not your problem?
(Y) (N) Do you think it's too bad that they're hurt or need help but they will probably be OK?
(Y) (N) Do you think it's too bad that they're hurt or need help but it's probably their own fault?
(Y) (N) Do you really just not care about them?
(Y) (N) Do you think they don't deserve help because it's really their own fault?
(Y) (N) Do you think they don't deserve help because they're making a big deal about minor or stupid problems?
(Y) (N) Do you feel angry or disgusted by them?
(Y) (N) Do you want them to just stop bothering you with their problems?
(Y) (N) Do you think they deserve to be yelled at or treated badly because they're so stupid?

☐ **YES** *(If Yes)* **How often did this happen in the past/worst month?**

☐ **Daily or almost daily** ☐ **2 - 3 times per week** ☐ **Once a week or less**

☐ **NO** *(If No)* Have there <u>ever</u> been any serious problems with this?

☐ **Yes (Lifetime)** ☐ **No**

PASS: ☐ **Prefers Not to Answer** ☐ **Does Not Understand** *(If Pass, move on to next item (D.6b.))*

Severity Rating of Symptom for D.6a.

Not Present – Developmentally normative sympathy for others

Threshold – Complete or consistent affective and cognitive indifference to, or inability or unwillingness to identify with, persons in distress or in need of help. Or active disgust/contempt for such individuals.

Past/Worst Month: ☐ **Not Present** ☐ **Threshold**

  NOTE: If symptom not present for Past Month, ask about it for Lifetime

Lifetime: ☐ **Not Present** ☐ **Threshold**

D.6b. Other times people might feel really bad when they see or know someone who is hurt or upset or needs help. They feel just as bad, or worse, than that person. Or they feel really horrible if they can't help the other person feel better. Or they worry that it's their fault. Have you felt that way? Who was upset? What did you do? What happened?

_____

_____

_____

_____

☐ YES *(If Yes)* How often did this happen in the past/worst month?

   ☐ Daily or almost daily ☐ 2 - 3 times per week ☐ Once a week or less

☐ NO *(If No)* Have there <u>ever</u> been any serious problems with this?

        ☐ Yes (Lifetime) ☐ No

PASS: ☐ Prefers Not to Answer ☐ Does Not Understand

     (If Pass, move on to conclude interview.)

When you felt really bad for someone who was hurt or upset or needed help…

(Y) (N) Did you give them emotional support?
(Y) (N) Did you feel better if you tried to help?
(Y) (N) Did you wish you could help but not feel guilty if you couldn't make things better?
(Y) (N) Did you think it's too bad they're hurt or need help and hope they will be okay?
(Y) (N) When you felt bad for them were you able to stay calm or to calm down before long?
(Y) (N) Did you feel so bad for them that you broke down and sobbed or cried?
(Y) (N) Did you feel so worried about them that you couldn't think about anything else?
(Y) (N) Did you feel so mad that you wanted to attack the people who were hurting them?
(Y) (N) Were you so upset that you were willing to do almost anything to help them feel better?
(Y) (N) Could you get along with friends, family, and other people at school/in the neighborhood?
(Y) (N) Could you still do activities you usually do, such as school, sports or clubs, or parties?
(Y) (N) Could you still enjoy TV or music?
(Y) (N) Could you sleep okay at night?
(Y) (N) Could you eat okay?

Severity Rating of Symptom for D.6b.

Not Present – Developmentally normative sympathy/compassion for others

Threshold – Intense and developmentally immature sympathetic sense of guilt or responsibility expressed in severe distress or emotionally dysregulated intentions or actions that lead to serious impairment

Past/Worst Month: ☐ Not Present ☐ Threshold

       <u>*NOTE: If symptom not present for Past Month, ask about it for Lifetime*</u>

Lifetime: ☐ Not Present ☐ Threshold

Box 6.7 Case Study: How PTSD Assessment Addresses Risks and Informs Treatment

This is a fictional case study based on some of the author's patients who have been assessed for PTSD. It illustrates the procedures and precautions necessary for PTSD assessment.

Mr. Williams is a 54-year-old African American man who sought treatment for panic attacks and depression at a Medical School community outpatient psychiatry clinic. He is a senior engineer working in the aerospace industry. He been married for 27 years, and he has an adult daughter and an adult son who are married and have children of their own. Mr. Williams described his sister and mother as having needed outpatient treatment for depression and a paternal grandfather who was a problem drinker. He had no previous mental health treatment, was medically healthy, and had no history of head injury, serious past medical illness, suicidality, or substance use problems.

Mr. Williams was making a deposit at his bank 2 months ago when the bank was robbed. Specifically, a noticeably agitated man walked into the bank with a gun and instructed the teller to give him $50,000. Mr. Williams attempted to reason with the robber and keep other customers calm, but the robber became upset and fired his gun, narrowly missing Mr. Williams but hitting another customer. The customer later died from the wounds. After shooting the customer, the armed man had quickly fled the scene and was never apprehended.

Mr. Williams spent 2 weeks on paid administrative leave, which he was instructed to do by his employer. He then returned to work for 4 weeks. Since the attempted robbery, he reported being depressed, feeling jumpy and tense all the time, having serious difficulty sleeping and concentrating, drinking 10–12 beers daily to cope, and going out on sick leave for the past 2 weeks. His wife urged him to get help because his symptoms were worsening. He reluctantly set up an appointment with a clinical psychologist who specialized in the treatment of PTSD.

At his first appointment, Mr. Williams was interviewed in depth about his current and past relationships, personal abilities and problems, educational and work experiences, illnesses, family history of illness, medical or mental treatments, and legal problems or other involvement with the legal system. This information was important in order for the therapist to understand Mr. Williams's overall life situation before evaluating the possible relationship between the recent traumatic event and his current feelings of "depression." He was asked these questions because there was a likely possibility of legal involvement, as the bank was being sued by the customer's family, and because of a possible worker's compensation case for his emotional condition. The psychologist gathered a detailed demographic, educational, employment, social, legal, family, mental health, and medical history.

In that "intake" interview, the TESI-A was used to carefully explore Mr. Williams's recollection of and reactions to the bank robbery, as well as to identify any other traumatic stressors that he had experienced before or since the event. The TESI was explained as questions that would help the evaluator and Mr. Williams to efficiently determine if other stressful experiences had happened to him that might affect how he was reacting to the bank robbery. The evaluator was careful to clarify that having prior stressful events would not mean that the robbery had not caused him distress or that his current emotional problems were "preexisting" disorders. He explained to Mr. Williams that when people experience a series of highly stressful or traumatic events, each new one may have a greater effect because of the buildup of stress reactions from the previous ones and that this was the body's normal, and even healthy, attempt to protect against harm by getting "mobilized for survival." The psychologist compared this to an airplane's wings that are always under stress and must have their structural integrity routinely assessed. By using a metaphor that Mr. Williams could relate to, the evaluator was able to reassure him that the inquiry about his trauma history (and next about any PTSD symptoms) was to diagnose fully the source of his current problems so that the best treatment could be provided, and not to point out any failings on his part or to minimize or discredit the distress he'd been feeling since the robbery.

On the TESI, Mr. Williams described having witnessed his father occasionally hit his mother as a child and of having been severely corporally punished (with a bat) and hit in fits of rage by his father. These incidents involved sufficient force that he and his mother had been knocked to the ground and in some instances had suffered broken bones. He also disclosed that he was afraid that his father would lose control so completely that he could kill one of them, even though this never actually happened. This evidence of physical harm and potential life threat meets PTSD's Criterion A1 for stressors that are objectively traumatic. Mr. Williams also described feeling terrified and helpless most of the times that his father was violent, although he said that he got to the point where he "just didn't care anymore if he kills one of us or not," and later felt "so angry that I grabbed the bat out of my father's hands the last time he tried to hurt her, and by then I was big enough so that he couldn't overpower me. I didn't feel scared anymore after that, but I had to be careful not to lose control, or I could have killed my father when he started to make threats." Mr. Williams thus might appear not to have qualified for PTSD's Criterion A2—subjective feelings of extreme fear, helplessness, or horror—in the last potentially traumatic violent incident with his father, but he clearly experienced subjective traumatic stress in most of the incidents.

Although he had been in motor vehicle accidents and some fistfights as a youth, and he had been scheduled to go to the World Trade Center on business the week after September 11, 2001, Mr. Williams did not describe any other events that met *DSM-IV-TR* criteria for traumatic stressors. When asked, he said that the robbery was more troubling to him currently than his father's abuse and domestic violence, but when memories of the robbery came to mind, he felt as if

(Continued)

Box 6.7 Continued

the robber "changed" and became his father, and then he'd feel almost as frightened as he did when he was a little boy. Mr. Williams was able to recall feeling terrified at first ("When I saw the gun and the crazy look in his eyes, I thought for sure he was going to kill somebody") but then felt unemotional detachment ("Like I was completely calm, and time slowed down so that everything happened in slow motion, and I could step outside my body and watch like it was just a movie"). Upon inquiry, he recalled having similar detached and unreal feelings that were actually quite pleasant in contrast to the earlier feeling of terror as a child when his father was violent. As he had many times after his father's violence, Mr. Williams said that when the robbery was over and he knew he wasn't going to be killed, he had to run to the restroom to vomit. These reactions qualify for PTSD's Criterion A2—subjective terror and horror—and include reactions probably indicative of dissociation. The veracity of Mr. Williams's account of the robbery was easily confirmed by checking newspaper reports of the incident.

The evaluator next used the CAPS to assess Mr. Williams's PTSD symptoms, focusing on his reactions to the recent attempted robbery as well as the additional intensification of these symptoms related to his earlier experiences of abuse and domestic violence. Mr. Williams endorsed three reexperiencing symptoms (intrusive thoughts, nightmares, and flashbacks of the bank robbery as if it was happening all over again; Criterion B), four avoidance and numbing symptoms (persistent avoidance of both thinking about and doing things or going places reminiscent of the robbery, anhedonia (loss of interest in formerly important activities such as his work and recreational activities), and social detachment (feeling emotionally distant from his wife); Criterion C), and three hyperarousal symptoms (difficulty sleeping and concentrating, and hypervigilance; Criterion D). Most symptoms were endorsed as occurring at least several times per week and were sufficiently intense to prevent him from being able to work or socialize. He reported that the symptoms had lasted for nearly 2 months (Criterion E) and that they clearly had disrupted his ability to work (Criterion F). Based on these results, a diagnosis of PTSD, Acute (less than 6 months in duration), was made. Although Mr. Williams described ongoing symptoms of dissociation similar to the dissociative reactions he experienced in the abuse and robbery incidents, he could not be diagnosed with Acute Stress Disorder because the most recent and currently primary traumatic stressor occurred more than 4 weeks before.

Based on the family history and the possibility that Mr. Williams had previously suffered or was currently suffering other psychiatric disorders, particularly depression, dysthymia, or anxiety disorders other than PTSD, Dr. Miller administered the MINI to explore comorbid psychopathology. Based on this interview, Mr. Williams additionally met diagnostic criteria for major depressive disorder, single episode, moderate; and alcohol dependence, without physiological dependence. There was no evidence of any previous occurrence of those disorders, which subsequently was corroborated in an interview with Mrs. Williams (with Mr. Williams's consent and approval). The evaluator asked Mr. Williams to complete two brief questionnaires assessing depression and alcohol use problems, which indicated that he was not suicidal (corroborating the intake interview's intensive questions about suicide, homicide, or self-injury risk as not currently present) and that he was experiencing primarily anxiety-related dysphoria (not a more persistent "vegetative" depression) and using alcohol excessively primarily to cope with these feelings and an inability to sleep.

Finally, because of the forensic implications of this case, the evaluator administered the Structured Interview of Reported Symptoms (SIRS) and MMPI-2. SIRS results demonstrated no significant indication of symptom overreporting. MMPI-2 results demonstrated a clinical profile that was consistent with how Mr. Williams described himself in the interviews and questionnaires. Although the MMPI-2 validity scale scores were outside the normal range ($L = 40$, $F = 85$, $K = 38$), the main potential threat to valid self-reporting was an elevated F score that was not more extreme than has been reported in numerous clinical research studies with people diagnosed with PTSD. An F score higher than normal ($>65/70$) but within three standard deviations of average (<90) has been shown to be suggestive of the extreme anxiety and distress accompanying moderate to severe PTSD.

Based on this assessment, the evaluator proposed a treatment plan beginning with education about PTSD and emotion regulation skills using the TARGET intervention in order to help Mr. Williams gain a greater sense of control over and acceptance of his stress reactions and to develop practical skills for managing stress reactions. Treatment also would use prolonged exposure and cognitive restructuring (PE/CR) to address his immediate traumatic stress reactions related to the recent robbery incident. TARGET and PE/CR also were planned to help Mr. Williams understand his acute dysphoria as an expectable "alarm reaction" and to provide him with skills for improving his mood. Referral to a psychiatrist for an evaluation of the possible benefits of medications that have been found to reduce anxiety and depression symptoms with many persons suffering from PTSD also was discussed with Mr. Williams. After meeting with the psychiatrist, Mr. Williams decided to take an antidepressant medication for a "trial period" of 3 months. With the psychiatrist's guidance, he eventually discontinued the medication because he was no longer experiencing greater than mild and manageable anxiety or depression symptoms.

items from a *DSM-IV* PTSD symptom questionnaire, modified to be answered as "yes" or "no" within the past week. With samples of adults who had experienced a train crash or crime victimization within the past month (on average, 21 days after the index trauma) and a second sample of assault victims identified in emergency department settings and screened 1–3 weeks later, the TSQ was more than 90% accurate in identifying PTSD cases. Carlson (2001) developed the Screen for Posttraumatic Stress Symptoms (SPTSS) as a brief self-report screening instrument for PTSD symptoms using a low reading level and without requiring a specific traumatic event. In a sample of adult psychiatric inpatients, the SPTSS was more than 80% accurate in identifying patients with undiagnosed PTSD. Zimmerman and Mattia (2001) developed a 15-item PTSD screen (PDSQ-P) for their 122-item Psychiatric Diagnostic Screening Questionnaire, and the screen was more than 80% accurate in identifying patients with undiagnosed PTSD.

The briefest PTSD screening questionnaires are two four-item questionnaires. The *DSM-IV* PTSD screen for primary care settings (PC-PTSD; Prins et al., 2003) asks a single question for each of the four factor-analytically derived categories of PTSD symptoms: intrusive reexperiencing, avoidance of trauma reminders, emotional numbing, and hyperarousal. The PC-PTSD was more than 80% accurate in identifying patients with undiagnosed PTSD with primary care (Prins et al., 2003) and addictions treatment (Kimerling, Trafton, & Ngyuen, 2006) patients, and incarcerated men and women (Ford, Trestman, Hogan, & Zhang, 2007; Ford, Trestman, Wiesbrock, & Zhang, 2009). The PC-PTSD is available from the National Center for PTSD (www.ptsd.va.gov), which also is leading the development of an updated version of the screen for *DSM*-5 PTSD.

Conclusion

Assessment of psychological trauma and PTSD must be done accurately and validly in order to enable clinicians to appropriately identify, diagnose, and treat adults and children with PTSD, and enable scientists to conduct research that advances our understanding of the psychosocial and biological impacts of psychological trauma and PTSD. PTSD assessment involves much more than simply asking people whether they have "had a trauma" or if they are suffering from the symptoms of PTSD. Careful thought must go into the exact wording of questions that are intended to elicit the true nature and extent of the respondents' exposure to the many different types of traumatic stressors and the frequency and intensity with which they are now, or have in the past, experienced each of the PTSD symptoms. Many years are required to develop and test the reliability and validity of questionnaires and structured interviews for complex psychological phenomena such as PTSD. The result is a valuable resource that may open the doors to help for tens of thousands of people who have suffered or are still suffering from PTSD, beginning with brief and nonstigmatizing screening instruments that can be administered on a large-scale basis and continuing with more in-depth questionnaire and structured interview assessments of PTSD.

A final caveat regarding assessment of traumatic stressors and PTSD: those who may benefit the most from PTSD screening and assessment are people who are known to have experienced severe traumatic stressors—such as children who receive protective services due to having been abused; women who are extricating themselves from domestically violent relationships; survivors of natural or humanmade disasters who have lost their homes, communities, or loved ones; and emergency first responders and military personnel who deal with death on a regular basis. There is little question that most if not all of these people have experienced psychological trauma; the only question is determining the exact nature of the traumatic stressor experience for each unique person and whether his or her recovery was impeded by PTSD. With this assessment information, treatment (see Chapters 7 and 8) and prevention (see Chapter 9) interventions can be directed in a sensitive and efficient manner to those who need them most.

References

Acierno, R., Kilpatrick, D. G., & Resnick, H. S. (1999). Posttraumatic stress disorder in adults relative to criminal victimization: Prevalence, risk factors, and comorbidity. In P. A. Saigh & J. G. Bremner (Eds.), *Posttraumatic stress disorder: A comprehensive text* (pp. 44–68). Boston, Massachusetts: Allyn and Bacon.

American Psychiatric Association. (2013). *Diagnostic and statistical manual of mental disorders* (5th ed.). Washington, DC: Author.

American Psychological Association. (2014). *Standards for educational and psychological testing*. Washington, DC: Author.

Breslau, N., Peterson, E., Kessler, R., & Schultz, L. (1999). Short screening scale for DSM-IV posttraumatic stress disorder. *American Journal of Psychiatry*, *156*, 908–911.

Brewin, C. R., Rose, S., Andrews, B., Green, J., Tata, P., McEvedy, C., et al. (2002). Brief screening instrument for post-traumatic stress disorder. *British Journal of Psychiatry*, *181*, 158–162.

Briere, J. (1996). *Trauma symptom checklist for children: Professional manual*. Odessa, Florida: Psychological Assessment Resources Inc.

Briere, J. (2004). *Psychological assessment of adult posttraumatic states: Phenomenology, diagnosis, and measurement*. Washington, DC: American Psychological Association.

Briere, J. (2005). *Trauma symptom checklist for young children: Professional manual*. Odessa, Florida: Psychological Assessment Resources Inc.

Briere, J. (2011). *Trauma symptom inventory-2 professional manual*. Odessa, Florida: Psychological Assessment Resources.

Briere, J., Kaltman, S., & Green, B. L. (2008). Accumulated childhood trauma and symptom complexity. *Journal of Traumatic Stress*, *21*, 223–226.

Briere, J., & Spinazzola, J. (2009). Assessment of complex posttramatic reactions. In C. A. Courtois & J. Ford (Eds.), *Treating complex traumatic stress disorders: An evidence-based guide*. New York, New York: Guilford.

Buckner, J. C., Mezzacappa, E., & Beardslee, W. R. (2009). Self-regulation and its relations to adaptive functioning in low income youths. *American Journal of Orthopsychiatry*, *79*(1), 19–30.

Bullock, B. M., & Dishion, T. J. (2007). Family processes and adolescent problem behavior: Integrating relationship narratives into understanding development and change. *Journal of the American Academy of Child and Adolescent Psychiatry*, *46*(3), 396–407.

Butcher, J. N., Graham, J. R., Ben-Porath, Y. S., Tellegen, A., Dahlstrom, W. G., & Kaemmer, B. (2001). *MMPI-2 (Minnesota Multiphasic Personality Inventory-2): Manual for administration, scoring, and interpretation* (Revised ed.). Minneapolis, Minnesota: University of Minnesota Press.

Carlson, E. B. (2001). Psychometric study of a brief screen for PTSD: Assessing the impact of multiple traumatic events. *Assessment, 8,* 431–441. http://dx.doi. org/10.1177/107319110100800408.

Copeland, W., Keeler, G., Angold, A., & Costello, E. J. (2007). Traumatic events and posttraumatic stress in childhood. *Archives of General Psychiatry, 64,* 577–584. http://dx.doi. org/10.1001/archpsyc.64.5.577.

Davidson, J. R. T., Kudler, H. S., & Smith, R. D. (1990). Assessment and pharmacotherapy of posttraumatic stress disorder. In J. E. L. Giller (Ed.), *Biological assessment and treatment of posttraumatic stress disorder* (pp. 205–221). Washington, DC: American Psychiatric Press.

Daviss, W. B., Mooney, D., Racusin, R., Ford, J. D., Fleischer, A., & McHugo, G. (2000). Predicting post-traumatic stress after hospitalization for pediatric injury. *Journal of the American Academy of Child and Adolescent Psychiatry, 39,* 576–583. http://dx.doi. org/10.1097/00004583-200005000-00011.

Demakis, G. J., & Elhai, J. D. (2011). Neuropsychological and psychological aspects of malingered posttraumatic stress disorder. *Psychological Injury and Law, 4,* 24–31. http://dx.doi. org/10.1007/s12207-011-9099-y.

D'Andrea, W., Ford, J., Stolbach, B., Spinazzola, J., & van der Kolk, B. A. (2012). Understanding interpersonal trauma in children: Why we need a developmentally appropriate trauma diagnosis. *American Journal of Orthopsychiatry, 82*(2), 187–200. http://dx.doi. org/10.1111/j.1939-0025.2012.01154.x.

Ehring, T., Klein, B., Clark, D., Foa, E. B., & Ehlers, A. (2007). Screening for posttraumatic stress disorder: What combination of symptoms predicts best? *Journal of Nervous and Mental Disease, 12,* 1004–1012.

Elhai, J. D., & Ford, J. D. (2007). Correlates of mental health service utilization intensity in the National Comorbidity Survey and National Comorbidity Survey Replication. *Psychiatric Services, 58,* 1108–1115.

Elhai, J. D., Ford, J. D., & Naifeh, J. A. (2010). Assessing trauma exposure and posttraumatic morbidity. In G. M. Rosen & B. C. Frueh (Eds.), *Clinician's guide to posttraumatic stress disorder* (pp. 119–151). Hoboken, New Jersey: John Wiley & Sons.

Elhai, J. D., Gray, M. J., Kashdan, T. B., & Franklin, C. L. (2005). Which instruments are most commonly used to assess traumatic event exposure and posttraumatic effects? A survey of traumatic stress professionals. *Journal of Traumatic Stress, 18,* 541–545. http://dx.doi. org/10.1002/jts.20062.

Elhai, J. D., Grubaugh, A. L., Kashdan, T. B., & Frueh, B. C. (2008). Empirical examination of a proposed refinement to DSM-IV posttraumatic stress disorder symptom criteria using the National Comorbidity Survey Replication data. *Journal of Clinical Psychiatry, 69,* 597–602. http://dx.doi.org/10.4088/JCP.v69n0411.

Elhai, J. D., & Naifeh, J. A. (2012). The missing link: A call for more rigorous PTSD assessment procedures. *Clinical Psychology: Science and Practice, 19,* 276–282. http://dx.doi. org/10.1111/cpsp.12005.

First, M. B., Spitzer, R. L., Gibbon, M., & Williams, J. B. (1996). *Structured Clinical Interview for DSM-IV Axis I Disorders, Clinician Version (SCID-CV).* Washington, DC: American Psychiatric Press.

Foa, E. B., Johnson, K. M., Feeny, N. C., & Treadwell, K. R. H. (2001). The Child PTSD Symptom Scale: A preliminary examination of its psychometric properties. *Journal of Clinical Child Psychology, 30,* 376–384. http://dx.doi.org/10.1207/S15374424JCCP3003_9.

Forbes, D. (2008). Minnesota Multiphasic Personality Inventory-2. In G. Reyes, J. D. Elhai, & J. Ford (Eds.), *Encyclopedia of psychological trauma* (pp. 430–433). Hoboken, NJ: Wiley.

Ford, J. D. (2008). Ethnoracial minority background, psychological trauma, and complex post-traumatic stress disorder among urban low-income women with severe mental illness. *Journal of Psychological Trauma*, *7*, 170–184.

Ford, J. D. (2011). Assessing child and adolescent complex traumatic stress reactions. *Journal of Child and Adolescent Trauma*, *4*(3), 217–232.

Ford, J. D. (2012). Posttraumatic stress disorder (PTSD) among youth involved in juvenile justice. In E. Grigorenko (Ed.), *Handbook of juvenile forensic psychology and psychiatry* (pp. 487–503). New York, NY: Springer.

Ford, J. D. (2013a). Posttraumatic stress disorder (PTSD) and substance abuse treatment. In P. Miller (Ed.), *Encyclopedia of addictive behaviors, volume 3. Interventions for addiction* (pp. 187–194). New York, NY: Elsevier.

Ford, J. D. (2013b). Enhancing emotional regulation with complex trauma survivors. In D. Murphy & S. Joseph (Eds.), *Trauma, and the therapeutic relationship* (pp. 58–77). New York, NY: Palgrave MacMillan.

Ford, J. D., Blaustein, M., Habib, M., & Kagan, R. (2013). Developmental trauma-focused treatment models. In J. D. Ford & C. A. Courtois (Eds.), *Treating complex traumatic stress disorders in children and adolescents: Scientific foundations and therapeutic models* (pp. 261–276). New York, NY: Guilford.

Ford, J. D., & Courtois, C. A. (2014). Complex PTSD, affect dysregulation, and Borderline Personality Disorder. *Borderline Personality Disorder and Emotion Dysregulation*, *1*, 9.

Ford, J. D., & Fournier, D. (2007). Psychological trauma, post-traumatic stress disorder, and health-related functioning among women in community mental health aftercare following psychiatric intensive care. *Journal of Psychiatric Intensive Care*, *3*, 27–34. http://dx.doi.org/10.1017/S1742646407001094.

Ford, J. D., & Gomez, J. M. (2015). Dissociation and posttraumatic stress disorder (PTSD) in non-suicidal self-injury and suicidality: A review. *Journal of Trauma and Dissociation*

Ford, J. D., Grasso, D., Greene, C., Levine, J., Spinazzola, J., & van der Kolk, B. (2013). Clinical significance of a proposed developmental trauma disorder diagnosis: Results of an international survey of clinicians. *Journal of Clinical Psychiatry*, *74*(8), 841–849. http://dx.doi.org/10.4088/JCP.12m08030.

Ford, J. D., Nader, K., & Fletcher, K. (2013). Assessment guidelines and instruments. In J. D. Ford & C. A. Courtois (Eds.), *Treating complex traumatic stress disorders in children and adolescents: An evidence-based guide*. New York, NY: Guilford.

Ford, J. D., Racusin, R., Ellis, C., Daviss, W. B., Reiser, J., Fleischer, A., et al. (2000). Child maltreatment, other trauma exposure, and posttraumatic symptomatology among children with Oppositional Defiant and Attention Deficit Hyperactivity disorders. *Child Maltreatment*, *5*, 205–217.Ford, J. D., et al. (2008). Traumatic victimization, post-traumatic stress disorder, suicidal ideation, and substance abuse risk among juvenile justice-involved youths. *Journal of Child and Adolescent Trauma*, *1*, 75–92. http://dx.doi.org/10.1080/19361520801934456.

Ford, J. D., Spinazzola, J., van der Kolk, B., & Grasso, D. (2014). Developmental Trauma Disorder (DTD) Field Trial: I. Evidence of reliability, structure, and validity of the DTD semi-structured interview (DTD-SI). *Symposium Developmental Trauma Disorder Field Trial: Scientific integrity and clinical utility of a developmentally-informed complex traumatic stress disorder for children*. J. Ford, Chair (11/8/14).

Ford, J. D., Trestman, R. L., Hogan, V., & Zhang, W. (2007). Development and initial validation of a brief screening instrument for newly incarcerated adults. *Assessment*, *14*, 279–299.

Ford, J. D., Trestman, R. L., Wiesbrock, V., & Zhang, W. (2009). Empirical validation of a brief mental health screening instrument for newly incarcerated adults. *Psychiatric Services*, *60*, 842–846.

Frueh, B. C., Elhai, J. D., Grubaugh, A., & Ford, J. D. (2012). *Assessment and treatment planning for PTSD.* Hoboken, NJ: John Wiley & Sons.

Frueh, B. C., Elhai, J. D., & Kaloupek, D. G. (2004). Unresolved issues in the assessment of trauma exposure and posttraumatic reactions. In G. M. Rosen (Ed.), *Posttraumatic stress disorder: Issues and controversies* (pp. 63–84). New York, New York: Wiley.

Goodman, L., Corcoran, C., Turner, K., Yuan, N., & Green, B. L. (1998). Assessing traumatic event exposure: General issues and preliminary findings for the Stressful Life Events Screening Questionnaire. *Journal of Traumatic Stress, 11,* 521–542. http://dx.doi.org/10.1 023/A:1024456713321.

Gray, M. J., Litz, B. T., Wang, J., & Lombardo, T. W. (2004). Psychometric properties of the Life Events Checklist. *Assessment, 11,* 330–341. http://dx.doi.org/10.1177/1073191104269954.

Guriel, J., & Fremouw, W. (2003). Assessing malingered posttraumatic stress disorder: A critical review. *Clinical Psychology Review, 23,* 881–904. http://dx.doi.org/10.1016/j. cpr.2003.07.001.

Haro, J. M., Arbabzadeh-Bouchez, S., Brugha, T. S., De Girolamo, G., Guyer, M. E., Jin, R., et al. (2006). Concordance of the Composite International Diagnostic Interview Version 3.0 (CIDI 3.0) with standardized clinical assessments in the WHO World Mental Health Surveys. *International Journal of Methods in Psychiatric Research, 15,* 167–180. http:// dx.doi.org/10.1002/mpr.196.

Harvey, M. (1996). An ecological view of psychological trauma and trauma recovery. *Journal of Traumatic Stress, 9,* 3–23. http://dx.doi.org/10.1002/jts.2490090103.

Josephson, A. M., & The AACAP Work Group on Quality Issues. (2007). Practice parameter for the assessment of the family. *Journal of the American Academy of Child and Adolescent Psychiatry, 46,* 922–937.

Keane, T. M., Brief, D. J., Pratt, E. M., & Miller, M. W. (2007). Assessment of PTSD and its comorbidities in adults. In M. J. Friedman, T. M. Keane, & P. Resick (Eds.), *Handbook of PTSD: Science and practice* (pp. 279–305). New York: Guilford.

Keane, T. M., Caddell, J. M., & Taylor, K. L. (1988). Mississippi Scale for Combat-Related Posttraumatic Stress Disorder: Three studies in reliability and validity. *Journal of Consulting and Clinical Psychology, 56,* 85–90. http://dx.doi.org/10.1037/0022-006X.56.1.85.

Kessler, R. C., Sonnega, A., Bromet, E., Hughes, M., & Nelson, C. B. (1995). Posttraumatic stress disorder in the National Comorbidity Survey. *Archives of General Psychiatry, 52,* 1048–1060.

Kim, S. H., & Hamann, S. (2007). Neural correlates of positive and negative emotion regulation. *Journal of Cognitive Neuroscience, 19*(5), 776–798.

Kimerling, R., Trafton, J., & Ngyuen, B. (2006). Validation of a brief screen for post-traumatic stress disorder with substance use disorder patients. *Addictive Behaviors, 31,* 2074–2079. http://dx.doi.org/10.1016/j.addbeh.2006.02.008.

King, D., & King, L. (2008). Research methodology. In G. Reyes, J. D. Elhai, & J. Ford (Eds.), *Encyclopedia of psychological trauma* (pp. 575–584). Hoboken, NJ: Wiley.

Ko, S., Ford, J. D., Kassam-Adams, N., Berkowitz, S., Saunders, B., Smith, D., et al. (2008). Creating trauma-informed child-serving systems. *Professional Psychology, 39,* 396–404.

Kubany, E. S., Haynes, S. N., Leisen, M. B., Owens, J. A., Kaplan, A. S., Watson, S. B., et al. (2000). Development and preliminary validation of a brief broad-spectrum measure of trauma exposure: The Traumatic Life Events Questionnaire. *Psychological Assessment, 12,* 210–224. http://dx.doi.org/10.1037/1040-3590.12.2.210.

Lang, A. J., & Stein, M. B. (2005). An abbreviated PTSD checklist for use as a screening instrument in primary care. *Behaviour Research and Therapy, 43,* 585–594. http://dx.doi. org/10.1016/j.brat.2004.04.005.

Lauterbach, D., & Vrana, S. (2001). The relationship among personality variables, exposure to traumatic events, and severity of posttraumatic stress symptoms. *Journal of Traumatic Stress*, *14*, 29–45.

Long, M. E., & Elhai, J. D. (2008). Posttraumatic stress disorder symptom scale. In G. Reyes, J. D. Elhai, & J. D. Ford (Eds.), *Encyclopedia of psychological trauma* (pp. 501). Hoboken, New Jersey: John Wiley & Sons.

Long, M. E., Elhai, J. D., Schweinle, A., Gray, M. J., Grubaugh, A. L., & Frueh, B. C. (2008). Differences in posttraumatic stress disorder diagnostic rates and symptoms severity between Criterion A1 and non-Criterion A1 stressors. *Journal of Anxiety Disorders*, *22*, 1255–1263. http://dx.doi.org/10.1016/j.janxdis.2008.01.006.

McLaughlin, K. A., Koenen, K. C., Hill, E. D., Petukhova, M., Sampson, N. A., Zaslavsky, A. M., et al. (2013). Trauma exposure and posttraumatic stress disorder in a national sample of adolescents. *Journal of the American Academy of Child and Adolescent Psychiatry*, *52*(8) 815–830.e814 http://dx.doi.org/10.1016/j.jaac.2013.05.011.

McLeer, S., Deblinger, E., Henry, D., & Orvaschel, H. (1992). Sexually abused children at high risk for posttraumatic stress disorder. *Journal of the American Academy of Child and Adolescent Psychiatry*, *31*, 876–879. http://dx.doi.org/10.1097/00004583-199209000-00015.

Mueser, T., Rosenberg, S. D., Fox, L., Salyers, M. P., Ford, J. D., & Carty, P. (2001). Psychometric evaluation of trauma and posttraumatic stress disorder assessments in persons with severe mental illness. *Psychological Assessment*, *13*, 110–117. http://dx.doi. org/10.1037/1040-3590.13.1.110.

Nader, K. (2008). *Understanding and assessing trauma in children and adolescents*. New York, NY: Routledge.

Newman, E., & Kaloupek, D. G. (2004). The risks and benefits of participating in trauma-focused research studies. *Journal of Traumatic Stress*, *17*, 383–394. http://dx.doi.org/10.1023/B:J OTS.0000048951.02568.3a.

Norris, F. (2008). Mississippi civilian scale for PTSD—revised. In G. Reyes, J. D. Elhai, & J. D. Ford (Eds.), *Encyclopedia of psychological trauma* (pp. 433). Hoboken, NJ: John Wiley & Sons.

Norris, F. H. (1990). Screening for traumatic stress: A scale for use in the general population. *Journal of Applied Social Psychology*, *20*, 1704–1718. http://dx.doi.org/10.1111/j.1559-1816.1990. tb01505.x.

Prins, A., Ouimette, P., Kimerling, R., Cameron, R., Hugelshofer, D., Shaw-Hegwer, J., et al. (2003). The Primary Care PTSD Screen (PC-PTSD): Development and operating characteristics. *Primary Care Psychiatry*, *9*, 9–14. http://dx.doi.org/10.1185/135525703125002360.

Reich, W. (2000). Diagnostic Interview for Children and Adolescents (DICA). *Journal of the American Academy of Child and Adolescent Psychiatry*, *39*, 59–66. http://dx.doi. org/10.1097/00004583-200001000-00017.

Rosen, G. M., & Taylor, S. (2007). Pseudo-PTSD. *Journal of Anxiety Disorders*, *21*, 201–210.

Saigh, P., Yaski, A. E., Oberfield, R. A., Green, B. L., Halamandaris, P. V., Rubenstein, H., et al. (2000). The Children's PTSD Inventory: Development and reliability. *Journal of Traumatic Stress*, *30*, 369–380. http://dx.doi.org/10.1023/A:1007750021626.

Scher, C. D., Stein, M. B., Asmundson, G. J. G., McCreary, D. R., & Forde, D. R. (2001). The Childhood Trauma Questionnaire in a community sample: Psychometric properties and normative data. *Journal of Traumatic Stress*, *14*, 843–857. http://dx.doi.org/10.102 3/A:1013058625719.

Shaffer, D., Fisher, P., Lucas, C., Dulcan, M., & Schwab-Stone, M. (2000). NIMH Diagnostic Interview Schedule for Children version IV (NIMH DISC-IV): Description, differences from previous versions, and reliability of some common diagnoses. *Journal of the American Academy of Child and Adolescent Psychiatry, 39*, 28–38. http://dx.doi. org/10.1097/00004583-200001000-00014.

Sheehan, D. V., Lecrubier, Y., Sheehan, K. H., Amorim, P., Janavs, J., Weiller, E., et al. (1998). The Mini-International Neuropsychiatric Interview (MINI): The development and validation of a structured diagnostic psychiatric interview for DSM-IV and ICD-10. *Journal of Clinical Psychiatry, 59*(Suppl. 20), 22–33.

Straus, M. A. (2012). Blaming the messenger for the bad news about partner violence by women: The methodological, theoretical, and value basis of the purported invalidity of the conflict tactics scales. *Behavioral Sciences & the Law, 30*(5), 538–556. http://dx.doi. org/10.1002/bsl.2023.

Straus, M. A., Hamby, S. L., Boney-McCoy, S., & Sugarman, D. B. (1996). The revised Conflict Tactics Scales (CTS2): Development and preliminary psychometric data. *Journal of Family Issues, 17*, 283–316.

Van der Kolk, B., Ford, J. D., & Spinazzola, J. (2014). Developmental Trauma Disorder (DTD) Field Trial Outcomes: III. Differential comorbidity of DTD and PTSD. *Symposium Developmental Trauma Disorder Field Trial: Scientific integrity and clinical utility of a developmentally-informed complex traumatic stress disorder for children*. J. Ford, Chair (11/8/14).

van der Kolk, B. A. (2005). Developmental trauma disorder: Toward a rational diagnosis for children with complex trauma histories. *Psychiatric Annals, 35*(5), 401–408.

Weathers, F. (2008). Posttraumatic stress disorder checklist. In G. Reyes, J. D. Elhai, & J. Ford (Eds.), *Encyclopedia of psychological trauma* (pp. 491–494). Hoboken NJ: Wiley.

Weathers, F. W., Blake, D. D., Schnurr, P. P., Kaloupek, D. G., Marx, B. P., & Keane, T. M. (2013). *The Clinician-Administered PTSD Scale for DSM-5 (CAPS-5)*. Interview available from the National Center for PTSD at <www.ptsd.va.gov>.

Weathers, F. W., Keane, T. M., & Davidson, J. R. (2001). Clinician-administered PTSD scale: A review of the first ten years of research. *Depression and Anxiety, 13*, 132–156. http:// dx.doi.org/10.1002/da.1029.

Wittchen, H. U., Gloster, A., Beesdo, K., Schonfeld, S., & Perkonigg, A. (2009). Posttraumatic stress disorder: Diagnostic and epidemiological perspectives. *CNS Spectrums, 14*(1 Suppl. 1), 5–12.

Wolpaw, J., Ford, J. D., Newman, E., Davis, J. L., & Briere, J. (2005). Trauma symptom checklist for children. In T. Grisso, G. Vincent, & D. Seagrave (Eds.), *Mental health screening and assessment in juvenile justice* (pp. 152–165). New York: Guilford.

Zajac, K., Ruggiero, K. J., Smith, D. W., Saunders, B. E., & Kilpatrick, D. G. (2011). Adolescent distress in traumatic stress research: Data from the National Survey of Adolescents-Replication. *Journal of Traumatic Stress, 24*(2), 226–229.

Zimmerman, M., & Mattia, J. I. (2001). The Psychiatric Diagnostic Screening Questionnaire: Development, reliability and validity. *Comprehensive Psychiatry, 42*, 175–189. http:// dx.doi.org/10.1053/comp.2001.23126.

Treatment of adults with PTSD

Posttraumatic stress disorder (PTSD) can be successfully treated, and it may even be preventable (see Chapter 9). Once PTSD has developed, two basic approaches have proven the best to address the needs and circumstances of the person seeking help. Psychotherapy is the best-researched treatment approach for PTSD, for adults as well as children (see Chapter 8). Pharmacotherapy—the use of therapeutic medications—is the other major approach for PTSD treatment (Bernardy & Friedman, 2015; Friedman & Davidson, 2014; Opler, Grennan, & Ford, 2009). Pharmacotherapy involves medicines prescribed by a medical doctor/psychiatrist or a specially qualified advanced practice nurse or psychologist. Medications that originally were used to treat depression, other anxiety disorders, seizure disorders, and medical conditions such as hypertension have shown promise in the treatment of adults with PTSD. In this chapter, we summarize the results of a number of randomized clinical trials (RCTs; scientifically rigorous research studies) that have been conducted to test the efficacy (the ability to achieve definite positive results) of approaches to psychotherapy and pharmacotherapy for PTSD (Box 7.1).

At the present time, the spectrum of evidence-based (i.e., having scientifically tested efficacy) PTSD treatments for adults is ever-broadening. There are a number of *trauma-focused psychotherapies* such as cognitive and behavioral therapies, emotion and interpersonal regulation therapies, psychodynamic and experiential therapies, marital and family therapies, and group therapies (Courtois & Ford, 2009, 2013). In addition, there are innovative variations to trauma-focused psychotherapies such as enhancement with computer-generated three-dimensional virtual reality (VR; Motraghi, Seim, Meyer, & Morissette, 2014; Rothbaum et al., 2014), neurofeedback to stimulate distinctive patterns of brain activity (Kluetsch et al., 2014).

As noted by McLean and Foa (2013) in a recent review on the topics of the diagnosis of PTSD and treatment with evidence-based treatments, new information about the effectiveness and the choice of trauma-focused treatments is being released all the time. To date, CBTs such as Prolonged Exposure therapy (PE), Cognitive Processing Therapy (CPT), Narrative Exposure Therapy (NET), and Eye Movement Desensitization and Reprocessing therapy (EMDR) have the strongest scientific evidence of efficacy—that is, research showing that the treatment is directly responsible for improvements in or recovery from PTSD. However, no one size fits all, and there is growing evidence that other psychotherapy approaches may be effective for (and in some cases, equally or better accepted by) persons of different backgrounds and circumstances who are seeking help for PTSD.

In addition to the many different specific methods of psychotherapy for PTSD, there are core treatment goals and practices that both clinicians and researchers have found to

Posttraumatic Stress Disorder. DOI: http://dx.doi.org/10.1016/B978-0-12-801288-8.00007-8

Box 7.1 Key Points

1. The spectrum of PTSD psychotherapies for adults is broad, including those with the strongest evidence base, cognitive behavior therapies (CBTs), and PTSD affect and interpersonal regulation (PAIR) therapies, as well as hypnotherapy, experiential and psychodynamic therapies, body and movement therapies, marital and family therapies, group therapies, and pharmacotherapy (medications).

2. Across all types of PTSD treatment for adults, a three-phase approach (of shorter or longer duration, depending on the needs and resources of the client) is the most standard, with each phase focused on a core treatment goal: (i) safety and preparation for therapy; (ii) modifying traumatic stress reactions, often (but not always) by a therapeutic reexamination of memories of specific traumatic experiences; and (iii) regaining or acquiring a productive and rewarding life by overcoming or managing PTSD symptoms.

3. The primary goal of PTSD treatment for adults is to reduce the intensity and frequency of PTSD symptoms to a level that is no longer troubling or is manageable (i.e., to no longer have the diagnosis). When other symptoms or disorders (such as depression or substance abuse) co-occur with PTSD, they also must be reduced or managed because improvements in PTSD are likely to be lost in conditions of psychological instability caused by other disorders. PTSD treatment also should enhance the person's social and emotion regulation skills and support personal effectiveness. Because there are differences in each person's capacities to engage in therapy and to tolerate and benefit from the emotional intensity of PTSD therapy, it is important to gauge the success of treatment according to goals that are achievable for each unique client and to collaboratively determine these goals.

4. Since 2000, a number of formal guidelines for adults with PTSD based on research findings (evidence-based treatments) have been published, including by the International Society for Traumatic Stress Studies (ISTSS), the US Department of Veterans Affairs, the American Psychiatric Association, the Institute of Medicine of the National Academies, the British National Institute for Clinical Excellence, the Northern Ireland Health Service, and the Australian Centre for Posttraumatic Mental Health.

5. The CBT approach to psychotherapy has strong scientific evidence of efficacy for the treatment of PTSD—that is, research showing that the treatment is directly responsible for improvements in the disease condition. The three principal components in CBT for PTSD are (i) education about PTSD and training in skills for managing stress reactions ("anxiety management" or "stress inoculation" training), (ii) therapist-guided recollection of specific past traumatic experiences (PE), and (iii) training in skills for modifying stress-related thoughts ("cognitive restructuring, CR").

6. Extensions of CBT for PTSD have been developed that address self-regulation problems such as emotional instability, impulsivity, anger and aggression, self-harm, and suicidality and are gathering consistent research support. These PAIR therapies have shown promise in addressing the complex problems of adults who have substance use disorders (SUDs) or borderline personality disorder (BPD) in combination with PTSD.

7. Group psychotherapy has been widely used clinically for adults with PTSD and appears to be promising as a method for conducting PE/CR with military veterans with PTSD. Pharmacotherapy involving medications originally developed to treat depression, anxiety, hypertension, and seizure disorders has been found to be associated with positive outcomes for adults with PTSD, with the strongest evidence for two antidepressant medications (sertraline and paroxetine) and an antihypertensive (prazosin). Medicines such as D-cycloserine have been investigated for use in enhancing exposure therapy for PTSD.

contribute to the successful resolution of PTSD. Therefore, before we discuss specific treatment methodologies, we first examine the fundamentals of PTSD treatment that form the foundation for all approaches to psychotherapy and pharmacotherapy for PTSD.

Best practice principles in the treatment of PTSD

The first principle of all therapeutic interventions is *primum non nocere* (translated from Latin, "first do no harm"). *Personal and interpersonal safety is an essential condition for successful treatment of PTSD*. Ensuring that clients are safe, in their lives as well as in therapy, to the fullest extent possible takes time and careful attention. Some clients with PTSD have lived and continue to live in conditions of danger or chaos that constantly threaten their safety (such as domestic or community violence). Others are involved in lifestyles or repetitive behaviors that place them at high risk for harm (such as due to persistent self-injury, suicidality, addictions, prostitution, or risk-taking). These conditions may become so second nature to them that they may seem "normal" (or unavoidable). When a therapist pays attention to and seeks to help the client to reduce these threats to safety, it may seem to the client that the therapist is being unrealistic due to not understanding or fully appreciating her or his life circumstances. Despite this, a first order of treatment is to help the client to (re-) consider the possibility that safety could be achieved and to help the client to establish conditions of safety to the fullest extent possible under the circumstances. If the client continues to be in a situation that is not safe (such as ongoing domestic violence, incest, sexual harassment, war, or political repression), the therapist should focus almost entirely on developing safety plans and should not move beyond the initial assessment and stabilization stage of treatment until the client's actual life circumstances can be made safe enough that further victimization and retraumatization are not imminent (http://www.nationalcenterdvtraumamh.org/wp-content/uploads/2013/03/NCDVTMH_EBPLitReview2013.pdf. Accessed 4/14/15).

The second key principle of PTSD treatment is that the therapy must enhance the client's ability to manage extreme bodily states at both ends of the spectrum from high arousal to being completely detached and shut down. As discussed in previous chapters, PTSD is characterized by alternating states of *hyper*arousal (such as panic, terror, impulsive risk-taking, rage, or addictive cravings) and *hypo*arousal (such as emotional and physical numbness, spiritual and interpersonal alienation, dissociation, or feeling utterly defeated and hopeless). All PTSD psychotherapies must help patients to recognize their physical state of hyper- or hypoarousal and teach skills for reducing and increasing arousal in order to achieve a midlevel or "window" of optimum tolerance (neither too much nor too little) of bodily and emotional arousal (Fosha, Paivio, Gleiser, & Ford, 2009; Ogden, Pain, & Fisher, 2006; Siegel, 2007). This may be done, for example, with anxiety management skills such as focused breathing or progressive muscle relaxation (PMR), mindfulness meditation practices, or emotion regulation and/or bodily awareness techniques. Learning to modulate (i.e., to adjust levels of) arousal is a prerequisite to being able to manage stress reactions sufficiently to be able to deal with day-to-day stressors, as well as to constructively and therapeutically face and come to terms with traumatic memories.

The third principle of PTSD treatment is that it must enhance the client's ability to approach and gain mastery, rather than avoid or shut off awareness, of internal bodily/ affective states and external events that trigger PTSD symptoms. Avoidance (and dissociation, a process that is a form of avoidance that is automatic and occurs without conscious intention on the part of the individual) is a hallmark of traumatic stress disorders. Resolving avoidance is a benchmark for successful PTSD treatment (Foa et al., 1999), as is enabling the client to regain conscious awareness when dissociation is a problem (van der Hart, Nijenhuis, & Steele, 2006). However, avoidance in PTSD initially is driven by a healthy motivation to not become overwhelmed when confronted by traumatic experiences. Avoidance thus must be understood in therapy as a reaction that is very difficult to stop, because it was adaptive for survival and may seem necessary to the client in order to not become overwhelmed by PTSD symptoms even when traumatic events no longer are placing her or his survival in jeopardy. Both conscious and unconscious forms of avoidance and dissociation become problematic when they develop into inflexible or automatic reactions that then generalize to other activities and behavior, causing emotional, relational, and behavioral constriction. A fundamental challenge, beginning in Phase 1 of PTSD treatment and continuing throughout all phases of treatment, is to enhance clients' awareness of both subtle and obvious forms of avoidance or dissociation s and to help them become aware of signs that they are safe enough to be able to pay attention to and handle upsetting reminders of past traumatic experiences.

A fourth key principle of PTSD treatment is to provide clients with useful new information as soon as possible and to continue to add to and reinforce this education throughout the therapy in order to enable them to understand PTSD and the recovery process in a way that engages their active participation and empowers them to take charge of their life. PTSD is a condition in which the individual perceives herself or himself as having become powerless and ineffective as a result of traumatic events that were (or seemed at the time to be) inescapable and uncontrollable. Therapeutic education validates the reality of these emotional reactions to traumatic events, while simultaneously helping the client to gain the knowledge and understanding that is necessary in order to (re)gain the power that comes from confidence in herself or himself and trustworthy other person—while recognizing that it also was understandable that she or he was actually (or felt) powerless in past traumatic experiences. This type of therapeutic education can demystify both the symptoms of PTSD and the process of psychotherapy and recovery from PTSD. Education about traumatic stress reactions and PTSD seeks to extend clients' understanding of the connection between experiences of traumatic stressors (whether in the more recent or distant past) and the development of symptoms of PTSD. It further aims to help clients understand and accept their own reactions as expectable and in important ways actually adaptive and at times even admirable, in the face of the complex, highly demanding, and abnormal circumstances created by traumatic events. Thus, therapeutic education does not "correct" the client's misunderstanding or "instruct" the client on how to better handle past traumatic experiences or current PTSD symptoms. Instead, therapeutic education enables the client to gain a fuller understanding of how she or he adapted to survive traumatic experiences and how those necessary adaptations can become PTSD symptoms now that they no longer are needed—or are not needed to the degree or constancy with which they have habitually become manifested—because survival is no longer at stake. Therapeutic education is designed to foster client self-understanding, realistic self-confidence, and self-compassion. Education thus lays the foundation for clients to learn and apply specific skills as therapy proceeds, in order to become able to manage and overcome PTSD symptoms.

The fifth principle of PTSD treatment is that the therapist must gain sufficient accurate information about the client in order to provide the client with guidance based upon respect for who the client is as a person; what the client values and believes in based on her or his formative family, cultural, and community experiences; and what the client has experienced that necessitated the survival adaptations that have become PTSD symptoms. As discussed in Chapter 6, this requires a thorough and sensitive assessment that involves learning from, as well as about, the client. In order for the therapist to achieve the other core goals of PTSD treatment, the assessment may also involve (with the adult client's consent) input from other key people in the client's life, records documenting the client's health and health care, achievements and problems in education and work, and legal or financial status. This information is used not simply to categorize whether the client has a PTSD diagnosis and needs treatment but to provide the therapist and client with a broader and deeper understanding of how surviving traumatic events has altered the client's life path (which may include symptoms of comorbid disorders as well as PTSD) and the strengths and personal characteristics that the client can draw upon to find a new (or regain a past) path that is safe, meaningful, and true to her or his values and identity.

The sixth principle of PTSD treatment is that every decision is made collaboratively, with neither the therapist nor the client making important choices about how the therapy shall proceed without reaching a shared consensus that honors the client's personal integrity and autonomy and the therapist's professional expertise and values. The client ultimately is the expert, and therefore the sole arbiter of all decisions regarding her or his life. Although the therapist can provide new knowledge and perspectives to inform the client's life choices, it is not within the purview of the therapist to make those choices for any client. By the same token, although the therapist has unique expertise about the nature of PTSD and the process of recovering from PTSD, the client also is an expert about her or his own life and therefore must have meaningful input into decisions regarding the treatment based upon her or his preferences, values, and cultural and spiritual beliefs. Whatever course the therapist recommends for PTSD treatment must therefore be informed by the input of both client and therapist.

The seventh principle of PTSD treatment is that treatment always follows a sequence of three-phases (Herman, 1992). Exactly how long each phase takes and the specific techniques utilized vary, depending on the needs and circumstances of each individual client and the therapeutic method being applied. However, the three phases are universal because each phase addresses an essential treatment goal.

1. The first phase of treatment focuses on safety, education, assessment, and treatment planning in order to accomplish the goal of enabling the client to achieve sufficient stability in her or his life to be able to fully engage in and benefit from treatment.
2. The second phase of treatment continues all of these foundational activities but also adds an important new dimension: trauma processing, which involves helping the client to shift from

avoiding awareness of traumatic memories and PTSD symptoms to becoming intentionally aware and (re)gaining a sense of self-confidence and empowerment.

3. The third phase of PTSD treatment continues the activities of the first two phases, with the addition of helping the client to apply her or his new knowledge and skills to (re)building a satisfying and successful (based on the client's personal standards and values) life—including healthy and fulfilling relationships, success in work or school, and meaningful personal and spiritual activities (Cloitre et al., 2011; Courtois & Ford, 2013; Ford & Courtois, 2009, 2013; Foa, Keane, Friedman, & Cohen, 2009).

In addition to the three-phase model proposed by Herman, the Stages of Change model proposed by Prochaska and DiClemente (1992) is useful in assessment and as an explanation for the client. Readiness to engage and motivation are important determinants of change; therapeutic gain therefore is dependent on the client's degree of motivation and effort. Motivational Enhancement Therapy (Miller & Rollnick, 2009), Dialectical Behavior Therapy (DBT; Harned, Korslund, Foa, & Linehan, 2012; Harned, Korslund, & Linehan, 2014; Linehan, 1993), and Acceptance and Commitment Therapy (ACT; Hayes, Luoma, Bond, Masuda, & Lillis, 2006) are models of psychotherapy originally developed for clients dealing with problems other than (but often comorbid with PTSD)—such as addictions, self-harm, and severe mental illness—by designed to enhancing clients' sense of autonomy, ability to manage extreme emotion states, and acceptance of the need for change and commitment to making changes. Although these treatments substantially differ from one another, they also have commonalities, such as an emphasis on increasing mindfulness, self-determination and self-management (empowerment), and self-regulation and interpersonal skills (Box 7.2).

Phases of therapy for PTSD

Phase 1. The first phase often is the longest portion of PTSD treatment and always the foundation for its success. At the outset, the therapist must explain how treatment will proceed and the client's rights and responsibilities in order to obtain a truly informed consent from the client to undergo the treatment (Box 7.3). This is the beginning of teaching not only about traumatic stress and PTSD but also what psychotherapy is about and how to participate most successfully and collaboratively.

Box 7.2 Informed Consent (and Refusal) for Trauma-Focused Treatment for PTSD

At the outset of therapy for PTSD, informed consent/refusal for participation in treatment is necessary for every client. Informed consent includes an explanation of protection of the client's privacy ("confidentiality" of personal information), which is the client's right (called "privilege," meaning that clients legally have control over what information is given by the therapist and to whom, with certain exceptions). The exceptions to confidentiality and to the client's privilege involve situations where "mandated reporting" is a legal requirement. This is particularly relevant in many PTSD cases, because the "mandate" is a requirement that therapists "report" (i.e., disclose) to proper authorities (usually state agencies responsible for protecting the safety and rights of people, such as the police and the public child protective services agency) any information that indicates that a vulnerable individual may be in serious danger. The most common example of mandated reporting is when a therapist learns that a child has been and may still be in danger of being physically or sexually abused or severely neglected. These cases are more common when children are in treatment (see Chapter 8), but they may occur with adults who reveal that they were abused or neglected as a child or that their child or a child they know is potentially being abused or severely neglected currently. In many states, therapists also are required ("mandated") legally to report situations in which they have reason to believe that an older adult is being physically harmed or is in life-threatening danger as the result of actions or neglect by persons responsible for their safety or care ("elder abuse").

Abuse, severe neglect, and the threat of being severely harmed or killed are likely in and of themselves to be psychologically traumatic, and the remedies for these dangers (typically an investigation by law enforcement or child welfare organizations) can be frightening despite their goal of protecting people from harm. Thus, when mandated reporting is necessary, traumatic stressors may be causing additional acute psychological stress that must be dealt with in the treatment process along with the issues that may originally have led the client to seek treatment in the first place.

Box 7.3 Everything You Wanted to Know About PTSD But Were Afraid to Ask

Educating clients at the beginning of psychotherapy for PTSD

Teaching clients about the effects of experiencing (directly or vicariously or witnessing) traumatic stressors, including PTSD, can be done in many ways. Most often, a description of the types of events that often are traumatic stressors is provided (such as the descriptions in the Traumatic Events Screening Inventory; see Chapter 6), followed by a review of the 20 symptoms that are included in the diagnosis of PTSD (such as the descriptions in the PTSD Checklist; see Chapter 6). It is very helpful for clients to know how therapists define traumatic stressors and PTSD in order to "demystify" these technical terms (which are commonly used but rarely well understood, even by professionals).

In addition, it can be helpful to teach clients about the changes in the body, emotions, and thought processes that occur as *adaptive* acute responses (i.e., beneficial ways of coping with) to traumatic stressors, and how and why these stress reactions can become chronic problems in the form of PTSD. This can help clients to feel more hopeful about benefiting from therapy, especially when the education includes explanations of how therapy can increase one's ability to overcome or manage PTSD symptoms. For example, Figure 7.1 is excerpted from the Trauma Affect Regulation: Guide for Education and Therapy (TARGET©) psychotherapy model for PTSD (Ford, 2015) (Figure 7.1).

(Continued)

Box 7.3 Continued

Normal Stress: The Brain and Body Working Together

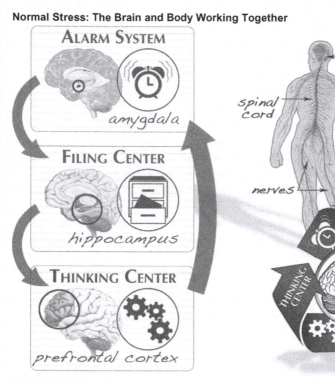

ALARM System
- Sends warning signal of potential problem
- Signals need for self-protection

FILING CENTER
- Organizes and files new information from the senses and the environment
- Accesses memory

THINKING CENTER
- Analyzes information
- Creates solutions
- Sends calming message to **ALARM**

Autonomic Nervous System
- Automatically creates right balance of arousal and calmness (accelerator/brake).

Figure 7.1 Understanding posttraumatic stress: TARGET© Education Sample. PTSD is the result of a healthy brain getting stuck in ALARM mode after ("post") a person faces extreme danger or injury (traumatic stress). The brain tries to protect you when you experience severe danger by staying highly alert and ready to deal automatically with any threat to your survival. PTSD happens when the brain gets stuck in survival or ALARM mode and this interferes with doing the ordinary things that we count upon our brain to do, like managing emotions, thinking clearly, and getting along with other people. So preventing or recovering from PTSD means helping the brain to shift out of ALARM mode and back to information processing, thinking, and taking charge of ordinary living. It means getting the THINKING CENTER back into action so you are not being automatically controlled by your ALARM System. The skills in TARGET are designed for that purpose.

Extreme Stress: The ALARM Takes Control

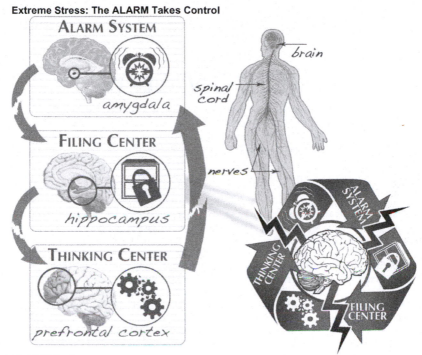

ALARM System
- Signals a crisis/emergency
- Goes on red alert to survive danger

FILING CENTER
- Slows down/becomes disorganized
- Fails to file incoming information
- Gets shut out of the decision-making process
- **THINKING CENTER**
- Shuts down normal thinking/problem-solving process
- Relies on automatic survival-related beliefs
- Gets shut out of the decision-making process

Autonomic Nervous System
- Goes into "**ALARM** Mode"
- Gets super-activated or shuts down

Figure 7.1 (Continued) Re-setting the alarm when it's stuck in survival mode doesn't happen by simply trying to "relax" or "calm down." However, it is possible to reset the ALARM system by using the THINKING CENTER in some ways that anyone can learn. If someone is routinely operating in survival mode and having extreme stress reactions, the one thing that can help is turning down the ALARM. To do this you have to turn on the THINKING CENTER so that it can make adjustments to the FILING SYSTEM; these adjustments actually turn down the ALARM. This takes specific skills that enable the THINKING CENTER to become focused so that information processing and affect regulation shift from being on automatic pilot to once again being guided by the THINKING CENTER.

(Continued)

Box 7.3 Continued

FREEDOM Steps

TARGET teaches a sequence of seven (7) skills described by the mnemonic FREEDOM. Each skill is designed to engage the THINKING CENTER and the Filing System in the brain, in order to directly counteract the bodily reactivity, mental confusion, emotional distress, and social isolation caused by an ALARM Center that is stuck in emergency/survival mode (PTSD).

Focus

Being focused helps you pay attention and think about what you know from your past experience that can help you figure out what's happening and what's most important to you instead of just reacting based on ALARM signals tied to past trauma. When you sweep your mind clear and focus on one thought that reminds you of who you are and what you value and believe, you are using your THINKING CENTER to guide you in deciding what you want to pay attention to. Then when you heighten your mental focus by concentrating on a single thought that you choose because it represents what is most important to you at this moment based on your core values, you're creating files of information in your FILING CENTER that help you pay attention to and remember what gives your life meaning and hope right now, instead of only creating and accessing the "ALARM" files that are about past danger and harm. Then you can mentally mark those new memory files by rating your Stress Level and your Personal Control Level using a quick and simple 10-point numerical rating scale. By carefully applying those three simple steps—which the TARGET model calls the "S-O-S"—you are mentally focused.

RECOGNIZE Triggers

Triggers are reminders of intensely negative experiences in the past. If you know specifically what Triggers set off your ALARM, this can help you prepare for and manage ALARM reactions. Most Triggers are not really a signal of life-or-death threats, but may be interpreted as such by a person's ALARM System. A Trigger can seem like an emergency to the ALARM System unless the THINKING CENTER is used to change the file in the brain from "horrible emergency" to "manageable stress." If you recognize Triggers in advance you are activating your THINKING CENTER and preparing your FILING CENTER to catch future ALARM reactions. This allows you to refile the information in categories that are helpful, such as *something that upsets me because it's a reminder of the past, but I can handle it now,* rather than based on the ALARM, such as "something too upsetting for me to handle" or "something that takes away all my personal control." Recognizing Triggers enables you to anticipate and reset ALARM signals as you learn to distinguish between a *real threat* and a *reminder*.

EMOTION Self-Check

Emotions come together in an area of the brain's THINKING CENTER that specializes in motivating us with positive emotions and guiding us to make changes with negative emotions. When the brain is in ALARM mode, negative emotions are dominant in both the THINKING CENTER and the FILING CENTER. As a result, positive emotions are not sufficiently available to help us feel hopeful and able to manage life. The purpose of identifying emotions is to jump-start the THINKING CENTER so the negative emotions produced by the ALARM System are balanced by positive

Figure 7.1 (Continued)

emotions that reflect the good as well as the stressful in life. The goal of this skill is to identify two types of emotions. The first are "ALARM" or "reactive" emotions such as terror, rage, shame, hopelessness, and guilt. Because these emotions are the most noticeable after a person has experienced trauma, they are the ALARM System's way of keeping you primed and ready to fend off further danger. Second, it is crucial to also identify "MAIN emotions" which include positive feelings (such as happiness, love, comfort, and compassion) and feelings that represent positive strivings (such as hope, interest, and confidence). By identifying both types of emotions, the THINKING CENTER is not disregarding input from the ALARM System but is balancing that input with awareness of emotions that reflect what a person values and hopes for in life instead of just the feeling of being in danger. This helps the FILING CENTER create folders for those positive feelings, values, and hopes so even when feeling danger or distress you can draw on positive emotions as well.

EVALUATE Thoughts

When the brain is in ALARM mode, thinking tends to be rigid, global, and automatic because your thoughts are based on categories in the Filing System that are very negative (such as, "I'll never be able to get through this," "I always mess things up," or "I can't trust anyone"). As with identifying emotions, achieving a healthier balance of positive as well as negative thinking requires two steps. It is important first to pay attention to reactive thoughts that reflect the ALARM Center's attempt to keep you focused on potential dangers. However, by labeling these as *reactive ALARM thoughts*, you are helping your THINKING CENTER get back in action. You are defining these thoughts as the product of an ALARM signal rather than as the absolute "truth." This puts these negative thoughts into new folders in the FILING CENTER; instead of being filed as "true facts about how dangerous or bad life is," these thoughts are filed in folders such as "this is my ALARM telling me that I may not be safe." Then it is possible to use the THINKING CENTER to evaluate these ALARM/reactive thoughts and decide what your *MAIN thoughts* are. For example, "I don't feel safe but I know that I've prepared for this situation, so I can handle it." Transforming reactive/ALARM thoughts into MAIN thoughts jump-starts the THINKING CENTER and enables it to both improve your filing categories and turn down the ALARM. This two-step process is "smart thinking"—moving from ALARM signals to evaluating the situation and your options with a focus on what you value most in life and how you choose to act. This is a fundamental change from the PTSD pattern, which causes problems by taking you straight from ALARM signals to automatic survival reactions. When trauma is no longer occurring, it is your MAIN thoughts that are most helpful. But to get those *MAIN* thoughts in focus it is first necessary to turn down the ALARM System by using the THINKING CENTER to think clearly about and appropriately file ALARM/reactive thoughts.

DEFINE Goals

When in survival/ALARM mode, goals tend to be limited to just making it through the immediate situation or away from the source of danger. These *reactive goals* are necessary in true emergencies, but they do not reflect a person's *MAIN goals* for doing worthwhile things right now and for ultimately achieving a good and meaningful life. As with emotions and thoughts, in order to turn down or reset the ALARM System and create a FILING CENTER system that can help you access your MAIN life goals, it is necessary to begin by paying attention to the ALARM System's input and define reactive goals as what they are: the product of your ALARM system, but not your MAIN goals in life. For example, reactive goals such as, "I want to never see this person again" or

Figure 7.1 (Continued)

(*Continued*)

Box 7.3 Continued

"I'm going to take off and never come back," may seem compelling in a crisis, but they don't include many other counterbalancing goals. Labeling these as ALARM/reactive goals (e.g., "I feel like running away but that's my ALARM trying to protect me and not my MAIN goal") helps the THINKING CENTER to turn down the ALARM System so you can begin to create or locate MAIN goals that reflect your deeper hopes and values (such as, "I want to build relationships in which I am respected and loved" or "I can take one step at a time to face and resolve my problems"). When you can learn to recognize both reactive and MAIN goals, your THINKING CENTER is using input from the ALARM System but balancing this with input from past experiences and hopes for the future. The result is not just more balanced and positive goals, but also an enhanced ability by the THINKING CENTER to signal to the ALARM System that you are able to deal with any potential dangers without having to be on automatic pilot in survival mode. This helps you to set goals based on what you realistically want and can achieve, instead of getting caught up in reacting primarily based on ALARM signals and the frightening things you are afraid might happen.

 Identify MAIN OPTIONS

The only options that are available when the ALARM is turned on and won't go off are automatic "fight or flight" reactive behaviors necessary in emergencies but often unhelpful in ordinary living. However, the ALARM System never completely overrides the THINKING CENTER. Even when a person seems to be reacting completely automatically their actions also reflect positive intentions based upon the "better judgment" of the THINKING CENTER. These positive intentions often are hidden by the more *extreme reactive options* that occur when automatic self-protective reactions dominate a person's choices under the influence of the ALARM System. TARGET is designed to help people to recognize these positive intentions so they can build on this underlying motivation and identify *MAIN options* instead of simply repeating the ALARM-based reactions. As you come to recognize your positive intent, your THINKING CENTER becomes more able to not only identify and choose a wider range of MAIN options but also to strengthen the FILING CENTER'S ability to remember those options. These changes signal the ALARM System you are safe enough to move away from survival mode, and thus can reset the ALARM so that it is less reactive. This helps you to make smart choices that have positive consequences for you and for others around you.

 MAKE a Contribution

When the ALARM is turned on and reacting to ordinary stressors as if they were emergencies, it is very difficult to come away from experiences with a feeling that you have made a positive difference. ALARM reactions can keep you from realizing you have made a positive contribution to the lives of your family members, friends, co-workers and neighbors. This can lead to feelings of alienation, worthlessness, or spiritual distress. This disconnect from one's own sense of self-worth and accomplishment and from feeling valued by others in the community is not an indicator of your real worth, your inherent ability to relate to others, or your true desire and ability to find and follow a spiritual path. If you are living in a constant state of ALARM, or are on the verge of being in ALARM/survival mode all of the time, you may be trying very hard to do things that make a positive difference and to figure out extremely difficult questions about morality, ethics, spirituality, and the value of your own life. Although you may feel you are failing at figuring out these questions because your beliefs and feelings have been deeply affected by a sense of never being safe or at peace, as a result of having a hypersensitive ALARM System. If you are able to turn down the inner ALARM, you may feel more able to recognize the true value you have as a person.

Figure 7.1 (Continued)

Turning down the ALARM System enables your THINKING CENTER to better recognize and build on the ways you have made—or could make—a contribution to the world. The ultimate goal of TARGET is to empower adults and young people to think clearly enough to stop and think under stress, recognizing triggers and mindfully handling ALARM reactions and, as a result, to be able to recognize the contribution they are making not only to their own lives but also to making other people's lives better.

Gaining the ability to reset the ALARM System by using the FREEDOM steps to fine-tune and energize the brain's THINKING CENTER is the most important way people who have experienced trauma and are trapped in ALARM reactions such as PTSD can develop a clear strong sense of being in control and feeling good about how they are handling personal life choices and relationships. Each FREEDOM step is a way the brain's THINKING CENTER sends a message to the ALARM System that you are in control and safe enough to shift your focus from reactive/survival issues to your MAIN feelings, thoughts, goals, and options. In order to do this, your brain has to first focus on reactive feelings, thoughts, goals, and options from the ALARM so that you can deal with any immediate dangers or problems. By intentionally paying attention to your survival reactions, you are *changing these from automatic reactions to reactions that you can think about and change*. You are then in a position to shift out of survival mode back to thinking clearly based on your MAIN feelings, thoughts, and goals, and to choose options based on what's most important to you rather than on survival and damage-control alone.

Figure 7.1 (Continued)

Careful listening and thoughtful reflection about what the client describes as her or his primary concerns and goals, and relevant life experiences (including successes as well as problems and stressors), are essential to encouraging client "buy-in" to treatment. The client needs to be motivated to actively participate in processes that are enhanced when enough trust and confidence in the therapist are developed to enable open disclosure of often painful and shameful experiences and feelings. When traumatic events have involved betrayal or trauma by other individuals and by institutions and have thus disrupted, compromised, exploited, or ended relationships, the risk of investing emotionally in yet another relationship—this time with the therapist—can be daunting. Trust and respect need to be earned by therapists and not automatically given or assumed by clients in PTSD treatment, even when they admire and value their therapists. PTSD therapists who are savvy to these dynamics know that the first sessions (and sometimes even the entire treatment) may constitute a test, whether deliberate or not, on the part of the client that should be expected and can be discussed openly and nondefensively. Traumatized individuals need to determine if the therapist has the ability and strength to undertake the therapeutic exploration of horrible experiences and extreme suffering that make up the client's personal history and day-to-day reality when living with the psychic pain of PTSD.

Some clients benefit so much from this "alliance-building," education, and personal acceptance (of them personally and of their story) during this first phase of psychotherapy that they feel able to resolve or manage their PTSD symptoms and those associated with depression or anxiety. In consequence, they and their therapist may choose to end therapy without a period of formal "retelling" or processing of the trauma. In such a case, Phase 1 is directly followed by Phase 3 and the closure of treatment. Whether Phase 1 must represents only a first step, or can be the basis for complete successful psychotherapy, is an important question.

Herman (1992) described how therapy for PTSD can be undertaken episodically rather than in one long progression. Others such as Courtois (2010) discussed how therapy for PTSD is often layered, and the resolution of one issue, while very important, may later cause the emergence of other issues. Internal and external triggers (including those that are *decremental*—that is, involving some sort of loss, reexposure to the trauma, and revictimization—and those that are *additive*—involving positive life events that in some way paradoxically serve as reminders of the trauma and its cost)—can cause the emergence or reemergence of PTSD symptoms. At those times, treatment that had been complete may need to be resumed in order to enable the person to manage and overcome the (re)emerging PTSD symptoms.

When clients drop out of treatment in the first phase, this often is due to avoidance of dealing with traumatic memories or distressing PTSD symptoms. Or it might be seen as constituting a "flight into health" (i.e., an attempt to deny inner distress and psychic conflict from a psychodynamic perspective). However, clients can greatly benefit even from a less than complete therapy. Some are highly comforted by the personal and emotional support received in this first phase, even to the point that they remain in Phase 1 and never move beyond or complete it. This sometimes occurs when they do not have the personal resources or motivation necessary to move on (sometimes due to the degree of their suffering and impairment, their age, and or health status). Whatever the case, the therapeutic challenge is not to "make" the client move forward into the next phase of therapy (or to graduate from therapy, for that matter), but to provide support and help the client with whatever resolution of emotional distress is possible so that she or he feels ready and actually is prepared to move to the next phase of therapy.

Although Phase 1 does not specifically focus on trauma memory reconstruction and processing, recollections of trauma are dealt with in other ways. The major difference between Phases 1 and 2 is that in Phase 1, the impact of past psychologically traumatic experiences is assessed (see Chapter 6), and clients are offered information about the impact of traumatic stressors, how traumatic stress reactions can lead to PTSD symptoms, and how PTSD symptoms can be overcome or managed (Box 7.4). This foundational knowledge may include body awareness and relaxation techniques, mindfulness practices, addiction recovery skills, and cognitive behavioral strategies for managing anger, depression, and anxiety. Once a relative degree of stabilization and active engagement in developing a therapeutic partnership ("alliance") has been achieved, assessment of the client's needs and readiness for Phase 2 can commence.

Phase 2 trauma processing is recommended if a client continues to be troubled by specific intrusive memories or has dissociative symptoms that continue to impair quality of life. Clients are ready for trauma processing if they understand how PTSD symptoms are adaptive stress reactions "gone-wrong," can apply skills for emotional modulation and self-management, have sufficient emotional stability and social support, and are not in immediate crisis or danger. Because Phase 2 is designed for clients to face and come to grips with trauma memories, they must be advised that they might feel worse for a period of time before they begin to get some relief; therefore, some

Box 7.4 CBT for PTSD: Necessary? Sufficient?

The evidence supporting the efficacy of CBT for adults with PTSD is quite strong and still growing (Jayawickreme et al., 2014; Powers, et al., 2010; Wang, 2014). However, it is important to also look carefully at who actually receives CBT treatments for PTSD and how much they improve in the scientific studies that comprise this evidence base, and also who might *not* be included and who does *not* complete or benefit from the standard approaches to CBT for PTSD—and how best to meet their needs.

A review of the results of more than 30 studies that were included as scientifically rigorous investigations of PTSD treatments in the first Practice Guidelines from the ISTSS (Foa, Keane, & Friedman, 2000) found that persons who were not permitted to participate to begin with had characteristics and problems that would tend to make them less likely to benefit from *any* treatment than persons who were included in the studies (Spinazzola, Blaustein, & van der Kolk, 2005). The studies tested several approaches to PTSD treatment, including CBT (both PE/CR and EMDR), group therapy, and pharmacotherapy. More than two-thirds of the studies excluded people who had a psychotic disorder or SUD, and more than one-quarter excluded persons with suicidal thoughts. Over one-third of the studies excluded people who had serious medical illnesses. People with chronic PTSD commonly have one or more of these serious psychiatric or health problems (see Chapter 4), so excluding them from studies testing the efficacy of PTSD treatments results in outcomes that do not necessarily apply to the use of these treatments with these more severely impaired adults. This is a problem of "external validity" or "generalizability," because study results may not be validly generalized to apply to people with characteristics different from those of the "included" participants in a study.

CBT for persons of ethnoracial minority backgrounds
Although no studies purposefully excluded persons of ethnoracial minority backgrounds, most (82%) had fewer than one in four participants from such a background. Fortunately, several rigorous scientific studies of PTSD treatment with adults have reported including a majority of participants who are of ethnoracial minority backgrounds (Cloitre et al., 2002, 2010; Ford et al., 2013, 2011). A particularly innovative study was conducted providing black African women in the Congo who had been sexually assaulted with CPT adapted to align with their cultural practices. The outcome tested also was culturally adapted, with the results showing that CPT resulted in women's increased involvement in social groups and likelihood of seeking emotional support in their local village (Hall et al., 2014).

Nevertheless, relatively few studies have been conducted to test the efficacy of PTSD treatments with persons of ethnoracial minority backgrounds, and it is not clear that even the PTSD treatments with the strongest evidence base will be accepted by and will produce improvements in PTSD for persons of ethnoracial minority backgrounds (Pole, Gone, & Kulkarni, 2008). It is important to note

(Continued)

Box 7.4 Continued

that there is no evidence that people of ethnoracial minority backgrounds do *not* benefit from PTSD treatment when they have been included in rigorous studies, but many questions remain unanswered that may influence the success of PTSD treatment with individuals of different backgrounds.

For example, in a recent study with men and women in treatment for SUDs, a psychotherapy for PTSD was found to be less effective than standard substance abuse treatment in preventing substance use relapse with African American men (Frisman et al., 2008). The PTSD psychotherapy was no less effective than standard substance abuse treatment in preventing substance use relapse with African American or Latina women or white men or women, and more effective than standard substance abuse treatment in sustaining all participants' self-efficacy. The finding concerning relapse and African American men also involved a very small number of participants (fewer than 10) and may have been due to factors other than the specific PTSD psychotherapy (such as the match of ethnoracial background between participants and counselors: no African American male counselors delivered the PTSD therapy, but there were ethnoracial minority female counselors).

CBT for adult survivors of childhood maltreatment

Additionally, most (79%) PTSD treatment studies included only persons whose PTSD was due to traumatic stressors experienced in adulthood, primarily accidental injuries. Although victims of assault or military veterans with PTSD were included in several studies of PTSD treatment efficacy, only one in five studies included adults with PTSD due to psychological trauma experienced in childhood (Spinazzola et al., 2005). However, a number of studies that either specifically recruited women with PTSD related to childhood abuse (Chard, 2005; Cloitre et al., 2002; Cloitre et al., 2010; Edmond, Rubin, & Wambach, 1999; McDonagh et al., 2005) or had a large subgroup of participants with PTSD related to childhood abuse (Ford et al., 2013, 2011; Resick, Nishith, & Griffin, 2003) have provided evidence that three approaches to CBT (PE/CR, EMDR, and CPT) and two emotion regulation psychotherapies (STAIR-PE and TARGET) are effective in reducing the severity of PTSD and associated psychiatric and psychosocial problems experienced by adult survivors of childhood abuse.

However, questions remain about how best to deliver PTSD psychotherapy to persons with the complex PTSD symptoms that often occur among survivors of childhood abuse and other forms of developmentally adverse interpersonal trauma (such as growing up in a violent family). CPT and skills training for affective and interpersonal regulation-prolonged exposure (STAIR-PE) have made adjustments to reduce the risk of clients becoming overwhelmed or incapacitated emotionally when doing Phase 2 trauma memory reconstruction (such as more extensive preparation in Phase 1 with emotion regulation skills, and using written recall of memories rather than vividly imagining trauma memories) (Jackson, Nissenson, & Cloitre, 2009). The study of PE/CR with women with histories of sexual abuse found that almost half dropped out of therapy, mostly when PE was beginning or at the midpoint when encouraged to reflect on how well the treatment was working for them (McDonagh et al., 2005).

A study of depressed men and women found that those with histories of childhood traumatic loss or abuse showed higher rates of remission from depression following either CBT or pharmacotherapy than participants with no childhood trauma history—but that pharmacotherapy was less efficacious in achieving remission from depression than CBT among the participants with childhood trauma histories (Nemeroff et al., 2006). Although most studies of PTSD with people with histories of childhood abuse involve only women, a sizable subgroup of military veterans with chronic PTSD have histories of childhood abuse. One study found that compared to those with no history of childhood abuse, male military veterans with histories of childhood abuse had a poorer response to intensive CBT treatment for chronic PTSD (Ford & Kidd, 1998).

Overall, there is evidence that CBT may be beneficial for adults with PTSD due to childhood abuse and potentially more beneficial than pharmacotherapy with childhood trauma survivors. However, in contrast to several studies showing that PE is the primary source of benefit to rape or assault survivors with PTSD (Foa et al., 2005), studies showing CBT to be beneficial with people with histories of childhood abuse or traumatic losses either did not include PE (Nemeroff et al., 2003) or included modified PE to reduce the risk of emotional destabilization (Chard, 2005; Cloitre et al., 2002, 2010; Edmonds et al., 1999; Resick et al., 2003). The one study that found that PE/CR to be effective with women with PTSD due to childhood sexual abuse did so with just over half of the PE/CR recipients because 43% dropped out and did not complete post-therapy assessments (McDonagh et al., 2005). Consistent with the view that intensive processing of traumatic memories can be beneficial but that caution is warranted with clients who have complex symptoms associated with childhood exposure to traumatic maltreatment (such as severe emotional and behavioral dysregulation, volatile or victimizing adult relationship, and flashbacks or dissociation), proponents of PE/CR and CPT recommend that the memory processing component of treatment should be adjusted in several ways in order to promote a sense of safety, trust, and empowerment for these clients. This includes encouraging clients to keep their eyes open, maintain eye contact with the therapist, and talk about trauma memories rather than vividly reliving them (Cook et al., 2004) or dealing with traumatic memories by developing cognitive strategies for handling the distressing effects of present-day reminders rather than reconstructing a memory narrative (Cook et al., 2014). For example, a client might be helped to describe a traumatic past experience by talking about how reminders of it now affect her or him while referring to the memory in the past tense as an observer rather than as a participant: "I get so upset that I can't think straight whenever I hear someone talking in an angry tone of voice, but I know now that that's because it was really scary when I was a kid, and I never knew how bad someone

(Continued)

Box 7.4 Continued

was going to get hurt when I saw my parents fighting." This is in contrast to the standard PE and CPT approach of describing or writing one's perceptions, feelings, and thoughts in the first-person, present tense as if the event was happening right at the present moment: "I can see them hitting each other, and I cover my ears so I can't hear them screaming; my body is feeling numb and my heart is pounding; I'm thinking that they're going to kill each other, and I can't do anything to stop it." For some clients, the immediacy and intensity of such recall can be a way to learn that they can face even very horrible memories and come away feeling stronger and no longer a helpless victim. For other clients, trauma memory exposure or narrative reconstruction can exceed their psychological and physical window of tolerance, and adaptations are necessary in order to ensure that therapy reduces rather than reactivates PTSD symptoms.

Patient-centered outcome research: guiding clinical flexibility with scientific methods

These adjustments to CBT procedures for PTSD clients tend to be based on clinical experience rather than scientific research, consistent with the basic requirement that clients' safety always is the first priority, including safety from psychological crises as well as from physical harm or danger. However, there is a paradigm shift in therapy outcome research that could provide a path to the best of both worlds: patient-centered outcome research (PCOR). PCOR is a set of research strategies to enable researchers, clinicians, and clients to partner together and answer critical research questions such as how they together can deal with the complex and often confusing choices involved in achieving and sustaining recovery from PTSD while accessing and navigating through complicated health care systems. Traditional treatment outcome research has produced powerful interventions for PTSD such as the CBT models, but it has not been intended or designed to enhance our understanding of how clients subjectively experience, participate in, and are affected by health care and interactions with treatment providers. Research shows clear linkages between clients' trust in and willingness to fully participate in PTSD treatment (McLaughlin, Keller, Feeny, Youngstrom, & Zoellner, 2014), but these findings have not been applied to systematically adapt how CBT is delivered to clients. PCOR takes on these critical questions that clients and their clinicians face daily in treatment and their personal lives.

PCOR is a systematic approach to patient-centered comparative clinical effectiveness research (CER), in which client and clinician preferences, choices, actions, and interactions are studied in order to determine tools, strategies, resources, and courses of action that are associated with cost-effective health care outcomes. For clients, PCOR involves testing and then providing guidance about which approaches to care work best, given their life circumstances, personal and familial concerns, socioeconomic circumstances, and sociocultural preferences. For clinicians, PCOR is designed to provide evidence-based guidance addressing the questions they face daily in practice. For insurers, PCOR produces evidence that can help them make the best decisions on how to improve PTSD outcomes while also containing costs, especially with high-impact health problems such as PTSD. For PTSD therapists and the broader mental health field, PCOR provides opportunities and an impetus to conduct real-world clinical research on topics such as:

- When, for whom, and how does CBT provide the most scientifically effective and personally acceptable way for trauma survivors to "talk about it" (Angelo et al., 2008)?
- What are the mechanisms—the subtle, step-by-step changes—that enable trauma survivors to benefit from CBT, and how do different CBT models activate these mechanisms?
- What sequencing of CBT's components—psychoeducation, coping and stress inoculation skills, trauma memory exposure or narrative reconstruction, or desensitization—best benefits and is most acceptable to different clients?
- Can CBT be adapted to incorporate or to work together with other approaches to PTSD therapy, and when and for whom does this enhance the acceptability or benefit of therapy?

Studies of CBT as delivered in clinical practice—as opposed to in the restrictive context of randomized controlled trial (RCT) studies in which therapists have little leeway to accommodate individualized needs or preferences of the client—indicate that clinicians tend to make numerous adaptations of the therapy in order to best fit different clients and treatment settings (Cook et al., 2014; Kaysen et al., 2014; Morland et al., 2014; Walter, Dickstein, et al., 2014; Walter, Varkovitzky, et al., 2014; Zoellner et al., 2011). If those critical decisions could be guided by scientific evidence that incorporates the perspectives of objective research, clinicians' field experience, and client's preferences and experiences, the chances of CBT—or any therapy for PTSD—benefitting most or all of the clients to whom it is provided—rather than only the subset for whom a good client–treatment match happens to occur by good luck—could be greatly increased, to the benefit of society as well as the individual.

Thus, by considering the limitations and cautionary findings from research studies, a highly effective treatment approach for adults with PTSD—CBT—potentially can be further improved. This is a good example of keeping the "baby" (the effective treatment) while "throwing out the bathwater" (developing adjustments to reduce potential adverse reactions to the therapy). In the PTSD field, as in all mental health and medical disciplines, there is no treatment that is beneficial for all recipients and completely free of potential adverse effects. The combination of good science (i.e., rigorous research testing treatments with the full range of clients to whom they are to be delivered) and good clinical practice (i.e., noting possible adverse reactions and creating and testing modifications to address these potential problems) results in continuous improvement in evidence-based treatments for PTSD such as CBT.

degree of relapse is to be expected, and safety and relapse planning is undertaken before moving forward. Clients are advised that they are not expected to "perfectly" face their memories and emotions—that is, without distress and occasional backward steps. Lapses and relapse are treated as opportunities for therapeutic problem solving and as normal parts of the growth and change process involved in recovering from PTSD.

Phase 2. Safely becoming able to face traumatic memories and gaining an understanding of how to overcome or manage the emotional reactions that reminders of memories trigger in daily life are the goals of Phase 2 PTSD treatment. This may result in a complete and emotionally manageable autobiographical narrative (i.e., a story with a beginning, middle, and end) of memories of specific traumatic events. Narrative reconstruction of memories must be timed and structured to support the client's ability to not only tolerate trauma memories and emotions but also to gain a sense of self-efficacy and a coherent life story that encompasses personal success and growth as well as the psychological trauma and PTSD symptoms.

In this phase, clients are encouraged to feel their emotions—first anxiety, but also fear, terror, grief, shame, anger, and guilt (to name but a few)—that are associated with psychologically traumatic events—that is, to become aware of rather than avoiding or dissociating from stress reactions and emotions triggered by trauma memories or reminders. Some treatment models specifically do not prescribe recalling traumatic memories, focusing instead on enhancing the client's capacities for self-regulation in their current lives (e.g., McDonagh et al.'s, 2005 present-centered therapy) or on strengthening the client's ability to reflectively examine many past and recent memories without focusing on traumatic experiences per se (Courtois, 1999; Ford & Russo, 2006). These therapies explicitly link the client's processing of *current* stressful or emotionally evocative experiences that involve reminders of past traumatic events (sometimes unbeknownst to the client) in order to enable the client to achieve a resolution of the sense of distress and helplessness related to those reminders and memories that can lead to avoidance of current experiences. Thus, Phase 2 trauma processing emphasizes helping the client be prepared for current situations in which reminders of past traumatic events trigger distress in order to counter the avoidance of feared or overwhelming memories by building confidence based on the ability to emotionally handle trauma reminders or triggers. When trauma processing involves recalling specific memories of traumatic events, this should always be done with the client's full and informed consent so that the client gains a sense of personal control and effectiveness and does not feel coerced into involuntarily "dredging up" trauma memories simply because the therapist dictates that this is a requirement of therapy. Therapists empower their clients to come to grips with their traumatic memories and/ or the distress that everyday reminders of such memories evoke, rather than prescribing memory recall as a required component of treatment.

It is important to emphasize that there is controversy in the PTSD field about whether therapy must include intensive recollection of specific trauma memories in order to be effective. Some CBTs for PTSD insist that this is essential and that therapy is incomplete without helping the client to therapeutically reexperience traumatic

memories through "exposure" or "narrative processing" or "desensitization" procedures. Other treatment models utilize a similar "narrative reconstruction" approach to
assist clients in gaining a sense of mastery or authority over their memories first in
relation to the full range of life experiences as a preparation for or alternative to systematically revisiting and reconstructing traumatic memories (e.g., Cloitre, Cohen, &
Koenen's, 2006, skills training for affect and interpersonal regulation (STAIR) in the
Life Skills Life Story model). That is, clients are guided in developing a more detailed
oral or written/drawn account of the events and circumstances that they feel have
been most important in their entire lives (e.g., the "lifeline" in the TARGET model
[Ford, 2015]). The goal of traumatic memory narrative reconstruction is to restore
clients' sense of authority over their own memories (Harvey, 1996) to desensitize
them to their traumatic memories, allowing them to become "normalized" (more like
memories of nontraumatic events), thus reducing their negative impact. Clients are
not encouraged to forget what happened to them but instead to be willing and able
to recognize when reminders are triggering the recall of distressing traumatic memories so that those triggers and memories no longer seem unmanageable but rather
become an accepted (although still unpleasant) part of their ongoing life experience.
Exposure therapy, often undertaken in prolonged format (PE; Foa & Kozak, 1986),
was the first systematic approach to therapeutic processing of traumatic memories.
PE involves detailed recounting of a traumatic event and emphasizes preparation for
this typically distressing activity. It is conducted in a variety of different formats and
offers the option of talking about the event rather than "reliving" it (Cook, Schnurr, &
Foa, 2004). PE involves the client recalling a specific traumatic memory as vividly as
possible in first-person mode (i.e., as if it was happening immediately at the present
moment), in imaginal form (with an audiotape of the trauma) (PEI), or *in vivo* form
(PEIV). Exposure therapy seeks to directly counter anxiety-based avoidance of traumatic recollection and to give the client a sense of self-determination and hardiness in
recalling traumatic memories with feelings of mastery (in contrast to feeling helpless
in the face of memories intruding in an unwanted and overwhelming manner—that is,
PTSD's intrusive reexperiencing symptoms). Clients are helped to experience emotions that arise and, with repeated exposure, to see that the intensity and distress of
these trauma-related emotions will lessen as the trauma is desensitized.

Since PE was developed, several approaches to traumatic memory desensitization
and reconstruction have been developed, including EMDR (Shapiro, 1995, 2002)
based on adaptive processing theory and CPT (Resick et al. 2008). These methods
are designed to help the client to experience and work through painful emotions, traumatic memories, and altered beliefs about self, others, and life meaning, in the process
bolstering the client's internal and external resources. Throughout the treatment, but
particularly during Phase 2 memory reconstruction and processing, the client must
be assisted in maintaining an adequate level of functioning consistent with past and
current lifestyles and circumstances and benefits from additional emotional support
of loved ones and the therapist.

Phase 3. PTSD psychotherapy concludes with a third phase in which the new
knowledge and ability to face and cope with reminders of troubling memories without

avoidance acquired in the first two phases are applied to all areas of the client's life. Common challenges include the development (or regaining) of trustworthy relationships and intimacy, healthy parenting, having a productive career, and dealing with continuing conflicts, limitations, or victimization in relationships. It is in this phase of the treatment that the client has many more resources to be more self-determined and empowered, free of some of the constraints of the past. Phase 3 PTSD treatment often involves refresher discussions to solidify the client's understanding and acceptance of PTSD symptoms as survival adaptations that have become an unnecessary demand on the body, emotions, and mind now that traumatic events are no longer occurring (assuming this is actually the case!). Phase 3 PTSD treatment also engages the client in using the self-regulation skills learned or strengthened in Phase 1 to continue to be aware of and actively manage reactions to current-day reminders of traumatic memories. Thus, in Phase 3 the client puts into practice in daily life the approach to dealing with traumatic memories and reminders that she or he learned in the therapy setting in Phase 2. In this way, PTSD therapy provides the client with a personal foundation for continuing to deal with reminders of traumatic experiences in a self-aware and confident manner so that avoidance and hypervigilance do not resume their domination of the client's life. Rarely, if ever, are traumatic memories "erased" because no memory is ever completely deleted from the brain (see Chapter 1), but successful PTSD treatment enables the client to gain mastery of those memories and to be able to handle distressing reminders effectively when they occur (Harvey, 1996).

PTSD treatment: practical issues

Treatment, like PTSD symptoms, is complex and multimodal. As just mentioned, the range of symptoms and comorbidities involved may require a number of treatment goals and a variety of treatment approaches. Thus, treatment should incorporate a variety of theoretical perspectives and clinical modalities individualized to best fit the client, rather than only one approach.

The client's development of a support system outside of therapy is essential. A personal support network outside of treatment and apart from the therapist is the best source of positive reinforcement of the gains achieved in therapy in the client's daily life. The greatest challenge to clients and therapists in PTSD therapy often is not addressing traumatic memories (as difficult and important as that can be) but helping the client to overcome PTSD's emotional numbing and social detachment/alienation symptoms in order to build relationships with trustworthy others and, in the process, to lessen dependence on the therapist and therapy as the sole source of support and understanding. This might also involve the client assessing the quality of his or her relationships and the ability of others to support their recovery. Especially in circumstances of embedded and ongoing family and community violence and addictions, the client may need to make a break from those who remain unhealthy, violent, and/or addicted, and develop more positive and trustworthy attachments.

Duration of treatment. One limitation of most research studies on PTSD treatment is that they impose a requirement that treatment must involve a predefined number of sessions, most often in the range of 9–12 sessions (Cook, Dinnen, Thompson, Simiola, & Schnurr, 2014), and as few as 4 or 5 sessions when treating clients with relatively recent traumatic events (see Chapter 9). In actual practice, PTSD therapy (especially when involving its complex variant) more often requires between 6 months and several years in order to provide sufficient time and therapeutic assistance to enable the client to traverse the three phases fully and without rushing. The more complex the client's trauma history, generally the more lengthy treatment is needed (e.g., when traumatic stressors include childhood abuse or family violence occurring over prolonged periods of time—including up to the present—than for a single assault or accident). Even PTSD therapies that are designed to be completed within 20–30 sessions or in a single episode of hospital treatment may require several repetitions of "cycles" or episodes of the intervention over many months or years.

Frequency of and type of services. Most therapy for PTSD occurs on a once or twice a week basis in an outpatient setting—that is, in a therapist's private practice office or a counseling clinic. Usually this is done in 50- to 75-minute sessions for one-to-one, couples, or family therapy and/or 75- to 120-minute sessions for group therapy (with groups usually including five to nine members). If pharmacotherapy is included in the treatment, after a 60- to 90-minute initial assessment for psychiatric medication, briefer sessions (usually 20–30 minutes) are then the norm for checkups. At times, patients will require specialized services and settings, including inpatient, partial hospital or day treatment, residential rehabilitation or supportive housing, or intensive outpatient programs (e.g., for substance abuse, eating disorders, sexual addiction, or suicidality). Such intensive treatment often provides, in addition to a secure environment for patient safety, groups on self-management or relationship skills, psychopharmacology services for medication evaluation and management; peer support programs (such as "12-step groups" sponsored by Alcoholics Anonymous, Narcotics Anonymous, Al-Anon, or Gamblers or Debtors Anonymous), and case management to address vocational, educational, residential, financial, and legal needs.

Treatment outcomes. The primary goal is to reduce the intensity and frequency of PTSD symptoms to a level that is no longer troubling to the client or that the client can manage well enough that they no longer substantially interfere with the client's life activities, goals, and well-being. When other symptoms or disorders (such as depression or substance abuse) co-occur with PTSD, these problems also must be reduced or managed concurrently because improvements in PTSD are likely to be delayed or lost if the other disorders cause psychological instability (Ford, Russo, & Mallon, 2007). Untreated traumatic stress symptoms also have been found to be associated with less positive outcomes in the treatment of other disorders, such as substance dependence, because they create a major risk for relapse (Anderson, Ziedonis, & Najavits, 2014; Ford, Hawke, Alessi, Ledgerwood, & Petry, 2007).

Additionally, a focus on clients' strengths or posttraumatic growth such as is advocated by the "positive psychology" orientation (Seligman, Rashid, & Parks, 2006) suggests that goals should include the enhancement of clients' social and emotional regulation skills and sense of personal effectiveness. Spiritual connection and healing and meaning-making are advocated in spiritually oriented treatments for trauma (Walker, Courtois, & Aten, 2015). Due to the differences in each client's capacities to engage in therapy and to tolerate and benefit from the often emotionally intense interactions that occur in PTSD therapy, it is important to gauge the success of treatment according to goals that are achievable for each unique client.

Evidence-based treatments for PTSD

PTSD, especially when chronic or complex in nature and due to its myriad symptoms and their varying manifestations, can be difficult to successfully treat. It is to be expected, therefore, that resourceful and creative therapists and trauma survivors will be searching for and experimenting with alternative or multimodal therapeutic approaches in order to increase the likelihood of successful treatment. It is important that a quest for new "tools in the tool kit" for the treatment of PTSD is encouraged publicly and politically (such as through governmental, foundation, and private industry grants for clinical innovation) while being scientifically and professionally scrutinized to ensure that the safety and health of those undergoing treatment are protected. There is no single best way to develop new or improved therapies for any psychiatric or medical disorder, but clinical practice guidelines are now available that have been designed to simultaneously encourage innovation while preserving the scientific and clinical integrity of the process and the resultant treatments. These guidelines initially were developed to ensure that ethical and legal/regulatory requirements were fulfilled in biomedical research, and have been adapted for psychological and psychiatric research on psychotherapy and for PTSD treatment research more specifically.

The guidelines for biomedical research include recommendations that scientific studies of human participants should be designed and conducted to achieve three principles that are articulated in the National Commission for the Protection of Human Subjects of Biomedical and Behavioral Research (1979) Belmont Report: respect for persons, beneficence, and justice. Definitions of these principles are excerpted from the report (italics added):

> *Respect for persons involves recognition of the personal dignity and autonomy of individuals, and special protection of those persons with diminished autonomy. Respect for persons is manifested in the informed consent process in which potential subjects are provided information about the study in a manner comprehensible to them and then allowed to choose whether or not they wish to participate.... Beneficence entails an obligation to protect persons from harm by maximizing anticipated benefits and minimizing possible risks of harm. Beneficence requires that investigators and IRB [institutional research review board] members engage in an analysis of the risks and benefits to the subjects, making sure that anticipated risks are proportional to the potential benefits. Risk should be minimized as much as possible.... Justice requires that the benefits and burdens of research be distributed equitable. The principle of justice instructs us that subjects should not be chosen simply because they are available and easy to manipulate. In addition it requires that subjects who are likely to benefit from a study should not be excluded. (pp. 4–7)*

It might seem that any attempt to help people recover from PTSD would, by defini-tion, automatically fulfill these criteria, but, in fact, that is not the case. An untested therapy for PTSD may be intended to provide recipients with relief from its symp-toms; however, until the therapy has been carefully tested, it is not possible to provide a recipient with sufficient information about its specific features (i.e., what exactly the therapy involves, including what the therapist will do and what the recipient is expected to do) and not only its potential benefits but also its risks/adverse effects and their likelihood. Informed consent (and refusal) requires an entirely voluntary and fully knowledgeable ("informed") agreement by the recipient to undertake the therapy ("consent") or to refuse it, and it is not possible without this information (see Box 7.2). Without the assurance of respect and beneficence, justice cannot be guaranteed, even if the intent of the therapist is to provide the best possible help to those who most stand to benefit.

The mental health professions have established rigorous scientific standards for research on psychotherapy treatments in order to address these issues. Therapies for psychological or psychiatric problems such as PTSD are evaluated according to these standards so that providers and recipients will know in advance the likelihood that a therapy will provide benefits and the degree of confidence that they can place in this estimate of beneficence. The term that is used to describe the adaptation of ethical and scientific principles to psychotherapy research is *evidence-based practices or treatments*. Per the American Psychological Association Statement Task Force on Evidence-Based Treatments (2006), the evidence based includes the best research evidence but also a consensus among clinicians and client values and preferences. There remains debate in the mental health and traumatic stress fields as to whether an entire treatment model can be considered "evidence-based" or whether the specific strategies or components "practices" that make up a treatment (that may be found in more than one treatment) are more appropriately certified as evidence-based.

For example, in PTSD psychotherapy, a core component in several treatment models is the "narrative reconstruction" of memories of traumatic event(s). This can involve a process described as "exposure therapy" or "prolonged exposure (PE)," during which the client is encouraged to repeatedly describe one or more memories of traumatic event(s) while imagining every detail of the experience as if the event(s) were occurring to the client at that moment (i.e., in the first-person, present tense— for example, "I was just about to fall asleep when I felt jolted by a loud noise, and the whole room was shaking"). Thus, the client is therapeutically being "exposed" in imagination (sometimes written out or audiotaped) or *in vivo* (i.e., in a similar real-life circumstance) to the traumatic event(s) or their reminders, not just once briefly, but for a "prolonged" number of repetitions. As discussed earlier in this chapter, trauma memory processing can be done in a number of different ways in different treatment models, typically in combination with other interventions (such as education about PTSD and learning skills for managing anxious thoughts and emotions). In some studies in which PE has been used to treat PTSD, recipients have discontinued treat-ment ("dropped out") in sizable numbers (McDonagh et al., 2005), while in other studies there has been no difference in dropout rates between treatments that include trauma memory processing and those that do not (Jayawickreme et al., 2014). Recent studies have found that trauma memory exposure may be effective in reducing PTSD symptom severity when done on a less prolonged basis, with fewer sessions of shorter length, and this may help some clients to tolerate the distress of the intensive memory recall (Foa, McLean, Capaldi, & Rosenfield, 2013).

The acceptability of intensive therapeutic recollection of traumatic memories to different clients in different formats thus requires additional study. However, studies of clients' preferences indicate that they often do want to talk about what happened to them, and they tend to prefer a talking therapy to the use of medication (Angelo, Miller, Zoellner, & Feeny, 2008). On the other hand, PE per se is not the only approach to talking about traumatic memories or current PTSD symptoms, and studies suggest that it is not as widely used by practicing therapists as it is studied in research investigations (Cook et al., 2014; Zayfert & Becker, 2007). Many therapists have not had the specialized training that is necessary in order to effectively use PE (Foa, Hembree, & Rothbaum, 2007), and others have reservations about using it for fear of retraumatizing their clients if the intensive recollection of traumatic memories overwhelms their capacities to cope (van Minnen, Harned, Zoellner, & Mills, 2012); this is true despite evidence that the majority of clients who agree to undertake PE report substantial benefits (Hagenaars & van Minnen, 2010; Ruzek et al., 2014). Due to its strong empirical substantiation, PE (and also CPT) is being used routinely in the US Department of Veteran Affairs (VA) after a systematic rollout of training for hundreds of VA mental health clinicians (Foa, Gillihan, & Bryant, 2013; Ruzek et al., 2014). Its use in other organizations and by private practice clinicians is much less systematized, although that may change with the emphasis being placed on cognitive-behavioral treatments in the professional curricula of many psychology, social work, counseling, marriage and family therapy, and psychiatry graduate clinical training programs (Courtois & Gold, 2009).

Since 2000, a number of formal guidelines for treating adults with PTSD have been published. Each has made recommendations based on the evaluation of the quality of the aggregate research database and on expert opinion. These PTSD clinical and practice guidelines published to date include a definitive set by the ISTSS based on reviews assessing the strength of the available evidence for a range of psychological and psychiatric treatments (Foa, Friedman, & Keane, 2000; Foa, Friedman, Keane, & Cohen, 2009); the US Department of Veterans Affairs and Department of Defense (US VA/DoD, 2010; see http://www.healthquality.va.gov/guidelines/MH/ptsd/cpg_PTSD-FULL-201011612.pdf); the Clinical Resource Efficiency Support Team (part of the Northern Ireland Health Service) (CREST, 2003); the American Psychiatric Association (APA, 2004); the British National Institute for Clinical Excellence (NICE, 2005); the Institute of Medicine of the National Academies (IOM, 2007); and the Australian Centre for Posttraumatic Mental Health at the University of Melbourne (ACPMH, 2007/2014) (see http://www.trauma-pages.com/s/tx_guides.php). Additional practice guidelines for complex forms of PTSD have been published by the ISTSS (2012) (see http://www.istss.org/AM/Template.cfm?Section=ISTSS_Complex_PTSD_Treatment_Guidelines&Template=%2FCM%2FContentDisplay.cfm&ContentID=5185) and the American Psychological Association's Division of Trauma Psychology (2015).

Each practice guideline system uses different criteria (standards and requirements) for judging the scientific and clinical evidence in support of each treatment model or practice, and designates several "levels" of support (such as "evidence-based," "promising," and "empirically informed," or grades ranging from A to F) with recommendations ranging from "strongly recommend" to "do not recommend." There is some consistency across the various systems in the interventions or best practices that are supported by the scientific research base, but there is much disagreement as well. There also is controversy as to the relative weight that clinicians' experiences in using treatment models or practices and clients' views of the treatments should have compared to scientifically rigorous research findings (American Psychological Association, 2006). And there is also debate about whether the physical science paradigm of experimental research of distinct treatment interventions is adequate to accurately and fully demonstrate the benefits of treatments for PTSD as well as other psychological or psychiatric disorders (Westen, Novotny, & Thompson-Brenner, 2004) and whether these give adequate attention to the values and preferences of clients. A major practical challenge is to actually get psychotherapists to fully utilize evidence-based interventions in their day-to-day treatment of clients with PTSD (Zayfert et al., 2005).

The most current PTSD treatment guidelines indicate that several versions of cognitive behavior therapy (CBT) with trauma memory processing have the strongest research evidence base for PTSD treatment with adults. PTSD affect and interpersonal regulation (PAIR) psychotherapies designed to facilitate the recognition and adaptive management of PTSD symptoms in current daily life without requiring in-depth processing of trauma memories also have developed a scientific evidence base. Medications developed for depression also have a growing scientific evidence base for the treatment of PTSD, including two selective serotonergic reuptake inhibitor (SSRI) antidepressants (fluoxetine and paroxetine), which are Food and Drug Administration (FDA) approved for adult (but not child) PTSD treatment.

CBT for PTSD

A long-held tenet in the PTSD field has been that memories of traumatic event(s), along with all of the associated bodily reactions, emotions, and thoughts or beliefs, must be faced directly until they are no longer incomplete, intrusive, and intolerable (Foa & Kozak, 1986). Memories of traumatic events are not expected to become less emotionally disturbing and painful—although this can occur—but the goal is to enable the client to gain a sense of mastery of the memories rather than feeling haunted, tortured, or too terrified to recall them (Harvey, 1996). This shift enables the client to stop, or reduce, her or his hypervigilance and avoidance of reminders of traumatic experiences, resulting in their being more like memories of nontraumatic events and less likely to perpetuate a vicious cycle of PTSD symptoms (intrusive memories triggering avoidance, dysregulated emotions and thinking, and hypervigilance, which in turn elicit stronger and more frequent intrusive memories). Interestingly, this view of the importance of facing and overcoming toxic memories was evident in psychoanalytic schools of psychotherapy for patients suffering from what was labeled as "hysteria" (symptoms currently understood as forms of dissociation, often related to traumatic experiences such as sexual assault or abuse; Nijenhuis & van der Hart, 2011).

CBT directly addresses the thoughts and beliefs that are often associated with fear and other negative emotions that occur when traumatic stress reactions persist and become a problem after the traumatic experiences have ended. It also addresses the avoidance of trauma-related thoughts, feelings, and situations that is often extensive. The general goal of CBT is to help the survivor process (remember and understand from a new perspective, often with new insight) and figure out what is most personally meaningful (for better or worse) in the memory of the traumatic event and to attain a realistic perspective on it. This, in turn, is believed to help the client develop or resume satisfying life activities by reducing or eliminating the avoidance behaviors and the posttraumatic symptoms (Hembree & Marinchak, 2008, pp. 126–127).

CBT for PTSD is based on the rigorously tested theoretical model that postulates that intrusive reexperiencing (unwanted memories and psychophysiological reminders of traumatic events) occurs as the paradoxical result of avoidance of thoughts or emotions about trauma memories or their reminders (Foa & Kozak, 1986). Common sense would indicate that avoiding trauma memories and reminders should provide relief, as suggested by advice such as "What you don't know can't hurt you," or "Don't dwell on the past." However, just the opposite has been found: the more someone tries *not* to think about something disturbing like a traumatic memory or *not* to feel upset when reminded of it, the more that individual actually is thinking about it (you have to think about something in order to know what you are trying to avoid), and the more bodily, mental, and emotional energy is being used to stay on guard for any signs of the memory or the reminders (i.e., being "hypervigilant," but in this case not watching out for the danger itself but rather for reminders of past danger or harm).

In order to reverse this cycle of instability, it is necessary to find a way to face rather than avoid the traumatic memory and reminders of it. In PE, the exposure is *not* to more actual trauma but instead to memories of traumatic events (in imagination—hence the term *imaginal exposure*) and to current (*in vivo*) situations that have reminders of the traumatic past event(s). As described earlier, by vividly recalling, imagining, or actually being in a situation that is strongly reminiscent of a past traumatic event (such as visiting the scene of a mass-casualty accident or disaster, or looking at pictures of an assailant or abuser), the client can therapeutically reexamine, clarify, and reconstruct a complete and emotionally manageable memory of what was previously overwhelmingly. The memory and reminders of it no longer evoke the same feelings of horror, terror, or helplessness that the person experienced at the time of its actual occurrence. The "emotion processing" involved in PE (Foa et al., 2007) thus may enable people to not just wish but to actually know and feel that "that was then, this is now." When a memory can be faced (with the support of an empathic and skilled guide in the person of the therapist) and the feelings it evokes can be felt fully but in a way that is emotionally manageable, the anxiety about being overwhelmed by the memory can be reduced to the point that it no longer seems (or is) necessary to fearfully avoid or defend against it.

CBT for PTSD involves careful preparation, including education about traumatic stress, PTSD, how facing rather than avoiding traumatic events and their memory can reduce its symptoms, and skills for managing anxiety (such as ways of breathing or tensing and relaxing muscles that enhance relaxation and counteract fear). This preparation typically is accomplished very efficiently in three 60- to 90-minute sessions in research-based CBT models (Hembree & Marinchak, 2008). Another six to eight sessions are devoted to PE, imaginal, and *in vivo*.

Imaginal exposure involves repeatedly revisiting the trauma memory in imagination. Imaginal exposure is designed to help the survivor to emotionally process her or his experience of the traumatic event(s) by vividly imagining the traumatic event(s) as if the event(s) were happening right at the current moment, while also being fully aware that the event(s) are not actually happening. This is typically done with the eyes closed and describing the event(s) aloud, including the thoughts, emotions, and physical sensations that were experienced during the event(s). This imaginal revisiting of the traumatic event(s) is typically repeated over and over throughout treatment or until the trauma memory ceases to elicit intense anxiety or distress.

In vivo exposure entails repeatedly facing safe but avoided situations, places, activities, or objects that evoke unrealistic anxiety because of their association with the trauma memory. *In vivo* exposure further enhances the processing of the traumatic experiences by asking the person to confront and remain in these planned situations until anxiety decreases or habituates significantly. Such therapeutic exposure provides powerful learning experiences that help the person to feel safer and attain more realistic views of the world (Hembree & Marinchak, 2008, p. 128). The "cognitive" aspect of CBT for PTSD involves the therapist helping the patient to identify thoughts or beliefs that increase rather than decrease anxiety and avoidance, as well as alternative thoughts that can be substituted to instead increase personal confidence and positive emotions. This "CR" is a dismantling of automatic anxiety-intensifying thoughts (such as "I'm helpless," or "Nobody will help me," or "There is no safe place in this world") and rebuilding new thoughts (such as "I can't stop every bad thing from happening, but I can handle those events and my own emotions in a way that helps to make things better," or "I can ask for help from people in my family and circle of friends who I know are trustworthy"). When new thoughts are practiced intentionally and repeatedly, they take the place of those that were automatic. The result is that the client may feel less anxiety and depression and more hope and confidence. He or she no longer needs to feel afraid of (and avoid) the anxiety-evoking thoughts. CR teaches that "thoughts are just thoughts—"sticks and stones can break my bones, but names can never hurt me"—similarly to how PE teaches that "memories and reminders are just memories and reminders." With PTSD, these are lessons that cannot only be talked about but must be experienced behaviorally. Hence, the name "cognitive *behavior* therapy": the therapy depends on the client experimenting with nonavoidant ways of facing and gaining mastery of the anxiety-evoking memories and thoughts that are at the core of PTSD—not just thinking positively or hoping not to feel so upset but taking decisive action to behave differently by choosing what to remember and what to think. In other words, insight is not enough. Application of new information to core beliefs that shape (or disrupt) a person's self-concept, emotions, and relationships and skill-building to develop the confidence and competence that enable a person to overcome adversity are the most important components and go a long way in undercutting anxiety and depression that so often co-occur with PTSD.

328	Posttraumatic Stress Disorder

PE/CR was developed originally by Foa, Rothbaum, Riggs, and Murdock (1991) in their work with rape trauma survivors. Two variations on this approach have been scientifically tested in numerous studies and are widely used by therapists. Some studies have shown benefits from adding CR (Bryant, Moulds, Guthrie, Dang, & Nixon, 2003), whereas others (Foa et al., 2005; Jayawickreme et al., 2014) have found no benefits. Another recent innovation has been the use of the drug D-cycloserine (de Kleine, Hendriks, Smits, Broekman, & van Minnen, 2014), as well as VR simulations of traumatic events (Rothbaum et al., 2014), to enhance PE for treatment of PTSD. Interestingly, recent research also suggests that PE leads to changes in trauma-related beliefs without the therapist formally attempting to do cognitive restructuring; careful therapeutic exposure may be sufficient to change PTSD cognitions (Zalta et al., 2014). RCT research studies have shown that PE leads to substantial reductions in PTSD and depression symptoms with a majority of adult clients who undertake the treatment after having developed PTSD as a result of experiencing traumatic sexual assault or abuse or community or military combat violence (Jayawickreme et al., 2014; Powers, Halpern, Ferenschak, Gillihan, & Foa, 2010).

CPT (Resick, Nishith, Weaver, Astin, & Feuer, 2002) is a particularly detailed method of CR for PTSD. Similar to PE, in CPT the client repeatedly replays the memory of a traumatic event in his or her mind, but the emphasis in CPT is on the therapist and client collaboratively developing a narrative—a step-by-step story-like description—that helps the client to figure out what is most meaningful personally rather than focusing primarily on becoming less emotionally distressed by the memory. The CPT trauma narrative also can be written rather than spoken or used with clients or cultures where oral storytelling and giving personal testimony (for healing rather than legal purposes) is traditional, it can be spoken as a way to give voice to the meaning that the experience has for the client and her or his family and community (Hall et al., 2014).

A primary goal that distinguishes CPT from PE is helping the client to learn how currently troubling and problematic thoughts and beliefs originated in the traumatic events or in their attempts to cope in the aftermath, and to adopt a more complete and less self-blaming or self-deprecating appraisal of the traumatic experience by providing corrective information that had been overlooked or dismissed as irrelevant or insignificant. Support for the proposed CR mechanism of change in CPT was provided by a study showing that depression and PTSD symptoms changed in tandem (Liverant, Suvak, Pineles, & Resick, 2012). Another study showed that PTSD clients receiving CPT were more likely than those receiving PE to report reduced thoughts of hopelessness, and the greatest reductions in PTSD symptoms achieved by CPT occurred when hopelessness also was reduced (Gallagher & Resick, 2012). PE showed similar overall benefits to those achieved by CPT, but in PE the apparent mechanism of change was a reduction in the overall level of distress that clients reported when recalling traumatic memories in therapy.

CPT has been shown to be effective in reducing PTSD in RCT scientific studies with both male (Mullen, Holliday, Morris, Raja, & Suris, 2014) and female (Hall et al., 2014; Jayawickreme et al., 2014; Suris, Link-Malcolm, Chard, Ahn, & North, 2013) survivors of sexual assault. A variation of CPT that does not involve creating a written narrative of a traumatic event but instead focuses on helping clients to rework their current beliefs contributing to PTSD—CPT-CR Only—has been shown to be equally as effective as the original CPT in reducing PTSD symptoms with combat veterans who had traumatic brain injuries but not as effective in reducing depression symptoms (Walter, Dickstein, Barnes, & Chard, 2014; Walter, Varkovitzky, Owens, Lewis, & Chard, 2014). Thus, as with PE, CR appears to have benefits, but it is the focused reconstruction of the narrative of the traumatic memory that seems to yield the greatest benefit. Both CPT and PE were found to be associated with reductions in suicidality in female sexual assault survivors over a 5- to 10-year period, with CPT showing a small but statistically significant greater benefit than PE (Gradus, Suvak, Wisco, Marx, & Resick, 2013).

EMDR is another exposure treatment based on an alternative theoretical model of *adaptive information processing* (EMDR; Shapiro, 1989, 1995). Following a detailed assessment that is part of an 8-step protocol, the client is encouraged to go through a specific traumatic memory silently ("imaginal exposure" in CBT terms), while simultaneously engaging in an alternative task that is somewhat distracting. This distractor task often involves simple movements or shifts in attention back and forth from left to right, such as side-to-side—or saccadic—eye movements, alternating audio tones in the left and right ear, or left-right finger or shoulder tapping. This dual bilateral attentional focusing occurs as the client replays the traumatic event in imagination and also pays attention to the accompanying thoughts, feelings, and bodily sensations in as vivid detail as possible.

Although similar to PE in its emphasis on intensive step-by-step recall of a traumatic event and reactions that occurred at the time, EMDR differs from PE not only in providing the bilateral distractor task but also in emphasizing careful examination of how all the parts of the event—especially thoughts that continue to be troubling to the client—form a logical narrative that makes sense in light of the specific sequence of events and the circumstances in which they occurred. In that respect, EMDR is more similar to CPT than PE. Also similar to CPT, EMDR systematically helps the client to challenge self-blaming or self-deprecating thoughts that occurred during the traumatic event (assessing the validity of cognitions, in EMDR terms) and to identify beliefs about personal strengths and supportive or protective relationships and keep those cognitions in focus (to install them as a positive resource, in EMDR terms) while recalling the traumatic event. EMDR differs from both PE and CPT in its brevity: as few as a single session and generally fewer than five to seven sessions are used to address each traumatic memory.

A statistical meta-analysis of the results of 26 RCT scientific studies demonstrated that EMDR resulted in moderate to large improvements in symptoms of PTSD, depression, and anxiety, and large reductions in overall personal distress with clients diagnosed with PTSD (Chen et al., 2014). In addition, the review concluded that therapy sessions longer than 60 minutes and experienced PTSD therapists were most likely to achieve the best outcomes, especially with depression and anxiety symptoms. The reason for the latter findings is not known, but one possibility is that clients often may need enough time and skillful therapeutic guidance to accomplish the multiple tasks involved in EMDR and to gain a sense of mastery of traumatic memories.

Although the exact mechanism by which EMDR achieves its results with PTSD clients is not yet fully understood, and early research casted doubt on whether the distractor tasks such as saccadic eye movements had any added value (Davidson & Parker, 2001), results of a more recent meta-analysis indicated that "the eye movements do have an additional value in EMDR treatments" (Lee & Culjpers, 2013, p. 239). Another meta-analysis concluded similarly that eye movements may help clients to access trauma memories more fully (as a more complete narrative), actively (rather than as a passive victim), and with more manageable distress (potentially enhancing self-confidence), but noted that most findings of benefit from distractor tasks came from studies of simulated therapy with healthy individuals rather than PTSD clients (Jeffries & Davis, 2013). While the fact that EMDR has been found to have similar neurobiological benefits to other CBT models for PTSD—reduced levels of hyperarousal in the body and brain—supports its use, the findings do not indicate that EMDR has any distinct effects compared to other CBT interventions on PTSD clients' stress reactivity or memory.

NET (Neuner, Schauer, Klaschik, Karunakara, & Elbert, 2004) is a generally briefer approach than PE or CPT (more comparable in length to EMDR) to CBT with both exposure therapy and cognitive restructuring. NET was designed for settings with limited socioeconomic or health care resources and politically traumatized individuals (including refugees, torture survivors, former political prisoners, sexual assault survivors, and military combatants). NET provides between 4 (Neuner et al., 2004) and 5 (Bichescu, Neuner, Schauer, & Elbert, 2007) to 10 (Halvorsen & Stenmark, 2010) or 12 (Hensel-Dittmann et al., 2011) individual therapy sessions in which the client creates a spoken or written narrative that encompasses not only memories of traumatic stressors but of his or her entire life that include detailed descriptions of traumatic events (similar to PE) and are recorded in writing by the therapist for the client to take home. Active listening, positive regard, and creative tasks (e.g., creating a lifeline by placing flowers and stones that represent positive and negative events along a rope to illustrate key events; reenacting body positions that were experienced or used to cope during traumatic events) also are used in helping the client to achieve therapeutic exposure to traumatic memories while constructing a life story that includes a reevaluation of basic beliefs that have been altered by traumatic experiences.

NET has been conducted with adults (and children; see Chapter 8) in some of the most severely traumatized nations and cultures in the world, both in the very middle of dangerous and chaotic communities and with displaced persons who have fled traumatic societies and are faced with the additional challenges (and potential traumatic stressors) of immigration as a refugee (see Chapter 10, Box 10.2 Evaluating Traumatic Stress Issues for Individuals Seeking Asylum). In several small RCT studies, NET's acceptability to clients and efficacy in reducing PTSD and depression symptoms with a majority of the adults (and children; see Chapter 8) receiving the treatment have been confirmed as lasting benefits with follow-up assessments up to a year after therapy ended (Dossa & Hatem, 2012; Hensel-Dittmann et al., 2011; Robjant & Fazel, 2010). In several creative studies, NET has also been shown to alter brain processing by increasing "top-down" (Adenauer et al., 2011) activation of the cortex—leading to active attention to reminders of danger rather than avoidance—and to enhance the body's immune system despite evidence of persistently low immune capacity to fight off illness even when PTSD improved (Morath, Gola, et al., 2014). In addition, when PTSD symptoms declined during the year following NET, there also was evidence that the breakdown of the body's basic genetic building blocks (DNA) was prevented (Morath, Moreno-Villanueva, et al., 2014). Thus, NET has demonstrated the ability not only to help traumatized adults recover from PTSD but also to enable them to shift from a survival brain to a learning brain (Ford, 2009) and to regain some of their bodies' vital healing capacities.

CBT interventions for special populations of adults with PTSD

CBT has been adapted for adults with three particularly problematic comorbid psychiatric disorders: SUDs, severe mental illness (including schizophrenia and bipolar disorder), and BPD. Each of these adaptations is discussed next.

CBT for PTSD and SUDs. From a cognitive-behavioral standpoint, PTSD and SUD both are the result of dysfunctional (i.e., threat-based or addiction-based) beliefs, cognitive biases, and reactive behavior patterns involving chronic avoidance that lead to an escalating sense of anxiety, anger, isolation, hopelessness, and helplessness (Ford et al., 2007). From a stress and coping perspective, PTSD and SUD involve maladaptive coping in response to stressors that range in intensity from mild to traumatic (Stewart & Conrod, 2003). From an empowerment or strengths-based perspective, PTSD and SUD involve a loss or breakdown of the person's psychological and interpersonal resources (e.g., sense of safety, trust in others, hope, self-efficacy, motivation) (Ford et al., 2007).

PTSD may negatively influence the course and outcome of SUD treatment. Najavits et al. (2007) found that cocaine-dependent outpatients with comorbid PTSD improved less than ASUD-only participants on measures of alcohol use and psychosocial problems. However, PTSD was not found to be a negative prognostic factor in several other studies (Ford, 2013). Pharmacotherapy, either associated depression symptoms with the SSRI antidepressant sertraline or for alcohol craving with disulfiram and naltrexone, has been shown to be safe and effective with adults with comorbid PTSD and alcohol use disorders. Clinically diagnosed PTSD was not associated with poorer opiate substitution treatment outcomes with military veterans or with treatment dropout in an adolescent residential therapeutic program. However, teens in the latter study who had experienced traumatic stressors (whether or not they had PTSD) were more likely to drop out of residential treatment for SUD. A comparing CBT for SUD and depression with a 12-step support group showed that clients with PTSD benefited as much as those without PTSD while they were in treatment and for several months thereafter. However, when reassessed 18 months after completing the treatment, those with PTSD reported achieving fewer days abstinent than clients who did not have PTSD (75% versus 91%).

A possibility suggested by the Cohen and Hien (2006) study of Seeking Safety (SS) for comorbid SUD and PTSD is that it may be the complex problems with self-regulation (such as depression, dissociation, social and sexual problems) rather than

PTSD per se that interferes with adherence and change in SUD treatment. Ford et al. (2007) conducted secondary analyses of data from a multisite study of the efficacy of a SUD treatment, called contingency management (CM), in community-based clinics and found that, over and above the strong benefits of CM intervention, the severity of self-regulation problems—but *not* history of traumatic stressor exposure, PTSD symptom severity, or overall psychiatric symptom severity—predicted poorer outcomes in terms of retention in treatment and objectively verified continuous abstinence from cocaine and heroin use during treatment, *only in the CM condition.* Self-regulation problems were the link between having witnessed violence in the past and premature termination from SUD treatment. Although PTSD and self-regulation problems were interrelated, only the self-regulation problems appeared to interfere with immediate treatment outcome, consistent with Ford and Kidd's (1998) findings with military veterans in treatment for chronic PTSD. Comorbid PTSD-ASUD often involves severe self-regulation problems (such as impulsivity, extreme emotion states, and abusive or empty relationships), and therefore treatments that address these complex outgrowths of PTSD may be needed when comorbid SUD and PTSD are treated.

Interestingly, clients who reported more severe self-regulation problems completed CM activities just as often as others, suggesting that self-regulation difficulties do not diminish their motivation or ability to engage in SUD treatment. Moreover, a high level of baseline PTSD symptoms actually was a positive predictor of achieving abstinence at 9-month follow-up assessments, in contrast to prior studies' findings suggesting that PTSD symptoms are a negative prognostic indicator in SUD treatment—here again, only for patients receiving CM. Thus, SUD treatment may provide a welcome distraction from and adaptive focus for persons experiencing intrusive trauma memories or hyperarousal and hypervigilance, or a source of predictability, controllability, and positive emotions in contrast to PTSD's negative cognitive biases and emotional distress and numbing. This hypothesis received indirect support from the results of three RCTs of SUD clients with childhood sexual abuse histories. These data showed that they were more likely than others to achieve abstinence (verified by urine tests) from substance use during treatment—and, only if they received CM, but not those receiving a less effective SUD treatment, clients with sexual abuse histories had significantly longer durations of abstinence during treatment than those without sexual abuse histories (Petry, Ford, & Barry, 2011). Highly structured SUD treatment may actually work best with clients who, as a result of severe childhood exposure to traumatic abuse, need to develop the kinds of self-regulation skills that interventions such as CM teach or strengthen. Gains in self-regulation skills may translate into reductions in PTSD symptoms, and this may help to explain the finding from several studies that as PTSD symptoms improve, SUD treatment outcomes also improve (Hien et al., 2010).

CBT interventions for co-occurring PTSD-SUD therefore consistently teach complementary cognitive and behavioral skills not only for overcoming PTSD and SUD symptoms but also for building or acquiring personal strengths or interpersonal resources and for coping with the effects of both current and past stressors without relying on substances or addictive behaviors. Psychotherapies with the strongest evidence of efficacy for treating comorbid PTSD and SUD extend CBT by adding affect and interpersonal regulation interventions.

Psychotherapy for comorbid PTSD and SUD begins with providing trauma-informed stabilization, safety, and education interventions (Phase 1 in PTSD psychotherapy), with the addition of a focus on understanding that stress reactions lead to and exacerbate substance use. Historically, treatment of addictions such as SUDs and PTSD developed independently and were kept in "silos," even as the common interrelationship (comorbidity) between PTSD and SUDs has been increasingly and incontrovertibly demonstrated (Fareed et al., 2013; Ford, 2012; Najavits & Hien, 2013). Contemporary approaches now stress the need for concurrent treatment of the addictive disorder and PTSD (Najavits & Hien, 2013). If one disorder remains active and untreated, it has a high probability of derailing recovery from the other. For example, achieving sobriety from alcohol or other substance use often is accompanied by a resurgence of PTSD symptoms, leading to an increased risk of relapse to the substance of choice. Or when clients find trauma memory processing distressing, they may be tempted to resume or increase their use of substances in order to quell or manage the distress they are experiencing.

Cognitive Behavior Therapy for Severe Mental Illness (CBT-SMI; Mueser, Descamps, Jankowsky, & Rosenberg, 2002; Mueser et al., 2008) is a 16-session one-to-one psychoeducation intervention for individuals with severe mental illness and PTSD in community mental health or in client psychiatric settings. In addition to teaching clients to recognize specific PTSD symptoms and ways they can intertwine with and exacerbate mental illness symptoms, CBT-SMI uses cognitive therapy to assist clients in challenging and revising distorted beliefs (similar to CPT) and anxiety management. CBT-SMI does not utilize PE but instead focuses on here-and-now coping skills to assist clients in managing intrusive memories. In an RCT research study, CBT-SMI was shown to be superior to standard community mental health center treatment in improving PTSD and psychiatric symptoms, reducing negative trauma-related beliefs, and enhancing clients' relationships with their case managers, particularly for clients who completed homework assignments that supported assertive methods of coping with stress reactions and trauma-related thoughts (Mueser et al., 2008). Similar to findings for PE, clients who reported less endorsement of trauma-related beliefs tended to also benefit the most in reducing severe PTSD symptoms.

Only 15% of the clients in the Mueser et al. (2008) study of CBT-SMI were diagnosed with a primary psychotic disorder. A European clinical research team demonstrated that adults with comorbid PTSD and psychotic disorders could not only safely tolerate exposure therapy for PTSD (de Bont, van Minnen, & de Jongh, 2013) but also showed evidence of benefits from both PE and EMDR in an RCT study comparing the two CBT treatments (van den Berg et al., 2015). In the first smaller feasibility and safety study with 10 outpatient clients, no serious adverse events were reported while the clients received 12 weekly sessions of therapy and over the next 3 months following PTSD therapy, nor was there any evidence of worsening of psychotic symptoms (hallucinations, delusions), other psychiatric symptoms, or interpersonal functioning. In a larger study with 155 outpatient clients who had past psychotic disorders and current PTSD, a briefer course (eight weekly sessions of 90 minutes in length) of PE or EMDR resulted in clinically significant reductions in PTSD symptoms for 57–60% of the clients (compared to less than half that percentage, 27%, for clients who received no PTSD treatment) that were generally sustained at a 6-month follow-up assessment. PE and EMDR were equally effective, and the number of serious adverse events (such as suicide attempts) was very low (occurring for only seven of the clients, less than 5%) and lower for PE and EMDR recipients than other clients. Although most of the clients in these studies had relatively mild psychotic symptoms, they were at risk for developing severe psychotic symptoms due to having had this occur in the past, and neither PE nor EMDR appeared to trigger this kind of relapse.

CBT for Comorbid PTSD and BPD. In the Mueser et al. (2008) study of CBT for SMI, 25% of the clients were diagnosed with BPD. This is consistent with evidence from nationally representative samples in the United States that approximately 30% of adults meeting criteria for either PTSD or BPD also met criteria for the other disorder, and closer to 40% of adults diagnosed with BPD had an episode of PTSD at some point in their lifetime (see Ford & Courtois, 2014 for a summary). A 10-year follow-up of adults diagnosed with BPD and PTSD found that even when they recovered from PTSD, almost half had a recurrence of PTSD, especially those who had a history of childhood sexual abuse (Zanarini et al., 2011). Thus, PTSD appears to be a persistent problem for adults who are dealing with the often severe emotional, behavioral, and interpersonal problems of BPD. This may be due in part to the toxic link between experiencing betrayal traumas such as sexual, physical, or emotional abuse in childhood and developing the severe self-regulation problems of BPD. DBT is well established as a treatment for preventing self-harm and enhancing interpersonal functioning with adults diagnosed with BPD (Neacsiu, Lungu, Harned, Rizvi, & Linehan, 2014). However, DBT did not show greater effectiveness than expert treatment as usual (TAU) with regard to symptoms that are strongly connected to PTSD and its self-regulation problems: guilt, shame, anger suppression, anxiety, core schemas, and impulse control. Therefore, an adaptation of DBT has been developed with a modified form of PE for PTSD. In a feasibility and safety study with women diagnosed with comorbid BPD and PTSD, DBT + PE yielded similar completion rates (67–70% when therapists had acceptable fidelity) and better outcomes for self-harm, depression, anxiety, guilt, and shame than DBT alone (Harned et al., 2014). A subsequent RCT study tested the efficacy of DBT + PE ("DBT-PTSD") with 74 women diagnosed with PTSD related to childhood sexual abuse (Bohus et al., 2013). Half of the participants met criteria for comorbid BPD. DBT-PTSD was associated with substantial reductions in PTSD severity for women with or without BPD, while those in a TAU condition showed almost no change: reductions on average of 33 versus 2 points on the Clinician Administered PTSD Scale. Dysfunctional behaviors such as self-harm were monitored carefully and did not increase for participants in DBT-PTSD. These findings provide an independent and well-controlled replication demonstrating the efficacy of combining PE for PTSD with DBT for women with that difficult-to-treat comorbidity.

Psychotherapies for Affect and Interpersonal Regulation (PAIR)

PTSD involves both a reduction in emotional experiencing (the "emotional numbing" and "social detachment" symptoms) and periodic "bursts" of distress in the form of unwanted trauma memories ("intrusive reexperiencing" symptoms) and intense anxiety and anger ("hyperarousal symptoms"). Experiential therapies are designed to help the client with PTSD to achieve a midlevel of emotional intensity and a full range of emotions by becoming more proactively aware of these symptomatic extremes of too little or too much emotion.

> *Living a life of vitality, resilience, and human connectedness in the face of*
> *adversity requires ready access to emotional experience. Access to basic emotions*
> *is necessary in order to harness adaptive resources (e.g., assertiveness, self-*
> *protection, humor, conscientiousness, creativity, self-efficacy, trust), as well as*
> *to be able to rely on others to help bolster these coping resources. Experiential*
> *psychotherapies are designed to systematically assist people in enhancing the*
> *ability to access emotions and the psychosocial resources linked to emotions.*
> *(Fosha, Siegel, & Solomon, 2009)*

Several approaches to psychotherapy for PTSD do not require clients to engage in therapeutic exposure or intensive narrative reconstruction of specific detailed memories of traumatic events, but focus instead on addressing the emotional difficulties and dysregulation and relationship problems that accompany severe stress reactions in the daily lives of people with PTSD. Although these PAIR psychotherapies originated between 1 and 2 decades after the first CBT models for PTSD, they are developing a scientific evidence base that is encouraging.

STAIR (Cloitre et al., 2006). STAIR-MPE provides an attachment-based (Cloitre, Stovall-McClough, Zorbas, & Charuvastra, 2008) and DBT-informed first phase of therapy aimed at enhancing affect and interpersonal regulation skills, followed by a modification of PE similar to that in DBT + PE, which carefully titrates trauma memory processing intensity to not exceed the client's affect regulation capabilities. Two RCT studies have demonstrated STAIR-MPE's efficacy in reducing severe PTSD, depression, and dissociation with women with chronic childhood victimization- or interpersonal violence–related PTSD (Cloitre, Koenen, Cohen, & Han, 2002; Cloitre, Petkova, Wang, & Lu Lassell, 2012; Cloitre et al., 2010; Koenen, Cohen, & Han, 2002).

Trauma Affect Regulation: Guide for Education and Therapy (TARGET). TARGET was developed in field tests with low-income women and men in mental health and SUD treatment programs (Ford & Russo, 2006) and with boys and girls in juvenile justice programs (Ford, Chapman, Hawke, & Albert, 2007). TARGET is applied in a 12-session individual therapy version and a 10-session group version and provides education and skills training for processing and managing trauma-related reactions triggered by current nontraumatic stressors. The skills are taught in a practical seven-step sequence summarized by a mnemonic ("FREEDOM"): *F*ocusing, *R*ecognizing current triggers; *E*motion identification and reappraisal; *E*valuation of reactive beliefs; *D*efining personal goals; *O*ptions for incrementally achieving goals; and *M*aking a contribution by managing traumatic stress reactions. The FREEDOM skill sequence is used as a basis for trauma/PTSD education, emotion regulation, cognitive reappraisal, goals/values clarification, and experimentation with new behavior in current stressor situations. A creative arts exercise—the personal "lifeline"—utilizes collage, drawing, poetry, music, and crafts to assist participants in developing a description of life experiences in a story-like narrative that includes traumatic events. In contrast to PE, traumatic events are neither recounted repeatedly nor treated as the primary focus. The goal in TARGET is to help participants recognize their personal strengths using the FREEDOM skills and to use these skills consistently and purposefully when they experience stress reactions in their current lives. In rigorous research studies, TARGET has shown evidence of effectiveness in rigorous research studies in reducing PTSD and trauma-related beliefs and psychiatric symptoms, sustaining the capacity for forgiveness and sobriety-related self-efficacy, and improving emotion regulation skills with women with chronic PTSD (Ford, Chang, Levine, & Zhang, 2013; Ford, Steinberg, & Zhang, 2011) and men and women with chronic comorbid PTSD and SUD (Frisman, Ford, Lin, Mallon, & Chang, 2008).

Interpersonal psychotherapy (IPT). IPT was developed to treat depression by enhancing social support and preventing acute crises in relationships. IPT is a one-to-one therapy typically involving between six and 20 sessions (with extended booster sessions to prevent relapse), in which skills for interpersonal decision-making and communication are taught, role played, and applied in carefully structured homework activities. A 14-session adaptation of IPT for adults with chronic PTSD was found to be equivalent to prolonged exposure (PE) in reducing PTSD symptoms, and almost two thirds of IPT recipients (compared to fewer than half of those receiving PE) achieving a clinically significant reduction in an independent assessor's ratings of PTSD symptoms (Markowitz *et al.*, 2015). IPT also had fewer drop-outs than PE, particularly among persons with major depressive disorder (who were nine times more likely to drop out of PE than those with PTSD but no depressive disorder). Both IPT and PE resulted in improvements in quality of life and interpersonal functioning that were superior to a relaxation skills intervention. IPT's approach of teaching social skills relevant to recovery from depression and PTSD does not involve intensive recall of trauma memories, yet it appears to be comparably effective to the PE trauma memory processing therapy, as well as possibly more tolerable or acceptable than PE for severely depressed adults.

Present Centered Therapy (PCT). PCT is a 12- to 14-session individual therapy that provides education about the links between psychologically traumatic events, PTSD symptoms, and problems in relationships, and teaches social problem-solving skills to address "traumagenic dynamics" of betrayal, stigma, powerlessness, and sexualization (found in child sexual abuse in particular, but applicable to other traumas as well) (Finkelhor, 1987). As in TARGET, PCT focuses on addressing current problems rather than trauma memory–based PE and uses a distinctive mnemonic to organize the skill set ("SIBEDR," pronounced "see better": *S*tate the problem, *I*nformation gathering, *B*rainstorm, *E*xperiment with alternatives, *D*ecide and *D*o it, *R*eview and *R*evise the plan). PCT also has the client keep a journal of relational stressors and responses as between-session homework. In a rigorous research study, PCT has been shown to be of comparable immediate benefit to PE/CR in reducing PTSD and psychiatric symptoms (although a lesser degree of continued improvement after treatment was concluded) and to have far fewer dropouts (9% versus 43%) in women with PTSD related to childhood sexual abuse (McDonagh et al., 2005). PCT also has been found to have comparable benefit to TARGET in reducing PTSD and anxiety symptoms and slightly greater benefit in reducing depression and guilt symptoms in a study of women with chronic PTSD (Ford et al., 2011). A different version of PCT, which shares the name but does not provide the systematic instruction in social problem-solving skills, has been found to be equally as effective as PE/CR as a group therapy with male military veterans with chronic PTSD (Schnurr et al., 2003) and less effective than PE/CR as an individual therapy with women military veterans with PTSD (Schnurr et al., 2007). Overall, the PCT social problem-solving skills component appears effective in improving present-day relationships (and reducing PTSD, depression, and related symptoms) in a manner that clients find helpful and engaging but not as directly beneficial in reducing PTSD intrusive reexperiencing symptoms and improving self-regulation as PE/CR and TARGET (Ford et al., 2011; McDonagh et al., 2005). A meta-analysis of five RCT research studies comparing PCT to PE or a comparable CBT for PTSD reported that PCT was equally effective across several measures of treatment outcome (including PTSD, depression, and anxiety symptoms) and had less than half the number of dropouts (14% versus 31%), indicating that PCT is efficacious for adults with PTSD.

Emotion Focused Therapy for Trauma (EFTT). Putting feelings into words enables a person to recognize and use the information provided by basic emotions, such as fear, anger, and sadness, that are experienced in wordless body feelings. In CBT, emotions are considered secondary to and largely defined by thoughts or beliefs. In contrast, in EFTT, emotions are seen as a basis for developing new ways of thinking and new beliefs about oneself and the world. This is particularly important in light of the strongly held negative beliefs that often accompany (and possibly intensify) PTSD. EFTT helps clients to reclaim rather than become desensitized to painful feelings and memories, while assisting them to create or regain positive beliefs about themselves, relationships, and the world. Although EFTT utilizes standard emotion management skills for severe emotion dysregulation (e.g., attention to breathing, relaxation, present-centered awareness), the primary focus in EFTT is empathic responding to client feelings and needs. Empathic responding fosters affect regulation capacities by increasing clients' awareness of their emotions, and in the process helping them to accurately label and express the meaning of each emotion. Feeling understood emotionally also helps to reduce distress. Empathic responses also help to adjust emotional intensity by reducing feelings of isolation and distress, as well as increasing physical and emotional arousal and making emotions more available to the person as useful information. Additionally, empathic responses set a model for appropriate emotional expression.

EFTT usually involves 16–20 weekly 1-hour sessions, individualized to each client. After initial sessions focused on ensuring safety, defining goals, and developing a therapeutic relationship through the use of empathic responding, EFTT uses an "imaginal confrontation" (IC) technique to reduce fear, avoidance, shame, and self-blame and improve emotion regulation. In IC, clients imagine perpetrators of abuse or neglect in an empty chair, observe their own thoughts and feelings, and express these directly to the imagined other. A third phase focuses on resolving issues with abusive/neglectful others and accessing adaptive anger and sadness. Finally, closure sessions help clients apply new learning in their daily lives. EFTT has been supported in scientific studies with both men and women with PTSD due to childhood traumatic abuse (Paivio, Jarry, Chagigiorgis, Hall, & Ralston, 2010; Paivio & Nieuwenhuis, 2001).

Seeking Safety (SS; Najavits, 2002) is a CBT intervention for the combination of PTSD and SUDs that provides up to 25 sessions that can be flexibly applied to teach more than 80 "safe coping skills" (such as "grounding" to detach from and cope with distress or dissociation; interpersonal assertiveness; self-monitoring; healthy self-nurturing; asking for help; and time management). Similar to CBT-SMI and CPT, SS uses cognitive therapy to challenge demoralizing or risky beliefs, including distortions specifically related to PTSD and addiction and the necessity of safety for healing. PE is also not used in SS. Instead, this method teaches skills for managing PTSD symptoms in daily life and in addiction recovery. Women completing SS in ongoing addiction treatment have improved on both addiction and PTSD symptoms comparably to an addiction-focused intervention (relapse prevention skills training) and better than in addiction treatment as usual, as well as of greater improvement in anxiety, depression, hostility, suicidality, and interpersonal problems than either relapse prevention or treatment as usual (Najavits, 2002). SS has shown evidence of efficacy in a scientifically rigorous study with adolescent girls with PTSD and SUD (Najavits, Gallop, & Weiss, 2006) and to have moderate benefits in a large but less scientifically rigorous study with homeless women (Desai, Harpaz-Rotem, Najavits, & Rosenheck, 2008). SS also is being adapted and appears to be suitable for men with PTSD and SUD (Weaver, Trafton, Walser, & Kimerling, 2007). Similar to work being done with STAIR, SS has been combined with a modified (abbreviated) version of PE, with promising results in case studies but no RCT evidence of efficacy as yet (Najavits, Schmitz, Gotthardt, & Weiss, 2005).

Anxiety Management Skills Training. Similar to PCT, anxiety management skills training, also known as "stress inoculation training" (SIT; Novaco, 1977), teaches specific skills that can be used to handle stress reactions in current life. SIT focuses on skills for managing anxiety or stress reactions, whereas PCT teaches skills for social problem-solving. SIT coping skills include relaxation, CR, self-dialogue, assertiveness, and behavioral rehearsal (role-playing, and covert modeling) skills (Hembree, 2008). Among several potential approaches to purposeful relaxation, the most commonly used is PMR. PMR involves tensing and then relaxing specific muscle groups throughout the body, while focusing attention on the difference in how these muscles feel when tense versus when relaxed. This learning is then applied to the recognition of physical tension in daily life. CR is taught as in the PE/CR approach to CBT for PTSD to enable the client to recognize and modify thoughts or beliefs that intensify stress reactions or reduce self-confidence and trust in relationships. Self-dialogue complements and extends CR by teaching ways to change an individual's internal dialogue—what the client "says" to herself/himself—in order to prepare for and cope with distressing feelings when confronted by stressful memories or current experiences. Self-dialogue also involves learning to offer internal praise and encouragement when challenging stressors and for the small as well as large successes. Assertiveness skills involve addressing conflicts or personal goals with others with direct, nonjudgmental, and respectful verbal and nonverbal communication. Finally, behavioral rehearsal involves practicing other anxiety management skills in order to be prepared and to feel confident before using the skills in real-life situations. Through rehearsal, the therapist provides modeling, and the client experiments with using the skills, either in imagination ("covert modeling") or by role playing (taking on different roles in simulated interactions). With repeated practice in a nonthreatening context, anxiety management skills can become well learned, and clients can become sufficiently confident to apply the skills. Behavior rehearsal enables clients to actually see the therapist and then see themselves (in imagination) and experience (both in imagination and in role playing) coping successfully with stressful situations. Despite its obvious logic and appeal, anxiety management skill training has been found to be less effective than PE or PE/CR in reducing PTSD symptoms in several research studies and to be generally ineffective when single skills are taught apart from the entire SIT package. When combined with biofeedback—a procedure in which the client and therapist get real-time feedback from machines that show the client's level of physiological arousal on several dimensions (such as heart rate, muscle tension, and brain wave patterns)—anxiety management skills have shown evidence of reducing PTSD symptoms, particularly hyperarousal (Clum, 2008). Therefore, SIT or anxiety management skills training is used primarily in Phase 1 preparation for either PE, CR, or both, except with clients who have particularly severe anxiety symptoms and may benefit from learning skills for symptom management and biofeedback.

Trauma Recovery and Empowerment Model (TREM; Ford, Fallot, & Harris, 2009; Harris & Fallot, 2001). TREM is a group psychoeducational intervention initially designed for women with co-occurring major mental illness and PTSD and was subsequently adapted for men with severe mental illness, women with severe addictive disorders and histories of victimization, and adolescent girls with addictive or psychiatric disorders. TREM has versions ranging from a 4-session introduction to a 24- to 33-session extended group. TREM focuses initially on the survivor's personal and relational experience in order to facilitate the reinstatement of psychosocial and psychosexual development that was interrupted by adversity (e.g., family and community poverty, racism, mental illness) and trauma. TREM then provides a supportive (gender-separated) group milieu in which each survivor can disclose memories of trauma to help overcome feelings of fear, grief, and shame while reintegrating those memories into a personal life narrative. TREM is similar to TARGET in teaching that symptoms originate as legitimate responses to trauma and to TARGET and STAIR PE in teaching skills for affect awareness and relational engagement. TREM was found to be associated with greater improvements in PTSD, SUD, and psychiatric symptoms than mental health or SUD treatment-as-usual in a multisite study of interventions for women in recovery from addiction and violence (Morrissey et al., 2005).

Hypnosis and hypnotherapy for PTSD

Hypnotic techniques have been used with ASD and PTSD for 200 years, and contemporary therapists use hypnosis within CBT or psychodynamic therapy rather than in isolation (Cardena, 2008). Hypnosis involves the therapist encouraging the client in focusing internally and suggesting that she or he is experiencing changes in body sensations, perception, thoughts, emotions, or behavior without the client intending or willing them to happen. The contrast between what the client is aware of consciously and intends to feel, think, or do and what the therapist suggests the client is feeling, thinking, or doing is the "induction" of (i.e., leads to) an altered state of consciousness (the hypnotic "trance," which is a mental "disconnect"). The hypnotic trance increases the ability to focus attention and thereby to make changes in dissociative symptoms such as PTSD intrusive reexperiencing (e.g., unwanted memories or flashbacks of traumatic experiences).

Hypnotic techniques such as self-hypnosis may be used in the first, stabilizing, phase of psychotherapy to achieve a calm mental focus or guided imagery to provide clients with an imaginary "safe place" and an altered view of themselves as effective ("ego strengthening"). During Phase 2, hypnotherapy techniques may be used to enhance clients' ability to vividly recall and successfully cope with the anxiety elicited by traumatic memories, including projective and restructuring techniques, age regression, and imaginal memory containment.

Research studies have shown that hypnotherapy was comparable to psychodynamic therapy in reducing PTSD and enhancing adjustment (Brom, Kleber, & Defares, 1989), and it increased the benefits when added to CBT for ASD (Bryant, Moulds, Guthrie, & Nixon, 2005). However, experts recommend that hypnosis *not* be to "recover" (i.e., enable clients to recall) traumatic memories that are not consciously available to them (Cardena, 2008; see Chapter 1). Hypnosis does not necessarily increase memories' accuracy or completeness, but it does increase the recaller's confidence in what they believe to be a memory—*even if this is not a valid memory* (Cardena, 2008). Hypnosis does not "cause" false memories, but it may lead therapists or clients to mistakenly believe they can purposefully search for and find lost memories when this is not the case (Courtois, 1999; Scoboria, Mazzoni, Kirsch, & Jimenez, 2006).

Psychodynamic therapies for PTSD

Psychodynamic therapy for PTSD is based on psychoanalytic theory and Freud's view that "hysteria" (in contemporary terms, dissociative and conversion symptoms) are the result of psychological defenses (such as denial, repression, or reaction formation) against the anxiety caused by memories of traumatic events. Freud distinguished traumatic neuroses from other neuroses, postulating that some psychic conflicts and anxiety were the result of actual traumatic events rather than a failure of the person to overcome psychological complexes. Psychodynamic psychotherapy for PTSD relies upon *interpretation* of defenses and of the anxiety that is being defended against (often due to an unacceptable wish or fear stimulated by a traumatic memory) to enable clients to relinquish or modify the defense and cope with anxiety in more adaptive ways (Kudler, 2008; Kudler, Krupnick, Blank, Herman, & Horowitz, 2008).

Psychodynamic psychotherapy involves helping the client to recognize unconscious defensive attempts to repress traumatic memories and associated thoughts and feelings when this occurs in the interaction with the therapist. This enables the client to understand and relinquish or modify these unconscious psychological defenses and "work through" (i.e., figure out how to live with) rather than perpetuating ("reenacting") the distress that they feel as a result of traumatic memories.

Psychodynamic psychotherapy has been tested for PTSD in only one study that meets rigorous scientific standards, in which Brom et al. (1989) showed that a brief form of psychodynamic psychotherapy was superior to placebo and equal or superior to hypnotherapy in reducing PTSD symptoms and improving clients' adjustment. Psychodynamic therapy is used by many PTSD therapists, but further research is needed to bolster its evidence base. The strongest scientific evidence for psychodynamic psychotherapies with adults who often have experienced severe childhood traumatization has been provided by an RCT study of a psychodynamic psychotherapy for BPD (Bateman & Fonagy, 2009). Fonagy and Bateman (2006) describe how attachment theory can be translated into an approach to regulating the extreme emotion states in BPD that they call "mentalization." To mentalize is to examine one's own thoughts and thought processes as if looking into one's own mind in order to sort out and organize those thoughts and mental processes. When adults with BPD were helped to develop this mentalization capacity in therapy, they were less likely to have suicidal incidents or to be hospitalized for psychiatric crises than if they were provided with the more standard form of therapy designed to help them manage their symptoms. While PTSD was not assessed in that study, it is likely that some, perhaps many, of the clients with BPD had comorbid PTSD, and the benefits of mentalizing psychotherapy for those individuals will be an important clinical and research question.

Integration of experiential and psychodynamic psychotherapies for PTSD

Accelerated Experiential Dynamic Psychotherapy (AEDP; Fosha et al., 2009; Gleiser, Ford, & Fosha, 2008) draws on research on emotional development in the caregiver–child attachment relationship in early childhood to hypothesize that PTSD psychotherapy should provide "(a) *dyadic affect regulation* of intense emotions in the context of an *attachment-based therapeutic relationship*" and "(b) a secure base through the therapist's actively and explicitly empathic, caring, emotionally engaged, affirming stance [so that the client does not feel] *alone with intense emotional experience*" (Fosha et al., 2009). Dyadic affect regulation means that therapists provide modeling and guidance while they interact in therapy sessions in order to work with the patient (the therapy "dyad") so the patient can observe and put bodily feelings into emotion words that make the emotions more manageable and livable.

AEDP accomplishes these goals with several therapeutic interventions, including "(a) somatic focusing (e.g., 'What are you feeling in your body right now?'), (b) explicit relational joining (e.g., 'We can work on how to make sense of these feelings together'), (c) affective mirroring (e.g., 'Before you turned away, I saw grief in your face'), and (d) deepening evocative portrayals (e.g., 'You felt you were drowning in terror')" (Fosha et al., 2009). Although AEDP has not been rigorously scientifically tested, it provides therapists with ways to help clients reduce avoidance of trauma-related memories, reminders, and emotional distress that are more detailed and fully defined than the general procedures for PE or NET (Gleiser et al., 2008).

A number of other "creative arts" and expressive therapies derived from the experiential and psychodynamic traditions have been adapted for PTSD treatment (Johnson, Lahad, & Gray, 2008). These include art therapy, involving the use of artistic forms of expression to describe and manage traumatic events, the emotions and beliefs that result, and the hopes and changes that can serve as a basis for recovery from PTSD. Music, dance, theater, and guided imagery (i.e., mentally visualizing traumatic stress reactions and adaptive ways of coping with or overcoming them) also have been creatively utilized in assisting trauma survivors to cope with or recover from PTSD. Creative arts modalities are used in a number of other PTSD psychotherapies, including some forms of CBT (e.g., guided imagery in the "resource installation" component of EMDR), hypnosis (which also uses guided imagery), and emotion regulation psychotherapies (such as the "lifeline" in TARGET). Creative arts therapies for PTSD have not been systematically tested.

Body-focused psychotherapy for PTSD

The distinctive changes in body physiology and brain structure and function that occur in PTSD (see Chapter 5) highlight the importance of helping people with PTSD to be aware of and regain healthy functioning in their bodies. *Sensorimotor Psychotherapy (SP)* is the most fully developed and widely practiced body-focused therapy for PTSD (Fisher & Ogden, 2009), along with the *Somatic Experiencing* method of Peter Levine. SP and SE, like hypnotherapy, provide other therapeutic interventions—most often experiential or psychodynamic therapies or CBT—rather than alone. Both techniques first guide clients in learning to recognize and nonjudgmentally observe rather than avoid being aware of bodily sensations and associated thoughts, emotions, and behaviors. Such "mindful" observation enables clients to notice that PTSD symptoms begin with subtle (or not so subtle) physiological changes, the foundation of emotional responses (such as fear, anger, or shame) and the thoughts that accompany them. These in turn lead to PTSD symptoms (such as an unwanted intrusive memory or reminder of the trauma). Mindful observation of body states and associated feelings, thoughts, and actions and modulation of these responses help clients learn to cope, thus assuaging their panic and perceived helplessness.

In addition to increasing internal awareness, SP and SE also teach skills for directly altering bodily arousal levels so that clients learn to restore states of calm and mobilize physical energy in productive ways. "Clients learn to decipher the body's signals: to notice impulses to move, to slow down, and to take self-protective action. When these impulses are noticed, the therapist helps the client to engage in conscious, intentional movements that increase the experience of the body as a resource, a body that can set a healthy boundary, stand its ground, or effectively fight and flee"

(Fisher & Ogden, 2009). SP and SE also use interventions to enable the client to "uncouple" traumatic memories from their intense emotional and somatic responses, thereby increasing the client's sense of safety in his or her body even when faced with reminders of past psychological traumas. The "uncoupling" process involves shifting mental focus away from the details of a memory to the way in which the body is responding currently during the remembering.

For example, as a client recalls being beaten by his father as a child, what is his internal experience of that event? Does recall trigger body sensations? Or a thought or belief? Some feelings or emotions? Or impulses to move in some way? With the guidance of the therapist, the client is asked to report "what is happening right here, right now." If one of the characteristics of trauma-related disorders is the loss of present time orientation, SP addresses that issue by helping clients to differentiate past and present: "When you remember that experience *then*, what happens here and *now* inside you?" (Fisher, 2008, p. 598).

Family and couples therapies for PTSD

The entire family is affected when a family member experiences psychological trauma and develops PTSD. When parents experience PTSD, whether due to experiencing psychological trauma directly or due to harm to their spouse or children, their ability to provide their spouse and children with a sense of security, nurturance, and healthy encouragement of growth is likely to be compromised despite their best efforts. Therefore, models of psychotherapy that focus on assisting couples or families recover from PTSD have been developed for both adults and children (Catherall, 1998; Figley, 1989; Ford, 2008; Ford & Courtois, 2013; Ford & Saltzman, 2009; Johnson & Courtois, 2009).

Family and couples therapies for PTSD have two common denominators that involve assisting family members in (i) establishing a functional "family system" or couple relationship by communicating with one another and solving problems in ways that enhance their actual and perceived sense of safety, respect, caring, trust, and healthy development, and (ii) accessing social support and resources (e.g., from neighbors and community members, or educational, governmental, or religious organizations or family/parent support programs) (Riggs, Monson, Glynn, & Canterino, 2008). Across a wide variety of psychosocial problems (e.g., family crises, psychiatric disorders, addictions, school failure) family therapy interventions have shown consistent evidence of effectiveness in achieving those goals (Diamond & Josephson, 2005).

However, few studies have investigated the efficacy of family therapy for those who have experienced psychological trauma or PTSD (Riggs et al., 2008). Although behavioral and cognitive behavioral approaches to marital therapy have shown some promise with couples in which one member has PTSD, only one scientifically valid study has been conducted to date in which participants were randomly assigned to receive family therapy or not. In that study, conducted on adult military veterans with PTSD, most of the subjects were adult partners in couple's therapy (a small number of cases involved a sibling or a parent), and the addition of family therapy to CBT for PTSD did not show evidence of incremental benefit (Glynn et al., 1999).

In the investigation of another population of interest, a family education and support intervention for families with a terminally ill adult member showed some evidence of benefiting the grieving process after 13 months of therapy (Kissane et al., 2006).

Group therapies for PTSD

Group therapies are widely utilized as a therapeutic and psychoeducational intervention for PTSD (Ford et al., 2009; Ready & Shea, 2008; Shea, McDevitt-Murphy, Ready, & Schnurr, 2008). Group therapy has been used with adult survivors of childhood abuse, domestic or community violence, traumatic military service, disasters, terrorism, and genocide and torture. Group therapies use many clinical models, including CBT, PAIR, and psychodynamic. In some cases, trauma-focused treatments such as PE and NET are being conducted and studied as to their efficacy in group settings.

Classen et al. reported on a study they conducted that compared supportive ("present-focused") and trauma memory ("trauma-focused") group modalities to a wait list with women survivors of childhood. They found both group therapies to be associated with reductions in self-reported dissociative and sexual symptoms, vindictiveness, and nonassertiveness, as well as with lowered risk of revictimization (Classen et al., 2011). Another study compared 10 sessions of individual or group psychotherapy for women who had experienced childhood sexual abuse, finding group and individual therapy to be associated with comparable benefits; however, half of the women sought additional treatment during the study, suggesting that neither therapy fully addressed their needs (Stalker & Fry, 1999). With incarcerated women, an emotion regulation group therapy was associated with improvements in PTSD and depression symptoms and reduced interpersonal problems compared to a treatment as usual—although 45% of the group participants dropped out, compared to 28% of the controls (Bradley & Follingstad, 2003).

With military veterans diagnosed with chronic PTSD, Schnurr et al. (2003) conducted a large ($N = 360$) study comparing group therapy using either PE/CR or "present centered" group therapy conducted during 35 sessions over the course of a year. Both therapies reduced PTSD symptom severity by 15–20%. The PE-based group therapy had a higher dropout rate treatment phase (23%) than PCT (13%), but participants receiving at least 24 group sessions showed evidence of greater reductions in PTSD symptom severity in the PE versus present centered treatment. Ready et al. (2008) later modified PE group therapy so that participants received more opportunities to therapeutically recall and recount traumatic memories both at home and in group sessions. In a field trial with 102 male veterans, clinically significant reductions in PTSD symptoms were found (based on therapist as well as client report) and were sustained, with few therapy dropouts.

A specialized brief CBT group therapy for insomnia associated with PTSD in women who were sexually assaulted as adults, Imagery Rehearsal Therapy (IRT) was found to be more effective in reducing nightmare frequency and PTSD symptom severity than a wait list condition (Krakow and Zadra, 2006). In an independent replication with an adaptation of IRT that included systematic trauma memory *Exposure* work (using nightmares as the focus), Rescripting of nightmares, and Relaxation training for sleep hygiene (EERT), researchers Davis and Wright (2007) found that after a three-session intervention, adult survivors of traumatic accidents and assaults reported reduced symptoms of PTSD and depression and improved sleep attributed to less fear of sleep, compared to a randomized control group who reported no changes. At a 6-month follow-up, 84% of the treatment completers reported no nightmares in the past week.

Pharmacological therapies (medication) for PTSD

Several new medication options for the treatment of symptoms of PTSD are being developed, researched, and reviewed by the US FDA and similar safety regulatory agencies in countries worldwide. Medications that are efficacious for depression are the most widely approved and used pharmacotherapy agents for PTSD, not surprising in light of the frequent comorbidity of PTSD and depression and the fact that PTSD emotional numbing symptoms overlap with the symptoms of depression (Bernardy & Friedman, 2015; Friedman & Davidson, 2014). Only two medications, both of which are selective serotonin reuptake inhibitors (SSRIs), sertraline (Zoloft) and paroxetine (Paxil) are FDA approved by the United States Food and Drug Administration (FDA) for the treatment of PTSD symptoms in adults, based on large studies demonstrating the medications' safety and efficacy for this purpose.

However, many other medications are being applied to PTSD treatment based on the growing research on the biology of PTSD (see Chapter 5). For example, an antihypertensive drug, prazosin, was first shown to help people with PTSD who suffer from nightmares. Recently, it has been found to be helpful to many with the chronic daytime anxiety and tension associated with the hyperarousal symptoms of PTSD (Opler et al., 2009). Pharmacotherapy for the treatment of PTSD follows a similar set of phases, as described earlier. It is most often applied in conjunction with psychotherapy because the anxiety, mood, and behavioral problems associated with PTSD require a number of different modalities.

Conclusion

In the four decades since the diagnosis of PTSD was codified, dozens of therapies have been developed for the treatment of its various problematic and often vexing symptoms. To date, both PE and EMDR, along with CPT, have the strongest empirical support as to their efficacy in symptom reduction. Many modifications to these treatments are now available and are being tested. Several medications—especially the SSRI class of antidepressants (Zoloft and Paxil in particular)—have been shown to ameliorate symptoms over short periods of time. Experiential, body-focused, expressive, hypnotic, and psychodynamic therapies provide additional tools that may enhance PTSD recovery in individuals, in couples, and in families, and need ongoing scientific investigation (Box 7.5).

Box 7.5 Case Example of Experiential Psychotherapy for PTSD

Angela, a pseudonym for a composite client, is a 37-year-old Caucasian woman who works as a paralegal for a criminal law firm. She grew up in a middle-class suburban family with two siblings. An average student, teachers observed her to be quiet and well behaved. She had no close friends and did not participate in extracurricular activities. However, Angela had an unwanted "secret life": her parents sexually and physically molested her and other young children while filming child pornography. She recalled feeling confused as a young child because her parents were either angry with or ignored her at home or in their group, but they acted "normal" in public. They frequently harshly punished her (drugging, starving, and forcing her to witness and participate in terrifying and humiliating sexual and physical violations) for offenses that she did not understand. In response, Angela tried not to draw attention to herself, and she understandably came to the belief that her parents truly hated her and wanted her dead.

To survive, Angela learned to empty her mind of all thoughts and erase all feelings; however, as a teenager, she increasingly could not hide feelings of rage and contempt. She escaped by setting fire to her family's house, whereupon she was placed in a juvenile correctional facility. At age 16, she became an emancipated minor, and she lived on the streets, where she survived by prostituting herself and selling drugs. Fortunately, the stage crew of a touring musical band too Angela under their wing and off the street. Angela got a GED and put herself through college, becoming a paralegal in order to "go after the bastards" who hurt innocent people. Despite achieving financial stability and feeling satisfaction in her work, Angela struggled with severe bouts of depression. Cutting herself and drinking or using drugs to the point of blackouts were her only means of relieving her depression. When promoted to oversee a paralegal office, she began—for the first time since childhood—to experience a deep sense of terror. She had increasing periods of "losing time" and was no longer able to numb herself by cutting. She was terrified of seeking therapy, believing she would be labeled crazy and institutionalized, a threat made repeatedly by her parents when she was a child. But after having a dissociative episode that led her boss to question her reliability, Angela decided that therapy might be her only way to forestall the complete breakdown that she'd always feared. She reluctantly made an appointment with a therapist, saying that she wanted therapy because she'd been depressed.

AEDP applied to the case example

Helping Angela to move from defensive avoidance, terror, and isolation to awareness, connection, and glimmers of core affective experience constitutes the first (step in AEDP).

A: *(avoiding eye contact and in a flat voice)* This incident at work has been so upsetting to me. My boss swears that she came into my office and found me huddled under my desk, crying, but I don't remember any of that ever happening. I don't know why she would possibly lie to me about something like that, but ...

Box 7.5 Continued

Th: (*in a soft, soothing voice*) That sounds very distressing on many levels. What's the worst part about it for you as you tell me right now? [empathy, specificity]

A: (*breathing increases and voice becomes shaky*) That she would see me in such a state. [shame and traumatic fear; hyperarousal]

Th: That brings up some strong feelings. [focus on immediate emotional experience]

A: No, I'm fine. [defense]

Th: You started to breathe faster just now and your voice trembled. It made me wonder if you weren't getting scared as you remembered it. [somatic focus, mirroring, empathy]

A: (*says nothing; looks dazed, staring off into space*)

Th: I get the sense that you have so many feelings inside right now that maybe they feel overwhelming. [anxiety/affect regulation]

A: I don't know. (*looks panicked*) [anxiety]

Th: (*very softly and gently*) Is there something scary about my seeing that in you? [empathic exploration of anxiety in the context of the relationship: N.B. the therapist's directly exploring the anxiety in the context of the here-and-now of the therapeutic relationship]

A: (*whispering*) It's dangerous. [the client takes the risk of sharing her authentic experience: the process is moving forward. Beginning of the first state of transformation.]

Th: Dangerous?

A: (*fragmented voice*) If people see, I'll get fired, or something terrible will happen.

Th: Angela, I see this profound terror in your face and hear it in your voice. I don't yet know what it's linked to—though I'm sure we'll get to that later when it's safe to —but right now, I'm so struck by your courage in coming here to talk to me even though you have all this fear inside of you. [going to the positive side of the fear: somatic mirroring in context of relationship; structuring; affirmation of courage]

A: (*looks surprised, fleeting smile, wary, but glances at therapist*) Really? [taking in the affirmation] I feel like such a spaz. I can barely talk, I don't know what's happening to me.

Th: Oh, you're anything but a spaz. This is what it's like for anyone to be terrified. You freeze, you feel confused, your mind goes blank. [empathy, affirmation, psycho-ed, normalizing]

A: (*making brief, intermittent eye contact*) Well, I feel a little better knowing that. A little bit less like a freak. [decrease in anxiety and shame: first state of transformation is proceeding]

Th: Quite the contrary. It takes a tremendous amount of strength to decide to start facing the terror of trauma and the other feelings that go along with it. [affirmative reframing]

A: (*soft, tremulous voice, tentative eye contact*) I don't feel very strong right now. [the client is taking the risk of allowing herself to feel vulnerable]

Th: Well, I don't think anybody can when they're facing these things alone. It's too much. [empathy, support, explicit about things being too much when one is alone]

(Continued)

Box 7.5 Continued

A: (*steadier voice, gaze down*) That's my life. One kind of hiding after another.

Th: Can I ask, I notice that you've been sneaking little peeks at me while we've been talking. What have you been seeing in me? What do you see in my eyes? [complex intervention: dyadic engagement, dyadic relational desensitization, facilitating new corrective experience; seeking to undo projection by inviting the client to track the therapist]

A: You look kind, like you want to help. But that's your job, right? And I've known a lot of people in my life who go from Dr. Jekyll to Mr. Hyde in a split second.

Th: Wow. That must make it so hard to feel safe around anyone, like any minute they could turn on you. Must make it even harder for you to be here. [empathy]

A: Yeah, that's why I've gotten so good at hiding.

Th: And yet, despite all the terror and the betrayal, here you are, starting to find a way to let me be with you. [recognizing, affirming, and amplifying positive healthy glimmers of healing, self-reparative tendencies coming to the fore]

A: (*half-jokingly*) Hopefully, I won't find myself dead in an alleyway somewhere. But I can't go on living this way either. (*starts to tear up*) [increase in the client's motivation for therapeutic exploration: very important green light. Beginning of State 2 work]

Th: What way?

At this early point in therapy, Angela has just begun to acknowledge, and to touch upon the actual experience of, her deeper emotions. With the therapist's consistent empathic and strength-based focus in the face of her dismissive and defensive stance, Angela is beginning to consider that the therapist might be genuinely respecting her competence rather than judging her based on what she presumes to be deficits or pathology (based on her abusive early life experiences and possible past encounters with trauma-insensitive professionals or systems). While the working alliance, the foundation for experiencing a secure attachment in therapy, is being formed, the therapist also is consistently tracking and mirroring Angela's moment-to-moment emotional experience, leading her closer to fuller, felt experience of her feelings.

As clients such as Angela become able to experience core emotions, they realize that they can do so without feeling overwhelmed or trapped; instead, they often feel a surprising sense of relief and the buoyant yet grounded feeling of rejuvenation, resilience, and resourcefulness. This is the beginning of the second state transformation, a shift from core emotion to core state, which has been described as *mentalization* (Allen, Fonagy, & Bateman, 2008) or *mindfulness* (e.g., Siegel, 2007).

The second state transformation is completed by *metaprocessing*—that is, discussing how it feels to be able to safely experience a range of emotions, which accesses *transformational affects* (e.g., pride, mastery, gratitude) and culminates in core state (Fosha, 2000; Fosha et al., 2009). The turbulence of intense emotions defines State 2, but calm, clarity, confidence, centeredness, curiosity, compassion, courage, and creativity define the core state. Work with core state phenomena culminates in the assertion of personal truth and strengthening of the individual's core identity. Next we see the client fluctuating between State 2 core emotions, transformational affects, anxiety about this change, and core state phenomena.

A: She's too afraid to let herself hope. (*cries harder*) [grief for the self; healing affects associated with positive transformational experience; second state transformation]

Th: She's been so, so hurt, and so, so scared. [empathy]

A: (*nods and continues to cry, sobbing now*) [strong affects associated with corrective experience, a corrective experience in its own right]

Th: (*waits until the crying slows down*) It's okay for her to be just where she's at right now. It's totally understandable given the fear. But can she let herself see your sadness and your tears? They are for her. [leading edge of exploring new experiences of intrarelational empathy and compassion for self: intrarelational State 2 work]

A: She sees, but she doesn't know what to do with it. [client able to tolerate a positive but very new experience, staying right on the edge of positive trepidation]

Th: That's okay; she doesn't have to do anything. Just take it in, as much as she can. (*moment of silence*) [relational intervention: helping, coaching, support, warmth]

Th: How are you feeling?

A: Calm. Less scared. Like I know I'm not going to be dragged out of my hiding place, but also maybe I'm not going to waste away there alone anymore. [postaffective breakthrough transformational affects of calm; increased capacity for coherent self-reflection; creation of safety and possibility of deeper connection. Beginning of core state]

Th: I sense your calm and the strength that you're accessing as you take the double risk of starting to let yourself feel some of this pain and aloneness and letting me be here with you and share in it with you. [affirmation with affective self-disclosure of admiration] What's that like for you right now? [metatherapeutic processing of therapeutic experience]

A: Well, if you'd asked me, I'd have said I'd never let it happen! But it just kind of did. And, well, I don't know if this makes any sense, but it feels kind of comforting. And at the same time scary. [transformational affects: the tremulous affects]

Th: Tell me about both. [addressing both bad and good, dread and hope, old and new]

A: Scary because the comfort is so foreign. Comforting because you saw something in me that it's never been safe to let anyone see, and so far I'm not hurt worse for it. But it's more than that. I actually feel better than I did before I came in here, and I never imagined that. It's like getting a balm for a very deep wound. It's not healed yet, but some of the sting is gone. Thank you for that. [Hallmark of core state: capacity for coherent and cohesive self-reflection]

(Continued)

Box 7.5 Continued

EFTT applied to the case example

During initial sessions, the real risk of danger from others (e.g., family members seeking retribution) will be assessed, and adequate resources for ensuring safety need to be ensured. Safety and trust in therapy will be fostered in several ways:

1. Validating her distrust and fear of disclosure ("Of course, you don't know me, so trust will take time. The things you've been though are very painful, so you want to be very careful about whom you share this with. My job is to understand how you see things and how you feel from your perspective, without judging you in any way.")
2. Providing information about therapy processes and roles ("We are not going to hammer away at your traumatic experiences session after session. I am interested in you, Angela, as a whole person. You are in the driver's seat. We will explore both past and present concerns, whatever is most important to you. My job is to ensure your safety and to support and promote your growth. That will mean helping you get in touch with painful feelings, but only so that you can work them through, here, in this safe environment, when you're ready, and at a pace you can handle.")
3. Communicating genuine compassion for her past and current suffering and acknowledgement and respect for her struggle to cope and build a life for herself ("I understand that depression is a major challenge for you, that it's a big struggle at times just to keep going. You also have been through incredibly difficult and painful experiences, and you've struggled to cope with these alone and for a very long time. I don't want you to be alone with this stuff anymore. Together we can work on whatever experiences are troubling to you, whatever you decide might be most helpful.")

Angela could fear and resist the therapist's efforts to help her approach painful and vulnerable feelings. This resistance could include the conscious or unconscious use of secondary anger to push the therapist away. In order to avoid alliance ruptures, the therapist must first communicate an understanding of Angela's fear of disclosure and her own painful experience and then collaborate with her on how best to deal with these issues in therapy.

Th: I understand it must be very difficult to get close to those painful feelings.

A: (*looking down*) I wish you would stop harping on my "painful feelings." It seems like your entire agenda is to make me cry, and I don't want to cry.

Th: Oh, I see. I appreciate you bringing this up so directly; it's important. I don't want to push you into feelings you don't want to feel or don't feel ready for. If I understand, right now you don't want to focus on things that could make you cry; you really don't want to go there.

A: Not now, not ever. I just don't want to get into all that past stuff. I need to forget it. I told you my only goal is to stop being so depressed and stop spacing out so I don't lose my job. In terms of the past, all I want is to make sure those "sickos" don't destroy any other kids' lives.

Th: We can focus on current difficulties to help you with spacing out and
        depression. But we have to understand those experiences better to change
        them, the thoughts, feelings, and memories that contribute to depression and
        shutting down. If some of that is connected to your past, it's going to be pretty
        hard to avoid the past entirely. Does that make sense?

A: Yes, I know that.

Th: Plus, many things that contribute to your current difficulties, I can only
        imagine, are extremely painful. It will take a lot of faith in yourself and your
        ability to handle it, as well as trust in me, in order to allow yourself to feel and
        open up about these things. But I think you know that continuing to push them
        away or keep them bottled up inside isn't working.

A: Yes, I know. I'm just scared (*eyes well up*) I don't think I can take it much
        longer. No one really knows what I've been through. I don't know if I have the
        strength to tell.

Th: I understand you must be very scared, and I respect your caution. You don't
        want to feel flooded by too many powerful feelings all at once. We can take all
        the time that you need to tell whatever you need to tell. But right now, I think
        you're saying that some of these feelings have just gotten to be such a burden
        that you're not sure how to carry them anymore. There are ways I can help, if
        you decide you maybe can trust me enough to share what you're feeling.

A: What could you understand? You don't know anything about my life, really.

T: I realize I know very little about your life, and it's always your choice what to
        share with me, but I'd like to understand and to know more about those deeper
        feelings and the experiences they come from. I also think it's good to focus
        not only on painful stuff but on your legitimate anger and healthy desire for
        justice, these are very important.

Promoting affect regulation and reducing fear, avoidance, and depression
will be the focus of the second phase of therapy. Difficulties with substance
abuse and cutting behavior are understood as maladaptive strategies for coping
with overwhelming affect. The primary source of fear and avoidance (including
dissociation) is understood as the activation of a core insecure and vulnerable
sense of self formed through childhood abuse experiences ("It's as if that scared,
helpless little kid gets activated, takes over, and you have no way of calming
her"). Similarly, depression is viewed as the activation of core sense of self as
weak, bad, and unlovable formed through childhood experiences of powerlessness, isolation, and sexual exploitation. A major focus of therapy therefore
involves exploring and changing this core sense of self. As current difficulties
(e.g., fear that her employer will find out about her past) or memories of abuse
are discussed in session, interventions with Angela empathically affirm her
vulnerability in approaching feelings such as shame and encourage her to stay
with, rather than run away from or immediately try to change, these feelings.
Therapeutic work with shame is particularly challenging because the associated

(*Continued*)

Box 7.5 Continued

action tendency is to hide. EFTT involves accessing and exploring the complex of thoughts, feelings, somatic experiences, and behaviors that contribute to depression and shame. During this process, healthy resources may emerge spontaneously ("I can't keep it all bottled up inside anymore; all those dirty secrets are poisoning me!") or can be initiated by the therapist ("Can you get in touch with yourself at that time, hating what was happening to you, feeling trapped?").

An important dual focus and aim is to monitor and strengthen Angela's capacity to regulate her emotions while at the same time encouraging her to gradually confront trauma-related emotions, thoughts, and memories. *Empathically Exploring* (EE) trauma feelings and memories exclusively in interaction with the therapist initially could be more tolerable for Angela than IC abusive and neglectful others in an empty chair. Later in therapy, IC could be introduced occasionally at the emergence of assertiveness and other healthy resources. It also could be advisable to initially confront less threatening others, such as a minimally threatening but neglectful mother than a cruel or sadistic other. For Angela, it could be easier to first fully express and feel entitled to her anger at injustice and violation before she can allow herself to fully experience vulnerability and emotional pain. Adaptive anger is associated with energy, vitality, protest, standing up for oneself, finding one's "backbone," and appropriately holding others, instead of self, responsible for harm.

The goal of IC or EE initially is to help Angela shift from expressions of undifferentiated hurt and global distress to more differentiated expression of adaptive anger and sadness. At in-session indicators of unresolved feelings toward perpetrators ("He was such a disgusting pervert. I feel sick every time I think about him" or "It just eats away at me; how could she let him do that stuff?"), Angela will be encouraged to imagine the relevant person either in an empty chair or in her "mind's eye," attend to her thoughts and feelings ("What happens to you on the inside as you imagine him/her [there]?") and express them either directly to this imagined other or to the therapist ("That's very important. Try saying that to your father [points to empty chair]: 'I don't want you near me.' And tell him why" or "Stay with that feeling; tell me more—what do you find so repulsive?" or "Tell her what she should have done, what a good mother would do").

Th:	I hear how much you hate him, despise him. Tell him, over there, what you hate, make him understand.
A:	Yes, I despise how you manipulated and corrupted innocent children for your own sick needs, and did it in the name of God! You perverted everything. I was innocent, and you ruined my childhood, made sex disgusting, destroyed my trust in humanity and my faith in God. Damn you! I hope you rot in hell. Oh, I sound just like him. I can't stand this!
Th:	But you're not him, Angela, you are justifiably angry and you want to see him punished for his despicable behavior, his crimes. Tell him.

A: Yes, I do want to see you punished; you deserve to be punished for all the harm you've done, and I'm going to find a way to see that that happens. You are not going to get away with it. You fucked me up royally. My life has been such a mess because of you, but I refuse to let you ruin my life anymore. This whole thing is about your sickness, not mine!

Th: How do you feel saying that?

A: It feels right. He was the adult, I was just a little kid. I deserved love and security, not that twisted life he imposed on me.

Th: How do you imagine your father over there would react [in his heart] if he knew how you really felt—defensive, remorseful, blaming, and angry?

A: It's funny, he used to seem so huge and powerful; now I see a sick, pathetic old man. I don't think he's capable of understanding. But it doesn't matter anymore. I know the truth.

These interventions support her anger and entitlement to justice and, like a victim impact statement, help her begin to articulate the effects of the abuse and hold the perpetrator(s) accountable for harm. One goal is for clients to arrive at a more differentiated perspective of perpetrators so they are seen as more human and life-size and less powerful. An important step is to elicit the client's understanding of perpetrators' responses to confrontation. Enacting or imagining the other also can elicit empathic resources. This can be particularly important in healing attachment relationships (if this is desirable for the client)—for example, coming to understand that one or both of her parents also were victims or would regret their behavior.

Allowing the pain of rejection and sadness of loss is also an important aspect of resolution. Accomplishing this is a gradual and complex process that involves the many emotions associated with traumatic experiences. Angela will need to face the pain of not being loved by her parents, all the losses and things she has missed out on (e.g., friends, healthy sexuality, security, self-esteem), and how profoundly she has been victimized by years of loneliness, exploitation, cruelty, and abuse. Allowing herself to fully feel the pain of these experiences (even for a moment) requires confidence in her ability to survive the pain as well as the therapist's supportive presence (e.g., soothing voice, hand on her hand or knee), encouraging statements (e.g., "Let it come"), and help in symbolizing the meaning of the pain (e.g., "Put words to your tears"; "What's the worst part of it for you?"; "So devastating—can you say more about what that meant to you?"). Accurate symbolization helps to create distance from the pain and to make her experience more comprehensible. Facing the emotional pain of traumatic experiences also includes facing associated but previously avoided aspects of self. Facing the pain of her isolation as a child, for example, could include feeling the shame associated with sexual abuse, prostitution, and self-destructive behavior; rage at years of victimization, violation, and abuse; and deep sadness at all the disappointments, losses, and suffering.

Finally letting go and allowing the self to fully feel the pain of traumatic experiences typically are followed by a sense of relief, an increased sense of agency or control, and an implicit challenging of beliefs that perpetuated avoidance (e.g., "I *can* handle it; it won't destroy me").

Excerpted and reprinted with permission from Fosha et al. (2009).

Other treatment methods and modalities (including hybrids, concurrent treatments, modifications of the original evidence-based treatment, application to new and more diverse populations, and new applications of a variety of medications) are under development and investigation. Many hold great appeal and show promise but are as of yet unproven. While innovation is a cornerstone for the development of increasingly effective PTSD therapies, therapists should exercise caution and should ensure that clients make an informed consent before and throughout their involvement in any treatment for PTSD (Box 7.6).

Box 7.6 A Cautionary Note About Popular PTSD Treatments That Are Not Evidence-Based

There are different degrees of being "evidence based," and there is controversy over what constitutes proper or sufficient evidence for a therapy or practice to be so designated. A treatment that is evidence-based for one purpose or population may not be for other purposes or populations, just as is the case for medications that are approved by the FDA only for certain illnesses until studies have validated the drug's therapeutic safety and efficacy with other illnesses. For example, in the case of PTSD, two SSRI antidepressants have been approved for use with adults (fluoxetine (Prozac) and sertaline (Zoloft)), but neither has been shown to have benefits with children who suffer from PTSD, and one actually was shown in a scientific study to *not* add to the benefit provided by CBT psychotherapy (see Chapter 8).

As a result, it is important not to assume that a PTSD treatment automatically is beneficial simply because it seems appealing or even is widely utilized. For example, several therapies have been described as "power" therapies for PTSD despite relatively little scientific evidence of their effectiveness. Power therapies include EMDR, which has developed a scientific evidence base for PTSD treatment, and several others that have not been scientifically tested: Thought Field Therapy, Trauma Incident Reduction, Emotional Freedom Therapy (also known as Tapping Therapy) (Poole, 1999), and, more recently, Visual/Kinetic Dissociation (based on "Neurolinguistic Programming"; Hossack & Bentall, 1996) and many other variants. These therapies use a variety of techniques similar to those of hypnosis (such as repetitive movements that interrupt emotional distress and refocus mental attention), experiential therapies (such as shifting mental focus from being absorbed in a memory to being a detached observer), body-focused therapies (such as teaching clients to notice shifts in physical arousal and to visualize energy flow ("meridians") in the body), and PE/CR or CPT (such as repeatedly recalling traumatic memories and reevaluating associated beliefs).

Thus, power therapies for PTSD largely involve creative but relatively minor adaptations of widely used and better-validated PTSD therapy methods. With the possible exception of EMDR (which has been modified extensively so that it is not a single uniform technique but a variety of options for PE/CR), the "power" in these therapies is largely due to therapists' beliefs that they confer unique benefits. With further careful scientific testing, some of the innovations of the power therapies may be shown to be reliably helpful (and safe) tools for PTSD psychotherapy, but until that is the case, caution is highly recommended in their use and promotion.

References

ACPMH (2007/2014). *Not a published document*. Available on-line <http://www.phoenixaus-tralia.org/resources/ptsd-guidelines/>Accessed 13.04.15.

Adenauer, H., Catani, C., Gola, H., Keil, J., Ruf, M., Schauer, M., et al. (2011). Narrative exposure therapy for PTSD increases top-down processing of aversive stimuli—evidence from a randomized controlled treatment trial. *BMC Neuroscience, 12*, 127. http://dx.doi.org/10.1186/1471-2202-12-127.

Allen, J. G., Fonagy, P., & Bateman, A. (2008). *Mentalizing in clinical practice*. Washington, DC: American Psychiatric Press.

American Psychiatric Association, (2004). *Practice guidleines for the treatment of patients with acute stress disorder and posttraumatic stress disorder*. Washington DC: American Psychiatric Association.

American Psychological Association, (2006). Evidence-based practice in psychology. *American Psychologist, 61*, 271–285.

American Psychological Association's Division of Trauma Psychology (2015). *Not a published document*. Available on-line <http://www.apa.org/about/offices/directorates/guidelines/ptsd-panel.aspx>Accessed 13.04.15.

Anderson, M. L., Ziedonis, D. M., & Najavits, L. M. (2014). Posttraumatic stress disorder and substance use disorder comorbidity among individuals with physical disabilities: Findings from the National Comorbidity Survey Replication. *Journal of Traumatic Stress, 27*(2), 182–191. http://dx.doi.org/10.1002/jts.21894.

Angelo, F. N., Miller, H. E., Zoellner, L. A., & Feeny, N. C. (2008). I need to talk about it: A qualitative analysis of trauma-exposed women's reasons for treatment choice. *Behavior Therapy, 39*(1), 13–21. http://dx.doi.org/S0005-7894(07)00057-3 [pii].

Bateman, A., & Fonagy, P. (2009). Randomized controlled trial of outpatient mentalization-based treatment versus structured clinical management for borderline personality disorder. *American Journal of Psychiatry, 166*(12), 1355–1364. http://dx.doi.org/10.1176/appi.ajp.2009.09040539.

Bernardy, N. C., & Friedman, M. J. (2015). Psychopharmacological strategies in the management of Posttraumatic Stress Disorder (PTSD): What have we learned? *Current Psychiatry Reports, 17*(4), 564. http://dx.doi.org/10.1007/s11920-015-0564-2.

Bichescu, D., Neuner, F., Schauer, M., & Elbert, T. (2007). Narrative exposure therapy for political imprisonment-related chronic posttraumatic stress disorder and depression. *Behaviour Research and Therapy, 45*(9), 2212–2220. http://dx.doi.org/S0005-7967(06)00293-2 [pii]; http://dx.doi.org/10.1016/j.brat.2006.12.

Bohus, M., Dyer, A. S., Priebe, K., Kruger, A., Kleindienst, N., Schmahl, C., et al. (2013). Dialectical behaviour therapy for post-traumatic stress disorder after childhood sexual abuse in patients with and without borderline personality disorder: A randomised controlled trial. *Psychotherapy and Psychosomatics*, *82*(4), 221–233. http://dx.doi.org/10.1159/000348451.

Bradley, R. G., & Follingstad, D. R. (2003). Group therapy for incarcerated women who experienced interpersonal violence: A pilot study. *Journal of Traumatic Stress*, *16*, 337–340.

Brom, D., Kleber, R. J., & Defares, P. B. (1989). Brief psychotherapy for posttraumatic stress disorders. *Journal of Consulting and Clinical Psychology*, *57*(5), 607–612.

Bryant, R. A., Moulds, M. L., Guthrie, R. M., & Nixon, R. D. V. (2005). The additive benefit of hypnosis and cognitive-behavioral therapy in treating acute stress disorder. *Journal of Consulting and Clinical Psychology*, *73*, 334–340.

Bryant, R. A., Moulds, M. L., & Nixon, R. V. (2003). Cognitive behaviour therapy of acute stress disorder: A four-year follow-up. *Behaviour Research and Therapy*, *41*(4), 489–494.

Cardena, E. (2008). Hypnotherapy. In G. Reyes, J. D. Elhai, & J. Ford (Eds.), *Encyclopedia of psychological trauma* (pp. 336–339). Hoboken NJ: Wiley.

Catherall, D. R. (Ed.). (1998). *Treating traumatized families*. Boca Raton, FL: CRC Press.Figley, C. R. (1989). *Helping traumatized families*. San Francisco: Jossey-Bass.

Chard, K. M. (2005). An evaluation of cognitive processing therapy for the treatment of posttraumatic stress disorder related to childhood sexual abuse. *Journal of Consulting Clinical Psychology*, *73*(5), 965–971. http://dx.doi.org/2005-13740-019 [pii]; http://dx.doi.org/10.1037/0022-006X.73.5.965.

Chen, Y. R., Hung, K. W., Tsai, J. C., Chu, H., Chung, M. H., Chen, S. R., et al. (2014). Efficacy of eye-movement desensitization and reprocessing for patients with posttraumatic-stress disorder: A meta-analysis of randomized controlled trials. *PLoS One*, *9*(8), e103676. http://dx.doi.org/10.1371/journal.pone.0103676.

Classen, C., Palesh, O. G., Cavanaugh, C., Koopman, C., Kaupp, J., Kraemer, H., et al. (2011). A comparison of trauma-focused and present-focused group therapy for survivors of childhood sexual abuse: A randomized controlled trial. *Psychological Trauma*, *3*, 84–93.

Cloitre, M., Cohen, L., & Koenen, K. C. (2006). *Treating survivors of childhood abuse: Psychotherapy for the interrupted life*. New York, NY: Guilford Press.

Cloitre, M., Courtois, C. A., Charuvastra, A., Carapezza, R., Stolbach, B. C., & Green, B. L. (2011). Treatment of complex PTSD: Results of the ISTSS expert clinician survey on best practices. *Journal of Traumatic Stress*, *24*(6), 615–627. http://dx.doi.org/10.1002/jts.20697.

Cloitre, M., Koenen, K. C., Cohen, L. R., & Han, H. (2002). Skills training in affective and interpersonal regulation followed by exposure: A phase-based treatment for PTSD related to childhood abuse. *Journal of Consulting and Clinical Psychology*, *70*(5), 1067–1074.

Cloitre, M., Petkova, E., Wang, J., & Lu Lassell, F. (2012). An examination of the influence of a sequential treatment on the course and impact of dissociation among women with PTSD related to childhood abuse. *Depression and Anxiety*, *29*(8), 709–717. http://dx.doi.org/10.1002/da.21920.

Cloitre, M., Stovall-McClough, C., Zorbas, P., & Charuvastra, A. (2008). Attachment organization, emotion regulation, and expectations of support in a clinical sample of women with childhood abuse histories. *Journal of Traumatic Stress*, *21*(3), 282–289. http://dx.doi.org/10.1002/jts.20339.

Cloitre, M., Stovall-McClough, K. C., Nooner, K., Zorbas, P., Cherry, S., Jackson, C. L., et al. (2010). Treatment for PTSD related to childhood abuse: A randomized controlled trial. *American Journal of Psychiatry*, *167*(8), 915–924. http://dx.doi.org/appi.ajp.2010.09081247 [pii]; http://dx.doi.org/10.1176/appi.ajp.2010.09081247.

Clum, G. (2008). Biofeedback. In G. Reyes, J. D. Elhai, & J. Ford (Eds.), *Encyclopedia of psychological trauma* (pp. 76–80). Hoboken NJ: Wiley.

Cohen, L. R., & Hien, D. A. (2006). Treatment outcomes for women with substance abuse and PTSD who have experienced complex trauma. *Psychiatric Services*, *57*(1), 100–106. http://dx.doi.org/10.1176/appi.ps.57.1.100.

Cook, J. M., Dinnen, S., Thompson, R., Simiola, V., & Schnurr, P. P. (2014). Changes in implementation of two evidence-based psychotherapies for PTSD in VA residential treatment programs: A national investigation. *Journal of Traumatic Stress*, *27*(2), 137–143. http://dx.doi.org/10.1002/jts.21902.

Cook, J. M., Schnurr, P. P., & Foa, E. B. (2004). Bridging the gap between posttraumatic stress disorder research and clinicalpractice: The example of exposure therapy. *Psychotherapy: Theory, Research, Practice & Training*, *41*, 374–387.

Courtois, C. A. (1999). *Recollections of sexual abuse: Treatment principles and guidelines*. New York: Norton.

Courtois, C. A. (2010). *Healing the incest wound* (2nd ed.). New York: W. W. Norton.

Courtois, C. A., & Ford, J. D. (Eds.). (2009). *Treating complex traumatic stress disorders: An evidence-based guide*. New York: Guilford.

Courtois, C. A., & Gold, S. (2009). The need for inclusion of psychological trauma in the professional curriculum. *Psychological Trauma*, *1*(1), 3–23.

Courtois, C. A., & Ford, J. D. (2013). *Treating complex trauma: A sequenced relationship-based approach*. New York: Guilford.

CREST, (2003). *The management of post traumatic stress disorder in adults*. Belfast: Clinical Resource Efficiency Support Team of the Northern Ireland Department of Health, Social Services and Public Safety.

Davidson, P. R., & Parker, K. C. (2001). Eye movement desensitization and reprocessing (EMDR): A meta-analysis. *Journal of Consulting and Clinical Psychology*, *69*(2), 305–316.

Davis, J. L., & Wright, D. C. (2005). Case series utilizing exposure, relaxation, and rescripting therapy: Impact on nightmares, sleep quality, and psychological distress. *Behavioral Sleep Medicine*, *3*(3), 151–157. http://dx.doi.org/10.1207/s15402010bsm0303_3.

de Bont, P. A., van Minnen, A., & de Jongh, A. (2013). Treating PTSD in patients with psychosis: A within-group controlled feasibility study examining the efficacy and safety of evidence-based PE and EMDR protocols. *Behavior Therapy*, *44*(4), 717–730. http://dx.doi.org/10.1016/j.beth.2013.07.002.

de Kleine, R. A., Hendriks, G. J., Smits, J. A., Broekman, T. G., & van Minnen, A. (2014). Prescriptive variables for D-cycloserine augmentation of exposure therapy for posttraumatic stress disorder. *Journal of Psychiatric Research*, *48*(1), 40–46. http://dx.doi.org/10.1016/j.jpsychires.2013.10.008.

Desai, R. A., Harpaz-Rotem, I., Najavits, L. M., & Rosenheck, R. A. (2008). Impact of the Seeking Safety program on clinicaloutcomes among homeless female veterans with psychiatric disorders. *Psychiatric Services*, *59*, 996–1003.

Diamond, G., & Josephson, A. (2005). Family-based treatment research: A 10-year update. *Journal of the American Academy of Child and Adolescent Psychiatry*, *44*, 872–887.

Dossa, N. I., & Hatem, M. (2012). Cognitive-behavioral therapy versus other PTSD psychotherapies as treatment for women victims of war-related violence: A systematic review. *Scientific World Journal*, *2012*, 181847. http://dx.doi.org/10.1100/2012/181847.

Edmond, T., Rubin, A., & Wambach, K. (1999). The effectiveness of EMDR with adult female survivors of childhood sexual abuse. *Social Work Research*, *23*, 103–116.

Fareed, A., Eilender, P., Haber, M., Bremner, J., Whitfield, N., & Drexler, K. (2013). Comorbid posttraumatic stress disorder and opiate addiction: A literature review. *Journal of Addictive Diseases*, *32*(2), 168–179. http://dx.doi.org/10.1080/10550887.2013.795467.

Finkelhor, D. (1987). The trauma of child sexual abuse: Two models. *Journal of Interpersonal Violence*, *2*, 348–366.

Fisher, J. (2008). Sensorimotor psychotherapy. In G. Reyes, J. D. Elhai, & J. Ford (Eds.), *Encyclopedia of psychological trauma* (pp. 597–599). Hoboken, NJ: Wiley.

Fisher, J., & Ogden, P. (2009). Sensorimotor psychotherapy. In C. A. Courtois & J. Ford (Eds.), *Treating complex traumatic stress disorders: An evidence-based guide*. New York: Guilford.

Foa, E. B., Dancu, C. V., Hembree, E. A., Jaycox, L. H., Meadows, E. A., & Street, G. P. (1999). A comparison of exposure therapy, stress inoculation training, and their combination for reducing posttraumatic stress disorder in female assault victims. *Journal of Consulting and Clinical Psychology*, *67*, 194–200.

Foa, E. B., Gillihan, S. J., & Bryant, R. A. (2013). Challenges and Successes in Dissemination of Evidence-Based Treatments for Posttraumatic Stress: Lessons Learned From Prolonged Exposure Therapy for PTSD. *Psychological Science in the Public Interest*, *14*(2), 65–111. http://dx.doi.org/10.1177/1529100612468841.

Foa, E. B., Hembree, E. A., & Rothbaum, B. O. (2007). *Prolonged exposure therapy for PTSD: Emotional processing of traumatic experiences: Therapist guide*. New York, NY: Oxford University Press.

Foa, E. B., Keane, T. M., & Friedman, M. J. (Eds.), (2000). *Effective treatments for PTSD*. New York: Guilford.

Foa, E. B., Keane, T. M., Friedman, M. J., & Cohen, J. A. (Eds.), (2008). *Effective treatments for PTSD* (2nd ed.). New York: Guilford.

Foa, E. B., & Kozak, M. J. (1986). Emotional processing of fear: Exposure to corrective information. *Psychological Bulletin*, *99*, 20–35.

Foa, E. B., McLean, C. P., Capaldi, S., & Rosenfield, D. (2013). Prolonged exposure vs supportive counseling for sexual abuse-related PTSD in adolescent girls: A randomized clinical trial. *JAMA: Journal of the American Medical Association*, *310*(24), 2650–2657. http://dx.doi.org/10.1001/jama.2013.282829.

Foa, E. B., Rothbaum, B. O., Riggs, D. S., & Murdock, T. B. (1991). Treatment of posttraumatic stress disorder in rape victims: A comparison between cognitive-behavioral procedures and counseling. *Journal of Consulting and Clinical Psychology*, *59*, 715–723.

Fonagy, P., & Bateman, A. W. (2006). Mechanisms of change in mentalization-based treatment of BPD. *Journal Clinical Psychology*, *62*(4), 411–430. http://dx.doi.org/10.1002/jclp.20241.

Ford, J. D. (2008). Family therapy. In G. Reyes, J. D. Elhai, & J. D. Ford (Eds.), *Encyclopedia of psychological trauma* (pp. 278–280). Hoboken, NJ: Wiley.

Ford, J. D. (2009). Neurobiological and developmental research: Clinical implications. In C. Courtois & J. D. Ford (Eds.), *Treating complex traumatic stress disorders: An evidence-based guide* (pp. 31–58). New York: Guilford.

Ford, J. D. (2012). Posttraumatic stress disorder and psychological trauma. In J. Verster, K. Brady, M. Galanter, & P. Conrod (Eds.), *Drug abuse and addiction in medical illness: Causes, consequences, and treatment* (pp. 335–342). Totowa, NJ: Springer/Humana Press.

Ford, J. D. (2013). Posttraumatic stress disorder (PTSD) and substance abuse treatment. In P. Miller (Ed.), *Encyclopedia of addictive behaviors, volume 3. Interventions for addiction* (pp. 187–194). New York, NY: Elsevier.

Ford, J. D. (2015). An affective cognitive neuroscience-based approach to PTSD psychotherapy: The TARGET model. *Journal of Cognitive Psychotherapy*, *29*, 69–91.

Ford, J. D., Chang, R., Levine, J., & Zhang, W. (2013). Randomized clinical trial comparing affect regulation and supportive group therapies for victimization-related PTSD with incarcerated women. *Behavior Therapy, 44,* 262–276. http://dx.doi.org/10.1016/j. beth.2012.10.003.

Ford, J. D., Chapman, J. F., Hawke, J., & Albert, D. (2007). *Trauma among youth in the juvenile justice system: Critical issues and new directions.* Albany, NY: National Center for Mental Health and Juvenile Justice.

Ford, J. D., & Courtois, C. (2009). Chapter 1. Defining and understanding complex trauma and complex traumatic stress disorders. In C. Courtois & J. D. Ford (Eds.), *Treating complex traumatic stress disorders: An evidence-based guide* (pp. 13–30). New York: Guilford.

Ford, J. D., & Courtois, C. A. (Eds.). (2013). *Treating complex traumatic stress disorders in children and adolescents: Scientific foundations and therapeutic models.* New York: Guilford.

Ford, J. D., & Courtois, C. A. (2014). Complex PTSD, affect dysregulation, and borderline personality disorder. *Borderline Personality Disorder and Emotion Dysregulation, 1,* 9.

Ford, J. D., Fallot, R., & Harris, M. (2009). Group therapy approaches to complex traumatic stress disorders. In C. Courtois & J. D. Ford (Eds.), *Treating complex traumatic stress disorders: An evidence-based guide.* New York: Guilford.

Ford, J. D., Hawke, J., Alessi, S., Ledgerwood, D., & Petry, N. (2007). Psychological trauma and PTSD symptoms as predictors of substance dependence treatment outcomes. *Behaviour Research and Therapy, 45*(10), 2417–2431. http://dx.doi.org/10.1016/j.brat.2007.04.001.

Ford, J. D., & Kidd, P. (1998). Early childhood trauma and disorders of extreme stress as predictors of treatment outcome with chronic PTSD. *Journal of Traumatic Stress, 11,* 743–761.

Ford, J. D., & Russo, E. (2006). Trauma-focused, present-centered, emotional self-regulation approach to integrated treatment for posttraumatic stress and addiction: Trauma adapative recovery group education and therapy (TARGET). *American Journal of Psychotherapy, 60,* 335–355.

Ford, J. D., Russo, E. M., & Mallon, S. D. (2007). Integrating treatment of posttraumatic stress disorder and substance use disorder. *Journal of Counseling and Development, 85,* 475–489.

Ford, J. D., & Saltzman, W. (2009). Family therapy aroaches to complex traumatic stress disorders. In C. A. Courtois & J. Ford (Eds.), *Treating complex traumatic stress disorders: An evidence-based guide.* New York: Guilford.

Ford, J. D., Steinberg, K., & Zhang, W. (2011). A randomized clinical trial comparing affect regulation and social problem-solving psychotherapies for mothers with victimization-related PTSD. *Behavior Therapy, 42,* 561–578. http://dx.doi.org/10.1016/j.beth.2010.12.005.

Fosha, D. (2000). The transforming power of affect: A model for accelerated change.

Fosha, D., Paivio, S., Gleiser, K., & Ford, J. D. (2009). Chapter 14: Experiential and emotion-focused therapy. In C. A. Courtois & J. D. Ford (Eds.), *Treating complex traumatic stress disorders: An evidence-based guide* (pp. 286–314). New York, NY: Guilford Press.

Fosha, D., Siegel, D., & Solomon, M. (Eds.), (2009). *The healing power of emotion: Affective neuroscience, development, & clinical practice.* New York: Norton.

Friedman, M. J., & Davidson, J. R. T. (2007). Pharmacotherapy for PTSD. In M. J. Friedman, T. M. Keane, & P. Resick (Eds.), *Handbook of PTSD: Science and practice* (pp. 245–268). New York: Guilford.

Friedman, M. J., & Davidson, J. R. T. (2014). Pharmacotherapy for PTSD. In M. J. Friedman, T. M. Keane, & P. Resick (Eds.), *Handbook of PTSD: Science and practice* (pp. 376–405) (2nd ed.). New York: Guilford.

Frisman, L. K., Ford, J. D., Lin, H., Mallon, S., & Chang, R. (2008). Outcomes of trauma treatment using the TARGET model. *Journal of Groups in Addiction and Recovery, 3,* 285–303.

Gallagher, M. W., & Resick, P. A. (2012). Mechanisms of Change in Cognitive Processing Therapy and Prolonged Exposure Therapy for PTSD: Preliminary Evidence for the

Differential Effects of Hopelessness and Habituation. *Cognitive Therapy and Research*, *36*(6)http://dx.doi.org/10.1007/s10608-011-9423-6.

Gleiser, K. A., Ford, J. D., & Fosha, D. (2008). Exposure and experiential therapies for complex post-traumatic stress disorders. *Psychotherapy: Theory, Research, Practice & Training*, *45*, 340–360.

Glynn, S. M., Eth, S., Randolph, E. T., Foy, D. W., Urbaitis, M., Boxer, L., et al. (1999). A test of behavioral family therapy to augment exposure for combat-related posttraumatic stress disorder. *Journal of Consulting and Clinical Psychology*, *67*(2), 243–251.

Gradus, J. L., Suvak, M. K., Wisco, B. E., Marx, B. P., & Resick, P. A. (2013). Treatment of posttraumatic stress disorder reduces suicidal ideation. *Depression and Anxiety*, *30*(10), 1046–1053. http://dx.doi.org/10.1002/da.22117.

Hagenaars, M. A., & van Minnen, A. (2010). Posttraumatic growth in exposure therapy for PTSD. *Journal of Traumatic Stress*, *23*(4), 504–508. http://dx.doi.org/10.1002/jts.20551.

Hall, B. J., Bolton, P. A., Annan, J., Kaysen, D., Robinette, K., Cetinoglu, T., et al. (2014). The effect of cognitive therapy on structural social capital: Results from a randomized controlled trial among sexual violence survivors in the Democratic Republic of the Congo. *American Journal of Public Health*, *104*(9), 1680–1686. http://dx.doi.org/10.2105/AJPH.2014.301981.

Halvorsen, J. O., & Stenmark, H. (2010). Narrative exposure therapy for posttraumatic stress disorder in tortured refugees: A preliminary uncontrolled trial. *Scandinavian Journal of Psychology*, *51*(6), 495–502. http://dx.doi.org/10.1111/j.1467-9450.2010.00821.x.

Harned, M. S., Korslund, K. E., Foa, E. B., & Linehan, M. M. (2012). Treating PTSD in suicidal and self-injuring women with borderline personality disorder: Development and preliminary evaluation of a Dialectical Behavior Therapy Prolonged Exposure Protocol. *Behaviour Research and Therapy*, *50*(6), 381–386. http://dx.doi.org/10.1016/j.brat.2012.02.011.

Harned, M. S., Korslund, K. E., & Linehan, M. M. (2014). A pilot randomized controlled trial of Dialectical Behavior Therapy with and without the Dialectical Behavior Therapy Prolonged Exposure protocol for suicidal and self-injuring women with borderline personality disorder and PTSD. *Behaviour Research and Therapy*, *55*, 7–17. http://dx.doi.org/10.1016/j.brat.2014.01.008.

Harris, M., & Fallot, R. D. (2001). *Using trauma theory to design service systems*. San Francisco, CA: Jossey-Bass.

Harvey, M. (1996). An ecological view of psychological trauma and trauma recovery. *Journal of Traumatic Stress*, *9*, 3–23.

Hayes, S. C., Luoma, J. B., Bond, F. W., Masuda, A., & Lillis, J. (2006). Acceptance and commitment therapy: Model, processes and outcomes. *Behaviour Research and Therapy*, *44*(1), 1–25. http://dx.doi.org/S0005-7967(05)00214-7 [pii].

Hembree, E., & Marinchak, J. (2008). Cognitive behavior therapy, adult. In G. Reyes, J. D. Elhai, & J. Ford (Eds.), *Encyclopedia of psychological trauma* (pp. 126–131). Hoboken, NJ: Wiley.

Hembree, E. A. (2008). Anxiety management training. In G. Reyes, J. D. Elhai, & J. Ford (Eds.), *Encyclopedia of psychological trauma* (pp. 41–44). Hoboken, NJ: Wiley.

Hensel-Dittmann, D., Schauer, M., Ruf, M., Catani, C., Odenwald, M., Elbert, T., et al. (2011). Treatment of traumatized victims of war and torture: A randomized controlled comparison of narrative exposure therapy and stress inoculation training. *Psychotherapy and Psychosomatics*, *80*(6), 345–352. http://dx.doi.org/10.1159/000327253.

Herman, J. L. (1992). *Trauma and recovery*. New York: Basic Books.

Hien, D. A., Jiang, H., Campbell, A. N., Hu, M. C., Miele, G. M., Cohen, L. R., et al. (2010). Do treatment improvements in PTSD severity affect substance use outcomes? A secondary analysis from a randomized clinical trial in NIDA's Clinical Trials Network. *American Journal of Psychiatry*, *167*(1), 95–101.

Hossack, A., & Bentall, R. P. (1996). Elimination of posttraumatic symptomatology by relaxation and visual-kinesthetic dissociation. *Journal of Traumatic Stress*, *9*(1), 99–110.

IOM (2007). *Not a published document*. Available on-line <https://www.iom.edu/Reports/2007/Treatment-of-PTSD-An-Assessment-of-The-Evidence.aspx> Accessed 13.04.15.

ISTSS (2012). *Not a published document*. Available on-line <http://www.istss.org/ISTSS_Main/media/Documents/ComplexPTSD.pdf>Accessed 13.04.15.

Jackson, C., Nissenson, K., & Cloitre, M. (2009). Cognitive behavioral therapy. In C. A. Courtois & J. Ford (Eds.), *Treating complex traumatic stress disorders: An evidence-based guide*. New York: Guilford.

Jayawickreme, N., Cahill, S. P., Riggs, D. S., Rauch, S. A., Resick, P. A., Rothbaum, B. O., et al. (2014). Primum non nocere (first do no harm): Symptom worsening and improvement in female assault victims after prolonged exposure for PTSD. *Depression and Anxiety*, *31*(5), 412–419. http://dx.doi.org/10.1002/da.22225.

Jeffries, F. W., & Davis, P. (2013). What is the role of eye movements in eye movement desensitization and reprocessing (EMDR) for post-traumatic stress disorder (PTSD)? A review. *Behavioural and Cognitive Psychotherapy*, *41*(3), 290–300. http://dx.doi.org/10.1017/S1352465812000793.

Johnson, D. R., Lahad, M., & Gray, A. (2008). Creative therapies for adults. In E. B. Foa, T. M. Keane, M. J. Friedman, & J. A. Cohen (Eds.), *Effective treatments for PTSD* (pp. 491–507) (2nd ed.). New York: Guilford.

Johnson, S., & Courtois, C. A. (2009). Couples therapy. In C. A. Courtois & J. Ford (Eds.), *Treating complex traumatic stress disorders: An evidence-based guide*. New York: Guilford.

Kaysen, D., Schumm, J., Pedersen, E. R., Seim, R. W., Bedard-Gilligan, M., & Chard, K. (2014). Cognitive processing therapy for veterans with comorbid PTSD and alcohol use disorders. *Addictive Behaviors*, *39*(2), 420–427. http://dx.doi.org/10.1016/j.addbeh.2013.08.016.

Kissane, D. W., McKenzie, M., Bloch, S., Moskowitz, C., McKenzie, D., & O'Neill, I. (2006). Family focused grief therapy: A randomized controlled trial in palliative care and bereavement. *American Journal of Psychiatry*, *163*, 1208–1218.

Kluetsch, R. C., Ros, T., Theberge, J., Frewen, P. A., Calhoun, V. D., Schmahl, C., et al. (2014). Plastic modulation of PTSD resting-state networks and subjective wellbeing by EEG neurofeedback. *Acta Psychiatrica Scandinavica*, *130*(2), 123–136. http://dx.doi.org/10.1111/acps.12229.

Krakow, B., & Zadra, A. (2006). Clinical management of chronic nightmares: Imagery rehearsal therapy. *Behavioral Sleep Medicine*, *4*(1), 45–70. http://dx.doi.org/10.1207/s15402010bsm0401_4.

Kudler, H. (2008). Psychodynamic psychotherapy, adult. In G. Reyes, J. D. Elhai, & J. Ford (Eds.), *Encyclopedia of psychological trauma* (pp. 528–531). Hoboken, NJ: Wiley.

Kudler, H., Krupnick, J., Blank, A., Herman, J. L., & Horowitz, M. (2008). Psychodynamic therapy for adults. In E. B. Foa, T. M. Keane, M. J. Friedman, & J. A. Cohen (Eds.), *Effective treatments for PTSD* (pp. 346–369) (2nd ed.). New York: Guilford.

Lee, C. W., & Cuijpers, P. (2014). What does the data say about the importance of eye movement in EMDR? *Journal of Behavior Therapy and Experimental Psychiatry*, *45*(1), 226–228. http://dx.doi.org/10.1016/j.jbtep.2013.10.002.

Linehan, M. (1993). *Cognitive behavioral treatment of borderline personality disorder*. New York, NY: Guilford Press.

Liverant, G. I., Suvak, M. K., Pineles, S. L., & Resick, P. A. (2012). Changes in posttraumatic stress disorder and depressive symptoms during cognitive processing therapy: Evidence for concurrent change. *Journal of Consulting and Clinical Psychology*, *80*(6), 957–967. http://dx.doi.org/10.1037/a0030485.

Markowitz, J. C., Petkova, E., Neria, Y., Van Meter, P. E., Zhao, Y., Hembree, E., et al. (2015). Is exposure necessary? A randomized clinical trial of Interpersonal Psychotherapy for PTSD. *American Journal of Psychiatry*. http://dx.doi.org/10.1176/appi.ajp.2014.14070908.

McDonagh, A., Friedman, M., McHugo, G., Ford, J. D., Sengupta, A., Mueser, K., et al. (2005). Randomized trial of cognitive-behavioral therapy for chronic posttraumatic stress disorder in adult female survivors of childhood sexual abuse. *Journal of Consulting and Clinical Psychology*, *73*(3), 515–524. http://dx.doi.org/10.1037/0022-006X.73.3.515.

McLaughlin, A. A., Keller, S. M., Feeny, N. C., Youngstrom, E. A., & Zoellner, L. A. (2014). Patterns of therapeutic alliance: Rupture-repair episodes in prolonged exposure for posttraumatic stress disorder. *Journal of Consulting and Clinical Psychology*, *82*(1), 112–121. http://dx.doi.org/10.1037/a0034696.

McLean, C. P., & Foa, E. B. (2013). Dissemination and implementation of prolonged exposure therapy for posttraumatic stress disorder. *Journal of Anxiety Disorders*, *27*(8), 788–792. http://dx.doi.org/10.1016/j.janxdis.2013.03.004.

Miller, W. R., & Rollnick, S. (2009). Ten things that motivational interviewing is not. *Behavioral and Cognitive Psychotherapy*, *37*(2), 129–140. http://dx.doi.org/S1352465809005128 [pii].

Morath, J., Gola, H., Sommershof, A., Hamuni, G., Kolassa, S., Catani, C., et al. (2014). The effect of trauma-focused therapy on the altered T cell distribution in individuals with PTSD: Evidence from a randomized controlled trial. *Journal of Psychiatric Research*, *54*, 1–10. http://dx.doi.org/10.1016/j.jpsychires.2014.03.01.

Morath, J., Moreno-Villanueva, M., Hamuni, G., Kolassa, S., Ruf-Leuschner, M., Schauer, M., et al. (2014). Effects of psychotherapy on DNA strand break accumulation originating from traumatic stress. *Psychotherapy and Psychosomatics*, *83*(5), 289–297. http://dx.doi.org/10.1159/000362739.

Morland, L. A., Mackintosh, M. A., Greene, C. J., Rosen, C. S., Chard, K. M., Resick, P., et al. (2014). Cognitive processing therapy for posttraumatic stress disorder delivered to rural veterans via telemental health: A randomized noninferiority clinical trial. *Journal of Clinical Psychiatry*, *75*(5), 470–476. http://dx.doi.org/10.4088/JCP.13m08842.

Morrissey, J. P., Jackson, E. W., Ellis, A. R., Amaro, H., Brown, V. B., & Najavits, L. M. (2005). Twelve-month outcomes of trauma-informed interventions for women with co-occurring disorders. *Psychiatric Services*, *56*, 1213–1222.

Motraghi, T. E., Seim, R. W., Meyer, E. C., & Morissette, S. B. (2014). Virtual reality exposure therapy for the treatment of posttraumatic stress disorder: A methodological review using CONSORT guidelines. [Review]. *Journal of Clinical Psychology*, *70*(3), 197–208. http://dx.doi.org/10.1002/jclp.22051.

Mueser, K. T., Rosenberg, S. D., Xie, H., Jankowski, M. K., Bolton, E. E., Lu, W., et al. (2008). A randomized controlled trial of cognitive-behavioral treatment for posttraumatic stress disorder in severe mental illness. *Journal of Consulting and Clinical Psychology*, *76*(2), 259–271. http://dx.doi.org/10.1037/0022-006X.76.2.259.

Mullen, K., Holliday, R., Morris, E., Raja, A., & Suris, A. (2014). Cognitive processing therapy for male veterans with military sexual trauma-related posttraumatic stress disorder. *Journal of Anxiety Disorders*, *28*(8), 761–764. http://dx.doi.org/10.1016/j.janxdis.2014.09.004ulll.

Najavits, L. M. (2002). *Seeking safety: A treatment manual for PTSD and substance abuse*. New York: Guilford.

Najavits, L. M., Gallop, R. J., & Weiss, R. D. (2006). Seeking safety therapy for adolescent girls with PTSD and substance use disorder: A randomized controlled trial. *Journal of Behavioral Health Services & Research, 33*, 453–463.

Najavits, L. M., Harned, M. S., Gallop, R. J., Butler, S. F., Barber, J. P., Thase, M. E., et al. (2007). Six-month treatment outcomes of cocaine-dependent patients with and without PTSD in a multisite national trial. *Journal of Studies on Alcohol, 68*(3), 353–361.

Najavits, L. M., & Hien, D. (2013). Helping vulnerable populations: A comprehensive review of the treatment outcome literature on substance use disorder and PTSD. *Journal of Clinical Psychology, 69*(5), 433–479. http://dx.doi.org/10.1002/jclp.21980.

Najavits, L. M., Schmitz, M., Gotthardt, S., & Weiss, R. D. (2005). Seeking safety plus exposure therapy: An outcome study on dual diagnosis men. *Journal of Psychoactive Drugs, 37*(4), 425–435.

National Commission for the Protection of Human Subjects of Biomedical and Behavioral Research (1979). *Not a published document.* Available on-line <http://www.hhs.gov/ohrp/policy/belmont.html>Accessed 13.04.15.

Neacsiu, A. D., Lungu, A., Harned, M. S., Rizvi, S. L., & Linehan, M. M. (2014). Impact of dialectical behavior therapy versus community treatment by experts on emotional experience, expression, and acceptance in borderline personality disorder. *Behaviour Research and Therapy, 53*, 47–54. http://dx.doi.org/10.1016/j.brat.2013.12.004.

Nemeroff, C. B., Bremner, J. D., Foa, E. B., Mayberg, H. S., North, C. S., & Stein, M. B. (2006). Posttraumatic stress disorder: A state-of-the-science review. *Journal of Psychiatric Research, 40*(1), 1–21.

Neuner, F., Schauer, M., Klaschik, C., Karunakara, U., & Elbert, T. (2004). A comparison of narrative exposure therapy, supportive counseling, and psychoeducation for treating posttraumatic stress disorder in an African refugee settlement. *Journal of Consulting Clinical Psychology, 72*(4), 579–587. http://dx.doi.org/10.1037/0022-006X.72.4.579 2004-16970-003 [pii].

NICE, (2005). *National Institute for Clinical Excellence (NICE) Posttraumatic stress disorder (PTSD): The management of PTSD in adults and children in primary and secondary care.* London: Author.

Nijenhuis, E. R., & van der Hart, O. (2011). Dissociation in trauma: A new definition and comparison with previous formulations. *Journal of Trauma and Dissociation, 12*(4), 416–445. http://dx.doi.org/10.1080/15299732.2011.570592.

Novaco, R. W. (1977). A stress inoculation approach to anger management in the training of law enforcement officers. *American Journal of Community Psychology, 5*(3), 327–346.

Ogden, P., Pain, C., & Fisher, J. (2006). A sensorimotor approach to the treatment of trauma and dissociation. *Psychiatric Clinics of North America, 29*(1), 263–279.

Opler, L., Grennan, M., & Ford, J. D. (2009). Psychopharmacological treatment of complex traumatic stress disorders. In C. A. Courtois & J. D. Ford (Eds.), *Treating complex traumatic stress disorders: An evidence-based guide.* New York: Guilford.

Paivio, S. C., Jarry, J. L., Chagigiorgis, H., Hall, I., & Ralston, M. (2010). Efficacy of two versions of emotion-focused therapy for resolving child abuse trauma. *Psychotherapy Research, 20*(3), 353–366. http://dx.doi.org/10.1080/10503300903505274.

Paivio, S. C., & Nieuwenhuis, J. A. (2001). Efficacy of emotion focused therapy for adult survivors of child abuse: A preliminary study. *Journal of Traumatic Stress, 14*(1), 115–133.

Petry, N. M., Ford, J. D., & Barry, D. (2011). Contingency management is especially efficacious in engendering long durations of abstinence in patients with sexual abuse histories. *Psychology of Addictive Behaviors, 25*, 293–300. http://dx.doi.org/10.1037/a0022632.

Pole, N., Gone, J. P., & Kulkarni, M. (2008). Posttraumatic stress disorder among ethnoracial minorities in the United States. *Clinical Psychology: Science and Practice, 15,* 35–61.

Poole, A. D., de Jongh, A., & Spector, J. (1999). Power therapies: Evidence versus emotion a reply to Rosen, Lohr, McNally and Herbert. *Behavioural and Cognitive Psychotherapy, 27*(1), 3–8.

Powers, M. B., Halpern, J. M., Ferenschak, M. P., Gillihan, S. J., & Foa, E. B. (2010). A meta-analytic review of prolonged exposure for posttraumatic stress disorder. *Clinical Psychology Review, 30*(6), 635–641. http://dx.doi.org/S0272-7358(10)00070-X [pii]; http://dx.doi.org/10.1016/j.cpr.2010.04.007.

Prochaska, J. O., & DiClemente, C. C. (1992). Stages of change in the modification of problem behaviors. *Progress in Behavior Modification, 28,* 183–218.

Ready, D., & Shea, M. T. (2008). Group therapy. In G. Reyes, J. D. Elhai, & J. D. Ford (Eds.), *Encyclopedia of psychological trauma* (pp. 301–303). Hoboken, NJ: Wiley.

Resick, P. A., Galovski, T. E., O'Brien Uhlmansiek, M., Scher, C. D., Clum, G. A., & Young-Xu, Y. (2008). A randomized clinical trial to dismantle components of cognitive processing therapy for posttraumatic stress disorder in female victims of interpersonal violence. *Journal of Consulting and Clinical Psychology, 76*(2), 243–258. http://dx.doi. org/2008-03290-007 [pii]; http://dx.doi.org/10.1037/0022-006X.76.2.243.

Resick, P. A., Nishith, P., & Griffin, M. G. (2003). How well does cognitive-behavioral therapy treat symptoms of complex PTSD? An examination of child sexual abuse survivors within a clinical trial. *CNS Spectrums, 8*(5), 340–355.

Resick, P. A., Nishith, P., Weaver, T. L., Astin, M. C., & Feuer, C. A. (2002). A comparison of cognitive-processing therapy with prolonged exposure and a waiting condition for the treatment of chronic posttraumatic stress disorder in female rape victims. *Journal of Consulting and Clinical Psychology, 70,* 867–879.

Riggs, D., Monson, C., Glynn, S., & Canterino, J. (2008). Couple and family therapy for adults. In E. B. Foa, T. M. Keane, M. J. Friedman, & J. A. Cohen (Eds.), *Effective treatments for PTSD* (pp. 458–478) (2nd ed.). New York: Guilford.

Robjant, K., & Fazel, M. (2010). The emerging evidence for Narrative Exposure Therapy: A review. *Clinical Psychology Review, 30*(8), 1030–1039. http://dx.doi.org/10.1016/j. cpr.2010.07.004.

Rothbaum, B. O., Price, M., Jovanovic, T., Norrholm, S. D., Gerardi, M., Dunlop, B., et al. (2014). A randomized, double-blind evaluation of D-cycloserine or alprazolam combined with virtual reality exposure therapy for posttraumatic stress disorder in Iraq and Afghanistan War veterans. *American Journal of Psychiatry, 171*(6), 640–648. http://dx.doi. org/10.1176/appi.ajp.2014.13121625.

Ruzek, J. I., Eftekhari, A., Rosen, C. S., Crowley, J. J., Kuhn, E., Foa, E. B., et al. (2014). Factors related to clinician attitudes toward prolonged exposure therapy for PTSD. *Journal of Traumatic Stress, 27*(4), 423–429. http://dx.doi.org/10.1002/jts.21945.

Schnurr, P. P., Friedman, M. J., Engel, C. C., Foa, E. B., Shea, M. T., Chow, B. K., et al. (2007). Cognitive behavioral therapy for posttraumatic stress disorder in women: A randomized controlled trial. *JAMA: Journal of the American Medical Association, 297*(8), 820–830.

Schnurr, P. P., Friedman, M. J., Foy, D. W., Shea, M. T., Hsieh, F. Y., Lavori, P. W., et al. (2003). Randomized trial of trauma-focused group therapy for posttraumatic stress disorder: Results from a department of veterans affairs cooperative study. *Archives of General Psychiatry, 60*(5), 481–489. http://dx.doi.org/10.1001/archpsyc.60.5.481.

Scoboria, A., Mazzoni, G., Kirsch, I., & Jimenez, S. (2006). The effects of prevalence and script information on plausibility, belief, and memory of autobiographical events. *Journal of Personality Assessment, 20,* 1049–1064.

Seligman, M. E. P., Rashid, T., & Parks, A. C. (2006). Positive psychotherapy. *American Psychologist, 61*, 774–788.

Shapiro, F. (1995). *Eye movement desensitization and reprocessing: Basic principles, protocols, and procedures.* New York: Guilford.

Shapiro, F. (2002). EMDR 12 years after its introduction: Past and future research. *Journal of Clinical Psychology, 58*(1), 1–22. http://dx.doi.org/10.1002/jclp.1126 [pii].

Shea, M. T., McDevitt-Murphy, M., Ready, D., & Schnurr, P. P. (2008). Group therapy. In E. B. Foa, T. M. Keane, M. J. Friedman, & J. A. Cohen (Eds.), *Effective treatments for PTSD* (pp. 306–327) (2nd ed.). New York: Guilford.

Siegel, D. J. (2007). *The mindful brain: Reflection and attunement in the cultivation of well-being.* New York, NY: W. W. Norton & Co.

Spinazzola, J., Blaustein, M., & van der Kolk, B. A. (2005). Posttraumatic stress disorder treatment outcome research: The study of unrepresentative samples? *Journal of Traumatic Stress, 18*(5), 425–436. http://dx.doi.org/10.1002/jts.20050.

Stalker, C. A., & Fry, R. (1999). A comparison of short-term group and individual therapy for sexually abused women. *Canadian Journal of Psychiatry, 44*(2), 168–174.

Stewart, S., & Conrod, P. (2003). Psychosocial models of functional associations between posttraumatic stress disorder and substance use disorder. In P. Ouimette & P. Brown (Eds.), *Trauma and substance abuse* (pp. 29–56). Washington, DC: American Psychological Association.

Suris, A., Link-Malcolm, J., Chard, K., Ahn, C., & North, C. (2013). A randomized clinical trial of cognitive processing therapy for veterans with PTSD related to military sexual trauma. *Journal of Traumatic Stress, 26*(1), 28–37. http://dx.doi.org/10.1002/jts.21765.

US VA/DoD (2010). *Not a published document.* Available on-line <http://www.healthquality.va.gov/guidelines/MH/ptsd/>. Accessed 13.04.15.

van den Berg, D. P., de Bont, P. A., van der Vleugel, B. M., de Roos, C., de Jongh, A., van Minnen, A., et al. (2015). Prolonged exposure vs eye movement desensitization and reprocessing vs waiting list for posttraumatic stress disorder in patients with a psychotic disorder: A randomized clinical trial. *JAMA Psychiatry, 72*(3), 259–267. http://dx.doi.org/10.1001/jamapsychiatry.2014.2637.

van der Hart, O., Nijenhuis, E. R. S., & Steele, K. (2006). *The haunted self: Structural dissociation and the treatment of chronic traumatization* (1st ed.). New York, NY: W. W. Norton & Co.

van Minnen, A., Harned, M. S., Zoellner, L., & Mills, K. (2012). Examining potential contraindications for prolonged exposure therapy for PTSD. *European Journal of Psychotraumatology*, 3.http://dx.doi.org/10.3402/ejpt.v3i0.18805.

Walker, D. F., Courtois, C. A., & Aten, J. (Eds.), (2014). *Spiritually oriented psychotherapy for trauma.* Washington, DC: American Psychological Association.

Walter, K. H., Dickstein, B. D., Barnes, S. M., & Chard, K. M. (2014). Comparing effectiveness of CPT to CPT-C among U.S. Veterans in an interdisciplinary residential PTSD/TBI treatment program. *Journal of Traumatic Stress, 27*(4), 438–445. http://dx.doi.org/10.1002/jts.21934.

Walter, K. H., Varkovitzky, R. L., Owens, G. P., Lewis, J., & Chard, K. M. (2014). Cognitive processing therapy for veterans with posttraumatic stress disorder: A comparison between outpatient and residential treatment. *Journal of Consulting and Clinical Psychology, 82*(4), 551–561. http://dx.doi.org/10.1037/a0037075.

Wang, Z. (2014). Adherence to a web-based intervention program for traumatized persons in mainland China. *European Journal of Psychotraumatology, 5*, 26526. http://dx.doi.org/10.3402/ejpt.v5.26526.

Weaver, C. M., Trafton, J. A., Walser, R. D., & Kimerling, R. E. (2007). Pilot test of seeking safety treatment with male veterans. *Psychiatric Services, 58*, 1012–1013.

Westen, D., Novotny, C. A., & Thompson-Brenner, H. (2004). The empirical status of empirically supported psychotherapies: Assumptions, findings, and reporting in controlled clini-
caltrials. *Psychological Bulletin*, *130*, 631–663.
Zalta, A. K., Gillihan, S. J., Fisher, A. J., Mintz, J., McLean, C. P., Yehuda, R., et al. (2014).
Change in negative cognitions associated with PTSD predicts symptom reduction in
prolonged exposure. [l]. *Journal of Consulting and Clinical Psychology*, *82*(1), 171–175.
http://dx.doi.org/10.1037/a0034735.
Zanarini, M. C., Horz, S., Frankenburg, F. R., Weingeroff, J., Reich, D. B., & Fitzmaurice,
G. (2011). The 10-year course of PTSD in borderline patients and axis II com-
parison subjects. *Acta Psychiatrica Scandinavica*, *124*(5), 349–356. http://dx.doi.
org/10.1111/j.1600-0447.2011.01717.x.
Zayfert, C., & Becker, C. B. (2007). *Cognitive-behavioral therapy for PTSD: A case formula-
tion approach*. New York: Guilford.
Zayfert, C., DeViva, J. C., Becker, C. B., Pike, J. L., Gillock, K. L., & Hayes, S. A. (2005).
Exposure utilization and completion of cognitive behavioral therapy for PTSD in a "real
world" clinicalpractice. *Journal of Traumatic Stress*, *18*, 637–645.
Zoellner, L. A., Feeny, N. C., Bittinger, J. N., Bedard-Gilligan, M. A., Slagle, D. M., Post, L.
M., et al. (2011). Teaching trauma-focused exposure therapy for PTSD: Critical clinical
lessons for novice exposure therapists. *Psychological Trauma*, *3*(3), 300–308. http://dx.doi.
org/10.1037/a0024642.

Treatment of children and adolescents with PTSD

Practice guidelines for the assessment and treatment of children and adolescents with PTSD were first developed by an expert panel convened more than a decade ago by the American Academy of Child and Adolescent Psychiatry (1998). Since the release of that seminal set of practice guidelines, substantial additional validation has been provided in scientific studies of the most robustly evidence-based treatment model: Trauma-Focused Cognitive Behavior Therapy (TF-CBT; Cohen, Mannarino, & Deblinger, 2006; Cohen, Mannarino, Deblinger, & Berliner, 2008). Other approaches to the treatment of children and adolescents with PTSD have been sufficiently clinically or scientifically tested to be included as actually or potentially evidence-based (Ford & Courtois, 2013; Nader, 2008; Saxe, MacDonald, & Ellis, 2007; Vickerman & Margolin, 2007) in the second edition of the International Society for Traumatic Stress Studies (ISTSSs) Practice Guidelines, *Effective Treatments for PTSD* (Foa, Keane, Friedman, & Cohen, 2008). These include Eye Movement Desensitization and Reprocessing (EMDR; Wesselman & Shapiro, 2013), school-based cognitive behavior therapies (Jaycox, Stein, & Amaya-Jackson, 2008), psychodynamic therapies (Lieberman, Ghosh Ippen, & Marans, 2008), creative arts therapies (Goodman, Chapman, & Gantt, 2008), and psychopharmacotherapy (treatment with therapeutic medications; Donnelly, 2008). Family systems therapies were included in the ISTSS Practice Guidelines only for adults, but promising approaches for family therapy with children with PTSD have been developed (Ford & Saltzman, 2009). Psychotherapies that focus on affective and interpersonal self-regulation also have been identified as promising for children with PTSD by the National Child Traumatic Stress Network (see Ford & Cloitre, 2009; Ford & Courtois, 2013).

This chapter provides an overview of the evidence-based and promising evidence-informed treatments for children and adolescents with PTSD. Case study examples illustrate the use of several of these treatments, with a discussion of the clinical and ethical considerations necessary to ensure the safe and effective application of PTSD treatment for children and adolescents (Box 8.1).

Evidence-based and empirically informed psychotherapy models for children with PTSD

The key elements in psychotherapy for children with PTSD have been summarized by the acronym, PRACTICE (Cohen et al., 2006): *P*arenting skills and *P*sychoeducation; *R*elaxation skills; *A*ffect modulation (helping the child and caregivers manage emotional distress); *C*ognitive coping skills; *T*rauma narrative reconstruction; *In vivo*

Posttraumatic Stress Disorder. DOI: http://dx.doi.org/10.1016/B978-0-12-801288-8.00008-X

Box 8.1 Key Points

1. Psychotherapy for children with PTSD follows the three-phase treatment model established for psychotherapy with adults with PTSD, including ensuring that the child is safe from further traumatization and prepared to engage in and benefit from therapy; reducing avoidance of memories of past traumatic experiences; and helping the child and family to restore or achieve a positive adjustment in as many walks of life as possible.

2. The core goal for the treatment of children with PTSD is to enable them (and their caregivers) to attain what Harvey (1996) described as mastery or "authority" in relation to their own memories—including but not limited to memories of traumatic events.

3. The essential elements in all approaches to psychotherapy for children with PTSD have been summarized by the acronym PRACTICE (Cohen et al., 2006): *P*arenting skills and *P*sychoeducation; *R*elaxation skills; *A*ffect modulation (helping the child and caregivers manage emotional distress); *C*ognitive coping skills; *T*rauma narrative reconstruction; *In vivo* application of skills (practicing skills and confronting reminders of traumatic experiences in daily life); *C*onjoint parent-child sessions (treatment sessions with the parent and child together); and *E*nsuring safety and posttherapy adjustment.

4. The PTSD psychotherapy for children with the strongest scientific evidence base is TF-CBT. TF-CBT consistently has been shown to be more effective than traditional supportive psychotherapy and was recently found to be equally effective alone as when combined with medication therapy.

5. Three other cognitive behavior therapy models for children and adolescents with PTSD have been sufficiently clinically or scientifically tested to be included as actually or potentially evidence-based: EMDR, cognitive behavioral intervention for traumatized students (CBITS—which is conducted in schools), and Parent-Child Interaction Therapy (PCIT [Parent Child Interaction Therapy]—which is conducted with parents of abused children, including parents who have been abusers).

6. A dyadic psychotherapy that takes a psychodynamic approach and emphasizes restoring or enhancing parent-child attachment (and that includes a parent as well as the traumatized child in all sessions) has been found in scientific studies to be effective with young children.

7. Creative arts therapies and family systems therapies are widely used clinically and were included in the ISTSS Practice Guidelines as promising treatments (although neither has demonstrated effective in scientific studies with traumatized children).

8. Psychotherapies that focus on affective and interpersonal self-regulation also have been identified as promising for children with PTSD by the National Child Traumatic Stress Network, including TARGET, Life Skills Life Story, Real Life Heroes, and Structured Psychotherapy for Adolescents Responding to Chronic Stress (SPARCS).

9. Treatment with children and families is always relational. PTSD is so debilitating for children that therapists may feel compelled to achieve large goals such as complete recovery in order to prevent the child and parent from suffering disappointment in the face of what may seem to be intractable problems. The challenge for therapists is to shift from emphasizing overcoming pathology or deficits as the goal of treatment to focusing on a series of smaller goals that are of immediate personal relevance to the child and caregiver.

(Continued)

10. Crises are not common but can occur during PTSD psychotherapy with children. Crisis deescalation with traumatized children requires the use of "grounding" strategies to counteract detachment, dissociation, and impulsivity, and affective engagement strategies to reestablish an immediate sense of emotional connection. In the aftermath of crises, therapeutic processing includes discussion of how the child used the self-regulation skills to successfully cope with the stress reactions involved in PTSD. Every crisis thus is an opportunity for PTSD treatment to highlight and enhance the traumatized child's competence and sense of efficacy in her or his self-regulation skills and her or his trust in healthy relationships.

application of skills (practicing skills and confronting reminders of traumatic experiences in daily life); Conjoint parent-child sessions (treatment sessions with the parent and child together); and, Ensuring safety and posttherapy adjustment. Each approach to psychotherapy provides these forms of assistance in different ways.

Over the past 20 years, several empirically supported psychotherapies have been developed for both acute and chronic pediatric PTSD (Berkowitz, Stover, & Marans, 2011; Chaffin, Funderburk, Bard, Valle, & Gurwitch, 2011; Ford, Blaustein, Habib, & Kagan, 2013; Stein et al., 2003). Common treatment elements that are empirically supported include (i) psychoeducation about PTSD; (ii) relaxation and coping skills; (iii) emotion awareness, expression, and regulation skills; (iv) cognitive processing of reactions to trauma; (v) helping the child to construct a therapeutic trauma narrative; (vi) *in vivo* exposure to trauma reminders and practicing of coping skills; (vii) conjoint parent-child sessions; and (viii) monitoring and enhancing individual safety (Carrion, 2013; Ford & Courtois, 2013; Schneider, Grilli, & Schneider, 2013).

Trauma-focused Cognitive Behavioral Therapy

The most extensively researched model of PTSD psychotherapy with children and adolescents is TF-CBT (Cohen, Berliner, & Mannarino, 2010, Cohen, Mannarino, & Iyengar; 2011). TF-CBT includes emotion identification, stress inoculation (e.g., breathing, relaxation) techniques, direct discussion of trauma experiences through gradual exposure exercises, cognitive restructuring, psychoeducation, and safety skill building. Several randomized clinical trials have demonstrated TF-CBT's superiority to supportive therapy with children (including ~33% adolescents) with PTSD following abuse, violence, and single-incident (e.g., severe accidents) traumatic stressors (Cohen et al., 2011; de Arellano et al., 2014). Outcomes for depression and behavioral problems have been mixed, with moderate effect sizes in some studies (Cohen et al. 2010; de Arellano et al., 2014). When children (or their parents) decline to engage in or cannot seem to emotionally tolerate the processing of specific trauma memories, there are evidence-based therapeutic options for either preparing the child and parents to feel sufficiently safe, confident, and able to modulate distressing emotions so that the child can experience the trauma narrative portion of treatment successfully (Cohen, Mannarino, Kliethermes, & Murray, 2012; Matulis, Resick, Rosner, & Steil, 2014) or to enable the child and parent to develop cognitive behavioral (Deblinger, Mannarino, Cohen, Runyon, & Steer, 2011) and self-regulation (Ford, Steinberg, & Zhang, 2011, Ford, Steinberg, Hawke, Levine, & Zhang; 2012) skills that address PTSD by reducing everyday traumatic stress reactivity and increasing emotion regulation, self-efficacy and social support.

For traumatized toddlers and preschoolers, adaptations of TF-CBT have shown promise and evidence that trauma memory work (exposure) and relaxation skill training are feasible as long as the protocol is developmentally appropriate and the parent is able to bind her anxiety sufficiently to be able to help the child with each step of the process (Scheeringa et al., 2007)—although to date this has been tested only with victims of disaster or motor vehicle accidents.

TF-CBT was developed to decrease symptoms of PTSD and depression by providing a combination of cognitive-behavioral skill building and gradual therapeutic exposure to trauma memories and reminders. TF-CBT follows a three-phase approach comparable to that used in psychotherapy with adults with PTSD (see Chapter 7). TF-CBT is designed to be conducted in 12–16 sessions of 90 minutes each (Cohen et al., 2006), although in community settings, session length may be shorter and treatment duration may be longer.

Phase one includes a careful assessment of potential current dangers (including possible further exposure to traumatic stressors such as abuse or family or community violence) and crises (including suicidality; other forms of self-injury; substance use; and parental psychiatric, substance abuse, or legal problems). If potential danger or the likelihood of crisis is high, treatment focuses on stabilizing the child's situation and support system before continuing on to the main therapeutic focus of Phase one TF-CBT. Phase one's therapeutic focus is on helping the child and parent(s) build a foundation of knowledge about psychological trauma and PTSD and skills for managing anxiety effectively. Education is provided to the child and to the parents separately about PTSD symptoms and how they may result when a child experiences a traumatic stressor. The child is taught skills for using physical relaxation, labeling specific emotion states, and effective thinking ("cognitive coping") to reduce anxiety. Simultaneously, during Phase one, separate sessions are held with parents to teach them skills for listening supportively, using positive reinforcement to motivate desired behaviors, and setting and keeping consistent rules and limits with their child. Periodic sessions with both the child and parent(s) are provided to help them learn from each other and to determine when to begin Phase two (Box 8.2).

The second phase of TF-CBT involves the therapist assisting the child in constructing a "narrative" (story-like) description of a specific traumatic event that has been identified as the most troubling event currently for the child. This "narrative reconstruction" is done in careful steps in order to enable the child to gradually confront the traumatic memory without feeling overwhelmingly frightened or otherwise distressed (ashamed, guilty, angry, sad, etc.). Based on Phase one history-taking with the child, parent(s), and other sources (such as child protective service workers, teachers, the child's pediatrician, or counselors), the therapist first identifies a specific traumatic

Box 8.2 Building a Trauma Story in TF-CBT

"Rachel" and "Julio" are composites (combinations) of several girls and boys who have made a personal story out of a traumatic memory while doing TF-CBT with the therapists at the University of Connecticut Health Center Child Trauma Clinic. Rachel is a 9-year-old African American girl who witnessed her biological father beating her mother and older siblings for "as long as I can remember" until her mother got a restraining order and divorced the father a year ago. Julio is a 15-year-old Latino boy who was sexually assaulted by a formerly trusted uncle at age 10 and who has been physically assaulted and threatened with murder repeatedly by his two older brothers. Rachel and Julio were assessed using the Clinician Administered PTSD Scale (CAPS-CA; see Chapter 6) and diagnosed with severe PTSD. Rachel also has severe depression symptoms, and Julio has had serious problems with anger outbursts and panic attacks. Portions of the beginning of their narrative reconstruction sessions are presented, without going into the precise traumatic details that they subsequently recounted. The dialogues illustrate how narrative reconstruction is explained and how the therapist helps the young person differently, depending on his or her age (in this case, a younger child and an adolescent) and the specifics of their experiences.

Rachel's picture book

Rachel was excited to learn how to relax her body using the Phase one progressive muscle relaxation and breathing skills, and she found the "emotion faces" game (figuring out a specific emotion state for each of several circular drawings depicting emotions) to be fun. Her therapist was able to use these pleasant activities both to build a trusting relationship and to teach Rachel about how bad experiences make the body tense and create upsetting feelings that she can cope with by using relaxation skills and labeling her specific emotion(s). The therapist then explained:

Therapist:	It's good to make a story out of bad experiences because that helps your body to relax so you can feel good emotions that you like. The story tells what happened, what you were thinking and doing, and what your body and emotions were feeling. Because it's a story, it means that it isn't happening anymore, and you don't have to think about it unless you want to.
Rachel:	I never want to think about when my daddy was beating up on my mommy and sister. I don't like it when I have dreams about that. I don't want to tell that story; it's awful.
Therapist:	Maybe if I help you to tell the story in a way that you think is good, you won't have to dream about it so much. You're very good at telling stories with words and pictures, like the story of the princess that you told, and those nice drawings you did. So maybe we could tell the unhappy story about your daddy and mommy and your sister together and draw it like you want to.

(Continued)

Box 8.2 Continued

Rachel:	Okay, I guess I could try. You start.
Therapist:	Here's a storybook you can draw and write in, and I'll help if you want. What do you want to call the story? We can put that on the front with a picture, just like on a book.
Rachel:	It's called *The Rachel Princess Wish Story*, because I'm a princess, and I get any wish I want. Here, I'll draw me with a princess dress and sparkly shoes and that shiny thing in my hair.
Therapist:	That's a beautiful picture! You look just like a princess. Do you want to write the name of the story on the cover? Do you want me to write some of it?
Rachel:	I'll write my name, "R A C H E L," and you write the rest. Okay, let's start the story. [*Turns the page*] I'll draw me before I was a princess, when I was little and daddy was hitting mommy and I didn't have any wishes so I felt very sad. See, I'm crying there, and my daddy's very big and my mommy's crying 'cause he's hurting her. He shouldn't do that.
Therapist:	That's right, your daddy shouldn't you're your mommy and make you and her cry, but it's just a story, so you can draw it any way that you want now. Let's pick just one time that you remember that story. Maybe one you dream about. We could make the bad dream into a story, and then you can tell it like you want to instead of it being a bad dream. How old are you in the story? Is it night or day? Is it cold or hot outside, like winter or summer? [Therapist asks questions to help Rachel locate the memory approximately in time, pausing after each question so Rachel can think about her answer and then tell or draw the story gradually in more detail.] Tell me when you want to turn the page, and we'll keep going on with the story, but only when you want to.
Rachel:	I'll tell some more about the story, and then I'll finish this picture. See, my daddy's face is very angry, and my mommy's face is very sad, and I'm still not a princess because my face is scared.
Therapist:	That's a good story because I can see how each person's face tells the emotion they're feeling. And you're writing that, too, "Daddy angry. Mommy is sad. Rachel scared face." In the story, is Rachel, thinking about being a princess or about something else?
Rachel:	I'm not a princess yet. I don't have my wish, so I can't be a princess.
Therapist:	So are you thinking about your wish, then? Is it a secret, or can you tell it?
Rachel:	[*Dramatically turning the page*] Here's the wish I'm thinking about. I wish my daddy would be a good king, and then I could be a princess. But he's too angry to be a good king.
Therapist:	He's so angry, he's hitting your mommy and your sister, too? And you and your mommy and sister are still crying because he's still angry and hitting?

Rachel: Yes, he's too angry and hitting. [*Draws a giant man hitting a smaller woman and little girl and another little girl in the corner, hiding behind a chair. Then draws red and black slashes all across the tableau.*] He's hurting them, I want him to stop, too scary. [*Starts to cry*]

Therapist: Okay, let's do the relaxation game now so you can feel better. Breathe in and out with me. Where do you want to make your muscles tense and relax? That's really good. You're helping your body to relax. Even though the story is really scary, you're telling and drawing the story really well, and you remembered to make the emotion faces really well, too. We can do the story some more next time so you can tell me the story of how you made your wish to be a princess come true. It must be true because you sure look like a real princess to me now!

Rachel: Well, I'm not a *real* princess, but I like being a pretend one. And I'll be a princess in the story when it's all done and I've colored every page.

Therapist: And princesses get to be happy even if they used to be scared or sad, and their mommies and sisters, too. Maybe the daddy gets to be a real king, or maybe he just has to stop hitting, but you can decide when you tell me more about the story next week, okay?

Rachel: Yes, I'll decide. And when I'm done, I'll show my princess wish story to my mommy.

Therapist: I'll bet she'll really like to see the story you're telling and drawing; it's a good one.

Julio's assault narrative

Julio: I don't really want anyone to know what my uncle did to me. If they do, they'll think I'm a punk who likes that kind of sex, and they'll have no respect for me. Then I'm really done.

Therapist: What happened to you is private, your business and no one else's. But it could help you to not lose respect for yourself—which you've said is an issue—if you know you can deal with the bad memory and put it into the past where it belongs. We can't change what happened or erase the memory completely, but we can make it into just a very bad memory by dealing with it.

Julio: But if I don't want to remember something, I just don't let myself think about it. I don't think about something like that on purpose; that just makes me feel worse!

Therapist: Remember how we talked about what happens when you try to not think about an emotion or tell yourself you're just not going to think about something and it won't bother you?

Julio: Yeah, I feel worse, and I think about it more. And I get real down on myself.

(Continued)

Box 8.2 Continued

Therapist: And that's nothing wrong about you; you're just not dealing with the first rule of thinking and emotions: if you can think it and you know what you're feeling, you're in control, but if you avoid a thought or feeling, then the negative thoughts and feelings take control. When you choose to deal with what you really think and what you're really feeling, you're in control.

Julio: Yeah, but what if what I think is that I'm a total f-up and I feel hopeless?

Therapist: That's what happens when you *stop* thinking and don't deal with something, Your natural thoughts and feelings aren't about giving up, they're about making things right. So one way to make something bad that happened right *now*, even if you can't make it right back then, is to just deal with the memory honestly, and then it's over and done, even if you still remember it.

Julio: Okay, like if you've got a beef with someone and you deal with them directly instead of pretending to make nice and waiting to get your revenge. But I really want to get revenge on my uncle for what he did to me; it was too bad to just let it go. He should die for that.

Therapist: I won't argue that it was really bad and that it's his responsibility and not yours. Before you decide for sure what you think about him or revenge, if you feel that you've handled the memory and it's behind you, then that won't interfere with your thinking clearly about the rest.

Julio: Like getting your mind clear before you make any big decisions, I can relate to that.

Therapist: Okay, so here's how we can do this. See how this sounds. You start with whatever you remember about what was happening—what you were doing and thinking and feeling, where you were, how you were dressed, who you were with—just before your uncle assaulted you. Then you take it just one step at a time, what happened first, then what happened next, and we break it down so that you don't dwell on the bad parts but you just tell the whole story in detail until it's over. And you get to decide when it ends and how you know it's over. I realize that emotionally it's still not over now. That's why dealing with the memory is important: to close the book on the bad parts of the memory without just sweeping them under the rug where they still bother you.

Julio: Well, they're still gonna bother me, no doubt, no matter what you say.

Therapist: Indeed, some bad parts may still bother you, but maybe not as many or as much. And we need to get the memory complete, so it may take several times to tell it right, but you're the judge. I'll just help you not skip over important parts and not get stuck in bad parts. When you're ready to tell the memory to the one person you've chosen, your mentor—and not to anyone else unless you decide you want to—then I'll be there for you while you do that, and you'll know that you've made the bad experience a regular—yes, as bad as it is, just a regular—memory and not something that makes you feel stressed and sick all the time.

Julio:	Okay, let's get on with it. I'll do the writing and the telling; that's the way I want it. I was just waking up on a Sunday morning after being out late at a party with friends the night before. I was wearing the shorts that I always used to sleep in. My first thought was that I had a huge headache. I definitely got wasted at that party, but it was a blast. Then I was rubbing my eyes, and I turned over and I about jumped a foot in the air because there's somebody else in my bed. I was like "What the hell, get out of here, you m-f." And then I felt an arm around my throat choking me and something was blocking my mouth so I couldn't yell. Then I got really scared.
Therapist:	Take a breath, and see if you need to tense or relax any muscles until you know that you're okay now, even though you're feeling really bad in the memory. Okay, how about stepping back and writing down what you just told me? Let's put it on paper so you can see it.

Summary

Although the details of the dialogue and the patients' memories differed in many ways, the common factors in these dialogues include (i) helping the young person to view the telling of his or her memory as a way to gain a sense of closure (albeit partial) and control (for Rachel, her wish to be a princess, and for Julio, his goal of not feeling or being viewed as a helpless victim); (ii) providing the young person with a way of telling the story and making a record of it that fits with their interests and preferences (for Rachel, a picture book with her as the artist and the therapist as the scribe; for Julio, a diary-like written record based on his visualized recollection); (iii) helping the young person to focus on details of the place, circumstances, actions, emotions, and thoughts in a step-by-step manner in which one thing leads to the next without any final stopping point until they decide that the "story" is over; (iv) helping the young person to use their self-management skills in order to keep their physical and emotional arousal within a tolerable "window" (not too much and not too little); and (v) highlighting the young person's ability and accomplishment in small consistent ways in order to teach them that they are capable of confronting distressing memories and feelings successfully and with a sense of pride and confidence in themselves despite also feeling distress.

event that either clearly is the most troubling memory currently for the child or that is a particularly vividly recalled example of several similar events. The child may not be able to recall every aspect of the traumatic event that will be the focus of "narrative reconstruction"—indeed, details that were not recalled originally often emerge as important features of the event—but the overall memory should be clear to the child from the outset, and the event should have a distinct beginning and end. Phase two memory-telling is not a "fishing expedition" or an attempt to retrieve or recover "lost" or "repressed" memories (see Chapter 1). The purpose is to enable the child to purposefully describe—in words and pictures—a very troubling experience in a manner that demonstrates to the child (and the parent(s)) that the child can choose to recall this memory and cope successfully with the distressing feelings associated with it. A related purpose is to enable the child to tell that memory in a way that is meaningful to the child to an adult who is consistently able to be both encouraging and empathic (the therapist), and then after using this first "telling" as practice, to also tell the memory to a parent or caregiver (whom the therapist has helped to prepare to communicate a similar blend of empathy and encouragement).

The goal of Phase two narrative reconstruction is to provide the child with a sense of self-confidence and mastery enables the child not to avoid the memory or reminders of it, and thus to be less troubled if the memory occurs (i.e., less severe "intrusive reexperiencing" symptoms), less emotionally shut down in general (i.e., less severe "emotional numbing" symptoms), and less worried about the traumatic event or the memory of the event occurring again (i.e., less severe hyperarousal and hypervigilance symptoms). The goal for the parent(s) is to enable them to similarly realize that their child can cope with a very troubling memory without having severe PTSD symptoms, and thus to enable them to be a role model and source of encouragement and emotional support for their child by communicating confidence as well as concern and empathy. The self-management skills learned in Phase one provide children (and parents) with tools they can use, with the therapist's guidance, to manage their anxiety and other distressing feelings as they separately and then together put a traumatic memory into the form of a story that can be told without anyone being emotionally overwhelmed or in any way harmed. PTSD involves memories of traumatic event(s) that have become so disturbing that children (and often the parents) believe they must simply keep them to themselves, often as shameful secrets that can cause chronic anxiety and depression. Narrative reconstruction demonstrates experientially to children and the parents that even the most troubling memory can be faced and turned into a real-life story that can be coped with and need not be a toxic secret or a permanently unhealed emotional wound.

In Phase three, the child and parent apply the new confidence and skills they have learned to deal with any remaining troubling memories (sometimes with a second round of narrative reconstruction) and to move forward with their lives and personal development. Problem-solving skills may be applied to address difficulties in school, with peers, in the family, or in parenting, as well as the self-management skills from Phase one. Activities that provide opportunities for success and positive interactions are encouraged by the therapist. Episodes of renewed anxiety or other PTSD symptoms are discussed using the storytelling technique from Phase two, so the child and parent further develop the skill of reflecting on stressful experiences, and thus feeling able to cope with rather than feeling overwhelmed by stressors in their daily lives.

TF-CBT has been well accepted by children, parents, and clinicians for the treatment of PTSD related to sexual abuse, traumatic loss, and, more recently, mass disaster (Cohen et al., 2008). However, when child patients do not have a clear specific memory of traumatic incidents that can serve as the focus for TF-CBT, or if their behavioral or psychosocial problems are of sufficient acuity or severity or their family/caregiver support systems are sufficiently unstable or fragmented (e.g., due to severe family violence, parental psychopathology, or multiple out-of-home placements) to require being addressed prior to group or individual PTSD education and trauma memory work, other psychotherapy models warrant consideration as an approach to stabilization prior to implementing TF-CBT or an alternative approach entirely (Box 8.3).

Box 8.3 Deciding When and with Whom to Use TF-CBT

In the real world, clinicians are faced with the question of when and how best to use TF-CBT as the sole therapeutic intervention or combined with other psychosocial or pharmacotherapy treatment modalities. Lang, Ford, and Fitzgerald (2010) summarized the following recommendations to guide this decision based on the published clinical research on TF-CBT.

For what age range is TF-CBT effective? Children from 3 to 17 years old have received TF-CBT in research studies, primarily school-age children and adolescents. Preschool children have been able to participate beneficially in all phases of TF-CBT (Scheeringa et al., 2007) as long as more extensive caregiver involvement and emphasis on teaching behavior management skills to parents are provided than with older children (Bouchard, Mendlowitz, Coles, & Franklin, 2004).

Is TF-CBT effective in the aftermath of traumatic stressors other than sexual abuse? A modified form of TF-CBT, called Cognitive Behavioral Therapy for Child Traumatic Grief (CBT-CTG), has also been shown to be associated with improvement in symptoms of PTSD and CTG in children following the traumatic death of a loved one, although no definitive research studies have been completed (Lang et al., 2010). When TF-CBT was provided in New York City to multiply traumatized children and adolescents after the September 11, 2001, terrorist incidents, the recipients showed a greater rate of improvement over 6 months than children who received other services, despite the TF-CBT group having more severe traumatic exposure (including physical abuse, sexual abuse, community violence, and painful medical procedures) and greater family adversity (CATS Consortium & Hoagwood, 2007). Thus, TF-CBT may be applied to children or adolescents who are troubled by specific memories of traumatic stressors when those memories include traumatic experiences of a wide variety of types.

Is TF-CBT effective without caregiver participation? Children who receive TF-CBT fare best when their parent(s) are able to participate and provide positive support without expressing high levels of distress. TF-CBT also may help parents improve their own depression symptoms, emotional reactions, and parenting practices. One study by King et al. (2000) found no significant differences in improvement on PTSD symptoms, depression, anxiety, or behavior problems when sexually abused children received TF-CBT with or without a participating parent. However, parent participation was related to greater reductions in the child's degree of emotional distress about having been sexually abused. Parents are not mere bystanders in TF-CBT but play a crucial role in providing acceptance and role modeling for their child, which may be a source of renewed hope, confidence, and self-worth for children who are emotionally wounded by abuse.

(Continued)

Box 8.3 Continued

Three special cases that arise unfortunately often with abused children and adolescents have not been formally studied in relation to whether TF-CBT can be done safely and effectively. The first is children who have no current primary caregiver or multiple temporary adult caregivers (such as due to placements in residential treatment or foster care, having an incarcerated parent). The second is children whose primary caregiver is significantly psychologically or emotionally impaired (such as due to mental illness or substance use disorders). The third is children whose primary caregivers significantly in conflict (such as an ongoing contentious divorce). In these cases, a clinical decision should be made about whether any reliable caregiver is psychologically stable enough to participate and support the child in TF-CBT. Parents expectably experience mixed feelings of anger, shock, guilt, shame, disbelief, avoidance, and minimization related to their child's traumatic experiences, and TF-CBT is designed to help the parent deal with their own distress in order to be emotionally available and supportive for their traumatized child. If a parent is unable to play that role and participate in TF-CBT, another adult caregiver (which may include foster parents, a mentor, a family member who is a surrogate parent) should be included as long as that caregiver is likely to be involved with the child for more than a temporary period. A caregiver's willingness to be consistently involved in the child's life and ability to understand the importance of making and following through with an emotional commitment to the child's full recovery and healthy development appear to be the crucial factors in determining whether TF-CBT can benefit the caregiver and, through the caregiver, benefit the child. However, the specifics of caregiver involvement remain a question in need of further scientific investigation.

When parental unavailability, conflict, or psychological or behavioral problems are sufficient to cause additional ongoing stress for a traumatized child, several alternative therapies described in this chapter may be helpful before or in lieu of TF-CBT. With young children, CPP and PCIT are designed to enhance caregiver empathy, responsiveness, consistency, and communication in relation to their child, potentially preparing the caregiver as well as the child for TF-CBT. When caregiver substance abuse may compromise the safety or emotional security of the child, Seeking Safety or TARGET may help the caregiver to simultaneously address their substance use issues.

Is TF-CBT effective without trauma memory work? A study with more than 200 children ages four to eleven years old who had experienced sexual abuse and had current posttraumatic stress symptoms found that TF-CBT was equally effective in reducing the children's PTSD and depression symptoms and increasing their ability to maintain safe relationships *without* the trauma narrative as when the trauma narrative was conducted (Deblinger et al., 2011). However, a relatively brief version (8 sessions) that included the trauma narrative was shown to be particularly effective in reducing the parents' and children's distress related to the past abuse. On the other hand, a lengthier (16 session) version that did not include the trauma narrative led to greater improvements in parenting practices and fewer "acting out" behavior problems by the children. Thus, there seem to be a number of potential active ingredients in TF-CBT that address different aspects of the adverse impact of traumatic stress reactions by children who have been sexually abused – including but not limited to the trauma narrative. There is evidence that other cognitive and behavioral components of TF-CBT may certainly be beneficial to children suffering from PTSD symptoms (Feeny, Foa, Treadwell, & March, 2004). For example, the CATS study (CATS Consortium & Hoagwood, 2007) showed that providing only the initial TF-CBT preparatory components (psychoeduation, parenting skills, relaxation, affective expression, cognitive coping) without the trauma narrative was as effective for children with mild PTSD symptoms as the full TF-CBT model was for children with severe PTSD symptoms.

Is TF-CBT effective for children with "complex traumatic stress disorders" or those with other ("comorbid") psychiatric conditions? TF-CBT studies have included children with other psychiatric symptoms, including problems with depression, panic, obsessions and compulsions, substance abuse, eating disorders, suicidality, and complex traumatic stress symptoms (such as dissociation, self-injury, and oppositional behavior). TF-CBT has been shown to be effective in reducing the severity of depression symptoms, but specialized interventions may be needed during or prior to Phase one in order to ensure that anxiety, addiction, suicidality or self-injury, dissociation, or oppositional-defiance do not interfere with Phase two narrative reconstruction. Specialized therapies designed for other psychiatric disorders or others designed to enhance children's or adolescents' emotion regulation skills may serve this purpose (such as Life Skills Life Story, Real Life Heroes, Seeking Safety, SPARCS, or TARGET; Ford & Courtois, 2014). Research is needed to identify if, when, and for whom different combinations of therapies lead to enhanced outcomes, and when and for whom TF-CBT's preparation for the child and caregiver prior to trauma narrative work is sufficient to address complex traumatic stress symptoms.

Therapies also have been developed to address dysregulation symptoms with traumatized adolescents, particularly when they also are heading for or involved in risky lifestyles and peer groups (e.g., school failure, delinquency, addiction, social isolation, dissociation, self-harm).

Trauma Affect Regulation: Guide for Education and Therapy

The most extensively validated self-regulation intervention for youth with PTSD is *Trauma Affect Regulation: Guide for Education and Therapy* (*TARGET*; Ford, 2015;

Ford et al. 2012; Ford & Hawke, 2011; Marrow, Knudsen, Olafson, & Bucher, 2012). TARGET teaches a seven-step sequence of self-regulation skills summarized by the acronym FREEDOM. The first two skills—focusing and recognizing triggers—provide a foundation for shifting from stress reactions driven by hypervigilance to proactive emotion regulation. The next four skills provide a dual-processing approach to differentiating stress-related and core value–grounded emotions, thoughts, goals, and behavioral options. The final skill teaches ways to enhance self-esteem and self-efficacy, recognizing how being self-regulated makes a contribution to the world. Youth also create a personal "lifeline" through drawing, collage, poetry, and other creative arts, in order to chart the course of their entire life, including traumatic events, losses, and times of success and happiness.

A randomized clinical trial with delinquent or justice-involved girls with dual diagnosis PTSD, substance use, and other (e.g., oppositional-defiant, depression, panic) disorders showed that a 10-session individual TARGET intervention was superior to relational psychotherapy in reducing PTSD and depression and improving emotion regulation (Ford et al. 2012). Additional evidence for TARGET's effectiveness as a group and milieu therapeutic intervention with detained or incarcerated boys and girls was provided by two quasi-experimental studies that showed reductions in violent behavioral incidents and coercive restraints and improvement in PTSD, depression, and hope/engagement in rehabilitation following TARGET (Ford & Hawke, 2012; Marrow et al. 2012). TARGet also has been shown to be effective in enhancing emotion regulation and reducing PTSD with traumatized mothers of young children (Ford et al., 2011).

A four-step skill set, T4, was developed based on the field trials for JJ facility and community (e.g., probation) staff. TARGET has been disseminated in several state juvenile justice and child protective services systems (e.g., Connecticut, Florida, Illinois, Ohio) and is being disseminated in Learning Communities in the New York City, Oakland (Alameda County), and San Jose (Santa Clara County) juvenile justice systems by the NCTSN Center for Juvenile Justice and Trauma Recovery. TARGET has been certified as an "effective" intervention (highest level of evidence) by the Office of Juvenile Justice and Delinquency Programs Model Programs website (http://www.ojjdp.gov/mpg/Program) and received the highest rating for dissemination infrastructure (and a positive rating for the science evidence base) by the National Registry of Evidence-Based Programs and Practices (www.nrepp.samhsa.gov).

Emerging evidence-based psychotherapies for children and youth with PTSD

Five manualized treatments originally developed and validated with adults with PTSD also have been adapted for and empirically evaluated in clinical trial studies with latency age children and adolescents: Prolonged Exposure (PE; an exposure-based trauma memory processing intervention; Foa, McLean, Capaldi, & Rosenfield, 2013; Gilboa-Schechtman et al., 2010), Cognitive Processing Therapy (CPT; a cognitive restructuring intervention but includes narrative memory processing; Matulis et al., 2014), EMDR (a modification of exposure and cognitive therapies; Shapiro, 2013), Trauma and Grief Components Therapy for Adolescents (TGCTA; a group therapy with exposure and narrative processing components; Saltzman, Pynoos, Layne, Steinberg, & Aisenberg, 2001), and KID Narrative Exposure Therapy (KIDNET; a modification of exposure and narrative processing therapies; Ruf et al., 2010). In addition, two school-based group therapy and psychoeducation programs (Cognitive Behavioral Intervention for Trauma in the Schools, CBITS; Kataoka et al., 2011; Stein et al., 2003; and Enhancing Resiliency Amongst Students Experiencing Stress, ERASE-Stress; Berger, Gelkopf, & Heineberg, 2012; Gelkopf & Berger, 2009) and a dyadic mother-child therapy for toddlers exposed to violence (Child-Parent Psychotherapy, CPP; Lieberman, Ghosh Ippen, & Van Horn, 2006) have been found to be effective in rigorous studies.

Prolonged Exposure Therapy

PE utilizes two primary therapeutic tools: imaginal exposure and *in vivo* exposure. Imaginal exposure involves "revisiting" the most currently distressing traumatic memory and providing a detailed verbal account of the traumatic memory that includes sensory information, thoughts, feelings, and reactions experienced. While recounting their traumatic memory in vivid detail, patients are instructed to verbalize subjective units of distress every 5–7 minutes on a scale from 0 to 100 or 0 to 10. *In vivo* activities outside of session involve actually having contact with feared people, places, and things that are reminders of past traumas but that are not currently dangerous. This is done starting with reminders that elicit a moderate level of anxiety (i.e., SUDS of 40) and keeping track of SUDS while remaining in the situation until distress decreases. A published manual provides detailed instructions for carrying out each PE phase (preparation, imaginal exposure, *in vivo* exposure, closure; Foa, Chrestman, & Gilboa-Schechtman, 2008). Two randomized clinical trial studies with girls who had experienced sexual abuse (Foa et al., 2013) and adolescent girls and boys who had experienced single-incident traumatic stressors (e.g., severe accidents; Gilboa-Schechtman et al., 2010) provided evidence of lasting therapeutic benefit (i.e., reduced PTSD and depression, improved psychosocial functioning) that was greater for 14-session PE than for supportive or psychodynamic therapies.

Cognitive Processing Therapy

CPT is an individual psychotherapy that was originally 10–12 sessions for adults with PTSD but has been adapted in a longer format for youth with PTSD. CPT involves first writing an impact statement of the personal meaning of the currently most distressing traumatic event, including the effect on beliefs about self, others, and the world, including themes such as trust, safety, self-esteem, and life goals. Subsequent

sessions focus on identifying maladaptive thoughts (stuck points), increasing awareness of connections between thoughts and feelings, and processing a traumatic event
by writing and reading a detailed narrative account and Socratic questioning designed
to help challenge maladaptive thinking patterns while reexamining and elaborating
or modifying the trauma memory's narrative description by "weighing the evidence"
for and against maladaptive thoughts. Two versions of CPT are available: the original
manual, which includes the creation of a detailed trauma narrative, and the CPT-C
manual, which involves the creation only of an "impact statement" regarding the
aftermath of the trauma without requiring a detailed narrative account. Research
suggests that the two versions are equally effective and that the CPT-C manual may
confer the advantages of demonstrating more rapid treatment gains with fewer clients
terminating prematurely (Resick et al., 2008; Walter, Dickstein, Barnes, & Chard,
2014). Although the manuals developed for adults have been used with success in
samples of traumatized youth (e.g., Chard, Weaver, & Resick, 1997), recently a
revised version of the CPT manual has been developed specifically for adolescents
(Matulis et al., 2014). Research to date shows that a brief group version of CPT with
incarcerated boys was superior to wait-list control in reducing PTSD and depression
symptoms (Ahrens & Rexford, 2002). In addition, the longer (31 session) developmentally adapted individual manual (which includes emotion regulation and interpersonal effectiveness skills) showed evidence of reduced PTSD and depression with 10
female and 2 male adolescents with abuse-related PTSD (Matulis et al., 2014).

Eye Movement Desensitization and Reprocessing

In EMDR, a currently distressing trauma memory is repeatedly described briefly
(unlike PE, typically for less than 1 minute), with titration of the exposure intensity (as
done in PE) and negative beliefs carefully identified (as done in CPT). In addition, a
distractor task is used during memory recall. Originally, as implied by the intervention's
name, the task was eye movements done back and forth, but it alternately can be any
form of bilateral (i.e., moving from left to right and vice versa) audio, visual, tactile, or
kinesthetic stimulation (such as tapping on alternate sides of the shoulders, or moving
the limbs alternately on each side of the body). The client then "blanks out" the memory
while refocusing on body awareness and breathing deeply. When trauma memory recall
is associated with little or no subjective distress, a cognitive exercise called resource
installation is conducted, with the client focusing on a positive belief rather than the
trauma memory while performing the distractor task. Positive beliefs (e.g., "I can handle this") also are identified and rated on a seven-point Validity of Cognitions scale.

Trauma and Grief Components Therapy for Adolescents

TGCTA is delivered in group sessions that comprise four modules. The first teaches
foundational knowledge and skills to enhance posttraumatic emotional, cognitive, and

behavioral regulation and interpersonal skills. Next, the group processes members' narratives of traumatic events (similar to CPT), followed by additional sessions in which grief and loss narratives are processed in order to facilitate the resolution of traumatic bereavement. A final module involves sessions to facilitate application of the knowledge and skills to current and future life challenges.

TGCTA was first developed, disseminated, and evaluated in a randomized trial for adolescent war survivors in Bosnia in the 1990s (Layne et al., 2008). It has since been implemented successfully for urban, gang-involved and at-risk youth in California (Saltzman et al., 2001) and for at-risk youth in the Delaware schools (Grassetti et al., 2014). It has been disseminated in NCTSN Learning Collaboratives and Learning Communities in many states since 2011 with trauma-informed milieu training (Think Trauma; see www.NCTSN.org) for facility staff. TGCTA's four modules address: (i) foundational knowledge and skills to enhance posttraumatic emotional, cognitive, and behavioral regulation and improve interpersonal skills; (ii) group sharing and processing of trauma experiences; (iii) group sharing and processing of grief and loss experiences; and (iv) resumption of adaptive developmental progression and future orientation. In both the randomized Bosnian trial and open trials with gang-involved US youth, TGCTA was associated with reduced PTSD, depression, and maladaptive grief reactions and improved school behavior (Layne et al., 2008; Saltzman et al., 2001). The manual is designed to be used not only by trained, masters-level clinicians but also by teachers, facility staff, and coaches. Each session contains step-by-step instructions for implementation, including suggested scripts for the exact language to use while conducting groups. Groups of 8–10 youth are generally led by two group leaders. Although single-gender groups are recommended, some facilities report successful implementation with mixed-gender groups. TGCTA's unique contributions for justice-involved youth are twofold: it includes group processing of trauma experiences (most often community violence exposure), which harnesses adolescent peer influence to promote greater self-regulation, and it has a full component for group processing of grief and loss. Because TGCTA is a modularized intervention, facilities that retain youth for briefer periods can implement only Modules I and IV, rather than implementing the full four-module version of 24 sessions, and the Bosnian research showed effectiveness for the briefer version (Layne et al., 2008).

KID Narrative Exposure Therapy

KIDNET is an adaptation of Narrative Exposure Therapy, a short-term therapy for individuals with PTSD symptoms due to traumatic exposure to organized violence (including refugees and asylum seekers) and natural disasters. KIDNET provides eight individual therapy sessions designed for refugee children with PTSD related to war and other types of organized violence. Rather than focusing only on trauma memories, the child is helped to build a chronological narrative of his or her entire life, including a detailed description of traumatic experiences (similar to PE) that is recorded in writing by the therapist and given to the child (as a form of personal "testimony" to underscore the child's resilience as a survivor) at the end of therapy. Active listening, unconditional positive regard, and creative tasks (e.g., constructing a lifeline with flowers and stones; representing positive and negative events along a rope to illustrate significant events; reenacting body positioning, during which children show therapists the ways they physically positioned their body during an event). Research studies testing KIDNET have shown its effectiveness in reducing children's PTSD symptoms even when traumatic violence is still ongoing or is an imminent danger (Robjant & Fazel, 2010). In one study, 26 children traumatized by organized violence were randomly assigned to KIDNET or to a waiting list. Children who received KIDNET group but not the controls showed a clinically significant improvement in PTSD, depression, and anxiety symptoms and in their functioning with their families, peers, and at school, with these gains continuing a year later (Ruf et al., 2010).

Seeking Safety

Seeking Safety is a 25- to 30-session multicomponent group or individual therapy designed originally for adults with co-occurring PTSD and substance use disorders. Seeking Safety teaches cognitive behavioral skills for coping with both PTSD symptoms (including complex symptoms such as emotion dysregulation, dissociation, and impulsivity) and addictive urges and habits involving alcohol or other drug use. Seeking Safety has shown promising results in numerous clinical field trial studies with generally comparable positive outcomes to those of comparison therapies such as relapse prevention and multimodal case management (Najavits & Hien, 2013). The most consistent findings for Seeking Safety with multiply disadvantaged and polyvictimized adults have been reduction in PTSD symptoms (Najavits & Hien, 2013). In a study with 33 primarily Caucasian female adolescents who reported multiple traumatic exposures (88% sexual abuse, 82% disaster/accident, 73% physical abuse) and met criteria for PTSD and one or more substance use disorders, Seeking Safety was associated with greater improvements than a wait-list control group on self-reported addiction and physical health problems. Seeking Safety's immediate posttreatment (but not 3-month follow-up) outcomes across a range of domains (including addictive disorders risk factors, depression, somatic/anorexic problems)—but not PTSD symptoms—surpassed those of SUD treatment-as-usual (Najavits, Gallop, & Weiss, 2006).

Cognitive Behavioral Intervention for Trauma In Schools

CBITS involves ten 60-minute weekly group sessions (with between six to eight children in each group) and one to three individual sessions to prepare the child for the group session in which group members each describe a trauma memory. Parents are provided with two education sessions and teachers with one education session so that they can support the child(ren) involved in the group. Six activities are included in C-BITS, including education about PTSD symptoms, relaxation training, skills for challenging anxious thoughts ("cognitive therapy"), trauma memory reconstruction ("stress or trauma exposure"), *in vivo* confrontation of reminders of traumatic or stressful experiences, and skills for solving problems in relationships ("social problem solving skills").

Thus, CBITS differs from TF-CBT in the setting (schools), format (group rather than individual and parent-child therapy), and age (10–15 years old, but not younger or older children) and types of traumatic stressors (including family and community violence, and disasters and severe accidents, but not sexual abuse) of the children for whom it was designed. CBITS is similar to TF-CBT in teaching self-management skills and assisting participants in trauma memory reconstruction, although the trauma memory work in CBITS is done in a much briefer manner (one to two sessions) and trauma narratives are shared with the entire group. CBITS has shown evidence of reducing youth- and parent-rated PTSD and depression symptoms in two studies, one with primarily ethnoculturally minority-group children and a comparison group of children from another location (Stein et al., 2003), and the second with an ethnoculturally diverse urban sample of children and delayed treatment comparison condition (Kataoka et al., 2011).

ERASE-Stress

ERASE-Stress involves 12–16 classroom sessions each lasting 90 minutes, with psychoeducation about PTSD, training in stress management and emotion regulation skills, and resiliency strategies. The intervention is unique in that it is delivered by homeroom teachers with training and supervision by traumatic stress clinician. In two studies (Berger et al., 2012; Gelkopf & Berger, 2009), middle school (early adolescence) students living in Israel who were exposed on an ongoing basis to the threat and actual occurrence of war-related violence received either the 12- to 16-session ERASE-Stress classroom education program or the school's usual classes. Almost half of the youths initially had a likely diagnosis of PTSD. In follow-up assessments 1 or 3 months after the ERASE-Stress intervention ended, students receiving ERASE-Stress reported reduced PTSD, anxiety, depression, and physical health symptoms and improved school, peer, and family functioning, but the usual curriculum students did not.

Child-Parent Psychotherapy

CPP engages mothers in verbal and nonverbal play with their infant or toddler in order to strengthen or restore the mother's capacity to be empathically and responsively available to her child (Klatzkin, Lieberman, & Van Horn, 2013). CPP therapists do not instruct or correct the mother or child, but instead provide developmental guidance through reflective comments that are hypotheses about what the child may be thinking and intending and the meaning that this has for the mother in light of the tension between her own posttraumatic reactions and her caring and affection for her child. CPP therapists also model appropriate protective behavior, provide the mother with emotional support, and assist her with crisis intervention and practical problem solving when stressors occur in the family's current life. CPP therapists pay special attention to helping the parent and child understand the impact of traumatic events on their individual and shared experience, as well as to access and share memories of positive experiences together (and for the mother, experiences of being cared for as a child or adult by her own parents) in order to sustain the mother as she cares for her child and both recover from the impact of trauma.

Other empirically based psychotherapy models for adolescents with PTSD

Several other psychotherapies for children or adolescents with PTSD have been developed (Ford & Courtois, 2013) or adapted from adult versions (Courtois & Ford, 2009) with detailed manuals and training programs to ensure that the intervention is delivered accurately.

Attachment, Self-Regulation, and Competency (ARC). ARC provides therapeutic activities to achieve goals within three domains: *attachment* (building and supporting safe and responsive care by primary caregivers, providers, and milieus); *self-regulation* (supporting youth capacity to identify, modulate, and express emotional and physiological experience); and *competency* (building self-reflective capacities, problem-solving skills, and a coherent and positive understanding of self). A published manual describes experiential activities to address each goal in psychotherapy and in modifications to the youth's milieu through staff training and family education (Blaustein & Kinniburgh, 2010).

PCIT (Urqiza & Timmer, 2013). PCIT is a behavioral parent management approach to family psychotherapy with traumatized young children and their parent(s) that takes a more behavioral approach to teaching parents skills for encouraging positive behaviors (such as active play and compliance with parental rules and requests) and reducing negative behaviors (such as angry defiance or impulsive acts) while they play with their child. PCIT has shown evidence of helping abusive parents to function more effectively in parenting (Timmer, Urquiza, Zebell, & McGrath, 2005), but it does not directly address traumatic stress reactions, and it has not been tested specifically with traumatized children with PTSD.

Real Life Heroes. Kagan (2008) developed and field tested Real Life Heroes as an therapy and educational intervention for young to school-age children. The therapy helps children identify their heroes, recognize how they have the same or similar qualities and skills as their heroes, and utilize this sense of "the hero within" to restore their confidence and overcome fear.

Sanctuary. Sanctuary is an organizational change model rather than an individual or group therapy (Bloom, 2013). Its aim is to establish a trauma-informed culture that supports youth in recovery from the impacts of traumatic stress, while simultaneously providing safety for clients, families, staff, and administrators. Seven features of the environment are addressed in order to build a culture of nonviolence, emotional intelligence, inquiry and social learning, shared governance, open communication, social responsibility, and growth and change.

Skills Training in Affect and Interpersonal Regulation (STAIR). STAIR is a well-validated individual psychotherapy for women with PTSD related to childhood maltreatment and violence (Cloitre et al., 2010) that was adapted as a group therapy (STAIR-A) for adolescents by Cloitre, Cohen, and Koenen (2006) to teach skills for emotion regulation and interpersonal effectiveness, and, with this as a base, to guide the youth in narrative reconstruction of the story of their entire life (including traumatic events). A psychoeducation module addressing psychological trauma and emotion identification is followed by modules on emotion regulation and interpersonal communication skills, with deep breathing and safety planning integrated into all sessions. A preliminary clinical study of the adolescent adaptation (Gudino et al., 2014) with 38 adolescent psychiatric inpatients reported decreases in PTSD and depression symptoms and increased coping self-efficacy after participating in between 3 and 36 group STAIR-A sessions.

SPARCS. SPARCS (DeRosa & Pelcovitz, 2008) is a group therapy that integrates key concepts from three evidence-based treatment models: Dialectical Behavior Therapy (DBT; DeRosa & Rathus, 2013), TARGET (Ford, 2015); and TGCTA. SPARCS is designed to enhance self-regulation, relationships, self-perception, and confidence in pursuing future goals.

Trauma Systems Therapy (TST; Saxe, Ellis, & Kaplow, 2007). TST takes a family systems perspective with a "wraparound" approach to providing the full range of services needed by children and families recovering from PTSD. The "wraparound" approach involves parents, teachers, counselors, pediatricians, child protection workers, mentors, probation officers, educational guidance professionals, recreational and occupational therapists, social workers, psychiatrists, and psychotherapists as a collaborative team working together to identify and address needs and stressors affecting each child and their family, school, and community. TST includes education about PTSD, cognitive behavior therapy skills for self-management of anxiety, affect and interpersonal regulation skills, and family therapy to these wraparound teams, thus helping a large array of providers to better help children with PTSD. TST is designed to help youths and families move through five phases of recovery from posttraumatic stress: "Surviving, Stabilizing, Enduring, Understanding, and Transcending." Ellis et al. (2012) reported positive results in a sample of 124 children and adolescents exposed to potentially traumatic events. Over the course of a 15-month follow-up, youth who received the TST intervention showed improvements in emotion regulation, general functioning, and social-environmental stability and were less likely to be hospitalized than children in routine mental health care.

Pharmacotherapy for children with PTSD

Pharmacological interventions are often considered as an adjunct to psychotherapy for PTSD. Medications can reduce symptoms when impairment disrupts daily functioning or help the child tolerate emotional pain associated with traumatic memories that may be augmented by psychotherapy (Connor, Ford, Arnsten, & Greene, 2014). Selective serotonin reuptake inhibitors (SSRIs) are often chosen for treating pediatric PTSD, but Cohen, Mannarino, Perel, and Staron (2007) found no evidence in a randomized clinical trial of added benefit when a SSRI (sertraline) was combined with TF-CBT for 10- to 17-year-old youth who had histories of sexual abuse. A 10-week randomized controlled trial using an independent sample of sertraline (50–150 mg/day, mean dose 115 mg/day) did not offer any advantage over placebo on a measure of PTSD symptom severity (Robb, Cueva, & Sporn, 2010). Although SSRIs may have a role in treating anxiety and depressive disorders comorbid with PTSD, their efficacy for children with PTSD is not evident. Adrenergic medications such as guanfacine extended release (which has shown promise in an open trial for traumatized children's daytime hyperarousal) and prazosin (which has demonstrated efficacy in reducing adults' PTSD hyperarousal) warrant clinical trial studies (Connor et al., 2014).

Many psychiatric medications have been used by clinicians to treat children with PTSD, but there is very little scientific evidence about either the efficacy or the safety of these medications for these children. The most widely used medications are antidepressants, particularly the SSRIs such as sertraline (Zoloft) or paroxetine (Paxil), both of which have been approved by the US Food and Drug Administration for the treatment of adults with PTSD but not for children, and the selective serotonergic/noradrenergic reuptake inhibitors (SSNRIs) such as nefazodone (Desyrel) or venlafaxine (Effexor). Medications that have shown benefit with anxiety (such as the antihypertensive medicines propanolol (Inderol) or clonidine), aggression (such as the antiseizure medication carbamazepine (Tegretol) or atypical antipsychogic medicines), and attention deficit hyperactivity disorder (such as the stimulant medicines methylphenidate (Ritalin or Concerta) or Adderall).

Concerns about the safety of antidepressant medications because of increased risk of suicide among children taking them for depression led the FDA to issue a warning on all such medications. However, when prescriptions of these medicines for childhood depression became less common, suicides among teens increased (Gibbons et al., 2007). Suicidality, although uncommon, is a risk for children with PTSD, but depression also increases the risk of suicide, so effective treatment of depression is important with children who suffer from PTSD. Unfortunately, the only scientific study of the efficacy of medication for children with PTSD reported disappointing results (Cohen et al. 2007). Sertraline had no benefit compared to placebo with child patients who also received TF-CB alone. Therefore, Connor and Fraleigh (2008) make the following recommendation:

> Medication therapy is considered adjunctive to other psychosocial treatments in childhood PTSD, and has two roles to play in the treatment of pediatric PTSD. These are to (a) target disabling PTSD symptoms so that daily impairment is diminished and the child may pursue a healthier developmental and psychosocial trajectory; and (b) help traumatized children tolerate emotionally painful material in order to participate in rehabilitative psychosocial therapy. Medication interventions should be considered for pediatric PTSD with the following characteristics: (a) severe PTSD symptoms that significantly interfere with daily

*functioning; (b) moderate PTSD symptoms with a marked physiological component
(autonomic nervous system hyperarousal, sleep disturbance, rage attacks,
irritability); (c) disabling PTSD symptoms that do not respond to 6 to 8 weeks
of psychosocial intervention with a family component; and (d) PTSD symptoms,
which are comorbid with other pharmacologically responsive psychiatric disorders
such as attention deficit/hyperactivity disorder, other anxiety disorders, psychotic
symptoms, and/or depression. (p. 473)*

No systematic studies of antipsychotics or mood stabilizers have been reported
with children with PTSD (Connor et al., 2014). For children with ASD due to burn
traumas, tricyclic and SSRI antidepressants have shown inconsistent evidence of efficacy, but a chart review study found a correlation between average morphine dose and
amount of decrease in PTSD symptoms. Thus, pharmacologic pain control may help
mitigate against ASD when traumatic events involve physical as well as psychological
injury (Connor et al., 2014).

Creative arts therapies

Art is a familiar mode of communication, interaction, and learning for most children.
Art therapy has been used as a means to help children express their observations,
feelings, and thoughts in a visual or auditory rather than verbal manner, potentially
providing a buffer against the intense emotional distress evoked by traumatic experiences and a way to experience mastery and competence as well as safety (Goodman
et al., 2008). Art therapy has been provided to children in the wake of natural disasters
(tsunamis, hurricanes, floods, fires), terrorism (the September 11 and Oklahoma City
bombings), traumatic illness or injury and hospitalization, war, and traumatic losses.
Although widely used, scientific research on the effectiveness of creative arts therapy
for children with PTSD has not been reported. Orr (2007) describes the many media
through which children can be engaged in art therapy:

*... crayons, oil pastels, clay, paint, lots of paper, pencils, colored pencils, felt
pens, paper, watercolor, tempera paint, watercolor paper and card stock, model
magic, Playdoh, plasticine, water-based clay, precut magazine images, construction
paper, tissue paper, string, yarn, glitter glue, and white glue. Materials were
chosen for their ease of transportation to the sites, as well as for their therapeutic
qualities. Drawing materials were brought to help children with storytelling of their
experiences because they allowed for control, while paint was used to increase
expression of feelings. Collage materials were used because they inherently provide
structure, are easy to control, and stimulate children's numbed imaginations.
Three-dimensional materials were used to provide children with the opportunity to
construct and reconstruct their environments and objects. (p. 355)*

Family systems therapies (Ford & Saltzman, 2009). Family therapy addresses the
impact of PTSD on all members of affected families, whether only one member (e.g.,
a rape) or the entire family (e.g., disaster or war in the family's community) was

exposed to traumatic events. Family therapy is designed to (i) establish a functional "family system" by enhancing family members' communication with one another and problem solving so as to increase the actual and perceived sense of safety, respect, caring, trust, and healthy development; and (ii) help family members get access to social support and resources (e.g., from neighbors and community members, or educational, governmental, or religious organizations or family/parent support programs). Family systems therapies have shown consistent evidence of effectiveness in achieving those goals with families in crisis due to losses, addiction, psychiatric illness, and legal and educational/work problems (Diamond & Josephson, 2005). However, few studies have investigated the efficacy of family therapy with families who have experienced psychological trauma or PTSD (Welch & Rothbaum, 2007). The only one scientific study of family therapy for PTSD did not involve children and failed to show any added benefit by family therapy when it was added to cognitive behavior therapy for PTSD (Glynn et al., 1999). However, an intervention for adolescents who have recovered from cancer and their families, and for children who are newly diagnosed with cancer and their families, has shown evidence of effectiveness in assisting the parents and children in reducing PTSD symptoms (Kazak et al., 2005) (Box 8.4).

Box 8.4 A Sample of Family Therapy for PTSD

The following simulated case vignette provides family therapy with a single-mother parent, her 15-year-old daughter from one prior relationship, and her 4- and 8-year-old daughter and son from a more recent relationship that ended 6 months ago due to the older daughter (*M*) reporting an incident of physical assault by her stepfather. *M* was described by her mother as oppositional-defiant at home since the age of 11. *M* accused her stepfather of emotional and sexual abuse at that age, but her mother had attributed the behavior to *M*'s "jealousy" toward her stepbrother and sister. *M* was born out of wedlock when her mother was 16 years old, and both lived with the maternal grandparents (with the truth of *M*'s parentage kept hidden) until her mother left home to marry *M*'s stepfather when *M* was 6 years old and brought *M* with her. When therapy began, *M*'s mother had called the police numerous times because *M* had stolen from her, was associating with friends who were using drugs, were several years older, and had dropped out of high school. Placement in a foster home was being recommended by the juvenile probation and child protective services professionals working with the family because there was no improvement in *M*'s "beyond parental control" behavior, and *M*'s mother was fearful that *M* would get pregnant and run away to live with one of the young men with whom she associated.

After six initial assessment and stabilization sessions in which the therapist (*T*) helped *M* and her mother to reframe their conflicts as mutually escalating stress reactivity, several altercations occurred between *M* and her mother, with the mother calling the police and *M* being arrested and placed in a juvenile detention facility. The following excerpts are from the next conjoint session.

T:	I'm glad to see you again after what I'm sure has been a stressful period for all of you.
Mother:	(*Sighs, looks at M with a combination of annoyance and resignation*): I don't think my daughter really wants to be a part of this family; she just wants her own way.
M:	(*Looks off into space with no expression; then looks down at her hands*)
T:	I can see that you're each in a reactive state, so we need to deal with the triggers for each of you right now to help you get back in focus. (*Turning to the younger children*) How about if you two help us by showing us how good you are at being really focused with the books and art stuff over on this table? Could you do that? That's great; we need you to just have fun and be really focused on whatever you like there, while your mom and *M* and I have a talk to help them get focused, too. So we'll all be working on being focused, and we'll check in with you so you two can show us how you do it, okay? (*Turns back to mother, while M intently watches her younger brother and sister play*) I can see how much you want *M* to be a part of this family, but I think your stress alarm is keeping you stuck in reactive feelings and thoughts. I can understand why you might be feeling very reactive, as a parent who loves your daughter and wants her to be safe and happy, and also to not make mistakes like ones that you feel you made at her age. Even though you're certainly feeling some reactive feelings, including maybe feeling hurt or worried when you think that *M* isn't going to be safe or be a part of the family. Would it be fair to say that love and hope for *M* are your main feelings underneath? It must be hard to get to those main feelings, and main thoughts like what you value about *M* and your relationship with her, when you're having these understandably strong reactions.
Mother:	Well, wouldn't any parent feel like this if she had a daughter who was disrespectful and selfish? She *is* making the same mistakes I made, and she's just as pigheaded as I was when I thought I knew everything as a teenager. Look what happened to me!
T:	You want *M* to be openminded and thoughtful about her choices, not stubbornly or impulsively doing things that aren't really what she wants or needs. Sounds like that's not easy for you to do either, even now, so maybe it's more that you and *M* both are very strong willed and emotionally intense, and that can look pigheaded or impulsive, but it's really just needing to not be controlled by your stress reactions. And you're working very hard to stay focused on making a good life for yourself and your children; as a single working mother, that's a lot of stress—especially when you had to choose to protect your children instead of staying in your marriage. That took a lot of courage and a real focus on doing the right thing.

(Continued)

Box 8.4 Continued

Mother: I know I should have ended that relationship a long time ago, when M said he was being abusive, but I just didn't know what to do or who to believe. (*M looks up intently at her mother*) I never wanted my daughter or any of my children hurt, but I didn't know it was so bad until the time when I left M with him while the kids and I visited my family. As soon as M told me what happened, I said that's it, enough, he's out. I won't let anyone hurt my daughter. (*Looks tearfully at M*) I wish she could stop being angry at me and accept that I really love her and will do whatever it takes so she's okay.

T: (*Turning to M, who looks down and away again after a pause*) Is it a trigger for you when your mom says things that might sound like she thinks you're the problem and maybe doesn't want you to be in this family? I'm not hearing your mom saying that exactly, but that could be what you're hearing now—or what you might have felt for a long time if you didn't know how to get your mom to understand how bad things were.

M: (*Pauses, looks intently at mother, who has her eyes closed, then looks down, nods yes*)

T: (*Turns to the younger children, who have stopped their previously active play and are looking wide-eyed at their mother and sister*) Well, this is some important stuff we're talking about, and I see that you two want to be sure that it all gets worked out okay. I'll make sure your mom and sister figure out how to make this okay, if you could just help us by showing us how to focus again? That's what I'm doing with your mom and sister, but since you two already are very good at focusing, it would be a very big help if you remind us how to be focused. You should focus on stuff that you like, like those books and toys and drawing, and that will help us focus really well on the talking we're doing. How does that sound? Is that a good plan, Mom? (*Mother refocuses on the younger children, smiles and nods yes*) Great, thanks, you guys for being such a good help to us by showing us how you focus. (*Younger children smile and resume play*) So I think maybe some of those really bad times are still bothering each of you, and you haven't known how to get your focus, together as well as individually, back on your main feelings and thoughts and goals. There are two ways to do that: one is to take some time, not a lot but some sessions, and just deal with the triggers and reactive emotions and thoughts that didn't get dealt with entirely in past stressful situations. I can help you do that in a way that is hard work but doesn't dredge up all the old stuff—just the specific triggers and reactions that you don't want to be bothered by all the time now. I can do that privately with each of you and both of you together, but we'll need to do that when the younger kids aren't here because it's really adult or young adult talk and not something that they are old enough to be involved in. Is that something you'd each be willing to do with me, maybe in some sessions in the next several weeks?

Mother and *M:*	(*Silently look pensive, then sigh and look accepting, and nod yes*)
T:	Okay, the other way we can do it right now, while you're both more focused than you were when we started—did you notice that? (*Pauses*) You're both very good at getting focused when you just do an SOS—slow your thoughts down, get oriented to what's really important to you, and then start thinking or doing things that give you more personal control—and I see the younger kids are very good at focusing in their own way, too. (*Everyone looks over at the younger children, who are playing happily and intently*) So what we can do to help you both deal with the triggers and reactive feelings and thoughts that are coming between you is to talk about a recent situation where you lost your focus, but we need to focus on figuring out the specific triggers right then for each of you and how you tried to keep your focus so you can do that again and maybe be able to succeed a little better in keeping your focus when something similar happens.
M:	Okay, how about the argument that happened between last night, when *M* took my phone and then wouldn't admit it. After I told her I couldn't trust her if she kept doing that, she turned around and didn't get up to go to school this morning. How about that?
T:	(*Turns to M*) Okay if we talk about that? Here's the ground rules: we're not just going to focus on what you did or didn't do; we'll include that, but we're also going to talk about how your mom got triggered and what she did or didn't do to be focused. The goal is for each of you to be able to keep your focus better, not to blame or punish anyone.
M:	(*Looks at mother, smiles*) That would be different. I usually get blamed and punished.
Mother:	(*Looks affronted, turns to T, who calmly gives her a look of curious interest*) I think a parent has to hold her daughter responsible and set limits. I don't call that blame and punishment. Am I supposed to just give up and let her do anything?
T:	You each make a good point. So it's important to *M* to not be blamed or punished, and it's important to your mom to be able to expect responsible behavior and set some limits. Those are good "main" goals, except *M*, I think that tells us more about what you don't want than what you do want in your relationship with your mom. If she isn't blaming or punishing you, do you just want her to let you do anything and totally leave you alone?
M:	Sometimes, yes. (*Turns to mom, smiles*) But no, not really. I know I can't just do what I want all the time, and I need to be responsible, but I try to do that, and she doesn't notice except when she gets stressed out, and then I'm always the one she blames.

(*Continued*)

Box 8.4 Continued

T: So what's your main goal in your relationship with your mom and your life? What do you want her to do, and what do you want for yourself?

M: (*Pauses*) I just want her to notice when I do good things and not send me away. (*Tears*)

Mother: (*Tears*) That's what I want, too, really. I never want you to go away, and I know I need to be better at noticing what you do that's good so you know I think you're great and I love you. I just get so stressed and worried. I know I shouldn't have such high expectations for *M*. I do want her to be able to be a girl and not have to be an adult and miss out on all the fun and freedom of being a teenager, but these days that seems to mean doing things that kids never would have dreamed of when I was that age—smoking marijuana, staying out to all hours, having a car of her own. It's just not what I think is right— it's really dangerous for her because the drug use gets her depressed.

T: Let's just slow down and take a moment to get focused, Mom. *M* seems very focused and is listening very carefully, so it's important that she hears your "main" feelings and goals right now, and that you do, too. The reactive feelings and thoughts are important, but we don't want them to take your focus away from what you really feel and want.

Mother: (*After an extended pause*) Okay, you're right; it's just hard. *M* always thinks very deeply about things, and she says she understands why I worry but that I should trust her and that I shouldn't try to keep her a child when she needs to grow up and be her own person. She's like me in that way: she wants her mom to trust her. And I want to, but I'm afraid I've failed her, and because of that, she's going to shut me out and just do whatever she wants—or thinks she has to—like I did when I was her age.

T: So things happened to you when you were *M*'s age or younger that made you feel unsafe or unprotected, and you shut people out and just did what you felt you had to.

Mother: (*Looks down, tearful*) It's not something I talk about, and it was different back then; the expectations were different, and some things could happen that you had to just keep secret. I thought I'd dealt with all that, and I don't want *M* to have that happen.

T: Sometimes feelings from bad experiences can get triggered even if you've tried to put the memories behind you, and if that interferes with your focus when you really want to do the right thing—as a parent or as a 15-year-old—and when you don't want it to turn into a conflict or hurt someone you care about—whether you're the daughter or the mother—then you may have dealt with it very well but just not quite finished by putting it all into focus so you know how to deal with triggers when they come up again now. I think that's what comes between you both now, more than anything else. *M*, do you sometimes have feelings or even memories that are from the past but all of a sudden can really bother you now? Maybe that's when you do things like taking stuff from your mom, which you know you shouldn't and don't even really want to, but those feelings can just take your focus away, and you're not really choosing but reacting?

M: (*Crying softly*) All the time, every day. I don't know why I do things like that when I really don't want to. I just feel like I have to do it and I do. That's not really what I'm like. I'm not really a liar or a thief, but I just stop thinking and feeling when I do that.

T: So even though you two are very different in some important ways, you share an ability to not just think but to care, very deeply, and to know that those you love always are with you and won't let you down. We can work on that if it makes sense to both of you that the challenge is to focus on what turns on your inner stress alarms and deal with that so you can be focused the way you want and really are capable of. That won't change everything, but it might give you back your most valuable resource: your ability to use your mind to focus, make good decisions, and feel good even when your stressed.

Summary. In this approach to family therapy based on the TARGET (Ford & Russo, 2006) affect regulation intervention for PTSD, family members together learn to identify both types of functioning—the "reactive" and the "main" (regulated)—in therapeutic interactions and in daily experiences and to see that they have a shared and solvable challenge—to regain or maintain self-regulation—rather than separate intractable dilemmas. Family therapy provides an opportunity for the therapist to model and engage family members in observing and practicing ways to respond to stressful encounters with one another—including those resulting from one or several members' PTSD—that provide them with increased confidence in their own and other family members' abilities to be emotionally caring, supportive, and respectful rather than adversarial and isolated.

Reprinted by permission from Ford and Saltzman (2009).

Real-world challenges in treating children with PTSD

In order to select, adapt, and successfully deploy available evidence-based or promising (evidence-informed) assessment and intervention protocols clinically with children with PTSD, several practical, therapeutic, and ethical considerations are essential (see Ford & Cloitre, 2009).

1. Identifying and addressing threats to the child or family's safety and stability are the first priority. The ethical principles of "*primum non nocere*" (first do no harm) and "*parens patriae*"(temporary guardianship) are crucial because potential threats to the safety of children with PTSD include (i) self-harm and suicidality; (ii) ongoing family violence, abuse, neglect, substance abuse, or psychopathology; or (iii) behavior that places the child or youth at risk for sexual victimization, community violence (e.g., physical assault, gang

conflicts), abduction or kidnapping, life-threatening accidents, life-threatening illness (e.g., sexually or needle-transmitted diseases), or legal problems and incarceration. When threats to safety are ongoing or imminent, treatment should concentrate on accessing resources (such as child protective services, legal protections such as restraining orders on violent adults or supervised visitation with past or potentially abusive adults, and in-home services such as multisystemic therapy (Henggeler, 1998) or multidimensional family therapy (Liddle, Rodriguez, Dakof, Kanzki, & Marvel, 2005)). If a youth is abusing substances, treatment for addiction and PTSD (such as Seeking Safety or TARGET) should be provided.

2. *The first step in treatment is developing a therapeutic relationship with the child and caregiver(s).* Traumatized children are young enough that they and their caregivers still are developing what Bowlby (1969) described as their "working models" of secure, responsive, helpful, and trustworthy primary relationships. When psychological trauma occurs, particularly developmentally adverse interpersonal trauma (Ford, 2005), children's working models (and associated capabilities for self-regulation of emotion, consciousness, impulses, and bodily functioning) may remain in flux and become chronically disorganized for the rest of childhood and adolescence (Miltenburg & Singer, 1999) and into adulthood (Lyons-Ruth, Dutra, Schuder, & Bianchi, 2006). The children's caregivers, often traumatized in their own lives (as well as stressed by their child's traumatization), may have difficulty in establishing and maintaining a secure and responsive relationship with their child and with the therapist. Thus, the therapeutic relationship with children with PTSD should be viewed as triadic rather than dyadic: bridges linking the child, caregiver, and therapist affectively to one another such that the therapist provides coregulation for the child and caregiver, empowering the caregiver to assume this role with the child while secure in the therapist's unconditional, nonintrusive, noncompetitive empathy and guidance. The therapist's role as coarchitect and cobuilder of these affective bridges with and between the child and caregiver is most evident in dyadic parent-child psychotherapies with young children such as CPP. However, creating and maintaining the triadic affective bridge is equally important with traumatized children and their attachment figures (who may be peers or mentors as well as, or instead of, the more obvious caregivers as the child grows into (pre)adolescence) at all ages.

3. *Treatment with children and families is always relational.* PTSD is so debilitating for children that therapists may feel compelled to achieve large goals such as complete recovery in order to prevent the child and parent from suffering disappointment in the face of what may seem to be intractable problems. The challenge for therapists is to shift from emphasizing overcoming pathology or deficits as the goal of treatment to focusing on a series of smaller goals that are of immediate personal relevance to the child and caregiver(s) (Ford & Russo, 2006). For example, rather than assuming that a child or caregiver will automatically agree that reducing avoidance of reminders of past traumatic experiences is a desirable treatment goal, the child's and caregiver's engagements and buy-ins to therapy are likely to be stronger if the therapist links reducing avoidance to the child's desire to be successful in school, sports, theater, dance, arts, auto mechanics, or video games and with the caregiver's hope that the child will be happier and more successful. Psychoeducation is important in every therapy for children with PTSD, and it is an opportunity to learn the child's and caregivers' goals, as well as to teach them about PTSD and recovery.

4. *Treatment for children with PTSD is always strengths-based.* The goals of psychotherapy for children and adolescents with PTSD include not only reducing the frequency and severity of PTSD symptoms but also enhancing biopsychosocial functioning. Existing or former strengths, resources, and resilience are the best predictor of children's recovery from complex traumatic stress disorders and socioeconomic adversity. It can be very

difficult to discern meaningful strengths or competences with children or youth who seem to be severely impulsive, withdrawn, oppositional, despondent, terrified, regressed, dissociative, or detached. Similarly, their parents or caregivers often seem to be reactive, dejected, resigned, confused, and easily narcissistically wounded, although this may be an understandable outcome of experiencing frustration, loss, isolation, and helplessness secondary to their child's past victimization and ongoing complex traumatic stress reactions. This requires a rigorous and disciplined focus on identifying and building on the capabilities that have made it possible for the child and caregiver(s) to continue to seek help (even if they seem to be rejecting or sabotaging that very help) and to pursue their personal goals (even if the goals seem to be primarily dysfunctional), beginning from the first therapeutic encounter and continuing in each subsequent assessment and treatment session. Interventions that explicitly orient the therapist and clients toward identifying the functional aspects of the clients' goals and behavioral choices (e.g., TARGET's distinction between "reactive" and "main" personal goals and behaviors; Real Life Heroes' emphasis on finding the inner hero; Life Skills Life Story's provisions for helping youths express their achievements as well as disappointments in a personal life story; ARC's competence interventions) can help therapists maintain a consistent strengths-based approach in treating children with PTSD.

5. *All phases of treatment should aim to enhance self-regulation competences.* In order to help the child shift from a posttraumatic "survival brain" to a "learning brain" (see Chapter 5), self-regulation skills are essential. Self-regulation requires a shift by the traumatized child (and the child's caregivers and role models) from emotional chaos to modulated emotion awareness and expression, from dissociation to planful and mindful goal-directed behavior, from neglect of their bodies to awareness and utilization of bodily cues as a guide to self-care and healthy growth, and from disorganized attachment models to responsible and healthy relationships.

6. With young children recovering from PTSD, dyadic psychotherapies such as CPP help caregivers to be a living example of emotion regulation. With school-age and preadolescent children, PTSD psychotherapies such as TF-CBT, CBITS, Real Life Heroes, SPARCS, and TARGET address emotion regulation by assisting children to develop a balance of autonomy, relatedness, and impulse control in peer interactions as well as in family. In adolescence, emotion dysregulation must be addressed in the form of eating disorders, conduct disorder, sexual and gender identity disorders, substance dependency, suicidality, and self-injurious behaviors that gravely complicate PTSD and compromise the youth's safety due to serious problems such as incarceration, truancy, teen pregnancy, gang involvement, and suicidality. Intensive psychotherapies such as Seeking Safety or TARGET, or integrative programs such as ARC and TST, are critical to successful treatment of PTSD with adolescents who are not only anxious but out of control.

7. Posttraumatic dissociation is a reflection of severely disturbed affect regulation that is very challenging to treat directly in children because, for most children until adolescence, the degree of reflective self-awareness necessary to recognize dissociation has not yet developed. Therefore, childhood dissociation and PTSD are best addressed by helping the child to learn how to be aware of different states of mind just as she or he is learning to be aware of anxiety, fear, anger, sadness, and troubling emotions as recognizable and manageable stress reactions. For example, labeling specific emotions in TF-CBT and role modeling (e.g., by "thinking out loud") a mindful or focused approach to defining immediate goals and behaviors that increase the child's access to positive feelings and reduce the intensity of negative affect in TARGET can help a child to be aware of and able to (re)gain the ability to change dissociative states into manageable emotions.

8. *Take steps to determine with whom, when, and how to address traumatic memories.* The core goal for the treatment of children with PTSD is to enable them (and their caregivers) to attain what Harvey (1996) described as mastery or "authority" in relation to their own memories—including but not limited to memories of traumatic events (Vickerman & Margolin, 2007). As children develop or regain affect and interpersonal regulation competences that they need in order to recognize and utilize their emotions, think and remember clearly, and cope with reminders of traumatic experiences, they become able to actually tolerate and understand traumatic memories. However, if memories remain troubling and avoided, PTSD is likely to persist. Thus, the answer to the first question—"With whom should traumatic memories be addressed in psychotherapy?"—clearly is *with every child (and as possible, caregiver) who is impaired as a result of PTSD or complex traumatic stress disorders* (Cohen et al., 2006; Saxe et al., 2007).

9. The answer to the second question—"When?"—depends on the answer to the third question—"How?" There are really three answers to the latter question: (i) the therapist recognizes the cues and reactions that indicate that a child is probably experiencing, or about to experience, traumatic stress reactions and associated self-dysregulation and guides the child and caregiver in anticipating, preparing for, and nonavoidantly coping with these posttraumatic sequelae in the course of therapeutic and daily activities; (ii) the therapist teaches the child and caregiver to recognize traumatic stress reactions as ways that they adaptively coped with past traumatic events and helps them to use self-regulation skills to mindfully choose how to modify unnecessary or unhelpful aspects of those reactions, while preserving and intentionally utilizing the currently egosyntonic and psychosocially adaptive aspects of those reactions (i.e., to keep the baby but not the bathwater); and (iii) the therapist guides the child and caregiver in story-building activities that enable the child to purposively recall and gain a sense of mastery in relation to memories of specific past troubling traumatic events.

10. The first option—sensitive psychotherapeutic management of clients' triggered distress—is at the core of Phase one in TF-CBT and all cognitive-behavioral, psychodynamic, and affect and interpersonal regulation psychotherapies for children with PTSD. Therefore, teaching self-management skills is the first step in PTSD treatment with any child or adolescent.

11. The second option—psychoeducation and self-regulation skills training to enhance clients' understanding of and ability to manage trauma-related stress reactions and self-dysregulation—is indicated when (i) a history of exposure to specific psychologically traumatic event(s) has been confirmed or is probable based upon credible (preferably multiple independent) sources, including archival (e.g., child protective services, legal, school) or clinical records, and child and caregiver self-reports on structured trauma history instruments (see Chapter 6); and (ii) the child's living arrangements and social support network are sufficiently stable to enable the child to regularly attend therapeutic sessions frequently enough to learn and practice self-regulation skills in emotionally and physically safe and relatively predictable and validating relationships.

12. When the third option—direct reconstruction of traumatic memories is undertaken—this typically is done with young children and caregiver(s) conjointly in spontaneous nonverbal activities (Van Horn & Lieberman, 2008). With older children (Cohen et al., 2006) and adolescents (Cloitre et al., 2006), traumatic memory reconstruction more often is done separately with the youth as a project in which the therapist assists the youth in repeatedly confronting a troubling memory (i.e., "exposure therapy") with the goal of enabling the youth to think of the memory as a past experience that is over and done and that can be recalled as fully (i.e., including self-validating as well as upsetting aspects) as other

memories and placed within the youth's larger personal story of her or his life (i.e., "narrative reconstruction"). With older children and adolescents, if possible, separate sessions are conducted with caregivers to prepare them and to help them address their own traumatic memories or stress reactions, followed by conjoint closure session(s) in which the child shares the reconstructed memory with the caregiver.

13. Therefore, trauma memory reconstruction requires (i) a physically and psychologically available permanent primary caregiver who is willing and able to help the child work through traumatic memories; (ii) a child with adequate core self-regulation capacities and environmental supports (in daily life settings and via a therapeutic safety net) to be able to manage episodically intense distress and stress reactions without becoming sufficiently affectively, dissociatively, or behaviorally destabilized to pose an immediate or chronic threat to the child's psychological health or safety (e.g., due to suicidality, psychosis, severe self-injury, substance dependence, or severe aggression); and (iii) a therapist with expertise in conducting traumatic memory reconstruction intervention with children of this age and developmental epoch who have significant complex traumatic stress disorder impairments and who has access to sufficient psychiatric and crisis backup (e.g., pharmacotherapy, acute crisis evaluation and hospitalization, case management wraparound resources, pediatric care) to be able to identify, prevent, or rapidly resolve treatment-related or -unrelated crises.

14. The overall approach involves progressing from options one to three, with each successive approach utilized only if (i) traumatic stress or potentially traumatic stress-related symptoms and impairments are present and not sufficiently resolved or managed, and (ii) the necessary resources and competences are in place to move to the next level. In practice, the progression from trauma-informed psychotherapy (option 1) to traumatic memory reconstruction (option 3) might occur as rapidly as within a single intake evaluation or initial treatment session (e.g., a child referred following or during a course of psychotherapy and pharmacotherapy in which the child and caregiver were stably and productively involved, but the child nevertheless was persistently troubled or impaired by PTSD or complex traumatic stress symptoms associated with well-documented traumatic experience(s) and the therapist did not feel qualified to conduct trauma memory reconstruction interventions). Alternately, therapy might progress from the trauma-informed to the trauma-focused (option 2) approach following a few or several sessions of initial assessment and therapeutic engagement, and then continue at that level while completing an affect and interpersonal regulation-based intervention for PTSD.

15. *Prevent and manage crises.* Many (but not all) children with PTSD have had to cope with chronic and often unpredictable discontinuities in their primary relationships and social support systems: losses due to deaths, out-of-home placements, institutionalization, family abandonment, and serial treatment providers (Faust & Katchen, 2004), as well as neglect and abuse due to parental and familial psychopathology, substance use disorders, violent or antisocial lifestyles, or severe socioeconomic adversities. They often have come to associate caring adults or positive peers and peer-group activities as undependable and likely to lead to disappointment or rejection; thus, even apparently positive events (e.g., birthday, holidays, field trips, family visits, recognition for accomplishments in school, sports, or arts, graduation ceremonies, new residence or school) may escalate PTSD symptoms. This may be misinterpreted in pathologizing terms as self-sabotage, psychopathy or incorrigibility, inability to tolerate delay of gratification, or passive dependency. However, such distress and dysregulation is predictable when traumatic memories are elicited by and reenacted in times of relational uncertainty. Therefore, the best approach to preventing or managing crises or deterioration is to assist the child and caregiver (including health

care, educational, judicial/legal, and mental health professionals and social/human service program staff) in anticipating and addressing the predictable dysregulation. This involves understanding the adaptive components (such as the attempt to protect against additional distress and demoralization and to communicate to responsible adults the importance of relational continuity), and collaboratively joining with the child in using self-regulation skills to increase everyone's sense of hope and trust. For example, to prepare for the transition from an intensive residential treatment program to a group or foster home, treatment for a child with PTSD might focus on helping the child to use affect regulation and relational skills to be able to remember that relationships don't end just because people can't see each other every day.

When crises cannot be prevented, a similar approach focused on restoring a sense of relational continuity and self-regulation provides a framework for helping to deescalate and stabilize the traumatized child or adolescent. This is an adaptation or special case of generic models of crisis intervention, which prescribe activating two key factors: (i) social support to reduce extreme spikes in the intensity of anxiety, dysphoria, anger, confusion, or detachment, and (ii) active problem solving in order to increase the sense of control, efficacy, and optimism. The primary threat to both objective and subjective social support for children with complex traumatic stress disorders is the loss of core relational (attachment) security, which the child experiences as a breakdown not just in relationships but in self-regulation of the body, emotions, impulse control, memory and thinking, and consciousness (dissociation). Thus, beyond the generic approaches to providing reassurance, immediate safety, structure, and limits (e.g., verbal deescalation tactics, time-out), crisis deescalation with traumatized children requires the use of several focal interventions: "grounding" strategies to counteract detachment, dissociation, and impulsivity (e.g., Cloitre et al., 2006; DeRosa & Pelcovitz, 2008; Ford, 2015) and affective engagement strategies to reestablish an immediate sense of emotional connection. In the aftermath of crises, therapeutic processing includes discussion of how the child used these self-regulation skills to successfully cope with PTSD's stress reactions. Every crisis thus is an opportunity for PTSD treatment to highlight and enhance the traumatized child's competence and sense of efficacy in her or his self-regulation skills and her or his trust in healthy relationships (Box 8.5).

Box 8.5 Real-World Challenges in Treating Children with PTSD: A Case Example

Danielle (whose name and specific identifying information have been disguised to protect privacy) is a 16-year-old girl referred for treatment after her adoptive mother called emergency mobile psychiatric services because Danielle was unable to calm down following an argument. Danielle was removed from her biological mother's care at the age of 4 due to her mother's neglect, substance use, and domestic violence between her mother and her boyfriend. She was placed in a series of foster homes, moving frequently between placements due to tantrums and accusations that she was stealing food and hiding it under her bed. At the age of 6, her biological father gained custody of her, but she was removed from his care and placed in a foster home at the age of 9 because he and her step-mother were physically and emotionally abusive toward her. She was adopted by her foster mother when she was 11 years old. Initially, Danielle got along well with her adoptive mother and did well in school, where she was a friendly and hard-working student. However, about 3 years ago, she began to exhibit a number of concerning behaviors. She started smoking cigarettes and marijuana and engaged in self-injurious cutting. She began wearing suggestive clothing and spending more time with a group of older adolescents, including a 16-year-old boy she referred to as her boyfriend. She became easily angered when she was told she could not do something, and she and her adoptive mother began to have increasingly heated arguments, often culminating in Danielle running away. Her adoptive mother reported that she did not feel able to control Danielle or keep her safe. In the past 2 years, Danielle has been involved in several individual outpatient and intensive outpatient therapy programs. She has been taken to the emergency department three times for evaluation due to behavioral concerns and has been hospitalized in an inpatient unit once due to an attempted overdose of pills. Her teachers report that she appears angry much of the time and seems to have difficulty paying attention in class. She is frequently defiant toward authority figures, and she has been suspended twice for fighting with other students. She often skips classes and leaves school grounds without permission, and she is at risk of failing several of her classes. Danielle frequently has trouble falling asleep, and in recent months she has had repeated nightmares of being murdered.

Alex was a typically developing boy before experiencing a single traumatic accident. He has had consistent social support and a stable and safe home environment. Immediately after the accident, he experienced symptoms of PTSD, including intrusive reexperiencing (nightmares and psychological distress at exposure to trauma reminders), avoidance of reminders of the accident (going outside to play), negative alterations in cognitions and mood (withdrawal from relationships, persistent sadness), and alterations in arousal and reactivity (irritable behavior and difficulty sustaining attention). Alex's pediatrician was notified by the emergency department following his visit on the day of the accident. An APRN in the pediatrician's office who was familiar with Alex and his family made a follow-up phone call to Alex's parents to see how he was recovering physically and emotionally and arranged follow-up office visits for Alex. The pediatrician and APRN observed and talked with Alex and his mother at each visit, initially identifying no posttraumatic behavioral or emotional changes. At a 1-month post-ED visit, Alex was noticeably more on edge than usual, and his mother reported the preceding changes. The pediatrician explained to Alex's mother that these were expectable reactions to the emotional shock of the accident and described how meeting with a therapist who specialized in

(Continued)

Box 8.5 Continued

helping children to recover from traumatic stress reactions could enable them to keep track of Alex's adjustment and provide a practical and efficient behavioral treatment if the symptoms did not improve. The APRN provided Alex's mother with contact information for two therapists who had evaluated and treated other patients in the practice successfully after traumatic events, and encouraged her to call back if she had any questions or concerns and, if she decided to have Alex see one of the therapists, to have the therapist contact the pediatric office to coordinate care.

Alex's mother decided to talk with both therapists and to take him to see the one with whom she felt most comfortable. To meet his needs, Alex's therapist developed a treatment plan that addressed not only his anxious response but also his significant attention problems and social withdrawal, and she chose TF-CBT, an evidence-based approach to addressing posttraumatic stress symptoms in children (Mannarino, Cohen, Deblinger, Runyon, & Steer, 2012) #5152 as her treatment modality. This involved a series of skill-based components presented to children and parents in parallel sessions and culminating in conjoint-sessions in which the child shares his or her "trauma story" with his parent(s). With the mother's release, the therapist immediately contacted the pediatric office and described the treatment plan to the APRN in order to enable the APRN and pediatrician to check with Alex and his mother about their satisfaction with the treatment and Alex's progress emotionally and behaviorally at a next visit.

Using this approach, the therapist first provided psychoeducation to both Alex and his mother about trauma and PTSD to help them understand Alex's symptoms and behaviors as common responses to stressful events. Next, Alex was taught relaxation skills to help him recognize, understand, and reduce the physiological reactivity he is experiencing. His parents were taught positive parenting techniques to help them address specific concerns and behaviors. Next, affective recognition and modulation (including feelings identification, intensity ratings, and positive self-talk) was addressed, and then cognitive coping skills were suggested. Once Alex was able to effectively identify and express his feelings, regulate his emotions, and use cognitive coping skills to address distressing thoughts, his therapist told him that he was ready to create his trauma narrative, which could take the form of any developmentally appropriate undertaking that engaged him in thinking about his traumatic experience, including creation of a story, comic, or song. Alex chose to create a book about his life, his family, and the accident. Through exposure and therapist-guided cognitive-processing, Alex increased his ability to tolerate thinking and talking about his accident and identified and altered unhelpful and inaccurate beliefs about what happened ("it was my fault"), himself ("I'm a bad boy"), and the world ("it's not safe to go outside"). When his trauma narrative was complete, Alex shared it with his parents, who had been carefully prepared by the therapist for this meeting, including engaging in role plays of supportive and validating responses, praise, and feedback for Alex, thus providing the family the opportunity to practice talking about the trauma together and simultaneously enhancing the parents' role as supportive and careful listeners for Alex. In addition to TF-CBT, an important piece of the intervention provided by the therapist was to work collaboratively with Alex's school to help them understand and address the ways that his PTSD affected his school functioning. The therapist also kept track with Alex's mother of subsequent pediatric visits and provided the APRN with a brief summary of the therapy and Alex's progress prior to each visit. With this information, the APRN and pediatrician were able to efficiently check with Alex's mother about her perception of Alex's recovery and therapy and to observe how Alex was doing behaviorally in each visit. There were no setbacks in this case, but had Alex experienced a worsening or resurgence of traumatic stress symptoms, the APRN was prepared to inform the therapist so the psychotherapy could be adapted to address the problems in a timely manner.

In contrast, Danielle endured multiple interpersonal victimization events and traumatic losses throughout her early childhood, including emotional and physical abuse at the hands of both her mother and father, twice being removed from her biological parents' home, and multiple placements in foster homes. While initially Danielle was relatively asymptomatic despite her significant trauma history, the onset of adolescence brought with it a delayed posttraumatic response. Danielle exhibited some of the more typical symptoms of PTSD, including intrusive reexperiencing (nightmares), avoidance of school, and hypervigilance (sleep and concentration problems), but her predominantly dysphoric, angry, and aggressive symptom presentations (including cutting herself) were not identified as associated with posttraumatic stress. However, as previously noted, the *DSM*-5 diagnosis of PTSD has added symptoms of pervasive blame, dysphoria, aggression, and self-harm, consistent with Danielle's pervasive difficulties with self-regulation and interpersonal relatedness that manifest as difficulties with emotion regulation, somatization, attention, impulse control, dissociation, interpersonal relationships, and self-attributions. Danielle had had limited and inconsistent pediatric care until she was adopted, but her adoptive mother recognized that this was essential in order to protect Danielle from developing chronic medical problems and to provide both her and Danielle with a consistent nonjudgmental source of support. Her adoptive mother identified a pediatric practice that specialized in adolescent female health issues and scheduled regular checkup visits twice yearly in order to help Danielle develop better self-care and physical hygiene.

Danielle had been required to undergo psychosocial and psychiatric treatment in several of her prior placements and on an emergency basis when she was hospitalized for crises. Danielle felt that none of these therapies had been helpful, because either the clinician seemed critical and "made me feel like there was something wrong with me that needed to be fixed" or the contact was only for a very limited time period and "as soon as I started to like [the therapists],

(Continued)

Box 8.5 Continued

I had to stop seeing them because I was moved to another group home or foster family." Danielle had been indifferent toward and unwilling to engage with two therapists who the Child Protective Services worker had required her to see, and her adoptive mother did not want to force Danielle to be in therapy. The adoptive mother talked privately about this dilemma with a nursing case manager in the pediatrics office, and the case manager then talked with both Danielle and her mother about what Danielle viewed as helpful in her positive past experiences with therapy and how they could identify therapists with a similar style and orientation whom Danielle could "audition" and then work with for as long as necessary without fear of untimely terminations. Danielle shifted from being unwilling to consider therapy to being skeptical but open to seeing if there was a therapist with whom she felt comfortable who could help—but not "fix"—her.

Once Danielle had decided to give one of the pediatric nurse's referrals a try, in order to meet Danielle's needs, her therapist developed treatment goals that addressed the multiple domains of self-regulation and relatedness that were affected by the emotional and physical violence and the disruption of primary attachment bonds that occurred within the context of her familial relationships. In addition, addressing the strained relationship between Danielle and her adoptive mother and helping her mother to provide consistent care, structure, and monitoring of Danielle's high-risk behaviors, while also supporting Danielle's normative adolescent strivings for autonomy and privacy were important components of her treatment. The therapist, with Danielle's knowledge and permission (and her mother's release), updated the nurse case manager on a monthly basis about the progress, and setbacks, in Danielle's therapy. When Danielle had her next semiannual pediatric visit, the pediatrician and the nurse case manager were able to ask her and her mother what seemed helpful or not in the therapy and how they each viewed Danielle's progress in dealing with emotional and behavioral challenges. With the preparation provided by the therapist's updates, this discussion was efficient and enabled the pediatric professionals to support Danielle's progress and her continued therapeutic involvement.

The mental health clinician used a combination of Parent Management Training and TARGET to achieve these goals. Danielle presented to therapy with the same defiant and angry presentation that her adoptive mother and teachers reported. She quickly told her therapist that she was "fine," that she would not talk about her past experiences, and that she didn't need any therapy. She followed this up with the assertion that she'd already been in lots of therapy and "it didn't help anyway." Danielle's therapist reassured her that she would not have to talk about her worst memories unless she chose to do so and that therapy would involve her and her mother learning about how coping with trauma turns on an alarm in the brain (the amygdala) that stays on even when it's not needed unless a trauma survivor knows how to reset it. Danielle liked the idea that her brain had become so proficient at protecting her when she was being abused that now it was stuck in a high alarm state, which was the source of her difficulty with anxiety and anger in relationships and school. As a result, now even small stressors were causing her brain to send out signals to prepare her body for extreme danger (the "fight-flight-freeze" response).

Danielle's therapist further explained to Danielle and her mother that therapy would help Danielle learn skills to deal with these extreme stress reactions by developing abilities that she already had—but hadn't known to apply to handle stress reactions—to think clearly and focus on her core values when she recognized that her brain and body were going back into "alarm mode." In subsequent sessions, Danielle (and her mother in parallel sessions) learned TARGET's mental focusing skills to help her clear her mind and think before acting and started to identify the triggers that activated her brain's alarm response. Together, these two skills were the first steps in helping Danielle learn how to prepare for and manage her alarm reactions. Next, Danielle's therapist introduced TARGET skills aimed at helping Danielle to become aware of her emotions and thoughts in order to identify and differentiate those that were "reactive" (generated by her alarm) from those that reflect her "main" values, hopes, and goals (those that occur when her alarm is reset by focused thinking). Danielle then worked with her therapist to define her "main" goals and identify the choices and behaviors that would help her achieve them. Once Danielle was able to recognize and modulate what had seemed to be uncontrollable stress reactions, she began to recognize her strengths and the many positive qualities she had to offer. As a result, she was able to become closer with her adoptive mother, enjoy her company, and earn her respect and trust, and ultimately regain a stabilizing sense of hope and self-esteem. While she still felt troubled and saddened by memories of trauma, her PTSD symptoms subsided.

Reprinted by permission from Connor et al. (2014).

Conclusion

Important innovations have been developed for the psychosocial treatment for children and adolescents with PTSD. Therapists who treat children and adolescents with PTSD have a responsibility to serve as a role model by personally using the affect and interpersonal regulation skills themselves that they teach to children and parents—that is, to not only "talk the talk" but also "walk the walk." This is not because therapists who treat children and adolescents with PTSD are "traumatized" by these patients or their families; it is quite the contrary because, despite the tough challenge that PTSD poses for recovery, most therapists working in this field are inspired by the children and families with whom they work (see Chapter 12). Advances in treatment for childhood PTSD also are developing at a very rapid pace as a result of innovative clinicians and increasingly rigorous scientific testing. However, most of the treatments now available for children and adolescents with PTSD have not been definitively proven to be effective, so there is much work to be done and many opportunities for creative and dedicated students and new professionals to make an important contribution to the treatment of children with PTSD.

References

Ahrens, J., & Rexford, L. (2002). Cognitive processing therapy for incarcerated adolescents with PTSD. *Journal of Aggression, Maltreatment & Trauma, 6*(1), 201–216.

American Academy of Child and Adolescent Psychiatry (1998). Not published. Available on-line <http://www.aacap.org/App_Themes/AACAP/docs/practice_parameters/PTSDT.pdf>Accessed 13.04.15.

Berger, R., Gelkopf, M., & Heineberg, Y. (2012). A teacher-delivered intervention for adolescents exposed to ongoing and intense traumatic war-related stress: A quasi-randomized controlled study. *Journal of Adolescent Health, 51*(5), 453–461.

Berkowitz, S. J., Stover, C. S., & Marans, S. R. (2011). The child and family traumatic stress intervention: Secondary prevention for youth at risk of developing PTSD. *Journal of Child Psychology and Psychiatry and Allied Disciplines, 52*(6), 676–685. http://dx.doi.org/10.1111/j.1469-7610.2010.02321.x.

Blaustein, M., & Kinniburgh, K. (2010). *Treating traumatic stress in children and adolescents: How to foster resilience through attachment, self-regulation, and competnecy.* New York: Guilford.

Bloom, S. (2013). The sanctuary model. In J. D. Ford & C. A. Courtois (Eds.), *Treating complex traumatic stress disorders in children and adolescents: Scientific foundations and therapeutic models* (pp. 277–294). New York: Guilford.

Bouchard, S., Mendlowitz, S. L., Coles, M. E., & Franklin, M. (2004). Considerations in the use of exposure with children. *Cognitive and Behavioral Practice, 11*, 56–65.

Bowlby, J. (1969). *Attachment and loss* (Vol. 1). London: Hogarth.

Carrion, V. G., Kletter, H., Weems, C. F., Berry, R. R., & Rettger, J. P. (2013). Cue-centered treatment for youth exposed to interpersonal violence: A randomized controlled trial. *Journal of Traumatic Stress, 26*(6), 654–662.

Chaffin, M., Funderburk, B., Bard, D., Valle, L. A., & Gurwitch, R. (2011). A combined motivation and parent-child interaction therapy package reduces child welfare recidivism in a randomized dismantling field trial. *Journal of Consulting and Clinical Psychology, 79*(1), 84–95. http://dx.doi.org/10.1037/a0021227.

Chard, K. M., Weaver, T. L., & Resick, P. A. (1997). Adapting cognitive processing therapy for child sexual abuse survivors. *Cognitive and Behavioral Practice, 4*(1), 31–52.

Cloitre, M., Cohen, L. R., & Koenen, K. C. (2006). *Treating survivors of childhood abuse: Psychotherapy for the interrupted life.* New York: Guilford.

Cloitre, M., Stovall-McClough, K. C., Nooner, K., Zorbas, P., Cherry, S., Jackson, C. L., et al. (2010). Treatment for PTSD related to childhood abuse: A randomized controlled trial. *American Journal of Psychiatry, 167*(8), 915–924. http://dx.doi.org/appi.ajp.2010.09081247 [pii]; http://dx.doi.org/10.1176/appi.ajp.2010.09081247.

Cohen, J. A., Berliner, L., & Mannarino, A. (2010). Trauma focused CBT for children with co-occurring trauma and behavior problems. *Child Abuse and Neglect, 34*(4), 215–224. http://dx.doi.org/10.1016/j.chiabu.2009.12.003.

Cohen, J. A., Mannarino, A. P., & Deblinger, E. (2006). *Treating trauma and traumatic grief in children and adolescents.* New York: Guilford.

Cohen, J. A., Mannarino, A. P., Deblinger, E., & Berliner, L. (2008). Cognitive-behavioral therapy for children and adolescents. In E. B. Foa, T. M. Keane, & M. J. Friedman (Eds.), *Effective treatments for PTSD* (pp. 223–245) (2nd ed.). New York: Guilford.

Cohen, J. A., Mannarino, A. P., & Iyengar, S. (2011). Community treatment of posttraumatic stress disorder for children exposed to intimate partner violence: A randomized controlled trial. *Archives of Pediatric and Adolescent Medicine*, *165*(1), 16–21. http://dx.doi. org/165/1/16 [pii]; http://dx.doi.org/10.1001/archpediatrics.2010.247.

Cohen, J. A., Mannarino, A. P., Kliethermes, M., & Murray, L. A. (2012). Trauma-focused CBT for youth with complex trauma. *Child Abuse and Neglect*, *36*(6), 528–541. http://dx.doi. org/10.1016/j.chiabu.2012.03.007.

Cohen, J. A., Mannarino, A. P., Perel, J. M., & Staron, V. (2007). A pilot randomized controlled trial of combined trauma-focused CBT and sertraline for childhood PTSD symptoms. *Journal of the American Academy of Child and Adolescent Psychiatry*, *46*, 811–819.

Connor, D. F., Ford, J. D., Arnsten, A. F., & Greene, C. A. (2014). An update on posttraumatic stress disorder in children and adolescents. *Clinical Pediatrics*. http://dx.doi. org/10.1177/0009922814540793.

Connor, D. F., & Fraleigh, L. (2008). Pharmacotherapy, child. In G. Reyes, J. D. Elhai, & J. Ford (Eds.), *Encyclopedia of psychological trauma* (pp. 471–474). Hoboken, NJ: Wiley.

Courtois, C. A., & Ford, J. D. (Eds.) *Treating complex traumatic stress disorders: An evidence-based clinician's guide*. New York, NY: Guilford Press.

Courtois, C. A., & Ford, J. D. (Eds.). (2009). *Treating complex traumatic stress disorders: An evidence-based guide*. New York: Guilford.

de Arellano, M. A., Lyman, D. R., Jobe-Shields, L., George, P., Dougherty, R. H., Daniels, A. S., et al. (2014). Trauma-focused cognitive-behavioral therapy for children and adolescents: Assessing the evidence. *Psychiatric Services*, *65*(5), 591–602. http://dx.doi. org/10.1176/appi.ps.201300255.

Deblinger, E., Mannarino, A. P., Cohen, J. A., Runyon, M. K., & Steer, R. A. (2011). Trauma-focused cognitive behavioral therapy for children: Impact of the trauma narrative and treatment length. *Depression and Anxiety*, *28*(1), 67–75. http://dx.doi.org/10.1002/da.20744.

DeRosa, R., & Pelcovitz, D. (2008). Group treatment for chronically traumatized adolescents: Igniting SPARCS of change. In D. Brom, R. Pat-Horenczyk, & J. D. Ford (Eds.), *Treating trauamatized children* (pp. 225–239). London: Routledge.

DeRosa, R. R., & Rathus, J. H. (2013). Dialectical behavior therapy with adolescents. In J. D. Ford & C. A. Courtois (Eds.), *Treating complex traumatic stress disorders in children and adolescents* (pp. 225–247). New York: Guilford.

Diamond, G., & Josephson, A. (2005). Family-based treatment research: A 10-year update. *Journal of the American Academy of Child and Adolescent Psychiatry*, *44*, 872–887.

Donnelly, C. (2008). Psychopharmacotherapy for children and adolescents. In E. B. Foa, T. M. Keane, M. J. Friedman, & J. A. Cohen (Eds.), *Effective treatments for PTSD* (pp. 269–278) (2nd ed.). New York: Guilford.

Ellis, B. H., Fogler, J., Hansen, S., Forbes, P., Navalta, C. P., & Saxe, G. (2012). Trauma systems therapy: 15-month outcomes and the importance of effecting environmental change. *Psychological Trauma: Theory, Research, Practice, and Policy*, *4*(6), 624–630.

Faust, J., & Katchen, L. (2004). Treatment of children with complicated Posttraumatic stress reaction. *Psychotherapy: Theory, Research, Practice, Training*, *41*, 426–437.

Feeny, N. C., Foa, E. B., Treadwell, K. R. H., & March, J. (2004). Posttraumatic stress disorder in youth: A critical review of the cognitive and behavioral treatment outcome literature. *Professional Psychology: Research and Practice*, *35*, 466–476.

Foa, E. B., Chrestman, K., & Gilboa-Schechtman, E. (2008). *Prolonged exposure manual for children and adolescents suffering from PTSD*. New York, NY: Oxford University Press.

Foa, E. B., Keane, T. M., Friedman, M. J., & Cohen, J. A. (Eds.), (2008). *Effective treatments for PTSD* (2nd ed.). New York: Guilford.

Foa, E. B., McLean, C. P., Capaldi, S., & Rosenfield, D. (2013). Prolonged exposure vs supportive counseling for sexual abuse-related PTSD in adolescent girls: A randomized clinical trial. *JAMA: Journal of the American Medical Association, 310*(24), 2650–2657.

Ford, J. D. (2005). Treatment implications of altered affect regulation and information processing following child maltreatment. *Psychiatric Annals, 35*(5), 410–419.

Ford, J. D. (2015). An affective cognitive neuroscience-based approach to PTSD psychotherapy: The TARGET model. *Journal of Cognitive Psychotherapy, 29,* 69–91.

Ford, J. D., Blaustein, M., Habib, M., & Kagan, R. (2013). Developmental trauma-focused treatment models. In J. D. Ford & C. A. Courtois (Eds.), *Treating complex traumatic stress disorders in children and adolescents: Scientific foundations and therapeutic models* (pp. 261–276). New York: Guilford.

Ford, J. D., & Cloitre, M. (2009). Psychotherapy for children and adolescents. In C. A. Courtois & J. D. Ford (Eds.), *Treating complex traumatic stress disorders: An evidence-based guide*. New York: Guilford.

Ford, J. D., & Courtois, C. A. (Eds.). (2013). *Treating complex traumatic stress disorders in children and adolescents: Scientific foundations and therapeutic models.* New York: Guilford.

Ford, J. D., & Courtois, C. A. (2014). Complex PTSD, affect dysregulation, and borderline personality disorder. *Borderline Personality Disorder and Emotion Dysregulation, 1,* 9.

Ford, J. D., & Hawke, J. (2012). Trauma affect regulation psychoeducation group and milieu intervention outcomes in juvenile detention facilities. *Journal of Aggression, Maltreatment & Trauma, 21*(4), 365–384. http://dx.doi.org/10.1080/10926771.2012.673538.

Ford, J. D., & Russo, E. (2006). Trauma-focused, present-centered, emotional self-regulation approach to integrated treatment for posttraumatic stress and addiction: Trauma adaptive recovery group education and therapy (TARGET). *American Journal of Psychotherapy, 60,* 335–355.

Ford, J. D., & Saltzman, W. (2009). Family therapy approaches to complex traumatic stress disorders. In C. A. Courtois & J. Ford (Eds.), *Treating complex traumatic stress disorders: An evidence-based guide*. New York: Guilford.

Ford, J. D., Steinberg, K., Hawke, J., Levine, J., & Zhang, W. (2012). Randomized trial comparison of emotion regulation and relational psychotherapies for PTSD with girls involved in delinquency. *Journal of Clinical Child and Adolescent Psychology, 41,* 27–37. http://dx.doi.org/10.1080/15374416.2012.632343.

Ford, J. D., Steinberg, K., & Zhang, W. (2011). A randomized clinical trial comparing affect regulation and social problem-solving psychotherapies for mothers with victimization-related PTSD. *Behavior Therapy, 42,* 561–578. http://dx.doi.org/10.1016/j.beth.2010.12.005.

Gelkopf, M., & Berger, R. (2009). A school-based, teacher-mediated prevention program (ERASE-Stress) for reducing terror-related traumatic reactions in Israeli youth: A quasi-randomized controlled trial. *Journal of Child Psychology and Psychiatry and Allied Disciplines, 50*(8), 962–971.

Gibbons, R. D., Brown, C. H., Hur, K., Marcus, S. M., Bhaurnik, D. K., Erkens, J. A., et al. (2007). Early evidence on the effects of regulators' suicidality warnings on SSRI prescriptions and suicide in children and adolescents. *American Journal of Psychiatry, 164,* 1356–1363.

Gilboa-Schechtman, E., Foa, E. B., Shafran, N., Aderka, I. M., Powers, M. B., Rachamim, L., et al. (2010). Prolonged exposure versus dynamic therapy for adolescent PTSD: A pilot randomized controlled trial. *Journal of the American Academy of Child and Adolescent Psychiatry, 49*(10), 1034–1042.

Glynn, S. M., Eth, S., Randolph, E. T., Foy, D. W., Urbaitis, M., Boxer, L., et al. (1999). A test of behavioral family therapy to augment exposure for combat-related posttraumatic stress disorder. *Journal of Consulting and Clinical Psychology, 67*(2), 243–251.

Goodman, R., Chapman, L., & Gantt, L. (2008). Creative arts therapies for children. In E. B. Foa, T. M. Keane, M. J. Friedman, & J. A. Cohen (Eds.), *Effective treatments for PTSD* (pp. 491–507) (2nd ed.). New York: Guilford.

Grassetti, S. N., Herres, J., Williamson, A. A., Yarger, H. A., Layne, C. M., & Kobak, R. (2014). Narrative focus predicts symptoms change trajectories in group treatment for traumatized and bereaved adolescents. *Journal of Clinical Child and Adolescent Psychology,* June 13, 1–9. http://dx.doi.org/10.1080/15374416.2014.913249.

Gudino, O. G., Weis, J. R., Havens, J. F., Biggs, E. A., Diamond, U. N., Marr, M., et al. (2014). Group trauma-informed treatment for adolescent psychiatric inpatients: A preliminary uncontrolled trial. *Journal of Traumatic Stress, 27*(4), 496–500.

Harvey, M. (1996). An ecological view of psychological trauma and trauma recovery. *Journal of Traumatic Stress, 9,* 3–23.

Henggeler, S. W. (1998). *Multisystemic treatment of antisocial behavior in children and adolescents.* New York: Guilford.

Hoagwood, K. E. (2007). CATS Consortium. *Journal of Clinical Child & Adolescent Psychology, 36,* 581–592.

Jaycox, L., Stein, B., & Amaya-Jackson, L. (2008). School-based treatment for children and adolescents. In E. B. Foa, T. M. Keane, M. J. Friedman, & J. A. Cohen (Eds.), *Effective treatments for PTSD* (pp. 327–345) (*2nd ed.*). New York: Guilford.

Kagan, R. (2008). Transforming troubled children into tomorrow's heros. In D. Brom, R. Pat-Horenczyk, & J. Ford (Eds.), *Treating traumatized children* (pp. 255–268). London: Routledge.

Kataoka, S., Jaycox, L. H., Wong, M., Nadeem, E., Langley, A., Tang, L., et al. (2011). Effects on school outcomes in low-income minority youth: Preliminary findings from a community-partnered study of a school-based trauma intervention. *Ethnicity and Disease, 21*(3 Suppl. 1), S1–71-77.

Kazak, A. E., Simms, S., Alderfer, M. A., Rourke, M. T., Crump, T., McClure, K., et al. (2005). Feasibility and preliminary outcomes from a pilot study of a brief psychological intervention for families of children newly diagnosed with cancer. *Journal of Pediatric Psychology, 30,* 644–655.

King, N. J., Tonge, B. J., Mullen, P., Myerson, N., Heyne, D., Rollings, S., et al. (2000). Treating sexually abused children with posttraumatic stress symptoms: A randomized clinical trial. *Journal of the American Academy of Child and Adolescent Psychiatry, 39*(11), 1347–1355. http://dx.doi.org/S0890-8567(09)60183-0 [pii]; http://dx.doi.org/10.1097/00004583-200011000-00008.

Klatzkin, A., Lieberman, A. F., & Van Horn, P. (2013). Child-Parent Psychotherapy and historical trauma. In J. D. Ford & C. A. Courtois (Eds.), *Treating complex traumatic stress disorders in children and adolescents* (pp. 295–314). New York: Guilford.

Lang, J. M., Ford, J. D., & Fitzgerald, M. M. (2010). An algorithm for determining use of trauma-focused cognitive-behavioral therapy. *Psychotherapy, 47*(4), 554–569.

Layne, C. M., Saltzman, W. R., Poppleton, L., Burlingame, G. M., Pasalic, M. S., Durakovic, E., et al. (2008). Effectiveness of a school-based group psychotherapy program for war-exposed adolescents: A randomized controlled trial. *Journal of the American Academy of Child and Adolescent Psychiatry, 47/9,* 1048–1062.

Liddle, H. A., Rodriguez, R. A., Dakof, G. A., Kanzki, E., & Marvel, F. A. (2005). Multidimensional family therapy: A science-based treatment for adolescent drug abuse. In J. Lebow (Ed.), *Handbook of clinical family therapy* (pp. 128–163). Hoboken, NJ: Wiley.

Lieberman, A., Ghosh Ippen, C., & Marans, S. (2008). Psychodynamic therapy for child trauma. In E. B. Foa, T. M. Keane, M. J. Friedman, & J. A. Cohen (Eds.), *Effective treatments for PTSD* (pp. 370–387) (2nd ed.). New York: Guilford. In.

Lieberman, A. F., Ghosh Ippen, C., & Van Horn, P. (2006). Child-parent psychotherapy: 6-month follow-up of a randomized controlled trial. *Journal of the American Academy of Child & Adolescent Psychiatry, 45*(8), 913–918.

Lyons-Ruth, K., Dutra, L., Schuder, M. R., & Bianchi, I. (2006). From infant attachment disorganization to adult dissociation: Relational adaptations or traumatic experiences? *Psychiatric Clinics of North America, 29*, 63–86.

Mannarino, A. P., Cohen, J. A., Deblinger, E., Runyon, M. K., & Steer, R. A. (2012). Trauma-focused cognitive-behavioral therapy for children: Sustained impact of treatment 6 and 12 months later. *Child Maltreatment, 17*(3), 231–241. http://dx.doi.org/10.1177/1077559512451787.

Marrow, M., Knudsen, K., Olafson, E., & Bucher, S. (2012). The value of implementing TARGET within a trauma-informed juvenile justice setting. *Journal of Child and Adolescent Trauma, 5*, 257–270.

Matulis, S., Resick, P. A., Rosner, R., & Steil, R. (2014). Developmentally adapted cognitive processing therapy for adolescents suffering from posttraumatic stress disorder after childhood sexual or physical abuse: A pilot study. *Clinical Child and Family Psychology Review, 17*, 173–190.

Miltenburg, R., & Singer, E. (1999). Culturally mediated learning and the development of self-regulation by survivors of child abuse: A Vygotskian approach to the support of survivors of child abuse. *Human Development, 42*, 1–17.

Nader, K. (2008). *Understanding and assessing trauma in children and adolescents: Measures, methods, and youth in context*. New York: Routledge.

Najavits, L. M., Gallop, R. J., & Weiss, R. D. (2006). Seeking safety therapy for adolescent girls with PTSD and substance use disorder: A randomized controlled trial. *Journal of Behavioral Health Services & Research, 33*, 453–463.

Najavits, L. M., & Hien, D. (2013). Helping vulnerable populations: A comprehensive review of the treatment outcome literature on substance use disorder and PTSD. *Journal of Clinical Psychology, 69*(5), 433–479.

Orr, P. P. (2007). Art therapy with children after a disaster: A content analysis. *The Arts in Psychotherapy, 34*, 350–361.

Resick, P. A., Galovski, T. E., Uhlmansiek, M. O., Scher, C. D., Clum, G. A., & Young-Xu, Y. (2008). A randomized clinical trial to dismantle components of cognitive processing therapy for posttraumatic stress disorder in female victims of interpersonal violence. *Journal of Consulting and Clinical Psychology, 76*(2), 243.

Robb, A. S., Cueva, J. E., & Sporn, J. (2010). Sertraline treatment of children and adolescents with posttraumatic stress disorder: A double-blind, placebo-controlled trial. *Journal of Child and Adolescent Psychopharmacology, 20*(6), 463–471.

Robjant, K., & Fazel, M. (2010). The emerging evidence for narrative exposure therapy: A review. *Clinical Psychology Review, 30*(8), 1030–1039.

Ruf, M., Schauer, M., Neuner, F., Catani, C., Schauer, E., & Elbert, T. (2010). Narrative exposure therapy for 7- to 16-year-olds: A randomized controlled trial with traumatized refugee children. *Journal of Traumatic Stress, 23*(4), 437–445.

Saltzman, W. R., Pynoos, R. S., Layne, C. M., Steinberg, A. M., & Aisenberg, E. (2001). Trauma- and grief-focused intervention for adolescents exposed to community violence: Results of a school-based screening and group treatment protocol. *Group Dynamics; Theory, Research, and Practice*, *5/4*, 291–303.

Saxe, G., Ellis, H., & Kaplow, J. (Eds.), (2007). *Collaborative treatment of traumatized children and teens: The trauma systems therapy approach*. New York: Guilford.

Saxe, G., MacDonald, H., & Ellis, H. (2007). Psychosocial approaches for children with PTSD. In E. B. Foa, M. J. Friedman, T. M. Keane, & P. Resick (Eds.), *Handbook of PTSD: Science and practice* (pp. 359–375). New York: Guilford.

Scheeringa, M., Salloum, A., Arnberger, R., Weems, C., Amaya-Jackson, L., & Cohen, J. A. (2007). Feasibility and effectiveness of cognitive-behavioral therapy for posttraumatic stress disorder in preschool children: Two case reports. *Journal of Traumatic Stress*, *20*(4), 631–636.

Schneider, S. J., Grilli, S. F., & Schneider, J. R. (2013). Evidence-based treatments for traumatized children and adolescents. *Current Psychiatry Reports*, *15*(1), 332. http://dx.doi. org/10.1007/s11920-012-0332-5.

Stein, B. D., Jaycox, L. H., Kataoka, S., Wong, M., Tu, W., Elliott, M. N., et al. (2003). A mental health intervention for schoolchildren exposed to violence: A randomized controlled trial. *Journal of the American Medical Association*, *290*(5), 603–611.

Timmer, S. G., Urquiza, A. J., Zebell, N. M., & McGrath, J. M. (2005). Parent-child interaction therapy: Application to maltreating parent-child dyads. *Child Abuse and Neglect*, *29*, 825–842.

Urqiza, A., & Timmer, S. (2013). Parent-child interaction therapy. In J. D. Ford & C. A. Courtois (Eds.), *Treating complex traumatic stress disorders in children and adolescents* (pp. 315–328). New York, NY: Guilford Press.

Van Horn, P., & Lieberman, A. (2008). Using dyadic therapies to treat traumatized children. In D. Brom, R. Pat-Horenczyk, & J. D. Ford (Eds.), *Treating traumatized children* (pp. 210–224). London: Routledge.

Vickerman, K. A., & Margolin, G. (2007). Posttraumatic stress in children and adolescents exposed to family violence: II. Treatment. *Professional Psychology: Research and Practice*, *38*, 620–628.

Walter, K. H., Dickstein, B. D., Barnes, S. M., & Chard, K. M. (2014). Comparing effectiveness of CPT to CPT-C among U.S. Veterans in an interdisciplinary residential PTSD/TBI treatment program. *Journal of Traumatic Stress*, *27*(4), 438–445. http://dx.doi.org/10.1002/ jts.21934.

Welch, S., & Rothbaum, B. A. (2007). Emerging treatments for PTSD. In M. J. Friedman, T. M. Keane, & P. Resick (Eds.), *Handbook of PTSD: Science and practice* (pp. 469–496). New York: Guilford.

Wesselman, D., & Shapiro, F. (2013). Eye movement desensitization and reprocessing. In J. D. Ford & C. A. Courtois (Eds.), *Treatment of complex traumatic stress disorders in children and adolescents* (pp. 203–224). New York: Guilford Press.

Prevention of PTSD

Preventing problems almost always is preferable to treating problems that have already become entrenched. As the saying goes, "An ounce of prevention is worth a pound of cure." This is very true in relation to PTSD, especially in light of the extremely debilitating and costly impact that chronic PTSD has not only for the individual victim but for his or her family, peer group, school or workplace, and society (see Chapters 1 and 2). Prevention requires innovative adaptations of the approaches to treatment that have been developed for PTSD, because dealing with the impact of exposure to traumatic stressors *before* PTSD has developed involves several new challenges over and above those posed by the treatment of chronic PTSD. In this chapter, the theoretical foundations and principles that guide PTSD prevention specialists and the relatively recently developed set of PTSD prevention interventions are described in detail, as well as a summary of the scientific research evidence for PTSD prevention (Box 9.1).

Box 9.1 Key Points

1. The best approach to prevention is to prevent psychological trauma from occurring, but this is not completely possible given the ubiquity of accidents, disasters, social upheavals, and violence. Programs designed to make workplaces, homes, schools, and roadways safe from accidents or violence are important forms of "primary" or "universal" prevention of PTSD because they may reduce the likelihood that traumatic stressors will occur in the first place.

2. Interventions developed specifically for people who are exposed to traumatic stressors and who have risk factors such as a prior history of substance use or psychiatric disorders, poor social support, or when the traumatic stressor involves abuse or violence in childhood (see Chapter 3) are forms of "secondary" or "selective" prevention. This is because these interventions are not designed to prevent traumatic stressors from occurring but instead to achieve the *secondary* goal of preventing PTSD among trauma-exposed persons who are *selected* because they are particularly likely to develop PTSD based on their risk factors.

3. Prevention of PTSD also may take the alternative form of "indicated" or "tertiary" prevention when the intervention is designed for people who already have developed PTSD and the intervention's goal is to prevent PTSD from becoming lasting or severe. For example, people who develop an acute stress disorder (ASD) in the first month after exposure to a traumatic stressor or who develop PTSD but have had the disorder only for a few months may be assisted in recovering before those disorders become chronic if provided with effective help. Although it would be preferable to prevent the traumatic exposure in the first place (primary prevention) or to prevent PTSD from ever developing (secondary prevention), this third-best (tertiary) approach can have great value by taking individuals who are "indicated" by their PTSD symptoms and helping them to recover before the disorder becomes chronic or severe.

(Continued)

Posttraumatic Stress Disorder. DOI: http://dx.doi.org/10.1016/B978-0-12-801288-8.00009-1

Box 9.1 Continued

4. Several theoretical models provide a blueprint for PTSD prevention, including Hobfoll's "conservation of resources (COR)" paradigm, De Jong and colleagues' "ecological" model, Saxe's "trauma systems therapy (TST)" paradigm, and Brom and Kleber's "minimal learning" model.

5. Sexual assault and youth violence primary prevention are two critically important areas in which a variety of widely used programs have been developed with a strong and growing scientific evidence base. Child abuse and accident primary prevention programs are examples of other "universal" approaches to the prevention of traumatic stress exposure.

6. Psychological First Aid (PFA) is a brief, efficient secondary prevention model for providing psychological and practical information, support, and resources "on-the-spot" (rather than in a clinic or office) and "on-the-fly" (rather than in formally scheduled appointments) to people affected by a disaster or mass-casualty incident (National Institute of Clinical Excellence, 2014). PFA is designed to help affected persons and families (i) better understand their own stress reactions as expectable and signs of coping (not as reactions to be feared, signs of personal failure or weakness, or signs of mental illness); (ii) get immediate help with their highest-priority practical and emotional needs; (iii) recognize the circumstances under which they should consider seeking formal counseling (such as when anxiety or alcohol use become a problem for them, their families, or their work); (iv) know how and where to access additional help, including mental health counseling; and (v) be able to help family members feel and be safe and cope with stress reactions. When individuals experience mild symptoms in the first 4 weeks after a traumatic stressor, "watchful waiting" also is recommended by the National Center of Clinical Excellence (2014). This involves providing access to a source of knowledgeable counseling or guidance that the person can contact if the symptoms become more severe or questions arise that have not been answered by PFA, as well as having a preset plan to recontact the individual within the first month (if the person consents to such contact) in order to ensure that any emergent treatment needs are addressed.

7. Critical Incident Stress Management (CISM; originally called critical incident stress "debriefing" or CISD) is another approach to secondary prevention of traumatic stress problems that was originally developed to assist emergency responders (such as police, fire, and paramedic personnel) in the immediate aftermath of traumatic work incidents. CISM involves several interventions in addition to emotional "debriefing" of critical incidents (i.e., a carefully structured discussion of the responders' recollections of what happened and what they felt, thought, and did during and after an emergency response operation). CISM is widely conducted with teams of adults who work together and have encountered a traumatic stressor event such as school personnel following a mass shooting or staff in a therapeutic program when a client commits suicide, as well as with teams of emergency first responders.

8. CISM is *not* recommended for individuals who have experienced a traumatic stressor and has not been demonstrated to be safe and effective with traumatized children or adolescents. The use of "debriefing" with individuals who have experienced a traumatic stressor such as a severe accident or assault, without including the other CISM interventions (such as assistance in accessing resources for further counseling, if needed), has been shown to be ineffective and potentially emotionally distressing in a small number of scientific studies. Therefore, CISM is most appropriately used with emergency responders and with the full set of interventions and not simply as a one-time (or "one-off") debriefing discussion.

9. Cognitive Behavior Therapy (CBT) is considered by the National Institute for Clinical Excellence in the United Kingdom, the International Society for Traumatic Stress Studies, the American Psychological Association, and the American Psychiatric Association, to be the only rigorously scientifically evidence-based intervention for the prevention of PTSD. CBT in the early postevent period (i.e., within 3–6 months of the event) tends to be done relatively briefly, typically in between one and five 60- to 90-minute sessions. When conducted within the framework of combined child and family therapy, or as a stepped collaborative health care intervention, CBT may prevent not only worsening PTSD symptoms but also associated problems such as depression and alcohol or substance abuse.

10. Studies have shown that most individuals who experience a traumatic event recover without developing PTSD by the 6-week postevent time-point, even if they have distressing stress reactions in the acute period. Therefore, CBT usually is not conducted until 1–3 months after a traumatic event has occurred, and only if PTSD symptoms are severe and persistent. However, individuals who develop serious impairment such as an ASD should receive immediate CBT both to assist them with their current posttraumatic stress (and related—e.g., depression or increased substance use) symptoms, because an estimated 80% of people who develop ASD go on to suffer PTSD (Figure 9.1).

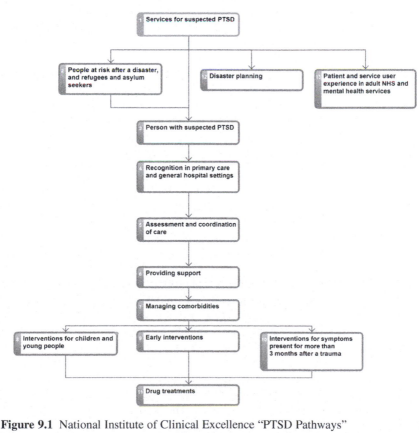

Figure 9.1 National Institute of Clinical Excellence "PTSD Pathways" recommendations for prevention and treatment of PTSD.
© NICE, 2014, last updated August 8, 2014 at http://pathways.nice.org.uk/pathways/post-traumatic-stressdisorder.

Overview of biopsychosocial approaches to prevention

Although the best approach to prevention is to prevent psychological trauma from occurring, this is not completely possible given the ubiquity of accidents, disasters, social upheavals, and violence. Programs designed to make workplaces, homes, schools, and roadways safe from accidents or violence are important forms of "primary" prevention of PTSD because they may reduce the likelihood that traumatic stressors will occur in the first place. For example, the Centers for Disease Control and Prevention has identified the prevention of sexual violence as a critical public health goal—that is, as a way to reduce the very serious harm and costs (to society as well as to the victimized person) of the injury and illness caused by sexual violence (Box 9.2).

Box 9.2 Prevention of Sexual Violence

Sexual violence is a public health epidemic because it is a source of medical and emotional harm that occurs to tens of thousands of people of all ages, races, socio-economic levels, and nationalities worldwide every year (Walsh, Koenen, Aiello, Uddin, & Galea, 2014; Walsh, Koenen, Cohen, et al., 2014). Myths and prejudices about women, sexuality, power, and violence can lead to a tragically misguided belief that sexual violence can be justified or overlooked, when nothing could be further from the truth (Chapleau & Oswald, 2014). Sexual violence is inherently a violation of the survivor's body and identity, and when sanctioned or tacitly permitted by groups or institutions, it is a fundamental betrayal of trust and the core values of humanism and social/moral responsibility (Smith & Freyd, 2014).

Four steps are necessary to develop an effective prevention program for a widespread public health problem such as sexual violence (Centers for Disease Control, 2004): (i) clearly defining the problem in terms that provide a basis for achieving meaningful improvements; (ii) identifying risk and protective factors (see Chapter 3) that can be modified or utilized to identify the people at greatest risk and the conditions needed in order to effect positive change; (iii) developing and testing specific prevention strategies; and (iv) ensuring the widespread dissemination and adoption of effective prevention strategies. These four steps to a public health approach to prevention are illustrated by the primary, secondary, and tertiary prevention approaches that have been proposed to address sexual violence.

Primary Prevention of Sexual Violence. The National Sexual Violence Resource Center describes an approach to primary prevention that emphasizes changing the basic attitudes that inadvertently permit or intentionally encourage sexual violence. Rather than defining the problem solely in terms of the traumatic behavior itself—sexual violence—they focus on the underlying conditions that promote or lead to an overlooking of sexual violence. Although they focus on women and girls as victims of sexual violence, this approach applies to preventing men and boys from being victimized by sexual violence as well. The attitudes that foster sexual violence can target boys (e.g., condoning predatory sexual behavior by trusted older males such as priests or teachers) or men (e.g., viewing gay men or men who are incarcerated as deserving to be victimized sexually) as well as women and girls.

Valuing the worth of each individual and the right of every person to safety and the pursuit of their own lifestyle and life goals is crucial to the prevention of rape, molestation, sexual trafficking, and other forms of sexual violence, regardless of the gender, age, sexual orientation, or other personal characteristics.

There are at least five kinds of damaging norms that contribute to an environment in which sexual violence can occur. They are norms about *women*—limited roles for and objectification and oppression of women; *power*—value placed on claiming and maintaining power (manifested as power over); *violence*—tolerance of aggression and attribution of blame to victims; *masculinity*—traditional constructs of manhood, including domination, control, and risk-taking; and *privacy*—notions of individual and family privacy that foster secrecy and silence. Our society glamorizes and sexualizes violence. Often sexual violence is ignored, excused, condoned, and even encouraged. While most people do not commit sexual violence, and therefore it is not *normal* behavior, these kinds of norms imply a level of acceptance and a sense of complacency about sexual violence. They promulgate a toxic environment in which sexual violence can take place *and* inhibit appropriate action, while condoning *in*appropriate *in*action. Given this, it is not surprising that some people commit sexual violence, and many bystanders don't speak up or intervene. We must acknowledge and change these norms if we are to make major strides in preventing sexual violence. The key is to create and sustain healthy norms in our communities. In addition to holding individual perpetrators accountable and providing quality services for victims, communities need a comprehensive prevention strategy. We must tip the balance in communities and replace current norms with norms that promote respect, safety, equality and healthy relationships and sexuality. This beckons for primary prevention … and a community-wide solution (The National Sexual Violence Resource Center. http://www.nsvrc.org/_cms/fileUpload/spectrum.html Accessed 29.10.08).

The national sexual violence resource center has developed a "spectrum" or set of levels of primary prevention that are necessary to stop sexual violence

	Level of spectrum	Definition of level
Level 1	Strengthening Individual Knowledge and Skills	Enhancing an individual's capability of preventing violence and promoting safety
Level 2	Promoting Community Education	Reaching groups of people with information and resources to prevent violence and promote safety
Level 3	Educating Providers	Informing providers who will transmit skills and knowledge to others and model positive norms
Level 4	Fostering Coalitions and Networks	Bringing together groups and individuals for broader goals and greater impact
Level 5	Changing Organizational Practices	Adopting regulations and shaping norms to prevent violence and improve safety
Level 6	Influencing Policies and Legislation	Enacting laws and policies that support healthy community norms and a violence-free society

(Continued)

Box 9.2 Continued

Secondary or Selected Prevention of Sexual Violence. Helping people who have experienced sexual violence in the immediate aftermath requires attention to all six levels of prevention. At the individual level, counseling for victims and other affected persons (such as their families) and medical treatment to protect their safety and reduce the extent of immediate or future harm are crucial. Community education is important (level 2) in order to reduce the likelihood that victims will be wrongly viewed as deserving or having caused sexual violence and to increase the likelihood that community members and organizations will support victims' recovery. At the third level, education is necessary to ensure that providers of services such as medical care and legal assistance are knowledgeable about the needs of sexual violence victims so services provided to victims enhance their recovery and restore lost resources (such as self-esteem, safety, financial losses; see Conservation of Resources section in this chapter). A variety of support and advocacy groups and organizations (such as rape crisis hotlines and counseling centers, shelters for battered partners, and victims' advocacy coalitions) have been established to meet the needs of sexual violence victims and to increase their legal rights and protections (levels 4–6).

Tertiary or Indicated Prevention of Sexual Violence. The most direct connection between sexual violence prevention and PTSD prevention is found in tertiary/indicated prevention, which involves the development and provision of specific interventions and services to reduce the long-term adverse consequences experienced by victims of sexual violence. These adverse reactions include PTSD symptoms that were first described by Burgess and Holmstrom (1974) as a "rape trauma syndrome," which involved two phases.

The initial, acute phase was distinguished by a high degree of disorganization in lifestyle, with prominent physical symptoms, a subjective state of fear or terror, and overwhelming fear of being killed. During the first several weeks after a rape, victims reported numerous physical problems, including soreness, bruising, tension headaches, sleep disturbances, stomach pains, and gynecological symptoms. In addition, many ... felt fear, humiliation, embarrassment, anger, and had thoughts of revenge and self-blame. The second phase typically began about 2–3 weeks after the rape and reflected the survivor's beginning to reorganize her life. During this long-term process of reorganization, an increase in physical activity was common, and many ... changed residences. In addition, ... women in the study routinely expressed fear of situations that reminded them of their rape. Finally, many women experienced sexual dysfunction and described nightmares related their traumatic experiences (Hembree & Cohen, 2008, p. 565).

Secondary prevention assistance provided by counselors, health care providers, and advocacy and support programs is crucial in the first hours and days following rape trauma, but more intensive (although potentially still quite brief) interventions have been found to be most helpful if the syndrome persists into Phase two. However, immediate support may be enhanced by offering rape trauma victims with immediate education and advice: a video developed for rape trauma victims to watch before they underwent a stressful forensic medical examination within 72 hours of the sexual assault was found to be superior to standard medical/legal services in reducing PTSD and depression symptoms 6 weeks later (Resnick et al., 2007).

Two CBT interventions that were originally developed and shown to be effective for the treatment of chronic PTSD following sexual assault have been adapted in briefer forms for recently traumatized sexual assault survivors. A variation of prolonged exposure (PE) therapy was designed to provide education about rape trauma and expectable stress reactions, skills for stress management (relaxation), cognitive therapy (CT) to reduce self-blame and enhance an assertive hopeful approach to recovery, and trauma memory exposure therapy both in session and in the woman's daily life (i.e., to help her purposefully repeatedly recall the rape incident in vivid detail in order to overcome anxiety and self-blame, and to selectively and safely encounter people (not including the rapist), places, and activities that reminded her of the incident in order to know that she can cope with the distress elicited by those reminders and that the incident is over). The CBT intervention resulted in immediate decreases in PTSD symptoms, depression, and anxiety that were somewhat greater than those achieved by supportive counseling (SC) (Foa et al., 2006).

A variation of cognitive processing therapy (CPT) for female survivors of sexual violence was compared to a program of individual emotional support in a cluster-randomized trial in villages in South Kivu province, Democratic Republic of the Congo (Hall et al., 2014). Local psychosocial assistants delivered the interventions from April through July 2011. We evaluated differences between CPT and individual support conditions for structural social capital (i.e., time spent with nonkin social network, group membership and participation, and the size of financial and instrumental support networks) and emotional support seeking. We analyzed intervention effects with longitudinal random effects models.

Results. We obtained small to medium effect size differences for two study outcomes. Women in the CPT villages increased group membership and participation at 6-month follow-up and emotional support seeking after the intervention compared with women in the individual support villages.

Conclusions. Results support the efficacy of group CPT to increase dimensions of social capital among survivors of sexual violence in a low-income conflict-affected context. Thus, even very brief CBT prevention interventions may accelerate recovery from rape trauma and potentially increase the social support that survivors are willing to seek and able to receive.

Within the traumatic stress fields, professionals have developed innovative interventions designed to prevent PTSD after traumatic stressors have occurred. This may be considered a form of "primary" prevention if the intervention enables people who are exposed to traumatic stressors to recover rapidly and fully from the expectable immediate stress reactions that occur for most people exposed to traumatic stressors. A 2013 review by Skeffington and colleagues (Skeffington, Rees, & Kane, 2013) of more than 1250 published articles that referred to PTSD prevention identified only 7 that described and evaluated primary prevention interventions. Two psychoeducation interventions on secondary/vicarious traumatization for military personnel immediately before deploying to serve in either a health care or combat role under dangerous circumstances were evaluated with self-report data collected data only postdeployment. Compared to personnel not receiving the intervention, no benefits in mental health, alcohol use, or social support were reported. Two other pretrauma interventions that added relaxation, cognitive, emotion regulation, and communication skills to education about traumatic stress for military personnel and police officers were evaluated. One study found no evidence of benefit, but the second, using a more scientifically rigorous methodology of randomly assigning participants to either receive the intervention or not, showed that the intervention was associated to reductions in anxiety and physical health problems and improvement in active planful coping strategies for stressful situations. A more extensive (14-week) program for primary school students in Israel (similar to the ERASE-Stress intervention provided following exposure to traumatic stressors; Gelkopf & Berger, 2009; see Chapter 8) provided traumatic stress education and taught skills for emotion regulation and adaptive stress management prior to the youth being exposed to rocket attacks. The more than 700 students receiving the intervention reported lower levels of PTSD symptoms 3 months after the rocket attacks than over 700 other students (Wolmer, Hamiel, & Laor, 2011). Finally, two studies provided 10–12 hours of stress management skills training for police officers who were either in training or in the field and demonstrated that recipients (versus officers who did not receive the training) showed superior behavioral performance or physiological stress coping in simulated stressful situations (as well as self-reported mood, confidence, and work skills 12 month after the intervention in one study). The review article concludes that there is no solid evidence to either support or contraindicate any approach to primary prevention of PTSD, although the models tested warrant further evaluation.

It may, however, be viewed as "secondary" or "selected" prevention (i.e., an intervention *selectively* provided to people who are at high risk for developing PTSD and therefore a *secondary* step when primary prevention is not possible or entirely effective), because people exposed to psychological trauma are particularly at risk for PTSD. If an intervention is developed specifically for people who have additional risk factors (such as a prior history of substance use or psychiatric disorders, poor social support, or when the traumatic stressor involves abuse or violence in childhood; see Chapter 3), this clearly constitutes selective or secondary prevention because these people are at especially high risk for PTSD. For example, children who witness domestic violence in their families are at high risk for significant impairment in adulthood despite not being identified as in need of therapeutic services or support because they cope resiliently or, tragically, are overlooked despite serious PTSD symptoms and related severe emotional, behavioral, school, addictive, and interpersonal problems (Box 9.3).

Box 9.3 Early Intervention with Children Exposed to Domestic Violence

A report by the US Attorney General's Defending Childhood Task Force in 2012 was released, ironically, on December 2, 2012 (http://www.justice.gov/defend-ingchildhood/cev-rpt-full.pdf), just 2 days before a horrific mass murder of 20 children and 6 adults at the Sandy Hook Elementary School. That report and the findings of a detailed investigation into the events leading up to the Sandy Hook shootings by the Connecticut Office of the Child Advocate, released 2 years later (http://www.justice.gov/defendingchildhood/cev-rpt-full.pdf), make the case very clearly that primary prevention of violence in children's lives always is the best way to prevent the often extreme and long-lasting adverse impact on children of exposure to violence.

Tragically, violence is prevalent in the lives of children, often in the form of witnessing as well as being directly victimized by physical abuse, assaults, or bullying. Turner, Finkelhor, and Ormrod (2006), using a predominantly African American sample, found that witnessing violence was associated with self-reported distress, but they also found that most respondents (about 75%) reported both witnessing and being directly victimized by violence. Young children (toddlers and preschool age) exposed to domestic violence are at risk for developing internalizing (anxious and depressed) and externalizing (disruptive behavior) problems (Briggs-Gowan et al., 2010; Briggs-Gowan, Carter, & Ford, 2012). A heightened tendency to react to repeated exposure to a variety of stressors (Grasso, Ford, & Briggs-Gowan, 2013) and PTSD symptoms (Miller, Howell, & Graham-Bermann, 2012) has been shown to connect violence exposure in early childhood to subsequent emotional and behavioral problems.

The traumatic impact of domestic violence on the lives of children

When violence occurs to, or is witnessed by, children in their own families, this can have a particularly pernicious traumatic impact that extends beyond childhood (Kitzmann, Gaylord, Holt, & Kenny, 2003) into adolescence (McLaughlin et al., 2013) and adulthood (Widom, Czaja, & Dutton, 2014). Children are exposed to domestic violence in many ways, including direct victimization by violent assaults by other family members (physical abuse, sibling or peer violence) and witnessing domestic violence (adult intimate partner violence (IPV), physical abuse, sibling or peer violence). Exposure to IPV has been repeatedly shown to be associated with the severity of behavior problems and cognitive and social competence deficits (Hungerford, Wait, Fritz, & Clements, 2012), yet some children exposed to IPV appear to be functioning well (Graham-Bermann, Gruber, Howell, & Girz, 2009). Children show different degrees of resilience when exposed to IPV, with less resilience on the part of those whose mothers had been abused in childhood and adopted a controlling style as a parent (Delker, Noll, Kim, & Fisher, 2014). In the latter study, the extent of IPV was greater for mothers who had been abused in childhood, suggesting that a negative cycle of childhood abuse, adult victimization by IPV, and attempts to cope by being controlling with one's children may be involved in the adverse psychosocial effects that witnessing IPV has on children.

(Continued)

Box 9.3 Continued

Children's appraisals of interparental conflict and their own emotional security also were shown to be, respectively, risk and protective factors for emotional and behavioral problems in childhood, adolescence, and adulthood after they had been exposed to IPV (Hungerford et al., 2012). Also, children who are exposed to IPV have been shown to have heightened physiological reactivity and difficulties in regulating stress reactions (Cummings, El-Sheikh, Kouros, & Buckhalt, 2009; Davies, Sturge-Apple, Cicchetti, & Cummings, 2007; Hibel, Granger, Blair, Cox, & The Family Life Project Key Investigators, 2009, 2011; Rigterink, Fainsilber Katz, & Hessler, 2010), consistent with a view that they develop a generalized psychobiological tendency toward hypervigilance and hyperarousal or dissociation that is PTSD's hallmark of being trapped in survival mode (Ford, 2009; see Chapter 5).

Schiff et al. (2014) used data from a longitudinal sample of children assessed periodically from birth to early adulthood to determine how witnessing parental IPV (involving physical violence, which may include conflicts and/or disagreements) or parental intimate partner conflict (IPC; conflictual interactions and disagreements) was related to the young adult's depression, anxiety, and substance use. IPC and IPV were measured at the 14-year follow-up. Children of women experiencing IPV at the 14-year follow-up were more likely to have anxiety, nicotine, alcohol, and cannabis disorders when assessed as young adults, independent of their mother's levels of anxiety or depression. Females typically are more likely to experience anxiety disorders and less likely to have alcohol use disorders than males. Yet, when these young adults had experienced IPV, the opposite result was found: the young men exposed to IPV were more likely to have anxiety disorders, and the young women exposed to IPV were more likely to have alcohol use disorders (and also depressive disorders). A study with inner-city youth found the expected gender difference for females exposed to domestic or community violence, with girls being more likely than boys to report higher levels of both anxiety and depression symptoms; however, there were no gender differences in violence-exposed youths' levels of PTSD or dissociative symptoms or disruptive behavior problems (Zona & Milan, 2011).

Franzese, Covey, Tucker, McCoy, and Menard (2014) found further evidence of a gender difference using data from the National Youth Survey Family Study or NYSFS, which involved 12 periodic assessments over a 27-year period based on a probability sample of households in the continental United States selected in 1976. The impact of exposure to violence in adolescence on mental health problems was more acute for males but, especially with respect to witnessing parental violence, was more long-lasting for females. In addition, it was exposure to domestic violence, and not more general exposure to violence, that was associated with seeking mental health services and being impaired socially or vocationally in adulthood. Thus, exposure to domestic violence has clear serious detrimental outcomes for children that may persist for decades into adulthood, but the adverse effects may differ importantly, depending on the victim's gender.

Ford, Gagnon, Connor, and Pearson (2011) assessed both witnessed and directly experienced violence victimization as reported by children in mental health treatment and their parents and found no gender differences. However, they found that directly experienced violence increased the likelihood of externalizing problems, but witnessed violence increased the likelihood of internalizing problems. In an inner-city sample of early adolescents, Reid-Quinones et al. (2011) found similar differences in reactions to witnessing violence versus being directly victimized: direct exposure to violence was associated with anger and externalizing reactions, while witnessing violence was associated with fearful reactions. Prevention interventions for children exposed to IPV thus must address the fear, anxiety, and dysphoria that being a helpless witness may produce, as well as the hyperarousal and impulse to react aggressively to perceived threats that may occur when a child is the direct victim of family violence.

Prevention interventions must address not only the victimized child but also the adults who are victimized by or perpetrate IPV. Widom et al. (2014) compared 497 midlife adults with documented histories of childhood physical and sexual abuse and/or neglect to 395 similar adults without such histories after first assessing them as primary and preschool-age children. Over 75% of both groups reported both victimization by and perpetration of IPV in the past year. Physical abuse or neglect in childhood predicted increased risk of being victimized in intimate partner physical violence as well as a more frequent and extensive IPV—but only for women, not for men. Childhood neglect (but not abuse) predicted greater likelihood of perpetrating physical injury to a partner. Further analyses of the previous data from the NYSFS showed that, for males, having been physically abused as a child predicted both perpetration of and victimization by IPV as an adult (Menard, Weiss, Franzese, & Covey, 2014). Adolescent exposure to violence did not predict adult IPV for females, and childhood physical abuse actually predicted avoiding intimate partner relationships (Menard et al., 2014). Although the results are not entirely consistent, it appears that females who are victimized in childhood or adolescence may be at risk for revictimization as adults by IPV if they become involved in marriage/cohabitating relationships, and males who are victimized in childhood may be at risk for perpetrating IPV as adults. Childhood neglect stands out as a risk factor for both genders for perpetrating IPV.

Preventing PTSD and building resilience in the wake of domestic violence

When children have been exposed to domestic violence, often this is first identified by the professionals who see them outside their homes. Pediatricians and other health professionals can play a vital role because they get to know both the child and the adult caregivers (Augustyn & Groves, 2005), ideally with regular periodic well-child checkups and evaluation and treatment when a physical

(Continued)

Box 9.3 Continued

illness or injury occurs. Dubowitz (2014) developed the Safe Environment for Every Kid (SEEK) model to help pediatric practitioners identify and help address risk factors for childhood maltreatment in families with young children. Children's safety has always been a top priority, so the SEEK model extends safety from tangible protections such as car seats and smoke alarms to checking with the child and caregiver(s) to ensure that they feel safe in their family home and relationships. Results of studies with both high- and low-risk families demonstrated that those whose pediatric provider had been trained in, and had access to parent education materials from, the SEEK program were less likely to engage in either major or minor abusive behaviors.

Screening in nonthreatening ways is recommended as a secondary or selective prevention approach by several national associations of pediatric and family medical and nursing professionals (https://www2.aap.org/pubserv/PSVpreview/pages/Files/Pediatric.pdf). Ford (2013) developed a practical guide for pediatric and family medical and nursing providers to enable them to efficiently educate children and parents about traumatic stress reactions and practical steps and skills to increase the child and caregivers' safety and well-being, as well as to understand when and how to access to evidence-based PTSD treatment for the child (and adult).

Schools are the place where children and youth spend the most time outside the home, and school personnel such as teachers, aides, counselors, social workers, and psychologists often are in a position to identify signs of distress or behavior problems that indicate that a student may be under stress or even experiencing traumatic stressors such as domestic violence. Mental health and guidance professionals such as school counselors play several key roles because they are immersed in the school environment (and therefore familiar and easily accessible to students and to other school personnel), yet have a distinct role and expertise that can make them a resource for students who want to seek help privately or school personnel who want guidance when they see signs of potential emotional or behavioral problems in their students. School counselors thus are observers, sources of therapeutic assistance, consultants to their school colleagues, and in the event of disclosures by a student of traumatic exposure such as domestic violence, crisis managers (https://www2.aap.org/pubserv/PSVpreview/pages/Files/Pediatric.pdf). Students who have been exposed to traumatic stressors such as domestic violence and who are experiencing PTSD symptoms can be further helped without ever having to leave the familiar school setting by secondary or tertiary prevention programs such as the evidence-based therapeutic interventions Cognitive Behavioral Intervention for Trauma in the Schools (C-BITS) or Enhancing Resiliency Among Students Experiencing Stress (ERASE-Stress; see Chapter 8).

When domestic violence is an ongoing danger, pediatric or school profession-als are not in a position to alone protect the child and other victimized family members. They are "mandated reporters," which means they are legally and ethically responsible for reporting potential child maltreatment to public agen-cies responsible for ensuring the safety of children (child protective services agencies) and the overall community (law enforcement agencies). Traumatic stress professionals play a vital role as consultants to child protection and law enforcement personnel, assisting them in recognizing and sensitively respond-ing to children and other family members who are being victimized by domestic violence (childstudycenter.yale.edu/community/cdcp.aspx)—as well as by pro-viding immediate access to evidence-based therapeutic interventions such as the Child and Family Traumatic Stress Intervention (CFTSI; see Chapter 8). The US Agency for Healthcare Research and Quality (AHRQ) conducted a systematic review in 2013 of the evidence of effectiveness of therapeutic interventions with children for both acute and chronic PTSD after maltreatment or domestic vio-lence (www.effectivehealthcare.ahrq.gov/reports/final.cfm).

Although the best time to implement secondary/selective or tertiary/targeted prevention interventions for children exposed to domestic violence is as early as possible in childhood, many of these children and adolescents are never identified because they cope effectively or find help in recovery from informal sources rather than from professional providers. Major life transitions in adult-hood often are sufficiently stressful to reactivate PTSD symptoms that may have been managed or even completely resolved earlier in childhood or adolescence. Such transitions do not have to be traumatic themselves to trigger delayed epi-sodes of full PTSD years or even decades after exposure to traumatic stressors and what appears to be a full recovery (Smid, Mooren, van der Mast, Gersons, & Kleber, 2009).

Early adulthood is just such a time of multiple potentially stressful life tran-sitions. Howell and Miller-Graff (2014) collected self-report measures from college students who experienced childhood violence, including maltreatment, community or family violence, or sexual assault. The students reported exten-sive histories of victimization, on average *nine* violent experiences reported from their childhoods. Childhood victimization was strongly associated with current depression and anxiety symptoms, yet many students who had experi-enced family or other forms of violence were highly resilient. Resilient young adults described themselves as having three key characteristics: spirituality, emotional intelligence, and support from friends. Thus, what Howell and Miller-Graff describe as "emerging adulthood" may be a transitional developmental period in which these and other potential protective factors against PTSD can be successfully addressed as a form of secondary or tertiary prevention (see also Taylor & Harvey, 2010).

Prevention of PTSD also may take the alternative form of "tertiary" or "indicated" prevention when the intervention is designed for people who already have developed a disorder and the intervention's goal is to prevent the disorder from becoming lasting or severe. For example, people who develop an ASD in the first month after exposure to a traumatic stressor or who develop PTSD but have had the disorder for only a few months may be assisted in recovering before those disorders become chronic if provided with effective help. The latter interventions are "tertiary" because they are third-best compared to either preventing the traumatic stressor from occurring (primary prevention) or preventing PTSD altogether (secondary or selected prevention). Tertiary prevention also may be described as "indicated," because the emergence of the early forms of PTSD (or ASD) *indicate* that timely intervention is needed to prevent the harm and cost that occur when PTSD becomes persistent and severe.

The opportunity to prevent PTSD is clearly suggested by the scientific evidence showing that most people who experience acute traumatic stress reactions do not develop PTSD (or do so gradually or only after a delay of months or years; see Chapter 2). The best time for prevention is either before a problem occurs or as soon afterward as possible. Perhaps the best example of widespread primary prevention interventions for PTSD is provided by violence prevention programs for children and adolescents in schools and communities. While these programs cannot entirely prevent violence and do not prevent exposure to other traumatic stressors that may lead to PTSD, they can be delivered on a very large scale to persons young enough that being spared the trauma of being victimized by violence could change the course of the next many decades of their (and their families') lives. Violence prevention also may save youths from the devastating consequences of becoming a perpetrator of violence (such as incarceration or traumatic guilt).

Selected or secondary prevention interventions for PTSD apply the therapeutic programs to children or adults who are likely to experience traumatic stressor(s) or who are seeking medical or psychological help following a recent acute traumatic stressor such as a disaster, assault, or injury, or chronic trauma such as ongoing family or community violence or abuse (Box 9.3). For example, "PFA" was developed for recent victims of disasters (such as a hurricane, flood, industrial explosion, or mass-terrorist incident) who have not yet developed ASD or any other disorder requiring therapeutic treatment. PFA involves providing basic forms of practical and psychological support to bolster the coping capacity of disaster survivors in the early aftermath when they often are experiencing acute stress reactions. Because PFA can be provided on a large-scale basis to people regardless of whether or not they are severely distressed, it can be used either as primary or secondary prevention. Several CBT approaches have been shown to prevent PTSD when provided to high-risk persons before they are exposed to traumatic stressors (e.g., with military personnel before they are deployed to a war zone) or when people have heightened levels of physiological arousal (e.g., a heart rate higher than 95 beats per minute) or significant psychological impairment (such as ASD) within a few hours or days after experiencing psychological trauma (Bryant, 2008).

Indicated or tertiary prevention interventions involve providing timely effective treatment for PTSD or related disorders if they develop acutely or emerge months or years later in order to prevent major life problems in the short term or chronic debilitating conditions in the long run. This third-line approach to prevention was discussed in detail in Chapters 7 and 8. The remainder of this chapter focuses on primary/universal and secondary/selective prevention of PTSD.

Theoretical foundations and principles of PTSD prevention

PTSD is a complex psychobiological condition that takes many forms, depending on the specific traumatic stressors and the larger life circumstances of the traumatized individual (see Chapters 3–5 and 11). Therefore, strategies and interventions for the prevention of PTSD must be grounded in well-reasoned and empirically supported theories of the disorder's causes (etiology) and how it develops or remits (changes for the better) over time (see Chapter 3). Several theories of the origins and course of PTSD are particularly relevant to the design of prevention strategies.

Hobfoll's Theory of COR. Stress is viewed in COR theory as the result of a threat or a loss of resources, rather than in terms of the direct injury or harm to the person (Walter, Hall, & Hobfoll, 2008). Resources include things that meet objective needs (such as food, clothing, and shelter), personal characteristics (such as self-esteem, knowledge, or skills), social support (such as practical or emotional help from family, friends, neighbors, or strangers), and services (such as medical or psychological care, law enforcement, schools, and stores). COR also defines certain "conditions" (such as being married or having a job) and "energies" (such as being well rested, having money, or having time available) that increase a person's access to resources as an indirect resource that may be lost or depleted when stressful events occur. COR theory postulates that bodily and psychological stress reactions are based on an inborn survival response that mobilizes the person to take action to regain the lost or reduced resources. COR theory therefore implies that prevention of PTSD must involve helping people to identify and restore or replace the most important resources that have been lost or depleted as the result of a traumatic event. This is an important shift in perspective from focusing on the stress reactions and distress caused by traumatic stressors to addressing losses in people's lives that occur when trauma strikes that, if restored or replaced, can be a source of recovery or resilience. COR theory views prevention programs as an investment in resources that, if effective, will help people and communities to recover or add to other resources that have been lost or temporarily made unavailable by a traumatic event such as a disaster or an encounter with violence.

COR theory has four corollaries that can guide PTSD prevention efforts. The first is that people with the fewest resources to begin with are more adversely affected and less able to regain lost resources in the wake of traumatic events than people with more resources. Second, those who lose the most resources initially during and after a traumatic event will lose even more over time. A third corollary is that people who have the most resources initially are most capable of restoring or gaining resources after a traumatic stressor. The fourth corollary is that people who have the least resources initially will fight to hold onto or defend whatever resources they can keep or find in the aftermath of a traumatic stressor. Therefore, PTSD prevention programs should selectively focus on people and communities who are impoverished or underserved—for example, the thousands of low-income families who are displaced from their homes by disasters such as hurricanes, tsunamis, or floods. Prevention interventions should be designed to support people in retaining the limited resources that they still possess—such as self-respect, the ability to make their own decisions, treasured personal items, their close relationships—in order to avoid creating unhelpful conflicts between "helpers" and "victims" (such as were evident in the "second disaster" that occurred for people stranded in New Orleans after Hurricane Katrina).

De Jong's Ecological Resilience Model. Resources exist in different forms within different aspects of the "ecosystem" in which people live. An ecosystem is an interconnected network of organisms that make up a social or physical environment. Ecology is the study of ecosystems, how they are formed and maintain or change their networks, and participating organisms. De Jong and colleagues (Tol, Jordans, Reis, & De Jong, 2008) draw on the work of the ecological psychologist Bronfenbrenner (1979) to identify four types or levels of ecosystems that are relevant to understanding and enhancing the resilience of children and families faced with pervasive traumatic events such as war or other forms of societal or institutional violence. The ecological environment is conceptualized as a nested number of systems around the individual child:

- the *microsystem*, consisting of the direct activities, roles, and interpersonal relations in a certain setting (e.g., the home, the school);
- the *mesosystem*, which is comprised of the interrelations among two or more of these settings (e.g., relations between home, school, and peer group);
- the *exosystem*, in which the child does not actively participate but that influences and is influenced by the developing person (e.g., the parents' workplaces);
- the *macrosystem*, which are consistencies in the form of culture or subculture in the micro-, exo-, and mesosystems (Tol et al., 2008, p. 166).

An ecological resilience perspective has several implications for prevention of PTSD. First, changes in how people behave that may seem small may nevertheless have a large impact for the better or worse in the wake of psychological trauma if these "microsystem" changes have ripple effects up through the meso-, exo-, and macrosystems. Second, the prevention interventions are most likely to have a powerful impact if they create positive changes at not just one or two but *all* of these ecosystem levels. Third, in order to influence the meso-, exo-, and macrosystems, prevention interventions must either directly or indirectly involve the family, peer group, work or school, and community systems as well as trauma survivors themselves. Fourth, aspects of trauma survivors' ecosystems that may seem only remotely related to their lives or recovery, such as exosystems in which they do not directly participate or the societal laws or cultural practices that constitute the macrosystem in which they live, must be changed if prevention interventions are to have large-scale sustained benefits.

Tol et al. (2008) provide several examples of innovative PTSD prevention interventions that follow these ecological principles:

> *In the case of Burundian child-headed households, when parents were killed during the civil war, sisters were observed to actively encourage education for siblings who were about to drop out from school. In northern Sri Lanka, extended family members, such as aunts and uncles, were often able to provide distraction from grief after the death or "disappearance" of fathers, as well as provide a stable supporting relationship when single mothers were focusing on their families' economic survival. (p. 169)*

Saxe's TST Model. Saxe, MacDonald, and Ellis (2007) translated Bronfenbrenner's (1979) ecological systems theory into not only a theoretical model but also a very practical technology for the prevention and treatment of PTSD. TST focuses on children who are experiencing multiple adversities (such as abuse or neglect, family violence, community violence, loss or separation from caregivers) and identifies ways in which the child is having difficulty in regulating emotions and the ways others in the child's family, school, and neighborhood are having difficulty helping the child with emotion regulation. TST proposes a developmental sequence in recovery from PTSD that begins with the child in a state of simply trying to survive and progresses through the three phases that are adopted by most PTSD treatment interventions (see Chapter 7): "stabilizing," "enduring" (dealing with troubling memories and reminders of traumatic experiences), and "understanding" (applying new skills and knowledge to engaging more successfully in activities and relationships). TST adds a novel final phase of recovery—"transcending"—which involves developing new strengths and directions in life (see "posttraumatic growth" in Chapter 2). TST addresses these recovery goals by utilizing techniques from three PTSD psychotherapy models, CBT, emotion regulation therapy, and narrative reconstruction therapy, and with pharmacotherapy (see Chapter 8).

TST has the potential to take PTSD therapy out of the therapist's office and into the communities and homes where traumatized children and families live and must attempt to both survive and transcend. TST is explicitly "disseminate-able" (Saxe et al., 2007, p. 6) with work sheets to guide providers and clients who use TST interventions such as "single point of contact" (p. 83), the "family collaborative meeting" (p. 156), "stabilization on site" (p. 170), and "systems advocacy screener" (p. 202). These interventions are adapted from the "systems of care" and "wraparound" approaches that have been developed and widely used nationally and internationally to provide child and family mental health services, but TST is the first systematic approach to such comprehensive services for severely traumatized children.

Brom and Kleber's Minimal Learning Model of Resilience. The ability to think clearly and accurately is one of the most crucial resources that may be compromised by psychological trauma (Ford, 2005). Effective "cognitive processing" (Brom & Kleber, 2008) also is an aspect of each person's microsystem that can have a major impact on their meso-, exo-, and even macrosystems. Brom and Kleber (2008) take this line of reasoning several steps further to theorize that the best form of cognitive processing to prevent PTSD in the wake of exposure to a traumatic stressor is what they describe as "minimal learning." It may seem strange to suggest that *less* learning is better than *more*, but recall that studies on the biology of PTSD indicate that what people who develop PTSD have learned is to *survive* rather than the ordinary kinds of knowledge acquisition that characterize learning under less dangerous or less threatening conditions. Although survival is paramount in traumatic events, when such events cause a shift from the "learning brain" to the "survival brain," the person can become trapped in the PTSD biological state of hyperarousal and mindset of alternating anxiety or emotional numbing, hypervigilance, and unstoppable unwanted memories (intrusive reexperiencing). If survival mode does not persist, the person is likely to be able to adjust without developing PTSD or recover from PTSD.

Therefore, Brom and Kleber (2008) propose that as far as learning is concerned, in the wake of psychological trauma, *less is more*. Specifically, they postulate that resilience in the wake of psychological trauma involves "minimal learning," which does not mean failing to learn from life experiences but instead a kind of learning that involves a "change [in] the meaning attributed to an event [rather] than change [in] one's deeper anchored belief system" (p. 143). They give the example of a man who is injured when a truck slams into his car from behind when he stops at a yellow light and whose son is in the car but is physically unhurt by the accident. If this man interprets the event as his fault for not having rushed through the yellow light and concludes that he can no longer trust himself as a father because he has failed to protect his son, he has adopted an interpretation of the meaning of the event that drastically changes his more deeply anchored belief about himself as a father. Such "survival" learning is typical among people with PTSD.

If, on the other hand, the person concludes that he handled the yellow light in a way that was the best way to protect his son (recognizing that more and worse accidents occur when people rush through yellow lights than when they obey the rules of the road and stop), he is likely to sustain (and possibly even strengthen) his belief in himself as a father and protector. This is what appears to happen when people are resilient and do not develop PTSD or recover from PTSD if traumatic stress reactions become sufficiently problematic to constitute a disorder: he has *minimally* changed his core sustaining beliefs. Therefore, prevention interventions should be designed to enable people to retain and strengthen positive core beliefs ("minimal learning"), while recognizing and coping with the shock and distress of a life-threatening event.

PTSD prevention interventions

PTSD prevention interventions include programs designed to prevent exposure to traumatic stressors (notably violence or crime/delinquency prevention interventions) or to mitigate against the development of acute or chronic PTSD before or in the immediate aftermath of exposure to traumatic stressors such as disasters, serious injuries, war, or family and community violence.

Community and School-Based Violence and Delinquency Prevention Programs. Youth violence and delinquency are widely recognized as serious and complex public health problems (Skeem, Scott, & Mulvey, 2014). While some information suggests that youth violence may be on the decline in the United States, recent studies indicate that it is no less prevalent today than it was at the peak of the youth violence epidemic and that rates of assault among youth have actually been on the rise since the mid-1990s (Maguire & Pastore, 1999).

When violence or other delinquent behaviors result in youths' involvement with law enforcement and the juvenile justice system, studies have shown that upwards of 90% of these children and adolescents have experienced psychological trauma and that they are more than 10 times more likely than other youths to suffer from PTSD (Ford, Chapman, Connor, & Cruise, 2012). While violence is only one of several types of psychological trauma that places children at risk for PTSD (Copeland, Keeler, Angold, & Costello, 2007), it is more strongly associated than nonviolent traumatic stressors with not only PTSD but also delinquent behaviors (such as substance abuse and other risky behaviors) and suicidality (Ford, Hartman, Hawke, & Chapman, 2008).

Several prospective longitudinal research studies have demonstrated a link between early aggressive and delinquent behavior in childhood and later violence and delinquency in adolescence and young adulthood (Farrington, 1991; Reid & Eddy, 1997). Therefore, violence and delinquency prevention programs ideally begin at the elementary school level or earlier. Schools have been identified as an ideal environment for implementing violence and delinquency prevention programs because children and adolescents spend more time and have more contact with peers, adult role models, and opportunities for learning at school than anywhere else. The FAST Track, Promoting Alternative THinking Strategies (PATH), and Second Step programs are examples of scientifically researched school-based prevention programs (Box 9.5).

However, without community-wide and family support and involvement in the intervention, any gains made in the school setting will quickly deteriorate as students leave the classroom and enter their homes and larger communities (Sherman et al., 1997). The most effective violence prevention interventions therefore involve families, schools, and community organizations (see, e.g., Functional Family Therapy, The Incredible Years, Multisystemic Therapy, and Multidimensional Treatment Foster Care; Box 9.4). Violence prevention programs also teach not only positive attitudes but also social skills to promote prosocial behavioral alternatives to aggression and delinquency (Frey, Hirschstein, & Guzzo, 2000; Gottfredson, 2000).

While thousands of violence prevention programs are available to American schools and internationally, few are broad-based, social skills–focused, and introduced in the earliest school grades. Fewer yet meet the most stringent criteria for violence prevention program effectiveness proposed by the Center for the Study and Prevention of Violence's *Blueprints* program. Of more than 600 programs evaluated by *Blueprints*, only 11 are considered "evidence-based," and another 18 are considered "promising." Unfortunately, many of these "model" programs are out of reach for the majority of school systems due to a low capacity for large-scaled implementation, high cost, or inappropriateness for the given population. However, the *Blueprints* programs and other widely disseminated violence prevention programs have reached tens of thousands of children, adolescents and their families, and schools (see Box 9.4).

Box 9.4 Youth Violence Prevention Programs

The Center for the Study and Prevention of Violence at the University of Colorado at Boulder has overseen a national violence prevention initiative to identify effective youth violence prevention programs for two decades. The Blueprints for Violence Prevention program has identified 11 scientifically validated violence prevention programs and 18 other promising violence prevention programs. These programs differ in many ways but share in common several of the characteristics associated with successful prevention program implementation, including addressing multiple risk and protective factors; intensive training and technical support; strong staff and administrative support; strong teacher buy-in; parent involvement; and community partnership and support (Gottfredson, 2000; Nation et al., 2003; Thornton, Craft, Dahlberg, Lynch, & Baer, 2000). Descriptions of several different youth violence and delinquency prevention programs have been abstracted from the Blueprints website (http://www.colorado.edu/cspv/blueprints/index.html).

Functional Family Therapy (FFT). FFT is delivered one family at a time, either in the home or in a clinic, following a three-phase model:

1. *Phase 1—Engagement and Motivation:* During these initial phases, FFT applies reattribution (e.g., reframing) and related techniques to impact maladaptive perceptions, beliefs, and emotions. This produces increasing hope and expectation of change, decreasing resistance, increasing alliance and trust, reducing the oppressive negativity within family and between family and community, and increasing respect for individual differences and values.
2. *Phase 2—Behavior Change:* This phase applies individualized and developmentally appropriate techniques such as communication training, specific tasks and technical aids, basic parenting skills, and contracting and response-cost techniques.
3. *Phase 3—Generalization:* In this phase, Family Case Management is guided by individualized family functional needs, their interaction with environmental constraints and resources, and the alliance with the therapist.

Each of these phases involves both assessment and intervention components. Family assessment focuses on characteristics of the individual family members, family relational dynamics, and the multisystemic context in which the family operates. The family relational system is described in regard to interpersonal functions and their impact on promoting and maintaining problem behavior. Intervention is directed at accomplishing the goals of the relevant treatment phase. For example, in the engagement and motivation phase, assessment is focused on determining the degree to which the family or its members are negative and blaming. The intervention would target the reduction of negativity and blaming. In behavior change, assessment would focus on targeting the skills necessary for more adaptive family functioning. Intervention would be aimed at helping the family develop those skills in a way that matched their relational patterns. In generalization, the assessment focuses on the degree to which the family can apply the new behavior in broader contexts. Interventions would focus on helping generalize the family behavior change into such contexts.

Multisystemic Therapy (MST). MST posits that youth antisocial behavior is multidetermined and linked with characteristics of the individual youth and his or her family, peer group, school, and community contexts. As such, MST interventions aim to attenuate risk factors by building youth and family strengths (protective factors) on a highly individualized and comprehensive basis. The provision of home-based services circumvents barriers to service access that often characterize families of serious juvenile offenders. An emphasis on parental empowerment to modify the natural social network of their children facilitates the maintenance and generalization of treatment gains. MST is a pragmatic and goal-oriented treatment that specifically targets those factors in each youth's social network that are contributing to his or her antisocial behavior:

- improve caregiver discipline practices;
- enhance family affective relations;
- decrease youth association with deviant peers;
- increase youth association with prosocial peers;
- improve youth school or vocational performance;
- engage youth in prosocial recreational outlets;
- develop an indigenous support network of extended family, neighbors, and friends to help caregivers achieve and maintain such changes.

Specific treatment techniques used to facilitate these gains are integrated from those therapies that have the most empirical support, including cognitive behavioral, behavioral, and the pragmatic family therapies. MST services are delivered in the natural environment (e.g., home, school, and community). The treatment plan is designed in collaboration with family members and is, therefore, family driven rather than therapist driven. The ultimate goal of MST is to empower families to build an environment that promotes health through the mobilization of indigenous child, family, and community resources. The typical duration of home-based MST services is approximately 4 months, with multiple therapist-family contacts occurring each week, determined by family need.

PATHS. PATHS is an educational curriculum designed to promote emotional and social competencies and reduce aggression and behavior problems in elementary school-aged children, while simultaneously enhancing the educational process in the classroom. The PATHS curriculum is taught three times per week for a minimum of 20–30 minutes per day and provides teachers with systematic, developmentally based lessons, materials, and instructions for teaching their students emotional literacy, self-control, social competence, positive peer relations, and interpersonal problem-solving skills. A key objective of promoting these developmental skills is to prevent or reduce behavioral and emotional problems. PATHS lessons include instruction in identifying and labeling feelings, expressing feelings, assessing the intensity of feelings, managing feelings,

(Continued)

Box 9.4 Continued

understanding the difference between feelings and behaviors, delaying gratification, controlling impulses, reducing stress, self-talk, reading and interpreting
social cues, understanding the perspectives of others, using steps for problem
solving and decision making, having a positive attitude toward life, self-
awareness, nonverbal communication skills, and verbal communication skills.
Teachers receive training in a 2- to 3-day workshop and in biweekly meetings
with the curriculum consultant.

The Incredible Years. Using three complementary training programs, trained
facilitators teach children, ages 2–10, at risk for and/or presenting with conduct problems (defined as high rates of aggression, defiance, or oppositional
and impulsive behaviors), and their parents and teachers, the following skills.
The BASIC program emphasizes parenting skills known to promote children's
social competence and reduce behavior problems such as how to play with
children, helping children learn, effective praise and use of incentives, effective
limit-setting, and strategies to handle misbehavior. The ADVANCE program
emphasizes parent interpersonal skills such as effective communication skills,
anger management, problem-solving between adults, and ways to give and get
support. The Supporting Your Child's Education program (known as SCHOOL)
emphasizes parenting approaches designed to promote children's academic
skills, such as reading skills, parental involvement in setting up predictable
homework routines, and building collaborative relationships with teachers.

Teacher training emphasizes effective classroom management skills, such
as the effective use of teacher attention, praise and encouragement, use of
incentives for difficult behavior problems, proactive teaching strategies, how to
manage inappropriate classroom behaviors, the importance of building positive
relationships with students, and how to teach empathy, social skills, and problem
solving in the classroom.

The Dinosaur Curriculum for children teaches skills such as emotional
literacy, empathy or perspective taking, friendship skills, anger management,
interpersonal problem solving, school rules, and how to be successful at school.
A treatment version is used by therapists with small groups of children exhibiting conduct problems. A prevention version is delivered to the entire classroom
by regular teachers, two to three times a week.

Multidimensional Treatment Foster Care (MTFC). MTFC was designed to
be a cost-effective alternative to group or residential treatment, incarceration,
and hospitalization for adolescents who have problems with chronic antisocial
behavior, emotional disturbance, and delinquency. Community families are
recruited, trained, and closely supervised to provide MTFC-placed adolescents
with treatment and intensive supervision at home, in school, and in the community; clear and consistent limits with follow-through on consequences; positive
reinforcement for appropriate behavior; a relationship with a mentoring adult;
and separation from delinquent peers. Training for community foster families

emphasizes behavior management methods to provide youth with a structured and therapeutic living environment. After completing a preservice training and placement of the youth, MTFC parents attend a weekly group meeting run by a program supervisor where ongoing support and supervision are provided. Foster parents are contacted daily during telephone calls to check on youth progress and problems. MTFC staff are available for consultation and crisis intervention 24/7.

Services to the foster family occur throughout the placement. Family therapy is provided for the biological (or adoptive) family, with the goal of returning the youth back to the home. The parents are supported and taught to use behavior management methods that are used in the MTFC foster home. Closely supervised home visits are conducted throughout the youth's placement in MTFC. Parents are encouraged to have frequent contact with the MTFC program supervisor to get information about their child's progress in the program. Frequent contact is maintained between the MTFC program supervisor and the youth's case workers, parole/probation officer, teachers, work supervisors, and other involved adults.

Families and Schools Together (FAST Track). This comprehensive and long-term prevention program aims to prevent chronic and severe conduct problems for high-risk children. It is based on the view that antisocial behavior stems from the interaction of multiple influences, and it includes the school, the home, and the individual in its intervention. FAST Track's main goals are to increase communication and bonds between these three domains; enhance children's social, cognitive, and problem-solving skills; improve peer relationships; and ultimately decrease disruptive behavior in the home and school. FAST Track has been implemented in rural and urban areas for boys and girls of varying ethnicity, social class, and family composition (i.e., the primary intervention is designed for all youth in a school setting). It specifically targets children identified in kindergarten for disruptive behavior and poor peer relations. The program spans grades 1–6, but it is most intense during the key periods of entry to school (first grade) and transition from grade school to middle school. It is multidimensional, including the following components: parent training, which occurs in first grade and emphasizes fostering children's academic performance, communicating with the school, controlling anger, and using effective discipline; home visitations, which occur biweekly to reinforce parenting skills, promote parents' feelings of efficacy and empowerment, and foster parents' problem-solving skills; social skills training, which enhances children's social-cognitive and problem-solving skills, peer relations, anger control, and friendship maintenance; academic tutoring, which is offered three times per week to improve children's reading skills; classroom intervention, which utilizes the PATHS curriculum, a program designed to be used in grades 1–5, to help children develop emotional awareness skills, learn self-control and problem-solving skills, foster a positive peer climate, incorporate home activities to allow parents' participation, and improve teachers' classroom management skills.

(Continued)

Box 9.4 Continued

Second Step. This school-based social-emotional curriculum was designed for children in grades prekindergarten through middle school. At the elementary school level, lessons are divided into three units that teach skills in anger and emotional management, empathy, and impulse control. The teaching methods employed in the Second Step curriculum include adult and peer modeling, role playing, and coaching and cueing. Each lesson includes a brief "Story and Discussion" led by a trained teacher using a photo and script, followed by opportunities for students to gain practice in targeted skills. Second Step has been implemented on a school district or citywide basis to promote consistent behavioral expectations for children and promote widespread use of modeling and verbal coaching/cueing by teachers, school staff, parents, and community workers who have regular contact with children: full-day training of all elementary school teachers and staff, including nonclassroom teachers (e.g., music, physical education, special education) and school administrators, is offered during a districtwide teacher workshop day and conducted by certified Second Step trainers; a series of three 45-minute training sessions on each of the three curriculum components (anger/emotional management, empathy, and impulse control) for noncertified school staff (e.g., custodial staff, teachers' aides, cafeteria staff) is offered at each school and conducted by certified Second Step trainers using an adaptation of the Supporting Second Step curriculum; a series of four 1.5-hour workshops for parents is offered at each school and one secondary location (public library) and conducted by a parent education consultant under the supervision of a certified Second Step trainer using an adaptation of the Second Step Family Guide; ongoing technical support is provided to each school by certified Second Step trainers, including weekly school visits, a Supporting Second Step bulletin board identifying the skills and concepts being taught at each grade level on a weekly basis, and periodic Second Step newsletters highlighting how teachers use creative approaches to reinforce Second Step and describing implementation tips for classroom and nonclassroom teachers; a series of four flyers is released through local newspapers in both English and Spanish to describe Second Step and identify ways in which parents and community members can model and reinforce the specific skills being taught in elementary schools; a 2.5-day "Training of Trainers," adapted to the needs of those working with children and families in the community, is held for members of community agencies and organizations, parents, and select members of the school system; and preimplementation meetings with principals, teachers, and other staff at each school, as well as with parent-teacher organizations, are offered to build support for Second Step, answer questions and concerns, and assist schools in developing site-based implementation plans based on their individual lesson schedules and to establish a school and community partnership team to ensure consistent application of Second Step language and principles throughout the school district and the community as a whole.

PFA in the Wake of Disaster and Terrorism. PFA has been defined as "the use of psychosocial interventions delivered during the immediate impact phase (first 4 weeks) following a disaster or other critical incident (such as a life-threatening accident or terrorist incident) to individuals experiencing acute stress reactions or problems in functioning, with the intent of aiding adaptive coping and problem-solving" (Watson, 2008a, 2008b, p. 535). PFA provides a guide for mental health–informed and trauma-informed assistance to affected children and families and first responders in the immediate wake of critical incidents. In the form of "second aid" and "third aid," PFA involves the delivery of brief mental health interventions in the first weeks and months after critical incidents and into the longer-term recovery phase. PFA is designed to be delivered in diverse settings. Sites may include shelters, schools, homes, family assistance centers, and other community settings. Following weapons of mass destruction (WMD) events, PFA may be delivered in mass-casualty collection points, hospitals, and at sites where decontamination and inoculation services are provided.

The National Child Traumatic Stress Network (NCTSN) and the National Center for PTSD (NCPTSD) developed the first *Psychological First Aid (PFA) Field Operations Guide* (NCTSN and NCPTSD, 2006) for emergency/disaster responders to use when providing PFA while working with persons immediately affected by disasters or mass-casualty incidents (such as the September 11 terrorist hijackings and March 11, 2003, Madrid training bombings).

The NCTSN/NCPTSD (2006) PFA field guide provides instructions for eight core actions:

1. *Contact and Engagement:* The initial step in PFA is identifying, making contact with, and beginning to build a trusting relationship with potentially traumatized children and adults in a nonintrusive, compassionate, and helpful manner. Most disaster or terrorism victims and their families never receive psychological assistance because the focus for services in the wake of disaster or mass-casualty incidents has been on physical safety, injuries, and damage to homes and property. However, increasingly over the past 25 years, humanitarian and disaster relief organizations and first responders (such as paramedics, law enforcement, and firefighters) have recognized the importance of supporting victims' psychological stability and coping resources as a means to enhance overall safety and to prevent subsequent stress-related disorders.
2. *Safety and Comfort:* Psychological recovery begins with regaining a sense of safety and access to basic needs that provide a sense of comfort in the midst of the painful and frightening events. For example, American Red Cross mental health volunteers are trained to first provide victims and emergency response co-workers with simple kinds of comfort such as liquids, snacks, blankets, a quiet place to sit, and a way to contact family and friends.
3. *Stabilization:* Crisis intervention techniques are used to calm and reorient distressed victims (and emergency response co-workers, who also may become distressed) (see Box 9.5).
4. *Information Gathering and Providing Practical Assistance:* The most helpful intervention in the wake of disaster or crises is that which addresses the affected person's current high-priority needs and concerns. Observing what the person is searching or asking others for help with (e.g., information about casualties and where they are being taken for treatment) or evidently in need of (e.g., a quiet place to sit, a brief break from filling out paperwork or caring for a distressed child) is a good way to be able to provide help without asking. However, it is always important to ask, "Would this be helpful?" before providing assistance, and also "Is there anything else I can do that would be most helpful to you with your main goal right now?"

5. *Connection with Social Supports:* The most reassuring thing for many disaster- or terrorism-affected persons is simply to be with familiar trusted persons such as family or friends. Often this is temporarily very difficult or even impossible in the wake of disaster—for example, when family members go to different emergency relief centers and cannot travel any further due to quarantine or curfew limitations. Providing a means for making contact (such as a cell phone and a working phone number at which a separated family member can be reached) or supplying accurate information about the safety of family members and when direct communication will be possible can be the most effective anxiety reduction interventions in crisis situations. If communication is impossible for the foreseeable future, even if this is only for a few hours, it is important to understand and supportively validate the victim's distress about this separation (e.g., "I can see how important it is to you to be able to know your children are safe and how upsetting it is not to be certain they're okay or to be able to talk or be with them now. I'll watch for any opportunity to get you more information or to help you get in contact or be with them").

6. *Information on Coping Support:* Victims of a recent disaster or mass-casualty incident and their families may not know, or may not think to remember, that stress reactions are normal and not a sign of something terribly wrong with them or the situation. Occasional brief supportive reminders can reduce affected persons' anxieties about feeling stressed. For example: "Feeling like your heart is pounding and your mind is racing is a sign that your body is gearing up to help you deal with the challenges this situation has caused; it's not pleasant, but it's just energy that your body needs your help in channeling productively. What are one or two things that you'd like to take care of that I could help you accomplish, or at least make a good start on, right now?"

7. *Linkage with Collaborative Services:* To use a metaphor from sports, helping people in the first hours and days after (or during) a disaster or mass-casualty incident is more like running one leg in a relay race than running an entire marathon all on one's own. Survivors and affected or bereaved families often feel as though they must endure an endless grueling race alone, with no clear finish line in sight and no one but themselves to run the course. First responders also can come to feel a sense of burden and isolation after several intense and demanding days of helping distressed victims and families. Therefore, whenever it is possible for a first responder to help an affected person or family to make a link to other supportive services (such as disaster relief organizations, food banks, insurance agents, health care professionals, child care programs, faith-based organizations, employment or educational consultants), this can reduce the sense of isolation and hopelessness for both the affected persons and the first responder.

PFA is provided by mental health providers from a variety of professions, such as social work, counseling, psychology, marriage and family therapy, and rehabilitation and educational counselors. Beyond the professional training and credentials required for practitioners in those professional fields, specialized training in PFA is recommended (Watson, 2008a,b).

PFA is a brief, efficient, nonpathologizing approach to providing psychological and practical information, support, and resources "on-the-spot" (rather than in a counseling clinic or office) and "on-the-fly" (rather than in formally scheduled appointments) to people affected by a disaster or mass-casualty incident. PFA is designed to help affected persons and families to (i) better understand their own stress reactions as expectable and signs of coping (not as reactions to be feared, signs of personal failure or weakness, or signs of mental illness); (ii) get immediate help with their highest-priority practical and emotional needs; (iii) recognize the circumstances under which they should consider seeking formal counseling (such as when anxiety or alcohol use becomes a problem for them, their families, or their work); (iv) know how and where to access additional help, including mental health counseling; and (v) be able to help family members feel and be safe and cope with stress reactions. PFA has not been scientifically tested to determine its effectiveness, but it is a translation of the best scientific evidence available about what is (and is not) helpful for disaster or mass-casualty incident survivors and affected families.

Box 9.5 Crisis Intervention Principles and Techniques for PFA

When first responders provide PFA, it is not unusual to encounter a small number of affected persons who are in crisis. This may be due to the immediate events (such as the death or severe injury of a loved one or close friend, or the loss of their home) or to preexisting vulnerabilities (such as having an anxiety disorder, substance use disorder, or depression that is worsened by the stress of the immediate incident or having limited or no social support system) or a combination of both. While working at disaster sites or relief/ services centers, it often is not possible to get the person in crisis to a clinic or emergency department for observation or treatment, and this may not be necessary or helpful in many cases (except when the person is an immediate risk to self or others, such as actually attempting suicide or threatening to harm someone else). The best help for acute emotional distress often is an immediate calming interaction, which may be guided by the following principles developed by the University of Connecticut School of Medicines' Center for Trauma Response, Recovery, and Preparedness (www.ctrp.org). © University of Connecticut.

1. *Protect* the person in crisis and everyone in the immediate situation, including yourself and other responders, by reorganizing the immediate environment to increase physical and emotional safety. Remove or modify any immediate sources of danger. For example:
   - remove broken glass or sharp objects, objects or furniture that could cause people to trip and fall, and liquids spilled on the floor;
   - assist persons who have been exposed to toxins to receive decontamination without inadvertently contaminating you or other persons;
   - cover or remove furniture with sharp corners;
   - place barriers to prevent intrusions by unauthorized persons;
   - reduce access to stairways by persons who could fall and injure themselves (such as children or individuals who have impaired balance or vision).

(Continued)

Box 9.5 Continued

Do not reassure people that they are safe *unless you have definite factual information that this is true.* If you do know factually that potential dangers are not imminent threats, explain this to affected persons or responders in a specific manner, *but do not say that "everything" or "everyone" is safe.* For example: "We've received an update from the FBI that the white powder was not anthrax or any other kind of poison," or "Every person is checked for any possible exposure to harmful chemicals or gas, and if this has happened or may have happened, they go through a decontamination procedure before they are allowed to enter this assistance center."

Physiological shock—If they are showing signs of physiological shock (pale, clammy skin, weak or rapid pulse, irregular breathing, dull or glassy eyes, unresponsive, no bladder or bowel control, restless or agitated), ask them to sit or lie down (and provide a suitably private and comfortable place to do so, even if this must be done in a crowded hectic setting), to look at you, and to listen to you.

Threat to harm self or others—Look for signs that they may hurt themselves or others (e.g., expresses intense anger toward self or others, exhibits extreme agitation). If so, seek immediate help from emergency medical or security personnel. Approach such persons gradually and cautiously in order to reduce intrusions on their personal space that might increase agitation, both for the person's safety and that of other persons (including you).

2. *Connect* affected persons and responders with one another and with immediate practical resources that enhance their safety, comfort, and ability to accomplish their goals. This includes providing information that is focused on how responders are making the situation safer without providing premature reassurance. Helping people get simple physical and social sources of comfort (e.g., food, beverages, blankets, quiet places, familiar supportive people, familiar routines and activities) is soothing and can enhance people's sense of safety and personal control. Helping people feel more connected may be accomplished in many ways:
   - Simply being in a comfortable place—consider the temperature, lighting, air quality, the furniture and how the furniture is arranged, access to other people in controllable ways.
   - Getting current accurate information while not being exposed to excessive inaccurate or retraumatizing information from the media, official updates, and informal conversations.
   - Doing things that are active (rather than passive waiting), practical (relying upon and utilizing immediately available resources), and familiar (drawing on well-learned behaviors that do not require new learning or deep thought) and that provide the person with a sense of being able to have some control over his situation by being able to simply make the situation safer or more tolerable or comfortable.
   - Being able to interact with other persons in the setting without feeling pressure to be upbeat or to talk to people simply because of being in the same situation.

People often are reluctant to talk to one another after being "thrown together" by the happenstance of being in the same disaster, or seeking aid in the same health care or family service center, because of feelings of acute psychological shock and also concerns about being burdened by others' fears, anger, or despair. However, talking to strangers can reduce the sense of isolation and helplessness that traumatic shock or loss causes, especially if the talk includes the discovery of common ground (e.g., a similar goal of trying to find children from whom they have been separated or coming from nearby neighborhoods) or enables people to help one another with moral support or new information.

- If family or friends are present, it may be helpful to enlist their aid in comforting or providing emotional support to the distressed person, while suggesting that this is an important way that they can help make the situation safer and more manageable for everyone involved (e.g., "By helping your daughter know that you're there for her now, you're making it possible for her to feel calm enough so that both of you can concentrate on what you need to do to find your other family members—and that also will help me to go and see if I can get you some information about your family and other families' missing persons"). Alternately, it may be best to take a distressed individual aside to a quiet place or to speak quietly with that person while family/friends are nearby (make sure the person, especially if a child, can see and be seen by family/friends at all times, unless contact with family increases the distress) so that you are helping the entire family by stepping in to help the distressed person regain a calmer and more focused state of mind.

- If the person seems overstimulated and in need of quiet and privacy, take her to a less hectic place. If they seem overwhelmed by listening to you, offer to stay with them without talking or to give them a few minutes alone, telling them that you will be available if they need you or that you will check back to see how they're doing and if there's anything you can do to help at that time. Stay nearby where you can observe without being intrusive. Offer to get them a drink, a snack, a chair, or a blanket. Don't try to talk directly if the person appears cognitively/ emotionally overloaded. Do not make it obvious that you are observing the person, because this can be embarrassing or elicit reactions such as suspiciousness, which can compound the person's distress. Make small talk, talk to other persons in the vicinity, do some paperwork, or in other ways demonstrate that you are occupied with other tasks but attentive should the person need or wish to receive further practical or emotional help.

   Do not judge your success in helping affected persons or responders by their immediate mood or state of mind, but instead focus on helping them to regulate extreme moods and negative states of mind (see Module 3). *Do not assume* that affected persons or responders will respond to your assistance with immediate positive reactions: it may take many hours, days, or even years before survivors or bereaved persons are able to feel more safety, confidence, trust, or hope after the shock, horror, and sense of helplessness/hopelessness caused by disaster or terrorism.

(Continued)

Box 9.5 Continued

3. Refocus the stressed person's attention toward calm confidence. The SOS mental focusing steps from the TARGET© PTSD prevention and treatment intervention provides three simple steps that can enable distressed individuals to rapidly reduce agitation and dissociation.

Stop, step back, and sweep your mind clear

- Suggest simple ways the person can be aware of body tension (e.g., "I can see that you are really gritting your teeth, and your feet and legs are bursting with energy"), and invite *but do not instruct* them to use that energy in other ways that recharge rather than drain their bodily energy (e.g., "If you take that physical energy and make it into mental energy, by relaxing your jaw and your legs, that may help you recharge your body and help you have more mental energy to solve these important problems," or "You may find that sitting in a more comfortable place/position will increase your efficiency").
- Comment when you observe any ways in which the person is letting go of bodily tension (e.g., "I can see you're releasing some of the tightness in your shoulders and your legs as you get more focused, and that will help you recharge your body's energy").
- Periodically describe salient aspects of the physical environment that may help the person feel more spatially oriented (e.g., "We're in a noisy room with fluorescent lights, but we can find a quiet corner that's near a window with some natural light," or "Have you noticed the posters on the walls or the view outside the windows?").
- Periodically comment on the other people in the setting to identify specific people rather than leaving the person with a sense of being lost in a crowd (e.g., "Those people are family service workers, and they're talking with other family members who are trying to locate people they care about, just like you're doing").
- Periodically comment on the purpose of the setting to help the person get or stay aware of what is happening and what he or she can accomplish by being in this particular place (e.g., "This is a Red Cross family assistance center where people can get help for themselves and for their families, and that's what we're working on for you right now").

Orient yourself

- Help individuals identify the one thing (or person) that is most important right at this moment.
- Help them build this orienting thought using core beliefs/values, as well as immediate needs—values that are calming, such as honesty, courage, kindness, fairness, and loyalty.
- Help them build this orienting thought based on the strengths they see in themselves as a person—characteristics that restore confidence, such as integrity, determination, and fairness.
- Help them to draw strength and courage from recalling how they feel about the people and relationships they most value and what they bring to those people's lives of most value.
- Help them to do one or two practical things that honor those core personal values, qualities, and relationships, while also serving as a practical step toward meeting immediate needs.

- Don't tell them to stop rushing, but help them channel their physical and emotional energies in a more focused manner, using the immediate goal(s) as the focus.
- Comment on even small examples of clear, logical, calm, confident, consequence-based thinking (e.g., "Now you're organizing a really practical plan for dealing with this," or "When you make choices based on who and what you value, you're regaining personal control, even if there's external forces and events that no one can control in this situation").

Self-check—keeping track of how much distress and control one is feeling right now
- Informally comment on or ask them how they're doing with feeling stressed, or use a "stress thermometer" (1 = No stress to 10 = Worst stress ever) to make easy numerical ratings.
- Informally comment on or ask them how they're doing with feeling in control in the current situation, or use a "personal control scale" (10 = In total control to 1 = No control over anything) to help them make an easy numerical rating.
- Comment on changes in how strong the stress reaction is that they are experiencing to help them recognize that even in terrible situations, the internal stress level can change for the better in spite of being much higher than usual and to highlight things they have done that may have led to a reduction in how stressed they feel (e.g., "Your stress level is still high, understandably in this situation, but I notice that as you are getting a plan organized for dealing with the immediate problems, your stress ratings actually are getting a little lower; that shows you that even under terrible stress, you're able to do things that bring your own stress level down so you can be effective").
- Comment on changes in how much personal control they are experiencing (from their own perspective, *not* making an external judgment) to help them recognize that even in terrible situations, they can do things mentally (such as making an organized plan or set of priorities) and behaviorally (such as making a long-distance phone call to family who may serve as contacts for reunifying separated family members) that actually increase their personal control in important ways, despite the fact that much of what has happened and is happening are beyond their control.

Critical Incident Stress Management (*CISM*) Jeffrey Mitchell developed critical incident stress debriefing (CISD) in the early 1980s to help emergency medical services personnel such as firefighters cope with occupational exposure to traumatic stressors such as threats to their own lives and severe injuries or suffering they observed in their work. CISD has become the most widely used prevention intervention internationally for people exposed to psychological trauma (McSweeney, Dickstein, & Litz, 2008). CISD typically is conducted as a single group session (usually between 2 and 4 hours in length, at times with a follow-up session in a week or two) by two facilitators: a mental health or human services professional and a "peer," who is an individual with similar professional training as the persons being debriefed *but who does not have a close personal or working relationship with the persons being debriefed and who was not exposed to the traumatic event being debriefed.*

For example, a law enforcement officer from a nearby city might serve as a peer facilitator for a group of other law enforcement officers who recently responded to a disaster or brutal assault or murder. The goal of CISD is to help participants learn about one another's recollections of and mental and emotional reactions to distressing event(s) in which they all were involved (directly or indirectly) and to clarify their own recollections and accept their own reactions (during and since the events) as expectable given the circumstances and the nature of normal stress reactions.

CISD involves seven phases. First, in an *introduction*, the facilitators and participants introduce themselves, and the facilitators explain the structure of the session—that it is different from an operational debriefing (because the emphasis is on personal closure, not on the team's or any participant's performance)—and emphasize the importance of each person's private disclosures being treated by every attendee as confidential. In the second "fact" phase, each participant is invited to take a turn describing what he or she recall happening in the critical incident, each from his or her own perspective, but "just the facts." Participants often learn about aspects of the events of which they had been unaware, thus acquiring a more complete memory of the events. The third or "thought" phase involves each participant describing the thoughts he or she had at the time of the incident and since. In the fourth "reaction" phase, each participant describes his or her emotional reactions at the time of the incident and current reactions and interpretations of the incident. The fifth phase is a description by participants of their stress "symptoms," followed by a sixth or "teaching" phase in which the facilitators describe how these symptoms are expectable and manageable stress reactions that do not indicate any lasting problems unless they persist and interfere significantly with work or personal life. Finally, the seventh or "reentry phase" involves a summing up of the session by the facilitators, any final questions or thoughts by the participants, and information from the facilitators about referrals and any follow-up session.

CISM was developed to address the limitations of CISD, in part as a result of research studies showing that a single session of CISD did not have any measurable benefit (McSweeney et al., 2008). CISM adds the following options before and after CISD (McSweeney et al., 2008):

- *Demobilization:* After a critical incident occurs, emergency personnel who served as first responders complete their work and officially are relieved of further duty, usually with formal operational "debriefing" of how the team handled the crisis incident.
- *Defusing:* Relatively early in the demobilization period (typically within 24–72 hours), a group or one-to-one session is conducted with responders by a trained facilitator. The general structure of CISD is followed, but in an abbreviated three-phase format (an introduction, an exploration of recollections and reactions, and information about stress reactions and their expectable nature and duration, examples of adaptive and problematic forms of coping, and resources for help if stress reactions become severe.
- *CISD* usually is conducted within 7–14 days of the incident or demobilization.
- *Individual or Family Crisis Intervention:* One-to-one sessions may be conducted with an individual responder or a responder and their family in order to help them safely deal with crises such as extreme alcohol or substance use, depression or suicidality, anger and aggressive behavior, panic attacks, or overwhelming grief or guilt.

No rigorous scientific study has shown CISD (or CISM) to be effective in reducing mental health problems after potentially traumatic incidents (McSweeney et al., 2008). However, this arguably was never the intent of CISD or CISM (Everly, Flannery, & Mitchell, 2000). Although CISM might be viewed as a way to prevent PTSD, the original intent and most common current usage of CISM is to help potentially traumatized individuals to regain (or keep) their confidence in themselves and in their work team and first responder colleagues. This occurs often enough that CISM has continued to be used and is widely recommended by first responders worldwide. However, there is the risk that the very detailed descriptions of traumatic events in the "fact" phase may increase rather than resolve some participants' stress reactions, and very intense acute stress reactions are associated with an increased risk of subsequent PTSD (see Chapter 2). Studies with an individual who very recently survived a life-threatening experience such as a (near) fatal vehicle accident or assault show that persons who were "debriefed" (usually in the form of a single one-to-one session in a hospital emergency department or similar acute care setting) reported more severe subsequent PTSD and anxiety symptoms (Ehlers, Mayou, & Bryant, 2003). It would not be appropriate to conclude from those findings that CISD or CISM are harmful—particularly because the context and structure of CISD is very different than a one-to-one "debriefing"—but it appears that CISM should be used with caution and should not be considered a viable prevention intervention if the goal is to prevent PTSD.

Sones, Thorp, and Raskind (2011, p. 84) offer a useful perspective on why CISD may be harmful or at best ineffective when done on a "one-off" (single session) basis with individual recipients:

> *First, all trauma victims are invited to the debriefing, regardless of their risk for developing PTSD. Risk for PTSD varies based on environmental and personal variables (Sones et al., 2011). Therefore, individuals attending CISD meetings may range from virtually unaffected by the event to severely traumatized. Those who have more severe symptoms may decline the invitation to attend because avoidance of trauma-related stimuli is a hallmark of psychological trauma, or, if they participate, they may have more difficulty seeing their response as normal when others report a less intense reaction. Conversely, there is the potential for those who are severely traumatized to cause distress in otherwise asymptomatic individuals when everyone in the group is sharing detailed personal accounts of the traumatic experience. As originally designed, CISD would gather people who know one another, such as firefighter units. However, sharing traumatic experiences with strangers, such as in mass-disaster sites, could be maladaptive. In single-session approaches there is little time to become familiar with others. There are potential ethical implications if all trauma victims are mandated to attend the session and disclose to others, as may happen in work-related incidents. In addition, single-session approaches may not provide sufficient opportunities to practice new skills.*

CBT Prevention Models. According to the National Institute for Clinical Excellence in the United Kingdom, the International Society for Traumatic Stress Studies, the American Psychological Association, and the American Psychiatric Association, CBT is the only rigorously scientifically evidence-based intervention for the prevention of PTSD. CBT usually is not conducted until 4–6 weeks after a traumatic event has occurred, except when the person develops severe impairment such as an ASD. Studies have shown that most individuals who experience a traumatic event recover without developing PTSD by the 6-week postevent time-point, even if they have distressing stress reactions in the acute period (McNally et al., 2003). However, an estimated 80% of people who develop ASD go on to suffer PTSD (Bryant, 2008). Whether the focus is on ASD or acute PTSD, CBT in the early postevent period (i.e., within 3–6 months of the event) tends to be done in five 60- to 90-minute sessions (National Institute of Clinical Excellence, 2014; Steenkamp, Papa, & Litz, 2008). Although CBT as a secondary prevention intervention follows the same general format and uses the same therapeutic and educational techniques as CBT for chronic PTSD (see Chapter 7), the psychoeducation focuses on acute stress reactions to traumatic events, and the exposure therapy component usually is much briefer (but no less intensive). The other CBT components for PTSD prevention are anxiety management skills training, cognitive restructuring, imaginal and *in vivo* therapeutic exposure, and relapse prevention (education to enable the individual to anticipate and successfully handle future stressors and symptoms).

In the imaginal exposure component, the person is helped to recall and retell her or his perceptions, emotions, thoughts, and actions as vividly as possible as if the event was happening at that moment. The therapist helps individuals to both focus intently on their actual experience and to know that they are actually safe and nothing bad really is happening. This is intended to experientially demonstrate to the trauma survivor that even very vivid recollections of the traumatic event, while initially anxiety provoking, are manageable and actually become less distressing the more they are purposefully recalled with an increasing awareness of the full range of perceptions, feelings, and thoughts that often happen so rapidly or are so intense that the individual has only a blurred or fragmentary memory. Exposure therapy in this acute posttrauma period thus may help the person to develop a reworked memory that is more complete and coherent than if they attempted to avoid recalling the memory. Paradoxically, the more that traumatic memories are recalled in this early phase, the less that they seem to intrude in ways and at times that are distressing—and the less hyperarousal and hypervigilance they trigger.

Rigorous scientific research studies have found CBT to be significantly more effective than SC or no treatment for ASD (Forneris et al., 2013; Kearns, Ressler, Zatzick, & Rothbaum, 2012). One study showed that five 90-minute weekly sessions of CBT was associated with substantially fewer participants who entered treatment with ASD developing PTSD (8–17%) than comparable individuals with ASD who received SC (67–83%) (Bryant, Harvey, Dang, Sackville, & Basten, 1998). Another study that enrolled motor vehicle accident survivors 4 months after the incidents found that only 11% who received 15 sessions of CBT developed PTSD at a 9-month follow-up, compared to 61% who received a self-help educational booklet (Ehlers et al., 2003). However, a study of CBT with female sexual and physical assault survivors within 1 month of the assault found it to have no greater benefit than SC (Foa, Zoellner, & Feeny, 2006). Several factors may have reduced the efficacy of CBT, including the timing of the intervention (relatively soon after the assault, rather than several months later as in the Ehlers et al. study), the inclusion of women who did not have ASD as well as those who did (potentially leading to more improvement than if all participants had sufficiently severe symptoms to warrant and ASD diagnosis), and the complex nature of interpersonal and sexual violence (which may require more extensive or adapted forms of CBT).

Zatzick et al. (2004) adapted the "stepped collaborative care" intervention, which has been shown to be cost-effective in treating mild to moderate depression with primary medical care patients (Katon et al., 2012) for acutely injured adults with PTSD symptoms. The intervention is adjusted ("stepped") by a clinical case manager who develops a treatment plan with coordinated medical and psychological services that are designed to match the nature and severity of the patient's symptoms. Instead of providing services only through periodic appointments or sessions at the hospital or clinic and requiring the patient to return to the emergency department for costly additional acute care if problems arise, the collaborative care model includes having the case manager available to be contacted at all times and helps the patient with related nonmedical/psychiatric issues such as problems with work or family. In addition, because alcohol abuse can severely complicate postinjury recovery and often is a comorbidity of PTSD (see Chapter 3), patients are screened for potential alcohol use problems and receive a brief motivational interviewing (Miller & Rollnick, 2009) intervention if they are at risk. A psychiatric evaluation was provided immediately to patients who expressed severe and sustained (for more than 24 hours) PTSD symptoms or related psychological distress. At a follow-up evaluation 3 months after the traumatic injury and subsequent follow-up assessments that continued until a year after the initial emergency admission, patients were assessed by structured interview, and those with PTSD could choose to receive CBT, pharmacotherapy, or both. Patients were randomly assigned to collaborative care or to a control condition in which they received standard emergency room and hospital care and a list of referrals to mental health providers in the community before leaving the hospital. Patients in the collaborative care condition had better mental health outcomes, less severe PTSD symptoms, and fewer symptoms of alcohol abuse/dependence than those in the control group. Collaborative care recipients did not develop PTSD or alcohol dependence disorders after receiving PTSD psychotherapy and/or pharmacotherapy, whereas a number of control patients developed or continued to experience those disorders. Additional statistical analyses were conducted to identify different trajectories (see Chapter 4) of PTSD and related problems over the follow-up period for these traumatized injured individuals, demonstrating that those with severe symptoms of PTSD, depression, or alcohol dependence and ethnoracial minority group members were at risk for chronic PTSD unless they received collaborative care—in which case they tended to be on a PTSD trajectory characterized by resilience (to have at most mild to moderate symptoms) or recovery (to reduce their severity of their symptoms to mild/moderate levels) (Osenbach et al., 2014). A replication study was conducted with traumatized injury survivors whose medical complications required hospitalization (Zatzick et al., 2013), with collaborative care recipients demonstrating greater reductions in PTSD symptoms and improvements in overall health and functioning than patients receiving usual care. Thus, the stepped collaborative care is an effective secondary prevention intervention for PTSD with both acutely traumatized adults with a range of severity of injuries.

Shalev et al. (2012) evaluated a similar PTSD secondary prevention program—the Jerusalem Trauma Outreach and Prevention—with patients who were survivors of traumatic events seen in the Hadassah Hospital emergency department. Structured interviews were done by telephone on average 10 days after the traumatic event(s), and individuals reporting symptoms of ASD were referred for clinical assessment; those who had moderate to severe levels of PTSD symptoms were invited to receive treatment that consisted of 12 weekly sessions of PE or CT, or pharmacotherapy with either a selective serotonin reuptake inhibitor antidepressant medication or a placebo, or 12 weeks in a wait-list group. Treatment started on average 1 month after the traumatic event. Assessment of PTSD using the Clinician-Administered PTSD Scale 5 and 9 months after the traumatic event showed a dramatic difference, with only one in five individuals who received PE (22%) or CT (20%) being diagnosed with PTSD at the 5-month assessment (versus almost 60% of the wait-list control participants). The PTSD prevalence rates did not differ between the antidepressant and placebo groups, both of which were comparable to the wait-list (62% versus 56% diagnosed with PTSD). At the 9-month follow-up assessment, 21% of participants who received PE had PTSD. The wait-list control participants received PE after the waiting period of 3 months, and at the 9-month assessment, only one in five of them had PTSD. Participants who reported symptoms of PTSD before treatment that were not sufficient to qualify as PTSD but that were a lesser or "partial" form of PTSD did similarly well with and without treatment. The results indicate that evidence-based psychotherapy for PTSD delivered a month following a traumatic stressor prevents the immediate development of PTSD, and when delivered at a 3- to 4-month delay, it effectively prevents longer-term development of PTSD. Antidepressant medication showed no evidence of benefit in preventing PTSD. The findings also suggest that many individuals with mild to moderate symptoms of PTSD in the first month after exposure to a traumatic stressor do not require preventive intervention.

Pharmacological Prevention of PTSD. Propranolol, an antihypertensive (blood pressure) medicine that blocks neurons that are receptors for noradrenaline-stimulated chemical signals, has been shown (when administered on average 4 hours after going to a hospital emergency department) to potentially reduce physiological reactivity to memories of traumatic events several months later. Pitman et al. (2002) prescribed propranolol or a placebo (inactive) pill to accident and violence victims for the next 10 days. One month later, those who received propanolol reported less severe PTSD symptoms. Three months later, there was no difference in PTSD symptoms, but the propanolol recipients were less physiologically reactive when listening to a vivid script of their traumatic experience than the placebo recipients. However, a recent study administered propanolol, a medication designed originally to prevent seizures (and more recently found to be effective with bipolar disorder; gabapentin), or placebo within 48 hours of injury to patients admitted to a medical-surgical trauma center. One, 4, or 8 months later, neither medication was associated with lower PTSD or depression symptom severity (Stein, Kerridge, Dimsdale, & Hoyt, 2007). Thus, the utility of blocking hyperarousal noradrenergically with medications such as propranolol soon after an injury remains uncertain.

Given the limited and inconsistent evidence (including most recently the Shalev et al., 2012, study), neither the International Society for Traumatic Stress Studies (Friedman & Davidson, 2008) nor the American Psychiatric Association currently recommends pharmacotherapy for the prevention of ASD or PTSD. However, there remain many potential biological pathways that contribute to the evolution of PTSD (see Chapter 5) that warrant further research in order to identify medications—or combinations of medications with promising psychotherapeutic approaches such as CBT—that may contribute to the secondary or tertiary prevention of PTSD.

PTSD Prevention with Children. A recent national survey of adults found that the median age of PTSD onset was 23 years of age (Kessler et al., 2005). Thus, many children and youth who experience traumatic stressors but are not identified as in need of treatment because of not developing severe PTSD symptoms may go on to develop delayed PTSD in adulthood unless preventive interventions are provided to those at risk. This underscores the value of identifying and delivering evidence-based treatment to adolescents with PTSD before they reach adulthood, as well as selective prevention interventions for children and adolescents who are at risk for PTSD before PTSD symptoms emerge, or on a targeted basis before posttraumatic symptoms crystallize into a disorder involving serious developmental and psychosocial impairment.

Although the development of interventions designed to prevent PTSD following trauma exposure is an emerging area, several approaches have been examined in the adult and child literature. Most selective and targeted prevention interventions include one or more of the following therapeutic approaches: psychoeducation to normalize posttraumatic stress reactions and symptoms, debriefing to promote emotional processing of the experience and impact of exposure to traumatic stressors, PFA, increased communication within the family, and enhanced coping skills (Marsac, Donlon, & Berkowitz, 2014). However, the evidence in support of each of these individual components is inconsistent.

Psychoeducation, for example, is a common component of many preventive interventions, but it has not been sufficiently studied independently to determine its comparative effectiveness in preventing PTSD (Forneris et al., 2013; Pfefferbaum, Varma, Nitiema, & Newman, 2014). Psychological debriefing in the immediate aftermath of a traumatic event had been widely espoused as a method of reducing distress and preventing PTSD. As just noted, reviews of randomized controlled studies of adults have concluded that this approach does not prevent PTSD and may, in fact, lead to an increased rate of PTSD by interfering with the natural recovery process (Forneris et al, 2013; Kearns et al., 2012). A review of debriefing studies with children found them to be methodologically inconsistent in terms of what constitutes "debriefing" and the timing of the intervention, with some studies describing delayed delivery up to several months following the traumatic event. Outcomes were also inconsistent, with some studies finding positive effects, and others no effect, although none found it to be harmful (as some adult studies have) (Pfefferbaum, Newman, & Nelson, 2014). However, the only study of debriefing with children who had experienced recent severe motor vehicle accidents found that the intervention had no discernible benefit in reducing subsequent PTSD (Stallard et al., 2006).

Although PFA has been adapted (Vernberg & Jacobs, 2008) or incorporated into crisis intervention programs (Brymer & Kassam-Adams, 2008; Marans, Smolover, & Hahn, 2012) for acutely traumatized children, it has not been systematically evaluated with children or adolescents (Marsac et al., 2014). Nevertheless, PFA's components (promoting safety and comfort, stabilization, connecting individuals with social and community supports, providing practical assistance, offering information about responses to trauma and coping) are each evidence-informed by current knowledge on the prevention and treatment of PTSD.

Two studies have evaluated the stepped collaborative care model with children. Zatzick et al. (2014) provided stepped collaborative care to injured adolescents during the year after screening and assessment for PTSD in the emergency room. Severe PTSD, depression, or alcohol and substance abuse symptoms were rare in this sample and were not improved more by the collaborative care intervention than by usual care. However, fully one-third of these teens carried weapons at the time of their injury, and by the 1-year follow-up assessment, only 7% receiving collaborative care were still carrying weapons (compared to three times as many, 21%, of youth receiving usual care). This reduction also was observed with youth who had sustained a traumatic brain injury. Kassam-Adams et al. (2011) evaluated a stepped collaborative care targeted prevention intervention with younger children hospitalized for injuries. Following universal screening, children identified at risk of developing PTSD were randomized to receive usual care or an intervention consisting of psychoeducation about traumatic stress, assessment of PTSD and other emotional and behavioral problems, and, as needed, one or more of the stepped care services: case management to ensure that the child's medical care and communication between the medical providers were meeting the child's needs and effectively engaging the child in adherence to medical regimens; brief therapy to parent-child intervention; psychiatric evaluation for severe emotional or behavioral problems, such as depression; and TF-CBT for children with PTSD. Similar to the Zatzick et al. (2014) findings, no differences in PTSD or depression symptoms emerged between the collaborative care and usual care groups.

The CFTSI (Berkowitz, Stover, & Marans, 2011) is a four-session child and caregiver intervention conducted within 30 days of a potentially traumatic event that utilizes psychoeducation and behavioral and cognitive approaches to managing traumatic symptoms, with the aim of increasing familial support, parent-child communication, and coping resources. A randomized controlled trial comparing CFTSI to a four-session supportive intervention found that intervention group had lower rates of PTSD and less severe PTSD and anxiety symptoms at a 3-month follow-up after the intervention was concluded. Thus, although the extensive intervention provided by stepped collaborative care may not be necessary if injured children are provided with effective medical care, a briefer focused PTSD prevention intervention for the child and family shows promise with acutely traumatized children and youth. It also is possible that stepped collaborative care may be needed, and effective, if the subgroup of acutely injured children and youth who are experiencing severe PTSD, depression, or alcohol/substance use problems are targeted rather than evaluating the intervention on a selective basis. The striking finding of reduced carrying of weapons by teens receiving stepped collaborative care suggests that the intervention has a positive impact with youth who are highly hypervigilant.

Pharmacotherapy generally has not proven effective as a prevention strategy for acutely injured children, with one exception. Studies of the use of propranolol with acutely injured children to prevent PTSD have not found evidence of effectiveness (Kearns et al., 2012; Nugent et al., 2010; Sharp, Thomas, Rosenberg, Rosenberg, & Meyer, 2010). A randomized controlled trial of sertraline use with severely burned children documented a decrease in children's PTSD symptoms as compared to placebo by parent report, but not by the child's self-report of PTSD symptoms (Stoddard et al, 2011).

However, studies of morphine use with acutely injured children suggest that reducing pain intensity may prevent PTSD (Marsac et al, 2014). Sheridan et al. (2014) reassessed children and adolescents 4 years after hospitalization for severe burns and found that PTSD symptoms were inversely correlated with the dose of morphine provided during acute burn care. While promising, these findings do not demonstrate that opiate (morphine) treatment effectively prevents PTSD but instead indicate that medical care for children who are in physical pain should carefully monitor and take timely steps to reduce the pain to tolerable levels in order to reduce the long-term severity of PTSD symptoms. The risk of chronic addictive opiate use after acute use of opiates in hospital care also requires extreme caution (Holman, Stoddard, & Higgins, 2013).

In addition to the selective and targeted early intervention approaches just described, resilience-enhancing pretrauma interventions aimed at preventing pediatric PTSD also are being developed. Pfefferbaum et al. (2014) identified five studies of predisaster preparedness interventions for children (three from the same group of investigators) largely conducted in school settings using a combination of PTSD psychoeducation and CBT techniques to increase disaster awareness, prevent exposure to hazardous conditions in disasters, and build resilience with cognitive and behavioral coping strategies. Although the results were not entirely consistent across the five studies, the general result was that preparedness programs were associated with less severe postdisaster PTSD symptoms.

Promising screening measures have been developed to identify children who recently experienced traumatic events and are at particular risk of developing PTSD (Kassam-Adams, 2008). For example, the Screening Tool for Early Predictors of PTSD (STEPP) provides seriously injured children and parents with a way to identify acute stress reactions and other potential indicators of risk of PTSD (such as prior behavioral problems, separation from parents at the time of the injury, fear and believing death might occur at the time of the trauma, injury or death of others in the same event, gender, having a fractured arm or leg, and high heart rate) with the help of emergency department clinicians. Tests of prevention interventions with children who not only have experienced traumatic stressors but are at greatest risk of developing PTSD offer an important avenue for potentially more effective selective prevention of PTSD.

Conclusion

Although most people who experience a traumatic stressor do not develop PTSD, "a salient and often silent minority will go on to develop chronic PTSD" (Steenkamp et al., 2008). In view of the debilitating and potentially lifelong impairment that can occur when PTSD develops and becomes chronic, early intervention to prevent PTSD is of substantial humanitarian, economic, and social as well as psychological importance. Brief targeted or stepped collaborative care CBT has a strong research and clinical track record and should be considered the front-line treatment for recently traumatized adults, youth, and children who are experiencing persistent impairment in their lives or well-being as a result of severe acute traumatic stress reactions. However, CBT is not a panacea (particularly for children who are experiencing acute but ongoing rather than time-limited traumatic stressors that involve bodily violation, such as sexual abuse or assault, or lengthy periods of helplessness and traumatization, such as childhood abuse, family violence, war, or political violence and torture). No medication as yet has been shown to prevent PTSD, either, despite promising research results suggesting that medication may interrupt the body's stress reactions (e.g., by reducing physical pain or depression symptoms) in ways that may prevent or begin to reverse the posttraumatic biological shift from healthy development (the "learning brain") to the "survival brain" (PTSD; see Chapter 5).

References

Augustyn, M., & Groves, B. M. (2005). Training clinicians to identify the hidden victims: Children and adolescents who witness violence. *American Journal of Preventive Medicine*, *29*(5 Suppl. 2), 272–278.

Berkowitz, S. J., Stover, C. S., & Marans, S. R. (2011). The child and family traumatic stress intervention: Secondary prevention for youth at risk of developing PTSD. *Journal of Child Psychology and Psychiatry and Allied Disciplines*, *52*(6), 676–685.

Briggs-Gowan, M. J., Carter, A. S., Clark, R., Augustyn, M., McCarthy, K. J., & Ford, J. D. (2010). Exposure to potentially traumatic events in early childhood: Differential links to emergent psychopathology. *Journal of Child Psychology and Psychiatry and Allied Disciplines*, *51*(10), 1132–1140. http://dx.doi.org/10.1111/j.1469-7610.2010.02256.x.

Briggs-Gowan, M. J., Carter, A. S., & Ford, J. D. (2012). Parsing the effects violence exposure in early childhood: Modeling developmental pathways. *Journal of Pediatric Psychology*, *37*(1), 11–22. http://dx.doi.org/10.1093/jpepsy/jsr063.

Brom, D., & Kleber, R. (2008). Resilience as the capacity for processing traumatic experiences. In D. Brom, R. Pat-Horenczyk, & J. Ford (Eds.), *Treating traumatized children* (pp. 133–149). London: Routledge.

Bronfenbrenner, U. (Ed.). (1979). *The ecology of human development: Experiments by nature and design*. Cambridge: Harvard University Press.

Bryant, R. (2008). Memory. In G. Reyes, J. D. Elhai, & J. D. Ford (Eds.), *Encyclopedia of psychological trauma* (pp. 424–426). Hoboken, NJ: Wiley.

Bryant, R. A., Harvey, A. G., Dang, S. T., Sackville, T., & Basten, C. (1998). Treatment of acute stress disorder: A comparison of cognitive-behavioral therapy and supportive counseling. *Journal of Consulting and Clinical Psychology*, *66*, 862–866.

Brymer, M., & Kassam-Adams, N. (2008). Crisis interventions, child. In G. Reyes, J. D. Elhai, & J. Ford (Eds.), *Encyclopedia of psychological trauma* (pp. 179–182). Hoboken, NJ: Wiley.

Burgess, A. W., & Holmstrom, L. L. (1974). Rape trauma syndrome. *American Journal of Psychiatry, 131*, 981–986.

Centers for Disease Prevention, (2004). *Sexual violence prevention: Beginning the dialogue.* Atlanta, GA: Author.

Chapleau, K. M., & Oswald, D. L. (2014). A system justification view of sexual violence: Legitimizing gender inequality and reduced moral outrage are connected to greater rape myth acceptance. *Journal of Trauma and Dissociation, 15*(2), 204–218.

Copeland, W. E., Keeler, G., Angold, A., & Costello, E. J. (2007). Traumatic events and posttraumatic stress in childhood. *Archives of General Psychiatry, 64*, 577–584.

Cummings, E. M., El-Sheikh, M., Kouros, C. D., & Buckhalt, J. A. (2009). Children and violence: The role of children's regulation in the marital aggression-child adjustment link. *Clinical Child and Family Psychology Review, 12*(1), 3–15. http://dx.doi.org/10.1007/s10567-009-0042-7.

Davies, P. T., Sturge-Apple, M. L., Cicchetti, D., & Cummings, E. M. (2007). The role of child adrenocortical functioning in pathways between interparental conflict and child maladjustment. *Developmental Psychology, 43*(4), 918–930. http://dx.doi.org/2007-09251-010 [pii]; http://dx.doi.org/10.1037/0012-1649.43.4.918.

Delker, B. C., Noll, L. K., Kim, H. K., & Fisher, P. A. (2014). Maternal abuse history and self-regulation difficulties in preadolescence. *Child Abuse and Neglect, 38*(12), 2033–2043.

Dubowitz, H. (2014). The Safe Environment for Every Kid (SEEK) model: Helping promote children's health, development, and safety: SEEK offers a practical model for enhancing pediatric primary care. *Child Abuse and Neglect, 38*(11), 1725–1733.

Ehlers, A., Clark, D. M., Hackmann, A., McManus, F., Fennell, M., Herbert, C., et al. (2003). A randomized controlled trial of cognitive therapy, a self-help booklet, and repeated assessments as early interventions for posttraumatic stress disorder. *Archives of General Psychiatry, 60*, 1024–1032.

Ehlers, A., Mayou, R. A., & Bryant, B. (2003). Cognitive predictors of posttraumatic stress disorder in children: Results of a prospective longitudinal study. *Behaviour Research and Therapy, 41*(1), 1–10. http://dx.doi.org/S0005796701001267 [pii].

Everly, G. S., Flannery, R. B., & Mitchell, J. T. (2000). Critical incident stress management: A review of the literature. *Aggression and Violent Behavior, 5*, 23–40.

Farrington, D. P. (1991). Childhood aggression and adult violence: Early precursors and life outcomes. In D. J. Pepler & K. H. Rubin (Eds.), *The development and treatment of childhood aggression.* Hillsdale, NJ: Lawrence Erlbaum.

Foa, E. B., Zoellner, L. A., & Feeny, N. C. (2006). An evaluation of three brief programs for facilitating recovery after assault. *Journal of Traumatic Stress, 19*, 29–43.

Ford, J. D. (2005). Treatment implications of altered affect regulation and information processing following child maltreatment. *Psychiatric Annals, 35*(5), 410–419.

Ford, J. D. (2009). Neurobiological and developmental research: Clinical implications. In C. A. Courtois & J. D. Ford (Eds.), *Treating complex traumatic stress disorders: An evidence-based guide* (pp. 31–58). New York: Guilford Press.

Ford, J. D. (2013). Identifying and caring for acutely traumatized children. *Consultant for Pediatricians, 12*(4), 182–187.

Ford, J. D., Chapman, J. C., Connor, D. F., & Cruise, K. C. (2012). Complex trauma and aggression in secure juvenile justice settings. *Criminal Justice & Behavior, 39*(5), 695–724.

Ford, J. D., Gagnon, K., Connor, D. F., & Pearson, G. (2011). History of interpersonal violence, abuse, and nonvictimization trauma and severity of psychiatric symptoms among children in outpatient psychiatric treatment. *Journal of Interpersonal Violence, 26*(16), 3316–3337.

Ford, J. D., Hartman, J. K., Hawke, J., & Chapman, J. (2008). Traumatic victimization posttraumatic stress disorder, suicidal ideation, and substance abuse risk among juvenile justice-involved youths. *Journal of Child and Adolescent Trauma, 1*, 75–92.

Forneris, C. A., Gartlehner, G., Brownley, K. A., Gaynes, B. N., Sonis, J., Coker-Schwimmer, E., et al. (2013). Interventions to prevent post-traumatic stress disorder: A systematic review. *American Journal of Preventive Medicine, 44*(6), 635–650.

Franzese, R. J., Covey, H. C., Tucker, A. S., McCoy, L., & Menard, S. (2014). Adolescent exposure to violence and adult physical and mental health problems. *Child Abuse and Neglect, 38*(12), 1955–1965.

Frey, K. S., Hirschstein, M. K., & Guzzo, B. A. (2000). Second step: Preventing aggression by promoting social competence. *Journal of Emotional and Behavioral Disorders, 8*, 102–112.

Friedman, M. J., & Davidson, J. R. T. (2008). Pharmacotherapy for PTSD. In M. J. Friedman, T. M. Keane, & P. Resick (Eds.), *Handbook of PTSD: Science and practice* (pp. 245–268). New York: Guilford.

Gelkopf, M., & Berger, R. (2009). A school-based, teacher-mediated prevention program (ERASE-Stress) for reducing terror-related traumatic reactions in Israeli youth: A quasi-randomized controlled trial. *Journal of Child Psychology and Psychiatry and Allied Disciplines, 50*(8), 962–971. http://dx.doi.org/10.1111/j.1469-7610.2008.02021.x.

Gottfredson, L. S. (2000). Skills gaps, not tests, make racial proportionality impossible. *Psychology Public Policy and Law, 6*(1), 129–143.

Graham-Bermann, S. A., Gruber, G., Howell, K. H., & Girz, L. (2009). Factors discriminating among profiles of resilience and psychopathology in children exposed to intimate partner violence (IPV). *Child Abuse and Neglect, 33*(9), 648–660.

Grasso, D. J., Ford, J. D., & Briggs-Gowan, M. J. (2013). Early life trauma exposure and stress sensitivity in young children. *Journal of Pediatric Psychology, 38*(1), 94–103. http://dx.doi.org/10.1093/jpepsy/jss101.

Hall, B. J., Bolton, P. A., Annan, J., Kaysen, D., Robinette, K., Cetinoglu, T., et al. (2014). The effect of cognitive therapy on structural social capital: Results from a randomized controlled trial among sexual violence survivors in the Democratic Republic of the Congo. *American Journal of Public Health, 104*(9), 1680–1686.

Hembree, E., & Cohen, S. (2008). Rape trauma. In G. Reyes, J. D. Elhai, & J. Ford (Eds.), *Encyclopedia of psychological trauma* (pp. 564–571). Hoboken, NJ: Wiley.

Hibel, L. C., Granger, D. A., Blair, C., Cox, M. J., & Family Life Project Key Investigators, (2009). Intimate partner violence moderates the association between mother-infant adrenocortical activity across an emotional challenge. *Journal of Family Psychology, 23*(5), 615–625. http://dx.doi.org/10.1037/a0016323.

Hibel, L. C., Granger, D. A., Blair, C., Cox, M. J., & Family Life Project Key Investigators, (2011). Maternal sensitivity buffers the adrenocortical implications of intimate partner violence exposure during early childhood. *Development and Psychopathology, 23*(2), 689–701. http://dx.doi.org/10.1017/S0954579411000010.

Holman, J. E., Stoddard, G. J., & Higgins, T. F. (2013). Rates of prescription opiate use before and after injury in patients with orthopaedic trauma and the risk factors for prolonged opiate use. *Journal of Bone and Joint Surgery, 95*(12), 1075–1080.

Howell, K. H., & Miller-Graff, L. E. (2014). Protective factors associated with resilient functioning in young adulthood after childhood exposure to violence. *Child Abuse and Neglect, 38*(12), 1985–1994.

Hungerford, A., Wait, S., Fritz, A., & Clements, C. M. (2012). Exposure to intimate partner violence and children's psychological adjustment, cognitive functioning, and social competence: A review. *Aggression and Violent Behavior, 17*, 373–382.

Kassam-Adams, N., Garcia-Espana, J. F., Marsac, M. L., Kohser, K. L., Baxt, C., Nance, M., et al. (2011). A pilot randomized controlled trial assessing secondary prevention of traumatic stress integrated into pediatric trauma care. *Journal of Traumatic Stress, 24*(3), 252–259.

Katon, W., Russo, J., Lin, E. H., Schmittdiel, J., Ciechanowski, P., Ludman, E., et al. (2012). Cost-effectiveness of a multicondition collaborative care intervention: A randomized controlled trial. *Archives of General Psychiatry, 69*(5), 506–514.

Kearns, M. C., Ressler, K. J., Zatzick, D., & Rothbaum, B. O. (2012). Early interventions for PTSD: A review. *Depression and Anxiety, 29*(10), 833–842.

Kessler, R. C., Berglund, P., Demler, O., Jin, R., Merikangas, K., & Walters, E. E. (2005). Lifetime prevalence and age-of-onset distributions of DSM-IV disorders in the national comorbidity survey replication. *Archives of General Psychiatry, 62*, 593–602.

Kitzmann, K. M., Gaylord, N. K., Holt, A. R., & Kenny, E. D. (2003). Child witnesses to domestic violence: A meta-analytic review. *Journal of Consulting and Clinical Psychology, 71*(2), 339–352.

Maguire, K., & Pastore, A. L. (1999). *Sourcebook of criminal justice statistics, 1998*. Albany, NY: Hindelang Criminal Justice Research Center.

Marans, S., Smolover, D., & Hahn, H. (2012). Responding to child trauma: Theory, programs, and policy. In E. L. Grigorenko (Ed.), *Handbook of juvenile forensic psychology and psychiatry* (pp. 453–466). New York: Springer.

Marsac, M. L., Donlon, K., & Berkowitz, S. (2014). Indicated and selective preventive interventions. *Child and Adolescent Psychiatric Clinics of North America, 23*(2), 383–397. x.

McLaughlin, K. A., Koenen, K. C., Hill, E. D., Petukhova, M., Sampson, N. A., Zaslavsky, A. M., et al. (2013). Trauma exposure and posttraumatic stress disorder in a national sample of adolescents. *Journal of the American Academy of Child and Adolescent Psychiatry, 52*(8) 815–830.e814. http://dx.doi.org/10.1016/j.jaac.2013.05.011.

McSweeney, L., Dickstein, B., & Litz, B. T. (2008). Critical incident stress management. In G. Reyes, J. D. Elhai, & J. D. Ford (Eds.), *Encyclopedia of psychological trauma* (pp. 183–186). Hoboken, NJ: Wiley.

Menard, S., Weiss, A. J., Franzese, R. J., & Covey, H. C. (2014). Types of adolescent exposure to violence as predictors of adult intimate partner violence. *Child Abuse and Neglect, 38*(4), 627–639.

Miller, L. E., Howell, K. H., & Graham-Bermann, S. A. (2012). Potential mediators of adjustment for preschool children exposed to intimate partner violence. *Child Abuse and Neglect, 36*(9), 671–675.

Miller, W. R., & Rollnick, S. (2009). Ten things that motivational interviewing is not. *Behavioral and Cognitive Psychotherapy, 37*(2), 129–140.

Nation, M., Crusto, C., Wandersman, A., Kumpfer, K. L., Seybolt, D., Morrissey-Kane, E., et al. (2003). What works in prevention – Principles of effective prevention programs. *American Psychologist, 58*, 449–456.

National Center of Clinical Excellence (2014). *Post-traumatic stress disorder overview.* <http://pathways.nice.org.uk/pathways/post-traumatic-stressdisorder>.

NCTSN and NCPTSD (2006). *This is not published.* Available on-line at <http://www.nctsn.org/content/psychological-first-aid>Accessed 14.04.15.

Nugent, N., Christopher, N., Crow, J., Browne, L., Ostrowski, S., & Delahanty, D. (2010). The efficacy of early propanolol administration at reducing PTSD symptoms in pediatric injury patients: A pilot study. *Journal of Traumatic Stress, 23*, 282–287.

Osenbach, J. E., Lewis, C., Rosenfeld, B., Russo, J., Ingraham, L. M., Peterson, R., et al. (2014). Exploring the longitudinal trajectories of posttraumatic stress disorder in injured trauma survivors. *Psychiatry, 77*(4), 386–397.

Pfefferbaum, B., Newman, E., & Nelson, S. D. (2014). Mental health interventions for children exposed to disasters and terrorism. *Journal of Child and Adolescent Psychopharmacology*, *24*(1), 24–31.

Pfefferbaum, B., Varma, V., Nitiema, P., & Newman, E. (2014). Universal preventive interventions for children in the context of disasters and terrorism. *Child and Adolescent Psychiatric Clinics of North America*, *23*(2), 363–382. ix-x.

Pitman, R. K., Sanders, K. M., Zusman, R. M., Healy, A. R., Cheema, F., Lasko, N. B., et al. (2002). Pilot study of secondary prevention of posttraumatic stress disorder with propranolol. *Biological Psychiatry*, *51*(2), 189–192.

Reid, J. B., & Eddy, J. M. (1997). The prevention of antisocial behavior. In D. M. Stoff, J. Breiling, & J. D. Maser (Eds.), *The handbook of antisocial behavior* (pp. 343–356). New York: Wiley.

Reid-Quinones, K., Kliewer, W., Shields, B. J., Goodman, K., Ray, M. H., & Wheat, E. (2011). Cognitive, affective, and behavioral responses to witnessed versus experienced violence. *American Journal of Orthopsychiatry*, *81*(1), 51–60.

Resnick, H., Acierno, R., Waldrop, A. E., King, L., King, D., Danielson, C., et al. (2007). Randomized controlled evaluation of an early intervention to prevent post-rape psychopathology. *Behaviour Research and Therapy*, *45*, 2432–2447.

Rigterink, T., Fainsilber Katz, L., & Hessler, D. M. (2010). Domestic violence and longitudinal associations with children's physiological regulation abilities. *Journal of Interpersonal Violence*, *25*(9), 1669–1683. http://dx.doi.org/10.1177/0886260509354589.

Saxe, G., MacDonald, H., & Ellis, H. (2007). Psychosocial approaches for children with PTSD. In E. B. Foa, M. J. Friedman, T. M. Keane, & P. Resick (Eds.), *Handbook of PTSD: Science and practice* (pp. 359–375). New York: Guilford.

Schiff, M., Plotnikova, M., Dingle, K., Williams, G. M., Najman, J., & Clavarino, A. (2014). Does adolescent's exposure to parental intimate partner conflict and violence predict psychological distress and substance use in young adulthood? A longitudinal study. *Child Abuse and Neglect*, *38*(12), 1945–1954.

Shalev, A. Y., Ankri, Y., Israeli-Shalev, Y., Peleg, T., Adessky, R., & Freedman, S. (2012). Prevention of posttraumatic stress disorder by early treatment: Results from the jerusalem trauma outreach and prevention study. *Archives of General Psychiatry*, *69*(2), 166–176. http://dx.doi.org/10.1001/archgenpsychiatry.2011.127.

Sharp, S., Thomas, C., Rosenberg, L., Rosenberg, M., & Meyer, W., III (2010). Propranolol does not reduce risk for acute stress disorder in pediatric burn trauma. *The Journal of Trauma*, *68*(1), 193–197.

Sheridan, R. L., Stoddard, F. J., Kazis, L. E., Lee, A., Li, N. C., Kagan, R. J., et al. (2014). Long-term posttraumatic stress symptoms vary inversely with early opiate dosing in children recovering from serious burns: Effects durable at 4 years. *Journal of Trauma and Acute Care Surgery*, *76*(3), 828–832.

Sherman, L. W., Gottfredson, D. C., MacKenzie, D. L., Eck, J., Reuter, P., & Bushway, S. D. (1997). *Preventing crime: What works, what doesn't, what's promising. A report to the United States Congress [NCH 171676]*. Washington, DC: US Department of Justice, Office of Justice Programs.

Skeem, J. L., Scott, E., & Mulvey, E. P. (2014). Justice policy reform for high-risk juveniles: Using science to achieve large-scale crime reduction. *Annual Review of Clinical Psychology*, *10*, 709–739. http://dx.doi.org/10.1146/annurev-clinpsy-032813-153707.

Skeffington, P. M., Rees, C. S., & Kane, R. (2013). The primary prevention of PTSD: A systematic review. *Journal of Trauma and Dissociation*, *14*(4), 404–422.

Smid, G. E., Mooren, T. T., van der Mast, R. C., Gersons, B. P., & Kleber, R. J. (2009). Delayed posttraumatic stress disorder: Systematic review, meta-analysis, and meta-regression analysis of prospective studies. *Journal of Clinical Psychiatry*, *70*(11), 1572–1582.

Smith, C. P., & Freyd, J. J. (2014). Institutional betrayal. *American Psychologist*, *69*(6), 575–587. http://dx.doi.org/10.1037/a0037564.

Sones, H. M., Thorp, S. R., & Raskind, M. (2011). Prevention of posttraumatic stress disorder. *Psychiatric Clinics of North America*, *34*(1), 79–94.

Stallard, P., Velleman, R., Salter, E., Howse, I., Yule, W., & Taylor, G. (2006). A randomised controlled trial to determine the effectiveness of an early psychological intervention with children involved in road traffic accidents. *Journal of Child Psychology and Psychiatry*, *47*, 127–134.

Steenkamp, M., Papa, A., & Litz, B. T. (2008). Prevention, adult. In G. Reyes, J. D. Elhai, & J. Ford (Eds.), *Encyclopedia of psychological trauma* (pp. 505–511). Hoboken NJ: Wiley.

Stein, M. B., Kerridge, C., Dimsdale, J. E., & Hoyt, D. B. (2007). Pharmacotherapy to prevent PTSD: Results from a randomized controlled proof-of-concept trial in physically injured patients. *Journal of Traumatic Stress*, *20*, 923–932.

Stoddard, F. J., Jr., et al., Luthra, R., Sorrentino, E. A., Saxe, G. N., Drake, J., Chang, Y., et al. (2011). A randomized controlled trial of sertraline to prevent posttraumatic stress disorder in burned children. *Journal of Child and Adolescent Psychopharmacology*, *21*(5), 469–477.

Taylor, J. E., & Harvey, S. T. (2010). A meta-analysis of the effects of psychotherapy with adults sexually abused in childhood. *Clinical Psychology Review*, *30*(6), 749–767.

Thornton, T. N., Craft, C. A., Dahlberg, L. L., Lynch, B. S., & Baer, K. (2000). *Best practices of youth violence prevention: A sourcebook for community action*. Atlanta, Georgia: Division of Violence Prevention, National Center for Injury Prevention and Control, Centers for Disease Control and Prevention.

Tol, W., Jordans, M., Reis, R., & De Jong, J. (2008). Ecological resilience: Working with child-related psychosocial resources in war-affected communities. In D. Brom, R. Pat-Horenczyk, & J. Ford (Eds.), *Treating traumatized children* (pp. 164–182). London: Routledge.

Turner, H. A., Finkelhor, D., & Ormrod, R. (2006). The effect of lifetime victimization on the mental health of children and adolescents. *Social Science and Medicine*, *62*(1), 13–27. http://dx.doi.org/10.1016/j.socscimed.2005.05.030.

Vernberg, E., & Jacobs, A. (2008). Psychological first aid, child. In G. Reyes, J. D. Elhai, & J. Ford (Eds.), *Encyclopedia of psychological trauma* (pp. 537–539). Hoboken, NJ: Wiley.

Walsh, K., Koenen, K. C., Aiello, A. E., Uddin, M., & Galea, S. (2014). Prevalence of sexual violence and posttraumatic stress disorder in an urban African-American population. *Journal of Immigrant and Minority Health*, *16*(6), 1307–1310.

Walsh, K., Koenen, K. C., Cohen, G. H., Ursano, R., Gifford, R. K., Fullerton, C. S., et al. (2014). Sexual violence and mental health symptoms among National Guard and Reserve soldiers. *Journal of General Internal Medicine*, *29*(1), 104–109.

Walter, K., Hall, B., & Hobfoll, S. (2008). Conservation of resources theory. In G. Reyes, J. D. Elhai, & J. Ford (Eds.), *Encyclopedia of psychological trauma* (pp. 157–159). Hoboken, NJ: Wiley.

Watson, P. J. (2008a). Psychological first aid, children. In G. Reyes, J. D. Elhai, & J. Ford (Eds.), *Encyclopedia of psychological trauma* (pp. 157–159). Hoboken, NJ: Wiley.

Watson, P. J. (2008b). Psychological first aid, adult. In G. Reyes, J. D. Elhai, & J. Ford (Eds.), *Encyclopedia of psychological trauma* (pp. 535–537). Hoboken, NJ: Wiley.

Widom, C. S., Czaja, S., & Dutton, M. A. (2014). Child abuse and neglect and intimate partner violence victimization and perpetration: A prospective investigation. *Child Abuse and Neglect, 38*(4), 650–663.

Wolmer, L., Hamiel, D., & Laor, N. (2011). Preventing children's posttraumatic stress after disaster with teacher-based intervention: A controlled study. *Journal of the American Academy of Child and Adolescent Psychiatry, 50*(4), 340–348. 348 e341–342.

Zatzick, D., Jurkovich, G., Rivara, F. P., Russo, J., Wagner, A., Wang, J., et al. (2013). A randomized stepped care intervention trial targeting posttraumatic stress disorder for surgically hospitalized injury survivors. *Annals of Surgery, 257*(3), 390–399.

Zatzick, D., Roy-Byrne, P., Russo, J., Rivara, F., Droesch, R., Wagner, A., et al. (2004). A randomized effectiveness trial of stepped collaborative care for acutely injured trauma survivors. *Archives of General Psychiatry, 61*(5), 498–506.

Zatzick, D., Russo, J., Lord, S. P., Varley, C., Wang, J., Berliner, L., et al. (2014). Collaborative care intervention targeting violence risk behaviors, substance use, and posttraumatic stress and depressive symptoms in injured adolescents: A randomized clinical trial. *JAMA Pediatrics, 168*(6), 532–539.

Zona, K., & Milan, S. (2011). Gender differences in the longitudinal impact of exposure to violence on mental health in urban youth. *Journal of Youth and Adolescence, 40*(12), 1674–1690. http://dx.doi.org/10.1007/s10964-011-9649-3.

Forensic issues in the traumatic stress field

Posttraumatic stress disorder (PTSD) plays an important role in the criminal, civil, and juvenile justice systems, because it is a serious and ubiquitous problem in the lives of many adults and children who are involved in these systems. Traumatic stress professionals therefore must be aware of the special issues involved in conducting research, providing expert and clinical evaluations and testimony, and conducting treatment, rehabilitation, and prevention interventions, in the legal (forensic) field.

This chapter provides an overview of the research and clinical challenges confronting traumatic stress professionals in several areas in the forensic field, including:

1. the child welfare and child protective services (CPS) systems (e.g., child abuse/neglect);
2. the family law courts (e.g., divorce and child custody, parental competence);
3. the juvenile justice system (e.g., juvenile courts, detention, probation, incarceration);
4. the adult criminal justice system (e.g., courts, jails, prisons, parole/probation).

We begin with an overview of the forensic mental health professional's roles in these systems and a discussion of the areas in which traumatic stress professionals working in them do research and provide expert assessments or treatment. Then, four key forensic issues related to PTSD are discussed, with an introduction to relevant research and clinical case studies:

1. determining if and when PTSD symptoms are being reported falsely or in an exaggerated manner for legal or disability compensation ("malingering");
2. determining whether PTSD should be a mitigating factor in criminal culpability;
3. determining the credibility of witnesses' and defendants' trauma memories;
4. determining the dangerousness and providing recommendations for treatment to support the rehabilitation and community reentry of incarcerated persons (Box 10.1).

Box 10.1 Key Points

1. Forensic PTSD assessment, treatment, and research include a large number of activities and studies in the child welfare and CPS systems with children who have been (or are at risk of being) severely maltreated (such as abuse or neglect).
2. Forensic PTSD assessment also is conducted in the family law court systems, related to civil law cases involving domestic violence (DV), divorce and child custody, and parental competence.
3. Forensic PTSD assessment, treatment, and research are being conducted in many juvenile justice system settings, such as with youths involved in juvenile courts, detention, probation, or incarceration.

(Continued)

Posttraumatic Stress Disorder. DOI: http://dx.doi.org/10.1016/B978-0-12-801288-8.00010-8

Box 10.1 Continued

4. Forensic PTSD assessment, treatment, and research also are being conducted in many adult criminal justice system settings, such as the courts, jails, prisons, and parole agencies.

5. Exposure to traumatic stressors and PTSD symptoms may be exaggerated or fabricated in order to obtain a more favorable outcome in civil or criminal legal proceedings or in disability compensation proceedings ("malingering").

6. Careful clinical observation and the use of psychological tests (particularly the Minnesota Multiphasic Personality Inventory, Second Edition (MMPI-2) make it possible for forensic assessors to identify many—but not all—persons who are falsely alleging PTSD for legal purposes. It is important not only to identify "malingerers" but also to distinguish people who report extremely severe traumatic stressors or PTSD symptoms that are *genuine* from those who are exaggerating or fabricating severe PTSD symptoms.

7. A diagnosis of PTSD may be a mitigating factor in court decisions concerning criminal culpability, most rarely as a basis for a "not guilty by reason of insanity, NGRI" plea and more often as a basis for negotiating a lesser charge (plea bargain) or punitive sentence.

8. The experience of traumatic stressors or PTSD before, during, or after an accidental injury or a criminal incident may reduce the credibility of witness and defendant memories.

9. PTSD may play a role in the acts of violent or sexual offenders and may increase their future potential dangerousness, but PTSD has not been shown to cause violence or sex offenses, and most persons with PTSD do not engage in violent or sexual offending acts.

10. Standards of practice are developing for forensic clinical and research work related to PTSD, but there are no formally accepted consensus standards and no legally regulated standards of care for the forensic assessment or treatment of PTSD.

Forensic mental health roles for traumatic stress professionals

The professional work of traumatic stress researchers and clinicians may lead them to be involved with persons who represent the legal system or are engaged in legal matters in a number of ways. Most traumatic stress professionals work within the mental health professions, and these professions designate the specialized activities that involve the legal system as "forensic" mental health. The American Board of Forensic Psychology (www.abfp.com) describes this as follows:

> *Forensic psychology is the application of the science and profession of psychology to questions and issues relating to law and the legal system. The word "forensic" comes from the Latin word forensis, meaning "of the forum," where the law courts of ancient Rome were held. Today, forensic refers to the application of scientific principles and practices to the adversary process where specially knowledgeable scientists play a role.*

Forensic mental health specialists conduct research and clinical activities in or related to courts of law and civil and criminal justice programs and facilities such as CPS agencies, adult jails and prisons, and juvenile justice detention and probation agencies. Civil legal proceedings are cases in which a person (the plaintiff) requests legal remedy for some harm, injury, or loss he or she believes another person(s) or an entity such as a business (the defendant) has caused him or her to experience (such as personal injury claims or workers' compensation cases). Civil law also involves requests to a court to provide legally mandated protection to a person (such as child custody cases) or to society (such as commitment cases in which a person is alleged to be a danger to self or others and to therefore require placement in a secure facility such as a psychiatric institution). Another branch of civil law consists of the federal immigration courts, in which individuals who are citizens of one country seek permission to enter and stay in another country, by gaining citizenship, temporary residency (in the United States, this is referred to as "green cards"), or asylum (i.e., protection from harm that they contend will happen if they are forced to return to their country of origin ("deported")) (see Box 10.2 for an asylum example).

Box 10.2 Evaluating Traumatic Stress Issues for Individuals Seeking Asylum

People can apply for asylum—that is, permission to remain in a country other than their country of citizenship for their safety and protection—as a means of immigrating to most countries internationally. In the United States, asylum applications are granted only if an individual can prove that he or she has been persecuted based on race, religion, nationality, political opinion, or membership in a social or cultural group, or will be persecuted if he or she is returned to his/her home country. Asylum may be sought in the United States either through *affirmative asylum* or *defensive asylum*. In affirmative asylum, the person applying submits documentation known as Form I-589 to the Bureau of Citizenship and Immigration Services (BCIS; an agency in the Homeland Security Department that formerly was called the Immigration and Naturalization Service, or INS). A BCIS asylum officer conducts an interview to determine whether the request will be granted. In defensive asylum, the individual already has been apprehended by law enforcement (e.g., an illegal or undocumented "alien" detained by the Homeland Security Department border patrol) and is legally required by the federal Immigration Court to appear before an immigration judge from the Executive Office for Immigration Review (EOIR). Article 3 of the United Nations Convention Against Torture (1999) states that no asylum seeker can be returned home if there is a credible threat of torture, but the BCIS asylum officers in danger of torture or persecution.

Students or protesters who engage in social or political activism face persecution such as violent assaults, imprisonment, and torture in some countries.

(Continued)

Box 10.2 Continued

Lesbian, gay, bisexual, and transsexual or transgender individuals are persecuted in a number of countries, especially those in which religions that ban other than heterosexual activity is an integral part of the government. Children and families who are fleeing community violence perpetrated by criminal organizations or groups that may or may not be covertly government sanctioned also may be eligible for asylum. Women or girls may be subject to severe punishment that constitutes persecution (including execution) for having a baby out of wedlock or for having been the victim of rape. They also may be targeted simply based upon their gender by organized criminal or political groups for sexual or physical violence, and a recent ruling in the Ninth Circuit Court of Appeals found that as such they constitute a social group eligible for asylum due to being subject to persecution, even if the group is not obviously visible or formally organized. Women who have been victimized by domestic or intimate partner violence have been less successful in seeking asylum because they have not been viewed as subject to public persecution; however, in a case still under review by the Immigration Court in Tacoma, the judge released a Honduran woman from detention after finding that her claim of persecution due to battering by her husband had merit because government protections against such abuse in that country are insufficient.

Based on the scientific and clinical evidence of prevalent and often severe PTSD among refugees and immigrants who are fleeing organized violence, an innovative collaboration has been developed at the University of Connecticut to provide PTSD evaluations by the Center for Trauma Recovery in the Medical School Department of Psychiatry for clients of the Law School's Asylum and Human Rights Clinic. The evaluations are done to provide an objective assessment of the extent of exposure to traumatic violence and the resultant harm caused to the asylum seeker by PTSD both currently and should the individual be forced to return to a country where they allege they will face additional persecution or persistent reminders of past traumatic persecution. A redacted composite example of the PTSD asylum evaluations illustrates how careful application of the PTSD criteria can provide immigration officers or courts with a basis for determining the psychological harm that has been done or could be done to asylum seekers.

I [clinical assessor], under penalty of perjury, affirm that the following information is true and correct to the best of my ability:

1. AA, a 47-year-old man from the Central African Republic (CAR), was referred by the University of Connecticut School of Law Asylum and Human Rights Clinic to the University of Connecticut Health Center Trauma Clinic to assess his current functioning in light of past traumatic events. The current evaluation focused on the psychological impact on Mr. A of being detained, interrogated, and tortured by the CAR National Intelligence Agency for his participation in an opposition political party.

2. Mr. A arrived on time to his appointment accompanied by a friend. The assessment, with only Mr. A present, was conducted in English. Mr. A presented as appropriately dressed and well groomed. Mr. A was alert and oriented. His thought processes were logical and coherent, and his thought content was appropriate. He was engaged throughout the evaluation, and maintained appropriate eye contact. Initially, Mr. A presented as detached, describing factual details of his life in the CAR and detailing his political views. He then slowly became more forthcoming about the psychological impact of his detentions, interrogations, and torture. Mr. A was noticeably anxious when discussing the possibility of returning to the CAR and tearful when reflecting on his separation from his wife and child after leaving his country.

3. Mr. A reported that, because of his participation in the United Democratic Party, he was repeatedly detained, interrogated, and tortured by the CAR National Intelligence Agency, starting in 1999. Mr. A described physical and psychological torture during his first detention in detail, which included being severely beaten with a baton, humiliated and degraded, and continually threatened with death. Subsequently, Mr. A reportedly lived in constant fear of further detention and torture for his political activities. He reported being detained and tortured, for days or weeks on an approximately yearly basis until 2012. He reported that with each episode, his fear and hypervigilance increased, which is consistent with scientific research on cumulative trauma exposure. Mr. A explained that the intensity of the physical and psychological violence escalated during his final detention in 2012, further heightening his fear for his safety and hypervigilance. Mr. A reported that throughout these years, his home was periodically raided and ransacked, and he and his family were under surveillance for extended periods of time. As such, Mr. A reportedly feared not only for his safety but also his family's well-being, and his fear became particularly salient after the birth of his first child.

4. Furthermore, Mr. A explained that because of the beatings and abuse during his detentions, his finger is scarred; he suffers from migraines and tinnitus; and he has neck, shoulder and back pain, among other physical ailments. He also stated that the torture that he experienced in the CAR has exacerbated the physical complications of his polio. He noted, for instance, increased swelling and pain in his legs and ankles following his final detention, during which he was beaten, electrocuted, buried waist deep, and malnourished. Mr. A's physical injuries and pains constitute daily reminders of his traumatic experiences, which compound and maintain the psychological effects of those experiences.

5. Mr. A described experiencing the following symptoms, which meet the diagnostic criteria of PTSD according to the *Diagnostic and Statistical Manual of Mental Disorder*, Fifth Edition. Mr. A reported feeling intense fear during and following his detentions, interrogations, and torture, which involved repeated incidents of serious physical harm and threatened death. He described intrusive reexperiencing of his traumas, avoidance of reminders of his traumatic experiences, negative alterations in his cognitions and mood (i.e., a pervasive negative emotional state, exaggerated negative perceptions of himself, and an inability to recall important aspects of his traumas), and negative alterations in his arousal and reactivity (i.e., disturbed sleep, hypervigilance, an exaggerated startle response). According to Mr. A, his symptoms of posttraumatic stress have caused a significant amount of distress. Mr. A reported

(*Continued*)

Box 10.2 Continued

that he first experienced posttraumatic stress symptoms after his initial detention, and his distress persisted throughout subsequent years, increasing immediately following each of his detentions. This timeline suggests that Mr. A's symptoms and distress are a direct consequence of his detentions, interrogations, and torture in the CAR.

6. Mr. A reported current persistent reexperiencing of his traumatic experiences, which include intrusive thoughts, nightmares, and dissociative reactions with triggers of his trauma. For instance, he described nightmares in which he is kidnapped and tortured while his family looks on, is unable to aid him, and reacts in horror. He also described dissociative reactions during which he smells one of his cells, as if detained in the CAR and not safely in the United States. Based on his report, Mr. A has expended great time and energy avoiding and planning to avoid reminders of his traumas. He described plans to surgically remove scars from his torture in order to lessen his daily triggers. He also stated that he has consistently engaged in a stream of activity through his years in the CAR and months in the United States in order to avoid the reminders of his traumatic exposures. Because fewer distractions are available, his symptoms of reexperiencing are reportedly more severe during the nighttime. Mr. A reported that intrusive thoughts and nightmares significantly disturb his sleep. He reportedly requires 3–4 hours to fall asleep and is awakened on a weekly basis by nightmares involving being tortured.

7. Mr. A stated that he has experienced pervasive fear and sadness since his initial detention in 1999. To cope with this intense distress, Mr. A described adopting a stance of indifference, which is consistent with the emotional numbing of PTSD. That is, he resigned himself to the possibility of detentions and torture in the CAR, and he became increasingly numb to his emotional experiences. Despite this emotional numbing, Mr. A continues to have moments of heightened fear and sadness with reminders of his trauma. He explained that while applying for asylum, he has been unable to avoid thinking about and discussing his traumatic experiences, and he has thus repeatedly been faced with feelings of intense anxiety and depression. Mr. A further explained that his emotional pain is accompanied by physical pains, including migraines and neck, shoulder, and back pain. Given the effort that Mr. A has expended to distance himself from his psychological distress, such physical manifestations of emotional pain are expectable.

8. As is typical for an individual who has experienced traumatizing events, Mr. A can describe the gist of his experiences, but he cannot consistently recall all of the details of his detentions, interrogations, and torture. He is able to recall some portions of his traumas with extreme detail and clarity, while others are vague and even confused. This inability to consistently remember aspects of his traumatic experiences is one symptom of PTSD and is not surprising given the nature and extent of the traumas that Mr. A experienced. For individuals with PTSD, it is often difficult to deliberately recall and describe their trauma, because their memories may be fragmented and disorganized. For those who have repeatedly experienced similar traumatic events, such as Mr. A, it can be particularly difficult to temporally organize and detail traumas. Mr. A acknowledged his general difficulties with memory and noted the specific limits of his recall during the current evaluation. For instance, he noted difficulty identifying if a series of events was confined to one detention or spanned several incidents.

Given Mr. A's openness regarding the limits of his memory, it is unlikely that inconsistencies in his recall reflect attempts to obscure the truth. Rather, his fragmented memory is likely a reflection of the repetitive nature of his exposure to traumatic stressors and the distress that he experienced during and afterward.

9. Despite his symptoms of posttraumatic stress, Mr. A has demonstrated a remarkable resilience. His resilience should not place the veracity of his statements regarding his history or current symptoms in doubt. Although he copes well enough to function adequately, his current functioning is attributable to his abilities to use avoidance to cope with his posttraumatic reexperiencing and to contextualize his traumatic experiences. Mr. A described a pattern of constant behavioral and cognitive avoidance, during which he consistently engages in activities and constantly redirects his thoughts to the present moment. When Mr. A is unable to avoid reminders of his trauma, he reflects on the potential for a regime change in the CAR as a consequence of his political opposition. That is, he focuses on the greater good that his past suffering may one day achieve. During the evaluation, these coping strategies were evident, as Mr. A repeatedly focused the conversation on the present need for reform in the CAR when asked about his reaction to his traumas. This redirection of the conversation should not be interpreted as an attempt to obscure the truth or be uncooperative. Rather, it is a reflection of Mr. A's efforts to cope with the distress associated with recalling his detentions and torture.

10. Mr. A uses avoidance and redirects his thoughts to cope not only with his individual symptoms of posttraumatic stress but also with his global state of distress. At the start of the evaluation, Mr. A requested that the results of the evaluation not be shared with him. He reportedly fears that his detentions, interrogations, and torture have created lasting psychological harm. Although Mr. A is aware of the psychological impact of his traumas, he avoids recognizing his distress. In an effort to deflect attention on his suffering, Mr. A also reportedly obscures his pain from his family and friends. For instance, he stated that he only disclosed his nightmares to his wife after she discussed her own nightmares, and, even then, he shielded her from his pain. Mr. A explained that he currently avoids situations in which he would tear up in front of others.

11. Mr. A's generally composed presentation therefore should not be mistaken for a lack of distress. Rather, his composure is a reflection of the coping strategies that he has employed for over a decade. Mr. A exerts substantial effort not only to manage his symptoms of posttraumatic stress but also to minimize his distress in front of those around him. Based on this evaluation, it appears likely that Mr. A will be able to describe his experiences in a calm and often unemotional manner that will actually understate the distress he has and is experiencing as a result of his traumatic experiences.

12. According to Mr. A, his decision to immigrate from the CAR was a difficult one. On the one hand, Mr. A perceived increased risk to his and his family's safety. He reported that his family's home began being watched, and the beatings during his last detention increased in intensity. On the other hand, Mr. A expressed devotion to his family and his country and intense guilt and sadness in leaving them behind. Indeed, Mr. A became tearful whenever he discussed his separation from his wife and child. He explained that, outside of the evaluation, he becomes depressed and is

(Continued)

Box 10.2 Continued

unable to hold back tears whenever he reflects on his separation from his family. Mr. A explained that he made the decision to leave the CAR in order to protect his family. That is, his fear of the CAR National Intelligence Agency outweighed the emotional cost of experiencing sadness and a sense of isolation due to being separated from his family and country.

13. Mr. A was noticeably anxious when discussing the possibility of returning to the CAR, and he reported being highly fearful of the prospect. From Mr. A's perspective, his return would inevitably result in either life in prison or death. As well, he believes that his return would significantly endanger his family. Mr. A described such fear of the CAR National Intelligence Agency that he monitors all of his communications online, via phone, and through mail with the CAR, so as not to reveal any information that could place him or his family at risk. Beyond the threat of physical harm, it is likely that returning to the CAR would be psychologically harmful for Mr. A, because he would be exposed to an increased number of direct and largely unavoidable traumatic reminders. In describing his life in the CAR, Mr. A noted that there are "painful reminders all around." Despite his resilience, Mr. A is less likely to effectively cope with ever-present triggers in the CAR if he returns, given his heightened fear that he and his loved ones would be targets of violence. It is likely that the frequency and/or intensity of his intrusive recollections, negative cognitions and affect, and hyperarousal would significantly increase if he returned to the CAR.

Criminal proceedings involve court hearings and trials in which someone has been charged with committing a crime. Forensic mental health evaluations and court testimony may be provided in criminal cases in which someone pleads not guilty of a crime by reason of insanity (NGRI). A forensic mental health evaluation also may be ordered by a criminal court to assist in determining if a person charged with a crime is mentally competent to stand trial. Alternately, a forensic mental health evaluation may be done to determine if a person represents a danger to others due to the possibility of committing violent acts or sexual offenses. Additionally, an evaluation may be ordered to enable the criminal court to determine if a person is in need of mental health treatment while confined in a jail, prison, or detention facility, or while living in the community but under supervision (by a diversion program or a probation officer) instead of being incarcerated, or on parole after release from having been incarcerated.

As a clinician, the traumatic stress professional may be involved in forensic mental health work by serving as an expert witness for either the plaintiff or the defendant in a civil case and for either the prosecution or the defense in a criminal case. Expert testimony may involve hiring the traumatic stress professional as a consultant by conducting a review of case records and presentation to the court of background factual information relevant to the case (such as defining what constitutes PTSD and how it may in general affect a person's behavior and mental state). Or testimony might involve assessing a person involved in a legal case and testifying about the results (such as assessing the trauma history and PTSD symptoms of a defendant charged with a crime or a plaintiff seeking damages from an accidental injury or assault).

As an expert witness, the traumatic stress professional may be called upon to estimate the likelihood that PTSD was a cause of an individual's behavior or compromised his or her ability to competently make decisions and act responsibly either at the time of an injurious act or crime or during a trial. The attorneys who represent the parties involved in a lawsuit or a defendant in a criminal trial or the judge may question the expert witness to make judgments of the extent to which harm sustained by a plaintiff or the victim of a crime includes PTSD as a result of the alleged incidents constituting a traumatic stressor that constitutes a psychological injury. The expert witness could also be asked to provide recommendations for services (such as mental health treatment generally or PTSD therapy specifically) or resources (such as foster or adoptive placement for a maltreated child or paid time off work for an injured employee) that will be needed in order to enable the person to recover from harm or to be able to competently stand trial or successfully complete incarceration and safely return to the community.

The clinical role for traumatic stress professionals in forensic settings also may include conducting pretrial or follow-up mental health assessments that are used by the judge to assist in decisions without having the professional actually testify in court. The forensic mental health role may involve directly providing or overseeing the provision of therapeutic services, such as a psychiatrist conducting pharmacotherapy or a psychologist, social worker, or counselor doing group or one-to-one psychotherapy for a legally detained, incarcerated, or paroled youth or adult. Traumatic stress clinicians also may conduct clinical quality assurance studies, such as reviewing court-ordered mental health assessment reports in order to determine if trauma history and PTSD were appropriately assessed and considered in the assessor's conclusions and recommendations.

Traumatic stress researchers also may be asked to serve as expert witnesses in legal cases in order to testify concerning scientific findings of relevance. For example, expert testimony may be requested concerning the scientific status of controversial matters such as whether traumatized persons can recall traumatic events accurately many years or decades after the fact, particularly if they did not recall the events for a period of time (see Chapter 1, the "false versus recovered or repressed memory" syndrome debate). Researchers also may be asked for expert testimony about the scientific status of specific assessment instruments, such as the accuracy of questionnaires or structured interviews for determining a plaintiff's or defendant's trauma history or PTSD. The reliability, validity, and predictive utility of tests and measures (see Chapter 6 on screening and assessment of PTSD) with persons involved in legal cases—such as how to determine if a plaintiff or defendant is falsely claiming or exaggerating the severity of his or her exposure to traumatic stressors or PTSD symptoms—"malingering" (Hall & Hall, 2006)—is an important forensic topic within the traumatic stress scientific research field.

Traumatic stress research includes a variety of lines of study that are being conducted within the civil and criminal justice systems. Scientific studies have been done to estimate the prevalence of past exposure to psychological trauma and current PTSD among men and women in jails and prisons (Ford, Trestman et al., 2007), as well as among youth in the juvenile justice system (Ford, Chapman, Hawke, & Albert, 2007). Studies have been conducted to empirically examine the role of exposure to traumatic stressors and PTSD in severe problems presented by incarcerated adults and youth, such as violent crimes, child maltreatment, and sexual offenses (Friel, White, & Hull, 2008). Research also has been conducted to test the efficacy or effectiveness of therapeutic treatments for incarcerated adults and youth involved in the juvenile justice system (Feierman & Ford, 2015; Ford, 2012). Research also is ongoing relevant to adults and youth in the criminal or juvenile justice systems to determine how exposure to traumatic stressors or PTSD affects the accuracy of memory (Scott et al., 2014; Wilker, Elbert, & Kolassa, 2014) and whether claims of PTSD symptoms are true or "malingered" (Wooley & Rogers, 2014).

Child welfare service and CPS

In 1974, the US Child Abuse Prevention and Treatment Act (CAPTA; PL 93-247) first provided federal funding to every state and established minimum standards and record-keeping systems to monitor child maltreatment nationally (Manly, 2008). Most recently in its reauthorized version, the Keeping Children and Families Safe Act of 2003 (PL 108-36), this law requires that each state adhere to federal standards that include that services be provided to address any instance of "at a minimum, any recent act or failure to act on the part of a parent or caretaker, which results in death, serious physical or emotional harm, sexual abuse or exploitation, or an act or failure to act which presents an imminent risk of serious harm" (42 U.S.C.A. §5106g). All 50 states in the United States and many nations have laws that require that suspected child abuse and neglect be reported and addressed in the best interest of the child.

The governmental agencies responsible for child abuse prevention and treatment in the United States are state or county CPS departments or divisions, with formal legal directives or guidance from the state's judicial branch and its courts of law. Both criminal and civil (e.g., family law) courts may be involved in child welfare or child protection cases—the criminal courts in order to impose punishments on perpetrators of child abuse and the civil/family courts in order to make determinations as to the circumstances (such as place of residence and legal custody) and services for the child (such as counseling or therapy for abuse-related PTSD or educational programming or assistance to remediate any ill effects of abuse on a child's ability to learn and succeed in school) and family (such as family therapy or economic or vocational assistance for a nonoffending parent). Each state may make its own interpretation of the federal definition of child abuse and of the federally mandated child protection and child welfare services (Manly, 2008), and this often changes over time. Thus, it is essential that traumatic stress professionals be familiar with the current local standards for what constitutes child abuse and what remedies and services can or must be provided to protect and assist abused children and their families.

Expert Witness Role. As an expert witness, a traumatic stress professional may be called upon to explain to the court the extent of occurrence of and the harm caused by child abuse. It is essential to draw upon the most current and scientifically valid sources of information in this controversial and ever-changing area. In the United States, CAPTA (PL 93-247) has mandated that "National Incidence Studies" (NIS) be conducted approximately once every decade to determine the scope of the problem of child maltreatment. The NIS defines child abuse using two different standards: "Harm" and "Endangerment." The Harm Standard requires showing that abuse has demonstrably injured the child, physically or psychologically. The Endangerment Standard is broader, including incidents that could potentially cause harm even if no actual harm can be definitively demonstrated, and was more inclusive of abuse or neglect that placed children at risk of harm. The fourth NIS, NIS-4 (Sedlak et al., 2010), found that 1.25 million children were maltreated according to the Harm Standard, which translates to 1 child per every 58 children in the United States (the "incidence" of child maltreatment). Using the Endangerment Standard, almost twice as many children were classified as maltreated (2.9 million, or 1 child per every 25 in the United States—i.e., more than 4% or one child in every 25).

The NIS website notes that its findings represent "the incidence of child maltreatment in the United States, including cases that are reported to the authorities as well as those that are not" (http://www.acf.hhs.gov/programs/opre/research/project/national-incidence-study-of-child-abuse-and-neglect-nis-4-2004-2009). In the United States, the National Child Abuse and Neglect Data System (NCANDS; http://www.acf.hhs.gov/programs/cb/resource/about-ncands) annually compiles official records from the CPS agencies in every state. According to NCANDS, in 2012, 3.4 million CPS referrals were received due to the alleged maltreatment of 6.3 million children. Of these, about 673,000 children were substantiated as victims of maltreatment—that is to say, an investigation was conducted by the CPS agency (usually by a BA or masters-level social worker employed by the agency), and there was sufficient evidence to conclude that abuse or neglect had in fact occurred. The most common form of maltreatment documented by the 2012 NCCANDS report was neglect (78% of all substantiated cases, or 3% of all children in the United States). Substantiated physical abuse (18% of all substantiated cases) and sexual abuse (9%) were less common. It is important to temper these findings in forensic testimony with the cautionary note that because these statistics are based only on officially reported and substantiated incidents of maltreatment, they likely underestimate the extent of maltreatment that actually occurs (Manly, 2008).

Forensic Testimony Related to Specific Cases. Traumatic stress professionals also are called upon to advise the court or the CPS agency as to the likelihood that a specific child has been subjected to abuse or neglect or the risk that the child will be subjected to maltreatment by parent(s) or other guardians in the future. In this role, the professional is in the more difficult role of not just providing an objective overview of the issues involved in a case that includes potential child maltreatment, but of making determinations and recommendations specific to a unique child and family. In the first instance, a determination of what *has already happened* to a child—that is, whether she or he was maltreated—requires a very thorough and precise assessment of events that tend to be very difficult for a child to describe, due to the emotional distress and confusion associated with abuse or neglect. Detailed guidelines have been developed by forensic child abuse assessment experts in order that substantial caution is taken to protect the child's psychological and physical safety and to support the child's privacy and sense of control when conducting a child abuse assessment (Herman, 2005; Werner & Werner, 2008).

Clinically and psychometrically sound assessment instruments and procedures also are essential to establish the specific event(s) that occurred and that were psychologically traumatic, including other traumatic experiences (such as severe accidents, community or family violence, and traumatic losses), as well as potential incidents of abuse or neglect (see Chapter 6 for a description of assessment instruments for establishing a history of exposure to traumatic stressors, such as the Traumatic Events Screening Instrument, Box 6.2). There is no single final source for determining what has happened to a child, so it also is crucial to gather information from as many independent sources as possible who may have knowledge of a child's experiences or of the potential signs of abuse or neglect (including parents, family members, teachers, health care professionals, CPS investigators, and medical and legal records).

In gauging the likelihood that maltreatment has occurred or will occur again, the forensic expert must be familiar with findings from the NIS and NCANDS that relate to the risk of abuse. The NIS-4 reported that children from families with single parents, large size, and low incomes were more likely to have been classified as maltreated than those from families that experience fewer stressors (such as divorce, unemployment and underemployment, and social prejudices) and have more socioeconomic resources (such as money to pay for children's needs and social support for parents' needs). The NCANDS data show that children under age 4 years old are most likely to be considered to have had substantiated maltreatment and that most maltreatment was done by a family member (82% of cases by a parent). While these findings suggest that parents or families that are subject to more stressors (including challenges related to caring for very young children) and that are likely to have fewer resources to assist them (see Hobfoll's Conservation of Resources model of stress vulnerability, Chapter 9) are more likely than other parents, families, or adults outside the family to maltreat a child, this is a statement of *risk* and not of *certainty*. Thus, it is not scientifically or clinically appropriate *ever* for a traumatic stress forensic assessor to conclude that a specific parent or family has maltreated a child or will in the future maltreat a child simply because these risk factors are present. The risk factors are appropriately used to focus the assessor's (and the court's and CPS agency's) attention on a heightened level of "endangerment" that should be addressed by careful assessment of the *actual harm* (if any) sustained by the child before maltreatment is considered to have occurred. Risk factors also provide a basis for the forensic assessor to recommend types of help that can *reduce* the child's endangerment (i.e., the likelihood of further maltreatment) by enhancing the parent's and family's resources (including their knowledge of early childhood development, their skills for developmentally sensitive caregiving, and their access to services and social support to assist them in meeting their family's needs) (Box 10.3).

Box 10.3 Forensic PTSD Research in the Child Protection System

Research on the nature and adverse impact of child maltreatment as a traumatic stressor has been ongoing for several decades (Manly, 2008). Scientific studies have demonstrated that maltreated children are at risk not only for PTSD but also for complex posttraumatic problems with depression, anger, guilt, shame, dissociative disorders, physical symptoms, suicidality, substance abuse, eating disorders, social isolation and extremely conflictual relationships, school problems, and sexual problems. Assessment measures with strong psychometric reliability and validity have been developed and are widely used clinically and in research to identify traumatized children (such as the Traumatic Events Screening Instrument; see Chapter 6) and their specific biopsychosocial symptoms and impairments (such as the Traumatic Stress Checklist for Children; see Chapter 6). The evidence base for efficacious PTSD psychotherapy is particularly strong with maltreated children, notably trauma-focused cognitive behavior therapy for sexually abused children (TF-CBT; see Chapter 8) and parent-child therapies for very young and school-age abused children (see Chapter 8).

An assessment of the adverse impact of maltreatment also is likely to be requested. Ford (2005) and Manly (2008) provide a thorough summary of the types of harm that may be caused by child abuse and neglect, including (i) developmental delays, including problems in acquiring competences and skills in the motoric (such as physical coordination), cognitive (such as language or reading), or social (such as interacting with peers or adults) domains; (ii) problems with emotion regulation (i.e., the ability to accurately identify, express, tolerate, and readjust negative and positive emotions) leading to fearfulness, dysphoria and hopelessness, rage and hostility, excessive shame and guilt, and emotional insecurity; (iii) problems with behavioral self-regulation due to difficulty in sustaining mental concentration, hyperactivity, impulsivity, forgetfulness, egocentrism, and diminished self-esteem; (iv) maladaptive social information processing such as a heightened sensitivity to anger, suspiciousness, distrust, and the belief that aggression or withdrawal (or both) are socially rewarded and necessary; (v) disorganized and insecure involvement in relationships, including both overinvolvement in unhealthy or even abusive relationships and underinvolvement or resistance to healthy relationships; and (vi) physical health problems that appear to be greatly exacerbated by day-to-day stressors (such as asthma, under/overeating, gastrointestinal problems, or impaired immune system activity).

In order to document the impact of maltreatment, a forensic psychological assessment must use scientifically and clinically validated measures of these psychological and behavioral problems (see Chapter 6) in order to establish that the child is functioning more poorly in some or all of these areas: (i) than expected given her or his age, gender, and family, educational, and sociocultural background, and (ii) than prior to the start (onset) of maltreatment, *if* there was a definite period of time in which maltreatment clearly was not occurring. Medical, school, and other (e.g., legal or treatment) records may provide useful corroborating information, especially if the child or responsible adults are not in a position (due to their age, stressors, or symptoms and impairments) to provide a credibly accurate report on these sensitive matters.

Recommendations for placement (such as reunification or remaining with one or both parents or other family members versus residence in a temporary respite or treatment program or with a foster or adoptive family) and treatment or rehabilitative services are a vital part of many case-specific forensic evaluations. The optimal placements and services for maltreated children and their families are those that foster a balance of responsible independence and self-reliance with physically and psychologically safe, dependable, and growth-oriented relationships. It is important for the traumatic stress professional to be knowledgeable of both the interventions that have a strong scientific evidence base for assisting maltreated children and their families with PTSD and associated psychological, behavioral, and interpersonal problems (see Chapter 8) and the actual services that are available and practically accessible to the particular child and family.

Family law courts

Family law courts are part of each state's Superior Court system in the United States, although they usually operate relatively autonomously within each county or large city. Family law courts hear civil law cases involving child maltreatment, juvenile delinquency, DV, legal separation and divorce, paternity, parental competence, child custody, adoption, legal guardianship, emancipation of a minor, spousal or child support, and community property.

Maltreatment and juvenile delinquency cases differ from most other family law cases in that they are initiated by a request ("petition") from a governmental agency on behalf of a child who is considered to be harmed or endangered (in the case of maltreatment, filed by the CPS agency) or to pose a danger or be unable to act within the bounds of the law (in the case of juvenile delinquency, filed by CPS or Juvenile Probation agency). Other family law cases begin with a petition for assistance from an individual, either on behalf of a child (such as requests to establish legal guardianship, adoption, or child support) on their own behalf (such as in matters involving divorce, separation, spousal support, paternity (a claim to recognition as the biological parent of a child), DV, or child custody).

Most family law cases do not necessarily involve psychological trauma or PTSD, but a thorough psychosocial assessment on behalf of a client petitioning for divorce, custody, support, adoption, legal guardianship, parental competence, or paternity should consider whether the adult (and the child, when children are involved) may have needs or limitations due to PTSD. Divorce, or the marital conflict and estrangement that often accompany it, is *not* automatically a traumatic stressor; indeed, while usually highly stressful, most marital conflicts and divorce proceedings fortunately are not life-threatening and do not involve sexual violation. Similarly, PTSD is *not* an *a priori* (i.e., definite) basis for judging any adult to be incompetent or otherwise unable to fulfill the responsibilities of parenting, custody, adoption, or legal guardianship.

However, family law cases that are not specifically filed based on DV may involve traumatic partner violence (including sexual as well as physical assault), and some family law cases are filed specifically by a spouse to gain protection from a domestically violent partner. Similarly, family law cases may involve child maltreatment even when neither abuse nor neglect has been formally alleged by a CPS agency. Therefore, a thorough clinical assessment using rigorous tools, such as the Conflict Tactics Scale-2 for potential unrecognized DV and the Childhood Trauma Questionnaire for potential child maltreatment, is advisable not only in formal cases of DV and child maltreatment but in any family law case in which recommendations about the best interests of children or the most beneficial resolution of marital or parental conflicts are provided by the traumatic stress professional.

DV is an often unrecognized and insidious form of psychological trauma in most if not all cases (Box 10.5). Unfortunately, informal coping strategies that involve staying in a domestically violent relationship tend not to stop the violence and abuse (M. Dutton, 2008). Treatment programs for perpetrators—most of whom are male but who also can be female—have had limited success in preventing the recurrence of violence, except when the perpetrator is able to achieve a fundamental shift from using aggressive dominance to cover up deep-seated insecurities to becoming sufficiently self-confident to genuinely empathize with and respect the partner as a separate individual (D. Dutton, 2008). Traumatic stress professionals have been involved in developing, conducting, and evaluating the effectiveness of psychosocial treatments for domestically violent individuals (D. Dutton, 2008).

Traumatic stress professionals also have worked in more nontraditional ways to partner with DV advocates in family law (and also criminal) courts, police departments, hotlines, shelters, respite housing, and counseling centers. Mental health professionals have had to learn from experience that many survivors of DV view psychosocial assessment or treatment as pathologizing. This is a counterreaction to the "disease model" of mental health services, which involves treating traumatized persons as if their distress is a sign of mental illness that requires treatment. Although psychosocial or psychiatric assessment and treatment may be beneficial when DV survivors experience PTSD or other psychiatric or substance use disorder symptoms, it is crucial to not inadvertently add to the sense of disrespect and devaluation that these individuals are recovering from in their primary relationship(s). Advocacy focuses on empowering DV survivors to make independent choices that increase their (and their loved ones') safety, self-worth, and trust in healthy, nonabusive relationships. Traumatic stress professionals have provided DV advocates with information about how PTSD can result from DV and cognitive behavioral strategies that they can share with their clients as practical "tools" for managing and recovering from PTSD without having to undergo any psychosocial assessments or treatment unless they choose to do so.

Thus, DV is not a single traumatic incident but typically a series of chronic exposures to potentially traumatic stressors and life circumstances that undercut the survivor's psychological, biological, and interpersonal resources. Traumatic stress researchers have shown that DV often—but not always—is preceded by childhood maltreatment and that women who are particularly vulnerable to this type of recurrent interpersonal violence have as much as a 17 times increased risk of developing PTSD (Schumm, Briggs-Phillips, & Hobfoll, 2006) and depression (Rayburn et al., 2005). Exposure to violence, particularly in the absence of a strong support system, is associated with persistent PTSD among women (Andrews, Brewin, & Rose, 2003; Gill, Vythilingam, & Page, 2008). Of particular concern is evidence that violence, abuse, addiction, and associated legal problems may occur in intergenerational cycles (McGloin & Widom, 2001). This does *not* mean that DV survivors abuse, traumatize, or psychologically harm their children, but rather that DV and child abuse can become a trap in which each new generation becomes caught until survivors can get the advocacy and resources they need to build new lives and new relationships for themselves and their children.

By providing educational assistance to family law courts, including to judges and all the court staff (Ford, Chapman, Mack, & Pearson, 2006) and to the advocates and professionals who offer help to parents, spouses, and children who are seeing assistance in the courts, traumatic stress clinicians are contributing to breaking these vicious cycles of conflict, abuse, and violence. PTSD therapies that have a strong research evidence base are being provided to children (see Chapter 8) and adults (see Chapter 7) as a resource that provides judges and court staff with a way to offer additional help when PTSD is complicating the already stressful process of legally addressing family problems.

Juvenile justice system

As many as one in nine (11%) of youth involved in the juvenile justice system currently suffer or have suffered from PTSD in the past year—10–20 times the number of PTSD cases as are found among similar-aged youth in the community (Ford et al., 2007). Youth in the juvenile justice system also are at higher risk than other youth for a variety of behavioral health disorders, many of which occur in combinations (i.e., as "comorbid disorders"). About 66% of girls and more than 80% of boys in a large juvenile detention center who had anxiety disorders also had an externalizing (e.g., ADHD, conduct disorder), internalizing (e.g., depression), or substance use disorder. Although not systematically tested for PTSD per se among juvenile justice–involved youths, research on the comorbidities of PTSD (see Chapter 4) suggest that they are likely to have one or more other behavioral health disorders.

Exposure to maltreatment or other interpersonal violence in childhood is common (> 67% prevalence) among youths in the juvenile justice system. Such "developmentally adverse interpersonal traumas" (Ford, 2005) are associated with the development of psychosocial adjustment problems that place youths at risk for entry into and recidivism in the juvenile and adult criminal justice systems: preoccupation with their own and other persons' anger (Pollak & Tolley-Schell, 2003); generalized expectancies of being physically or sexually harmed (Gully, 2003); a hostile/aggressive information processing style (Dodge, Pettit, Bates, & Valente, 1995);

problems with complex cognitive operations necessary for selective or sustained attention, hypothesis testing and problem solving, and semantic organization (Beers & De Bellis, 2002); deficits in short-term and delayed verbal memory (Cordón, Pipe, Sayfan, Melinder, & Goodman, 2004), and detailed and overinclusive memories of traumatic events (Cordón et al., 2004). In adolescence and adulthood, youth who have experienced traumatic childhood adversity are at risk for not only mental health and behavior problems but also for medical conditions such as diabetes, heart disease, and immune system disorders and revictimization.

Traumatic victimization may tip the scales for many youths and put them on—or lock them into—a path to delinquency. When exposed to coercion, cruelty, violence, neglect, or rejection, youths may cope by resorting to indifference, defiance of rules and authority, or aggression as self-protective counterreactions. The youth may feel so terrified, alone, and powerless in the face of traumatic victimization that the best way she or he can find to cope may take the form of anger, defiance, callousness, or aggression. In these cases, risk taking, breaking rules, fighting back, and hurting others who are perceived to be powerful (e.g., authority figures) or vulnerable (e.g., younger children, animals) may become ways to survive emotionally (or literally).

Fundamentally, these defensive attempts to overcome or resist the helplessness and isolation caused by victimization are motivated by the desire to regain the ability to regulate the extreme bodily and emotional states (e.g., terror, confusion, despondency, rage) and to process information and behave in ways that provide a sense of control and accomplishment (e.g., thinking clearly enough to make and act on choices that are based on prior learning and future consequences) (Ford, 2005). Delinquency has been hypothesized to result from a fundamental dysregulation of emotion (e.g., fits of rage, difficulty expressing or even feeling love or happiness, intense frustration, desperate anxiety, or inconsolable despair; Ford et al., 2007) and information processing (e.g., excessive suspiciousness, lack of consideration of prosocial options or adverse consequences of deviant behavior, acting without foresight or planning). As a result, for delinquent youths, emotions may seem unmanageable or absent, and thinking tends to be reactive, rigid, impulsive, and defiant. This in turn leads to distorted views of self, peers, and relationships (e.g., low self-worth, anticipating frustration or harm) and difficulty solving ordinary social problems (Dodge et al., 1995).

Thus, while *not* suggesting that every delinquent youth is emotionally dysregulated due to traumatic victimization, these findings suggest that by focusing on sanctions and services that address *emotional dysregulation* and *distorted information processing*, the juvenile justice system can play a vital role in both helping children who have been traumatically victimized and reducing the likelihood of recidivism and escalating danger to society by youthful offenders whether they have or have not been traumatically victimized. This formulation is consistent with the legal concepts of restorative justice (Secker et al., 2004) and zero tolerance (Bazemore, Zaslaw, & Riester, 2005). Zero tolerance is an approach to criminal justice policy that emphasizes personal responsibility and societal safety, while restorative justice emphasizes the need to integrate community and offender and allow the offender to recognize and repair damage to the community. If delinquent youths are behaving dangerously as a result of dysregulated emotions and distorted information processing, they will best be able to take responsibility and to show respect for other people and the law if they are assisted in *gaining the capacity to manage their emotions and think clearly enough to act responsibly* (Ford, Chapman, Connor, & Cruise, 2012).

Juvenile justice systems have not routinely addressed PTSD. However, in the past decade, as traumatic stress researchers have demonstrated that psychological trauma exposure and PTSD are prevalent among juvenile justice–involved youth, there has been a push to improve the juvenile justice system's response to traumatized youths (Feierman & Ford, 2015; Ford & Blaustein, 2013). At the same time, new approaches to identifying and treating traumatic stress disorders among youth have emerged. The resources include two related but distinct approaches to services for justice-involved youths: *trauma-informed services* (e.g., screening for trauma history and traumatic stress symptoms; providing education for youths, families, and legal and health care professionals and staff about how to recognize and manage traumatic stress) and *trauma-specific services* (e.g., in-depth assessment and evaluation of trauma history and traumatic stress disorders; psychological or psychiatric treatment for PTSD) (Ford, 2012).

Because behaviors associated with PTSD often look very similar to common delinquent behaviors, it is important for juvenile justice staff (and mental health staff working within juvenile justice systems) to recognize that there are multiple pathways to similar symptom patterns. Some juvenile justice systems (e.g., in Connecticut; Ford et al., 2012; Ford & Hawke, 2012) routinely screen youth to identify those with a history of trauma exposure, PTSD symptoms, and related risks such as suicidality, depression, and substance abuse. In terms of exposure, it is important to determine what specific traumatic stressors have occurred at what ages, and in what circumstances, in each youth's life. In terms of symptoms, it is important to determine what specific PTSD or associated traumatic stress reactions or trauma-exacerbated symptoms are interfering with a youth's ability to think clearly and demonstrate healthy choices and positive growth. Screening instruments include comprehensive trauma history measures such as the Traumatic Events Screening Instrument (see Box 6.3), PTSD symptom measures such as the UCLA PTSD Index (see Chapter 6), and brief yet broad measures of associated symptoms such as Massachusetts Youth Screening Instrument, Version 2 (MAYSI-2; Grisso, Barnum, Fletcher, Cauffman, & Peuschold, 2001), or the Traumatic Symptom Checklist for Children (TSCC; see Chapter 6).

Screening should be followed by education for all youth, particularly those who are identified as having histories of exposure to traumatic stressors and PTSD or related symptoms (which unfortunately represents 75% or more of the juvenile justice population; Ford, Hartman, Hawke, & Chapman, 2008), with education about how traumatic stressors can lead to PTSD and how to cope with stress reactions so that PTSD does not occur or is manageable. Connecticut has a relatively small juvenile justice population proportionate to the state's overall population, with juvenile justice services concentrated in 13 courts and associated probation offices, 5 detention centers (three primarily for boys, two exclusively for girls), and a training school for incarceration of boys. Connecticut has adopted a systematic screening and educational protocol for traumatic stress and associated behavioral and socioemotional impairments based upon the TARGET model (Ford, 2015; Ford & Hawke, 2012). TARGET is serving as a foundation for making every detention center, every probation officer working with girls (those working with boys expected to soon follow), and other youth programs trauma-informed. Administrators, line staff, health care staff, probation officers, and community program providers and consulting clinicians have received training and are receiving ongoing consultation to enable them to adapt the TARGET model to each distinct setting with gender sensitivity and cultural competence. A field study funded by the Office of Juvenile Justice and Delinquency Programs involved a several-year evaluation that showed that youth in juvenile detention centers who received TARGET in groups and in the day-to-day center milieu were less likely to be involved in disruptive incidents or to have correctional sanctions than youth who did not receive TARGET (Ford & Hawke, 2012).

Ohio has a vastly larger juvenile justice system than Connecticut—one of the largest in the country—and is implementing a trauma initiative incrementally due to the size of the system. Ohio's Department of Children, Youth, and Families has determined that trauma exposure is of sufficient prevalence that trauma-informed services are a top priority for all youth involved in the system. Staff within six juvenile justice mental health residential treatment programs for youths with psychiatric as well as legal problems have received intensive training in the TARGET model and are receiving ongoing consultation as they revise their policies and procedures and implement milieu and group programs using the self-regulation skills taught in TARGET. A quasi-experimental evaluation study comparing similar programs that do not adopt the TARGET educational curriculum has shown that units on which TARGET is provided have as much as 75% fewer disruptive incidents and restraints than other units (Marrow, Knudsen, Olafson, & Bucher, 2012). Boys and girls who participated in the TARGET intervention reported significantly greater reductions in depression and anger, and increases in self-efficacy and engagement in rehabilitative services, compared to youth on units that did not provide TARGET.

From a fiscal perspective, the development of PTSD screening and secondary or tertiary prevention services (see Chapter 9) in existing juvenile justice programs and settings can be achieved cost effectively. Ford et al. (2007) describe how this can be done using blended funding strategies, such as with the federal low-income subsidies provided by Medicaid, mental health "block grants," and Temporary Assistance to Needy Families. Providing educational, rehabilitative, and therapeutic programs designed to reduce posttraumatic dysregulation (see Chapter 6) can shift the entire culture of juvenile justice programs (Bloom, 2013; Ford & Blaustein, 2013) and the larger systems in which they operate (Feierman & Ford, 2015; Ford et al., 2012) toward fostering self-regulation and away from punishment.

Adult criminal justice system

An estimated 2 million adults (http://www.bjs.gov/content/pub/press/cpus12pr.cfm) are incarcerated in the United States (in 2012), with an estimated 58% in state prisons, 9% in federal prisons, and 32% in local jails. Sixteen percent, of state prison inmates, 7% of federal inmates, and 16% of jail inmates suffer from a psychiatric disorder (Ditton, 1999). More precise epidemiological research estimates of current and lifetime prevalence of psychiatric disorders among men (Trestman, Ford, Zhang, & Wiesbrock, 2007) and women (Jordan, Schlenger, Fairbank, & Caddell, 1996; Teplin, Abram, & McClelland, 1997) in jail or prison indicate that psychiatric disorders are substantially more prevalent among incarcerated adults than in community studies. Most incarcerated adults with psychiatric disorders have comorbid substance use disorders (Abram, Teplin, McLelland, & Dulcan, 2003), yet fewer than 25% receive any (Teplin, Abram, & McClelland, 1997) or adequate treatment (Jordan et al., 2002).

Despite the many risk factors for exposure to violence and other traumatic stressors faced by incarcerated adults, PTSD has only recently been studied in adult correctional populations. A study of a representative sample of newly incarcerated adults who had not been identified as having any psychiatric disorder found that 12% met criteria for current PTSD and 29% for lifetime PTSD (Trestman et al., 2007), with women having double the risk of men, comparable to findings from studies of pretrial female jail detainees (Teplin et al., 1996) and newly incarcerated female felons (Jordan et al., 1996). Goff, Rose, Rose, and Purves (2007) identified four studies of adults incarcerated in prison from four countries (Australia, Canada, New Zealand, United States) that estimated the current prevalence of PTSD to be between 4% and 21% for men and 10% and 21% for mixed-gender samples. These current PTSD prevalence estimates, while varying in their definition of timing (e.g., past month, 6 months, or year), consistently exceed the 2% (Stein, Walker, Hazen, & Forde, 1997) to 2.8% (Kessler, Sonnega, Bromet, Hughes, & Nelson, 1995) estimates for current PTSD prevalence in the community. Screening incarcerated adults for PTSD and providing them with education and access to preventive or treatment services regarding PTSD therefore may be an important unmet need.

Brief screening measures have been developed to identify persons with or at risk for PTSD and have been tested in psychiatric, medical, community, and school settings (see Chapter 6). A brief screen originally developed to detect PTSD in primary care medical care, the four-item PC-PTSD, has shown consistent evidence of clinical utility in identifying adults with PTSD in primary medical care settings (Ouimette, Wade, Prins, & Schohn, 2008; Prins et al., 2003) and substance abuse treatment (Kimerling, Trafton, & Ngyuen, 2006) populations. When tested in a research study with more than 2000 newly incarcerated adult jail admissions, the PC-PTSD was able to more than 70% accurately identify the 3% of men and 15% of women who were found to meet diagnostic criteria for PTSD using the Clinician Administered PTSD Scale (CAPS; see Chapter 6; Ford, Trestman, et al., 2007; Ford, Trestman, Wiesbrock, & Zhang, 2009).

Despite the apparent prevalence of PTSD among incarcerated adults and the availability of a brief screening instrument to identify those most likely to need assistance with (or to prevent) PTSD, few published scientific studies of PTSD treatment for this vulnerable "captive" audience exist. Pilot studies have been reported with incarcerated women, including an integrative group cognitive-behavioral therapy ("Seeking Safety"; see Chapter 7) that was found to be associated with reduced PTSD and substance use among incarcerated women with substance abuse disorders, although 33% were reincarcerated within 3 months (Zlotnick, Najavits, Rohsenow, & Johnson, 2003). A different cognitive-behavioral group therapy for incarcerated women with histories of childhood sexual and/or physical abuse (including Dialectical Behavior

Therapy (see Chapter 7) skills and writing assignments) resulted in gains on the Beck Depression Inventory, Inventory of Interpersonal Problems, and Trauma Symptom Inventory (Bradley & Follingstad, 2003). However, the dropout rate from the group therapy was high (46%), and effects on reincarceration were not tested. Two forms of cognitive-behavioral therapy delivered in one-to-one sessions—relaxation therapy and eye movement desensitization reprocessing (EMDR; see Chapter 7)—were not effective in reducing the anxiety of four of five battered incarcerated women (Colosetti & Thyer, 2000). Only the first of these pilot studies systematically investigated the ability of the intervention to engage women in the program (Zlotnick et al., 2003), and none used a comparison condition or randomized assignment.

Recently, a PTSD treatment for incarcerated women was shown to be efficacious in a scientific outcome study (Ford, Chang, Levine, & Zhang, 2013). The treatment was a group therapy designed to enhance women's skills for managing reactive emotions in their current lives as well as to educate them about how using these skills can enhance their personal effectiveness and help them to gain control of posttraumatic stress reactions (Trauma Affect Regulation: Guide for Education and Therapy, TARGET; Ford, 2015). TARGET, which had demonstrated efficacy as a group therapy for adults in substance abuse treatment (Frisman et al., 2008), was compared to a supportive group therapy (SGT) that previously had shown evidence of modest benefits with women survivors of childhood abuse (Wallis, 2002). Incarcerated women who participated in TARGET groups reported significant decreases in PTSD, depression, dissociation, self-harm, and sexual problems and increased hope. TARGET recipients also showed significantly greater increases in forgiveness towards others who had harmed them than SGT recipients.

Incarcerated women (Wolff et al., 2011) and men (Wolff, Huening, Shi, & Frueh, 2014) often face complex rehabilitation challenges due to experiencing the combination of PTSD and substance abuse or dependence. Wolff, Frueh, Shi, and Schumann (2012) conducted groups with the Seeking Safety intervention for co-occurring PTSD and substance abuse (see Chapter 8) with incarcerated women and found evidence of clinically significant reductions in PTSD symptom levels after completion of the group for a subset of participants who, prior to the group, had severe PTSD symptoms. Substance use problems could not be directly assessed due to the women's incarceration status, but the majority of group attendees reported substantial reductions in general psychological distress. Thus, providing systematic treatment for the combined problems of PTSD and substance abuse is a potentially valuable role that traumatic stress professionals can play in the rehabilitation of incarcerated women. Because similar findings have been reported with the TARGET intervention with men as well as women in recovery from substance use disorders (Frisman et al., 2008), these services may be an important contribution to rehabiliting incarcerated men as well.

Forensic challenges for PTSD clinicians and researchers

Exaggeration of PTSD symptoms for legal or disability compensation ("malingering"). Malingering is defined in *DSM-5* as "the intentional reporting of symptoms for personal gain (e.g., money, time off work)" (American Psychiatric Association, 2013, p. 326). Factitious Disorder (300.19 in the *DSM-5*) is a similar condition that involves the "falsification of physical or psychological signs or symptoms, or induction of injury of disease, associated with identified deception," except that in this case there is an "absence of obvious external rewards" (American Psychiatric Association, 2013, p. 324). Soliman and Resnick (2008) conclude that:

> *PTSD is relatively easy to feign, since the symptoms are largely subjective and the criteria are widely available. Each malingerer is like an actor playing a role, and the key to detecting malingering is having a detailed understanding of the symptoms that they might fake. Some clues to malingered PTSD include the verbatim recitation of PTSD criteria, an inability to explain how PTSD symptoms affect daily activities, alleging constant or worsening symptoms, and incongruence between reported symptoms and observed signs during the interview. (p. 284)*

Resnick, West, and Payne (2008) hypothesized that there actually are three distinct types of malingering related to PTSD. "Pure" malingering involves inventing both a false history of exposure to traumatic stressors and false PTSD symptoms. "Partial" malingering is subtler, involving the falsely reporting or exaggerating of PTSD symptoms by individuals who actually have experienced traumatic stressors but in reality are not sufficiently symptomatic to warrant a PTSD diagnosis. The "false imputation" variant is a rarer subtype, involving true experiences of traumatic stressors and true PTSD symptoms, but making a false claim that the symptoms were caused by specific traumatic exposures (e.g., asserting that an automobile accident or workplace injury was the source of PTSD symptoms when they actually were due to childhood exposures to traumatic stressors). A study by Wooley and Rogers (2015) tested this model with men and women incarcerated due to criminal histories in a mental health inpatient facility who were asked to either honestly report or falsify their trauma histories and PTSD symptoms. The pure malingerers and the false imputation malingerers were relatively easy to detect because they reported much higher levels of PTSD symptoms than the honest PTSD subgroup, and their answers to a personality questionnaire revealed that they were distorting their descriptions of themselves in a manner designed to accentuate negative characteristics. The partial malingerers were more difficult to detect, because they tended to report their PTSD symptoms accurately, and they did not distort their descriptions of themselves generally as much as the other malingering subtypes (although they did negatively distort their personality descriptions sufficiently to be potentially distinguishable from the true PTSD subgroup). These intriguing findings suggest that the greatest challenge to PTSD forensic assessors when called upon to detect malingering is not to identify individuals who completely fabricate their trauma history and PTSD or the link between specific traumatic exposures and PTSD symptoms, but instead those who have genuine trauma histories but are inaccurately reporting symptoms that either are not real or that are due to other problems (such as a preexisting depression or anxiety disorder) and not traumatic stress.

In addition to clinical observation, psychometric testing has been scientifically studied as a basis for detecting false or exaggerated claims of PTSD. Elhai and colleagues conducted a series of studies with military veterans using the MMPI-2 and found that several subscales (F, F-Fb, F-K, Ds$_2$, O-S, and OT) provided over 80% accuracy (80% sensitivity, 86% specificity) in detecting individuals who claimed to have PTSD but were found to be exaggerating or fabricating the symptoms (Elhai & Frueh, 2001; Elhai, Gold, Sellers, & Dorfman, 2001; Elhai et al., 2004, 2002). Veterans with very extreme scores on the MMPI-2 validity scales associated with exaggerating (Infrequency [F] ≥ 120) or fabricating (Dissimulation [Ds] ≥ 97) were most likely to be malingering. A meta-analysis (i.e., a statistical summary of the findings of numerous independent scientific investigations) of 73 studies using the MMPI-2 to detect psychiatric malingering found that most individuals who actually had PTSD scored within the mildly to moderately distressed range on most of the test's scales, except for having extremely high scores on the F scale and a related subscale that assesses exaggerated responses (Fb) (Rogers, Sewell, Martin, & Vitacco, 2003).

Elhai et al. (2002) also identified a set of MMPI-2 items (Fptsd) that better discriminated from true PTSD than the F scale or two variants, Fb and Fp (the latter subscale has items that are infrequently endorsed by persons with genuine psychiatric disorders). Subsequent research demonstrated that Fp was the best detector of malingered PTSD among civilian adults, while Fptsd was best with military veterans (Elhai et al., 2004). Other studies suggest that it is important to use several MMPI-2 validity scales in order to confirm malingered PTSD (Box 10.4; Franklin, Repasky, Thompson, Shelton, & Uddo, 2002). It also is important to note that very different cutoff scores for what constitutes evidence of malingered PTSD have been reported with the MMPI-2 validity scales, depending on the specific population (such as military veterans versus civilian accident victims or childhood abuse survivors) and circumstances (such as a civil or criminal trial or an application for disability) (Hall & Hall, 2006). It also is possible that savvy attorneys or litigants can use knowledge of the nature of the MMPI-2 validity scales to not only fake PTSD but also to fool the forensic tester (Hall & Hall, 2007).

Box 10.4 Case Study: PTSD, Real or Malingering?

The following case illustrates the importance and difficulty of distinguishing between true PTSD and exaggerated or fabricated claims of PTSD.

A 50-year-old Vietnam veteran applied for [disability benefits] for PTSD shortly after his discharge from the Army and was initially denied. After a minor traffic accident (no injury or obvious threat to life) many years after his discharge, he again applied for VA benefits, claiming the accident had activated a delayed PTSD related to his military service. On this attempt, he received a 50% disability rating and an explanation, in writing, as to why he did not qualify for 70% disability. A higher evaluation of 70% impairment is not warranted unless there are deficiencies in most areas such as work, school, or family relations; judgment, thinking, or mood due to such symptoms as suicidal ideation; obsessive rituals, which interfere with routine activities; speech intermittently

(Continued)

Box 10.4 Continued

illogical, obscure, or irrelevant; near-continuous panic or depression affecting the ability to function independently, appropriately, and effectively; impaired impulse control (such as unprovoked irritability with periods of violence); spatial disorientation; neglect of personal appearance and hygiene; difficulty in adapting to stressful circumstances (including work or a work-like setting); and inability to establish and maintain effective relationships. After receiving the above information, the veteran presented to a VA hospital and reported that he had not shaved for the last 2 weeks; was having crying spells; was irritable and hypervigilant; had low frustration tolerance; had difficulty sleeping; felt suicidal; was having flashbacks ([that were] not dissociative in nature), heard voices, and had nightmares; could not communicate at work or with family; felt distant; could not remember things; had to keep checking for weapons; and had continuous panic attacks. He also reported that his wife told him that he did not make sense intermittently. On appeal of his second PTSD disability claim, he was approved for 70% disability.

After receiving the additional disability, he filed a civil suit claiming the minor accident had caused *de novo* [new] PTSD. The civil case was dismissed when it became apparent that he had lied about his previous medical history, records, and disability status; that he had psychometric testing suggestive of malingering; that he had extreme and inconsistent symptoms at the time of his evaluation, which were out of proportion to the level of trauma he experienced; and that he did not have commonly seen risk factors preceding the event or at the time of the event. This case demonstrated the patient-driven subjective nature of the symptoms of PTSD; clear secondary gain (the desire to benefit from being or acting "sick") as motivation for malingering; the ease with which additional symptoms were generated from a prompting/symptom checklist; the importance of verifying the history; and the importance of the clinician's understanding of the symptoms which usually occur in true PTSD and how they differ from those seen in malingering, as well as the ambiguity of what constitutes a traumatic event.

The case report does not describe the military veteran's experiences while in the Army, which may have been legitimately psychologically traumatic in some cases or may have never risen to the level of traumatic stressors. It also is not clear whether the recent motor vehicle accident was psychologically traumatic and whether the accident (even if not itself actually traumatic) reactivated traumatic stress symptoms sufficiently to constitute a delayed case of military-related PTSD. These are plausible possibilities that may be overlooked when there is a strong possibility of malingering, particularly because PTSD often involves avoidance symptoms that may include an avoidance of disclosing the full extent of distressing (intrusive) memories and associated emotional or physiological (hyperarousal) distress, as well as emotional numbing and social detachment symptoms that may lead to understatement or diminished awareness of the posttraumatic memories and distress. It is important to have evidence that is as clearcut as in the present case to show that the person is merely "reciting" a list of symptoms (particularly that the symptoms are not consistently reported over time) and of actions or circumstances that are distinctly inconsistent with the reported symptoms (such as not actually showing evidence of an extreme startle response in an interview despite stating that being severely startled was common).

Note, however, that extreme, and at times inconsistent, responses regarding potentially traumatic events or PTSD symptoms should *not* be assumed to reflect malingering. It is only after a thorough assessment of past history (verifying specific traumatic incidents with public records whenever possible), current symptoms and problems in living (verified whenever possible by other persons who know the individual well and can provide relatively objective appraisals), and psychological testing for signs of malingering (such as with the MMPI-2) that a conclusion can be drawn with a reasonable degree of accuracy in a forensic evaluation of the validity of an individual's claim to be suffering from PTSD.

MMPI-2 Scales and Sub-scales Used to Identify Malingering

1. Cannot Say (? Or CS): number left unanswered or answered as both true and false
2. Correction or Defensiveness (K): attempts to portray self favorably, but more subtle than L
3. Deceptive Subtle (DS): subset of the subtle questions noted for high face validity, but minimal predictive value for pathology
4. Ego Strength (ES): original indicated prognosis for psychotherapy, extremely low (ES with normal mental status suggests overreporting psychopathology)
5. Fake Bad (FBS): designed to detect simulated emotional stress in personal injury claimants, obvious items endorsed versus more subtle items not listed
6. Back F (FB): infrequently endorsed items, indicating extreme pathology, cry for help, symptom exaggeration (questions 280 on)
7. F-FB: consistency of answers for first half of test and second half
8. Gough Dissimulation Index (F-K): high scores correlate with overreporting, low scores with underreporting
9. Gough Dissimulation Scale for the MMPI-2 (Ds2): infrequently endorsed affective items
10. Infrequency (F): infrequently endorsed items, indicating extreme pathology, cry for help, symptom exaggeration (first 361 questions)
11. Infrequency-Psychopathology (Fp): infrequent responses in a psychiatric population
12. Infrequency-PTSD (Fptsd): infrequently endorsed responses in sample of veterans diagnosed with PTSD
13. Lie (L): unsophisticated attempt to portray favorable impression
14. Keane PTSD (PK): combat-related PTSD, (norm versus treatment-seeking military veterans)
15. Obvious Items (Ob): selections with high face value of pathology
16. Obvious Minus Subtle (OS): index of symptom exaggeration

(Continued)

Box 10.4 Continued

17. Other Subtle (Os): subset of subtle questions more predictive of pathology
18. Schlenger PTSD (PS): difference between subtle and obvious, suggests overreporting combat-related PTSD (norm versus untreated vets)
19. Subtle items (Su): 100-question subscale
20. Superlative Self-Presentation (S): test of defensiveness for people presenting self in highly virtuous manner
21. Total Obvious (OT): obvious symptoms associated with pathology reported
22. True Response Inconsistency (TRIN): 20 pairs of questions to which same response is inconsistent
23. Variable Response Inconsistency (VRIN): sum of inconsistent responses

MMPI Results from Meta-analysis Study by Rogers et al. (2003)

Presumptively genuine PTSD patients	Feigners of all conditions
L scale 52.67 ± 1 SD 9.31	L scale 49.42.67 ± 1 SD 11.47
F 86.31 ± 1 SD 21.58	F 108.09 ± 1 SD 23.82
K 38.30 ± 1 SD 7.31	K 38.24 ± 1 SD 7.90
Fb 92.31 ± 1 SD 24.55	FB 107.52 ± 1 SD 25.50
F-K 8.70 ± 1 SD 10.60	F-K 25.49 ± 1 SD 20.55
Fp 69.02 ± 1 SD 21.00	Fp 86.41 ± 1 SD 25.22
O-S 182.24 ± 1 SD 71.79	O-S 200.84 ± 1 SD 73.77
Ds 68.40 ± 1 SD 14.60	Ds 87.49 ± 1 SD 15.70
FBS 80.36 ± 1 SD 14.51	FBS 80.71 ± 1 SD 16.43

Case study and Tables from Hall and Hall (2007), reprinted with permission.

It is tempting to seek a solution to forensic malingering of PTSD in the form of a polygraph-like test of physiological reactivity, because hyperarousal is a central feature of PTSD. However, like polygraph testing, psychophysiological testing for stress reactivity can be faked and is not infallible (Hall & Hall, 2006). A study in which participants who did not have PTSD were instructed to produce extreme states of physical tension in order to simulate the PTSD hyperarousal state showed that the simulators could produce heart rate elevations comparable to those of military veterans with PTSD but could not produce a full range of psychophysiological reactivity shown by most of the veterans with PTSD (see Chapter 5). Thus, testing that shows multichannel stress reactivity might be a candidate for a physiological test for PTSD. However, studies of the physiological reactivity of persons with or without PTSD consistently have shown that approximately one in four persons with PTSD do *not* show some or all of the classic stress reactivity that typically is associated with PTSD (Hall & Hall, 2006). Therefore, physiological testing of stress reactivity may contribute evidence to support a forensic diagnosis of PTSD but cannot be used to definitively rule out PTSD or to demonstrate malingering of PTSD.

PTSD as a mitigating factor in criminal culpability. PTSD may be alleged to have caused a person to commit criminal acts or to have diminished capacity to have understood the criminal nature of such actions. This is based upon the clinical observation that PTSD often involves episodes of disorientation, confusion, and erratic or poorly considered behavior, and may involve severe dissociative flashbacks in which the person is only partially (or not at all) aware of their current circumstances and actions. Sparr (1996) notes that in the United States criminal justice system, "individuals are considered responsible, and therefore accountable or culpable for their behavior if there [is] … (1) a criminal act (*actus reas*) and (2) criminal intention (*mens reas*)" (p. 405). Therefore, if a psychiatric disorder such as PTSD can be shown to have interfered with the person's capacity for intentional thought (the insanity plea), it is possible for defense attorneys to argue that a defendant who has been shown to have committed a criminal act may nevertheless be NGRI. PTSD also may be a basis for a pretrial plea bargain (such as an agreement to plead guilty to a lesser crime with more serious charges waived) or during the penalty phase to negotiate for a sentence of lesser severity by the court (Sparr, 1996).

When PTSD is considered as a diagnosis by a forensic mental health expert on behalf of a criminal trial defendant, it is always essential to consider alternative explanations for the defendant's apparent suffering and behavior (Sparr, 1996). First and foremost, the possibility that the defendant is exaggerating or fabricating alleged past traumatic events, or the PTSD symptoms from a bona fide or fabricated trauma, at the time of the crime must be thoroughly examined (see Box 10.4). Second, it is possible that the defendant had PTSD at the time of crime but it was unrelated to the intent or acts involved in the crime. PTSD symptoms such as anger, difficulties with mental concentration, and hypervigilance may make a person more susceptible to impulsive acts or may interfere with the ability to judge the consequences of risk or harmful actions, but a specific connection must be established between the PTSD symptom(s) and the absence or diminishment of the ability to make a rational judgment before and during the commission of a criminal act. Sparr (1996) describes this as showing a "causal" relationship between PTSD and the commission of criminal acts, but there is no scientific evidence that PTSD "causes" any specific acts or types of behavior (see Chapter 3). Therefore, at most, a forensic PTSD assessor may be able to establish that PTSD likely contributed to a failure of judgment or behavioral control and thus may be sufficient to be considered a basis for ruling out criminal intention or for reducing the severity of a crime (e.g., from murder to involuntary manslaughter) or of punitive sentencing (e.g., from incarceration to a suspended sentence with mandatory participation in treatment for PTSD).

A special case of this issue involves survivors of DV who injure or kill their battering partner. Expert testimony that the survivor experienced "battered woman syndrome" (a variation of the rape trauma syndrome that involves the symptoms of PTSD; see Box 10.5) was found to lead mock jurors (college students serving as jury members in a simulated trial) to be more lenient in their decisions about criminal culpability than when the expert testimony did not describe the survivor as suffering

Box 10.5 PTSD and Domestic Violence (DV)

According to M. Dutton (2008), DV, also known as intimate partner violence, is:

… an abusive pattern of physical, sexual, or psychological behaviors, and may include stalking. Its severity can range from mild to extreme life-threatening acts. Although DV may involve a single incident, more commonly there is an ongoing pattern over time. DV occurs in heterosexual and same-sex relationships. In heterosexual relationships, women typically experience more severe injury than do men. (p. 231)

According to the Centers for Disease Control and Prevention, DV may include:

- Physical violence, defined as intentional use of physical force with the potential for causing death, disability, injury, or harm, includes pushing, shoving, throwing, slapping, beating, hair pulling, hitting with a fist or object, twisting arms, kicking, strangling, using a weapon, and other acts of physical aggression.
- Sexual abuse involves intentional touching of the genitalia, anus, groin, breast, inner thigh, or buttocks of any person against his or her will, or of any person who is unable to understand the nature or condition of the act, to decline participation, or to communicate unwillingness to be touched, as well as forced witnessing of sexual acts.
- Sexual violence is defined as the use of physical force to compel a person to witness or engage in a sexual act against his or her will (e.g., forcible rape). It also includes an attempted or a completed sex act involving a person who is unable to understand the nature or condition of the act because of illness, disability, use of alcohol or other drugs, or intimidation or pressure.
- Threat of physical or sexual violence involves words, gestures, or weapons to communicate the intent to cause death, disability, injury, or physical harm, or to compel a person to engage in sex acts or abusive sexual contact when the person is either unwilling or unable to consent. In addition to direct verbal threats ("I'm going to kill you"), threats include brandishing a weapon or firing a weapon into the air, gestures, or grabbing for genitalia or breast.
- Psychological abuse includes other verbal threats, intimidation, isolation, victim blaming, humiliation, control of daily activities and money, stalking (repeated unwanted contacts), and manipulation of children in order to demean or instill fear in an adult partner.

Many forms of DV are potentially traumatic events, because they involved threatened or actual harm to self or others and elicit emotions of intense fear, helplessness or horror. DV typically occurs repeatedly, and the threat of recurrence often persists for years because the possibility of contact with an abusive partner rarely ends (M. Dutton, 2008). DV has been associated with a wide range of mental and physical health problems, including PTSD in as many as 33% to more than 80% of survivors (M. Dutton, 2008). Greater severity and frequency of physical violence (especially that which is life threatening), use of a weapon, more severe psychological abuse, sexual abuse, and a history of childhood sexual abuse have been shown to predict greater severity and frequency of PTSD symptoms (M. Dutton, 2008). Women who were living in a shelter due to having experienced DV were most likely to seek mental health services if they were not experiencing general psychological distress, but specifically if they had PTSD symptoms that were severe (Klopper, Schweinle, Ractliffe, & Elhai, 2014). PTSD symptoms may reflect an awareness on the part of individuals who subjected to DV that they are not simply suffering from ordinary blues or worries (which might seem insufficient to warrant seeking help) but that they are being traumatized by the violence and entrapment and need to get help for themselves.

Depression (major depressive disorder) has been found to occur in more than 50% of women survivors of DV (M. Dutton, 2008). The factors that predict who is at risk to develop depression among women survivors of DV are similar to those for PTSD. Women survivors of DV also were found to be approximately twice as likely as other women to develop panic or eating disorders and suicidality, but men survivors of DV were not (Romito & Grassi, 2007).

Women survivors of DV also are more likely than those who have not both to experience physical health problems and to perceive their overall health as poor, including due to headaches, insomnia, chocking sensations, hyperventilation, gastrointestinal symptoms, and chest, back, and pelvic pain (M. Dutton, 2008). A study found that men who had experienced DV also were more than twice as likely as other men to report their health as "less than good" compared to men who did not report having experienced DV (Romito & Grassi, 2007).

Witnessing DV in childhood is reported by more than 10% of adults, 14% of women, and 11.5% of men (Dube et al., 2001). Children who are exposed to DV are more likely than other children to have PTSD, suicidality, and substance use problems (D'Andrea, Ford, Stolbach, Spinazzola, & van der Kolk, 2012), with adverse effects as early as infancy (Bogat, DeJonghe, Levendosky, Davidson, & von Eye, 2006) and toddlerhood (Schechter et al., 2011). Children who grow up in a family scarred by DV are at risk for psychological, interpersonal, and substance use problems, as well as a variety of physical illnesses, both during childhood and adolescence (Bayarri Fernandez, Ezpeleta, Granero, de la Osa, & Domenech, 2011; Jun et al., 2012; Swanston, Bowyer, & Vetere, 2014) and into adulthood (Jucksch et al., 2011; Roos et al., 2013; Sareen et al., 2013). Sensitive parenting can reduce the psychological harm to children caused by DV but not completely prevent it (Gustafsson, Cox, & Blair, 2012).

from that syndrome (Schuller & Rzepa, 2002). Notably, the increased leniency only occurred when "jurors" were instructed to make their own decisions without necessarily following the exact letter of the law. The study findings cannot be assumed to hold true in actual trials, but they suggest that expert testimony concerning PTSD or similar posttraumatic syndromes may lead jurors to have greater empathy for defendants accused of doing harm as a form of self-defense.

Credibility of witness and defendant memories of potentially traumatic events.
Whether witnesses or defendants in legal proceedings can accurately recall psychologically traumatic events is a matter of continuing controversy. PTSD involves several problems with memory, including memories of traumatic events that are paradoxically both exceptionally vivid and yet often fragmented and incomplete. These "intrusive" memories may have broader effects on the person's memory, potentially compromising attention and concentration, short-term memory, and long-term (i.e., for distant past events) memory (Bryant, 2008). However, it is possible that memory problems may precede the experiencing of traumatic stressors and the onset of PTSD, thus constituting "a *risk factor* for PTSD's development (in addition to serving as a consequence)" (Bryant, 2008). People with PTSD often have difficulty recalling specific memories about their personal past ("autobiographical memory"), as is the case with other psychiatric disorders such as major depressive disorder. Additionally, people with PTSD tend to ruminate, and this activity can lead them to have trouble selectively recalling specific experiences because they are preoccupied with vague memories that are distressing and difficult to screen out.

Most relevant to forensic determinations of the accuracy of memory is the controversy described by Bryant (2008, p. 425):

> ... *over the extent to which memory for traumatic events is enhanced or depleted*
> *relative to memories for other events. Much of this debate has focused on the*
> *so-called "repressed memory" issue, which involves the proposition that people*
> *can suppress traumatic memories for prolonged periods (maybe many years)*
> *and then can recall these events later. Also termed dissociative amnesia, this*
> *phenomenon purportedly occurs when people dissociate memory of a trauma*
> *so that it is no longer accessible. Many surveys have been reported concerning*
> *trauma survivors' tendency to have amnesia, but these are sometimes unreliable*
> *sources of information because they often confuse amnesia with normal forgetting,*
> *intentional cognitive avoidance, impaired encoding of an event into memory which*
> *precludes being able to remember it, and reluctance to report a memory that is*
> *retrieved. Experimental approaches have been applied to adults who have survived*
> *childhood sexual abuse. For example, the directed forgetting paradigm is a common*
> *cognitive task in which the subject is presented with trauma-related, positive, or*
> *neutral words, and after each presentation they are asked to forget or remember the*
> *word. Using this paradigm, there is no evidence of superior forgetting in survivors*
> *of childhood sexual abuse; in fact, these individuals tend to recall trauma-related*
> *information very well. In contrast, there is some evidence that people with acute*
> *stress disorder do have a proficiency in forgetting trauma-related information using*
> *a directed forgetting paradigm. Notably, these people display dissociative reactions*
> *to the trauma and have been affected by the trauma only very recently. There is also*
> *evidence that people with PTSD may not retrieve some trauma-related information*
> *adequately because their focus on trauma-related memories may lead to automatic*
> *inhibition of other trauma information. Whereas people tend to have good recall of*
> *traumatic events, their recall is likely to be as flawed, in terms of its accuracy, as*
> *with most memories. Although some theorists have argued that trauma memories*
> *are indelibly imprinted in our memories, and that their recollection is an accurate*
> *account of exactly what transpired, this is far from the truth. Longitudinal studies*

that have assessed trauma survivors at different periods after trauma exposure have found that memory for details of the traumatic event is often not accurate. Similarly, memory for earlier stress reactions is not accurately recalled at later times. As with most memory, studies have found that memory for details of the traumatic event, and of one's reactions, is influenced by the emotional state at the time of recall; people with severe PTSD tend to exaggerate how bad their trauma and their reactions were, whereas those who have fewer stress reactions tend to minimize their experience (McNally, 2003). In summary, our knowledge about how people manage severely distressing trauma memories is limited. At the present time, there is not sound empirical evidence that people do dissociate trauma memories to the extent proposed by dissociative amnesia theories. The general conclusion is that people tend to recall their trauma memories too vividly, although there may be some mechanisms that result in preferential forgetting of other trauma-related information.

Lindblom and Gray (2008) describe a number of normal "mechanisms" or causes for incomplete or inaccurate memory that must be ruled out before PTSD or dissociation are assumed to be even a partial contributor, let alone the cause, of memory problems. These include the normal "decay" (or fading) of memory over time, the incompleteness of initial memory imprints (because total recall is a rare exception rather than the rule), and interference due to intervening events that may disrupt or modify the memory. They describe the conflict that began in the late 1980s when adults who were suffering from emotional distress or conflict and estrangement in their current or past relationships were encouraged by popular media to believe that these problems were due to "repressed" memories of abuse that had to be "recovered" in order to restore emotional health. The "recovered-memory therapy movement," notably spurred by the book *The Courage to Heal* (Bass & Davis, 1988), led to increasing numbers of adults claiming recovered memories of abuse and a backlash from the parents, families, and others who felt accused as abusers and who formed groups such as the now international False Memory Syndrome Foundation. The controversy was fueled by claims of widespread cult abuse, such as in the case of the McMartin Preschool trial, in which allegations against numerous teachers and staff were initially upheld and subsequently found to be false.

The most unfortunate aspect of the overzealous attempts to uncover repressed abuse memories and the countermovement to discredit adults who come forward with memories of abuse from years or decades earlier is that two extreme views have become relatively entrenched despite neither being scientifically valid nor clinically helpful to people who are attempting to recall sensitive and distressing experiences under highly stressful forensic circumstances (such as testifying publicly in court against a violent or sexual assailant). Memory by definition is incomplete and only partially accurate, so the critical goal for forensic assessors with witnesses or defendants who are asked to recall potentially traumatic events is to provide these clients with assistance in clarifying what they can and cannot recall and with what degree of confidence, while also educating them and attorneys and judges on how PTSD can affect—but neither destroys nor invalidates—a person's memory of both traumatic and other experiences.

Lindblom and Gray (2008) provide recommendations including that forensic and other clinicians should not automatically assume psychogenic amnesia to be operating when memories of potentially traumatic events are nonexistent or incomplete. When trauma-related memories are the focus of treatment, clinicians should *not* use "memory recovery" techniques (such as hypnosis) because the validity of "new" or "recovered" memories under those conditions is not established. Additionally, only forensic interviewers with proper training should gather evidence to be used in a court of law.

Dangerousness (and rehabilitation) of sexual and violent offenders. Until recently, the prediction of who will actually commit sexual or violent offenses has been considered to be largely impossible. Past acts of sexual misconduct or physical violence have been viewed as the best—albeit very imperfect—predictors of future acts (McDermott et al., 2008).

However, in the past decade, "actuarial" risk assessment tools have been developed that have shown promise for the identification of persons who are at risk for future sexual offending, including adults (such as the Sexual Offender Risk Assessment Guide, SORAG; Harris & Rice, 2003) and youth (such as the Estimate of Risk of Adolescent Sex Offender Recidivism, ERASOR; Worling, 2004), and for violence, including adults (such as the Violence Assessment Risk Guide, VRAG; Quinsey, Harris, Rice, & Cormier, 2006) and youth (such as the Structured Assessment of Violence Risk in Youth, SAVRY; Borum, Bartel, & Forth, 2003). Actuarial tests are constructed by identifying the specific questions or factors from a wide variety of prior clinical and scientific studies that most consistently are associated with the problem of concern, and then conducting new scientific studies to hone in on a subset of factors that best predict the problem's future occurrence. For example, McDermott et al. (2008) collected interview, clinician rating, and questionnaire assessments for 108 forensically committed adult psychiatric inpatients, most of whom were placed in the locked facility following a trial in which they were judged to be NGRI. The researchers found that in two risk assessment tests (the HCR-20 and the VRAG), severe symptoms of impulsivity, social detachment, hostility, and depression, and secondarily psychopathy (an absence of empathy or concern for other people or their rights or welfare) were predictive of actual acts of aggression over a 1- to 4-year time period.

Risk factors assessed with adult offenders for actuarial purposes to predict the likelihood of reoffense tend to include (from the VRAG, #1–12, the SORAG, #13 and 14, or both #15 and 16):

1. did not live with both parents until age 18;
2. elementary school maladjustment;
3. history of alcohol problems;
4. unmarried;
5. nonviolent offense history (other criminal offenses than violent ones);
6. severity of physical injury to primary victim;
7. male gender of primary victim;
8. *DSM-III* personality disorder;
9. *DSM-III* schizophrenia diagnosis;
10. Psychopathy Checklist-Revised (PCL-R), a measure of severe psychopathy;
11. victims other than girls under the age of 14;

12. deviant sexual interests in phallometric testing (physiological measures of sexual arousal in response to pictures or films depicting abusive sexual activities);
13. failure to successfully return to the community after prior conditional release from incarceration or secure treatment;
14. younger age at time of the offense.

Some adult risk assessments and most of those developed for youth, such as the SAVRY and ERASOR, sample a broader array of risk factors, including individual risk characteristics (such as impulsivity and poor emotion regulation), social risk factors (such as the absence of an intimate peer group or involvement in a peer group that endorses sexual offending or violence), familial risk factors (such as chaotic family relationships and conflict with or little involvement from parents), and protective factors (such as supportive peer, family, or parental relationships, and involvement in school or prosocial extracurricular activities).

Assessment of history of traumatic stressor exposure and PTSD are conspicuously absent from the hundreds of recent studies on the prediction of violence and sexual offending. When trauma history or PTSD has been considered as a potential risk factor for violence, it tends to be associated with violence risk but less strongly than factors such as impulsivity, psychosis, and dissociation—with the exception of exposure to violence as a victim in childhood or in atrocities during military service, and severe neglect (Fehon, Grilo, & Lipschitz, 2005; Taft et al., 2005).

In addition, many of the actuarial risk factors that have been identified as predictors of future sexual or violent offending are likely to be associated with exposure to traumatic stressors and PTSD (such as alcohol problems, hostility, impulsivity, and personality disorders) (Box 10.6).

Box 10.6 PTSD and Criminal Behavior

PTSD can be linked to criminal behavior in two primary ways. First, symptoms of PTSD can incidentally lead to criminal behavior. Second, offenses can be directly connected to the specific trauma that an individual experienced.

PTSD symptoms can lead to an individual to be vulnerable to engaging in criminal behavior and/or sudden outbursts of violence. Individuals with PTSD are often plagued by memories of the trauma and are chronically on edge (or in the new dissociative subtype of PTSD, emotionally tuned out). Often, attempts are made to self-medicate with drugs and alcohol. The emotional numbness many trauma survivors experience can lead the survivor to engage in sensation-seeking behavior in an attempt to experience some type of emotion. Some combat veterans also may seek to recreate the adrenaline rush experienced during combat. Feeling the need to be always "on guard" can cause veterans to misinterpret benign situations as threatening and cause them to respond with self-protective behavior. Increased baseline physiological arousal results in violent behavior that is out of proportion to the perceived threat. It is common for

(Continued)

Box 10.6 Continued

trauma survivors to feel guilt, which can sometimes lead them to commit crimes that will likely result in their apprehension, punishment, serious injury, or death.

A direct link between a particular traumatic stressor and a specific crime can be indicated in three primary ways. First, crimes at times literally or symbolically recreate important aspects of a trauma. *State v. Gregory* (1. State v. Gregory, No. 19205 (Cr. Ct. Montgomery County, Md. 1979)) provides an example of this type of case. Mr. Gregory, a Vietnam combat veteran, was charged with eight counts of kidnapping and assault after an incident at a bank in Silver Springs, Maryland, on February 9, 1977. He entered the bank dressed in a suit with his military decorations pinned on it and armed with two M-16 automatic rifles, the weapon used by US forces in Vietnam. He announced that he was not robbing the bank, let the women and children go, and took the remaining occupants hostage. Over a 5-hour period, Mr. Gregory fired over 250 rounds of ammunition into the air and at inanimate objects before the police apprehended him without serious injury to anyone.

Mr. Gregory was initially convicted, but the conviction was later overturned on appeal. The examining psychiatrist determined that Mr. Gregory had been one of very few survivors of an ambush in Vietnam, and the psychiatrist testified that the defendant's behavior in the bank was an attempt to recreate an ambush situation. Also, his behavior was viewed as an attempt at passive suicide in order to relieve the intense guilt he felt about having survived the ambush in Vietnam when so many others perished.

The second way that traumatic stressors can be linked to specific crimes is that environmental conditions similar to those existing at the time of the trauma can induce behavior (in particular, violent responses) similar to that exhibited during the trauma. *People v. Wood* (People v. Wood, 80-7410 (Cir. Ct. Cook County, Ill., May 5, 1982)) is an example of this type of case. Mr. Wood was charged with attempted murder after shooting his foreman during a dispute. His prior diagnosis of PTSD and his history of combat duty in Vietnam were documented. Testimony and actual tape recordings were introduced that showed a similarity between the noises in the factory and noises Mr. Wood heard during combat, and it was argued that these conditions set the stage for Mr. Wood's violent behavior. The jury returned a verdict of NGRI.

The final way that traumatic stressors can be linked to specific crimes is that life events immediately preceding the offense can realistically or symbolically force the individual to face unresolved conflicts related to the trauma. This creates a disturbed psychological state in which otherwise unlikely behaviors emerge. *State v. Heads* (State v. Heads (1980) http://www.ecases.us/case/la/1742227/ state-v-heads) is an example of this type of case. Mr. Heads, a Vietnam combat veteran with no prior criminal history, was convicted of second-degree murder in 1978 after breaking into his sister-in-law's house and repeatedly firing a .45 caliber automatic pistol. One of the bullets killed the sister-in-law's husband.

Mr. Heads had recently separated from his wife and had entered his sister-in-law's home in an attempt to locate her. Because he had experienced the loss of many friends in Vietnam, the severe emotional threat of losing his wife disrupted his psychological equilibrium and resulted in extremely violent behavior. In addition, the scene of the shooting in Louisiana was described as "Vietnam-like," which was seen as contributing to his violence. His conviction was over-turned on appeal in 1981 when a jury returned a verdict of NGRI.

Crimes that are directly linked to traumatic stressors usually have certain characteristics. Often, the defendant has no criminal history and cannot offer a coherent explanation for the behavior. Others may also find it difficult to discern any current motivation for the crime. The choice of a victim may seem acci-dental, and an apparently benign situation may result in violence. There may be amnesia surrounding all or part of the crime, and the individual may report that there were numerous stressors prior to the crime that related literally or psycho-logically to the original trauma. The act itself may also be linked symbolically or realistically to the original trauma. However, the individual is usually unaware of this connection.

The presence of PTSD can be considered by a court during sentencing. If a defendant is diagnosed with PTSD, this information can be introduced as a miti-gating factor in the penalty phase of a capital case. In states with versions of the "three strikes" law and in federal cases, the presence of PTSD may be a reason for the court to depart from mandatory sentencing guidelines.

Various issues pertaining to an individual's traumatic experience and subsequent adjustment are relevant when PTSD is introduced in sentencing proceedings:

- Was any type of treatment made available to the defendant either immediately after the event or in the months afterward?
- At what age did the trauma occur, and what are the ramifications for the defendant's personality development? Although trauma at an early age can have a more pervasive effect on an individual's functioning, it is easier to document pre- and posttrauma personality changes when the stressors have been experienced at a later age.
- If a defendant has a history of criminal convictions or poor adjustment during prior incarcerations, what is the role that undiagnosed PTSD may have played in this behav-ior? Because being in prison requires a person to be constantly vigilant regarding the threat of violence, an individual with PTSD who is in prison can be profoundly retraumatized, and his or her PTSD symptoms may be exacerbated to the point where he or she will act out with violence.
- Finally, what is the psychiatric prognosis? Although PTSD is a chronic condition, with the proper treatment and education, its symptoms can usually be successfully managed. It is unlikely that survivors receive the proper treatment for PTSD during incarceration. In fact, because prison life may retraumatize a person, a lengthy incar-ceration will likely seriously exacerbate PTSD symptoms and cause the person's level of functioning to deteriorate.

Adapted from "Criminal Behavior and PTSD: A National Center for PTSD Fact Sheet," by C. Baker & C. Alfonso, with permission from the National Center for PTSD (www.ncptsd.org).

Thus, while neither exposure to psychological trauma nor PTSD can be used to identify adults or youth who are likely to commit violent or sexual offenses, both should be considered as potential contributors to the severity of risk or offending when other risk factors are present. Rather than viewing psychological trauma or PTSD as causes of violence or sexual offending—which has *not* been demonstrated scientifically or clinically—it is best to consider them as risks that, if addressed in treatment and rehabilitation, may contribute to reducing the risk of violence and sexual offending among persons who pose a high risk to society.

Forensic mental health standards of care and standards of practice

Although most PTSD assessment and treatment protocols and research questions that are addressed in civil or criminal law programs or populations are similar or identical to those found in other areas of PTSD clinical work and scientific study, the forensic context involves special considerations related to both the rights of patients or participants and the safety of the clinician or scientist. Adults and youth involved in civil or criminal justice proceedings or programs are a "vulnerable" population, because they are subject to stressors (such as the impact of harm that some have sustained as a victim or the curtailment of their rights mandated by legal detention, incarceration, parole, or probation) and pressures (such as coercion to disclose otherwise private information and the threat of potentially severe legal consequences) that are extraordinary. Thus, it is essential that the traumatic stress clinician or researcher not intentionally or inadvertently create additional stressors or pressures, and particularly not violate any fundamental legal rights.

Crucial areas of caution for traumatic stress clinicians and researchers in forensic contexts involve the protection of patients' or participants' confidentiality and informed consent, safety of self and others, and right to an accurate diagnosis and appropriate treatment (Heilbrun, DeMatteo, Marczyk, & Goldstein, 2008). In addition, Soliman and Resnick (2008) note that it is important to be aware of and avoid "dual relationships" that may involve conflicts of interest for the forensic traumatic stress professional.

Preserving confidentiality requires attention to not releasing personally identifying information without the written informed consent of the adult (or the legal guardian of a minor). The only possible exceptions are the use of private information for the exact purposes for which the information has been gathered—typically to assist in the legal proceedings, as authorized by the person's legal representative—or if either officially ordered by the court or required in order to prevent harm to the person or others. Any information that is legally commanded to be disclosed without the consent of the person and the approval of his or her legal representative should be checked with an independent legal advisor (such as the attorney representing the researcher's university or the clinician's clinic or hospital) before being disclosed, even if formally required by a subpoena.

Traumatic stress research in forensic settings always should have received approval for all study procedures and for the specific methods of obtaining fully informed consent by an independent research review committee (often called an "Institutional Review Board," or IRB). The IRB not only scrutinizes the study protocol carefully but also includes representative(s) who are specifically knowledgeable about the rights and potential threats to confidentiality and free choice faced by legally involved persons. For example, these special reviewers are designated "prisoner advocates" for research studies involving incarcerated youth or adults. Fully informed consent may not be possible in many legal contexts such as juvenile detention, jail, or prison, because the person is subject to pressures that may not be obvious to the researcher or clinician (such as coercion to participate in an assessment or a research study in order to not forfeit certain privileges or to improve the chance of parole or release). Therefore, precautions may be needed—and often already are in place—to prevent assessment, treatment, or research from offering choices that cannot be made with full freedom of choice. For example, a randomized clinical trial testing therapeutic treatments may be required to provide equally beneficial alternative therapies rather than using a no-treatment or minimal-treatment control condition (Ford et al., 2013).

When testing or interviewing legally involved persons, they may disclose past incidents of harm done to themselves or others or thoughts of doing harm to self or others in the future. In any clinical or research work, there is an ethical and (in most states in the United States) a legal obligation to report to the legal authorities any information indicating that a person is likely to severely harm self or others. These ethical and legal duties include a duty to warn any person who is likely to be seriously endangered by the patient or study participant and a mandate to report to the legally authorized child protection agency if a child is likely to be maltreated. They also include ensuring that a person who is likely to follow through on a suicide attempt or other potentially severe self-injury is immediately confined and treated in a mental health or medical facility that is authorized to provide emergency crisis intervention.

These requirements and duties regarding protecting the safety of the person and others vary, depending on the exact governmental regulations in different locales, and it is not clear that they are in effect in court proceedings or in assessments, services, or research conducted in criminal justice facilities (Heilbrun et al., 2008). When assessment is done at the request of a criminal defense attorney or a civil plaintiff's attorney, all information is protected by the client-attorney privilege and therefore should not be released without the client's consent and the attorney's concurrence. However, Heilbrun et al. (2008) suggest a basis for providing information about imminent harm or danger directly to the court in order to fulfill the duty to warn, citing the American Bar Association's *Criminal Justice Mental Health Standards*. When making difficult decisions about how best to protect individuals from harm in any clinical or research context, and particularly in the often high-risk court and correctional forensic context, the best general guideline promulgated by all mental health professions is to consult first with knowledgeable colleagues or supervisors and with an impartial legal expert before any action.

Traumatic stress research does not necessarily involve diagnosing PTSD or other mental health conditions, or providing appropriate treatment, but clinicians conducting assessment or treatment with legally involved individuals are responsible ethically (and potentially legally) to develop an accurate diagnostic summary and to offer or recommend treatment that is appropriate to the diagnostic findings. In research, it also often is important to account for the effects of other psychiatric disorders or symptoms beyond PTSD—and doing so requires careful information gathering with reliable and valid assessment instruments that address not only PTSD but the full spectrum of psychiatric and psychosocial problems (Koch, O'Neill, & Douglas, 2005). For clinical purposes, an accurate diagnostic report based on psychometrically and clinically rigorous assessment tools is always essential—even if the primary focus of the assessment is PTSD. So, too, providing or recommending treatment that addresses the client's or patient's full needs—and not just PTSD—is important. Accurate and complete diagnosis and treatment are particularly crucial in forensic work because a failure to do so may be grounds for a complaint to the professional's licensure board or for a lawsuit for malpractice against the professional (Heilbrun et al., 2008). A failure to conduct a comprehensive assessment is problematic in any clinical context, but when this undermines the accuracy or credibility of forensic evaluations and testimony, there may be adverse consequences not only for the person being evaluated but also for the evaluator as a result of the heightened level of legal scrutiny in forensic cases.

"Dual roles" are situations in which a clinician or researcher has a duty to or alliance with more than one client or research collaborator/funder, which may lead to a failure to fulfill the duty to each party if the interests of the clients or collaborator/funders are in conflict. For example, if treatment is being provided to a patient with PTSD, the clinician would not be able to provide expert witness testimony in a legal proceeding involving that patient because it would not be possible to be fully objective and impartial (as is required in forensic expert testimony) due to the therapeutic alliance with the patient. However, there are many "gray area" instances in which there are dual roles, but it may be possible to perform the forensic role as long as the clinician openly discloses her or his primary allegiance. For example, the clinician treating the patient for PTSD could potentially serve as a case-specific forensic witness if he or she makes it clear to all parties (especially the judge) that any testimony or reports provided to the court will be based upon an objective analysis of information obtained in the treatment—but that this is not equivalent to a fully impartial forensic mental health evaluation due to the therapeutic alliance.

PTSD research in forensic contexts also may involve dual roles and conflicts of interest. For example, if a researcher is studying the effects of a medication for PTSD with the sponsorship and funding of the pharmaceutical company that manufactures the medication, the potential conflict of interest must be fully disclosed to all parties (e.g., the administrators in the court or correctional facility in which the study is taking place, and all participants), and the researcher must take stringent precautions to ensure that the study's findings are not biased by the influence of the pharmaceutical company's desire to obtain positive results to support future sales of the medication. Researchers also may encounter dual role situations in forensic contexts that cannot be managed with open disclosure and technical precautions. For example, results of brain scans or neuropsychological or interview testing for studies of the psychobiological features of PTSD with detained youth or incarcerated adults should not be provided to facility clinicians or administrators, attorneys, or the court without the participant's fully informed consent.

Although the stakes are high in forensic traumatic stress clinical work and research studies, unfortunately there are no definitive standards of practice or care to guide the forensic mental health clinician or researcher (Heilbrun et al., 2008). Standards of practice are guidelines set by professional associations that recommend, but do not require, precautions for clinicians and researchers in their professional studies. Standards of care are governmentally mandated rules and regulations that are enforced legally (e.g., through malpractice lawsuits). Standards of care tend to have a higher bar for proving misconduct by a forensic mental health professional—for example, requiring that there be evidence not only of a failure to adequately protect or provide for the welfare of an incarcerated person or litigant but also of intentional misconduct that directly causes harm to the individual (Heilbrun et al., 2008). In the absence of clearcut forensic mental health standards of practice or care, the traumatic stress clinician or researcher working in a forensic context is advised to bear in mind the particular areas of vulnerability of people in the legal system and to carefully follow general standards of practice that apply to clinical practice and scientific research in all settings (Heilbrun et al., 2008). Comprehensive proposals for addressing the clinical and research challenges of forensic PTSD work are provided in a recently published handbook of forensic psychology and neuropsychology (Heilbrun, DeMatteo, & Goldstein, 2015).

References

Abram, K. M., Teplin, L. A., McLelland, G. M., & Dulcan, M. K. (2003). Comorbidity of severe psychiatric disorders and substance use disorders among women in jail. *American Journal of Psychiatry*, *160*, 1007–1010. http://dx.doi.org/10.1176/appi.ajp.160.5.1007.

American Psychiatric Association, (2013). *Diagnostic and statistical manual of mental disorders* (5th ed.). Washington, DC: Author.

Andrews, B., Brewin, C. R., & Rose, S. (2003). Gender, social support, and PTSD in victims of violent crime. *Journal of Traumatic Stress*, *16*, 421–427.

Bass, E., & Davis, L. (1988). *The Courage to Heal*. New York: Harper & Row Publisher.

Bayarri Fernandez, E., Ezpeleta, L., Granero, R., de la Osa, N., & Domenech, J. M. (2011). Degree of exposure to domestic violence, psychopathology, and functional impairment in children and adolescents. [Research Support, Non-U.S. Gov't]. *Journal of Interpersonal Violence*, *26*(6), 1215–1231.

Bazemore, G., Zaslaw, J. G., & Riester, D. (2005). Behind the walls and beyond: Restorative justice, instrumental communities, and effective residential treatment. *Juvenile and Family Court Journal*, *56*(1), 53–73.

Beers, S. R., & De Bellis, M. D. (2002). Neuropsychological function in children with maltreatment-related posttraumatic stress disorder. *American Journal of Psychiatry*, *159*(3), 483–486.

Bloom, S. (2013). The sanctuary model. In J. D. Ford & C. A. Courtois (Eds.), *Treating complex traumatic stress disorders in children and adolescents: Scientific foundations and therapeutic models* (pp. 277–294). New York, NY: Guilford.

Bogat, G. A., DeJonghe, E., Levendosky, A. A., Davidson, W. S., & von Eye, A. (2006). Trauma symptoms among infants exposed to intimate partner violence. *Child Abuse & Neglect*, *35*, 109–125.

Borum, R., Bartel, P., & Forth, A. (2003). *Manual for the structured assessment of violence risk in youth, version 1.1*. Tampa: University of South Florida.

Bradley, R. G., & Follingstad, D. R. (2003). Group therapy for incarcerated women who experienced interpersonal violence: A pilot study. *Journal of Traumatic Stress*, *16*, 337–340.

Bryant, R. (2008b). Memory. In G. Reyes, J. D. Elhai, & J. D. Ford (Eds.), *Encyclopedia of psychological trauma* (pp. 424–426). Hoboken, NJ: Wiley.

Colosetti, S. D., & Thyer, B. A. (2000). The relative effectiveness of EMDR versus relaxation training with battered women prisoners. *Behavior Modification*, *24*, 717–737.

Cordón, I. M., Pipe, M. -E., Sayfan, L., Melinder, A., & Goodman, G. S. (2004). Memory for traumatic experiences in early childhood. *Developmental Review*, *24*, 101–132.

D'Andrea, W., Ford, J., Stolbach, B., Spinazzola, J., & van der Kolk, B. A. (2012). Understanding interpersonal trauma in children: Why we need a developmentally appropriate trauma diagnosis. *American Journal of Orthopsychiatry*, *82*(2), 187–200. http://dx.doi.org/10.1111/j.1939-0025.2012.01154.x.

Ditton, P. M. (1999). Corporate Author U. S. & Bureau of Justice Statistics. *Mental health and treatment of inmates and probationers*. Special report; Variation: Special report. United States. Bureau of Justice Statistics.

Dodge, K. A., Pettit, G. S., Bates, J. E., & Valente, E. (1995). Social information-processing patterns partially mediate the effect of early physical abuse on later conduct problems. *Journal of Abnormal Psychology*, *104*(4), 632–643.

Dube, S. R., Anda, R. F., Felitti, V. J., Chapman, D. P., Williamson, D. F., & Giles, W. H. (2001). Childhood abuse, household dysfunction, and the risk of attempted suicide throughout the life span: Findings from the Adverse Childhood Experiences Study. *Journal of the American Medical Association*, *286*(24), 3089–3096.

Dutton, D. (2008). Perpetration-induced trauma. In G. Reyes, J. D. Elhai, & J. D. Ford (Eds.), *Encyclopedia of psychological trauma* (pp. 466–467). Hoboken, NJ: Wiley.

Dutton, M. A. (2008). Domestic violence. In G. Reyes, J. D. Elhai, & J. D. Ford (Eds.), *Encyclopedia of psychological trauma* (pp. 231–235). Hoboken, NJ: Wiley.

Elhai, J. D., & Frueh, B. C. (2001). Subtypes of clinical presentations in malingerers of posttraumatic stress disorder: An MMPI-2 cluster analysis. *Assessment*, *8*(1), 75–84.

Elhai, J. D., Gold, S. N., Sellers, A. H., & Dorfman, W. I. (2001). The detection of malingered posttraumatic stress disorder with MMPI-2 fake bad indices. *Assessment*, *8*(2), 221–236.

Elhai, J. D., Naifeh, J. A., Zucker, I. S., Gold, S. N., Deitsch, S. E., & Frueh, B. C. (2004). Discriminating malingered from genuine civilian posttraumatic stress disorder: A validation of three MMPI-2 infrequency scales (F, Fp, and Fptsd). *Assessment*, *11*, 139–144. http://dx.doi.org/10.1177/1073191104264965.

Elhai, J. D., Ruggiero, K. J., Frueh, B. C., Beckham, J. C., Gold, P. B., & Feldman, M. E. (2002). The Infrequency-posttraumatic stress disorder scale (Fptsd) for the MMPI-2: Development and initial validation with veterans presenting with combat-related PTSD. *Journal of Personality Assessment*, *79*(3), 531–549.

Fehon, D. C., Grilo, C. M., & Lipschitz, D. S. (2005). A comparison of adolescent inpatients with and without a history of violence perpetration: Impulsivity, PTSD, and violence risk. *Journal of Nervous and Mental Disease*, *193*, 405–411.

Feierman, J., & Ford, J. D. (2015). Trauma-informed juvenile justice systems and approaches. In K. Heilbrun, D. DeMatteo, & N. Goldstein (Eds.), *Handbook of psychology and juvenile justice*. Washington, DC: American Psychological Association.

Ford, J. D. (2005). Treatment implications of altered affect regulation and information processing following child maltreatment. *Psychiatric Annals*, *35*(5), 410–419.

Ford, J. D. (2012). Posttraumatic Stress Disorder (PTSD) among youth involved in juvenile justice. In E. Grigorenko (Ed.), *Handbook of juvenile forensic psychology and psychiatry* (pp. 487–503). New York, NY: Springer.

Ford, J. D. (2015). An affective cognitive neuroscience-based approach to PTSD psychotherapy: The TARGET model. *Journal of Cognitive Psychotherapy, 29*(1), 68–91.

Ford, J. D., & Blaustein, M. E. (2013). Systemic self-regulation: A framework for trauma-informed services in residential juvenile justice programs. *Journal of Family Violence, 28*, 665–677.

Ford, J. D., Chang, R., Levine, J., & Zhang, W. (2013). Randomized clinical trial comparing affect regulation and supportive group therapies for victimization-related PTSD with incarcerated women. *Behavior Therapy, 44*(2), 262–276. http://dx.doi.org/10.1016/j.beth.2012.10.003.

Ford, J. D., Chapman, J., Mack, M., & Pearson, G. (2006). Pathway from traumatic child victimization to delinquency: Implications for juvenile and permanency court proceedings and decisions. *Juvenile and Family Court Journal, 57*(1), 13–26.

Ford, J. D., Chapman, J. F., Connor, D. F., & Cruise, K. C. (2012). Complex trauma and aggression in secure juvenile justice settings. *Criminal Justice & Behavior, 39*, 695–724.

Ford, J. D., Chapman, J. F., Hawke, J., & Albert, D. (2007). *Trauma among youth in the juvenile justice system: Critical issues and new directions.* Albany, NY: National Center for Mental Health and Juvenile Justice.

Ford, J. D., Hartman, J. K., Hawke, J., & Chapman, J. (2008). Traumatic victimization, posttraumatic stress disorder, suicidal ideation, and substance abuse risk among juvenile justice-involved youths. *Journal of Child and Adolescent Trauma, 1*, 75–92. http://dx.doi.org/10.1080/19361520801934456.

Ford, J. D., & Hawke, J. (2012). Trauma affect regulation psychoeducation group and milieu intervention outcomes in juvenile detention facilities. *Journal of Aggression, Maltreatment & Trauma, 21*(4), 365–384.

Ford, J. D., Steinberg, K. L., & Zhang, W. (2011). A randomized clinical trial comparing affect regulation and social problem-solving psychotherapies for mothers with victimization-related PTSD. *Behavior Therapy, 42*(4), 560–578. http://dx.doi.org/S0005-7894(11)00048-7 [pii]; http://dx.doi.org/10.1016/j.beth.2010.12.005.

Ford, J. D., Trestman, R. L., Wiesbrock, V. H., & Zhang, W. (2009). Validation of a brief screening instrument for identifying psychiatric disorders among newly incarcerated adults. *Psychiatric Services, 60*, 842–846. http://dx.doi.org/10.1176/appi.ps.60.6.842.

Franklin, C. L., Repasky, S. A., Thompson, K. E., Shelton, S. A., & Uddo, M. (2002). Differentiating overreporting and extreme distress: MMPI-2 use with compensation-seeking veterans with PTSD. *Journal of Personality Assessment, 79*, 274–285. http://dx.doi.org/10.1207/S15327752JPA7902_10.

Friel, A., White, T., & Hull, A. (2008). Posttraumatic stress disorder and criminal responsibility. *Journal of Forensic Psychiatry & Psychology, 19*, 64–85.

Frisman, L. K., Ford, J. D., Lin, H., Mallon, S., & Chang, R. (2008). Outcomes of trauma treatment using the TARGET model. *Journal of Groups in Addiction and Recovery, 3*, 285–303.

Gill, J., Vythilingam, M., & Page, G. G. (2008). Low cortisol, high DHEA, and high levels of stimulated TNF-alpha, and IL-6 in women with PTSD. *Journal of Traumatic Stress, 21*, 530–539.

Goff, A., Rose, E., Rose, S., & Purves, D. (2007). Does PTSD occur in sentenced prison populations? A systematic literature review. *Criminal Behavior and Mental Health, 17*(3), 152–162.

Grisso, T., Barnum, R., Fletcher, K. E., Cauffman, E., & Peuschold, D. (2001). Massachusetts youth screening instrument for mental health needs of juvenile justice youths. *Journal of the American Academy of Child and Adolescent Psychiatry, 40*, 541–548.

Gully, K. J. (2003). Expectations test: Trauma scales for sexual abuse, physical abuse, exposure to family violence, and posttraumatic stress. *Child Maltreatment, 8,* 218–229.

Gustafsson, H. C., Cox, M. J., & Blair, C. (2012). Maternal parenting as a mediator of the relationship between intimate partner violence and effortful control. *Journal of Family Psychology, 26*(1), 115–123.

Hall, R. C., & Hall, R. C. (2006). Malingering of PTSD: Forensic and diagnostic considerations, characteristics of malingerers and clinical presentations. *General Hospital Psychiatry, 28*(6), 525–535.

Hall, R. C. W., & Hall, R. C. W. (2007). Detection of malingered PTSD: An overview of clinical, psychometric, and physiological assessment: Where do we stand? *Journal of Forensic Sciences, 52,* 717–725. http://dx.doi.org/10.1111/j.1556-4029.2007.00434.x.

Harris, G. T., & Rice, M. E. (2003). Actuarial assessment of risk among sex offenders. *Sexually Coercive Behavior: Understanding and Management, 989,* 198–210.

Heilbrun, K., DeMatteo, D., & Goldstein, N. (Eds.), (2015). *Handbook of psychology and juvenile justice.* Washington, DC: American Psychological Association.

Heilbrun, K., DeMatteo, D., Marczyk, G., & Goldstein, A. M. (2008). Standards of practice and care in forensic mental health assessment: Legal, professional, and principles-based consideration. *Psychology, Public Policy, and Law, 14*(1), 1–26.

Herman, S. (2005). Improving decision making in forensic child sexual abuse evaluations. *Law and Human Behavior, 29,* 87–120.

Jordan, B. K., Federman, E. B., Burns, B. J., Schlenger, W. E., Fairbank, J. A., & Caddell, J. M. (2002). Lifetime use of mental health and substance abuse treatment services by incarcerated women felons. *Psychiatric Services, 53,* 317–325.

Jordan, B. K., Schlenger, W. E., Fairbank, J. A., & Caddell, J. M. (1996). Prevalence of psychiatric disorders among incarcerated women: Convicted felons entering prison. *Archives of General Psychiatry, 53,* 513–519.

Jucksch, V., Salbach-Andrae, H., Lenz, K., Goth, K., Dopfner, M., Poustka, F., et al. (2011). Severe affective and behavioural dysregulation is associated with significant psychosocial adversity and impairment. *Journal of Child Psychology and Psychiatry, 52*(6), 686–695.

Jun, H. J., Corliss, H. L., Boynton-Jarrett, R., Spiegelman, D., Austin, S. B., & Wright, R. J. (2012). Growing up in a domestic violence environment: Relationship with developmental trajectories of body mass index during adolescence into young adulthood. *Journal of Epidemiology and Community Health, 66*(7), 629–635.

Kessler, R. C., Sonnega, A., Bromet, E., Hughes, M., & Nelson, C. B. (1995). Posttraumatic stress disorder in the National Comorbidity Survey. *Archives of General Psychiatry, 52,* 1048–1060.

Kimerling, R., Trafton, J., & Ngyuen, B. (2006). Validation of a brief screen for post-traumatic stress disorder with substance use disorder patients. *Addictive Behaviors, 31,* 2074–2079. http://dx.doi.org/10.1016/j.addbeh.2006.02.008.

Klopper, J. J., Schweinle, W., Ractliffe, K. C., & Elhai, J. D. (2014). Predictors of mental healthcare use among domestic violence survivors in shelters. *Psychological Services, 11*(2), 134–140.

Koch, W. J., O'Neill, M., & Douglas, K. S. (2005). Empirical limits for the forensic assessment of PTSD litigants. *Law and Human Behavior, 29*(1), 121–149.

Lindblom, K., & Gray, M. (2008). Memories of traumatic experiences. In G. Reyes, J. D. Elhai, & J. D. Ford (Eds.), *Encyclopedia of psychological trauma* (pp. 412–424). Hoboken, NJ: Wiley.

Manly, J. (2008). Child maltreatment. In G. Reyes, J. D. Elhai, & J. Ford (Eds.), *Encyclopedia of psychological trauma* (pp. 119–124). Hoboken, NJ: Wiley.

Marrow, M., Knudsen, K., Olafson, E., & Bucher, S. (2012). The value of implementing TARGET within a trauma-informed juvenile justice setting. *Journal of Child and Adolescent Trauma, 5,* 257–270.

McDermott, B. E., Edens, J. F., Quanbeck, C. D., Busse, D., & Scott, C. L. (2008). Examining the role of static and dynamic risk factors in the prediction of inpatient violence: Variable- and person-focused analyses. *Law and Human Behavior*, *32*(4), 325–338.

McGloin, J. M., & Widom, C. S. (2001). Resilience among abused and neglected children grown up. *Development and Psychopathology*, *13*, 1021–1038.

Ouimette, P., Wade, M., Prins, A., & Schohn, M. (2008). Identifying PTSD in primary care: Comparison of the Primary Care-PTSD Screen (PC-PTSD) and the General Health Questionnaire-12 (GHQ). *Journal of Anxiety Disorders*, *22*, 337–343.

Pollak, S. D., & Tolley-Schell, S. A. (2003). Selective attention to facial emotion in physically abused children. *Journal of Abnormal Psychology*, *112*(3), 323–338.

Prins, A., Ouimette, P., Kimerling, R., Cameron, R. P., Hugelshofer, D. S., Shaw-Hegwer, J., et al. (2003). The primary care PTSD screen (PC-PTSD): Development and operating characteristics. *Primary Care Psychiatry*, *9*(1), 9–14.

Quinsey, V. L., Harris, G. T., Rice, M. E., & Cormier, C. (Eds.), (2006). *Violent offenders: Appraising and managing risk* (2nd ed.). Washington DC: American Psychological Association.

Rayburn, N. R., Wenzel, S. L., Elliott, M. N., Hambarsoomians, K., Marshall, G. N., & Tucker, J. S. (2005). Trauma, depression, coping, and mental health service seeking among impoverished women. *Journal of Consulting and Clinical Psychology*, *73*, 667–677. http://dx.doi.org/10.1037/0022-006X.73.4.667.

Resnick, P. J., West, S., & Payne, J. W. (2008). Malingering of posttraumatic disorders. In R. Rogers (Ed.), *Clinical assessment of malingering and deception* (pp. 109–127) (3rd ed.). New York, NY: Guilford Press.

Rogers, R., Sewell, K. W., Martin, M. A., & Vitacco, M. J. (2003). Detection of feigned mental disorders: A meta-analysis of the MMPI-2 and malingering. *Assessment*, *10*, 160–177. http://dx.doi.org/10.1177/1073191103010002007.

Romito, P., & Grassi, M. (2007). Does violence affect one gender more than the other? The mental health impact of violence among male and female university students. *Social Science and Medicine*, *65*(6), 1222–1234. http://dx.doi.org/10.1016/j.socscimed.2007.05.017.

Roos, L. E., Mota, N., Afifi, T. O., Katz, L. Y., Distasio, J., & Sareen, J. (2013). Relationship between adverse childhood experiences and homelessness and the impact of axis I and II disorders. *American Journal of Public Health*, *103*(Suppl. 2), S275–S281.

Sareen, J., Henriksen, C. A., Bolton, S. L., Afifi, T. O., Stein, M. B., & Asmundson, G. J. (2013). Adverse childhood experiences in relation to mood and anxiety disorders in a population-based sample of active military personnel. *Psychological Medicine*, *43*(1), 73–84.

Schechter, D. S., Willheim, E., McCaw, J., Turner, J. B., Myers, M. M., & Zeanah, C. H. (2011). The relationship of violent fathers, posttraumatically stressed mothers and symptomatic children in a preschool-age inner-city pediatrics clinic sample. *Journal of Interpersonal Violence*, *26*(18), 3699–3719.

Schuller, R. A., & Rzepa, S. (2002). Expert testimony pertaining to battered woman syndrome: Its impact on jurors' decisions. *Law and Human Behavior*, *26*, 655–673.

Schumm, J. A., Briggs-Phillips, M., & Hobfoll, S. E. (2006). Cumulative interpersonal traumas and social support as risk and resiliency factors in predicting PTSD and depression among inner-city women. *Journal of Traumatic Stress*, *19*, 825–836.

Scott, J. C., Matt, G. E., Wrocklage, K. M., Crnich, C., Jordan, J., Southwick, S. M., et al. (2014). A quantitative meta-analysis of neurocognitive functioning in posttraumatic stress disorder. *Psychological Bulletin*. http://dx.doi.org/10.1037/a0038039.

Secker, J., Benson, A., Balfe, E., Lipsedge, M., Robinson, S., & Walker, J. (2004). Understanding the social context of violent and aggressive incidents on an inpatient unit. *Journal of Psychiatric and Mental Health Nursing*, *11*(2), 172–178.

Sedlak, A. J., Mettenburg, J., Basena, M., Petta, I., McPherson, K., Greene, A., et al. (2010). *Fourth National incidence study of child abuse and neglect (NIS–4): Report to congress.* Washington, DC: U.S. Department of Health and Human Services, Administration for Children and Families.

Soliman, S., & Resnick, P. (2008). Forensic assessment. In G. Reyes, J. D. Elhai, & J. D. Ford (Eds.), *Encyclopedia of psychological trauma* (pp. 283–285). Hoboken, NJ: Wiley.

Sparr, L. F. (1995). Post-traumatic stress disorder: Does it exist? *Neurologic Clinics, 13,* 413–429.

Stein, M. B., Walker, J. R., Hazen, A. L., & Forde, D. R. (1997). Full and partial posttraumatic stress disorder: Findings from a community survey. *American Journal of Psychiatry, 154,* 1114–1119.

Swanston, J., Bowyer, L., & Vetere, A. (2014). Towards a richer understanding of school-age children's experiences of domestic violence: The voices of children and their mothers. *Clinical Child Psychology and Psychiatry, 19*(2), 184–201.

Taft, C. T., Pless, A. P., Stalans, L. J., Koenen, K. C., King, L. A., & King, D. W. (2005). Risk factors for partner violence among a national sample of combat veterans. *Journal of Consulting and Clinical Psychology, 73,* 151–159.

Teplin, L. A., Abram, K. M., & McClelland, G. M. (1997). Mentally disordered women in jail: Who receives services? *American Journal of Public Health, 87,* 604–609.

Trestman, R. L., Ford, J., Zhang, W., & Wiesbrock, V. (2007). Current and lifetime psychiatric illness among inmates not identified as acutely mentally ill at intake in Connecticut's jails. *Journal of the American Academy of Psychiatry and the Law, 35,* 490–500.

Wallis, D. A. N. (2002). Reduction of trauma symptoms following group therapy. *Australian and New Zealand Journal of Psychiatry, 36,* 67–74.

Werner, J., & Werner, M. C. M. (2008). Child sexual abuse in clinical and forensic psychiatry: A review of recent literature. *Current Opinion in Psychiatry, 21,* 499–504.

Wilker, S., Elbert, T., & Kolassa, I. T. (2014). The downside of strong emotional memories: How human memory-related genes influence the risk for posttraumatic stress disorder—a selective review. *Neurobiology of Learning and Memory, 112,* 75–86.

Wolff, N., Frueh, B. C., Shi, J., Gerardi, D., Fabrikant, N., & Schumann, B. E. (2011). Trauma exposure and mental health characteristics of incarcerated females self-referred to specialty PTSD treatment. *Psychiatric Services, 62*(8), 954–958.

Wolff, N., Frueh, B. C., Shi, J., & Schumann, B. E. (2012). Effectiveness of cognitive-behavioral trauma treatment for incarcerated women with mental illnesses and substance abuse disorders. *Journal of Anxiety Disorders, 26*(7), 703–710.

Wolff, N., Huening, J., Shi, J., & Frueh, B. C. (2014). Trauma exposure and posttraumatic stress disorder among incarcerated men. *Journal of Urban Health, 91*(4), 707–719.

Wooley, C. N., & Rogers, R. (2014). The effectiveness of the personality assessment inventory with feigned PTSD: An initial investigation of Resnick's model of malingering. *Assessment.* http://dx.doi.org/10.1177/1073191114552076.

Wooley, C. N., & Rogers, R. (2015). The effectiveness of the personality assessment inventory with feigned PTSD: An initial investigation of Resnick's model of malingering. *Assessment.* http://dx.doi.org/10.1177/1073191114552076.

Worling, J. R. (2004). The Estimated of Risk of Adolescent Sexual Offense Recidivism (ERASOR): Preliminary psychometric data. *Sexual Abuse, 16*(3), 235–254.

Zlotnick, C., Najavits, L. M., Rohsenow, D. J., & Johnson, D. M. (2003). A cognitive-behavioral treatment for incarcerated women with substance abuse disorder and posttraumatic stress disorder: Findings from a pilot study. *Journal of Substance Abuse Treatment, 25*(2), 99–105.

Social, cultural, and other diversity issues in the traumatic stress field

This chapter describes how the impact of psychological trauma and posttraumatic stress disorder (PTSD) differ, depending on individual differences and the social and cultural context and culture-specific teachings and resources available to individuals, families, and communities. We use the framework (Kira et al., 2011) formulated to differentiate the impact on the individual's or group's (i) personal, unique physical characteristics, including skin color, racial background, gender, and sexual orientation; and (ii) family, ethnocultural, and community membership, including majority or minority group status, religious beliefs and practices, socioeconomic resources, and political and civic affiliations. While personal and social factors can be a positive resource contributing to safety and well-being, they also can be a basis for placing the person or group in harm's way.

Disadvantaged persons and communities—such as those in poverty or who face stigma and discrimination, disabilities, homelessness, political repression, communal/societal violence (including paramilitary, military, and gang warfare), forced immigration (refugees and asylum seekers), interrogation and torture, terrorism, genocide, and catastrophic disasters—are particularly vulnerable both to being exposed to traumatic stressors and to developing PTSD and associated psychiatric disorders and psychosocial problems (Betancourt et al., 2015; Brown, 2008; Goldsmith, Martin, & Smith, 2014; Herrera Rivera, De Jesus Mari, Baxter Andreoli, Ines Quintana, & Pacheco De Toledo, 2008; Seedat, Nyamai, Njenga, Vythilingum, & Stein, 2004). This vulnerability largely is explained by exposure to chronic and cumulative stressors (such as stigma, discrimination, and poverty), ongoing interpersonal and group victimization, intergroup conflict, systems of belief and tradition, and exposure to chronic or particularly horrific traumatic stressors (including the often lengthy aftermath of catastrophic disasters, and societal conflicts), rather than being due solely to ethnic or cultural differences (Kira et al., 2011).

Racially or ethnoculturally based discrimination is widely recognized as having been a scourge on the human race for millennia. Genocide—the attempt to eradicate an entire racial, ethnic, or cultural group—has caused untold suffering and cost the lives of hundreds of millions of people across the planet throughout human history. The term *historical trauma* has been coined to describe the traumatic impact that racially or ethnoculturally based genocide has on not only the immediate targets but moreover on their progeny for generations afterward. The living memory of traumatic assaults on the survival and human dignity of entire groups or societies can persist as a form of vigilance against any sign of a potential recurrence of the genocide.

Posttraumatic Stress Disorder. DOI: http://dx.doi.org/10.1016/B978-0-12-801288-8.00011-X

This is an adaptive response in one sense, providing an awareness and readiness to respond should the genocide or any associated forms of stigma, discrimination, or violence ever recur with impunity. However, it can also become a form of persistent hypervigilance similar to that seen in PTSD, placing a strain upon the individual's or group's daily life that may compromise their well-being. Our discussion of the impact of exposure to traumatic stressors and PTSD on ethnoracial groups and individuals whose forebears have experienced historical trauma will bear this fact in mind.

In addition, gender-based biases and beliefs, many of which are based on long-standing religious and cultural traditions, have caused women to be systematically discriminated against and subject to routine physical and sexual assault. Gender-based discrimination and violence against females (whether intra- or extrafamilial) have been so widespread as to be implicated in what Kristof and WuDunn (2009) term "gendercide." In their recent book, they cite examples of selective abortions based on a fetus's gender and differential nutrition and care beginning in infancy also based on gender preference. They are then often followed by lifelong major disparities in education and restricted role and career opportunities for females as compared to males. Unfortunately, even today, with all the advances that have occurred predominantly in Western societies, these same issues remain in place around the world. The increased recognition of the underclass status of the majority of women and girls and the discrimination they face, along with the violence perpetrated against them (often seemingly with impunity), in countries around the world (whether industrialized and "advanced," or relatively primitive) has led to the recent development of major initiatives against global violence and discrimination against women. Malala Yousafzai, who was shot by the Taliban for her espousal of universal education for girls, was awarded the Nobel Peace Prize, the youngest recipient to date. The brutality of the attack against her was shocking, yet it served to highlight the traumatic threat to which many girls and women across the world are exposed when targeted for hateful acts by those who believe this is necessary to maintain the status quo and the subservience of females.

Discrimination and violence based on sexual orientation and transgender/intergender status are yet other sources of traumatic victimization that must be well recognized. Sexual orientation is both a personal and social characteristic that is more complex than the gender that a person inherits based on inborn sexual characteristics. When socially ascribed gender and culturally promulgated expectations for gender-based activities, such as mating, are a mismatch to an individual's sense of his or her own true sexual preferences and identity, the conflict can be psychologically devastating. Global initiatives therefore are underway to prevent or ameliorate the adverse impact of discrimination, stigma, and violence based on sexual orientation and identity providing an essential foundation for the basic liberties, freedom from assault, and the right to marry to gay, lesbian, bisexual, and transgendered (GLBT) individuals.

It should also be noted that boys and men are also subject to abuse and assault at rates that are not yet adequately researched. Males may be more subject to violence when they are in a position of vulnerability of some sort due to being a member of a group that is targeted and/or of lesser status/lesser strength. Depending on their cultural background and its traditions and beliefs, individuals may also have "multiple vulnerability status"—that is, to be members of more than one group or to have characteristic that cause them to be even more susceptible to discrimination or victimization (i.e., adolescent black male in the United States; a baby born with physical or developmental disabilities in a culture that endorses selective resources to the ablebodied; a gay man or lesbian woman of color in a highly homophobic and racist society).

Age is yet another vulnerability factor dimension that has not received adequate recognition, with individuals at either end of the life span as most vulnerable. Research has substantiated that children and adolescents are the most at-risk segment of the population globally (Finkelhor, 2014). Victimization of the elderly and the less-abled/disabled members of the population is now documented as widespread in many societies and is increasingly under investigation. Like other forms of abuse, victimization of the elderly and less-abled is often based on the victim's relative degree of dependence and his powerlessness to defend himself.

The extent and impact of exposure to traumatic stressors experienced by each of these vulnerable populations is discussed in this chapter, as are the efforts of international non-governmental organizations (NGOs) to provide them with resources to reduce their exposure to traumatic stressors or to mitigate the adverse effects of traumatic exposure and PTSD (Box 11.1).

Box 11.1 Key Points

1. Culture, ethnicity, gender, sexual orientation, and disability are potential sources of resilience, but they also may lead to chronic stressors such as social stigma, discrimination, and oppression, which can increase psychological trauma and PTSD.
2. Cumulative adversities are faced by many persons, communities, ethnocultural minority groups, and societies that may lead to—as well as worsen the impact of—PTSD:
   - persons of ethnoracial minority backgrounds;
   - persons discriminated against due to gender or sexual orientation;
   - persons with developmental or physical disabilities;
   - economically impoverished persons and groups, including the homeless;
   - victims of political repression, genocide, "ethnic cleansing," or torture;
   - persons chronically or permanently displaced from their homes and communities due to catastrophic armed conflicts or disasters.
3. Members of ethnoracial minority groups have been found to be more likely in some cases to develop PTSD than other persons, but in other cases they are *less* likely to develop PTSD (e.g., persons of Asian or African descent).
4. Members of ethnoracial minority groups often encounter disparities in access to social, educational, economic, and health care resources; it is these disparities that are the most likely source of the increased vulnerability of these persons to psychological trauma and PTSD.

(Continued)

Box 11.1 Continued

5. PTSD therapists must avoid stereotypic assumptions in order to ensure that assessment and treatment are genuinely collaborative and sensitive to each client's ethnocultural and other expectations, goals, and preferences. A culturally competent approach to treating PTSD begins with a collaborative discussion in which the therapist adopts the stance of a respectful visitor to the client's outer and inner world—clarifying the client's expectations and preferences, and the meaning of sensitive interpersonal communication modalities (such as spatial proximity, gaze, choice of names, private versus public topics, synchronizing of talk and listening, use of colloquialisms, providing advice or education).

6. A systematic assessment of trauma history and PTSD thus should include not only a listing of events and symptomatic or resilient responses in the aftermath but how the person interpreted these events and reactions based on his or her cultural framework, beliefs, and values.

7. In contrast to the general pattern of stigma-related violence being directed toward girls and women, gay and bisexual boys and men were more likely to report violent victimization or threats than lesbian or bisexual women or girls. The findings from a survey of gay, lesbian, and bisexual (GLB) adolescents suggest that stigma and victimization begin early in life, with physical and sexual attacks occurring as early as ages 8–9 years old. One in 11 GLB adolescents have been found to have PTSD, as much as 20 times more than other children and adolescents.

8. Poverty puts people at risk for traumatic violence, and not having a stable residence (homelessness) compounds this risk and further increases the likelihood of developing PTSD and associated mental health distress and health conditions.

9. Political repression, genocide, and mass armed conflicts involve psychological (and often physical as well) assaults by the people and institutions in power on people, families, communities, and organizations who are deprived of access to political power and socioeconomic resources—and therefore also on their fundamental freedoms and values. Without access to self-determination and the resources necessary to sustain independence, people are vulnerable not just to traumatic exploitation and violence but also to the traumatic loss of their intimate relationships, their families, their way of life, and their values.

10. Refugees and "internally displaced" or "stateless" persons who have been displaced from or lost their families, homes, and communities due to armed conflicts or mass disasters (such as tsunamis, hurricanes, or earthquakes) are at least 10 times (and as much as 30 times) more likely than other children or adults to develop PTSD, with as many as one in three refugees or disaster survivors developing Acute Stress Disorder (ASD) or PTSD.

The role of gender, ethnicity, culture, and social resources in PTSD

Every individual, family, and community has a heritage that includes a distinctive blend of personal, racial, ethnic, cultural, and national characteristics. Not infrequently, within this heritage, there often is a legacy of personal or familial exposure to psychological trauma in the immediate or most distant past, or both. Psychological trauma and PTSD occur across the full spectrum of gender, racial, ethnic, and cultural groups in the United States (Pole, Gone, & Kulkarni, 2008). Psychological trauma and PTSD are epidemic internationally as well, particularly for ethnoracial minority groups (which include a much broader range of ethnicities and cultures and manifestations of PTSD than typically recognized in studies of PTSD in the United States; de Jong, Komproe, Spinazzola, van der Kolk, & Van Ommeren, 2005; de Jong, Komproe, & Van Ommeren, 2003). The scientific and clinical study of PTSD and its treatment among gender and ethnoracial majority and minority groups is of great importance, especially given the disparities, adversities, and traumas to which they have been subjected historically (Miranda, McGuire, Williams, & Wang, 2008)—and to which they are still exposed in health and health care, education and income, and adult criminal and juvenile justice (Ford, 2008).

Although Latinos (and possibly African Americans) persons are at greater risk than European Americans for PTSD based on available research findings (Pole, Gone, & Kulkarni, 2008), it is possible that the elevated prevalence may be due to differences in the extent or types of exposure to psychological trauma (including prior traumas that often are not assessed in PTSD clinical or epidemiological studies; Eisenman, Gelberg, Liu, & Shapiro, 2003) or to differences in exposure to other risk or protective factors such as poverty, education, or gender-based violence (Turner & Lloyd, 2003, 2004). In addition, there is sufficient diversity (in norms, beliefs, values, roles, practices, language, and history) *within* categorical ethnocultural groups such as African Americans or Latinos to call into question any sweeping generalizations about their exposure and vulnerability or resilience to psychological trauma (Pole et al., 2008).

Race, ethnicity, gender and sexual identity, and culture tend to be described with shorthand labels that appear to distinguish homogeneous subgroups but that actually obscure the true heterogeneity within as well as between different groups (Marsella, Friedman, Gerrity, & Scurfield, 1996). One partial antidote for this problem is for clinicians and researchers to be curious about these issues and to ask study participants or clinical patients to self-identify their own racial, ethnic, and cultural background and to essentially educate them about their unique characteristics and associated belief systems and traditions (Brown, 2008; Brown, Hitlin, & Elder, 2006). It also is important to carefully assess factors that are associated with differential exposure to adverse experiences (such as racial-ethnic discrimination) or differential access to protective resources (such as income, health care, education, police protection), rather than assuming that each member of an ethnocultural group is identical on these crucial dimensions. However, when systematic disparities in exposure to stressors or deprivation of resources are identified for specific groups, such as persons from indigenous cultures— the original inhabitants of a geographic area who have been displaced or marginalized by colonizing national/cultural groups—are found to have a generally increased risk of discrimination, poverty, addiction, family violence, and poor health (Harris et al., 2006; Liberato, Pomeroy, & Fennell, 2006), it is crucial not to mistakenly conclude that those persons are less resilient than others when they are confronted with traumatic stressors. Commonly, the very opposite is true: persons and groups who are subjected to chronic stressors or deprivations tend to be *more* resilient than others, but they also are more exposed to and less protected from traumatic stressors (Pole et al., 2008).

Racism and associated discrimination and mistreatment are particularly chronic stressors faced by many members of ethnoracial and other minority groups. Racism may constitute a form of psychological trauma in and of itself, increasing the risk of exposure to psychological trauma, and exacerbating its impact by increasing the risk of PTSD (Ford, 2008). As of yet, few systematic studies have directly examined racism as a risk factor for exposure to psychological trauma, although the connection is increasingly recognized (Carter & Forsyth, 2009; Hunter & Schmidt, 2010; Miller, 2009). Perhaps, the Holocaust and other forms of genocide have been the most investigated to date. Studies of survivors of the Holocaust and other types of ethnic annihilation provide particularly graphic and tragic evidence of the infliction of psychological trauma en masse in the name of racism (Staub, 2005; Yule, 2000). Studies are needed that systematically compare persons and groups who are exposed to different types and degrees of racism in order to test whether (and under what conditions) racism is a form of, or leads to exposure to other types of, traumatic stressors (Ford, 2008).

When racism leads to the profiling and targeting of ethnoracial minority groups for violence, dispossession, dislocation, or annihilation, the risk of PTSD increases in proportion to type and degree of the traumatization involved (Pole et al., 2008). For example, studies based in the United States (Pole et al., 2008) and internationally (MacDonald, Chamberlain, & Long, 1997) suggest that racial discrimination may have played a role in placing military personnel from ethnoracial minority groups at risk for more extensive and severe combat trauma exposure. One study found that self-reported experiences of racial discrimination increased the risk of PTSD among Latino and African American police officers (Pole, Best, Metzler, & Marmar, 2005).

Another study with Asian American military veterans from the Vietnam War era showed that exposure to multiple race-related stressors that met PTSD criteria for psychological trauma was associated with more severe PTSD than when only one or no such race-related traumas were reported (Loo, Fairbank, & Chemtob, 2005). This study more precisely operationalized racism than any prior study, utilizing two psychometrically validated measures of race-related stressors and PTSD. However, as in the Pole et al. (2005) study, the stressors/traumas and PTSD symptoms were assessed by contemporaneous self-report, so the actual extent of racism experienced by the participants cannot be definitely determined. The Loo et al. (2005) study also did not control for traumatic stressor exposure other than that which was related to racism. In order to extend the valuable work these studies have begun, it will be important to utilize measures based on operationally specific criteria for categorizing and quantifying exposure to discrimination (e.g., Wiking, Johansson, & Sundquist, 2004) as a distinct class of stressors that can be assessed separately as well as concurrently with exposure to psychological trauma.

Research also is needed to determine to what extent the adverse outcomes of racial disparities are the direct result of racism as a stressor (e.g., racially motivated stigmatization, mistreatment, subjugation, and deprivation resulting in personal and community depression and destabilization), as opposed to the indirect effects of racism (such as microaggressions that accrue over time). Racism can also indirectly reduce access to protective factors (adequate nutrition and other socioeconomic and community resources) that protect against the adverse effects of stressors (such as poverty, pollution, disaster) and traumatic stressors (such as accidents, crime, or violence). Hurricane Katrina and its aftermath provided just such an example. It is important to determine whether PTSD is the product of either the direct or indirect effects of racism, or both, particularly given its demonstrated association with other psychiatric conditions (such as depression, anxiety, and addiction) and with increased risk of physical illness (such as cancer and cardiovascular disease) in ethnoracial minorities (e.g., among American Indians; Sawchuk et al., 2005).

Education is a particularly relevant example of a socioeconomic resource to which ethnoracial minorities often have restricted access as that as a protective factor mitigating against the risk of PTSD (Dirkzwager, Bramsen, & Van Der Ploeg, 2005) and overall health status (Wiking et al., 2004). Racial disparities in access to education are due both to direct influences (such as lower funding for inner-city schools that disproportionately serve minority students) and indirect associations with other racial disparities (such as disproportionate juvenile and criminal justice confinement of ethnoracial minority persons). Racial disparities in education are both the product of and a contributor to reduced access by minorities to other socioeconomic and health resources (such as income, health insurance, adequate nutrition) (Harris et al., 2006). When investigating risk and protective factors for PTSD, it is essential therefore to consider race and ethnicity in the context not only of ethnocultural identity and group membership but also of racism and other sources of racial disparities in access to socioeconomic resources.

Although all ethnoracial minority groups tend to be disproportionately disadvantaged with regard to the more privileged majority population, particularly severe disparities in access to vital resources often are complicated by exposure to pervasive (both intrafamilial and community) violence and by the loss of ties to family, home, and community. When family and community relationships are severed—as occurs with massive political upheaval, war, genocide, slavery, colonization, or catastrophic disasters—racial and ethnocultural groups may find themselves scattered and subject to further victimization and exploitation. For example, there continue to be massively displaced populations in Central and South America, the Balkans, central Asia, and Africa. When primary social ties are cut or diminished as a result of disaster, violence, or political repression, the challenge expands beyond survival of traumatic life-threatening danger to preserving a viable life, community, and culture in the face of life-altering losses and suppression of those very factors needed to maintain (Garbarino & Kostelny, 1996; Rabalais, Ruggiero, & Scotti, 2002). Ethnoracial groups that have been able to preserve or regenerate core elements of their original cultural norms, practices, and relationships within intact or reconstituted families may actually be particularly resilient to traumatic stressors and protected against the development of PTSD. For example, persons of Asian or African descent have been found to be less likely than those of other ethnocultural backgrounds to develop PTSD. Whether this is due to factors other than ethnicity per se, such as having cultural practices and beliefs that sustain family integrity and social ties, is a question that has not been scientifically studied and should be a focus for research (Pole et al., 2008).

A recurring theme is that the psychological trauma inflicted in service of racial discrimination may lead not only to PTSD but also to a range of insidious psychosocial problems that result from adverse effects upon the psychobiological development of the affected persons. When families and entire communities are destroyed or displaced, the impact on the psychobiological development of children and young adults may lead to complex forms of PTSD that involve not only persistent fear and anxiety but also core problems with relatedness and self-regulation of emotion, consciousness, and bodily health that are described as "complex PTSD" (Herman, 1992) or "Disorders of Extreme Stress" (de Jong et al., 2005).

A critical question not yet answered by studies of PTSD and racial discrimination (Pole et al., 2005) and race-related stress (Loo et al., 2005), as well as by the robust literature that shows evidence of intergenerational transmission of risk for PTSD (Kellerman, 2001), is whether racism constitutes a "hidden" (Crenshaw & Hardy, 2006) or "invisible" (Franklin, Boyd-Franklin, & Kelly, 2006) form of traumatization that may be transmitted across generations. Recent research findings demonstrating highly adverse effects of emotional abuse in childhood (Teicher, Samson, Polcari, & McGreenery, 2006) are consistent with a view that chronic denigration, shaming, demoralization, and coercion may constitute a risk factor for severe PTSD and associated psychobiological problems. Research is needed to better describe how emotional violence or abuse related to racism may (along with physical violence) constitute a form of traumatic stress and how this may adversely affect not only current but also future generations.

A fully articulated conceptual model for the scientific study and social/clinical prevention and treatment of the adverse impact of psychological trauma and PTSD requires principles and practices informed by this diversity of factors, rather than a "black and white" view of race, ethnicity, or culture that misrepresents the individual's and group's heritage, nature, and needs. Treatment preferences, in terms of characteristics of the therapist as well as the therapy model, differ substantially not only across but also within ethnoracial groups (Pole et al., 2008).

As a result, it is not possible as yet—and may never be possible—to precisely prescribe how best to select or train therapists and design or adapt therapies to fit different ethnocultural groups and the individuals within them. A culturally competent (Brown, 2008, 2009a, 2009b) approach to treating PTSD (Ford, 2008) begins with a collaborative discussion in which the therapist adopts the stance of a respectful visitor to the client's outer and inner world—clarifying the client's expectations and preferences, and the meaning of sensitive interpersonal communication modalities (such as spatial proximity, gaze, choice of names, private versus public topics, synchronizing of talk and listening, use of colloquialisms, providing advice or education). PTSD therapists thus must avoid stereotypic assumptions and become both a host and guest in the client's psychic world in order to ensure that assessment and treatment are genuinely collaborative and sensitive to each client's ethnocultural traditions, expectations, goals, and preferences (Parson, 1997; Stuart, 2004). At times, it is helpful to involve other members of the family or culture in assisting with the treatment. Religious beliefs and spirituality are other dimensions of culture that have not yet been given sufficient focus in most psychotherapy but must also be assessed and understood by the therapist (Walker, Courtois, & Aten, 2014).

Cultural competence means many things to many people, and unfortunately, it is often mistakenly equated with being of the same racial, ethnic, cultural, religious, or national background as the persons involved in a study or receiving services, or knowing *in advance exactly* what each person believes and expects, how they communicate with and are most receptive to learning from others, and what their experience has been in relation to sensitive matters such as psychological trauma or PTSD. This is likely to be a serious mistake for several reasons. Sharing some general racial, ethnic, cultural, or national features (or an apparently identical language or religion) is not synonymous with shared identity, knowledge, or history. Even persons from as virtually identical backgrounds as monozygotic twins raised in the same family have substantial differences in physical and temperamental characteristics as well as often quite distinct social learning histories, and thus rarely if ever can reliably read one another's minds or exactly know one another's vulnerabilities and strengths. Therefore, cultural competence should not be defined in terms of stereotypic assumptions about identity or prescience but instead based upon a respectful interest in learning from each person and community what they have experienced and how they understand and are affected by psychological trauma and PTSD.

We should also note that the idioms of distress can differ by culture and tradition. Professionals from industrialized nations and Anglo cultures must be cautious and respectful in working with individuals and communities from other cultures that are challenged by PTSD in the aftermath of exposure to violence or disasters. Before offering or providing education or therapeutic assistance, it is essential to become aware of how the potential recipients understand and prefer to communicate about traumatic stress and the process of healing from traumatization.

The implication for psychometric assessment of psychological trauma and PTSD with clients of ethnocultural minority groups (Hall, 2001; Marsella et al., 1996) is that it is essential to carefully select protocols that do not confront individuals with questions that are inadvertently disrespectful of their values or practices (e.g., including peyote as an example of an illicit drugs in a Native American tribe that uses it for religious rituals), irrelevant (e.g., distinguishing blood family from close friends in a group that considers all community members as family), or incomplete (e.g., limiting health care to Western medical or therapeutic services, to the exclusion of traditional forms of healing). A systematic assessment of trauma history and PTSD thus should include not only a recitation of events in a person's life and symptomatic or resilient responses in the aftermath but how the person interpreted these events and reactions based on their cultural framework, beliefs, and values (Manson, 1996).

Interventions for prevention or treatment of PTSD typically have been developed within the context of the Western medical model (Parson, 1997; but see Andres-Hyman, Ortiz, Anez, Paris, & Davidson, 2006; Hinton et al., 2005; Hwang, 2006, for examples of culturally sensitive adaptations). Evidence-based PTSD treatment models are not necessarily incompatible with culturally specific healing practices and have in common the goal of fostering not just symptom reduction but a bolstering of resilience and mastery (see Chapters 7 and 8). The integration of culturally specific methods and rituals in prevention or treatment interventions for PTSD, however, requires careful ethnographic study (i.e., observing and learning about the values, norms, beliefs, and practices endorsed and enforced by different cultural subgroups and their particular idioms (ways of describing and explaining) traumatic stress and

PTSD) so the PTSD clinician and researcher can truly work collaboratively with—rather than imposing external assumptions and standards upon—the members of the wide range of ethnic and cultural communities.

Discrimination due to gender or sexual orientation and PTSD

In most cultures, girls and women are subject to discrimination in the form of limitations on their access to crucial socioeconomic resources. Women earn 30–40% lower wages or salaries than men in most job classes in the United States (http://www.pay-equity.org/info.html) and Europe (http://www.eurofound.europa.eu/ewco/2007/01/ES0701049I.htm). Although girls and women are approaching parity with boys and men in access to education in most areas of the world (and exceed the enrollment of boys or men in secondary and college/university education), in sub-Saharan Africa and Asia, women and girls are as much as 33% less likely to be able to enroll in education and to have achieved literacy as adults (http://www.uis.unesco.org/template/pdf/EducGeneral/UISFactsheet_2008_No%201_EN.pdf).

Girls and women also may be systematically subjected to extreme forms of psychological and physical trauma as a result of their gender being equated with second-class citizenship and social norms that permit or even encourage exploitation. Sexual exploitation of women and girls is an international epidemic, including abuse and molestation, harassment, rape and punishment of rape victims, forced marriage, genital mutilation, and sex trafficking or slavery (Box 11.2). Physical abuse or assault of women and girls is tolerated—and in some cases actually prescribed as a form of social control—in both mainstream cultures and subcultures that span the globe and include most religions and developed as well as developing or preindustrial societies.

Similar potentially traumatic forms of violence are directed at many GLBT persons as a result of both formal and informal forms of social stigma and discrimination. Epidemiological studies have been conducted with samples of GLBT youth (D'Augelli, Grossman, & Starks, 2006) and adults (Herek, 2009) in the United States, suggesting that they are often subjected to potentially traumatic violence as a result of their nontraditional sexual orientation and behavior. Instances of violence *specifically related to sexual orientation* include:

- 5–10% of gay men and 10% of lesbians who were physically assaulted in the past year;
- 20–32% of GLB adults who were subjected to actual or threatened violence toward their person or a property crime at some point in their lives;
- 9–11% of GLB adolescents reported past incidents of physical or sexual violence.

In contrast to the general pattern of stigma-related violence being directed toward girls and women, gay and bisexual boys (D'Augelli et al., 2006) and men (Herek, 2009) were more likely to report violent victimization or threats than lesbian or bisexual women or girls. The findings from the survey of GLB adolescents suggest that stigma and victimization begin early in life, with physical and sexual attacks occurring as early as ages 8–9 years old. One in eleven GLB adolescents met criteria for PTSD,

Box 11.2 "Making the Harm Visible": Sexual Exploitation of Women and Girls

Women from every world region report that the sexual exploitation of women and girls is increasing. All over the world, brothels and prostitution rings exist underground on a small scale, and on an increasingly larger scale, entire sections of cities are informally zoned into brothels, bars, and clubs that house, and often enslave, women for the purposes of prostitution. The magnitude and violence of these practices of sexual exploitation constitute an international human rights crisis of contemporary slavery. In *Prostitution: A Form of Modern Slavery*, Dorchen Leidholdt, the coexecutive director of the Coalition Against Trafficking in Women, examines the definitions of slavery and shows how prostitution, and related forms of sexual exploitation, fit into defined forms of slavery.

In some parts of the world, such as the Philippines, prostitution is illegal but well entrenched from providing "recreational services" to military personnel. In "Blazing Trails, Confronting Challenges: The Sexual Exploitation of Women and Girls in the Philippines," Aida F. Santos describes the harmful conditions for women and girls in prostitution in the Philippines, with problems related to health, violence, the legal system, and services. In other regions, such as northern Norway, organized prostitution is a more recent problem, stemming from the economic crisis in Russia. In "Russian Women in Norway," Asta Beate Håland describes how an entire community is being transformed by the trafficking of women for prostitution from Russia to campgrounds and villages across the border in Norway.

Political changes combined with economic crises have devastated entire world regions, increasing the supply of vulnerable women willing to risk their lives to earn money for themselves and their families. Aurora Javate de Dios, president of the Coalition Against Trafficking in Women, discusses the impact of the Southeast Asian economic crisis on women's lives in "Confronting Trafficking, Prostitution and Sexual Exploitation: The Struggle for Survival and Dignity." Economic globalization controlled by a handful of multinational corporations located in a few industrialized countries continues to shift wealth from poorer to richer countries. In her paper "Globalization, Human Rights and Sexual Exploitation," Aida F. Santos shows us the connection between global economics and the commodification and sexual exploitation of women and girls, especially in the Philippines. Structural adjustment programs implemented by international financial institutions impose loan repayment plans on poor countries, which sacrifice social and educational programs in order to service their debt to rich nations and banks. Fatoumata Sire Diakite points to structural adjustment programs as one of the factors contributing to poverty and sexual exploitation in her paper "Prostitution in Mali." Zoraida Ramirez Rodriguez writes in "Report on Latin America" that the foreign debt and policies of the International Monetary Fund are primary factors in creating poverty for women and children. These forces leave women with few options, increasing the supply of women vulnerable to recruitment into bride trafficking and the prostitution industry.

(Continued)

Box 11.2 Continued

Social problems such as sexual and physical abuse within families force girls and women to leave in search of safety and a better life, but often they find more exploitation and violence. Physical and sexual abuse of girls and women in their families and by intimate partners destroys girls' and women's sense of self and resiliency, making them easy targets for pimps and traffickers who prey on those who have few options left to them. These factors are evident in many of the papers from all world regions in this volume, such as Jill Leighton and Katherine DePasquale's, "A Commitment to Living," and Martha Daguno's, "Support Groups for Survivors of the Prostitution Industry in Manila."

Government policies and practices also fuel the demand for prostitution, as they legalize prostitution or refuse to enforce laws against pimps, traffickers, and male buyers. In *Making the Harm Visible*, we see how countries with governmental structures and ideological foundations as different as the Netherlands and Iran, both promote and legalize sexual violence and exploitation of girls and women. In "Legalizing Pimping, Dutch Style," Marie-Victoire Louis exposes the liberal laws and policies that legalize prostitution and tolerate brothels in the Netherlands. At the other extreme, religious fundamentalists in Iran have legalized the sexual exploitation of girls and women in child and temporary marriages and the sexual torture of women in prison. Sarvnaz Chitsaz and Soona Samsami document this harm and violation of human rights in "Iranian Women and Girls: Victims of Exploitation and Violence."

Global media and communication tools, such as the Internet, make access to pornography, catalogs of mail-order brides, advertisements for prostitution tours, and information on where and how to buy women and girls in prostitution widely available. This open advertisement normalizes and increases the demand by men for women and girls to use in these different forms of exploitation. Donna M. Hughes describes her findings on how the Internet is being used to promote the sexual exploitation of women and children in "The Internet and the Global Prostitution Industry." In this milieu, women and girls become commodities— bought and sold locally and trafficked from one part of the world to another.

How do we make the harm of sexual exploitation visible? In a world where sexual exploitation is increasingly normalized and industrialized, what is needed to make people see the harm and act to stop it? The women in *Making the Harm Visible* recommend four ways to make the harm of sexual exploitation visible: listen to the experiences of survivors, expose the ideological constructions that hide the harm, expose the agents that profit from the sexual exploitation of women and children, and document harm and conduct research that reveals the harm and offers findings that can be used for policy initiatives.

Reprinted with permission from the Introduction to *Making the Harm Visible*, Edited by D. Hughes & C. Roche (1999). Kingston, RI: The Coalition Against Trafficking in Women. http://www.uri.edu/ artsci/wms/hughes/mhvtoc.htm.

3–20 times the prevalence of children (Copeland, Keeler, Angold, & Costello, 2007) and adolescents (Kilpatrick et al., 2000) in national samples in the United States.

Although gender and sexual orientation may seem intuitively to be simpler phenomena than race or ethnicity, in reality they are quite complex in terms of referring to not just biological characteristics but many aspects of psychological identity and social affiliations. Being a female or a male, let alone gay, lesbian, bisexual, or transgendered/intergendered, means many different things to different people. Although more stable than changeable, sexual orientation and even gender may be changed for the same person over time. It is inaccurate to assume that all or even most people of a given gender or sexual orientation are identical or even similar without careful and objective assessment of how they view themselves and how they actually act, think, and feel.

In relationship to psychological trauma and PTSD, therefore, the broad generalizations that have been suggested by research concerning gender and sexual orientation relate more to the way in which people of a gender or sexual orientation are generally viewed and treated (which varies, depending on the society and culture) than to inherent qualities of a given gender or sexual orientation (which is highly individual across all societies and cultures). The finding that girls and women are more often subjected to sexual and intrafamilial traumatic stressors, while boys and men more often experience physical, accidental, combat, and assaultive traumatic stressors is consistent with stereotypic sex roles that are found in many (but not all) cultures that assign females to the role of subservient helper and caregiver, while males are assigned to the role of leader and warrior. There are biological foundations for these differences—such as due to distinct levels of the sex-linked hormones estrogen and testosterone, and brain chemicals that differentially affect females and males (oxytocin and vasopressin; see Chapter 5). However, biology need not dictate a person's or a group's destiny, so it is inaccurate to assume that males or females must always fill these sex role stereotypes, particularly when there are severe adverse consequences, such as the epidemics of abuse of girls and women and of boys and men killed as violent combatants or as the "spoils of war."

Stereotypes can be even more insidious and damaging in relation to sexual orientation. Only in the past 3 decades has homosexuality been rescued from the status of a psychiatric disorder (as it was in the first three editions of the *Diagnostic and Statistical Manual*). Stigma and harassment evidently are still experienced, potentially with traumatic results when violent acts are tolerated or even encouraged, by GLBT adults and youth. It is not surprising that the prevalence of PTSD is greater among persons with other than heterosexual sexual identities, and the extent to which this is the result of the pernicious stigma directed at such individuals in most cultures or of outright traumatic violence, or both, remains to be tested.

Physical and developmental disabilities and PTSD

Persons with physical or developmental disabilities are another group of persons who unfortunately may be subjected to stigma and discrimination. Physical disabilities are more common in developing countries than in more industrialized and affluent nations in which medical technology and accident and illness prevention have reduced the risk of severe injury or genetically based physical disabilities (Mueser, Hiday, Goodman, & Valentini-Hein, 2003). Persons with physical disabilities may be at risk for exposure to traumatic accidents or maltreatment as children and as adults due to limitations in their abilities to care for themselves and live independently, particularly if they have cognitive impairment due to conditions such as mental retardation or serious mental illness.

Only one study that examined the prevalence of exposure to potentially traumatic events among physically disabled persons could be located. That was a national survey of women with physical disabilities by the Center for Research on Women with Disabilities (Nosek, Howland, & Young, 1997). On the one hand, the study found that disabled women were no more likely to report exposure to physical or sexual abuse than women without physical disabilities. However, in more detailed interviews with a subsample, more than 80% reported instances of abuse, on average two incidents per woman (each often lasting for a lengthy time period). For example, the report provides verbatim quotations:

> *My mother wasn't around much, and I always felt in my sisters' way, like I held them back from things they wanted because they had to help care for me. My sisters would slap me and shut me in my room. —32-year-old woman with congenital osteogenesis imperfecta*
>
> *After my child was born, my husband became jealous and didn't want me to get up and take care of her. He would take my chair away from me and tied me up when I pulled myself out of bed. I left him the first chance I had. —49-year-old woman with spinal cord injury since age 17*

More than half of all respondents (52% with disabilities, 51% with no disability) reported a history of either physical or sexual abuse, or both, which is a substantially higher prevalence than that reported in epidemiological surveys of nationally representative samples of women. Notably, women with disabilities were more likely than women without disability to report emotional abuse from a caregiver or family member and to have experienced all forms of abuse for a longer time period than women without disability. Although PTSD was not assessed, women younger than 50 years old with spina bifida (39%), amputation, traumatic brain injury (TBI), or multiple sclerosis (>25%) were highly likely to be diagnosed with depression than women with no disability. In light of the extensive histories of potentially traumatic abuse and of depression, it appears that women with physical disabilities—particularly those in early to midlife adulthood with disabilities that involve progressive deterioration or mental or psychological disfiguration—may be at risk for having experienced traumatic interpersonal violence and other forms of abuse and suffering from undetected PTSD.

TBI is a special case of physical disability because it involves physical injury that specifically compromises mental functioning. TBI ranges from mild (no more than 30 minutes of unconsciousness and 24 hours of amnesia) to severe (coma of at least 6 hours or amnesia for more than 24 hours). Studies with adults and children of both genders who have sustained TBI demonstrate that they are as likely to develop PTSD as persons in equally severe accidents or assaults who have not (McMillan, Williams, & Bryant, 2003). Fewer studies have been conducted with persons with severe than mild TBI, but they have not been found to be *less* likely to develop PTSD, as was originally hypothesized—due to not being able to experience or later recall the psychologically traumatic aspects of the injury as vividly as a person who does not lose consciousness or have amnesia. A subsequent study confirmed that adults with TBI were less likely to report acute traumatic stress symptoms immediately after the injury and to recall having felt helpless when interviewed several weeks later but that 3 months after the accident, they were equally likely to report PTSD symptoms as injury survivors with no TBI (Jones, Harvey, & Brewin, 2005). TBI definitely exacerbates, and indeed may cause, PTSD, as tragically is illustrated by the extremely high estimates of prevalence of PTSD among military veterans of the Iraq and Afghanistan wars with TBI. Thus, PTSD warrants careful assessment when TBI has occurred.

Concerning developmental disabilities, similarly, only one published study of PTSD could be located (Ryan, 1994). In that study, 51 adults receiving services for learning disability were more likely than other adults (Kessler, Sonnega, Bromet, & Hughes, 1995) to report exposure to traumatic stressors (100% prevalence, on average two past traumatic events). However, they had no greater risk than adults in the general population when exposed to traumatic stressors. The most frequently reported types of traumatic exposures were multiple experiences of sexual abuse by multiple perpetrators (commonly starting in childhood), physical abuse, or life-threatening neglect. Traumatic losses involving a caregiver or close relative or friend (including witnessing the death in several instances (such as witnessing a sibling dying in a fire, a close friend die during a seizure or an accident, or a parent commit suicide by shooting himself in the head with a gun)) were also reported by at least 10% of the participants.

Most of the learning-disabled adults who met criteria for PTSD had been referred for treatment for violent or disruptive behavior, typically with no psychiatric diagnosis or a diagnosis of schizophrenia, autism, or intermittent explosive disorder. When PTSD was diagnosed, major depression was a frequent comorbid disorder; yet, neither PTSD nor depression typically had been identified prior to the clinical assessment study. The findings of this study suggest that adults with developmental disorders often have been targets for abuse or neglect in childhood or have sustained severe traumatic losses and that their PTSD and depression tend to go undiagnosed as clinicians make their behavioral difficulties the focus of treatment services (Box 11.3).

Poverty, psychological trauma, and PTSD

Poverty is an adverse result of having low "social status." This does not mean that a person or group is objectively deficient but rather that he or she is identified socially and politically as either not deserving or not possessing the social mandate to have access to resources such as money, safety, housing, transportation, health care and nutrition, education, and gainful employment. Kubiak's (2005) social location theory states that each individual possesses identities within their society that are defined

Box 11.3 Developmental Disabilities and PTSD: Case Studies

Two cases taken from McCarthy (2001)[1] show the adverse impact of undetected PTSD: "A 15-year-old girl with a learning disability has suffered early abuse of a physical and sexual nature, including neglect. She presented [for medical evaluation] in early childhood with behavioral problems of aggression. She settled in a residential school from age 12 to 13 before an act of arson. She later revealed that she had experienced inappropriate sexual behaviors with peers at school. She complained of intrusive thoughts and images, along with depressive symptoms. At times she shows sexually inappropriate behavior and self-harm."

"A 40-year-old man with a moderate learning disability who had been sexually assaulted by a care[giver] presented [for medical evaluation] in [an] acute state with disturbance of appetite, sleep, loss of skills, and emotional numbness, but the abuse was revealed only months later. On being exposed to the perpetrator at a later date, he showed a deterioration in mental state with acute symptoms of anxiety, and later developed a depressive disorder requiring medication. His level of functioning never returned to that prior to the traumatic event."

A third case illustrates the therapeutic gains that a PTSD perspective can provide:

A 32-year-old woman with learning disabilities and pervasive developmental disorder had been diagnosed at age 11 with schizophrenia and subsequently had been diagnosed with schizoaffective disorder, bipolar disorder, and borderline personality disorder. For 20 years after the first psychiatric diagnosis and hospitalization, she had been psychiatrically hospitalized more than 50 times due to episodes of acute suicidality complicated by auditory command hallucinations (i.e., she believed she was hearing voices telling her to kill herself) and compulsive self-harm behavior (she used sharp objects to cut virtually every area on both arms and legs). Treatment included high doses of antipsychotic, antiseizure, antidepressant, and antianxiety medications and two courses of electroconvulsive therapy, with periods of relative stabilization sufficient for her to live in an assisted living residential home and on two occasions to live in an independent apartment with in-home daily case management and nursing care. Each period of improvement was relatively brief, lasting no longer than 3–6 months, at which time she experienced severe worsening in the apparently psychotic, depressive, and anxiety symptoms, requiring multiple rehospitalizations and progressive loss of social and cognitive abilities. For several years, family therapy was conducted, and the patient's history of traumatic stressors was assessed gradually in order not to lead to further destabilization. In addition to potential episodes of sexual assault as an adolescent and young adult, her mother disclosed that her biological father had been severely domestically violent during the patient's first 2 years of life, until the mother ended that relationship. When PTSD was confirmed and accepted by the treatment team and the patient and her family as the primary diagnosis, the patient felt that she finally understood why she was experiencing the cyclic surges in distress and was able to utilize affect regulation skills (taught using *Dialectic Behavior Therapy and Trauma Affect Regulation: Guide for Education and Therapy*; see Chapter 7). Over the next year, her medications were carefully reduced to the lower therapeutic range for attentional problems and anxiety, with a sustained improvement in mood and social and cognitive functioning such that she was able to successfully work as a skilled volunteer in an assisted living center for older adults.

[1]Case vignettes reprinted with permission from McCarthy (2001, p. 167).

by factors such as their race, socioeconomic class, gender, age, residential status, and legal status. The greater the number of oppressed identities that one possesses, the more likely one will be "poor," including not only low income but also living in neighborhoods plagued with high crime, gang violence, abandoned buildings, drugs, teen pregnancy, high unemployment rate, underfunded schools, housing shortage, food of limited nutritional value, and unresponsive police. Thus, poverty fundamentally is a breakdown of the social order as well as a resultant deprivation of resources for some people.

The relationship between low income and exposure to psychological trauma and PTSD has been studied primarily in relationship to women and families, including those who currently have stable housing and those who do not. Morrell-Bellai, Goering, and Boydell (2000) identify poverty as a core risk factor for homelessness, because the socioeconomic benefits provided by a diminishing societal safety net and the typically insufficient employment wages provided by marginal jobs force people to rely on an increasingly limited pool of subsidized housing or to become homeless. Associated risk factors include a lack of education, lack of work skill, physical or mental disability, substance abuse problem, minority status, sole support parent status, or the absence of an economically viable support system (Fischer & Breakey, 1991; Morrell-Bellai et al., 2000). Snow and Anderson (1993) found that the most common reasons for homelessness reported in a survey of men and women living "on the street" were family-related problems such as marital breakup; family caregivers becoming unwilling or unable to care for a mentally ill or substance-abusing family member; escape from a dysfunctional and/or abusive family; or not having a family to turn to for support.

Poverty and homelessness involve a vicious cycle in which socioeconomic adversities are compounded by the experience of homelessness, leading to psychological disaffiliation, hopelessness, and loss of self-efficacy, and often substance dependence (Bentley, 1997; Hopper & Baumohl, 1994; Morrell-Bellai et al., 2000)—which thus tends to perpetuate poverty and homelessness. A recent study by Frisman, Ford, Lin, Mallon, and Chang (2008) reported that 91% of a sample of very low-income homeless women caring for children had experienced at least one type (and on average, five different types) of psychologically traumatic events, usually repeatedly and over long periods of time, with one in three having experienced full or partial PTSD at some time in their lives. In addition, Ford and Frisman (2002) found that one in three of these homeless women with children had experienced a complex variant of PTSD involving problems with dysregulated affect or impulses, dissociation, somatization, and alterations in fundamental beliefs about self, relationships, and the future (i.e., "complex PTSD" or "disorders of extreme stress"; Ford, 1999). More than half of the sample had a history of either or both PTSD and its complex variant.

Exposure to violence and other forms of victimization begins in childhood for many homeless individuals, in part due to their exposure and the vulnerability of their living conditions (North, Smith, & Spitznagel, 1994). Rates of childhood physical abuse as high as 52% among homeless adolescents have been reported (MacLean, Paradise, & Cauce, 1999), and this figure may be on the low end. Extremely poor women, whether homeless or not, have elevated rates of lifetime PTSD or other mental illness, and a history of such disorders is associated with having grown up in family and community environments with violence, threat, and anger (Bassuk, Dawson, Perloff, & Weinrub, 2001; Davies-Netzley, Hurlburt, & Hough, 1996). However, homelessness per se may confer additional risk: homeless mothers and their children have higher lifetime rates of violent abuse and assault than equally impoverished housed mothers (Bassuk et al., 1998). Thus, poverty puts people at risk for traumatic violence, but not having a stable residence compounds this risk and the likelihood of developing PTSD.

Victims of political repression, genocide ("ethnic cleansing"), and torture

When political power is used to repress free speech and citizens' self-determination, there is an increase in the risk to members of that nation or community and its neighbors and associates of psychological trauma. Domestic violence (see Box 10.5) is a microcosm that shares much in common with large-scale political repression, because physical, psychological, and economic power is used to entrap, systematically break down, and coercively control the thoughts as well as the actions and relationships of the victim. On a larger scale, political repression involves similar psychological (and often physical as well) assaults by the people and institutions in power on the people, families, communities, and organizations that are deprived of access to political power and socioeconomic resources—and therefore also on their fundamental freedoms and values. Without access to self-determination and the resources necessary to sustain independence, people are vulnerable to not just traumatic exploitation and violence but also to the traumatic loss of their intimate relationships, their families, their way of life, and their values (Box 11.4).

Genocide (also described as "ethnic cleansing") involves the planned and systematic elimination of an entire collectivity of people, based on discrimination against them. Historically, genocide has occurred often when conquering nations not only dominated and subjugated other nations but sought to eradicate their core culture and its leaders and teachers and to kill off or enslave the entire population. Examples in the twentieth century include the Armenian genocide in Turkey, the Holocaust

Box 11.4 The Lost Boys of Sudan: Complex PTSD in the Wake of Societal Breakdown

In the book *What Is the What?*, by Dave Eggers (2005), Valentino Achak Deng (a fictional character based upon a real person) provides an autobiography that includes his trials and tribulations in his current home in Atlanta, Georgia, after a traumatic journey of many years as a "lost boy" fleeing from his family's home in a rural village in Southern Sudan to refugee camps in Ethiopia and Kenya. Valentino graphically describes a relentless series of traumatic experiences that include his village becoming a war zone, the deaths of family and friends, starvation and continual threats of being killed while traveling by foot with thousands of other "lost" children to escape Sudan, witnessing brutal acts of violence by children as well as adults (e.g., a boy beating another boy to death in a fight over food rations), and being robbed and beaten unconscious in his own home in Atlanta by a predatory African American couple.

Valentino is a good example of a person who suffers from chronic and complex PTSD, yet is extremely articulate, intelligent, and resourceful. Valentino struggles with both unwanted memories and the need to keep his memories so that he ultimately can make sense of what has happened to him: *What Is the What?* By writing his autobiography, he did what the therapy for children or adults with PTSD is intended to do: making sense of, rather than attempting to avoid, memories and reminders of traumatic experiences as a part—albeit horrible or tragic—of one's complete life story (see Chapters 7 and 8).

For example, in trauma-focused cognitive behavior therapy, the therapist helps the child to write (or in other creative ways to depict, such as by drawing pictures; using puppets, dolls, or action figures; or using collage or music) a "story" of what happened to them before, during, and after traumatic experience(s) and to share this "story" with a parent who can help the child with feelings of guilt and fear so that the traumatic memory can be "over" in the child's mind. Because Valentino was not able to get that kind of help, his autobiography as an adult (the book) is a kind of second attempt to achieve a sense of resolution by telling his story. But we see how this is very difficult to do when current life involves new problems and dangers that interfere with achieving a sense of safety. Whether Valentino succeeds in achieving some degree of emotional resolution about what he and his loved ones have suffered is an open question. What is clear is that he never stops trying to do so.

It also is apparent that Valentino's ethnic identification and heritage as an African man from the Dinka tribe is very important as a protective factor enabling him to retain a small but significant fragment of his sense of personal identity and his intimate ties to his family and community. He experiences an odyssey as a victim fleeing the scene of horrific trauma, an initially reluctant but eventually drug-induced savage combatant, and a refugee "stranger in a strange land" when he is able to escape to what seems like an entirely different planet in the cosmopolitan urban setting of Atlanta and the southern United States. It is the psychological trauma that he experiences on this odyssey, and the chronic stressors and societal breakdown and oppression that led him—and millions of others of all ages and a multiplicity of ethnocultural groups—on this journey of crisis and survival, and not his ethnicity or cultural background that is responsible for the profound symptoms of PTSD that he develops.

inflicted on Jewish people in Europe by the Nazis, the "ethnic cleansing" in Bosnia and Serbo-Croatia in the 1980s, and the massacres and mass starvation and epidemics perpetrated in Rwanda in 1994, in Sudan beginning in 2003, and in Somalia, Kenya, and Zimbabwe most recently. *Genocide* was first used as a term in 1944 by Raphael Lemkin, combining the words *genos*, from the Greek for "race" or "kind," and *cidere*, which is Latin and can be translated as "kill" (Brom & Kleber, 2008). In 1948, the term was adopted by the United Nations General Assembly and defined by the United Nations Convention on the Prevention and Punishment of the Crime of Genocide (CPPCG) as follows:

> *[Genocide is] any of the following acts committed with intent to destroy, in whole or in part, a national, ethnical, racial, or religious group, as such:*
> a. *Killing members of the group;*
> b. *Causing serious bodily or mental harm to members of the group;*
> c. *Deliberately inflicting on the group conditions of life calculated to bring about its physical destruction in whole or in part;*
> d. *Imposing measures intended to prevent births within the group;*
> e. *Forcibly transferring children of the group to another group. (http://www. unhchr.ch/html/menu3/b/p_genoci.htm)*

Gregory Stanton, the president of Genocide Watch, described "8 Stages of Genocide"; http://www.genocidewatch.org/aboutgenocide/8stagesofgenocide.htm. Accessed 4/14/15:

1. Classification—earliest stage, dividing people into "us" and "them" (the victim group).
2. Symbolization—assigning particular symbols to designate the victim group members.
3. Dehumanization—equating certain people with subhuman animals, vermin, or insects.
4. Organization—militias or special units created for the purpose of genocide.
5. Polarization—broadcasting of propaganda aimed at marginalizing the out-group.
6. Preparation—out-group members are physically separated or confined in a "ghetto."
7. Extermination—murder, starvation, infection, or other forms of inflicting pain and death.
8. Denial—refusal to accept responsibility or admit wrongdoing, maintaining the self-righteous position that the victim group deserved annihilation and were subhuman.

These stages are approximate and vary in each separate incident, but they demonstrate how genocide differs from other forms of even very horrific violence (such as war) because the aim is not simply to subdue, harm, or exploit but to dehumanize, exterminate, and annihilate. Genocide thus involves several traumatic features, including loss of self-worth and allegiance to core values and institutions; prolonged pain and suffering; bereavement; terror and horror of annihilation; injury; helplessness while witnessing demeaning, cruel, and violent events; and confinement.

Survival responses to genocide are described by Brom and Kleber (2008) as:

> ... *a narrowing of functioning and awareness in order to maximize the chances of survival [often involving] psychic closing off (also called robotization—that is, acting and feeling emotionally and mentally empty or on "automatic pilot" like a "robot"), [and] regression—that is, feeling, thinking, and acting like a child (or in the case of children, like a much younger age than actual chronological age). Often victims also experience a strong dependence on perpetrators who decide on life*

and death. The "muselman effect" … manifested by complete physical decrepitude, apathy, slowing of movement, and gradual disintegration of personality (including loss of the capacity for rational reasoning) may result when individuals have been exposed to long-term and extreme circumstances. An additional phenomenon that is well documented is the so-called "death imprint" resulting when substantial witnessing of death continues to haunt the survivor.

These reactions closely parallel the symptoms of both ASD (such as dissociation and regression) and PTSD (such as intrusive reexperiencing and emotional numbing).

The adverse long-term effects of experiencing genocide are severe and pervasive. More than one in three survivors become clinically depressed and develop PTSD. The social support of caring family members (and for children, parents, or other caregivers) and relationships and activities that individuals to retain their spiritual or religious beliefs and their sense of self-respect are crucial protective factors against PTSD and depression. However, even the most resilient and socially supported person is likely to experience distressing memories and survivor guilt years or even decades later. Studies with elderly Holocaust survivors who are physically and emotionally very hardy (often well into their 80s and 90s) have documented significant persisting emotional distress and PTSD symptoms 60 or more years later (Brom & Kleber, 2008). Moreover, the offspring of Holocaust survivors with PTSD are more likely than offspring whose parents do not have PTSD to themselves experience PTSD as adults (Yehuda et al., 2000, 2012).

Genocide often involves physical hardships that compromise physical health and may lead to long-term illnesses and depletion of the body's immune system. For example, the physical exertion and pain involved in torture, untreated physical illnesses, insufficient sleep, starvation, exposure to extreme temperatures, and forced labor may accelerate the aging process (Brom & Kleber, 2008). Genocide also often includes separating individuals from their families and community groups. This not only deprives the survivor of crucial social support but engenders a sense of isolation, distrust, and shame and of being permanently psychologically damaged (Herman, 1992). Survivors also are faced with a choice of holding to their allegiance to their family, nation, culture, and racial identity, despite the punishment inflicted by the perpetrators, or abandoning these basic commitments and rejecting themselves and people like them. Faced with this impossible choice (as epitomized in William Styron's classic novel, *Sophie's Choice*), survivors often believe that they failed utterly and let down not only themselves but their family and culture *no matter how resiliently they coped and the integrity of their efforts.* Survivor guilt is an expression of a sense of grief, powerlessness, and failure, including questioning why they survived and others did not.

Torture. Torture is a terrible special case of political repression that involves "malicious intent and a total disregard for the recipient's dignity and humanity. Thus, torture is among the most egregious violations of a person's fundamental right to personal integrity and a pathological form of human interaction" (Quiroga & Jaranson, 2008).

The 1984 United Nations (UN) Office of High Commissioner for Human Rights established a "Convention against Torture and Other Cruel, Inhuman or Degrading

Treatment or Punishment (CAT)," which has been endorsed by 210 nations and defines torture as follows:

> *For the purpose of this Convention, the term "torture" means any act by which severe pain or suffering, whether physical or mental, is intentionally inflicted on a person for such purpose as obtaining from him or a third person information or a confession, punishing him for an act he or a third person has committed, or is suspected of having committed, or intimidating or coercing him or a third person, or for any reason based on discrimination of any kind, when such pain or suffering is inflicted by, or at the instigation of, or with the consent or acquiescence of, a public official or other person acting in an official capacity. It does not include pain or suffering arising only from, inherent in, or incidental to lawful sanctions. (http://www.unhchr.ch/html/menu3/b/h_cat39.htm accessed 01/19/09)*

An Amnesty International 2000 worldwide survey found that 75% of countries practice torture systematically, despite the absolute prohibition of torture and cruel and inhuman treatment under international law. Torture may be euphemistically referred to as "enhanced interrogation techniques" and condoned in order to obtain "intelligence" from designated enemies of the nation, although this is completely prohibited by the UN resolution (Quiroga & Jaranson, 2008). Widespread controversy has attended the use of such techniques by the US Central Intelligence Agency in response to the September 11, 2001, terrorism incidents, controversy that peaked in 2014 with the presidential decision to close the Guantanamo Bay military prison, and the release of the US Senate report revealing and questioning the legality and morality of torture tactics used in interrogation and incarceration. Basoglu, Livanou, and Crnobaric (2007), in a sample from the Balkan War (1991–2001) studied from 2000 to 2002, showed that the torture need not inflict physical pain in order to produce PTSD.

Psychological assessment of torture survivors was systematized by the *Istanbul Protocol*, a manual on the effective investigation and documentation of torture and other cruel, inhumane, or degrading treatment or punishment that includes modules for medical, psychological, and legal professionals United Nations resolution 55/89 on December 4, 2000 (Quiroga & Jaranson, 2008). The psychological problems most often reported by torture survivors are emotional symptoms (anxiety, depression, irritability/aggressiveness, emotional liability, self-isolation, alienation from others, withdrawal); cognitive symptoms (confusion/disorientation, memory and concentration impairments); and neuro-vegetative symptoms (lack of energy and stamina, insomnia, nightmares, sexual dysfunction) (Quiroga & Jaranson, 2008). The most frequent psychiatric diagnoses are PTSD and major depression, other anxiety disorders such as panic disorder and generalized anxiety disorder, and substance use disorders. Longer-term effects include changes in personality or worldview, consistent with complex PTSD (Quiroga & Jaranson, 2008). The greater the degree of distress and loss of sense of control during torture, the greater the likelihood of PTSD and depression. Resilience, through being able maintain a sense of personal control, efficacy, and hope while enduring torture, is associated with less distress during torture and lower risk of PTSD (Quiroga & Jaranson, 2008).

However, Quiroga and Jaranson (2008) cited a study by Olsen showing that 10 years after torture, physical pain was still prevalent even if torture was primarily psychological in nature. Based on this finding and related studies, they conclude the following (p. 655):

The most important physical consequence of torture is chronic, long-lasting pain experienced in multiple areas of the body. All [physical] torture victims show some acute injuries, sometimes temporary, such as bruises, hematomas, lacerations, cuts, burns, and fractures of teeth or bones, if examined soon after the torture episode. Permanent lesions, such as skin scars on different parts of the body, have been found in 40% to 70% of torture victims. ... Falanga, beating the sole of the feet with a wooden or metallic baton, has been studied extensively. Survivors complain of chronic pain, a burning sensation. ... Acute renal failure secondary to rhabdomyolysis, or destruction of skeletal muscle, is a possible consequence of severe beating involving damage to muscle tissue. This condition can be fatal without hemodialysis. ... A severe traumatic brain injury that is caused by a blow or jolt to the head or a penetrating head injury may disrupt the function of the brain by causing a fracture of the skull, brain hemorrhage, brain edema, seizures, and dementia. The effects of less severe brain injury have not been well studied. Damage to peripheral nerves has been documented in cases where victims have been suspended by their arms or tightly handcuffed.

Treatment for torture survivors must be multidisciplinary and involves a long-term approach. Several treatment modalities have been developed, but little consensus exists concerning the standard of practice, and treatment effectiveness has not been scientifically validated by treatment outcome studies (Quiroga & Jaranson, 2008). A key element that is widely agreed upon is to pay careful attention to not inadvertently replicating in benign ways aspects of torture in the treatment (such as by pressing a survivor to recount traumatic memories without the survivor's informed and voluntary consent; by encouraging or discouraging political, family, and social activities except as initiated by the survivor; or by behaving in authoritarian ways rather than seeking to be collaborative with the survivor). It also is best to use medical, psychiatric medication, and psychotherapy modalities to address the PTSD symptoms of impaired sleep, nightmares, hyperarousal, startle reactions, and irritability. Quiroga and Jaranson (2008) also recommend using groups for socializing and supportive activities to reestablish a sense of family and cultural values, and supporting the traditional religious and cultural beliefs of the survivor. Currently, nearly 250 torture survivor treatment centers exist worldwide, 134 of them accredited by the International Rehabilitation Council of Torture Victims (Quiroga & Jaranson, 2008). Most of these centers also involve the survivors' families and communities in developing shared approaches to recovery and reparation of the harm done to all.

The controversy concerning the use of torture on detainees in the so-called "war on terror" has led to deep concern on the part of not only the public at large but specifically by mental health professionals. The issue is that psychiatry and psychology professionals who are in the military or consult to the military have been involved in the detention and interrogation of suspected terrorists at high-security facilities such as the military base at Guantanamo Bay and the military prison in Iraq, Abu Ghraib. As a result, guidelines for mental health professionals working in these or similar facilities in which prolonged detention and interrogation may involve practices that constitute torture have been developed by a special committee of the American Psychological Association's Division (56) on Trauma Psychology (Box 11.5).

Box 11.5 Excerpts from American Psychological Association Division 56 Task Force Examining Psychologists' Role in Interrogation from the Perspective of Trauma

The involvement of psychologists in national security interrogations in places like Abu Ghraib, Guantanamo Bay, CIA black sites, and other undisclosed secret prisons has become a matter of considerable controversy. The issue has not only been addressed in the popular media as evidenced by articles in venues such as the *New York Times*, *Vanity Fair*, *The New Yorker*, and *Psychology Today*, but it has also received widespread attention in diverse professional publications as *Journal of the American Medical Association*, *New England Journal of Medicine*, *Lancet*, *British Medical Journal*, *Journal of Psychiatry & Law*, *Psychiatric News*, *Military Medicine*, *The Chronicle of Higher Education*, ... and *Congressional Quarterly*.

The APA Council of Representatives ... included in its "unequivocal condemnation" all techniques considered torture or cruel, inhuman or degrading treatment or punishment under the United Nations Convention Against Torture and Other Cruel, Inhuman, or Degrading Treatment or Punishment; the Geneva Conventions; the Principles of Medical Ethics Relevant to the Role of Health Personnel, particularly physicians, in the Protection of Prisoners and Detainees against Torture and Other Cruel, Inhuman, or Degrading Treatment or Punishment; the Basic Principles for the Treatment of Prisoners, the McCain Amendment, the United Nations Principles on the Effective Investigation and Documentation of Torture and Other Cruel, Inhuman, or Degrading Treatment or Punishment an "absolute prohibition against mock executions; waterboarding or any other form of simulated drowning or suffocation; sexual humiliation; rape; cultural or religious humiliation; exploitation of fears, phobias, or psychopathology; induced hypothermia; the use of psychotropic drugs or mind-altering substances; hooding; forced nakedness; stress positions; the use of dogs to threaten or intimidate; physical assault, including slapping or shaking; exposure to extreme heat or cold; threats of harm or death; isolation; sensory deprivation and overstimulation; sleep deprivation; or the threat [of these] to an individual or to members of an individual's family. Psychologists are absolutely prohibited from knowingly planning, designing, participating in, or assisting in the use of all condemned techniques at any time and may not enlist others to employ these techniques.

We have come to the conclusion that the United States' harsh interrogation-detention program is potentially trauma-inducing both in general (e.g., indefinite detention, little contact with lawyers, no contact with relatives or significant others, prolonged absence of due process, awareness that other prisoners have been tortured, lack of predictability or control regarding potential threats to survival or bodily integrity) and in terms of some of its specific components (e.g., prolonged isolation, waterboarding, humiliation, painful stress positions). In other words, these potentials for trauma extend beyond the narrow procedures that meet international definitions of torture. The evidence for risk of psychological trauma to detained enemy combatants is particularly compelling and well grounded in formal research, but there is also suggestive anecdotal and theoretical evidence of trauma induction in interrogators and the broader society. We were particularly struck by the fact that the potentially traumatic elements include not only activities designed to extract information from prisoners but also much of the detention process as it is currently conceived, beyond much oversight, or compliance with international law. Given the pervasiveness of these traumatogenic elements, it is questionable whether psychologists can function in these settings without participating in, or being adversely affected by, heightened risk for trauma. Nonetheless, as a group of psychologists with expertise in preventing traumatic stress and ameliorating debilitating posttraumatic sequelae, we believe that certain steps could ... minimize the risk of psychological trauma. They are as follows:

1. We believe that the risk of traumatic stress and negative posttraumatic sequelae will be reduced if psychologists adhere to both the APA *Ethical Standards* and subsequent refinements of APA policies pertaining to interrogation, detention, and torture. Such adherence would be more likely if the APA ethics code were revised to incorporate, as enforceable standards, the specific interrogation and torture-related policy refinements that have occurred since 2002.

2. Psychologists should promote situations that maintain the risk of traumatic stress at acceptably low levels and avoid situations that heighten the risk for traumatic stress occurring. Among other things, this means that psychologists should not provide professional services in secret prisons that appear to be beyond the reach of normal standards of international law or in settings in which torture and other human rights abuses have been credibly documented to be permitted on the basis of local laws. It also suggests that psychologists should not support or participate in any detention or interrogation procedure that constitutes cruel or inhumane treatment or that otherwise has been shown to elevate risk of traumatic stress (e.g., prolonged isolation).

3. If psychologists work in settings in which detention and interrogations are conducted, then they should conduct or seek an assessment of the potential traumatic features of the treatment of detainees before, during, and after interrogation. This assessment can be informal or formal, depending on whether other systems of oversight are in place. This assessment should include an examination of the social psychological factors that could elevate risk of trauma. Because not all psychologists have expertise in assessing traumatic stress risk and/or social psychological

(Continued)

Box 11.5 Continued

factors, the assessment should be conducted by psychologists who have this specific expertise. Such assessments could inform decisions not only by psychologists but also by others working in facilities in which detention and interrogation occur. It is recommended therefore that APA advocate for appropriate governmental authorities to appoint an independent oversight committee for each facility of this type and that the oversight committees include psychologists identified by APA as having relevant expertise.

4. If psychologists work in settings in which risk of traumatic stress is found to be elevated then they should (i) formally recommend alterations that could reduce the traumatogenic potential of the detention and interrogation process (n.b. some recommendations may be aimed at policy makers rather than local authorities); (ii) conduct or seek an assessment of posttraumatic stress symptoms and associated features (e.g., depression, dissociation) in detainees, interrogators, and other directly or indirectly involved staff; (iii) recommend appropriate psychological interventions for any detainees or personnel found to be suffering from clinically significant psychological difficulties; and (iv) refuse to participate in any activities that significantly increase risk of traumatic stress. If a psychologist working in such settings does not have specific expertise required to meet some of the above recommendations, then she or he should consult with psychologist(s) who have this expertise to make the appropriate determination.

5. Because some detainee abuses have been credibly linked to an absence of appropriate training and/or expertise, psychologists should advocate for, participate in designing, and/or assist with providing appropriate and comprehensive training to all personnel involved in interacting with detainees. This training should include (i) clear ethical guidelines emphasizing the prohibition of causing harm and the importance of protecting detainee rights, (ii) a research-based overview of the nature and consequences of traumatic stress and posttraumatic impairment as they relate to the interrogation and confinement process and all parties involved in layperson terms with practical implications, and (iii) detailed review of research on false confessions, in layperson terms, with practical implications for enhancing the validity and utility of information gathered in the course of interrogation and detention. Because not all psychologists have expertise in these specific matters, APA should develop standardized training materials that cover the current state of psychological knowledge and practices on these important topics, and ensure that these materials are regularly updated by qualified psychologists in consultation with experts from other fields such as law enforcement, the military, and human rights.

6. Because protecting human rights reduces the risk for traumatic stress and posttraumatic impairment, psychologists should collaborate with legal, military, and other colleagues to advocate for due process for all detainees, including providing clear guidelines about finite lengths of detention prior to formal hearing or trial and enforcing the recent Supreme Court decision to reinstate habeas corpus and other international standards of human rights. Psychologists' support for these actions should not come from a blanket support for adherence to law but rather from an informed judgment that these … laws reduce the risk for harm. Psychologists should be prepared to disagree with any future international laws or US Supreme Court decisions that heighten risk for traumatic stress.

7. Psychologists should support increased transparency during the detention and interrogation process. Such increased transparency could reduce the likelihood of traumatizing practices, increase the likelihood that traumatizing practices will be identified and stopped as early as possible, and protect ethical psychologists and other workers within the system from being falsely accused of acting unethically. We recognize that this recommendation raises an apparent conflict with the goal of secrecy commonly endorsed by national security organizations. We concur that full transparency is unreasonable and counterproductive. Yet, we do believe that increased transparency is a safeguard against traumatizing practices. Though the details of resolving this conflict are beyond the scope of this task force's expertise, we believe that reasonable, knowledgeable intelligence experts, in consultation with psychologists, can construct a system of oversight that will both retain credible independence from the military chain of command and guard classified information. One suggestion may be to establish a greater presence of psychological expertise within a framework of oversight protection.

8. If psychologists are going to continue to be involved in interrogations, then it will be important to continue to segregate the function of interrogation consultant from that of mental health provider to reduce risk of perceived or actual betrayal by the detainee. It is unknown whether betrayal of trust due to dual roles can constitute a direct form of traumatization under these circumstances, but it is likely that betrayal in this context could exacerbate traumatic stress that occurs of other aspects of detention and interrogation (especially in light of the ways that such detention appears to disrupt attachment as outlined in the body of our report). Maintaining separate roles also may enable the psychologist to more effectively assist detainees with traumatic stress reactions by fostering a trusting therapeutic relationship.

9. Psychologists should advocate for extra protections for detainees who are from vulnerable populations such as minors, ethnic minorities, or other groups that have limited access to socioeconomic or political resources or are potentially subject to societal discrimination or prejudice because such groups may be more likely to receive coercive interrogations and/or excessive force and less likely to be sympathetically viewed by the general public. For this purpose, psychologists may work within sponsor/authorizing organizations to institute developmental, gender, and culture sensitivity trainings for interrogators and should review evidence concerning the impact of different forms of traumatic stressors and differential sensitivity to the interrogation/detention setting/process on different (and particularly vulnerable) ages, genders, and cultural backgrounds. Such psychologists should, to whatever extent possible, guard against such information being used to exploit vulnerable populations and instead emphasize ways to enhance safety and psychological well-being in the interrogation process. If psychologists lack relevant expertise to meet the recommendations, ... they should seek or advocate for outside expert consultation.

10. Psychologists should collaborate with colleagues from a variety of professions and organizations, including the military and intelligence organizations, to conduct ethical research on several aspects of the detention and interrogation process, especially its potential for inducing trauma. Recent reviews suggest that most of the interrogation procedures used today have not received recent rigorous study (Intelligence Science Board, 2006). Furthermore, very little of the recent study has been directed toward understanding the psychological effects of interrogation on not only the detainees but also the people working within and outside the interrogation and detention system.

Refugee survivors of political violence and catastrophic disasters

Political violence not only leads to traumatic harm to people while they are living in their communities but also often when victims are forced to flee their homes either to another country or while remaining within their country. Refugees are defined by the United Nations High Commissioner for Refugees (UNHCR) as persons who have left their nation of origin to escape violence. Article one of the 1951 United Nations Convention Relating to the Status of Refugees defines a refugee as someone who "owing to well-founded fear of being persecuted for reasons of race, religion, nationality, membership of a particular social group or political opinion, is outside the country of his nationality and is unable or, owing to such fear, is unwilling to avail himself of the protection of that country; or who, not having a nationality and being outside the country of his former habitual residence as a result of such events, is unable or, owing to such fear, is unwilling to return to it" (UNHCR, p. 16; http:// www.unhcr.org/home/PUBL/3b5e90ea0.pdf; accessed 19.01.09).

Therefore, refugees are distinct from both legal and illegal immigrants, economic migrants, environmental migrants, and labor migrants (Weine, 2008). Refugees must involuntarily leave home, community, and family and friends, often with limited resources or preparation and usually without knowing whom they can trust and where they can find safe passage and a safe haven. Thus, both prior to and during the displacement, refugees often suffer psychologically traumatic experiences, including having their community or homes attacked or destroyed due to war; racially, gender-based, or ethnically targeted genocide or terrorism; institutionally orchestrated deprivation and violence; along with torture, atrocities, rape, witnessing violence, fear for their lives, hunger, lack of adequate shelter, separation from loved ones, and destruction and loss of property (Weine, 2008).

Estimating the number of refugees is very difficult. A minimum estimate that is probably much lower than the actual number is calculated by the United Nations based on the number of persons in resettlement camps or individually recognized by a host country. Based on this definition, there were 16 million refugees worldwide in 2007 (www.unhcr.org) (Figure 11.1).

UNHCR's "Global Trends 2011" report details for the first time the extent of forced displacement from a string of major humanitarian crises that began in late 2010 in Côte d'Ivoire, and was quickly followed by others in Libya, Somalia, Sudan, and elsewhere. In all, 4.3 million people were newly displaced, with a full 800,000 of these fleeing their countries and becoming refugees. "2011 saw suffering on an epic scale. For so many lives to have been thrown into turmoil over so short a space of time means enormous personal cost for all who were affected," said the UNHCR António Guterres. "We can be grateful only that the international system for protecting such people held firm for the most part and that borders stayed open. These are testing times."

Worldwide, 42.5 million people ended 2011 either as refugees (15.2 million), internally displaced (26.4 million), or in the process of seeking asylum (895,000).

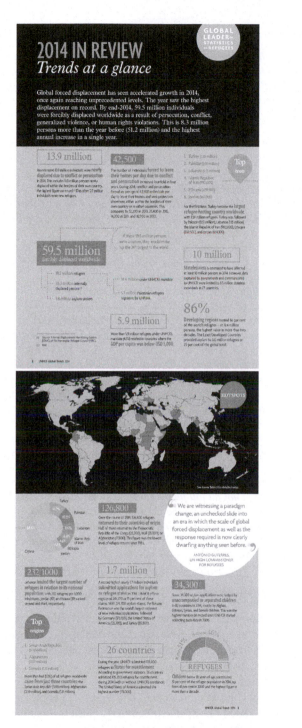

Figure 11.1 Refugees, internally displaced persons (IDPs), and stateless persons worldwide. © 2015 United Nations High Commissioner for Refugees. All rights reserved.

Despite the high number of new refugees, the overall figure was lower than the
2010 total of 43.7 million people, due mainly to the offsetting effect of large
numbers of IDPs returning home: 3.2 million, the highest rate of returns of IDPs in
more than a decade. Among refugees, and notwithstanding an increase in voluntary
repatriation over 2010 levels, 2011 was the third lowest year for returns (532,000)
in a decade.

Viewed on a 10-year basis, the report shows several worrying trends. One is
that forced displacement is affecting larger numbers of people globally, with the
annual level exceeding 42 million people for each of the last 5 years. Another is
that a person who becomes a refugee is likely to remain one for many years—often
stuck in a camp or living precariously in an urban location. Of the 10.4 million
refugees under UNHCR's mandate, almost three-quarters (7.1 million) have been in
exile for at least 5 years awaiting a solution.

Overall, Afghanistan remains the biggest producer of refugees (2.7 million),
followed by Iraq (1.4 million), Somalia (1.1 million), Sudan (500,000), and the
Democratic Republic of the Congo (491,000).

Around four-fifths of the world's refugees flee to their neighboring countries,
reflected in the large refugee populations seen, for example, in Pakistan (1.7 million
people), Iran (886,500), Kenya (566,500), and Chad (366,500).

Among industrialized countries, Germany ranks as the largest hosting country
with 571,700 refugees. South Africa, meanwhile, was the largest recipient of
individual asylum applications (107,000), a status it has held for the past 4 years.

UNHCR's original mandate was to help refugees, but in the six decades since
the agency was established in 1950, its work has grown to include helping many of
the world's internally displaced people and those who are stateless (those lacking
recognized citizenship and the human rights that accompany this).

The Global Trends 2011 report notes that only 64 governments provided data on
stateless people, meaning that UNHCR was able to record numbers for only around
a quarter of the estimated 12 million stateless people worldwide.

Of the 42.5 million people who were in a state of forced displacement as of
the end of last year, not all fall under UNHCR's care. Some 4.8 million refugees,
for example, are registered with the UN Relief and Works Agency for Palestine
Refugees. Among the 26.4 million internally displaced, 15.5 million receive
UNHCR assistance and protection. Overall, UNHCR's refugee and IDP caseload of
25.9 million people grew by 700,000 people in 2011.

http://www.unhcr.org/4fd9e6266.htm, accessed 4/14/15

Most reside in neighboring countries, fleeing from conflict-torn places such as
Burundi, Congo, Somalia, and Sudan in Africa; Palestine and Iraq in the Middle
East; Afghanistan, China, Nepal, Myanmar, and Malaysia in Asia; Colombia in South
America; and the Balkans and Russian federation. Others seek asylum in or immi-
grate to Western countries in Europe and America.

Many people displaced from their communities by violence remain in their home
country. They are not considered refugees, but "IDPs": "people or groups … who have
been forced to leave their homes" due to "armed conflict, situations of generalized violence, violations of human rights, or natural- or human-made disasters, and who have
not crossed an international border" (www.unhcr.org). As of 2007, there were more than
three times as many IDPs as refugees, an estimated 51 million worldwide, 26 million

due to armed conflict and 25 million due to mass natural disasters (www.unhcr.org). Between one and more than 3 million IDPs were known to be in several countries in 2007, including Colombia, Congo, Iraq, Somalia, Sudan, and Uganda. Azerbaijan, Cote due N'Orde, and Sri Lanka had more than 500,000 known IDPs each.

At least another 3 million persons are considered "stateless"—that is, to not be citizens of any nation, in 2007. Nepal and Bangladesh have the majority of the stateless persons in the world, although nearly 3 million persons in those two countries were made citizens in 2007. Palestine and Iraq are the other countries with large numbers of stateless persons. There may be millions more stateless individuals, because only 54 countries assisted the United Nations in its census of stateless persons in 2007 (www.unhcr.org).

The impact of forced displacement often is not just extremely stressful but traumatic. Refugees, IDPs, and stateless persons have few protections and often must live in confined camps or crowded public shelters, where they are vulnerable to assaults (including rape), robbery, and illness. Many have witnessed horrific violence associated with wars, genocide, or other forms of mass armed conflict that caused them to flee. Loss of family and friends due to violence or illness is common, as well as due to being separated with no way to communicate. Studies have documented high prevalence levels of PTSD and depression among refugees or IDPs from armed conflicts in central America, southeast Asia, the Middle East, and the Balkans (Fazel, Wheeler, & Danesh, 2005; Marshall, Schell, Elliott, Berthold, & Chun, 2005) at least 10 times higher than the 1–3% prevalence estimates from epidemiological surveys (see Chapter 3). PTSD prevalence estimates that are more than three times higher than these very high levels, as high as 30–34%, have been reported among disabled central American refugees (Rivera, Mari, Andreoli, Quintana, & Ferraz, 2008) and among Afghan mothers (Seino, Takano, Mashal, Hemat, & Nakamura, 2008).

Other studies have more specifically investigated physical displacement in the traumatic stress experienced by refugees. Displacement may involve many stressors, and a research review found that "living in institutional accommodation, experiencing restricted economic opportunity, [being] displaced internally within their own country [or] repatriated to a country they had previously fled or whose initiating conflict was unresolved" were particularly problematic. This review of 56 reports involving 67,294 participants (22,221 refugees and 45,073 persons who were not displaced) showed that displacement alone was associated with more severe mental health problems, including PTSD (Porter & Haslam, 2005). In contrast to most research findings on the etiology (see Chapter 3) and epidemiology (see Chapter 4) of PTSD, "refugees who were older, more educated, and female and who had higher predisplacement socioeconomic status and rural residence also had worse outcomes" (Porter & Haslam, 2005, p. 602).

People become "internally displaced" as often due to mass natural disasters as to armed violence. In the United States, several hundred thousand people had to leave the New Orleans area following Hurricane Katrina in August 2005. Almost 400,000 received medical care at American Red Cross Shelters within the next month (Mills, Edmondson, & Park, 2007). Many displaced persons already were severely disadvantaged due to living in poverty (roughly 28% of the population of New Orleans), having limited access to quality health care, and exposure to community violence (Mills et al., 2007). In a study of 132 adult evacuees from New Orleans and surrounding parishes (56% men, average age 43 years old, 74% black, 82% low income (annual income less than $30,000), 67% reporting a prehurricane psychiatric disorder (33% depression, 20% anxiety disorder, 8% bipolar disorder)), most (95%) waited several days to be evacuated, and a majority reported sustaining minor to severe injuries (63%) and mild to severe illness (71%) in the hurricane or evacuation process. One in seven lost a loved one due to death in the hurricane or its aftermath, and most (85%) were separated from a family member for a day or more. Many (70%) lost their home, two-thirds of whom were without property insurance. Almost two in three (62%), particularly women, people with a prior psychiatric disorder, and those who recalled feeling their lives were in danger during the hurricane or its aftermath, were injured physically, or felt they had limited control over their current life circumstances, reported symptoms sufficient to qualify for a diagnosis of ASD.

Natural disasters of several magnitudes greater have occurred in less developed and affluent areas of the world. For example, the tsunami that struck on December 26, 2004, in the wake of the Sumatra-Andaman earthquake killed an estimated 250,000 people along the coastlines of the Indian Ocean, including 130,000 Indonesians. Another half a million Indonesians were displaced from their communities. Studies of survivors of this tsunami from Indonesian areas such as Aceh and North Sumatra (Frankenberg et al., 2008), as well as from Thailand (van Griensven et al., 2006) and Sri Lanka (Hollifield et al., 2008), have demonstrated that posttraumatic stress, anxiety, and depression are suffered by hundreds of thousands, and perhaps millions, of people who experienced psychological trauma due to the tsunami (Box 11.6).

Box 11.6 Refugee Posttraumatic Stress in the Wake of Mass Natural Disaster

Frankenberg et al. (2008) reported a unique study of the impact of a massive natural disaster: the Indian Ocean tsunami that struck the day after Christmas 2004. Unlike most research on mental health after disasters, this study began with a survey of a representative sample of persons in the host country (Indonesia) almost 2 years before the disaster. This "National Socioeconomic Survey (SUSENAS)" provided a registry of respondents and predisaster data on health and socioeconomic characteristics of people throughout Indonesia. The "Study of the Tsunami Aftermath and Recovery (STAR)" attempted to recontact 39,500 persons interviewed in 585 communities by the SUSENAS.

The study also was able to determine the extent of damage caused to each community by the tsunami. The researchers got data from the National Aeronautics and Space Administration's Moderate Resolution Imaging Spectroradiometer sensor collected 1 year prior to the tsunami, and again immediately after the tsunami, to assess the degree to which the pretsunami ground cover visible in the first image had been replaced by bare earth in the second image. Communities with at least 20% loss of ground cover were classified as heavily damaged (15%

of the 585 surveyed communities). Those with some loss of ground cover were categorized as moderately damaged (50% of all locales), and 35% with no loss of ground cover were classified as undamaged by the tsunami. Community leaders' and field observers' estimates of damage strongly correlated ($r=0.84$ and 0.79) with these satellite-based estimates.

One in three of the survey respondents (average age 36 years old) heard the tsunami wave or people screaming. Fewer sustained injuries (3%), lost a spouse (3%), lost a parent or child (5%), or witnessed family or friends "struggle or disappear" (6%), but 25% lost a family member or friend, 25% lost their home, and 15% lost their farming land, livestock, or equipment.

Posttraumatic stress was assessed by asking every respondent 15 years or older to answer seven of the items from the PTSD Checklist (see Chapter 6), as follows:

Since the tsunami, have you ever experienced (never, rarely, sometimes, or often) and do you now experience (no, sometimes, often):

A. *Repeated, disturbing memories, thoughts, dreams, or experiences of THE tsunami*
B. *Feeling very upset when something reminded you of THE tsunami*
C. *Avoiding activities or situations because they reminded you of a stressful experience*
D. *Feeling as if your future will somehow be cut short*
E. *Trouble falling or staying asleep*
F. *Feeling irritable or having angry outbursts*
G. *Being "super-alert," watchful, or on guard*

Exposure to probable traumatic stress due to hearing the wave or screams, being injured, or seeing friends or family members "struggle or disappear," doubled the severity of PCL-C scores. Consistent with this finding, compared to the sleep difficulties reported before the tsunami, after the tsunami, there was a large increase in the likelihood of sleep difficulties only in the most heavily damaged areas. PCL-C scores increased the most in the worst damaged locales, followed by the moderately damaged ones, with little change in the nondamaged communities. PCL-C scores averaged 5.77, 4.71, and 2.98 for the heavily, moderately, and undamaged areas, respectively, at the time of the interview and had been 33% higher at their peak after the tsunami (based on respondents' recollections). This is consistent with other studies that have reported persistent PTSD symptoms among the worst exposed persons but a substantial decline in PTSD symptom severity over time even among heavily exposed persons (see Chapter 2).

Women reported higher PCL-C scores than men, but primarily only in the heavily damaged areas. Age was a factor in all communities: persons younger than 30 years reporting an increase after the tsunami and persons 50 years and older reporting lower PCL-C scores after the tsunami. Interestingly, respondents who had a parent alive before the tsunami had lower PCL-C scores after the tsunami, but marital status, education, and income were not related to posttsunami PCL-C scores. Property damage also correlated with posttsunami PCL-C scores.

(Continued)

Box 11.6 Continued

As Frankenberg et al. (2008) noted, these findings probably understate the severity and widespread nature of the harm, including posttraumatic stress, caused by a massive disaster such as this tsunami. However, the study provides the strongest evidence to date that a disaster that is not only life threatening for many but that displaces tens or hundreds of thousands of persons from their homes, families, neighbors, and way of life has the strongest adverse impact on communities that are most directly affected.

Another study (van Griensven et al., 2008) conducted 8 weeks after the tsunami in six southwestern provinces of Thailand (where more than 8000 persons died or were unaccounted for and another 8500 were injured) included random samples of 371 displaced persons and 321 nondisplaced persons from the most heavily hit area and 368 persons from less damaged areas. Even though the extent of death and destruction was less in the worst-hit areas of Thailand than in Indonesia, symptoms of PTSD were reported by 12% of displaced and 7% of nondisplaced persons in the most damaged area of Thailand (and by 3% in the less damaged areas). Anxiety or depression symptoms were reported by three times as many persons, with similar proportions depending on displacement and the severity of damage to the community. Thus, this study adds to the findings of the study from Indonesia by demonstrating that displacement from home and community was a factor in PTSD and related symptoms soon after a mass natural disaster.

The Thailand study also resurveyed participants from the worst-damaged area 7 months later (9 months after the tsunami) and confirmed that displaced persons continued to be more likely than nondisplaced persons to suffer from PTSD, anxiety, and depression symptoms. Consistent with other studies (Ford, Adams, & Dailey, 2007) of postdisaster recovery (including the Indonesia study), as the first anniversary of the disaster approached, about 40% of each group had recovered sufficiently to no longer report severe symptoms.

Whereas the Indonesia study examined the extent of damage to participants' homes and (for most) the source of their incomes (farmland, animals, and equipment), the Thailand study inquired directly as to whether respondents had lost their source of income and found that loss of livelihood was the strongest correlate of PTSD, anxiety, and depression symptoms. Thus, the Thailand study showed that losing not only home or community but also one's ability to generate an independent income through gainful work may contribute to the development and persistence of PTSD and related anxiety and depression symptoms. The defining characteristics of becoming a refugee in the wake of disaster therefore include (i) exposure to life-threatening catastrophe; (ii) loss of or separation from family and friends, (iii) loss of home and community; and (iv) loss of one's personal or family livelihood. Each of these factors may result in acute posttraumatic distress, and the combination of several places people at risk for persistent PTSD.

As Weine (2008) describes, resettlement of refugees is a substantial challenge not only for displaced persons themselves but also for the host country. Relatively stable and affluent countries in Asia (such as Pakistan, due to Afghan refugees), the middle east (such as Lebanon and Syria, due to Palestinian refugees), and Africa (such as Kenya and South Africa), as well as most European and British Commonwealth nations and the United States, have had a large influx of refugees. The half of all refugees who are resettled in cities experience economic pressures due to poverty and low-wage work and must live in communities that are crowded, segregated economically and culturally, and often adversely affected by crime, gangs, drugs, AIDS, and troubled schools (Weine, 2008). Another half of all refugees are resettled in suburban and rural areas, which are more isolated (www.unhcr.org). In either case, refugees often face prolonged separations from family, friends, and loved ones, as well as the burden of having to find a way to subsist while saving money to bring others to their new home and to provide support to those back home who have stayed behind.

Refugee children have additional needs and challenges, including having to survive life-threatening experiences without adult help or guidance and then, if they are fortunate enough to be permanently resettled, having to return to being a "child" with a new family, community, and culture (Henderson, 2008). Refugee children often display not only the symptoms of PTSD but also behavior problems (such as control, aggression, or defiance of authority), profound bereavement, and developmental, learning, or educational delays or deficits that are understandable in light of their often chronic deprivations before and during displacement. However, children also can be particularly resilient in the face of the psychological losses and traumas of being a refugee, and often they are a key source of hope for their families in the resettlement process (Weine, 2008).

Many refugees have opportunities to receive mental health services, either in the context of a refugee camp or after resettlement, but many do not seek or utilize these services. Survival; getting stable and predictable access to food, money, housing, transportation, and safety; renewing communication with friends and family; and sustaining or regaining connection to cultural and religious traditions, values, and practices may take precedence over mental health treatment (and may in fact be the best form of therapy for many, under the circumstances).

In resettlement settings, clinical treatment for refugee trauma is typically organized through refugee mental health clinics or specialized torture victim treatment centers, with services including crisis intervention, psychopharmacology, individual psychotherapy, group psychotherapy, and self-help groups and activities (Weine, 2008). To deliver culturally appropriate services, many programs involve traditional healers, socialization or mutual support groups, multifamily groups, and culturally based activities (Weine, 2008). Services also tend to be provided by staff who themselves are members of the refugees' ethnic community, in collaboration with traumatic stress specialists and mental health professionals. The traditional model of Western professional "expert" doctor or consultant who unilaterally tells local staff or clients how best to do assessment, diagnosis, or treatment has been justly criticized as culturally insensitive and potentially harmful rather than helpful (Weine, 2008). Instead, the joint experience and expertise of the refugee client, local professional and paraprofessional alike, traditional healers, and traumatic stress professionals are taken together in a team approach that validates the client's and local helpers' cultures and traditions. This approach enhances the providers' ability to make a true cross-cultural assessment of symptoms and diagnoses, to adapt interventions to reflect different cultural beliefs and practices, and to engage not just individual clients but families and communities in recovery from PTSD. Such an approach is consistent with new theoretical views of refugee traumatic stress, which include "the concepts of cultural bereavement, cultural trauma, family consequences of refugee trauma, community trauma, and social suffering" (Weine, 2008). This more culturally grounded view of refugees' experiences of traumatic stress and recovery from PTSD has led to the development of innovative therapy approaches (such as incorporating personal testimony and reconciliation into treatment) that address refugees' psychological vulnerabilities but strongly acknowledge their (and their families' and communities') hopes and strengths (Weine, 2008).

Programs addressing the social and political aspects of catastrophic traumatic stressors

When mass catastrophes, whether human-made or "Acts of God" in origin, including natural disasters such as tsunamis, tornadoes, hurricanes, floods, or earthquakes, or public health emergencies, such as AIDS, severe acute respiratory syndrome (SARS), pandemic influenza, Ebola, or human-made disasters such as terrorist attacks, airline crashes, ferry capsizes, and train derailments, cause tens or hundreds of thousands or even millions of people and families to experience psychological trauma, the resultant suffering and needs are generally beyond the capacities of traditional mental health services and other forms of government-sponsored services. NGOs play a critical role supporting and assisting persons and communities affected by catastrophic disaster or violence, including providing psychological support through clinical and nonclinical behavioral health services (Hamilton & Dodgen, 2008).

NGO responses to the mental health needs of mass-disaster survivors are based on the core belief that "all disasters are local" (Hamilton & Dodgen, 2008). This means that local responders such as law enforcement, police, emergency medical teams, and professionals from the health care facilities, schools, and government are invariably first on the scene and frequently remain involved for months or years afterward. When insufficient resources are available, a local community may request help from the country, state, or provincial governments, which in turn may request regional or national assistance from both government and private sectors. For that reason, NGOs that provide assistance following disasters, such as the American Red Cross, the National Voluntary Organizations Active in Disaster (NVOAD), the United Way, and the Salvation Army do so through their local chapters, which organize the initial relief efforts to provide shelter, food, legal aid, health and mental health care, and humanitarian assistance. Organized in 1970, NVOAD is the umbrella organization coordinating all disaster relief services provided by volunteer organizations such as the American Red Cross throughout the United States.

NGOs also work closely with faith-based organizations (FBOs) in the United States (such as Catholic Charities United States, Church World Service, Lutheran Disaster Response, National Association of Jewish Chaplains) within the National Response Framework of the Federal Emergency Management Agency (FEMA), which guides the nation's "all-hazards incident response" (Hamilton & Dodgen, 2008). For example, American Red Cross disaster mental health (DMH) volunteers provide mental health services to people in shelters, while the Church of the Brethren provides crisis intervention to young children through their Disaster Child Care program (Hamilton & Dodgen, 2008).

The American Red Cross is the most widely recognized NGO providing DMH services in the United States. In 1905, Congress chartered the American Red Cross to "carry on a system of national and international relief in time of peace" to reduce and prevent the suffering caused by national calamities program (Hamilton & Dodgen, 2008). In 1990, the American Red Cross established a formal DMH Services program and began training licensed and certified mental health professionals to volunteer and assist other Red Cross workers to cope with and recover from the traumatic stress (or "vicarious trauma") of their disaster relief work. Initially only licensed psychologists and social workers were permitted to become Red Cross DMH volunteers, but recently professionals from other disciplines, such as psychiatry and masters-level marriage and family therapy or counseling professions, also have become eligible.

The American Red Cross has set up formal agreements with the American Psychiatric Association, the American Psychological Association, the National Association of Social Workers, the American Counseling Association, and the American Association of Marriage and Family Therapy. The agreements provide that in the event of a mass disaster, the Red Cross will notify each professional associations to put out a call to their memberships for professionals who have completed Red Cross preparatory training and who can take time out from their ordinary work to serve as DMH volunteers for 2 weeks or more at Red Cross disaster services sites.

The American Red Cross sets up and oversees Family Assistance Centers for disaster-affected communities, provides crisis and grief counseling through its DMH volunteers, and coordinates with federal agencies such as FEMA and the National Transportation Safety Board (for airline or mass transportation disasters) to provide child care services and interfaith memorial services. The Red Cross also works closely with disaster-focused NGOs such as the National Organization for Victim Assistance, Disaster Psychiatry Outreach, and the International Critical Incident Stress Foundation, Inc. (ICISF). Founded in 1989, the ICISF trains mental health professionals, emergency responders, clergy, and chaplains to conduct Critical Incident Stress Management (see Chapter 9) teams to support disaster services personnel.

In 2005, the American Red Cross broadened the scope of DMH services to include assisting disaster-affected persons who are seeking Red Cross assistance, as well as Red Cross volunteers. All DMH volunteers now are trained in Psychological First Aid (see Chapter 9) so that they will provide mental health services to disaster victims in an appropriately circumscribed manner that is therapeutic without attempting to conduct psychotherapy at a disaster relief site.

Two other freestanding programs participating in a DMH response are the Green Cross Assistance Program, which provides trained traumatology specialists and the Association of Traumatic Stress Specialists, an association of mental health professionals and paraprofessionals who assist survivors of psychological trauma (Hamilton & Dodgen, 2008). A number of US NGOs also work internationally to provide psychosocial support and traumatic stress counseling to survivors of disasters and mass conflicts. These include the International Services of the American Red Cross, the United Methodist Committee on Relief, Church World Services, Green Cross, Action Aid—the United States, the American Refugee Committee, The Center for Victims of Torture, and Doctors Without Borders (Hamilton & Dodgen, 2008). The International Federation of Red Cross and Red Crescent Societies also assist many nations' Red Cross organizations in serving their own and neighboring countries.

A 2006 analysis by the United States Homeland Security Institute found that FBOs and NGOs had a significant beneficial impact during and after Hurricanes Katrina and Rita, with mental health and spiritual support among 10 types of services (Hamilton & Dodgen, 2008). The study reported that while FBOs and NGOs faced significant limitations and challenges in providing services, mental health and spiritual support was one of the three best-applied special practices, particularly services designed to preserve family unity within disaster relief shelters.

Hamilton and Dodgen (2008, p. 451) describe how NGOs can work together to meet critical needs in times of mass crisis, using the September 11, 2001, terrorist attacks in New York, Washington, and Pennsylvania, as a case in point:

Local mental health providers working in mental health settings mobilized quickly, but needs were expected to surpass local capability. The American Red Cross dispatched DMH providers from local and adjacent communities to provide mental health support and stress reduction assistance. National volunteers recruited from across the country arrived within a few days to augment that mission. Concurrently, ICISF-trained volunteers, some of whom were already part of military mental health systems, also arrived to provide assistance. Other agencies, such as FBOs, also organized support for victims. In Washington, the military was the gatekeeper for volunteers and worked closely with the American Red Cross to coordinate mental health support. In New York, civilian authorities collaborated with the American Red Cross. As family assistance centers were set up to aid grieving families, national DMH volunteers continued providing mental health support. Because the terrorist attacks created a crime scene, access was controlled and NGOs needed official standing to provide assistance. Incorporating lessons learned from 9/11, a similar event today would be different in several ways: all NGOs and government agencies would organize their response under the National Incident Management System (NIMS) and the NRF, thus creating a more centralized, coordinated response and reducing overlapping or competing activities on the part of NVOADs. Because of ongoing coordination and outreach efforts since 9/11, a greater array of disciplines and specific types of expertise would be available through NGOs. The benefits of these efforts were seen during the responses to Hurricanes Katrina and Rita in 2005.

Conclusion

Personal and community characteristics that reflect ethnocultural, national, gender, age, and disability factors are crucial in defining the identity of every human being. When traumatic stress occurs in a person's or community's life, its impact is influenced by these identity factors. When identity is used as a basis for stigma, discrimination, or socioeconomic disadvantage, those stressors compound the effect of traumatic stressors and can be traumatic in and of themselves. By addressing the vulnerability that this combination in a scientifically and clinically responsible manner (Alcantara, Casement, & Lewis-Fernandez, 2013; C'De Baca, Castillo, & Qualls, 2012; Ghafoori, Barragan, Tohidian, & Palinkas, 2012) to assist rather than stigmatize persons and communities (Ruglass et al., 2014), the traumatic stress professional can play a crucial role in our society's quest for social justice.

References

Alcantara, C., Casement, M. D., & Lewis-Fernandez, R. (2013). Conditional risk for PTSD among Latinos: A systematic review of racial/ethnic differences and sociocultural explanations. *Clinical Psychology Review*, *33*(1), 107–119. http://dx.doi.org/10.1016/j.cpr.2012.10.005.

Andres-Hyman, R. C., Ortiz, J., Anez, L. M., Paris, M., & Davidson, L. (2006). Culture and clinicalpractice: Recommendations for working with Puerto Ricans and other Latinas(os) in the United States. *Professional Psychology: Research and Practice*, *37*, 694–701.

Basoglu, M., Livanou, M., & Crnobaric, C. (2007). Torture vs other cruel, inhuman, and degrading treatment - Is the distinction real or apparent? *Archives of General Psychiatry*, *64*(3), 277–285.

Bassuk, E. L., Dawson, R., Perloff, J. N., & Weinrub, L. F. (2001). Post-traumatic stress disorder in extremely poor women: Implications for health care clinicalicians. *Journal of the American Medical Women's Association*, *56*(2), 79–85.

Betancourt, T. S., Abdi, S., Ito, B. S., Lilienthal, G. M., Agalab, N., & Ellis, H. (2015). We left one war and came to another: Resource loss, acculturative stress, and caregiver-child relationships in Somali refugee families. *Cultural Diversity & Ethnic Minority Psychology*, *21*(1), 114–125. http://dx.doi.org/10.1037/a0037538.

Brom, D., & Kleber, R. (2008). Resilience as the capacity for processing traumatic experiences. In D. Brom, R. Pat-Horenczyk, & J. Ford (Eds.), *Treating traumatized children* (pp. 133–149). London: Routledge.

Brown, D. (2009). Assessment of attachment and abuse history, and adult attachment style. In C. Courtois & J. D. Ford (Eds.), *Treating complex traumatic stress disorders: An evidence-based guide*. New York: Guilford.

Brown, J. S., Hitlin, S., & Elder, G. H. (2006). The greater complexity of lived race: An extension of Harris and Sim. *Social Science Quarterly*, *87*, 411–431.

Brown, L. (2009). Cultural competence. In C. A. Courtois & J. D. Ford (Eds.), *Treatment of complex traumatic stress disorders* (pp. 166–182). New York: Guilford.

Carter, R. T., & Forsyth, J. M. (2009). A guide to the forensic assessment of race-based traumatic stress reactions. *Journal of the American Academy of Psychiatry and the Law*, *37*(1), 28–40.

C'De Baca, J., Castillo, D., & Qualls, C. (2012). Ethnic differences in symptoms among female veterans diagnosed with PTSD. *Journal of Traumatic Stress*, *25*(3), 353–357. http://dx.doi.org/10.1002/jts.21709.

Copeland, W. E., Keeler, G., Angold, A., & Costello, E. J. (2007). Traumatic events and post-traumatic stress in childhood. *Archives of General Psychiatry*, *64*, 577–584.

Crenshaw, D. A., & Hardy, K. V. (Eds.). (2006). *Understanding and treating the aggression of traumatized children in out-of-home care*. New York: Guilford.

D'Augelli, A. R., Grossman, A. H., & Starks, M. T. (2006). Childhood gender atypicality, victimization, and PTSD among lesbian, gay, and bisexual youth. *Journal of Interpersonal Violence*, *21*, 1462–1482.

Davies-Netzley, S., Hurlburt, M. S., & Hough, R. L. (1996). Childhood abuse as a precursor to homelessness for homeless women with severe mental illness. *Violence and Victims*, *11*, 129–142.

de Jong, J., Komproe, I. H., Spinazzola, J., van der Kolk, B. A., & Van Ommeren, M. H. (2005). DESNOS in three postconflict settings: Assessing cross-cultural construct equivalence. *Journal of Traumatic Stress*, *18*, 13–21.

de Jong, J. T. V. M., Komproe, I. H., & Van Ommeren, M. (2003). Common mental disorders in postconflict settings. *The Lancet*, *361*(9375), 2128–2130.

Dirkzwager, A. J. E., Bramsen, I., & Van Der Ploeg, H. M. (2005). Factors associated with posttraumatic stress among peacekeeping soldiers. *Anxiety, Stress & Coping*, *18*, 37–51.

Eisenman, D. P., Gelberg, L., Liu, H., & Shapiro, M. F. (2003). Mental health and health-related quality of life among adult Latino primary care patients living in the United States with previous exposure to political violence. *Journal of the American Medical Association*, *290*, 627–634.

Fazel, M., Wheeler, J., & Danesh, J. (2005). Prevalence of serious mental disorder in 7000 refugees resettled in western countries: A systematic review. *Lancet*, *365*(9467), 1309–1314.

Finkelhor, D. (2014). *Childhood victimization: Violence, crime, and abuse in the lives of young people*. New York, NY: Oxford University Press.

Fischer, P. J., & Breakey, W. R. (1991). The epidemiology of alcohol, drug, and mental disorders among homeless persons. *American Psychologist*, *46*, 1115–1128.

Ford, J. D. (1999). Disorders of extreme stress following war-zone military trauma: Associated features of posttraumatic stress disorder to comorbid but distinct syndromes? *Journal of Consulting and Clinical Psychology*, *67*(1), 3–12.

Ford, J. D. (2008). Trauma, posttraumatic stress disorder, and ethnoracial minorities: Toward diversity and cultural competence in principles and practices. *Clinical Psychology: Science and Practice*, *15*, 62–67.

Ford, J. D., Adams, M. L., & Dailey, W. F. (2007). Psychological and health problems in a geographically proximate population time-sampled continuously for three months after the September 11th, 2001 terrorist incidents. *Anxiety, Stress & Coping*, *20*, 129–146.

Frankenberg, E., Friedman, J., Gillespie, T., Ingwersen, N., Pynoos, R., Rifai, I. U., et al. (2008). Mental health in Sumatra after the tsunami. *American Journal of Public Health*, *98*, 1671–1677.

Franklin, A. J., Boyd-Franklin, N., & Kelly, S. (2006). Racism and invisibility: Race-related stress, emotional abuse and psychological trauma for people of color. *Journal of Emotional Abuse*, *6*(2), 9–30.

Frisman, L. K., Ford, J. D., Lin, H., Mallon, S., & Chang, R. (2008). Outcomes of trauma treatment using the TARGET model. *Journal of Groups in Addiction and Recovery*, *3*(285-303)

Garbarino, J., & Kostelny, K. (1996). The effects of political violence on Palestinian 'children's behavior problems: A risk accumulation model. *Child Development*, *67*, 33–45.

Ghafoori, B., Barragan, B., Tohidian, N., & Palinkas, L. (2012). Racial and ethnic differences in symptom severity of PTSD, GAD, and depression in trauma-exposed, urban, treatment-seeking adults. *Journal of Traumatic Stress*, *25*(1), 106–110. http://dx.doi.org/10.1002/jts.21663.

Goldsmith, R. E., Martin, C. G., & Smith, C. P. (2014). Systemic trauma. *Journal of Trauma and Dissociation*, *15*(2), 117–132.

Hall, G. C. N. (2001). Psychotherapy research with ethnic minorities: Empirical, ethical, and conceptual issues. *Journal of Consulting and Clinical Psychology*, *69*, 502–510.

Hamilton, S., & Dodgen, D. (2008). Nongovernmental organizations. In G. Reyes, J. D. Elhai, & J. D. Ford (Eds.), *Encyclopedia of psychological trauma* (pp. 448–451). Hoboken, NJ: Wiley.

Harris, R., Tobias, M., Jeffreys, M., Waldegrave, K., Karlsen, S., & Nazroo, J. (2006). Racism and health: The relationship between experience of racial discrimination and health in New Zealand. *Social Science and Medicine*, *63*, 1428–1441.

Henderson, S. (Ed.). (2008). Child and adolescent mental health. *Child and adolescent psychiatry clinicalics of North America*. New York: Elsevier.

Herek, G. M. (2009). Hate crimes and stigma-related experiences among sexual minority adults in the United States: Prevalence estimates from a national probability sample. *Journal of Interpersonal Violence*, *24*, 54–74.

Herman, J. L. (1992). *Trauma and recovery*. New York: Basic Books.

Herrera Rivera, W., De Jesus Mari, J., Baxter Andreoli, S., Ines Quintana, M., & Pacheco De Toledo, M. (2008). Prevalence of mental disorder and associated factors in civilian Guatemalans with disabilities caused by the internal armed conflict. *International Journal of Social Psychiatry*, *54*, 414–424.

Hinton, D. E., Chhean, D., Pich, V., Safren, S. A., Hofmann, S. G., & Pollack, M. H. (2005). A randomized controlled trial of cognitive-behavior therapy for Cambodian refugees with treatment-resistant PTSD and panic attacks: A cross-over design. *Journal of Traumatic Stress*, *18*, 617–629.

Hollifield, M., Hewage, C., Gunawardena, C. N., Kodituwakku, P., Bopagoda, K., Weerarathnege, K., et al. (2008). Symptoms and coping in Sri Lanka 20-21 months after the 2004 tsunami. *British Journal of Psychiatry*, *192*, 39–44.

Hopper, K., & Baumohl, J. (1994). Held in Abeyance - Rethinking Homelessness and Advocacy. *American Behavioral Scientist*, *37*(4), 522–552.

Hunter, L. R., & Schmidt, N. B. (2010). Anxiety psychopathology in African American adults: Literature review and development of an empirically informed sociocultural model. *Psychological Bulletin*, *136*(2), 211–235. http://dx.doi.org/2010-03383-009 [pii]; http://dx.doi.org/10.1037/a0018133.

Hwang, W. C. (2006). The psychotherapy adaptation and modification framework - Application to Asian Americans. *American Psychologist*, *61*, 702–715.

Intelligence Science Board, (2006). *Educing information: Interrogation: Science and art*. Washington, DC: National Defense Intelligence College Press.

Jones, C., Harvey, A., & Brewin, C. (2005). Traumatic brain injury, dissociation, and post-traumatic stress disorder in road traffic accident survivors. *Journal of Traumatic Stress*, *18*, 181–191.

Kellerman, N. P. (2001). Psychopathology in children of Holocaust survivors: A review of the research literature. *Israeli Journal of Psychiatry and Related Sciences*, *38*(1), 36–46.

Kessler, R. C., Sonnega, A., Bromet, E., & Hughes, M. (1995). Posttraumatic stress disorder in the National Comorbidity Survey. *Archives of General Psychiatry*, *52*, 1048–1060.

Kilpatrick, D. G., Acierno, R., Saunders, B., Resnick, H. S., Best, C. L., & Schnurr, P. P. (2000). Risk factors for adolescent substance abuse and dependence: Data from a national sample. *Journal of Consulting and Clinical Psychology*, *68*, 19–30.

Kira, I., Templin, T., Lewandowski, L., Ramaswamy, V., Bulent, O., Abu-Mediane, S., et al. (2011). Cumulative tertiary appraisal of traumatic events across cultures: Two studies. *Journal of Loss and Trauma, 16*(1), 43–66. http://dx.doi.org/10.1080/15325024.2010.519288.

Kristof, N. D., & WuDunn, S. (2009). *Half the sky: Turning oppression into opportunity for women worldwide.* New York, NY: Vintage Books.

Kubiak, S. (2005). Trauma and cumulative adversity in women of a disadvantaged Social location. *American Journal of Orthopsychiatry, 75*, 451–465.

Liberato, A. S. Q., Pomeroy, C., & Fennell, D. (2006). Well-being outcomes in Bolivia: Accounting for the effects of ethnicity and regional location. *Social Indicators Research, 76*, 233–262.

Loo, C. M., Fairbank, J. A., & Chemtob, C. M. (2005). Adverse race-related events as a risk factor for posttraumatic stress disorder in Asian American Vietnam veterans. *Journal of Nervous and Mental Disorders, 193*, 455–463.

MacDonald, C., Chamberlain, K., & Long, N. (1997). Race, combat, and PTSD in a community sample of New Zealand Vietnam War veterans. *Journal of Traumatic Stress, 10*, 117–124.

MacLean, M. G., Paradise, M. J., & Cauce, A. M. (1999). Substance use and psychological adjustment in homeless adolescents: A test of three models. *American Journal of Community Psychology, 27*(3), 405–427.

Manson, S. M. (1996). The wounded spirit: A cultural formulation of post-traumatic stress disorder. *Cultural and Medical Psychiatry, 20*, 489–498.

Marsella, A. J., Friedman, M. J., Gerrity, E. T., & Scurfield, R. M. (Eds.), (1996). *Ethnocultural aspects of posttraumatic stress disorder: Issues, research, and clinical applications.* Washington, DC: American Psychological Association.

Marshall, G. N., Schell, T. L., Elliott, M. N., Berthold, S. M., & Chun, C. A. (2005). Mental health of Cambodian refugees 2 decades after resettlement in the United States. *Journal of the American Medical Association, 294*, 571–579.

McCarthy, J. (2001). Post-traumatic stress disorder in people with learning disability. *Advances in Psychiatric Treatment, 7*, 163–169.

McMillan, T. M., Williams, W. H., & Bryant, R. (2003). Post-traumatic stress disorder and traumatic brain injury: A review of causal mechanisms, assessment, and treatment. *Neuropsychological Rehabilitation, 13*, 149–164.

Miller, G. H. (2009). The trauma of insidious racism. *Journal of the American Academy of Psychiatry and the Law, 37*(1), 41–44. http://dx.doi.org/37/1/41 [pii].

Mills, M. A., Edmondson, D., & Park, C. L. (2007). Trauma and stress response among Hurricane Katrina evacuees. *American Journal of Public Health, 97*(Suppl. 1), S116–123.

Miranda, J., McGuire, T. G., Williams, D. R., & Wang, P. (2008). Mental health in the context of health disparities. *American Journal of Psychiatry, 165*, 1102–1108.

Morrell-Bellai, T., Goering, P. N., & Boydell, K. M. (2000). Becoming and remaining homeless: A qualitative investigation. *Issues in Mental Health Nursing, 21*, 581–604.

Mueser, K., Hiday, V., Goodman, L., & Valentini-Hein, D. (2003). Persons with physical and mental disabilities. In B. L. Green (Ed.), *Trauma interventions in war and peace: Prevention, practice, and policy* (pp. 129–154). New York: Kluwer Academic/Plenum Publishers.

North, C. S., Smith, E. M., & Spitznagel, E. L. (1994). Violence and the homeless: An epidemiologic study of victimization and aggression. *Journal of Traumatic Stress, 7*(1), 95–110.

Nosek, M., Howland, C., & Young, M. (1997). Abuse of women with disabilities: Policy implications. *Journal of Disability Policy Studies, 8*, 157–175.

Parson, E. R. (1997). Posttraumatic child therapy (P-TCT) - Assessment and treatment factors in clinicalwork with inner-city children exposed to catastrophic community violence. *Journal of Interpersonal Violence, 12*, 172–194.

Pole, N., Best, S. R., Metzler, T., & Marmar, C. R. (2005). Why are hispanics at greater risk for PTSD? *Culture, Diversity, Ethnicity, and Minority Psychology*, *11*(2), 144–161.

Pole, N., Gone, J. P., & Kulkarni, M. (2008). Posttraumatic stress disorder among ethnoracial minorities in the United States. *Clinical Psychology: Science and Practice*, *15*, 35–61.

Porter, M., & Haslam, N. (2005). Predisplacement and postdisplacement factors associated with mental health of refugees and internally displaced persons - A meta-analysis. *Journal of the American Medical Association*, *294*(5), 602–612.

Quiroga, J., & Jaranson, J. (2008). Torture. In G. Reyes, J. D. Elhai, & J. D. Ford (Eds.), *Encyclopedia of psychological trauma* (pp. 654–657). Hoboken, NJ: Wiley.

Rabalais, A. E., Ruggiero, K. J., & Scotti, J. R. (2002). Multicultural issues in the response of children to disasters. In W. K. Silverman & A. M. La Greca (Eds.), *Helping children cope with disasters and terrorism* (pp. 73–99). Washington, DC US: American Psychological Association.

Rivera, W. H., Mari, J. D., Andreoli, S. B., Quintana, M. I., & Ferraz, M. P. D. (2008). I prevalence of mental disorder and associated factors in civilian guatemalans with disabilities caused by the internal armed conflict. *International Journal of Social Psychiatry*, *54*, 414–424.

Ruglass, L. M., Hien, D. A., Hu, M. C., Campbell, A. N., Caldeira, N. A., Miele, G. M., et al. (2014). Racial/ethnic match and treatment outcomes for women with PTSD and substance use disorders receiving community-based treatment. *Community Mental Health Journal*, *50*(7), 811–822. http://dx.doi.org/10.1007/s10597-014-9732-9.

Ryan, R. (1994). Posttraumatic stress disorder in persons with developmental disabilities. *Community Mental Health Journal*, *30*, 45–54.

Sawchuk, C. N., Roy-Byrne, P., Goldberg, J., Manson, S., Noonan, C., Beals, J., et al. (2005). The relationship between post-traumatic stress disorder, depression and cardiovascular disease in an American Indian tribe. *Psychological Medicine*, *35*, 1785–1794.

Seedat, S., Nyamai, C., Njenga, F., Vythilingum, B., & Stein, D. J. (2004). Trauma exposure and post-traumatic stress symptoms in urban African schools: Survey in CapeTown and Nairobi. *British Journal of Psychiatry*, *184*, 169–175.

Seino, K., Takano, T., Mashal, T., Hemat, S., & Nakamura, K. (2008). Prevalence of and factors influencing posttraumatic stress disorder among mothers of children under five in Kabul, Afghanistan, after decades of armed conflicts. *Health and Quality of Life Outcomes*, *6*, 19–32.

Snow, D. A., & Anderson, L. (1993). *Down on their luck: A study of homeless street people*. Berkeley, CA, US: University of California Press.Bentley, A. (1997). The psychological effects of homelessness and their impact on the development of a counselling relationship. *Counselling Psychology Quarterly*, *10*(2), 195–210.

Staub, E. (2005). The roots of goodness: The fulfillment of basic human needs and the development of caring, helping and non-aggression, inclusive caring, moral courage, active bystandership, and altruism born of suffering. *Nebraska Symposium on Motivation*, *51*, 33–72.

Stuart, R. B. (2004). Twelve practical suggestions for achieving multicultural competence. *Professional Psychology: Research and Practice*, *35*, 3–9.

Teicher, M. H., Samson, J. A., Polcari, A., & McGreenery, C. E. (2006). Sticks, stones, and hurtful words: Relative effects of various forms of childhood maltreatment. *American Journal of Psychiatry*, *163*, 993–1000.

Turner, R. J., & Lloyd, D. A. (2003). Cumulative adversity and drug dependence in young adults: Racial/ethnic contrasts. *Addiction*, *98*, 305–315.

Turner, R. J., & Lloyd, D. A. (2004). Stress burden and the lifetime incidence of psychiatric disorder in young adults: Racial and ethnic contrasts. *Archives of General Psychiatry*, *61*, 481–488.

van Griensven, F., Chakkraband, M. L. S., Thienkrua, W., Pengjuntr, W., Cardozo, B. L., Tantipiwatanaskul, P., et al. (2006). Mental health problems among adults in tsunami-affected areas in southern Thailand. *JAMA: Journal of the American Medical Association, 296*(5), 537–548.

Walker, D. F., Courtois, C. A., & Aten, J. (Eds.), (2014). *Spiritually oriented psychotherapy for trauma*. Washington, DC: American Psychological Association.

Weine, S. (2008). Refugees. In G. Reyes, J. D. Elhai, & J. D. Ford (Eds.), *Encyclopedia of psychological trauma* (pp. 571–574). Hoboken, NJ: Wiley.

Wiking, E., Johansson, S. E., & Sundquist, J. (2004). Ethnicity, acculturation, and self reported health. A population based study among immigrants from Poland, Turkey, and Iran in Sweden. *Journal of Epidemiology and Community Health, 58*, 574–582.

Yehuda, R., Bierer, L. M., Schmeidler, J., Aferiat, D. H., Breslau, I., & Dolan, S. (2000). Low cortisol and risk for PTSD in adult offspring of Holocaust survivors. *American Journal of Psychiatry, 157*, 1252–1259.

Yule, W. (2000). From pogroms to "ethnic cleansing": Meeting the needs of war affected children. *Journal of Child Psychology and Psychiatry, 41*, 695–702.

Careers and ethical issues in the traumatic stress field

A rich array of opportunities and challenges can be found in careers that focus on traumatic stress, including the scientist/researcher (in basic, clinical, and translational sciences), the mental health and social work clinician, the public health and medical professional, the educator, the social/humanitarian advocate, and the criminal justice professional. In this chapter, real-life examples are used to illustrate the kinds of work, rewards, and dilemmas involved in each career path.

Particular focus is placed on understanding the impact that working with persons or communities suffering from posttraumatic stress disorder (PTSD) has on the professional. PTSD is not contagious, but helping or studying people who are experiencing PTSD often brings clinicians and scientists face-to-face with the painful reality that psychological trauma can strike at any time and can have a devastating effect on anyone who is victimized. Compassionate therapists and researchers are affected by the distress that their patients and study participants are experiencing due to PTSD. This is called vicarious or secondary trauma, or compassion fatigue. Approaches to maximizing the benefits of working in careers in the PTSD field are discussed, including ways to understand and prevent vicarious/secondary trauma and compassion fatigue from turning into professional burnout and workplace problems that can spill over into all areas of personal life.

Professionals working in the PTSD field have remarkable personal and professional resilience, and these strengths provide a basis for making careers in the PTSD field a source of lasting satisfaction and fulfillment, as well as an important contribution to bettering the world.

A number of challenging ethical issues face traumatic stress clinicians and scientists as they seek to provide services, conduct research, and influence policy regarding these and other vulnerable groups (e.g., children, older adults, incarcerated persons). These ethical issues are inherent in all mental health research, assessment, and treatment, but they are especially evident and relevant when vulnerable traumatized persons or populations are being studied or helped. Thus, a discussion of the ethical challenges facing traumatic stress clinicians and researchers, and the ethical principles that guide them in their work, is a fitting way to close this book.

Several career paths are available to the aspiring traumatic stress scientist, clinician, or educator. Each path begins with specialized graduate (postbaccalaureate) training in one of a number of potential professional disciplines that intersect with the traumatic stress field. These disciplines and their overlap with one another and shared connection to the traumatic stress field are depicted in Figure 12.1. Within the many professional disciplines that study traumatic stress and PTSD as a "subspecialty," there are opportunities to learn from and work with scientists, clinicians, educators,

Posttraumatic Stress Disorder. DOI: http://dx.doi.org/10.1016/B978-0-12-801288-8.00012-1

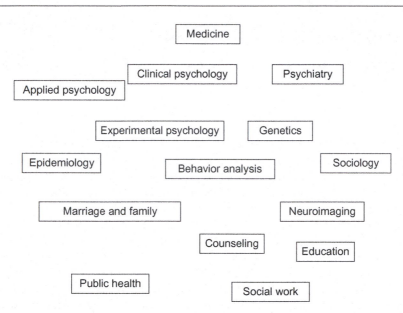

Figure 12.1 Professional disciplines intersecting with the traumatic stress field.

and administrators who can provide mentoring and guidance to the new professional. This can begin as early as in undergraduate college or university studies (and in some cases even in high school), typically by attending relevant classes and then working as a research, clinical, or teaching assistant on projects or cases conducted by the mentor. With this experience comes the chance to read more deeply and develop new ideas (hypotheses) that can be tested in mentored research or clinical studies or educational projects. Based on this combination of book and experiential learning, the trainee can contribute to the preparation and writing of research or clinical reports that may be presented at professional meetings (often as "posters" that summarize the background, methods, results, and conclusions of a project; see Figure 12.2 for a sample) and then written up as articles for publication in scholarly journals (the professional magazines that publish clinical and scientific studies). When the trainee provides not only hard work but also new ideas and original writing to such a presentation or publication, she or he can become a coauthor and share in the professional or scientific recognition associated with scholarly clinical or research communications. Serving as a coauthor, and ultimately as the lead author, on presentations and publications is an important way to both contribute to the traumatic stress field and to become qualified for jobs (and later for promotion) as a research or clinical faculty member who mentors other new professionals.

There are several career paths within the traumatic stress field, including ones that are primarily focused on clinical service or developing and administering clinical services, as well as ones that are more oriented toward research or teaching—and combinations of all of the above. For the sake of illustration, five general career paths are presented, using the careers of actual clinicians, scientists, educators, and program

Mothers with PTSD: Understanding the Role of Negative Mood State as a Mechanism of Treatment Change

Matthew Stimmel, PhD[1]; Keith Cruise, PhD, MLS[2];Julian Ford, PhD[3].

[1]Veterans Justice Programs, Department of Veterans Affairs; [2]Fordham University; [3]University of Connecticut Health Center

Introduction

Background:

➢ Impairment in mood and affect regulation is part of new DSM-5 criteria for PTSD and is related to poor health, depression and SUD in adults and violence and risk taking among adolescents (Black, Gunter, Allen, et al., 2007; Miller, Vachon, & Aalsma, 2012).

➢ Appraisal of traumatic events can influence emotional responding, including automatic responses based on past emotional responding and biological cues (Dalgleish, 2004).

➢ Trauma Affect Regulation: Guide for Education and Therapy (TARGET) is an emotion regulation based intervention for PTSD with demonstrated efficacy in reducing PTSD symptomatology and negative mood (Ford et al., 2011, 2013; Stimmel, et al., 2013).

➢ There is limited understanding of the relationship among negative mood, affect regulation and PTSD, and how affect regulation impacts treatment drop out

Objectives:

➢ Investigate whether negative mood state (as a proxy for negative affect regulation) is a mechanism of change in TARGET or Present Centered Therapy (PCT) reducing PTSD symptoms

➢ Investigate whether this relationship is moderated by specific treatments.

Method

Sample:

➢ 146 low-income mothers:
➢ 41% Caucasian; 40% African American; 18% Latina
➢ 57% high school education or less
➢ 72% with co-occurring psychiatric diagnoses and 43% with co-occurring substance use disorder
➢ Participants randomizec to receive TARGET or PCT

Measures:

➢ Clinician Administered PTSD Scale (CAPS total score)
➢ General Expectancies for Negative Mood Regulation (NMR total score)

➢ Assessed at baseline, post-treatment, and 3 month follow-up

Mediators:

➢ Positive and Negative Affect Schedule (NA total score)
➢ Assessed at baseline, session 4 and session 10, post-treatment, and 3 month follow-up

Analytic Plan:

➢Hierarchical linear modeling (Bauer, Preacher, & Gil 2006);
➢Level 1: measures within persons
➢Level 2: persons within groups

Results

Table 2. Mediation Effect of Negative Mood State on Time and Negative Affect Regulation Without Controlling for Axis I Diagnoses

	B	SE	t (96)	p
PANAS-NA	23.39	0.81	28.73	< .001
NMR	126.06	2.44	51.67	< .001
Time – NMR (c paths)	2.25	0.33	6.66	< .001
Time – PANAS NA (a paths)	-0.59	0.15	-4.10	< .001
PANAS NA-NMR (b path)	-0.88	0.10	-9.53	< .001

	B	CI
Direct effect size (c)	2.29ᵃ	1.61, 2.98
Indirect effect size	0.58	0.19, 0.98
Proportion mediated	25.7%	

*Note: NMR = Negative Mood Regulation Scale; PANAS (NA) = Positive and Negative Affect Scale.
ᵃNegative Affect. Proportion mediated = indirect effect/direct effect*
ᵃ p < .001

Negative Mood State as Mechanism of Change

➢ Negative mood state accounted for 20.3% of improvement in PTSD symptoms in the total sample (Table 1).

➢ Negative mood state accounted for 25.7% of improvement in affect regulation in the total sample (Table 2).

Table 1. Mediation Effect of Negative Mood State on Time and PTSD Symptoms Severity Without Controlling for Axis I Diagnoses

	B	SE	t (96)	p
PANAS NA	23.39	0.81	28.76	< .001
CAPS	30.44	4.01	7.60	< .001
Time – CAPS (c paths)	-4.62	0.48	-9.54	< .001
Time – PANAS NA (a paths)	1.20	0.15	8.24	< .001
Time – CAPS (c' paths)	-3.69	0.47	-7.85	< .001

	B	CI
Direct effect size (c)	-4.62ᵃ	-5.57, -3.67
Indirect effect size	-0.94	-1.51, -0.36
Proportion mediated	20.3%	

*Note: CAPS = Clinician Administered PTSD Scale; PANAS NA = Positive and Negative Affect Scale, Negative Affect; Proportion mediated = indirect effect/direct effect.
ᵃ p < .001*

Figure 1. Conceptual model for moderated mediation

Treatment groups as moderators of negative mood state

➢ 40.8% of the total effect of time on PTSD symptoms in the TARGET group was mediated by negative mood state, while only 17.3% of total effect of time on PTSD symptoms in the PCT group was mediated by negative mood state (Table 3).

➢ 29.7% of the total effect of time on affect regulation in the TARGET group was mediated by negative mood state, while there was no significant indirect effect of negative mood state on affect regulation in the PCT group (Table 3).

Table 3. Moderated Mediation Effect of Negative Mood State on Time, PTSD and Negative Affect Regulation

	Outcome: PTSD		Outcome: NMR	
	TARGET	PCT	TARGET	PCT
Direct effect size	-6.19ᵃ	-4.50ᵃ	2.36ᵃ	2.14ᵃ
Indirect effect size	-2.53ᵃ	-0.78ᵃ	0.70ᵃ	0.45
Proportion mediated	40.8%	17.3%	29.7%	--

ᵃp < .001

Conclusions

➢ TARGET is effective at reducing PTSD symptoms and improving affect regulation among low-income mothers with PTSD
➢ Specific improvements in negative mood state mediates treatment outcomes, supporting theoretical underpinnings of TARGET, and providing practical application of affect regulation strategies in brief manualized treatment
➢ Multiple benefits for using TARGET including
➢ providing cognitive strategy for managing stress response
➢ addressing victimization and symptoms of trauma without requiring exposure
➢ increasing affect regulation that can lead to improved emotional and behavioral functioning

Figure 12.2 Sample presentation poster in the traumatic stress field.

administrators in the traumatic stress field to show how each path actually has been taken and the contributions that can be made by taking that path. After these descriptions of career paths, the chapter concludes with a discussion of the core ethical (value) issues that confront traumatic stress professionals on all of these career paths.

Careers in the traumatic stress field: 1. The research scientist

Two scientists who have made exceptional contributions to the PTSD field provide very different examples of how a focus on research can advance our understanding of the nature and impact of traumatic stressors from the level of molecules and genes to complex life challenges.

> *Kerry Ressler, MD, PhD, a Howard Hughes Medical Institute investigator, researches the molecular and cellular mechanisms of fear learning and the process of extinction of fear in mouse models. The primary objective of the work in the Ressler lab is to use the power of molecular genetics to understand the molecular biology, neural circuitry, and behavioral biology of fear and extinction of fear in mouse models. Dr. Ressler is also a practicing psychiatrist with an interest in translational and clinical research on fear-based psychiatric disorders; he focuses on posttraumatic stress disorder (PTSD) at Grady Memorial Hospital. Dr. Ressler hopes that by understanding how fear works in the mammalian brain in the laboratory, it will improve understanding of and provide translational treatments and possibly prevention for fear-based disorders, such as PTSD, phobic disorders, and panic disorder. (http://www.psychiatry.emory.edu/faculty/ressler_kerry.html)*

Research scientists in the traumatic stress field often begin their careers by working as undergraduate research assistants in a major professor's laboratory, frequently on studies that have little to do with PTSD but that provide invaluable experience in the subtleties of "bench" research. Kerry Ressler, MD, PhD, is a good example, having contributed sufficiently as a graduate student to Professor Linda Buck's groundbreaking research on the genetics of smell in mice to serve as coauthor several papers on this topic, including as lead author on two (Ressler, Sullivan, & Buck, 1993, 1994). While remaining involved in the scientific study of biological phenomena, when Dr. Ressler became a postdoctoral fellow at Emory University School of Medicine, he had shifted his focus to investigating the biology of anxiety, fear, and depression.

Dr. Ressler utilized funding for his fellowship to learn about his new field of study, and he launched a program of scientific study by publishing a series of articles in leading biological psychiatry and neuroscience journals that provided a "literature review"—that is, a scholarly summary and critique of the methods and findings of all available published studies—on a specialized topic warranting further research. The topic was the role in depression and anxiety of two types of brain chemicals (norepinephrine and serotonin) and their receptors in the brain (Ressler & Nemeroff, 2001). Dr. Ressler continued to do "bench" research working in the animal laboratory of a senior scientist, Dr. Michael Davis. In this research, Drs. Ressler, Davis, and colleagues demonstrated that a brain area long associated with learning and remembering ("memory consolidation") fear, the amygdala, was actually part of a "broad neural circuit" that involved connections among several areas of the brain based upon complex activities of genes, proteins, and molecules (Ressler & Davis, 2003; Ressler, Paschall, Zhou, & Davis, 2002). Their research team studied extinction of fear, the key to recovery from PTSD—that is, learning that when a fear or anxiety reaction is not adaptive (or to no longer be fearful when danger is not imminent). They found that extinction learning was enhanced by injecting rats (or directly infusing into their amygdalas) a chemical (D-cycloserine) that increases neural activation if this was done just before experimental tasks designed to achieve extinction of fear memories (Walker, Ressler, Lu, & Davis, 2002). Dr. Ressler has continued to study learning and overcoming fear with animals, showing that other brain chemicals are essential to different aspects of both learning and remembering to both be afraid and not be afraid—including a wide range of brain chemicals that play diverse roles such as promoting the survival of neurons (brain-derived neurotrophic factor), regulating and remodeling neural synapses (β-catenin), inhibiting neural activity (benzodiazepines, GABAA), activating stress responses (corticotrophin releasing factor), and increasing anxiety (endogenous cannabinoids, cholecsystokinin).

Moreover, Dr. Ressler has taken the important step of "translating" findings from animal research studies into clinical research with humans, leading to several important advances in the treatment of PTSD. The same chemical (D-cycloserine) that increased extinction of fear learning in rats was shown to enhance the effects of exposure therapy (see Chapter 7) for height-phobic adults (Ressler et al., 2004). A "virtual reality" treatment that incorporates many of the features of laboratory fear extinction procedures along with a vivid three-dimensional recreation of real dangers (in a safe and well-controlled therapeutic environment) has been shown to be efficacious for military veterans with combat-related PTSD, particularly when combined with D-cycloserine (Rothbaum et al., 2014). Gene variations have been identified that contribute to the risk of developing PTSD due to childhood abuse (Mehta et al., 2013), and these studies also have demonstrated the potential protective role of friendship in reducing this risk (Powers, Ressler, & Bradley, 2008). Barriers to receiving treatment for PTSD among low-income ethnoracial minority group women also have been identified in order to promote policies that better provide the necessary treatment for this often underserved group of PTSD survivors (Davis, Ressler, Schwartz, Stephens, & Bradley, 2008; see Chapter 11). These three lines of research were joined together in an innovative study that demonstrated that a brief PTSD psychotherapy intervention (three sessions of prolonged exposure therapy) delivered to socioeconomically disadvantaged and acutely traumatized individuals beginning in their emergency department patients was efficacious in reducing PTSD symptoms when reassessed 12 weeks later—and patients with a profile of genes that had been previously identified as potential risk factors for PTSD were most likely to actually have PTSD at the 12-week assessment unless they received the brief therapy (Rothbaum et al., 2014). Animal research findings from Ressler's lab and other collaborating research laboratories, and the implications for and potential translations to improved treatment for PTSD in human beings, were summarized in literature review papers by Morrison and Ressler (2014) and Dias, Banerjee, Goodman, and Ressler (2013).

Jennifer Freyd, PhD, is a cognitive psychologist by training who originally con-ducted laboratory research on how people think that led to a landmark theory of dynamic mental representation (Freyd, 1987) in which she postulated that cognitive representations (such as ideas or mental images) could gain a kind of momentum over time (Freyd & Johnson, 1987). For this work, Dr. Freyd received a Presidential Young Investigator Award from the National Science Foundation in 1985. After conducting laboratory psychology research at Stanford University and Cornell University in the 1980s, she joined the faculty of the University of Oregon Department of Psychology (where she has been a professor for more than 2 decades) and launched a very dif-ferent line of research in the PTSD field that was based on personal experience, as well as a logical extension of her laboratory studies on how ideas can take on a life of their own—or become lost and die on the vine—in the face of directly contradictory evidence.

Since the early 1990s, Dr. Freyd has directed a laboratory investigating the impact of interpersonal and institutional trauma on mental and physical health, behavior, and society. In 1994, Freyd published a paper describing the concept of "betrayal trauma," followed by a book with the same title, which has come to be one of the most widely used and researched constructs in the PTSD and dissociation fields. She and more than 50 graduate students who have worked in her Dynamics Lab and gone on to successful clinical and research careers in psychology, as well as dozens of clinical researchers internationally, have explored the ways in which exposure to traumatic stressors in the context of trusting relationships can alter a child's entire development and change the course of their life for decades or even permanently (Delker & Freyd, 2014; Goldsmith, Chesney, Heath, & Barlow, 2013; Goldsmith, Freyd, & DePrince, 2012; Mackelprang et al., 2014; Martin, Cromer, Deprince, & Freyd, 2013). This line of research has required great courage both from the investigators such as Dr. Freyd and the participants, many of whom have disclosed—under the protection of pro-cedures designed to protect their privacy and safety—heartrending experiences of betrayal and traumatization (Smith & Freyd, 2014a). In 2013, Dr. Freyd and Pamela Birell coauthored a controversial book describing the dynamics of denial of childhood sexual abuse by survivors and by society: *Blind to Betrayal.*

Freyd has led an initiative to prevent what she has described as "institutional betrayal" (Smith & Freyd, 2014b), including twice speaking at the White House (as a member of a Presidential Task Force to Protect Students from Sexual Assault) in 2014 on how institutional betrayal can take the form of cover-ups of sexual abuse and sexual assault by our most trusted institutions such as schools and colleges. Dr. Freyd also led a group of more than 60 academic scholars in advocating that the Association of American Universities adopt a plan for a transparent and scientifically designed investigation of the incidence and prevalence of sexual assault and sexual harassment experienced by university students at all levels.

Dr. Freyd's impact on the clinical and scientific fields of PTSD and dissociation also has been substantial through her role as founder (in 1999) and editor of the *Journal of Trauma & Dissociation* for almost 2 decades. The *Journal* is the offi-cial scholarly publication of the International Society for the Study of Trauma and Dissociation (ISSTD) and publishes a range of theoretical, clinical, and scientific articles that have encouraged practitioners and researchers to work toward a better understanding of the complex phenomenon of posttraumatic dissociation.

Careers in the traumatic stress field: 2. The clinician practitioner

The careers of three clinicians who have had a major impact on the PTSD field exemplify the challenges, opportunities, and achievements that are possible for clinician practitioners who work "in the trenches" providing therapeutic aid to people suffering from PTSD.

Judith Lewis Herman, MD, trained as a psychiatrist in the 1970s and specialized in the treatment of incest survivors and battered women. Dr. Herman began publishing clinical findings and recommendations in the early 1980s with a groundbreaking book, *Father-Daughter Incest* (Herman, 1981). In that and subsequent writings, Dr. Herman also described social and cultural factors—such as traditional norms and practices, as well as formal legal and political policies—that contributed to the oppression and violence directed at marginalized subgroups such as women and persons living in poverty or of ethnoracial or sexual identity minority backgrounds.

While serving as a faculty member in clinical psychiatry at Harvard University Medical School, Dr. Herman also cofounded and served as Director of Training at the Victims of Violence Program in the Cambridge Hospital Department of Psychiatry and as a founding member of the Women's Mental Health Collective. As a clinician providing pharmacotherapy and psychotherapy for PTSD and associated psychiatric conditions, and as a supervisor, clinical consultant, and teacher for graduate trainees in psychiatry, psychology, and other mental health professions, Dr. Herman assisted not only female incest victims but survivors of a wide range of types of severe traumatic stress such as military combat, torture, domestic violence, physical and emotional abuse, and community violence. She formulated a new variation of PTSD—complex PTSD (later known as disorders of extreme stress not otherwise specified (DESNOS); see Chapter 1)—in a book titled *Trauma and Recovery* (Herman, 1992), which has been the most widely read source on PTSD for laypersons as well as professionals for 2 decades. The complex PTSD condition was translated into a diagnostic interview (Pelcovitz et al., 1997) and tested in a field trial study—that is, a research investigation with patients and people not seeking treatment who were interviewed at several sites in the United States (van der Kolk, McFarlane, & Weisaeth, 1996)—while being considered for inclusion as a new diagnosis in the *DSM-IV* (see Chapter 1). Although the complex PTSD diagnosis was not officially included in the *DSM-IV*, it again is under consideration for the *DSM-5* and has been the inspiration for countless clinicians who seek to understand and provide treatment to survivors of psychological trauma whose symptoms are more severe and extensive than those included in the *DSM-IV* definition of PTSD (Herman, 2009). Based on her work as a clinician and as a recognized leader by all mental health professions and specifically within the American Psychiatric Association, Dr. Herman was asked to provide the expert summary of the rationale for a complex PTSD diagnosis for adults by the Association's *DSM*-5 task force.

Dr. Herman's writings also illustrate how a practicing clinician can develop new insights through careful observation and a willingness to put old assumptions to the test in the therapy process rather than simply holding to them unquestioningly. Her writings also demonstrate the importance of thoroughly reading the works of other clinicians, not just in recent publications but from many years and decades in the past. For example, a 1993 article with Liebowitz and Harvey acquainted readers with the concept of PTSD therapy occurring in "phases," as had been described a century earlier by the French psychiatrist Pierre Janet. By updating Janet's model for contemporary PTSD clinicians, this paper led to what is now considered the "standard of care" in PTSD psychotherapy with children (see Chapter 8) as well as adults (see Chapter 7). In a 2008 editorial, Dr. Herman challenged the notion that psychotherapy for PTSD must only be based on science and, while acknowledging the importance of scientific testing of treatment methods, described how the creativity of the craftsperson is equally essential so that therapy is provided with sensitivity and respect for the unique dilemmas and strengths of each PTSD patient or client.

Bessel A. van der Kolk, MD, also is a clinician (and like Dr. Herman, a psychiatrist by training) who, beginning in the late 1970s, worked extensively with patients who suffered from what in 1980 was first formally recognized as PTSD (see Chapter 1). Dr. van der Kolk specialized in pharmacotherapy and psychotherapy, publishing the first article summarizing medication treatment options for PTSD (van der Kolk, 1984a), and brought together experts on the biology as well as the psychology of PTSD in a symposium at the American Psychiatric Association's 1982 convention that was the basis for the first comprehensive text on PTSD (van der Kolk, 1984b). Dr. van der Kolk, Greenberg, Boyd, and Krystal (1985) also pioneered the use of animal research on extreme stress—specifically the "learned helplessness" paradigm of inescapable shock—as a basis for developing hypotheses that could be tested clinically through the use of medications that affect relevant brain chemicals ("neurotransmitters") and psychotherapy methods that increase the person's sense of being able to exert meaningful control over both PTSD memories and current-day stress reactions. These are now fundamental concepts in the treatment of PTSD (see Chapter 7).

While conducting treatment with military veterans, Dr. van der Kolk had observed that their traumatic memories were distinctly different in quality from ordinary memories. This began a series of clinical studies and reports by Dr. van der Kolk and his colleagues that over the next 3 decades established the foundational view that PTSD treatment involves reducing the extreme intensity and fragmentation of "intrusive reexperiencing" (memories and reminders of traumatic experiences; van der Kolk, 2009). For example, in 1984, Dr. van der Kolk and colleagues published an article in the *American Journal of Psychiatry* describing how PTSD nightmares differed from ordinary nightmares. Van der Kolk and Ducey (1989) published a report demonstrating vividly through a clinical study using the Rorschach projective test that memories of traumatic stressor events involve "an unmodified reliving of traumatic material [with] biphasic cognitive processing of traumatic experiences of rigidly defended, affective numbing versus overwhelmed intrusive reliving" (p. 259). They hypothesized that this "lack of integration of the traumatic experience" accounts for two key aspects of PTSD: "extreme reactivity to environmental stimuli" and the "disorganizing effects on the psyche" (p. 259).

Through his clinical work with Vietnam War veterans, Dr. van der Kolk also noted that the stage of psychological development at which psychological trauma occurs and the impact of traumatic stressors on the person's ability to successfully meet the developmental challenges of that stage have a profound impact on the development of PTSD. Specifically, many Vietnam War veterans were developmentally still in the throes of adolescence when they were thrust into the dangers and traumatic losses of war, and the psychological traumas to which they were exposed appeared to have blocked or severely disrupted their progress in resolving the developmental challenges of adolescence. For example, those with PTSD often struggled with confusion about their identity and values as an adult, as well as had difficulty taking on the independent adult roles of an intimate partner in a couple relationship, a parent to young children, and a responsible worker on a self-actualizing career path (van der Kolk, 1985). This theme of psychological trauma leading to not only to the persistent fear, anxiety, and depression symptoms of PTSD but also to much broader psychosocial problems due to interrupting or even completely halting psychological development is another foundational concept for the PTSD field currently.

Over the next 3 decades, Dr. van der Kolk combined intensive involvement in providing ongoing clinical treatment of a wide variety of people suffering from PTSD with collaborative presentations and publications with many of the leading experts in the PTSD field. In 1987, his edited book *Psychological Trauma* included several coauthored chapters that foreshadowed some of the most important and controversial developments in the PTSD field. Writing with Dr. Herman (Herman & van der Kolk, 1987), they proposed that "PTSD is often undiagnosed in cases in which secrecy or stigma prevent recognition of the traumatic origins of [borderline personality] disorder. Such patients often improve dramatically when the connection between symptoms and trauma is recognized and appropriate treatment is instituted. We believe that some of the negative therapeutic reactions so frequently observed in borderline patients might be avoided by early and appropriate recognition of the relationship between the patient's current symptomatology and its origins in a traumatic history" (p. 111). Subsequently, Drs. van der Kolk and Herman were leaders in the formulation of the "DESNOS" syndrome and its assessment (Pelcovitz et al., 1997) and field testing for the *DSM-IV*, and Dr. van der Kolk was lead author on the first publication describing the results of the field trial (van der Kolk, Roth, Pelcovitz, Sunday, & Spinazzola, 1996, 2005). In 2014, he published a landmark book describing the results of his clinical, scientific, and philosophic investigations into PTSD, *The Body Keeps the Score: Brain, Mind, and Body in the Healing of Trauma.*

Focusing on children with PTSD due to having experienced abuse, Dr. van der Kolk and colleagues (Fish-Murray, Koby, & Van der Kolk, 1987) proposed that these children suffered not only from anxiety but from altered patterns of thinking that involved a preoccupation with threat that interfered with their ability to form trusting relationships with caregivers. The hypothesis that abuse leads children to become preoccupied with potential threats (to the detriment of healthy cognitive and social development) has been validated and refined in a number of experimental studies by researchers with abused children (Pine, 2007). The hypothesis that psychological trauma may fundamentally disrupt the development of secure "attachment" bonds with caregivers and that the resultant "disorganization" of the child's core beliefs about trust and safety in nurturing relationships constitutes a crucial and often life-long problem in addition to PTSD has been extensively researched (Lyons-Ruth, Dutra, Schuder, & Bianchi, 2006) and translated into innovations in treatment for both children (Ford & Cloitre, 2009) and adults (Courtois, Ford, & Cloitre, 2009) with complex forms of PTSD. Dr. van der Kolk founded a center for the treatment of traumatized children within the National Child Traumatic Stress Network and has led the effort of a task force within the Network that has formulated the complex PTSD syndrome of Developmental Trauma Disorder (see Chapter 1; Ford et al., 2013) for children and adolescents.

With regard to the treatment of PTSD, Dr. van der Kolk has been an advocate for the use of psychotherapies that promote the integration of thinking, emotion, and bodily self-regulation (Green berg & van der Kolk, 1987; van der Kolk, 2009). He and his colleagues (Spinazzola et al., 2005) have argued that cognitive behavior therapies such as prolonged exposure, cognitive processing therapy, and trauma-focused cognitive behavior therapy have strong research support in part because they are not used with patients with the most severe or complex forms of PTSD and associated disorders. They showed in a clinical research study (van der Kolk et al., 2007) that a cognitive behavior therapy (EMDR; see Chapter 7) and pharmacotherapy (the antidepressant fluoxetine) were beneficial primarily with adults whose PTSD was due to traumatic stressors experienced in adulthood but not with those whose trauma exposure began in childhood.

Steven Gold, PhD, is a clinical psychologist and a professor at Nova Southeastern University (NSU) Center for Psychological Studies in Fort Lauderdale, Florida. More than 25 years ago, in 1990, he founded and still continues to serve as director of the Trauma Resolution Integration Program (TRIP) at NSU's Psychology Services Center. This is an innovative clinical services and training program that has prepared more than 200 advanced graduate trainees in clinical psychology to provide evidence-based and theoretically grounded assessment, coping skills training groups, and individual, couples, and family therapy for adults with PTSD and/or dissociative disorders. The Child and Adolescent Traumatic Stress Program at NSU, directed by Dr. Gold's colleague and cotrainer/supervisor, clinical psychologist Jan Faust, PhD, provides complementary clinical training and PTSD psychotherapy services for children and adolescents. His leadership in bringing a PTSD perspective to the graduate training of masters- and doctoral-level professionals is exemplified by an article he wrote on the importance of providing training that ensured that psychotherapists would recognize and know how to treat sequelae of childhood sexual abuse (Gold, 1997) and a subsequent article coauthored with one of the authors of this book that made a powerful case for expertise in assessment and treatment of PTSD as essential—not optional—in the training of every mental health professional (Courtois & Gold, 2009).

While developing the clinical services and training programs at the TRIP and conducting psychological assessment and psychotherapy with traumatized adults as a practicing clinician, Dr. Gold conducted and published a series of clinical assessment studies on psychometric measures (see Chapter 6), such as the MMPI for forensic screening (see Chapter 10) and therapeutic treatment planning of individuals with PTSD and dissociative disorders. He focused initially on adult survivors of childhood sexual abuse, identifying specific patterns of psychiatric, dissociative, and PTSD symptoms that were associated with different characteristics of their abuse experiences and their memories of the abuse (Gold, Hill, Swingle, & Elfant, 1999; Gold, Hughes, & Swingle, 1999; Gold, Lucenko, Elhai, Swingle, & Sellers, 1999; Gold, Swingle, Hill, & Elfant, 1998; Klotz Flitter, Elhai, & Gold, 2003). Dr. Gold also conducted studies with one of this book's coauthors that have helped psychological assessors take a scientifically grounded approach to dealing with one of the most difficult challenges in the PTSD field, determining when PTSD is a genuine problem versus "malingering" (see Chapter 10; Elhai, Frueh, Gold, Gold, & Hamner, 2000; Elhai, Gold, Frueh, & Gold, 2000; Elhai, Gold, Sellers, & Dorfman, 2001).

In the course of his clinical practice and research, Dr. Gold developed a new approach to psychotherapy for PTSD, which he called Contextual Therapy (Gold, 2009), specifically for the treatment for adult survivors of prolonged child abuse (PCA). He and therapists he supervised at the TRIPP Center were working with adult survivors of childhood sexual abuse and severe PCA, and they found that PTSD therapies that emphasized reworking memories of traumatic stressors often not only did not achieve positive outcomes but had clients reporting escalating distress and a worsening of problem behaviors. They changed their approach and worked with their clients on what was important to *them*, which, despite often having had horrific traumatic exposures, instead "was the unremittingly bleak tenor of their everyday lives growing up. Whether or not their abuse had been by a family member, they described formative years bereft of the conditions that many would like to believe are universally present for children: consistently loving and supportive parents, predictable routine and structure, and sufficient supervision and guidance. Additionally, there were features in their backgrounds that made them especially vulnerable to abuse. In the absence of reliable nurturance and affection, they were eager for attention and caring. Having adapted to capricious and constantly shifting 'rules,' they had also learned that the overarching rule was to obey immediately and without questioning" (Gold, 2009, p. 230). Contextual therapy helps clients to develop skills in three key areas of day-to-day living: relationships; maintaining basic routines and accomplishing goals in school or work; and thinking clearly about the choices, values, and view of themselves and the world that guide them toward a safe and satisfying life. PTSD symptoms such as avoidance, hypervigilance, and flashbacks or other kinds of dissociation can prevent a person from using and building these life skills and, when traumatic stressors are pervasive in childhood, from even developing the skills in the first place. Contextual therapy thus was designed to enable trauma survivors to not just get over PTSD but to (re)build their lives.

Dr. Gold also has played an important role in advancing the field of PTSD clinical science and services by founding and serving as the editor of two peer-review journals that publish scholarly articles on clinical research (*Psychological Trauma: Theory, Research, Practice and Policy*, founding editor since 2009) and clinical practice (*Journal of Trauma Practice*, cofounding coeditor with Dr. Faust from 2002 to 2008).

Like Drs. Herman, van der Kolk, and Gold, many dedicated and effective clinician practitioners devote their careers to working "in the trenches" while providing psychological assessment and treatment for children and adults with PTSD (and complex PTSD). While these eminent clinician practitioners have been honored by being elected to the presidency of the major professional organizations in the PTSD field—the International Society for Traumatic Stress Studies (Drs. Herman and van der Kolk), the ISSTD (Dr. Gold), and the American Psychological Association Division (i.e., "Division 56 ") of Trauma Psychology (Dr. Gold)—most of the clinicians treating clients with PTSD are truly "unsung heroes" who do not publish and make professional presentations as prolifically and influentially as these three icons in the field. However, their accomplishments in helping deeply troubled people find paths to recovery from PTSD—and the hope, self-respect, and supportive relationships that make it possible to find meaning and satisfaction in life even while still suffering from PTSD for years or even decades—is a source of deep fulfillment that can be found only very rarely in most other careers. Even small reductions in the psychological distress and strain on the body and relationships caused by PTSD can be a turning point for the better for the victim and a source of great benefit and reduced burden for the family and society.

Careers in the traumatic stress field: 3. The scientist practitioner

The career paths discussed to this point are (as illustrated by the case examples) not necessarily compartmentalized purely into the role of either the scientist or the clinician, but it is more common for professionals in the traumatic stress fields to specialize primarily or even exclusively on one role or the either. In every mental health field, however, there are people who deliberately make science and clinical practice equivalent priorities. Indeed, the field of clinical psychology specifically holds the "scientist-practitioner" paradigm as its fundamental role model.

Bonnie Lepper Green, PhD, is a clinical psychologist and a professor of psychiatry at Georgetown University Medical School. After completing a masters thesis on children's creativity, she became involved in two large postdisaster recovery projects that led to a career in the traumatic stress field. The massive failure of a large earthen dam almost instantly flooded the small town of Buffalo Creek, West Virginia, in 1972. Over the next 5 years, Dr. Green was a member of a team of psychological assessors from the University of Cincinnati Traumatic Stress Study Center who interviewed and collected questionnaire data from most (600 in all) of the surviving townspeople as a part of a class action lawsuit filed to provide them with reparations for damages and losses they sustained. The assessments were conducted soon after the disaster, 2 years later, and 5 years later and reported first in a book (Gleser, Green, & Winget, 1981) and in a series of scholarly articles published over the next 15 years (including results of interviews done 14–17 years after the disaster with affected adults and children; Green, Grace, Lindy, & Leonard, 1990; Green et al., 1994).

On Memorial Day weekend in 1977, a large "supper club" in a small town in Kentucky in which 3000 people were dining suddenly became engulfed in flames. Hundreds of people were trapped and terrified, 200 were seriously injured, and 165 died. Dr. Green and colleagues interviewed more than 100 of the survivors twice (1 and 2 years after the incident), as well as employees and family members who had not been at the disaster, in a study for Dr. Green's PhD dissertation that became a landmark publication describing differences in the course of recovery over time of people subjected to different levels of exposure to disaster (Green, Grace, & Gleser, 1985). Dr. Green and faculty mentor Dr. Jacob Lindy and his clinical team also conducted psychotherapy with 30 survivors, and published their observations on the treatments and patients' varied responses (Lindy, Green, Grace, & Titchener, 1983).

In addition to conducting scientific studies based on clinical assessment and delivering clinical treatments to assist traumatized individuals, Dr. Green had the opportunity to conduct clinical assessment and treatments with Vietnam War veterans while still a graduate student at the University of Cincinnati Traumatic Stress Study Center. This was before the advent of cognitive behavior therapy for PTSD, so treatment was provided from a psychoanalytic perspective but with an emphasis on frequently assessing outcomes using scientific as well as clinical measures and constantly using clinical observations to identify what approaches to outreach and treatment led to benefits and what did not with military war trauma as well as disaster trauma survivors. From a more primarily scientific perspective, standardized assessment instruments (see Chapter 6) were administered repeatedly over time to as many survivors (and unaffected persons, to provide quasi-experimental "control" samples) as possible in order to objectively describe the course of posttraumatic stress (Green, Lindy, & Grace, 1988), predict who was at greatest risk of developing different combinations of problems (Green, Lindy, Grace, & Gleser, 1989), and assess treatment outcomes (Lindy, Grace, & Green, 1984). These continue to be key questions for scientists and clinicians in the traumatic stress field (see Chapters 3 and 7–9).

In the subsequent 2 decades, Dr. Green has continued to conduct both treatment and research studies on topics of relevance to traumatic stress scientists and clinicians, such as the impact of psychological trauma and PTSD on physical health and illness (Green & Schnurr, 2004), and life-threatening illness as a potential traumatic stressor (Green et al., 1998). She also has conducted extensive studies on the differences in the effects of exposure to psychological trauma, depending on the exact type of traumatic stressor (particularly whether it was prolonged or repeated and involved sexual violation or other intentional harm by a human being) and the stage of psychological development at which it first occurred (Ford, Green, Kaltman, & Stockton, 2006), and the victim's race (Green et al., 1990) and legal status (Green, Miranda, Daroowalla, & Siddique, 2005). As an editor of the *Journal of Traumatic Stress*, Dr. Green established a standard of scientific rigor and clinical relevance that has made the journal not only the flagship publication of the International Society for Traumatic Stress Studies but also the scholarly publication most widely read by both clinicians and researchers in the field.

Edna Foa, PhD, also a clinical psychologist, is a professor of clinical psychology in psychiatry at the University of Pennsylvania and director of the Center for the Treatment and Study of Anxiety. For more than a decade after completing her PhD in 1971, with a dissertation research study on the relationship of frustration and aggression (Foa, Turner, & Foa, 1972), she conducted treatment and research studies focused on a very difficult-to-treat psychiatric disorder—obsessive-compulsive disorder—pioneering the use of the behavioral approach of "exposure therapy and response prevention" that has become the standard of care for OCD psychotherapy

(Foa, Steketee, & Milber, 1980). In the 1980s, she published scholarly reviews of the research literatures on the core processes involved in posttraumatic stress (Foa & Kozak, 1986) and clinical interventions for the treatment of survivors of violence and other traumatic stressors (Foa & Rothbaum, 1989). Dr. Foa developed a variation of exposure therapy (called "flooding" or "prolonged exposure") for rape survivors with PTSD, and after clinical pilot testing conducted a rigorous "randomized controlled trial" study that demonstrated that prolonged exposure was more efficacious in reducing PTSD symptom severity among rape survivors than stress management or supportive counseling interventions (Foa, Rothbaum, Riggs, & Murdock, 1992).

Since that pioneering clinical research study, Dr. Foa and her colleagues and trainees have conducted several further scientific studies to both replicate their initial findings and to clarify the "active ingredients" and the "process of change" that occur in behavior therapy for PTSD. Exposure therapy was found to produce changes in trauma-related cognitions equally well when delivered alone as when a "cognitive restructuring" component was added to the treatment (Foa, Rothbaum, & Furr, 2003) and potentially to be less effective when "diluted" with other methods such as cognitive therapy. Exposure therapy also was found to be most effective when the recipient was both emotionally engaged and able to gradually lower the level of anxiety associated with the traumatic memory being recalled ("habituation"; Jaycox, Foa, & Morral, 1998). However, a briefer (30 minutes rather than 60 minutes) approach to conducting exposure therapy within each session was found to be equally as effective as longer exposure sessions despite not achieving habituation (van Minnen & Foa, 2006).

Exposure therapy also was found to generally be as well tolerated (if not better) by patients than psychotherapies for PTSD that involve less distress during trauma memory recall (such as EMDR or cognitive processing therapy) or no trauma memory recall at all (such as cognitive therapy or stress inoculation training) based on a review of studies of the rates of dropouts from PTSD therapy (Hembree et al., 2003) and a study that showed that only a minority of survivors of traumatic violence experienced persistently exacerbated PTSD symptoms during exposure therapy—and those persons ultimately benefited no less than others who did not have persistently worsened symptoms (Foa, Zoellner, Feeny, Hembree, & Alvarez-Conrad, 2002). A minority of patients do not improve or benefit only slightly from exposure therapy in terms of reduced PTSD symptoms, particularly those who describe themselves as "alienated and mentally defeated" (Ehlers et al., 1998) or who suffered interpersonal trauma in childhood or physical injury along with psychological trauma as an adult (Hembree, Gordon, Riggs, & Foa, 2004) or who were diagnosed with borderline personality disorder (Feeny, Zoellner, & Foa, 2002).

Although exposure therapy "augments" (i.e., leads to additional benefits from) antidepressant medication (Rothbaum et al., 2006), providing antidepressant medication does not appear to provide a solution for patients who do not fully benefit from exposure therapy (Simon et al., 2008). Therefore, several creative adaptations to the treatment have been developed by Dr. Foa and colleagues (Cahill, Foa, Hembree, Marshall, & Nacasch, 2006; Cook, Schnurr, & Foa, 2004), as well as published guides for therapists (Foa, Hembree, & Rothbaum, 2007) and trauma survivors (Rothbaum, Foa, & Hembree, 2007) describing how to use exposure therapy and its principles in daily living.

Clinicians and researchers need rigorous and relevant assessment measures to evaluate their patients' or study participants' problems with PTSD and the improvements
that occur in treatment. Dr. Foa has led the development and psychometric validation
of several widely used assessment measures for obsessive-compulsive disorder and
for PTSD (Treadwell & Foa, 2004), including structured interviews and questionnaires for adults and children to measure the severity of PTSD symptoms (and with
the interview, to determine whether they qualify for a diagnosis of PTSD) and the
beliefs that they hold about themselves and the world that may have been distorted by
PTSD—the Posttraumatic Cognitions Inventory.

Dr. Foa also has developed several influential theoretical models to explain how
PTSD originates and why it persists, beginning with the classical and operant conditioning paradigms (Foa & Kozak, 1986) and the uncontrollable and unpredictable
stressor paradigm (Foa, Zinbarg, & Rothbaum, 1991). She incorporated a review of
research on human emotion and information processing in order to formulate a fear
network model of emotion processing and an integrated cognitive model, which have
been the foundation for many subsequent theoretical advances in the understanding
of PTSD (Dalgleish, 2004). Dr. Foa's research includes numerous studies on how
PTSD develops following exposure to psychological trauma (Orth, Cahill, Foa, &
Maercker, 2008) and how people recover from psychological traumatization and
PTSD (Gilboa-Schechter & Foa, 2001). Thus, Dr. Foa's career illustrates how the
rigorous and creative search for a better understanding of and effective treatments for
PTSD by a clinically expert researcher can lead to innovations that can greatly benefit
many persons who see help in recovering from PTSD by providing therapists with
evidence-based tools for accurate assessment and effective treatment.

Careers in the traumatic stress field: 4. The health services researcher

As an undergraduate student, Nnamdi Pole, PhD, worked as a research assistant on
studies of alcohol's effects on mice (Wagner, Fisher, Pole, Borve, & Johnson, 1993)
before completing a PhD in clinical psychology at the University of California at
Berkeley. As a graduate student, he began to study the process of psychotherapy using
detailed analyses of the therapist-patient dialogue and the patient's physiological
responses, as measured during actual therapy sessions (Pole et al.,, 2009). Working
with expert PTSD researchers at the University of California, San Francisco, and
nationally, Dr. Pole undertook a series of studies with police officers (Pole et al.,
2001, Pole, Neylan, Best, Orr, & Marmar; 2003) and cadet trainees (Pole et al., 2007)
that demonstrated that the actual level and types of physiological and biological
reactivity in PTSD are related to but nevertheless differ from people's own subjective
accounts of emotion state and tendency to become hyperaroused (such as "startle"
responses). The studies also showed that having a stressful ongoing work environment and limited social support, strong peritraumatic reactions of distress or dissociation, and a history of childhood psychological trauma were associated with greater
risk of future PTSD as well as more extreme physiological reactivity and emotional

numbing. In 2007, Dr. Pole published a comprehensive review of the psychophysiology of PTSD, describing his own and many other researchers' findings, with recommendations for further scientific research and improved treatment services.

Dr. Pole also has conducted a parallel line of research on the controversial topic of the relationship of race, ethnicity, and culture on the development of, recovery from, and treatment of PTSD. As summarized in his definitive 2008 review of more than 175 publications:

> With respect to prevalence, Latinos were most consistently found to have higher PTSD rates than their European American counterparts. Other groups also showed differences that were mostly explained by differences in trauma exposure. Many prevalence rates were varied by subgroup within the larger ethnoracial group, thereby limiting broad generalizations about group differences. With regard to treatment outcome, some studies of veterans found lower utilization among some minority groups, but community-based epidemiological studies following a traumatic event found no differences. Finally, in terms of treatment, the literature contained many recommendations for culturally sensitive interventions but little empirical evidence supporting or refuting such treatments. Taken together, the literature hints at many important sources of ethnoracial variation but raises more questions than it has answered. (Pole, Gone, & Kulkarni, 2008, p. 35)

Several insights and cautions were raised by Dr. Pole's own research and his reviews of clinical and scientific studies. Psychotherapy, whether for PTSD or for other mental health conditions such as depression (Pole, Ablon, & O'Connor, 2008), involves subtle interactions between the therapist and patient that occur on a physiological and emotional level as well as in their explicit verbal exchange, and concepts from several theoretical models (such as cognitive-behavior and psychodynamic therapies) are needed to fully describe how the therapist and patient together help the patient to gain an increased ability to exert personal control and a concomitant sense of mastery over symptoms and life stressors. Similarly, the experience of traumatic stress and resistance, resilience, recovery, or chronic PTSD involves a complex interplay of physiologic and cognitive/affective reactivity and self-regulation. Both psychotherapy and posttraumatic stress may differ substantially for persons of different ethnocultural backgrounds, although many of these differences are not due to race, ethnicity, or culture per se but to the stressfulness of the person's ongoing life circumstances, the resources such as social support that they can call upon, and, with regard to PTSD, the magnitude and subjective shock of the traumatic stressor(s). These foundational principles provide a basis for more precise scientific research and more thoughtful responses by clinicians and by policy makers to the impact of psychological trauma on vulnerable persons and groups. Dr. Pole translated the results of his clinical and research work and literature reviews into overseeing a task force's development of an important report for the American Psychological Association Division of Psychological Trauma on the potentially traumatic consequences of detainment and interrogation of suspected terrorists and recommendations for psychologists' participation in, or abstention from, these activities (see Chapter 11).

Jon Elhai, PhD, worked with expert mentors Drs. Steven Gold and B. Christopher Frueh on a series of studies as a clinical psychology graduate student at Nova Southeastern University and a predoctoral intern at the Medical University of South Carolina, describing personality characteristics of adult survivors of childhood sexual abuse and of combat military veterans (Elhai et al., 2000), in particular identifying differences distinguishing false ("malingering") from true PTSD cases (Elhai et al., 2004). In these studies, Dr. Elhai and colleagues have debunked the "common wisdom" that scores thought to reflect exaggeration of emotional distress on the best validated psychological questionnaire, the MMPI-2, are an indication of "faking" PTSD symptoms. Instead, these studies point to the need for the use of different MMPI-2 scores designed specifically to detect exaggerated or false claims of PTSD symptoms with military veterans or with adult survivors of childhood abuse.

The factors that are associated with, and may lead to, seeking and continued use of health care services by persons with histories of psychological trauma and PTSD has been a second line of research by Dr. Elhai and colleagues, beginning with studies of military combat veterans and abuse survivors in the United States (Elhai, North, & Frueh, 2005), and subsequently including Canadian military (Richardson, Elhai, & Pedlar, 2006) and peacekeeping (Elhai, Richardson, et al., 2007) personnel, American Red Cross disaster responders (Elhai, Jacobs, et al., 2006), adult primary care (Elhai, Patrick, Anderson, Simon, & Frueh, 2006) and general community samples (Elhai & Ford, 2007), and adolescents in the juvenile justice system (Grijalva, Ford, Docherty, Fricker-Elhai, & Elhai, 2007). Across this wide range of potentially trauma-exposed adolescents and adults, the use of mental health services was consistently associated with exposure to psychological trauma and PTSD, and PTSD was associated with the use of medical care. These findings suggest that screening for psychological trauma history and PTSD, and preventive interventions such as education about PTSD (Gray, Elhai, & Frueh, 2004) or telehealth consultations (i.e., talking with a health care provider long-distance using video conferencing technology; Elhai, 2008), are needed in order to help people recover from PTSD without excess utilization of health care. The statistical techniques utilized in these studies also provide for more precise scientific conclusions, particularly by correcting inaccuracies that may occur when large numbers of study participants do not utilize any health care services (as is typically the case) (Elhai, Calhoun, & Ford, 2009).

Dr. Elhai also has conducted research studies on the clinical assessment and diagnosis of PTSD. Although the PTSD diagnosis in *DSM-IV* involves three groups of symptoms—intrusive reexperiencing, avoidance and emotional numbing, and hyperarousal (see Chapter 1)—studies with college students (Elhai, Gray, et al., 2007) and national samples of adults (Elhai, Frueh, et al., 2007) and adolescents (Elhai, Ford, Ruggiero, & Frueh, 2009) in the United States have demonstrated that either a two- or four-factor model may better account for PTSD symptoms. The two-factor model eliminates symptoms that overlap with depression and generalized anxiety and as a result may better distinguish PTSD from those disorders. The four-factor model retains all the *DSM-IV* PTSD symptoms but separates active avoidance symptoms and emotional numbing symptoms into two separate "criterion" sets (i.e., groups of related symptoms). This foreshadowed the change that has occurred in the *DSM-5*, in which PTSD avoidance symptoms are now a separate criterion set apart from emotional numbing symptoms.

Careers in the traumatic stress field: 5. The educator

Patricia Watson, PhD, and Josef Ruzek, PhD, work in the US Department of Veterans Affairs National Center for PTSD, respectively as the deputy to the executive director for Education and the director of the Education Division. In these complementary roles, Drs. Watson and Ruzek have led the development of a number of large-scale education initiatives for mental health, medical, nursing, and social work professionals in the United States and globally. Prior to the September 11, 2001, terrorist incidents, they led the development of disaster mental health response teams by providing intensive training seminars at Veterans Affairs medical centers and veterans centers nationally. After 9/11, they initiated a collaborative national work group with experts from the Departments of Health and Human Services and Veterans Affairs. The result was an evolving set of consensus guidelines for the mental health response to chemical, biological, and radiologic attacks (Ritchie et al., 2004), pandemic influenza (Reissman, Watson, Klomp, Tanielian, & Prior, 2006), and mass disasters generally (Gibson et al., 2006; Hobfoll et al., 2007; Ritchie, Watson, & Friedman, 2006; Ruzek, 2006; Watson, Gibson, & Ruzek, 2007), as well as a clinician's guide to Psychological First Aid (see Chapter 9; Watson, 2008a, 2008b; Gibson et al., 2006).

A second educational initiative related to PTSD in the Department of Veterans Affairs led by the National Center's Education Division has been the dissemination of evidence-based psychotherapies for chronic PTSD (Whealin, Ruzek, & Southwick, 2008) and PTSD with comorbid substance use disorders (Cook, Walser, Kane, Ruzek, & Woody, 2006). Designed as a pilot project of the VA Best Practices and Knowledge Management committee (Ruzek, Friedman, & Murray, 2005), this initiative began with the identification of psychotherapy models with the strongest research evidence base for the treatment of chronic PTSD, prolonged exposure and cognitive processing therapy, and for PTSD with comorbid substance use disorders, Seeking Safety (see Chapter 7). The developers of these PTSD treatment models worked with Dr. Ruzek to establish procedures for training and providing ongoing supervision to Veterans Affairs mental health clinicians working in PTSD programs, and as a result, several dozen teams and hundreds of clinicians were trained and supervised in conducting these treatments with men and women.

The education programs of the National Center for PTSD led by Drs. Watson and Ruzek include a number of ongoing resources that are unique in the traumatic stress field. The National Center website (www.ncptsd.org) provides updated information for military veterans, families, and health care professionals in the form of fact sheets, video education seminars, descriptions of treatment models and assessment measures, samples of published articles, and the most extensive bibliographic database (i.e., a listing of all published articles and books) in the traumatic stress field, the Published International Literature on Traumatic Stress (PILOTS), which is overseen by Dr. Frederick Lerner. National Center newsletters for clinicians (the *Clinical Quarterly*, published through 2003) and researchers (the *Research Quarterly*, edited by Drs. Matthew Friedman and Paula Schnurr), which also are available at www.ncptsd.org, provide reviews and commentaries on the most pressing issues for PTSD treatment and science. An in-residence intensive training program for PTSD clinicians is provided under Dr. Ruzek's supervision at the Education Division site.

Many more PTSD professionals are educators who teach undergraduate and graduate students in colleges, universities, medical schools, schools of marriage and family therapy, nursing, professional psychology, public health, and social work. These educators review the scientific, clinical, theoretical, and public policy literatures in scholarly journals and books, and teach seminars and lecture classes that typically do not focus primarily on PTSD but include PTSD as one of several topics. Although there are several recent books that provide a thorough overview of the traumatic stress and PTSD field (such as the 2007 *Handbook of PTSD*, edited by Friedman, Keane, and Resick, and the 2008 *Encyclopedia of Psychological Trauma*, edited by Reyes, Elhai, and Ford), until the present book there has not been a textbook for educators to use in teaching a complete seminar or lecture to undergraduate and graduate students on PTSD.

Careers in the traumatic stress field: 6. The program director

Sandra Bloom, MD, is a psychiatrist who developed and directs the "Sanctuary" program for organizations that seek to provide safe and effective therapeutic services to persons with PTSD. In 1998, as chair in Child and Family Mental Health at the Jewish Board of Family and Children's Services of New York, Dr. Bloom began to oversee implementation of the Sanctuary Model, as described in her 1997 book *Creating Sanctuary: Toward the Evolution of Sane Societies*, in three residential treatment centers for children and domestic violence shelters. She was a coinvestigator on a 2000–2003 National Institute of Mental Health grant evaluating this implementation (Rivard et al., 2003).

Dr. Bloom developed the Sanctuary Model "as an antidote to recurrent stress and systemic dysfunction," and as described on www.sanctuaryweb.com, the model's aims are to:

- Increase community/cohesiveness by creating a nonviolent environment.
- Increase the degree of "social immunity" to the spread of violence—that is, people's ability to retain their core values and support one another when confronted by violence, and reduce the frequency and severity of episodes of interpersonal violence, including verbal, physical, and sexual forms of harassment; bullying; and violence by staff and clients.
- Increase capacity for "social learning"—that is, the ability to learn by being with people.
- Increase democratic decision making and shared responsibility in problem solving and conflict resolution, and provide safe environments for all clients and staff.
- Provide an opportunity for troubled clients to have corrective emotional, relational, and environmental experiences—that is, therapeutic experiences when they are most troubled.
- Reduce crises.
- Improve staff/leader job satisfaction.
- Reduce staff turnover.
- Improve client satisfaction.

In 2005, working as a senior fellow at the Andrus Center for Learning and Innovation, Dr. Bloom initiated the "Sanctuary Institute" in order establish a network of sanctuary programs that now includes residential, group home, juvenile justice, inpatient and outpatient centers for children, and substance abuse and inpatient programs for adolescents and adults in seven states and three countries outside the United States (www.sanctuaryweb.com). The Sanctuary Model has ambitious goals intended to enable organizations to achieve a "trauma-informed" environment for clients, staff, and administrators—that is, to create policies and awareness that help people to recognize and cope with traumatic stress reactions without causing further harm.

Dr. Bloom has taken a nontraditional career path after working for many years as a psychiatrist conducting pharmacotherapy and psychotherapy in programs treating persons with chronic mental illness. The Sanctuary Institute that she directs teaches entire organizations how to appreciate the importance of healthy relationships ("secure attachment"; see Chapter 8), recognize and helpfully respond to episodes of dissociation by recognizing the "social legacy of trauma" that leads people to protect themselves by shutting down mentally when highly stressed, and how to create a "therapeutic community" in which recovery from PTSD can safely occur. Dr. Bloom has developed a "tool kit" for implementing the Sanctuary Model, which includes an educational curriculum described as the "SELF" model and the "Seven Commitments." SELF stands for creating an organization in which Safety is protected, Emotions are respected, Loss is responded to with support, and the Future is imbued with a realistic sense of hope. The seven commitments are to develop skills for personal safety, emotion management, learning from other people, democratic decision making, flexible but firm personal boundaries, responsible participation in relationships, and coping positively with change.

Maxine Harris, PhD, is chief operating officer for Clinical Affairs and cofounder of Community Connections, a nonprofit agency in inner-city Washington, DC, that specializes in treating low-income ethnoracial minority women with serious mental illness, most of whom have extensive histories of interpersonal psychological trauma, and many of whom are or have been homeless and substance abusers. With her Community Connections colleagues, Dr. Harris developed a new approach to group treatment of women with complex psychiatric and posttraumatic impairments: the Trauma Recovery and Empowerment Model (TREM; Harris, Anglin, & Community Connections Trauma Work Group, 1998).

TREM uses a combination of therapeutic methods derived from interpersonal, relational, client-centered, cognitive-behavioral, and psychodynamic models, including (i) psychoeducation about psychological trauma, PTSD, and recovery from complex trauma stress disorders; (ii) teaching skills for cognitive reevaluation, self-efficacy, mood and arousal regulation, and interpersonal effectiveness; (iii) mobilizing peer validation and support; and (iv) assisting clients in developing an understanding of their lives to foster hope and change.

TREM teaches several core assumptions, as described by Fallot and Harris (2002):

- Some current difficulties may have originated as legitimate, even courageous, coping responses to traumatic events.
- Repeated childhood trauma deprives women of the opportunity to develop life skills.
- Trauma severs connections to one's family, one's community, and oneself.
- Repeatedly abused women feel powerless and unable to advocate for themselves.

The TREM group curriculum originally was designed to involve 29 weekly sessions of 75 minutes in length, divided into four phases: mpowerment (9 sessions), trauma recovery (10 sessions), advanced trauma recovery issues (8 sessions), and closing rituals (2 sessions). The TREM trauma recovery skills include (Fallot & Harris, 2002):

- Self-awareness
- Self-protection
- Self-soothing
- Emotional modulation
- Relational mutuality
- Accurate labeling of self and others
- Sense of agency and initiative taking
- Consistent problem solving
- Reliable parenting
- Possessing a sense of purpose and meaning
- Judgment and decision making

In collaboration with social scientists from Dartmouth Medical School, Dr. Harris has been coinvestigator on federally funded grants to study the lives, traumatic stress histories, and psychosocial strengths and impairments of homeless women, substance-addicted homeless persons, and persons with serious mental illness, and to implement vocational and therapeutic services for their recovery. With Dr. Roger Fallot, Dr. Harris coedited the first published book on trauma-informed services in 2001. As described cogently in the Fallot and Harris (2008) entry in the *Encyclopedia of Psychological Trauma*, trauma-informed services are based upon:

> *... an understanding of the prevalence and consequences of psychological trauma and of the factors that facilitate recovery from traumatic stress shapes the activities, physical settings, and relationships involved in providing help to people in need. For example, because trauma disrupts one's core belief that the world is a safe and secure place, trauma survivors are acutely sensitive to issues of safety and security. Consequently, trauma-informed human services, whether they are delivered in a psychological, medical, or even a criminal justice service system, should be provided in a physically safe setting and delivered by staff who are trained to maintain appropriate emotional and physical boundaries.*
>
> *"Trauma-informed" approaches are generally contrasted with "trauma-specific" services (Harris & Fallot, 2001). The primary tasks of the latter are to address directly the impact of trauma and to facilitate healing and recovery [such as] therapeutic interventions focusing on PTSD. ... In contrast, any service or program can be trauma-informed, regardless of its primary goal or its size and complexity. Individual or group interventions can be trauma-informed by taking an understanding of trauma into account in their structure or content. Substance abuse groups, for example, may address connections between trauma and addictions. Most commonly, though, the trauma-informed approach applies to larger programs, agencies, or systems of care. These service contexts, characterized by a special awareness of the particular strengths, challenges, and vulnerabilities of trauma survivors, arrange their settings and activities to be safe, welcoming, and engaging for service recipients.*

A unique aspect of trauma-informed services, whether at the level of the individual practitioner or the human service program, is the effort to minimize the possibility of reenacting trauma-related dynamics and causing retraumatization. Trauma-related dynamics refer to the interpersonal patterns that characterize relationships in which psychological trauma occurs (such as abusive or violent families) or that have been adversely impacted by psychological trauma (such as families whose members have experienced war, disaster, or community violence).

Finkelhor (1987) describes four "traumagenic dynamics" that arise from sexual abuse, which are relational dilemmas that survivors struggle to overcome and that services must not replicate: stigma, powerlessness, betrayal, and sexualization. For example, a typical abuse dynamic occurs when the victim of abuse is forced to do things against his or her will, potentially replicating the traumagenic dynamic of powerlessness. In such an instance, the person has no say in making decisions nor in preventing the abuse and consequently may feel frightened and threatened rather than safe and able to regain healthy functioning.

Any human service system that replicates traumagenic dynamics such as disempowerment is inadvertently causing the individual to feel revictimized in the service/care relationship. A trauma-informed knowledge of this dynamic might result in providers paying special attention to giving consumers an active voice in the services they receive and to providing consumers a standard mechanism whereby they might appeal decisions they did not like without fear of reprisal. Thus, trauma informed services do not have to specifically provide treatment for traumatic stress disorders, but they recognize the impact that traumatic stress has had upon the consumers of their services and develop approaches to delivering their services that enhance trauma survivors' sense of safety, trust, and empowerment.

In this model, psychological trauma is viewed as a core event (or series of events) around which the person's subsequent life experiences are shaped. A trauma survivor's "symptoms" tend to be seen as extensions of understandable attempts to cope with traumatic events rather than as an illness or other deficit. Survivors' skills and strengths are assessed, affirmed, and enhanced. Collaborative rather than hierarchical service relationships are valued, built around recovery goals and a timeline comfortable for the consumer. Consumer-survivors therefore play a central role in planning, implementing, and evaluating trauma-informed services. Based on the experiences and priorities of trauma survivors, trauma-informed programs adopt guiding principles that offer consistent alternatives to potentially harmful traumagenic-dynamics (Finkelhor, 1987): safety, trustworthiness, choice, collaboration, and empowerment.

Trauma-informed approaches attend to all aspects of programmatic culture: informal activities and the physical environment as well as formal policies and procedures; support staff as well as direct service staff; and direct services as well as systems-level processes. Universal screening for psychological trauma and traumatic stress is expected in trauma-informed services. Providers then, as appropriate, may discuss with individuals their particular history of trauma exposure and their specific responses to trauma in a more extensive assessment as well as ensuring that service planning takes into account this history and the strengths and vulnerabilities that each survivor has as a result of having experienced psychological trauma. … In terms of staff education, training in trauma-informed principles and practices is offered for all staff (including administrators). The primary goal of such general training is to enhance all staff members' understanding of traumatic stress so that they may respond more positively to trauma survivors in their own work roles. For example, reception and other support staff may focus on becoming more hospitable and engaging with consumers and on handling difficult situations in ways that minimize the possibility of escalation and inadvertent retraumatization. Residential staff learn about the potential "triggers" for trauma-related responses that are part of many living arrangements (such as limited privacy, shared spaces, staff access to bedrooms). Administrators actively support trauma-informed changes in organizational policies and in the physical and interpersonal setting. Where the human service agency is also a mental health service provider, administrators provide the capacity to deliver effective, accessible, trauma-specific interventions. Human resource practices also prioritize sensitivity to the experience of psychological trauma. Interviews of prospective staff include questions about their knowledge of psychological trauma. Orientation for all new staff may present basic information about trauma and emphasize the centrality of trauma-informed approaches in the agency's mission. Employee performance evaluation and promotion policies also may give weight to continuing education in the field of psychological trauma or to on-the-job accomplishments that enhance the program's ability to deliver trauma-informed services. Finally, and very importantly, trauma-informed agencies emphasize the necessity of staff support and care in order to help providers and other staff members identify and deal with their own work-related stress in serving trauma survivors. (pp. 660–662)

From this description, it is clear that Dr. Harris has given a great deal of thought to how to create and sustain therapeutic programs that, at all levels and in all activities, support recovery from PTSD (and that mitigate against the effects on employees or staff of vicarious trauma). While providing therapeutic services to hundreds of women, and in recent years men and adolescents of both genders as well, the Community Connections program that Dr. Harris leads also has provided her with insights that have enabled her to create a model for other programs and for the treatment of people with complex forms of PTSD (Harris, Graham, & Ennis, 2003).

Thus, the careers and work of both Dr. Bloom and Dr. Harris epitomize the creative accomplishments that come from applying trauma-informed principles to a home organization, and extending those principles and practices in the form of models such as Sanctuary and TREM that can be a foundation for other programs.

Ethical issues in PTSD research and treatment

Professional organizations such as the American Psychological and Psychiatric Associations, the National Association of Social Workers, the American Association of Marriage and Family Therapy, and the American Counseling Association have created standards and codes of ethics for their members in order to ensure competence and protect recipients of services and participants in scientific studies (Courtois, 2008). Professional ethical standards are designed to be consistent with applicable civil and criminal laws (see Chapter 10), but they are guidelines and benchmarks and guidelines for acceptable practice within the profession rather than legally binding regulations (such as the legal requirements for licensure as a mental health practitioner).

Different professional organizations hold their members to different standards, according to the particular professional activities considered to be within the profession's scope (such as clinical assessment, psychotherapy, scientific research with human participants or animal subjects, Internet-delivered services, or forensic evaluations and expert witness testimony). Professional ethical standards and codes tend to have a core set of principles that is relatively unchanging and many specific rules or guidelines that are subject to revision and updating as new areas and modes of practice, new legal requirements, and new research findings emerge.

Pope and Vasquez (1998) describe the importance of thoughtful and diligent application of ethical guidelines and standards by the scientist, professional, educator, and student:

> *Ethics codes cannot do our questioning, thinking, feeling, and responding for us. Such codes can never be a substitute for the active process by which the individual therapist or counselor struggles with the sometimes bewildering, always unique constellation of questions, responsibilities, contexts, and competing demands of helping another person.... Ethics must be practical. Clinicians confront an almost unimaginable diversity of situations, each with its own shifting questions, demands, and responsibilities. Every clinician is unique in important ways. Ethics [must stay in] touch with the practical realities of clinical work, with the diversity and constantly changing nature of the therapeutic venture. (p. xiii)*

Ethical professional and scientific practice requires personal stability, maturity, and flexibility on the part of the therapist or scientist and the ability to be reflective rather than simply reactive. Ideally, personal values and professional ethics will be consistent, but in some situations that is not possible (Courtois, 2008). Therapists and scientists therefore must be mindful of their own personal values and of their professional organizations' ethical standards, decision making, and practice—while never assuming that the two are identical (Courtois, 2008).

In clinical practice settings, such as private practice psychotherapy or counseling, hospitals or outpatient behavioral health agencies, or school or child guidance clinics, professional standards and ethical codes address issues including (Courtois, 2008):

- Conducting all services honestly and so as to maximize client safety (as summarized by the medical professional's responsibility to "first do no harm"). This includes fully informing clients about professional fees and payment requirements, and when and how health care insurance may cover the costs.
- Client confidentiality and the client's right to make a fully informed consent to participate in the assessment or treatment must be safeguarded. This includes ensuring that the Health Insurance Portability and Accountability Act legal regulations designed to safeguard each client's privacy of his or her "personal health information" are complied with fully. It also includes advising clients of the limits of confidentiality, such as legal requirements that helpers report child or elder abuse.

- Therapists must have adequate qualifications, including professional training, supervised experience, licensure or certification, and expertise in specialties (such as in conducting exposure therapy for PTSD or providing forensic evaluations).
- Assessment and treatment practices must be consistent with what is considered the "standard of practice"—that is, with the practices that reflect the current scientific and clinical evidence of how best to achieve positive outcomes and prevent harm.
- Professional impartiality and fairness must govern all actions. This includes fully disclosing any conflict of interest that might prevent a clinician from putting the client's interest completely ahead of any competing priorities. It also includes not engaging in "dual relationships," which are relationships that involve a conflict between the clinician's personal and professional commitments (such as providing treatment to family members and/or seeking or accepting financial or other benefits from clients beyond the agreed-upon fees).
- Professional integrity and boundaries must be maintained—especially the prohibition against becoming involved in romantic relationships or sexual contact with clients.
- Finally, collegial and respectful relationships should be maintained with professional colleagues who may participate in, consult on, or make referrals for clients' services.

With regard to the ethical conduct of scientific research, key principles include:

- Informed consent must be obtained from all participants or from their legal guardian if they are not old enough or otherwise competent to make a fully informed decision as to whether to participate in each activity required by the research study. This includes informing participants of potential alternative procedures or treatments that may be of equal benefit to them and any new information that might affect their decision to participate in or withdraw from the research study.
- The benefits to the participant and to society must always outweigh the costs to the participants of engaging in research activities, and the costs must not cause harm to the participants unless this is fully remedied by the study procedures and has been fully disclosed and consented to by the participants or guardians in advance.
- Research procedures must always match or exceed accepted standards for scientific conduct, including using procedures, tests, interventions, and equipment that have been scientifically demonstrated to accurately achieve their intended purpose.
- Coercion to participate must be prevented, particularly in the case where potential participants may feel pressured to participate due to fear of adverse consequences if they decline (such as in a study conducted with students by their academic mentor or advisor, or with incarcerated prisoners who may fear loss of legal standing if they decline to participate or hope to improve their legal standing by participating).
- Impartiality and fairness must govern all actions. This includes fully disclosing any conflict of interest that might prevent a researcher from putting the participant's interest completely ahead of any competing priorities. It also includes not engaging in "dual relationships," which are relationships that involve a conflict between the researcher's personal and professional commitments (such as having family members serve as participants or attempting to gain commercial funding for research by making research findings or reports more favorable to the sponsor than is objectively true).

Although professional standards and ethics are important in all areas of professional practice and scientific research, they are particularly important in work with traumatic stress disorders because traumatized persons already have been injured psychologically (and often also physically) and therefore must be treated in a way that minimizes the possibility of further injury. In fact, the core ethical principle of professional practice "first do no harm" can be amplified to "do no *more* harm" in the work with persons with traumatic stress disorders.

The psychological trauma and PTSD that have been experienced by clients or research participants also can be emotionally distressing for clinicians or scientists to learn about. Even the most professionally impartial and scientifically rigorous traumatic stress specialist is still a human being, and both anxiety and fear ("If it happened to them, it could happen to me or to those whom I most care about") or caring and compassion can cloud clinical or scientific judgment. This type of reaction has been described as "vicarous trauma" or "secondary trauma," or "compassion fatigue," as described by Pearlman and Caringi (2009):

> *Supporting the recovery of people who have been affected by severe, prolonged, or early violence, neglect, or abuse is an honor and a challenge. It is an honor because it requires earning the trust of those whose trust has been compromised in other relationships. It is also a challenge because it requires the therapist to maintain self-awareness and attention to emotional reactions and behaviors while remaining attuned to the client's needs. The empathic engagement necessary for truly therapeutic relationships with [persons suffering from PTSD] often has transformative negative personal repercussions for the therapist. ... When the helper opens himself or herself to another's pain, s/he may experience personal distress [arising] from imagining personally experiencing the traumatic event, resulting in negative feelings [and changes in personal outlook, because] empathy arises from imagining what the client experienced.*

The result of vicarious trauma can take the form of under- or overresponding in clinical or research work with traumatized clients or participants, as described by Courtois (2008):

> *Overresponse can result in "rescuing" of the client that, in turn, can result in a failure to maintain appropriate boundaries and the development of dual relationships. For example, a therapist might meet with the client on a daily basis, have numerous phone calls between appointments, give the client advice on how to handle personal problems, or in more extreme cases provide practical or financial help to the client, arrange meetings outside of the office setting, or in general do a variety of special things for the client that could be as egregious as having sexual contact with the client.*
>
> *Underresponse can paradoxically be related to overresponse.... As the [scientist or] practitioner becomes overwhelmed by the demands of the work and the client, he or she might become angry and detach or blame the client [or participant] as a result. In some cases, this results in hostility toward the client and abrupt and unplanned endings (abandonment) based on these feelings. Underresponse can also be the result of dislike of and stigmatization of the client [or research participant] and his or her psychological trauma history and traumatic stress symptoms. All of these reactions are ethically compromised in that they have the potential to add to the client's [or research participant's] distress and to cause further emotional harm. (p. 525)*

Vicarious trauma is a "normal" (i.e., expectable) reaction, and more likely a sign of caring and compassion that of any failing or weakness on the part of the traumatic stress professional. Vicarious trauma may involve psychological or physical reactions that are similar to symptoms of PTSD, but it is *not* PTSD, with only two rare exceptions. The exceptions are if a patient or research participant actually is severely harmed or unexpectedly is killed or dies or acts in a manner that causes the clinician or scientist to experience life-threatening harm or the imminent threat of such severe harm. Patients have assaulted or otherwise threatened or attempted to harm the professionals caring for them, and they also may be accidentally harmed or killed or take their own lives. Such an experience can be psychologically traumatic for the clinician or scientist, and this is fundamentally different that feeling the indirect ("vicarious") impact of a patient's or study participant's traumatic experiences and posttraumatic distress. Thus, only very rarely do patients or research participants actually "traumatize" the professionals working with them, and vicarious trauma refers to the much more common instance in which the patient or participant does nothing directly to harm or traumatize the professional but simply has an effect on the professional by openly disclosing their traumatic experiences or showing the adverse impact that PTSD has had.

The experience of vicarious trauma is an opportunity for personal and professional growth on the part of the traumatic stress professional (Pearlman and Caringi, 2009). Although there is no definitive research on vicarious trauma or ways to cope with it, the experience of many traumatic stress professionals is that vicarious trauma provides a window to recognize one's own capacity for courage and integrity—because although the courage required of people who actually survive psychological trauma is far greater than that required of the professional who is attempting to learn from or help them, it nevertheless is a daunting experience to learn "up close and personal" about terrible events or the suffering that such events can cause. Therefore, self-reflection is the single most important antidote for vicarious trauma: careful thought about how the patient's or research participant's traumatic experiences or suffering is affecting one's own feelings and thinking, and gradually gaining a better understanding of oneself through awareness of these reactions. Personal therapy can be a part of this self-reflection, but it is not necessarily required, and it is best undertaken *before* vicarious trauma reactions become a problem personally or professionally. In addition, healthy activities like exercise, taking a break to meditate between professional appointments or research procedures, discussing personal reactions in a separate forum such as with a clinical supervisor in a professional support group with other clinicians, and maintaining active involvement in positive relationships and activities outside "work," are important ways in which to not only maintain a healthy lifestyle but also to "process" (that is, privately think about) reactions that are expectable but nevertheless distressing.

Ultimately, the best approach to ethical science and clinical practice and to being aware of and coping positively with vicarious trauma is to develop a career path that is personally meaningful and rewarding. Almost any career in the traumatic stress field brings with it many unique opportunities to make a difference in the lives of people, and that is a reward that is only rarely available in most other careers. The challenges facing traumatic stress professionals are substantial, personally as well as clinically and scientifically, but the opportunity to help solve one of the most serious problems facing the world and to contribute to making the lives of courageous trauma survivors more satisfying and successful is the chance of a lifetime (Box 12.1).

Box 12.1 Key Points

1. Careers in the traumatic stress (PTSD) field begin with specialized graduate training in one or more of several interrelated professional disciplines, including clinical, applied, or experimental psychology; medicine; psychiatry; public health; social work; counseling; marriage and family therapy; education; sociology; or behavior analysis.

2. The research scientist career path in the traumatic stress field involves conducting technically rigorous studies of the biological, behavioral, and social impact of exposure to extreme stressors on animals or of exposure to traumatic stressors on human beings. Traumatic stress research scientists tend to work as faculty members in universities, medical schools, or research institutes such as the Rand Corporation.

3. The clinician practitioner career path in the traumatic stress field involves conducting assessment and treatment of children or adults who have, or are suspected of having, histories of psychological trauma and impairments in their social, occupational, school, or family functioning, or health—or legal problems when the practitioner is a forensic specialist (see Chapter 10). Traumatic stress clinicians tend to work in private practice (i.e., as independent practitioners in their own office or with a group of affiliated clinicians in a "group" practice) or in clinics, hospitals, or counseling centers.

4. The scientist practitioner career path in the traumatic stress field involves balancing research and clinical work as equivalent priorities, usually with a focus on developing and scientifically testing innovative approaches to the assessment, treatment, or prevention of PTSD. Traumatic stress scientist practitioners tend to, as faculty in universities or medical schools, supervise graduate clinical research trainees who are learning to conduct psychotherapy or pharmacotherapy and research studies on assessment or treatment.

5. The health services researcher path in the traumatic stress field involves conducting research studies on when, why, and how people seek professional help of different kinds due to PTSD and how to make these services most beneficial and cost-effective. Traumatic stress health services researchers tend to work in positions that are funded by grants they obtain from the federal or state government or private foundations, while on the faculty of university or medical schools or scientific institutes such as the Evaluation Division of the National Center for PTSD or the New York State Psychiatric Institute.

6. The educator career path in the traumatic stress field involves developing and providing training to professionals who want to specialize in traumatic stress studies or services, or teaching undergraduates or graduate students in college or university programs.

7. The program director career path in the traumatic stress field involves developing or managing clinical services programs (such as serving as the clinical director of a mental health clinic or substance abuse treatment program). Traumatic stress program directors often work in nonprofit or for-profit mental health or human services organizations.

8. The most fundamental ethical principle for all helping professions and sciences is to "first do no harm"—that is, to always protect the safety, privacy, and well-being of every client or research participant (animal as well as human). This is particularly important when involving people who have experienced psychological trauma and are troubled by PTSD in research studies or clinical services, because these people—although usually highly resilient—are vulnerable to having PTSD symptoms worsened by additional stressors.

9. Vicarious trauma is a reaction of empathy and compassion that can mimic the symptoms of PTSD, but that is not the same as PTSD. Understanding and being continuously aware of the emotional impact of working with traumatized individuals and communities, and that this is an expectable and manageable reactions, are essential responsibilities of every professional who does scientific or clinical work in the traumatic stress field.

10. Careers in the traumatic stress field bring substantial personal and professional challenges, and with this comes an unprecedented opportunity to contribute to making not only traumatized people's lives safer and more successful but also those of their families and all the members of their—our—communities.

References

Cahill, S. P., Foa, E. B., Hembree, E. A., Marshall, R. D., & Nacash, N. (2006). Dissemination of exposure therapy in the treatment of posttraumatic stress sisorder. *Journal of Traumatic Stress, 19*, 597–610.

Cook, J. M., Schnurr, P. P., & Foa, E. B. (2004). Bridging the gap between posttraumatic stress disorder research and clinicalpractice: The example of exposure therapy. *Psychotherapy: Theory, Research, Practice, Training, 41*, 374–387.

Cook, J. M., Walser, R. D., Kane, V., Ruzek, J. I., & Woody, G. (2006). Dissemination and feasibility of a cognitive-behavioral treatment for substance use disorders and posttraumatic stress disorder in the Veterans Administration. *Journal of Psychoactive Drugs, 38*(1), 89–92. http://dx.doi.org/10.1080/02791072.2006.10399831.

Courtois, C. A. (2008). Complex trauma, complex reactions: Assessment and treatment. *Psychological Trauma: Theory, Research, Practice, and Policy, 1*(1), 86–100. http://dx.doi.org/10.1037/1942-9681.s.1.86.

Courtois, C. A., Ford, J. D., & Cloitre, M. (2009). Best practices in psychotherapy for adults. In C. A. Courtois & J. D. Ford (Eds.), *Treating complex traumatic stress disorders: An evidence-based guide* (pp. 82–103). New York, NY: Guilford Press.

Courtois, C. A., & Gold, S. (2009). The need for inclusion of psychological trauma in the professional curriculum. *Psychological Trauma, 1*(1), 3–23.

Dalgleish, T. (2004). Cognitive approaches to posttraumatic stress disorder: The evolution of multirepresentational theorizing. *Psychological Bulletin, 130*, 228–260.

Davis, R. G., Ressler, K. J., Schwartz, A. C., Stephens, K. J., & Bradley, R. G. (2008). Treatment barriers for low-income, urban African Americans with undiagnosed posttraumatic stress disorder. *Journal of Traumatic Stress, 21*, 218–222.

Delker, B. C., & Freyd, J. J. (2014). From betrayal to the bottle: Investigating possible pathways from trauma to problematic substance use. *Journal of Traumatic Stress, 27*(5), 576–584.

Dias, B. G., Banerjee, S. B., Goodman, J. V., & Ressler, K. J. (2013). Towards new approaches to disorders of fear and anxiety. *Current Opinion in Neurobiology, 23*(3), 346–352.

Ehlers, A., Clark, D. M., Dunmore, E., Jaycox, L., Meadows, E., & Foa, E. B. (1998). Predicting response to exposure treatment in PTSD: The role of mental defeat and alienation. *Journal of Traumatic Stress, 11*, 457–471.

Ehring, T., Klein, B., Clark, D., Foa, E. B., & Ehlers, A. (2007). Screening for posttraumatic stress disorder: What combination of symptoms predicts best? *Journal of Nervous and Mental Disease, 12*, 1004–1012.

Elhai, J. D., Calhoun, P. C., & Ford, J. D. (2008). Statistical procedures for analyzing mental health services data. *Psychiatric Research, 160*, 129–136.

Elhai, J. D., & Ford, J. D. (2007). Correlates of mental health service utilization intensity in the National comorbidity survey and National comorbidity survey replication. *Psychiatric Services, 58*, 1108–1115.

Elhai, J. D., Ford, J. D., & Naifeh, J. (2009). Assessing traumatic event exposure and posttraumatic morbidity. In G. M. Rosen & B. C. Frueh (Eds.), *Assessment and treatment of psychiatric disorders*. New York: Guilford.

Elhai, J. D., Ford, J. D., Ruggiero, K. J., & Frueh, B. C. (in review). *Diagnostic alterations for posttraumatic stress disorder: Examining data from the National Comorbidity Survey Replication and National Survey of Adolescents*.

Elhai, J. D., Ford, J. D., Ruggiero, K. J., & Frueh, C. B. (2009). Diagnostic alterations for post-traumatic stress disorder: Examining data from the National Comorbidity Survey Replication and National Survey of Adolescents. *Psychological Medicine, 39*(12), 1957–1966. http://dx.doi.org/10.1017/S0033291709005819.

Elhai, J. D., Frueh, B. C., Gold, P. B., Gold, S. N., & Hamner, M. B. (2000). Clinical presentations of posttraumatic stress disorder across trauma populations: A comparison of MMPI-2 profiles of combat veterans and adult survivors of child sexual abuse. *Journal of Nervous and Mental Disease, 188*, 708–713.

Elhai, J. D., Gold, P. B., Frueh, B. C., & Gold, S. N. (2000). Cross-validation of the MMPI-2 in detecting malingered posttraumatic stress disorder. *Journal of Personality Assessment, 75*, 449–463.

Elhai, J. D., Gold, S. N., Sellers, A. H., & Dorfman, W. I. (2001). The detection of malingered posttraumatic stress disorder with MMPI-2 fake bad indices. *Assessment, 8*, 217–232.

Elhai, J. D., Gray, M. J., Kashdan, T. B., & Franklin, C. L. (2005). Which instruments are most commonly used to assess traumatic event exposure and posttraumatic effects?: A survey of traumatic stress professionals. *Journal of Traumatic Stress, 18*, 541–545.

Elhai, J. D., Grubaugh, A. L., Kashdan, T. B., & Frueh, B. C. (2008). Empirical examination of a proposed refinement to DSM-IV posttraumatic stress disorder symptom criteria using the National Comorbidity Survey Replication data. *Journal of Clinical Psychiatry, 69*(4), 597–602.

Elhai, J. D., Naifeh, J. A., Zucker, I. S., Gold, S. N., Deitsch, S. E., & Frueh, B. C. (2004). Discriminating malingered from genuine civilian posttraumatic stress disorder: A validation of three MMPI-2 infrequency scales (F, Fp, and Fptsd). *Assessment, 11*, 139–144.

Elhai, J. D., Ruggiero, K. J., Frueh, B. C., Beckham, J. C., Gold, P. B., & Feldman, M. E. (2002). The infrequency-posttraumatic stress disorder scale (Fptsd) for the MMPI-2:

Development and initial validation with veterans presenting with combat-related PTSD. *Journal of Personality Assessment, 79*, 531–549.

Fallot, R., & Harris, M. (2002). The Trauma Recovery and Empowerment Model (TREM): Conceptual and practical issues in a group intervention for women. *Community Mental Health Journal, 38*(6), 475–485.

Fallot, R., & Harris, M. (2008). Trauma-informed services. In G. Reyes, J. D. Elhai, & J. Ford (Eds.), *The encyclopedia of psychological trauma* (pp. 660–662). Hoboken, NJ: Wiley.

Feeny, N. C., Foa, E. B., Treadwell, K. R. H., & March, J. (2004). Posttraumatic stress disorder in youth: A critical review of the cognitive and behavioral treatment outcome literature. *Professional Psychology-Research and Practice, 35*, 466–476.

Feeny, N. C., Zoellner, L. A., & Foa, E. B. (2002). Treatment outcome for chronic PTSD among female assault victims with borderline personality characteristics: A preliminary examination. *Journal of Personality Disorders, 16*, 30–40.

Finkelhor, D. (1987). The trauma of childhood sexual abuse: Two models. *Journal of Interpersonal Violence, 2*(2), 348–366.

Fish-Murray, C., Koby, E., & Van der Kolk, B. A. (1987). Evolving ideas: The effect of abuse on children's thoughts. In B. A. Van der Kolk (Ed.), *Psychological trauma* (pp. 89–110). Washington DC: American Psychiatric Association Press.

Foa, E. B., Dancu, C. V., Hembree, E. A., Jaycox, L. H., Meadows, E. A., & Street, G. P. (1999). A comparison of exposure therapy, stress inoculation training, and their combination for reducing posttraumatic stress disorder in female assault victims. *Journal of Consulting and Clinical Psychology, 67*, 194–200.

Foa, E. B., Davidson, J. R. T., Frances, A., Culpepper, L., Ross, R., & Ross, D. (1999). The expert consensus guideline series: Treatment of posttraumatic stress disorder. *Journal of Clinical Psychiatry, 60*, 4–76.

Foa, E. B., Ehlers, A., Clark, D. M., Tolin, D. F., & Orsillo, S. M. (1999). The Posttraumatic Cognitions Inventory (PTCI): Development and validation. *Psychological Assessment, 11*, 303–314.

Foa, E. B., Hembree, E. A., Cahill, S. P., Rauch, S. A., Riggs, D. S., Feeny, N. C., et al. (2005). Randomized trial of prolonged exposure for posttraumatic stress disorder with and without cognitive restructuring: Outcome at academic and community clinicalics. *Journal of Consulting and Clinical Psychology, 73*, 953–964.

Foa, E. B., Hembree, E. A., & Rothbaum, B. O. (2007). *Prolonged exposure therapy for PTSD: Emotional processing of traumatic experiences: Therapist guide.* New York: Oxford University Press.

Foa, E. B., & Jaycox, L. H. (Eds.). (1999). *Cognitive-behavioral theory and treatment of posttraumatic stress disorder.* Arlington, VA: American Psychiatric Publishing.

Foa, E. B., Johnson, K. M., Feeny, N. C., & Treadwell, K. R. H. (2001). The child PTSD symptom scale: A preliminary examination of its psychometric properties. *Journal of Clinical Child Psychology, 30*, 376–384.

Foa, E. B., Keane, T. M., & Friedman, M. J. (Eds.), (2000). *Effective treatments for PTSD.* New York: Guilford.

Foa, E. B., Keane, T. M., Friedman, M. J., & Cohen, J. A. (Eds.), (2008). *Effective treatments for PTSD* (2nd ed.). New York: Guilford.

Foa, E. B., & Kozak, M. J. (1986). Emotional processing of fear: Exposure to corrective information. *Psychological Bulletin, 99*, 20–35.

Foa, E. B., & Rothbaum, B. O. (1989). Behavioural psychotherapy for post-traumatic stress disorder. *International Review of Psychiatry, 1*, 219–226.

Foa, E. B., & Rothbaum, B. O. (1998). *Treating the trauma of rape: Cognitive-behavioral therapy for PTSD*. New York: Guilford.

Foa, E. B., Rothbaum, B. O., & Furr, J. M. (2003). Augmenting exposure therapy with other CBT procedures. *Psychiatric Annals, 33*(1), 47–53.

Foa, E. B., Rothbaum, B. O., Riggs, D. S., & Murdock, T. B. (1991). Treatment of posttraumatic stress disorder in rape victims: A comparison between cognitive-behavioral procedures and counseling. *Journal of Consulting and Clinical Psychology, 59*, 715–723.

Foa, E. B., Steketee, G., & Milby, J. B. (1980). Differential effects of exposure and response prevention in obsessive-compulsive washers. *Journal of Consulting and Clinical Psychology, 48*, 71–79.

Foa, E. B., Turner, J. L., & Foa, U. G. (1972). Response generalization in aggression. *Human Relations, 25*, 337–350.

Foa, E. B., Zinbarg, R., & Rothbaum, B. O. (1992). Uncontrollability and unpredictability in post-traumatic stress disorder: An animal model. *Psychological Bulletin, 112*, 218–238.

Foa, E. B., Zoellner, L. A., & Feeny, N. C. (2006). An evaluation of three brief programs for facilitating recovery after assault. *Journal of Traumatic Stress, 19*, 29–43.

Foa, E. B., Zoellner, L. A., Feeny, N. C., Hembree, E. A., & Alvarez-Conrad, J. (2002). Does imaginal exposure exacerbate PTSD symptoms? *Journal of Consulting and Clinical Psychology, 70*, 1022–1028.

Ford, J. D., & Cloitre, M. (2009). Best practices in psychotherapy for children and adolescents. In C. A. Courtois & J. D. Ford (Eds.), *Treating complex traumatic stress disorders: An evidence-based guide* (pp. 59–81). New York: Guilford.

Ford, J. D., Grasso, D., Greene, C., Levine, J., Spinazzola, J., & van der Kolk, B. (2013). Clinical significance of a proposed developmental trauma disorder diagnosis: Results of an international survey of clinicians. *Journal of Clinical Psychiatry, 74*(8), 841–849. http://dx.doi.org/10.4088/JCP.12m08030.

Ford, J. D., Stockton, P., Kaltman, S., & Green, B. L. (2006). Disorders of extreme stress (DESNOS) symptoms are associated with type and severity of interpersonal trauma exposure in a sample of healthy young women. *Journal of Interpersonal Violence, 21*, 1399–1416.

Freyd, J. (1994). Betrayal trauma: Traumatic amnesia as an adaptive response to childhood abuse. *Ethics & Behavior, 4*(4), 307–329.

Freyd, J. J. (1987). Dynamic mental representations. *Psychological Review, 94*(4), 427–438.

Freyd, J. J., & Johnson, J. Q. (1987). Probing the time course of representational momentum. *Journal of Experimental Psychology. Learning, Memory, and Cognition, 13*(2), 259–268.

Gerardi, M., Rothbaum, B. O., Ressler, K., Heekin, M., & Rizzo, A. (2008). Virtual reality exposure therapy using a virtual Iraq: Case report. *Journal of Traumatic Stress, 21*, 209–213.

Gibson, L. E., Ruzek, J. I., Naturale, A. J., Watson, P. J., Bryant, R. A., Rynearson, T., et al. (2006). Interventions for individuals after mass violence and disaster: Recommendations from the roundtable on screening and assessment, outreach, and intervention for mental health and substance abuse needs following disasters and mass violence. *Journal of Psychological Trauma, 5*(4), 1–28.

Gleser, G., Green, B. L., & Winget, C. (Eds.), (1981). *Prolonged psychosocial effects of disater*. New York, New York: Academic Press.

Gold, S. N. (1997). Training professional psychologists to treat survivors of childhood sexual abuse. *Psychotherapy, 34*, 365–374.

Gold, S. N. (2009). Contextual therapy. In C. A. Courtois & J. D. Ford (Eds.), *Treating traumatic stress disorders: An evidence-based guide* (pp. 227–242). New York, NY: Guilford Press.

Gold, S. N., Hill, E. L., Swingle, J. M., & Elfant, A. S. (1999). Relationship between childhood sexual abuse characteristics and dissociation among women in therapy. *Journal of Family Violence, 14,* 157–171.

Gold, S. N., Hughes, D. M., & Swingle, J. M. (1999). Degrees of memory of childhood sexual abuse among women survivors in therapy. *Journal of Family Violence, 14,* 35–46.

Gold, S. N., Lucenko, B., Elhai, J., Swingle, J. M., & Sellers, A. (1999). A comparison of psychological/psychiatric symptomatology of women and men sexually abused as children. *Child Abuse & Neglect, 23,* 683–692.

Gold, S. N., Swingle, J. M., Hill, E. L., & Elfant, A. S. (1998). Acts of childhood sexual abuse: An empirically derived typology. *Journal of Family Violence, 13,* 233–242.

Goldsmith, R. E., Chesney, S. A., Heath, N. M., & Barlow, M. R. (2013). Emotion regulation difficulties mediate associations between betrayal trauma and symptoms of posttraumatic stress, depression, and anxiety. *Journal of Traumatic Stress, 26*(3), 376–384.

Goldsmith, R. E., Freyd, J. J., & DePrince, A. P. (2012). Betrayal trauma: Associations with psychological and physical symptoms in young adults. *Journal of Interpersonal Violence, 27*(3), 547–567.

Gray, M. J., Elhai, J. D., & Frueh, B. C. (2004). Enhancing patient satisfaction and increasing treatment compliance: Patient education as a fundamental component of PTSD treatment. *Psychiatric Quarterly, 75*(4), 321–332.

Green, B. L. (2003). *Trauma interventions in war and peace: Prevention, practice, and policy.* New York: Kluwer Academic/Plenum Publishers.

Green, B. L., Grace, M., Lindy, J. D., & Leonard, A. (1990). Race differences in repsonse to traumatic stress. *Journal of Traumatic Stress, 3,* 379–393.

Green, B. L., Grace, M. C., & Gleser, G. C. (1985). Identifying survivors at risk: Long-term impairment following the Beverly Hills Supper Club fire. *Journal of Consulting and Clinical Psychology, 53,* 672–678.

Green, B. L., Grace, M. C., Vary, M. G., Kramer, T. L., Gleser, G. C., & Leonard, A. C. (1994). Children of disaster in the 2nd decade - a 17-year follow-up of buffalo creek survivors. *Journal of the American Academy of Child and Adolescent Psychiatry, 33,* 71–79.

Green, B. L., Lindy, J. D., & Grace, M. C. (1988). Long-term coping with combat stress. *Journal of Traumatic Stress, 1,* 399–412.

Green, B. L., Lindy, J. D., Grace, M. C., & Gleser, G. C. (1989). Multiple diagnosis in posttraumatic stress disorder. The role of war stressors. *Journal of Nervous and Mental Disorders, 177,* 329–335.

Green, B. L., Miranda, J., Daroowalla, A., & Siddique, J. (2005). Trauma exposure, mental health functioning, and program needs of women in jail. *Crime and Delinquency, 51,* 133–151.

Green, B. L., Rowland, J. H., Krupnick, J. L., Epstein, S. A., Stockton, P., Stern, N. M., et al. (1998). Prevalence of posttraumatic stress disorder in women with breast cancer. *Psychosomatics, 39,* 102–111.

Green, B. L., & Schnurr, P. P. (Eds.). (2004). *Trauma and Health.* Washington DC: American Psychological Association.

Grijalva, F. E., Ford, J. D., Docherty, A. R., Fricker-Elhai, A. E., & Elhai, J. D. (2008). Sociodemographic associations with mental health and residential care utilization among juvenile delinquents. *Psychological Services, 5*(2), 153–160.

Harris, M., Anglin, J. D., & Community Connections Trauma Work Group, (1998). *Trauma recovery and empowerment: A clinician's guide for working with women in groups.* New York: Free Press.

Harris, M., & Fallot, R. D. (2001). *Using trauma theory to design service systems.* San Francisco, CA: Jossey-Bass.

Harris, M., Graham, T., & Ennis, M. (Eds.), (2003). *The twenty-four Carar Buddha and other fables: Stories of self discovery.* Baltimore: Sidran Institute.

Harris, R., Tobias, M., Jeffreys, M., Waldegrave, K., Karlsen, S., & Nazroo, J. (2006). Racism and health: The relationship between experience of racial discrimination and health in New Zealand. *Social Science and Medicine, 63,* 1428–1441.

Herman, (2009). Foreword. In C. A. Courtois & J. D. Ford (Eds.), *Complex traumatic stress disorders: An evidence-based clinicalician's guide.* New York, New York: Guilford.

Hobfoll, S. E., Watson, P., Bell, C. C., Bryant, R. A., Brymer, M. J., Friedman, M. J., et al. (2007). Five essential elements of immediate and mid-term mass trauma intervention: Empirical evidence. *Psychiatry: Interpersonal and Biological Processes, 70*(4), 283–315.

Klotz Flitter, J. M., Elhai, J. D., & Gold, S. N. (2003). MMPI-2 F scale elevations in adult victims of child sexual abuse. *Journal of Traumatic Stress, 16,* 269–274.

Lyons-Ruth, K., Dutra, L., Schuder, M. R., & Bianchi, I. (2006). From infant attachment disorganization to adult dissociation: Relational adaptations or traumatic experiences? *Psychiatric Clinics of North America, 29,* 63–86.

Mackelprang, J. L., Klest, B., Najmabadi, S. J., Valley-Gray, S., Gonzalez, E. A., & Cash, R. E. (2014). Betrayal trauma among homeless adults: Associations with revictimization, psychological well-being, and health. *Journal of Interpersonal Violence, 29*(6), 1028–1049.

Martin, C. G., Cromer, L. D., Deprince, A. P., & Freyd, J. J. (2013). The role of cumulative trauma, betrayal, and appraisals in understanding trauma symptomatology. *Psychol Trauma, 52*(2), 110–118.

Mehta, D., Klengel, T., Conneely, K. N., Smith, A. K., Altmann, A., Pace, T. W., et al. (2013). Childhood maltreatment is associated with distinct genomic and epigenetic profiles in posttraumatic stress disorder. *Proceedings of the National Academy of Sciences of the United States of America, 110*(20), 8302–8307.

Morrison, F. G., & Ressler, K. J. (2014). From the neurobiology of extinction to improved clinical treatments. *Depression and Anxiety, 31*(4), 279–290.

Norris, F. H., Friedman, M. J., & Watson, P. J. (2002). 60,000 disaster victims speak: Part II. Summary and implications of the disaster mental health research. *Psychiatry, 65,* 240–260.

Orth, U., Cahill, S. P., Foa, E. B., & Maercker, A. (2008). Anger and posttraumatic stress disorder symptoms in crime victims: A longitudinal analysis. *Journal of Consulting and Clinical Psychology, 76,* 208–218.

Pearlman, L. A., & Caringi, J. (2009). Living and working self-reflectively to address vicarious trauma. In C. A. Courtois & J. D. Ford (Eds.), *Treating complex traumatic stress disorders: An evidence-based guide* (pp. 202–222). New York: Guilford Press.

Pelcovitz, D., van der Kolk, B., Roth, S., Mandel, F., Kaplan, S., & Resick, P. (1997). Development of a criteria set and a structured interview for disorders of extreme stress (SIDES). *Journal of Traumatic Stress, 10,* 3–16.

Pine, D. S. (2007). Research review: A neuroscience framework for pediatric anxiety disorders. *Journal of Child Psychology and Psychiatry, 48*(7), 631–648.

Pole, N., Best, S. R., Metzler, T., & Marmar, C. R. (2005). Why are hispanics at greater risk for PTSD? *Culture, Diversity, Ethnicity, and Minority Psychology, 11*(2), 144–161.

Pole, N., Best, S. R., Weiss, D. S., Metzler, T., Liberman, A. M., Fagan, J., et al. (2001). Effects of gender and ethnicity on duty-related posttraumatic stress symptoms among urban police officers. *Journal of Nervous and Mental Disease, 189*(7), 442–448.

Pole, N., Gone, J. P., & Kulkarni, M. (2008). Posttraumatic stress disorder among ethnoracial minorities in the United States. *Clinical Psychology: Science and Practice, 15,* 35–61.

Pole, N., Neylan, T., Otte, C., Henn-Hasse, C., Metzler, T. J., & Marmar, C. R. (2009). Prospective prediction of posttraumatic stress disorder symptoms using fear potentiated auditory startle responses. *Biological Psychiatry*, 65(3), 235–240.

Pole, N., Neylan, T. C., Best, S. R., Orr, S. P., & Marmar, C. R. (2003). Fear-potentiated startle and posttraumatic stress symptoms in urban police officers. *Journal of Traumatic Stress*, 16(5), 471–479.

Pole, N., Neylan, T. C., Otte, C., Metzler, T. J., Best, S. R., Henn-Haase, C., et al. (2007). Associations between childhood trauma and emotion-modulated psychophysiological responses to startling sounds: A study of police cadets. *Journal of Abnormal Psychology*, 116(2), 352–361. http://dx.doi.org/10.1037/0021-843X.116.2.352.

Pope, K., & Vasquez, M. (Eds.). (1998). *Ethics in psychotherapy and counseling: A practical guide* (2nd ed.). New York: John Wiley & Sons..

Powers, A., Ressler, K. J., & Bradley, R. G. (2008). The protective role of friendship on the effects of childhood abuse and depression. *Depression and Anxiety*

Reissman, D. B., Watson, P., Klomp, R., Tanielian, T., & Prior, S. (2006). Pandemic influenza preparedness: Adaptive responses to an evolving challenge. *Journal of Homeland Security and Emergency Management*, 3(2) [Article 13].

Ressler, K., & Davis, M. (2003). Genetics of childhood disorders: L. Learning and memory, part 3: Fear conditioning. *Journal of the American Academy of Child and Adolescent Psychiatry*, 42(5), 612–615.

Ressler, K. J., & Mayberg, H. S. (2007). Targeting abnormal neural circuits in mood and anxiety disorders: From the laboratory to the clinicalic. *Nature Neuroscience*, 10, 1116–1124.

Ressler, K. J., & Nemeroff, C. B. (2001). Role of norepinephrine in the pathophysiology of neuropsychiatric disorders. *CNS Spectrums*, 6(8) 663–666, 670.

Ressler, K. J., Paschall, G., Zhou, X. L., & Davis, M. (2002). Regulation of synaptic plasticity genes during consolidation of fear conditioning. *Journal of Neuroscience*, 22, 7892–7902.

Ressler, K. J., Rothbaum, B. O., Tannenbaum, L., Anderson, P., Graap, K., Zimand, E., et al. (2004). Cognitive enhancers as adjuncts to psychotherapy: Use of D-cycloserine in phobic individuals to facilitate extinction of fear. *Archives of General Psychiatry*, 61, 1136–1144.

Ressler, K. J., Sullivan, S. L., & Buck, L. B. (1993). A zonal organization of odorant receptor gene expression in the olfactory epithelium. *Cell*, 73, 597–609.

Ressler, K. J., Sullivan, S. L., & Buck, L. B. (1994). A molecular dissection of spatial patterning in the olfactory system. *Current Opinion in Neurobiogy*, 4, 588–596.

Richardson, J. D., Elhai, J. D., & Pedlar, D. J. (2006). Association of PTSD and depression with medical and specialist care utilization in modern peacekeeping veterans in Canada with health-related disabilities. *Journal of Clinical Psychiatry*, 67(8), 1240–1245.

Ritchie, E. C., Friedman, M., Watson, P., Ursano, R., Wessely, S., & Flynn, B. (2004). Mass violence and early mental health intervention: A proposed application of best practice guidelines to chemical, biological, and radiological attacks. *Military Medicine*, 169(8), 575–579.

Rivard, J. C., Bloom, S. L., Abramovitz, R., Pasquale, L. E., Duncan, M., McCorkle, D., et al. (2003). Assessing the implementation and effects of a trauma-focused intervention for youths in residential treatment. *Psychiatric Quarterly*, 74(2), 137–154.

Rothbaum, B. O., Cahill, S. P., Foa, E. B., Davidson, J. R. T., Compton, J., Connor, K. M., et al. (2006). Augmentation of sertraline with prolonged exposure in the treatment of posttraumatic stress disorder. *Journal of Traumatic Stress*, 19, 625–638.

Rothbaum, B. O., Foa, E. B., & Hembree, E. A. (2007). *Reclaiming your life from a traumatic experience: Workbook*. New York: Oxford University Press.

Rothbaum, B. O., Foa, E. B., Riggs, D. S., & Murdock, T. (1992). A prospective examination of post-traumatic stress disorder in rape victims. *Journal of Traumatic Stress*, *5*, 455–475.

Rothbaum, B. O., Kearns, M. C., Reiser, E., Davis, J. S., Kerley, K. A., Rothbaum, A. O., et al. (2014). Early intervention following trauma may mitigate genetic risk for PTSD in civilians: A pilot prospective emergency department study. *Journal of Clinical Psychiatry*, *75*(12), 1380–1387. http://dx.doi.org/10.4088/JCP.13m08715.

Rothbaum, B. O., Price, M., Jovanovic, T., Norrholm, S. D., Gerardi, M., Dunlop, B., et al. (2014). A randomized, double-blind evaluation of D-cycloserine or alprazolam combined with virtual reality exposure therapy for posttraumatic stress disorder in Iraq and Afghanistan War veterans. *American Journal of Psychiatry*, *171*(6), 640–648. http://dx.doi.org/10.1176/appi.ajp.2014.13121625.

Ruzek, J. I., Friedman, M. J., & Murray, S. (2005). Toward a knowledge management system for posttraumatic stress disorder treatment in. veterans healthcare. *Psychiatric Annals*, *35*(11), 911–920.

Smith, C. P., & Freyd, J. J. (2014a). The courage to study what we wish did not exist. *Journal of Trauma and Dissociation*, *15*(5), 521–526.

Smith, C. P., & Freyd, J. J. (2014b). Institutional betrayal. *American Psychologist*, *69*(6), 575–587.

Tolin, D. F., & Foa, E. B. (2006). Sex differences in trauma and posttraumatic stress disorder: A quantitative review of 25 years of research. *Psychological Bulletin*, *132*, 959–992.

Treadwell, K., & Foa, E. (2004). Assessment of post-traumatic stress disorder. In W. T. O'Donohue & E. R. Levensky (Eds.), *Handbook of forensic psychology: Resource for mental health and legal professional* (pp. 347–366). New York: Elsevier Science.

van der Kolk, B. (Ed.). (1987). *Posttraumatic stress disorder: Biological and psychological sequelae*. Washington DC: American Psychiatric Association Press.

van der Kolk, B., Blitz, R., Burr, W., Sherry, S., & Hartmann, E. (1984). Nightmares and trauma: A comparison of nightmares after combat with lifelong nightmares in veterans. *American Journal of Psychiatry*, *141*, 187–190.

van der Kolk, B., Greenberg, M., Boyd, H., & Krystal, J. (1985). Inescapable shock, neurotransmitters, and addiction to trauma: Toward a psychobiology of post traumatic stress. *Biological Psychiatry*, *20*, 314–325.

van der Kolk, B. A. (1985). Adolescent vulnerability to posttraumatic stress disorder. *Psychiatry*, *48*, 365–370.

van der Kolk, B. A. (Ed.). (1987). *Psychological trauma*. Washington DC: American Psychiatric Association Press.

van der Kolk, B. A., & Courtois, C. A. (2005). Editorial comments: Complex developmental trauma. *Journal of Traumatic Stress*, *18*, 385–388.

Van der Kolk, B. A., & Ducey, C. (1989). The psychological processing of traumatic experience: Rorschach patterns in PTSD. *Journal of Traumatic Stress*, *2*, 259–274.

van der Kolk, B. A., McFarlane, A. C., & Weisaeth, L. (Eds.), (1996). *Traumatic stress: The effects of overwhelming experience on mind, body, and society*. New York, US: Guilford.

van der Kolk, B. A., Pelcovitz, D., Roth, S., Mandel, F. S., McFarlane, A., & Herman, J. L. (1996). Dissociation, somatization, and affect dysregulation: The complexity of adaptation to trauma. *American Journal of Psychiatry*, *153*, 83–93.

van der Kolk, B. A., Roth, S., Pelcovitz, D., Sunday, S., & Spinazzola, J. (2005). Disorders of extreme stress: The empirical foundation of a complex adaptation to trauma. *Journal of Traumatic Stress*, *18*(5), 389–399.

van der Kolk, B. A., Spinazzola, J., Blaustein, M. E., Hopper, J. W., Hopper, E. K., Korn, D. L., et al. (2007). A randomized clinical trial of eye movement desensitization and reprocessing

(EMDR), fluoxetine, and pill placebo in the treatment of posttraumatic stress disorder: Treatment effects and long-term maintenance. *Journal of Clinical Psychiatry*, *68*(1), 37–46.

van Minnen, A., & Foa, E. B. (2006). The effect of imaginal exposure length on outcome of treatment for PTSD. *Journal of Traumatic Stress*, *19*, 427–438.

Wagner, G. C., Fisher, H., Pole, N., Borve, T., & Johnson, S. K. (1993). Effects of monoaminergic agonists on alcohol-induced increases in mouse aggression. *Journal of Studies on Alcohol Supplement*, *11*, 185–191.

Walker, D. L., Ressler, K. J., Lu, K. T., & Davis, M. (2002). Facilitation of conditioned fear extinction by systemic administration or intra-amygdala infusions of D-cycloserine as assessed with fear-potentiated startle in rats. *Journal of Neuroscience*, *22*, 2343–2351.

Watson, P., Gibson, L., & Ruzek, J. I. (Eds.), (2007). *Public mental health interventions following disasters and mass violence*. New York: Guilford Press.

Watson, P. J. (2008a). Psychological first aid, adult. In G. Reyes, J. D. Elhai, & J. Ford (Eds.), *Encyclopedia of psychological trauma* (pp. 535–537). Hoboken, NJ: Wiley.

Watson, P. J. (2008b). Psychological first aid, children. In G. Reyes, J. D. Elhai, & J. Ford (Eds.), *Encyclopedia of psychological trauma* (pp. 157–159). Hoboken, NJ: Wiley.

Whealin, J. M., Ruzek, J. I., & Southwick, S. (2008). Cognitive-behavioral theory and preparation for professionals at risk for trauma exposure. *Trauma, Violence, & Abuse*, *9*(2), 100–113.

Afterword

Posttraumatic stress disorder (PTSD) is an extraordinarily costly and complex condition that causes incalculable suffering for tens of millions of people worldwide. Although commonly believed to be mainly an aftereffect experienced by military personnel exposed to the horrors of war, PTSD has been recognized as a much more pervasive problem that can affect literally any human being. In wars or other military conflicts, it is not only the warriors who are traumatized but also the much larger population of civilian children and adults who are directly harmed or have to witness death and destruction while having to live for weeks, months, or years in the dark shadow of the imminent threat of death, destruction, or loss of their homes, families, and friends, schools and workplaces, and often their entire community.

Separately from the ravages of war, or tragically in many cases as yet another layer added on to the traumatization caused by war, women or girls (and also men and boys) who are sexually assaulted, or exploited and trafficked (forced into prostitution), children who are maltreated, families or communities living with life-threatening violence, survivors of disasters or life-threatening accidents, victims of political violence or genocide—all of these people are at risk for PTSD. When these types of psychological trauma lead to PTSD, the adverse impact on the person and the cost to society is comparable to—or greater than—that of the most severe medical illnesses (such as heart disease or cancer). For each victim, and their family and community, the cost of PTSD is not just a matter of poor health and expensive health care but a much greater tragedy of profound personal suffering that may last for many years or even a lifetime.

Therefore, understanding how and why exposure to certain "traumatic" stressors causes psychological trauma, and how and for whom this leads to the debilitating disorder of PTSD, is an essential challenge for health care researchers and clinicians and for social and economic policy makers. Thousands of researchers, clinicians, and educators internationally therefore devote their careers to working scientific and therapeutic studies related to PTSD and to informing the public and preparing students for careers in the field by teaching about PTSD. The problems and challenges facing PTSD scientists, clinicians, and educators are daunting, but the opportunities are greater. These include the scientific opportunity to learn intricately about the inner workings of the body and mind from the level of molecules and genes to families and entire organizations and societies, and the humanitarian opportunity to provide crucial help to millions of children and adults—and their families and communities—who suffer from PTSD.

As you have learned in this book, literary and historical accounts of war, disaster, abuse, family violence, and tragic untimely deaths actually are descriptions of psychological trauma and PTSD that have existed since the earliest days of humanity many millennia ago. Although most people never experience most types of psychological trauma, research in the past 50 years has shown that *the majority of adults (and almost as many children) will experience at least one psychologically traumatic event at some time*. Fortunately, for most the immediate ("acute") stress reactions that are an almost universal response (although highly individual in their specific nature) dissipate to a large extent within a matter of a few days or weeks. Unfortunately, this is *not* true for 7–10% who develop persistent stress reactions in the form of Acute Stress Disorder or subsequently as PTSD. In addition, an equal or greater number will develop an anxiety disorder, depression, a substance use disorder, a behavioral disorder of childhood or adolescence, or another psychiatric disorder—or experience a worsening of preexisting symptoms in those disorders—following exposure to psychological trauma. There are many paths or trajectories that may lead to experiencing psychological trauma and to recovery or to the development of PTSD (see Chapter 2). Studies of the etiology (causes or risk factors; see Chapter 3) and the epidemiology (form and extent of occurrence in populations; see Chapter 4) of PTSD have shown the disorder to be more widespread than previously thought and to be the product of not only exposure to psychological trauma but also of factors such as genetic and environmental vulnerability and resilience. Scientists and clinicians are reporting fascinating new findings every week concerning how and for whom psychological trauma and PTSD occur, and the biological (see Chapter 5) as well as psychological causes and impact of PTSD—including the tragic contribution of PTSD to the vulnerability and severity of serious medical illnesses. The need for further research in this area is likely to grow for many decades to come, as is the need for creative translations of the scientific findings into the development of therapeutic and prevention interventions for PTSD.

PTSD can be successfully treated, and it may be preventable. The starting point for treatment is screening and clinical assessment (see Chapter 6). Over the past 4 decades, the PTSD field has gone from having a few preliminary assessment measures—mostly questionnaires and structured interviews—to the development of a wide array of well-researched tools for screening to detect potential problems with PTSD and assessment to determine the nature and extent of exposure to traumatic stressors and of PTSD and many related problems. As these screening and assessment instruments continue to be refined and scientifically tested, new approaches are on the horizon that include sophisticated biological measures (such as brain imaging and genetic assays) and behavioral measures (such as techniques for assessing a person's activity level, state of mind, and interactions at the very time that they are occurring or soon after). The field is just beginning to understand how the brain actually functions when PTSD is occurring, how genes affect (and are affected by—epigenetics) people's highly individual reactions to psychological trauma, and how people feel, think, and act on a moment-to-moment basis "24/7" when they are challenged by the symptoms of PTSD (and the additional challenges of sustaining recovery when PTSD has been successfully managed or overcome).

Once PTSD has developed, there are two basic approaches to treatment, each with many specific options that can be deployed to best address the needs and circumstances of the person who is seeking help (see Chapters 7 and 8). Psychotherapy is the best researched treatment approach for PTSD, for children as well as adults. The spectrum of PTSD psychotherapies is broad, including cognitive behavioral therapies (CBTs), PTSD affect and interpersonal regulation therapies (PAIR), psychodynamic and experiential therapies, body and movement therapies, marital and family therapies, and group therapies. CBT and PAIR have the strongest scientific evidence of efficacy as a treatment of PTSD—that is, research showing that the treatment is directly responsible for improvements in the disease condition, in this case PTSD. However, no one size fits all, and there is growing evidence that other psychotherapy approaches may be efficacious for (and in some cases, better accepted by) persons of different circumstances seeking help for PTSD.

A three-phase approach to PTSD psychotherapy has become standard. Each phase represents a core treatment goal: first, ensuring that the recipient is sufficiently safe and psychologically prepared to be free from further exposure to traumatic stressors (such as abuse or domestic or community violence) or serious crises (such as suicide or relapse into alcohol or drug addiction); second, enabling the recipient to understand and therapeutically change the persistent stress reactions that are the biological and psychological source of PTSD; and third, empowering the recipient to begin, or resume, living a fuller and more personally rewarding life by utilizing psychological capacities and social resources (such as family relationships, friendships, and work and recreation pursuits) with which PTSD has interfered.

Pharmacotherapy—the use of therapeutic medications—is the other major approach to treating PTSD, with many medicines now in use. Most medications used to treat PTSD originally were developed to treat affective or psychotic disorders, and medical conditions (such as hypertension or seizure disorders). As the biology of PTSD is becoming clearer (see Chapter 5), exciting new medication options are being developed and researched in scientific studies with animals and humans at the level of the basic molecules, proteins, DNA and genes, neurons and synapses, and neurochemicals that are involved in the body's stress response system and related systems in the brain and body (such as the reward, perceptual, memory, and immune systems). Extensive research on the basic biological mechanisms of PTSD in the next several decades is likely to lead to completely new drugs that must then be carefully tested before they can be approved for PTSD treatment by the US Food and Drug Administration and similar safety regulatory agencies in countries worldwide. Because PTSD involves many bodily systems and interconnected areas in the brain, it is unlikely that any single drug or biological agent will be shown to be the "cure" for PTSD; rather, it is more likely that drugs will be developed that help certain groups of people who share very specific genetic and psychological attributes (both strengths as well as vulnerabilities) and for whom PTSD takes an equally specific biological form.

It also is likely that the single most direct and effective method of altering the brain's patterns of activity—that is, psychological interventions that help people to think and act in ways that directly depend on and activate the brain's circuits—will continue to be developed in the form of psychotherapies that change how people use their brains. Thus, treatment and prevention of PTSD (see Chapters 7–9) in the future are likely to involve combinations of psychotherapy and pharmacotherapy rather than only one or the other. Ideally, combinations of these two modalities will substantially bolster each other's effectiveness (Ressler et al., 2004).

Whether psychological trauma has (or may have) occurred and whether PTSD is (or may be) a source of impairment for a person are key questions not only for treatment and prevention but also for legal purposes. In both civil and criminal law, PTSD assessors and researchers play an important role by addressing the difficult question of what role psychological trauma and PTSD have had in the evolution of legal problems and how legal decisions, penalties, and remedies should be determined by public safety personnel (including law enforcement and child protection professionals) and legal professionals, judges, and juries (see Chapter 10). Neither exposure to a traumatic stressor nor PTSD has been shown to "cause" criminal or harmful behavior (such as child abuse, family violence, or assault), but they may play mitigating or exacerbating roles when people commit such acts or are victimized by them. The question of "malingering"—making up or exaggerating symptoms or problems in order to justify receiving compensation or excuse illegal or otherwise harmful acts— remains a major challenge for PTSD assessors and researchers. Continued research and clinical innovation regarding the nature and detection of real versus malingered PTSD with vulnerable populations such as war veterans and survivors of abuse or violence is likely to be an important point of convergence of the PTSD and legal fields.

The impact of psychological trauma and the risk of developing PTSD differs, depending on the social and cultural context in which traumatic stressors occur, and the social and cultural resources available to individuals, families, and communities who are exposed to psychological trauma (see Chapter 11). Disadvantaged persons and communities such as those experiencing poverty, stigma, and discrimination; incarceration; homelessness; political repression; communal/societal violence (including military and gang warfare); forced immigration (refugees); interrogation and torture; terrorism; and genocide are particularly likely to be victims of psychological trauma and to develop PTSD. The social, economic, political, and cultural challenges facing vulnerable groups whose members also often are subjected to traumatic stressors pose several fundamental ethical challenges for clinicians and scientists who conduct assessment, treatment, and prevention services addressing PTSD. The PTSD field is ably represented by a number of researchers, clinicians, educators, and advocates who have taken on the extremely tough challenge of partnering with people (including entire communities and societies) who have been subjected to racism, political violence, and stigma all over the world. Such work represents the best combination of science, professionalism, and humanitarianism.

With all these challenges and exciting new developments, the PTSD field offers many paths to a highly rewarding career (see Chapter 12). The goal of this book has been to spark each reader's interest in learning more about the fascinating insights and vital discoveries that have emerged from the study of PTSD. Although the topic is very serious, and in many cases tragic, there is no career path more important than understanding and helping to treat or prevent PTSD.

References

Ressler, K. J., Rothbaum, B. O., Tannenbaum, L., Anderson, P., Graap, K., Zimand, E., et al. (2004). Cognitive enhancers as adjuncts to psychotherapy: Use of D-cycloserine in phobic individuals to facilitate extinction of fear. *Archives of General Psychiatry, 61*(11), 1136–1144. http://dx.doi.org/10.1001/archpsyc.61.11.1136.

Index